D1250606

HANDBOOK OF RUSSIAN ROOTS

COLUMBIA SLAVIC STUDIES

A SERIES OF THE DEPARTMENT OF SLAVIC LANGUAGES
COLUMBIA UNIVERSITY

HANDBOOK OF RUSSIAN ROOTS

COMPILED BY

CATHERINE A. WOLKONSKY

AND

MARIANNA A. POLTORATZKY

COLUMBIA UNIVERSITY PRESS

NEW YORK

The preparation and publication of this work was originally made possible by a grant from the Rockefeller Foundation to the Department of Slavic Languages of Columbia University and by grants from the Salmon Fund of Vassar College.

Printed in the United States of America

c 10 9 8 7

ACKNOWLEDGMENTS

The authors could never have completed this work without assistance and encouragement from many sources. First of all, we are grateful to Professor Ernest J. Simmons, General Editor of the Slavic Studies and Executive Officer of a grant from the Rockefeller Foundation to the Department of Slavic Languages of Columbia University, who made possible the preparation and publication of the *Handbook of Russian Roots*. We are also grateful to the Committee on Research of Vassar College, whose generous grant from the Salmon Fund enabled us to secure the necessary technical help and contributed to the costs of publication. The Flagg Foundation, under the presidency of Mrs. Henry H. Villard, also gave a substantial grant.

Our colleagues at Vassar College have helped us greatly with the various semantic problems which had to be solved in the translation of the Russian text into English. Foremost among these is Professor Jane J. Swenarton, whose scholarship and enthusiasm were a real inspiration. Associate Professor Mary E. Giffin encouraged us by advice during the preliminary stages of our work.

Our sincere appreciation is due to Mrs. Chebysheva who helped in the initial work of collecting material. Finally we are very thankful to Professor Alexander D. Bilimovich, formerly of the University of Kiev, for assistance in the research.

Catherine A. Wolkonsky
Marianna A. Poltoratzky

GENERAL PLAN

The pattern of roots is more clearly preserved in Russian than in any other Slavic or indeed Indo-European tongue. Consequently, it is obvious that a knowledge of the roots will be helpful to anyone working with the language. So far, no dictionary of roots has appeared in this country, except for a small volume by the late Professor George Patrick of the University of California, published in 1938. This was the first attempt to bring this characteristic of the language to the attention of students. Even in Russia, there is only Reiff's *Korneslov,* published in St. Petersburg in 1835.

The present handbook gives over 500 of the most productive roots with their derivatives and compounds. It is at the same time a dictionary of literary, conversational, and colloquial Russian as written and spoken throughout the nineteenth century and down to the present day, including the neologisms introduced since 1917. The aim of the authors is to provide not only a reference book but, more important, a systematic and practical teaching aid for vocabulary building, especially designed for English-speaking students in this country or elsewhere. It should be of special value for training translators and students in Russian Area courses working in source material. Also it is hoped that teachers will use this handbook as an etymological reference. This handbook may be of help to students: (1) in mastering the language through the development of "root consciousness" and through a more systematic approach to vocabulary building, and (2) in discovering the spirit of the language, understanding more easily its grammar, syntax, and phraseology, and learning its most characteristic idioms, proverbs, and sayings.

The roots are given in alphabetical order and according to the following plan:

1. The basic root with all its variants, for example:

БРОС-, БРОШ-, throw, toss

2. The root cluster or group of words derived from that root follow. Within the root cluster, the *verb* comes first in its infinitive form (perfective and imperfective aspects):

брóс-ить, *v.p.,* брос-áть, *v.i.*

3. The *passive* voice of the verb; the reflexive and reciprocal verbs:

брóс-ить-ся, *v.p.r.,* брос-áть-ся, *v.i.r.*

4. The participles and gerunds.

5. The same verb with its various prefixes in alphabetical order, each of which is followed by its derivatives:

в-брóс-ить,	*v.p.,* to throw in
вы́-брос-ить,	*v.p.,* to throw out
до-брóс-ить,	*v.p.,* to throw as far as, to add by throwing
за-брóс-ить,	*v.p.,* to throw behind, beyond; abandon
на-брóс-ить,	*v.p.,* to throw on
пере-брóс-ить,	*v.p.,* to throw over
с-брóс-ить,	*v.p.,* to throw off, etc.

6. The verb and its derivatives are followed by the nouns, adjectives, and other parts of speech derived directly from the root.

In those cases in which the root is not clearly expressed in a verb or there is no verb formed by this root, as in орёл, истина, then the root cluster begins with that part of speech in which the root is most clearly expressed.

The words are divided into morphemes, i.e., into their component parts, for example:

Prefix	Root	Suffix	End suffix	
вы-	брос-	и-	ть	вы-брác-ыва-ть

The verb is always followed by the case or cases which it governs, and also the prepositions, if necessary:

брóс-и-ть + acc., + dat.

All the verbs are given in the infinitive, and if there is a change in the root, then the 1st person singular is added:

брóс-и-ть, inf., брош-ý, 1st person sing., future

The declinable parts of speech are given in the nominative case, masculine singular.

Most words are illustrated by an example, often an idiomatic expression, a proverb, or a saying. The examples have been carefully chosen with the purpose of illustrating the exact meaning of the word.

Obsolete words are occasionally included if found often in poetic and literary works and source material.

The Russian text is accented throughout and translated into English. Every effort has been made to give the correct semantic value, and in the case of figurative speech, the idiomatic English rendition. When no idiomatic equivalent can be found, then the emphasis is on the accuracy of the translation.

RUSSIAN WORD FORMATION

Components of the Word

In the Russian language, a word may consist only of the root, but the greater part of Russian words consists chiefly of several defining parts, namely:

1. the root
2. the stem
3. the suffix ⎫
4. the prefix ⎬ affixes
5. the inflectional ending. ⎭

1. The basic part of the word, from which other words related to it in meaning are derived, is called the *root*. The root contains the chief meaning of the word.

Related words, formed from a single root, make up one family or cluster of words, for example, from the root "ВОД-" we may form the following cluster of words: вод-а, вод-яной, под-вод-ный, вод-ник, на-вод-нить, на-вод-нение, etc.

Words consisting of a root, or of a root and an ending, are called nonderived words. Words formed from a root with the addition of affixes (prefixes, suffixes) are called derivatives.

2. That part of the word which remains when the ending is discarded is called the *stem*. The stem represents the important defining part of the word because it broadens and refines the meaning of the root.

In the word "вода," the root "вод-" is also the stem of the word. In the word "вод-ян-ой," "водян-," which consists of the root "вод-" plus the suffix "-ян-," is the stem. In the word "под-вод-н-ый," "под-вод-н-," which consists of the root "вод-" plus the prefix "под-" and the suffix "-н-," forms the stem.

Consequently, in nonderived words the stem is identical with the root, for example, стол, дом, вода. In derivatives the stem always consists of two or several elements, namely, of a root with affixes added to it.

3. The part of the stem which follows the root is called the *suffix*. The role of the suffix is twofold:

(a) the suffix gives a new shade of meaning to the word, for example, in стол-ик, дом-ик, the suffix "-ик" gives a diminutive and affectionate meaning.

(b) suffixes perform a word-forming function, namely they enable different parts of speech to be formed from the same root, for example, from the root свет:

свéт-л-ый, *adj.*	With the aid of the suffix "-л-" an adjective is formed.
свет-и́-ть, *v.*	With the aid of the suffix "-и-" a verb is formed.
свет-и́-вш-ий, *part.*	With the aid of two suffixes "-и-" and "-вш-" a participle is formed, etc.

4. The part of the stem which precedes the root and gives the word a new shade of meaning is called the *prefix,* for example, нос-и́ть, *v.*

в-нос-и́ть, *v.*	The prefix "в-" signifies that the action is directed inward (ВНОСИ́ТЬ В ДОМ).
вы-нос-и́ть, *v.*	The prefix "вы-" signifies that the action comes out from within (ВЫНОСИ́ТЬ ИЗ ДО́МА).

The root, prefix, and suffix are the unchanging parts of the word.

5. The *ending* or inflection is the changeable part of the word. The ending indicates the link between words, and usually defines the gender, number, person, and case, for exampe, дом, *n.,* sing. *nom*:

дом-á	The ending "a" may mean a noun that is in the nominative case, masculine plural.
дом-óв	The ending "-ОВ" signifies a noun in the genitive case, masculine plural.
бéл-ый, *adj.*	The ending "-ЫЙ" means an adjective in the nominative case, masculine singular.

In the Russian language, compound derivatives are also used. They may consist of two roots, for example: пар(root)-о-воз (root) — locomotive; земл (root)-е-коп(root) — digger. The vowel "o" or "e" serves as the link vowel between the two roots.

Table of Word Components

	Stem			
Prefix	*Root*	*Suffix*		*Ending*
	лёт			
по-	лёт			
	лёт-	чик		
по-	лет-	а-		-ю
пере-	лёт-	н-		-ый

THE MAIN SUFFIXES

Noun suffixes

denoting profession, occupation, or agency:

-тель	учи́-тель
-чик	лёт-чик
-щик, -льщик	ка́мен-щик, носи́-льщик
-ец, -лец	бо-éц, корми́-лец

-арь	пéк-арь
-яр	стол-я́р
-ник	уче-ни́к
-ак, -як	рыб-áк, мор-я́к
-ок	стрел-óк

2. The following suffixes form nouns referring to persons, denoting nationality, religion, social stratum, or place of habitation:

-ец	америкáн-ец
-анин	англич-áнин
-янин	кресть-я́нин
-ин	болгáр-ин
-ич	москв-и́ч

3. Nouns referring to persons of feminine gender are formed with the help of the following suffixes:

-ниц-а	added to masc. form	-тель	учи́тель, учи́тель-ниц-а
-к-а		-ец	америкáнец, америкáн-к-а
		-ак	рыбáк, рыбáч-к-а
		-ич	москви́ч, москви́ч-к-а
		-анин	англичáнин, англичáн-к-а
		-янин	крестья́нин, крестья́н-к-а
		-ин	болгáрин, болгáр-к-а
иц-а		-ец	певéц, пев-и́ц-а

4. The following suffixes form nouns denoting qualities:

-ость	хрáбр-ость
-есть	свéж-есть
-от-а	добр-от-á
-ет-а	нищ-ет-á
-ств-о	богáт-ств-о
-изн-а	бел-изн-á

5. The following suffixes form nouns denoting actions:

-к-а	прогу́л-к-а
-н-я	воз-н-я́
-отн-я	бег-отн-я́
-овн-я	болт-овн-я́
-ани-е	пис-áни-е
-ени-е	уч-éни-е
-ств-о	устрóй-ств-о
-ьб-а	ход-ьб-á

6. The following suffixes show singleness:

-ин-а	горóш-ин-а (one pea)
-инк-а	снеж-и́нк-а (one snowflake)

7. Nouns denoting young animals are formed with the aid of the suffix "-ёнок" ("-онок" after sibilants):

-ёнок	кот-ёнок
-онок	волч-óнок
	медвеж-óнок

8. The following suffixes form diminutives of affection:

-ик	до́м-ик
-чик	стака́н-чик
-ок, -ёк	лес-о́к, огон-ёк
-к-	ру́ч-к-а
-оч-к-а	де́в-оч-к-а
-еч-к-а	кни́ж-еч-к-а
-ец	хле́б-ец
-ц-о, -ц-е	дерев-цо́, око́н-це
-иц-е	пла́ть-иц-е
-еньк-а	дерев-е́ньк-а
-ушк-а, -юшк-а	ма́т-ушк-а, во́л-юшк-а
-ышк-о	со́лн-ышк-о

9. The following suffixes are derogatory:

-ишк-о, -ишк-а	город-и́шк-о, мальч-и́шк-а
-ёнк-а, -онк-а	девч-о́нк-а, коров-ёнк-а

10. Magnifying suffixes:

-ище	дом-и́щ-е
-ищ-а	руч-и́щ-а

Adjective suffixes

1. With the aid of the following suffixes, adjectives are formed from nouns:

Suffix	Noun	Adjective
-н-	кни́г-а	кни́ж-н-ый
-енн-	пле́м-я	пле́м-енн-ой
-ин-	го́лубь	голуб-и́н-ый
-ан-, -ян-	ко́ж-а, серебр-о́	ко́ж-ан-ый, серебр-я́н-ый
-ов-, -ев-	час, бой	час-ов-о́й, бо-ев-о́й
-ск-	го́род	город-ск-о́й
-овит-	де́ло	дел-ови́т-ый
-ат-	бород-а́	бород-а́т-ый
-аст-	зуб	зуб-а́ст-ый
-ист-	ка́мень	камен-и́ст-ый
-ив-	ложь	лж-и́в-ый
-лив-	сон	сон-ли́в-ый
-ин	тёт-я	тёт-ин

2. With the aid of the following suffixes, adjectives are formed from verbs:

Suffix	Verb	Adjective
-уч-, -юч-	лет-е́ть, кол-о́ть	лет-у́ч-ий, кол-ю́ч-ий
-ач-, -яч-	леж-а́ть, вис-е́ть	леж-а́ч-ий, вис-я́ч-ий
-к-	ре́з-ать	ре́з-к-ий
-лив-	терпе́-ть	терпе-ли́в-ый
-чив-	придир-а́ть-ся	приди́р-чив-ый

Verb suffixes

1. With the aid of the following suffixes, verbs are formed from nouns:

Suffix		Noun	Verb	
Infinitive	Present Tense		Infinitive	Present Tense
-ов-	-у-	бесе́да	бесе́д-ов-ать	бесе́д-у-ю
-ев-	-ю-	го́ре	гор-ев-а́ть	гор-ю́-ю
-ыв-, -ив-	-ыв-а, -ив-а	докла́д	докла́д-ыв-ать	докла́д-ыв-а-ю
-а-	-а-	пло́тник	пло́тнич-а-ть	пло́тнич-а-ю
-и-		рыба́к, сор	рыба́ч-и-ть, сор-и́-ть	

2. With the aid of the following suffixes, verbs are formed from adjectives:

Suffix	Adjective	Verb
-е- (for v. intrans.)	бе́л-ый	бел-е́-ть
-и- (for v. trans.)		бел-и́-ть

Participle suffixes

1. Active participles of the present tense are formed with the aid of suffixes:

Suffix	Participle
-ущ-, -ющ- (from verbs of the 1st conjugation)	пи́ш-ущ-ий, пита́-ющ-ий
-ащ-, -ящ- (from verbs of the 2d conjugation)	леж-а́щ-ий, ви́д-ящ-ий

2. Active participles of the past tense are formed with the aid of suffixes:

Suffix	Infinitive	Participle
-вш-	писа́ть	писа́-вш-ий
-ш-	нести́	нёс-ш-ий

3. Passive participles are formed with the aid of suffixes:

Suffix		Infinitive	Participle
-ем- (1st conjugation verbs) } present		чита́ть	чита́-ем-ый
-им- (2d conjugation verbs) } tense		люби́ть	люб-и́м-ый
-енн- } past		унести́	унес-ённ-ый
-нн- } tense		прочита́ть	прочи́та-нн-ый
-т- }		запере́ть	за́пер-т-ый

The Formation of Verbs

FORMING THE ASPECTS OF THE VERB

All the ways of forming verbal aspects that follow are shown in the *Handbook* in actual practice; the examples in the text show how to form verbs of various aspects from basic Russian roots.

General commentary

1. The majority of simple verbs, i.e., without prefixes, belong to the imperfective aspects; писать, читать, нести, спать are examples.

2. However, the verbs дать, лечь, сесть, стать, деть, and many verbs ending in "-ить," including, купить, бросить, кончить, простить, пустить, решить, belong to the perfective aspect.

3. Several simple verbs can have both perfective and imperfective aspects, depending on the context, for example, ра́нить, жени́ть.

Perfective	Imperfective
За́втра в сраже́нии ра́нят мно́гих.	Ка́ждый день на фро́нте ра́нят мно́гих.
Мы обяза́тельно же́ним сы́на.	Ско́ро бу́дем жени́ть сы́на.

4. Verbs with prefixes in most cases belong to the perfective aspect, for example, написать, прочитать, принести, уйти.

5. However, compound verbs which are formed from prefixes and indeterminate verbs of motion, for example, носить, водить, ходить, бегать, летать, are in most cases imperfective; examples include приносить, уносить, вносить, переносить, приводить, уводить, привозить, увозить, заходить, уходить, приходить, находить.

Verbs of the imperfective aspect

1. From almost every verb of the perfective aspect, a verb of the imperfective aspect with the same meaning may be formed. For example:

Perfective	Imperfective
дать	дава́ть
нача́ть	начина́ть
привезти́	привози́ть

2. A verb of the imperfective aspect may be formed from the corresponding verbs of the perfective aspect by means of suffixes. Most frequently used is the suffix "-ыва," "-ива-," in which the root "-о-" in the perfective aspect often changes to "-а-" in the imperfective aspect, for example:

Perfective	Imperfective
списа́ть	спи́сывать
прочита́ть	прочи́тывать
заказа́ть	зака́зывать
опозда́ть	опа́здывать
вы́толкнуть	выта́лкивать
сбро́сить	сбра́сывать

3. Another way of forming verbs of the imperfective aspect is to change the suffix "-и-" (perfective) into "-я-" (imperfective) or "-а-" after sibilants, for example:

Perfective	Imperfective
реш-и́-ть	реш-а́-ть
ко́нч-и-ть	конч-а́-ть
окруж-и́-ть	окруж-а́-ть
употреб-и́-ть	употребл-я́-ть
бро́с-и-ть	брос-а́-ть

4. A fourth way of forming the imperfective aspect is to use the suffix "-a-," in which case the root "-e-" or "-я-" ("a-" after sibilants) may alternate with "-и-," for example:

Perfective	Imperfective
растере́ть	растира́ть
умере́ть	умира́ть
запере́ть	запира́ть
вы́честь	вычита́ть
нача́ть	начина́ть

5. A fifth way of forming verbs of the imperfective aspect is to take the suffix "-ва-" and use it in those cases where the *root* ends in a vowel, for example:

Perfective	Imperfective
разби́ть	разби-ва́-ть
слить	сли-ва́-ть
дать	да-ва́-ть
разда́ть	разда-ва́-ть
узна́ть	узна-ва́-ть
созна́ть	созна-ва́-ть
согре́ть	согре-ва́-ть

6. Sometimes, in rare cases, a completely different verb serves as the imperfective aspect for verbs of a perfective aspect, for example:

Perfective	Imperfective
взять	брать
положи́ть	класть
пойма́ть	лови́ть
сказа́ть	говори́ть

7. Several verbs have an imperfective aspect which is distinguished from a perfective aspect only by the change of stress, for example:

Perfective	Imperfective
посы́пать	посыпа́ть
рассы́пать	рассыпа́ть
разре́зать	разреза́ть
обре́зать	обреза́ть

Semelfactive and frequentative verbs

1. With the help of the suffix "-ну-," the perfective aspect of semelfactive or momentous verbs is formed from the imperfective aspect, for example:

Imperfective	Perfective Semelfactive
пры́гать	пры́г-ну-ть
крича́ть	кри́к-ну-ть
свисте́ть	сви́ст-ну-ть
кида́ть	ки́-ну-ть
плева́ть	плю́-ну-ть
клева́ть	клю́-ну-ть

2. With the aid of the suffix "-ыва-," "-ива-," the frequentative or iterative verbs are formed. They express action and may be formed from several verbs, for example:

Imperfective	Frequentative
ходи́ть	ха́ж-ива-ть
заходи́ть	заха́ж-ива-ть
сиде́ть	си́ж-ива-ть
чита́ть	чи́т-ыва-ть
носи́ть	на́ш-ива-ть
писа́ть	попи́с-ыва-ть
говори́ть	гова́р-ива-ть
	погова́р-ива-ть [1]

VERBS OF MOTION: DETERMINATE AND INDETERMINATE VERBS WITH DIFFERENT STEMS

Determinate	Indeterminate
бежа́ть	бе́гать
вести́	води́ть
везти́	вози́ть
е́хать	е́здить
лете́ть	лета́ть
нести́	носи́ть
плыть	пла́вать
ползти́	по́лзать

All these verbs of motion belong to the imperfective aspect, but their meaning depends on whether they are determinate or indeterminate. Determinate verbs signify action or movement in one direction, done only once in a determinate or definite period, for example: Куда вы идёте? Я иду в библиотеку. Завтра мне надо ехать в Москву. Сейчас мне надо бежать на почту. Indeterminate verbs signify actions and movements which either usually take place, for example, птицы летают, рыбы плавают, люди ходят, or an action or movement which is repeated and takes place at different times or in different directions, for example; Ученики ходят в школу каждый день. Дети бегают по саду.

Alternations of Letters in Word Formation

The term "alternation" signifies the tendency of certain consonants and vowels to change into another particular letter in accordance with a very definite pattern peculiar to that letter. This phenomenon can take place in the root and in the suffix. This phonetic characteristic was inherited from the protoslavic period and is preserved to a great extent in modern Russian. Following a historical phonetic law, the alternations in consonants take place when certain consonants are united with soft vowels or with the original *jod* (*j*), which in writing may be expressed by the soft sign; sometimes it is not written at all, as in the suffixes к, н, б, (originally ьк, ьн,

---

[1] The prefix "по-" reinforces the character of iterativeness in the verb.

ьб). It is important to know that until the fourteenth century all sibilants were considered as soft consonants; that is why the alternations are preserved in sibilants even when they precede hard vowels.

There are some special alternations, such as д becoming жд (instead of ж) and т becoming щ, which have been preserved in words of specifically Church Slavonic origin; for example, from the verb водить we have two forms for the nouns: one purely Russian, вожатый, and the other, Church Slavonic, вождь.

ALTERNATIONS OF CONSONANTS

Gutturals with sibilants

1. Before soft vowels and the soft reduced vowel "ь":

Gutturals	Sibilants	Hissing Sibilants	Examples
г	ж	з	друг, дрýжеский, друзья́
к	ч	ц	лик, ли́чико, лицевóй
х	ш		у́хо, у́ши; пух, пуши́нка
х		с	тряхнýть, трясéние, тряси́на

2. Before the а, о, у, which were originally ja, jo, ju:

Gutturals	Sibilants	Hissing Sibilants	Examples
г	ж		друг, дружóк; сапóг, сапожóк; луг, лужóк
к	ч	ц	грек, гречáнка, рука, ручóнка; клик, кли́чý, восклицáние
х	ш		дух, душá; у́хо, ушáстый; пахáть, пашý

3. In front of the suffixes н, к, б, which were originally ьн, ьк, ьб:

Gutturals	Sibilants	Hissing Sibilants	Examples
г	ж		друг, дрýжный
к	ч	ц	рыбáк, рыбáчка, рыбáцкий
х	ш		пáхарь, пáшня, вспáшка; вóздух, воздýшный, дыхáние, оды́шка
х		с	встряхнýть, встря́ска

Dentals with sibilants in words of Church Slavonic:

Dentals	Russian Alternation	Church Slavonic Alternation	Examples
д	ж	жд	ход, хожý, хождéние; суд, сужý, суждéние
т	ч	щ	свет, свечá, освещéние, свечнóй

Hissing sibilants with sibilants:

Hissing Sibilants	Sibilants	Examples
с	ш	высокó, вы́ше, вышинá; проси́ть, прошéние
з	ж	францýз, францýженка; морóз морóженое
ц	ч	отéц, отéческий, отчи́зна

Consonant groups

Alternations			Examples
ск	ст	щ	блеск, блестя́щий, бле́щет
зг	зж		визг, визжа́ние; бры́згать, бры́зжет
зд	зж		проéзд, проéзжий

Labials

1. The labials б, в, м, п, ф alternate with the labial plus the letter л before soft vowels:

Alternations		Examples
б	бл	любóвь, люблю́, влюблённый; гребу́, грéбля
в	вл	лов, лóвля, ловлю́, налóвлено
м	мл	корм, кормлéние, кормлю́
п	пл	покýпка, кýпля, куплю́, кýпленный
ф	фл	графá, графлю́, графлéние

ALTERNATIONS OF VOWELS

Verb stems

Alternating Vowels			Examples
о	á		Only in verbs with suffixes -ива-, -ыва-, and their derivatives: устрóить, устрáивать; уговорúть, уговáривать; сбрóсить, сбрáсывать
е	а		лезть, лáзить
е	ё	я	лечь, лёг, ля́гу
и	е		брить, брéю
и	е	я	сидéть, сесть, ся́ду

Alternating vowels which sometimes drop out are called mobile or fleeting vowels.

Noun stems

Alternating Vowels		Examples
о	—	сон, сна; ложь, лжи, лживый
е	—	отéц, отцá; день, дня

Verb and noun stems

Alternating Vowels				Examples
е и о а —				умерéть умирáть, мор, вымарывать, умру́
е и о —				заперéть, запирáть, запóр, запру́
и ь ей ой				бить, бью, бей, бой
и ь е ов —				шить, шью, шей, шов, шва
ы о у				вздыхáть, вздох, воздух; засыхáть, сóхнуть, сухóй
ы о ов				крыть, крой, кров; рыть, рой, ров
ы ов ав				плыть, пловéц, плáвать
у ов				кузнéц, ковáть
ю ев				клюв, клевáть

After prefixes ending in a hard consonant, и alternates with ы:

и	ы	игрáть, разыгрáть, сыгрáть; отыгрáться, обыгрáть; искáть, обыскáть, подыскáть, отыскáть, разыскáть, рóзыск; именнóй, безымённый

ALTERNATIONS IN THE CONJUGATIONS OF VERBS

The formation of various verbal forms follows definite patterns of alternations. The following categories cover most verbal alternations which will be encountered in Russian.

First conjugation (3d person plural ending in -ут, -ют)

1. In verbs with the suffix "-a-" which lose this suffix in the stem of the present imperfective and the future perfective, the following alternations take place in all persons:

Alternations	Examples
с — ш	пис-а́-ть, пиш-у́, пи́ш-ешь, пи́шет, пи́ш-ут; чес-а-ть, чеш-у, чеш-ешь, чеш-ут
з — ж	сказ-а́-ть, скаж-у́, ска́ж-ешь, ска́ж-ут; ре́з-а-ть, ре́ж-у, ре́ж-ешь, ре́ж-ут; вяз-а́-ть, вяж-у́, вя́ж-ешь, вя́ж-ут
т — ч	мет-а́-ть, меч-у́, ме́ч-ешь, ме́ч-ут
т — щ	ропт-а́-ть, ро́пщ-у, ро́пщ-ешь, ро́пщ-ут; клевет-а́-ть, клевещ-у́, клеве́щ-ешь, клеве́щ-ут
к — ч	скак-а́-ть, скач-у́, ска́ч-ешь, ска́ч-ут; пла́к-а-ть, пла́ч-у, пла́ч-ешь, пла́ч-ут
х — ш	пах-а́-ть, па́ш-у́, па́ш-ешь, па́ш-ут
д — ж	глод-а́-ть, гло́ж-у, гло́ж-ешь, гло́ж-ут
г — ж	бры́зг-а-ть, бры́зж-у, бры́зж-ешь, бры́зж-ут
ск — щ	пле́ск-а-ть, плещ-у́, пле́щ-ешь, плещ-ут; полоск-а́-ть, полощ-у́, поло́щ-ешь, поло́щ-ут
ст — щ	хлест-а́-ть, хлещ-у́, хле́щ-ешь, хле́щ-ут; свист-а́-ть, свищ-у́, сви́щ-ешь, сви́щ-ут

2. After the labials б, м, п, the letter л is added:

Alternations	Examples
б — б + л	колеб-а́-ть, коле́б-л-ю, коле́б-л-ешь, коле́б-л-ют
п — п + л	сы́п-а-ть, сы́п-л-ю, сы́п-л-ешь, сы́п-л-ют
м — м + л	дрем-а́-ть, дрем-л-ю́, дре́м-л-ешь, дре́м-л-ют

3. In monosyllabic verbs there are no systematic alternations, for example, лг-а-ть, лг-у, лж-ёшь, лж-ёт, лж-ём, лж-ёте, лгут (no alternation in 1st person singular and 3d person plural). As an exception there is no alternation in the verb тк-а-ть, тк-у, тк-ёшь, тк-ут.

4. In verbs of the 1st conjugation with the infinitive ending in -сти, -сть, the following alternations take place in all persons of the present imperfective and the future perfective:

Alternations	Examples
ст(и) — д	брест-и́, бред-у́, бред-ёшь, бред-у́т; вест-и́, вед-у́, вед-ёшь, вед-у́т
ст(и) — т	мест-и́, мет-у́, мет-ёшь, мет-у́т; цвест-и́, цвет-у́; плест-и́, плет-у́, плет-ёшь, плет-у́т
ст(и) — б	грест-и́, греб-у́, греб-ёшь, греб-у́т; скрест-и́, скреб-у́, скреб-ёшь, скреб-у́т
ст(ь) — д	клас-ть, клад-у́, клад-ёшь, клад-у́т; крас-ть, крад-у́, крад-ёшь, кра́д-ут; пряс-ть, пряд-у́, пряд-ёшь, пряд-у́т; (у)пас-ть, (у)пад-у́, (у)пад-ёшь, (у)пад-у́т

5. In the verbs of the 1st conjugation with infinitives ending in -чь, the following alternations take place:

Alternations	Examples
ч — к — ч — к	печ-ь, пек-у́, печ-ёшь, печ-ёт, печ-ём, печ-ёте, пек-у́т; теч-ь, тек-у́, теч-ёшь, теч-ёт, теч-ём, теч-ёте, тек-у́т
ч — г — ж — г	бере́ч-ь, берег-у́, береж-ёшь, береж-ёт. береж-ём, береж-ёте, берег-у́т; стере́ч-ь, стерег-у́, стереж-ёшь, стереж-ёт, стереж-ём, стереж-ёте, стерег-у́т; стрич-ь, стриг-у́, стриж-ёшь, стриг-у́т; жеч-ь, жг-у, жж-ёшь, жг-ут; моч-ь, мог-у́, мо́ж-ешь, мо́г-ут

In this group of verbs, in the 1st person singular, and the 3d person plural, the -у- cannot follow a sibilant.

Second conjugation (3d person plural ending in -ат, -ят)

1. In the 2d conjugation, the same alternations from dentals to sibilants take place as in the 1st conjugation, but only in the 1st person singular of the present imperfective and future perfective: ходи́ть, хож-у́, хо́д-ишь, хо́д-ят.

2. An -л- is added to the labials only in the 1st person singular: люб-л-ю́, лю́б-ишь, лю́б-ят; лов-и́ть, лов-л-ю́, ло́в-ишь, ло́в-ят; лом-и́ть, лом-л-ю́, ло́м-ишь, ло́м-ят; граф-и́ть, граф-л-ю́, граф-и́шь, граф-я́т.

Alternations	Examples
д — ж	сид-е́ть, сиж-у́, сид-и́шь, сид-я́т; ви́д-еть, виж-у, ви́д-ят
з — ж	воз-и́ть, вож-у́, во́з-ишь, во́з-ят
с — ш	прос-и́ть, прош-у́, про́с-ишь, про́с-ят
т — ч	верт-е́ть, верч-у́, ве́рт-ишь, ве́рт-ят
ст — щ	блест-е́ть, блещ-у́, блест-и́шь, блест-я́т; льст-ить, льщ-у, льст-ишь, льст-ят
б — б + л	люб-и́ть, люб-л-ю́, лю́б-ишь, лю́б-ят
в — в + л	лов-и́ть, лов-л-ю́, ло́в-ишь, ло́в-ят
м — м + л	корм-и́ть, корм-л-ю́, ко́рм-ишь, ко́рм-ят
п — п + л	сп-а-ть, сп-л-ю, сп-ишь, сп-ят; терп-е́ть, терп-л-ю, те́рп-ишь, те́рп-ят
ф — ф + л	граф-и́ть, граф-л-ю́, граф-и́шь, граф-я́т

3. The following alternations occur in verbs of the 2d conjugation in the formation of aspects: д — жд, д — ж, т — щ, т — ч, ст — щ.

4. The alternation д-жд (inherited from the Church Slavonic) has been preserved in some verbs which have the suffix -и- in the perfective and -а- in the imperfective:

Perfective	Imperfective
о-суд-и́-ть	о-сужд-а́-ть
по-бед-и́-ть	по-бежд-а́-ть
на-град-и́-ть	на-гражд-а́-ть
у-бед-и́-ть	у-бежд-а́-ть

It has also been preserved in the participles осуждённый, побеждённый, награждённый, убеждённый.

5. The alternation д — ж is characteristic of original Russian verbs:

Perfective	Imperfective
провод-и́-ть	провож-а́-ть
ссуд-и́-ть	ссуж-а́-ть
разря́д-и́-ть	разряж-а́-ть

5. The alternation т — щ, like д — жд, was also inherited from the Church Slavonic:

Perfective	Imperfective
преврат-и́-ть	превращ-а́-ть
освят-и́-ть	освящ-а́-ть
просвет-и́-ть	просвещ-а́-ть
смут-и́-ть	смущ-а́-ть

7. The alternation с — ш occurs especially in verbs borrowed from the Church Slavonic:

Perfective	Imperfective
воскрес-и́-ть	воскреш-а́-ть
искус-и́-ть	искуш-а́-ть
укра́с-и-ть	украш-а́-ть

8. The alternation т — ч is of Russian origin:

Perfective	Imperfective
заме́т-и-ть	замеч-а́-ть
отве́т-и-ть	отвеч-а́-ть
наме́т-и-ть	намеч-а́-ть

9. The alternation ст — щ:

Perfective	Imperfective
извест-и́-ть	извещ-а́-ть
прост-и́-ть	прощ-а́-ть
очи́ст-и-ть	очищ-а́-ть

10. The alternation з — ж:

Perfective	Imperfective
вы́груз-и-ть	выгруж-а́-ть
вы́раз-и-ть	выраж-а́-ть

11. The alternation ст — ск:

Perfective	Imperfective
пуст-и́-ть	пуск-а́-ть

THE MAIN PREFIXES

Prefixes derived from prepositions

без- (бес- before voiceless consonants), without, less; dis-, ir-, un-
без-ру́кий, armless
бес-поко́ить, disturb

в-, во- (въ- before soft vowels), in, into
в-ход, entrance
во-шёл, he came in, into
въ-е́хать, to drive in

до-, until, to the end, pre-

до-чита́ть (кни́гу), to read (a book) to the end
до-истори́ческий, prehistoric
до-жда́ться, to wait until

за-, beyond, behind, for, for a short period; (can express inception of action); (with *v.r.*) to be lost in, to forget oneself in doing something

за-ходи́ть, to drop in, look in on
за-гро́бный, beyond the grave
за-че́м? what for?
за-пла́кать, to start weeping
за-чита́ться, to be lost in reading

из-, изо- (ис- before voiceless consonant; изъ- before a soft vowel, из-ы when и follows in root); from, out of

из-бра́ть, to elect
изо-дра́ть, to tear to shreds
ис-ключи́ть, to expel
изъ-ясня́ть, to explain
изъ-ы́сканный, exquisite; farfetched

между-, inter- (never used with verb)
на-, on, upon
над-, over, super-

между-наро́дный, international
на-кле́ить, to glue on
над-стро́ить, to build upon, to erect a superstructure

о-, об-, обо- (объ- before a soft vowel), about, round, over

о-смотре́ть, to look over, examine
об-ду́мать, to think over
обо-йти́, to go around, to circumvent
объ-ясни́ть, to explain

от-, ото- (отъ before a sof vowel; от-ы when и follows in root); away from

от-ходи́ть, to withdraw
отъ-е́хать, to drive away from
от-ыска́ть, to find by dint of searching

по- (mostly used to make verb perfective); for a bit, in the style of

по-е́хать, to go (by vehicle)
по-говори́ть, to have a chat, to talk for a short while
по-ру́сски, in Russian

под-, подо- (подъ- before a soft vowel), under

под-зе́мный, underground
подо-бра́ть, to pick up
подъ-езжа́ть, to drive up to

пред-, перед- (предъ- before a soft vowel), before, fore-, pre-; пред-ы when и follows in root)

пред-сказа́ть, to foretell
предъ-явля́ть, to present a document, a claim
пред-ыду́щий, preceding

при- (with verbs expresses nearness, motion towards, application of one thing close to another)
про-, through, past

при-ши́ть, to sew to
при-е́хать, to arrive at

про-е́хать, to drive through
про-лете́ть, to fly past

с-, со- (съ- before a soft vowel), with, down, off, or to make the verb perfective; с-ы when и follows in root)

с-шить, to sew together
со-йти́ с крыльца́, to come off the porch
с-де́лать, to make, do
съ-езд, convention
с-ыгра́ть, to play

у- (to make the verb perfective), away

у-е́хать, to depart, to go away
у-ви́деть, to see suddenly, catch sight of

чрез-, excessive, extra (never used with verb)

чрез-выча́йный, extraordinary

Inseparable prefixes

воз-, вос-, вз-, вс-, взо- (взъ- when word begins with vowel), up

воз-буди́ть, to arouse (feelings)
вос-ста́ние, uprising, revolt
взо-рва́ть, to blow up

вы-, out (under stress if used with a perfective verb)

вы́-слать, *perf.*, to send out
вы-ража́ть, *imperf.*, to express

низ-, (нис-; (before voiceless consonant), down

низ-ве́ргнуть, to throw down
нис-посла́ть, to send from heaven

пере-, пре-, over, across, afresh; to excess, high degree

пере-вози́ть, to transport
пере-ступи́ть, to transgress
пере-соли́ть, to oversalt
пре-вос-ходи́ть, to excel
пре-кра́сный, splendid

раз- (разо-; рас- before voiceless consonant; разъ- before a soft vowel; becomes ро́з- when accented), dis-, un-, asunder

разо-рва́ть, to tear apart
раз-да́ть, to distribute
рас-пада́ться, to disintegrate
разъ-единя́ть, to disunite
раз-ыска́ть, to find
они́ ро́з-дали, they distributed

ABBREVIATIONS

acc., accusative case
act., active
adj., adjective
adj., part. act. past, adjectival active past
  participle
adj., part. act. pres., adjectival active
  present participle
adj., part. pass. past, adjectival passive
  past participle
adj., part. pass. pres., adjectival passive
  present participle
adj., pred., adjective predicate
adv., adverb
ad. express., adverbial expression
adv., part. perf., adverbial perf. participle
adv., part. imperf. adverbial imperf.
  participle
anat., anatomical, anatomy
astr., astronomical, astronomy
colloq., colloquial
comp., comparative
conj., conjugation
dat., dative case
derog., derogatory
det., determinate
dim., diminutive
eccl., ecclesiastical
fig., figurative
folk, folk expression
gen., genitive case
geom., geometrical, geometry
gram., grammar
hist., historical, history
imperf., imperfective
indet., indeterminate
inf., infinitive
instr., instrumental case
interj., interjection
intrans., intransitive
lit., literally
math., mathematical, mathematics

med., medical
mil., military
myth., mythological, mythology
n., noun
naut., nautical
n.f., noun feminine
n.m., noun masculine
n.n., noun neuter
num., numeral
num. card., cardinal numeral
num. ord., ordinal numeral
obs., obsolete
part., participle
pass., passive
perf., perfective
phon., phonetics
pl., plural
poet., poetic, poetical
prep., prepositional case
pre-Rev., prerevolutionary
pres., present
pron., pronoun
prov., proverb
rel., religion
sing., singular
smf., semelfactive
tech., technical
trans., transitive
v., verb
v.i., verb imperfective
v.i.iter., verb imperfective iterative
v.i.r., verb imperfective reflexive (or
  reciprocal)
v.p., verb perfective
v.p.r., verb perfective reflexive (or reciprocal)
v.p.r.smf., verb perfective reflexive semelfactive
v.p.smf., verb perfective semelfactive
v.r., verb reflexive (or reciprocal)
zool., zoological, zoology

THE RUSSIAN ALPHABET

А	а	К	к	Х	х
Б	б	Л	л	Ц	ц
В	в	М	м	Ч	ч
Г	г	Н	н	Ш	ш
Д	д	О	о	Щ	щ
Е	е	П	п	Ъ	ъ
Ё	ё	Р	р	Ы	ы
Ж	ж	С	с	Ь	ь
З	з	Т	т	Э	э
И	и	У	у	Ю	ю
Й	й	Ф	ф	Я	я

SELECTED REFERENCE WORKS

Akademiia nauk SSSR, Institut iazykoznaniia. Slovar' sovremennogo russkogo litera-turnogo iazyka. Moscow-Leningrad, Izdat. Akademii nauk SSSR, 1951.

Aleksandrov, A. Polnyi russko-angliiskii slovar'. Berlin, Verlag Ges. Glucksmann, 1923.

Dal', Vladimir. Poslovitsy russkogo naroda. 3d edition. St. Petersburg, M. O. Vol'f, 1914.

——, Tolkovyi slovar' zhivogo velikorusskogo iazyka. St. Petersburg, M. O. Vol'f, 1880.

Oxford English Dictionary. Oxford, Clarendon Press, 1933.

Patrick, George Z. Roots of the Russian Language. New York, Pitman, 1938.

Preobrazhenskii, A. G. Etymological Dictionary of the Russian Language. New York, Columbia, 1951.

Smirnitskii, A. I., et al. Russko-angliiskii slovar'. Moscow, Gosizdat., 1952.

Sreznevskii, Izmail Ivanovich. Materialy dlia slovaria drevne-russkogo iazyka po pismennym pamiatnikam. St. Petersburg, Izd. Imperatorskoi Akademii nauk, 1893-1906.

Ushakov, Dmitrii N., et al. Tolkovyi slovar' russkogo iazyka. Moscow, Gosizdat "Sovetskaia entsiklopediia," 1933-40.

Vasmer, Max. Russisches Etymologisches Wörterbuch. Heidelberg, Carl Winter, 1953.

A

AЗ-, THE LETTER A IN CHURCH SLAVONIC

аз, *n.*, (*obs.*), the letter A. Аз-ы́, *pl.*, rudiments, beginnings. Не знать ни аза́, (*saying*), not to know A from B. Нача́ть изуче́ние с азо́в, to begin the study of something from its rudiments. Аз, *pron.*, *from Ch.-Slav.*, I; Russian, я. "Аз есмь Госпо́дь Бог Твой" (*Bib.*), "I am the Lord thy God."

а́з-бук-а, *n.f.*, alphabet. Ру́сская а., the Russian alphabet. А. глухонемы́х, alphabet for deafmutes. А. Мо́рзе, Morse code (alphabet). Но́тная а., music notation. Аз-буч-ный, *adj.*, alphabetical. А. указа́тель, alphabetical index, guide. А-ая и́стина, a truism. В а́збучном поря́дке, in alphabetical order.

АЛ-, SCARLET, BRIGHT RED

а́л-ый, *adj.*, scarlet, bright red. Алые гу́бы (щёчки), red lips (cheeks). Алая ле́нта, a scarlet ribbon. Алая ро́за, a red rose.

ал-е́-ть, *v.i.*, **по-ал-е́ть**, *v.p.*, to redden, become bright red. Восто́к але́л, the East was glowing, aglow. Её щёки поале́ли, her cheeks turned scarlet. Ал-е́ть-ся, *v.i.r.*, за-ал-е́ть-ся, *v.p.r.*, to grow, become, bright red. Алость, *n.f.*, redness. Ал-е́ющий, *adj.*, *part. act. pres.*, reddening; *see* а́лый.

АЛК-, АЛЧ-, HUNGER, CRAVING; GREED

алк-а́-ть, **а́лч-у**, *v.i.*, вз-алк-а́ть, *v.p.*, + *gen.*, *obs.*, to crave, be hungry, hunger for; *fig.*, long for. Они́ а́лчут зна́ний, they long for knowledge. Алч-ность, *n.f.*, cupidity, greed, avidity. А. к де́ньгам, сла́ве, cupidity, desire for money, glory. Алч-ный, *adj.*, greedy, grasping, avid. А. челове́к, greedy man. Алчущий, *adj.*, *part. act. pres.*, hungry, famished. "Алчущие и жа́ждущие пра́вды" (*Bib.*), "they that hunger and thirst after righteousness."

АУ-, HALLOO, ECHO

ау́, *interj.*, ho! halloo! В лесу́ раздава́лись де́тские голоса́: ау, ау! chil-dren's voices rang through the wood: halloo! halloo! Уже́ ау́, брат: пре́жнего не воро́тишь, (*saying*), it's all gone, old man; you will not bring back the past.

ау́-к-а-ть, *v.i.*, ау́-к-нуть, *v.p.*, to halloo, shout, hail. Ау́-кать-ся, *v.i.r.*, Ау́-кнуть-ся, *v.p.r.*, to shout to each other. Как ау́кнется, так и откли́кнется (*prov.*), as you sow, so shall you reap. Я совсе́м бы́ло получи́л рабо́ту, да в после́дний моме́нт она́ мне ау́кнулась, (*colloq.*), I almost got the job, but at the last moment it fell through. Ау́-канье, *n.n.*, hallooing, shouting to each other. В лесу́ раздава́лось ау́канье, hallooing was heard in the wood.

АХ, ALAS! OH!

ах, *interj.*, *also used as n.*, oh! alas! ah! Ах, как хорошо́, oh, how wonderful! Ах, я забы́ла, oh, I have forgotten! Ах, ты, лентя́й, oh, you idler! lazybones! Пойду́т вся́кие а́хи да о́хи, people will begin to complain. Ах-ти́, *interj.* oh! ah! Не ахти́ како́й, (*colloq.*), not so very wonderful. Не ахти́, как бога́т, (*colloq.*), not so very rich.

а́х-а-ть, *v.i.*, а́х-нуть, *v.p.*, (*colloq.*), to groan, oh and ah, exclaim; + *acc.*, (*colloq.*), to hit somebody. Не успе́л а́х-нуть, (*colloq.*), before he could say Jack Robinson. Он его́, как а́хнет по голове́, suddenly he gave him a blow on the head.

по-а́х-а-ть, *v.p.*, *see* а́хать. Раз-а́х-ать-ся,, *v.p.r.*, to indulge in complaining. Ах-анье, *n.n.*, sighing, groaning, complaining. Ах-овый, *adj.*, (*colloq.*), no good whatever, shameless, impudent. А. па́рень, impudent young man. А-ая рабо́та, inferior work.

Б

БАБ-, WOMAN

ба́б-а, *n.f.*, woman, country woman; (*fig.*), milksop, sissy (of a man); (*tech.*), ram-block, pole driver, rammer. Дере́венская ба́ба, peasant, village woman. Он не мужчи́на, а настоя́щая ба́ба, he is not a man, he is a sissy. Б.-Яга́, (*folklore*), Baba-Yaga, a witch. Бой-б., (*colloq.*), quarrelsome woman. Ка́менная б., ancient rough-hewn stone statue. Ро́мовая б., rum cake. Сне́жная б., snow woman (*equiv. of* snow man). Ба́б-ка, *n.f.*, (*obs.*) grandmother. Пови-ва́льная б., midwife; pastern (of horse). Игра́ в ба́бки, game of knucklebones. Баб-ёнка, *n.f.*, (*colloq.*), young woman. Ба́б-очка, *n.f.*, butterfly. Ночна́я б., night butterfly, moth. Ба́б-ушка, *n.f.*, grandmother, old woman. Это ещё б. на́двое сказа́ла, (*colloq.*), we shall see! Ба́бушкины ска́зки, old wives' tales. Баб-ье, *n.n.*, (*colloq.*), women. Ба́б-ий, *adj.* (*colloq.*), woman's, femine. Со́рок лет — ба́бий век (*saying*), 40 years is the span of a woman's life. Ба́бье ца́рство, kingdom of women. Ба́бье ле́то, Indian summer.

баб-н-ич-а-ть, *v.i.,* (*obs., colloq.*), to work as a midwife.

БАВ-, AMUSEMENT; ADDITION; RIDDANCE

за-ба́в-а, *n.f.,* amusement, entertainment, sport, fun; pastime. Де́тская з. *fig.,* child's play. За-ба́в-ник, *n.m.,* За-ба́в-ница, *n.f.,* an amusing, entertaining person. За-ба́в-ный, *adj.,* amusing, entertaining, diverting, droll. З. слу́чай, a funny incident. Он ужа́сно з., he is so funny, he is simply priceless. За-ба́в-но, *adv.,* funnily, amusingly.

за-бав-л-я́-ть, *v.i.,* за-ба́в-ить, *v.p.,* + *acc.,* + *instr.,* to amuse, entertain. З. гостей шу́тками (анекдо́тами), to amuse guests with jokes (anecdotes). За-бав-л-я́ть-ся, *v.i.r.,* за-ба́в-ить-ся, *v.p.r.,* to amuse, entertain oneself, be amused.

по-за-ба́в-и-ть, *v.p.,* + *acc.,* to amuse for a while. П. ребёнка, to amuse a child. По-за-ба́в-ить-ся, *v.p.r.,* to amuse oneself, have some fun.

до-бав-л-я́-ть, *v.i.,* до-ба́в-ить, *v.p.,* + *gen.,* + *dat.,* to add, append, annex, throw in. Доба́вьте мне су́пу, give me some more soup. До-бав-л-я́ть-ся, *v.i.r.,* до-ба́в-ить-ся, *v.p.r.,* to be added. До-ба́в-ка, *n.f.,* до-бав-л-е́ние, *n.n.,* addition, supplement, appendix. Д. к газе́те, supplement to the newspaper. До-ба́в-очный, *adj.,* supplementary, additional, extra, surplus. Д. нало́г, surtax. Д-ая сто́имость, surplus value. В-до-ба́в-ок, *adv.,* besides, in addition, moreover, more than that.

из-бав-л-я́-ть, *v.i.,* из-ба́в-ить *v.p.,* + *acc.,* to free, deliver, save, rescue, spare; get rid of. И. от сме́рти, to save from death. Изба́вить от хлопо́т, to spare someone much trouble. Изба́ви

Бог! Heaven forbid! Из-ба́в-л-я́ть-ся, *v.i.r.,* из-ба́в-ить-ся, *v.p.r.,* от + *gen.,* to get rid of; escape. Из-ба́в-итель, *n.m.,* из-бав-и́тельница, *n.f.,* liberator, rescuer, redeemer. Из-ба-и́тельный, *adj.,* delivering, liberating. Из-бав-ле́ние, *n.n.,* deliverance, rescue, release, liberation.

на-бав-л-я́-ть, *v.i.,* на-ба́в-ить, *v.p.,* + *acc.,* to increase in price. Н. це́ну, to raise the price. На-бав-л-я́ть-ся, *v.i.r.,* to be increased in price.

над-бав-л-я́-ть, *v.i.,* над-ба́в-ить, *v.p.,* + *acc.,* (*colloq.*), to outbid; *see also* на-бавля́ть. Над-ба́в-ка, *n.f.,* increase; outbidding. Над-ба́в-очный, *adj.,* outbidding, overbidding.

от-бав-л-я́-ть, *v.i.,* от-ба́в-ить, *v.p.,* + *gen.,* to take out; decrease, diminish. О. муки́ из мешка́, to take some flour out of the bag. У него́ де́нег хоть отбавля́й (*colloq.*), he has so much money that if he lost some he would never miss it. От-ба́в-ка, *n.f.,* taking away. decrease, diminution.

под-бав-л-я́-ть, *v.i.,* под-ба́в-ить, *v.p.,* + *gen.,* to add a small amount. П. спи́рту в напи́ток, to fortify a liquor, beverage. Под-бав-л-я́ть-ся, *v.i.r.,* под-ба́в-ить-ся, *v.p.r.,* to be added.

при-бав-л-я́-ть, *v.i.,* при-ба́в-ить, *v.p.,* + *acc.,* + *gen.,* to add, augment, supply. П. жа́лование, to raise wages. П. ша́гу, to walk faster. При-бав-л-я́ть-ся, *v.i.r.,* при-ба́в-ить-ся, *v.p.r.,* to be added, increased. Дни прибавля́ются, the days are lengthening. При-ба́в-ка, *n.f.,* при-бав-л-е́ние, *n.n.,* addition, supplement, increase. Приба́вка жа́лования, increase, raise in wages. При-бавле́ние семе́йства, an increase in the family. При-ба́в-очный, *adj.,* additional. П. проду́кт, surplus product. П-ая сто́имость, surplus value.

раз-бав-л-я́-ть, *v.i.,* раз-ба́в-ить, *v.p.,* + *acc.,* + *instr.,* to dilute, mix. Р. вино́ водо́й, to water one's wine. Раз-бав-л-я́ть-ся, *v.i.r.,* раз-ба́в-ить-ся, *v.p.r.,* to be mixed, diluted. Раз-ба́в-л-енный, *adj., part. pass. past,* diluted, mixed, watered.

с-бав-л-я́-ть, *v.i.,* с-ба́в-ить, *v.p.,* + *acc.,* to reduce, abate, lower. С. вес трениро́вкой, to lose weight while training. С. жа́лование, to cut wages. С-ба́в-ка, *n.f.,* cut in price, reduction; *antonym of* приба́вка. С. цен, cut in prices.

у-бав-л-я́-ть, *v.i.,* у-ба́в-ить, *v.p.,* + *acc.,* to diminish, lessen, shorten, abate. У. длину́, to shorten the length. У-бав-л-я́ть-ся, *v.i.r.,* у-ба́в-ить-ся, *v.p.r.,* to be diminished, decreased. Луна́ убавля́ется, the moon is on the wane. У-ба́вка, *n.f.*, shortening, reduction, diminution. У-бав-л-éние, *n.n.*, diminishing, lessening, reducing. У. луны́, the waning of the moon.

про-бав-л-я́ть-ся, *v.i.r.*, + *instr.*, (*colloq.*), to subsist, get along, be satisfied with small amounts. П. ча́ем и хле́бом, to live on tea and bread.

БАЛ-, INDULGENCE, LENITY

бал-ова́-ть, бал-у́ю, *v.i.*, + *acc.*, из-бал-ова́ть, *v.p.*, to pet, spoil; (*colloq.*), to play, dally. Б. дете́й, to spoil children. Бал-ова́ть-ся, *v.i.r.*, по-бал-ова́ть-ся, *v.p.r.*, to be up to mischief, be naughty, indulge in having fun. Б. с огнём, to play with fire. Бал-овни́к, *n.m.*, бал-овни́ца, *n.f.*, naughty child; one who spoils children. Ба́л-овень, *n.m.*, pet, spoiled child. Б. судьбы́, minion of fortune. Бал-овство́, *n.n.*, overindulgence; mischievousness, naughtiness. Бал-о́ванный, из-бал-о́ванный, *adj.*, spoiled. И. ребёнок, spoiled child.

БАН-, BATHING

ба́н-я, *n.f.*, Russian bath, steam bath. Парова́я б., steam bath. Крова́вая б., blood bath, carnage. Кака́я у вас ба́ня, how terribly hot it is in your room. Пойти́ в ба́ню; мы́ться в ба́не, to take a steam bath. Ба́н-щик, *n.m.*, ба́н-щица, *n.f.*, bathhouse attendant. Ба́нный, *adj.*, bath-. Приста́л, как ба́нный лист, (*colloq.*), he is a nuisance, I cannot get rid of him. Ба́нное заведе́ние, baths (establishment). Пред-ба́н-ник, *n.m.*, dressing room in bathhouse.

ба́н-и-ть, *v.i.*, + *acc.*, (*colloq.*), to bathe, wash, steep in water.

БАР-, БОЯР-, NOBILITY, GENTILITY

ба́р-ин, *n.m.*, *obs.*, gentleman, nobleman, squire, landowner; sir (*in addressing*). Жить ба́рином, to live like a lord. Бар-чо́нок, бар-чу́к, ба́р-ич, *n.m.*, (*obs.*), young nobleman; nobleman's, squire's son. Ба́р-ыня, *n.f.*, lady, nobleman's wife; madam, my lady (*in addressing*). Ба́р-ышня, *n.f.*, girl, young lady, unmarried daughter of a squire. Ба́р-е, *pl.*, (*obs.*), noblemen, squires. Ба́р-ский, *adj.*, lord's, lordly, squire's. Жить на ба́рскую но́гу, to live like a lord. По-ба́рски, *adv.*, lordly, in grand style.

ба́р-ство, *n.n.*, rank of gentleman; gentility. Ба́р-ственный, *adj.*, lordly. Б. вид, lordly appearance.

ба́р-ств-ова-ть, *v.i.*, по-ба́р-ствовать,

v.p., to live in a lordly way for a short while. Ба́р-ствующий, *adj.*, *part. act. pres.*, living like a lord.

ба́р-щина, *n.f.*, (*hist.*), work done by a serf for the lord. Ба́р-щинный, *adj.*, of ба́рщина.

бо́яр-ин, *n.m.*, (*hist.*), boyar, old Russian nobleman. Правле́ние бо́яр, the rule of the Boyars. Боя́р-ыня, *n.f.*, (*hist.*), Russian noblewoman; (*in addressing*), ма́тушка-боя́рыня. Боя́р-ышня, *n.f.*, unmarried daughter of a boyar. Боя́р-е, *n. pl.*, see боя́рин. Боя́р-щина, *n.f.*, rule of boyars, work done for boyars. Боя́р-ский, *adj.*, noble's, boyar's. Боя́рский двор, homestead of a boyar. Боя́рская Ду́ма, (*hist.*), Council of Boyars. Боя́рское сосло́вие, the Boyar class.

БАРАБАН, DRUM

бараба́н, *n.m.*, drum; (*tech.*), reel. Бить в б., to beat the drum. Б. для за́писей, recording drum. Б. для нама́тывания про́волоки, coiling drum. Бараба́н-щик, *n.m.*, drummer. Бараба́н-ный, *adj.*, drum-. Б. бой, beating of the drums. Б-ая па́лочка, drumstick. Б-ая перепо́нка, eardrum.

бараба́н-и-ть, *v.i.*, за-бараба́н-ить, *v.p.*, to drum, beat a drum. Б. на роя́ле, to strum on the piano; bang the piano. Б. па́льцами, to drum on the table.

БАРАН-, БАРАШ-, RAM, SHEEP

бара́н, *n.m.*, ram, sheep. Бара́н-ина, *n.f.*, mutton. Молода́я б., lamb. Туше́ная б., stewed lamb. Бара́н-ка, *n.f.*, ring-shaped roll, Russian doughnut. Бара́н-ий, *adj.*, ram's, mutton-. Б. жир, mutton fat. Бара́нья котле́та, mutton chop. Согну́ть в бара́ний рог, (*colloq.*), to subjugate by ill-treating and oppressing.

бара́ш-ек, *n.m.*, (*dim.*), young ram, lamb. Бара́ш-ки, *n. pl.*, (*dim.*), young rams, lambs (*see* бара́шек); fleece; crests of foam on waves, whitecaps. Не́бо, покры́тое бара́шками, fleecy clouds. Зави́ться бара́шком, to curl like lamb's wool. Бара́ш-ковый, *adj.*, lambskin. Б-ая ша́пка (Б. воротни́к), astrakhan or lambskin cap (collar).

БАС(Н)-, FABLE, FAIRY TALE

ба́с-н-я, *n.f.*, fable, fairy tale; idle talk. Расска́зывать ба́сни, to invent stories, tell tall tales. Соловья́ ба́снями не ко́рмят, (*prov.*), a fine cage won't feed the bird. Ба́с-енка, по-бас-ёнка, *n.f.*, (*dim.*), *see* басня. Бас-енный, fabulous. Бас-н-о-писец, *n.m.*, writer of fables. Крылов — знаменитый баснописец, Krylov is a famous fabulist. Бас-н-о-словие, *n.n.*, invention of tall tales. Бас-н-о-словный, *adj.*, fabulous, legendary, incredible, beyond belief. Б-ые цены, fabulous prices. Бас-н-о-словно, *adv.*, fabulously.

БАТР-, FARM, LABOR

батр-ак, *n.m.* (*hist.*), farm hand, hired farm laborer; (*fig.*), mere hireling. батр-ачка, *n.f.*, workwoman, female farm laborer. Батр-ацкий, *adj.*, farm hand's, farm laborer's.

батр-ач-и-ть, *v.i.*, to work as a farm hand, do hack work. Батр-ачество, *n.n.*, status of farm laborer. Батр-аческий, *adj.*, *see* батрацкий.

БАЮ-, БАЙ, LULLING

баю, *interj.*, баю-бай, баю-шки-баю, bye! hush! Баю-шки-баю, баю-бай, lullaby, baby. Дети, пора бай-бай, children, it's time to go to bed.

баю-к-а-ть, *v.i.* + *acc.*, to rock to sleep with a lullaby. **Баю-кание**, *n.n.*, lulling to sleep.

у-баю-к-а-ть, *v.p.*, у-баю-кивать, *v.i.*, + *acc.*, + *instr.*, to lull, rock one to sleep. Убаюкивать несбыточными надеждами, to quiet with false hopes. У. пением (чтением), to sing, (read) to sleep. У-баю-кивание, *n.n.*, lulling, rocking. У-баю-канный, *adj.*, *part. pass. past*, lulled to sleep.

БД-, БУД-, БУЖ-, БУЖД-, VIGIL

бд-е-ть, *v.i.*, (*obs.*), to watch. Бд-ение, *n.n.*, vigilance, watchfulness. Всенощное бдение, all-night religious service. Бд-ительность, *n.f.*, vigilance, watchfulness. Усыпить чью-нибудь б., to make unaware of danger, lull someone's vigilance. Бд-ительный, *adj.*, vigilant, watchful, wakeful, alert. Б. надзор, close supervision. Бд-ительно, *adj.*, vigilantly, watchfully, with open eyes.

буд-й-ть, буж-у, *v.i.*, раз-буд-йть, *v.p.*, + *acc.*, to wake up, call, rouse from sleep. Рано утром меня разбудил звонок, the bell woke me up early in the morning. Буд-ильник, *n.m.*, alarm clock.

воз-буд-й-ть, *v.p.*, воз-бужд-а-ть, *v.i.*, to excite, stimulate, arouse, provoke. В. аппетит, to whet the appetite. В. вопрос, to raise a question. В. дело, to bring suit. В. гнев, to anger. В. жа-лость, to stir pity. Воз-буд-йть-ся, *v.p.r.*, воз-бужд-ать-ся, *v.i.r.*, to become excited. Воз-буд-имость, *n.f.*, excitability. Воз-буд-итель, *n.m.*, stimulant. Воз-бужд-ение, *n.n.*, excitement, stimulation. Воз-бужд-ающее средство, medical stimulant. Воз-бужд-ённый, *adj.*, *part. pass. past*, excited.

по-буд-й-ть, *v.p.*, по-бужд-ать, *v.i.*, + *acc.*, to incite, urge, instigate, stir, rouse. П. к занятиям, to urge to work. П. к. преступлению, to incite to crime. Что побудило его так поступить? what prompted him to act this way? Побужд-ать-ся, *v.i.r.*, to be prompted, incited. По-бужд-ение, *n.n.*, motive, incitement, spur, prompting, impulse. Следовать побуждению совести, to follow the dictates of one's conscience.

про-буд-й-ть, *v.p.*, про-бужд-ать, *v.i.*, + *acc.*, to wake up, awaken, arouse. П. охоту к изучению литературы, to arouse a desire to study literature. Про-буд-йть-ся, *v.p.r.*, про-бужд-ать-ся, *v.i.r.*, to become awakened. У него пробудилось желание, в нём пробудилось желание, a desire awoke in him. Про-бужд-ение, *n.n.*, waking up, awakening. Весеннее пробуждение природы, spring, awakening of nature.

до-буд-йть-ся, *v.p.r.*, to succeed in awakening. Вы так крепко спали, что еле вас добудился, you were sleeping so soundly that I hardly succeeded in waking you up.

буд-ни, *n.pl.*, workdays, weekdays, humdrum days. Буд-ничность, *n.f.*, drabness. Буд-ничный, *adj.*, everyday, drab. Б. день, workday. Б-ая жизнь, drab life, routine. Б-ое платье, everyday dress.

БЕГ-, БЕЖ-, FLIGHT

бег, *n.n.*, run, double (quick) time. Состязание в беге, foot race. Бег-а, *n.pl.*, races. Пускать лошадь на бега, to enter in a race. Быть в бегах, to be in hiding, be a fugitive. Бег-ом, *adv.*, running, on the run. Он прибежал б., he came running fast.

бег-а-ть, бег-аю, *v.i.*, *indet.*, от + *gen.*; за + *instr.*, to run, flee. Б. от кого-либо, to avoid someone. Б. за кем-либо, to run, dangle after. Б. взапуски, to chase each other. Часы бегут, the clock is fast. Бег-анье, *n.n.*, running, racing. Б. на коньках, skating. Бег-ающий, *adj.*, *part. act. pres.*, running. Б-ие глаза, restless eyes. Бег-лец, *n.m.*, fugitive, runaway, deserter. Б. из тюрьмы, prison breaker. Бег-лянка, *n.f.*, *see* беглец. Бег-лый, *n.m.*, *see* беглец. Бег-лый, *adj.*, fluent; superficial. Б. взгляд, glance, momentary look. Б. осмотр, cursory inspection. Б-ое чтение, fluent reading. Бег-ло, *adv.*, fluently. Бег-лость, *n.f.*, fluency. Бег-овой, *adj.*, racing. Беговой ипподром, race course. Б-ая лошадь, race horse. Бег-ство, *n.n.*, flight, hasty retreat, desertion. Позорное б., shameful flight. Б. войск, (*mil.*), rout. Обратиться в б., спасаться бегством, to take to flight, flee. Бег-отня, *n.f.*, scampering, bustle, running about. У меня много беготни, I've such a lot of running to do. Бег-ун, *n.m.*, runner; race horse, trotter.

беж-а́-ть, бег-у́, *v.i.*, *det.*, see бегать. Он бежал из тюрьмы, he escaped from prison. Б. рысью, to trot. Б. сломя голову, (*idiom*), to run at breakneck speed. Б. со всех ног, as fast as one can run. Время бежит, time flies. Беженец, *n.m.*, беж-енка, *n.f.*, refugee.

в-беж-а́-ть, *v.p.*, в-бег-а́ть, *v.i.*, в + *acc.*, to run in, rush into. В. в комнату, to rush into the room.

вз-беж-а́-ть, *v.p.*, вз-бег-а́ть, *v.i.*, на + *acc.*, to run up. В. на́ гору, to run up a hill.

вы́-беж-а-ть, *v.p.*, вы-бег-а́ть, *v.i.*, из + *gen.*, to run out. В. из комнаты, из дому, to run out of a room, house.

до-беж-а́-ть, *v.p.*, до-беж-а́ть, *v.i.*, до + *gen.*, to reach, run as far as. Он добежал до реки первым, he was the first to reach the river. До-бег-ать-ся, *v.p.r.*, до + *gen.*, to become exhausted from running. Д. до изнеможения, to run oneself out.

за-беж-а́-ть, *v.p.*, за-бег-ать, *v.i.*, к + *dat.*, to drop in. Забегать к кому-нибудь, to drop in on someone. Забегать вперёд, (*fig.*), to forestall.

за-бег-ать, *v.p.*, to begin to run.

из-беж-а́-ть, *v.p.*, из-бег-ать, *v.i.*, + *gen.*, из-бег-нуть, *v.p.*, *smf.*, to avoid, escape, elude, shrink from, evade, И. наказания, to evade, escape a penalty. Избегать общества, to avoid society. Из-беж-ание, *n.n.*, avoidance. Во и., in order to avoid.

на-беж-а́-ть, *v.p.*, на-беж-а́ть, *v.i.*, + *acc.*, to run against; fall upon; fold (*e.g.*, a dress). На-бег, *n.m.*, raid, foray, inroad, invasion. Произвести набег, to raid.

о-беж-а́-ть, *v.p.*, о-бег-ать, *v.i.*, + *acc.*, to run around. О-бег-ать, *v.p.*, see обежать. Он обегал и объездил весь город, he went all over the city walking and driving.

от-беж-а́-ть, *v.p.*, от-бег-ать, *v.i.*, от + *gen.*, to run off a few steps. Отбежать

от дороги, to run off a road. От-бегать, *v.p.*, + *acc.*, *only in expression*: отбегать пятки (ноги), (*colloq.*), to tire one's feet (by running).

пере-беж-а́-ть, *v.p.*, пере-бег-ать, *v.i.*, + *acc.*, to cross, run across. П. улицу, to run across the street. П. кому-либо дорогу, (*fig.*), to forestall someone. Пере-беж-ка, *n.f.*, (*mil.*), bound, rush; flight over to the enemy. Делать п-у, (*mil.*), advance by bounds from cover to cover. Пере-беж-чик, *n.m.*, turncoat, deserter.

по-беж-а́-ть, *v.p.*, в + *acc.*, to run, start running. Он побежал в аптеку, he ran to the drug store.

по-бег-а́-ть, *v.p.*, to run for a little while. Он побегал 10 минут, he ran for 10 minutes. По-бег, *n.m.*, escape, flight, desertion; (*bot.*), shoot, sprout, sprig. По-бег-ушки, *n.pl.*, running to and fro. Быть на побегушках, (*colloq.*), to run errands.

под-беж-а́-ть, *v.p.*, под-бег-ать, *v.i.*, к + *dat.*, to run up to.

при-беж-а́-ть, *v.p.*, при-бег-ать, *v.i.*, в + *acc.*; к + *dat.*, to come running to, into. Он прибежал в школу, he came running to school. При-бег-нуть, *v.p.*, *smf.*, при-бег-ать, *v.i.*, к + *dat.*, to resort to. П. к силе, to resort to force. При-беж-ище, *n.n.*, refuge. Находить в чём-либо п., to take, find refuge in something.

про-беж-а́-ть, *v.p.*, про-бег-ать, *v.i.*, + *acc.*, to run over, pass over, run through, look over. Пробежать книгу, to run through a book. Про-бег-ать, *v.p.*, to spend a certain time in running. Дети пробегали всё утро в саду, the children ran around the garden all morning. Про-бег, *n.m.*, run, distance covered, race.

с-беж-а́-ть, *v.p.*, с-бег-ать, *v.i.*, to run down, rush down, come running down; run away. У него краска сбежала с лица, he became pale. С-беж-ать-ся, *v.p.r.*, с-бег-а́ться, *v.i.r.*, to run, come running together; to shrink (*e.g.*, material); to flock, crowd, troop. С-бег-ать, *v.p.*, to run and come back. Сбегай за папиросами! run and get me some cigarettes.

у-беж-а́-ть, *v.p.*, у-бег-ать, *v.i.*, to run away, make away, make off. Он убежал из тюрьмы, he ran away from prison. У-бег-ать-ся, *v.i.r.*, to get tired out with running. Дети убегались за целый день и заснули, the children became tired from running all day and fell asleep. У-беж-ище, *n.n.*, refuge, retreat, shelter, asylum. Бомб-о-у-беж-ище, bomb shelter.

раз-бе́г, *n.m.*, run, start, momentum in running. С разбе́га, at a run.

раз-беж-а́-ть-ся, *v.p.r.*, to start running preparing for a jump; раз-бег-а́ть-ся, *v.i.r.*, to start running (e.g., in a running jump), gather momentum; disperse (running). Не́где разбежа́ться, there is no room for a running jump. У меня́ глаза́ разбежа́лись, I was dazzled.

БЕД- (БѢД-), БЕЖД- (БѢЖД-), БИД-, БИЖ-, POVERTY, MISERY, DISTRESS

бед-а́, *n.f.*, misfortune, distress, bad luck, misery, calamity. Б. не прихо́дит одна́ (*prov.*), it never rains but it pours. Не велика́ б.; что за б.; это ещё не б., there is no great harm in it. На беду́, unfortunately. Попа́сть в беду́, to get into trouble. Семь бед — оди́н отве́т (*prov.*), in for a penny, in for a pound.

бед-н-е́-ть, *v.i.*, о-бед-не́ть, *v.p.*, to become poor. Бе́дность, *n.f.*, poverty, destitution. Бе́дность не поро́к (*prov.*), poverty is no crime. Бед-нота́, *n.f.*, poverty, destitution; the poor. Бед-ня́к, *n.m.*, бед-ня́га, бед-ня́жка, *n.m. and f.*, poor fellow, poor soul, poor peasant. Бе́д-ный, *adj.*, poor, indigent, needy; miserable, unfortunate. Б. по за́мыслу содержа́ния, barren of ideas. Бед-ня́цкий, *adj.*, poor.

бед-о́вый, *adj.*, mischievous; dangerous, unmanageable. Б. ребёнок, naughty child.

бед-о-ку́рить, *v.i.*, на-бед-о-ку́рить, *v.p.*, to be up to mischief. Бед-о-ку́р, *n.m.*, one who is up to mischief, prankster.

бе́д-ств-овать, *v.i.*, to live in great poverty, be destitute. Бе́д-ствие, *n.n.*, calamity, disaster, misery, distress. Б. причинённое неурожа́ем, misery caused by a poor harvest. Стихи́йное б., a calamity due to an act of God, due to natural causes.

по-бе́д-а, *n.f.*, victory, triumph, conquest. Лёгкая п., an easy victory. Одержа́ть побе́ду, to win a victory.

по-бед-и́-ть, *v.p.*, по-бежд-а́ть, *v.i.*, + *acc.*, to conquer, defeat, vanquish, win a victory. П. число́м голосо́в, to outvote. П. врага́, to conquer an enemy. Побед-и́тель, *n.m.*, по-бед-и́тельница, *n.f.*, conqueror, victor, winner. Победи́телей не су́дят (*prov.*), a conquerer is always right. По-бе́д-ный, *adj.*, triumphant, victorious. По-бед-о-но́сец, *n.m.*, (*obs.*), conqueror. По-бед-о-но́сный, *adj.*, victorious, triumphant. П-ое во́йско, victorious army. По-бед-о-но́сно, *adv.*, victoriously, triumphantly. По-бежд-ённый, *adj.*, *part. pass. past*, conquered, defeated. Быть побеждённым,

to be defeated. Призна́ть себя́ побеждённым, to admit defeat.

у-бед-и́-ть, *v.p.*, у-бежд-а́ть, *v.i.*, + *acc.*, to convince, persuade. Дать у. себя́, to let oneself be convinced. У-бед-и́ть-ся, *v.p.r.*, у-бежд-а́ть-ся, *v.i.r.*, в + *prep.*, to be convinced; persuade oneself. Я убеди́лся в том, что я прав, I am convinced that I am right. У-бед-и́тельность, *n.f.*, persuasiveness. Отлича́ться большо́й убеди́тельностью, to be very convincing. У-бед-и́тельный, *adj.*, persuasive, convincing, earnest. У-ая про́сьба, earnest request. У-ое красноре́чие, persuasive eloquence. У-бед-и́тельно, *adv.*, persuasively, convincingly, earnestly. Говори́ть убеди́тельно, to speak convincingly. У-бежд-е́ние, *n.n.*, conviction. Не поддаю́щийся убежде́нию, unyielding. У-бежд-ённый, *adj.*, *part. pass. past*, convinced, positive. Сле́по у. в чём-либо, cocksure.

пере-у-бед-и́-ть, *v.p.*, пере-у-бежд-а́ть, *v.i.*, + *acc.*, to cause someone to change his mind.

пред-у-бед-и́-ть, *v.p.*, пред-у-бежд-а́ть, *v.i.*, to prejudice. Пред-у-бежд-е́ние, *n.n.*, prejudice. Пред-у-бежд-ённый, *adj.*, *part. pass. past*, prejudiced.

раз-у-бед-и́-ть, *v.p.*, раз-у-бежд-а́ть, *v.i.* + *acc.*, to dissuade, advise against.

о-би́д-а, *n.f.*, offense, insult, outrage, wrong. Кро́вная о., deadly insult. Не в оби́ду будь ска́зано, no offense meant. Он себя́ в оби́ду не даст, he is not slow to defend himself. О-би́д-ный, *adj.*, offensive, insulting. О-би́д-но, *adv.*, offensively, insultingly. О., что он не пришёл, what a pity he didn't come.

о-би́д-е-ть, *v.p.*, о-биж-а́ть, *v.i.*, + *acc.*, + *instr.*, to offend, insult, injure, wrong. Я оби́дел его́. I hurt his feelings. О-би́д-еть-ся, *v.p.r.*, о-биж-а́ть-ся, *v.i.r.*, на + *acc.*, to take offense, feel hurt, feel wronged, resent. Он обиде́лся на бра́та (на его́ слова́), he took offense at his brother (his words). О-би́д-чивость, *n.f.*, susceptibility, touchiness. О-би́д-чик, *n.m.*, о-би́д-чица, *n.f.*, an insulting person. О-би́д-чивый, *adj.*, susceptible to offense, touchy, easily offended. О-би́ж-енный, *adj.*, *part. pass. past*, offended, hurt, injured. О. приро́дой, ill-favored, physically handicapped.

БЕЛ- (БѢЛ-), WHITENESS

бе́л-ый, *adj.*, white. Б. гриб, a kind of fungus; mushroom. Б. лист бума́ги, a blank sheet of paper. Б. у́голь, white coal, water power. На бе́лом све́те, in the wide world. Бе́лые стихи́, blank verse. Бе́лая Гва́рдия, *n.f.*, белогвар-де́ец, *n.m.*, White Guard, anti-Bolshevik army; soldier of White Guard. Бел-енький, *adj., dim.*, white. Б. цвето́чек, little white flower. Бел-изна́, *n.f.*, whiteness. Б. ко́жи, whiteness of skin. Бел-есова́тость, *n.f.*, whitishness. Бел-есова́тый, *adj.*, whitish. Бел-ёсый, *adj.*, whitish. До-бел-а́, *adv.*, heated to incandescence, until something (*e.g.*, metal) is white hot, to a white heat. На́-бел-о, *adv.*, clean, fair. Переписа́ть н., to write out a fair copy. Бел-о-бры́сый, *adj.*, (*colloq.*), with very light eyelashes and eyebrows. Беловоло́сый, *adj.*, fair-haired. Белоку́рый, *adj.*, fair, blond. Белока́менный, white-stoned. Москва́ Белока́менная, Moscow built of white stone. Белору́чка, *n.f.*, kid glove; idler, lazy man or woman. Белосне́жный, *adj.*, snow-white. Бел-о́к, *n.m.*, the white. Бело́к яйца́, white of an egg. Белки́ глаз, the whites of the eyes. Бел-ко́вина, *n.f.*, albumen. Бел-ь-мо́, *n.n.*, cataract. Бе́л-ка, *n.f.*, (zool.), squirrel. Бе́л-ичий, *adj.*, of a squirrel. Б. мех, squirrel fur. Б-чья шу́бка, coat of squirrel fur. Бел-я́к, *n.m.*, (zool.), white hare. Бел-я́нка, *n.f.*, kind of mushroom; fair-faced woman.

бел-ь-ё, *n.n.*, linen; underclothing. Пос-те́льное б., bed linen. Столо́вое б., table linen. Бел-ь-ево́й, *adj.*, linen. Б. магази́н, linen store. Бел-ь-евщи́ца, бел-о-швейка, *n.f.*, seamstress, needlewoman. Белошве́йная мастерска́я, linen workshop, seamstress's establishment.

бел-е́-ть, *v.i.*, по-бел-е́ть, *v.p.*, to appear white, to become white; blanch, fade. "Беле́ет па́рус одино́кий" (Lermontov), "a lonely sail shimmers." У неё во́лосы побеле́ли, her hair became white. За-бел-е́ть, *v.p.*, to loom white suddenly. Бел-е́ть-ся, *v.i.r.*, за-бел-е́ть-ся, *v.p.r.*, to shimmer, appear white. Вдали́ забеле́лись сне́жные верши́ны, the snow-clad peaks shimmered in the distance. Про-бе́л, *n.m.*, gap, blank, omission; flaw, deficiency. П. в кни́ге, omission in a book. Восполня́ть про-бе́лы, meet the deficiency.

бел-и́-ть, *v.i.*, по-бел-и́ть, *v.p.*, + *acc.*, to whiten, bleach. Б. зда́ние (сте́ну), to whitewash a building (wall). Б. ткань, to bleach material. Бел-и́ть-ся, *v.i.r.*, на-бел-и́ть-ся, *v.p.r.*, to powder one's face. Бел-е́ние, *n.n.*, bleaching. Б. тка́-ней, bleaching of material. Бел-ёный, *adj.*, bleached. По-бе́л-ка, *n.f.*, white-

washing. П. стен, whitewashing of walls. Бел-и́ла, *n.pl.*, white (cosmetic). Б. для полиро́вки, Paris white. Б. свинцо́вые, white lead. Бел-и́льщик, *n.m.*, one who bleaches, bleacher, blancher, whitewasher. Бел-и́льня, *n.f.*, bleachery, bleach works. Бел-и́льный порошо́к, б-ая и́звесть, bleaching powder.

вы́-бел-и-ть, *v.p.*, see бели́ть.

за-бел-и́-ть, *v.p.*, за-бе́л-ивать, *v.i.*, + *acc.*, to whiten, whitewash. З. суп (чай) молоко́м, to put milk into soup (tea). З. потоло́к, to whitewash a ceiling.

под-бел-и́-ть, *v.p.*, под-бе́л-ивать, *v.i.*, + *acc.*, to whiten up, bleach slightly. Под-бе́л-ка, *n.f.*, whitening, bleaching.

у-бел-и́-ть, *v.p.*, у-бел-я́ть, *v.i.*, + *acc.*, (*poet.*), to whiten. "Убели́л твой ку́дри моро́з" (Nekrasov), "the frost has whitened your locks." Убелённый седина́ми, grey with age.

БЕРЕГ- БЕРЕЖ-, БРЕГ-, БРЕЖ-, SHORE, BANK

бе́рег, *n.m.*, shore, coast, bank. Б. мо́ря, seashore, coast. Отло́гий б. мо́ря, beach. Б. реки́, bank of a river. Берег-ово́й *adj.*, shore-. Б-а́я ли́ния, coastline. Б-а́я оборо́на, coast defense.

брег, *n.m.*, (*obs., poet.*), see бе́рег. Брега́ реки́, the banks of a river.

без-бре́ж-ность, *n.f.*, boundless space. Без-бре́ж-ный *adj.*, boundless, unlimited.

на́-береж-ная, *n.f.*, embankment, quay. На́-береж-ный, *adj.*, quay-. По-бере́жье, *n.n.*, shore, coast, coastal region. По-бере́ж-ный, *adj.*, along the shore. При-бре́ж-ье, *n.n.*, coast, coastal region. При-бре́ж-ный, *adj.*, near the shore, near the bank of a river. П-ая полоса́ (у мо́ря), seaboard, coast line. Прибре́жные во́ды, waters close to the shore.

БЕРЕЗ-, БЕРЕСТ, BIRCH

берёз-а, *n.f.*, birch tree. Плаку́чая б., weeping birch. Берёз-ка, *n.f., dim. of* берёза. Берез-ня́к, *n.m.*, birch grove. Берёз-овик, *n.m*, a brown edible mushroom growing at foot of birch trees. Берёз-овый, *adj.*, birchen, birch. Бе-рёзовая ро́ща, birch grove. Угости́ть берёзовой ка́шей, (*colloq.*), to thrash with birch switches. Под-берё́з-ник, *n.m.*, see берёзовик.

берёс-та, *n.f.*, birch bark. Берёст-овый, берест-яно́й, *adj.*, birchbark.

БЕРЕЧ-, БЕРЕГ-, БРЕЧ-, БРЕГ-, БЕРЕЖ-, БРЕЖ-, PRESERVATION, DEFENSE, PROTECTION

береч-ь, берег-у́, береж-ёт, *v.i.,* + *acc.,* to take care of, look after, respect, spare. Б. своё здоро́вье, to take care of one's health. Б. свои́ си́лы, to spare oneself. Копе́йка рубль бережёт (*prov.*), look after the pence and the pounds will take care of themselves. Бере́ч-ь-ся, *v.i.r.,* to guard against, beware, mind. Берег-и́сь, *v.i., imper.* + *gen.,* look out, take care, beware of; *see* бере́чься.

о-береч-ь, *v.p.,* о-берег-а́ть, *v.i.,* + *acc.,* to guard, defend, protect, preserve. О-бере́ч-ь-ся, *v.p.r.,* о-берег-а́ть-ся, *v.i.r.,* от + *gen.,* to look after, protect oneself from, defend.

при-береч-ь, *v.p.,* при-берег-а́ть, *v.i.,* + *acc.,* to reserve, preserve. При-берег-а́ть-ся, *v.i.r.,* to be preserved. П. запа́сы для зимы́, to reserve stocks for the winter.

с-береч-ь, *v.p.,* с-берег-а́ть, *v.i.,* + *acc.,* to save, lay up, reserve, conserve. С. на чёрный день, (*idiom*), to lay up for a rainy day. С-берег-а́тельный, *adj.,* saving. Сберега́тельная ка́сса, savings bank. С-бер-ка́сса, *n.f.* (*recent*), savings bank. С-береж-е́ния, savings. Скро́мные сбереже́ния, small savings.

у-береч-ь, *v.p.,* у-берег-а́ть, *v.i.,* + *acc.,* от + *gen.,* to preserve, guard, protect, keep safe. У. ребёнка от просту́ды, to guard a child from a chill. У-бере́ч-ь-ся, *v.p.r.,* у-берег-а́ть-ся, *v.i.r.,* от + *gen.,* to keep oneself safe, preserve, protect oneself.

пре-не-бре́ч-ь, *v.p.,* пре-не-брег-а́ть, *v.i.,* + *instr.,* to neglect, scorn, disregard, pay no regard to. П. ста́рым дру́гом, to scorn an old friend. П. сове́том, to scorn advice. Пре-не-бреж-е́ние, *n.n.,* neglect, disregard, scorn, disdain. П. до́лгом, neglect of duty. Говори́ть с пренебреже́нием, to disparage, slight, to talk with disdain, set at naught. Пре-не-бреж-и́тельный, *adj.,* disdainful, neglectful, slighting. П. тон, a disdainful tone. Пре-не-бреж-и́тельно, *adv.,* disdainfully.

береж-ли́вость, *n.f.,* thrift, economy, frugality. Береж-ли́вый, *adj.,* thrifty, parsimonious. Береж-ли́во, *adv.,* thriftily.

бе́реж-н-ость, *n.f.,* caution, heed, prudence. Бе́реж-ный, *adj.* cautious, careful. Бе́реж-но, *adv.,* cautiously. Береж-ёный, *adj.,* (*used as n.*), well protected. Бережёного Бог бережёт (*prov.*), the Lord takes care of him who takes care of himself.

не-бре́ж-н-ость, *n.f.,* carelessness, negligence. Не-бре́ж-ный, *adj.,* negligent, neglectful, careless, slipshod. Небре́жная рабо́та, careless, slipshod work. Не-бре́ж-но, *adv.,* negligently, carelessly.

БЕС- (БѢС-), БЕШ- (БѢШ-), DEMON, DEVIL

бес, *n.m.,* demon, devil. Рассыпа́ться ме́лким бе́сом, (*idiom*), to wheedle, cajole, flatter. Бес-ёнок, *n.m.,* little devil, imp; *pl.,* бес-еня́та.

бес-и́-ть, беш-у́, *v.i.,* + *acc.,* to enrage, vex, provoke, madden. Он бе́сит меня́, he drives me mad. Бес-и́ть-ся, *v.i.r.,* to fly into a passion, rave, rage. Бес-нова́ть-ся, *v.i.r.,* to be possessed, fume, rage. Сумасше́дший бесновался це́лый день, the madman raged all day long. Бес-нова́ние, *n.n.,* rage, raving, frenzy. Бес-нова́тый, *adj. used as n.,* demoniac, possessed. Бес-о́вский, *adj.,* devilish, diabolical, fiendish. Бес-о́вщина, *n.f.,* (*colloq.*), devilry.

беш-ен-ство, *n.n.,* rage, madness, fury; hydrophobia. Бе́ш-еный, *adj.,* angry, furious, raging. Б-ая ско́рость, mad speed. Б-ая соба́ка, mad dog. Б. ве́тер, raging wind. Плати́ть б-ую це́ну, to pay an exorbitant price. Бе́ш-ено, *adv.,* madly, furiously. Б. мча́ться, to rush madly.

вз-бес-и́-ть, *v.p.,* + *acc.,* to enrage. Вз-бес-и́ть-ся, *v.p.r.,* to become enraged. Соба́ка взбеси́лась, the dog became rabid. Вз-беш-ённый, *adj., part. pass. past,* furious, in a rage.

пере-бес-и́ть-ся, *v.p.r.,* (*used only in pl.*), to have hydrophobia; (*fig.*), to have sown one's wild oats. Все соба́ки перебеси́лись, all the dogs have run mad.

по-бес-и́ть-ся, *v.p.r.,* to be angry, have a fit of anger. Де́ти побеси́лись и успоко́ились, the children raised pandemonium for a while and then quieted down.

БЕСЕД-, CONVERSATION

бесе́д-а, *n.f.,* conversation, talk, discussion. Провести́ бесе́ду, to lead a discussion. Бесе́д-ка, *n.f.,* bower, arbor, summer house.

бесе́д-ова-ть, бесе́д-ую, *v.i.,* по-бесе́д-овать, *v.p.,* о + *prep.,* с + *instr.,* to converse, talk together; preach. Б. с дру́гом, to talk with a friend. Бесе́д-ование, *n.n.,* conversation; preaching.

со-бесе́д-ова-ть, *v.i.,* (*obs.*), to converse with. Со-бесе́д-ование, *n.n.,* conversation, talk. Со-бесе́д-ник, *n.m.,* со-бесе́д-ница, *n.f.*, conversationalist, talker. Он интере́сный собесе́дник, he is an interesting talker.

БИ-, БЬ-, БОЙ-, БО-, COMBAT, BATTLE; BEAT

би-ть, бь-ю, *v.i.*, + *acc.*, + *instr.*, to beat, flog, thrash. Бить посу́ду, to smash china. Б. трево́гу, to sound an alarm. Б. баклу́ши, to dawdle, to idle. Б. хвосто́м, to lash the tail. Б. струёй, to spout. Би́-ть-ся, *v.i.r.* + *instr.*, to fight. Б. голово́й об сте́ну, to knock one's head against the wall. Б. из-за куска́ хле́ба, to struggle for one's living. Б. над чем-ли́бо, to take much trouble about something. Б. над реше́нием зада́чи, to struggle with a problem. Б. об закла́д, to bet, wager. Би-е́ние, *n.n.*, beat, pulse, throb, palpitation (of the heart). Би-тьё, *n.n.*, beating, flogging. Б. посу́ды, smashing of china. Би́-тый, *adj.*, *part. pass. past*, beaten, cracked. Би́тые стёкла, smashed glass. Я вас жду би́тый час, (*colloq.*), I've been waiting for you a full hour. Би́тые сли́вки, whipped cream. Би́-тва, *n.f.*, battle, fight, combat. Би-то́к, *n.m.*, chopped meat patty. Битко́м наби́тый, crowded. Трамва́й, битко́м наби́тый, a crowded streetcar.

в-би-ть, *v.p.*, в-би-ва́ть, *v.i.*, + *acc.*, to hammer in, drive in. В. гво́зди, to hammer, drive nails. В-би́-тый, *adj.*, *part. pass. past*, driven in. Вбива́ть в зе́млю кол, to drive a stake fast in the ground.

вз-би-ть, *v.p.*, вз-би-ва́ть, *v.i.*, + *acc.*, to beat up; to whip (*e.g.*, cream), to fluff. Взбить во́лосы, to fluff up one's hair. Вз-би́-тый, *adj.*, *part. pass. past*, whipped up, fluffed up. Взби́тые сли́вки, whipped cream.

вы́-би-ть, *v.p.*, вы-би-ва́ть, *v.i.*, + *acc.*, to smash, break; из + *gen.*, to beat out, knock out. Вы́бить око́нное стекло́, to smash the window glass. Вы́бить из седла́, to throw from the saddle. Вы́-би-ть-ся, *v.p.r.*, вы-би-ва́ть-ся, *v.i.r.*, to be exhausted. Вы́биться из сил, to be exhausted. Вы́биться на доро́гу, (*fig.*), to elbow one's way.

до-би́-ть, *v.p.*, до-би-ва́ть, *v.i.*, + *acc.*, to dispatch, kill, finish. Доби́ть ра́неного (пле́нного), to kill a wounded man (prisoner). До-би́-ть-ся, *v.p.r.*, до-би-ва́ть-ся, *v.i.r.*, + *gen.*, to struggle for and succeed; struggle, strive for. Доби́ться своего́, to attain what one was struggling for. Добива́ться невозмо́жного, to strive after the impossible

за-би́-ть, *v.p.*, за-би-ва́ть, *v.i.*, + *acc.*, to hammer in, drive in. З. гво́зди в сте́ну,

to drive nails into a wall. З. го́лову уче́ньем, (*colloq.*), to stuff one's head with learning. Путь забит ваго́нами, the way is blocked with railway cars. За-би́-ть-ся, *v.p.r.*, за-би-ва́ть-ся, *v.i.r.*, в + *acc.*, to cringe. Заби́ться в у́гол, to hide, cringe, in a corner. Пульс наконе́ц заби́лся, the pulse began to beat at last. За-би́-вка, *n.f.*, driving in, down. Заби́вка свай, pile driving. За-би-я́ка, *n.m.*, squabbler, quarrelsome person. Забия́ка ле́зет пе́рвый в дра́ку, a squabbler starts the fight.

из-би́-ть, *v.p.*, из-би-ва́ть, *v.i.*, + *acc.*, to beat unmercifully; massacre. Избива́ть кого́-нибу́дь до поте́ри созна́ния, to beat someone into unconsciousness. Из-би-е́ние, *n.n.*, beating; massacre. Избие́ние младе́нцев (*Bib.*), Massacre of the Innocents. Из-би́-тый, *adj.*, *part. pass. past*, beaten; (*fig.*), hackneyed. Не говори́те изби́тыми фра́зами: это ску́чно, do not talk in hackneyed phrases; it's boring.

на-би́-ть, *v.p.*, на-би-ва́ть, *v.i.*, to fill, pack, stuff; print. Набить ва́той, + *instr.*, to wad; набить каблуки́, + *acc.*, to heel (a shoe). Набить це́ну, to raise the price. На-би́-ть-ся, *v.p.r.*, на-би-ва́ть-ся, *v.i.r.*, в + *acc.*, to crowd oneself in, to jam in. Наби́ться битко́м, (*emphatic*), to crowd. Пассажи́ры битко́м наби́лись в ваго́н, the passengers crowded into the railway car. Наби́ться на знако́мство, to force an acquaintance. На-би́-вка, *n.f.*, padding, stuffing. На-би-вно́й, *adj.*, printed. На-би́вно́й си́тец, printed cotton. На-би́-тый, *adj.*, *part. pass. past*, packed. Н. зо́лотом кошелёк, a purse full of gold. Н. дура́к, (*colloq.*), an utter fool.

пере-би́-ть, *v.p.*, пере-би-ва́ть, *v.i.*, + *acc.*, to beat to pieces; interrupt; cross someone's path; reupholster. Переби́ть неприя́теля, to annihilate the enemy. Переби́ть посу́ду, to smash all the dishes. Слу́шатель переби́л расска́зчика свои́ми вопро́сами, the listener interrupted the storyteller with his questions. Переби́ть кого́-ли́бо, to interrupt someone who is speaking. Пере-би́-ть-ся, *v.p.r.*, пере-би-ва́ть-ся, *v.i.r.*, to struggle, live from hand to mouth for a short while, tide oneself over. Перебива́ться с хле́ба на квас, (*idiom.*), to live from hand to mouth.

по-би́-ть, *v.p.*, по-би-ва́ть, *v.i.*, + *acc.*, + *instr.*, to massacre, beat, kill, defeat. П. кого́-ли́бо его́ же ору́жием, to beat someone with his own weapon. П. реко́рд, to beat a record. П. ко́зырем, to trump (cards). Все я́блоки в саду́ поби́ты моро́зом, all the apples in the garden have been spoiled by frost. По-бй-ть-ся, *v.p.r.*, to be beaten, damaged. Яйца побились в доро́ге, the eggs were broken on the way.

под-бй-ть, *v.p.,* под-би-ва́ть, *v.i.,* + *instr.,* + *acc.,* to line; incite. Подби́ть ме́хом, + *instr.,* to line with fur. Под-би́ть ору́дие, to damage a gun. Ло́дку подби́ло под мост, the boat was driven under the bridge. Под-бй-ть-ся, *v.p.r.,* под-би-ва́ть-ся, *v.i.r.,* to be lined with. Под-бй-вка, *n.f.,* lining. Шу́бка на бе́личьей подби́вке, a fur coat with squirrel lining.

при-бй-ть, *v.p.,* при-би-ва́ть, *v.i.,* + *acc.,* + *instr.,* to beat, thrash; fasten tight; drive to the shore. Приби́ть гвоздь, + *acc.,* to nail fast. Приби́ть гвоздя́ми доще́чку, + *instr.,* to nail a small board. Посе́вы приби́ло гра́дом, the hail has damaged the crops. При-бй-ть-ся, *v.p.r.,* при-би-ва́ть-ся, *v.i.r.,* + *instr.,* to be fastened, nailed; to be driven to shore. При-би-ва́ние, *n.n.,* fastening, nailing.

про-бй-ть, *v.p.,* про-би-ва́ть, *v.i.,* + *acc.,* to make a hole in, go through, pierce. Проби́ть доро́гу, to open a way. Про-би́ть лёд, to break the ice. Про-бй-ть-ся, *v.p.r.,* про-би-ва́ть-ся, *v.i.r.,* to force one's way. Трава́ начина́ет пробива́ть-ся, the grass is beginning to grow. Свет проби́лся сквозь гря́зные о́кна, the light was coming in through dirty panes.

раз-бй-ть, *v.p.,* раз-би-ва́ть, *v.i.,* + *acc.,* to break, smash; defeat. Р. вдре́безги, to smash to pieces. Раз-бй-ть-ся, *v.p.r.,* раз-би-ва́ть-ся, *v.i.r.,* to bruise oneself badly; be wrecked. Раз-бй-вка, *n.f.,* laying out, planning, arranging. В раз-би́вку, haphazardly, with no continuity. Спра́шивать слова́ в разби́вку, to ask words at random (during a lesson).

с-би-ть, *v.p.,* с-би-ва́ть, *v.i.,* + *acc.,* с + *gen.,* to knock down; beat together. С. ма́сло, to churn. С. самолёт, (*mil., aviation*), to down a plane. С. с ног, to send flying. С. спесь, (*colloq.*), to take down a peg or two. С-бй-ть-ся, *v.p.r.,* с-би-ва́ть-ся, *v.i.r.,* to be lost, confused, disconcerted; huddle. С. в ку́чу, to huddle together. С. с ног, to be dead tired, to walk or run one's feet off. С. с пути́, to stray, lose the way. С-би-ва́ние, *n.n.,* churning (*e.g.,* butter); whipping (*e.g.,* cream); beating (*e.g.,* eggs). С-бй-вчивость, *n.f.,* confusedness. С-бй-вчивый, *adj.,* confused, indistinct. С-ые показа́ния, conflicting statements. С-бй-вчиво, *adv.,* confusedly, indistinctly. Говори́ть сби́вчи-во, to ramble (in speaking). С-бй-

тень, *n.m.,* Russian hot drink of water, honey, and spices.

у-бй-ть, *v.p.,* у-би-ва́ть, *v.i.,* + *acc.,* to kill, murder, assassinate. У. медве́дя, to kill a bear. У. наде́жды, (*fig.*), to crush hopes. Хоть убе́й, ничего́ не ви́дно, (*colloq.*), you could kill me, but I still cannot see anything. У. вре́мя, (*fig.*), to kill time, У-бй-ть-ся, *v.p.r.,* у-би-ва́ть-ся, *v.i.r.,* to be fatally injured; (*colloq.*), to hurt oneself; lament, grieve. Мать убива́ется по уме́р-шему сы́ну, the mother is disconsolate over the death of her son. У-бй-й-ство, *n.n.,* murder, assassination. У-бй-й-ца, *n.m.,* assassin, murderer. У-бй-й-ственный, *adj.,* deadly, killing; (*fig.*), boring, wearisome. У. кли́мат, deadly climate. У-бй-й-ственно, *adv.,* deadly, extremely.

бой, *n.m.,* battle, fight; striking (of a clock). Бой быко́в, bullfight. Взять с бо́я, to take by storm. Бой-кий, *adj.,* clever, bright, alert. Б. ма́льчик, alert little boy. Б-ая у́лица, busy street, thoroughfare. Бой-кость, *n.f.,* alertness, pertness; glibness, fluency. Б. пера́, facility, readiness, in writing. Бой-ня, *n.f.,* slaughterhouse. На бо́йне би́ли быко́в, steers were killed at the slaughterhouse. Бой-ни́ца, *n.f.,* loophole; embrasure.

бо-ев-о́й, *adj.,* battle-, fighting, combat. Б. самолёт, combat aircraft. Б-ая зада́ча, strategic task. Бо-е-спосо́бность, *n.f.,* fighting potential. Бо-е-спосо́б-ный, *adj.,* fit for combat. Бо-е́ц, *n.m.,* fighter, warrior, soldier.

От-бо́й, *n.m., (mil.),* cease-firing signal. Бить отбо́й, to sound a retreat signal. Дать отбо́й, to ring off (telephone). Мне от них отбо́я нет, I can't get rid of them. У э́той де́вушки отбо́я (ю) нет от женихо́в, this girl has loads of suitors.

пере-бо́й *n.m.,* interruption, stoppage (of work in industry); misfire (engine). Пульс с перебо́ями, intermittent pulse.

при-бо́й, *n.m.,* surf; high tide. Прибо́й волн, breakers.

про-бо́й, *n.m.,* cramp iron; catch; screw ring; (tech.), mandrel; punch; *see* про-бо́йник. Про-бо́-ина, *n.f.,* hole in armor plate; shell hole, damage done to sides of ship. Пробо́ина в ши́не, puncture in a tire. Про-бо́й-ник, *n.m.,* (*tech.*), piercer, punch.

раз-бо́й, *n.m.,* brigandage, robbery, пира́су. Раз-бо́й-ник, *n.m.,* brigand, bandit, robber.

раз-бо́й-нич-ать, *v.i.,* to rob, take to the highway. Раз-бо́й-ничество, *n.n.,* robbery, pillage. Раз-бо́й-нический, *adj.*

piratic. Раз-бо́й-ничий, *adj.*, piratic. Р. прито́н, den of robbers, pirates' den.

БУЙ-, БУ-, БУШ-, FURY, RAGE

бу́й-н-ый, *adj.*, бу́-ен, *adj. pred.*, violent, furious, tempestuous, raging. Бу́йность, *n.f.*, fury, raging, wildness, violence. Бу́й-но, *adv.*, violently, furiously, tempestuously. Бу́й-н-ый, *adj.*, stormy. Б ве́тер, raging wind. Б-ое мо́ре, stormy sea. Бу́йный сумасше́дший, violently insane man.

бу́й-ство-ва-ть, *v.i.*, to rage, storm, act violently. Бу́й-ство, *n.n.*, tumult, uproar. Солда́та наказа́ли за бу́йство, the soldier was punished for his boisterousness, rowdiness.

бу-я́н-и-ть, *v.i.*, на-бу-я́нить, *v.p.*, to build up violence. Пья́ный всегда́ буя́нит, a drunken man is always violent. Бу-я́н, *n.m.*, ruffian, bully.

буш-ева́-ть, *v.i.*, to storm, rage; make an uproar. Ве́тер бушева́л, the wind was raging. Буш-ева́ние, *n.n.*, storm, raging. Буш-у́ющий, *adj., part. act. pres.*, raging. Б-ие во́лны, raging waves.

за-бу-ш-ева́-ть, *v.p.* бушева́ть, *v.i.*, to break into a storm. Вдруг мо́ре забушева́ло, the sea suddenly became stormy.

вз-буш-ева́-ть-ся, *v.p.r.*, to break into a tempest, rage, storm. Мо́ре взбушева́лось, the sea suddenly became stormy.

раз-буш-ева́-ть-ся, *v.p.r.*, to run wild, storm violently. Толпа́ разбушева́лась, the crowd was in a turmoil.

БЛАГ-, БЛАЖ-, WELL, GOOD; WELFARE

бла́г-о, *n.n.*, blessing, welfare. О́бщее б., common welfare. Обще́ственное б., public welfare. Призна́ли за б., (*obs.*), they judged it right to do so. (*Colloq., as a conjunction*), since. Пользу́йтесь слу́чаем, бла́го вы здесь, don't miss your chance, since you are here. Благо-ве́рный, -ая, *adj. used as n.*, (*jokingly*), husband; wife. Бла́го-вест, *n.m.*, ringing of church bells. Благо-ве́щение, *n.n.*, (*rel.*), Annunciation. Благо-ви́дность, *n.f.*, comeliness; plausibility. Благо-ви́дный, *adj.*, comely, fair. Б. предло́г, a plausible excuse.

благо-воли́ть, *v.i.*, со-благо-воли́ть, *v.p.*, к + *dat.*, to favor, regard with good will; deign. Нача́льник к нему́ благоволи́т, he is favored by his superior. Благо-воле́ние, *n.n.*, benevolence, graciousness, favor, kindness. Выка́зывать б., to show favor (to). Благо-воспи́танность, *n.f.*, good breeding, politeness. Благо-воспи́танный, *adj.*, well-bred, polite. Он ведёт себя́ благовоспи́танно, he has good manners.

благо-гове́ть, *v.i.*, перед + *instr.*, to venerate. Благ-о-гове́ние, *n.n.*, reverence, veneration, awe. Внуша́ть б., to strike with awe, imbue with reverence. Благоговейный, *adj.*, reverent, reverential. Благ-о-гове́йно, *adv.*, reverently, reverentially.

благо-дари́ть, *v.i.*, по-благо-дари́ть, *v.p.*, + *acc.*, за + *acc.*, to thank, give thanks. Я благодарю́ вас за кни́гу, thank you for the book. Благо-да́рность, *n.f.*, gratitude, thanks. В б., in acknowledgment, as a token of gratitude. Не сто́ит благода́рности, don't mention it. Благо-да́рный, *adj.*, thankful (for), grateful. Б. труд, gratifying work. Я вам о́чень благода́рен, I am much obliged to you. Благо-да́рно, *adv.*, thankfully, gratefully. Благода́рственное письмо́, letter of thanks. Благо-даря́, *adv. part. pres.*, thanks to, owing to. Благо-да́ть, *n.f.*, grace, blessing; abundance. Благо-да́тный, *adj.*, beneficial, blissful; abundant. Б. кли́мат, a beneficial climate.

благо-де́тельствовать, *v.i.*, о-благо-де́тельствовать, *v.p.*, + *acc.*, to shower presents or favors on someone. Благоде́тель, *n.m.*, б-ница, *n.f.*, benefactor, benefactress. Благо-де́тельный, *adj.*, beneficial, beneficient. Б-ое влия́ние ю́жного кли́мата, the beneficial influence of the southern climate. Благожела́тель, *n.m.*, -ница, *n.f.*, well-wisher. Благо-жела́тельный, *adj.*, well disposed toward; benevolent. Благо-жела́тельно, *adv.*, benevolently. Благозву́чие, *n.n.*, euphony. Благо-зву́чный, *adj.*, euphonious, harmonious, melodious. Б. го́лос, a melodious voice. Благо-зву́чно, *adv.*, euphoniously. Благ-о́й, *adj.*, good, beneficial. Б. сове́т, good advice. Б-а́я мысль, a happy idea. Крича́ть благи́м ма́том (*colloq.*), to shout at the top of one's voice. Благо-надёжность, *n.f.*, reliability, dependability. Благо-надёжный, *adj.*, reliable, dependable. Благо-наме́ренный, *adj.*, well-meaning, well-intentioned. Благо-обра́зие, *n.n.*, comeliness. Благо-обра́зный, *adj.*, comely. У него́ б. вид, he has a pleasant appearance. Благо-обра́зно, *adv.*, in a comely manner. Благо-полу́чие, *n.n.*, well-being, security, happiness, felicity. Благо-полу́чный, *adj.*, safe, secure, fortunate. Благо-полу́чно, *adv.*, all right. Всё обсто́ит б., everything is all right. Благо-приобре́тение, *n.n.*, acquisition by honorable means. Благоприобретённый, *adj.*, acquired by honorable means.

благо-прия́тствовать, *v.i.* + *dat.*, to favor, foster; (*fig.*), to smile on. Всё ему благоприя́тствует, all things conspire to please him. Благо-прия́тный, *adj.*, favorable, auspicious, propitious. Б. ве́тер, propitious wind. Б. моме́нт, propitious opportunity. Благо-прия́тные усло́вия, favorable conditions. Благо-прия́тные о́тзывы, favorable references. Благо-прия́тно, *adv.*, auspiciously. Благо-разу́мие, *n.n.*, prudence, common sense. Благо-разу́мный, *adj.*, wise, prudent, sensible, cautious. Б. посту́пок, sensible action.

о-благо-ро́дить, *v.p.*, о-благо-ра́живать, *v.i.*, + *acc.*, to ennoble, develop noble qualities, exalt, uplift morally. Благоро́дие, *n.n.*, (*obs.*, *used only in form of address*), Ваше Благоро́дие, your honor. Благо-ро́дный, *adj.*, noble, honorable, generous. Б. мета́лл, precious metal. Б. челове́к, generous, noble, honorable man. Благо-ро́дство, *n.n.*, nobility. Благо-ро́дно, *adv.*, nobly, honorably, generously. Благо-скло́нность, *n.f.*, affability. Заслужи́ть чью-либо́ б., to find favor in the eyes of. Благо-скло́нный, *adj.*, favorably inclined toward, favorable, benevolent. Б. чита́тель, *in addressing*, gentle reader, courteous reader. Благо-скло́нно, *adv.*, favorably, benevolently. Относи́ться б., to favor.

благо-слови́ть, *v.p.*, благо-словля́ть, *v.i.*, + *acc.*, to bless, give one's blessing. Б. свою́ судьбу́, to thank one's fate, Благо-слове́ние, *n.n.*, blessing, benediction. Благо-слове́нный, *adj.*, blessed, blest. Б. край, blessed country.

благо-твори́тельствовать, *v.i.*, + *dat.*, to be active in philanthropy, be philanthropic, be a benefactor to someone. Благо-твори́тель, *n.m.*, б-ница, *n.f.*, philanthropist. Благо-твори́тельность, *n.f.*, philanthropy, charity. Благо-твори́тельный, *adj.*, philanthropic, charitable. Б-ые учрежде́ния, charitable institutions. Благо-тво́рный, *adj.*, beneficial, salutary. Благо-тво́рно, *adv.*, beneficiently. Это де́йствует на меня́ благотво́рно, it has a salutary effect on me. Благо-устро́йство, *n.n.*, good order; public welfare. Благоустро́йство го́рода (больни́цы), good order, organization of the city (of the hospital). Благо-устро́енный, *adj.*, well arranged, well managed. Б-ая кварти́ра, a well-appointed apartment.

благо-уха́ть, *v.i.*, to emit fragrance. Благо-уха́ние, *n.n.*, fragrance, perfume. Б. цвето́в, fragrance of flowers. Благо-

уха́ющий, *adj.*, *part. act. pres.*, sweet-smelling, fragrant.

Благо-че́стие, *n.n.*, piety, devotion. Благо-чести́вый, *adj.*, pious, religious, devout. Благо-чести́во, *adv.*, piously.

блаж-е́н-ствовать, *v.i.*, to enjoy felicity, be blissfully happy. Блаж-е́нство, *n.n.*, beatitude, blessedness, felicity. Быть на верху́ блаже́нства, (*fig.*), to be in seventh heaven. Блаж-е́нный, *adj.*, blessed, blissful, beatific; (*fig.*), silly. Б-ое состоя́ние, state of blissful happiness.

блаж-и́-ть, *v.i.*, (*colloq.*), to be freakish. (*fig.*), to have a bee in one's bonnet. Блаж-ь, *n.f.*, fad, fancy. Блаж-но́й, *adj.*, (*colloq.*), freakish, cranky.

у-блаж-и́-ть, *v.p.*, у-блаж-а́ть, *v.i.*, + *acc.*, (*colloq.*), to make happy, pamper. У. больно́го, to pamper a sick person. По-бла́ж-ка, *n.f.*, pampering. Де́лать п-и, to be indulgent, pamper.

БЛЕД-(БЛѢД-), PALENESS, WAN

блед-н-ый, *adj.*, pale, wan, pallid. Б., как полотно́, as white as a sheet. Б. стиль, insipid, colorless style. Бледнова́тый, *adj.*, somewhat pale. Блед-н-Бледно-ли́цый, pale-faced.

блед-н-е́-ть, *v.i.*, по-блед-не́ть, *v.p.*, to grow pale, turn pale, to pale. Он сме́ртельно побледне́л, he turned pale as death. Блед-ность, *n.f.*, paleness, pallor. Блед-н-о, *adv.*, pale, light; (*fig.*), insipid, colorless. Бледно-ро́зовый, pale pink. Бледно-голубо́й, pale blue. Бледно-ли́цый, pale faced.

блед-н-и́-ть, *v.i.*, + *acc.*, to cause to look pale. Этот цвет вас бледни́т, this color makes you look pale.

БЛЕСК-, БЛЕСТ-, БЛЕЩ-, БЛИСТ-, БЛЕС-, GLITTER, LUSTER, BRILLIANCE

блеск, *n.m.*, luster, glitter, gloss, brilliance. Б. остроу́мия, brilliance of wit. Б. сла́вы, blaze of glory. От-блеск, *n.m.*, reflection, gleam. О. зари́, reflection of sunset. Про́-блеск, *n.m.*, ray of light, gleam, flash, spark. П. наде́жды, a ray of hope. П. созна́ния, moment of consciousness.

блест-е́-ть, блещ-у́, *v.i.* + *instr.*, to shine, glitter, flash. Он бле́щет умо́м, he sparkles with wit. Огни́ блестя́т, the fires gleam. Не всё то зо́лото, что блести́т, (*prov.*), all that glitters is not gold. Блёст-ка, *n.f.*, spangle, tinsel. Осыпа́ть блёстками, to bespangle. Ёлка осы́пана блёстками, the Christmas tree is covered with tinsel. Блест-я́щий, *adj., part. act. pres.*, lustrous, shining, brilliant, resplendent. Б-ее о́бщество, the most fashionable society. Блест-я́ще, *adv.*, brilliantly. Ора́тор говори́л блестя́ще, the orator spoke brilliantly.

за-блест-е́-ть, *v.p.*, to begin to shine, sparkle. Вода́ заблесте́ла на со́лнце, the water sparkled in the sunshine. Её глаза́ ра́достно з-ли, her eyes began to shine with pleasure.

блес-ну́-ть, *v.p.smf.*, + *instr.*, to flash: *see* блесте́ть. Б. красноре́чием, to display geat eloquence. Мо́лния блесну́ла, there was a flash of lightning.

про-блес-ну́-ть, *v.p.smf.*, to flash through. У меня́ проблесну́ла мысль, an idea flashed across my mind. Сигна́льная раке́та проблесну́ла, (*aviation*), a signal flare flashed.

до́-блест-ь, *n.f.*, valor, heroism. До́блест-ный, *adj.*, valiant. Д-ое во́йско, a valiant army. До́-блест-но, *adv.*, valiantly, Солда́ты д. сража́лись на фро́нте, the soldiers fought valiantly at the front.

блист-а́-ть, *v.i.*, to shine; *see* блесте́ть. Она́ блиста́ла в о́бществе, she shone in society. Блист-а́ние, *n.n.*, glitter, scintillation; (*fig.*), splendor. Блист-а́тельность, *n.f.*, brilliance. Блист-а́тельный, *adj.*, resplendent, brilliant. Блист-а́тельно, *adv.*, brilliantly. Блиста́ющий красото́й (мо́лодостью), shining with beauty (youth). Го́род, блиста́ющий вече́рними огня́ми, the city shining with evening lights.

БЛИЗ-, БЛИЖ-, NEARNESS, PROXIMITY

близ, *prep.* + *gen.*, near, close to. Близ бе́рега, off the coast. Бли́з-ость, *n.f.*, nearness, proximity, neighborhood, intimacy. Бли́з-кий, *adj.*, near, nigh, close by. Б. и дорого́й, close and dear. Б. друг, close, intimate, friend. Бли́зкое знако́мство с + *instr.*, intimate knowledge of, acquaintance with. На бли́зком расстоя́нии, at short distance, range. Его́ бли́зкие, his own people, his close relatives. Бли́з-ко, *adv.*, near at hand. Б. его́ се́рдцу, (*fig.*), close to the heart. Б. меня́ каса́ется, it concerns me closely. В-близ-и́, *adv.*, near, not far from, in the neighborhood of. Близнецы́, *n.m.pl.*, twins. Близ-лежа́щий, *adj., part. act. pres.*, adjacent, neighboring, near. Близ-о-ру́кий, *adj.*, nearsighted. Близ-о-ру́кость, *n.f.*, myopia, nearsightedness.

бли́ж-е, по-бли́ж-е, *adv.* (*compar.*), nearer, closer. Подойди́ ко мне побли́же, come closer to me. Я с ним бли́же знако́м, чем ты, I know him better than you do. Бли́ж-ний, *adj.*, *also used as n.*, fellow man, neighbor. Б. го́род, nearby town. Люби́ть бли́жнего, to love one's fellow man, neighbor.

бли́з-ить-ся, *v.i.r.*, to approach, draw nearer. Бли́зится о́сень, autumn is approaching.

при-бли́з-и-ть, *v.p.*, при-ближ-а́-ть, *v.i.*, + *acc.*, к + *dat.*, to bring near to, draw something nearer. Бино́кль приближа́ет предме́ты, field glasses bring objects nearer. При-бли́з-ить-ся, *v.p.r.*, при-ближ-а́ть-ся, *v.i.r.*, к + *dat.*, to approach, draw near. Вре́мя приближа́ется к зиме́, winter is drawing near. Кри́зис приближа́ется, the crisis is imminent. Мы приближа́лись к бе́регу, we were nearing land. При-ближ-е́ние, *n.n.*, approach, drawing near, approximation. При-бли́ж-ённость, *n.f.*, nearness, proximity. При-бли́ж-ённые, *n. pl.*, those belonging to the intimate circle; *adj., part. pass. part.*, drawn near. При-близ-и́тельность, *n.f.*, proximation. При-близ-и́тельный, *adj.*, approximate. П. подсчёт, approximate total, calculation, figure. При-близ-и́тельно, *adv.*, approximately, roughly.

с-бли́з-и-ть, с-бли́ж-у, *v.p.*, с-ближ-а́ть, *v.i.*, + *acc.*, to bring together, near, make persons better acquainted with each other. С. показа́ния, to compare evidence. С-бли́з-ить-ся, *v.p.r.*, с-ближ-а́ть-ся, *v.i.r.*, + *instr.*, to make friends. Они́ познако́мились и сбли́зились друг с дру́гом, they met and became friends. С-ближ-е́ние, *n.n.*, bringing together, rapprochement. В 1939 произошло́ сближе́ние СССР с Герма́нией, in 1939 a rapprochement was effected between the USSR and Germany.

БЛИН-, PANCAKE

блин, *n.m.*, Russian pancake. Блины́-люби́мое ку́шанье ру́сского наро́да, Russian pancakes are the favorite dish of the Russian people. Ма́сленичные блины́, carnival pancakes. Пло́ский, как блин, flat as a pancake. Блин-о́к, *n.m.*, small pancake. Бли́н-чик, *n.m.*, pancake filled with cottage cheese, jam. На сла́дкое по́дали бли́нчики с варе́ньем, for dessert they served small pancakes with jam. Бли́н-ник, *n.m.*, блин-ница, *n.f.*, person who makes, sells, pancakes. Бли́н-чатый, *adj.*, made with layers of pancakes. Б. пиро́г, pie made with layers of pancakes and minced meat or eggs.

БЛЮД-, DISH

блюд-о, *n.n.,* dish, course; charger. выкла́дывать ку́шанье на блю́до, to dish up. За ры́бой сле́довало мясно́е блю́до, the fish was followed by a meat dish. Обе́д в три блю́да, a three-course dinner. Блюд-е́чко, *n.n.,* (*dim.*), блю́дце. Ча́йное б., saucer.

блюдо-ли́з, *n.m.,* (*colloq.*), toady, sycophant. Блюдо-ли́зничать, *v.i.,* to toady.

БОГ-, БОЖ-, GOD, WEALTH

Бог, *n.m.,* God. Бог-и́ня, *n.f.,* goddess. Бог-о-ма́терь, *n.f.,* Бог-о-ро́дица, *n.f.,* Mother of God. Бог-о-мо́лец, *n.m.,* бог-о-мо́лка, *n.f.,* pilgrim. Бог-о-мо́лье, *n.n.,* pilgrimage. Бог-о-мо́льный, *adj.,* devout, religious. Бог-о-мо́льно, *adv.,* devoutly, religiously, prayerfully. Бог-о-сло́в, *n.m.,* theologian. Бог-о-сло́вие, *n.n.,* theology. Бог-о-сло́вский, *adj.,* theological. Бог-о-служе́ние, *n.n.,* divine service, worship. Бог-о-служе́бный, *adj.,* of or pertaining to a divine service. Б-ые кни́ги, books for worship.

бог-о-твори́ть, *v.i.,* + *acc.,* to deify, idolize, worship. Боготвори́ть своего́ ребёнка, (*fig.*), to idolize one's child.

бог-о-ху́льствовать, *v.i.,* to blaspheme, use profane language. Бог-о-ху́льство, *n.n.,* blasphemy, profanity. Бог-о-ху́льник, *n.m.,* blasphemer. Бог-о-ху́льный, *adj.,* blasphemous, profane. Б-ые кля́твы, blasphemous oaths.

бож-еств-о́, *n.n.,* deity, divinity, god. Бо́ж-е, *n.m., voc. of* Бог. Бо́же мой, My God! Oh, dear me! Good heavens! Бо́же, помоги́ мне, Oh, God, help me. Бож-е́ственность, *n.f.,* divinity, heavenliness. Бож-е́ственный, *adj.,* divine, godlike, heavenly. Бож-е́ственно, *adv.,* divinely. Бо́ж-ий, *adj.,* God's, of God. Бо́жий Про́мысел, Divine Providence. Бо́жья коро́вка, (*zool.*), ladybird, lady bug. Без-бо́ж-ие, *n.n.,* atheism. Без-бо́ж-ник, *n.m.,* atheist. На́-бож-ность, *n.f.,* devotion, piety. На́-бож-ный, *adj.,* devout, pious.

бож-и́-ть-ся, *v.i.r.,* по-бож-и́ть-ся, *v.p.r.,* to swear in God's name. Бож-ни́ца, *n.f.,* ikon case. Бож-о́к, *n.m.* (*dim.*), idol.

о-бож-а́-ть, *v.i.,* + *acc.* (*fig.*), to adore, worship. Обожа́ть свою́ мать, to adore one's mother. О-бож-а́ние, *n.n.,* extreme fondness, admiration for someone, (something).

У-бо́ж-ество, *n.n.,* poverty, wretchedness, scantiness. У. мы́сли, triviality, pettiness, mediocrity of mind. У-бо́г-ий, *adj.,* miserable, poor wretched. У-ая стару́шка, miserable, poor, old woman. У-бо́г-о, *adv.* scantily, poorly. Жить у., to live wretchedly.

бог-ат-е́-ть, *v.i.,* раз-бог-ате́ть, *v.p.,* to become rich. Бог-а́тство, *n.n.,* richness, wealth, fortune, money, gold. Большо́е б., opulence. Есте́ственные б-а, natural resources. Бог-а́тый, *adj.,* rich, wealthy, opulent. Б-ая расти́тельность, rich vegetation. Бог-а́то, *adv.,* richly, sumptuously. Жить б., to live sumptuously. Бог-а́ч, *n.m.,* rich man. Бога́чка, n.f., rich woman.

о-бог-ат-и́-ть, *v.p.,* о-бог-аща́ть, *v.i.,* + *acc.,* to enrich. О. сумму зна́ний, to enrich the sum of knowledge. О-бог-ати́ть-ся, *v.p.r.,* о-бог-аща́ть-ся, *v.i.r.,* to enrich oneself; enrich oneself at someone else's expense. О-бог-аще́ние, *n.n.,* enrichment. О. за счёт войны́, war profiteering. О-бог-ати́тельный, *adj.,* enriching.

бог-ат-ы́р-ь, *n.m.,* a robust, vigorous man; hero of the Russian ballads and folklore. Бог-аты́рский, *adj.,* athletic, heroic, valiant. Б. сон, (*fig.*), a very sound sleep. Б-ое здоро́вье, (*fig.*), exuberant health.

БОДР-, БАДР-, COURAGE

бо́др-ост-ь, *n.f.,* courage, nerve; cheerfulness. Б. ду́ха, alertness; high spirits; courage. Придава́ть бо́дрости, to hearten. Бо́др-ый, *adj.,* cheerful, alert, hale. Б. на вид, of vigorous appearance. Б. ду́хом, cheerful. Бодр-я́щий, *adj., part. act. pres.,* enlivening, bracing, invigorating.

бодр-и́-ть, *v.i.,* + *acc.,* to brace, stimulate. Бодр-и́ть-ся, *v.i.r.,* to take courage, brace oneself.

о-бодр-и́-ть, *v.p.,* о-бодр-я́ть, *v.i.,* + *acc.,* to encourage, hearten, inspire. О-бодр-и́ть-ся, *v.p.r.,* о-бодр-я́ть-ся, *v.i.r.,* to take heart, become encouraged. О-бодр-е́ние, *n.n.,* encouragement. О-бодр-я́ющий, *adj., part. act. pres.,* encouraging. О. взгляд, an encouraging look.

под-бодр-и́-ть, *v.p.,* под-бодр-я́-ть, под-ба́др-ивать, *v.i.,* + *acc.,* to encourage. Под-бодр-и́ть-ся, *v.p.r.,* под-ба́др-ивать-ся, *v.i.r.,* to be slightly encouraged, brace up.

при-о-бодр-и́-ть, *v.p.,* при-о-бодр-я́ть, *v.i.,* + *acc.,* to put spirit into, hearten a little. П. студе́нтов пе́ред экза́менами, to encourage students before an examination. При-о-бодр-и́ть-ся, *v.p.r.,*

при-о-бодр-я́ть-ся, *v.i.r.*, to recover one's spirits, become somewhat encouraged.
бо́др-ство-ва-ть, *v.i.*, to keep awake. Бо́др-ствование, *n.n.*, vigilance, watchfulness, wakefulness. Изнурённый бо́дрствованием, exhausted by watching. Бо́др-ствующий, *adj., part. act. pres.*, awake, wide awake.

БОК-, БОЧ-, БЕК-, SIDE

бок, *n.m.*, side, flank. Б. зда́ния, side of a building. Пра́вый (ле́вый) бок, right (left) side. Бок-о́-бок, *adv.*, side by side, alongside. Под бо́ком, at hand. Сбо́ку, by the side. Лежа́ть на боку́, *(fig.)*, to do nothing, be lazy. Взять кого-либо за бока́, *(colloq.)*, to put the screws on someone. Намя́ть бока́, *(colloq.)*, to cudgel. По бока́м, on each side. Бок-ово́й, *adj.* lateral, sidelong, of or pertaining to a side. Б-а́я дверь, side door. Б-а́я ка́чка, *(fig.)*, rolling (of a boat). Пора́ на боковую, *(colloq.)*, it's time to go to bed. Бо́ком, *adv.*, sideways, sidewise. Подходи́ть б., to approach sidewise, sidle. Бочко́м, *adv.*, *(colloq.)*, *see* бо́ком.
под-боч-ён-и-ть-ся, *v.p.r.*, под-боч-ёнивать-ся, *v.i.r.*, to lie down on one's side; set one's arms akimbo. Стоя́ть подбоченя́сь, to stand with one's arms akimbo. Бек-р-е́нь, *n.m.*, *used only in expression*: набекре́нь, on one side, at an angle.

БОЛ-, БАЛ-, ILLNESS, HURT, PAIN, ACHE

бол-е́-ть, *v.i.*, + *instr.*, to ache, hurt; ail, be ill; suffer from. У меня́ боли́т голова́, my head aches, I have a headache. Боле́ть душо́й, to be anxious about. Бол-е́зн-ь, *n.f.*, illness, disease, sickness. Душе́вная б., mental illness. Зара́зная б., contagious disease. Морска́я б., sea sickness. Бол-е́зненность, *n.f.*, unhealthiness; sickliness; painfulness. Бол-е́зненный, *adj.*, ailing, sickly; painful. Болезненный на вид, pallid, sickly looking. Болезненное состоя́ние, condition of being sick. Боле́зненно, *adv.*, painfully.
за-бол-е́-ть, *v.p.*, за-бол-ева́ть, *v.i.*, to become sick, be taken sick, begin to ache, + *instr.*, to catch, contract, come down with. Заболе́ть лихора́дкой, to catch a fever, come down with a fever. У меня́ заболе́л зуб, my tooth began to ache. За-бол-ева́ние, *n.n.*, case (of a disease).

на-бол-е́-ть, *v.p.*, to become very sore. От нарыва вся рука́ наболе́ла, the whole hand has become very sore from the abscess. На душе́ наболе́ло, I have suffered a great deal. На-бол-е́вший, *adj., part. act. past,* painful, aching, sore. Н. вопро́с, a sore subject.
пере-бол-е́-ть, *v.p.*, + *instr.*, to be taken ill one after another; to suffer. Все де́ти переболе́ли ко́рью, all the children one after the other had measles. П. душо́й за кого́-нибудь, to suffer with someone.
при-бол-е́-ть, *v.p.*, to be sick for a while. Де́ти приболе́ли немно́го, the children were sick for a while.
по-бол-е́-ть, *v.p.*, по-ба́л-ивать, *v.i.*, to ache for a short time. Голова́ поболе́ла и прошла́, I had a headache for a little while, but it is all over. Зу́бы поба́ливают, my teeth ache off and on.
про-бол-е́-ть, *v.p.*, to be ill. Он проболе́л всю о́сень, he was sick the whole autumn.
раз-бол-е́ть-ся, *v.p.r.*, раз-ба́л-ивать-ся, *v.i.r.*, *(rare)*, to ache all over; to become very ill. Я совсе́м разболе́лся, I have become quite ill.
бол-ь, *n.f.*, pain, ache, soreness. Причиня́ть б., to cause pain, hurt. Зубна́я б., toothache. Головна́я б., headache. Боль-но́й, *adj., also used as n.m.*, patient, sick person. Психи́чески б., mental patient. Больно́й вопро́с, *(fig.)*, sore subject. Свали́ть с больно́й головы́ на здоро́вую, *(idiom)*, to lay the fault at another man's door. Бо́л-ь-но, *adv.*, painfully, very, terribly, awfully. Мне бо́льно слы́шать, it grieves me to hear. Он бо́льно горя́ч, *(colloq.)*, he is very hot-tempered. Бол-я́чка, *n.f.*, *(colloq.)*, sore. Кака́я-то боля́чка на лице́, some kind of sore on the face.
бол-ь-ни́ца, *n.f.*, hospital, infirmary. Его́ отвезли́ в городску́ю больни́цу, they took him to the city hospital. Боль-ни́чный, *adj.*, hospital-. Больни́чный служи́тель, orderly. Больни́чная ка́сса, hospital fund at a factory. Больни́чная пала́та, hospital ward.
со-бол-езн-ова́-ть, *v.i.*, + *dat.*, to condole, pity, sympathize. С. го́рю, to sympathize with someone's grief. Со-болезнова́ние, *n.n.*, condolence, pity, sympathy. Выража́ть с., to express condolence. Письмо́, выража́ющее с., letter of condolence.
серд-о-бо́л-ие, *n.n.*, pity, compassion. Серд-о-бо́л-ь-ный, *adj.*, compassionate, tender-hearted.

БОЛ-, БОЛ(ЬШ)-, MORE, LARGE, GREAT

бол-ьш-о́й, *adj.,* large, big, bulky. Б. па́лец, thumb; the big toe. Б. свет, society, high life. Б-а́я бу́ква, capital letter. Бо́л-ьш-ий, *adj. (comp.),* greater, larger, major. С. бо́льшим внима́нием, with more attention. Бо́льшая часть, the greater part. Са́мое бо́льшее, the utmost. Бо́льшей ча́стью, for the most part. Бол-ьш-у́щий, *adj., (colloq.),* uncommonly large, huge, enormous. Б-и́е ру́ки и но́ги, enormous, uncommonly large limbs, Бо́л-ьш-е, *adj., comp., also used as adv.,* larger; more, any more, again. Фра́нция бо́льше Швейца́рии, France is larger than Switzerland. Я бо́льше не бу́ду э́того де́лать, I will not do it any more. Бо́л-ее, *adv. (comp.),* more (modifying an adjective). Бо́льш-е-голо́вый, *adj.,* macrocephalic, unusually large-headed. Бо́льш-инство́, *n.n.,* majority, plurality. Б. так ду́мает, the majority thinks so. В б-ве́ слу́чаев, in most cases. По б-у́ голосо́в, by a majority of votes.

бол-ьш-еви́к, *n.m.,* бол-ьш-еви́чка, *n.f.,* Bolshevik. Ру́сская соц.-дем. па́ртия раздели́лась на большевико́в и меньшевико́в, the Russian Social Democratic Party divided into Bolsheviks and Mensheviks.. Бол-ьш-еви́стский, *adj.,* Bolshevist.

бол-ьш-ев-изи́рова-ть, *v.i.,* + *acc.,* to make Bolsheviks of. Бол-ьш-евизи́рова-ть-ся, *v.i.r.,* to become a Bolshevik. Бол-ьш-евиза́ция, *n.f.,* conversion to Bolshevism. Бол-ьш-еви́зм, *n.m.,* Bolshevism.

БОЛОТ-, MOOR, SWAMP

боло́т-о, *n.n.,* bog, swamp, marsh. Вся́кий кули́к своё б. хва́лит *(prov.),* every dog praises his own kennel. Меща́нское б., mediocrity of middle-class life. Боло́т-истый, *adj.,* swampy, marshy. Б-ая ме́стность, marshland. Боло́тный, *adj.,* see боло́тистый. Б. газ, marsh gas. Б-ые огни́, will-o'-the-wisp.

БОЛТ-, БАЛТ-, CHATTER, TALK, DANGLE

болт-а́-ть, *v.i.,* + *acc.,* to shake, stir; chat, chatter, babble; dangle. Б. о пустяка́х, to chatter. Б. жи́дкость, to stir a liquid. Болт-а́ть-ся, *v.i.r.,* to dangle, lounge about, swing. На верёвке болта́лось бельё, the laundry was swinging on a line. Что ты тут болта́ешься? why are you lounging about here?

Болт-ли́вость, *n.f., (colloq.),* undue talkativeness, loquacity. Болт-ли́вый, *adj.,* chatty, talkative, gossipy. Болтовня́, *n.f.,* chatter, gossip, talk. Болт-у́н, *n.m.,* болт-у́нья, *n.f.,* chatterbox.

вз-болт-а́-ть, *v.p.,* вз-ба́лт-ывать, *v.i.,* + *acc.,* to shake up. В. лека́рство, to shake well (as medicine), Вз-ба́лт-ывание, *n.n.,* shaking up a liquid.

вы́-болт-а-ть, *v.p.,* вы-ба́лт-ывать, *v.i.,* + *acc., (colloq.),* to disclose, let out. Вы́болтать та́йны, to disclose secrets.

за-болт-а́-ть, *v.p.,* to break into chatter. За-ба́лт-ывать, *v.i.,* + *acc.,* to dissolve. Заболта́ть (забалтывать) дро́жжи, to dissolve yeast in water. За-болт-а́ть-ся, *v.p.r.,* to chat too much. Я заболта́лся и опозда́л, I chatted so long that I was late.

про-болт-а́-ть, *v.p.,* про-ба́лт-ывать, *v.i.,* + *acc., (obs.),* to divulge; chatter, talk. П. секре́т, та́йну, to divulge a secret. проболта́ть весь день, to talk the whole day, spend the day talking. Про-болт-а́ть-ся, *v.p.r.,* про-ба́лт-ывать-ся, *v.i.r.,* to idle, loiter; divulge a secret, let the cat out of the bag.

раз-болт-а́-ть, *v.p.,* раз-ба́лт-ывать, *v.i.,* + *acc.,* to shake, stir up; divulge, let out, spill *(e.g.,* a secret). Р. муку́ в воде́, to mix flour with water. Р. секре́т, to give away a secret.

БОР-, БОР-(Ь)-, WRESTLE, STRUGGLE

бор-о́ть-ся, бор-ю́-сь, *v.i.r.,* с + *instr.,* за + *acc.,* to wrestle, struggle; champion, fight for. Боро́ться за и́стину, to fight for truth. Б. с кем-ли́бо, to wrestle. Б. с искуше́нием, to struggle against temptation. Б. с поро́ками, to strive against vices. Борь-ба́, *n.f.,* fight, contest, struggle, combat, wrestling. Б. за ка́чество, *(recent),* the drive for quality, Б. за овладе́ние те́хникой, struggle for the mastery of technical skill. Б. за существова́ние, the struggle for existence. Б. кла́ссов, class strife. Бор-е́ц, *n.m.,* wrestler, athlete; champion. Б. за свобо́ду, fighter for freedom. Дух-о-бо́ры, *n. pl.,* Dukhobors (religious sect). Дух-о-бо́р-ство, *n.n.,* the teachings of the Dukhobors.

един-о-бо́р-ство-вать, *v.i., (obs.),* to combat singly. Един-о-бо́р-ство, *n.n.,* single combat, duel. Рат-о-бо́р-ец, *n.m., (obs.),* warrior. Рат-о-бо́р-ствовать, *v.i.,* to wage war.

пере-бор-о́ть, *v.p.,* + *acc.,* to overcome. П. в себе́ страх, to overcome one's fear.

по-бор-о́ть, *v.p.,* + *acc.,* to overcome, conquer. Поборо́ть проти́вника, to defeat an opponent. П. в себе́ чу́вство стра́ха (тоски́), to overcome a feeling of terror (distress).

по-бо́р-ство-вать, *v.i.,* uphold, support. П. за ве́ру, to uphold a faith. По-бо́р-ник, *n.m.,* по-бо́р-ница, *n.f.,* advocate, supporter, champion, upholder. П. пра́вды и справедли́вости, a champion of truth and justice. Не-пре-о-бор-и́-мый, *adj.* (*obs.*), invincible, unconquerable. Н-ая си́ла, *force majeure.*

БР-, БЕР-, БИР-, БОР-, TAKE, SEIZE; CLIMB; ELECT; COLLECT

бр-а-ть, бер-у́, *v.i.,* взять, *v.p.,* + *acc.,* to take, seize, capture. Б. уро́ки, to take lessons. Б. в аре́нду, to take a lease on, to rent. Б. в жёны, to take a wife, marry. Б. в плен, to take prisoner. Б. на пору́ки, to bail someone out. Б. приме́р с кого́-либо, to follow someone's example. Бр-а́ть-ся, *v.i.r.,* взя́ть-ся, *v.p.r.,* за + *acc.,* to take up, undertake, begin, turn to. Б. (в.) за рабо́ту, to start work on. Б. (в.) за ору́жие, to take up arms. Б. (в.) за ум, to come to one's senses. Отку́да мо́гут взя́ться э́ти слу́хи? where can such rumors originate?

в-бир-а́-ть, *v.i.,* во-бр-а́ть, *v.p.,* + *acc.,* to suck in, absorb, imbibe, drink in. В. све́жий во́здух, to inhale fresh air. В. в себя́ зна́ния, to absorb knowledge.

вз-бир-а́ть-ся, *v.i.r.,* взо-бр-а́ть-ся, *v.p.r.,* to climb up, ascend, mount, clamber up. В. на́ гору, to climb a mountain.

вы-бир-а́-ть, *v.i.,* вы́-бр-ать, *v.p.,* + *acc.,* to choose, elect, select, pick out. В. себе́ пла́тье, to choose, select, a dress. В. председа́теля, to elect a chairman. В. удо́бный моме́нт, to time well. Вы-бир-а́ть-ся, *v.i.r.,* вы́-бр-ать-ся, *v.p.r.,* to get out, remove from. В. из затрудне́ний, to get out of a predicament. В. из кварти́ры, to move out of an apartment. Вы́-бор, *n.m.,* choice, option, selection. Большо́й в. чего́-либо, a great choice, large selection. Останови́ть свой вы́бор, to make a choice. У меня́ нет вы́бора, I have no choice. Вы́-бор-ка, *n.f.,* excerpt. Де́лать в-и, to excerpt. Вы́-бор-ность, *n.f.,* eligibility. Вы́-бор-ный, *adj.,* chosen, elective; — *used as n.,* deputy, delegate. Вы́-бор-щик, *n.m.,* elector. Вы́-бор-ы, *n. pl.,* elections. Всео́бщие в., general elections.

до-бир-а́-ть, *v.i.,* до-бр-а́ть, *v.p.,* + *acc.,* + *gen.,* to gather what is left; finish gathering. Э́той мате́рии не хвата́ет, на́до добра́ть ещё метр, there is not enough material; we must get another

meter. До-бир-а́ть-ся, *v.i.r.,* до-бр-а́ть-ся, *v.p.r.,* до + *gen.,* to attain, reach. Д. до́ дому, to reach home. Д. до и́стины, to find out the truth.

за-бир-а́-ть, *v.i.,* за-бр-а́ть, *v.p.,* + *acc.,* to take, grab. З. вперёд, в креди́т, to take in advance, on credit. З. всё в свои́ ру́ки, to take control of everything. З. в солда́ты, (*colloq.*), to draft. За-бир-а́ть-ся, *v.i.r.,* за-бр-а́ть-ся *v.p.r.,* to come in stealthily, steal into. З. в ко́мнату, to steal into somebody's room. З. на де́рево, to climb a tree. За-бо́р-ный, *adj.,* pertaining to a charge account, *in expression*: З-ая кни́жка, charge account book. За-бо́р-истый, *adj.,* tenacious, strong; interesting. З. моти́в, a racy tune. З-ое вино́, heady wine. За-бо́р, *n.m.,* fence.

из-бир-а́-ть, *v.i.,* из-бр-а́ть, *v.p.,* + *acc.,* + *instr.,* to elect, choose, adopt (*e.g.,* a career). И. представи́теля, to elect a representative. Из-бир-а́тель, *n.m.,* elector, voter. Избира́тели, body of electors. Из-бир-а́тельный, *adj.,* electoral. И. го́лос, vote. И-ая у́рна, ballot box. И-ая кампа́ния, election campaign. Из-бр-а́ние, *n.n.,* election, choice. Из-бр-а́нник, *n.m.,* из-бр-а́нница, *n.f.,* incumbent, chosen one. Он мой избра́нник, he is my choice. Из-бр-анный, *adj., part. pass. past,* chosen. Избранное о́бщество, select society, elite. Избранные сочине́ния Пу́шкина, selected works of Pushkin.

на-бир-а́-ть, *v.i.,* на-бр-а́ть, *v.p.,* + *acc.,* to collect, gather; compose, set up; to pile up. Н. рабо́чих, to contract workers. Н. солда́т, во́йско, to enlist soldiers, levy troops. На-бир-а́ть-ся, *v.i.r.,* на-бр-а́ть-ся, *v.p.r.,* + *gen.,* to accumulate, acquire. Н. но́вых сил, to acquire new strength. Н. сме́лости (ума́), to grow bold (wise). На-бо́р, *n.m.,* collection, set, assemblage; (*mil.*), conscription, recruitment, levy of troops; typesetting, composition. Н. рабо́чих, hiring of workers. Н. слов, mere verbiage. Набо́рная маши́на, typesetting machine. На-бо́р-щик, *n.m.,* на-бо́р-щица, *n.f.,* typesetter.

о-бир-а́-ть, *v.i.,* обо-бр-а́ть, *v.p.,* + *acc.,* to pick; rob; (*fig.*), fleece, plunder. Обобра́ть магази́н, to rob a store. О-бир-а́ние, *n.n.,* gathering, picking, despoiling. О-бир-а́ла, *n.m.,* (*colloq.*), cheat, swindler, sharper. О-бо́р-ка, *n.f.,* flounce, trimming.

от-бир-а́-ть, *v.i.,* ото-бр-а́ть, *v.p.,* + *acc.,* to take away, confiscate; sort out, select, pick out. О. зре́лые я́блоки, to pick out the ripe apples. О. иму́щество, to confiscate property. От-бир-а́ние, taking away, confiscation. От-бо́р, *n.m.*, selection, choice. Есте́ственыый о., natural selection. Сде́лать о., to make a selection. От-бо́р-ный, *adj.*, choice, select, the best, first-rate.

пере-бир-а́-ть, *v.i.*, пере-бр-а́ть, *v.p.*, + *acc.*, to look over, examine, sort; turn over (*e.g.*, the leaves of a book); finger. П. де́ньги из ба́нка, to overdraw one's bank account. П. стру́ны, to pluck the strings. П. про́шлое, (*fig.*), to brood over the past; to rehash grievances. Пере-бир-а́ть-ся, *v.i.r.*, пере-бр-а́ть-ся, *v.p.r.*, to cross over, pass over. П. на кварти́ру, to move to an apartment. П. че́рез у́лицу, to cross the street. Пере-бо́р, *n.m.*, overdraft; surplus receipts. Пере-бо́р-ка, *n.f.*, partition, *see* перегоро́дка; sorting, looking over; resetting (*typography*).

под-бир-а́ть, *v.i.*, подо-бр-а́ть, *v.p.*, + *acc.*, to pick up, gather; select, assort, match. П. люде́й на слу́жбу, to pick ┬men for service. П. во́жжи, to pull, take up the reins. П. моти́в на роя́ле, to pick out a tune. П. под цвет, to match a color. Под-бир-а́ть-ся, *v.i.r.*, Подо-бр-а́ть-ся, *v.p.r.*, к + *dat.*, to be selected, be matched; steal up to, approach. П. к врагу́, to creep up to, approach, the enemy. Под-бир-а́ние, *n.n.*, gathering, picking up. Под-бо́р, *n.m.*, selection, assortment, matching. П. ка́дров, selection of personnel. Това́р, как на подбо́р, (*saying*), high quality selection of goods.

при-бир-а́-ть, *v.i.*, при-бр-а́ть, *v.p.*, + *acc.*, to put in order, arrange, clean. П. ко́мнату (ку́хню), to tidy a room (kitchen). Прибери́те кни́ги, put the books away. При-бо́р, *n.m.*, apparatus, instrument set; cover. Пи́сьменный п., writing set. Ча́йный п., tea set. Столо́вый п., table silver.

про-бир-а́-ть, *v.i.*, про-бр-а́ть, *v.p.*, + *acc.*, to scold, reprove, reprimand; penetrate through and through (as cold). Меня́ пробира́ет хо́лод, I am cold. Про-бир-а́ть-ся *v.i.r.*, про-бр-а́ть-ся, *v.p.r.*, в + *acc.*, to make one's way, steal into. П. сквозь толпу́, to thread one's way, force one's way, through the crowd. Про-бо́р, *n.m.*, parting (hair). Де́лать п., to part one's hair.

раз-бир-а́-ть, *v.i.*, разо-бр-а́ть, *v.p.*, + *acc.*, to dismantle, take to pieces; read (*e.g.*, music); to decipher (handwriting); analyze, knock down, sort (things, papers). Р. чемода́н, to unpack a suitcase. Р. де́ло, to try, examine, discuss a case. Р. по ко́сточкам, (*colloq.*), to pick to pieces, criticize severely. Его́ разбира́ет зло́ба, he is

seething with anger. Раз-бир-а́ть-ся, *v.i.r.*, разо-бр-а́ть-ся, *v.p.r.*, в + *prep.*, to discriminate, appraise. Р. в де́ле (в запу́танном вопро́се), to analyze a case (an involved question). Раз-бир-а́тельство, *n.n.*, examination, investigation, discussion. Раз-бо́р, *n.m.*, choice, selection; criticism; grammatical analysis. Р. де́ла, trial. Р. кни́ги, статьи́, criticism, review of books, article. Де́лать разбо́р, (*grammar*), to parse, analyze. Придти́ к ша́почному разбо́ру, to come late. Раз-бо́р-ка, *n.f.*, (маши́ны), taking to pieces, dismantling (a machine); analysis. Раз-бо́р-ный, *adj.*, that can be taken apart, collapsible. Р. дом, prefabricated house. Раз-бо́рчивость, *n.f.*, fastidiousness, discernment. Раз-бо́р-чивый, *adj.*, squeamish, fastidious; clear, legible. Р. по́черк, legible handwriting. Раз-бо́р-чиво, *adv.*, clearly, legibly. Писа́ть р., to write legibly.

со-бир-а́-ть, *v.i.*, со-бр-а́ть, *v.p.*, + *acc.*, to gather, collect. С. ре́дкие кни́ги, to collect rare books. С. цветы́ (я́годы), to pick flowers (berries). С. маши́ну, to assemble a machine. Со-бир-а́ть-ся, *v.i.r.*, со-бр-а́ть-ся, *v.p.r.*, в + *acc.*, с + *instr.*, to be gathered, collected; to congregate; plan. С. в да́льний путь, to prepare for a long journey. С. с мы́слями, to collect one's thoughts. Мы собира́емся идти́ в теа́тр, we plan to go to the theater. Со-бир-а́ние, *n.n.*, gathering, collecting. С-бор, *n.m.*, gathering, collection (*e.g.*, for church, charities). С-бо́р-ка, *n.f.*, assemblage of mechanical parts, of parts of mechanism; flounce, crease, tuck. С-и на пла́тье, tucks on a dress. С-бо́р-ы, *n.m. pl.*, preparations for a journey. С-бо́рище, *n.n.*, crowd, mob. С-бо́р-щик, *n.m*,. assembler, fitter; collector. Собр-а́ние, *n.n.*, gathering, reunion, assembly, meeting. По́лное с. сочине́ний, complete, collected works. С-бо́р-ник, *n.m.*, collection, symposium. С. стихо́в, a collection of verse. С-бо́р-ный, *adj.*, miscellaneous, heterogeneous; assembling, gathering. С. цех, assembling workshop. С. пункт, С-ое ме́сто, gathering place. Со-бо́р, *n.m.*, cathedral, church council, assembly, synod. Со-бо́р-ный, *adj.* cathedral, conciliar.

у-бир-а́-ть, *v.i.*, у-бр-а́ть, *v.p.*, + *acc.*, to remove, take off, away; trim, adorn, decorate; clean. У. ко́мнату, to tidy up a room. У. со стола́, to clear a table. У. хлеб с по́ля, to gather in the harvest. У. цвета́ми, to adorn with flowers. У-бир-а́ть-ся, *v.i.r.*, у-бр-а́ть-ся, *v.p.r.*, to be put in order; be decorated; be gone. Де́рево убира́ется ли́стьями, the tree is coming out in leaf. Убра́ться по добру́, по здоро́ву, (*idiom*), to get away safely. Убира́йся! begone, get out of here! У-бо́р, *n.m.*, attire, dress, finery. Головно́й у., headdress, hat, cap. У-бр-а́нство, *n.n.*, adornment, ornament, decoration. У-бо́р-истость, *n.f.*, closeness, compactness (of print, handwriting). У-бо́р-истый *adj.*, close, compact. У-бо́р-исто, *adv.*, closely, compactly. Писа́ть у., to write compactly, closely. У-бо́р-ка, *n.f.*, putting in order, arranging; removal; harvest, gathering in; storing. У-бо́р-ная, *n.f.*, lavatory, toilet. У-бо́р-щик, *n.m.*, у-бо́р-щица, *n.f.*, charwoman, attendant, janitor. Убо́рочный *adj.*, harvesting У-ая кампа́ния (*recent*), harvest campaign. У-ые маши́ны, harvesting machines.

БРАН-, БОРОН-, БРОН-, SCOLD, ABUSE

бран-ь, *n.f.*, bad language, scolding; (*obs.*), warfare. Пал на по́ле бра́ни, (*poet.*), he fell on the field of battle. Бра́н-ный, *adj.*, abusive, libelous; (*obs.*), martial, warlike. Б-ое по́ле, battlefield. Б-ая речь, abusive speech.

бран-и́-ть, *v.i.*, по-бран-и́ть, *v.p.*, + *acc.*, to scold, chide, berate, abuse. Бран-и́ть-ся, *v.i.r.*, по-бран-и́ть-ся, *v.p.r.*, to quarrel; use bad, insulting language, swear. Он брани́тся, как изво́зчик, he is swearing like a cabman.

воз-бран-и́-ть, *v.p.*, воз-бран-я́ть, *v.i.*, + *dat.*, + *acc.*, to forbid, prohibit. В. иностра́нцу въезд в страну́, to refuse a foreigner entrance into a country. Воз-бран-я́ть-ся, *v.i.r.*, to be forbidden, prohibited. Ходи́ть по траве́ возбраня́ется, it is forbidden to walk on the grass.

вы́-бран-и-ть, *v.p.*, бран-и́ть, *v.i.*, + *acc.*, (*colloq.*), to scold. Отец вы́бранил сыни́шку за ша́лость, the father scolded his son for his pranks.

пере-бра́н-ивать-ся, *v.i.r.*, пере-бран-и́ть-ся, *v.p.r.*, с + *instr.*, to quarrel, abuse one another. П. со слу́жащими, to quarrel with one's employees. Пере-бра́н-ка, *n.f.*, quarrel, wrangle, altercation.

раз-бран-и́-ть, *v.p.*, + *acc.*, to abuse, give a sharp scolding; (*colloq.*), to blow up, fly up. Раз-бран-и́ть-ся, *v.p.r.*, с + *instr.*, to quarrel, wrangle, have a row with.

о-боро́н-а, *n.f.*, defense. О. го́рода (пози́ций), the defense of a town (of trenches). О-боро́н-ный, *adj.*, defensive,

О-борон-и́тельный, *adj.*, defensive. О-ая война́, defensive war. О-ые мероприя́тия, defensive measures.

о-борон-я́-ть, *v.i.*, о-борон-и́ть, *v.p.*, + *acc.*, to defend, stand up for. О-борон-я́ть-ся, *v.i.r.*, от + *gen.*, to defend oneself, stand on the defensive.

бро́н-я, *n.f.*, armor. Б. на кварти́ру, (*recent*), special order for securing an apartment. Брон-е-но́сный, *adj.*, armored. Брон-е-ви́к, *n.m.*, armored car. Брон-е-но́сец, *n.m.* dreadnought, battleship. Брон-е-по́езд, *n.m.*, armored train. Брон-е-та́нковые войска́, armored tank troops.

брон-и́р-ова́-ть, *v.i.*, за-брон-ирова́ть, *v.p.*, + *acc.*, to cover with armor plate; (*recent*) to book, reserve. Б. биле́ты (места́), to book tickets (seats). Б. *v.p.*, + *acc.*, to cover with armor plate; Б. креди́ты, to assure credits. Брон-и́р́ованный, за-брони́р́ованный, *adj.*, *part. pass. past*, armored, covered with armored plate; (*recent*) booked, reserved. Заброни́р́ованное ме́сто в ваго́не, reserved seat in railroad car.

БРАТ-, BROTHER

брат, *n.m.*, brother; *pl.*, бра́тья. Это мой родно́й б., this is my own brother. Двою́родный б., first cousin. Наш б., (*colloq.*), we, ваш б., (*colloq.*), you, your kind. Наш б. актёр, we actors. Ну, б.! well, my friend! По рублю́ на б-а, one ruble to each. Бра́т-ец, *n.m.*, (*dim., colloq.*), young brother; *in addressing*, my dear brother. Бра́т-ия, *n.f.*, brotherhood, fraternity; (*Bib.*), brethren. Ни́щая б., beggars. Мона́сты́рская б., brotherhood, fraternity. Свобо́да, ра́венство и бра́тство, liberty, equality, and fraternity. Бра́т-ский, *adj.*, brotherly, fraternal. Б-ая любо́вь, brotherly love. Бра́т-ний, *adj.*, brother's. По-бра́тски, *adv.*, fraternally, like brothers. Бра́тски пожа́ть ру́ку, to shake hands in a very friendly way. Брат-о-уби́йство, *n.n.*, fratricide. Брат-о-уби́йца, *n.m.*, brother's murderer, fratricide. Брат-о-уби́йственный, *adj.*, fratricidal, Б-ая война́, fratricidal war, civil war. Собра́т, *n.m.*, companion, fellow, brother by profession. С. по ору́жию, brother-in-arms. С. по ремеслу́, fellow-craftsman. Собра́тья по профе́ссии, brethren, fellow-workers, colleagues. Побрат-и́м, *n.m.*, (*obs.*), sworn brother. По-бра́тски (бра́тски), in brotherhood.

брат-а́ть-ся, *v.i.r.*, по-брат-а́ть-ся, *v.p.r.*, с + *instr.*, to fraternize. Брат-а́ние, *n.n.*, fraternization.

БРЕД-, БРЕЖ-, БРЕС-, БРОД-, БРОЖ-, WANDERING

бред, *n.m.,* delirium, frenzy, raving. Бред сумасшéдшего, the raving of a madman. Впасть в брел. to become delirious. Быть в бредý, to be delirious.
брéд-и-ть, брéж-у, *v.i.,* + *instr.,* to dream, be delirious, rave, wander in one's mind. Б. чем-лúбо, to be mad about, have a fixation. Брéд-ни, *n.pl.,* nonsense, raving. Брéд-ящий, *adj., part. act. pres.,* delirious.
брес-тú, бред-ý, *v.i.,* побрестú, *v.p.,* to wander, roam, drag along. Старýха едвá бредёт, the old woman can hardly drag her feet. "Откýда, ýмная, бред·ёшь ты, головá?" (Krylov), "Where have you dragged yourself in from, bright boy?" Брéд-ень, *n.m.,* drag net.
вз-брес-тú, *v.p.,* на + *acc.,* в + *acc.,* to come into, *only in expression*: в. в гó- лову, на ум, to come into one's head, one's mind. Говорúть, что взбредёт на ум, to say whatever comes to one's mind, talk without thinking.
за-брес-тú, *v.p.,* to go astray, stroll in, stroll far. Мы забрелú далекó в лес, we strolled far into the forest.
на-брес-тú, *v.p.,* на + *acc.,* (*obs.*), to come across, strike against. Н. на мысль, to chance upon an idea. Н. на открытие, to make a discovery by chance.
по-брес-тú, *v.p.,* to plod along. Нúщий побрёл по дорóге, the beggar plodded along the road.
брод-ú-ть, брож-ý, *v.i.,* to wander, rove, ramble, stroll; ferment. Б. пó лесу, to wander in the forest. Пúво брóдит, the beer is fermenting. Брож-éние, *n.n.,* fermentation (chemistry); (*fig.*), discontent, ferment. Вызывáть брожéние, to produce fermentation, cause discontent.
брод, *n.m.,* ford. Переходúть в брод, to ford, cross by a ford. Не спросясь брó- ду, не сýйся в вóду (*prov.*), look before you leap. В-раз-брóд, *adv.,* separately, without order. Идтú вразбрóд, to walk helter-skelter. С-брод, *n.m.,* rabble. Всякий сброд, rag, tag, and bobtail.
брод-яж-ить, брод-яжничать, *v.i.,* to go about as a tramp. Брод-яга, *n.m.,* vagabond, tramp. Брод-яжничество, *n.n.,* vagrancy. Брод-ячий, *adj.,* wandering, vagrant. Вестú бродячий óбраз жúз- ни, to lead the life of a tramp. Б-ая соб- áка, a stray dog.
по-брод-ú-ть, *v.p.,* to wander, roam for a while. П. по свéту, to wander in the wide world. Квас достáточно побро-

дúл, the kvass has fermented sufficiently.
пере-брод-úть, *v.p.,* to complete fermentation. Пúво перебродúло, the beer has fermented, the process of fermentation is completed. К тридцатú годáм он перебродúл, by the age of thirty he had sown his wild oats.

БРЕМ-, БЕРЕМ-, BURDEN, LOAD, WEIGHT

брéм-я, *n.n.,* burden, load, weight. Снять б. винý, to exonerate. Разрешéние от брéмени, delivery,' birth. Под брéме- нем, under the burden of.
о-брем-ен-ú-ть, *v.p.,* о-брем-енять, *v.i.,* + *acc.;* + *instr.,* to burden, overburden, cumber. О. рабóтой, to overwhelm with work. О-брем-енéние, *n.n.,* load, burden, charging, overloading, overburdening. О-брем-енённый, *adj., part. pass. past.,* overloaded, overburdened. О. долгáми, burdened with debts. О- брем-енúтельность, *n.f.,* heavy burden, onus, burdensomeness. О-брем-енú- тельный, *adj.,* burdensome, onerous, heavy. О-ое поручéние, onerous task, mission.
берéм-енность, *n.f.,* pregnancy, gestation period. Лóжная б., false pregnancy. Шестóй мéсяц берéменности, sixth month of pregnancy.
берéм-ен-е-ть, *v.i.,* за-берéм-енеть, *v.p.,* to become pregnant, conceive. Берéм- енная, *adj.,* pregnant, *used as a n.,* pregnant woman.

БРОС-, БРОШ-, БРАС-, PROPULSION, THROWING

брóс-и-ть, *v.p.,* брос-á-ть, *v.i.,* + *acc.,* to throw, cast, fling; abandon, give up. Б. злóбный взгляд, to cast an angry look. Б. кáрты, to throw down one's cards. Брóсить мýзыку, to give up music. Брóсьте егó, leave him alone. Брóс-ить-ся, *v.p.r.,* брос-áть-ся, *v.i.r.,* на + *acc.,* to rush, throw oneself, dash. Б. вверх (вниз) по лéстнице, to rush, run up (down) the stairs. Б. комý-лúбо на шéю, to throw oneself on somebody's neck. Кровь бросáется в гóлову (лицó), blood rushes to the head (face). Брос-áющийся в глазá, conspicuous, manifest, evident, obvious. Брóш-енный, *adj., part. pass. past,* deserted, abandoned; thrown.
вы-брос-и-ть, *v.p.,* вы-брáс-ывать, *v.i.,* + *acc.,* из + *gen.,* to throw out, cast away, reject. В. лóзунг, to launch a slogan. В. товáр на рынок, to dump goods

on the market. В. из головы́, to put out of one's mind. Вы́-брос-ить-ся, *v.p.r.*, вы́-бра́с-ывать-ся, *v.i.r.*, to be thrown out; throw oneself out. Вы́броситься из окна́, to throw oneself out of a window.

за-бро́с-и-ть, *v.p.*, за-бра́с-ывать, *v.i.*, + acc., to throw beyond; abandon, neglect. З. мяч, to throw a ball.

за-брос-а́ть, *v.p.*, за-бра́с-ывать, *v.i.*, to throw at; load, heap; overwhelm with. З. вопро́сами, to ply with questions. З. камня́ми, to stone. За-бро́ш-ен-ность, *n.f.*, neglect, desertion. За-бро́ш-енный, *adj., part. pass. past,* deserted, abandoned. З. дом, uninhabited, deserted house, З. ребёнок, neglected, abandoned child.

на-бро́с-и-ть, *v.p.*, на-бра́с-ывать, *v.i.*, + acc., to throw over. Н. оде́жду на себя́, to throw clothing (*e.g.*, a coat) over one's shoulders.

на-брос-а́ть, *v.p.*, на-бра́с-ывать, *v.i.*, + acc., to pile up by throwing repeatedly in large quantities; sketch, draft, outline. Он наброса́л камне́й в я́му, he threw quantities of stone into the pit. На-бро́с-ить-ся, *v.p.r.*, на-бра́с-ывать-ся, *v.i.r.*, на + acc., to fall on, attack. Н. на кни́гу, to grab or throw oneself on a book; read voraciously. Н. на врага́, to fall on the enemy. Набра́сываться на еду́, to eat greedily. Набро́сок, *n.m.*, sketch, rough draft.

от-бро́с-и-ть, *v.p.*, от-бра́с-ывать, *v.i.*, + acc., to throw aside, toss away, sweep away. О. снег от поро́га, to sweep the snow off from the doorstep. Отбро́сьте вся́кие церемо́нии, (*imperat.*), waive all ceremony, don't stand on ceremony. От-бро́с-ы, *n.pl.*, waste, garbage, scraps. О. о́бщества, (*fig.*), the dregs of society. От-бро́ш-енный, *adj., part. pass. past,* thrown away, rejected. Эта отбро́шенная тео́рия, a rejected, discarded theory.

пере-бро́с-и-ть, *v.p.*, пере-бра́с-ывать, *v.i.*, + acc., to throw over, transfer swiftly. П. на другу́ю рабо́ту, to transfer someone to other work. П. войска́, to transfer troops swiftly. Пере-бро́с-ить-ся, *v.p.r.*, пере-бра́с-ывать-ся, *v.i.r.*, + instr., to be transferred rapidly; exchange rapidly. П. не́сколькими слова́ми, to exchange a few words. Пере-бра́с-ывание, *n.n.*, пере-бро́с-ка, *n.f.*, throwing over; swift transfer.

по-брос-а́ть, *v.p.*, + acc., to throw; forsake, desert.

под-бро́с-и-ть, *v.p.*, под-бра́с-ывать, *v.i.*,

+ *instr.*, to throw, toss up; expose. П. мяч, to throw a ball up. П. ребёнка кому́-либо, to leave, abandon, a child on someone's doorstep.

раз-брос-а́ть, *v.p.*, раз-бра́с-ывать, *v.i.*, + acc., to scatter, throw around, squander. Не разбра́сывайте книг, do not scatter the books around. Раз-бра́с-ывать-ся, *v.i.r.*, to lack singleness of purpose. Раз-бро́с-анность, *n.f.*, dispersion, disconnectedness. Раз-бро́с-анный, *adj., part. pass. past,* dispersed, disconnected. Р-ное населе́ние, sparse population. Раз-бро́с-анно, *adv.*, disconnectedly.

с-бро́с-и-ть, *v.p.*, с-бра́с-ывать, *v.i.*, + acc., to throw off, discard. С. вса́дника с седла́, to throw a rider, unhorse someone. С. ма́ску, to unmask, С. оде́жду, to slip off one's clothes. С-бра́с-ывание, *n.n.*, throwing down, off.

БУР-, STORM

бу́р-я, *n.f.*, storm, tempest. Снѐжная бу́ря, snowstorm. Бу́ря в стака́не воды́, (*fig.*), tempest in a teacup. Бур-а́н, *n.m.*, snowstorm in the steppes. Бур-е-ло́м, *n.m.*, windfallen trees. В лесу́ валя́лось мно́го бурело́ма, the forest was strewn with windfallen trees. Бур-е-ве́стник, *n.m.*, (*zool.*), stormy petrel. Бу́р-ность, *n.f.*, storminess, violence, impetuosity, boisterousness. Бу́рность поры́вов, impetuosity of emotions.

бу́р-ный, *adj.*, stormy, tempestuous, wild, rough, impetuous. Б. поры́в ве́тра, strong gust of wind. Б-ные стра́сти, impetuous passions. Бу́р-но, *adv.*, stormily, wildly.

бур-у́н, *n.m., mar.*, breaker, bow wave; буру́ны, *pl.*, surf.

бур-л-и́-ть, *v.i.*, to bubble, storm, boil. Мо́ре бурли́т, the sea is writhing. Ре́вность в нём бурли́т, jealousy is seething within him. Бур-л-я́щий, *adj., part. act. pres.*, seething. Бурля́щие поро́ги, the seething rapids (of a river).

за-бур-л-и́-ть, *v.p.*, to begin to bubble. Кипя́щая вода́ забурли́ла, the boiling water started to bubble. Бур-л-и́вость, *n.f.*, tempestuousness, storminess. Бур-л-и́вый, *adj.*, stormy, tempestuous.

о-бур-ева́-ть, *v.i.*, + acc., to agitate. Его́ обурева́ют стра́сти, he is agitated by violent passions. О-бур-ева́емый, *adj., part. pass. pres.*, passionately overwhelmed by. О. честолю́бием, a prey to ambition.

БЫ·, БЫ(Т)-, БУ(Д)-, БВ-, BEING, EXISTENCE

бы-ть, *v.i.,* to be, exist. Б. в отсу́тствии, to be absent. Б. в по́ру, to fit. Б. в си́лах, to have the strength, the power to. Б. в состоя́нии, to be able, be in a condition to. Б. знако́мым, to be acquainted. Как быть? what is to be done? Мо́жет быть, maybe, perhaps.

бы-ва́-ть, *v.i. iter.,* to occur, happen; visit frequently; *see* быть. Вы ре́дко быва́ете здесь, you are quite a stranger here. Быва́ют и таки́е слу́чаи, there are, indeed, cases like that. Бы́-вший, *adj.,* former, late, ex-. Б-ие лю́ди, former people of consequence. Бы-ва́ло, *v.i., past* (*impersonal*), it used to happen frequently. Он, б., слу́шал, he used to listen. И вдруг его́ как не быва́ло, and in a moment he was gone. Как ни в чём не быва́ло, as if nothing were the matter. Бы-ва́лый, *adj.,* that happened; experienced, worldly wise. Б. челове́к, one who has had considerable experience.

вы́-бы-ть, *v.p.,* вы-бы-ва́ть, *v.i.,* из + *gen.,* to leave, quit. В. из стро́я, (*mil.*), to be a casualty.

за-бы́-ть, *v.p.,* за-бы-ва́ть, *v.i.,* + *acc.,* to forget, forgive. З. оби́ду, to forgive an offense. Я забы́л ваш а́дрес, I have forgotten your address. За-бы́-ть-ся, *v.p.r.,* за-бы-ва́ть-ся, *v.i.r.,* + *instr.,* to forget oneself, doze, become unconscious; be lost in reveries. З. тяжёлым (лёгким) сном, to fall into a heavy (light) sleep. За-б-в-е́ние, *n.n.,* oblivion. Преда́ть забве́нию, (*poet.*), to forget. За-бы-тьё, *n.n.,* slumber, drowsiness, unconsciousness. Впада́ть в з., to fall into a heavy slumber, lose consciousness. За-бы́-в-чивость, *n.f.,* forgetfulness, carelessness, inattentiveness. За-бы́-в-чивый, *adj.,* forgetful, careless, inattentive.

до-бы́-ть, *v.p.,* до-бы-ва́ть *v.i.,* + *acc.,* to extract, mine; obtain, acquire, gain. Д. де́ньги (све́дения), to secure money (information). До-бы-ва́ть-ся, *v.i.r.* + *instr.,* to be extracted, mined. На Ура́ле добыва́ется мно́го мета́лла, in the Urals many metals are mined. До-бы́-ча, *n.f.,* extraction (*mining*); profit, loot, gain, prey. Сде́латься добы́чей пла́мени, to fall a prey to the flames.

из-бы́-ть, *v.p.,* из-бы-ва́ть, *v.i.,* + *acc.,* (*obs., used mostly in expression*): И. го́ре, to recover from grief. Из-бы́-ток, *n.m.,* superabundance, plenty. И. населе́ния, overpopulation. И. здоро́вья, exuberant health. Возмеща́ть с избы́тком, to overcompensate. Из-бы́-точный,

adj., superfluous, surplus. И. урожа́й, superabundant harvest.

о-бы-ва́-тель, *n.m.,* inhabitant, resident, man in the street. О-бы-ва́тельский, *adj.,* resident; philistine. О-бы-ва́тельщина, *n.f.* (*derog.*), philistinism. О. заса́сывает, the philistine environment swallows one up.

от-бы́-ть, *v.p.,* от-бы-ва́ть, *v.i.,* to depart, set out; + *acc.,* to serve (term, sentence). Парохо́д отбыва́ет в 6 часо́в утра́, the boat leaves at 6 A.M. Отбыва́ть во́инскую пови́нность, to serve one's time in the army. Отбыва́ть срок наказа́ния, to serve one's sentence (in prison). От-бы-ва́ние, *n.n.,* serving of a term. О. сро́ка слу́жбы, term of service in the army. От-бы́-тие, *n.n.,* departure (as a train). От-бы-ва́ющий, *adj., part. pres. act.,* departing.

по-бы́-ть, *v.p.,* по-бы-ва́ть, *v.i.,* to stay, stay for a little while, visit, make a sojourn. Побыва́ть в Евро́пе, to visit Europe. По-бы́-вка, *n.f.* (*colloq.*), furlough, leave of absence. На п-у, on leave, for a stay. Солда́т прие́хал домо́й на п-у, the soldier came home on furlough.

пере-бы́-ть, *v.p.,* пере-бы-ва́ть, *v.p.,* + *acc.,* to have been in many places, to spend time. На Но́вый Год я перебыва́ю у всех знако́мых, I shall visit all my friends on New Year's Day. В Ри́ме перебыва́ло мно́го тури́стов, many tourists visited Rome. Придётся пере-бы́ть ночь под откры́тым не́бом, we shall have to spend the night in the open.

пре-бы́-ть, *v.p.,* (*obs.*), пре-бы-ва́ть, *v.i.,* to stay, reside, sojourn; continue. Пребыва́ть в неве́дении, to be in the dark, not know. Пребыва́ть в ве́ре, to walk in faith, Пре-бы-ва́ние, *n.n.,* stay, sojourn. Постоя́нное п., permanent address, residence.

при-бы́-ть, *v.p.,* при-бы-ва́ть, *v.i.,* to arrive, come; increase, rise, swell. По́езд прибыл, the train is in, has arrived. Вода́ в реке́ прибыла́, the river has swollen. При́-бы-ль, *n.f.,* profit. Чи́стая п., net profit. При-бы-ва́ние, *n.n.,* rising, swelling, increase. При-бы́-тие, *n.n.,* arrival. При-бы-ва́ющий по́езд, incoming train.

про-бы́-ть, *v.p.,* to stay, remain. Я про́был там до среды́, I stayed there till Wednesday.

с-бы-ть, *v.p.,* с-бы-ва́ть, *v.i.,* + *acc.,* to dispose of, rid oneself of, to sell off. С. това́р, to sell off merchandise. Он сбыл свои́ ве́щи, he disposed of his belongings. С-бы́-ть-ся, *v.p.r.,* с-бы-ва́ть-ся, *v.i.r.,* to be sold, disposed of, to happen, occur, turn out. Хоро́шие сны не сбыва́ются, beautiful dreams don't come true. С-бы-т, *n.m.*, sale market, outlet for goods. Име́ть с., to have a market for. С-бы́-точный, *adj.*, possible, probable, *only in expression*: Сбы́точное ли э́то де́ло? is it possible? Не-с-бы́-точный, *adj.*, unrealizable. Н-ые мечты́, unrealizable dreams, wishes.

у-бы́-ть, *v.p.*, у-бы-ва́ть, *v.i.*, to decrease, diminish, lessen, sink to a lower level. Луна́ убыва́ет, the moon is on the wane. Вода́ убыва́ла в реке́, the water was receding in the river. У-бы́-ль, *n.f.*, decrease, diminution. Вода́ идёт на у., water is getting low, receding. У-бы-ва́ние, *n.n.*, decrease, waning. У-бы́-ток, *n.m.*, damage, loss. У. причинён-ный бу́рей (пожа́ром), the damage done by storm (fire). Чи́стый у., dead loss. Возмеща́ть у-и, to pay damages. У-бы́-точность, *n.f.*, lack of profit, loss (in business). У-бы́-точный, *adj.*, losing, unprofitable.

бы-т, *n.m.*, mode of life, manners and customs. Но́вый б., new way of life. Бы-т-ово́й, *adj.*, taken from life; referring to the life of a people. Б-ы́е усло́вия, living conditions. Бы́-т-ность, *n.f.*, stay, sojourn. В бы́тность мою студе́нтом, when I was a student. Само-бы́тность, *n.f.*, originality. С. нату́ры, originality of nature, character. Само-бы́тный, *adj.*, original. С. писа́тель, original writer. Быт-иé, *n.n.*, being, existence. Б. определя́ет созна́ние, existence determines consciousness. Кни́га Бытия́, (*Bib.*), Genesis. Житьё-бытьё, *n.n.* (*colloq.*), life, living, mode of existence. Со-бы́т-ие, *n.n.*, event, fact, occurrence. Неожи́данное с., sudden event. От-пра́здновать с., celebrate the occasion. Междунаро́дные собы́тия, international events.

Бы-л-ь, *n.f.*, fact, true story, Бы-л-и́на, *n.f.*, bylina (a metrical Russian legend). Были́нный э́пос, old Russian epic. Бы-л-и́нка, *n.f.*, blade of grass. Бы-л-ьё, *n.n.*, herbs, plants. Бы-ло́е, *n.n.*, bygone. Бы-л-о́й, *adj.*, past, bygone. В былы́е времена́, in olden days. Бы́-л-о, *past used as adv.*, nearly, on the point of, almost. Его́ чуть бы́ло не уби́ло, he was within a hair's breadth of being killed. Я чуть бы́ло не ушёл (не сказа́л), I was just about to go (say).

бу́-д-у, *1st pers. sing., fut., of* быть. Бу́д-ущность, *n.f.*, the future prospects, coming ages. Бу́д-ущий, *adj., part. act. pres.*, (*imperfective future*), next. Бу́д-ущее, *adj. used as n.n.*, the future. Б.

вре́мя, (*gram.*), future tense. Б-ое поколе́ние, the next generation. У него́ блестя́щее бу́дущее, he has a brilliant future. Бу́д-учи, *adv., part. pres.*, while being. Бу́д-ет, *fut. impers.*, it will be enough. Бу́дет вам разгова́ривать, спать пора́, enough talking, it's time to go to bed. Получи́ли по рублю́ и бу́дет с вас, you've each received a ruble and that's enough. Буд-ь, *2d pers. sing., imperat.*, be. Будь здоро́в; (*polite form*), бу́дьте здоро́вы, be in good health, I wish you good health. Будь благоразу́мен, be sensible. Бу́д-то, *conj.* (from бу́дь-то), as if it were, as though. Лежи́т, бу́дто мёртвый, he is lying there as if he were dead. Уж бу́дто он так умён? is he really so smart?

В

ВАГ-, ВАЖ-, WEIGHT, IMPORTANCE, DARING

от-ва́г-а, *n.f.*, daring, courage, audacity. Этот солда́т изве́стен свое́й отва́гой, this soldier is known for his daring.

от-ва́ж-ива-ть-ся, *v.i.r.*, от-ва́ж-ить-ся, *v.p.r.*, to dare, venture, risk. Неприя́тель не отва́жится на при́ступ, the enemy will not venture an assault. От-ва́ж-ность, *n.f.*, daring, fearlessness. От-ва́ж-ный, *adj.*, daring, bold. Мой брат отва́жный матро́с, my brother is a courageous sailor. От-ва́ж-но, *adv.*, boldly, courageously.

ва́ж-ность, *n.f.*, importance, significance, weight; pretentiousness. Напуска́ть на себя́ в., to assume airs. Не велика́ в., it's of no consequence. Ва́ж-ный, *adj.*, important, significant, grave, grand. В-ая персо́на, a man of consequence. В-ое де́ло, important business. Ва́ж-но, *adv.*, importantly, significantly, gravely. Это о́чень в., it is very important.

ва́ж-нич-а-ть, *v.i.*, за-ва́ж-ничать, *v.p.*, + *instr.*, to put on airs, give oneself airs. Ва́жничать чи́ном (происхожде́нием), to give oneself airs because of rank (high lineage). Ва́ж-ничание, *n.n.*, giving oneself airs.

у-важ-а́-ть, *v.i.* + *acc.*, to respect, esteem, honor. У. себя́, to have self-respect. У. ста́рших, to respect one's elders. У-важ-а́емый, *adj., part. pass. pres.*, respected (*form of address in letters*). У. Ива́н Ива́нович, Dear (Respected) Ivan Ivanovich. Мно́го-уважа́емый, very respected. Глубоко-уважа́емый, highly respected. У-важ-е́ние, *n.n.*, respect, esteem, deference. По́льзоваться у-ем, to be held in respect.

у-ва́ж-и-ть, *v.p.*, + *acc.*, (*colloq.*), to consider, take into consideration. У. про́сьбу, to comply with a request. У-важ-и́тельный, *adj.*, justifiable, justified, valid. По уважи́тельной причи́не, for a justifiable reason.

ВАЛ-, ВОЛ-, ROLL, SURGE; BULWARK, HEAP

вал, *n.m.*, billow, surge; bulwark, shaft (*tech.*); heap. Окружа́ть ва́лом, to bank. Ва́л-ик, *n.m.*, bolster, cylinder.

вал-и́-ть, *v.i.*, по-вал-и́-ть, с-вал-и́-ть, *v.p.*, + *acc.*, + *instr.*, to throw down, overthrow, topple, fell; to fall heavily. Снег вали́т, the snow falls in heavy flakes. Вали́ть (свали́ть) свою вину́ на друго́го, to put the blame on someone else. Ве́тер ва́лит дере́вья, the wind is blowing down the trees. Ему́ сча́стье вали́т, he is having a run of luck. Вали́ть ва́лом, (*idiom*) to throng. Вали́ть-ся, *v.i.r.*, с-вал-и́ть-ся, *v.p.r.*, to fall, tumble down. В. от уста́лости, to drop with fatigue. На бе́дного Мака́ра все ши́шки ва́лятся (*prov.*), an unfortunate man would be drowned in a teacup. Всё ва́лится из рук, (*idiom*), everything falls out of his hands, he is very clumsy, he never succeeds. Ва́л-ка, *n.f.*, falling, cutting down. Ва́л-кий, *adj.*, faltering, tottering. Ва́л-ко, *adv.*, unsteadily. Ни ша́тко, ни ва́лко, (*saying*), just middling.

за-вал-и́-ть, *v.p.*, за-ва́л-ивать, *v.i.*, + *acc.*, + *instr.*, to heap up, block up, cover up. З. вход камня́мн, to block up the entrance with stones. З. я́му, to fill up a hole, pit. З. рабо́той, to overburden, swamp with work. За-вал-и́ть-ся, *v.p.r.*, за-ва́л-ивать-ся, *v.i.r.*, to be obstructed; fall in, fall behind. З. спать, в посте́ль, (*idiom*), to go to bed. Кни́га завали́лась за дива́н, the book has fallen behind the sofa. За́-вал-ь, *n.f.*, (*colloq.*), old merchandise, old rubbish. За-вал-я́щий, *adj.*, (*colloq.*), lying about, useless. За-ва́л, *n.m.*, obstruction. З. в ша́хте, obstruction in a mine. З. в кишка́х, (*med.*), obstruction in the intestines.

на-вал-и́ть, *v.p.*, на-ва́л-ивать, *v.i.*, + *acc.*, to heap, pile up, fill, load, put on. Н. дрова́ на воз, to load a cart with firewood. Н. рабо́ту на кого́-ли́бо (*colloq.*), to overload a person with work. На я́рмарку навали́ло тьма наро́ду (*colloq.*), the fair was overcrowded. На-вал-и́ть-ся, *v.p.r.*, на-ва́л-ивать-ся, *v.i.r.*, на + *acc.*, to lean, bend heavily. Н. на дверь и проломи́ть её,

to lean heavily on the door and break it in.

об-вал-и́ть, *v.p.*, об-ва́л-ивать, *v.i.*, + *acc.*, to crumble; heap around. Бу́ря обвали́ла дом, the storm has reduced the house to rubble. Об-вал-и́ть-ся, *v.p.r.*, об-ва́л-ивать-ся, *v.i.r.*, to crumble down. Стена́ обвали́лась, the wall has fallen. Об-ва́л, *n.m.*, crumbling, fall, landslide. Сне́жный о., avalanche.

от-вал-и́ть, *v.p.*, от-ва́л-ивать, *v.i.*, + *acc.*, от + *gen.*, to put off, push off, leave the shore, pull off. Отвали́ть ка́мень от воро́т, to push a stone away from the gate. О. полмиллио́на на богаде́льни, (*colloq.*), to donate half a million for old people's homes. Паро-хо́д отвали́л в 3 ч., the steamer pushed off at 3 o'clock. От-вал-и́ть-ся, *v.p.r.*, от-ва́л-ивать-ся, *v.i.r.*, to fall off by itself. Штукату́рка отвали́лась, the plaster fell off. От-ва́л, *n.m.*, mold board, earth board (of plow). Нае́сться до отва́ла, (*colloq.*), to eat one's fill.

пере-вал-и́ть, *v.p.*, пере-ва́л-ивать, *v.i.*, за + *acc.*, через + *acc.*, to pass. Перевали́ть за по́лночь (по́лдень), to be past midnight (noon). Ему́ перевали́ло за́ со́рок, (*colloq.*), he is over 40. Перевали́ть че́рез го́ры, to cross a range of mountains. Пере-вал-и́ть-ся, *v.p.r.*, пере-ва́л-ивать-ся, *v.i.r.*, to waddle. Пере-ва́л, *n.m.*, mountain pass.

по-вал-и́ть, *v.p.*, + *acc.*, to throw down, overthrow; go (come) in crowds. Ве́тер повали́л мно́го дере́вьев, the wind blew down many trees. Дым повали́л из трубы́, the smoke poured out of the chimney. Вал-и́ть-ся, *v.i.r.*, по-вал-и́ть-ся, *v.p.r.*, to fall, be thrown down. Забо́р повали́лся, the fence has fallen. Впо-ва́л-ку, *adv.*, huddled, in a huddle. Спать вповáлку, to sleep on the floor side by side. Напо-ва́л, *adv.*, outright, on the spot. Солда́т был уби́т напова́л, the soldier was killed outright. По-ва́л-ь-ный, *adj.*, general, epidemic. П-ая боле́знь, epidemic disease. По-ва́л-ь-но, *adv.*, without exception, all. Заболе́ли ти́фом все пова́льно, they all came down with typhus without exception.

под-вал-и́-ть, *v.p.*, под-ва́л-ивать, *v.i.*, + *acc.*, to pile up to, heap up to. П. дрова́ к стене́, to pile wood up to the wall. Под-ва́л, *n.m.*, basement, cellar. Под-ва́л-ь-ный, *adj.*, basement, of or pertaining to a basement. П. эта́ж, basement. П-ое помеще́ние, a basement apartment.

при-вал-и́-ть, *v.p.*, при-ва́л-ивать, *v.i.*, + *acc.*, to lean something against an object, heap up. Привали́ть камень к стене to lean a stone against the wall. Какое ему счастье привалило! how fortunate he is При-ва́л, *n.m.*, halt. Де́лать п. to halt.

про-вал-и́-ть, *v.p.,* про-ва́л-ивать, *v.i.,* + *acc.,* to collapse, reject, send off, chase out. Провали́ть законопрое́кт, to kill a bill. Снег провали́л кры́шу, the snow caused the roof to collapse. Прова́ливай! *imperat.,* off! away with you! get away! Про-вал-и́ть-ся, *v.p.r.,* про-ва́л-ивать-ся, *v.i.r.,* to fall through, in; break down, fail. Студе́нт провали́лся на экза́менах, the student failed his examinations. Провали́ться сквозь зе́млю, to fall through, disappear. Прова́л, *n.m.,* downfall; large gap.

раз-вал-и́ть, *v.p.,* раз-ва́л-ивать, *v.i.,* + *acc.,* to undo, unmake, disorganize. Р. зда́ние (дом), to pull down a building (house). Р. рабо́ту, to disorganize work. Раз-вал-и́ть-ся, *v.p.r.,* раз-ва́л-ивать-ся, *v.i.r.,* to fall; go to pieces, go to ruin. Де́ло развали́лось, the business went to ruin. Он сел и развали́лся на дива́не, he sat down and sprawled on the sofa. Раз-ва́л, *n.m.,* disorganization, collapse, downfall. Был по́лный разва́л, everything was going to pieces. Разва́л-ина, *n.f.,* ruin, wreck. Он стал совсе́м разва́линой, he is a wreck of his former self. Разва́лины, *n.pl.,* ruins. Р. за́мка, the ruins of a castle. Ро́звал-ь-ни, *n.f.pl.,* a wide, low country sledge.

с-вал-и́ть, *v.p.,* с-ва́л-ивать, *v.i.,* + *acc.,* to throw down. С. бре́мя, (отве́тственность), to shift off a burden, responsibility. С. воз, to unload a cart. С-вал-и́ть-ся, *v.p.r.,* с-ва́л-ивать-ся, *v.i.r.,* to fall, tumble down, collapse. С. с ле́стницы, to tumble downstairs. С., как снег на́ голову, to come like a bolt from the blue. Он свали́лся, he became sick. С-ва́л-ка, *n.f.,* dump, scrapheap; (*fig.*), scramble; (*colloq.*), fight. Свезти́ му́сор на сва́лку, to cart away trash to the dump. Быть в са́мой сва́лке, to be in the thick of the fight.

вал-я́-ть, *v.i.,* вы́-вал-ять, *v.p.,* + *acc.,* to roll, full felt or cloth. В. шля́пы (ва́ленки), to full felt for hats (boots). В. дурака́, (*colloq.*), to play the fool. Вал-я́ть-ся, *v.i.r.,* to roll about, loll. В. в посте́ли, to loll in bed. В. в беспоря́дке, to be scattered about. В. в снегу́, to roll in snow. В. в грязи́, to wallow in the mire. Валя́й! (*colloq.*), begin! go ahead! Ва́л-енки, *n.pl.,* *valenki*, felt boots. Ва́л-еный *adj.,* felt.

об-вал-я́-ть, *v.p.,* об-ва́л-ивать, *v.i.,* в + *prep.,* to roll (*e.g.,* in flour). О. котле́ту в муке́, to roll a cutlet in

flour. У-ва́л-ень, *n.m.,* lump, clumsy fellow.

вол-н-а́, *n.f.,* wave, billow, surge, sea. Волна́ захлестну́ла су́дно, the waves flooded the vessel. Звукова́я в., sound wave. Светова́я в., light wave. Ста́чечная в., (*fig.*), a wave of strikes. Цве́та морско́й волны́, sea-green color. Волн-ова́я тео́рия, wave theory. Волни́стый, *adj.,* wavy, undulating, rippling. В-ая ткань, crimped material. В-ые во́лосы, wavy hair. В-ое желе́зо, corrugated iron. В-ая ме́стность, undulating country. Вол-н-о-ло́м, *n.m.,* breakwater. Вол-н-о-обра́зный, *adj.,* undulating, wavy. В-ое движе́ние, wave motion. Вол-н-о-указа́тель, *n.m.,* radio wave detector.

вол-н-ова́-ть, *v.i.,* вз-вол-нова́ть, *v.p.,* + *acc.,* to agitate, disturb, upset, alarm. Ве́тер волну́ет морску́ю гладь, the wind disturbs the calm of the sea's surface. Эти ве́сти волну́ют меня́, this news upsets, alarms me. Бу́ря взволнова́ла мо́ре, the storm stirred up the sea Вол-н-ова́ть-ся, *v.i.r.,* вз-вол-нова́ть-ся, *v.p.r.,* to wave, billow, surge, rise in waves; be agitated, excited. Река́ взволнова́лась, the river became stormy. Мо́ре си́льно волну́ется, the sea is very stormy. Нельзя́ волнова́ться из-за пустяко́в, one should not be upset by trifles. Вол-не́ние, *n.n.,* rough sea, heavy sea; agitation, emotion; commotion, unrest; disturbance, В. в наро́де, unrest among the people.

за-вол-н-ова́-ть-ся, *v.p.r.,* to become agitated. Пу́блика зашуме́ла, заволнова́лась, the audience became noisy, excited.

раз-вол-н-ова́-ть, *v.p.,* + *acc.,* (*colloq.*), to agitate, move, stir. Ве́тер разволнова́л мо́ре, the wind has stirred up the sea. Это письмо́ разволнова́ло его́, this letter has upset him. Раз-вол-нова́ть-ся, *v.p.r.,* to become agitated. Р. из-за пустяко́в, to fuss over trifles.

ВАР-, COOKING

вар, *n.m.,* pitch; cobbler's wax; boiling water. Каше-ва́р, *n.m.,.* regimental cook. На-ва́р, *n.m.,* broth, stock. Нава́р-истый, *adj.,* concentrated (*e.g.,* broth). Н. бульо́н, strong broth. От-ва́р, *n.m.,* decoction. Де́лать о., to decoct. Ри́совый о., rice water. От-варно́й, *adj.,* boiled, cooked. О-бе мя́со, boiled meat. По́-вар, *n.m.,* cook, chef. По-ва́р-енный, *adj.,* culinary. П-ая кни́га, cookbook. П-ая соль, salt; (*chem.*), sodium chloride. По-вар-ёнок, *n.m.,* kitchen boy, scullion. По-вар-и́ха, *n.f.,* cook. По-вар-ско́й, *adj.,* cook's. П. нож, kitchen knife. Само-ва́р, *n.m.,* samovar. Ездить в Ту́лу со свои́м самова́ром *(saying),* to carry coals to Newcastle. Ва́р-ево, *n.n.,* concoction, soup, broth. Вар-ене́ц *n.m.,* boiled, fermented, milk. Вар-е́ники, *n.m.pl.,* cottage cheese dumplings. Вар-ёный, *adj.,* boiled. Вар-е́нье *n.n.,* jam, preserve. Ва́р-ка, *n.f.,* cooking. В. варе́нья, making jam, preserves. В. пи́ва, brewing beer. Не-с-вар-е́ние, *n.n.,* *(med.),* indigestion. Пищ-е-вар-е́ние, *n.n., (med.),* digestion. Плохо́е п., poor digestion. Пище-вар-и́тельный *adj., (med.),* digestive.

вар-и́-ть, *v.i.,* с-вар-и́ть, *v.p.,* + *acc.,* to boil, cook. В. суп, to make soup. В. обе́д, to cook dinner. Вар-и́ть-ся, *v.i.r.,* с-вар-и́ть-ся, *v.p.r.,* to be boiled, cooked. В. в со́бственном соку́ *(fig.),* to stew in one's own juice.

вы́-вар-и-ть, *v.p.,* вы-ва́р-ивать, *v.i.,* + *acc.,* to boil down, extract, decoct. Вы́-вар-ить-ся, *v.p.r.,* вы-ва́р-ивать-ся, *v.i.r.,* to be boiled down. Вся вода́ вы́варилась, the kettle has boiled dry.

до-вар-и́-ть, *v.p.,* до-ва́р-ивать, *v.i.,* + *acc.,* to boil enough, to the necessary degree. До-вар-и́ть-ся, *v.p.r.,* до-ва́р-ивать-ся, *v.i.r.,* to be boiled enough.

за-вар-и́-ть, *v.p.,* за-ва́р-ивать, *v.i.,* + *acc.,* to brew, start boiling, cooking. З. бельё, to boil clothes in washing. З. чай (ко́фе), to make, brew, tea (coffee). Сам завари́л ка́шу, сам и рас-хлёбывай *(prov.),* he who breaks, pays. За-вар-и́ть-ся, *v.p.r.,* за-ва́р-ивать-ся, *v.i.r.,* to be boiled, brewed. Вот завари́-лась ка́ша! *(colloq.),* the fat's in the fire! Чай зава́ривается кипятко́м, tea is brewed with boiling water. За-вар-но́й, *adj.,* boiled. З. крем, custard.

на-вар-и́-ть, *v.p.,* на-ва́р-ивать, *v.i.,* + *gen.,* to cook in quantities. Н. щей на не́сколько дней, to cook enough cabbage soup for several days.

об-вар-и́-ть, *v.p.,* об-ва́р-ивать, *v.i.,* + *acc.,* + *instr.,* to scald. О. о́вощи, to scald vegetables. О. ру́ку чём-нибудь, to scald the hand with something. Об-вар-и́ть-ся, *v.p.r.,* об-ва́р-ивать-ся, *v.i.r.,* + *instr.,* to scald oneself. Он обвари́лся кипятко́м, he scalded himself with boiling water.

от-вар-и́-ть, *v.p.,* от-ва́р-ивать, *v.i.,* + *acc.,* + *gen.,* to boil, cook; *see* вари́ть.

пере-вар-и́-ть, *v.p.,* пере-ва́р-ивать, *v.i.,* + *acc.,* to boil to excess, overcook; to cook over again; to digest. Перева́ри-вать пи́щу, to digest food. Я не перева́риваю э́того челове́ка, I cannot stand this man. Пере-вар-и́ть-ся, *v.p.r.,*

пере-ва́р-ивать-ся, *v.i.r.,* to be digested; be overcooked. Пере-ва́р-ивание, *n.n.,* digestion. Пере-ва́р-енный, *adj., part. pass. past,* overdone, overcooked; digested. П-ое мя́со, overcooked meat. П-ая вода́, boiled water. Пере-вар-и́мый, *adj., part. pass. pres.,* digestible. Легко́ п., easily digestible.

под-вар-и́-ть, *v.p.,* под-ва́р-ивать, *v.i.,* + *acc.,* to boil, adding new ingredients.

при-вар-и́ть, *v.p.,* при-ва́р-ивать, *v.i.,* + *acc.,* to boil an additional quantity of; *(tech.),* to weld together. Привари́ть пла́нку, to weld a strip of metal on. Привари́ть су́пу, to cook more soup. При-ва́р-ка, *n.f.,* welding to. При-ва́р-ок, *n.m.* supplementary ration.

про-вар-и́-ть, *v.p.,* про-ва́р-ивать, *v.i.,* + *acc.,* to boil thoroughly. Ры́бу на́до сле́дует провари́ть, it is necessary to cook fish thoroughly. Про-вар-и́ть-ся, *v.p.r.,* про-ва́р-ивать-ся, *v.i.r.,* to be boiled thoroughly.

раз-вар-и́-ть, *v.p.,* раз-ва́р-ивать, *v.i.,* + *acc.,* to boil soft, stew. Раз-ва́р-енный, *adj., part. pass. past,* boiled until soft, overcooked, stewed thoroughly. Раз-варно́й, *adj.,* boiled until soft. Р. карто́фель, boiled potatoes. Р-а́я ры́ба, boiled fish.

с-вар-и́-ть, *v.p.,* + *acc.,* to boil, cook. С-ва́р-ивать, *v.i.* + *acc.,* to weld. С-вар-и́ть-ся, *v.p.r.,* с-ва́р-ивать-ся, *v.i.r.,* to boil, be boiled; be welded. Суп свари́лся, the soup is ready. С-ва́р-ка, *n.f., (tech.),* welding. Автоге́нная с. мета́ллов, arc welding. С-ва́р-щик, *n.m,.* welder. Сва́рочная мастерска́я, welding workshop.

у-вар-и́-ть, *v.p.,* у-ва́р-ивать, *v.i.,* + *acc.,* to boil down, stew, cook to a turn. У. сиро́п, чтобы стал гу́ще, to cook syrup until it thickens. У-вар-и́ть-ся, *v.p.r.,* у-ва́р-ивать-ся, *v.i.r.,* to be cooked to a turn. У-ва́р-ка, *n.f.,* boiling down, loss through boiling.

ВЕ-, WAFT, BLOW, FAN

ве́-я-ть, *v.i.,* to blow softly; wave; + *acc.,* to fan; winnow. Ве́тер ве́ет, the wind blows. В окно́ ве́ет прохла́дой, cool air blows through the window. Ве́-ялка, *n.f.,* winnowing machine. Ве́-яние. *n.n.,* breathing, blowing; winnowing; *fig.,* tendency. В. ве́тра, soft blowing of the wind. Ве́янье зерна́, winnowing. Но́вые ве́яния, new ideas.

за-ве́-я-ть, *v.p.,* за-ве-ва́ть, за-ве́-ивать, *v.i.,* + *acc.,* to begin to blow, to drift over, to blow, (as snow or sand). Заве́ял лёгкий ве́тер, a light wind began to blow. Мете́ль завева́ла доро́гу, the snowstorm was blowing snow over the road.

на-ве́-я-ть, *v.p.,* на-ве-ва́ть, *v.i.,* + *acc.,* to drift, heap up, blow together. Н. печа́ль, грусть, to sadden, make one melancholy.

об-ве́-я-ть, *v.p.,* об-ве-ва́ть, *v.i.,* + *instr.,* + *acc.,* to winnow, fan. О. хо́лодом (ве́тром), to feel a gust of cold air (wind).

по-ве́-я-ть, *v.p.,* по-ве-ва́ть, *v.i.,* + *instr.,* to begin to blow. Ве́тер пове́ял с мо́ря, the wind began to blow from the sea. На меня́ пове́яло мину́вшим, (*fig.*), memories of the past came over me.

про-ве́-я-ть, *v.p.,* про-ве-ва́ть, про-ве́-вать, *v.i.,* + *acc.,* to winnow. Прове́ять зерно́, to winnow the grain through. Про-ве́-ять-ся, *v.p.r.,* про-ве-ва́ть-ся, про-ве́-ивать-ся, *v.i.r.,* to be winnowed. Зерно́ хорошо́ прове́ялось, the grain has been thoroughly winnowed.

раз-ве́-я-ть, *v.p.,* раз-ве-ва́ть, раз-ве́-ивать, *v.i.,* + *acc.,* to blow about, scatter, disperse. Ве́тер разве́ял облака́, the wind dispersed the clouds. Раз-ве́-ять-ся, *v.p.r.,* раз-ве́-ивать-ся, раз-ве-ва́ться, *v.i.r.,* от + *gen.,* to wave, flutter, fly, be dispersed by wind. Пыль разве́ялась, the dust blew away. Флаг развева́ется, the flag is waving. Сомне́ния разве́ялись, doubts vanished. Пла́мя развева́ется от ве́тра, the flame is fanned by the wind.

с-ве́-я-ть, *v.p.,* с-ве-ва́ть, с-ве́-ивать, *v.i.,* + *acc.,* + *instr.,* to blow off, away. Ве́тром све́яло с я́блони лепестки́ цвето́в, the wind blew the petals off the apple tree.

ве́-тер, *n.m.,* ве́-тры, *pl.,* из ветр, (*obs., poet.*), wind. Ве-тер-о́к, *n.m., dim.,* breeze. Ве́тер поднима́ется, the wind is rising. Попу́тный ве́тер, fair, favorable, wind. Сквозно́й в., draft. У него́ ве́тер в голове́, (*colloq.*), he is a thoughtless fellow. Ве-три́ло, *n.n.,* (*poet.*), sail. "Без руля́ и без ветри́л" (*Lermontov*), "without rudder or sail." Ве́-тр-еный, *adj.,* windy; light-minded, giddy, flighty. В. день, windy day. В. челове́к, flighty man. Ве́-тр-ено, *adv.,* windy; giddily, in a flighty manner. На дворе́ ве́трено, it is windy outdoors. Ветр-о-дви́гатель, *n.m.,* wind motor, wind-driven generator. Ветр-я́к, *n.m.,* (*colloq.*), windmill. Ветр-ян-о́й, *adj.,* wind-. Ветряно́й дви́гатель, see ветродви́гатель. Ве́тряная о́спа, chicken pox.

ве́-тр-ен-ич-а-ть, *v.i.,* to be flighty, act thoughtlessly. Ве́-треник, *n.m.,* ве́-треница, *n.f.,* flighty or giddy person.

Ве́-тр-еность, *n.f.,* giddiness, lightheadedness, thoughtlessness.

вы́-ве-тр-ить, *v.p.,* вы-ве́-тр-ивать, *v.i.,* + *acc.,* to air. В. мехову́ю оде́жду, to air fur coats. Вы-ве́-тр-ивание, *n.n.,* airing. По-ве́-тр-ие, *n.n.,* epidemic, infection. П. на о́спу, epidemic of smallpox.

про-ве́-тр-ить, *v.p.,* про-ве́-тр-ивать, *v.i.,* + *acc.,* to air thoroughly, ventilate. П. ко́мнату, to air, ventilate, a room. Про-ве́-трить-ся, *v.p.r.,* про-ве́-триваться, *v.i.r.,* to be aired. Про-ве́-тривание, *n.n.,* airing, ventilation.

ВЕД-, (ВѢД-), ВЕЖ- (ВѢЖ-), ВЕЖД- (ВѢЖД-), ВЕСТ- (ВѢСТ-), ВЕЩ- (ВѢЩ-), KNOWLEDGE

ве́д-а-ть, *v.i.* + *instr.,* to know. Ве́дать чем-ли́бо, to manage, control. Она́ ве́дает хозя́йством, she is in charge of housekeeping. Ве́д-ение, *n.n.,* knowledge, *only in expression*: в чьём-либо в-и, within someone's jurisdiction, under someone's management. Не-ве́д-ение, *n.n.,* ignorance. Не-ве́д-омый, *adj., part. pass. pres.,* (*poet.*), unknown. Неве́домые стра́ны, unknown countries. Ве́д-и, *n.n.* (*Ch. Slav.*), the letter В. Ве́д-ома, *adv., only in expression*: с ве́дома, with (someone's) knowledge; без его́ ве́дома, without one's knowledge. За-ве́д-омо, *adv.,* known to be. Заве́домо зна́я, knowing beforehand. Ве́д-омость, *n.f.,* journal, report; list; payroll. Ве́д-омости, *n.p.,* newspaper, Ве́д-омство, *n.n.,* department, office. Вое́нное в., war office, department. Суде́бное в., department of justice. Вед-ь, *emphatic particle*, well, but; why! Да ведь я же не зна́л, well, but I did not know about it. Но ведь э́то так, well, but it's so. Ве́д-ь-ма, *n.f.,* witch, hellcat.

вы́-вед-а-ть, *v.p.,* вы-ве́д-ывать, *v.i.,* + *acc.,* to investigate, find out. Выве́дывать чьи-ли́бо наме́рения, to sound out a person's intentions.

за-ве́д-ыва-ть, *v.i.,* + *instr.,* to manage, superintend. З. ру́сским отде́лом, to be head of the Russian Department. За-ве́д-ующий, *m.,* за-ве́д-ующая, *f., adj., part. act. pres., used as n.,* manager, chief, director. З. гости́ницей, head clerk. З. магази́ном, store manager. З. канцеля́рией, director. З. хозя́йством, housekeeper. З. шко́лой, headmaster, principal.

за-по-ве́д-а-ть, *v.p.,* за-по-ве́д-ывать, *v.i.,* + *acc.,* to command, order. За́-по-вед-ь, *n.f.,* commandment, order. Де́сять за́-поведей, the Ten Commandments, De-

calogue. За-по-вѐд-ник, *n.m.*, preserve, forest in which shooting is prohibited. Рыбный з., fishing preserve. Лесной з., forest where felling of trees is prohibited, national park. За-по-вѐд-ный, *adj.*, interdicted, forbidden, prohibited. Заповѐдные зѐмли, state reservations.
из-вѐд-а-ть, *v.p.*, из-вѐд-ывать, *v.i.*, + *acc.*, to learn, find out, investigate; try. И. счастье (гóре), to taste, drink, the cup of happiness (sorrow). Из-вѐд-анный, *adj.*, *part. pass. past*, tested, proved to be efficient. И. путь, a well-known way, an acknowledged method.
ис-по-вѐд-ывать, *v.i.*, + *acc.*, to profess a religion. И. христианство, to profess Christianity. Ис-по-вѐд-ание, *n.n.*, faith, religion. Вер-о-исповѐдание, *n.n.*, confession of faith. Христианское вероисповѐдание, Christian religion.
ис-по-вѐд-а-ть, *v.p.*, ис-по-вѐд-ывать, *v.i.*, + *acc.*, to hear confession. Свящѐнник исповѐдывал вѐрующих, the priest confessed the believers. Ис-по-вѐд-ать-ся, *v.p.r.*, ис-по-вѐд-ывать-ся, *v.i.r.*, to confess, to go to confession. Ис-по-вед-ь, *n.f.*, confession. Ис-по-вѐд-ник, *n.m.*, confessor, father confessor.
на-вѐд-ать-ся, *v.p.r.*, на-вѐд-ывать-ся, *v.i.r.*, о + *prep.*, к + *dat.*, to call on, visit; inquire about, after. Н. о здорóвье, to inquire about the health. Н. к больнóму, to visit a sick man.
о-с-вѐд-ом-и-ть, *v.p.*, ос-вед-омлять, *v.i.*, + *acc.*, to inform. О. присýтствующих о случившемся, to inform those present of what has happened. Ос-вѐд-омить-ся, *v.p.r.*, ос-вед-омлять-ся, *v.i.r.*, о + *prep.*, to inquire, ask about, inform oneself of, secure information on. О. о причине отсýтствия, to inquire about the reason for absence. Ос-вед-омлѐние, *n.n.*, information. Ос-вед-омлённость, *n.f.*, knowledge. Ос-вед-омлённый, *adj.*, *part. pass. past*, informed. Хорошó (плóхо) осведомлённый, well (ill) informed. Ос-вед-омитель, *n.m.*, informant. Ос-вед-омительный, *adj.* informative, instructive. О-ое бюрó, information bureau.
от-вѐд-а-ть, *v.p.*, от-вѐд-ывать, *v.i.*, + *acc.*, + *gen.*, (*obs.*), to taste, try, experience. Не отвѐдав гóря, не познáешь и счастья, (*prov.*), not having tasted grief, thou shalt not know happiness.
по-вѐд-а-ть, *v.p.*, + *acc.*, + *dat.*, (*obs.*, *poet.*), to tell, relate, communicate, disclose. Повѐдать дрýгу свою тáйну, to disclose one's secret to a friend.
про-вѐд-а-ть, *v.p.*, про-вѐд-ывать, *v.i.*, + *acc.*, о + *prep.*, to visit, call on;

find out, learn. П. больнóго, to visit a sick man. П. о чём-либо, to find out something.
раз-вѐд-а-ть, *v.p.*, раз-вѐд-ывать, *v.i.*, + *acc.*, to inquire about; investigate, explore. Р. расположѐние сил неприятеля, to reconnoiter the location of the enemy forces. Раз-вѐд-ка, *n.f.*, search, exploration; (*mil.*), reconnaissance. Воздýшная р., (*mil.*), air observation, reconnaissance. Производить р-у, to reconnoiter, scout. Раз-вѐд-чик, *n.m.*, scout; (*mining*), prospector. Раз-вѐд-ывательный, *adj.*, раз-вѐд-очный, *adj.*, reconnoitering, prospecting. Р. самолёт, reconnaissance plane.
с-вѐд-а-ть, *v.p.*, + *acc.*, to learn, get to know. С-вѐд-ение, *n.n.*, knowledge, information, intelligence. Принять к свѐдению, to take notice of. Давáть свѐдения, to impart information. С-вѐдущий, *adj.*, versed in, expert in. Быть свѐдущим в чём-либо, to be versed in.
с-вид-ѐтель-ство-вать (*from* "с-вѣд-етельствовать"), *v.i.*, за-с-вид-ѐтельствовать, *v.p.*, + *acc.*, to bear witness to, testify to, give evidence of, attest, certify, authenticate (documentarily). Свидѐтельствовать, засвидѐтельствовать свою личность, to prove one's identity. З. своё почтѐние, (*obs.*), to pay one's respects. С-вид-ѐтель, *n.m.*, с-ница, *n.f.*, witness. Свидѐтель на судѐ, witness in a lawsuit, at a trial. С-вид-ѐтельство, *n.n.*, evidence, testimony; certificate. Свидѐтельство об окончáнии школы, school diploma.
у-вѐд-ом-и-ть, *v.p.*, у-вед-омлять, *v.i.*, + *acc.*, о + *prep.*, to inform, notify, give notice. У. о дне экзáмена, to inform of the day of the examination. У. о получѐнии письмá, to notify of the receipt of a letter. У-вед-омляться *v.i.r.*, to be informed, secure information, be notified. У-вед-омлѐние, *n.n.*, information, notice. Получить у. из бáнка, to receive notice from the bank.
пред-у-вѐд-ом-и-ть, *v.p.*, преду-вед-омлять, *v.i.*, + *acc.*, to inform beforehand, advise of, warn. Преду-вед-омлѐние, *n.n.*, notice, notification, forewarning.
вѐж-лив-ость, *n.f.*, civility, courtesy, politeness. Не-вѐж-ливость, *n.f.*, incivility, bad manners. Не-вѐж-а, *n.m.*, ill-mannered person, boor, churl. Не-вѐжд-а, *n.m.*, know-nothing, ignoramus. Не-вѐж-ество, *n.n.*, ignorance. Вѐжливо, politely. Не-вѐж-ливо, rudely.
вест-ь, *v.i.*, *3d pers. sing. of* вѣсти, (*Ch. Slav.*), to know, *only in expression*: Бог весть, Heaven knows what; *syn.*, Бог знáет что. Не весть что, *obs.*, неизвѐстно что, no one knows what. Вест-ь,

n.f., news, message, information. Ра́-
достные ве́сти, good news. Худы́е
ве́сти не лежа́т на ме́сте (*prov.*),
bad news travels fast. Ве́ст-очка, *n.f.*,
(*dim.*), news. Да́йте о себе́ ве́сточку,
let me hear from you, drop me a line.
Вест-и́мо, *adv.*, (*obs.*), surely certainly.
"Отку́да дрови́шки? — Из ле́су вест-
и́мо" (Nekrásov), "Whence the firewood? — From the forest, certainly."
Ве́ст-ник, *n.m.*, ве́ст-ница, *n.f.*, messenger, bearer, forerunner, precursor. Вест-
ово́й, *adj.*, *used as n.*, orderly. У офице́-
ра бы́ло два вестовы́х, the officer had
two orderlies. Вещ-а́-ть, *v.i.*, + *acc.*
(*obs.*), to prophesy. Вещ-а́ние, *n.n.*,
prophesying, foretelling, predicting.
Радиовеща́ние, radio broadcasts. Ве́щ-
ий, *adj.*, (*obs.*), weird, prophetic, un-
canny. "Ве́щий Оле́г" - стихотворе́ние
Пу́шкина, the "Lay of the Wise Oleg"
is a poem by Pushkin.

воз-вест-и́ть, *v.p.*, воз-вещ-а́ть, *v.i.*, +
acc., to inform, communicate, announce.
Воз-вещ-е́ние, *n.n.*, announcement.

из-вест-и́ть, *v.p.*, из-вещ-а́ть, *v.i.* + *acc.*,
to let know, announce, inform, com-
municate. И. студе́нтов о нача́ле
заня́тий, to announce to the students
the beginning of classes. Извеща́ем
вас, we beg to inform you. Из-вещ-
е́ние, *n.n.*, notification, information.
Извеще́ние о нача́ле экза́менов, notice
about the beginning of examinations.
Из-ве́ст-ие, *n.n.*, information, news,
tidings. После́дние изве́стия, the latest
news. Из-ве́ст-но, *pred. adj.*, *used as
parenthetical expression*: as is known.
Как изве́стно, as everyone knows.
Изве́стно-ли вам? do you know? Мне
всё об э́том изве́стно, I am well aware
of it. Из-ве́ст-ность, *n.f.*, reputation,
fame. По́льзоваться гро́мкой изве́ст-
ностью, to be well known, be famous.
Поста́вить в и., to inform of. Из-ве́ст-
ный, *adj.*, certain; well known, famous,
notorious. И. арти́ст, a famous artist.
В изве́стных слу́чаях, in certain cases.
Без-ве́ст-ность, *n.f.*, obscurity. Без-
ве́ст-ный, *adj.*, unknown, obscure. Без-
ве́ст-но, *adv.*, *only in expression*: б.
пропа́вший, a missing person.

на-вест-и́ть, *v.p.*, на-вещ-а́ть, *v.i.*, + *acc.*,
to visit, call in.

о-по-вест-и́ть, *v.p.*, опо-вещ-а́ть, *v.i.*, +
acc., о + *prep.* to inform, declare, announce. О. студе́нтов о собра́нии, to
announce a meeting to the students.
Опо-вещ-е́ние, *n.n.*, announcement, declaration.

по-вест-в-ова́-ть, *v.i.*, о + *prep.*, to relate,
narrate, recount, tell. Повествова́ть о
мину́вших собы́тиях, to relate past

events. По́-вест-ь, *n.f.*, short novel, no-
velette. По-вест-вова́ние, *n.n.*, narrative, relation. По-вест-вова́тель, *n.m.*,
повествова́тельница, *n.f.*, narrator. По-
вест-вова́тельный, *adj.*, narrative.

пред-вещ-а́ть, *v.i.*, пред-вест-и́ть, *v.p.*, +
acc., (*obs.*), to forebode, presage, foretell. Пред-вещ-а́ние, *n.n.*, (*obs.*), pre-
diction, foretelling. Пред-ве́ст-ие, *n.n.*,
presage, omen. Пред-ве́ст-ник, *n.m.*,
предве́стница, *n.f.*, forerunner, precursor. Чёрные ту́чи - предве́стники бу́ри,
dark clouds are the forerunners of a
storm.

пред-воз-вещ-а́ть, *v.i.*, пред-воз-вест-
и́ть, *v.p.*, + *acc.*, to foretell, prophesy,
predict. Пред-воз-ве́ст-ник, *n.m.*,
предвозве́стница, *n.f.*, prophet, one
who foretells. Пред-воз-вещ-е́ние, *n.n.*,
foretelling, prophesy.

со́-вест-ить, *v.i.*, у-со́-вест-ить, *v.p.*, +
acc., (*colloq.*), to admonish, exhort. С.
шалуна́, to admonish a scamp. со́-вест-
ить-ся, *v.i.r.*, по-со́-вест-ить-ся, *v.p.r.*,
+ *inf.*, to have scruples. Он сове́стится
проси́ть по́мощи, he has scruples
about asking for help. Со́-вест-ь, *n.f.*,
conscience. Угрызе́ния с-и, remorse.
По со́вести говоря́, honestly speaking.
Со́-вест-ливость, *n.f.*, conscientious-
ness, scrupulousness. Со́-вест-ливый,
adj., conscientious, scrupulous. Со́-
вест-но, *adv.*, contritely. Мне со́вест-
но, I am ashamed, contrite about it. Бес-
со́-вест-ность, *n.f.*, unscrupulousness,
dishonesty. Бес-со́-вест-ный, *adj.*, unscrupulous. disgraceful. Б. посту́пок,
a shameful deed. Бес-со́-вест-но, *adv.*,
shamefully, disgracefully.

благо-вест-и́ть, *v.i.*, to ring for church.
Бла́говест, *n.m.*, ringing for church.
Благо-ве́щ-ение, *n.n.* (*rel.*), Annuncia-
tion.

**ВЕЛ-, ВОЛ-, ВОЛЬ-, ВЛ-, WILL, COM-
MAND, ORDER**

вел-е́-ть, *v.p.*, *v.i.*, + *dat.* (*in past used
only as v.p.*) to order, command, bid,
tell. Я веле́л им уйти́, I told them to
go away. Веле́ть что́-нибудь сде́лать,
to have something done. Ему́ не веля́т
есть мя́са, he is not allowed to eat
meat. Де́лать, как ве́лено, to do as one
is told. Вел-е́ние, *n.n.* (*obs.*), decree,
order.

по-вел-е́-ть, *v.p.*, по-вел-ева́ть, *v.i.*, +
dat., + *instr.*, to command, order, enjoin. Повелева́ть миллио́нами люде́й,
to rule over millions of people. Мой
долг повелева́ет мне сде́лать э́то, my
duty compels me to do it. По-вел-е́ние,
n.n., (*obs.*), command, order, injunc-

tion, decree. По-вел-и́тельный, *adj.*, imperative, authoritative, dictatorial. П. тон, authoritative voice. П-ое накло-не́ние, (*gram.*), imperative mood. По-вел-и́тельно, *adv.*, imperatively.

во́л-я, *n.f.*, will; freedom, liberty; *see,* свобо́да. Во́ля ва́ша; на то ва́ша до́брая во́ля, (*coll.*), as you please; as you like. Во́лей-нево́лей, willy-nilly. Дава́ть во́лю воображе́нию, to give free rein to one's imagination. Дава́ть во́лю стра́сти, to let loose one's passions. Дава́ть во́лю языку́, to loose one's tongue. Отпуска́ть на во́лю, to set free, liberate. Во́ль-ная, *adj. used as n.,* (*hist.*), document releasing from serfdom. Дава́ть во́льную, to release from serfdom.

во́ль-нич-а-ть, *v.i.,* to take liberties with; be wilful. Во́ль-ничание, *n.n.,* the taking of liberties. Во́ль-но, *adv.,* freely; (*mil.*), at ease! Вольно́ ему́ бы́ло ходи́ть туда́, (*colloq.*), what business had he to go there? Воль-н-о-ду́мец, *n.m.,* freethinker. Воль-н-о-ду́мный, *adj.,* freethinking. Воль-н-о-ду́мство, *n.n.,* freethinking. Воль-н-о-ду́мствовать, *v.i.,* to be a free thinker. Воль-н-о-наёмный, *adj.,* hired. Воль-н-о-слу́шатель, *n.m.,* unmatriculated university auditor. Во́ль-н-ость, *n.f.,* freedom, liberty. Поэти́ческая в., poetic license. Позволя́ть себе́ во́льности, to take liberties with. Во́ль-ный, *adj.,* free. В. го́род, free city. В. перево́д, free translation. В-во́л-ю, *adv.,* to one's heart's content. Нае́сться ввво́лю, to eat to one's heart's content. Вдо́-воль, *adv.,* to one's heart content.

до-з-во́л-и-ть, *v.p.,* до-з-вол-я́ть, *v.i.,* to permit, allow, authorize, grant, give leave. До-з-вол-е́ние, *n.n.,* authorization, permission, leave. До-з-во́л-енный, *adj., part. pass. past,* permitted, legal.

из-во́л-и-ть, *v.i.,* + *gen.,* (*obs.*), to desire, grant, wish; deign. Чего́ изво́лите? (*obs.*), what can I do for you? What is your wish? Не изво́льте беспоко́иться, do not trouble yourself. Изво́льте вы́йти, pray go out.

со-из-во́л-и-ть, *v.p.,* со-из-вол-я́ть, *v.i.,* (*obs.*), to assent, agree, consent, authorize. Со-из-вол-е́ние, *n.n.* (*obs.*), assent, sanction, consent, authorization. С соизволе́ния нача́льства, (*obs.*), by permission of the authorities.

со-благ-о-вол-и́-ть, *v.p.,* to deign; to have the kindness to. Она́ не соблаговоли́ла отве́тить, (*sarcastic*) she did not deign to answer.

благ-о-вол-и́ть, *v.i.,* к + *dat.* (*obs.*), to regard with favor, have kind feelings.

Благоволи́те отве́тить, kindly answer. Нача́льник благоволи́т к нему́, the director regards him with favor. Благ-о-вол-е́ние, *n.n.,* good will, kindness.

по-з-во́л-и-ть, *v.p.,* по-з-вол-я́ть, *v.i.,* + *acc.,* + *dat.,* to allow, permit, let, give leave to, suffer. П. себе́ во́льности, to take liberties with. Если пого́да позво́лит, weather permitting. Я охо́тно позволя́ю ему́ по́льзоваться мои́ми кни́гами, I am perfectly willing to have him use my books. По-з-вол-е́ние, *n.n.,* permission, leave. С позволе́ния сказа́ть, saving your presence. По-з-во́л-ено, it is allowed. По-з-вол-и́тельный, *adj.,* permissible.

при-во́ль-е, *n.n.,* freedom; plenty. Приво́ль-ный, *adj.,* affording freedom; plentiful.

про-из-во́л, *n.m.,* arbitrariness, abuse. Про-из-во́ль-ный, *adj.,* arbitrary. Не-про-из-во́ль-ный, *adj.,* involuntary. Про-из-во́ль-но, *adv.,* arbitrarily, voluntarily. Не-про-из-во́ль-но, *adv.,* involuntarily.

не-во́л-и-ть, *v.i.,* при-не-во́л-ить, *v.p.,* + *acc.,* (*colloq.*), to force, constrain, compel. Не-во́ль-ник, *n.m.,* не-во́ль-ница, *n.f.,* slave. Торго́вля нево́льниками, slave trade. Не-во́ль-ный, *adj.,* involuntary, unintentional. Не-во́л-я, *n.f.,* bondage, captivity; necessity.

у-во́л-и-ть, *v.p.,* у-воль-ня́ть, *v.i.,* + *acc.,* to discharge, dismiss, furlough; turn away, expel. Меня́ уво́лили по сокраще́нию шта́тов, I was dismissed because of reduction of personnel. У-во́л-ить-ся, *v.p.r.,* у-воль-ня́ть-ся, *v.i.r.,* to be dismissed, discharged, retire. У-воль-не́ние, *n.n.,* discharge, dismissal. У-во́ль-ни́тельное свиде́тельство, discharge certificate.

до-во́ль-ство-вать, *v.i.,* + *acc.,* (*mil.*), to provide, supply. Д. войска́, to supply troops with food, to provision troops. до-во́ль-ство-вать-ся, *v.i.r.,* у-до-во́ль-ствоваться, *v.p.r.,* + *instr.,* to be content with, be satisfied with. Д. ма́лым, to be satisfied with the minimum. У. отве́том, to be satisfied with the answer. До-во́ль-ствие, *n.n.,* ration, allowance. До-во́ль-ство, *n.n.,* ease, prosperity, contentment; *see* зажи́точность, Жить в дово́льстве, to live in clover. До-во́ль-ный, *adj.,* contented, pleased, satisfied with. До-во́ль-но, *adv.,* enough, sufficiently; rather. Она́ д. хорошо́ поёт, she sings well enough, pretty well. Дово́льно! Enough! Enough of this! У-до-во́ль-ствие, *n.n.,* pleasure, enjoyment. Это для него́ грома́дное у., it affords him the greatest pleasure. Я сде́лаю э́то с больши́м удово́льствием, I shall be pleased to do it. Не-удово́льствие, *п.п.*, displeasure, discontent, dissatisfaction. Про-до-во́ль-ствие, *п.п.*, supply, provisions, food. Продо-во́ль-ственный, *adj.*, feeding, providing food. П. пункт, emergency food station. П. магази́н, food store. П-ая ка́рточка, ration card.

у-до-вл-е-твори́ть, *v.р.,* у-до-вл-е-тво-ря́ть, *v.i.,* + *acc.,* + *dat.,* to satisfy. У. жела́ния, to satisfy one's wishes. У. тре́бованиям, to come up to the mark, meet demands, requirements. У-до-вл-е-твори́ть-ся, *v.р.r.,* у-до-вл-е-творя́ть. ся, *v.i.r.,* + *instr.,* to be satisfied with, content oneself with. У-до-вл-е-творе́ние, *п.п.*, satisfaction, reparation. У-до-вл-е-творённость, *п.f.*, satisfaction, contentment. У-до-вл-е-творён-ный, *adj., part. pass. past,* satisfied, content. У-до-вл-е-творённо, *adv.,* with satisfaction. У-до-вл-е-твори́тель-ность, *п.f.*, satisfactoriness. Удовле-твори́тельный, *adj.*, satisfactory. Удо-влетвори́тельно, *adv.*, satisfactorily, passing, pretty well. По фи́зике он получи́л "удовлетвори́тельно", he received a passing mark in physics.

ВЕЛИК-, ВЕЛИЧ-, ВЕЛ-, GREAT

вели́к, в-а́, в-о́, *adj. pred.,* large; *see* вели́к-ий. Башмаки́ мне вели́кий, the shoes are large for me. У стра́ха глаза́ велики́, (*prov.*), a thing looms larger, if you are frightened. От ма́ла до вели́ка, men, women, and children, from oldest to youngest. Вели́к-ий, *adj.,* great. Вели́кие Держа́вы, the Great Powers. Пётр Вели́кий, Peter the Great. Вели́кий пост, Great Lent. Велик-ова́т, *adj.,* rather large. Сапоги́ немно́го в-ы, the boots are rather large Велик-а́н, *п.п.*, giant. Велик-а́нша, *п.f.*, giantess. Велик-о-ду́шие, *п.п.*, magnanimity, generosity. Велик-о-ду́шный, *adj.,* magnanimous, generous. Велик-о-ле́пие, *п.п.*; magnificence, splendor. Велик-о-ле́пный, *adj.*, magnificent, splendid. Велик-о-му́ченик, *п.т.*, велик-о-му́ченица, *п.f.*, great martyr. Велик-о-по́стный, *adj.*, Lenten. Велик-о-све́тский, *adj.*, distinguished, genteel, refined. Велик-о-ро́ссы, Велик-о-ру́сы, *п.т.pl.*, Great Russians. Велик-о-ру́сские го́воры, Great Russian dialects.

велич-а́-ть, *v.i.,* + *acc.,* to glorify, extol; call a person by his patronymic. Как вас велича́ть? (*obs.*), what is your name? Велич-а́вость, *п.f.*, stateliness. Велич-а́вый, *adj.*, stately, majestic. Велич-а́во, *adv.*, loftily, majestically, with dignity. Велич-а́йший, *superl.,*

adj., greatest, extreme, superb. Де́ло велича́йшей ва́жности, a matter of the greatest importance. Велич-е́ствен-ность, *п.f.*, majestic air, stateliness, grandeur. Велич-е́ственный, *adj.,* grand, majestic, stately. Велич-е́ствен-но, *adv.*, grandly, majestically. Вели́ч-ество, *п.п.*, majesty. Вели́ч-ие, *п.п.*, grandeur, greatness. Велич-ина́, *п.f.*, size, dimension.

воз-вели́ч-ить, *v.р.,* воз-вели́ч-ивать, *v.i.,* + *acc.,* to exalt, raise. Воз-вели́ч-ение, *п.п.*, glorification, exaltation.

пре-у-вели́ч-и-ть, *v.р.,* пре-у-вели́ч-ивать, *v.i.,* + *acc.,* to exaggerate, over-state, heighten. Пре-у-вели́ч-е́ние, *п.п.*, exaggeration, overstatement. Пре-у-вели́ч-енный, *adj.*, exaggerated, hyperbolical.

у-вели́ч-и-ть, *v.р.,* у-вели́ч-ивать, *v.i.,* + *acc.,* to increase, augment, enlarge. У-вели́ч-ить-ся, *v.р.r.,* у-вели́ч-ивать-ся, *v.i.r.,* to be increased, augmented, enlarged. То увели́чиваться, то умень-ша́ться, to wax and wane. У-вели́ч-ение, *п.п.*, increase, augmentation, enlargement, magnification. У. произ-води́тельности труда́, a rise in the production of labor. У. числа́ безра-бо́тных, an increase in the number of unemployed. У-вели́ч-ительный, *adj.*, magnifying, augmentative. У. су́ффикс, (*gram.*), augmentative suffix. У-ое стекло́, magnifying glass.

вельм-о́жа, *п.т.,* (*from Ch. Slav.,* ве́льми, very much, *obs.*), magnate, lord. Вельмо́жный, *adj.,* (*obs.*), lordly.

ВЕР-, (ВѢР-), TRUST, FAITH

ве́р-а, *п.f.*, faith, belief, religion. Ве́ра в Бо́га, belief in God. Си́мвол Ве́ры, the Nicene Creed. Приня́ть на ве́ру, to take on faith. Ве́р-ность, *п.f.*, faithful-ness, loyalty, fidelity; truth. В. го́лоса, true voice. В. в любви́, faithfulness in love. В. прися́ге, loyalty to one's oath. Вер-н-о-по́дданство, *п.п.*, loyalty, al-legiance to a monarch. Вер-н-о-по́д-данный, *adj., also used as n.,* (*hist.*), loyal to a monarch; loyal subject. Вер-н-о-по́дданнический, *adj.*, loyal to a monarch. В-ие чу́вства, feelings of loyalty towards a monarch. Не-ве́р-ность, *п.f.*, falseness, infidelity, unfaith-fulness. Ве́р-ный, *adj.*, faithful, loyal; true. В. до гро́ба, true unto death. В. слух, good ear. Быть в-ным своему́ сло́ву, to be true to one's word. В-ая жена́, faithful wife. Не-ве́р-ный, *adj.*, untrue, false, wrong, unfaithful, in-fidel. Ве́р-но, *adv.*, faithfully, truly, cor-rectly. В.! that's right. В. как два́жды два четы́ре, (*saying*), as true as 2 and 2 make 4. Вер-нѐе, *adj. comp.*, more correct, more sure. Не-ве́р-но, *adv.*, incorrectly, wrong. Н. называ́ть, to miscall, misname. Н. рассчи́тывать, to miscalculate.

ве́р-и-ть, *v.i*, по-ве́р-ить, *v.p.*, to believe, have faith. Ве́р-ить кому́-ли́бо, + *dat.*, to have confidence in. Не ве́рить слу́хам, to disbelieve rumors. Мне не ве́рится, I can hardly believe.

в-ве́р-и-ть, *v.p.*, в-вер-я́ть, *v.i.*, + *dat.*, + *acc.*, to entrust, trust to. Вверя́ть кому́-ли́бо что-ли́бо, to entrust someone with something. Вве́рить та́йну дру́гу, to trust one's friend with a serect. В-ве́р-енный, *adj.*, *part.* *pass.* *past*, entrusted. В-ое мне учрежде́ние, the institution entrusted to me. В-ве́р-ить-ся, *v.p.r.*, в-вер-я́ть-ся, *v.i.r.*, + *dat.*, to confide in.

до-ве́р-и-ть, *v.p.*, до-вер-я́ть, *v.i.*, to believe, credit, + *acc.*, entrust (*e.g.*, a secret). + *dat.*, to trust someone. Дове́рить кому́-нибудь та́йну, to entrust a secret to someone. Недоверя́ть, *v.i.*, + *dat.*, to mistrust. Я недове́ряю э́тому челове́ку, I mistrust this man. До-ве́р-ие, *n.n.*, trust, confidence, faith. Не-дов-е́рие, *n.n.*, mistrust, incredulity, lack of confidence. Лиша́ть дове́рия, to discredit, deprive of confidence. До-вер-и́тель, *n.m.*, client, constiutent. До-вер-и́тельный, *adj.*, confidential. До-ве́р-ить-ся, *v.p.r.*, до-вер-я́ть-ся, *v.i.r.*, + *dat.*, to trust, confide. До-ве́р-енность, *n.f.*, power of attorney, voucher. По дове́ренности, by proxy, by power of attorney. Получи́ть де́ньги по дове́ренности, to receive money by power of attorney.

за-ве́р-и-ть, *v.p.*, за-вер-я́ть, *v.i.*, to assure, witness. З. счёт (ко́пию), to certify a bill (a copy). За-вер-е́ние, *n.n.*, assurance. За-вер-и́тель, *n.m*, за-вер-и́тельница, *n.f.*, witness.

из-ве́р-ить-ся, *v.p.r.*, из-ве́р-ивать-ся, *v.i.r.*, to lose faith, belief, in. И. в свои́х си́лах, to lose confidence in oneself.

по-ве́р-ить, *v.p.*, + *acc.*, + *dat.*, to believe; credit; *see* ве́рить. П. слу́ху, to believe a rumor Пове́рьте мне, believe me. По-ве́р-ье, traditional belief. Ста́ринное п., ancient belief. По-ве́р-ить, *v.p.*, по-вер-я́ть, *v.i.*, + *acc.*, + *dat.*, to confide, entrust. П. та́йну, to confide a secret. По-ве́р-енный, *n.m.*, attorney. П. в дела́х, chargé d'affaires. Прися́жный п., (*pre-Rev.*), lawyer. По-ве́р-ить, *v.p.*, по-вер-я́ть, *v.i.*, + *acc.*, to check, verify; *see* прове́рить. По-ве́р-ка, *n.f.*, check; (*mil.*), visit, roll, call.

П. зна́ний (вре́мени), a check of knowledge (time-check).

про-ве́р-и-ть, *v.p.*, про-вер-я́ть, *v.i.*, + *acc.*, to verify, check, examine. П. часы́, to verify a clock. П. на о́пыте, to check by experience. Про-ве́р-ка, *n.f.*, verification, examinaton, check. П. исполне́ния, a check of work completed. Прове́рочная коми́ссия, control committee.

раз-у-ве́р-и-ть, *v.p.*, раз-у-вер-я́ть, *v.i.*, + *acc.*, в + *prep.*, to dissuade, disabuse. Он разуве́рил меня́ в мои́х подозре́ниях, he has dissuaded me from my suspicions.

с-ве́р-и-ть, *v.p.*, с-вер-я́ть, *v.i.*, + *acc.*, с + *instr.*, to compare, check with. С. часы́, to regulate a watch, clock. С-ве́р-ить-ся, *v.p.r.*, с-вер-я́ть-ся, *v.i.r.*, с + *instr.*, to be compared with, be verified. С-ве́р-ка, *n.f.*, revision, collation. С. часо́в, regulation of a clock.

у-ве́р-и-ть, *v.p.*, у-вер-я́ть, *v.i.*, + *acc.*, to assure. Я уверя́ю вас, I assure you. Бу́дьте уве́рены! be assured! У-ве́р-ить-ся, *v.p.r.*, у-вер-я́ть-ся, *v.i.r.*, в + *prep.*, to assure oneself, become convinced, make sure. У-вер-е́ние, *n.n.*, assertion, assurance.

ВЕРТ-, ВЕРЧ-, ВЕР-, ВЕРЕТ-, ВРАТ-, ВРАЩ-, ВОРОТ-, ВОРОЧ- (ВОРАЧ-), ВОРОШ-, ВОРОЖ, ROTATION: REVOLUTION, GYRATION, CIRCULATION

верт-е́-ть, **верч-у́**, *v.i.*, + *acc.*, + *instr.*, to turn, whirl, twirl. В. колесо́, to turn a wheel. В. па́льцами, to twiddle one's thumbs. Верт-е́ть-ся, *v.i.r.*, to turn around, whirl, spin. Ве́ртится в голове́, it's on the tip of my tongue. Земля́ верти́тся вокру́г со́лнца, the earth revolves around the sun. Верч-е́ние, *n.n.*, twisting, boring, turning (*e.g.*, on a lathe). Верт-ля́вость, *n.f.*, restlessness. Верт-ля́вый, *adj.*, restless, fidgety. Верт-у́шка, *n.f.*, whirligig; flirt. Верет-ено́, *n.n.*, spindle.

в-верт-е́ть, *v.p.*, в-вёрт-ывать, *v.i.*, + *acc.*, to screw in.

в-вер-ну́ть, *v.p.*, *smf.*, + *acc.*, в-вёрт-ывать, *v.i.*, to screw in. В. словцо́, to put in a word, get a word in edgewise.

вы-верт-еть, *v.p.*, вы-ве́рч-ивать, (*colloq.*), *v.i.*, + *acc.*, to unscrew.

вы́-вер-ну-ть, *v.p.*, вы-вёрт-ывать, *v.i.*, + *acc.*, to unscrew. В. карма́ны, to turn out pockets. В. ру́ку, to wrench someone's hand.

за-верт-е́ть, *v.p.*, + *acc.*, + *instr.*, to screw up; begin to spin. За-верт-е́ть-ся, *v.p.r.*, to begin to whirl, spin. Завертелись колёса машины, the wheels of the machine began to spin.

за-вер-ну́-ть, *v.p.*, за-вёрт-ывать, *v.i.*, + *acc.*, to envelop, roll, wrap up, muffle, enfold; turn. З. покупку в бумагу, to wrap a purchase in paper. Автомобиль завернул направо, the car turned to the right. З. в гости, (*colloq.*), to drop in, call on someone.

за-вер-ну́ть-ся, *v.p.r.*, за-вёрт-ывать-ся, *v.i.r.*, в + *acc.*, to be wrapped, wrap oneself (in). Он завернулся в одеяло, he wrapped himself in a blanket. За́ворот кишо́к, *n.m.*, (*med.*), volvulus. Заворо́т доро́ги, a turn in a road.

на-верт-е́ть, *v.p.*, на-вёрт-ывать, *v.i.*, + *acc.*, to screw on, turn on, twist around, wind.

на-вер-ну́-ть, *v.p.*, на-вёрт-ывать, *v.i.*, + *acc.*, to wind on. Н. гайку, to screw a nut onto a bolt.

об-верт-е́ть, *v.p.*, об-вёрт-ывать, *v.i.*, + *acc.*, to screw on, turn on, twist around, wind.

об-вер-ну́-ть, *v.p.*, об-вёрт-ывать, *v.i.*, to wrap up, wind around.

от-верт-е́ть, *v.p.*, от-вёрт-ывать, *v.i.*, to turn back, unscrew. От-верт-е́ть-ся, *v.p.r.*, to become unscrewed, disengaged (from). Ручка отвертелась, the handle has come unscrewed. От-вёртка, *n.f.*, screw driver.

от-вер-ну́-ть, *v.p. smf.*, от-вёрт-ывать, *v.i.*, to turn back, unscrew. Отвернуть одеяло, to turn back a blanket. От-вер-ну́ть-ся, *v.p.r.*, от-вёрт-ывать-ся, *v.i.r.*, от + *gen.*, to turn away from, be unscrewed.

от-вора́ч-ива-ть, *v.i.*, *see* отвёртывать. От-вора́ч-ивать-ся, *see* отвёртывать-ся.

пере-вер-ну́-ть, *v.p. smf.*, пере-вёрт-ывать, *v.i.*, пере-вора́ч-ивать, *v.i.*, to reverse, turn over, invert. Перевернуть страницу, to turn over a page. Перевора́чивать всё вверх дном, to turn everything upside down. Пере-вер-ну́ть-ся, *v.p.r.*, пере-вёрт-ывать-ся, *v.i.r.*, Пере-вора́ч-ивать-ся, *v.i.r.*, to upset, overturn. Перевёртываться в воздухе, to turn a somersault. Переворо́т, *n.m.*, overthrow, coup d'état. П. в науке, a revolution in science. Полити́ческий п., a political upheaval, coup d'état.

по-вер-ну́-ть, *v.p.*, по-вёрт-ывать, повора́чивать, *v.i.*. + *acc.*, to turn around. П. кого-нибудь лицом к свету, to turn someone to face the light. П. направо, to turn to the right. По-вер-ну́ть-ся, *v.p.r.*, по-вёрт-ывать-ся, *v.i.r.*, to turn around. П. кругом, to face about. Здесь негде повернуться, there is not enough room to turn around in,

here. По-вора́ч-ивать-ся, *see* повёртываться. П. лицом к свету, to turn to face the light. Повора́чивайся живей, (*colloq.*), hurry up. По-воро́т, *n.m.*, turn, turning, bend. П. к лучшему, a change, turn for the better. Круто́й п., a sharp turn.

по-воро́т-ить, *v.p.*, (*colloq.*), *see* повернуть. По-воро́т-ливость, *n.f.*, nimbleness, agility. Не-по-воро́т-ливость, *n.f.*, clumsiness. По-воро́т-ливый, *adj.*, nimble, agile. Не-по-воро́т-ливый, *adj.*, clumsy, slow. По-воро́т-ный, *adj.*, of or pertaining to a turn. П. круг, turntable. П. пункт, a turning point, crisis.

под-вер-ну́-ть, *v.p.*, под-вёрт-ывать, *v.i.*, + *acc.*, to screw, tuck in, turn under. П. рукава, to roll up one's sleeves. П. брюки до колен, to turn one's pants up to the knees. П. себе ногу, to sprain an ankle. Под-вер-ну́ть-ся, *v.p.r.*, под-вёрт-ывать-ся, *v.i.r.*, + *dat.*, to turn up. Подвернулся удобный случай, an opportunity turned up. Он кстати подвернулся, he turned up at the right moment.

под-воро́т-ить, *v.p.*, *see* подвернуть. Под-вора́ч-ивать, *v.i.*, (*colloq.*), *see* подвёртывать. Под-вора́ч-ивать-ся, *see* подвёртываться.

при-верт-е́ть, *v.p.*, при-вёрт-ывать, *v.i.*, +*acc.*, to screw tight, shut.

раз-вер-ну́-ть, *v.p.*, раз-вёрт-ывать, *v.i.*, + *acc.*, to open, unwrap, unfold, unroll, spread; develop. Р. ковёр, to unroll a carpet. Р. знамя, to unfurl, fly a banner. Р. работу, на производстве (*recent*), to expand industry. Раз-вер-ну́ть-ся, *v.p.r.*, раз-вёрт-ывать-ся, *v.i. r.*, to expand, develop; come out. Раз-вёрт-ка, *n.f.*, (*tech.*), reamer. Раз-вёрт-ывание, *n.n.*, opening, unfolding, unwrapping, development.

с-вер-ну́-ть, *v.p.*, с-вёрт-ывать, *v.i.*, + *acc.*, to roll up, wrap. С. бумагу, ковёр, to roll up paper, a rug. С. в улицу, (*colloq.*), to turn into a street. С-вер-ну́-ть-ся, *v.p.r.*, с-вёрт-ывать-ся, *v.i.r.*, + *instr.*, to roll up, be rolled up; curdle; coil; (*med.*), coagulate. Змея свернулась кольцом, the serpent coiled itself up. Листья свернулись, the leaves dried up. С-вер-нувшийся, *adj. part. act. past*, curdled, set, coagulated. Свернувшееся молоко, soured milk. С-вёр-нутый, *adj. part. pass. past*, rolled up, folded. С. пакетом, made into a parcel.

с-вер-т-е́ть, *v.p.*, *see* с-вёрт-ывать. С-вёрт-ок, *n.m.*, package, packet, roll. С-вёрт-ывание, *n.n.*, coagulation; rolling, coiling; shriveling; curtailment.

у-вер-ну́-ть-ся, *v.p.r.*, у-вёрт-ывать-ся,

v.i.r., от + *gen.*, to evade, escape, avoid, shirk. У. от прямо́го отве́та, to avoid a direct answer. У. от исполне́ния до́лга, to shirk one's duties. У-ве́рт-ка, *n.f.*, subterfuge, evasion, dodging. У-вёрт-ливость, *n.f.* evasiveness, shiftiness. У-вёрт-ливый, *adj.*, evasive, shifty.

врат-а́ (воро́т-а), *n.pl.*, (*rel.*), gate, gates. Ца́рские врата́, the Holy Gates of the altar in the Greek Orthodox Church, Врат-а́рь, *n.m.*, goalkeeper (in *soccer*); (*rel.*), warden, gatekeeper. При-вра́т-ник, *n.m.*, gatekeeper, porter.

вращ-а́-ть, *v.i.*, + *acc.*, + *instr.*, to revolve, turn, rotate. Стано́к враща́ет колесо́, the lathe turns the wheel. Вращ-а́ть-ся, *v.i.r.*, to revolve, rotate. Земля́ враща́ется, the earth rotates. В. в о́бществе, to move in society, social circles. Вращ-а́ющийся, *adj.*, *part. act. pres.*, revolving. В. стул, a swivel chair. Вращ-е́ние, *n.n.*, rotation, gyration, revolution. В. земли́, the rotation of the earth.

воз-вращ-а́ть, *v.i.*, воз-врат-и́ть, *v.p.* + *acc.*, to return, give back. В. де́ньги, to return money. Воз-вращ-а́ть-ся, *v.i.r.*, воз-врат-и́ть-ся, *v.p.r.*, to return. В. домо́й, to return home. В. на ро́дину, to return to one's native land. Воз-вра́т, *n.m.*, return, returning, giving back. Воз-вра́т-ный, *adj.*, of or pertaining to returning; recurring. В. глаго́л, (*gram.*), reflexive verb. На возвра́тном пути́, on the way back. Воз-вращ-е́ние, *n.n.*, return; restitution.

из-вращ-а́ть, *v.i.*, из-врат-и́ть, *v.p.*, + *acc.*, to pervert, corrupt; misinterpret; distort. И. и́стину, to distort the truth. Из-вращ-е́ние, *n.n.*, perversion, distortion. И. смы́сла, a distortion of meaning. Из-вращ-ённость, *n.f.*, perversity. Из-вращ-ённый, *adj. part. pass. past*, perverted.

об-ращ-а́ть, *v.i.*, (*from* об-вращ-а́ть), об-рат-и́ть, *v.p.* (*from* об-врат-и́ть), + *acc.*, to turn, change, transform, convert; put into circulation. О. взгляд на, to look at. О. в ра́бство, to enslave. О. внима́ние, to turn one's attention to. О. пусты́ню в сад, to turn a desert into a garden. Об-ращ-а́ть-ся, *v.i.r.*, об-рат-и́ть-ся, *v.p.r.*, to turn, revert; apply; appeal to. О. в бе́гство, to take to flight. О. в ко́нсульство, to apply to a consulate. О. с ре́чью, to address, speak. О. с ке́м-либо ду́рно (хорошо́), to treat someone badly (well). Об-ращ-е́ние, *n.n.*, a conversion to a faith; treatment; manner of handling. О. к чита́телю, the act of addressing a reader. Пусти́ть в о., to put into circu-

lation. Изъя́ть из обраще́ния, to withdraw from circulation.

об-орот-и́-ть, *v.p.*, (*from* об-ворот-и́ть), об-ора́ч-ивать, *v.i.*, (*colloq.*), + *acc.*, to turn round; change, transform. Об-орот-и́ть-ся, *v.p.r.*, об-ора́ч-ивать-ся, *v.i.r.*, to be turned, changed; turn around. О. на себя́, (*fig.*), to look at oneself. Об-орот-ень, (*from* о́б-ворот-ень), *n.m.*, werewolf. Об-оро́т-истый, *adj.*, resourceful. Об-оро́т-ливый, *adj.*, clever. Об-оро́т-ливость, *n.f.*, resourcefulness, dexterity, ability, cleverness. Об-оро́т, *n.m.*, turn, direction, revolution, revolving О. ре́чи, locution. Де́нежный о., turnover of money. Смотри́ на оборо́те, see the reverse side, (over), please turn over Об-оро́т-ный, *adj.*, circulating. О. капита́л, circulating capital. О-ная сторона́, the reverse side.

от-вращ-а́ть, *v.i.*, от-врат-и́ть, *v.p.*, + *acc.*, to turn away, aside. О. опа́сность, to ward off danger. О. беду́, несча́стье, to ward off misfortune. От-вращ-е́ние, *n.n.*, aversion, disgust, repugnance, horror. Внуша́ть о., to fill with disgust. Чу́вствовать к чему́-нибудь о., to loathe, have an aversion for something. От-врат-и́тельный, *adj.*, abominable, shocking, repulsive, disgusting. О-ая пого́да, foul weather. О-ое зре́лище, a forbidding, disgusting sight. От-врат-и́тельно, *adv.*, abominably, disgustingly.

пре-вращ-а́ть, *v.i.*, пре-врат-и́ть, *v.p.*, + *acc.*, to turn into, change, transform, convert. П. в пыль, to reduce to dust. П. в у́голь, to carbonize, reduce to ashes. Пре-вращ-а́ть-ся, *v.i.r.*, пре-врат-и́ть-ся, *v.p.r.*, в + *acc.*, to turn into, change, be converted. Гу́сеница преврати́лась в ба́бочку, the caterpillar turned into a butterfly. Пре-вращ-е́ние, *n.n.*, transformation, metamorphosis, change, transmutation. Пре-вра́т-ность, *n.f.*, vicissitude. Превра́тности судьбы́, the reverses of fortune, ups and downs. Пре-вра́т-ный, *adj.*, changeful; wrong; adverse. Пре-вра́т-но, *adv.*, adversely. Истолкова́ть п., to misinterpret.

раз-вращ-а́ть, *v.i.*, раз-врат-и́ть, *v.p.*, + *acc.*, to deprave, corrupt, debauch, pervert. Раз-вращ-а́ть-ся, *v.i.r.*, раз-врат-и́ть-ся, *v.p.r.*, + *acc.*, to become depraved, corrupt.

раз-вра́т-нич-ать, *v.i.*, to lead a depraved life. Раз-вра́т-ник, *n.m.*, раз-вра́т-ница, *n.f.*, debauchee, libertine. Раз-вра́т, *n.m.*, corruption, debauchery, vice. Раз-вращ-ённость, *n.f.*, perversion. Раз-вра́т-ный, *adj.*, corrupt, debauched, depraved, perverse. Раз-вращ-ённый, *adj. part. pass. past,* perverted. Раз-вращ-éние, *п.п.,* corruption, seduc-tic.1.

со-вращ-а́ть, *v.i.,* со-врат-и́ть, *v.p.,* + *acc.,* с + *gen.,* to corrupt, debauch, lead astray. С. с пути́ и́стинного, to pervert. Со-врат-и́тель, *п.m.,* perverter, seducer, corrupter. Со-вращ-а́ть-ся, *v.i.r.,* со-врат-и́ть-ся, *v.p.r.,* с + *gen.,* to become perverted. Со-вращ-éние, *п.п.,* corruption, leading astray.

воро́т-а *n.pl.,* gate, gates. Стоя́ть в воро́тах (под воро́тами), to stand in the gateway. Под-воро́т-ня, *п.f.,* space under a gate.

ворот-и́-ть, *v.p., (colloq.),* + *acc.,* to call back. В. кого́-нибудь с полдоро́ги, to cause someone to turn back midway. Сде́ланного не вороти́шь, *(saying),* what's done cannot be undone. Ворот-и́ть-ся, *v.p.r.,* to come back, return.

вы́-ворот-ить, *v.p.,* вы-вора́ч-ивать, *v.i.,* + *acc.,* to turn out, inside out. В. карма́ны, to turn one's pockets inside out (as proof that one is out of funds). Всю ду́шу вывора́чивает, *(fig.),* it breaks one's heart. Вы́-вороч-енный, *adj. part. pass. past,* turned out, inside out.

за-ворот-и́ть, *v.p.,* за-вора́ч-ивать, *v.i., see* завёртывать. З. наза́д (напра́во), to turn back, (to the right). З. рукава́, to turn up one's sleeves.

из-вора́ч-ивать-ся, *v.i.r., see* из-верну́ть-ся, to shift, elude, avoid. Из-воро́т-ливость, *п.f.,* resourcefulness. Из-воро́т-ливый, *adj.,* resourceful.

на-ворот-и́ть, *v.p.,* на-вора́ч-ивать, *v.i.,* + *acc.,* to pile up, heap up. Н. гру́ду камне́й, to make a pile of stones.

от-ворот-и́ть, *v.p.,* от-вора́ч-ивать, *v.i.,* + *acc.,* to turn back, off. От-воро́ч-ивать-ся, *v.i.r.,* to turn away. О. от кого́-либо, to turn one's face away from someone. От-воро́т-ы, *п.m.pl.,* lapels; tops of boots.

пере-ворот-и́ть, *v.p.,* пере-вора́ч-ивать, *v.i.,* + *acc.,* to turn over, upside down. П. всё, to turn everything over and upside down. Пере-вора́ч-ивать-ся, *v.i.r., see* перевёртываться.

по-ворот-и́ть, *v.p.,* по-вора́ч-ивать, *v.i., see* пове́ртывать. По-ворот-и́ть-ся, *v.p.r.,* по-вора́ч-ивать-ся, *v.i.r., (slang),* to turn around; *see* пове́ртывать-ся.

раз-ворот-и́ть, *v.p.,* раз-вора́ч-ивать, *v.i.,* + *acc.,* to unwrap, unfold, unroll; upset, destroy, shatter, undo. Ядро́ развороти́ло сте́ну, the cannonball shattered the wall. Раз-вороч-енный, *adj. part. pass. past,* destroyed, shattered.

с-ворот-и́ть, *v.p.,* с-вора́ч-ивать, *v.i.,* +

acc., to displace, remove, turn aside. С. с пра́вильного пути́, to turn from the right path. С-вора́ч-ивание, *п.п.,* turning, shunting.

во́рот, *п.m.,* opening for neck, collar; *(tech.),* windlass, winch, Ворот-ни́к, *п.m.,* collar. Отложно́й (стоя́чий) в., turned-down (turned-up) collar. Во-рот-ничо́к, *п.m., (dim.),* a small collar. Косо-воро́т-ка, *n.f.,* a Russian shirt. Ши́-ворот *(obs.),* collar. Ш. навы́во-рот *(idiom),* upside down, inside out. Взять за ш., *(idiom),* to take someone by the scruff of the neck. Водо-воро́т, *п.m.,* whirlpool, swirl. Кружи́ться в водоворо́те, to swirl, eddy.

ворош-и́-ть, *v.i.,* ворох-ну́ть, *v.p. (colloq.),* + *acc.,* to stir, turn; disturb, make uneasy. В. сéно, to turn hay over. Ве́тер вороши́л бума́гу на столе́, the wind stirred the paper on the table. Ворош-и́ть-ся, *v.i.r.,* ворох-ну́ть-ся, *v.p.r.,* to stir. Не вороши́сь! Don't move! Смотри́, не ворохни́сь, когда́ бу́дешь фотографи́роваться, take care not to move when you are being photo-graphed. За-вороши́ть-ся, *v.p.r.,* to begin to stir, move. Ребёнок завороши́лся в свое́й посте́льке, the child began to move in its cot.

ВЕРХ-, ВЕРШ-, ВОРОХ-, ВОРОШ-, SUMMIT; SUPREMACY

верх, *п.m.,* top, upper part. В. горы́, the summit of a mountain. В. ве́жливости (соверше́нства), the acme, peak of politeness (perfection). В. глу́пости, the height of folly, stupidity. В. шу́бы, the exterior of a fur-lined coat. Ве́рх-ний, *adj.,* upper. В. я́щик, top drawer. В-ее пла́тье, clothes.

на-ве́рх, *adv.,* upstairs. Пойти́ н., to go upstairs. На-верх-у́, *adv.,* upstairs. Он живёт н., he lives upstairs. Верх-о́вье, *п.п.,* a riverhead, the source of a river. В. Во́лги, the Upper Volga. Верх-о́вный, *adj.,* supreme, sovereign. В. влады́ка, a sovereign, overlord. В. главнокома́ндующий, commander-in-chief. В. суд, Supreme Court. Верх-ово́й, *adj. used as n.,* mounted rider; *adj.,* of or pertaining to riding. В-а́я ло́шадь, saddle horse. Верх-о́м, *adv.,* on horseback, mounted. Е́здить в., to ride. Ве́рх-ом, *adv.,* full to the brim. Ча́йная ло́жка са́хару с ве́рхом, a heaping teaspoonful of sugar. Верх-у́шка, *п.f.,* top, upper part, (summit). В. бугра́, top of a hillock.

верх-о-во́дить, *v.i.,* to lord it over. Верхо-во́д, *п.m., (colloq.),* a leader through influence and personality, rather than legal right.

верш-и́-ть, *v.i.,* + *instr.,* to rule over. В. дела́ми, to manage affairs. В. судь-бо́й люде́й, (*fig.*), to shape people's destinies. Верш-и́тель, *n.m.,* верш-и́тельница, *n.f.,* one who shapes destinies. Верш-и́на, *n.f.,* top, summit, peak. Дости́гнуть верши́ны холма́, to reach the top of a hill. Верш-о́к, *n.m.,* (*obs.*), a measure of approximately 1½ inches; upper part; superficial knowledge, smattering. Вершки́ хвата́ть, (*idiom*), to acquire a smattering of.

за-верш-и́ть, *v.p.,* за-верш-а́ть, *v.i.,* + *acc.,* to complete, crown, finish. З. пятиле́тку, to complete a Five-Year Plan. За-верш-а́ющий, *adj., part. act. pres.,* concluding, closing, final, crowning. З. год, concluding year. За-верш-е́ние, *n.n.,* completion.

с-верш-и́ть, *v.p.,* с-верш-а́ть, *v.i.,* + *acc.,* (*obs.*), to complete, accomplish, achieve. С-верш-и́ть-ся, *v.p.r.,* с-верш-а́ть-ся, *v.i.r.,* to be completed, done.

со-верш-и́ть, *v.p.,* со-верш-а́ть, *v.i.,* to accomplish, effect, perform. С. по́двиг, to accomplish a feat, heroic action. С. преступле́ние, to commit a crime. Со-верш-и́ть-ся, *v.p.r.,* со-верш-а́ть-ся, *v.i.r.,* to occur, be accomplished, performed. Со-верш-е́ние, *n.n.,* accomplishment, completion; performance. С. преступле́ния, the committing of a crime. Со-верш-е́нно, *adv.,* quite, completely, entirely. С. ве́рно, precisely, quite so, completely true. С. незнако́мый, a complete stranger. Со-верш-еннолетие, *n.n.,* coming of age. Дости́гнуть совершеннолетия, to come of age. Со-верш-еннолетний, *adj.,* of age. Со-верш-е́нство, *n.n.,* perfection, ideal. Верх совершенства, the peak of perfection. В совершенстве, to perfection. Он зна́ет ру́сский язы́к в совершенстве, he knows the Russian language perfectly. Со-верш-е́нствование, *n.n.,* perfecting.

со-верш-е́н-ств-ова-ть, *v.i.,* у-со-верш-е́нствовать, *v.p.,* + *acc.,* to improve, to perfect. С. свои зна́ния (свои изобрете́ния), to perfect one's knowledge (inventions). Со-верш-е́нствовать-ся, *v.i.r.,* у-со-верш-е́нствовать-ся, *v.p.r.,* в + *prep.,* to achieve perfection; improve, perfect oneself. Он уе́хал в Москву́, чтобы у. в зна́нии ру́сского языка́, he went to Moscow to perfect his knowledge of Russian.

во́рох, *n.m.,* heap, pile. В. соло́мы, a heap of straw. В. но́востей, a great quantity of news. В. пла́тья, a pile of clothes.

ворош-о́к, *n.m., dim. of* во́рох.

ВЕСЕЛ-, CHEER, CHEERFULNESS, JOY, GAIETY

ве́сел, *adj. pred.,* весел-а́, *f.,* ве́сел-о, *n., see* весёлый. Весёлый, *adj.,* cheerful, merry, amusing, funny. В. расска́з, an amusing story, tale. В-ая жизнь, a merry life. В-ое настрое́ние, high spirits. Ве́сел-о, *adv.,* gaily, merrily. В. проводи́ть вре́мя, to have a good time. Как ве́село! What fun! Мне в., I am in a cheerful mood.

весел-и́ть, *v.i.,* по-весел-и́ть, *v.p.,* + *acc.,* to cheer, gladden, enliven. В. о́бщество, to cheer a group of people. В. ребёнка, to amuse a child. Весел-и́ть-ся, *v.i.r.,* по-весел-и́ть-ся, *v.p.r.,* to enjoy oneself, have a good time. Весёл-ость, *n.f.,* gaiety, cheerfulness. Весе́ль-е, *n.n.,* mirth, gaiety, cheerfulness. Весел-ь-ча́к, *n.m.,* merrymaker. Весел-я́щий, *adj. part. act. pres.,* of or pertaining to laughter, pleasure, cheer. В. газ, laughing gas. В-яся пу́блика, pleasure seekers. На-весел-е́, *adv.,* slightly drunk. По́сле буты́лки вина́ он чу́вствует себя н., after one bottle of wine, he feels slightly intoxicated.

весел-е́-ть, *v.i.,* по-весел-е́ть, *v.p.,* to become merry, cheerful. Выздора́вливающие больны́е повеселе́ли, the convalescents became more cheerful.

у-весел-и́ть, *v.p.,* у-весел-я́ть, *v.i.,* + *acc.,* to amuse, entertain. У-весел-я́ть-ся, *v.i.r.,* to amuse oneself. У-весел-е́ние, *n.n.,* entertainment, merrymaking, amusement. У-весел-и́тельный, *adj.,* entertaining. У-весел-и́тель, *n.m.,* у-весел-и́тельница, *n.f.,* clown, buffoon, entertainer.

ВЕС-, (ВЕСЬ-), ВС-, ENTIRETY

вес-ь, *adj., also used as pron.,* all, whole, total. вся, *f.,* всё, *n.;* все, *pl.* Весь свет, the whole world. Весь день, the whole day. Руба́шка вся изо́рвана, the shirt is all torn. Я всю ночь не спала́, I didn't sleep all night. Хлеб у нас весь вы́шел, we are all out of bread. Вся су́мма, sum total. Все де́ньги растра́чены, all the money has been spent. Они все жи́вы, they are all alive. Я весь ваш, I am all yours. Со всех ног, (*idiom*), at top speed. Крича́ть во всю Ива́новскую, (*hist.*), to shout at the top of one's voice. Смея́ться во всё го́рло, (*colloq.*), to laugh uproariously.

вес-ь-ма́, *adv.,* very, very much, extremely. Я весьма́ рад, что вы прие́хали, I am very glad you came.

вез-дé (*from* весь-де), *adv.*, everywhere. Он побывáл везде, и в Москвé, и в Парѝже, he travelled all over: he was in both Moscow and Paris. Везде-сýщность, *n.f.*, omnipresence. Вéзде-сýщий, *adj.*, omnipresent. ∗ В. Бог, God the Omnipresent.

вс-ё, *pron. n.*, all, anything. Да и всё тут; вот вам и всё, that's all. Мне всё равнó, it's all the same to me. Ему всё нипочём, (*colloq.*), nothing disturbs him. И это всё? — Is that all? Они всё ссóрятся, they are always quarrelling. Он всё ещё в постéли, he is still in bed. Всё бы вам веселѝться, you think only of diversions. Всё-таки, *adv.*, just the same, still, no matter what, notwithstanding. Я в.-таки испóлнил свой долг, still, I have done my duty. Я в.-таки пойдý гулять, no matter what, I'm going for a walk. вс-егó нá-вс-его, *adv.*, in all, all told. Он получѝл всегó нáвсего тóлько э́то, all told, he only received this. Всегó бóлее, *adv.*, the most, most of all. Обыкновéнно бóлее всегó говорѝт тот, кто мéнее всегó мóжет чтó-нибудь доказáть, he who has the least to say usually talks the most. Всегó мéнее, *adv.*, the least. Всегó лýчше, *adv.*, the best. Всегó дешéвле, *adv.*, the cheapest of all. Всегó чáще, *adv.*, the most frequently.

вс-е-гдá, *adv.*, always, at all times, constantly, on occasions, ever. Всегдá день сменяется нóчью, night always follows the day. Я всегдá рáд вас вѝдеть, I'm always glad to see you. Всегдáшний, *adj.*, usual, habitual. Со своéй всегдáшней любéзностью, with his usual courtesy. В-ие жáлобы, the usual complaints. Вс-е-благѝй, *adj.*, everlasting goodness (*as* God). Вс-е-вéдение, *n.n.*, omniscience. Все-вéдущий, *adj.*, *also used as n.*, all-knowing, omniscient. В. вѝдящий, *adj.*, all-seeing. Все-вѝдящее óко, (*rel.*), all-seeing eye. Все-возмóжный, *adj.*, all possible, every conceivable kind of. Всевозмóжные кнѝги, all kinds of books, every conceivable kind of book. Цветы́ всевозмóжных стран, flowers of every land. Вс-е-держѝтель, *n.n.*, the Almighty. Всемѝрный, *adj.*, universal. Всемогýщество, *n.n.*, omnipotence. Всемогýщий, *adj.*, almighty, all-powerful; omnipotent. Всенарóдный, *adj.*, national, public, general. Всенарóдно, *adv.*, nationally, publicly, generally. Всéнощная, *n.f.*, vespers, evening service. Всеóбщий, *adj.*, common, general, universal. Всеóбщая вóинская повѝнность, universal military service. В.

забастóвка, general strike. В-ее избирáтельное прáво, universal suffrage. В-ее негодовáние, general indignation. Всеóбщность, *n.f.*, universality. Всеобъéмлющий, *adj.*, universal, all-embracing. В. ум, a universal mind. Человéк в-го умá, a man of wide mental grasp. Всеорýжие, *n.n.*, complete armor. Во всеорýжии, fully armed. Всепрощéние, *n.n.*, forgiveness. Всеуслы́шание, *n.n.*, *in expression*: во всеуслы́шание, within everyone's hearing. Всецéло, *adv.*, entirely, wholly, exclusively. В. поглощён, wholly absorbed in. Это в. принадлежѝт вам, this is entirely yours.

вс-як-ий, *pron. and adj.*, всяк, *short form*, everyone, every, each. В. мóжет э́то сдéлать, anyone can do it. В. встрéчный и поперéчный, (*idiom*), every Tom, Dick and Harry. Как другóй, like anyone else. На в. слýчай, in any case. Во в-ое врéмя, at any time. Всяк за себя отвечáет, (*idiom.*), everyone is responsible for himself. Всячески, *adj.*, of all kinds. Вс-ячески, *adv.*, in every way. Вс-ячина, *n.f.*, hodgepodge, medley. Всякая всячина, (*idiom*), a little of everything.

вс-ю́ду, повсю́ду, *adv.*, everywhere, anywhere. На сéвере всю́ду растёт соснá, pinetrees grow everywhere in the North. Повсю́ду тишь да гладь, да Бóжья благодáть, (*saying*), all is peace and quiet.

ВЕТ-, ВЕЩ-, ВЕЧ-, UTTERANCE, SPEECH

за-вéт, *n.m.*, covenant, will. За-вéтный, *adj.*, sacred; cherished. За-вéтные мы́сли, желáния, cherished thoughts, desires.

за-вещ-á-ть, *v.p.*, + *acc.*, + *dat.*, to leave, bequeath, pass on. За-вещ-áтель, *n.m.*, testator. За-вещ-áтельница, *n.f.*, testatrix. За-вещ-áние, *n.n.*, will, testament. Сдéлать з., to make a will.

на-вéт, *n.m.*, (*obs.*), slander, calumny. Злой н., vile slander. На-вéт-чик, *n.m.*, на-вéт-чица, *n.f.*, slanderer, calumniator.

об-éт, (*from* об-вéт), *n.m.*, vow, promise. Монáшеский о., monastic vow. Дать о., to make a vow. Обет-óванный, *adj.*, (*obs.*), promised. Земля́ Обетовáнная, the Promised Land. О. край, a region of fabulous wealth and fertility.

об-ещ-áн-ие, *n.n.*, a promise. Дать о., to make a promise. Сдержáть о., to keep a promise. Кля́твенное о., an oath, vow. Нарýшить о., to break a promise.

об-ещ-á-ть, *v.i.*, + *acc.*, + *dat.*, to promise. Мне обещáют хорóшее мéсто, they promise me a good position. Об-éщ-анный, *adj. part. act. pres.*, promised. Обéщанного ждут три гóда, (*prov.*), one does not hope to soon receive something promised.

на-об-ещ-áть, *v.p.*, + *gen.*, to make extravagant promises. Наобещáл с три кóроба и ничегó не сдéлал, (*colloq.*), he promised much and did nothing. по-об-ещ-áть, *v.p., see* обещáть.

от-вéт, *n.m.*, answer, reply. Держáть о., (*obs.*), to render an account. Быть в отвéте, (*obs.*), to be responsible for.

от-вéт-и-ть, от-вéч-у, *v.p.*, от-веч-áть, *v.i.*, + *acc.*, + *dat.*; на + *acc.*; за + acc., to answer, reply; be responsible for. О. урóк учúтелю, to recite one's lesson to a teacher О. на вопрóс, to answer a question. Я отвечáю за негó, I am responsible for him. О. на чýвство, to reciprocate one's feelings. От-вéт-ный, *adj.*, responsive. О-ое чýвство, requited feeling. Без-отвéтный, *adj.*, mild, timid, fainthearted. Ответ-ственность, *n.f.*, responsibility. Нестú за что-либо о., to be responsible for something. Без-отвéтственность, *n.f.*, irresponsibility. От-вéт-ственный, *adj.*, responsible. Без-отвéтственный, *adj.*, irresponsible, unaccountable. Без-отвéт-ственно, *adv.*, irresponsibly, unaccountably. Поступáть б., to act irresponsibly. От-вéт-чик, *n.m.*, от-вéт-чица, *n.f.*, defendant, respondent.

при-вéт, *n.m.*, welcome, greeting, compliments. Шлю вам сердéчный привéт, I send you my heartfelt greetings. Передáйте привéт вáшей сестрé, extend my compliments to your sister.

при-вéт-ствовать, *v.i.*, + *acc.*, to salute, hail, greet, welcome. При-вéт-ствие, *n.n.*, greeting, salute, salutation. Привéт-ственный, *adj.*, welcoming. П-ая речь, welcome speech.

со-вéт, *n.m.*, council, soviet; advice, counsel, opinion. С. минúстров, council of ministers. Воéнный с., council of war. Надёжный с., sound advice.

со-вéт-ова-ть, *v.i.*, по-со-вéт-овать, *v.p.*, + *acc.*, + *dat.*, to advise, counsel, recommend. С. лечéние вóдами, to recommend a water-cure. Я вам совéтую прочитáть эту кнúгу, I advise you to read this book. Со-вéт-овать-ся, *v.i.r.*, по-совéт-овать-ся, *v.p.r.*, с + *instr.*, to consult, advise, confer with. С. с друзьями, to consult with friends. Со-вéт-ник, *n.m.*, adviser, counselor; councilor. С. посóльства, counselor of an embassy. Со-вéт-чик, *n.m.*, (*colloq.*), adviser, one who gives advice. Со-вет-

изáция, *n.f.*, sovietization. Со-вет-úзм, *n.m.*, sovietism. Со-вéт-ский, *adj.*, Soviet. С-ая влáсть (правúтельство), the Soviet government, the government of the U.S.S.R. С-ое прáво, Soviet law.

со-вещ-áть-ся, *v.i.r.*, с + *instr.*, о + *prep.*, to deliberate, confer, take counsel. С. с минúстрами (юрúстом, дóктором), to consult with the ministers (a lawyer, doctor). С. о текýщих делáх, to discuss current affairs. Со-вещ-áние, *n.n.*, council, conference. Со-вещ-áтельный, *adj.*, consultative, deliberative. С. гóлос, deliberative vote. С-ое собрáние, deliberative assembly.

со-от-вéт-ствовать, *v.i.*, + *dat.*, to correspond to (with). С. своемý назначéнию, своéй цéли, to serve the purpose. Со-от-вéт-ственность, *n.f.*, со-отвéт-ствие, *n.n.*, conformance, conformity, suitability. В соотвéтствии, с + *instr.*, in accordance with. Со-от-вéт-ствующий, *adj., part. act. pres.*, appropriate. Со-от-вéт-ственно, *adv.*, according to, correspondingly, appropriately. С. требóваниям, in accordance with requirements. Со-от-вéт-ственный, *adj.*, proper, suitable, corresponding.

ВИ-, ВЬ-, WEAVING

ви-ть, вь-ю, *v.i.*, с-ви-ть, *v.p.*, + *acc.*, to twist, twine, spin, wind. В. венкú, to weave wreaths. В. верёвки, to twist ropes. В. верёвки из когó-нибудь (*idiom*), to twist someone around one's little finger. В. гнёзда, to build nests. Вú-ть-ся, *v.i.r.*, to be curled. У неё вьются вóлосы, she has curly hair. Витóй, *adj.*, twisted. В-áя колóнна, wreathed column. В-áя лéстница, winding staircase. За-ви-тóк, *n.m.*, lock, curl; flourish (*in writing*). За-ви-тýшка, *n.f.*, braided bread. Вь-ющийся, *adj., part. act. pres.*, climbing, twining, creeping; curly, frizzy, crisp. В. плющ, ivy. Вьющиеся вóлосы, curly hair. В-иеся растéния, climbing plants. Вú-лы, *n.pl.*, pitchfork. Вú-л-ка, *n.f.*, fork. Столóвая в., a table fork.

вз-вú-ть-ся, *v.p.r.*, вз-ви-вá-ть-ся, *v.i.r.*, to rise in the air, fly up. Зáнавес взвúлся, the curtain rose.

за-вú-ть, *v.p.*, за-ви-вá-ть, *v.i.*, + *acc.*, to wave, curl, frizzle, crimp. За-вúть-ся, *v.i.r.*, за-вивá-ть-ся, *v.i.r.*, to have one's hair waved, wave one's hair. За-вú-вка, *n.f.*, waving, wave, curling. Щипцы для завúвки, curling iron.

из-вú-ть-ся, *v.p.r.*, из-ви-вá-ть-ся, *v.i.r.*, to wriggle, wind, coil, cringe, writhe with pain. Дорóга извивáлась по гóрным склóнам, the road wound over the mountain slopes. Змея извива́ется, а snake coils. Он извива́лся пе́ред нача́льством, (derog.), he cringed in the presence of his superiors. Из-ви́-лина, n.f., bend, crook, sinuosity, tortuousness. И. доро́ги, a bend in a road. Мозговы́е изви́лины, convolutions of the brain. Из-ви́-листый, adj., sinuous, tortuous, winding, meandering.

об-ви́-ть, v.p., об-ви-ва́-ть, v.i., + acc., + instr., to wind round. Плющ обви́л де́рево, the ivy wound itself around the tree. Об-ви́ть-ся, v.p.r., об-ви-ва́ть-ся, v.i.r., to be wound around.

пере-ви́-ть, v.p., пере-ви-ва́ть, v.i., + acc., + instr., to entwine, wind over, interweave, intertwine, intertwist. П. косу́ ле́нтой, to entwine a ribbon into a braid of hair. Пере-вито́й, пере-ви́тый, adj. part., entwined, interwoven, intertwined, intertwisted.

по-ви́-ть, v.p., по-ви-ва́ть, v.i., + acc., to swathe, swaddle, twine. П. новорож-дённого, to swaddle a newborn baby. Повива́льный, adj., swaddling. П. институ́т, obstetrics institute. П-ая ба́б-ка, (obs.), midwife. Повиту́ха n.f., (obs.), midwife.

под-ви́-ть, v.p., под-ви-ва́ть, v.i., + acc., see зави́ть, завива́ть. Под-ви́-ть-ся, v.p.r., под-ви-ва́ть-ся, v.i.r., to curl one's hair slightly, have one's hair curled.

при-ви́-ть, v.p., при-ви-ва́ть, v.i., + acc., + dat., to graft; inoculate, vaccinate; (fig.), indoctrinate. П. я́блоню, to graft on an apple tree. П. де́тям о́спу, to vaccinate children against smallpox. При-ви́-ть-ся, v.p.r., при-ви-ва́ть-ся, v.i.r., to be grafted; vaccinated. Эти взгля́ды здесь не привили́сь, these views found no followers here. Это выраже́ние не привило́сь, this expression did not find favor with the public. Приви-ва́ние, n.n., при-ви́-вка, n.f., при-ви́-тие, n.n., grafting; inoculation, vaccination. При-ви́-вочный, adj., serving as a graft, as an inoculation. П. отря́д, (recent), inoculation unit.

раз-ви́-ть, v.p., раз-ви-ва́ть, v.i., + acc., to develop, evolve; untwist, wind off, uncurl. Р. бе́шеные те́мпы (на произво́дстве), (recent), to develop breakneck speed (e.g., in production, output). Р. во́лосы, to uncurl hair. Р. план, иде́ю, to develop a plan, an idea. Р. ско́рость, to develop speed. Раз-ви́-ть-ся, v.p.r., раз-ви-ва́ть-ся, v.i.r., to be developed, develop oneself. Р-ся у́мственно, to develop mentally, mature. У него́ развива́ется туберкулёз, he is developing tuberculosis. Раз-ви́-тие, n.n., development, growth, progress, evolution.

Ра́ннее р., precocity. Р-ие промы́шленности, growth, development of industry. Р. свои́х спосо́бностей, self-development. Раз-ви-то́й, adj., intelligent, well-developed mentally, physically. Р-а́я мускулату́ра, well-develeped musculature. Р-а́я те́хника, well-developed technology. Раз-ви́-лина, n.f., fork, bifurcation. Раз-ви́-листый, adj., forked.

с-ви́-ть, v.p., с-ви-ва́ть, v.i., + acc., see вить. с-ви́-ток, n.m., roll, scroll. с-ви́-тый, adj., part. pass. past, coiled, convoluted.

у-ви́-ть, v.p., у-ви-ва́ть, v.i., + acc., + instr., to entwine, twine, wreathe, wrap around. У. ро́зами коло́нну, to entwine a column with roses. У-ви-ва́ть-ся, v.i.r., за + instr., to court.

ви-л-я́ть, v.i., ви-ль-ну́ть, v.p., wag, dodge; (fig.), lie.

у-ви-ль-ну́ть, v.p., у-ви́-ливать, v.i., от + gen., to elude, evade, dodge. У. от исполне́ния обя́занностей, to evade one's duties, obligations. У. от уро́ка, to cut a class. У-ви́-ливание, n.n., evasion, dodging. У. от пра́вды, an evasion of truth.

ви-хрь, n.m., whirlwind. ви́-хрем, used as adv., suddenly, impetuously.

вь-ю́га, n.f., snowstorm. Зимо́й быва́ют си́льные вью́ги, in winter violent snowstorms occur.

вь-юн, n.m., loach; restless person.

вь-ю́ч-ить, v.i., на-вь-ю́чить, v.p., + acc., на + acc., to burden, load, pack. Вь-юк, n.m., pack, burden. Вь-ю́чный, adj., of burden. В-ая ло́шадь, pack-horse. В-ое живо́тное, a beast of burden.

вь-ю́шка, n.f., damper.

ВИД-, ВИЖ-, ВИСТ-, VISION, SIGHT, VISIBILITY

вид, n.m., aspect, look, appearance, air, view, landscape, sight; form, kind, sort, species; intention, purpose; (gram.), aspect. В. на́ мо́ре, a view of the sea. Вне́шний в., outward appearance. В. на жи́тельство, passport; permit for residence. Де́лать в., to pretend. Потеря́ть (упусти́ть) из ви́ду, to lose sight of. Это хорошо́ на в., it looks fine. В ви́де, in the form of. Откры́тка с ви́дом, a picture postcard. Соверше́нный (несоверше́нный) в., (gram.), perfective (imperfective) aspect. Видово́й, adj., of or pertaining to species. В-о́е измене́ние, a modification of a species. В-о́е разли́чие, a specific difference. Ви́д-ный, adj., noticeable, conspicuous, prominent. В. мужчи́на, (colloq.), a handsome man. На са́мом ви́дном ме́сте, in the most conspicuous place. Занима́ть ви́дное ме́сто (положе́ние), to occupy a high post, position. Ви́д-но, *adv.*, apparently, evidently. Не-ви́д-ный, *adj.*, plain, unsightly. Мило-ви́д-ный, *adj.*, comely, pretty. Оче-ви́д-ец, *n.m.*, оче-ви́д-ица, *n.f.* an eyewitness. Оче-ви́д-ность, *n.f.*, obviousness. Оче-ви́д-ный, *adj.*, obvious, evident, apparent. Оче-ви́д-но, *adv.*, apparently, evidently. Бы́ло о., что он не придёт, it was obvious that he would not come. Разно-ви́д-ность, *n.f.*, variety. Р. расте́ний (живо́тных), a variety of plants (animals).

вид-о-изменя́ть, *v.t.*, вид-о-измени́ть, *v.p.*, + *acc.*, to modify. Вид-о-изменя́ть-ся, *v.i.r.*, вид-о-измени́ть-ся, *v.p.r.*, to undergo a change, modification. Видо-измене́ние, *n.n.*, a change, modification.

вид-е́-ть, ви́ж-у, *v.i.*, у-ви́д-еть, *v.p.*, + *acc.*, to see, behold, view, perceive. В. во сне́, to dream of, see in a dream. В. ме́льком, to have a glimpse of. Его́ нельзя́ в., he cannot be seen. Я ви́жу его́, как живо́го, (*idiom., fig.*), I see him as if he were before my eyes. Ви́д-еть-ся, *v.i.r.*, у-ви́д-еть-ся, *v.p.r.*, to see one another.

вид-а́-ть, *v.i.*, у-вид-а́ть, *v.p.*, + *acc.*, (*colloq.*), *see* ви́деть, уви́деть. По-вид-а́ть, *v.p.*, to visit. Давно́ хоте́л повида́ть земляка́, I have long wanted to visit one of my countrymen. Вид-а́ть-ся, *v.i.r.*, по-вид-а́ть-ся, *v.p.r.*, to visit one another. Вид-не́ть-ся, *v.i.r.*, за-вид-не́ть-ся, *v.p.r.*, to appear, be seen. Уже́ завидне́лись на не́бе звёзды, stars have already begun to appear in the sky. Вид-е́ние, *n.n.*, vision, apparition. Сно-ви́д-е́ние, *n.n.*, dream, vision in a dream. Теле-ви́д-ение, *n.n.*, television. Ясно-ви́д-ение, clairvoyance, second sight. Ясно-ви́д-ец, *n.m.*, ясно-ви́д-ящая, *n.f.*, a clairvoyant. Ви́д-имость, *n.f.*, visibility; semblance. Ви́д-имый, *adj. part. pass. pres.*, seen, visible; *ant.*, не-ви́д-имый, unseen, invisible. Без ви́димой причи́ны, without an apparent reason. Ви́д-имо, *adv.*, evidently. По-ви́димому, *adv.*, apparently. Она́, ви́димо, (пови́димому) хо́чет изуча́ть ру́сский язы́к, she evidently wishes to study Russian. Не-ви́д-имо, *adv.*, invisibly. Наро́ду бы́ло ви́димо-неви́димо, (*idiom.*), there was an immense crowd of people. Не-вид-и́мка, *n.f.*, an invisible being. Ша́пка-невиди́мка, *n.f.*, (*folklore*), a cap which makes one invisible.

вз-ви́д-еть, *v.p.*, + *acc.*, *used only in ex-* *pression*: От бо́ли он не взви́дел све́та, from pain, everything went black before his eyes.

за-ви́д-еть, *v.p.*, + *acc.*, (*colloq.*), to see, get a glimpse of. Лишь бе́рег зави́дит во мгле... (*Lermontov*), as soon as he sees the shore through the mist...

пред-ви́д-еть, *v.i.*, + *acc.*, to foresee, have forebodings. Предви́деть свою́ судьбу́, to foresee one's fate. Пред-ви́д-еть-ся, *v.i.r.*, + *acc.*, used only in 3d pers., to be foreseen, be in sight. Вака́нсии не предви́дится, there is no vacancy in sight.

при-ви́д-еть-ся, *v.i.r.*, (*colloq.*), to imagine having seen, to appear to. Дурно́й сон приви́делся мне, I had a nightmare. При-ви́д-е́ние, *n.n.*, ghost, spectre, apparition.

с-вид-а́ние, *n.n.*, meeting, appointment, rendezvous. Назна́чить с., to make an appointment, date. До свида́ния, good-by, au-revoir.

за-ви́д-овать, *v.i.*, по-за-ви́д-овать, *v.p.*, + *dat.*, to envy, be envious. За-ви́д-ный, *adj.*, enviable. З-ое положе́ние, a desirable position. Глаза́ завиду́щие, ру́ки загребу́щие (*saying*), he has envious eyes and greedy hands. За-ви́д-но, *adv.*, with envy, enviably. Мне з., I am envious.

за́-вист-ь, *n.f.*, envy, jealousy. З. к сла́ве, к почёту, к бога́тству, envy of glory, honor, riches. Возбужда́ть з., to excite jealousy, envy. За-ви́ст-ник, *n.m.*, за-ви́ст-ница, *n.f.*, envious person. За-ви́ст-ливый, *adj.*, envious, jealous. За-ви́ст-ливо, *adv.*, enviously, jealously. Смотре́ть на что-ли́бо з., to look upon something with envy.

не́-на-вист-ь, *n.f.*, hatred, abhorrence. Смотре́ть с не́навистью, to eye with hatred. Предме́т мое́й не́нависти, the object of my hatred. Не-на-ви́ст-ник, *n.m.*, не-на-ви́ст-ница, *n.f.*, hater. Не-на-ви́ст-ный, *adj.*, hateful, odious, detestable.

не-на-ви́д-еть, *v.i.*, воз-не-на-ви́д-еть, *v.p.*, + *acc.*, to hate, to conceive a hatred for.

ВИН-, BLAME, CULPABILITY, GUILT, FAULT

вин-а́, *n.f.*, fault, guilt. Моя́ в., it is my fault. Сва́ливать вину́ на друго́го, to blame someone else. Вин-о́вник, *n.m.*, вин-о́вница, *n.f.*, the guilty one, culprit; (*fig.*), cause, author, instigator. Вино́вник всех несча́стий, one who is blamed for all misfortunes. В. торжества́, celebrant, one in whose honor a celebration is held. Вин-о́вность, *n.f.*, guilt, culpability. Отрица́ть свою́ в., to plead not guilty. Вин-о́вный, *adj.*, guilty, culpable, at fault. В. в госуда́рственной изме́не, guilty of high treason. Объявля́ть вино́вным, to convict. Вин-ова́тый, *adj.*, guilty, culpable. Име́ть в. вид, to have a guilty look. Вин-ова́т! *adj. pred.*, I'm sorry! Excuse me! В э́том, он не винова́т, it isn't his fault. Вини́тельный, *adj.*, accusative. В. паде́ж, (*gram.*), accusative case. Не-вин-о́вность, *n.f.*, guiltlessness. Не-вин-о́вный, *adj.*, innocent, guiltless, blameless. Не-ви́н-ный, *adj.*, innocent, virgin.

вин-и́-ть, *v.i.*, + *acc.*, to accuse, blame. Не вини́те его́, don't blame him. Я виню́ себя́ во всём, I blame no one but myself. По-вин-и́ть-ся, *v.p.r.*, (*obs.*), to plead guilty.

из-вин-и́ть, *v.p.*, из-вин-я́ть, *v.i.*, + *acc.*, to excuse, forgive, pardon. Извини́те меня́, Excuse me! Forgive me! I beg your pardon! Из-вин-и́ть-ся, *v.p.r*, из-вин-я́ть-ся, *v.i.r.*, to excuse oneself, apologize. Из-вин-и́тесь за меня́, make my excuses. Из-вин-е́ние, *n.n.*, apology, excuse; pardon. Прошу́ извине́ния, I beg your pardon. Я не могу́ приня́ть ва́шего извине́ния, I cannot accept your apology. Из-вин-и́тельный, *adj.*, excusable, pardonable. И. посту́пок, a pardonable action.

об-вин-и́ть, *v.p.*, об-вин-я́ть, *v.i.*, + *acc.*, в + *prep.*, to accuse, charge. О. во лжи, to accuse of lying. Об-вин-я́ть-ся, *v.i.r.*, to be tried for, be charged with. О. в кра́же, to be accused of theft. Об-вин-е́ние, *n.n.*, accusation, charge. Об-вин-и́тель, *n.m.*, об-вин-и́тельница, *n.f.*, accuser, prosecutor. Госуда́рственный (обще́ственный), о., state (public) prosecutor. Об-вин-и́тельный, *adj.*, accusatory, incriminatory. О. акт, indictment. Вы́нести о. пригово́р, to find guilty, convict.

по-вин-ова́-ть-ся, *v.p.r.* and *v.i.r.*, + *dat.*, to obey, comply with. На́до п. ста́ршим one must obey one's elders. По-вин-ове́ние, *n.n.*, obedience. Слепо́е п., (*fig.*), implicit, blind obedience. По-ви́н-ность, *n.f.*, duty, obligation, service. Во́инская п., obligation to military service. По-ви́н-ная, *adj. used as n. only in expression:* Принести́ пови́нную, (*obs.*), to confess one's guilt. Пови́нную го́лову и меч не сечёт, (*prov.*), a fault confessed is half redressed.

про-вин-и́ть-ся, *v.p.r.*, to commit an offence; be guilty. Про-ви́н-ность, *n.f.*, misdemeanor. Про-вин-и́вшийся, *adj.*

part. pass. past, guilty; guilty of having committed an offence.

ВИС-, ВИШ-, ВЕС-, ВЕШ-, SUSPENSION, WEIGHT

вис-е́-ть, виш-у́, *v.i.*, в, на + *prep.*, над + *instr.*, to hang, be hanging, be suspended. По-вис-е́ть, *v.p.*, to hang awhile, for a while. Карти́на виси́т на стене́, the picture is hanging on the wall. В. в во́здухе, to hang in the air. Плащ пови́сит и вы́сохнет, the raincoat will hang awhile and dry. Вися́чий, *adj.*, pendant, pendulous. В. мост, suspension bridge. В. замо́к, padlock. Вис-я́щий, *adj.*, *part. act. pres.*, hanging. Портре́т, вися́щий на стене́, the portrait hanging on the wall. Ви́селица, *n.f.*, gallows, gibbet. Избежа́ть ви́селицы, to escape the gallows; save one's neck. Ви́с-ельник, *n.m.*, hanged man, person fit to be hanged.

за-ви́с-еть, *v.i.*, от + *gen.*, to depend on. Урожа́й зави́сит от кли́мата, the harvest depends on the climate. Наско́лько от меня́ зави́сит, (*express.*), as far as it depends on me. За-ви́с-ящий, *adj. part. act. pres.*, depending. За-ви́симый, *adj. part. pass. pres.*, dependent. Не-зави́симый, *adj.*, independent. Н-ое госуда́рство, independent state, nation. За-ви́с-имость, *n.f.*, dependence. Экономи́ческая з., economic dependence. В зави́симости от обстоя́тельств, depending on circumstances. Не-зави́симость, *n.f.*, independence. Н. Аме́рики от Англии была́ объя́влена 4-го июля 1776 го́да, America's independence from England was declared on the 4th of July, 1776. Не-за-ви́с-имо, *adv.*, independently.

ви́с-ну-ть, *v.i.*, по-ви́с-нуть, *v.p.*, на + *prep.*, над + *instr.*, to hang, drop. В. на ше́е, (*colloq.*), to hang on the neck, embrace.

на-ви́с-ну-ть, *v.p.*, на-вис-а́ть, *v.i.*, на + *acc.*, над + *instr.*, to impend, hang over, overhang; hover. Ве́тви нави́сли над ручьём, the branches hung over the brook. На-ви́с-ший, *adj. part. act. past*, hanging over, impending, suspended over. Н-ие бро́ви, beetle-brows.

об-ви́с-ну-ть, *v.p.*, об-вис-а́ть, *v.i.*, to hang loose, droop, be flabby. Ко́жа обви́сла на его́ изможжённом лице́, the skin hung loose on his emaciated face.

от-ви́с-ну-ть, *v.p.*, от-вис-а́ть, *v.i.*, to hang down, hang baggily, loosely. От-ви́с-лый, *adj.*, baggy, loose-hanging. С отви́слыми уша́ми, *or* вислоу́хий, lop-eared.

по-ви́с-ну-ть, *v.p.,* по-вис-а́ть, *v.i.,* в + *prep.,* на + *acc.,* над + *instr.,* to hang, be suspended, hang down, droop; flag. Ребёнок пови́с на ше́е у ма́тери и не хоте́л уходи́ть, the child clung to his mother's neck and did not want to go away. Де́ло пови́сло в во́здухе, (*fig.*), the case hung in the air. пере-вис-а́ть, *v.i.,* to overhang. Ро́зы перевиса́ли че́рез огра́ду са́да, the roses hung over the garden fence.

с-вис-а́ть, *v.i.,* to hang over, down; dangle, droop; bend aside. С-вис-а́ющий, *adj. part. act. pres.,* hanging, dangling, drooping. С-ие усы́, walrus moustache.

вес, *n.m.,* weight. Продава́ть на в., to sell by weight. Изли́шек ве́са, overweight. Приба́вить в ве́се, to gain in weight. Име́ть в., (*fig.*), to carry weight. Вес-ы́, *n.pl.,* scales; weighing machine. Ве́с-кость, (*fig.*), weightiness. В. до́вода, weightiness of an argument. Ве́с-кий, *adj.,* weighty, significant. В-ое сло́во, significant word. Ве́ско, *adv.,* weightily, significantly.

вес-и-ть, ве́ш-у, *v.i.,* to weigh. Этот хлеб ве́сит 2 фу́нта, this bread weighs 2 pounds.

вз-ве́с-ить, *v.p.,* вз-ве́ш-ивать, *v.i.,* + *acc.,* to weigh; (*fig.*), consider. В. мя́со, са́хар, ма́сло, to weigh meat, sugar, butter. В. свои́ слова́, to weigh one's words. В. все до́воды за и про́тив, the weigh the pros and cons. Вз-ве́с-ить-ся, *v.p.r.,* вз-ве́ш-ивать-ся, *v.i.r.,* to weigh oneself. Вз-ве́ш-ивание, *n.n.,* weighing.

вы́-вес-ить, *v.p.,* вы-ве́ш-ивать, *v.i.,* + *acc.,* to hang out. В. бельё для просу́шки, to hang clothes out to dry. В. объявле́ние, to put up a notice. Вы-ве́ш-ивать-ся, *v.i.r.,* to hang from, be hung from, be posted. Расписа́ние уро́ков выве́шивается во всех кла́ссах, the schedule of lessons is posted in all the classes. Вы́-вес-ка, *n.f.,* sign-board. В. магази́на, a store sign-board, store sign. Вы́-веш-енный, *adj. part. pass. past,* hung out, posted, exhibited.

до-ве́с-ить, *v.p.,* до-ве́ш-ивать, *v.i.,* + *gen.,* to make up weight. Д. са́хару, муки́, to make up the weight of sugar, flour. Не-до-ве́с, *n.m.,* short weight.

за-ве́с-ить, *v.p.,* за-ве́ш-ивать, *v.i.,* + *acc.,* to curtain, conceal with curtains. З. окно́, to curtain a window. За-ве́ш-ивание, *n.n.,* covering, curtaining. За-ве́ш-енный, *adj. part. pass. past,* curtained. З-ые о́кна, curtained windows. За-ве́с-а, *n.f.,* curtain; (*rel., used without adj.*), veil, screen. Дымова́я з., smoke screen.

за-на-ве́с-ить, *v.p.,* за-на-ве́ш-ивать, *v.i.,* + *acc.,* to curtain, cover with a curtain. За́-на-вес-ь, *n.f.,* (*obs.*), за-на-ве́с-ка, *n.f.,* curtain, drapery. За́навеси (зана-ве́ски) на о́кнах, window curtains. Подня́ть з. to raise a curtain. Задёрнуть з., to draw a curtain. За́-на-вес, *n.m.,* stage curtain. Театра́льный з., theatre, stage curtain. Желе́зный з., (*fig.*), Iron Curtain. Стра́ны за желе́зным за́навесом, the countries behind the Iron Curtain.

на-ве́с-ить, *v.p.,* на-ве́ш-ивать, *v.i.,* + *acc.,* to hang, suspend. Н. дверь, to hang a door. На-ве́с, *n.m.,* shed.

об-ве́с-ить, *v.p.,* об-ве́ш-ивать, *v.i.,* + *acc.,* + *instr.,* to give short weight; hang round. Продаве́ц обве́сил покупа́теля, the salesman gave the customer short weight. Об-ве́с-ить-ся, *v.p.r.,* об-ве́ш-ивать-ся, *v.i.r.,* + *instr.,* to be given short weight; cover, adorn oneself, be covered, adorned with trinkets. Об-ве́ш-ивание, *n.n.,* the giving of short weight. Об-ве́с, *n.m.,* short weight.

от-ве́с-ить, *v.p.,* от-ве́ш-ивать, *v.i,* + *acc.,* to weigh out. О. кило́ муки́, to weigh out a kilogram of flour. О. покло́ны, (*obs.*), to make deep bows, bow low, deeply. О. уда́ры, (*colloq.*), to strike blows. От-ве́с, *n.m.,* vertical drop. По отве́су, perpendicularly, vertically. От-ве́с-ный, *adj.,* perpendicular, vertical. О-ая скала́, steep cliff, rock. От-ве́с-но, *adv.,* vertically, steeply. Па́дает о. с высоты́ 1000 футов, there is a vertical drop of 1000 feet. От-ве́ш-ивание, *n.n.,* weighing out.

пере-ве́с-ить, *v.p.,* пере-ве́ш-ивать, *v.i.,* + *acc.,* to weigh again; outbalance, overbalance; hang in a different place; prevail. На́до сно́ва п. все я́щики с фру́ктами, it is necessary to reweigh all the boxes of fruit. Ча́шка с това́ром переве́сила ча́шку с ги́рями, the goods outbalanced the weights. Переве́сьте пальто́ из шка́фа на ве́шалку, transfer the overcoat from the closet to the clothes rack. Его́ до́воды переве́сили все возраже́ния, his evidence outweighed all the objections. Пере-ве́с-ить-ся, *v.p.r.,* пере-ве́ш-ивать-ся, *v.i.r.,* to suspend oneself over; hang over, stoop over. Рыболо́в переве́сился че́рез пери́ла моста́, the fisherman hung over the railing of the bridge. Пере-ве́с, *n.m.,* overweight, overbalance; (*fig.*), preponderance. П. в на́шу по́льзу, the odds are in our favor. П. голосо́в, the majority of votes. Брать ружьё на п., (*mil.*), to trail arms.

под-ве́с-ить, *v.p.,* под-ве́ш-ивать, *v.i.,* +

асс., to suspend, hang under. П. кóло-кол, to hang a bell. Под-вéш-ивание, *n.n.,* suspension, hanging. Под-вéс-ить-ся, *v.p.r.,* под-вéш-ивать-ся, *v.i.r.,* to be suspended; hang under, from, on. П. на трапéции, to hang on a trapeze. Под-вéс-ок, *n.m.,* под-вéс-ка, *n.f.,* pendant, earring. Под-вéс-ный, под-вес-нóй. *adj.,* suspended, pendulous. П-áя желéзная дорóга, suspension railway.

при-вéс-ить, *v.p.,* при-вéш-ивать, *v.i.,* + *асс.,* to suspend, hang, append, attach, add to the weight. При-вéш-ивать-ся, *v.i.r.,* к + *dat.,* to be appended, attached, added. При-вéс-ка, *n.f.,* additional weight.

раз-вéс-и-ть, *v.p.,* раз-вéш-ивать, *v.i.,* + *асс.,* to weigh out, hang about, out; suspend. Р. мешóк мукú на кило-грáммы, to weigh out a sack of flour in packets of a kilogram. Р. бельё на верёвке, to hang out the wash on a line. Р. ýши, (*idiom.*), to listen attentively, be spellbound. Раз-вéш-ивать-ся, *v.i.r.,* to be weighed out, suspended, hung out. Табáчные лúстья развéши-ваются для просýшки, tobacco leaves are hung out for drying. Раз-вéс, *n.m.,* weighing. На развéс, by weight. Раз-вес-нóй, *adj.,* by weight, in bulk. Р. чай, loose tea sold in bulk. Раз-но-вéс, *n.m.,* small weights.

с-вéс-ить, *v.p.,* с-вéш-ивать, *v.i.,* + *асс.,* to weigh; hang down. *see* взвéсить. Свéсьте мне одúн фунт мукú, weigh me a pound of flour. С-вéс-ить-ся, *v.p.r.,* с-вéш-ивать-ся, *v.i.r.,* to be weighed; hang down; overhang; *see* взвéшиваться.

вéш-ать, *v.i.,* по-вéс-ить, *v.p.,* + *асс.,* to hang, hang up, suspend; weigh. В. бельё для просýшки, to hang up clothes to dry. В. престýпника, to hang a criminal. В. гóлову, (*fig.*), to be downcast. Вéш-ать-ся, *v.i.r.,* по-вéс-ить-ся, *v.p.r.,* to hang oneself; be suspended. Со скýки хоть вéшайся! To be bored to death! Вéш-алка, *n.f.,* clotheshanger, coat hanger, stand. По-вéш-ение, *n.n.,* hanging. Казнь чéрез п., execution by hanging. По-вéш-енный, *adj. part. pass. past,* hanged (*e.g.,* on a gibbet).

по-вéс-н-ич-ать, *v.i.,* to behave wildly, rant, play the madcap. По-вéс-а, *n.m.,* madcap.

ВЛАД-, ВЛАСТ-, ВОЛОСТ-, AUTHORITY, RULE, POWER, POSSESSION

влад-é-ть, *v.i.,* + *instr.,* to own, possess; have authority, rule, hold, master. В. богáтством, to possess wealth. В.

морями, to rule over the seas. В. орýжием (инструмéнтом), to wield a weapon (an instrument). В. иност-рáнным языкóм, to speak a foreign language. Он хорошó владéет рýс-ским языкóм, he speaks fluent Russian. Влад-éние, *n.n.,* possession, domain, estate, dominion, ownership. Коллек-тúвное в., (*recent*), collective ownership. Вступáть во в., to take possession legally. Лишáть прáва в-я, to dispossess. Влад-éлец, *n.m.,* влад-éлица, *n.f.,* owner, landlord, master, holder. В. дóма, имéния, landlord, landowner. Влад-éтель, *n.m.,* влад-éтельница, *n.f.,* possessor; sovereign. Влад-éтельный, *adj.,* sovereign. В. князь, (*hist.*), ruling prince.

за-влад-éть, *v.p.,* за-влад-евáть, *v.i.,* + *instr.,* to seize, take possession. Не-прúятель завладéл мнóгими крéпост-ями, the enemy seized many fortresses.

о-влад-éть, *v.p.,* о-влад-евáть, *v.i.,* + *instr.,* to seize, take possession, secure, master, conquer. О. собóй, to regain one's composure. О. внимáнием, to hold some one's attention. О. тéхникой рабóты, искýсства, to master the technique of work, art. О-влад-евáние, *n.n.,* seizing, mastering. Со-влад-éлец, *n.m.,* со-влад-éлица, *n.f.,* joint owner, proprietor. Со-влад-éние, *n.n.,* joint ownership.

со-влад-á-ть, *v.p.,* с + *instr.,* to overpower, conquer; succeed. С. со свойм чýвством, to master one's feeling.

влад-ы́ч-еств-ова-ть, *v.i.,* (*obs.*), над + *instr.,* to rule, dominate, lord. В. над морями, to dominate, rule the seas. Влад-ы́ка, *n.m.,* (*hist.*), lord, ruler; (*rel.*,) bishop. Преосвящéнный Вла-ды́ка, Archbishop of the Greek Orthodox Church. Влад-ы́чество, *n.n.,* lordship, sovereignty. Под егó влады́че-ством, under his dominion, rule, lordship Влад-ы́чица, *n.f.,* (*hist.*), sovereign; (*rel.*), Our Lady.

власт-ь, *n.f.,* power, authority, rule; dominion, lordship. Верхóвная в., supreme power. Исполнúтельная в., executive power. Быть во влáсти, to be at the mercy (of someone). Влáсть имýщие, (*iron.*), the powers that be; those in power. Пáртия, стоящая у влáсти, the party in power. Влáст-ный, *adj.,* commanding, dictatorial, authoritarian; imperative. Влáстной рукóй, with an authoritative hand. Влáстный харáктер, dictatorial person. Влáстно, *adv.,* comandingly, dictatorially. Без-влáст-ие, *n.n.,* anarchy. Без-влáст-ный, *adj.,* powerless. Едино-влáстие, *n.n.,* dictatorial rule, absolute monarchy.

Едино-вла́стный, *adj.*, monarchic. Едино-вла́стно, *adv.*, monarchically. Подвла́ст-ность, *n.f.*, subjection, dependence. Под-вла́ст-ный, *adj.* subject to, dependent on. Само-вла́стие, *п.п.*, absolute power, despotism. Само-вла́стный, *adj.*, absolute, unlimited, despotic. **вла́ст-вовать**, *v.i.*, над + *instr.*, to dominate, lord over, rule, reign. Вла́ст-вование, *п.п.*, domination. Власт-ели́н, *п.т.* (*obs.*), lord, sovereign. Власт-и́тель, *п.т.* (*obs.*), potentate. Власт-о-лю́бец, *п.т.*, one who loves power. Власт-о-лю́бие, *п.п.*, love of power. Власт-о-люби́вый, *adj.*, power-mad.

об-лад-а́ть, (*from* об-влад-а́ть), *v.i.*, + *instr.*, to possess, have, be master of. О. прекра́сным здоро́вьем, to enjoy excellent health. О. тала́нтом, умо́м, to be talented, gifted, clever; possess talent. О. пра́вом, to have the right. Об-лад-а́ние, *п.п.*, possession, mastery. Об-лад-а́тель, *п.т.*, об-лад-а́тельница, *n.f.*, possessor, owner, master, (mistress).

пре-об-лад-а́ть, *v.i.*, to predominate. Пре-об-лад-а́ние, *п.п.*, predominance. Пре-об-лад-а́ющий, *adj. part. act. pres.*, predominant. Ру́сские составля́ют преоблада́ющее населе́ние в Сиби́ри, the Russians form the predominant population in Siberia.

о́б-ласт-ь (*from* о́б-власть), *n.f.*, province, region, territory, district; field, domain. Моско́вская о., Moscow Province. В о́бласти а́томной нау́ки име́ются больши́е достиже́ния, in the realm of atomic science, great achievements have been made. Об-ласт-но́й, *adj.*, pertaining to a district, region; provincial, regional. О. суд, district court.

во́лост-ь, *n.f.*, (*obs.*), volost, a small administrative division containing several villages. Волост-но́й, *adj.*, pertaining to a district. В. старшина́, (*obs.*), district village elder. В. сход, (*obs.*), district meeting. Волко́м, (*recent*), *abbr. of* Волостно́й Комите́т, District Committee.

ВОД-, ВОЖ-, ВОЖД-, ВЕД-, ВЕС(ТИ)-, CONDUCT, GUIDANCE, DIRECTION

вод-и́ть, вож-у́, *v.i. indet.*, вес-ти́, вед-у́, *v.i. det.*, + *acc.*, + *instr.*, to conduct, lead. Води́ть дете́й в шко́лу, to take children to school. В. слепо́го, to lead a blind man. Вести́ войну́, to wage war, conduct a war, be at war. Герма́ния вела́ войну́ с СССР, Germany waged war with the USSR. В. де́ло, to manage a business. В. кни́ги, to keep account

books. В. себя́, to behave, conduct oneself. Води́ть за́ нос, (*colloq.*), to fool, to lead by the nose. Води́ть смычко́м по стру́нам, to draw a bow over the strings (as of an instrument). Веди́те себя́ прили́чно! Behave yourself! Вод-и́ть-ся, *v.i.*, to associate with; inhabit, live. Води́ться с вора́ми, (*colloq.*), to associate with thieves. В э́тих леса́х во́дятся медве́ди, bears inhabit these forests. Вод-и́тель, *п.т.*, (*recent*), chauffeur, driver. В. маши́ны, (*recent*), chauffeur, driver. Лес-о-во́д, *п.т.*, forester. Лес-о-во́д-ство, *п.п.*, forestry. Кон-е-во́д, *п.т.*, horse breeder. Кон-е-во́д-ство, *п.п.*, horse breeding. Овц-е-во́д, *п.т.*, sheep breeder. Овц-е-во́д-ство, *п.п.*, sheep breeding. Птиц-е-во́д, *п.т.*, poultry breeder. Птиц-е-во́д-ство, *п.п.*, poultry breeding. Скот-о-во́д, *п.т.*, cattle breeder. Скот-о-во́д-ство, *n.n.*, cattle breeding. Сад-о-во́д, *п.т.*, horticulturalist. Сад-о-во́д-ство, *п.п.*, horticulture. Цвет-о-во́д, *п.т.*, nurseryman. Цвет-о-во́д-ство, *п.п.*, floriculture. Овце-во́д-ческий, *adj.*, pertaining to sheep breeding.

вожд-ь, *п.т.*, leader, chief; captain. В. па́ртии, party chief. Вож-а́к, вожа́тый, *п.т.*, leader (*e.g.*, of a conspiracy, mutiny).

вож-жа́, *n.f.*, во́жж-и, *pl.*, reins. Натяну́ть во́жжи, (also used *fig.*), to tighten the reins. Опуска́ть (опусти́ть) во́жжи, (also used *fig.*), to give a horse its head.

в-вод-и́ть, *v.i.*, в-вес-ти́, *v.p.*, + *acc.*, to bring in, introduce, lead in. Ввести́ зако́н в де́йствие, to put a law into enforcement, operation. В. су́дно в га́вань, to bring a ship into a harbor. В. в расхо́д; в заблужде́ние, to put one to expense; to mislead. В-во́д-ный, *adj.*, introductory, prefatory; parenthetic. В-во́д-ное сло́во, предложе́ние, parenthetic word, clause. В-вед-е́ние, *n.m.*, introduction, preface.

вз-вод-и́ть, *v.i.*, вз-вес-ти́, *v.p.*, + *acc.*, to impute; cock a gun. В. куро́к, to set the hammer (*e.g.*, of a gun). В. обвине́ние, to accuse. Вз-вод, *п.т.*, platoon. Вз-во́д-ный, *adj.*, of a platoon; *also used as n.*, platoon commander. В. команди́р, platoon commander.

вы-вод-и́ть, *v.i.*, вы́-вес-ти, *v.p.*, + *acc.*, to lead, take, bring out; to destroy (*e.g.*, insects); draw a conclusion. В. на прогу́лку, to take for a walk. В. пятно́, to remove a stain. В. цыпля́т, to hatch chickens. В. кого́-либо из себя́, to make someone lose his temper. Вы-вод-и́ть-ся, *v.i.r.*, вы́-вес-ти-сь, *v.p.r.*, to be led, taken, brought out; be hatched; become extinct (of animals). Эти пятна ничём не выводятся, nothing will remove these stains. Вы-вод, *n.m.*, conclusion. Сделать в., to draw a conclusion. Ложный в., faulty conclusion. Вы-вод-ок, *n.m.*, brood. В. утят, гусят, brood of ducklings, goslings.

До-вод-и́ть, *v.i.,* до-вес-ти́, *v.p.,* + *acc.,* до + *gen.,* to lead up to; bring, drive, reduce to; escort. Д. детей до школы, to escort children to school. Д. дело до конца, to bring a matter to an end. Д. до отчаяния, to drive to despair. До-вод-и́ть-ся, *v.i.r.,* до-вес-ти́-сь, *v.p.r.,* (*colloq.*), to happen, chance to be. Он мне дово́дится двою́родным бра́том, he happens to be my cousin. Прика́з дово́дится до све́дения всего́ полка́, the order is directed to the whole regiment. До́-вод, *n.m.,* reason, argument. Неопровержи́мый д., irrefutable argument. Все до́воды за и про́тив, all the pros and cons.

за-вод-и́ть, *v.i.,* за-вес-ти́, *v.p.,* + *acc.,* to wind, start; acquire; establish. З. буди́льник, to wind, set an alarm clock. З. дру́жбу (знако́мство), to make a friendship (acquaintance). З. лошаде́й, to acquire horses. З. кого́-нибудь куда́-нибудь, to take someone out of the way. За-вод-и́ть-ся, *v.i.r.,* за-вес-ти́-сь, *v.p.r.,* to be wound, set; be acquired; be established. У него́ завели́сь де́ньги, he has acquired money. Здесь уж так заведено́, it is the custom here. За-во́д, *n.m.,* works, factory, plant, mill; (*colloq.*) custom. Сталелите́йный з., steel plant. Автомоби́льный з., automobile plant. У нас э́того нет и в заво́де, (*colloq., obs.*), it is not our custom. За-во́д-ка, *n.f.,* за-во́д, *n.m.,* winding mechanism. Автомати́ческий з. у мото́ра, starter, self-starter. за-вод-но́й, *adj.,* pertaining to winding. за-вод-о-управле́ние, *n.n.,* (*recent*), factory management. За-во́д-ский (о́й), *adj.,* pertaining to a factory, plant. За-во́дчик, *n.m.,* owner of a factory. Ко́нный заво́д, horse breeding farm. Конн-о-заво́дчик, *n.m.,* horse breeder.

из-вод-и́ть, *v.i.* из-вес-ти́, *v.p.,* + *acc.,* + *instr.,* to exhaust; overwork, exasperate; spend, use up, consume. И. де́ньги, to squander money. Из-вод-и́ть-ся, *v.i.r.,* из-вес-ти́-сь, *v.p.r.,* to be exhausted, overworked; be exasperated; be spent, used up, consumed. И. от рабо́ты, (*colloq.*), to be overworked. И. от го́ря, to eat one's heart out.

на-во́д-и́ть, *v.i.,* на-вес-ти́, *v.p.,* + *acc.,* to direct, point out; lead, lay out. Н. гля́нец, to glaze. Н. мост, to construct a bridge. Н. поря́док, to tidy up. Н. тоску́, to bore to death. На-важд-е́ние, *n.n.,* (*obs.*), enticement, allurement. На-во́д-чик, *n.m.,* marksman, gunner. На-вод-я́щий, *adj., part. act. pres.,* leading, conducting, conductive. Н. вопро́с, leading question.

об-вод-и́ть, *v.i.,* об-вес-ти́, *v.p.,* + *acc.,* + *instr.,* to lead round, encircle, surround; outline. О. глаза́ми, to look around. Об-во́д-ка, *n.f.,* об-во́д, *n.m.,* the action of enclosing, surrounding, encircling; outlining; by-passing. Об-во́д-ный, *adj.,* enclosing, surrounding, encircling, outlining, by-passing.

об-за-вод-и́ть, *v.i.,* об-за-вес-ти́, *v.p.,* + *instr.,* to provide; acquire. Об-за-вод-и́ть-ся, *v.i.r.,* об-за-вес-ти́-сь, *v.p.r.,* + *instr.,* to be provided with; settle. О. семьёй и до́мом, to settle down to domestic life. Об-за-вед-е́ние, *n.n.,* acquisition, provision.

пере-вод-и́ть, *v.i.,* пере-вес-ти́, *v.p.,* + *acc.,* с + *gen.,* to translate; transfer; cross; (*idiom*), to catch one's breath. П. с ру́сского языка́ на англи́йский, to translate from Russian into English. П. часову́ю стре́лку вперёд (наза́д), to set a clock ahead (back). Пере-вод-и́ть-ся, *v.i.r.,* пере-вес-ти́-сь, *v.p.r.,* to be translated, transferred; become extinct. У него́ де́ньги не перево́дятся, he is never without money. Пере-во́д, *n.m.,* translation; transfer; interpretation. П. пи́сьменный, written translation. П. у́стный, oral translation, interpretation. П. вре́мени (де́нег), (*colloq.*), waste of time (money). П. из Москвы́ на Кавка́з, to transfer from Moscow to the Caucasus. П. часо́в вперёд, the setting of a clock ahead (*e.g.,* for daylight saving time). Де́нежный п., money order; transfer. Почто́вый п., postal money order. Пере-во́д-чик, *n.m.,* пере-во́д-чица, *n.f.,* translator, interpreter. Пере-во́дный, *adj.,* translated; pertaining to a translation. П. рома́н, translated novel. П. бланк, money order.

по-вод-и́ть, *v.i.,* по-вес-ти́, *v.p.,* + *instr.,* to move. П. глаза́ми, to roll one's eyes. П. уша́ми, (of animals) to move, wiggle one's ears. Конь повсди́л уша́ми, the horse was moving its ears.

по-вод-и́ть, *v.p.,* + *acc.,* to walk an animal for a while, to lead. П. коня́ по двору́, to walk a horse in a yard for a short while. П. слепо́го по у́лицам, to lead a blind man through the streets for a while. По-вод-ы́рь слепо́го, a blind man's lead. По́-вод, *n.m.,* по-во́дья, *n.m.pl.,* rein, reins (as of a saddle horse). Натяну́ть п., to draw the reins. Быть на поводу́, (*idiom.*), to be under

someone's thumb. Бу́дьте самостоя́-
тельны, не бу́дьте на поводу́ у други́х,
be independent, stop being led by
others. По́-вод, *n.m.,* по́-вод-ы, *n.m.pl.,*
occasion, ground, cause. По́воды к
войне́, cause of war (*casus belli*). Из-
бега́ть по́водов для ссо́ры, to avoid
occasions for quarrelling. По по́воду,
in connection with, on the occasion of,
for the purpose of. Собра́ние по по́-
воду вы́боров но́вого правле́ния, a
meeting for the purpose of electing a
new administration. По-вед-е́ние, *n.n.,*
behavior. Дурно́е (хоро́шее) п., bad
(good) behavior.

под-вод-и́ть, *v.i.,* под-вес-ти́, *v.p.,* + *acc.,*
to lead up to; place under; underpin
(*e.g.,* a building); strike a balance, balance, sum up; undermine; let down.
П. ито́г, to sum up. Под-вод-и́ть-ся,
v.p.r., to be led up to, placed under.
Под-во́д-а, *n.f.,* a horse and cart. Под-
во́д-чик, *n.m.,* driver of a cart.

при-вод-и́ть, *v.i.,* при-вес-ти́, *v.p.,* +
acc. в + *acc.,* to bring, lead to; (*math.*),
reduce to; cite, quote. П. дете́й в шко́лу,
to bring children to school. П. в восто́рг
(в у́жас), to delight (horrify, frighten).
П. в исполне́ние, to carry out, put into
practice. При-вод-и́ть-ся, *v.i.r.,* при-
вес-ти́-сь, *v.p.r.,* to be brought, led to;
to chance, happen. Маши́на приво́-
дится в де́йствие па́ром, the machine
is activated by steam. Мне не приве-
ло́сь быва́ть там, (*colloq.*), I've never
had the occasion to be there. При-во́д,
n.m., the action of bringing; (*tech.*),
drive, gear. Ременно́й п., (*tech.*), belt
drive. При-вод-но́й, *adj.,* pertaining to
driving. П. вал, driving shaft.

про-вод-и́ть, *v.i.,* про-вес-ти́, *v.p.,* + *acc.,*
to lead through; conduct, spend, pass;
deceive, trick. П. желе́зную доро́гу,
to construct a railroad. П. законо-
прое́кт, to pass a bill. П. в жизнь, to
put into practice. Про-вод-и́ть-ся, *v.i.r.,*
to be led through; realized. Про́-вод,
n.m., wire. Про-во́д-ка, *n.f.,* installation. П. электри́чества, installation of
electricity. Про-вод-ни́к, *n.m.,* guide;
porter, conductor.

про-вож-а́ть, *v.i.,* про-вод-и́ть, *v.p.,* +
acc., to see someone off; to escort
home; accompany. Со-про-вожд-а́ть,
v.i., + *acc.,* to escort. Вре́мя-пре-про-
вожд-е́ние, *n.n.,* a pastime. Ра́ди в-ия.,
as a pastime, to pass the time, for the
sake of passing time. Про́-вод-ы, *n.pl.,*
send-off.

про-из-вод-и́ть, *v.i.,* про-из-вес-ти́, *v.p.,*
+ *acc.,* to produce, make, perform, effect; drive. П. ремо́нт до́ма, to make
repairs on a house. П. впечатле́ние, to
make an impression. П. о́пыты, to conduct experiments. П. сенса́цию, to
create a sensation. П. сло́во от ко́рня,
to derive a word from a root. Про-из-
вод-и́ть-ся, *v.i.r.,* to be produced, made,
performed, derived. Про-из-вед-е́ние,
n.n., work, composition; production. П.
иску́сства, work of art. П-ия Пу́шкина,
Pushkin's works. Про-из-во́д-ный, *adj.,*
(*gram.*), derivative. П-ое сло́во,
(*gram.*), derivative, derived word. Про-
из-во́д-ственный, *adj.,* pertaining to
production, manufacture. П-ая про-
гра́мма, production schedule. П-ое со-
веща́ние, (*recent*), conference dealing
with production. Про-из-во́д-ство, *n.n.,*
production. П. ста́ли, production of
steel. П. в офице́ры, promotion to an
officer's rank.

раз-вод-и́ть, *v.i.,* раз-вес-ти́, *v.p.,* + *acc.,*
to separate, divorce; raise, cultivate;
dilute. Р. по места́м, to escort, direct
people to their seats. Р. мост, to raise,
swing open a bridge. Р. ого́нь, to build
a fire. Р. рога́тый скот, to raise cattle.
Раз-вод-и́ть-ся, *v.i.r.,* раз-вес-ти́-сь,
v.p.r., to divorce, be divorced. Они́
развели́сь в про́шлом году́, they were
divorced last year. Раз-во́д-ка, *n.f.,* a
drawing apart; (*tech.*), saw-set; tooth
setter. Р. моста́, the swinging open,
drawing up of a bridge. Разводно́й
мост, a drawbridge. Раз-во́д, *n.m.,* divorce; (*mil.*), trooping of the colors,
posting of the guard. Получи́ть р., to
obtain a divorce. Оста́вить на р., to
keep for the purpose of breeding. Раз-
вод-но́й, *adj.,* pertaining to separation,
divorce. Раз-во́д-ы, *n.pl.,* arabesque
designs. Си́тец в развода́х, printed
cotton.

с-вод-и́ть, *v.i.,* с-вес-ти́, *v.p.,* + *acc.,* to
settle; pay, draw together. С. концы́,
to join ends. С. дете́й в сад, to take
children to a garden. С. дру́жбу, (*colloq.*), to make a friendship. С. концы́
с конца́ми, (*fig.*), to make both ends
meet. С. с ума́, to drive mad; fascinate.
С-вод-и́ть-ся, *v.i.r.,* с-вес-ти́-сь, *v.p.r.,*
to be brought together. Всё э́то сво́-
дится к пустяка́м, it all comes to
nothing. С-вед-е́ние, *n.n.,* cramp, contraction; reduction, settling; squaring
of accounts. С. ли́чных счёто́в, squaring of accounts with somebody. С. на
нет, (*fig.*), to bring to naught. С-вед-
ённый, *adj. part. pass. past,* contracted,
cramped; settled. С-вод, *n.n.,* vault,
arch; statute. С. зако́нов, statute, code
of laws. Готи́ческий с., gothic arch.
С-во́д-ка, *n.f.,* resumé, summary. Опе-
рати́вная с., (*mil.*), summary of opera-
tions, communiqué. В газе́те ежедне́в-

но печа́тается операти́вная сво́дка с фро́нта, a communiqué from the front is published daily in the newspaper. С-во́д-ный, *adj.*, compound; collated; combined; summarized. С. брат, stepbrother. С. указа́тель, summarized index. С-во́д-чатый, *adj.*, (*arch.*), arched, vaulted.

у-вод-и́ть, *v.i.*, у-вес-ти́, *v.p.*, + *acc.*, to lead away, walk off with, steal, kidnap, rustle. У. дете́й, to lead away children. У. скот, to lead away, to rustle cattle. У-во́д, *n.m.*, leading away, stealing, rustling; (*mil.*), withdrawal of troops.

рук-о-вод-и́ть, see рук-.

ВОД-, WATER

вод-а́, *n.f.*, water. В. вы́шла из берего́в, the water has flooded the banks. По́лая в., high water. Пре́сная (солёная) в., fresh (salt) water. Водо́й не разольёшь, (*saying*) thick as thieves. ... И концы́ в во́ду, (*saying*), ... and it will never be discovered. Мно́го воды́ утекло́ с тех пор, (*fig.*), much water has flowed under the bridge. Как ры́ба в воде́, (*fig.*), as happy as a fish in water. Вод-и́ца, вод-и́чка, *n.f.*, (*dim.*), water. Во́д-ка, *n.f.*, vodka. Дать на во́дку, to tip, leave a tip. Во́д-очный, *adj.*, pertaining to vodka. В. заво́д, vodka distillery. Во́д-ник, *n.m.*, water transport worker. Сою́з во́дников, (*recent*), water transport workers' union. Во́д-ный, *adj.*, pertaining to water. В. тра́нспорт, water transport. Вод-о-боя́знь, *n.f.*, hydrophobia, rabies. Вод-о-во́з, *n.m.*, one who distributes water from a barrel cart. Вод-о-воро́т, *n.m.*, whirlpool. Кружи́ться в водоворо́те, to pe caught in a vortex, whirlpool. Вод-о-ка́чка, *n.f.*, water tower. Вод-о-ла́з, *n.m.*, diver; Newfoundland dog. Вод-о-ла́зный, *adj.*, pertaining to diving. В. ко́локол, diving bell. Вод-о-лече́ние, hydrotherapy. Вод-о-лече́бный, *adj.*, hydrotherapeutic. Вод-о-па́д, *n.m.*, waterfall, falls, cascade. Вод-о-по́й, *n.m.*, watering place. Вод-о-прово́д, *n.m.*, water pipe; plumbing. Вод-о-прово́дчик, *n.m.*, plumber. Вод-опрово́дная ста́нция, waterworks. Вод-о-разде́л, *n.m.*, watershed. Вод-о-ро́д, *n.m.*, hydrogen. Во́д-о-росль, *n.f.*, water plants. Вод-о-свя́тие, вод-о-освяще́ние, *n.n.*, blessing of water. Вод-о-снабже́ние, *n.n.*, water supply. Вод-о-храни́лище, *n.n.*, reservoir, cistern. Вод-яно́й, *adj.*, aquatic. Вод-яно́й, *adj. used as n.*, (*myth.*), water sprite. В-а́я ли́лия, water lily. В-а́я турби́на, water turbine. В-о́е отоп-

ле́ние, hot-water heating. В-о́е расте́ние, aquatic plant. Вод-яни́стость, *n.f.*, wateriness. Вод-яни́стый, *adj.*, watery. Вод-я́нка, *n.f.*, dropsy.

на-вод-н-и́-ть, *v.p.*, на-вод-ня́ть, *v.i.*, + *acc.*, to inundate, flood; (*fig.*), to overrun. На-вод-не́ние, *n.n.*, flood, inundation.

под-во́д-ный, *adj.*, submarine, submersed. П. флот, submarine fleet. П. ка́мень, underwater rock. П-ое расте́ние, underwater plant.

пол-о-во́дье, *n.n.*, high water during spring floods. Весе́ннее п., spring floods.

ВОЗ-, ВОЖ-, ВЕЗ-, CONVEYANCE, TRANSFERENCE

воз, *n.m.*, cart, wagon. В. дров, a cart of firewood. Что с во́зу упа́ло, то пропа́ло, (*prov.*), what is lost is lost. Возни́ца, *n.m.*, driver; coachman. Из-во́з, *n.m.*, carrier's trade. Из-во́з-чик, *n.m.*, cabman, cabby. Взять изво́зчика, to take a cab. Лес-о-во́з, (*recent*), freighter for lumber transportation. Пар-о-во́з, *n.m.*, locomotive, steam engine. Пар-о-во́з-ный, *adj.*, pertaining to a locomotive, steam engine. П-ая брига́да, a locomotive crew. Пар-о-воз-о-строе́ние, *n.n.*, locomotive building industry. По-во́з-ка, *n.f.*, vehicle, carriage.

воз-и́-ть, вож-у́, *v.i. indet.*, вез-ти́, *v.i. det.* по-вез-ти́, *v.p.*, + *acc.*, to convey, transport, carry; drive. Ка́ждый день мать во́зит дете́й в шко́лу, the mother drives her children to school every day. Врач повёз больно́го в больни́цу, the doctor drove the sick man to a hospital. Ему́ везёт в любви́ (в ка́ртах), he is lucky in love (in cards). Воз-и́ть-ся, *v.i.r.*, по-воз-и́ть-ся, *v.p.r.*, + *acc.*, с + *instr.*, to take trouble, fuss over; romp. Мне пришло́сь мно́го вози́ться с ребёнком, I had a lot of trouble with the child. Де́ти вози́лись на полу́, the children were romping on the floor. Воз-ня́, *n.f.*, trouble; noise, rumpus; romping. Подня́ть возню́, to create a rumpus.

в-воз-и́ть, *v.i.*, в-вез-ти́, *v.p.*, + *acc.*, to import. Англия ввозит хлеб, England imports wheat. В-воз-и́ть-ся, *v.i.r.*, to be imported. В-воз, *n.m.*, import. Незако́нный в., smuggling. Ввозный, *adj.*, pertaining to imports, importing. В-ые по́шлины, import duties.

вы-воз-и́ть, *v.i.*, вы́-вез-ти, *v.p.*, + *acc.*, to export; remove. Кана́да вывозит хлеб заграни́цу, Canada exports grain. Вы́-воз, *n.m.*, export, exporting. вывоз-но́й, *adj.*, pertaining to export, exporting. Вывозны́е по́шлины, export duties.

до-воз-и́ть, *v.i.,* до-вез-ти́, *v.p.,* + *acc.,* до + *gen.,* to drive, convey to. Изво́зчик довёз нас до вокза́ла, the cabdriver drove us to the station.

за-воз-и́ть, *v.i.,* за-вез-ти́, *v.p.,* + *acc.,* to drive, convey; leave. З. кого́-ли́бо домо́й, to drive someone home. За-воз-и́ть-ся, *v.p.r.,* to bustle about; be restless; *see* вози́ться, Мы́ши завози́лись под поло́м, the mice were bustling about under the floor.

на-воз-и́ть, *v.i.,* на-вез-ти́, *v.p,* + *gen.,* to gather in large quantities. Н. дров на́ зиму, to gather wood for the winter. Наво́з, *n.m.,* dung, manure. Наво́з-ный, *adj.,* pertaining to dung, manure. Н. жук, dung beetle. Н-ая ку́ча, a dunghill, dungheap.

от-воз-и́ть, *v.i.,* от-вез-ти́, *v.p.,* + *acc.,* to transport; return; escort. О. кого́-ли́бо домо́й, to drive someone home. О. в больни́цу, to take to a hospital.

пере-воз-и́ть, *v.i.,* пере-вез-ти́, *v.p.,* + *acc.,* to convey, carry, transport. Пере-воз-и́ть-ся, *v.i.r.,* to be transported, carried, conveyed. Пере-во́з-ка, *n.f.,* transportation. Сто́имость перево́зки, cost of transporation. Пере-во́з-чик, *n.m.,* ferryman. Пере-во́з-очный, *adj.,* pertaining to transportation. Перево́зочные сре́дства, means of transportation. Пере-во́з, *n.m.,* ferry transportation. П. на реке́, river ferry.

под-воз-и́ть, *v.i.,* под-вез-ти́, *v.p.,* + *acc.,* to convey, transport, bring up to. Под-воз-и́ть-ся, *v.i.r.,* to be brought, carried, transported. Хлеб подво́зится на ссыпно́й пункт, grain is transported to the collecting station. Под-во́з, *n.m.,* transport of supplies.

при-воз-и́ть, *v.i.,* при-вез-ти́, *v.p.,* + *acc.,* to bring, transport; import. При-воз-и́ть-ся, *v.i.r.,* to be brought, transported; imported. При-во́з, *n.m.,* bringing, transporting; supplying; importing. При-во́з-ный; при-воз-но́й, *adj.,* pertaining to bringing, transporting; supplying; importing.

раз-воз-и́ть, *v.i.,* раз-вез-ти́, *v.p.,* + *acc.,* to distribute by conveyance. Раз-воз-и́ть-ся, *v.i.r.,* to be transported; to frolic, gambol. Пи́сьма развозятся почто́вым автомоби́лем, letters are distributed by mail car. Де́ти развози́лись в саду́, the children were playing in the garden. Раз-во́з, *n.m.,* distribution. Раз-во́з-ка, *n.f.,* (*slang*), distribution by means of a conveyance.

с-воз-и́ть, с-вож-у́, *v.i.,* с-вез-ти́, *v.p.,* + *acc.,* to convey to a given place. Свез-

ти́ молоко́ в го́род, to transport milk to the city.

у-воз-и́ть, у-вож-у́, *v.i.,* у-вез-ти́ *v.p.,* + *acc.,* to cart away. Ра́неных увезли́ в го́спиталь, the wounded were taken away to the hospital.

ВОЛОК-, ВОЛОЧ-, ВЛЕЧ-, ВЛЕК-, ВЛАК-, ВЛАЧ-, ВОЛАК-, TRACTION, DRAWING, HAULING; FIBRE

во́лок, *n.m.,* portage. Тащи́ть во́локом, (*obs.*), to transport by portage. Волоки́та, *n.f.,* red tape, procrastination; *n.m.,* a ladies' man, gallant Канцеля́рская в., red tape. Волок-но́, *n.n.,* fibre. Волок-о́нце, *n.n.,* minute fibre. Волокни́стый, *adj.,* fibrous, fibroid. На́-волок-а, *n.f.,* pillowcase, pillowslip. Про́волок-а, *n.f.,* wire. Колю́чая п., barbed wire. Про́-волоч-ка, *n.f.,* small, thin wire. Про́-волоч-ный, *adj.,* pertaining to wire, made of wire. П. кана́т, wire cable. П-ая сеть, wire netting. П-ое загражде́ние, (*mil.*), wire entanglement.

волоч-и́-ть, волок-у́, *v.i.,* + *acc.,* to drag, trail, lug. В. но́ги, to drag one's feet. В. про́волоку, to draw wire. Волоч-и́ть-ся, *v.i.r.,* to drag, trail; court (за + *instr.*). Волоч-е́ние, *n.n.,* dragging. В. про́-волок-и, drawing of wire.

вы́-волоч-ить, *v.p.,* вы-вола́к-ивать, *v.i.,* + *acc.,* to drag out. В. се́ти из воды́, to draw nets out of water.

за-волоч-и́ть, *v.p.,* за-вола́к-ивать, *v.i.,* to cloud, darken; sadden. Ту́чи заволокли́ всё не́бо, clouds have covered the whole sky. За-вола́к-ивать-ся, *v.i.r.,* to become beclouded. З. вла́гой, to become enshrouded in vapor, mist.

об-волоч-и́ть, *v.p.,* об-вола́к-ивать, *v.i.,* + *acc.,* + *instr.,* (*obs.*), to envelope. Об-вола́к-ивать-ся, *v.i.r.,* to become shaded in mist. Луна́ обвола́кивается ту́чами, the moon is becoming covered by a mist. Об-вола́к-ивание, *n.n.,* enveloping, beclouding.

про-волоч-и́ть, *v.p.,* про-вола́к-ивать, *v.i.,* + *acc.,* to draw through; delay (*as* a lawsuit). П. кана́т, to draw a cable across. Про-воло́ч-ка, *n.f.,* protraction, delay, procrastination. Напра́сная п. вре́мени, useless procrastination.

влеч-ь, влек-у́ *v.i.,* + *acc.,* to involve; necessitate; bring; attract. Война́ влечёт за собо́й мно́го жертв, war involves many victims. Влеч-е́ние, *n.n.,* inclination, bent; craving. В. к му́зыке, inclination towards music. Сле́довать своему́ влече́нию, to follow one's inclination.

за-влеч-ь, *v.p.,* за-влек-а́ть, *v.i.,* + *acc.,* to entice, lure.

из-влеч-ь, *v.p.,* из-влек-а́ть, *v.i.,* + *acc.,* to extract, draw out, elicit. И. пу́лю из ра́ны, to extract a bullet from a wound. И. ко́рень из числа́ (*math.*), to extract the root of a quantity. И. вы́году, to derive profit. Из-влеч-е́ние, *п.п.,* extraction. И. из кни́ги, abstract of a book.

на-влеч-ь, *v.p.,* на-влек-а́ть, *v.i.,* + *acc.,* to draw, bring on; cause. Н. на себя́ гнев (опа́сность, подозре́ние), to incur anger (danger, suspicion).

от-влеч-ь, *v.p.,* от-влек-а́ть, *v.i.,* + *acc.,* to distract, divert; abstract. О. внима́ние, to divert one's attention. От-влеч-ь-ся, *v.p.r.,* от-влек-а́ть-ся, *v.i.r.,* от + *gen.,* to digress, be distracted. От-влеч-е́ние, *п.п.,* abstraction. От-влеч-ён-ность, *n.f.,* abstractness. От-влеч-ён-ный, *adj. part. pass. past,* abstract. О-ая величина́, иде́я, abstract quantity, idea. От-влеч-ённо, *adv.,* abstractly.

при-влеч-ь, *v.p.,* при-влек-а́ть, *v.i.,* + *acc.,* к + *dat.,* to attract. П. внима́ние, to attract one's attention. П. к суду́, to sue, take to court. При-влек-а́ть-ся, *v.i.r.,* к + *dat.,* за + *acc.,* to be attracted. П. к отве́тственности за что́-нибудь, to be prosecuted for something. При-влеч-е́ние, *п.п.,* attraction. П. к уча́стью в чём-нибудь, to be drawn into participating in something. При-влек-а́тельность, *n.f.,* attractiveness, charm. При-влек-а́тельный, *adj.,* attractive, winsome. П-ая улы́бка, winning smile. При-влек-а́тельно, *adv.,* winsomely, attractively.

раз-влеч-ь, *v.p.,* раз-влек-а́ть, *v.i.,* + *instr.,* to amuse, entertain, divert. Р. ребёнка и́грами, to amuse a child with games. Раз-влеч-ь-ся, *v.p.r.,* раз-влек-а́ть-ся, *v.i.r.,* + *instr.,* to play, have a good time. Раз-влеч-е́ние, *п.п.,* amusement, diversion, entertainment. Он занима́ется му́зыкой для развле-че́ния, he has taken up music as a diversion. Наро́дные развлече́ния, national pastimes.

у-влеч-ь, *v.p.,* у-влек-а́ть, *v.i.,* + *acc.,* to carry away; fascinate. У-влеч-ь-ся, *v.p.r.,* у-влек-а́ть-ся, *v.i.r.,* + *instr.,* to be carried away, take a fancy to. У-влеч-е́ние, *п.п.,* enthusiasm, passion. у-влек-а́тельность, *n.f.,* attractiveness, fascination. У-влек-а́тельный, *adj.,* absorbing, captivating, thrilling. У. расска́з, a thrilling narrative. У-влек-а́тельно, *adv.,* absorbingly, fascinatingly.

влач-и́ть, *v.i.,* + *acc.,* (*poet.*), to drag; see волочи́ть. В. жа́лкое существова́ние, to lead a miserable existence. Влач-и́ть-ся, (*poet.*), see волочи́ться.

об-лач-и́ть, (from об-влач-и́ть), *v.p.,* об-лач-а́ть, *v.i.,* + *acc.,* to put on priestly vestments, robe. О. свяще́нника, to put vestments on a priest. Об-ле́ч-ь-ся, *v.p.r.,* об-лач-а́ть-ся, *v.i.r.,* в + *acc.,* to array oneself; don vestments. О. в ри́зы, to put on church vestments. Об-лач-е́ние, *п.п.,* priestly vestments, canonicals. Церко́вное о., church vestments.

о́б-лак-о (*from* о́б-(в)-лак-о), *п.п.,* cloud. Не́бо затяну́лось облака́ми, the sky became overcast. Об-лач-ность, *n.f.,* cloudiness. Об-лач-ный, *adj.,* clouded, beclouded, cloudy.

об-лек-а́-ть (*from* об-влек-а́ть), *v.i.,* об-ле́ч-ь, *v.p.,* + *acc.,* в + *acc.,* to clothe, give the shape of. О. в бе́лые оде́жды, to clothe in white garments. О. полно-мо́чиями, to invest with authority, a mission.

об-лек-а́ть-ся, *v.i.r.,* об-ле́ч-ь-ся, *v.p.r.,* (*fig.*), to assume, adopt the form of. *see* облача́ться. Об-оло́ч-ка (*from* об-воло́ч-ка), *n.f.,* envelope, cover, wrapper. Сли́зистая о., (*anat.*), mucous membrane. О. снаря́да, shell of a projectile. Водонепроница́емая о., (*tech.*), waterproof casing.

ВОЙ-, ВО-, WARFARE

вой-на́, *n.f.,* war, warfare. Мирова́я в., world war. Гражда́нская в., civil war. Партиза́нская в., guerilla warfare. Объявля́ть войну́, to declare war. Во́й-ск-о, *п.п.,* army, troops, forces. Де́йствующие в-а́, combat forces. Регуля́рные в-а́, regular forces. Сою́з-ные в-а́, allied forces. Вой-сково́й, *adj.,* military, pertaining to the army. В-а́я канцеля́рия, military office.

во́-ин, *п.т.,* (*obs., poet.*), warrior, soldier. В сраже́нии он показа́л себя́ и́стин-ным во́ином, he proved himself a splendid fighter in action. Во́-ин-ство, *п.п.,* (*obs.*), army, host. Во-ин-ствен-ность, *n.f.,* warlikeness, combativeness, belligerence. Во-ин-ственный, *adj.,* warlike, combative, belligerent, martial. В. дух, warlike spirit. В. наро́д, a bellicose, martial people, nation. Во-ин-ствующий, *adj., part. act. pres.,* militant, warring, martial. В-ий материа-ли́зм, (*recent*), militant materialism. Во́-ин-ский, *adj.,* military. В. биле́т, military train ticket. В-ая пови́нность, compulsory military service. Во-я́ка, *n.т.,* (*derog.*), warrior.

во-е-вóд-а, *n.m.*, (*hist., obs.*), commander in chief; governor of a province. Во-е-вóд-ство, *n.n.*, government of a province.

во-éн-ный, *adj.*, military, martial, pertaining to war. В-ая слýжба, military service. Поступйть на воéнную слýжбу, to enlist. В-ое министéрство, Ministry of War. В-ый комиссариáт, (*recent*), war commissariat. В. коммунйзм, (*recent*), war, war-time communism. В. завóд, munitions factory. В-ое положéние, martial law. Во-éн-ные, *adj.*, *used as n.*, the military; men in uniform. Воéн-щина, *n.f.*, (*derog.*), soldiery; militarists. Военкóм, *n.m.*, (*recent, abbr. of* воéнный комиссáр), army commissar. Военкóр, *n.m.*, (*recent, abbr. of* военный корреспондéнт), war correspondent. Военмóр, *n.m.*, (*recent, abbr. of* воéнный морáк), Navy man. Военрýк, *n.m.*, (*recent, abbr. of* воéнный руководйтель), military instructor. Воéнно-обáзанный, *adj.*, *used as n.*, liable to military service. Воéнно-плéнный, *adj. used as n.*, prisoner of war. Военно-полевóй суд, court martial. Воéнно-слýжащий, military man, army man. Воéнно-слýжащий флóта, navy man. Военизáция, *n.f.*, (*recent*), militarization, preparation for aggressive war. Военизйровать, *v.p., and v.i.*, + *acc.*, (*recent*), to militarize, prepare for aggressive war. В. промышленность, to mobilize industry for military purposes.

во-евáть, *v.i.*, по-во-евáть, *v.p.*, с + *instr.*, to wage war, war. Итáлия воевáла во 2-ую мировýю войнý, Italy fought in the 2nd World War. Он ужé с утрá воюет с женóй, (*colloq.*), he has been quarreling with his wife since morning.

за-во-евáть, *v.p.*, за-во-ёвывать, *v.i.*, + *acc.*, to conquer. З. странý to conquer a country. З. себé положéние, to secure a position. З. довéрие, to earn someone's confidence. За-во-евáние, *n.n.*, conquest. За-во-евáтель, *n.m.*, conqueror. За-во-евáтельный, *adj.*, aggressive. З-ая войнá war of conquest; aggressive, offensive war.

от-во-евáть, *v.p.*, от-во-ёвывать, *v.i.*, + *acc.*, to acquire, gain through warfare. Нарóд отвоевáл прáво на свобóду, by fighting the people earned the right to freedom. Я цéлых три гóда провоевáл на передовóй лйнни, I fought at the front for three years.

раз-во-евáть-ся, *v.p.r.*, (*colloq.*), to storm, bluster, tangle, engage one another.

ВОР- THIEVERY; DEXTERITY, CLEVERNESS

вор, *n.m.*, thief, burglar, pickpocket. Ворйшка, *n.m.*, pilferer. Вор-óвка, *n.f.*, thief. Вор-овствó, *n.n.* thievery, theft, stealing. Вор-óванный, *adj. part. pass. past*, stolen. Вор-овскóй, *adj.*, of or pertaining to thieves. В. притóн, thieves' den.

вор-овá-ть, *v.i.*, у-вор-овáть, *v.p.*, по-вор-овáть, *v.p.*, + *acc.*, to steal, thieve, rob, commit burglary.

на-вор-овáть, *v.p.*, на-вор-óвывать, *v.i.*, + *acc.*, + *gen.*, to steal in quantity. Он наворовáл себé цéлое состояние, he acquired a fortune by stealing.

об-вор-овáть, *v.p.*, об-вор-óвывать, *v.i.*, + *acc.*, to rob. Вчерá нóчью обворовáли нáших сосéдей, last night our neighbors were burglarized.

про-вор-овáть-ся, *v.p.r.*, to embezzle. Кассйр проворовáлся, (*colloq.*), the cashier embezzled some money.

раз-вор-овáть, *v.p.*, раз-вор-óвывать, *v.i.*, + *acc.*, (*colloq.*), to steal, pilfer everything. Разворовáли дровá, all the firewood was stolen bit by bit.

про-вóр-ить, *v.i.*, с-про-вóр-ить, *v.p.*, + *acc.*, (*folk.*), to do something adroitly, expeditiously, dexterously. Про-вóрность, *n.f.*, *see* про-вóр-ство. Про-вóрный, *adj.*, dexterous, adroit, swift. Про-вóр-но, *adv.*, dexterously, adroitly, expeditiously. Про-вóр-ство, *n.n.*, adroitness, dexterity, expeditiousness.

ВОРОЖ-, ВОРАЖ-, ВРАЧ-, CHARM, ENCHANTMENT, CURE

ворож-й-ть, *v.i.*, по-ворож-йть, *v.p.* (*obs.*), to tell fortunes. Цыгáнки ворожáт, gypsies foretell the future. Ворож-бá, *n.f.*, fortune-telling. Ворож-éй, *n.m.*, ворож-éя, *n.f.*, (*obs., poet.*), fortune-teller.

за-ворож-йть, *v.p.*, за-ворáж-ивать, *v.i.*, + *acc.*, to charm, bewitch, cast a spell over. "Свойми чýдными очáми тебя старйк заворожйл" (Pushkin), "With his beautiful eyes the old man has bewitched you."

об-ворож-йть, *v.p.*, об-ворáж-ивать, *v.i.*, + *acc.*, + *instr.*, to fascinate, bewitch, charm completely. Обворáживать свойм обращéнием, свойми манéрами, to charm with one's behavior, manners. Об-ворож-йтельность, *n.f.*, fascination, charm. Об-ворож-йтельный, *adj.*, fascinating, bewitching, charming. О. человéк, a charming person. О-ая жéнщина, a fascinating woman. О-ая улыбка, a charming smile.

при-ворож-и́ть, *v.p.,* при-вораж-ивать, *v.i.,* + *acc.,* to bewitch, enchant.

врач, *n.m.,* physician, doctor. Врач-хиру́рг, surgeon. Дома́шний в. family doctor.

врач-ева́ть, *v.i.,* (*obs.*), + *acc.,* to doctor, treat, cure. В. не́дуги, to treat illnesses, infirmities. Врач-ева́ние, *n.n.,* doctoring, treatment, cure. Врач-е́бный, *adj.,* pertaining, to doctoring, treating, curing; medical. В-ая по́мощь, medical aid. В-ый осмо́тр, medical examination.

ВРАГ-, ВОРОГ-, ВРАЖ-, ВРАЖД-, HOSTILITY, ENMITY

враг, *n.m.,* enemy, foe. В. перешёл грани́цу, the enemy has crossed the border. Иде́йный в., an ideological enemy. Во́рог (враг) *n.m.,* (*obs., poet.*), enemy.

вра́ж-еский, *adj.,* hostile, pertaining to an enemy. Вра́ж-ий, *adj.,* (*obs., poet.*), hostile. Вра́жеское наше́ствие, an enemy invasion. Вра́жеский стан, enemy camp.

вражд-а́, *n.f.,* enmity, hostility; feud. Кро́вная в., blood feud. Вражд-е́бность, *n.f.,* state of hostility, animosity. Вражд-е́бный, *adj.,* hostile, inimical. В-ые наме́рения, hostile intentions. В-ые отноше́ния, unfriendly, inimical relations.

вражд-ова́-ть, *v.p.,* and *v.i.,* с + *instr.,* to be hostile, be at loggerheads; at variance, up in arms against. Сосе́дние стра́ны вражду́ют ме́жду собо́й, the neighboring countries are hostile to one another. Вражд-у́ющий, *adj. part. act. pres.,* conflicting, hostile, inimical, antagonistic. В-ие сто́роны, conflicting parties.

ВР-, ВИР-, FALSEHOOD, UNTRUTH, MISPRESENTATION

вр-ать, *v.i.,* со-вр-а́ть, *v.p.,* + *acc.,* to lie, fib. Врать - грешно́, it is a sin to lie. Врёт, как си́вый ме́рин, (*colloq.*), he lies like a trooper. Вра́-ки, *n.pl.,* idle talk, lies. Вра-ль, *n.m.,* liar. Вр-анье́, *n.n.,* lying. Вр-ун, *n.m.,* вр-у́нья, *n.f.,* liar, prevaricator.

за-вр-а́ть-ся, *v.p.r.,* to lie without restraint.

за-вир-а́ть-ся, *v.i.r.,* to talk nonsense. Так завра́лся, что ему́ переста́ли ве́рить, he lied so much, they all stopped believing him.

на-вр-а́ть, *v.p.,* + *acc.,* + *gen.,* в + *prep.,* to lie to excess; tell tall tales. Н. вся́ких небыли́ц, to tell tall tales.

Н. в перево́де (*colloq.*), to err in translating.

пере-вр-а́ть, *v.p.,* пере-вир-а́ть, *v.i.,* (*colloq.*), to outdo, surpass in lying; to make a mistake, error. П. фами́лию, to make a mistake in some one's last name. П. все фа́кты, to mix up all the facts.

при-вр-а́ть, *v.p.,* при-вир-а́ть, *v.i.,* (*colloq.*), to exaggerate, romanticize. ...и к бы́лям небыли́ц без счёту привира́л (*Krylov*), and to real stories added innumerable tall tales.

ВТОР-, DUALITY, TWO; REPETITION, DUPLICATION

вто́р-ник, *n.m.,* Tuesday.

втор-о́й, *num. ord.,* the second. Вто́рник - второ́й день неде́ли, Tuesday is the second day of the week. Второ́й час, the hour between one and two o'clock; past one o'clock. Екатери́на Втора́я, Catherine II, Empress of Russia. В-а́я скри́пка, second fiddle; (*fig.*), a subordinate role, part. В-о́е блю́до, second course, dish. Втор-и́ч-ный, *adj.,* secondary; reiterative. В-ая пове́стка second notice. Втор-и́чно, *adv.,* again, a second time, once more. В. затре́бовать, to demand a second time. Втор-о-го́дник, *n.m.,* a pupil who is repeating a course, class for the second year in a row. Втор-о-кла́ссник, *n.m.,* a pupil, student in the second class, grade. Втор-о- кла́ссный, *adj.,* pertaining to the second class, grade. Втор-о-разря́дный, *adj.,* second-rate, inferior, mediocre. Втор-о-степе́нный, *adj.,* secondary, of minor importance. Во-втор-ы́х, secondly, in the second place.

вто́р-и-ть, *v.i.,* + *dat.,* to echo, accompany, harmonize; (*fig.*), repeat. Она́ хорошо́ вто́рит в хо́ре, she sings the second part in the choir well. В. глу́пым спле́тням, to repeat stupid gossip.

по-втор-и́ть, *v.p.,* по-втор-я́ть *v.i.,* + *acc.,* to repeat, reiterate. П. вслух, to repeat aloud. П. уро́к, to repeat (prepare) a lesson. Кра́тко п., to recapitulate, repeat briefly. По-втор-и́ть-ся, *v.p.r.,* по-втор-я́ть-ся, *v.i.r.,* to be repeated, repeat oneself. Он повторя́ется, в свои́х реча́х, he repeats himself in his speeches. Ста́рое не повтори́тся, the past will never repeat itself.

пол-тор-а́, *num.,* (*from* пол-(в)тор-а́), one and a half. Он учи́л уро́к полтора́ часа́, he studied his lesson for an hour and a half.

пол-тор-а́-ста, *num.,* one hundred and fifty. У меня́ полтора́ста рубле́й на сберега́тельной кни́жке, I have one hundred and fifty rubles in my savings account.

по-втор-е́ние, *п.п.,* repetition, iteration, reiteration. Кра́ткое п., a short review. Повторе́ние - мать уче́ния, (*saying*), repetition is the mother of learning. По-втор-и́тельный, *adj.,* iterative, reiterative. П-ое упражне́ние, a review exercise. П. курс, refresher course. По-втор-ный, *adj.,* second, repeated. П-ая приви́вка о́спы, (*med.*), re-vaccination against small-pox. По-втор-но, *adv.,* repeatedly, again, once more.

ВЫС-, ВЫШ-, HEIGHT, ALTITUDE, ELEVATION

выс-ота́, *n.f.,* height, altitude, elevation. В. над у́ровнем мо́ря, altitude above sea level. Быть на высоте́ положе́ния, to rise to the occasion. Выс-ь, *n.f.,* (*poet.*), height. Жа́воронок лети́т в небе́сную высь, the lark is soaring upward into the sky. Выс-о́кий, *adj.,* high, lofty, towering, tall. В. рост, tallness. В-ая ко́мната, a high room (ceiling). В в-ой сте́пени, highly, to a high degree. Выс-око́, *adv.,* high, aloft. Вы́ш-е, *adj. and adv. comp.,* higher, taller; above. В. на́ших сил, beyond our strength. Смотри́ вы́ше, see above. Вы́с-ший, *adj. superl.,* higher, superior, highest, supreme. В-ая матема́тика, higher mathematics. В-ие уче́бные заведе́ния, institutions of higher education. Выс-о́чество, *п.п.,* (*title*), Highness. Выс-оча́йший, *adj.,* highest (*as a sovereign*), supreme. Выс-оче́нный, *adj.* (*derog.*) (*colloq.*), very high, tall. Выс-ок-о-ме́рие, *п.п.,* haughtiness, arrogance. Выс-ок-оме́рный, *adj.,* haughty, arrogant. В. челове́к, a haughty man. Выс-ок-о-ме́рно, *adv.,* haughtily, arrogantly. Выс-ок-о-па́рность, *n.f.,* grandiloquence, pompousness. Выс-ок-о-па́рный, *adj.,* pompous, grandiloquent. Выс-ок-о-па́рно, *adv.,* pompously, bombastically. Говори́ть в., to speak pompously. Выс-ок-о-торже́ственный, *adj.,* most solemn. В. день, a solemn day, holiday.

выш-ин-а́, *n.f.,* height. В. ба́шни, the height of a tower. Вы́ш-ка, *n.f.,* watch tower. На вы́шке стоя́л часово́й, a sentinel stood on the watch tower.

воз-вы́с-и-ть, *v.р.,* воз-выш-а́ть, *v.i.,* + *acc.,* to raise, lift, elevate, exalt. В. го́лос, to raise one's voice. Воз-вы́с-ить-ся, *v.р.r.,* воз-выш-а́ть-ся, *v.i.r.,* + *instr.,* to be raised, rise above. Воз-выш-е́ние, *п.п.,* elevation; eminence. Воз-вы́ш-енность, *n.f.,* elevation,

height, loftiness. Воз-вы́ш-енный, *adj. part. pass, past,* elevated; lofty, exalted, sublime. Воз-вы́ш-енно, *adv.,* loftily.

по-вы́с-и-ть, *v.р.,* по-выш-а́ть, *v.i.,* + *acc.,* to raise, increase, heighten. П. по слу́жбе, to promote. П. го́лос, to raise one's voice. П. производи́тельность труда́, to increase the productivity of labor. По-вы́с-ить-ся, *v.р.r.,* по-выш-а́ть-ся, *v.i.r.,* to be raised, rise. Температу́ра у больно́го повыша́ется, the patient's temperature is rising. По-выше́ние, *п.п.,* rise, promotion, advancement. П. цен, a rise in prices. Он получи́л повыше́ние, he was promoted.

пре-вы́с-и-ть, *v.р.,* пре-выш-а́ть, *v.i.,* + *acc.,* to exceed, surpass. П. свой полномо́чия, to exceed one's commission, authority. Пре-выш-а́ть-ся, *v.i.r.,* to be exceeded, surpassed. Пре-выш-е́ние, *п.п.,* excess. П. вла́сти, to overreach one's authority.

ВЯЗ- ВЯЖ-, УЗ-, ЮЗ-, JUNCTION, JOINING, KNITTING, TYING

вяз-а́ть, *v.i.,* с-вяз-а́ть, *v.р.,* + *acc.,* to bind, tie; knit. В. снопы́, to bind into sheaves. В. из верёвок се́ти, to make a net. В. кру́жево, to make lace. Вяз-а́ть-ся, *v.i.r.,* used only impers., to be tied, bound, knitted; to be in harmony, agreement with. Это не вя́жется с, (*express.*), this does not agree with. Его́ расска́з не вя́жется с действи́тельностью, his story does not correspond with reality. Вяж-ущий, *adj. part. act. pres.,* binding. Же́нщина, в-ая чулки́, a woman knitting stockings. В. вкус, a tart taste. Вяз-а́нка, *n.f.,* truss, bundle. В. хво́роста, bundle of faggots. Вя́з-анка, *n.f.,* (*recent*), sweater, cardigan. Вяз-а́ние, *п.п.,* binding, tying, knitting. Вяз-а́льщик, *п.т.,* binder. Вяз-а́льный, *adj.,* pertaining to knitting. В-ая маши́на, knitting machine. В-ая спи́ца, knitting needle. Вя́з-ка, *n.f.,* tying, binding; bundle. Вязь, *n.f.,* a set of letters interwoven into a design. Писа́ть вя́зью, (*hist.*), to write in a special style used for the preparation of state documents. Ве́нзель, *п.т.,* monogram.

в-вяз-а́ть, *v.р.,* в-вя́з-ывать, *v.i.,* + *acc.,* to tie in, knit in; (*fig.*), to involve. В. цветну́ю поло́ску в носки́, to knit a colored stripe into a sock. В. кого́-нибудь в неприя́тное де́ло, (*colloq.*), to involve someone in an unpleasant business. В-вяз-а́ть-ся, *v.р.r.,* в-вя́з-ывать-ся, *v.i.r,* в + *acc.,* to meddle, interfere. В. в разгово́р, (*colloq.*), to join, butt into a conversation without being invited. В. в чужи́е дела́, (*col-*

loq.), to meddle in others' affairs.

вы́-вяз-а́ть, *v.p.,* вы́-вя́з-ывать, *v.i.,* +
acc., to knit. В. шерстяно́й шарф, to
knit a woolen scarf.

за-вяз-а́ть, *v.p.,* за-вя́з-ывать, *v.i.,* +
acc., to tie, tie a knot. З. ве́щи в у́зел,
to tie things into a bundle. З. га́лстук,
to tie a tie. З. отноше́ния, to enter into
relations. За-вя́з-ка, *n.f.,* tie; string,
band; (*literary*: initial point, plot).
Завя́зки на пере́днике развяза́лись,
the apron strings became untied. З.
расска́за, the focal point of a story.

на-вяз-а́ть, *v.p.,* на-вя́з-ывать, *v.i.,* +
acc., + *dat.,* to attach, fasten, tie on;
(*fig.*), impose. Н. своё мне́ние кому́-
нибудь, to impose one's opinion on
someone. На-вяз-а́ть-ся, *v.p.r.,* на-вя́з-
ывать-ся, *v.i.r.,* to intrude, obtrude. Н.
на знако́мство, to foist one's acquaintance on someone. На-вя́з-чивость,
n.f., intrusion, obtrusion; importunity.
На-вя́з-чивый, *adj.,* obtrusive. Н-ая
иде́я, a fixed idea.

над-вяз-а́ть, *v.p.,* над-вя́з-ывать, *v.i.,* +
acc., to knit, reknit; repair by knitting.

об-вяз-а́ть, *v.p.,* об-вя́з-ывать, *v.i.,* +
acc., to bind, tie, bandage. О. го́лову
платко́м, to tie a kerchief round one's
head. Об-вя́з-ка, *n.f.,* the action of
tying, binding.

от-вяз-а́ть, *v.p.,* от-вя́з-ывать, *v.i.,* +
acc., от + *gen.,* to let loose, release,
untie, unfasten. О. ло́шадь, to untie a
horse. От-вяз-а́ть-ся, *v.p.r.,* от-вя́з-
ывать-ся, *v.i.r.,* to become unfastened;
(*fig.*), rid oneself of. От-вяж-и́тесь!
Leave me alone!

пере-вяз-а́ть, *v.p.,* пере-вя́з-ывать, *v.i.,*
+ *acc.,* + *dat.,* to bind, tie, dress a
wound. П. ра́ну, to dress a wound. П.
паке́т верёвкой, to tie a parcel with
string. Пере-вя́з-ка, *n.f.,* binding, dressing, bandage. Врач сде́лал перевя́зку
ра́неному, the doctor dressed the man's
wound. Пере-вя́з-очный, *adj.,* pertaining to binding, tying. П. материа́л,
(*med.*), dressing, bandage cloth. П.
пункт, dressing station. На перевя́зоч-
ном пу́нкте ока́зывают пе́рвую по́-
мощь ра́неным, at a dressing station
the wounded are given first aid. Пе́ре-
вяз-ь, *n.f.,* sling, belt, Sam Brown. Рука́
на пе́ревязи, a hand in a sling.

под-вяз-а́ть, *v.p.,* под-вя́з-ывать, *v.i.,*
+ *acc.,* + *instr.,* to bind, tie up. П. ве́т-
ки куста́ (де́рева), to tie up the
branches of a bush (tree). Под-вя́з-ка,
n.f., garter. Под-вя́з-ывание, *n.n.,* binding, tying up.

при-вяз-а́ть, *v.p.,* при-вя́з-ывать, *v.i.,*
+ *acc.,* к + *dat.,* to tie, bind to; attach. П. ло́шадь к забо́ру, to tie a

horse to a fence. П. ребёнка к себе́
ла́ской, (*fig.*), to gain a child's affection through kindness, gentleness.
При-вяз-а́ть-ся, *v.p.r.,* при-вя́з-ывать-
ся, *v.i.r.,* к + *dat.,* to become tied,
bound to; become attached, devoted.
Сирота́ привяза́лся к опекуну́, как к
родно́му отцу́, the orphan became attached to his guardian like to his own
father. При-вя́з-анность, *n.f.,* attachment. При-вя́з-анный, *adj. part. pass.
past,* tied, bound; attached. При-вя́з-
чивость, *n.f.,* tendency to attach oneself to someone; lovingness; quarrelsomeness. При-вя́з-чивый, *adj.,* affectionate, loving; faultfinding, captious,
quarrelsome. При́-вяз-ь, *n.f.,* tie, string,
rope. Соба́ка на при́вязи, a dog on a
leash.

раз-вяз-а́ть, *v.p.,* раз-вя́з-ывать, *v.i.,* +
acc., to untie, unbind, let loose, release,
set free. Р. ру́ки, to untie one's hands;
(*fig.*), to release, give full scope to.
Раз-вяз-а́ть-ся, *v.p.r.,* раз-вя́з-ывать-
ся, *v.i.r.,* с + *instr.,* to become untied,
undone, unfastened; to undo, get rid of.
Мой га́лстук развяза́лся, my necktie
is untied. Р. с. долга́ми, (*colloq.*), to
clear one's debts. Раз-вя́з-ка, *n.f.,* outcome; clarification, denouement; climax.
Р. рома́на, the climax of a novel, romance. Де́ло идёт к развя́зке, the affair is approaching a climax. Раз-вя́з-
ность, *n.f.,* (*derog.*), jauntiness, ease of
manner, behavior. Р. мане́р, ease of
manner, behavior. Раз-вя́з-ный, *adj.,*
free, easy, jaunty. Этот молодо́й чело-
ве́к сли́шком р., that young man is a
bit too jaunty.

с-вяз-а́ть, *v.p.,* с-вя́з-ывать, *v.i.,* + *acc.,*
to tie, bind together; connect; knit. С.
сноп, to bind a sheaf. С. себя́ обеща́-
нием, to pledge oneself, bind oneself
by a promise. С. кого́-либо по рука́м
и нога́м, (*also fig.*), to bind someone
hand and foot. С-вяз-а́ть-ся, *v.p.r.,*
с-вя́з-ывать-ся, *v.i.r.,* с + *instr.,* to be
tied, bound. Не свя́зывайся с плохи́ми
людьми́, (*colloq.*), don't have anything
to do with bad people. С-вя́з-ка, *n.f.,*
bundle, roll, sheaf, bunch. С. ключе́й,
a bunch of keys. Голосовы́е свя́зки,
vocal cords. С-вя́з-ывание, *n.n.,* tying,
binding together. С-вя́з-ность, *n.f.,*
connectedness, coherence. В сочине́нии
должна́ быть с. мы́слей, in a composition there must be coherence of thought.
С-вя́з-ный, *adj.,* connected, coherent.
Не-с-вя́з-ный, *adj.,* disconnected, in-
coherent. С-вя́з-очный, *adj.,* (*med.*),
pertaining to ligaments. С-вяз-у́ющий,
adj. part. act. pres., binding, connective. Догово́ры, с-ие э́ти стра́ны, the

treaties binding these countries. С-вя́з-анный, *adj. part. pass. past,* tied, bound, linked. С. обеща́нием, bound by a promise. С. у́зами родства́, related by birth. С-вяз-ь, *n.f.,* tie, bond; junction, connection, liaison. Подде́рживать (порва́ть) связь, to uphold, (sever) a bond, connection. Ро́дственные свя́зи, blood ties, family ties. В связи́ с э́тим, (*express.*), in connection with this. С хоро́шими свя́зями, well connected, having influential contacts. Офице́р свя́зи, liaison officer, signal corps officer. С-вяз-и́ст, *n.m.,* (*recent*), signal corpsman.

у-вяз-а́ть, *v.p.,* у-вя́з-ывать, *v.i.,* + *acc.,* + *instr.,* to tie, bind up; pack; (*fig.*), bring into agreement, harmony. У. тео́рию с пра́ктикой, to combine theory with practice. У-вяз-а́ть-ся, *v.p.r.,* у-вя́з-ывать-ся, *v.i.r.,* to be tied, bound up; be packed; be brought into agreement, harmony. У. за ке́м-либо, (*colloq.*), to follow someone without being asked.

вяз-ну-ть, *v.i.,* в + *prep.,* to become bogged in mud, mire, bog. Колёса вя́знут в грязи́, the wheels are sinking in the mud. Вя́з-кий, *adj.,* sticky, swampy. В-ая грязь, sticky mud. Вя́з-кость, *n.f.,* stickiness, swampiness, viscosity.

за-вя́з-нуть, *v.p.,* за-вяз-а́ть, *v.i.,* в + *prep.,* to stick, sink in a mire, bog. З. в грязи́, to stick in mire. З в долга́х, to be bogged down in debts, be head over heels in debt.

у-вя́з-нуть, *v.p.,* у-вяз-а́ть, *v.i.,* в + *prep.,* to sink, stick, in a mire. У. в боло́те, to become bogged down. У. в неразреши́мых вопро́сах, to become bogged down in unsolvable problems.

об-яз-а́ть, (*from* об-вяз-а́ть), *v.p.,* об-я́з-ывать (*from* об-вя́з-ывать), *v.i.,* + *acc.,* to bind; obligate, engage. Это вас ни к чему́ не обя́зывает, this does not obligate you. Вы меня́ о́чень обя́жете, you will do me a great favor. Об-яз-а́ть-ся, *v.p.r.,* об-я́з-ывать-ся, *v.i.r.,* + *dat.,* to bind, obligate oneself; pledge oneself. Я обяза́лся ему́ помо́чь, I pledged myself to help him. Я не люблю́ никому́ обя́зываться, I dislike being under an obligation to anyone. Об-я́з-анность, *n.f.,* obligation, duty. Исполня́ющий обя́занности дире́ктора, acting director. Об-я́з-анный, *adj.,* under obligation, obligated; indebted to. Очень обя́зан, I'm much obliged. Я обя́зан э́то сде́лать, it is my duty to do this. Об-яз-а́тельный, *adj.,* obligatory, compulsory. О-ая вое́нная слу́жба, compulsory military service. Об-яз-а́тельно, *adv.,* without fail, com-

pulsorily. Об-яз-а́тельство, *n.n.,* obligation; bond, engagement, pledge. Вы́полнить свои́ обяза́тельства, to meet one's obligations.

у́з-ел, *n.m.,* knot; bundle, pack. У. на верёвке, a knot in string. Железнодоро́жный у., rail road junction. Увя́зывать ве́щи в у́зел, to tie things in a bundle. Уз-ело́к, *n.m.,* small knot, bundle. Уз-лово́й, *adj.,* knotty. У. вопро́с, (*recent*), a key question, issue. У-áя ста́нция, junction station.

уз-д-а́, *n.f.,* bridle; (*fig*), curb, check, restraint. Ло́шадь на узде́, a bridled horse. Держа́ть в узде́, to keep in check. Уз-д-е́чка, *n.f.,* bridle, bit. Уз-д-цы́, *n.pl., in expression:* держа́ть ло́шадь под у., to hold a horse by the bridle. Недо-у́з-док, *n.m.,* halter. Надева́ть н., to put on a halter.

взн-уз-д-а́-ть, *v.p.,* взн-у́з-дывать, *v.i.,* + *acc.,* to put on a bit; curb. В. коня́, to bridle a horse.

об-уз-д-а́-ть, *v.p.,* об-у́з-дывать, *v.i.,* + *acc.,* to bridle; curb, hinder, restrain. О. коня́, to break in, tame a horse. О. свой язы́к, (*colloq*.), to curb one's tongue. Об-уз-да́ние, *n.n.,* об-у́з-дывание, *n.n.,* breaking in of a horse; restraint. Не-об-у́з-данность, *n.f.,* unrestraint; licentiousness. Не-об-у́з-данный, *adj. part. pass. past,* unbridled, unrestrained.

разн-уз-д-а́-ть, *v.p.,* разн-у́з-дывать, *v.i.,* + *acc.,* to unbridle. Разнузда́й лоша-де́й и поста́вь в коню́шню, unbridle the horses and put them in the stable. Разн-у́з-данность, *n.f.,* unruliness, lack of restraint. Разн-у́з-данный, *adj. part. pass. past,* unbridled, unruly, uncontrollable. Р-ая ло́шадь пасла́сь на лугу́, a horse without a bridle was grazing in the meadow. Р-ая страсть, unbridled passion.

у́з-ник, *n.m.,* (*obs., poet.*), prisoner, captive. Шильо́нский У́зник, (Byron), *The Prisoner of Chillon.*

у́з-ы, *n.pl.,* bonds, ties. У. кро́ви, blood ties. Бра́чные у., bonds of marriage. Об-у́з-а, *n.f.,* burden, encumbrance; nuisance.

со-ю́з, *n.m.,* union, association, coalition, alliance, league, (*gram.*), conjunction. С. госуда́рств, an alliance, federation of states. С. оборони́тельный (наступа́тельны) defensive (offensive) alliance. Со-ю́з-ник, *n.m.,* со-ю́з-ница, *n.f.,* ally, associate, confederate. Со-ю́з-ный, *adj.,* allied, confederate. С. сове́т, allied council. Сове́тский Сою́з, Soviet Union. Профсою́з (*abbr. of* Профессиона́льный Сою́з), trade union.

Г

ГАД-, SUPPOSITION, CONJECTURE, GUESS

гад-а́-ть, *v.i.,* по-гад-а́ть, *v.p.,* по + *dat.,* to tell one's fortune. Г. по ка́ртам, to read cards, tell one's fortune from cards. Г. по руке́, to read the palm. Гад-а́лка, гад-а́льщица, *n.f.,* fortune-teller. Гад-а́ние, *n.n.,* fortune - telling, divination. Нежда́нно-негада́нно, (*idiom.*), unexpectedly, against all expectations. Гад-а́тельный, *adj.,* conjectural, hypothetical. Гад-а́тельно, *adv.,* conjecturally, hypothetically. Ду́мать и гада́ть, (*idiom.*), to think and to guess.

до-гад-а́ть-ся, *v.p.r.,* до-га́д-ывать-ся, *v.i.r.,* to guess, conjecture. До-га́д-ка, *n.f.,* surmise, conjecture, guess. Выска́зывать дога́дку, to surmise, conjecture. До-га́д-ливость, *n.f.,* quick-wittedness, shrewdness, ingenuity. До-га́д-ливый, *adj.,* quick-witted, shrewd, ingenious.

за-гад-а́ть, *v.p.,* за-га́д-ывать, *v.i.,* + *acc.,* to pose a riddle. З. зага́дку, to pose a riddle. За-га́д-ка, *n.f.,* riddle, enigma, mystery. За-га́д-очность, *n.f.,* mysteriousness. За-га́д-очный, *adj.,* mysterious, enigmatic. З-ая ли́чность, a mysterious person. За-га́д-ывание, *n.n.,* riddles, guessing games.

от-гад-а́ть, *v.p.,* от-га́д-ывать, *v.i.,* + *acc.,* to guess. О. зага́дку, to guess a riddle. О. та́йное наме́рение, to guess a secret intention. От-га́д-ка, *n.f.,* answer to a riddle. От-га́д-чик, *n.m.,* от-га́д-чица, *n.f.,* guesser. От-га́д-ывание, *n.n.,* guessing.

пред-у-гад-а́ть, *v.p.,* пред-у-га́д-ывать, *v.i.,* + *acc.,* to guess beforehand, foresee. П. наме́рение врага́, to foresee the enemy's intentions.

раз-гад-а́ть, *v.p.,* раз-га́д-ывать, *v.i.,* + *acc.,* to unriddle, divine, guess, puzzle out; *see* отгада́ть. Р. зага́дку (шара́ду), to unriddle a puzzle (charade). Р. мы́сли, to read one's thoughts. Раз-га́д-ка, *n.f.,* answer, solution, key. Раз-га́д-чик, *n.m.,* diviner.

у-гад-а́-ть, *v.p.,* у-га́д-ывать, *v.i.,* + *acc.,* to guess, divine. У. пого́ду на сего́дня, to forecast the weather for today. Угада́йте, кто мне присла́л письмо́, guess who sent me a letter. У-га́д-ывание, *n.n.,* guessing, divining, divination.

на-у-га́д, *adv.,* at random, at a guess, by guesswork. Пу́тники потеря́ли доро́гу и пошли́ науга́д, the travelers lost their way and went on by guess work.

ГАД-, ГАЖ-, REPTILE, VILENESS, MEANNESS, EVIL

гад, *n.m.,* га́д-ина, *n.f.,* (*zool.*), reptile; (*fig.*), a mean, base person. Га́д-кий, *adj.,* bad, evil, wicked; foul, disgusting. Г. челове́к, an evil person. Г. посту́пок, a disgusting, vile action. Га́д-ко, *adv.,* wickedly, vilely, disgustingly. Га́ж-е, *adj. and adv. comp.,* more disgusting, more disgustingly. Гад-ли́вость, *n.f.,* a feeling of aversion, contempt. Гад-ли́вый, *adj.,* easily nauseated, disgusted. Г-ое чу́вство, a feeling of disgust. Га́д-ость, *n.f.,* (*colloq.*), muck, abominable, repulsive thing, object; a vile action. Он спосо́бен на вся́кую г., he is capable of anything vile. Гад-ю́ка, *n.f.,* (*zool.*), adder, viper.

га́д-и-ть, га́ж-у, *v.i.,* на-га́д-ить, *v.p.,* + *acc.,* + *dat.,* to spoil, defile, corrupt, befoul.

за-га́д-ить, *v.p.,* за-га́ж-ивать, *v.i.,* + *acc.,* (*colloq.*), to soil, besmear, befoul. За-га́ж-ивание, *n.n.,* soiling, besmearing, befouling.

из-га́д-ить, *v.p.,* из-га́ж-ивать, *v.i.,* + *acc.,* (*colloq.*); *see* зага́дить.

под-га́д-ить, *v.p.,* под-га́ж-ивать, *v.i.,* + *dat.,* (*colloq.*), to spoil, botch, bungle, mess, fail. Спе́ли бы хорошо́, да басы́ нам подга́дили, (*colloq.*), we would have sung well, but the bass section failed us.

ГАР-, ГОР-, ГРЕ-, BURNING, HEAT, CALEFACTION

гар-ь, *n.f.,* smell of burning.

гор-е́-ть, *v.i.,* to burn, glow, blaze. Дом гори́т, the house is on fire. Ла́мпа гори́т, the lamp is burning. Г. жела́нием, to burn with desire. Рабо́та гори́т в его́ рука́х, he works at high speed. От моро́за щёки горя́т, cheeks burn from cold. Гор-я́щий, *adj. part. act. pres.,* burning. Г. го́род, a city in flames. Гор-ю́чее, *adj., used as n.,* (*tech.*), gasoline, fuel. Пополне́ние горю́чим, fueling. Запра́вка горю́чего, refueling. Гор-ю́чий, *adj.,* combustible. Г. материа́л, combustible fuel. Г-ие слёзы, bitter tears. Гор-ю́честь, *n.f.,* combustibility. Гор-н, *n.m.,* furnace, forge. Гор-ни́ло, (*poet.*), *n.n., see* горн.

воз-гор-е́ть-ся, *v.p.r.,* воз-гор-а́ть-ся, *v.i.r.,* + *instr.,* to become inflamed; be roused, stirred. В. жела́нием, to be seized with a desire.

вы́-гор-еть, *v.p.,* вы-гор-а́ть, *v.i.,* to burn out, be consumed. Дом вы́горел до тла, the house burned to the ground.

до-гор-е́ть, *v.p.,* до-гор-а́ть, *v.i.,* to burn

low, burn out. Свеча́ догоре́ла, the candle burned out.

за-гор-е́ть, *v.p.,* за-гор-а́ть, *v.i.,* to acquire a tan, become sunburned, bask. З. на со́лнце, to tan oneself in the sun. За-гор-а́ние, *п.п.,* sunburn. За-га́р, *п.т.,* tan, sunburn. За-гор-е́лый, *adj.,* tanned, sunburned. З-ое лицо́, sunburned face. За-гор-е́ть-ся, *v.p.r.,* за-гор-а́ть-ся, *v.i.r.,* to begin to burn, burst into flames. Загоре́лся дом, the house caught fire. З-ся восто́к, (*fig.*), dawn appeared in the east. З-ся спор, an argument flared up. На-гор-е́ть, *v.p.,* на-гор-а́ть, *v.i.,* to burn to a snuff. Свеча́ нагоре́ла, the candle burned to a snuff. Ей нагоре́ло за лень, (*colloq.*), she was reprimanded for laziness. На-га́р, *п.т.,* snuff of a candle. Снима́ть нагар, to snuff a candle.

об-гор-е́ть, *v.p.,* об-гор-а́ть, *v.i.,* to become scorched, charred, burned. Сте́ны обгоре́ли, the walls were charred. Об-гор-е́лый, *adj.,* burned, scorched, charred. О-ое поле́но, a charred log. О-га́р-ок *п.т.,* a candle end.

пере-гор-е́ть, *v.p.,* пере-гор-а́ть, *v.i.,* to burn through, out. Электри́ческая ла́мпочка перегоре́ла, the electric bulb burned out. Пере-гор-а́ние, *п.п.,* a burning through, out. Пере-га́р, *п.т.,* a product of combustion. От него́ несёт ви́нным перега́ром, (*colloq.*), he reeks of alcohol.

по-гор-е́ть, *v.p.,* по-гор-а́ть, *v.i.,* to burn (*as* a house), be destroyed by fire. Во вре́мя войны́ мно́гие города́ погоре́ли, during the war many cities were destroyed by fire. По-гор-е́лец, *п.т.,* a victim of a fire. По-гор-е́лый, *adj.,* burned out.

под-гор-е́ть, *v.p.,* под-гор-а́ть, *v.i.,* to be scorched, burned (*as* food in a pot). Ка́ша подгоре́ла, the porridge has burned. Под-гор-е́лый, *adj.,* burned (*as* the bottom of a pan, food in a pot).

при-гор-е́ть, *v.p.,* при-гор-а́ть, *v.i.,* to burn, be burned lightly. Мя́со пригоре́ло, the meat is slightly burned, scorched. При-гор-е́лый, *adj.,* burned, scorched slightly.

про-гор-е́ть, *v.p.,* про-гор-а́ть, *v.i.,* to burn through, down, be destroyed by fire; (*fig.*), become bankrupt. Дно в котле́ прогоре́ло, the bottom of the cauldron has burned through. Это акционе́рное о́бщество прогоре́ло-this stock company is bankrupt.

раз-гор-е́ться, *v.p.r.,* раз-гор-а́ть-ся, *v.i.r.,* to burst into flames; become increasingly hotter. Ого́нь разгоре́лся, the fire is beginning to burn well.

Би́тва разгоре́лась, the battle became more heated. У неё глаза́ разгоре́лись, her eyes are all aglow. Раз-га́р, *п.т.,* peak, height (*as of a season*); the state of being in full swing. В разга́ре ле́та, at the height of summer. Экза́мены в по́лном разга́ре, the examinations are in full swing.

с-гор-е́ть, *v.p.,* с-гор-а́ть, *v.i.,* до + *gen., instr.,* + to burn out, be consumed by fire. С. до тла, to reduce to ashes. С. жела́нием, любо́вью, to be consumed with desire, love. С со стыда́, to be consumed with shame. С-гор-а́ние, *п.п.,* combustion. Дви́гатель вну́треннего сгора́ния, internal combustion engine. С-гор-яча́, *adv.,* rashly, angrily, in a moment of extreme anger. Ска́зано с., said in a moment of anger.

у-гор-е́ть, *v.p.,* у-гор-а́ть, *v.i.,* от + *gen.,* to be asphyxiated. У. от га́за, to become asphyxiated by gas. У-гор е́вший, *adj. part. act. past,* asphyxiated *used as n.,* one who has become asphyxiated. Ты что, угоре́л? (*colloq.*), Are you out of your mind? У-гор-е́лый, *adj.,* possessed, mad. Ме́чется, как угоре́лая, (*colloq.*), she is throwing herself about like one possessed. У-га́р, *п.т.,* asphyxiation. Пья́ный у., intoxication, drunkenness. У-га́р-ный, *adj.,* asphyxiating.

гор-я́ч-ий, *adj.,* hot; (*fig.*), ardent, fervent, passionate; hasty. Г. исто́чник, a hot spring. Г-ая печь, a hot stove. Г-ая ло́шадь, a fiery horse, steed. Г-ее вре́мя, the busiest time. Г-ее се́рдце, a warm heart.

гор-яч-и́ть, *v.i.,* раз-гор-ячи́ть, *v.p.,* + *acc.,* to irritate, excite. Р. коня́, to excite a horse. Р. кровь, to stir the blood. Гор-я́чка, *n.f.,* a fever. Бе́лая г., delirium tremens. Поро́ть горя́чку, (*colloq.*), to be in an extreme hurry. Гор-я́чность, *n.f.,* fiery, feverish zeal; passion. Гор-яч-о́, *adv.,* hotly; (*fig.*), ardently, fervently, passionately, eagerly. Докла́дчик говори́л г., the lecturer spoke ardently. Гор-яч-и́ть-ся, *v.i.r.,* to become excited. Не горячи́тесь! Don't get excited.

по-гор-яч-и́ть-ся, *v.p.r.,* to lose one's temper; forget oneself; be short-tempered. Она́ погорячи́лась и успоко́илась, she lost her temper and then calmed down.

раз-гор-яч-и́ть-ся, *v.p.r.,* to become inflamed, excited. Р. от та́нцев, to become hot from dancing. Р. от вина́, to get a glow from wine.

гре-ть, *v.i.,* по-гре-ть, *v.p.,* + *acc.,* to warm, heat. Г. ру́ки у огня́, to warm one's hands over a fire. Гре́-ть-ся, *v.i.r.*, по-греть-ся, *v.p.r.*, to warm oneself. Г. у пе́чки, to warm oneself at a stove. Г. на со́лнце, to bask in the sun. Гре́-л-ка, *n.f.*, hot-water bottle; foot warmer.

на-гре́-ть, *v.p.*, на-гре-ва́ть, *v.i.*, + *acc.*, to warm, heat. Со́лнце нагре́ло песо́к, the sun has warmed the sand. Он нагре́л меня́ на 50 рубле́й, (*slang*), he did me out of fifty rubles. На-гре́-ть-ся, *v.p.r.*, на-гре-ва́ть-ся, *v.i.r.*, to become warm, be heated. Вода́ бы́стро нагре́лась на пе́чке, the water heated quickly on the stove. На-гре́-в, *n.m.*, (*tech.*), heating, heat. На-гре-ва́тельный, *adj.*, generating heat, heating. Н. аппара́т, heating apparatus.

обо-гре́-ть, *v.p.*, обо-гре-ва́ть, *v.i.*, + *acc.*, to warm, heat thoroughly. О. ко́мнату, to heat a room. О. но́ги, to warm one's feet. Обо-гре́-ть-ся, *v.p.r.*, обо-гре-ва́ть-ся, *v.i.r.*, to warm up, become warm, warm oneself. О. у огня́, to warm oneself before a fire. Обо-гре-ва́ние, *n.n.*, warming.

ото-гре́-ть, *v.p.*, ото-гре-ва́ть, *v.i.*, + *acc.*, to thaw, take the chill out. О. замёрзшего, to warm one who has been chilled through. Ото-гре́-ть-ся, *v.p.r.*, ото-гре-ва́ть-ся, *v.i.r.*, to get warm, warm oneself, take the chill off. О. у пе́чки, to warm oneself over a stove. Ото-гре-ва́ние, *n.n.*, a warming up.

пере-гре́-ть, *v.p.*, пере-гре-ва́ть, *v.i.*, + *acc.*, to overheat. П. молоко́, to overheat milk. Пере-гре́-ть-ся, *v.p.r.*, пере-гре-ва́ть-ся, *v.i.r.*, to be overheated. Пере-гре-ва́ние, *n.n.*, overheating (*as of an engine*). Пере-гре́-тый, *adj.*, *part. pass. past,* overheated. П-ая пе́чка, an overheated stove.

подо-гре́-ть, *v.p.*, подо-гре-ва́ть, *v.i.*, + *acc.*, to warm up. П. обе́д, to warm up dinner. Подо-гре-ва́ние, *n.n.*, a warming up. Подо-гре-ва́тель, *n.m.*, (*tech.*), heater. Подо-гре́-тый, *adj. part. pass. past,* warmed up.

При-гре́-ть, *v.p.* при-гре-ва́ть, *v.i.*, + *acc.*, to offer warmth, shelter; treat kindly. Со́лнце пригрева́ет, the sun warms. П. сироту́, to treat an orphan with kindness.

про-гре́-ть, *v.p.*, про-гре-ва́ть, *v.i.*, + *acc.*, to warm through, penetrate with heat. П. ко́мнату, to heat a room. Про-гре-ва́ние, *n.n.*, the action of warming, heating through; (*med.*), thermotherapy.

разо-гре́-ть, *v.p.*, разо-гре-ва́ть, *v.i.*, + *acc.*, to warm thoroughly. Р. ку́шанье,

to heat, warm up food. Разо-гре-ва́ние, *n.n.*, the action of heating through.

со-гре́-ть, *v.p.*, со-гре-ва́ть, *v.i.*, + *acc.*, to warm, heat. Со-гре́-ть-ся, *v.p.r.*, со-гре-ва́ть-ся, *v.i.r.*, to become warm. Со-гре-ва́ние, *n.n.*, the action of becoming warm, hot. Со-гре-ва́тельный, *adj.*, creating warmth, heat. С. компре́сс, a hot compress.

ГИБ-, ГУБ-, DESTRUCTION

ги́б-ну-ть, *v.i.*, от + *gen.*, to perish, die. Всхо́ды ги́бнут от за́морозков, shoots perish from early autumn frosts. Лю́ди ги́бнут от чумы́, people perish from plague. Ги́б-ель, *n.f.*, catastrophe, ruin, destruction, wreck, loss. Г. корабля́, a shipwreck. Г. наро́ду, (*fig.*, *colloq.*), an immense crowd of people. Ги́б-ельный, *adj.*, ill; fatal, disastrous, ruinous. Г-ые после́дствия пья́нства, the curse of drink.

по-ги́б-ну-ть, *v.p.*, по-гиб-а́ть, *v.i.*, от + *gen.*, to perish, be lost, ruined. Мой оте́ц поги́б на фро́нте, my father was killed at the front. Цветы́ погиба́ют от моро́за, flowers perish from the frost. По-ги́б-ель, *n.f.*, ruin, destruction; perdition. Согну́ться в три поги́бели, (*idiom*), to become stooped, crooked; (*fig.*), to fawn, be subservient. По-ги́б-ельный, *adj.*, ruinous, fatal, destructive. По-ги́б-ший, *adj. part. act. past,* lost, perished; *also used as n.,* those who have perished, been lost. В газе́те помещён спи́сок поги́бших в возду́шной катастро́фе, the list of those who perished in the plane wreck has been published in the paper. П. челове́к, a lost man, soul.

губ-и́ть, губ-л-ю́, *v.i.*, по-губ-и́ть, *v.p.*, + *acc.*, to ruin, destroy. Г. жизнь люде́й, to ruin peoples, lives. Г. вре́мя, to waste time. Г. себя́, to ruin oneself. Губ-и́тель, *n.m.*, one who destroys, ruins; spoiler. Губ-и́тельность, *n.f.*, balefulness, destructiveness. Губ-и́тельный, *adj.*, destructive, ruinous, injurious; fatal. Г. ого́нь неприя́теля, the destructive fire of the enemy.

за-губ-и́ть, *v.p.*, + *acc.*, (*colloq.*), to ruin, destroy, cause to perish. З. свою́ жизнь, to ruin one's life. З. свой тала́нт, to waste one's talent. За-гу́б-ленный, *adj. part. pass. past,* lost, ruined, perished. З-ая душа́, a lost soul.

с-губ-и́ть, *v.p.*, + *acc.*, to ruin, spoil, destroy; waste. Пья́нством он сгуби́л себя́, he destroyed himself through drink.

ГЛАВ-, ГОЛОВ-, HEAD, SOVEREIGN-TY, SUPREMACY

глав-а́ (голов-а́), *n.f.,* head, chief, master; foreman; chapter. Г. семьи́, the head of a family. Г. до́ма, the head of a household. Во главе́ госуда́рственного управле́ния, at the head of state affairs. Глава́ седьма́я, том пе́рвый, chapter seven, volume one. Дели́ть кни́гу на гла́вы, to divide a book into chapters. Глав-а́рь, *n.m.,* leader. Г. за́говора, ring leader. Глав-е́нство, *n.n.,* (*obs.*), supremacy, mastership. Гла́в-ный, *adj.,* chief, principal, main. Г. инжене́р, chief engineer. Г. вино́вник, chief culprit. Г-ая кварти́ра, headquarters. Теа́тр - гла́вная те́ма разгово́ров, the theatre is the chief topic of conversation. Гла́вным о́бразом, chiefly, mostly, mainly; above all. Загла́в-ие, *n.n.,* title. З. кни́ги, the title of a book. За голов-о́к, *n.m.,* title, headline, rubric. За-гла́в-ный, *adj.,* pertaining to a title. З. лист, title page. З-ые бу́квы, initials, capital letters. О-глав-ле́ние, *n.n.,* table of contents, index. Стрем-гла́в, *adv.,* headlong, rashly, impetuously.

воз-гла́в-и-ть, *v.p.,* воз-глав-ля́ть, *v.i.,* + *acc.,* to head. В. во́йско, to command troops. В. экспеди́цию, to head an expedition.

о-за-гла́в-ить, *v.p.,* о-за-гла́в-ливать, *v.i.,* + *acc.,* to entitle. О. статью́, to entitle an article.

голов-а́, *n.f.,* head, pate. У госуда́рственного де́ятеля должна́ быть у́мная голова́, a statesman must be intelligent. Городско́й г., (*obs.*), mayor. Г. проце́ссии, the head of a procession. Све́тлая (пуста́я) г., a clear (empty) head. У меня́ боли́т г., I have a headache. Уйти́ с голово́й в рабо́ту, to be engrossed in one's work. Голо́в-ка, *n.f.,* (*dim.*), a small head. Г. була́вки (гвоздя́), the head of a pin (nail). Г. чеснока́, (лу́ка), head of garlic (an onion). Голов-а́стик, *n.m.,* tadpole. (*fig.*), large head. Голов-е́шка, *n.f.,* (*dim.*), see головня́. Голов-ня́, *n.f.,* fire-brand, brand; blight. Голов-но́й, *adj.,* pertaining to the head. Г. мозг, brain. Г. убо́р, hat, headgear. Г-ая боль, headache. Голов-о-круже́ние, *n.n.,* giddiness, dizziness; (*med.*), vertigo. Г. от успе́хов, (*fig.*), intoxication with one's own success. Голов-о-кружи́тельный, *adj.,* causing dizziness. Г. успе́х, a giddy success. Г-ая высота́, giddy height. Голов-о-ло́мка, *n.f.,* puzzle. Голов-о-ло́мный, *adj.,* puzzling. Голов-о-мо́йка, *n.f.,* scolding, rebuke,

reprimand. Зада́ть головомо́йку, to reprimand, rebuke, scold. Голов-о-ре́з, *n.m.,* cut-throat, roughneck. Голов-о-тя́п, *n.m.,* (*derog.*), blockhead, dunce. Голов-о-тя́пство, *n.n.,* stupidity. Голов-о-тя́пничать, *v.i.,* to behave stupidly; bungle. Из-голо́в-ье, *n.n.,* head of a bed; headboard. Сиде́ть у изголо́вья, to sit at a bedside. На́-голов-у, *adv.,* (*mil.*), by frontal attack *in the expression*: Разби́ть неприя́теля н., to rout an enemy.

у-голо́в-ный, *adj.,* criminal, penal. У. ро́зыск, (*recent*), criminal investigation department. У. суд, criminal court. У-ое пра́во, criminal law. У-голо́в-ник, *n.m.,* criminal. У-голо́в-щина, *n.f.,* a criminal act.

ГЛАД-, ГЛАЖ-, SMOOTHNESS

глад-ь *n.f.,* smooth surface of water; satin stitch. Гладь о́зера, smooth surface of a lake. Тишь, да гладь, (*saying*), all is peace and calm. Вы́шитый гла́дью, embroidered in satin. Гла́д-кий, *adj.,* smooth, even, sleek, polished. Г-ая доро́га, a smooth, even road. Г-ая мате́рия, solid-color material. Г. лоб, (*fig.*), a smooth forehead. Г-ая причёска, a smooth hairdo. Г-ая речь, fluent speech. Гла́д-ко, *adv.,* smoothly, evenly, sleekly, in a polished manner. Г. отко́рмленный, well-fed. Гла́ж-е, *adv., comp.,* more smoothly.

глад-и-ть, гла́ж-у, *v.i.,* + *acc.,* to iron, press, smooth. Г. бельё, to iron the laundry. Г. про́тив ше́рсти, (*fig.*), to irritate. По голо́вке, to pat on the head; to approve. Глад-и́льщик, *n.m.,* presser. Глад-и́льный, *adj.,* pertaining to ironing. Г-ая доска́, ironing board.

вы́-глад-ить, *v.p.,* вы-гла́ж-ивать, *v.i.,* + *acc.,* to iron out folds, creases; smooth out.

за-гла́д-ить, *v.p.,* за-гла́ж-ивать, *v.i.,* + *acc.,* to even, level; (*fig.*), to efface, expiate, blot out. З. скла́дку, to iron a pleat. З. вину́, to make amends. З. грехи́, to expiate, atone for one's sins.

от-гла́д-ить, *v.p.,* от-гла́ж-ивать, *v.i.,* + *acc.,* to iron out.

пере-гла́д-ить, *v.p.,* + *acc.,* to complete one's ironing. Она́ прегла́дила всё бельё, she ironed all the laundry.

пере-гла́д-ить, *v.p.,* пере-гла́ж-ивать, *v.i.,* + *acc.,* to iron again.

по-гла́д-ить, *v.p.,* по-гла́ж-ивать, *v.i.,* + *acc.,* to stroke, caress. П. ребёнка по голо́вке, to pat a child on the head.

при-гла́д-ить, *v.p.,* при-гла́ж-ивать, *v.i.,* + *acc.,* to smooth down. П. во́лосы, to smooth one's hair. при-гла́д-ить-ся,

v.p.r., при-гла́ж-ивать-ся, *v.i.r.,* to make oneself tidy; smooth one's hair.
раз-гла́д-ить, *v.p.,* раз-гла́ж-ивать, *v.i.,* + *acc.,* to iron, press out; smooth. Раз-гла́ж-ивание, *n.n.,* ironing, pressing, smoothing. Раз-гла́ж-енный, *adj. part. pass. past,* ironed, pressed out; smoothed out.
с-гла́д-ить, *v.p.,* с-гла́ж-ивать, *v.i.,* + *acc.,* to level off; smooth, plane; (*fig.*), to reconcile. С. нерóвности, to smooth off uneven areas. С. неприя́тное впечатлéние, to wipe out an unpleasant impression. С-гла́д-ить-ся, *v.p.r.,* с-гла́ж-ивать-ся, *v.i.r.,* to be leveled, planed. С-гла́ж-ивание, *n.n.,* pressing, ironing, leveling, planing.

ГЛАД-, ГОЛОД-, HUNGER

глад, *n.m.,* (*Ch.-Sl.*), *see* гóлод.
гóлод, *n.m.,* hunger, famine, starvation. Чу́вствовать г., to be hungry. Морúть когó-нибудь г-ом, to starve someone. Умира́ть с г-у, to die of hunger, starve to death. Голóд-ный, *adj.,* hungry, famished, ravenous. Г-ая смерть, death from starvation. Голод-а́ние, *n.n.,* starvation. Голод-а́ющий, *adj. part. act. pres.,* starving. Голод-óвка, *n.f.,* starvation; hunger strike, fast. Объявля́ть г-у, to declare a hunger strike, fast.
голод-а́-ть, *v.i.,* по-голод-а́ть, *v.p.,* to starve, hunger, famish.
из-голод-а́ть-ся, *v.p.r.,* to become very hungry. Он изголода́лся в пути́, he became very hungry on the way. Изголода́лся по хорóшей му́зыке, I have become hungry for good music.
про-голод-а́ть, *v.p.,* to suffer from hunger over a period of time. Дерéвня прогологола́ла всю зиму́, the village starved through the entire winter.
про-голод-а́ть-ся, *v.p.r.,* to become hungry. Проголода́ешься, так хлéба доста́ть догада́ешься (*prov.*), if one becomes hungry enough, one finds a way to obtain bread. В-прó-голод-ь, *adv.,* starving, half-starving. Жить в., to live from hand to mouth.

ГЛАЗ-, EYE

глаз, *n.m.,* eye. Глаза́ - óрган зрéния, the eyes are organs of sight. Опытный г., a practiced eye. На-гла́з, approximately. В глаза́, to one's eyes. С глаз долóй, из сéрдца вон (*saying*), out of sight, out of mind. С гла́зу на́ глаз, privately, without witnesses. Пуска́ть пыль в глаза́, to throw dust in (someone's) eyes. Глаз-óк, *n.m., dim. of* глаз. Одни́м глазкóм, out of the corner of

one's eye. Дéлать гла́зки, to flirt. Аню́тины гла́зки, pansies. Глаз-нóй, *adj.,* ocular; pertaining to the eye. Г. зуб, eye-tooth. Г-óе я́блоко, eyeball. Глаз-а́стый, *adj.,* (*colloq.*), having large eyes. За-гла́з-ный, *adj.,* in the absence of, in one's absence. З-óе решéние, judgment by default. За-гла́зно, *adv.,* without seeing. Заг-ла́з-а́, *adv.,* behind one's back; sight unseen. Купи́ть з., to buy a pig in a poke. Глаз-о-мéр, *n.m.,* measurement by eye. Глаз-у́нья, *n.f.,* a dish of fried eggs. На-гла́з-ник, *n.m.,* blinker.
глаз-é-ть, *v.i.,* по-глаз-éть, *v.p.,* на + *acc.,* to stare, gaze. Толпа́ глазéла на слона́, the crowd gazed at the elephant.
с-гла́з-ить, *v.p.,* + *acc.,* to throw an evil spell on; overlook. Не с. бы! Touch wood!

ГЛАС-, ГЛАШ-, ГОЛОС-, VOICE

глас (гóлос), *n.m.,* voice. Г. Бóга, the Lord's voice, the voice of the Lord. Г. вопию́щего в пусты́не, a voice crying in the wilderness. Гла́с-ность, *n.f.,* publicity. Преда́ть гла́сности, to make public, announce publicly, publicize. Гла́с-ный, *adj.,* public, open; *used as n.,* (*gram.*), vowel. Г-óе ведéние суда́, an open trial, hearing. "А" - гла́сный звук, "A" is a vowel. Не-гла́с-ный, *adj.,* private, unpublicized. Н-óе обсуждéние дéла, a private hearing. Н-ым óбразом, privately, secretly. Гла́с-но, *adv.,* publicly. Не-гла́с-но, *adv.,* privately.
глас-и́-ть, глаш-у́, *v.i.,* + *acc.,* to say, mean. Послóвица гласи́т, the proverb says. Глаш-а́тай, *n.m.,* (*hist.*), herald, town-crier. Глаша́таи объявля́ли ца́рские ука́зы, the Tsar's decrees were announced by heralds.
воз-глас-и́ть, *v.p.,* воз-глаш-а́ть, *v.i.,* + *acc.,* to proclaim. Вóз-глас, *n.m.,* exclamation, cry. Воз-глаш-éние, *n.n.,* the act of proclaiming.
едино-гла́с-ие, *n.n.,* unanimity in voting. Едино-гла́сный, *adj.,* unanimous. Едино-гла́сно, *adv.,* unanimously. Председа́тель был вы́бран е., the chairman was elected unanimously.
о-глас-и́ть, *v.p.,* о-глаш-а́ть, *v.i.,* + *acc.,* to make public, announce; publish the banns. О. резолю́цию, to announce a resolution. О-гла́с-ка, *n.f.,* publicity. Избега́ть о-и, to avoid publicity. О-глаш-éние, *n.n.,* proclamation; publication of the banns. О. прави́тельственного распоряжéния, the announcement of a government decree. Не подлежа́щее оглашéнию, strictly confidential,

not for publication. Секре́тный прика́з, не подлежа́щий оглаше́нию, a secret order, not for publication. О-глас-и́ть-ся, *v.p.r.*, о-глаш-а́ть-ся, *v.i.r.*, + *instr.*, to resound. Лес оглаша́лся пе́нием птиц, the forest resounded with the singing of birds.

при-глас-и́ть, *v.p.*, при-глаш-а́ть, *v.i.*, + *acc.*, to invite. П. на обе́д, to invite to dinner. П. врача́, to call a doctor. При-глаш-а́ть-ся, *v.i.r.*, to invite oneself, be invited. На собра́ние приглаша́ются то́лько чле́ны профсою́за, only members of the trade union are invited to the meeting. При-глаш-е́ние, *n.n.*, invitation. При-глаш-ённый, *adj. part. pass. past,* invited; *used as n.*, a person who has received an invitation. На ве́чере бы́ло мно́го приглашённых, there were many guests at the party.

про-воз-глас-и́ть, *v.p.*, про-воз-глаш-а́ть, *v.i.*, + *acc.*, to proclaim, announce. П. тост за кого́-нибудь, to propose a toast ᶜto someone. Про-воз-глаш-а́ть-ся, *v.i.r.*, to be proclaimed, announced. Про-воз-глаш-е́ние, *n.n.*, proclamation, declaration, announcement. П. незави́симости, a declaration of independence.

раз-глас-и́ть, *v.p.*, раз-глаш-а́ть, *v.i.*, + acc., to disseminate, proclaim, divulge, publish. Р. та́йну, to divulge a secret. Раз-глас-и́ть-ся, *v.p.r.*, раз-глаш-а́ться, *v.i.r.*, to be widely proclaimed; be divulged, announced. Секре́ты не разглаша́ются, secrets are not divulged. Раз-глаш-е́ние, *n.n.*, public proclamation, advertisement, dissemination.

со-глас-и́ть-ся, *v.p.r.*, со-глаш-а́ть-ся, *v.i.r.*, с + *instr.*, to agree, consent, comply with. Согласи́тесь со мной, что вы непра́вы, admit that you are wrong. Я согласи́лся на его́ про́сьбу, I complied with his request. со-глас-ие, *n.n.*, agreement, assent, consent. Дать с., to agree, consent. В согла́сии, in harmony, agreement. Муж и жена́ живу́т в по́лном согла́сии, husband and wife live in perfect harmony. С ва́шего согла́сия, with your consent. С ва́шего согла́сия, я возьму́ э́ту кни́гу, with your consent I'll take this book. Молча́ние - знак согла́сия, (*saying*), silence is a sign of consent. Со-глас-и́тельный, *adj.*, conciliatory. С-ая коми́ссия, board of conciliation, board of arbitration. Со-гла́сный, *adj.*, agreeing, consenting, consistent with, harmonious; in accordance with; (*gram.*), consonant. Со-гла́с-ен, *adj. pred.*, agreed, in agreement. Я с ва́ми вполне́ с., I'm in complete agreement with you. Ко́пия согла́сна с по́длинником, the copy agrees with the original. Со-гла́с-но, *adv.*, in conformance with, according to, in accordance with. С. мо́де, in fashion. Костю́м сде́лан с. мо́де, the suit is made according to the latest fashion. Мы поём с., we are singing in perfect harmony. Не-согла́с-ие, *n.n.*, disagreement, discord, dissent. Не-со-гла́с-ный, *adj.*, disagreeing, discordant, out of accord with. Я не согла́сен на э́то, I do not agree to this. Не-со-гла́с-но, *adv.*, in discord, out of accord with, discordantly. Соглаш-а́тель, *n.m.* (*derog.*), conciliator. Со-глаш-а́тельство *n.n.*, (derog.), conciliation. Полити́ческое с., a conciliatory policy. Со-глаш-е́ние, *n.n.*, agreement, understanding, arrangement. Та́йное с., a secret agreement. Прийти́ к взаи́мному соглаше́нию, to come to a mutual agreement.

со-глас-ова́ть, *v.p.*, со-глас-о́вывать, *v.i.*, + *acc.*, to agree, make agree. С. прилага́тельное с существи́тельным, to make an adjective agree with a noun. Со-глас-ова́ть-ся, *v.p.r.*, со-глас-о́вывать-ся, *v.i.r.*, + *instr.*, to be in agreement, be coordinated. Со-глас-ова́ние, *n.n.*, agreement, concordance. Со-гласо́ванность, *n.f.*, coordination of action. Не-со-глас-о́ванность, *n.f.*, lack of coordination. Со-глас-о́ванный, *adj.*, coordinated. Не-со-глас-о́ванный, *adj.*, uncoordinated. Со-глас-о́ванно, *adv.*, with coordination. Не-со-глас-о́ванно, *adv.*, without coordination.

разно-гла́с-ие, *n.n.*, discord, disharmony, difference of opinion, outlook. Разногла́с-ный, *adj.*, dissonant, conflicting, discordant.

го́лос *n.m.*, voice. Сла́бый г., a weak voice. Си́льный г., a strong voice. Мужско́й, же́нский г., a masculine, feminine voice. Возвыша́ть г., to raise one's voice. Быть в го́лосе, to be in good voice. В оди́н г., unanimously. Сказа́ть в оди́н г., to say something all together, to speak with one voice. Голос-и́стый, *adj.*, vociferous, stentorian. Г. солове́й, a melodious nightingale. Голос-ово́й, *adj.*, vocal. Г-а́я щель, (*anat.*), glottis. Г-ы́е свя́зки, the vocal chords. Без-голо́с-ый, *adj.*, voiceless (*e.g., an inferior singer*). От-голо́с-ок, *n.m.*, echo. От-голо́с-ки войны́, the aftermath of war. От-голо́ски в печа́ти, press comments. Разно-голо́с-ица, *n.f.*, discordance, dissonance. Разно-голо́сный, *adj.*, many-voiced.

голос-и́ть, *v.i.*, (*obs.*), to wail, lament. Г. по поко́йнику, (*folk.*), to lament over a corpse. Голос-и́льщица, *n.f.*, wailer.

голос-ова́ть, *v.i.*, про-голос-ова́ть, *v.p.*, + *acc.*, to vote. П. резолю́цию, (*re-*

cent), to pass a resolution. Голосова́ние, *п.п.,* voting. Поста́вить вопро́с на голосова́ние, to put an issue to a vote.

ГЛУБ-, DEPTH

глуб-ин-а́, *n.f.,* depth, profundity, profoundness. Г. моря́, depth of the sea. Г. ра́ны, depth of a wound. Г. мы́сли, profundity of thought. Г. чу́вства, depth of feeling. В глубине́ души́, at heart, in the depths of one's heart. Измере́ния глубины́, soundings.

глуб-о́к-ий, *adj.,* deep, profound; thoughtful. Г-ое о́зеро, мо́ре, a deep lake, sea. Г-ая таре́лка, soup plate. Г-ий сон, deep, sound sleep. Г. ум, a profound mind. Г-ая ночь, a dark night. Г-ая ста́рость, extreme old age. Г-ое неве́жество, dense ignorance. Глубок-о́, *adv.,* deeply, profoundly. Г. на дне мо́ря, deep at the bottom of the sea, ocean. Г. сидя́щее су́дно, a vessel of deep draught. Глубоко-мы́слие, *п.п.,* depth of thought. Г.-мы́сленный, *adj.,* thoughtful. Г. уважа́емый, *adj., form of address in letters,* highly esteemed.

глуб-ь, *n.f.,* depth; *see* глубина́. Морска́я глубь, (*poet.*), the deep. В-глуб-ь, *adv.,* deeply. Уйти́ в. леса́, to go into the heart of a forest. В. страны́, inland. Проника́ть в. чего́-либо, to penetrate deeply into something.

у-глуб-и́ть, *v.p.,* у-глуб-л-я́ть, *v.i.,* + *acc.,* to deepen; excavate. У. кана́ву, коло́дец, to deepen a ditch, a well. У. свои́ зна́ния, to deepen one's knowledge. У-глуб-и́ть-ся, *v.p.r.,* у-глуб-л-я́ть-ся, *v.i.r.,* to become deeper, deepen; go deeply into. У. в лес, to go deep into a forest. У. в рабо́ту, to become absorbed in work. У. в размышле́ния, to plunge into meditation. У-глубле́ние, *п.п.,* deepening; hollow, hole, cavity. У. дна реки́, deepening of a river bed. У. в по́чве, hollow in the earth, ground. У. зна́ний, a deepening, extension of one's knowledge. У-глуб-л-ённый, *adj., part. pass. past,* deepened. У. в размышле́ния, deep in thoughts. У-ое изуче́ние како́го-нибудь предме́та, a thorough study of some subject.

ГЛУХ-, ГЛУШ-, ГЛОХ-, DEAFNESS, REMOTENESS, WILDERNESS

глух-о́й, *adj., used also as n.,* deaf, hard of hearing; (*gram.*), voiceless, unvoiced. Г. челове́к, a deaf man. Не кричи́те, я не глухо́й! You needn't shout, I'm not deaf. Г. лес, a thick forest. Г.

переу́лок, lonely side-street, alley. Г-а́я ночь, a dark night. Г-о́е вре́мя го́да, a dull season, time of the year. Глух-о-немо́й *adj., used also as n.,* deaf-mute. А́збука глухонемы́х, deaf-and-dumb alphabet. Глух-ота́, *n.f.,* deafness, hardness of hearing. На́-глух-о, *adv.,* hermetically, tightly. Заколоти́ть дверь на́глухо, to nail a door tightly. Н. застегну́ться, to button oneself tightly.

глуш-и́-ть, *v.i.,* + *acc.,* to deafen. Г. ры́бу, to stun fish. Г. ра́дио, (*recent*), to jam a broadcast. Глуш-и́тель, *п.т.,* (*tech.*), silencer, muffler. Глуш-ь, *n.f.,* a thicket; solitary, remote place. Провинциа́льная г., provincial, rustic remoteness. Лесна́я г., remote depths of a forest.

за-глуш-и́ть, *v.p.,* за-глуш-а́ть, *v.i.,* + *acc.,* to drown, deaden, smother, stifle, suppress. Орке́стр заглуша́л го́лос певца́, the orchestra drowned out the singer's voice. З. боль, to soothe a pain.

о-глуш-и́ть, *v.p.,* о-глуш-а́ть, *v.i.,* + *acc.,* + *instr.,* to deafen, stun, stupefy. Гром оглуши́л меня́, the thunder deafened me. О. уда́ром по голове́, to stun someone with a blow on the head. О-глуш-е́-ние, *п.п.,* deafening, stunning, О-глуш-и́тельный, *adj.,* deafening, stunning. О. уда́р гро́ма, a deafening clash of thunder. О. крик, a deafening scream.

гло́х-ну-ть, *v.i.,* to grow deaf; run wild (*of vegetation*). Старики́ с года́ми гло́хнут, old people grow deaf with age. Города́ пусте́ют и гло́хнут, cities are becoming deserted and are fading out.

о-гло́х-ну-ть, *see* гло́хнуть. По́сле скарлати́ны ребёнок огло́х, the child became deaf after an attack of scarlet fever. О-гло́х-ший, *adj. part. pass. past,* grown deaf.

за-гло́х-ну-ть, *v.p.,* to be choked, smothered; be overgrown with. Сад загло́хнул, the garden is overgrown with weeds. Слу́хи загло́хли, the rumors have stopped.

ГЛЯД-, ГЛЯЖ-, ГЛЯ-, GLANCE, LOOK, VIEW

гляд-е́-ть, *v.i.,* по-гляд-е́ть, *v.p.,* на + *acc.,* to look, glance. Он гляде́л на меня́ в упо́р, he stared at me. Г. при́стально, to gaze, stare. Того́ и гляди́ он придёт, (*colloq., idiom*), I fear he may come at any moment. Гляд-е́ть-ся, *v.i.r.,* по-гляд-е́ть-ся, *v.p.r.,* в + *acc.,* (*obs.*), to look at oneself, look at oneself in the mirror. Г. в зéркало, to look at oneself in the mirror.

вы́-гляд-еть, *v.i.,* to appear to be, look. В. молóже, стáрше свои́х лет, to look younger, older than one's age. В. хорошó, to look well. Больнóй плóхо вы́глядит, the sick man does not look well.

вы-гля́д-ывать, *v.i.,* вы́-гля-нуть, *v.p.,* из + *gen.,* to peer, look out; peep out. Мáльчик вы́глянул из окнá, the boy looked out of the window.

до-гляд-éть, *v.p.,* до-гля́д-ывать, *v.i.,* + *acc.,* to observe, notice, note; to see to something; to see to something to the end, watch over till the end. Ня́ня догля́дывает детéй, *(colloq.),* the nurse is looking after the children. Не доглядéть, to neglect, overlook. Не доглядéли ребёнка и он утону́л, they failed to watch the child and he drowned.

о-гляд-éть, *v.p.,* о-гля́д-ывать, *v.i.,* о-гля-ну́ть, *v.p. smf.,* + *acc.,* to examine, look over. О. с ног до головы́, to scrutinize someone from head to foot. О-гля́д-ывать-ся, *v.i.r.,* о-гля-ну́ть-ся, *v.p.r. smf.,* to look back, behind; look around; accustom oneself. О-гля́д-éть-ся, *v.p.,* to orientate oneself, find one's bearings. Они́ ужé огляди́лись в Амéрике, they've already settled down and accustomed themselves to life in America.

пере-гляд-éть, *v.p.,* пере-гля́д-ывать, *v.i.,* + *acc.,* *(colloq.),* to look through. Он переглядéл все карти́ны на вы́ставке, he looked at all the paintings at the exhibition. Пере-гля́д-ывать-ся, *v.i.r.,* пере-гля-ну́ть-ся, *v.p.r.,* to exchange glances.

по-гляд-éть, *v.p.,* по-гля́д-ывать, *v.i.,* на + *acc.,* в + *acc.,* за + *instr.,* to glance, look at for a moment; look after, watch over. Погляди́те на себя́ в зéркало, look at yourself in the mirror. То и дéло он погля́дывал на часы́, he was constantly looking at his watch. Погляди́те за детьми́, look after the children.

под-гляд-éть, *v.p.,* под-гля́д-ывать, *v.i.,* за + *instr.,* to examine furtively; watch, spy, peep. П. сквозь замóчную сквáжину, to peep through a keyhole. Под-гля́д-ывание, *n.n.,* peeping, spying, observing.

при-гляд-éть, *v.p.,* при-гля́д-ывать, *v.i.,* + *acc.,* *(colloq.),* to seek until one finds. Я приглядéл себé нóвый дом, I've succeeded in finding a new house. При-гля́д-éть-ся, *v.p.r.,* при-гля́-дываться, *v.i.r.,* к + *dat.,* to learn by

observing, looking, watching; to look at something closely. Когдá я пригляделся к нему́, он мне понрáвился, When I looked at him more closely, I took a liking to him. Я так пригляделся к э́тому ви́ду, что ужé не замечáю егó красоты́, I am so accustomed to this view I no longer notice its beauty. При-гля-ну́ть-ся, *v.p.r.,* + *dat.,* *(colloq.),* to catch someone's fancy, to please. Онá ему́ приглянýлась, *(folk.)* she caught his fancy.

про-гляд-éть, *v.p.,* про-гля́д-ывать, *v.i.,* + *acc.,* to look, skim through; П. кни́гу, газéту, to look through a book, a newspaper. Про-гля́д-ывать, *v.i.,* про-гля-ну́ть, *v.p.,* + *acc.,* peep out; overlook. В егó словáх прогля́дывает иро́ния, there is a touch of irony in his words. Сóлнце прогляну́ло из-за облакóв, the sun peeped out through the clouds. Учи́тель проглядéл оши́бку в тетрáди ученикá, the teacher overlooked a mistake in the pupil's notebook.

раз-гляд-éть, *v.p.,* раз-гля́д-ывать, *v.i.,* + *acc.,* to view, examine, scrutinize, consider in detail. Р. хорошéнько, to examine closely, thoroughly. Р. когó-нибудь, чтó-нибудь со всех сторóн, to look someone, something over from all sides, angles.

у-гляд-éть, *v.p.,* + *acc.,* to watch over *(used more frequently in the negative).* Не у., to overlook, miss, neglect. Всегó не угляди́шь, *(saying),* one can't foresee everything.

вз-гля́д-ывать, *v.i.,* вз-гля-ну́ть, *v.p. smf.,* на + *acc.,* to cast a glance at; look at furtively. Он взгляну́л на меня́ и прошёл мимо, he glanced at me and passed by. Вз-гляд, *n.m.,* look, glance, gaze; view, opinion. Брóсить в. на когó-нибудь, чтó-нибудь, to glance at someone, something. Здрáвый в. на вéщи, a healthy attitude, sound judgment. Взгля́ды на жизнь, an attitude towards life; point of view.

за-гля́д-ывать, *v.i.,* за-гля-ну́ть, *v.p. smf.,* в + *acc.,* to look, peep in; have a look. З. в гóсти, to call on, visit. За-гля́д-éть-ся, *v.p.r.,* за-гля́д-ывать-ся, *v.i.r.,* to gape, stare, lose oneself in admiration of something. З. на красáвицу, to gaze in admiration at a beautiful woman. За-гля́д-éние, *n.n.,* contemplation. Это прóсто з.! This is simply a feast for the eyes!

в-гля́д-éть-ся, *v.p.r.,* в-гля́д-ывать-ся, *v.i.r.,* в + *acc.,* to peer, look closely. В. в когó-либо, to observe someone closely. В. в темноту́, to peer into darkness.

на-гляд-е́ть-ся, *v.p.r.,* на + *acc.,* to have one's fill of looking. Я не могу́ нагляде́ться на э́тот вид, I cannot see enough of this view. Я уже́ нагляде́лся на э́ту карти́ну, она́ мне надое́ла, I've seen more than enough of this painting, I'm tired of it. На-гля́д-ный, *adj.,* graphic, descriptive. Н. уро́к an object lesson. Н-ое посо́бие, visual aid. На-гля́д-но, *adv.,* graphically, visually. Не-на-гля́д-ный, *adj.,* (*fig.*), dear, beloved. Мой н-ые де́ти! My dearest children!

ГН-, ГОН-, PURSUIT, CHASE, HUNT, DRIVE

гн-а-ть, *v.i.,* по-гн-а́-ть, *v.p.,* в + *acc.,* с + *gen.,* из + *gen.,* to pursue, chase, hunt, drive. Г. в по́ле, с по́ля, to drive into a field, off a field. Г. автомоби́ль, велосипе́д, (*v.i. only*), to drive at top speed. Г. неприя́теля, to pursue an enemy. Г. кого́-нибудь из до́му, to turn someone out of a house. Гн-а́ть-ся, *v.i.,* по-гн-а́ть-ся, *v.p.,* за + *instr.,* to pursue; strive. Г. за во́ром, to pursue a thief. Г. за сла́вой, to strive for fame.

гон-я́-ть, *v.i. indet.,* + *acc.,* с + *gen.,* to drive away; chase, hunt. Ка́ждое у́тро он гоня́ет скот на па́стбище, every morning he drives the cattle to pasture. Г. с ме́ста на ме́сто, (*colloq.*), to drive from place to place. Г. кого́-либо за что́-либо, (*colloq.*), to reprimand, scold someone for something. Гон-я́ть-ся, *v.i.r.,* to chase; seek after. Г. по пята́м, to pursue closely. Г. за по́честями, to seek honors. Гон-е́ние, *n.n.,* persecution, oppression. Полити́ческое, рели-гио́зное г., political, religious persecution. Го́н-ка, *n.f.,* race, pursuit, chase; hurry; distillation. Г. вооруже́ний, armament race. Го́н-ки, *n.pl.,* races. Автомоби́льные г., auto races. Го́н-щик, *n.m.,* racer. Гон-е́ц, *n.m.,* despatch-rider, messenger. Гон-и́тель, *n.m.,* persecutor. Гон-и́мый, *adj. part. pass. pres.,* persecuted. Го́н-чая (соба́ка), hound, fox hound. Го́н-очный, *adj.,* pertaining to racing. Г. автомоби́ль, racing car. Г-ая я́хта, racing yacht.

во-гн-а́ть, *v.p.,* в-гон-я́ть, *v.i.,* в + *acc.,* to drive in. В. гво́зди в сте́ну, to drive nails into a wall. Он меня́ в гроб вго́нит, he will be the death of me (*literally*: he will drive me into my grave). В. в кра́ску, to put to shame.

вы́-гн-ать, *v.p.,* вы-гон-я́ть, *v.i.,* + *acc.,* из + *gen.,* to turn out, oust, expel. В. ста́до в по́ле, to turn a herd out into a field В. из шко́лы, to expel

from school. Вы́-гон, *n.m.,* communal pasture. Пра́во на обще́ственный в., the right to the use of a communal pasture. Вы́-гон-ка, *n.f.,* distillation.

до-гн-а́-ть, *v.p.,* до-гон-я́ть, *v.i.,* + *acc.,* to overtake; join. Я вас догоню́, I'll catch up with you. Д. кого́-либо в уче́нии, to catch up with someone in studies.

за-гн-а́ть, *v.p.,* за-гон-я́ть, *v.i.,* + *acc.,* to drive in, pen; (*fig.*), harass. З. скот, to drive cattle into a pen, enclosure. З. ло́шадь, to tire out a horse. З. кого́-либо рабо́той, (*colloq.*), to work someone to death. За-го́н, *n.m.,* enclosure, corral. Быть в заго́не, (*fig.*), to be kept in the background. За-го́н-щик, *n.m.,* drover, beater (*in hunting*).

из-гн-а́ть, *v.p.,* из-гон-я́ть, *v.i.,* + *acc.,* to banish, exile. Из-гн-а́ние, *n.n.,* exile, banishment, expatriation. Из-гн-а́нник, *n.m.,* exile. Из-гн-а́нный, *adj. part. pass. past,* exiled, banished, expatriated, expelled.

на-гн-а́-ть, *v.p.,* на-гон-я́ть, *v.i.,* + *acc.,* to overtake; drive. Н. смерте́льную тоску́, to bore to death. Н. страх, to terrorize, frighten. На-гон-я́й, *n.m.,* rebuke, reprimand. Дава́ть н., to reprimand, rebuke. Получа́ть н., to be reprimanded, scolded, rebuked.

обо-гн-а́-ть, *v.p.,* об-гон-я́ть, *v.i.,* + *acc.,* to outstrip, surpass. Автомоби́ль обогна́л изво́зчика, the car overtook the horse cab.

ото-гн-а́-ть, *v.p.,* от-гон-я́ть, *v.i.,* + *acc.,* to drive, chase away. О. му́ху, to chase a fly away. О. мра́чные мы́сли, to drive away gloomy thoughts.

пере-гн-а́ть, *v.p.,* пере-гон-я́ть, *v.i.,* + *acc.,* to surpass, outstrip, outspeed, outrun. П. кого́-либо в чём-нибудь, to surpass someone in something. Пере-го́н, *n.m.,* stage; driving of cattle. Де́лать небольши́е перего́ны, to make gradual progress, travel by easy stages. Пере-го́н-ка, *n.f.,* distillation. П. не́фти, oil refining. Бе́гать наперего́нки (вперего́нки), (*colloq.*), to run foot races, to race (not for formal sport).

по-гн-а́-ть, *v.p.,* + *acc.,* to drive, chase. П. кого́-либо вон, to drive someone away. П. лошаде́й, to urge horses on. П. ста́до в по́ле, to drive cattle out to pasture. По-гн-а́ть-ся, *v.p.r,* за + *instr.,* to chase. П. за за́йцем, to chase a hare.

по-гон-я́ть, *v.i.,* + *acc.,* to urge, spur on. П. ло́шадь кнуто́м, apply the whip to a horse. По-го́н-я, *n.f.,* pursuit, chase. По-го́н-щик, *n.m.,* driver (*e.g.,* of a mule team).

подо-гн-а́ть, *v.p.,* под-гон-я́ть, *v.i.,* + *acc.,* to urge on, hurry. П. под оди́н разме́р, to gauge; to make conform in size. Под-гон-я́ть-ся, *v.i.r.,* + *instr.,* to be urged on; be adjusted.

при-гн-а́ть, *v.p.,* при-гон-я́ть, *v.i.,* + *acc.,* to drive; fit, adjust, close. П. пле́нных, (*colloq.*), to bring in prisoners. П. пальто́, (*colloq.*), to fit an overcoat. При-го́н-ка, *n.f.,* fitting, adjustment.

про-гн-а́ть, *v.p.,* про-гон-я́ть, *v.i.,* + *acc.,* to drive, turn out, away; dismiss. П. ученика́ из шко́лы, to expel a pupil from school. П. печа́ль, to drive away melancholy. Ве́тер прогна́л ту́чи, the wind dispersed the clouds. Про-го́н, *n.m.,* the run between two points (of a railroad), the distance between two points (in travel). Про-го́н-ные де́ньги, allowance for travelling.

разо-гн-а́ть, *v.p.,* раз-гон-я́ть, *v.i.,* + *acc.,* to drive away, dispel, disperse. Р. толпу́, to disperse a crowd. Разо-гн-а́ть-ся, *v.p.r.,* to acquire momentum. Раз-гон-я́ть-ся, *v.i.r., used in 3d pers. only:* to be dispersed. Толпа́ разгоня́ется милиционе́рами, the crowd is being dispersed by the militia. Раз-го́н, *n.m.,* momentum; dispersal.

со-гн-а́ть, *v.p.,* с-гон-я́ть, *v.i.,* + *acc.,* с + *gen.,* to drive off; round up. С. со двора́, (*folk.*), to drive out of a house. С. скоти́ну, to round up cattle. С-гон-я́ть-ся, *v.i.r.,* to be driven together.

у-гн-а́ть, *v.p.,* у-гон-я́ть, *v.i.,* + *acc.,* to drive away, blow away; rustle. Табу́н угна́ли в ночно́е, the herd of horses was driven to pasture for the night. У-гн-а́ть-ся, *v.p.r.,* у-гон-я́ть-ся, *v.i.r.,* за + *instr.,* to overtake. За ним не угна́ться, (*idiom.*), there is no keeping up with him.

ГН-, ГИБ-, CURVATURE, BEND, FLEXIBILITY

гн-у-ть, *v.i.,* + *acc.,* to bend, curve, flex. Г. желе́зо, to bend iron bars. Г. спи́ну пе́ред ке́м-нибудь, to cringe, bow before someone. Я. ви́жу, куда́ вы гнёте, (*colloq.*), I see what you're driving at. Гн-у́ть-ся, *v.i.r.,* to bend, stoop. Дере́вья гну́тся от ве́тра, the trees are bending in the wind. Гн-у́тый, *adj. part. pass. past,* bent, curved. Г-ая-ме́бель, furniture made of curved wood, curved furniture.

во-гн-у́ть, *v.p.,* в-гиб-а́ть, *v.i.,* + *acc.,* to curve inwards, render concave. Во́-гн-утость, *n.f.,* concavity. Во́-гн-утый, *adj. part. pass. past,* concave, rendered concave.

вы́-гн-уть, *v.p.,* вы-гиб-а́ть, *v.i.,* + *acc.,* to curve out, render convex. В. спи́ну, to hog one's back. Вы́-гиб, *n.m.,* outward curve, convexity. Вы-гиб-а́ние, *n.n.,* curving, arching out; convexity.

за-гн-у́ть, *v.p.,* за-гиб-а́ть, *v.i.,* + *acc.,* to fold, bend, turn in, down, back. З. па́лец, to bend down one's finger. З. у́гол в кни́ге, to bend down the corner of a page in a book. З. кре́пкое словцо́, (*colloq.*), to use strong language. За-ги́б, *n.m.,* fold, bend. З. реки́, a bend in a river.

изо-гн-у́ть, *v.p.,* из-гиб-а́ть, *v.i.,* + *acc.,* to bend, curve. Изо-гн-у́ть-ся, *v.p.r.,* из-гиб-а́ть-ся, *v.i.r.,* to bend, bow very low. Во́лга изгиба́ется у Жигулёвских гор, the Volga makes a bend near the Zhigulev Hills. Из-ги́б, *n.m.,* winding, fold, bend, crook; tortuousness. Изо́-гн-утость, *n.f.,* curvature, flexion. Изо́-гн-утый, *adj. part. pass. past,* bent, curved.

на-гн-у́ть, *v.p.,* на-гиб-а́ть, *v.i.,* + *acc.,* to bend down, incline. Н. ве́тку, to bend a branch. Н. го́лову, to bend one's head. На-гн-у́ть-ся, *v.p.r.,* на-гиб-а́ть-ся, *v.i.r.,* to stoop, bow. Ве́тви нагну́лись, the branches became bent.

обо-гн-у́ть, *v.p.,* о-гиб-а́ть, *v.i.,* + *acc.,* to bend around, go around a corner.

ото-гн-у́ть, *v.p.,* от-гиб-а́ть, *v.i.,* + *acc.,* to turn, bend back, unbend. О. у́гол страни́цы, to unbend the corner of a page. От-ги́б, *n.m., see* сгиб. От-гиб-а́ние, *n.n.,* unbending, straightening.

пере-гн-у́ть, *v.p.,* пере-гиб-а́ть, *v.i.,* + *acc.,* to twist, bend over. П. па́лку, (*fig.*), to go too far. Пере-гн-у́ть-ся, *v.p.r.,* пере-гиб-а́ть-ся, *v.i.r.,* to be bent over, bend over. П. че́рез пери́ла, to lean over the banisters. Пере-ги́б, *n.m.,* bend, twist. П. криво́й, (*geom.*), inflection. Парти́йные переги́бы, (*recent*), party deviations.

по-гн-у́ть, *v.p.,* + *acc.,* to bend. Лев погну́л пру́тья кле́тки, the lion bent the bars of the cage. По-гн-у́ть-ся, *v.p.r.,* to be bent. Ось погну́лась, the axle is bent.

подо-гн-у́ть, *v.p.,* под-гиб-а́ть, *v.i.,* + *acc.,* под + *acc.,* to tuck in, tuck under, turn in. Он сел и подогну́л но́ги под себя́, he sat down and tucked his feet under him. Подо-гн-у́ть-ся, *v.p.r.,* под-гиб-а́ть-ся, *v.i.r.,* to bend under. У старика́ подгиба́ются но́ги, the old man's legs are failing him.

при-гн-у́ть, *v.p.,* при-гиб-а́ть, *v.i.,* + *acc.,* to bend down; close. Бу́рей пригну́ло де́рево к земле́, the storm bent the tree to the ground. При-гн-у́ть-ся, *v.p.r.,* при-гиб-а́ть-ся, *v.i.r.,* to bend to; close.

разо-гн-у́ть, *v.p.,* раз-гиб-а́ть, *v.i.,* + acc., to unbend, straighten out, smooth out. Р. пружи́ну, to straighten out a spring. Р. спи́ну, to unbend one's back. Разо-гн-у́ть-ся, *v.p.r.,* раз-гиб-а́ть-ся, *v.i.r.,* to straighten up, unbend oneself. Раз-гиб-а́ющий, *adj. part. act. pres.,* unbending. Р. му́скул, (*anat.*), extensor muscle. Раз-гиб-а́я, *adj. part. act. pres.,* unbending. "День и ночь, не разгиба́я спины́, я зубри́л"(*Chekhov*), I studied day and night without unbending my back.

со-гн-у́ть, *v.p.,* с-гиб-а́ть, *v.i.,* + acc., to bend, flex, curve, crook. со-гн-у́ть-ся, *v.p.r.,* с-гиб-а́ть-ся, *v.i.r.,* to bend down, stoop. У меня́ коле́но не сгиба́ется, my knee does not bend. Сгиба́ться под тя́жестью но́ши, to sink under the weight of a burden. С-гиб, *n.m.,* flection. С-гиб-а́ние, *n.n.,* flexure, flection. С. суста́вов, the flection of the joints.

ги́б-к-ость, *n.f.,* pliability, flexibility, suppleness. Ги́б-кий, *adj.,* flexible, pliable, supple, willowy; elastic; slender, svelte. Г. стан, (*poet.*), a slender figure.

ГНЕВ-, ANGER, WRATH

гнев, *n.m.,* anger, ire, rage, wrath. Взрыв гне́ва, a gust of anger. В припа́дке гне́ва, in a burst of rage, anger. гне́вный, *adj.,* angry, angered, irate, enraged. Г. взор, an angry look. Гне́вно, *adv.,* angrily. Г. взгляну́ть на кого́-либо, to glance angrily at someone.

гне́в-ать-ся, *v.i.r.,* (*obs.*), на + acc., to be angry, chafe, fume, rage. Оте́ц си́льно гне́вался на сы́на, the father became very angry at his son.

гнев-и́ть, *v.i.,* про-гнев-и́ть, *v.p.,* + acc., (*obs.*), to make angry, incense, enrage. П. Бо́га, to bring the wrath of God down upon oneself. "Скажи́те, что вас так гневи́т?" (*Griboedov*), Tell me, what angers you so?

про-гне́в-ать, *v.p.,* + acc., to displease; anger, irritate. Про-гне́в-ать-ся, *v.p.r.,* to be displeased; angered, irritated. Не прогне́вайтесь, (*obs.*), don't be angry.

раз-гне́в-ать, *v.p.,* + acc., (*obs.*), to anger, enrage. Раз-гне́в-ать-ся, *v.p.r.,* (*obs.*), на + acc., to become angry. Ба́тюшка разгне́вался и прогна́л францу́за, (*Pushkin*), Father became angry and dismissed the Frenchman. Раз-гне́в-анный, *adj. part. pass. past,* angered, enraged, incensed. Р. го́лос, жест, an enraged voice, angry gesture.

ГНЕТ-, PRESSURE

гнёт, *n.m.,* oppression, yoke; press, weight; depression, worry. Г. суро́вого режи́ма, the oppression of a severe regime. Под гнётом нищеты́, under the yoke of poverty.

гнес-ти́, *v.i.,* + acc., to depress, oppress. Мысль о сме́рти гнетёт люде́й, the thought of death depresses people. Гнетёт меня́ тоска́ по ро́дине, I am oppressed by a longing for home. Гнету́щий, *adj. part. act. pres.,* depressing, oppressing. Г-ие мы́сли, depressing thoughts, ideas.

на-гнет-а́ть, *v.i.,* + acc., to force, compel, press. На-гнет-а́тельный, *adj.,* (*tech.*), pertaining to forcing by pumping. Н. кла́пан, a delivery valve. Н. насо́с, a force pump.

у-гнет-а́ть, *v.i.,* + acc., to depress, weigh down, oppress. Победи́тели угнета́ли побеждённых, the conquerors were oppressing the conquered. Безде́нежье угнета́ло его́, lack of money depressed him. У-гнет-а́тель, *n.m.,* oppressor. У-гнет-е́ние, *n.n.,* oppression. У-гнет-ённость, *n.f.,* depression; state of being depressed. У-гнет-ённый, *adj. part. pass. past,* depressed, oppressed. У-ые наро́ды, oppressed nations, peoples. У-ое настрое́ние, a depressed mood. Быть в угнетённом состоя́нии, to be in a depressed mood, in the dumps, blues.

ГНИ-, ГНО-, ГНОЙ-, DECOMPOSITION, DECAY, PUTREFACTION

гни-ль, *n.f.,* rot, decay; a rotten, decayed object. Гни-ло́й, *adj.,* putrid, corrupt, rotten. Г. апельси́н, a rotten orange. Г. кли́мат, a damp climate. Г. режи́м, a corrupt regime. Гни́-лость, *n.f.,* rottenness, putrefaction. Гни-лу́шка, *n.f.,* a piece of rotten wood.

гни-ть, *v.i.,* по-гни́-ть *v.p.,* to rot, decay, decompose. До́ски бы́стро гнию́т под дождём, boards rot quickly in the rain. Заключённые гни́ли в тюрьме́, (*fig.*), the prisoners were rotting in prison. Гни-е́ние, *n.n.,* decay, putrefaction. Гни-ю́щий, *adj. part. act. pres.,* putrescent, rotting, decaying. Г. пень, a rotting stump of a tree.

за-гни́-ть, *v.p.,* за-гни-ва́ть, *v.i.,* с + gen., to begin to rot, decay. Ры́ба загнива́ет с головы́, (*saying*), a fish starts to rot at the head.

пере-гни́-ть, *v.p.,* пере-гни-ва́ть, *v.i.,* to rot through. Столб перегни́л и слома́лся, the post rotted through and broke.

про-гни́-ть, *v.p.,* про-гни-ва́ть, *v.i.,* to rot through. Ба́лки прогни́ли, the beams have rotted through.

с-гни-ть, *v.p.,* с-гни-ва́ть, *v.i.,* see **гнить.**
гной, *n.m.,* pus, matter. Гной-ни́к, *n.m.,* abscess; (*fig.*), a group of corrupt people. Гно́й-ный, *adj.,* purulent. Г-ая ра́на, a purulent wound. Гно-е-ви́дный, *adj.,* (*med.*), puriform. Пере-гно́й, *n.m.,* humus. Пере-гно́-йная по́чва, humus.
гно-й-ть, *v.i.,* с-гно-й-ть, *v.p.,* + *acc.,* to cause to rot, decay. Дождь гнойт сéно, rain causes hay to rot.
гно-й́ть-ся, *v.i.r.,* to suppurate, fester; discharge pus. Ра́на гнойтся, the wound is festering.
за-гно-й́ть-ся *v.p.r.* to become festered.
на-гно-й́ть-ся, *v.p.r.,* to become festered. *v.i.r.,* see гнойться. На-гно-éние, *n.n.,* festering, suppuration. Вы́звать н., to cause suppuration.

ГОВОР-, ГОВАР-, LANGUAGE, SPEECH

говор-и́ть, *v.i.,* + *acc.,* сказа́ть, *v.p.,* to speak, say, tell. Г. по-ру́сски, to speak Russian. Г. бы́стро, to speak rapidly. Г. пра́вду в глаза́, to speak the truth to one's face. Г. речь, to deliver a speech. Как говорится, as the saying goes; as they say. Вообще́ говоря́, generally speaking. Здесь говоря́т по-англи́йски, English is spoken here. Го́вор, *n.m.,* talk, rumor; dialect, patois. Ме́стный г., local dialect. Говори́льный, *adj.,* pertaining to speech. Г. аппара́т, organ of speech, voice box. Говор-и́льня, *n.f.,* a gathering at which much is said and little accomplished. Говор-ко́м, *adv.,* in the style, manner of recitative. Говор-ли́вость, *n.f.,* talkativeness, loquacity. Говор-ли́вый, *adj.,* talkative, chatty. Говор-я́щий, *adj. part. act. pres.,* talking, speaking. Говор-у́н, *n.m.,* говору́нья, *n.f.,* (*colloq.*), talker, chatterer.
вы́-говор-ить, *v.p.,* вы-гова́р-ивать, *v.i.,* + *acc.,* to articulate, utter, pronounce; lecture, scold, reprimand. Вы́-говор-ить пéрвое сло́во, to utter one's first word. Пра́вильно в., to pronounce correctly. Мать вы́говорила ма́льчику за ша́лость, (*colloq.*), the mother scolded the boy for his pranks. Он вы́говорил себé пра́во на беспла́тное обучéние, he stipulated for himself the right to free tuition. Вы́-говор, *n.m.,* pronunciation, accent; lecture, rebuke, reprimand. Моско́вский в., a Moscow accent. Сде́лать в., to reprimand, rebuke, reprove.
до-говор-и́ть, *v.p.,* до-гова́р-ивать, *v.i.,* + *acc.,* to talk to the end; finish speaking. Он договори́л свою́ мысль, he expressed his thought completely. Он

не договори́л чего́-то, he hasn't expressed himself fully. До-гова́р-иваться, *v.i.r.,* до-говор-и́ть-ся, *v.p.r.,* о + *prep.,* to negotiate, treat, contract, agree. Д. о пла́те, to negotiate about payment. Д. до хрипоты́, to talk oneself hoarse. Д. о ми́ре, to make a treaty of peace. До-гова́р-ивающийся, *adj. part. act. pres.,* negotiating, contracting. Д-иеся сто́роны, contracting parties. До-гово́р, *n.m.,* agreement, contract; treaty, pact. Д. о нейтралитéте и не-нападéнии, treaty of neutrality and non-aggression. Торго́вый д., a commercial treaty. Заключа́ть д., to come to terms; make a treaty. До-говор-ённость, *n.f.,* agreement on a point in question. Не-до-говор-ённость, *n.f.,* lack of agreement, understanding. До-гово́р-ный, *adj.,* pertaining to a contract, agreement; contractual, stipulated.
за-говор-и́ть, *v.p.,* to recover one's speech; begin to talk. Ребёнок заговори́л, the child has begun to speak. По́здно занима́ться разгово́рами, когда́, заговори́ли пу́шки, (*express.*), it is too late to argue after the guns have begun to speak. Он вас заговори́т, he will talk your ear off. Он заговори́л с ним по-ру́сски, he started a conversation in Russian with him.
за-гова́р-ивать, *v.i.,* + *acc.,* с + *instr.,* to begin to speak; to exercise, cast a spell; to charm away (*e.g.,* a pain). З. зу́бы, to charm away a toothache, (*fig.*), to evade a question. Нéчего зу́бы загова́ривать: говори́ пря́мо! (*colloq.*), there is no use evading the question: speak up! З. с кéм-нибудь, to begin a conversation with someone.
за-говор-и́ть-ся, *v.p.r.,* to become lost in a conversation with someone. Мы заговори́лись и пропусти́ли пóезд, we were absorbed in talk and missed the train. За-гова́р-ивать-ся, *v.i.r.,* to rave, dote, talk nonsense. Больно́й стал загова́риваться, the patient began to rave. Говори́, да не загова́ривайся, (*saying*), talk away, but don't lose your head. За́-говор, *n.m.,* plot, conspiracy, secret design; charm, exorcism. Раскры́ть з., to disclose a plot. Полити́ческий з., a political conspiracy. Загово́р на любо́вь (на кровь, на доро́гу), an incantation to induce love (to stop bleeding, to insure a happy journey), За-говор-ённый, *adj. part. pass. past,* bewitched. З. клад, (*obs.*), a bewitched treasure. За-гово́р-щик, *n.m.,* conspirator. Стать загово́рщиком, to become a conspirator.
на-говор-и́ть, *v.p.,* на-гова́р-ивать, *v.i.,*

+ *acc.*, + *gen.*, на + *acc.*, to talk someone's head off; slander. Н. патефо́нную пласти́нку, (*recent*), to record. Н. неприя́тностей, to say many unpleasant things to someone. На него́ наговори́ли, он не винова́т, they have slandered him, he is not guilty. На-гово́р, *n.m.*, slander, calumny; charm, enchantment.

о-говор-и́ть, *v.p.*, о-гова́р-ивать, *v.i.*, + *acc.*, to slander, blame, defame; stipulate. О. неви́нного, to slander an innocent man. О-гово́р-и́ть-ся, *v.p.r.*, о-гова́р-ивать-ся, *v.i.r.*, to make a reservation; to use a word inadvertently. О-гово́р, *n.m.*, slander, denunciation, defamation. О-гово́р-ка, *n.f.*, reservation; clause. С огово́ркой, with reservation. Без огово́рок, without reservation. Без-о-гово́р-очно, *adv.*, without reservations, unconditionally. Приня́ть усло́вия б., to accept a contract unconditionally. О-гово́р-щик, *n.m.*, о-гово́р-щица, *n.f.*, slanderer, informer, denunciator.

от-говор-и́ть, *v.p.*, от-гова́р-ивать, *v.i.*, + *acc.*, от + *gen.*, to dissuade. Я её отговори́л от её реше́ния, I talked her out of her decision. От-гово́р-и́ть-ся, *v.p.r.*, отгова́р-ивать-ся, *v.p.r.*, + *instr.*, to feign, pretend. О. нездоро́вьем, незна́нием, to feign illness, ignorance. От-гово́р-ка, *n.f.*, pretext, pretense, subterfuge. Пуста́я о., a flimsy pretext. Он всегда́ найдёт отгово́рку, что́бы не рабо́тать, he will always find an excuse for not working. Без-от-гово́р-очно, *adv.*, literally. Вы́полнить прика́з б., to fulfill an order literally.

пере-говор-и́ть, *v.p.*, с + *instr.*, о + *prep.*, to discuss. П. с кем-ли́бо по телефо́ну, to discuss something with someone by telephone. П. о де́ле, to discuss a matter. Пере-гова́р-ивать-ся, *v.i.r.*, с + *instr.*, to converse, exchange remarks. Пере-гово́р-ный, *adj.*, negotiatory. П-ая бу́дка, telephone booth. П-ая ста́нция, telephone exchange. Пере-гово́р-ы, *n.pl.*, negotiations; parley. Вести́ п., to conduct negotiations, negotiate. Ми́рные п., peace negotiations.

по-говор-и́ть, *v.p.*, с + *instr.*, о + *prep.*, to have a short conversation, talk. Мне на́до бу́дет поговори́ть с мои́м сотру́дником о но́вом уче́бнике, I shall have to talk with my collaborator about our new textbook.

по-гова́р-ивать, *v.i.*, о + *prep.*, to talk from time to time (about something that might happen). Он погова́ривает об отъе́зде, from time to time he talks of leaving. Погова́ривают о войне́,

there are rumors of war. По-гово́р-ка, *n.f.*, a saying. Воше́дший в погово́рку, proverbial; that has become proverbial.

под-говор-и́ть, *v.p.*, под-гова́р-ивать, *v.i.*, + *acc.*, to incite, instigate. П. забастова́ть, to instigate a strike.

при-говор-и́ть, *v.p.*, при-гова́р-ивать, *v.i.*, + *acc.*, к + *dat.*, to sentence, condemn, convict. П. кого́-нибудь к сме́рти, to sentence someone to death. При-гово́р, *n.m.*, sentence, conviction, judgment. Вы́нести п., to bring in a verdict. Отмени́ть п., to reverse a judgment. П. суда́ прися́жных, (*obs.*), the verdict of a jury. При-гово́р-ённый, *adj. part. pass. past*, sentenced, convicted, condemned.

раз-гова́р-ивать, *v.i.*, с + *instr.*, to talk, speak, converse. Они́ разгова́ривают по-ру́сски, they are conversing in Russian. Переста́ньте р.! Stop talking! Раз-гово́р-и́ть-ся, *v.p.r.*, to indulge in endless talk. Я разговори́лся со свои́м сосе́дом, I got into a long conversation with my neighbor. Раз-гово́р, *n.m.*, talk, conversation. Р. о пого́де, a conversation about the weather; (*fig.*), a conversation without purpose. Р. по душа́м, a heart-to-heart talk. Раз-гово́р-ный, *adj.*, conversational. Р. язы́к, spoken language; vernacular. Р. кружо́к, a conversational circle . Раз-гово́р-чивость, *n.f.*, talkativeness. Раз-гово́р-чивый, *adj.*, talkative, garrulous.

с-говор-и́ть-ся, *v.p.r.*, с-гова́р-ивать-ся, *v.i.r.*, о + *prep.*, to agree, settle; arrange, make an appointment. С. о цене́, to agree on a price. С-гово́р, *n.m.*, agreement. С-гово́р-чивость, *n.f.*, compliancy, tractability, manageability. С-гово́р-чивый, *adj.*, compliant, tractable, agreeable, manageable.

у-говор-и́ть, *v.p.*, у-гова́р-ивать, *v.i.*, + *acc.*, to urge, persuade, induce. У. больно́го сде́лать опера́цию, to persuade a sick person to undergo an operation. У-гово́р-и́ть-ся, *v.p.r.*, у-гова́р-ивать-ся, *v.i.r.*, с + *instr.*, to agree, come to an agreement. Мы уговори́лись е́хать вме́сте, we agreed to travel together. У-гово́р, *n.m.*, agreement, understanding. С угово́ром, on condition; with the understanding. У. доро́же де́нег, (*saying*), a promise is a promise. У-гова́р-ивание, *n.n.*, persuasion, inducement, urging.

ГОД-, ГОЖ-, ГОЖД-ГАД-, SUITABILITY; YEAR; PROPITIOUSNESS

год, *n.m.*, year, twelvemonth. Бу́дущий г., next year. Про́шлый, г., last year.

Ка́ждый г., every year. Но́вый, г., the New Year, New Year's Day. Уче́бный г., school year. Ему́ 22 го́да, he is twenty-two years old. Быть разви́тым не по года́м, to be developed beyond one's years. Год-и́на, *n.f.*, (*obs.*), time, year. Тяжёлая г., hard times. Год-овщи́на, *n.f.*, anniversary. Г. сме́рти, the anniversary of a death. Год-ово́й, *adj.*, annual, yearly. Г. дохо́д, annual income. Год-и́чный, *adj.*, annual, yearly. Г. отчёт, an annual report. Год-ова́лый, *adj.*, aged one year; yearling. Г. ребёнок, a year-old child; yearling. Еже-го́д-ный, *adj.*, yearly, annual; occurring once a year. Е. докла́д, an annual lecture. Еже-го́д-ник, *n.m.*, yearbook; annual. Еже-го́д-но, *adv.*, yearly, annually, once a year. По-год-и́ть, *v.p. used only in the imperative case*: Погоди́те! Wait a moment! Just a moment! По-го́д-ки, *n.pl.*, children born at intervals of one year. По-го́д-но, *adv.*, (*obs.*), annually, yearly.

по-го́д-а, *n.f.*, weather. Дождли́вая п., rainy weather. Мя́гкая п., mild weather. По-го́ж-ий, *adj.*, (*folk*), serene, fine. П. день, a fine day. Не-по-го́д-а, *n.f.*, foul weather. Не-вз-го́д-а, *n.f.*, misfortune, adversity.

год-и́ть-ся, гож-у́сь, *v.i.*, to suit, fit. Так поступа́ть не годи́тся, such behavior is unbecoming. Она́ не годи́тся в учи́тельницы, she is not fit to be a teacher. Го́д-ность, *n.f.*, fitness, suitability. Го́д-ный, *adj.*, fit, suitable, proper; available. Г. для питья́, drinkable. Г. к слу́жбе, fit for service. Не-го́д-ный, *adj.*, unfit, improper, unsuited. Н. челове́к, a worthless person. Н. для вое́нной слу́жбы, unfit for military service.

не-год-ова́ть, *v.i.*, на + *acc.*, to be indignant. Н. на судьбу́, to resent one's fate. Не-год-ова́ние, *n.n.*, indignation. Взрыв н-ия, an outburst of indignation. Не-го́д-ник, *n.m.*, не-го́д-ница, *n.f.*, *milder than* негодя́й. Не-год-я́й, *n.m.*, wretch, villain, scoundrel.

воз-не-год-ова́ть, *v.p.*, на + *acc.*, to become indignant.

при-год-и́ть-ся, *v.p.*, + *dat.*, to be of use, be useful. Гра́моте учи́ться - всегда́ пригоди́тся (*saying*), literacy is always useful. Не плюй в коло́дец: пригоди́тся воды́ напи́ться (*prov.*), don't spit in the well—you may need to drink the water. При-го́д-ность, *n.f.*, fitness, suitability. П. к рабо́те, fitness for work. Не-при-го́д-ность, *n.f.*, unfitness, uselessness, unsuitability. При-го́д-ный, *adj.*, fit, suitable, good for. П. к

употребле́нию, fit for use. Не-при-го́д-ный, *adj.*, не-го́ж-ий, *adj.*, (*colloq.*), unfit, useless, ineffective. При-го́жий, *adj.*, (*colloq.*), comely, good-looking. П-ая де́вушка, a pretty girl.

у-год-и́ть, *v.p.*, у-гожд-а́ть, *v.i.*, + *dat.*, в + *acc.*, to humor; gratify, please. У. роди́телям, to please and obey one's parents. У. и на́шим, и ва́шим, (*derog.*), to run with the hare and hunt with the hounds. Ей не угоди́шь, she is hard to please. У-го́д-а, *n.f.*, *used only in expression*: В уго́ду, in order to please, to oblige. У-го́д-ливость, *n.f.*, officiousness; fawning; *see also* у-го́д-ничество. У-го́д-ник, *n.m.*, saint. Св. Уго́дник Никола́й, St. Nicholas. У-го́д-ничать, *v.i.*, пе́ред + *instr.*, to be officious. У-го́д-ничество, *n.n.*, officiousness; fawning. У-го́д-ный, *adj.*, officious. У-го́д-но, *adv.*, used only impersonally: Как вам у., as you please, wish. Ско́лько у., as much as you wish. Что вам у.? What will you have? Неуго́дно-ли вам хле́ба? Won't you have some bread? У-гожд-е́ние, *n.n.*, humoring; compliance.

вы́-гад-ать, *v.p.*, вы-га́д-ывать, *v.i.*, + *acc.*, to profit; save, spare; derive profit or advantage. Он вы́гадал 20 рубле́й на э́той поку́пке, he saved twenty rubles on this purchase. В. вре́мя, to save time. Вы́-год-а, *n.f.*, profit, advantage. Получа́ть вы́году, to derive profit from. Вы́-год-ность, *n.f.*, utility, advantageousness. Вы́-год-ный, *adj.*, profitable, advantageous. В-ое ме́сто, a well-paying job. В-ое де́ло, a lucrative business. Представля́ть в в-ом све́те, to show something to its best advantage, in the best light. Вы́-год-но, *adv.*, profitably.

про-гад-а́ть, *v.p.*, про-га́д-ывать, *v.i.*, (*colloq.*), на + *prep.*, to sustain a financial loss. П. при обме́не валю́ты, to lose in an exchange of currency. Купе́ц прогада́л на э́том това́ре, the merchant sustained a loss on these goods.

ГОЛ-, NUDITY

го́л-ый, *adj.*, bare, naked, nude; bald; poor, indigent. Г-ое те́ло, naked body. Г-ая пусты́ня, a barren desert. Г-ая и́стина, (*fig.*), the naked truth. Спать на го́лой земле́, to sleep on the bare ground. Гол, как соко́л (*saying*), as poor as a church mouse. Гол-ытьба́, *n.f.*, (*colloq.*), the poor, indigent. Гол-ы́ш, *n.m.* naked child; pebble. Гол-ышо́м, *adv. express.*, (*colloq.*), stark naked. Ребёнок бе́гал г., the child ran around naked. Гол-ь, *n.f.*, nakedness, nudity; bareness; poverty, the poor. Голь на вы́думки хитра́ (*prov.*), necessity is the mother of invention.

о-гол-и́ть, *v.p.,* о-гол-я́ть, *v.i.,* to denude, bare, uncover. О-гол-и́ть-ся, *v.p.r.,* о-гол-я́ть-ся, *v.i.r.,* to denude, bare oneself, strip. О-гол-ённый, *adj. part. pass. past,* nude, naked, bare, uncovered. Зимо́й дере́вья стоя́т оголённые, in winter the trees are bare.

гол-о-ле́дица, *n.f.,* glazed frost, icecrusted ground.

гол-о-сло́вный, *adj.,* unfounded, without proof. Г-ое обвине́ние, an unfounded accusation. Гол-о-сло́вность, *n.f.,* unfoundedness. Г. обвине́ния, unfoundedness of an accusation. Гол-о-сло́вно, *adv.,* without proof.

о-гол-те́лый, *adj.,* (*folk*), frantic, shameless. Что ты но́сишься, как о.? Why are you behaving so frantically?

ГОЛУБ(Ь), PIGEON, DOVE; BLUENESS

го́луб-ь, *n.m.,* pigeon, dove. Лесно́й г., wood pigeon. Почто́вый г., carrier pigeon. Си́зый г., rock dove. Голуб-о́к, *n.m.,* young pigeon, dove. Голу́б-ка, *n.f.,* female pigeon (*fig.*), see голу́бушка. Новобра́чные живу́т, как г-ки, the newly-weds live like a pair of turtledoves. Голуб-и́ца, *n.f.,* (*obs.*), hen pigeon, little dove. Голуб-я́тник, *n.m.,* pigeon breeder, pigeon fancier. Голуб-я́тня, *n.f.,* pigeon house, dovecote. Голуб-и́ный, *adj.,* dovelike. Г-ое гнездо́, pigeon nest. Г-ая по́чта, mail delivery by carrier pigeon; pigeon post. Г-ая кро́тость, dovelike meekness.

голу́бить, *v.i.,* при-голу́б-ить, *v.p.,* + *acc.,* to caress, fondle. Приходи́ ко мне, мой ми́лый, приголу́бь и обогре́й... (*folksong*), come to me, my dear, caress and comfort me. Голу́б-чик, *n.m.,* голу́б-ка, *n.f.,* голу́б-ушка, *n.f.,* darling, dear.

голуб-е́-ть, *v.i.,* по-голуб-е́ть, за-голуб-е́ть,, *v.p.,* to become sky-blue in color. Вдали́ голубе́ли го́ры, in the distance the mountains appeared a soft bluegrey. Голубо́й, *adj.,* blue, azure, skyblue. Г-о́е мо́ре, не́бо, a blue sea, sky. Г-а́я кра́ска, azure, blue paint, color. Голубова́тый, *adj.,* bluish grey. Г-о́е пла́тье, a bluish-grey dress. Голуб-о-гла́зый, *adj.,* blue-eyed. Г-ый ребёнок, a blue-eyed child. Голуб-изна́, *n.f.,* azure blue. Г. не́ба, the azure blue of the sky. Голуб-и́ца, *n.f.,* blackberry.

ГОР-, HILL, MOUNTAIN

гор-а́, *n.f.,* mountain, mount. Высо́кая г., high mountain. Г. книг, a pile of books. В го́ру, uphill. Поднима́ться в го́ру тяжело́, it is difficult to go uphill. Идти́ в го́ру, (*fig.*), to rise in one's career. Под гору, downhill. Он за меня́ горо́й, he defends me in every way. Го́р-ец, *n.m.,* гор-я́нка, *n.f.,* mountaineer, highlander. Го́р-ка, *n.f.,* small hill, hillock; cabinet, whatnot. Кра́сная г., (*fig.*), the first week after Easter. Гор-и́стый, *adj.,* mountainous. Г-ая ме́стность, a mountainous region. Гор-н-о-заво́дчик, *n.m.,* proprietor of a foundry. Гор-н-о-заво́дский, *adj.,* pertaining to the metallurgical and mining industries. Гор-н-о-рабо́чий, *n.m.,* miner. Го́р-ный, *adj.,* mountainous. Г. инжене́р, mining engineer. Г. прохо́д, mountain pass. Г. хруста́ль, rock crystal. Г-ая цепь, mountain chain. Гор-ня́к, *n.m.,* mining engineer, student. Лы́жник-горня́к, skier specializing in mountain skiing. На-го́р-ный, *adj.,* upland, mountainous; pertaining to highlands. Н. бе́рег реки́, the hilly bank of a river. Вз-го́р-ье, *n.n.,* на-го́р-ье, *n.n.,* upland, highlands. Под-го́р-ье, *n.n.,* lowland. Пред-го́р-ье, *n.n.,* foothills. Предго́рья Кавка́за, the foothills of the Caucasus Mountains. При-го́р-ок, *n.m.,* hillock, small hill.

го́р-ница, *n.f.,* (*obs.*), chamber, room. Го́р-ничная, *n.f.,* chambermaid, servant.

ГОР-, ГОР(ЬК)-, ГОР(К)-, ГОР(Ч)-, BITTERNESS, GRIEF, WOE

го́р-е, *n.n.,* grief, sorrow, misfortune, woe. Безуте́шное г., inconsolable grief. Обезу́меть от го́ря, to be beside oneself with grief. Мы́кать г., (*folk*), to live poorly. С го́ря, out of grief. Запи́ть с го́ря, to drown one's sorrow in drink. Го́рю слеза́ми не помо́жешь, (*saying*), you will not help your sorrow with tears. Го́р-есть, *n.f.,* (*obs.*), sorrow, grief, misfortune, woe. Го́р-естный, *adj.,* sorrowful, sad, distressing. Го́р-естно, *adv.,* sadly, sorrowfully.

гор-ева́ть, *v.i.,* по-гор-ева́ть, *v.p.,* о + *prep.,* to grieve, be sick at heart. Он горю́ет о поко́йной жене́, he is grieving for his deceased wife. Погорева́л, да и уте́шился, his sorrow was shortlived. Гор-е-мы́ка, *n.m.,* (*folk., poet.*), poor wretch. Гор-е-мы́чный, *adj.,* wretched, miserable. за-гор-нва́ть *v.p.,* to begin to grieve.

при-гор-ю́н-ить-ся, *v.p.r.,* (*folk*), to become sad, be dejected. Кра́сная де́вица пригорю́нилась, (*folksong*), the beautiful maiden became sad.

го́р-ьк-ий, *adj.*, bitter; (*fig.*), sad, painful. Г. минда́ль, bitter almond. Г. пья́ница, a hard drinker. Г-ая до́ля, bitter fate. Г-ая и́стина, the bitter truth. Г-ие воспомина́ния, sad memories. Го́р-ьк-о, *adv.*, bitterly; (*fig.*), painfully. У меня́ во рту г., I have a bitter taste in my mouth.

го́р-к-ну-ть, *v.i.*, про-го́рк-нуть, *v.p.*, to grow rancid. От жары́ ма́сло го́ркнет, butter becomes rancid from heat. Го́р-еч-ь, *n.f.*, bitter taste, bitterness. Г. жи́зни сиро́тской, the bitterness of an orphan's life.

гор-ч-и́ть, *v.i.*, to have a bitter taste. Несве́жее ма́сло горчи́т, rancid butter has a bitter taste. Гор-ч-и́ца, *n.f.*, mustard. Гор-ч-и́ч-ник, *n.m.*, mustard plaster. Ста́вить кому́-либо горчи́чник на грудь, to apply a mustard plaster to someone's chest. Гор-ч-и́чница, *n.f.*, mustard pot. Гор-чи́чный, *adj.*, pertaining to mustard. Г. газ, mustard gas. Г-ое зерно́, mustard seed.

о-гор-ч-и́ть, *v.p.*, о-гор-ч-а́ть, *v.i.*, + *acc.*, to distress, chagrin; vex, afflict. Изве́стие о боле́зни ма́тери меня́ огорчи́ло, the news of my mother's illness grieved me. О-гор-ч-и́ть-ся, *v.p.r.*, о-гор-ч-а́ть-ся, *v.i.r.*, + *instr.*, to be grieved; feel sorry, sad. О. неуда́чей, to be grieved by failure. Мы о́чень огорчи́лись, узна́в о ва́шей поте́ре, we were sorry to hear of your loss. О-горч-е́ние, *n.n.*, distress, chagrin, grief. С глубо́ким огорче́нием, with deep regret. О-гор-чё́нный, *adj.*, *part. pass. past*, distressed, grieved, embittered. О. отка́зом от рабо́ты, grieved by the refusal of a job.

ГОРЛ-, ЖЕРЛ-, ORIFICE, MOUTH, THROAT

го́рл-о, *n.n.*, throat. Дыха́тельное г., windpipe. Быть сы́тым по го́рло (*idiom*), to have had one's fill. У меня́ боли́т г., I have a sore throat. Крича́ть во всё г., (*colloq.*), to shout at the top of one's voice. Нае́сться по г., (*colloq.*), to stuff oneself. Го́рл-ышко, *n.n.*, throat; neck (*of a vessel*). Г. буты́лки, the neck of a bottle. Горл-ово́й, *adj.*, pertaining to the throat. Г. ка́шель, a throat cough. Горл-о-дё́р, *n.m.*, (*slang*), alcoholic beverage that burns the throat.

горл-а́н-ить, *v.i.*, (*colloq.*), to bawl, yell, squall. Горл-а́н, *n.m.*, brawler, noisy person.

о-жере́л-(ь)-е, *n.n.*, necklace. Жемчу́жное о., a pearl necklace.

жерл-о́, *n.n.*, crater, *syn.*, отве́рстие. Ж. вулка́на, the crater of a volcano. Ж. пу́шки, ору́дия, muzzle (of a cannon).

ги́рл-а, *n.pl.*, delta. Г. Днепра́, Дуна́я, the delta of the Dnieper, Danube.

ГОРОД-, ГРАД-, ГОРОЖ-, ГРАЖД-, ГОРАЖ-, ENCLOSURE, CITY

го́род, *n.m.*, град, (*Ch.-Sl.*, *obs.*), town, city. Гла́вный г., chief city, capital. Жить за́ городом, to live out of town, in the suburbs. Город-и́шко, *n.n.*, provincial town. Город-о́к, *n.m.*, small town. Город-ни́чий, *adj. used as n.*, (*obs.*), the prefect of a town. Городово́й, *n.m.*, (*obs.*), policeman. Городско́й, *adj.*, urban, metropolitan, pertaining to a city. Г. голова́, (*obs.*), mayor. Г-ая ду́ма, (*obs.*), city council. Г-ое населе́ние, urban population. Гóрисполко́м, (*recent, abbr. of* городско́й исполни́тельный комите́т) city council (*literally*; city executive committee). Пред-гор-ко́м, (*recent, abbr. of* председа́тель городско́го комите́та) mayor (*literally*: chairman of the city committee). Гор-оно́, (*recent, abbr. of* городско́й отде́л наро́дного образова́ния), city department of education (*literally*: city department of national enlightenment). При-го́род, *n.m.*, suburb. При́-город-ный, *adj.*, suburban. П. по́езд, suburban train. П-ое сообще́ние, suburban railroad. Вин-о-гра́д, *n.m.*, grapes, grapevine. Вин-о-гра́дник, *n.m.*, vineyard.

горож-а́нин, *n.m.*, townsman, city dweller. Горож-а́нка, *n.f.*, townswoman. Горож-а́не, *n.pl.*, townsfolk; city dwellers.

гражд-а́нин, *n.m.*, гражд-а́нка, *n.f.*, citizen. Гра́жд-ане, *n.pl.*, citizens. Гражд-а́нство, *n.n.*, citizenship. Получи́ть права́ гражда́нства, to obtain one's citizenship. Гражд-а́нский, *adj.*, civil, social, civic. Г. долг, civic duty. Г. брак, civil marriage. Г-ая война́, civil war. Г-ое пра́во, civil law.

город-и́-ть, **горож-у́**, *v.i.*, + *acc.*, to hedge, fence. Г. огоро́д (*fig.*), to make a fuss. Не́чего бы́ло огоро́д г., it was no use making such a fuss. Г. чушь, (*colloq.*), to talk nonsense. Город-ки́, skittles, *used in the expression*: игра́ть в городки́, to play skittles.

вы́-город-ить, *v.p.*, вы-гора́ж-ивать, *v.i.*, + *acc.*, to support; justify; excuse. В. себя́, to justify oneself.

за-город-и́ть, *v.p.*, за-гора́ж-ивать, *v.i.*, + *acc.*, to enclose, fence, block. З.

путь, to block, obstruct a way. З. свет, to stand in someone's light. За-город-и́ть-ся, *v.p.r.*, за-гора́ж-ивать-ся, *v.i.r.*, to barricade oneself. За-горо́д-ка, *n.f.*, partition, fence. За́-город-ный, *adj.*, suburban. З. дом, a house in the suburbs. За-гора́ж-ивание, *n.n.*, enclosure, enclosing.

за-град-и́ть, *v.p.*, за-гражд-а́ть, *v.i.*, + *acc.*, to barricade, obstruct. З. прохо́д, to block a passageway, stand in someone's way. За-гражд-е́ние (про́волоч-ное), *n.n.*, (wire) entanglement, barrier. За-град-и́тельный, *adj.*, protective; blocking a way. З. отря́д, (*mil.*), defensive detachment of troops.

на-град-и́ть, *v.p.*, на-гора́ж-ивать, *v.i.*, + *acc.*, + *gen.*, to pile, heap. Н. перего́род-ки, to build numerous partitions. Н. вздо́ру, (*colloq.*), to talk nonsense.

на-град-и́ть, *v.p.*, на-гражд-а́ть, *v.i.*, + *acc.*, to reward, decorate, recompense. Он награждён о́рденом за хра́брость, he was decorated for bravery. Приро́да награди́ла его́ больши́ми спосо́бностями к матема́тике, nature endowed him with great mathematical abilities. На-гра́д-а, *n.f.*, reward, prize. На-град-ны́е, *adj. pl. used as n.*, bonus. На-гражд-е́ние, *n.n.*, reward, decoration (with an order, medal).

воз-на-град-и́ть, *v.p.*, воз-на-гражд-а́ть, *v.i.*, + *acc.*, + *instr.*, за + *acc.*, to reward, remunerate. В. кого́-либо за убы́тки, to recompense someone for damages, losses. В. за слу́жбу, to reward someone for services. Воз-на-град-и́ть-ся, *v.p.r.*, воз-на-гражд-а́ть-ся, *v.i.r.*, + *instr.*, to be rewarded. Воз-на-гражд-е́ние, *n.n.*, reward, recompense. Доба́вочное в., supplementary reward.

о-град-и́ть, *v.p.*, о-гражд-а́ть, *v.i.*, + *acc.*, to enclose, fence; defend, guard. О. го́род стена́ми, to surround a city with walls. О. себя́ от волне́ний, to protect oneself from worries.

о-град-и́ть-ся, *v.p.r.*, огражд-а́ть-ся, *v.i.r.*, от + *gen.*, to defend, guard oneself; to be defended, guarded from, against. О-гра́д-а, *n.f.*, fence, enclosure, wall. О. кла́дбища, cemetery fence, wall. О-град-и́тельный, *adj.*, defensive, protective. О-гражд-е́ние, *n.n.*, enclosure, defense.

о-город-и́ть, *v.p.*, о-гора́ж-ивать, *v.i.*, + *acc.*, to enclose, fence. О. сад забо́ром, to fence in a garden.

о-город-и́ть-ся, *v.p.r.*, о-гора́ж-ивать-ся, *v.i.r.*, + *instr.*, to fence oneself in, be fenced in with, by. О-горо́д, *n.m.*, kitchen garden. О-горо́д-ник, *n.m.*, gardener. О-горо́д-ный, *adj.*, pertaining to gardening. О-горо́ж-енный, *adj. part. pass. past*, enclosed, fenced in. Из-город-ь, *n.f.*, fence. Жива́я и., hedge.

пере-город-и́ть, *v.p.*, пере-гора́ж-ивать, *v.i.*, + *acc.*, to partition, screen. Пере-город-и́ть-ся, *v.p.r.*, пере-гора́ж-ивать-ся, *v.i.r.*, + *instr.*, to be partitioned. Пере-горо́д-ка, *n.f.*, partition, screen.

пре-град-и́ть, *v.p.*, пре-гражд-а́ть, *v.i.*, + *acc.*, to obstruct, block up. П. путь, to block the way. Пре-гражд-а́ть-ся, *v.i.r.*, to be obstructed, barred, impeded. Пре-гражд-е́ние, *n.n.*, hindering, blocking up. Пре-гра́д-а, *n.f.*, obstacle, obstruction, bar. П. на пути́, road barrier. Воображе́ние прегра́д не зна́ет, imagination knows no obstacles.

раз-город-и́ть, *v.p.*, раз-гора́ж-ивать, *v.i.*, + *acc.*, to take down a fence; to hedge off; separate, divide. Р. и́зго-родь, to take down a fence. Р. дом, ко́мнату, to divide a yard, room into sections. Раз-город-и́ть-ся, *v.p.r.*, раз-гора́ж-ивать-ся, *v.i.r.*, + *instr.*, to hedge, fence oneself off.

ГОСПОД-, ГОСПОЖ-, ГОСУД-, (СУД-), MASTERY, DOMINANCE; THE LORD

Гос-по́д-ь, *n.m.*, God, the Lord. Г. Бог, the Lord God. Го́споди! *interj.*, Lord! Oh, Lord! Г. его́ зна́ет, (*express.*), the Lord only knows. Го́споди! да что́-же э́то тако́е! (*interj.*), Lord! how can this be! Не дай Го́споди! God forbid! Гос-по́д-ень, *adj.*, pertaining to the Lord. Моли́тва Госпо́дня, the Lord's prayer.

гос-под-и́н, *n.m.*, lord, master; mister; gentleman, господа́, *n.pl.*, Sirs, gentlemen; (*obs.*), the masters, squires. Я сам себе́ господи́н, I am my own master. Быть господи́ном своего́ сло́ва, (*express.*), to keep one's promises. Господа́, пойдёмте обе́дать, gentlemen, let us dine. Госпо́д-ский, *adj.*, (*obs.*), manorial. Г. дом, (*obs.*), manor house.

госпож-а́, *n.f.*, lady, mistress; Mrs.

госпо́д-ствовать, *v.i.*, над + *instr.*, to dominate, predominate, rule, reign, sway. Здесь госпо́дствуют ю́го-за́падные ве́тры, here southwesterly winds prevail. Госпо́д-ство, *n.n.*, domination, predominance, prevalence, sway. XX век — век госпо́дства челове́ка над во́здухом, the twentieth century is the century of man's mastery over the air. Госпо́д-ствующий, *adj. part. act. pres.*, predominant, dominating, prevalent. Заня́ть г-ее положе́ние, to occupy a dominant position. Г-ее (преоблада́ющее) мне́ние, predominating opinion.

госуд-а́рь, *n.m.,* Tsar, sovereign prince; Sire (*in direct address*). Государь всея Руси́ (*hist.*), Sovereign of all Russia. Ми́лостивый г., (*obs.*), *form of polite address,* Sir. Госуд-а́рство, *n.n.,* state, country, body politic; realm, empire, kingdom, republic. Госуд-а́рыня, *n.f.,* tsarina. Ми́лостивая г., (*obs.*), Madam (*in direct address*). Госуд-а́рственный, *adj.,* pertaining to a state, country. Г. де́ятель, statesman. Г. ум, a statesman's mind. Г. долг, a national debt. Г. переворо́т, a coup d'état. Г-ая Ду́ма (*hist.*), Duma (*pre-Rev. parliament*). Гос-, *abbr. of* государственный, a *combining form meaning* (Soviet) governmental, state, *in such expressions as:* Госаппара́т, *abbr. of* госуда́рственный аппара́т, machinery of State. Госба́нк, *abbr. of* госуда́рственный банк, State bank. Госизда́т, *abbr. of* госуда́рственное изда́тельство, government printing house.

су́д-арь, *n.m.,* (*obs.*), Sir; *abbr. of* государь. Суд-а́рыня, *n.f.,* (*obs.*), Madam; *abbr. of* госуда́рыня.

ГОСТ-, ГОЩ-, GUEST, HOST

гост-ь, *n.m.,* го́ст-(ь)-я, *n.f.,* guest, visitor; (*hist.*), merchant. Незва́ный гость ху́же тата́рина, (*prov., hist.*), an uninvited guest is worse than a Tartar. Го́ст-и, *n.pl.,* guests, company. Идти́ в го́сти, to go visiting. Обе́дать в гостя́х, to dine out. В гостя́х хорошо́, а до́ма лу́чше, (*saying*), East or West, home is best. Гост-и́н-ая, *adj., used as n.,* living room, parlor. Гости́ный двор, (*pre-Rev.*), stores, arcades, bazaars in Russian cities. Гост-и́н-иц-а, *n.f.,* hotel, inn. Содержа́тель г-ы, *n.m.,* innkeeper. Гост-е-прии́мство, *n.n.,* hospitality. Ру́сский наро́д сла́вится г-ом, the Russian people are renowned for their hospitality. Гост-е-прии́мный, *adj.,* hospitable. Гост-е-прии́мно, *adv.,* hospitably. Гост-и́н-ец, *n.m.,* present, gift.

гост-й-ть, **гощ-у́,** *v.i.,* + *acc.;* у + *gen.,* to be on a visit, stay with. Мы всё ле́то гости́ли у ро́дственников, we stayed with relatives all summer. Я гощу́ у своего́ дру́га, I am visiting my friend. За-гост-и́ть-ся, *v.p.r.,* to visit too long, overstay one's welcome.

по-гост-и́ть, *v.p.,* to visit for a short time. Мы погости́м у них два, три дня, we shall visit them for two or three days. По-го́ст, *n.m.,* country church-yard.

у-гост-и́ть, *v.p.,* у-гощ-а́ть, *v.i.,* + *acc.,* + *instr.,* to treat, regale, entertain. Нас угости́ли хоро́шим обе́дом, they entertained us with a good dinner. Пожа́луйста, угоща́йтесь! Please, help yourself У-гощ-е́ние, *n.n.,* refreshments; treat. Вку́сное у., a real treat, tasty refreshments.

ГОТОВ-, ГОТАВ-, READINESS, PREPARATION

гото́в-и-ть, *v.i.,* при-гото́в-ить, *v.p.,* + *acc.,* to prepare, make ready; provide, cook; dress (*e.g.,* food). Г. обе́д, to prepare dinner. Г. кни́гу к печа́ти, to prepare a book for publication. Г. уро́к, to prepare, learn a lesson. "Что день гряду́щий мне гото́вит?" (Pushkin), "The day to come, what is it preparing for me?" Гото́в-ить-ся, *v.i.r.,* при-гото́в-ить-ся, *v.p.r.,* к + *dat.,* to prepare oneself, to be preparing. Г. к экза́мену, to prepare for an examination. Пригото́виться к путеше́ствию, to prepare for a trip. Гото́в-ность, *n.f.,* readiness, preparedness; disposition. Выража́ть с гото́вности, to consent, offer. В боево́й гото́вности (*mil.*), in fighting trim. Гото́в-ый, *adj.,* ready, prepared, apt. Г. к услу́гам (*obs.*), Yours truly. Г-ое пла́тье, ready-made clothing. Будь гото́в к труду́ и оборо́не! (*recent; Soviet slogan*), be prepared for work and defense. Гото́в-о, *adv.,* ready.

за-гото́в-ить, *v.p.,* за-гото́в-ля́ть, *v.i.,* за-гота́в-ливать, *v.i., iter.,* + *acc.,* to purvey, procure supplies, store, stock. З. дрова́ на́ зиму, to store wood for the winter. За-гото́в-ка, *n.f.,* purveyance, provision of stocks of food, supply of provisions. Хле́бо-загото́вка, (*recent*), the storing of grain. За-готов-ле́ние, *n.n.,* storing, stocking, providing.

из-гото́в-ить, *v.p.,* из-готов-ля́ть, *v.i.,* из-гота́в-ливать, *v.i., iter.,* + *acc.,* to prepare, make, manufacture. И. зака́з, to carry out an order. Из-готов-ле́ние, *n.n.,* preparation, manufacture, production. На-из-гото́в-ку, in readiness. Держа́ть винто́вку н., (*mil.*), to keep a rifle in readiness.

на-гото́в-ить, *v.p.,* на-гота́в-ливать, *v.i.,* + *acc.,* + *gen.,* to prepare in great quantities, make ready, keep a store of. Н. це́лый склад дров, to prepare a whole stock of firewood. Н. к обе́ду вся́кой вся́чины, to prepare a lot of all kinds of food for dinner. На-гото́в-ить-ся, *v.p.r.,* to prepare oneself. На всех не наготовишься, (*idiom*), no matter how much one prepares, one will never be ready. На-гото́в-е, *adv.,* on call.

Быть н., to be ready. Держа́ть во́йско н., to keep troops in readiness.

под-гото́в-ить, *v.p.*, под-готов-ля́ть, *v.i.*, под-гота́в-ливать, *v.i.*, *iter.*, + *acc.*, to prepare, make ready beforehand. П. ученика́ к экза́мену, to prepare a pupil for an examination. Под-готов-и́тель-ный, *adj.*, preparatory. П-ые рабо́ты, preparatory work. Под-гото́в-ить-ся, *v.p.r.*, под-готов-ля́ть-ся, *v.i.r.*, к + *dat.*, под-гота́в-ливать-ся, *v.i.r.*, *iter.*, to prepare oneself for a definite objective. Под-гото́в-ка, *n.f.*, preparation. П. ка́дров, (*recent*), personnel training. П. к войне́, preparation for war. Под-гото́в-ленный, *adj. part. pass. past*, prepared. Хорошо́ п. студе́нт, well grounded student.

при-гото́в-ить, *v.p.*, при-готов-ля́ть, *v.i.*, + *acc.*, to prepare. П. лека́рство, to prepare a medicine. При-гото́в-ить-ся, *v.p.r.*, при-готов-ля́ть-ся, *v.i.r.*, к + *dat.*, при-гота́в-ливать-ся, *v.i.r.*, *iter.*, to prepare oneself, be prepared. П. к наступле́нию, to prepare for an offensive. При-готов-ле́ние, *n.n.*, preparation. Без приготовле́ния, off hand, impromptu. При-гото́в-ленный, *adj. part. pass. past*, prepared, ready. При-гото́в-и́тельный, *adj.*, preparatory. П. класс, preparatory class. П-ая шко́ла, preparatory school. При-гото́в-и́шка, *n.m. or f.*, (school, *slang*), a preparatory school pupil.

у-гото́в-ить, *v.p.*, у-готов-ля́ть, *v.i.*, + *acc.*, (*obs., poet.*), to prepare, make ready. Судьба́ уготовила мне тяжё́лую жизнь, fate has prepared a hard life for me.

ГРЕБ-, ГРЕС-, ГРАБ-, ГРОБ-, INTERMENT, BURIAL, EXCAVATION; THIEVERY, SPOLIATION

гре́б-ень, *n.m.*, греб-ё́нка, *n.f.*, comb. Петуши́ный г., cock's comb. Ча́стый г., a fine-tooth comb. Г. волны́, the crest of a wave. Стричь под гребё́нку, to cut hair close to the scalp, crop. Греб-ё́нчатый, *adj.*, comb-like. Греб-енщи́к, *n.m.*, comb maker. Греб-ешо́к, *n.m.*, a small comb.

греб-е́ц, *n.m.*, oarsman. Греб-но́й, *adj.*, pertaining to rowing. Г. спорт, rowing. Г-а́я ло́дка, rowboat.

грес-ти́, греб-у́, *v.i.*, + *instr.*, to row, pull, stroke. Г. одни́м весло́м, to paddle.

вы́-грес-ти, *v.p.*, вы-греб-а́ть, *v.i.*, + *acc.*, to rake together out. В. золу́ из пе́чки, to rake ashes out of a stove. Вы́-гребна́я, *adj.*, *in expression*: в-а́я я́ма, cesspool.

за-грес-ти́, *v.p.*, за-греб-а́ть, *v.i.*, + *acc.*, to rake together. З. се́но, to rake hay Он загреба́ет больши́е де́ньги (*colloq.*), he rakes in a lot of money. Чужи́ми рука́ми жар загреба́ть (*saying*), to make someone else pull one's chestnuts out of the fire.

от-грес-ти́, *v.p.*, от-греб-а́ть, *v.i.*, + *acc.*, to rake away; shovel away; row away. О. снег от двере́й. to shovel snow away from a door.

под-грес-ти́, *v.p.*, под-греб-а́ть, *v.i.*, + *acc.*, to rake up, scrape up.

раз-грес-ти́, *v.p.*, раз-греб-а́ть, *v.i.*, + *acc.*, to rake, scrape away, shovel away. Р. снег лопа́той, to shovel snow away.

с-грес-ти́, *v.p.*, с-греб-а́ть, *v.i.*, + *acc.*, to rake off. С. снег с кры́ши, to shovel snow from a roof. С. в оха́пку (*colloq.*), to grab. Су-гро́б, *n.m.*, snowdrift.

гра́б-арь, *n.m.*, digger; *see* землеко́п. Гра́б-ли, *n.pl.*, rake. Ко́нные г., horsedrawn rake.

гроб, *n.m.*, coffin, casket. Класть в г., to place into a coffin. Свести́ в г., (*fig.*), to cause some one's death (*literally*: to drive someone into his grave. По́мнить до гро́ба, to remember something to one's dying day. Гроб-ни́ца, *n.f.*, tomb, sepulchre, reliquary, sarcophagus. Гроб-овщи́к, *n.m.*, coffin maker; undertaker. Гроб-ово́й, *adj.*, sepulchral; pertaining to a coffin, grave. До гробово́й доски́, (*fig.*), to one's dying day. Г-о́е молча́ние, deathly silence.

за-гро́б-ный, *adj.*, beyond the grave. З. го́лос, a voice from the dead. З-ая жизнь, the hereafter.

по-греб-а́ть, *v.i.*, по-грес-ти́, *v.p.*, + *acc.*, to bury, inter. По-греб-е́ние, *n.n.*, interment, funeral. По-греб-а́льный, *adj.*, funeral. П. звон, funeral bell, toll. П-ое пе́ние, choral singing at a funeral. По́-греб, *n.m.*, cellar. Ви́нный п., wine cellar. Порохово́й п., powder magazine.

гра́б-и-ть, *v.i.*, + *acc.*, to rob, plunder, strip, loot, sack. Граб-ё́ж, *n.m.*, robbery, plunder, pillage; burgláry. Граб-и́тель, *n.m.*, robber, burglar, plunderer. Ггаб-и́тельский, *adj.*, predatory.

на-гра́б-ить, *v.p.*, + *gen.*, to amass through robbery, plunder. Н. де́нег, to amass a fortune illegally.

о-гра́б-ить, *v.p.*, *see* гра́бить. О-гра́б-ленный, *adj. part. pass. past*, robbed, plundered, looted. Он был огра́блен до после́дней руба́шки, he was robbed even of the shirt off his back. О-граб-ле́ние, *n.n.*, burglary, theft, robbery, plunder.

раз-гра́б-ить, *v.p.,* раз-граб-ля́ть, *v.i.,* + *acc.,* to plunder, ransack, loot. Р. ла́вку, иму́щество, to loot a shop, property. Раз-граб-ле́ние, *n.n.,* plunder, pillage, looting.

ГРЕМ-, ГРОМ-, THUNDER, DESTRUCTION, RUIN

грем-е́-ть, *v.i.,* to thunder, roll, rattle, roar; (*fig.*), resound. Гром греми́т, it is thundering. Пу́шки гремя́т, the cannons are roaring. Не греми́ посу́дой, don't rattle the dishes! Грем-я́щий, *adj. part. act. pres.,* thundering. Грему́чий,* *adj.,* rattling. Г-ая змея́, rattlesnake.

за-грем-е́ть, *v.p.,* of греме́ть. Вдруг загреме́л гром, suddenly it began to thunder.

от-грем-е́ть, *v.p., used only in 3d pers.,* to become silent after rumbling.

по-грем-е́ть, *v.p. of* греме́ть. По-грему́шка, *n.f.,* a baby rattle.

про-грем-е́ть, *v.p. of* греме́ть. Его́ сла́ва прогреме́ла по всей Евро́пе, his fame resounded through all Europe.

гром, *n.m.,* thunder, thunderbolt. Г. аплодисме́нтов, thunderous applause. Г. пу́шек, the thunder of cannons. Гром-о-ве́ржец, *n.m.,* The Thunderer (Jupiter). Гром-о-отво́д, *n.m.,* a lightning conductor. Гром-ово́й, *adj.,* thunderous.

гро́м-кий, *adj.,* loud, sonorous, stentorian; (*fig.*), famous. Г. го́лос, a loud voice. Г-ое и́мя, a well-known, famous name. Гро́м-ко, *adv.,* loudly, aloud. Гром-ко-говори́тель, *n.m.,* loud-speaker. Гром-о-гла́сный, (from гром-ко-гла́сный), *adj.,* loud, loud-voiced. Гром-о-гла́сно, *adv.,* openly, loudly, in a loud voice. Объявля́ть что-ли́бо г., to declare, announce something openly.

гром-ых-а́-ть, *v.i.,* to rumble, rattle. Вдали́ громыха́ет гром, thunder is rumbling in the distance. Подво́да громыха́ла по доро́ге, the wagon rattled along the road. Гром-ыха́ние, *n.n.,* rumble, rumbling. Гром-ыха́ющий, *adj. part. act. pres.,* rumbling, rattling.

гром-и́-ть, *v.i.,* по-гром-и́ть, раз-гром-и́ть, *v.p.,* + *acc.,* to destroy, ruin; thunder. Г. врага́, *n.m.,* rout the enemy. Погро́м, *n.m.,* destruction. Раз-гро́м, *n.m.,* destruction, rout, defeat. Р. в дому́ (*colloq.*), havoc in one's home. Гром-и́ла, *n.m.,* burglar.

ГРЕХ-, ГРЕШ-, SIN

грех, *n.m.,* sin, transgression, fault. Соверши́ть грех, to commit a sin. Г.

сказа́ть, it would be unjust to say. С грехо́м попола́м (*idiom*), with difficulty; so-so. Грех-о́вность, *n.f.,* sinfulness, peccability. Грех-о́вный, *adj.,* sinful, peccable. Грех-о-во́дник, *n.m.,* (*obs.*), sinner, transgressor. Грех-о-паде́ние, *n.n.,* the Fall of man.

греш-и́-ть, греш-у́, *v.i.,* про́тив + *gen.,* to do wrong, err. Г. про́тив здра́вого смы́сла, to sin against common sense. Гре́ш-ник, *n.m.,* гре́ш-ница, *n.f.,* sinner, transgressor, offender. Гре́ш-ный, *adj.,* sinful, peccable. Греш-о́к, *n.m.* (*colloq.*), peccadillo, a trifling offense.

на-греш-и́ть, *v.p.,* to accumulate sins.

по-греш-и́ть, *v.p.,* по-греш-а́ть, *v.i.,* про́тив, + *gen.,* to err, sin, make mistakes. П. про́тив и́стины, to sin against truth. Не-по-греш-и́мость, *n.f.,* infallibility, impeccability. До́гмат па́пской непогреши́мости, the doctrine of Papal infallibility. Не-по-греш-и́мый, *adj. part. pass. pres.,* infallible, impeccable. По-гре́ш-ность, *n.f.,* error, mistake.

пре-греши́ть, *v.p.,* пре-греш-а́ть, *v.i.,* (*rel.*), to commit great sins. П. про́тив за́поведей, to sin against the commandments. Пре-греш-е́ние, *n.n.,* grave sin.

со-греш-и́ть, *v.p.,* со-греш-а́ть, *v.i.,* to sin, trespass, offend; *see* греши́ть. Со-греш-е́ние, *n.n.,* act of committing a sin, transgression; sin.

ГРОЗ-, ГРОЖ-, THUNDER, THREAT, MENACE, TERROR

гроз-а́, *n.f.,* thunder-storm; (*fig.*), danger; calamity, misfortune, disaster; terror. Г. с ли́внем, a thunder shower. Этот учи́тель - гроза́ всех шко́льников, this teacher is the terror of the school. Гро́з-ный, *adj.,* threatening, menacing, terrible. Г. при́знак, a threatening symptom. Ива́н Гро́зный, Ivan the Terrible. Гроз-ово́й, *adj.,* pertaining to storm, thunder. Г-ые ту́чи, thunder clouds.

гроз-и́-ть, грож-у́, *v.i.,* + *dat.,* + *instr.,* грози́ть, + *instr.* Грози́ть палко́й (кулако́м), to shake a stick (fist) at someone.

по-гроз-и́ть, при-гроз-и́ть, *v.p. of* грози́ть, + *instr.* Пригрози́ть наказа́нием, to threaten with punishment.

у-грож-а́ть, *v.i. syn.* грози́ть. У-грожа́ющий, *adj. part. act. pres.,* threatening, menacing. У. ме́стью, threatening vengeance. У-ая опа́сность, imminent danger. У-грож-а́юще, *adv.,* threateningly, menacingly. Смотре́ть у., to look menacingly. У-гро́з-а, *n.f.,* threat, menace, danger. У. дождя, threat of rain. У. войны, threat of war.

ГРОМАД-, ГРОМОЗД-, ГРОМОЖД-, MULTITUDE, MAGNITUDE; IMMENSITY, ENORMITY

громáд-а, *n.f.,* mass, bulk, heap, pile; social group, political party, assembly. Громáда дворцóв, the grandeur of many palaces. Громáда гор, a great mass of mountains. Громáд-ина, *n.f.,* a huge object; a very tall person. Что за г. э́тот борéц, what a huge man this wrestler is. Громáд-ность, *n.f.,* hugeness, enormity. Громáд-ный, *adj.,* huge, enormous, vast.

громозд-и́-ть, *v.i.,* на-громозд-и́ть, *v.p.,* + *acc.,* to heap, pile one thing upon another. Г. мéбель, to crowd furniture. Г. кни́ги, to pile up books. Громозд-и́ть-ся, *v.i.r.,* to tower. Г. оди́н на другóм, to be piled up one on top of another. Громóзд-кий, *adj.,* cumbersome, unwieldy. Г-ая мéбель, heavy, cumbersome furniture.

вз-громозд-и́ть, *v.p.,* вз-громожд-á́ть, *v.i.,* + *acc.,* на + *acc.,* to pile up high. Взгромозди́ли все сундуки́ на воз, they piled all the trunks on the cart. Вз-громозд-и́ть-ся, *v.p.r.,* вз-громожд-á́ть-ся, *v.i.r.,* на + *acc.,* to clamber up. "... на ель ворóна взгромоздя́сь..." (Krylov), "...the crow, having perched on a spruce tree...".

за-громозд-и́ть, *v.p.,* за-громожд-á́ть, *v.i.,* + *acc.,* to barricade. Кáмни загромождáли вход в пещéру, the entrance to the cave was barricaded by a pile of stones.

на-громозд-и́ть, *v.p.,* на-громожд-á́ть, *v.i.,* + *acc.,* + *gen.,* to pile, heap up one on top of the other. Н. сундуки́, to pile up trunks. На-громожд-éние, *n.n.,* piling, heaping.

о-грóм-ность, *n.f.,* hugeness, enormity. О. госудáрственных задáч, hugeness of state problems. О-грóм-ный, *adj.,* (*syn.* громáдный), huge, enormous. О. кáмень, huge stone. О. успéх, great success.

ГРУБ-, COARSENESS, RUDENESS

грýб-ост-ь, *n.f.,* rudeness, coarseness. Г. натýры, coarse nature. Говори́ть грýбости, to speak rudely. Грýб-ый, *adj.,* rough, rude, crude, coarse, ill-mannered. Г. человéк, a rude man. Г. гóлос, a gruff voice. Г-ая лесть, gross flattery. Г-ое обращéние, rude behavior. Г-ая оши́бка, serious mistake. Грýб-о, *adv.,* rudely, roughly, harshly. Груб-

овáтый, *adj.,* somewhat coarse, loutish.

груб-é-ть, *v.i.,* о-груб-éть, *v.p.,* to harden, roughen; become coarse, rude. Он огрубéл, живя́ в глуши́, living in remote places, he became coarse.

за-груб-é-ть, *v.p. of* грубéть, от + *gen.,* to become hard, callous. Ру́ки загрубéли от рабóты, my hands became hardened from work. За-груб-éние, *n.n.,* hardening. За-груб-éлый, *adj.,* rough, horny, coarse. З-ые ру́ки, calloused, rough hands.

по-груб-é-ть, *v.p. of* грубéть. По-грубéлый, *adj.,* grown hard, coarse, callous. П-ая кóжа, a leathery, coarse skin.

груб-и́-ть, *v.i.,* на-груб-и́ть, *v.p.,* + *dat.,* to talk rudely. Н. своемý учи́телю, to be rude to one's teacher.

груб-ия́н-ить, *v.i.,* на-груб-ия́нить, *v.p.,* + *dat.,* (*syn.* груби́ть, нагруби́ть). Груб-ия́н, *n.m.,* rude, impertinent man; ruffian. Груб-ия́нство, *n.n.,* impertinence, rudeness. За г. накáзывают, rudeness is punishable.

ГРУЗ-, ГРУЖ-, WEIGHT, LOAD, BURDEN

груз, *n.m.,* load, burden, weight, cargo. Тяжёлый г., heavy cargo. Г. состоя́л из кóфе и сáхара, the cargo consisted of coffee and sugar. Грýз-ный, *adj.,* corpulent, massive, heavy. Г-ая фигýра, a heavy, corpulent figure. Г-ые вéщи, heavy things. Груз-ови́к, *n.m.,* truck, lorry. Груз-овóй, *adj.,* pertaining to freight. Г. парохóд, freighter, cargo ship. Г-óе движéние, freight traffic. Груз-о-оборóт, *n.m.,* freight turnover. Груз-о-отправи́тель, *n.m.,* consigner of freight, shipper. Груз-о-подъёмность, *n.f.,* carrying power. Груз-о-получáтель, *n.m.,* consignee.

груз-и́-ть, **груж-ý,** *v.i.,* по-груз-и́ть, *v.p.,* + *acc.,* + *instr.,* to load, ship, embark. Г. парохóд товáрами, to load goods on a freighter. Г. пшени́цу в вагóны, to load cars with wheat. Грýз-чик, *n.m.,* loader, longshoreman, stevedore. Груз-и́ть-ся, *v.i.r.,* по-груз-и́ть-ся, *v.p.r.,* to be loaded with freight. Г. ýглем, to coal (*e.g.,* ships). Начáть г., to start loading. Груж-ёный, *adj.,* loaded, laden. Г. вагóн, loaded freight car.

вы́-груз-ить, *v.p.,* вы-груж-áть, *v.i.,* + *acc.,* из + *gen.,* to unload. В ýголь из вагóнов, to unload coal from freight cars. Вы́-груз-ить-ся, *v.p.r.,* вы-груж-áть-ся, *v.i.r.,* to be unloaded. Вы́-груз-ка, *n.f.,* debarkation, unloading.

за-груз-и́ть *v.p.,* за-груж-áть, *v.i.,* + *acc.,* + *instr.,* to burden, load, overload, overburden. З. подвáлы картóшкой, to fill a cellar with potatoes. З. рабóтой, to overburden with work.

на-груз-и́ть, *v.p.*, на-груж-áть, *v.i.*, to load in quantity; *see* грузи́ть. На-грузи́ть-ся, *v.p.r.*, на-груж-áть-ся, *v.i.r.*, to carry a large load, undertake much work. На-грýз-ка, *n.f.*, loading; work load. Н. продолжáлась два часá, the loading lasted two hours. Непóлная н., (*recent*), part-time job. Двойнáя н., (*recent*), double duties.

по-груз-и́ть, *v.p.*, + *acc.*, to load, ship; plunge, immerse, dip, submerge; *see* погружáть. По-груж-áть-ся, *v.i.r.*, по-груз-и́ть-ся, *v.p.r.*, to be immersed, dipped, submerged. Корáбль погрузи́лся в вóду, the ship sank in the water. П. в отчáяние, to plunge into despair. По-груж-éние, *n.n.*, immersion, sinking. По-груж-ённость, *n.f.*, state of being immersed, submerged, absorbed in something. По-груж-ённый, *adj. part. pass. past*, absorbed in. П. в изучéние кáрты, absorbed in the study of a map. П. в размышлéние, deep in thought. П. в свою рабóту, intent on one's work. По-грýз-ка, *n.f.*, loading. П. войск в эшелóн, the loading of troops on a military train.

пере-груз-и́ть, *v.p.*, пере-груж-áть, *v.i.*, + *acc.*, + *instr.*, to overload; transfer goods. П. товáры с однóго сýдна на другóе, to transfer goods from one craft to another. П. рабóтой, to overwork, overburden. Пере-груз-и́ть-ся, *v.p.r.*, пере-груж-áть-ся, *v.i.r.*, + *instr.*, to be transferred (goods); overloaded. Пере-грýж-енность, *n.f.*, overload, overwork. Пере-грýж-енный, *adj. part. pass. past*, overladed, overworked. Пере-грýз-ка, *n.f.*, transfer of freight; overloading; *see* перегрýженность. Пере-грýз-очный, *adj.*, of перегрýзка. П-ое сýдно, transfer freighter.

раз-груз-и́ть, *v.p.*, раз-груж-áть, *v.i.*, + *acc.*, to unload. Раз-груз-и́ть-ся, *v.p.r.*, раз-груж-áть-ся, *v.i.r.*, to be unloaded, unburden oneself. Раз-грýз-ка, *n.f.*, unloading. Р. от рабóты, (*recent*), relief from work. Раз-грýз-очный, *adj.*, pertaining to unloading. Раз-грýз-чик, *n.m.*, stevedore.

с-груз-и́ть, *v.p.*, с-груж-áть, *v.i.*, + *acc.*, to take a load down, off.

ГУЛ-, WALKING, PERAMBULATION, STROLL, SAUNTER, PROMENADE

гул-я́ть, *v.i.*, в + *prep.*, to walk, stroll, promenade; celebrate, make merry. Мы гуляем кáждый день, we take a walk every day. Мы гуляли в садý (в

пáрке, на берегý), we walked in the garden (in the park, on the shore). Я ужé недéлю гуляю по слýчаю ремóнта мастерскóй, I have not worked for a week because they are making repairs in the workshop. Вся дерéвня три дня гуляла на свáдьбе, (*colloq.*), the entire village made merry for three days after the wedding. Гулянье, *n.n.*, walking, strolling, promenading; outdoor life, festivity. Сегóдня большóе гулянье в пáрке, today there is a festival in the park. Гул-яка, *n.m.*, idler, reveller, rake. Гул-яющий, *adj. part. pass. pres.*, walking, strolling; used as *n.*, stroller, walker.

за-гул-я́ть, *v.p.*, за-гýл-ивать, *v.i.*, (*colloq.*), to go off on a spree. Он загулял и не пришёл на рабóту, he went on a spree and did not turn up for work.

на-гул-я́ть, *v.p.*, на-гýл-ивать, *v.i.*, + *acc.*, (*colloq.*), to feed, fatten (*e.g.*, cattle). Н. аппети́т прогýлкой, to work up a good appetite by walking. На-гуля́ть-ся, *v.p.r.*, to walk at will, as much as one likes. В выходнóй день нагуляюсь ввóлю, on my day off I'll walk to my heart's content.

по-гул-я́ть, *v.p.*, to take a walk. По-гýл-ивать, *v.i.*, (*colloq.*), to be fond of carousing.

под-гул-я́ть, *v.p.*, (*colloq.*), to get drunk; (*fig.*), to be unsatisfactory. Обéд подгулял, (*colloq.*), the dinner was rather bad.

про-гул-я́ть, *v.p.*, про-гýл-ивать, *v.i.*, (*colloq.*), + *acc.*, to walk for pleasure, spend time in idleness; squander; shirk work. П. весь день в лесý, to spend the whole day strolling in the forest. П. дéньги, to squander money. П. урóк, to miss a lesson. Про-гул-я́ть-ся, *v.p.r.*, про-гýл-ивать-ся, *v.i.r.*, to take a walk; promenade, stroll. Пéред сном полéзно прогуля́ться, it is good to take a stroll before going to bed. Про-гýл, *n.m.*, (*recent*), absenteeism, truancy. Борьбá с прогýлами, (*recent*), the battle against absenteeism. Про-гýл-ка, *n.f.*, a walk, stroll. П. верхóм, a ride on horseback. П. в автомоби́ле, a drive in an automobile. Увесели́тельная п., a pleasure trip, excursion. Про-гýл-ь-щик, *n.m.*, (*recent*), shirker.

раз-гул-я́ть, *v.p.*, + *acc.*, to drive away, dissipate. Р. сон, тоскý, to drive away sleep (sadness). Раз-гýл-ивать, *v.i.*, по + *dat.*, to walk, stroll about, saunter, loiter. Р. по бульвáру, to stroll along a boulevard. Раз-гул-я́ть-ся, *v.p.r.*, to amuse oneself; become gay; be on the loose; to clear up, become fine (*of weather*). Гóсти так разгуля́лись, что пустились танцовать, the guests became so gay, they began to dance. Погода разгулялась, the weather has brightened. Разгул, *n.m.*, revelry, debauchery. Предаваться разгулу, to give oneself over to revelry. Раз-гул-ьный, *adj.*, loose, rakish.

ГУСТ-, ГУЩ-, DENSITY, THICKNESS

густ-é-ть, *v.i.,* по-густ-éть, *v.p.,* to thicken, condense; become thick, dense. Крахмал густеет, starch thickens. Густ-отá, *n.f.,* thickness, density. Г. раствора, condensation of a solution. Густ-ой, *adj.,* thick, dense. Г. дым, dense smoke. Г. лес, a thick forest. Г-ое население, a dense population. Г-ые волосы, thick hair. Густ-о, *adv.,* thickly, densely. Не густо (*fig.*), not much. Угостили нас не густо, (*colloq.*), they entertained us rather poorly. Густ-о-лиственный, *adj.,* having dense foliage. Густ-о-растущий, *adj. part. act. pres.,* luxuriant (*e.g.,* a tree, bush). **за-густ-é-ть,** *v.p., see* густеть. Сироп загустел, the syrup has thickened. **гущ-а,** *n.f.,* dregs, lees, grounds. Кофейная г., coffee grounds. В гуще леса, in the thick of the forest. Быть в самой г. толпы, to be in the thick of a crowd. Гущ-е, *adj. comp.,* thicker, denser. **с-густ-й-ть,** *v.p.,* с-гущ-ать, *v.i.,* + *acc.,* to thicken, condense. С. жидкость, to concentrate, thicken a liquid. С. краски (*fig.*), to exaggerate. С-густ-йть-ся, *v.p.r.,* с-гущ-ать-ся, *v.i.r.,* to become thick, thicken, condense. Туман сгустился, the fog has become dense. С-гущ-ённый, *adj. part. pass. past,* condensed. С-ое молоко, condensed milk. С-ые сливки, heavy cream. С-гущ-ающийся, *adj. part. pass. pres.,* thickening, becoming thick. С-неся сумерки, the gathering darkness. С-гущ-аемость, *n.f.,* condensability. С-гущ-ение, *n.n.,* thickening, condensation. С-густ-итель, *n.m.,* condenser. С-густ-ок, *n.m.,* clot. С. крови, blood clot.

Д

ДА-, ДАР-, ДАТ-, GIVING

да-ть, *v.p.,* да-вать, *v.i.,* + *acc.,* + *dat.,* to give, present, donate, bestow, grant; permit, allow, let. Д. взаймы, to lend money. Д. книгу, to give a book. Этому мальчику нельзя дать больше десяти лет, this boy does not look more than ten years old. Давайте! (+ *inf. imp. or 1ste pers. pl. perf.*), Let us! Д. рабо-

тать! Let's work! Д. погуляем, let's take a walk. Да-нь, *n.f.,* tribute, tax. Дá-н-ный, *adj. part. pass. past,* given; present. В данное время, at present, at this time. Данные, *pl.,* facts, data. Его д. несомненны, his data is undisputable. Дат-ельный падеж (*gram.*), dative case. Благ-о-дать, *n.f.,* grace, blessing, abundance. Благ-о-дат-ный, *adj.,* beneficial, blissful, abundant. Б. климат, beneficial climate. **дá-ча,** *n.f.,* the giving of something; single ration; villa. Д. взаймы, the giving, as a loan. Д. показаний, deposition. Д. овса, ration of oats. Дач-е-владелец, *n.m.,* the owner of a villa. Дáч-ник, *n.m.,* дáч-ница, *n.f.,* a summer resident. **в-дá-ть-ся,** *v.p.r.,* в-да-вáть-ся, *v.i.r.,* в + *acc.,* to become addicted to, give in to. В. в крайности, to rush to extremes. В. в подробности, to go into details. Залив вдаётся в сушу, the gulf juts inland. **воз-дá-ть,** *v.p.,* воз-да-вáть, *v.i.,* + *acc.,* to render; remunerate, reward. В. должное, to do justice. Воз-дá-ть-ся, *v.i.r.,* + *acc.,* to be rewarded. Ему воздастся за это, he will be repaid accordingly. **вы́-да-ть,** *v.p.,* вы-да-вáть, *v.i.,* + *acc.,* to betray; give away. В. вексель, to sign a note, give an IOU. В. замуж, to give in marriage. В. друга, to betray a friend. В. секрет, to betray (divulge) a secret. В. жалование, to pay a salary. Вы-да-вáть-ся, *v.i.r.,* to protrude, project, jut out; to be issued, distributed. Жалование выдаётся, wages are paid. Скала выдаётся в море, the rock juts out into the sea. Вы́-да-ча, *n.f.,* distribution. Завтра в. жалования, tomorrow is payday. Вы-да-ющийся, *adj. part. act. pres.,* prominent, outstanding, distinguished. В. учёный нашего времени, the outstanding scientist of our time. В-ая победа, a signal victory. **до-дá-ть,** *v.p.,* до-да-вáть, *v.i.,* + *acc.,* to add, make up a balance; pay up. Я не додал вам двух рублей, I've given you two rubles less. До-дá-ча, *n.f.,* addition to make up a balance. **за-дá-ть,** *v.p.,* за-да-вáть, *v.i.,* + *acc.,* + *dat.,* to set, assign; propound. З. вопрос, to ask a question. З. урок, to assign a lesson. З. тон, (*mus.*), to give the pitch; (*fig.*), to set the fashion. За-дá-ть-ся, *v.p.r.,* за-да-вáть-ся, *v.i.r.,* + *instr.,* to be conceited, give oneself airs; to make up one's mind to do something. З. целью изучить русский язык, to set oneself the task of learning the Russian language. За-дá-ние, *n.n.,* task, assignment. Вы́-полнить з., to carry out an assignment. За-да́т-ок, *n.m.*, deposit. Я дал пять рубле́й в зада́ток, I gave a deposit of five rubles. За-да́т-ки, *n.pl.*, disposition, inclination; instincts. Музыка́льные з., talent for music. Зада́-ча, *n.f.*, problem, proposition, undertaking. Реша́ть з-у, to solve a problem, proposition. Боева́я з., an urgent task; (*mil.*), combat assignment. За-да́-чник, *n.m.*, (*math.*), a book of problems, practice book. Не-за-да́-ча, *n.f.*, (*colloq.*), ill luck.

о-за-да́-ч-ить, *v.p.*, о-за-да́-чивать, *v.i.*, + *acc.*, + *instr.*, to embarrass; perplex, puzzle. О. неожи́данным вопро́сом, to embarrass, perplex by asking an unexpected question. О-за-да́-ченный, *adj. part. pass. past,* embarassed, perplexed, puzzled.

из-да́-ть, *v.p.*, из-да-ва́ть, *v.i.*, + *acc.*, to produce; utter, emit; publish, issue, proclaim; establish. И. звук, to emit a sound. И. за́пах, to exhale an odor. И. постановле́ние, to issue a regulation. И. газе́ту, to publish a newspaper. Из-да-ва́ть-ся, *v.i.r.*, to be published. "Пра́вда" издаётся в Москве́, "Pravda" is published in Moscow. Изда́-ние, *n.n.*, edition, publication, issue. Дешёвое и., a cheap edition. Из-да́-тель, *n.m.*, publisher. Из-да́-тельство, *n.n.*, publishing house.

над-да́-ть, *v.p.*, над-да-ва́ть, *v.i.*, + *acc.*, (*colloq.*), to add. Н. ско́рость, to increase speed. Н. це́ну, to outbid. Над-да́-ча, *n.f.* addition, outbidding.

об-да́-ть, *v.p.*, об-да-ва́ть, *v.i.*, + *instr.*, to scald, drench. О. водо́й, to drench with water. О. кипятко́м, to scald with boiling water. Об-да́-ть-ся, *v.p.r.*, об-да-ва́ть-ся, *v.i.r.*, to be drenched, scalded.

от-да́-ть, *v.p.*, от-да-ва́ть, *v.i.*, + *acc.*, + *instr.*, to give away; return, restore. О. за́нятые де́ньги, to give back borrowed money. Эта буты́лка отдаёт кероси́ном, this bottle gives off a smell of kerosene. О. в шко́лу, to send to a school. О. под суд, to prosecute. От-да́-ть-ся, *v.p.r.*, от-да-ва́ть-ся, *v.i.r.*, + *dat.*, to yield, give oneself; be devoted. Мать вся отдава́лась воспита́нию дете́й, the mother devoted herself completely to the education of her children. От-да́-ние, *n.n.*, return, giving back. О. че́сти, (*mil.*), a salute, saluting.

пере-да́-ть, *v.p.*, пере-да-ва́ть, *v.i.*, + *acc.*, to transmit, convey, relay, pass on. П. поруче́ние, to relay, transmit a message. П. приказа́ние, to relay an order. П. по ра́дио, to broadcast. П. ли́шнее, to give more than necessary. Переда́й-те приве́т ва́шей сестре́, please convey my regards to your sister. Пере-да́-ть-ся, *v.p.r.*, пере-да-ва́ть-ся, *v.i.r.*, to be transmitted, conveyed, relayed. П. проти́внику, to go over to the enemy, defect. Электри́ческая эне́ргия мо́жет передава́ться на большо́е расстоя́ние, electrical energy can be transmitted over long distances. Пере-да́-ча, *n.f.*, rendering, transmission; parcel of food. Аресто́ванному принесли́ переда́чу, (*recent colloq.*), they brought the prisoner a parcel of food. Пере-да́-точный, *adj.*, intermediary, pertaining to transmission. П. пункт, a transmitting station. Пере-да́-тчик, *n.m.*, transmitter. Ра́дио-переда́ча, *n.f.*, radio broadcasting, broadcast.

по-да́-ть, *v.p.*, по-да-ва́ть, *v.i.*, + *acc.*, to give, present, serve. П. го́лос, to vote, cast one's vote. П. заявле́ние, to file an application. П. на стол, to wait at table. По-да́-ть-ся, *v.p.r.*, по-да-ва́ть-ся, *v.i.r.*, to be served (a dish); draw, move, give away; yield. Он си́льно пода́лся, his health gave way. По-да́-тель, *n.m.*, по-да́-тельница, *n.f.*, (*obs.*), petitioner, applicant. П. сего́ проше́ния, (*obs.*), petitioner. По-да́т-ливость, *n.f.*, pliability. По-да́т-ливый, *adj.*, yielding, pliable. П. на лесть, susceptible to flattery. По́-дать, *n.f.*, tax, duty. По-да́-ча, *n.f.*, giving, presenting, service. П. пе́рвой по́мощи, first aid. По-да́-чка, *n.f.*, sop, pittance. По-да-я́ние, *n.n.*, dole, alms, charity.

под-да́-ть, *v.p.*, под-да-ва́ть, *v.i.*, + *acc.*, to grow, increase; reinforce. П. мяч раке́ткой, to strike a ball upwards with a racket. П. хо́ду, to add speed. Под-да́-ть-ся, *v.p.r.*, под-да-ва́ть-ся, *v.i.r.*, + *dat.*, to succumb, yield. П. обма́ну (угро́зам), to yield to deceit (threats). П. влия́нию, to be influenced, succumb to influence. П. внуше́нию, to be susceptible to hypnotic suggestion. Это не поддаётся описа́нию, this is indescribable. Под-да́-нство, *n.n.*, citizenship (*in a kingdom*). По́д-да-нный, *adj. used as a n.*, subject. Брита́нский п., a British subject.

пре-да́-ть, *v.p.*, пре-да-ва́ть, *v.i.*, + *acc.*, + *dat.*, to betray, play foul. П. дру́га, to betray one's friend. П. забве́нию, to bury in oblivion. П. оте́чество, to betray one's fatherland. Пре-да́-ть-ся, *v.p.r.*, пре-да-ва́ть-ся, *v.i.r.*, + *dat.*, to give, abandon oneself to. П. мечта́м, to fall into a reverie. П. го́рю, to give way to grief. Пре-да́-ние, *n.n.*, tradition, legend. Наро́дные преда́ния, folk legends. Пре-да́-ние земле́, burial, interment. П. суду́, a bringing to trial. Пре́-да-н-ность, *n.f.*, devotion, attachment. Пре́-да-н-ный, *adj.*, devoted, attached. Пре́данный Вам, Yours truly, devotedly. П. сын, a dutiful son. Пре́-да-н-но, *adv.*, devotedly. Солда́т до́лжен пре́данно служи́ть свое́й ро́дине, a soldier must serve his country devotedly. Пре-да́-тель, *n.m.*, пре-да́-тель-ница, *n.f.*, traitor, betrayer. Пре-да́-тельство, *n.n.*, treachery, betrayal, treason. Пре-да́-тельский, *adj.*, treacherous, traitorous. Пре-да́-тельски, *adv.*, treacherously, traitorously. Поступи́ть п., to act treacherously.

пре-по-да-ва́-ть, *v.i.*, + *acc.*, + *dat.*, to teach, instruct. П. биоло́гию студе́нтам, to teach biology to students. Пре-по-да-ва́тель, *n.m.*, teacher, instructor. П. ру́сского языка́, a teacher of Russian. Пре-по-да-ва́ние, *n.n.*, teaching, instruction. П. иностра́нных языко́в, the teaching of foreign languages.

при-да́-ть, *v.p.*, при-да-ва́ть, *v.i.*, + *acc.*, + *dat.*, to augment, add, supplement. П. вкус, to add zest. П. си́лы, to increase the strength. П. лоск, to polish. Я не придаю́ значе́ния его́ слова́м, I attach no importance to his words. При-да-ва́ть-ся, *v.i.r.*, to be increased, augmented. При-да́-ное, *adj.*, *used as n.*, dowry, trousseau. При-да́т-ок, *n.m.*, appendage. При-да́т-очный, *adj.*, additional. П-ое предложе́ние (*gram.*), subordinate clause. При-да́-ча, *n.f.*, supplement. В прида́чу, in addition.

про-да́-ть, *v.p.*, про-да-ва́ть, *v.i.*, + *acc.*, to sell. П. кни́гу (ма́сло, ло́шадь), to sell a book (butter, a horse). Про-да́-ть-ся, *v.p.r.*, про-да-ва́ть-ся, *v.i.r.*, to be sold, change hands. Дом продаётся, the house is for sale. Про-да-ве́ц, *n.m.*, про-да-вщи́ца, *n.f.*, salesman, saleswoman, sales_ clerk. Про-да́-жа, *n.f.*, sale, selling. Про-да́-ж-ность, *n.f.*, venality. Про-да́-ж-ный, *adj.*, for sale; venal, corrupt, mercenary.

рас-про-да́-ть, *v.p.*, рас-про-да-ва́ть, *v.i.*, + *acc.*, to sell, auction off. Рас-про́-дан, *adj. pred. part. pass. past,* sold out. Весь това́р распро́дан, all the goods are sold. Биле́ты распро́даны, all the tickets are sold. Рас-про-да-ва́ть-ся, *v.i.r.*, to be sold, auctioned off. Рас-про-да́-жа, *n.f.*, sale, clearance.

раз-да́-ть, *v.p.*, раз-да-ва́ть, *v.i.*, + *acc.*, to distribute, portion out, deal out. Р. жа́лование to distribute a payroll. Р. награ́ды, to distribute decorations, awards. Р. ку́шанье, to dish out food. Раз-да́-ть-ся, *v.p.r.*, раз-да-ва́ть-ся, *v.i.r.*, to be distributed, apportioned; grow wider, stretch; resound, arise. Изда́ли раздава́лись вы́стрелы, shots resounded in the distance. Толпа́ раз-

дала́сь, the crowd made way. Раз-да́-ча, *n.f.*, distribution, delivery. Раз-да́т-чик, *n.m.*, distributor. Раз-да́-гочный, *adj.*, distributory. Р. пункт, distribution center.

с-да́-ть, *v.p.*, с-да-ва́ть, *v.i.*, + *acc.*, to give up, part with; check (*as* luggage). С. ка́рты, to deal cards. С. кварти́ру, to rent an apartment. С. кре́пость, to surrender a fortress. С. экза́мены, to pass an examination. С. рабо́ту, to deliver a completed piece of work. С. чемода́н в бага́ж, to check a suitcase. С-да́-ть-ся, *v.p.r.*, с-да-ва́ть-ся, *v.i.r.*, to surrender, acknowledge defeat. С. в плен, to surrender as a prisoner of war. Этот дом сдаётся, this house is for rent. С-да́-ча, *n.f.*, small change; surrender; checking, deal (*in cards*). Вот с. с десяти́ рубле́й, here is the change from ten rubles. Возьми́те сда́чу на чай, keep the change as a tip. С. кре́пости, the surrender of a fortress.

у-да́-ть-ся, *v.p.r.*, у-да-ва́ть-ся, *v.i.r.*, to succeed, turn out well. Не у., to fail. О́пыт уда́лся, the experiment was successful. Мне не удало́сь его́ повида́ть, I failed to see him. У-даль, *n.f.*, у-да́-ль-ство́, *n.n.*, daring, boldness. У-да́-ча, *n.f.*, success; good luck, good fortune. У-да-л-е́ц, *n.m.*, daring, bold fellow, У-да-л-о́й, *adj.*, daring, bold. На-уда́чу, at random. Пожела́ть уда́чи, to wish one good luck. Уда́чи и неуда́чи, ups and downs. У-да́-чливый, *adj.*, lucky, fortunate. У. челове́к, a lucky man. У-да́ч-ник, *n.m.*, a lucky man. Неуда́ч-ник, *n.m.*, failure, unlucky man. У-да́-чный, *adj.*, successful, well done. У. перево́д, a good translation. Не-у-да́-чный, *adj.*, unsuccessful. Н-ое выраже́-ние, an unfortunate, unfelicitous remark. У-да́-чно, *adv.*, successfully, well. Не-у-да́-чно, *adv.*, unsuccessfully, unfortunately.

дар-и́ть, *v.i.*, по-дар-и́ть, *v.p.*, + *acc.*, + *dat.*, to give, present, grant. По-да́р-ок, *n.m.*, gift, present.

дар, *n.n.*, gift, donation, grant. Дары́ церко́вные, holy communion. Дар красноре́чия, the gift of eloquence. Дар-е́ние, *n.n.*, donation, giving, present. Дар-и́тель, *n.m.*, giver, donor, grantor. Дарёный, *adj. part. pass. past,* given. Дарёному коню́ в зу́бы не смо́трят (*saying*), one does not look a gift horse in the mouth. Да́р-ом, *adv. express.*, gratis, free; to no purpose, in vain. Получи́ть д., to receive free of charge. Я прошёл в кино́ да́ром, без биле́та, I went into the movies without a ticket. Тра́тить д. вре́мя, to waste one's time. Это ему́ не д., доста́лось, he did not get this for nothing. Недаром, *adv.*, not without cause, reason. Дар-м-о-éд, *n.m.*, (*derog.*), sponger, parasite. Дáр-ственный, *adj.*, *in expression*: Д-ая зáпись, settlement, deed for the gift of property. Без-дáрность, *n.f.*, lack of talent, ability. Без-дáр-ный, *adj.*, lacking talent, ability.

благо-дар-и́ть, *v.i.,* по-благо-дар-и́ть, *v.p.,* + *acc.,* to thank. Благодарю́ вас, thank you. Благо-дáр-ность, *n.f.,* thanks, gratitude. В б., in gratitude. Не стóит благодáрности, don't mention it. Благо-дáр-ный, *adj.,* grateful. Не-благо-дáр-ный, *adj.,* ungrateful. Н. труд, unrewarding work. Я вам óчень благодáрен, I am very grateful to you. Благо-дáр-но, *adv.,* gratefully. Благо-дáр-ственное письмó, a letter of thanks. Благо-дар-я́, *adv., part. pres., also used as prep.,* thanks to, owing to, due to. Б. мои́м учителя́м, я получи́л хорóшее образовáние, thanks to my teachers, I had a good education.

за-дар-и́ть, *v.p.,* за-дáр-ивать, *v.i.,* + *acc.,* to load with presents. Новобрáчных задари́ли подáрками, the newlyweds were showered with gifts.

о-дар-и́ть, *v.p.,* о-дар-я́ть, *v.i.,* + *acc.,* to overwhelm with gifts. О-дар-ённость, *n.f.,* talent. О-дар-ённый, *adj. part. pass. past,* gifted, talented. О. музыкáнт, a talented musician.

от-дар-и́ть, *v.p.,* от-дáр-ивать, *v.i.,* + *acc.,* to give presents in return; reciprocate.

раз-дар-и́ть, *v.p.,* раз-дáр-ивать, *v.i.,* + *acc.,* to distribute, give presents. Раз-дáр-ивание, *n.n.,* distribution of gifts.

дар-овáть, *v.p.,* + *acc.,* (*obs.*), to confer, grant. Д. прощéние, to pardon, Д. свобóду, to grant freedom, reprieve. Дар-овáние, *n.n.,* donation, gift, talent; granting. Дар-óванный, *adj. part. pass. past,* granted, donated. Дар-ови́тость, *n.f.,* ability, capacity, talent. Дар-ови́тый, *adj.,* gifted, clever, endowed with talents. Дар-овóй, *adj.,* gratuitous, free of charge. На дар-овщи́нку, (*colloq.*), without payment.

ДАВ-, ДАВ(Л)-, GRAVITY, PRESSURE

дав-и́-ть, дав-л-ю́, *v.i.,* + *acc.,* to squeeze, press, squash; oppress; run over, hurt by pressure. Д. виногрáд, to press grapes. Этот воротни́к дáвит мне шéю, this collar hurts my neck. Дав-и́ть-ся, *v.i.r.,* по-дав-и́ть-ся, *v.p.r.,* + *instr.,* от + *gen.,* to be pressed; choke. Д. кóстью, to choke on a bone. Волк кóстью чуть не подави́лся, (*Krylov*), the wolf almost choked on the bone.

Д. от кáшля, to choke from coughing. Дáв-ка, *n.f.,* press, throng, crowd. Дав-л-éние, *n.n.,* pressure, stress, enforcement; thrust. Атмосфéрное д., atmospheric pressure. Высóкое (ни́зкое) д., high (low) pressure. Окáзывать д., to enforce. Под давлéнием обстоя́тельств, under the pressure of circumstances.

в-дав-и́-ть, *v.p.,* в-дáв-л-ивать, *v.i.,* + *acc.,* в + *acc.,* to press, smash in. В. прóбку в буты́лку, to press a cork into a bottle. В-дáв-л-ивание, *n.n.,* pressing, caving in. В-дав-и́ть-ся, *v.p.r.,* в-дáв-л-и-вать-ся, *v.i.r.,* в + *acc.,* to be pressed in. Кáмень вдави́лся в зéмлю, the stone sank (dug itself) into the earth.

вы́-дав-и-ть, *v.p.,* вы-дáв-л-ивать, *v.i.,* + *acc.,* to press, squeeze out. В. сок из лимóна, to squeeze the juice out of a lemon. Вы́-дав-л-енный, *adj. part. pass. past,* pressed, forced out. В-ое окóнное стеклó, a forced window pane. Вы́-дав-ить-ся, *v.p.r.,* вы-дáв-л-ивать-ся, *v.i.r.,* + *instr.,* из + *gen.,* to be pressed, squeezed out. Сок выдáвливается прéссом из виногрáда, the juice is squeezed out of the grapes by a press.

за-дав-и́ть, *v.p.,* + *acc.,* to crush, run over, knock down and kill. З. человéка автомоби́лем, to run over a person, and crush him to death.

на-дав-и́ть, *v.p.,* на-дáв-л-ивать, *v.i.,* + *acc.,* на + *acc.,* + *gen.,* to press on; squeeze in quantity; exercise pressure. Н. кнóпку звонкá, to press the button of a bell, buzzer. На-дáв-л-ивать-ся, *v.i.r.,* + *instr.,* to be pressed.

от-дав-и́ть, *v.p.,* + *acc.,* + *dat.,* to tread, press, crush. О. нóгу кому-нибýдь, to tread heavily on somebody's toes.

по-дав-и́ть, *v.p.,* по-дав-л-я́ть, *v.p.* + *acc.,* to suppress, crush; depress. П. восстáние, to quell an uprising. П. чýвство стрáха, to suppress the feeling of fear. По-дав-и́ть-ся, *v.i.r.,* + *instr.,* to be suppressed. Мятéж подавля́ется си́лой орýжия, the mutiny is being suppressed by force of arms. По-дав-л-я́ющий, *adj. part. act. pres.,* crushing. П-ее большинствó голосóв, a large majority of votes (voices). По-дав-л-éние, *n.n.,* suppression crushing, repression. По-дáв-л-енность, *n.f.,* depression, repression, despondency, blues. По-дáв-л-енный, *adj. part. pass. past,* depressed, dejected, despondent.

при-дав-и́ть, *v.p.,* при-дáв-л-ивать, *v.i.,* + *acc.,* + *instr.,* to press, squeeze tightly. П. к землé, to crush to the ground. При-дáв-л-ивать-ся, *v.i.r.,* + *instr.,* to be pressed down, against.

про-дав-и́ть, *v.p.*, про-да́в-л-ивать, *v.i.*, + *acc.*, to break through, crush in. П. сиде́ние сту́ла, to break through the seat of a chair. Про-дав-и́ть-ся, *v.p.r.*, про-да́в-л-ивать-ся, *v.i.r.*, + *acc.*, to be crushed, broken in.

раз-дав-и́ть, *v.p.*, раз-да́в-л-ивать, *v.i.*, + *acc.*, to crush, smash; run over; squash. Р. паука́, to crush a spider. Раз-дав-и́ть-ся, *v.p.r.*, to be crushed, smashed. В су́мочке зе́ркало мо́жет раздави́ться, the mirror might be smashed in the bag. Раз-да́в-ленный, *adj. part. pass. past*, crushed, run over. Р. на́ смерть, crushed to death.

с-дав-и́ть, *v.p.*, с-да́в-л-ивать, *v.i.*, + *acc.*, to squeeze, press together, squash. С. ру́ку до бо́ли, to squeeze a hand until it hurts. С-дав-и́ть-ся, *v.p.r.*, to become crushed. Ве́щи в чемода́не сдави́лись, the things in the suitcase were crushed. С-да́в-л-ивание, *n.n.*, squeezing; compression. С-да́в-л-енный, *adj. part. pass. past*, compressed, constrained. С. го́лос, a constrained voice.

у-дав-и́ть, *v.p.*, + *acc.*, to strangle, throttle. У-дав-и́ть-ся, *v.p.r.*, to strangle (hang) oneself. У-дав-л-е́ние, *n.n.*, strangling. У-да́в-л-енник, *n.m.*, (*colloq.*), one who has hanged himself.

у-да́в, *n.m.*, (*zool.*), boa constrictor. Волк-о-да́в, *n.m.*, wolfhound.

ДАВН-, PRETERITION, THE PAST, PAST TIME

давн-о́, *adv.*, long ago; (*synonymous with the expression*: мно́го вре́мени тому́ наза́д). Э́то бы́ло давно́: сто лет тому́ наза́д, it was a long time ago: one hundred years ago. Д. проше́дшие времена́, remote times. Я давно́ его́ не вида́л, I haven't seen him for a long time. Давнопроше́дшее вре́мя (*gram.*), pluperfect tense. Давн-е́нько, *adv.*, (*colloq.*), *see* давно́. Не-да́вно, *adv.*, recently, not long ago. Да́вн-ость, *n.f.*, remoteness; (*law*), prescription. Пра́во да́вности, prescriptive right. Да́вн-ий, *adj.*, ancient, old, of long standing. Д-ие собы́тия, events of long ago. Давн-и́шний, *adj.*, (*obs.*), *see* да́вний. Не-да́в-ний, *adj.*, recent. Давны́м-давно́, *adv.*, a very long time ago; long, long ago. Ки́ев был осно́ван давны́м-давно́: бо́лее ты́сячи лет тому́ наза́д, Kiev was founded a long time ago: more than one thousand years ago. С да́вних времён (пор), from very remote times.

из-давн-а́, *adv.*, long since; ages ago. Э́то и. заведено́, this was established a long time ago.

по-да́вн-о, *adv.*, (*colloq.*), so much the more; let alone. Хоро́шие ученики́ не могли́ реши́ть зада́чи, а плохи́е и пода́вно, the good students could not solve the problem, let alone the poor ones.

ДВ-А-, DUALITY, DUPLICITY, TWO

дв-а, *num. card.*, *m. and n.*, дв-е, *f.*, two. Два гла́за, two eyes. Две ру́ки, two hands. В двух слова́х, briefly, in a word. Расскажи́ коро́тко, в двух слова́х, tell us briefly, in a word. В двух шага́х, nearby (*literally*, in two steps).

дв-а́-дцать, *num. card.*, twenty, a score. Два-дца́тый, *num. ord.*, the twentieth. Д. уро́к, the twentieth lesson. Д-ая до́ля, a twentieth, a twentieth part. Два-дцат-и-ле́тие, *n.n.*, a period of twenty years' duration; twentieth anniversary. Два-дцат-и-пятиле́тие, *n.n.*, a period of twenty-five years' duration; twenty-fifth anniversary. Два-дцат-и-пятиле́тний, *adj.*, pertaining to twenty-five years. Два́-жды, *adv.*, twice. Д. два четы́ре, two times two is four.

дв-е-на́-дцать, *num. card.*, twelve. Дв-е-на́-дцатый, *num. ord.*, twelfth.

дв-е́-сти, *num. card.*, two hundred. Дв-о́е, *num. coll.*, two. Дв-ое-вла́стие, *n.n.*, a diarchy. Дв-ое-то́чие, *n.n.*, (*gram.*), colon.

дв-о-и́ть-ся, *v.i.r.*, to be doubled. У меня́ двои́тся в глаза́х, I see double.

раз-дво-и́ть, *v.p.*, раз-два́-ивать, *v.i.*, + *acc.*, to bisect, bifurcate. Раз-дво-и́ть-ся, *v.p.r.*, раз-два́-ивать-ся, *v.i.r.*, to be divided in two parts; be forked, bifurcated. В э́том ме́сте доро́га раздва́ивается, the road forks in this place. Раз-дво-е́ние, *n.n.*, fork, bifurcation. Раз-дво́-енный, *adj. part. pass. past*, forked, bifurcated, split. Р-ое копы́то, cleft hoof. Р-ая ли́чность, split personality.

с-дво-и́ть, *v.p.*, с-два́-ивать, *v.i.*, + *acc.*, to double up, combine in pairs. С. ряды́, to double the ranks. С-два́-ивание, *n.n.*, a doubling. С-дво́-енный, *adj.*, *part. pass. past*, doubled.

у-дво́-ить, *v.p.*, у-два́-ивать, *v.i.*, + *acc.*, to redouble; (*gram.*), reduplicate. У. це́ну, to double a price. У. стара́ние, to redouble one's efforts. У-дво́-ить-ся, *v.p.r.*, у-два́-ивать-ся, *v.i.r.*, to be redoubled. Си́ла ве́тра удво́илась, the force of the wind has redoubled. У-дво-е́ние, *n.n.*, redoubling, reduplication. У-дво́-енный, *adj. part. pass. past*, redoubled. Нача́ть рабо́тать с удво́енной эне́ргией, to begin to work with redoubled energy.

двóй-ка, *n.f.,* two, a pair. Д. пик (*in cards*), the two of spades.

двой-нúк, *n.m.,* a double, twin, the very image. Двой-нóй, *adj.,* double, twofold. Д. подбородок, a double chin. Вести д-ýю игрý, to be two-faced. Двóй-ня, *пит. coll.,* twins.

двóй-ственность, *n.f.* duality, duplicity. Двóй-ственный, *adj.,* dual, two-faced. Д. харáктер, a two-faced person. Д-ое числó (*gram.*), dual number. Д-ая полúтика, a policy of non-committance.

двою́-рóдный, *adj., in expressions:* д. брат, *m.,* first cousin. Д-ая сестрá, *f.,* first cousin. Дво-я́кий, *adj.,* of two kinds, double. Д-ого рóда, of two kinds. Дво-я́ко, *adv.,* in two ways. Двубóртный, *adj.,* double-breasted (*as a coat*). Дву-глáвый, *adj.,* two-headed. Дву-глáсный, *adj.,* containing two sounds. Д. звук, (*gram.*), a diphthong. Дву-лúчный, *adj.,* two-faced, hypocritical. Двух-этáжный, *adj.,* two-storied (*of a building*). Дву-язы́чный, *adj.,* bilingual.

ДВЕР-, ДВОР-, DOOR, COURT, YARD

двер-ь, *n.f.,* door. Входнáя д., entrance door. В дверя́х, in the doorway. Двернóй, *adj.,* pertaining to a door. Д. порóг, threshold. Д. рýчка, door handle. Двéр-ца, *n.f.,* (*dim.*), the door of a vehicle, car, closet, etc. Пред-двéр-ие, *n.n.,* (*fig.*), beginning, eve, introduction, threshold. Мы стоúм у преддвéрия велúких собы́тий, we are on the threshold of great events.

двор, *n.m.,* yard, courtyard; royal court. За дóмом нахóдится д., there is a yard behind the house. Гостúный д., (*obs.*), arcades. На дворé, out of doors. Во дворé, in a yard. Королéвский д., a king's court. При дворé, at court. При-двóр-ный, *adj., used as n.,* courtier. П. этикéт, court etiquette. Царя́ окружáли придвóрные, the Tsar was surrounded by courtiers. Крестья́нский д., a peasant farmstead. Нет ни колá, ни дворá (*idiom*), to have neither house, nor home. Двóр-ник, *n.m.,* caretaker. Двóр-ня, *n.f.,* (*obs.*), domestic staff, household servants. Двор-ня́га, *n.f.,* mongrel, cur. Двор-óвый, *adj.,* pertaining to a farmstead, courtyard; (*hist.*), menial, pertaining to a squire's estate. Д. человéк, (*obs.*), servant in a country estate. Д-ая собáка, a watchdog. За-двóр-ки, *n.m.pl.,* a backyard. Жить на задвóрках, to live in a tenement. По-двóр-ье, *n.n.,* a town-house belonging to an absentee landlord. Монасты́рское п., a monastery's church

and quarters in a city. По-двóр-ный, *adj.,* pertaining to a homestead, estate. П. спúсок, a record of homesteads. На-двóр-ный, *adj.* located in a courtyard. Н. совéтник, (*obs.*), a court counselor; a rank in civil service. Н-ое строéние, an outbuilding.

двор-éц, *n.m.,* palace. Цáрский д., the Tsar's palace. Дворéц Трудá, (*recent*), Palace of Labor. Двор-цóвый, *adj.,* palatial, pertaining to a palace. Д. переворóт, a palace revolution. Дворéцкий, *adj., used as n.,* (*obs.*), steward, butler.

двор-яни́н, *n.m.,* (двор-я́не, *n.m.pl.*), nobleman, squire. Двор-я́нский, *adj.,* noble; patrician; pertaining to nobility, gentry. Д-ого происхождéния, of noble, gentle birth. Двор-я́нство, *n.n.,* nobility, gentry. Жáловать дворя́нством (*obs.*), to ennoble, bestow knighthood.

во-двор-úть, *v.p.,* во-двор-я́ть, *v.i.,* + *acc.,* to settle, install. В. тишинý, to restore quiet. В. поря́док, to enforce order. Во-двор-úть-ся, *v.p.r.,* во-двор-я́ть-ся, *v.i.r.,* to become settled, settle. Он водворúлся на нóвой квартúре, he has settled in a new apartment. Водвор-éние, *n.n.,* installation, settling.

вы́-двор-ить, *v.p.,* вы-двор-я́ть, *v.i.,* + *acc.,* (*derog.*), to turn out, fire, expel. В. из дóма, to turn out of the house. В. со слýжбы, to fire from a job. Выдвор-éние, *n.n.,* turning out, firing. вы́-двор-ить-ся, *v.p.r.,* вы-двор-я́ть-ся, *v.i.r.,* to be turned out, fired, expelled.

ДВИГ-, ДВИ-, ДВИЖ-, ДВИЗ-, MOTION, MOVEMENT

двúг-а-ть, *v.i.,* двú-нуть (*from* двúгнуть), *v.p., smf.* + *acc.,* + *instr.,* to move, stir, set in motion. Д. стол (стул), to move a table (a chair). Д. горáми (*fig.*), to move mountains. С егó талáнтами горáми мóжно д., with his talent, it is possible to move mountains. Двúг-ать-ся, *v.i.r.,* двú-нуть-ся, *v.p.r., smf.,* to move, stir; begin to move, start out. Двúгаться взад и вперёд, to move back and forth. Д. толпóй, to move in unison, in mass. Двúг-ание, *n.n.,* moving, stirring. Двúг-атель, *n.m.,* engine, motor. Д. внýтреннего сгорáния, internal combustion engine. Нефтянóй д., oil burning engine. Двúг-ательный, *adj.,* impelling, locomotive, motive. Д-ая сúла, motive power. Движ-éние, *n.n.,* motion, movement; traffic; circulation. Д. планéт, the motion of the planets. Ýличное д., street traffic. Железнодоро́жное (парохо́дное) д., rail (ship) traffic. Д. по слу́жбе, a promotion to a higher position. Вам на́до побо́льше движе́ния, you need more exercise. Приводи́ть в д., to put into motion. Дви́ж-имость, *n.f.*, goods and chattels; personal property. Не-дви́ж-имость, *n.f.*, immobility; real estate. Дви́ж-имый, *adj. part. pass. pres.*, movable. Д-ое иму́щество, movable property. Не-дви́ж-имое иму́щество, immovable property, real estate. Дви́ж-ущий, *adj. part. act. pres.*, moving, propelling. Д-ая си́ла, motive force.

в-двиг-а́ть, *v.i.*, в-дви́-нуть, *v.p.*, + *acc.*, to push, shift, squeeze in. В. я́щик в стол, to close a table drawer. В-двиг-а́ть-ся, *v.i.r.*, в-дви́-нуть-ся, *v.p.r.*, to be pushed, squeezed in.

воз-двиг-а́ть, *v.i.*, воз-дви́г-нуть, *v.p.*, + *acc.*, to erect, raise. В зда́ние (кре́пость), to erect a building (a fortress). Во́з-двиг-а́ть-ся, *v.i.r.*, воз-двиг-ну́ть-ся, *v.p.r.*, to be built, erected. В Москве́ воздвига́ется па́мятник геро́ям войны́, in Moscow a monument is being erected to the heroes of the war. Воз-двиг-а́ние, *n.n.*, Воз-движ-е́ние, *n.n.*, (*Ch.-Sl.*), erection, raising. Пра́здник Воздви́жения, the Greek Orthodox holy day of finding and raising the Cross.

вы-двиг-а́ть, *v.i.*, вы́-дви-нуть, *v.p.*, + *acc.*, to draw, pull out; to sponsor, promote. В. я́щик, to pull out a drawer. В. законопрое́кт в парла́менте, to introduce a bill in Parliament. В. кандидату́ру, to sponsor a candidate, a candidacy. Вы-двиг-а́ть-ся, *v.i.r.*, вы́-дви-нуть-ся, *v.p.r.*, to rise, make one's way in the world. Вы-движ-е́ние, *n.n.*, вы-движ-е́нчество, *n.n.*, (*recent*), promotion, advancement. Вы-движ-е́нец, *n.m.*, one promoted, advanced by the Soviet authorities. Вы-движ-е́нка, *n.f.*, the same (feminine).

за-двиг-а́ть, *v.i.*, за-дви-нуть, *v.p.*, + *acc.*, to bolt, bar, close. З. я́щик, to close a drawer. За-движ-ка, *n.f.*, bolt, latch. Око́нная з., window latch. За-движ-но́й, вы-движ-но́й, *adj.*, sliding.

за-двиг-а́ть, *v.p.*, see дви́гать.

на-двиг-а́ть, *v.i.*, на-дви́-нуть, *v.p.*, + *acc.*, to move, push towards. Н. шля́пу на лоб, to pull a hat down over one's eyes. На-двиг-а́ть-ся, *v.i.r.*, на-дви́-нуть-ся, *v.p.r.*, to approach, draw near, gather, to be drawn. Ту́чи надвига́ются, clouds are gathering. Ночь (ста́рость) надвига́ется, night (old age) is approaching. На-двиг-а́ющийся, *adj. part. act. pres.*, approaching,

impending. Н-аяся опа́сность, imminent danger.

ото-двиг-а́ть, от-двиг-а́ть, *v.i.*, ото-дви́-нуть, *v.p.*, + *acc.*, to move away, aside. О. стол от стены́, to move a table away from a wall. Ото-двиг-а́ть-ся, *v.i.r.*, ото-дви́-нуть-ся, *v.p.r.*, to be moved, pushed back. Ото-двиг-а́ние, *n.n.*, the action of moving, pushing back.

пере-двиг-а́ть, *v.i.*, пере-дви́-нуть, *v.p.*, + *acc.*, to move about, shift. П. обстано́вку, to shift furniture, furnishings. Едва́ п. но́ги, to scarcely drag one's feet. Пере-двиг-а́ть-ся, *v.i.r.*, пере-дви́-нуть-ся, *v.p.r.*, to be moved, shifted. П. с ме́ста на ме́сто, to move from place to place. Пере-движ-е́ние, *n.n.*, travel, locomotion; shifting; dislodging. Сре́дства передвиже́ния, means of transportation. Пере-дви́ж-ка, *n.f.*, (*recent*), передвижна́я библиоте́ка, mobile, traveling library. Ки́но-передви́жка, (*recent*), mobile movies. Пере-движ-но́й, *adj.*, mobile, movable; traveling. П-а́я вы́ставка, traveling exhibition.

по-двиг-а́ть, *v.i.*, по-дви́-нуть, *v.p.*, + *acc.*, to move on, advance. П. стол (кре́сло) к окну́, to push a table (an armchair) to the window. По-двиг-а́ть-ся, *v.i.r.*, по-дви́-нуть-ся, *v.p.r.*, to move, advance, make progress, to be moved to. Рабо́та подвига́ется, the work is progressing.

по-дви́г-ать, *v.p.*, to move slightly; *see* дви́гать. П. бровя́ми (па́льцами), to move one's eyebrows (fingers) slightly. По-дви́г-ать-ся, *v.p.r.*, to move slightly. Больно́й застона́л и слегка́ подви́гался, the patient moaned and moved slightly. По-дви́ж-ность, *n.f.*, mobility, liveliness. Не-по-дви́ж-ность, *n.f.*, immobility, fixedness. По-движ-но́й, *adj.*, movable, mobile. П. соста́в желе́зных доро́г, rolling stock. П-а́я ра́ма, sliding frame. По-дви́ж-ный, *adj.*, active, lively. П. ребёнок, an active, lively child. Не-по-дви́ж-ный, *adj.*, motionless, immobile. Н. взгляд, a fixed look, expression.

по-дви́г-ну-ть, *v.p.*, на + *acc.*, (*obs.*), to affect, move. П. кого́-нибудь на сострада́ние (милосе́рдие), to move to compassion. По́-двиг, *n.m.*, exploit, great deed. П. геро́я, a heroic deed. Вели́кий п., noble deed. Сла́вный п., glorious exploit.

по-дви́ж-ничать, *v.i.*, to lead an ascetic life. По-дви́ж-ник, *n.m.*, an ascetic. По-дви́ж-ничество, *n.n.*, asceticism. По-дви́ж-нический, *adj.*, ascetic. П-ая жизнь Свято́го Се́ргия Ра́донежского, the ascetic life of St. Sergius of

Radonezh. С-по-движ-ник, *п.т.*, с-под-виж-ница, *n.f.*, (*obs., poet.*), supporter, one who makes common cause with.

По-двиз-а́ть-ся, *v.i.*, на (в) + *prep.*, to proceed along a given line of action, work for an ideal. Подвиза́ться на обще́ственном по́прище, to work devotedly for the benefit of a community. П. на сце́не, to devote oneself to the stage.

подо-двиг-а́ть, *v.i.*, подо-дви́-нуть, *v.p.*, + *acc.*, to pull up, nearer. П. стул, to pull, draw up a chair.

при-двиг-а́ть, *v.i.*, при-дви́-нуть, *v.p.*, + *acc.*, to draw near, up to. П. стул к столу́, to draw a chair up to a table. При-двиг-а́ть-ся, *v.i.r.*, при-дви́-нуть-ся, *v.p.r.*, to be drawn nearer. Слу́шатели придви́нулись к расска́зчику, the listeners drew nearer to the story-teller.

про-двиг-а́ть, *v.i.*, про-дви́-нуть, *v.p.*, + *acc.*, to move forward; (*fig.*), to promote, advance. П. де́ло, to promote a cause. П. кого-ли́бо в председа́тели, to promote someone to the presidency. Про-двиг-а́ть-ся, *v.i.r.*, про-дви́-нуть-ся, *v.p.r.*, to be moved forward, advance, make one's way. П. с трудо́м, to advance with difficulty. П. вперёд, to forge ahead. Про-движ-е́ние, *п.п.*, advancement, furtherance, progress, promotion. П. по слу́жбе, promotion in the service.

раз-двиг-а́ть, *v.i.*, раз-дви́-нуть, *v.p.*, + *acc.*, to separate, draw apart. Р. стол, to pull a table apart (to remove, put in leaves). Раз-двиг-а́ть-ся, *v.i.r.*, раз-дви́-нуть-ся, *v.p.r.*, to be pulled, drawn apart; separate. Толпа́ раздви́нулась и пропусти́ла милиционе́ра, the crowd drew apart and made room for the policeman. Раз-движ-но́й, *adj.*, extensible. Р. стол, an extension table.

с-двиг-а́ть, *v.i.*, с-дви́-нуть, *v.p.*, + *acc.*, to pull, draw together; displace. С. ряды́, to close ranks. С-двиг-а́ть-ся, *v.i.r.*, с-дви́-нуть-ся, *v.p.r.*, to be drawn together. Ряды́ солда́т сдви́нулись, the soldiers closed ranks. Он не сдви́нулся с ме́ста, he didn't move from the spot. С-двиг, *п.т.*, displacement; dislocation; (*fig.*), landslide. С. пласто́в земли́, the shifting of the Earth's strata. С. в рабо́те, (*recent*), improvement in the work.

ДЕЛ-, ДЕ-, ДЕЙ-, ACTION, ACTIVITY, DOING, MAKING

де́л-о, *п.п.*, business, affair, matter; case; concern; file; act, deed. У меня́ ва́жное де́ло в ба́нке, I have some important business at the bank. Д. вку́са, a matter of taste. Д. че́сти, a point of honor. Д. обще́ственного значе́ния, a matter for public concern. Суде́бное д., a law suit. В чём де́ло? What's the matter? Не ва́ше де́ло! (*colloq.*), It's none of your business! Не вме́шивайтесь не в свои́ дела́! Mind your own business! Министе́рство Иностра́нных Дел, Ministry of Foreign Affairs. В са́мом де́ле, in reality, truly. Пе́рвым де́лом, first of all, in the first place. Дела́, *п.pl.*, business, affairs. Де́нежные дела́, financial, money matters. Как ва́ши дела́? How are things? How's business? Не-де́л-я, *n.f.*, a week. Не-де́л-ь-ный, *adj.*, weekly. Н. за́работок, a week's wages. Еже-не-де́л-ьный, *adj.*, occurring every week, weekly. Еже-не-де́л-ьно, *adv.*, occurring every week, weekly. По-не-де́л-ьник, *п.п.*, Monday. Де́л-ь-ный, *adj.*, efficient, clever, capable; sensible. Д. челове́к, a capable man. Де́л-ь-но, *adv.*, capably, efficiently, sensibly. Он говори́т д., he talks sensibly. Дел-о-ви́тость, *n.f.*, business-like methods; business ability. Дел-о-ви́тый, *adj.*, business-like. Дел-о-во́й, *adj.*, business-like, business. Дел-о-производи́тель, *п.т.*, executive secretary, administrator. Дел-о-произво́дство, *п.п.*, secretarial work, administration of office work, correspondence.

де́л-а-ть, *v.i.*, с-де́л-ать, *v.p.*, + *acc.*, to make, do; render. Д. столы́ и сту́лья, to make tables and chairs. Д. успе́хи, to make progress. Д. вид, to pretend, feign. Д. вы́говор, to rebuke, reprimand. Что де́лать? What can one do? Парохо́д де́лает 30 узло́в в час, the steamer makes 30 knots. Де́л-ать-ся, *v.i.r.*, с-де́л-ать-ся, *v.p.r.*, to be made; become, grow, wax, turn; occur, happen. Сде́латься злым, to become malicious, wicked. Сде́латься знамени́тым худо́жником, to become a famous painter. Сде́латься же́ртвою престу́пника, to become the victim of a criminal. С-де́лка, *n.f.*, agreement, arrangement, transaction. Вы́годная с., a bargain, profitable transaction. Незако́нная с., an illegal transaction. Соверша́ть сде́лку, to strike a bargain, make a deal. С-де́л(ь)ный, *adj.*, of or pertaining to piecework. С-ая пла́та, payment by the piece. С-ая систе́ма, piecework labor. С-де́л(ь)-щина, *n.f.*, piece work. С-де́л-ь-но, *adv.*, by the job, piece.

в-де́л-ать, *v.p.*, в-де́л-ывать, *v.i.*, + *acc.*, to fit, insert; set, put in. В. драгоце́нный ка́мень в кольцо́, to mount a precious stone in a ring. В. шкаф в сте́ну, to install a closet in a wall. В-де́л-анный, *adj. part. pass. past*, installed; set, built in. В-дел-ывание, *п.п.*, fitting, setting in.

воз-дел-ать, *v.p.*, воз-дел-ывать, *v.i.*, + *acc.*, to cultivate, till. В. зéмлю, to till land; plow. Воз-дел-ывание, *п.п.*, cultivation, tillage. Воз-дел-анный, *adj. part. pass. past*, tilled, cultivated. В-ое пóле, a cultivated field.

вы-дел-ать, *v.p.*, вы-дел-ывать, *v.i.*, + *acc.*, to make, produce, manufacture. В. кóжу, to dress leather.

до-дел-ать, *v.p.*, до-дел-ывать, *v.i.*, + *acc.*, to finish, complete, put finishing touches to. До-дел-ывание, *п.п.*, completion, finish.

за-дел-ать, *v.p.*, за-дел-ывать, *v.i.*, + *acc.*, to block, wall up. З. стéну, to block up a hole in a wall. За-дел-ывать-ся, *v.i.r.*, to be blocked, walled up.

на-дел-ать, *v.p.*, + *gen.*, to make in great quantities; cause. Н. ошúбок, to make many mistakes. Н. хлопóт, to cause trouble.

об-дел-ать, *v.p.*, об-дел-ывать, *v.i.*, + *acc.*, to finish off; shape, set, mount; (*fig.*), inveigle, take advantage of some one's credulity. О. кóжу, to tan leather. О. драгоцéнный кáмень, to cut a precious stone. О. свои делишки, (*derog.*), to engage in shady deals, practices. Об-дéлка, *n.f.*, shaping, fashioning.

от-дел-ать, *v.p.*, от-дел-ывать, *v.i.*, + *acc.*, to finish off, trim, adorn, decorate; (*fig.*), abuse. О. плáтье кружевом, to trim a dress with lace. О. квартúру, to decorate, renovate an apartment. От-дéл-ать-ся, *v.p.r.*, от-дел-ывать-ся, *v.i.r.*, to be trimmed, finished off, adorned, decorated; (*colloq.*), to get rid of. Еле отделался от кредитóров (*colloq.*), I barely managed to get rid of my creditors.

пере-дел-ать, *v.p.*, пере-дел-ывать-ся, *v.i.*, + *acc.*, to remake, alter; reform, revise. Этот костюм нáдо передéлать, this suit must be altered. П. стихотворéние, to revise a poem. П. харáктер, to reform. Пере-дéл-ка, *n.f.*, alteration. Отдáть в передéлку, to have altered. Попáсть в передéлку (*colloq.*), to get into hot water.

под-дел-ать, *v.p.*, под-дел-ывать, *v.i.*, + *acc.*, to counterfeit, forge, falsify. П. докумéнт (чужую пóдпись), to forge a document (someone's signature). Под-дéл-ать-ся, *v.p.r.*, к + *dat.*, to be subservient. Под-дéл-ывать-ся, *v.i.r.*, под + *acc.*, к + *dat.*, to be subservient; to be counterfeited, imitated. П. под стиль, to imitate a style in art. П. к комý-либо, to be subservient to someone. Под-дéл-ка, *n.f.*, an imitation, for-

gery. П. докумéнта, a forgery of a document. П. драгоцéнных камнéй, to make imitation, fake jewelry. Под-дéл-ь-ный, *adj.*, counterfeit; artificial, false; forged. П-ая пóдпись, a forged signature. П-ые цветы, artificial flowers. Не-под-дéл-ь-ный, *adj.*, genuine, sincere.

по-дел-ать, *v.p.*, + *acc.*, to do; also *in expressions*: Ну что подéлаешь? Well, what can you do? Ничегó не подéлаешь! There is nothing you can do! По-дéл-ывать, *v.i.*, + *acc.*, to be doing; also *in expression*: Что вы подéлываете? What are you doing? По-дел-óм, *adv.*, *in expression*: подéлóм емý, it serves him right!

при-дел-ать, *v.p.*, при-дел-ывать, *v.i.*, + *acc.*, к + *dat.*, to add, attach, join, affix. П. замóк к двéри, to install a lock in a door. При-дéл-ывать-ся, *v.i.r.*, к + *dat.*, to be attached, affixed, joined. При-дéл, *п.т.*, a chapel in a large church, cathedral.

про-дел-ать, *v.p.*, про-дел-ывать, *v.i.*, + *acc.*, to perform, accomplish. П. дверь в стенé, to build a door in a wall. П. огрóмную рабóту, to perform a large job of work. Про-дéл-ка, *n.f.*, a prank, escapade.

раз-дел-ать, *v.p.*, раз-дел-ывать, *v.i.*, + *acc.*, to dress (*e.g.*, fowl); cultivate; stain, grain (*e.g.*, wood); scold, reprimand. Р. дверь под орéх, to grain a door in imitation of walnut. Р. когó-нибудь под орéх, (*colloq.*), to reprimand, scold, someone. Раз-дéл-ать-ся, *v.p.r.*, раз-дéл-ывать-ся, *v.i.r.*, с + *instr.*, to get rid of something; have done with, be through with. Р. с долгáми, to get rid of debts. Р. с кредитóрами, to pay off one's creditors. Он дéшево со мной не разделается (*colloq.*), he will not get off easily with me.

вино-дéл-ие, *п.п.*, wine growing, making. Вино-дéл, *п.т.*, winegrower, maker. Вино-дéл-ательный, *adj.*, of or pertaining to wine making.

земл-е-дéл-ие, *п.п.*, agriculture. Земл-е-дéлец, *п.т.*, farmer, tiller of the soil. Земл-е-дéл-ь-ческий, *adj.*, agricultural.

из-дéл-ие, *п.п.*, a manufactured article. Из-дéл-ия, *n.pl.*, wares. Желéзные (мéдные) издéлия, iron (copper) wares. Кустáрные и., articles of handicraft.

рук-о-дéл-ь-ничать, *v.i.*, to do needlework.

рук-о-дéл-ие, *п.п.*, needlework. Рук-о-дéл-ь-ница, *n.f.*, woman who does needlework, embroidery, needlewoman. Рук-о-дéл-ь-ный, *adj.*, of or pertaining to needlework.

без-дёл-ь-ничать, *v.i.,* to idle, loaf. Без-дёл-ь-ничание, *п.п.,* idleness, loafing. Без-дёл-ь-ник, *п.т.,* без-дёл-ь-ница, *п.f.,* an idler, loafer. Без-дёл-ь-е, *п.п.,* idleness, loafing. Без-дёл-ь-ица, *п.f.,* a trifle. Без-дел-ýшка, *п.f.,* a knick-knack; bagatelle; toy.

благо-дё-тель-ство-вать, *v.i.,* о-благо-дё-тельствовать, *v.p.,* + *acc.,* (*obs.*), to be a benefactor. О. бедняка́, to be a benefactor to a poor man. Благо-дё-тель, *п.т.,* (*obs.*), a benefactor. Благо-дё-тельный, *adj.,* beneficial.

де-я́ни-е, *п.п.,* (*obs.*), deed, work. Бес-смёртное д., an immortal deed, act. Дея́ния Апо́столов (*Ch. Sl.*), the Acts of the Apostles. Благо-де-я́ние, *п.п.,* benefaction, blessing, boon. Зло-де-я́ние, *п.п.,* crime, misdeed.

дё-ятель, *п.т.,* дё-ятельница, *п.f.,* a person active in some activity. Госуда́рственный д., statesman. Общёственный д., social worker; public-spirited man. Дё-ятельность, *п.f.,* activity, work (*usually for the benefit of the community*); profession, vocation. Общёственная д., social, public work. Дё-ятельный, *adj.,* active, energetic. Дё-ятельно, *adv.,* actively, energetically. Само-дё-ятельность, *п.f.,* independent action, spontaneous activity. Вёчер самодеятельности (*recent*), an evening program of local talent.

дей-ствúт-ельность, *п.f.,* reality, actuality; validity. В действúтельности, in reality, in fact, actually. Дей-ствúтель-ный, *adj.,* real, actual, valid; effective. Д. зало́г, (*gram.*), the active voice of a verb. Д. член Акадéмии Нау́к, an active member of the Academy of Sciences. Д-ое собы́тие, an actual happening. Дей-ствúтельно, *adv.,* actually, really, truly; indeed.

дéй-ство-ва-ть, *v.i.,* по-дéй-ство-ва-ть, *v.p.,* на + *acc.,* to proceed; operate, work, function, be effective, effect. Машúна хорошо́ дéйствует, the machine works well. Д. на нéрвы, to affect the nerves. Алкого́ль дéйствует на мозг, alcohol affects the brain. Лека́рство не поде́йствовало, the medicine proved ineffective. Дéй-ству-ющий, *adj. part. act. pres.,* active, acting. Д-ие ли́ца, the characters in a play (*dramatis personae*). Дéй-ствие, *п.п.,* action; act (*in a play*); work, operation, effect, efficacy, influence; deed. Д. происхо́дит в дерéвне, the action takes place in the country. Приводúть в дéйствие, to put into action, start (*e.g., a motor*). Вое́нные д-ия, hostilities.

без-дéй-ствовать, *v.i.,* to be inactive.

Без-дéй-ствие, *п.п.,* inaction, inactivity.

со-дéй-ствовать, *v.i.,* по-со-дé-ство-вать, *v.p.,* + *dat.,* to help, assist, cooperate, collaborate. С. успéху, to contribute to the success of something. Со-дéй-ствие, *п.п.,* assistance, help, cooperation. С. в преступлéнии, complicity in a crime. Оказáть с., to lend support; sustain.

зло-дéй-ствовать, *v.i.,* to act in a criminal manner. Зло-дéй-ство, *п.п.,* a crime; evil, cruel, deed. Зло-дéй, *п.т.,* malefactor, evildoer, villain. Зло-дéй-ский, *adj.,* villainous, criminal, wicked, malevolent.

лиц-е-дéй-ствовать, *v.i.,* (*obs.*), to play. Лиц-е-дéй, *п.т.,* (*obs.*), actor, faker.

ДЕ-, ДЕЖД-, (ДЁЖ-), PLACING, PUT-TING ON, HOPING

де-ть, *v.p.,* де-вáть, *v.i.,* + *acc.,* to put, place. Куда́ вы девáли (дéли) мою́ кнúгу? Where have you put my book? Ему́ нéкуда девáть (деть) свой си́лы, he cannot find an outlet for his energies. Дé-ть-ся, *v.p.r.,* де-вáть-ся, *v.i.r.,* (*colloq.*), to disappear, hide, take refuge. Куда́ она́ девáлась? What has become of her? Ей нéкуда девáться, she has nowhere to go.

в-де-ть, *v.p.,* в-де-вáть, *v.i.,* + *acc.,* в + *acc.,* to put, draw through. В. нúтку, to thread a needle. В-де-вáние, *п.п.,* the action of threading.

воз-дé-ть, *v.p.,* воз-де-вáть, *v.i.,* (*obs.*), + *acc.,* to raise, lift. В. о́чи горé (*rel.,* Ch.-Sl.*), to raise one's eyes heavenward.

за-дé-ть, *v.p.,* за-де-вáть, *v.i.,* + *acc.,* + *instr.,* to be caught in, knock, brush against, graze; tease, provoke, hurt, sting. Задéл за гвоздь и порвáл рука́в, I caught my sleeve on a nail and tore it. З. самолю́бие, to hurt one's feelings, ego. З. за живо́е (*idiom*), to sting to the quick.

из-де-вáть-ся, *v.i.r.,* над + *instr.,* to mock, ridicule. И. над оши́бками и про́махами кого́-нибудь, to laugh at someone's errors and blunders. Из-де-ва́тельство, *п.п.,* mockery. Из-де-ва́тельский, *adj.,* provoking, mocking; contemptuous. И-ое отношéние, contemptuous treatment of someone.

на-дé-ть, *v.p.,* на-де-вáть, *v.i.,* + *acc.,* to don, put on. Н. чехо́л на мéбель, to place slip covers on furniture. Н. пла́тье на дéвочку, to put a dress on a little girl. Н. пальто́, to put on a coat.

о-дé-ть, *v.p.,* о-де-вáть, *v.i.,* + *acc.,* в + *acc.,* + *instr.,* to dress, clothe. О. и накорми́ть всю семью́, to clothe and feed an entire family. Зима́ оде́ла лес сне́гом, (*poet.*), winter has clothed the forest in snow. О-де́ть-ся, *v.p.r.*, о-де-ва́ть-ся, *v.i.r.*, to dress oneself, be dressed. О. по мо́де, to dress in the fashion. О. чи́сто, опря́тно, to dress neatly. О-де-ва́ние, *n.n.*, the act of dressing. О-де́жд-а, *n.f.*, clothes, clothing, garments, attire. Фо́рменная о., a uniform. Ве́рхняя о., outer clothing. О-дёж-а, *n.f.*, о-дёж-ка, *n.f.* (*in proverbs*). По оде́жке протя́гивай но́жки, (*saying*), to cut one's clothes according to one's cloth.

пере-о-де́-ть, *v.p.*, пере-о-де-ва́ть, *v.i.*, + *acc.*, to change clothes. П. ребёнка, to change a child's clothes. Пере-о-де́-ть-ся, *v.p.r.*, пере-о-де-ва́ть-ся, *v.i.r.*, в + *acc.*, to change one's clothes, dress; disguise oneself. П. в но́вое пла́тье (но́вый костю́м), to change into a new suit.

под-де́-ть, *v.p.*, под-де-ва́ть, *v.i.*, + *acc.*, to place, put under; (*colloq.*), ridicule, laugh at someone's expense. П. плато́к под пальто́, to put on a shawl under one's coat. П. ры́бу у́дочкой, to hook a fish. Как ло́вко я его́ подде́л (*colloq.*), how cleverly I fooled him. Под-дё-вка, *n.f.*, a sleeveless jacket.

при-о-де́-ть, *v.p.*, при-о-де-ва́ть, *v.i.*, + *acc.*, (*colloq.*), to dress up. П. дете́й по слу́чаю пра́здника, to dress children for a holiday. При-о-де́-ть-ся, *v.p.r.*, при-о-де-ва́ть-ся, *v.i.r.*, to dress oneself, be dressed. Приоде́лся и пошёл в теа́тр, he dressed and went to the theatre.

про-де́-ть, *v.p.*, про-де-ва́ть, *v.i.*, + *acc.*, to pass, put through; thread. П. кана́т че́рез кольцо́, to pass a rope through a ring. П. ни́тку в иго́лку, to thread a needle. Про-де-ва́ние, *n.n.*, the action of passing through, threading.

раз-де́-ть, *v.p.*, раз-де-ва́ть, *v.i.*, + *acc.*, to undress, unclothe, disrobe. Р. больно́го, to undress a sick person. Граби́тели разде́ли прохо́жего, the thieves took the clothes of the passerby. Раз-де́-ть-ся, *v.p.r.*, раз-де-ва́ть-ся, *v.i.r.*, to undress, disrobe. Раз-де-ва́ние, *n.n.*, the action of undressing, unclothing, disrobing. Раз-де-ва́льня, раз-де-ва́лка, (*slang*), *n.f.*, a cloakroom in a school.

разо-де́-ть, *v.p.*, разо-де-ва́ть, *v.i.*, + *acc.*, to dress, adorn. Раз-о-де́-ть-ся, *v.p.r.*, разо-де-ва́ть-ся, *v.i.r.*, to dress, adorn oneself, put on one's best. Р. во всё но́вое, to dress in new finery. Р. в пух и прах (*idiom*), to dress to kill. Раз-о-де́-тый, *adj. part. pass. past*, dressed in one's best.

на-де́-ять-ся, *v.p.r.*, по-на-де́-ять-ся, *v.i.r.*, на + *acc.*, to hope, trust, be confident, rely on. Н. на успе́х, to hope for success. Наде́юсь за́втра верну́ться, I hope to be back tomorrow. На него́ вполне́ мо́жно н., one can rely on him completely.

на-де́жд-а, *n.f.*, hope, trust, reliance; promise, expectation. Н. на спасе́ние, hope for salvation. После́дняя н., the last hope. В наде́жде на, in the hope of. На-дёж-ность, *n.f.*, reliability, trustworthiness. На-дёж-ный, *adj.*, reliable, trustworthy, secure, safe. Н-ое предприя́тие, safe, secure undertaking. Н. рабо́тник, a reliable worker. Н-ое убе́жище, a safe shelter. На-дёж-но, *adv.*, safely, reliably, securely.

об-на-дёж-ить, *v.p.*, об-на-дёж-ивать, *v.i.*, + *acc.*, to encourage, give hope. О. больно́го, to give a sick person hope.

без-на-дёж-ность, *n.f.*, hopelessness, despair, a hopeless state. Без-на-дёж-ный, *adj.*, hopeless, despairing. Б-ая боле́знь, a fatal illness, hopeless case. Без-на-дёж-но, *adv.*, hopelessly.

ДЕЛ-, ДОЛ-, SHARING, DIVIDING

дел-и́ть, *v.i.*, по-дел-и́ть, *v.p.*, to divide, divide into parts, shares; apportion). Д. на ча́сти, to divide into parts. Д. попола́м, to halve. Д. шесть на три, to divide six by three. Дел-и́ть-ся, *v.i.*, по-дел-и́ть-ся, *v.p.*, to share; be divided, divisible. Де́сять де́лится на два, ten is divisible by two. Д. впечатле́ниями, to share one's impressions. Д. мы́слями, to share one's ideas. Дел-и́мое, *n.n.*, (*math.*), dividend. Дел-и́мость, *n.f.*, divisibility. Дел-и́мый, *adj. part. pass. pres.*, divisible. Дел-и́тель, *n.m.*, (*math.*), divisor.

вы́-дел-ить, *v.p.*, вы-дел-я́ть, *v.i.*, + *acc.*, to distinguish, single out, particularize; isolate; secrete, discharge, exude. В. вещество́ из сме́си, (*chem*), to isolate a substance from a compound. В. вла́гу, to ooze, exude moisture. В. курси́вом, to italicize. В. часть, to extract, isolate a part.

вы́-дел-ить-ся, *v.p.r.*, вы-дел-я́ть-ся, *v.i.r.*, + *instr.*, из + *gen.*, to stand out; to receive one's share; to be discharged, exuded, secreted. Институ́т вы́делился из университе́та, the institute has become independent of the university. Среди́ студе́нтов он выделя́ется свои́ми спосо́бностями, his abilities make him stand out among the students. Вы-дел-е́ние, *n.n.*, secretion, discharge. Гно́йное в., (*med.*), pus. Вы-дел-и́тельный, *adj.*, secretory.

на-дел-и́ть, *v.p.*, на-дел-я́ть, *v.i.*, + *acc.*, + *instr.*, to impart, endow, consign, dispense. Приро́да ще́дро надели́ла его́ тала́нтами, nature has bountifully endowed him with talent. Н. землёй, to give each his share of land. На-де́л, *n.m.*, share, portion of land. Земе́льный н., plot of land. На-дел-е́ние, *n.n.*, apportionment, allotment of land. Н. землёй, allotment of land.

об-дел-и́ть, *v.p.*, об-дел-я́ть, *v.i.*, + *acc.*, + *instr.*, (*colloq.*), to deprive of a share, allot shares unfairly. Оте́ц рассерди́лся на сы́на и обдели́л его́ в завеща́нии, the father was angry with his son and deprived him of his share in his will. Жизнь обдели́ла его́, и он влачи́л жа́лкое существова́ние, he received less than his due from life, and he dragged out a miserable existence.

о-дел-и́ть, *v.p.*, о-дел-я́ть, *v.i.*, + *acc.*, + *instr.*, to present, endow. Мать одели́ла всех дете́й по́ровну сластя́ми, the mother divided the sweets evenly among all the children. Приро́да одели́ла его́ спосо́бностями к му́зыке, nature endowed him with musical talent.

от-дел-и́ть, *v.p.*, от-дел-я́ть, *v.i.*, + *acc.*, + *instr.*, to separate, detach, isolate, disjoin. О. мя́со от кости́, to separate meat from a bone. О. перегоро́дкой часть ко́мнаты, to partition off part of a room. От-дел-и́ть-ся, *v.p.r.*, от-дел-я́ть-ся, *v.i.r.*, от + *gen.*, to be separated, detached. О. от компа́нии, to be separated from the rest-of the company. От-де́л, *n.m.*, department, section, division. О. ка́дров (*recent*), personnel, staff department. Ру́сский Отде́л, Department of Russian (*in schools*). От-дел-е́ние, *n.n.*, section; discharge, separation; train compartment. О. це́ркви от госуда́рства, the separation of Church from State.

пере-дел-и́ть, *v.p.*, пере-дел-я́ть, *v.i.*, + *acc.*, to redivide, reapportion. П. ко́мнату, to partition, divide a room. Пере-де́л, *n.m.*, a redivision. П. земли́, a re-allotment of land.

раз-дел-и́ть, *v.p.*, раз-дел-я́ть, *v.i.*, + *acc.*, to redivide, reapportion. П. ко́мсеparate into parts, sections; share. Р. кни́гу на гла́вы, to divide a book into chapters. Р. насле́дство, to divide an inheritance. Р. де́сять на пять, to divide ten by five. Р. с ке́м-нибудь ра́дости и печа́ли, to share one's joy and grief with someone. Раз-дел-и́ть-ся, *v.p.r.*, раз-дел-я́ть-ся, *v.i.r.*, to be divided. Раз-де́л, *n.m.*, division, partition. Р. насле́дства, division of an in-

heritance. Водо-раз-де́л, *n.m.*, a water divide. Раз-дел-е́ние, *n.n.*, the action of division, distribution. Р. на сло́ги, syllabication, division into syllables. Р. труда́, division of labor. Раз-де́л-ьный, *adj.*, of or pertaining to division, separation. Р. акт, deed of partition (*as of an estate*). Раз-дел-ённый, *adj. part. pass. past*, partitioned, divided.

у-дел-и́ть, *v.p.*, у-дел-я́ть, *v.i.*, + *acc.*, + *dat.*, to spare, give; apportion. Он удели́л часть своего́ состоя́ния на постро́йку больни́цы, he apportioned a part of his holdings for the construction of a hospital. У. внима́ние, to heed, pay attention. Я не могу́ у. вре́мени на э́то, I cannot spare any time for this. У-де́л, *n.m.*, lot, portion; destiny, fate; (*hist.*), an independent principality in mediaeval Russia. У-де́л-ь-ный, *adj.*, (*phys.*), specific. У. вес, specific gravity, weight. У. князь, (*hist.*), Russian mediaeval prince. У-ая теплота́, specific heat.

до́л-я, *n.f.*, part, piece; fate. Дочь получи́ла пя́тую до́лю насле́дства, the daughter received one fifth of the inheritance. "Хоте́л объе́хать це́лый свет и не объе́хал со́той до́ли" (Griboedov), I wanted to travel all over the world, but I did not cover even one hundredth of it. Ей вы́пало на до́лю мно́го несча́стий, much misfortune fell to her lot. Несча́стная д. сироты́, the sad fate of an orphan. До́л-ь-ка, *n.f.*, section. Д. чеснока́ (лимо́на), a clove of garlic (section of lemon).

ДЕН-, ДН-, DAY

ден-ь, *n.m.*, (дн-я, *gen.*), day. Понеде́льник - пе́рвый день неде́ли, Monday is the first day of the week. Д. но́вого го́да, New Year's Day. Д. о́тдыха, a day of rest. Д. рожде́ния, a birthday, day of one's birth. Бу́дний д., a workday, weekday. Выходно́й д., a day off. До́брый день! Good day! Це́лый д., the whole day. Д. денско́й (*folk*), the day long. Тре́тьего дня, the day before yesterday. На-дня́х, the other day, some days ago. Днём, during the day. Ден-щи́к, *n.m.*, (*mil., obs.*), an officer's orderly.

по-дён-ный, *adj.*, designated by the day. П-ая зарпла́та (*recent*), wages by the day. По-дён-но, *adv.*, by the day. По-дён-щик, *n.m.*, по-дён-щица, *n.f.*, day-laborer, workman hired by the day. К нам прихо́дит подёнщица убира́ть дом, a woman hired by the day comes to clean our house. По-дён-щина, *n.f.*, work by the day. Ходи́ть на подёнщину (*obs.*), to work as a day laborer. **дн-ева́-ть, дн-ю́ю,** *v.i.,* в + *prep.,* to spend the whole day. Он дню́ет и ночу́ет в э́том до́ме, he is at this house day and night. Дн-ева́лить, *v.i.,* (*mil., colloq.*), to be on duty (*of privates only*). Дн-ева́льный, *adj. used as n., (mil.*), orderly, a soldier on duty. Д. по бара́ку, an orderly on duty in the barracks. Дн-евни́к, *n.m.,* diary, journal. Д. путеше́ствия, diary of a journey. Вести́ д., to keep a diary. Он ведёт д. свое́й жи́зни, he keeps a diary of his life. Дн-евно́й, *adj.,* of or pertaining to the day; diurnal. Д. свет, daylight. Д. за́работок, a day's wages. Еже-дн-е́вный, *adj.,* daily, occurring every day. Е-ая газе́та, a daily newspaper. Е-ые уро́ки, daily lessons. Еже-дн-е́вно, *adv.,* daily, every day. Одно-дн-е́вный, *adj.,* of one day's duration; (*fig.*), ephemeral. Много-дн-е́вный, *adj.,* of many days' duration.

по́л-ден-ь, *n.m.,* noon, noonday, midday. Вре́мя до полу́дня, forenoon. Вре́мя о́коло полу́дня, noonday, noontime. Вре́мя по́сле полу́дня, afternoon. Пол-дн-е́вный, *adj.,* of or pertaining to a half-day's duration. П. час (*poet.*), noon hour. П. за́работок, a half-day's earnings. Пол-у́-ден-ный, *adj.,* of or pertaining to noon, noontime. П. зной, noon blaze, heat. По-пол-у́-дн-и, *adv.,* in the afternoon.

ДЕНЬГ- (ДЕНЬЖ-), ДЕНЕ́Ж-, CURRENCY, MONEY

де́ньг-и, *n.pl.,* money, currency; coins. Бума́жные д., paper money. Карма́нные д., pocket money. Командиро́вочные д., travelling allowance. Ни за каки́е д. (*idiom*), not for all the money in the world. Д. на була́вки (*obs.*), pin money. Он всегда́ при деньга́х, he always has money. У меня́ нет с собо́й де́нег, I have no money on me. Де́ньж-а́та, (*colloq.*), деньж-о́нки, *pl.,* (*derog.*), money.

де́неж-ный, *adj.,* pecuniary, monetary, of or pertaining to money; (*fig.*), well-to-do. Д. знак, a monetary token. Д. мешо́к, moneybag. Д. перево́д, a postal order, money order. Д. штраф, a fine. Д-ая едини́ца, a monetary unit. Д-ая по́мощь, financial assistance. Д-ое затрудне́ние, financial difficulty. Д-ые дела́, financial, money matters. Де́неж-ка, *n.f.,* (*dim., obs.*), a small copper coin called a half-kopek. Де́неж-ки, *n.pl.,* (*dim., colloq.*), cash. **без-де́неж-ье,** *n.n.,* lack of money. Без-де́неж-ный, *adj.,* penniless, moneyless.

о-без-де́неж-и-ть, *v.p.,* + *acc.,* (*colloq.*), to deprive of money.

ДЕРЕ́В-, ДРЕВ-, ДРОВ-, TIMBER, WOOD, TREE

де́рев-о, *n.n.,* tree, wood. Плодо́вое д., fruit tree. Хво́йное д., coniferous tree. Ли́ственное д., deciduous tree. Дерев-о-обде́лочная промы́шленность, woodworking industry. Дерев-о-обде́лочник, *n.m.,* woodworker. Дерев-цо́, *n.n.,* a small tree, sapling. **дерев-ен-е́ть,** *v.i.,* о-дерев-ене́ть, *v.p.,* to become wooden; (*fig.*), to stiffen. От моро́за но́ги деревене́ют, feet stiffen with cold. О-дерев-ене́лость, *n.f.,* stiffening, hardening. Дерев-я́нный, *adj.,* wooden, made of wood. Д. дом, a wooden house. Д-ое ма́сло, inferior olive oil. Дерев-я́шка, *n.f.,* a piece of wood. **дре́в-о,** *n.n.,* (*Ch.-Sl.*), tree. Д. позна́ния добра́ и зла (*Bib.*), the tree of knowledge of good and evil. Генеалоги́ческое д., a genealogical tree. Древо-ви́дный, *adj.,* tree-like. Не́рвы име́ют древови́дные отро́стки, nerves have tree-like branches. Древ-о-ви́дное расте́ние, a tree-like plant. Древ-о-насажде́ние, *n.n.,* tree planting. **древ-еси́на,** *n.f.,* wood. Древ-е́сный, *adj.,* arborous, arboreal; woody. Д. спирт, wood alcohol. Д. у́голь, charcoal. Дре́в-ко, *n.n.,* shaft, pikestaff, staff. **дров-а́,** *n.pl.,* firewood, wood. Дро́в-ни, *n.pl.,* a peasant sledge. Дров-о-загото́вка, *n.f.,* (*recent*), the storing of wood. Дров-о-се́к, *n.m.,* wood-cutter; woodsman; lumberjack. В лесу́ раздава́лся топо́р дровосе́ка (*Nekrasov*), The sound of the woodcutter's ax was heard in the forest. Дров-яно́й, *adj.,* of or pertaining to firewood. Д. сара́й, woodshed. Д. склад, storehouse for firewood.

ДЕРЖ-, MAINTENANCE, HOLD; PRESERVATION; RETENTION

держ-а́-ть, *v.i.,* + *acc.,* to hold, keep. Д. каранда́ш в руке́, to hold a pencil in one's hand. Д. ла́вку, to maintain a shop. Д. речь, to make a speech. Д. пари́, to bet. Д. экза́мен, to take an examination. Д. язы́к за зуба́ми, (*idiom.*), to hold one's tongue. Он не уме́ет себя́ д., he does not know how to behave. Держ-а́ть-ся, *v.i.r.,* + *instr.,* за + *acc.,* to hold on; stand up. Д. рука́ми за пери́ла, to hold on to a banister. Д. пря́мо, to hold oneself straight, erect. Держи́тесь кре́пко! Hold tight!

держ-а́ва, *n.f.,* power; orb. Мирова́я д., a world power. Вели́кие держа́вы, the great powers. Держ-а́вный, *adj.,* sovereign, potent, powerful; reigning. Само-держ-а́вие, *n.n.,* autocracy. Само-де́рж-ец, *n.m.,* autocrat. Само-держ-а́вный, *adj.,* autocratic.

воз-держ-а́ть-ся, *v.p.r.,* воз-де́рж-ивать-ся, *v.i.r.,* от + *gen.,* to abstain, restrain oneself. В. от гне́ва, to suppress anger. В. от голосова́ния, to abstain from voting. Воз-держ-а́ние, *n.n.,* abstinence. В. от алкого́ля, abstinence, temperance. Воз-де́рж-анность, *n.f.,* abstinence, forbearance. Воз-де́рж-анный, *adj.,* abstinent, temperate, forbearing. В. челове́к, a temperate man.

вы́-держ-ать, *v.p.,* вы-де́рж-ивать, *v.i.,* + *acc.,* to endure; sustain; undergo. В. испыта́ние, to pass a test. В. хара́ктер, to be firm. В. экза́мен, to pass an examination. Не в. уда́ра, to fail to withstand a blow, shock. Вы́-держ-ка, *n.f.,* extract; self-control, firmness, endurance. Вы́-держ-анный, *adj. part. pass. past,* seasoned. В-ое вино́, seasoned wine. В. челове́к, a self-controlled person.

за-держ-а́ть, *v.p.,* за-де́рж-ивать, *v.i.,* + *acc.,* to detain, stop; retain; arrest, delay. З. жа́лование, to withhold a salary. З. кора́бль в порту́, to lay an embargo on a ship. За-де́рж-ка, *n.f.,* delay, impediment. За-держ-а́ть-ся, *v.p.r.,* за-де́рж-ивать-ся, *v.i.r.,* to be delayed, to stay longer than planned.

из-держ-а́ть, *v.p.,* из-де́рж-ивать, *v.i.,* + *acc.* (*obs.*), to spend money; use, consume. Я издержа́л все де́ньги на пое́здку в Крым, I spent all my money on a trip to the Crimea. Из-держ-а́ть-ся, *v.p.r.,* из-де́рж-ивать-ся, *v.i.r.,* to have spent one's money. Из-де́рж-ка, *n.f.,* expense, cost. Суде́бные изде́ржки, court costs.

о-держ-а́ть, *v.p.,* о-де́рж-ивать, *v.i.,* + *acc.,* to overcome, gain an advantage. О. верх, to gain an advantage over someone; prevail, overcome. О. побе́ду, to conquer, win a victory. О-держ-и́мый, *adj. part. pass. pres.,* possessed, frantic. О. навя́зчивой иде́ей, obsessed by a fixed idea.

пере-держ-а́ть, *v.p.,* пере-де́рж-ивать, *v.i.,* + *acc.,* to overexpose (*in photography*); keep too long; overdraw (*in banking*). Пере-де́рж-ка, *n.f.,* overdraft; (*fig.*), reexamination.

по-держ-а́ть, *v.p.,* + *acc.,* to hold, keep for a period of time. П. ребёнка на рука́х, to hold a child in one's arms. Подержи́те мою́ су́мку, пока́ я доста́ну биле́т, hold my bag while I get a ticket. Подерж-а́ть-ся, *v.p.r.,* за + *acc.,* to hold on to something for a while. По-де́рж-анный, *adj.,* used; secondhand. П. автомоби́ль, a used car.

под-держ-а́ть, *v.p.,* под-де́рж-ивать, *v.i.,* + *acc.,* to support, sustain. П. жизнь, to sustain life. П. наде́жду, to keep up hope. П. семью́, to support a family. Под-де́рж-ивать-ся, *v.i.r.,* + *instr.,* to be supported, sustained. Под-де́рж-ка, *n.f.,* support; maintenance.

при-держ-а́ть, *v.p.,* при-де́рж-ивать, *v.i.,* + *acc.,* to hold, keep, check, restrain. П. язы́к, to hold one's tongue. При-де́рж-ивать-ся, *v.i.r.,* за + *acc.,* + *gen.,* to hold on to, hold to. П. за пери́ла, to hold on to a banister. П. осо́бых мне́ний, to have one's own opinions. П. пра́вила, to follow a rule. П. те́мы, to keep to a subject.

про-держ-а́ть, *v.p.,* + *acc.,* to keep, detain. Он продержа́л меня́ два часа́, he detained me for two hours. Про-держ-а́ть-ся, *v.p.r.,* to hold out, endure. Кре́пость продержа́лась 11 ме́сяцев, the fortress held out for eleven months.

с-держ-а́ть, *v.p.,* с-де́рж-ивать, *v.i.,* + *acc.,* to hold back, restrain. С. гнев, to suppress one's anger. С. сло́во, обеща́ние, to stand by one's word, keep one's promise. С-де́рж-анность, *n.f.,* reserve, restraint, reticence. С-де́рж-анный, *adj. part. pass. past,* reserved, discreet, restrained, self-controlled. С-ая я́рость, composed, pent up fury. С-держ-а́ть-ся, *v.p.r.,* с-де́рж-ивать-ся, *v.i.r.,* + *instr.,* to control oneself, restrain oneself. С-де́рж-ивание, *n.n.,* check, restraint, suppression.

со-держ-а́ть, *v.p.,* + *acc.,* to keep, support, maintain; contain. С. дом в чистоте́, to keep a house clean. С. двух дете́й, to support two children. С. под аре́стом, to keep under arrest. Со-держ-а́ть-ся, *v.i.r.,* to be kept, supported, maintained; be contained. В э́той кни́ге соде́ржатся все его́ тео́рии, his book contains all his theories. Со-держ-а́ние, *n.n.,* contents; salary, maintenance. С. и фо́рма, content and form. Челове́к без вну́треннего содержа́ния, a shallow-minded person. Со-держ-и́мое, *n.n.,* contents. С. буты́лки, the contents of a bottle. Со-держ-а́тельность, *n.f.,* meaningful contents (*e.g.,* of a book). Со-держ-а́тельный, *adj.,* meaningful. Со-держ-а́тель ресто-ра́на, proprietor, keeper of a restaurant.

у-держ-а́ть, *v.p.,* у-де́рж-ивать, *v.i.,* + *acc.,* to hold, keep back, restrain, retain.

У. в па́мяти, to retain in one's memory. У. зево́к, to suppress a yawn. У. пять рубле́й из жа́лования, to deduct five rubles from one's salary. У-держ-а́ть-ся, *v.p.r.*, у-де́рж-ивать-ся, *v.i.r.*, от + *gen.*, to restrain oneself, abstain. Я не мог у. от сме́ха, I couldn't restrain myself from laughter. У-держ-а́ние, *n.n.*, reservation, retention, restraining. Без у́-держ-у, *adv.*, immoderately, without restraint. Без-у́-держ-ный, *adj,*. impetuous. Б. поры́в, an overwhelming, uncontrollable impulse. Б. смех, uncontrollable laughter.

ДЕРЗ-, ДРАЗ-, ДРАЖ-, ANNOYANCE, VEXATION, IRRITATION; AUDACITY, DARING

дерз-а́-ть, *v.i.*, дерз-ну́ть, *v.p.*, + *inf.*, (*obs.*), to dare, presume. Я не дерзну́л нару́шить его́ поко́й, I did not dare to disturb him, to upset his composure. Дерз-но-ве́ние, *n.n.*, audacity, daring. Дерз-но-ве́нный, *adj.*, audacious. Дерз-но-ве́нно, *adv.*, audaciously, daringly. Дерз-а́-ющий, *adj. part. act. pres.*, audacious.

дерз-и́-ть, *v.i.*, на-дерз-и́ть, *v.p.*, + *dat.*, to talk impertinently. Д. учи́телю, to be rude to one's teacher. Де́рз-ость, *n.f.*, audacity, impertinence, rudeness. Наговори́ть де́рзостей, to talk impertinently, rudely. Де́рз-кий, *adj.*, impertinent, insolent, rude. Дерз-я́щий, *adj. part. act. pres.*, impertinent, insolent, daring, rude. Де́рз-ко, *adv.*, rudely, impertinently, insolently.

драз-н-и́ть, *v.i.*, + *acc.*, + *instr.*, to tease, provoke, mock. Д. соба́ку, to tease a dog. Д. ло́жными наде́ждами (*fig.*), to tantalize, tease with false hopes.

пере-драз-ни́ть, *v.p.*, пере-дра́з-нивать, *v.i.*, + *acc.*, to ape, imitate, mimic. Обезья́ны, говоря́т, передра́знивают люде́й, it is said that monkeys imitate people.

раз-драз-ни́ть, *v.p.*, раз-дра́з-нивать, *v.i.*, + *acc.*, (*colloq.*), to provoke, tease. Р. аппети́т, to provoke one's appetite.

раз-драж-а́ть, *v.i.*, раз-драж-и́ть, *v.p.*, + *acc.*, + *instr.*, to annoy, irritate, try one's patience. Р. желу́док (не́рвы), to irritate one's stomach (nerves). Р. кого́-нибудь назо́йливыми про́сьбами, to annoy someone with constant requests. Р. глаза́, to make one's eyes smart. Раз-драж-а́ть-ся, *v.i.r.*, + *instr.*, to lose one's temper, to become irritated. Ко́жа раздража́ется тепло́м, the skin is irritated by heat. Больно́й легко́ раздража́ется, a sick man is easily irritated. Раз-драж-е́ние, *n.n.*, annoy-

ance, exasperation, irritation. Припа́док раздраже́ния, a fit of bad humor, temperament. Раз-драж-и́мость, *n.f.*, irritability. Раз-драж-и́мый, *adj. part. pass. pres.*, irritable. Раз-драж-и́тель, *n.m.*, (*med.*), irritant. Раз-драж-и́тельность, *n.f.*, irritability, fretfulness. Раз-драж-и́тельный, *adj.*, irritable, fretful. Раз-драж-и́тельно, *adv.*, irritably, fretfully.

ДИВ-, (ДИВ-Л-), WONDER, MARVEL; ASTONISHMENT, AMAZEMENT, WONDERMENT, SURPRISE

ди́в-о, *n.n.*, (*obs.*), marvel, wonder, prodigy. Что за д., what a wonder! На д., wonderfully. Ди́ву даёшься его́ глу́пости (*colloq.*), it's amazing how stupid he is. Ди́в-ный, *adj.*, wonderful, marvelous, delightful. Д. за́пах, a delicious odor. Д-ая пого́да, wonderful weather. Ди́в-но, *adv.*, wonderfully, delightfully.

див-и́ть-ся, див-л-ю́сь, *v.i.r.*, + *dat.*, to wonder, marvel, be surprised. Мы диви́лись его́ успе́хам, we marvelled at his success.

на-див-и́ть-ся, *v.p.*, + *dat.*, + *acc.*, to admire sufficiently; wonder. Я не могу́ надиви́ться его́ успе́хам, I cannot get over his success.

по-див-и́ть-ся, *v.p.r.*, + *dat.*, to admire; wonder. Я нема́ло подиви́лся стра́нностям э́того челове́ка, I wondered greatly at this man's strange ways.

у-див-и́ть, *v.p.*, у-див-ля́ть, *v.i.*, + *acc.*, to astonish, surprise, amaze. У-див-л-я́ть-ся, *v.i.r.*, у-див-и́ть-ся, *v.p.r.*, + *dat.*, to be astonished, surprised; wonder, marvel. Я удивля́юсь ва́шим спосо́бностям к иностра́нным языка́м, I am amazed at your ability in foreign languages.

у-див-л-е́ние, *n.n.*, wonder, surprise, astonishment, amazement. Приводи́ть в у., to astonish, amaze. Обе́д вы́шел на у., the dinner turned out to be a wonder. К моему́ удивле́нию, to my surprise.

у-див-и́тельный, *adj.*, wonderful, astonishing, surprising, striking, marvelous. Что у-ого в э́том? what's so wonderful about this? Ничего́ у-ого, no wonder. У-див-и́тельно, *adv.*, wonderfully, astonishingly, surprisingly, strikingly, marvelously. У. хорошо́, surprisingly well!

ДИК-, ДИЧ-, SAVAGERY, WILDNESS

дик-а́рь, *n.m.*, savage, wild man; shy, unsociable person. Дик-а́рка, *n.f.*, a woman savage; shy, unsociable woman. Она́ стра́шная д., she is incredibly shy (unsociable). Ди́к-ость, *n.f.*, savagery, wildness; absurdity; shyness, unsociability. Ди́к-ий, *adj.*, wild, savage; odd, extravagant, absurd; unsociable, shy. Д-ая у́тка, a wild duck. Д-ие племена́, savage tribes. Ди́к-о, *adv.*, wildly; violently; oddly, absurdly. Дик-обра́з, *n.п.*, porcupine. Дик-о́вин(к)а, *n.f.*, a wonder, prodigy; rarity; curiosity. Что за дико́вина! How strange! What a strange thing! Трамва́й ему́ в дико́винку, he has never seen a streetcar. Дик-о́винный, *adj.*, odd; outlandish, bizarre, unusual, uncommon.

дич-ь, *n.f.*, game, wild fowl; thicket, remote spot; nonsense. И дичь, forest wild-life. Кака́я д.! What nonsense! Поро́ть дичь, to talk nonsense.

дич-а́ть, *v.i.*, о-дич-а́ть, *v.p.*, to become wild, savage, unsociable. В э́той глуши́ лю́ди ско́ро дича́ют, in this remote place people quickly become like savages. Дич-и́ть-ся, *v.i.r.*, + *gen.*, to be shy, unsociable. Д. всех, to shy away from everyone.

о-дич-а́-лость, *n.f.*, wildness; shyness. О-дич-а́лый, *adj.*, wild, unsociable; untamed. О-дич-а́вший, *adj. part. act. past*, one who has become shy, wild, unsociable.

ДЛИН-, ДЛ-, ДОЛГ-, ДОЛОГ-, ДОЛЖ-, ДАЛ-Ь-, ДОЛ-, LENGTH

длин-а́, *n.f.*, length. Ме́ра длины́, measure of length. В длину́, lengthwise. Растяну́ться в длину́, to fall lengthwise. Длина́ реки́ (доро́ги), length of a river (road). Дли́н-ный, *adj.*, long, lengthy. Д. Ура́льский хребе́т тя́нется от Се́верного Ледови́того океа́на почти́ до Каспи́йского мо́ря, the long Ural range stretches from the Arctic Ocean to the Caspian Sea. Дли́н-н-о-, *a combining form meaning* long. Длин-н-оволо́сый, *adj.*, long-haired. Длин-н-о-но́гий, *adj.*, long-legged. Длиннопо́лый сюрту́к, (*obs.*), long-skirted frock coat. Дли́н-н-о, *adv.*, lengthily, at length.

по́-длин-ник, *n.т.*, original. Это не ко́пия, а п., this is not a copy, but the original. Чита́ть поэ́му в по́длиннике, to read a poem in the original. По́длин-но, *adv., also adj. pred. neut.*, genuinely, truly, really, originally. Пу́шкин п. ру́сский поэ́т, Pushkin is a true Russian poet. По́-длин-ный, *adj.*, genuine, true, authentic, original. П. текст, original text. Это его́ по́длинные слова́, these are his very own words. По́-длин-ность, *n.f.*, authenticity, originality. П. э́того докуме́нта

дока́зана, the authenticity of this document has been proved. До-по́-длин-но, *see* подлинно. Д. ве́рно, true to the original. До-по́-длин-ный, *adj., see* по́длинный.

у-длин-й-ть, *v.p.*, у-длин-я́ть, *v.i.*, to lengthen, elongate. У. рука́в, to lengthen a sleeve. У-длин-е́ние, *n.п.*, lengthening. У. рабо́чего дня, lengthening of a work day. У-длин-и́ть-ся, *v.p.r.*, у-длин-я́ть-ся, *v.i.r.*, to be lengthened, become longer. Осенью вечера́ удлиня́ются, the evenings become longer in autumn.

дли́-тельность, *n.f.*, prolongation, lengthiness. Дли́-тельный, *adj.*, protracted, long, lingering. Д. пери́од, prolonged period. Дли́-тельно, *adv.*, a long time, at length.

дли-ть, *v.i.*, про-дли́-ть, *v.p.*, + *асс.* (*obs.*), to protract, prolong, draw out. Заседа́ние дли́лось це́лый день, the session lasted a whole day. Продли́ть заня́тия, to prolong classes. Продли́ть о́тпуск, to prolong, extend a vacation. Дли́-ть-ся, *v.i.r.*, про-дли́-ть-ся, *v.p.r.*, to last, be continued. Про-дл-е́ние, *n.п.*, prolongation, extension.

до́л-гий, *adj.*, long, prolonged. Д. пери́од, prolonged period. Откла́дывать в до́лгий я́щик, (*saying*), to defer, delay. Не откла́дывай дела́ в до́лгий я́щик, don't procrastinate. До́л-ог, *adj. pred.*, (*obs.*), long. Во́лос до́лог, да ум коро́ток, (*saying*), beautiful, but dumb. До́лг-о, *adv.*, long, a long time. Нам пришло́сь д. ждать по́езда, we had to wait a long time for the train. До́лго-ли до беды́, (*express.*), a misfortune can easily occur. До́лг-о, *a combining form meaning* long (*with reference to time*). Долг-о-ве́чность, *n.f.*, longevity, permanence. Долг-о-ве́чный, *adj.*, long-lived; lasting. Долг-о-жда́нный, *adj.*, long-awaited. Долг-от-а́, *n.f.*, longitude; (*ling.*), length. Долг-о-терпе́ние, *n.п.*, long-suffering. Долг-о-терпели́вый, *adj.*, long-suffering. Долг-о-сро́чный, *adj.*, long-term. За-до́лг-о, *adv.*, long before. Не з., shortly. Не з. пе́ред отъе́здом, shortly before his departure. На-до́лг-о, *adv.*, for a long time. До́л-ь-ше, *adj. comp. and adj. comp.*, longer. Я до́льше вас в э́том го́роде живу́, I have been living in this city longer than you. До́л-е, *adj. comp.*, (*obs.*), longer. Я уезжа́ю надо́лго, I am leaving for a long time. Про-долг-ова́тость, *n.f.*, oblong. Про-долг-ова́тый, *adj.*, oblong. П. мозг, (*anat.*), medulla oblongata.

про-долж-а́-ть, *v.i.*, про-долж-ить, *v.p.*, + *асс.*, to continue, proceed. П. ли́нию, to prolong a line. Продолжа́йте писа́ть, write on, continue to write. Про-долж-а́ть-ся, *v.i.r.*, про-до́лж-ить-ся, *v.p.r.*, to continue, last, be prolonged. Холода́ мо́гут продолжа́ться до ма́я, the cold weather may last until May. Про-долж-а́тель, *n.m.*, successor. Про-долж-е́ние, *n.n.*, continuation, prolongation. П. сле́дует, to be continued. В п., during, in the course of. Ученики́ реша́ли зада́чи в продолже́ние всего́ уро́ка, the pupils worked on problems for the whole lesson. Про-долж-и́тель-ность, *n.f.*, duration, continuance, lengthiness. Про-долж-и́тельный, *adj.*, prolonged, long.

дал-ь, *n.f.*, distance. Это така́я даль! It is such a long way off! В-дал-ь, *adv.*, *used with verbs of motion,* far away, a long way off. В-дал-и́, *adv.*, far away, a long way off. Да́л-ь-ность, *n.f.*, far distance. Бег на д. расстоя́ния, marathon, long distance race. Д. полёта, (*mil.*), flight range. Да́л-ь-ний, *adj.*, far off, away; remote, distant. Д. ро́дственник, distant relative. Даль-не́йший, *adj.*, furthest, further-most. В. дальне́йшем, in the future, В. д. я не повторю́ э́той оши́бки, in the future I shall not repeat this mistake. Д-ие подро́бности, further particulars. Да́л-ь-но-, *a combining form meaning* far, distant. Дально-бо́йный, *adj.*, long-range (of artillery). Д-ое ору́дие, long-range gun. Дально-ви́дность, *n.f.*, foresight, farsightedness. Дально-ви́дный, *adj.*, farsighted, farseeing. Даль-не-восто́чный, Far Eastern. Д-ая а́рмия, Far Eastern army. Да́льний Восто́к, the Far East. Да́льно-зо́р-кость, *n.f.*, farsightedness. Дально-зо́ркий, *adj.*, farsighted. Очки́ для д-их, glasses for farsighted people. Дал-ё-кий, *adj.*, distant, remote. Д. го́род, a distant city, town. Д. от и́стины (це́ли), far from the truth (purpose). Дал-е-ко́, *adv.*, far, afar, far off; abroad. Д. за по́лночь, long after midnight. Д. не дура́к, (*colloq.*), far from being a fool. Да́л-ее, *adv.*, *comp.*, further, farther. И так да́лее (и т.д.), and so forth (etc.). Да́л-ь-ше, *adv. comp.*, further, farther. И что́-же да́льше? And what next? Не ви́деть д. своего́ но́са, (*idiom*), not to see beyond one's own nose. В-дал-еке́, *adv.*, in the far distance.

от-дал-и́ть, *v.p.*, от-дал-я́ть, *v.i.*, + *acc.*, to estrange; postpone; remove. О. разлу́ку, to postpone a separation. От-дал-и́ть-ся, *v.p.r.*, от-дал-я́ть-ся, *v.i.r.*, от + *gen.*, to withdraw; be postponed, removed, rendered distant, remote.

Парохо́д отдали́лся от бе́рега, the ship was moving away from the shore. О. от друзе́й, to shun friends. От-дал-е́ние, *n.n.*, removal, estrangement. От-дал-ённость, *n.f.*, remoteness, aloofness. В. отдале́нии, far off, in the far distance. От-дал-ённый, *adj. part. pass. past,* remote, distant. О-ая дере́вня, a remote village. О-ое схо́дство, remote likeness.

у-дал-и́ть, *v.p.*, у-дал-я́ть, *v.i.*, + *acc.*, to move, move off, away; remove. У. свечу́ от глаз, to move a candle away from the eyes. У. безбиле́тных из ваго́-на, to remove ticketless passengers from a car. У. больно́й зуб, to extract a bad tooth. У. пятно́ с пла́тья, to remove a stain from a dress. У-дал-и́ть-ся, *v.p.r.*, у-дал-я́ть-ся, *v.i.r.*, от + *gen.*, в + *acc.*, to move off, away, withdraw. У. от го́рода (от люде́й), to leave a city (shun people, withdraw from society). У. от дел (на поко́й), to retire. У-дал-е́ние, *n.n.*, the action of moving off, away; removal, withdrawal. У-дал-ённый, *adj. part. pass. past,* withdrawn, removed.

дол-е-во́й, *adj.*, (*tech.*), lengthwise, longitudinal; *see* продо́льный. Д. разре́з де́рева, longitudinal section of a tree, of wood. В долево́м направле́нии, lengthwise.

в-дол-ь, *prep. and adv.*, + *gen.*, lengthwise, along. В. бе́рега, along the shore. В. по у́лице, along the street. В. и поперёк, far and wide. Отря́д распо-ложи́лся на о́тдых вдоль доро́ги, the detachment settled down for a rest along the road.

про-до́л-ь-ный, *adj.*, lengthwise, longitudinal. П-ая сторона́ до́ма, the long side of a house. П-ая пила́, rip saw. Про-до́л-ь-но, *adv.*, lengthwise.

дол, *n.m.*, (*poet.*), dale. По гора́м и до́лам, up hill and down dale. Дол-и́на, *n.f.*, valley. Д. реки́ Те́река, the valley of the river Terek.

ДОБ-, SUITABILITY, APPROPRIATE-NESS

на́-доб-но, *impers. expression,* it is necessary. На́-доб-ность, *n.f.*, (*obs.*), necessity, need. Кра́йняя н., exigency. Име́ть н., to require. В слу́чае на́доб-ности, in case of need. На́-доб-ный, *adj.*, (*obs.*), necessary.

по-на́-доб-ить-ся, *v.p.r.*, (*colloq.*), to be necessary. Мне э́то понадо́билось, I needed this.

у-до́б-ный, *adj.*, convenient, handy; comfortable, cosy. У-ая кварти́ра, a comfortable apartment. У. слу́чай, a

suitable occasion, opportunity. Пóльзо-
ваться удóбным слýчаем, to seize, take
advantage of an opportunity. У-дóб-но,
adv., conveniently, comfortably. У.-ли
вам? Are you comfortable? Не-у-дóб-
но, *adv.*, inconveniently, uncomfortably.
Не-у-дóб-ный, *adj.*, inconvenient, uncomfortable. У-дóб-ство, *п.п.*, conve-
nience, comfort. Квартúра со всéми
удóбствами, an apartment with all con-
veniences. Не-у-дóб-ство, *п.п.*, inconvenience, discomfort. Не имéть теле-
фóна в квартúре - э́то большóе н., it
is a great inconvenience not to have a
telephone in one's apartment. По-доб-
áть, *v.i., used impers., (obs.)*, to become, suit, be worthy of. Не подобáет
вам так говорúть, it does not become
you to speak this way. По-доб-áющий,
adj. part. act. pres., appropriate, becoming.

по-дóб-ие, *п.п.*, similarity. По подóбию,
in the image of. По-дóб-ный, *adj.*,
similar, alike, equal. Подóбным óбразом, likewise, in a similar manner.
Ничегó подóбного, nothing of the kind.
И тому подóбное, (и т. п.), and so forth
(etc.). По-дóб-но, *adv.*, similarly. П.
томý как, the same as.

с-по-дóб-и-ть, *v.p.*, с-по-доб-лять, *v.i.*,
(obs.), to consider one worthy of. С-
по-дóб-ить-ся, *v.p.r.*, с-по-доб-л-ять-
ся, *v.i.r.*, to be thought, considered,
worthy.

у-по-дóб-ить, *v.p.*, у-по-доб-л-ять, *v.i.*,
+ *acc.*, + *dat.*, to liken to, compare.
Гóголь уподóбил Россию быстро
несýщейся трóйке, Gogol compared
Russia to a swiftly rushing troika (team
of three horses). У-по-дóб-ить-ся,
v.p.r., у-по-доб-л-ять-ся, *v.i.r.*, to be
likened to, compared to something,
someone. У-по-доб-л-éние, *п.п.*, comparison, likening.

ДОБР-, ДАБР-, GOODNESS, KIND-
NESS

добр-ó, *п.п.*, the letter D in Church Slavonic; good; property, goods. Добрó -
пятая бýква в церкóвно-славянс-
ком алфавúте, *dobro* is the name of
the fifth letter in the Church Slavonic
alphabet. Дéлать д., to do good.
Платúть добрóм за зло, to render
good for evil. Добр-óм, *adv.*, in a
friendly way. Лýчше добрóм отдáть,
better return it willingly. Добр-о-, *a
combining form meaning* good. Добр-о-
вóлец, *п.т.*, volunteer. Добр-о-вóль-
ный, *adj.*, voluntary. Д-ая пóмощь,
voluntary aid. Добр-о-дéтель, *n.f.*, virtue. Добр-о-дéтельный, *adj.*, virtuous,

pious. Добр-о-дýшный, *adj.*, good-
natured. Добр-о-сóвестный, *adj.*, conscientious. Добр-отá, *n.f.*, kindness,
goodness. Добр-óтный, *adj.*, of good
quality. Дóбр-ый, *adj.*, kind, good;
genial, gentle. Д. день! Good day!
В д. час! Good luck! Д-ое úмя, a good
name, reputation. Добр-ó, *adv. in the
expression*: Д. пожáловать! Welcome!
Добр-як, *n.m.*, good-natured man.

добр-é-ть, *v.i.*, по-добр-éть, *v.p.*, to become kinder. Наш хозяин добрéет:
обещáет прибáвку дать, our employer
is becoming kinder: he promises us an
increase. Добр-éть, *v.i.*, раз-добр-éть,
v.p., (colloq.), to become corpulent, put
on weight, flesh. На хорóшей пúще
нетрýдно и раздобрéть, it is not difficult to put on weight with good food.

за-дóбр-ить, *v.p.*, за-дáбр-ивать, *v.i.*, +
acc., to cajole, coax; bribe.

о-дóбр-ить, *v.p.*, о-добр-ять, *v.i.*, + *acc.*,
to approve, sanction; applaud. О. предложéние, to approve an offer. О-добр-
éние, *п.п.*, approval, approbation; applause. О-дóбр-енный, *adj., part. pass.
past*, approved, sanctioned. О-добр-
úтельный, *adj.*, approving. О-добр-
úтельно, *adv.*, approvingly.

раз-дóбр-ить, *v.p.*, + *acc.*, to persuade
to be generous, kind. Р. скупóго человéка, to persuade a miser to be generous. Раз-дóбр-ить-ся, *v.p.r.*, to have a
spell of kindness, generousness.

с-добр-úть, *v.p.*, с-дáбр-ивать, *v.i.*, +
acc., to spice, flavor, enrich (*as* food).
С. тéсто сáхаром, to enrich dough
with sugar. С-дóб-а, (*from* с-дóбр-а),
n.f., ingredients which enrich dough.
Положúть в тéсто сдóбу, to enrich
dough, add butter to dough. С-дóб-
ное тéсто, rich dough containing much
butter and eggs.

с-добр-овáть, *v.p., only in expression*:
Тебé не сдобровáть, it will turn out
badly for you.

у-дóбр-и-ть, *v.p.*, у-добр-ять, у-дóбр-
ивать, *v.i.*, + *acc.*, to manure; to enrich
land with fertilizer. У-добр-éние, *п.п.*,
the process of fertilizing with manure,
fertilizer. Перегнóй - хорóшее у. для
пóчвы, humus is a good fertilizer for
the soil. Чернозём не трéбует удобрéния, black soil does not require
fertilizer.

ДОЛГ-, ДОЛЖ-, DEBT, OBLIGATION,
DUTY

долг, *n.m.*, debt, duty. Выплатить д., to
pay a debt. Д. платежóм крáсен,
(*saying*), one good turn deserves
another. Д. чéсти, debt of honor. Госу-

да́рственный д., national debt. Испо́лнить свой д., to fulfill one's duty. Быть в долгу́, как в шелку́, (*saying*), to be head over heels in debt. Долгово́й, *adj.*, pertaining to a debt. Д-а́я распи́ска, promissory note. Д-о́е обяза́тельство, promissory note.

долж-а́ть, *v.i.,* за-долж-а́ть. *v.p.,* + *acc.,* + *dat.,* to contract a debt, owe money, run into debt. Он мне задолжа́л 100 рубле́й, he owes me 100 rubles. Задо́лж-енность, *n.f.,* debt, indebtedness. Долж-ни́к, *n.m.,* долж-ни́ца, *n.f.,* debtor. Несостоя́тельный д., insolvent debtor, bankrupt.

долж-ен-ство-ва́-ть, *v.i.,* (*obs.*), to be obligated, indebted. Он до́лж-ен, она́ долж-на́, они́ долж-ны́, he, she owes; he, she, they must, + *inf.*; he, she, they ought to, + *inf.* Он мне до́лжен 5 рубле́й, he owes me 5 rubles. Она́ должна́ ему́ написа́ть, she ought to write to him. Подожди́те немно́го, он до́лжен быть здесь в 8 часо́в, wait a little, he should be here at 8 o'clock. Он до́лжен был предви́деть э́то, he ought to have foreseen this. До́лж-ное, *adj. used as n.,* that which is due. Воздава́ть д., to do justice. До́лж-ный, *adj.,* due, proper, right, just. До́лжным о́бразом, properly, duly. На д-о́й высоте́, up to the mark. Долж-но́, *adv.,* properly, duly; from a sense of obligation, duty. Должно́ быть, *parenthetical expression,* probably, in all likelihood, very likely. Он, должно́ быть, забы́л об э́том, very likely, he has forgotten about it. До́лжность, *n.f.,* office, function, post, position. Занима́ть д., to hold an office. Должностно́й, *adj.,* official. Д. просту́пок, breach of trust, confidence. Д-о́е лицо́, official, officer, functionary.

о-долж-а́ть, *v.i.,* о-долж-и́ть, *v.p.,* + *acc.,* + *dat.,* to lend, loan, (*fig.*), oblige. Сдолжи́те мне 10 рубле́й, lend me 10 rubles. О-долж-и́ть-ся, *v.p.r.,* о-должа́ть-ся, *v.i.r.,* + *dat.,* + *instr.,* to become obligated, indebted. О. табачко́м, (*colloq. obs.*), to borrow tobacco. О-долж-е́ние, *n.n.,* favor, service, kindness. Сде́лайте мне о., do me a favor. Я сочту́ э́то за о., I shall consider it a favor.

ДОМ-, DOMICILE, HOME

дом, *n.m.,* house, home. Жило́й д., dwelling house. Д. о́тдыха, rest home. Торго́вый д., commercial house, trading firm. Иго́рный д., gambling house. До́ма, *adv.,* at home. Быть, как до́ма, to feel at home. У него́ не все до́ма,

(*slang*), he's not all there. Верну́ться домо́й, to return home.

дом-а́шний, *adj.,* domestic, home-made. Д. телефо́н, home telephone. Д-яя пти́ца, poultry. Д-яя рабо́тница (дом-рабо́тница), (*recent*), domestic servant, maid. Д-ее хозя́йство, housekeeping. Д-ие живо́тные, domestic animals. Доми́шко, *n.m.,* (*derog.*), small house, hovel. Ста́ренький д. стоя́л на краю́ дере́вни, an old hovel stood at the edge of the village. До́м-ик, *n.m.,* little house, cottage. Дом-ови́тость, *n.f.,* thriftiness, economy. Дом-ови́тый, *adj.,* thrifty, economical. Д-ая хозя́йка, a good housewife. Дом-о-владе́лец, *n.m.,* home owner. Дом-о-владе́ние, *n.n.,* ownership of a house, home. Дом-о-хозя́ин, *n.m.,* *see* домовладе́лец.

дом-о́в-нич-ать, *v.i.,* (*colloq.*), to stay at home and keep house. Все ушли́ рабо́тать, домо́вничать оста́лась то́лько ба́бушка, everyone went to work in the field, only the grandmother remained to keep house. Дом-ово́й, *adj., used as n.,* goblin; brownie. По наро́дным пове́рьям домово́й живёт за пе́чкой, according to popular belief the house-elf lives behind the stove. Дом-о́вый, *adj.,* (*recent*), housing trust. Дом-о́вая кни́га, house register.

Дом-о-стро́й, *n.m.,* (*hist.*), a medieval code of rules for managing a household. Кни́га Домостро́й была́ напи́сана в 16 ве́ке, the Domostroj was written in the 16th century.

дом-о-ча́дец, *n.m.,* member of a household.

дом-о-се́дничать, *v.i.,* to stay at home, spend time at home. Моя́ жена́ лю́бит домосе́дничать, а не ходи́ть по гостя́м, my wife likes to stay at home rather than go visiting. Дом-о-се́д, *n.m.,* домосе́дка, *n.f.,* home-loving person, stay-at-home. Дом-о-се́дство, *n.n.,* the state of being a stay-at-home.

ДОРОГ-, ДОРОЖ-, ROUTE, COURSE, ROAD

доро́г-а, *n.f.,* road, way, Больша́я д., highway. Желе́зная д., railroad. Дать доро́гу кому́-либо, to let someone pass. Пойти́ не по свое́й доро́ге, (*fig.*), to miss one's vocation. Я про́был три дня в доро́ге, the journey took me three days. Доро́ж-ка, *n.f.,* path, walk; track. До́брая сла́ва за пе́чкой лежи́т, а худа́я сла́ва по доро́жке бежи́т, (*prov.*), a good deed remains hidden, but a bad report travels fast. Доро́ж-ный, *adj.,* pertaining to travel, to a road. Д. мешо́к, handbag. Д. костю́м, traveling suit. Д-ое строи́тельство, road construction. Д-ые расхо́ды, travelling expenses, costs. Железно-доро́ж-ник, railroad worker. Железно-доро́ж-ный, *adj.*, railway, railroad. При-доро́ж-ный, *adj.*, pertaining to the roadside, wayside. П-ые столбы́, milestones, road markers. Авто-доро́ж-ный Институ́т, (*recent*), Institute for the Construction of Highways. Без-доро́ж-ье, *п.п.*, impassability (*e.g.*, of a road). Осе́ннее (весе́ннее), б., the condition of roads in autumn (spring), precluding travel. Без-доро́ж-ный, *adj.*, pathless, impassable.

по-доро́ж-ная, *adj. used as n.f.*, (*obs.*), order for post horses. По-доро́ж-ный, *adj. used as n.m.*, (*obs.*), fellow traveller. По-доро́ж-ник, *п.m.*, (*bot.*), plantain. В ру́сских степя́х растёт подоро́жник, plantain grows on the steppes of Russia.

ДР-, ДЕР-, ДОР-, ДАР-, ДИР-, ДЫР-, RENDING, TEARING; QUARRELING

др-а́к-а, *n.f.*, scuffle, fight, brawl. Ма́льчики затея́ли дра́ку, the boys started a scuffle. Др-ач-ли́вость, *n.f.*, pugnaciousness. Др-ач-ли́вый, *adj.*, pugnacious, disposed to fight. Др-ачу́н, *п.m.*, pugnacious man. Др-ачу́нья, *n.f.*, pugnacious woman.

др-а-ть, дер-у́, *v.i.*, по-др-а́ть, *v.p.*, + *acc.*, to tear; whip, flog, thrash. Д. кору́ с де́рева, to strip the bark from a tree. Д. го́рло, to bawl, roar. Д. шку́ру, (*colloq.*), to flay; (*fig.*), exploit. Эта му́зыка дерёт у́ши, this music hurts one's ears. Дер-ёв-ня, *n.f.*, village, the country. Др-а́ный, *adj.*, torn, tattered, ragged. Д. рука́в, а torn sleeve. Др-а́нка, *n.f.*, shingles. Кро́вельная д., roof shingles. Др-а́ть-ся, *v.i.r.*, по-др-а́ть-ся, *v.p.r.*, с + *instr.*, за + *acc.*, to fight, scuffle; tear. Д. с ке́м-нибудь, to fight with someone. Ле́нский дра́лся на дуэ́ли с Оне́гиным, Lenskii fought a duel with Onegin. Д. за свои́х друзе́й, to fight for one's friends.

вы́-др-ать, *v.p.*, вы-дир-а́ть, *v.i.*, + *acc.*, to tear out; thrash, whip. В вори́шку, to thrash a young thief. В. клок воло́с, to tear out a tuft of hair.

за-др-а́ть, *v.p.*, за-дир-а́ть, *v.i.*, + *acc.*, to begin to tear; provoke, tease; pick a quarrel. З. за живо́е, to cut to the quick. З. нос, to be haughty. З. це́ну, (*colloq.*), to ask an exorbitant price. За-ди́р-а, *n.f.*, a quarrelsome, contentious person. За-до́р, *п.m.*,

brashness; impetuousness. Юноше́ский з., youthful brashness. За-до́р-ный, *adj.*, impetuous, provoking. З. взгляд, provocative look. З-ые ре́чи, provocative words, speeches.

изо-др-а́ть, *v.p.*, из-дир-а́ть, *v.i.*, + *acc.*, (*slang*), to tear apart, rend. И. пла́тье (брю́ки), to tear one's dress (trousers) to tatters. Изо́-др-анный, *adj. part. pass. past*, torn apart, rent.

на-др-а́ть, *v.p.*, + *acc.*, (*colloq.*), to spank. Н. у́ши, to pull some one's ears. Н. берёзовой коры́, to strip a quantity of birchbark.

обо-др-а́ть, *v.p.*, об-дир-а́ть, *v.i.*, + *acc.*, to peel, strip; (*fig.*), fleece. Ободра́ть ячме́нь, на крупу́, to pearl barley. О. как ли́пку, (*saying*), to strip some one to the skin. Обо́-др-анный, *adj. part. pass. past*, ragged, in tattered clothes. Обо-др-а́нец, *п.m.*, tramp. Об-дир-а́ла, *п.m.*, (*colloq.*), one who fleeces people.

ото-др-а́ть, *v.p.*, от-дир-а́ть, *v.i.*, + *acc.*, to tear, rip off. О. переплёт от кни́ги, to tear the binding off a book. О. за́ у́ши, to whip soundly. От-дир-а́ние, *п.п.*, tearing off.

при-др-а́ть-ся, *v.p.*, при-дир-а́ть-ся, *v.i.*, к + *dat.*, to nag, find fault with. П. к пустяка́м, to quibble over trifles. П. к слу́чаю, to use as a pretext. При-ди́р-а, *n.f.*, fault-finder. При-ди́р-ка, *n.f.*, captious objection. При-ди́р-чивость, *n.f.*, captiousness. При-ди́р-чивый, *adj.*, captious, nagging, fault-finding. При-ди́р-чиво, *adv.*, captiously.

про-др-а́ть, *v.p.*, про-дир-а́ть, *v.i.*, + *acc.*, to tear through; wear out. П. ло́кти, to wear out the elbows (*e.g.*, of a jacket). С трудо́м продра́ть глаза́, (*idiom*), to wake up with difficulty. Про-др-а́ть-ся, *v.p.r.*, про-дир-а́ть-ся, *v.i.r.*, to tear, break through. П. сквозь ча́щу, to break through a thicket.

раз-о-др-а́ть, *v.p.*, раз-дир-а́ть, *v.i.*, + *acc.*, to tear to pieces, rend; (*fig.*), to torture. Во́лки разодра́ли овцу́ на куски́, the wolves tore the sheep to pieces. Его́ раздира́ли на ча́сти, (*fig.*), he was being torn in all directions. Печа́ль раздира́ет ду́шу, (*poet.*), sorrow tears at the heart. Раз-дир-а́ющий, *adj. part. act. pres.*, rending. Р-ие ду́шу кри́ки, heart-rending screams. Раз-до́р, *п.m.*, discord, dissension. Се́ять р., to sow dissension; behave mischievously. Я́блоко раздо́ра, (*fig.*), the apple of discord.

со-др-а́ть, *v.p.*, с-дир-а́ть, *v.i.*, + *acc.*, to flay, excoriate; skin. С. ко́жу, to skin. С. шку́ру с уби́того медве́дя, to skin a bear. С-дир-а́ть-ся, *v.i.r.*, to be torn off. С-дир-а́ние, *п.п.*, flaying, excoriation; skinning.

у-дир-а́ть, *v.p.*, у-др-а́ть, *v.i.*, to scamper off, take to one's heels, run away.

вз-до́р-ить, *v.i.*, по-вз-до́р-ить, *v.p.*, с + *instr.*, to quarrel, argue. Вз-дор, *п.т.*, nonsense, rubbish. Моло́ть в., to talk nonsense. Вз-до́р-ность, *n.f.*, absurdity, quarrelsomeness. Вз-до́р-ный, *adj.*, absurd, quarrelsome.

дыр-а́, ды́рка, *n.f.*, hole, tear; wretched place. Зашто́панная дыра́, a mended hole. Ды́р-очка, *n.f.*, (*dim.*), a little hole, tear. У меня́ в зу́бе д., I have a cavity in my tooth. Дыр-я́вый, *adj.*, full of holes. Д. чуло́к, a stocking full of holes.

у-да́р-ить, *v.p.*, у-дар-я́ть, *v.i.*, + *acc.*, + *instr.*, to hit, strike. У. кого́-нибудь па́лкой, to strike someone with a cane. У. на врага́, (*mil.*), to attack the enemy. У. по рука́м, to strike a bargain. У-да́р-ить-ся, *v.p.r.*, у-дар-я́ть-ся, *v.i.r.*, о + *acc.*, to hit, knock, hurt oneself. У. о ка́мень, to strike a stone.

у-да́р, *п.т.*, blow, stroke, hit, shock. У. гро́ма, thunder clap. Со́лнечный у., sunstroke. Уда́ры судьбы́, (*fig.*), reverses of fortune. Одни́м уда́ром уби́ть двух за́йцев, (*saying*), to kill two birds with one stone. У-дар-е́ние, *п.п.*, accent, stress. У. па́дает на второ́й слог, the accent falls on the second syllable. У-да́р-ник, *п.т.*, (*tech.*), pellet; (*recent*), shock worker. Рабо́чий-уда́рник награждён пре́мией, the shock worker was awarded a prize. У-да́р-ничество, *п.п.*, (*recent*), shock work. На заво́де объя́влено у., it has been announced that shock work has been introduced at the plant. У-да́р-ный, *adj.*, pertaining to shock. У-ые те́мпы, (*recent*), speed-up of labor. Рабо́тать уда́рными те́мпами, (*recent*), to work at an increased speed.

ДРОГ-, ДРОЖ-, ДРАГ-, ДОРОГ-, ДОРОЖ-, ДРЫГ-, SHAKE, SHUDDER, TREMBLE

дро́г-ну-ть, *v.p.*, to shudder, tremble; hesitate. Войска́ дро́гнули и потесни́лись наза́д, the troops wavered and retreated.

вз-дро́г-нуть, *v.p.smf.*, вз-дра́г-ивать, *v.i.*, от + *gen.*, to start, flinch, shudder. В. от ра́дости, to jump with joy. В. от испу́га, to shudder with fear.

пере-дро́г-нуть, *v.p.*, на + *prep.*, от + *gen.*, to become chilled through and through. П. на моро́зе, to become chilled from exposure to cold.

про-дро́г-нуть, *see* передро́гнуть.

со-дрог-а́ть-ся, *v.i.r.*, со-дрог-ну́ть-ся, *v.p.r.*, от + *gen.*, to shudder, shiver. С. от стра́ха (у́жаса), to shiver with terror (fright). Су́-дорог-а, *n.f.*, cramp, spasm, convulsion, Су́-дорож-ный, *adj.*, convulsive, spasmodic. С-ое сжа́тие ноги́, leg cramp.

дрож-а́ть, *v.i.*, за-дрож-а́ть, *v.p.*, от + *gen.*, + *instr.*, to tremble, shake, shiver, shudder. Д. всем те́лом, to shake all over. Д. над чём-либо, (*fig.*), to take excessive care of. От взры́ва задрожа́ли стёкла, the window panes rattled from the explosion. Дрож-ь, *n.f.*, trembling, shivering, shuddering, tremor, quiver. От стра́ха дрожь пробежа́ла по мои́м жи́лам, a shiver ran down my spine. Д. в го́лосе, a tremor in one's voice. Лихора́дочная д., chills, fever. Дрож-а́ние *п.п.*, trembling, tremor, vibration.

дры́г-ать, *v.i.*, дры́г-нуть, *v.p.*, + *instr.*, to twitch, jerk. Д. ного́й, to twitch one's foot. Дры́г-ание, *п.п.*, jerking, twitching.

ДОРОГ-, ДОРОЖ-, ДРАГ-, ДРАЖ-, DEARNESS, EXPENSIVENESS; ENDEARMENT

дорог-о́й, *adj.*, dear, expensive, costly; darling, dear. Д. сын! Dear Son! До́рог-о, *adv.*, dear, dearly, costly, expensively. Этот автомоби́ль сто́ит д., this automobile is expensive. Дорог-ови́зна, *n.f.*, high cost, high prices.

дорож-а́ть, *v.i.*, по-дорож-а́ть, *v.p.*, to rise in price. Хлеб дорожа́ет, the price of wheat is rising. Доро́ж-е, *adj. comp.*, dearer, more expensive.

вз-дорож-а́ть, *v.p.*, дорожа́ть, *v.i.*, to rise in price. Все това́ры вздорожа́ли, all goods have become more expensive. Вз-дорож-а́ние, *п.п.*, a rise in price.

дорож-и́ть, *v.i.*, + *instr.*, to value, prize, esteem. Он дорожи́т э́той кни́гой, he values this book. Им на слу́жбе о́чень дорожа́т, they value him highly at his job. Не дорожи́ть, to think little of. Дорож-и́ть-ся, *v.i.r.*, (*colloq.*), to overcharge, ask an excessively high price. Прода́йте ваш дом деше́вле, не дорожи́тесь, sell your house more reasonably, don't ask too high a price.

драго-це́нный, *adj.*, precious, invaluable. Д. ка́мень, gem, jewel, precious stone. Драго-це́нность, *n.f.*, treasure; jewel, gem. Драго-це́нности, *n.f.pl.*, jewelry, valuables, precious things.

драж-а́йший, *adj. superl.*, (*obs.*), most expensive, dearest. Моя́ дража́йшая полови́на, (*iron.*), my better half.

ДРУГ-, ДРУЖ-, ДРУЗ-, FRIENDSHIP, AMITY

друг, *n.m.,* friend. друз-ья́, *pl.,* friends. Д. де́тства, childhood friend. Мой лу́чший д., my best friend. Друг дру́га, each other. Друг за дру́гом, one after the other. Писа́ть друг дру́гу, to write to one another. Бли́зкие друзья́, intimate friends. Друж-о́чек, *n.m.,* (*dim.*), dear; (*colloq.*), ducky. Друж-и́ще, *n.m.,* old friend. По-дру́г-а, *n.f.,* girl friend; playmate. Дру́ж-ка, *n.f.,* (*colloq.*), best man, groom's man. Не́друг, *n.m.,* (*obs.*), enemy.

дру́ж-ба, *n.f.,* friendship, amity. Быть в дру́жбе, to be friends. Не в слу́жбу, а в дру́жбу, (*saying*), out of friendship. Дру́ж-ный, *adj.,* harmonious, unanimous; friendly. Д. отпо́р, unanimous resistance. Д-ая семья́, a close-knit family. Дру́ж-но, *adv.,* harmoniously, in concord. Рабо́тать д., to work together. Друж-е-лю́бие, *n.n.,* friendliness. Друже-лю́бный, *adj.,* friendly. Друж-е-лю́бно, *adv.,* amicably, friendlily. Дру́ж-еский, *adj.,* friendly, amicable. Дру́ж-ественный, *adj.,* friendly, amicable. Д-ая услу́га, a good turn, friendly gesture. Быть на дру́жеской ноге́, (*express.*), to be on friendly terms with someone. По-дру́ж-ески, *adv.,* in a friendly way. Друж-и́на, *n.f.,* (*hist.*), armed entourage of a medieval prince. Пожа́рная, д., fire brigade. Боева́я д., volunteer brigade. Друж-и́нник, *n.m.,* (*hist.*), a member of a medieval prince's armed retinue. Дружи́нники кня́зя Святосла́ва, the members of Prince Sviatoslav's retinue.

друж-и́-ть, *v.i.,* по-друж-и́ть, *v.p.,* с + *instr.,* to be friendly with. Они́ дружи́ли с са́мого де́тства, they were friends from childhood. По-друж-и́ть-ся, *v.p.r.,* с + *instr.,* to make friends, make acquaintance.

раз-друж-и́ть-ся, *v.p.r.,* с + *instr.,* to sever friendly relations.

с-друж-и́ть, *v.p.,* to effect a friendship. Слу́жба в а́рмии сдружи́ла нас, we became friends while serving together in the army. С-друж-и́ть-ся, *v.p.r.,* со + *instr.,* to become friendly with. Учени́к сдружи́лся со все́ми одноклассниками, the pupil made friends of all his classmates. Со-дру́ж-ество, *n.n.,* friendly union, community, commonwealth. С. наро́дов, commonwealth of nations.

у-друж-и́ть, *v.p.,* у-друж-а́ть, *v.i.,* + *dat.,* to render a friendly service, befriend.

друг-о́й, *adj.,* other, another, different.

В д. раз, another time, the next time. Други́ми слова́ми, in other words. Никто́ друго́й, no other, no one else. Други́е времена́, други́е нра́вы, (*saying*), other times, other customs.

ДУ-, ДУХ-, ДУШ-. ДЫХ-, ДЫШ-, ДОХ-, (ДМ-, ДЫМ-), SOUL, SPIRIT; BREATH; FRAGRANCE; SMOKE; BLOWING

ду́-ть, *v.i.,* ду́-ну-ть, *v.p.smf.,* to blow. Д. на ого́нь, to blow on a fire. Ду-нове́ние, *n.n.,* whiff, breath, waft, puff. Д. ветерка́, a breath of wind. Ду-ть, *v.i.,* по-ду́-ть, *v.p.,* to blow; thrash soundly; drink deep. Ду́ет ве́тер с мо́ря, the wind is blowing from the sea. У окна́ ду́ет, there is a draft from the window. Поду́л холо́дный ве́тер, a cold wind began to blow. Дуть стекло́, to blow glass. Он и в ус не ду́ет! (*idiom*), he doesn't care a rap! Ду́-ть-ся, *v.i.r.,* to pout, be sulky. Что ты ду́ешься на меня́? Why are you pouting at me? Ду-тьё, *n.n.,* (*tech*), blowing. Д. стекла́, glass blowing. Ду́-тый, *adj.,* part. *pass. past,* blown, blown up. Брасле́т из ду́того зо́лота, a solid gold bracelet. Д-ые це́ны, exorbitant prices. Д-ые ши́ны, pneumatic tires., Ду́-ло, *n.n.,* muzzle of a gun, artillery piece.

в-ду́-ну-ть, *v.p.,* в-ду́-вать, *v.i.,* + *acc.,* to blow in, upon; breathe upon; insufflate. В-ду-ва́ние, *n.n.,* insufflation.

вз-ду́-ть, *v.p.,* вз-ду-ва́ть, *v.i.,* + *acc.,* to inflate, blow up. В. ого́нь, to fan a fire. Вз-ду-ть, *v.p.,* вз-ду-ва́ть, *v.i.,* + *acc.,* to inflate; raise (*as prices*). Вздуй хороше́нько э́того озорника́, (*fig.*), give this little mischief maker a good drubbing. Вз-ду́-ть-ся, *v.p.r.,* вз-ду-ва́ть-ся, *v.i.r.,* to swell, become swollen, inflated. Це́ны вздули́сь, prices have become inflated. Вз-ду́-тие, *n.n.,* swelling. В. живота́, flatulence. Вз-ду́-тый, *adj.* part. *pass. past,* swollen, inflated. В-ые расце́нки, inflated estimates.

вы́-ду-ть, *v.p.,* вы-ду-ва́ть, *v.i.,* + *acc.,* to blow out; blow (*e.g., glass*); (*slang*), drink. В. стекло́, to blow glass. Он вы́дул 5 буты́лок вина́, (*slang*) he polished off 5 bottles of wine.

за-ду́-ть, *v.p.,* за-ду-ва́ть, *v.i.,* + *acc.,* to put out, extinguish. З. свечу́, to extinguish a candle. За-ду́ть-ся, *v.p.r.,* за-ду-ва́ть-ся, *v.i.r.,* to be extinguished.

за-ду́-ть, *v.p.,* to begin to blow. Заду́л си́льный ве́тер, a strong wind began to blow.

на-ду́-ть, *v.p.,* на-ду-ва́ть, *v.i.,* to cause to swell, distend, inflate; cheat, dupe. Н. шар, to inflate a balloon. Н. гу́бы, (*colloq.*), to pout. Н. покупа́телей, (*colloq.*), to cheat customers, buyers. На-ду́-ть-ся, *v.p.r*, на-ду-ва́ть-ся, *v.i.r.*, to be inflated; swell out (*as* sails); sulk, pout. На-ду-ва́ла, *n.m.*, (*colloq.*), swindler, deceiver. На-ду-ва́ние, *n.n.*, inflation (*e.g.*, of a balloon, bag). На-ду-ва́тельство, *n.n.*, cheating, swindling. На-ду-вно́й, *adj.*, inflated. Н-а́я поду́шка, air cushion. На-ду́-тый, *adj.*, *part. pass. past*, inflated, bloated, puffed up; (*fig.*), sulky. Н-ые гу́бы, pouting lips. Н-ый шар, inflated balloon.

об-ду́-ть (об-ду́-нуть), *v.p.*, об-ду-ва́ть, *v.i.*, + *acc.*, to blow off. Он обду́л запылённую кни́гу со всех сторо́н, he blew the dust off the book. Об-ду-ва́ла, *n.m.*, (*slang*), cheat, crook. О-ду-ва́нчик, *n.m.*, dandelion, blowball.

от-ду́-ть, *v.p.*, от-ду́-нуть, *v.p.*, от-ду-ва́ть, *v.i.*, + *acc.*, to blow away; beat. Ве́тром отду́ло все пе́рья в сто́рону, all the feathers were blown away by the wind. За ша́лости его́ отду́ли, (*colloq.*), they beat him for his pranks. От-ду-ва́ть-ся, *v.i.r.*, + *acc.*, to puff, pant. О. за кого́-либо, (*slang*), to do another's work, to be responsible for another.

про-ду́-ть, *v.p.*, про-ду-ва́ть, *v.i.*, + *acc.*, to blow through. П. тру́бку, to blow through a pipe. П. все де́ньги, (*slang*), to lose, squander all one's money. Про-ду́-ть-ся, *v.p.r.*, про-ду-ва́ть-ся, *v.i.r.*, to be blown through; lose. П. в ка́рты, (*slang*), to lose at cards. Про-ду́-вка, *n.f.*, (*tech.*), a blowing through. Про-ду-вно́й, *adj.*, (*colloq.*), sly, roguish, crafty. П. моше́нник, rogue, crook.

раз-ду́-ть, *v.p.*, раз-ду-ва́ть, *v.i.*, + *acc.*, to disperse, blow in all directions; fan; distend. Р. ого́нь в пе́чке, to fan a fire in a stove. Ве́тер раздува́л лепестки́ я́блонь, the wind was blowing the petals off the apple blossoms. Р. де́ло (успе́х), to exaggerate a matter (success). Раз-ду́-ть-ся, *v.p.r.*, раз-ду-ва́ть-ся, *v.i.r.*, to become swollen, inflated. Щека́ разду́лась, the cheek became swollen. Раз-ду-ва́ние, *n.n.*, blowing; exaggeration. Раз-ду-ва́льный, *adj.*, pertaining to blowing, inflating. Р. мех, (*tech.*), bellows.

с-ду-ть, (с-ду́-ну-ть), *v.p.*, с-ду-ва́ть, *v.i.*, + *acc.*, с + *gen.*, to blow away, off. С. пе́пел с папиро́сы, to blow the ashes off a cigarette.

дух, *n.m.*, spirit, mind; ghost; odor, smell. Свято́й Дух, the Holy Ghost. Д. вре́мени, the spirit of the times.

Во весь д., at full speed. Переводи́ть д., to catch one's breath. Быть в ду́хе, to be in good spirits. Быть не в ду́хе, to be out of sorts, out of humor. О ней ни слу́ху, ни ду́ху, nothing is heard of her. Па́дать ду́хом, to lose heart, become discouraged, despondent. В леса́х и река́х живу́т ду́хи, (*myth.*), spirits dwell in forests and rivers. Дух-и́, *n.m.pl.*, perfume, scent; essence.

дух-о-ве́нство, *n.n.*, clergy, priesthood. Дух-овни́к, *n.m.*, confessor. Духо́вный, *adj.*, spiritual, unworldly, ecclesiastical. Д-ая, *adj.*, sacred; pertaining to a church. Д-ая му́зыка, sacred, church music. Д-ое лицо́, clergyman, priest. Дух-о́вно, *adv.*, spiritually.

дух-ово́й, *adj.*, (*mus.*), brass, woodwind. Д. инструме́нт, wind instrument. Д. орке́стр, brass band. Д-а́я печь, oven. Дух-о́вка, *n.f.*, oven. Спечь пиро́г в духо́вке, to bake a pie in an oven. Дух-от-а́, *n.f.*, oppressive heat, lack of air. Ду́ш-ный, *adj.*, close, hot, oppressive. Д-ая ко́мната, stuffy room. Ду́шно, *adv.*, close, stuffy. Мне д., I feel hot, I am suffocating. От-ду́ш-ина, *n.f.*, ventilator, air-hole; (*tech.*), safety valve.

о-дух-о-твори́ть, *v.p.*, о-дух-о-творя́ть, *v.i.*, + *acc.*, to spiritualize, inspire. О-дух-о-творённость, *n.f.*, spirituality, inspiration. О-дух-о-творённый, *adj.*, spiritual, inspired. О-ое лицо́, an inspired face.

душ-а́, *n.f.*, soul, mind, spirit; heart. Я тро́нут до глубины́ души́ ва́шим внима́нием, I am deeply touched by your attention. Ни живо́й души́, (*fig.*), not a soul. Мать в сы́не души́ не ча́ет, (*idiom*), a mother dotes upon her son. Разгово́р по душе́, a heart-to-heart talk. Жить душа́ в ду́шу, to live in perfect harmony. Быть душо́й о́бщества, to be the life of a party. Мёртвые Ду́ши, Dead Souls, title of the novel by Gogol. Душ-е́вный, *adj.*, sincere, cordial; mental, psychical. Д-ая боле́знь, mental illness. Д-ое споко́йствие, peace of mind. Душ-е́вно, *adv.*, sincerely. По-ду́ш-ный, *adj.*, per person. П. нало́г, (*hist.*), poll tax, capitation. Душ-е-гре́йка, *n.f.*, woman's warm, sleeveless jacket. Ду́ш-енька, ду́ш-ечка, *n.f.*, darling, dear, sweetheart. Душ-о́нка, *n.f.*, (*derog.*), weakling, a person with a small, mean soul. Велик-о-ду́шие, *n.n.*, magnanimity. Тще-ду́ш-ие, *n.n.*, feebleness, weakness. Тще-ду́ш-ный, *adj.*, feeble, weak, infirm. За-душ-е́вность, *n.f.*, cordiality, intimacy, sincerity. За-душ-е́вный, *adj.*, cordial, hearty, sincere. За-душ-е́вно, *adv.*, heartily, cordially, sincerely.

душ-и́-ть, *v.i.,* за-душ-и́ть, *v.p.,* + *acc.,* to stifle, strangle, suffocate. З. челове́ка, to strangle a person. Д. свобо́ду, to stifle liberty. Душ-и́тель, *n.m.,* strangler, suffocator.

душ-и́-ть, *v.i.,* на-душ-и́ть, *v.p.,* + *acc.,* + *instr.,* to perfume, scent. Д. плато́к, to perfume a handkerchief. Душ-и́ть-ся, *v.i.r.,* на-душ-и́ть-ся, *v.p.r.,* + *instr.,* to perfume oneself. Д. дороги́ми духа́ми, to perfume oneself with expensive perfume. Душ-и́стый, *adj.,* fragrant, sweet-smelling. Д. ла́ндыш, a fragrant lily of the valley. Душ-о́к, *n.m.,* musty smell. Мя́со с душко́м, tainted meat.

о-душ-ев-и́ть, *v.p.,* о-душ-евля́ть, *v.i.,* + *acc.,* + *instr.,* to inspire, animate. О-душ-евлённый, *adj. part. pass. past,* animated, inspired. Не-о-душ-евлённый, *adj.,* inanimate, uninspired.

во-о-душ-ев-и́ть, *v.p.,* во-о-душ-евля́ть, *v.i.,* + *acc.,* + *instr.,* to inspire, fill with enthusiasm; *see* одушевля́ть. О. войска́, to raise an army's spirit.

при-душ-и́ть, *v.p.,* + *acc.,* + *instr.,* to smother, choke. Уби́йца придуши́л свою́ же́ртву, the murderer smothered his victim.

у-душ-и́ть, *v.p.,* у-душ-а́ть, *v.i.,* + *acc.,* + *instr.,* to asphyxiate. У-душ-е́ние, *n.n.,* stifling, suffocation, choking, asphyxiation. У-душ-и́тель, *n.m.,* strangler, smotherer; *(fig.),* oppressor. У-ду́ш-ливый, *adj.,* stifling. У. газ, suffocating, asphyxiating gas. У-ду́ш-ье, *n.n.,* asthma.

дых-а́ние, *n.n.,* breathing, respiration, breath. Затаи́ть д. to bate one's breath. Иску́сственное д., artificial respiration. Дых-а́тельный, *adj.,* respiratory. Д-ое го́рло, *(anat.),* windpipe.

дыш-а́-ть, *v.i.,* + *instr.,* to breathe, respire. Д. све́жим во́здухом, to breathe fresh air. Тяжело́ д., to puff, gasp. Дыши́те! Inhale! Take a deep breath!

на-дыш-а́ть, *v.p.,* на + *acc.,* to warm by breathing. Н. на зе́ркало (на стекло́), to breathe upon a mirror (glass). На-дыш-а́ть-ся, *v.p.r.,* + *instr.,* to breathe in at length. Н. морски́м во́здухом, to fill one's lungs with sea air.

от-дыш-а́ть-ся, *v.p.r.,* to catch one's breath. Да́йте мне о., let me catch my breath.

по-дыш-а́ть, *v.p.,* + *instr.,* to breathe a little. Я хоте́л-бы п. све́жим во́здухом, I would like a breath of fresh air.

дох-ну́-ть, *v.p.smf.,* *see* дыша́ть. Он дохну́л на очки́ и вы́тер их, he breathed on his glasses and wiped them.

до́х-ну-ть, *v.i.,* to die *(of animals).* Д. с

го́лода, to be dying of hunger. До́хлый, *adj.,* dead *(of animals).* Д-ая ко́шка, a dead cat. Дох-ля́тина, *n.f.,* carrion.

в-дох-ну́-ть, *v.p. smf.,* в-дых-а́ть, *v.i.,* + *acc.,* to breathe in, inhale; inspire. В. во́здух, to inhale. В. му́жество, to inspire courage, manliness. В-дых-а́ние, *n.n.,* inhaling, inhalation. Аппара́т для вдыха́ния, inhalator.

в-дох-н-ов-и́ть, *v.p.,* в-дох-новля́ть, *v.i.,* + *acc.,* to inspire. В-дох-нове́ние, *n.n.,* inspiration. В-дох-нове́нный, *adj. part. pass. past,* inspired. В-дох-нове́нно, *adv.,* with inspiration. В-дох-нови́-тель, *n.m.,* one who inspires. В-дох-нови́ться, *v.p.r.,* во-дох-новля́ть-ся, *v.i.r.,* to be inspired, carried away. В-дохновля́ющий, *adj. part. act. pres.,* inspiring. В-им о́бразом, in an inspiring manner.

вз-дох-ну́ть, *v.p.smf.,* вз-дых-а́ть, *v.i.,* to sigh, take a breath, long for. В. свобо́дно, to breathe freely. Тяжело́, в., to sigh deeply. Вздох, *n.m.,* sigh. Испусти́ть после́дний в., *(fig.),* to breathe one's last. Вз-дых-а́тель, *n.m., (colloq.),* suitor, wooer.

вы́-дох-нуть, *v.p.smf.,* вы-дых-а́ть, *v.i.,* to breathe out, exhale. Вы́-дох, *n.m.,* exhalation, breathing out. Вы́-дох-нуть-ся, *v.p.r.,* вы-дых-а́ть-ся, *v.i.r.,* to evaporate, become exhausted. Чай выдыха́ется, the tea is losing its aroma. Тала́нт выдыха́ется, his talent is on the wane. Вы́-дох-ший-ся, *adj. part. act. past,* played out, evaporated, exhausted. Вы-дых-а́ние, *n.n.,* expiration, evaporation, exhaustion; exhaling.

за-дох-ну́ть-ся, *v.p.r,* за-дых-а́ть-ся, *v.i.r.,* to choke, suffocate, be out of breath. Мы задыха́лись в ду́шной ко́мнате, we were suffocating in a stuffy room. З. от зло́сти, to choke with anger.

из-до́х-нуть, *v.p.,* из-дых-а́ть, *v.i.,* to die *(of animals).* Из-дых-а́ние, *n.n.,* loss of breath; death, dying *(of animals).* До после́днего издыха́ния, to one's last breath. Быть при после́днем издыха́нии, to be dying.

от-дох-ну́ть, *v.p.,* от-дых-а́ть, *v.i.,* to rest. Я уста́ла и се́ла отдохну́ть, I was tired and sat down to rest. Зимо́й земля́ отдыха́ет, in winter the earth rests. От-дых, *n.m.,* rest, repose, relaxation. Дава́ть о., to give rest. День о́тдыха, *(recent),* day off. Рабо́тать без о́тдыха, to work without rest.

пере-до́х-нуть, *v.p.,* *see* до́хнуть, Все на́ши ку́ры передо́хли, all our hens died.

пере-дох-ну́ть, *v.p.,* to stop to take a

breath. Пу́тник сел у доро́ги п., the traveler sat down by the road to take a rest. Пере-ды́ш-ка, *n.f.*, respite. Дава́ть переды́шку, to give respite.

по-до́х-нуть, *v.p.,* по-дых-а́ть, *v.i.,* (*colloq.*), to die (*of animals*).

с-до́х-нуть, *v.p.,* с-дых-а́ть, *v.i.,* (*colloq., vulgar*), to die.

дым, *n.m.,* smoke. Из трубы́ идёт д., smoke is coming out of the chimney. Пуска́ть д., to puff out smoke. Нет ды́ма без огня́, (*saying*), there's no smoke without a fire.

дым-и́ть, *v.i.,* на-дым-и́ть, *v.p.,* to smoke, fill with smoke. Пе́чка надыми́ла, the stove has filled the room with smoke. Дым-и́ть-ся, *v.i.r.,* to smoke, steam, reek. Ды́м-ка, *n.f.,* haze, mist. Ды́м-ный, *adj.,* smoky. Дым-ово́й снаря́д, smoke shell. Д-а́я заве́са, smoke screen. Д-а́я труба́, smoke stack, chimney, funnel. Дым-о́к, *n.m.,* puff of smoke. Дым-о-хо́д, *n.m.,* flue. Ды́м-чатый, *adj.,* smoky, hazy.

за-дым-и́ть, *v.p.,* to begin to smoke.

вз-дым-а́ть, *v.p.,* + *acc.,* (*poet.*), to raise. Бу́ря вздыма́ла во́лны, the storm whipped up the waves. Вз-дым-а́ть-ся, *v.i.r.,* to rise, heave, swell. Тума́н вздыма́ется над о́зером, a fog is rising over the lake.

на-дм-е́н-ность, *n.f.,* haughtiness, superciliousness. На-дм-е́нный, *adj.,* haughty, supercilious. Н. челове́к, a haughty person. На-дм-е́нно, *adv.,* haughtily, high-handedly, disagreeably.

ДУМ-, THOUGHT

ду́м-а, *n.f.,* thought, meditation; (*hist.*), council; (*poet.*), ballad, elegy. Тяжё-лые ду́мы овладе́ли мно́ю, heavy thoughts overwhelmed me. Городска́я Ду́ма, City Hall; city council. Госуда́рственная Ду́ма, Duma (representative state assembly in pre-revolutionary Russia). Ду́м-ец, *n.m.,* (*hist.*), a member of the Duma. Ду́м-ка, *n.f.,* (*dim.*), small pillow.

ду́м-а-ть, *v.i.,* по-ду́м-ать, *v.p.,* о + *prep.,* to think of, about; suppose; intend, mean. Д. о чём-либо, to be thinking of something, have somthing on one's mind Д. ду́му, (*folklore*), to meditate, brood. Мно́го д. о себе́, to be conceited. Ду́м-ать-ся, *v.i.r.,* по-ду́м-ать-ся, *v.p.r.,* used only in 3d pers. pl., in expressions: Мне ду́мается, I think; I believe; it seems to me; it occurs to me. Мне поду́малось, it occurred to me; it has occurred to me; it seemed to me.

вз-ду́м-ать, to conceive a thought, take it into one's head, decide suddenly. Не вздумайте кури́ть в кла́ссе, don't dare to smoke in class. Вз-ду́м-ать-ся, *v.p.r.,* + *dat., used only in 3d pers.,* to occur suddenly to someone. Ему́ взду́-малось купи́ть балала́йку, he suddenly decided to buy a balalaika.

в-ду́м-ать-ся, *v.p.,* в-ду́м-ывать-ся, *v.i.,* в + *acc.,* to consider carefully, to meditate, to ponder. В. в смысл ре́чи (кни́ги), to ponder over the meaning of a speech (a book). В-ду́м-чивость, *n.f.,* meditativeness, thoughtfulness. В-ду́м-чивый, *adj.,* meditative, pensive, thoughtful. В-ое лицо́, a thoughtful face, pensive expression. В-ду́м-чиво, *adv.,* meditatively, pensively, thoughtfully.

вы́-дум-ать, *v.p.,* вы-ду́м-ывать, *v.i.,* + *acc.,* to invent, think up; lie, fib. В. но́вую маши́ну, (*colloq.*), to invent a new machine. Он по́роха не вы́ду-мает, (*fig.*), he's not bright. Вы́-дум-ка, *n.f.,* invention, fiction, fable, rumor, Вы́-дум-щик, *n.m.,* boaster, liar, faker. Вы-ду́м-ывание, *n.n.,* invention, fiction, excogitation; devising.

до-ду́м-ать-ся, *v.p.r.,* до-ду́м-ывать-ся, *v.i.r.,* + *dat.,* to come to a conclusion.

за-ду́м-ать, *v.p.,* за-ду́м-ывать, *v.i.,* + *acc.,* to intend, conceive, plan. З. дурно́е, to conceive an evil deed. Хорошо́ заду́манный прое́кт, well conceived, well planned project. За-ду́м-ать-ся, *v.p.r.,* за-ду́м-ывать-ся, *v.i.r.,* to be thoughtful; be sad; muse. Глубоко́ з., to plunge into a deep reverie. О чём вы заду́мались? what are you thinking about? За-ду́м-чивость, *n.f.,* thoughtfulness, pensiveness; musing; reverie. За-ду́м-чивый, *adj.,* thoughtful. З. взгляд, pensive look. За-ду́м-чиво, *adv.,* pensively.

на-ду́м-ать, *v.p.,* на-ду́м-ывать, *v.i.,* + *acc.,* (*colloq.*), to devise, make up one's mind. Он наду́мал жени́ться, he made up his mind to marry. На-ду́м-анный, *adj. part. pass. past,* far-fetched. Н. расска́з, a far-fetched story.

об-ду́м-ать, *v.p.,* об-ду́м-ывать, *v.i.,* + *acc.,* to consider. О. план, to consider a plan. О. отве́т, to consider, think over an answer. Об-ду́м-ывание, *n.f.,* thoughtfulness. Об-ду́м-анный, *adj. part. pass. past,* well thought out. О-ые реше́ния, thoughtful decisions. Убийст-во с зара́нее обду́манным наме́ре-нием, premeditated murder. Не-об-ду́м-анный, *adj.,* heedless, rash, thoughtless. Н. посту́пок, rash action. Об-ду́м-анно, *adv.,* following long consideration. Не-об-ду́м-анно, *adv.,* heedlessly, thoughtlessly. Поступа́ть н., to act rashly.

о-ду́м-ать-ся, *v.p.r.*, о-ду́м-ывать-ся, *v.i.r.*, to bethink, reflect. Оду́майтесь, пока́ не по́здно, think a little, before it's too late.

пере-ду́м-ать, *v.p.*, пере-ду́м-ывать, *v.i.*, + *acc.*, to change one's mind; think a matter over. Мы переду́мали е́хать в сре́ду, пое́дем в пя́тницу, we have changed our minds about going on Wednesday, we are going on Friday. Я переду́мал мно́гое за э́то вре́мя, I did a lot of thinking during this time.

по-ду́м-ать, *v.p.*, по-ду́м-ывать, *v.i.*, *iter.*, to think of, contemplate. На́до бы́ло ра́ньше об э́том поду́мать, you should have thought of it earlier. Поду́май то́лько! Just fancy! Мы уже́ поду́мываем об отъе́зде отсю́да, we are already considering leaving.

при-ду́м-ать, *v.p.*, при-ду́м-ывать, *v.i.*, + *acc.*, to devise, imagine, fabricate, invent, conceive. П. расска́з, to think up a story П. вы́ход из положе́ния, to find a way out of a situation.

про-ду́м-ать, *v.p.*, про-ду́м-ывать, *v.i.*, + *acc.*, to think over thoroughly. П. отве́т, to think an answer over thoroughly. П. вопро́с, to consider a question, think over a question thoroughly.

раз-ду́м-ать, *v.p.*, to change one's mind. Хоте́л пойти́ в теа́тр, да разду́мал, I wanted to go to the theatre, but changed my mind.

раз-ду́м-ывать, *v.i.*, to waver, hesitate, be irresolute. Разду́мываю, купи́ть дом или нет, I am wavering about buying a house. Не́чего р., (*colloq.*), there is no reason to hesitate. Раз-ду́м-ывание, *n.n.*, indecision, faltering, wavering. Раз-ду́м-ье, *n.n.*, hesitation, wavering; deep thought. Погрузи́лся в р., he fell into deep thought. Его́ взяло́ разду́мье, he is in doubt.

ДУР-, FOLLY, IMBECILITY

дур-ь, *n.f.*, foolishness, folly, nonsense. Д. в голове́, (*colloq.*), a head full of nonsense, weak in the head. Вы́бить из кого́-либо д., to beat the nonsense out of someone. С при́-дур-ью, crack-brained. Ду́р-а, *n.f.*, Ду́р-ища, *n.f.*, (*aug.*), fool, stupid woman. Дур-а́к, *n.m.*, blockhead, fool. Дурака́м сча́стье (*saying*), fools are lucky. Оста́ться в дурака́х, (*saying*), to be left holding the bag. Дур-але́й, *n.m.*, дур-ачи́на, *n.m.*, (*aug.*), see дура́к. Дур-ачо́к, *n.m.*, (*dim.*), halfwit. Ива́нушка-дурачо́к, Ivan the Fool. Дур-ачки́, *n.pl.*, a card game. Игра́ть в д., to play at durachki (*a card game*). Дур-ачьё,

n.n., (*coll.*), fools. Ду́р-ень, *n.m.*, simpleton, fool. Дур-а́цкий, *adj.*, stupid, foolish. Д. колпа́к, fool's cap. Дура́шливый, *adj.*, (*colloq.*), stupid, foolish. По-дур-а́цки, *adv.*, foolishly, stupidly. Поступа́ть п., (*colloq.*), to act stupidly. С-ду́р-у, *adv.*, foolishly, out of stupidity. С. он наговори́л вся́кого вздо́ру, out of foolishness, he talked our heads off with every kind of nonsense. Ду́р-ий, *adj.*, (*colloq.*), foolish. Ду́рья башка́, blockhead.

дур-а́ч-и-ть, *v.i.*, о-дур-а́ч-ить, *v.p.*, + *acc.*, to fool, make a fool of, ridicule. Фо́кусник одура́чил всех ло́вкостью рук, the magician fooled everyone with his manual agility. Дур-а́чить-ся, *v.i.r.*, to play the fool. Молодёжь дура́чилась весь ве́чер, the young people fooled around the whole evening long. По-дур-а́чить-ся, *v.p.r.*, над + *instr.*, to ridicule. Они́ подура́чились над новичко́м, they made fun of the new student.

дур-е́-ть, *v.i.*, о-дур-е́ть, *v.p.*, (*colloq.*), to become stupid, crazy, insane. От пья́нства он уже́ одуре́л, he has become mentally deranged from drinking.

о-дур-я́-ть, *v.i.*, о-дур-и́ть, *v.p.*, + *acc.*, to stupefy. О́-дур-ь, *n.f*, mental torpor, stupefaction. О-дур-е́ние, *n.n.*, mental torpor, process of becoming mentally deranged, stupefied. Рабо́тать до одуре́ния, to work one self into a daze. О-дур-е́лый, *adj.*, stupid, meaningless, stupefied. О-дур-я́ющий, *adj. part. act. pres.*, stupefying. О. за́пах духо́в (цвето́в), heavy scent of perfume (flowers).

дур-и́-ть, *v.i.*, о-дур-и́ть, *v.p.*, + *acc.*, to fool. Никто́ не позво́лит д. себя́, no one will permit himself to be deluded. Не дури́, говори́ то́лком. Don't be a fool, speak seriously.

с-дур-и́ть, *v.p.*, (*colloq.*), to blunder, commit a folly.

дур-ма́н-ить, *v.i.*, о-дур-ма́н-ить, *v.p.*, + *acc.*, + *instr.*, to intoxicate, stupefy. О. нарко́тиками, to stupefy with narcotics. Дур-ма́н, *n.m.*, narcotic, intoxicant. Дур-ма́н-ить-ся, *v.i.r.*, о-дур-ма́н-ить-ся, *v.p.r.*, to be stupefied, doped. От ды́ма я совсе́м одурма́нился, I was overcome by smoke.

дур-н-е́-ть, *v.i.*, по-дур-не́ть, *v.p.*, to grow ugly, wicked. Дур-но́й, *adj.*, bad, evil, wicked, vicious. Д-а́я пого́да, bad weather. Д-а́я сла́ва, ill fame, repute. Д-о́е поведе́ние, misbehavior. Ду́р-но, *adv.*, badly. Д. воспи́танный, ill bred. Д. говори́ть о ко́м-либо, to slander someone, speak evil of someone. Мне д., I feel dizzy, faint. Дур-нота́, *n.f.*, giddiness, faintness. Чу́вствовать дурноту́, to feel faint, swoon. Дур-ну́шка, *n.f.*, an ugly woman.

Е

ЕДИН-, ОДИН-, ОДН-, ONE, UNITY, ONENESS

еди́н, *num. card.,* (*Ch.-Sl.*), one.

един-и́-ть, *v.i.,* (*obs.*), unite. Един-е́ние, *n.n.,* unity, accord, union. В едине́нии си́ла, in union there is strength. Един-и́ца, *n.f.,* unit, one; low mark. Администрати́вная е. administrative unit. Е. длины́, unit of length. Е. измере́ния, unit of measure. Едини́ца - са́мая плоха́я отме́тка, a one is the lowest mark (in the USSR school grading system). Еди́ничность, *n.f.,* singleness. Един-и́чный, *adj.,* single; isolated. Е. слу́чай, isolated case. Еди́н-ый, *adj.,* single, sole, only, unique. Е. фронт, a single, united front. Он не произнёс ни еди́ного сло́ва, he didn't utter a single word. Там не́ было ни еди́ной души́, there wasn't a soul there. Еди́н-о-, *a combining form meaning* one. Един-о-бо́жие, *n.n.,* monotheism. Един-о-бра́чие, *n.n.,* monogamy. Един-о-вла́стие, *n.n.,* monarchy. Един-о-гла́сие, *n.n.,* unanimity. Един-о-гла́сный, *adj.,* unanimous. Един-о-гла́сно, *adv.,* unanimously. Един-о-ду́шие, *n.n.,* unanimity, accord. Един-о-ду́шный, *adj.,* unanimous. Един-о-ду́шно, *adv.,* unanimously. Един-о-мы́слие, *n.n.,* agreement in opinion, concord, harmony. Един-о-мы́шленник, *n.m.,* adherent, partisan. Еди́нство, *n.n.,* unity, oneness. Е. ме́ста (вре́мени, де́йствия), unity of place (time, action). Еди́н-ственность, *n.f.,* uniqueness, singularity. Еди́н-ственный, *adj.,* only, single, sole, unique, singular. Е. в своём ро́де, the only of its kind, unique. Е. ребёнок, an only child. Е-ая моя́ наде́жда, my one and only hope. Е-ое число́ (*gram.*), singular number. Еди́н-ственно, *adv.,* only, solely, exclusively, uniquely.

вос-со-един-и́-ть, *v.p.,* вос-со-един-я́ть, *v.i.,* + *acc.,* to reunite, reintegrate. Вос-со-един-и́ть-ся, *v.p.r.,* вос-со-един-я́ть-ся, *v.i.r.,* с + *instr.,* to rejoin. Вос-со-един-е́ние, *n.n.,* reunion, reintegration. В. церкве́й, reunion of Christian churches; ecumenical movement.

объ-един-и́ть, *v.p.,* объ-един-я́ть, *v.i.,* + *acc.,* to unite, consolidate. О. мир, to unite the world. Объ-един-и́ть-ся, *v.p.r.,* объ-един-я́ть-ся, *v.i.r.,* с + *instr.,* to be united; rally. Объ-един-е́ние, *n.n.,* union, unification. Всесою́зное о., (*recent*), All-Union Combine.

Объ-един-ённый, *adj. part. pass. past,* united. О-ые На́ции, United Nations. Объ-един-я́ющий, *adj. part. act. pres.,* uniting, combining, consolidating.

со-един-и́ть, *v.p.,* со-един-я́ть, *v.i.,* + *acc.,* + *instr.,* to unite, connect, link. С. абоне́нтов по телефо́ну, to connect two parties by telephone. С. войска́, to unite troops. С. мосто́м, to bridge. Со-един-и́ть-ся, *v.p.r.,* со-един-я́ть-ся, *v.i.r.,* + *instr.,* to unite, join, become associated. Войска́ сою́зников соедини́лись под о́бщим кома́ндованием, the Allied troops united under one command. Со-един-е́ние, *n.n.,* union, junction, combination, fusion. С. концо́в про́волоки, splicing of wires. Хими́ческое с., chemical fusion. Со-един-ённый, *adj., part. pass. past,* united, joined, combined, fused. Соединённые Шта́ты Аме́рики, the United States of America. Со-един-и́тель, *n.m.,* connector. Со-един-и́тельный, *adj.,* connective, conjunctive; (*gram.*), copulative. С. сою́з, (*gram.*), conjunction. С-ая ткань (*anat.*), connective tissue.

при-со-един-и́ть, *v.p.,* при-со-един-я́ть, *v.i.,* + *acc.,* к + *dat.,* to add; incorporate, join. П. про́вод к магистра́ли, to connect a wire to the main line. При-со-един-и́ть-ся, *v.p.r.,* при-со-единя́ть-ся, *v.i.r.,* к + *dat.,* to be added, joined; join. П. к друзья́м, to join friends. П. к реше́нию, to join in a resolution. При-со-един-е́ние, *n.n.,* addition, incorporation, joining; annexation.

разъ-един-и́ть, *v.p.,* разъ-един-я́ть, *v.i.,* + *acc.,* to disconnect, separate. Судьба́ нас разъедини́ла, we have been separated by fate. Разъ-един-и́ть-ся, *v.p.r.,* разъ-едни-я́ть-ся, *v.i.r.,* to be separated, disconnected. Провода́ разъедини́лись, the wires were disconnected. Разъ-един-е́ние, *n.n.,* disjunction, separation, disconnection. Разъ-един-и́тель, *n.m.,* breaker, interrupter, disconnector. Разъ-един-я́ющий, *adj. part. act. pres.,* disconnecting, disjunctive.

у-един-и́ть-ся, *v.p.r.,* у-един-я́ть-ся, *v.i.r.,* to retire, seclude oneself. У. для бесе́ды с дру́гом, to retire for a chat with one's friend. У-един-е́ние, *n.n.,* solitude, retirement. Жить в уедине́нии, to live in solitude. Скло́нный к уедине́нию, retiring. У-един-ённость, *n.f.,* isolation, seclusion. У-един-ённый, *adj. part. pass. past,* secluded, isolated, solitary. У. о́стров, a lonely island. У-ое ме́сто, a secluded spot. У-един-ённо, *adv.,* alone, in seclusion. На-един-е́, *adv.,* privately, alone.

по-един-о́к, *n.m.,* (*obs.*), duel, single

combat. Вы́звать на п., to challenge to a duel. Слове́сный п., a verbal duel.
оди́н, *num. card.,* одн-а́, *f.,* одн-о́, *neut.,* one; a certain; only, alone. Он оди́н, only he; he is alone. Оди́н друго́го сто́ит, (*idiom*), one is just as bad as the other. О. за други́м, one after another; single file. За о. раз, in one go. Нельзя́ всё сде́лать за оди́н раз, one should not do everything in one go. Одни́м сло́вом, in a word. За-одно́, *adv.,* all together, simultaneously. Де́йствовать всем з., to act all together. Одно́ и то́ же, the same thing. Одинёхонек, оди́н-одинёхонек, *adj.,* quite alone. Оста́лся я оди́н-одинёхонек: без семьи́, без друзе́й, I remained all alone, without family, without friends.
один-о́к-ий, *adj.,* solitary, single, lonely; unmarried. О. ху́тор, a solitary farm. Один-о́чество, *n.n.,* solitude, loneliness. Один-о́чка, *n.f.,* singleton, single. Жить одино́чкой, to live alone. Один-о́чный, *adj.,* one man; solitary. О-ое заключе́ние, solitary confinement. О-ая ка́мера, a cell for solitary confinement. Один-а́ково, *adv.,* equally. Говори́ть о. свобо́дно по-ру́сски и по-англи́йски, to speak Russian and English equally fluently. Один-а́ковость, *n.f.,* uniformity, sameness, identity. Один-а́ковый, *adj.,* same, identical, equal.
оди́н-на-дцать, *num. card.,* eleven. Оди́н-на-дцатый, *num. ord.,* the eleventh. Одн-а́жды, *adv.,* once, once upon a time. О. но́чью, once in the night. Одн-о, *a combining form meaning* one. Одн-о-а́ктный, *adj.,* one-act (*e.g.,* a play, drama). Одн-о-вре́менность, *n.f.,* simultaneousness. Одн-о-вре́менный, *adj.,* simultaneous. Одн-о-вре́менно, *adv.,* simultaneously, at the same time. Одн-о-дне́вный, *adj.,* of one day's duration. Одн-о-кла́ссник, *n.m.,* classmate. Одн-о-ку́рсник, *n.m.,* classmate. Одн-о-ле́тки, *pl.,* persons born in the same year, contemporaries. Одн-о-ле́тний, *adj.,* (*bot.*), annual. Оди-о-обра́зие, *n.n.,* uniformity, monotony. Одн-о-обра́зный, *adj.,* monotonous, unvaried. Одн-о-ро́дный, *adj.,* homogeneous, uniform; similar; of the same origin. Одн-о-сторо́нний, *adj.,* one-sided. О-ее наруше́ние догово́ра, breach of contract by one party. Одн-о-сторо́нность, *n.f.,* one-sidedness.

ЕЗД-, ЕЗЖ-, ЕХ-, ЕД-, LOCOMOTION (BY MEANS OF A CONVEYANCE)

езд-и-ть, е́зж-у, *v.i. indet.,* to ride, drive; go, travel by vehicle. Е. на лошадя́х, to drive in a horse and carriage. Е.

па́рой (одино́чкой), to drive a pair of horses (one horse). Е. по всему́ све́ту, to travel all over the world. Езд-а́, *n.f.,* drive, driving; ride, riding. Е. на велосипе́де, bicycling. Бы́страя е., fast driving, riding. Ме́дленная е., slow driving, riding. Е. верхо́м, horseback riding. Езд-о́к, *n.m.,* rider, horseman.
е́х-а-ть, е́д-у, *v.i.det.,* to drive, ride, go. Е. в о́тпуск, to go on leave, furlough. Е. на по́езде, to ride in a train. Е. верхо́м, to ride horseback. Е. на охо́ту, to go hunting. Е. по желе́зной доро́ге, to travel by train.
въ-е́х-ать, *v.p.,* въезж-а́ть, *v.i.,* в, на + *acc.,* to enter, ride into; drive, move into. В. во двор, to drive into a courtyard. В. на́ гору, to drive up a mountain. Въ-езд, *n.m.,* approach, entrance; avenue, drive. При въе́зде в город, at the entrance to the town. Пра́во въе́зда, right of entrance.
вы́-ех-ать, *v.p.,* вы-езж-а́ть, *v.i.,* из + *gen.,* to leave, depart; ride, drive out. В. из го́рода, to drive out of a town. В. за грани́цу, to go abroad. Выезжа́ть на други́х, to exploit others.
вы́-езд, *n.m.,* departure: turn out. В. из страны́, departure from a country. Вы́-езд-ка, *n.f.,* breaking in, schooling (*as* of horses). В. молоды́х лошаде́й, the breaking in of young horses. Выездно́й лаке́й, (*obs.*), footman.
до-е́х-ать, *v.p.,* до-езж-а́ть, *v.i.,* до + *gen.,* to drive as far as, reach. Мы ещё не дое́хали до ста́нции, we have not reached the station yet, До-езж-а́чий, *adj. used as n.,* whipper-in (hunting).
за-е́х-ать, *v.p.,* за-езж-а́ть, *v.i.,* в + *acc.,* за + *instr.,* к + *dat.,* to go beyond, pass; to call for, upon; go astray, lose one's way. З. в глушь, to drive to a remote place. З. во двор, to drive into a yard, courtyard. Я зае́ду за ва́ми, I'll call for you.
за-е́зд-ить, *v.p.,* + *acc.,* to ruin, wear out. З. ло́шадь, to ruin, wear out a horse. З. челове́ка, (*fig.*), to wear out a person. За-е́зж-енный, *adj., part. pass. past,* worn out. За-е́зд, *n.m.,* an event in horse-racing, at a horse-show.
на-е́х-ать, *v.p.,* на-езж-а́ть, *v.i.,* на + *acc.,* to gather in numbers; come occasionally; collide with, strike against. На́ехало мно́го госте́й, many guests gathered. Автомоби́ль нае́хал на прохо́жего, the car struck a passerby. На-е́зд, *n.m.,* inroad, inrush; flying visit. Быва́ть нае́здом, to visit occasionally for a short time. На-е́зд-ник, *n.m.,* rider, horseman, jockey, equestrian. Черке́сы - уда́лые нае́здники, Circassians are daring horsemen.

объ-е́х-ать, объ-е́зд-ить, *v.p.,* объ-езж-а́ть, *v.i.,* + *acc.,* to travel over; make the rounds; make a tour of; detour, make a detour. О. весь свет, to travel all over the world. Объе́хать боло́то, to make a detour around a marsh. До́ктор объе́хал свои́х больны́х, the doctor made the rounds of his patients. Объ-е́зд, *n.m.,* tour, circult. Ехать в о., to go by a roundabout route, make a detour. Объ-е́зд-чик, *n.m.,* mounted forest ranger.

объ-е́зд-ить, *v.p.,* объ-езж-а́ть, *v.i.,* + *acc.,* to school, break in a horse. О. ло́шадь, to break in a horse. Объ-е́здка, *n.f.,* schooling of a horse.

отъ-е́хать, *v.p.,* отъ-езжа́ть, *v.i.,* to drive off, away; depart. Отъ-е́зд, *n.m.,* departure, leaving. Че́рез неде́лю по́сле моего́ отъе́зда из Москвы́, a week after my departure from Moscow. Отъ-езж-а́ющий, *adj. part. act. pres.,* departing; *used as n.,* one who is departing.

пере-е́х-ать, *v.p.,* пере-езж-а́ть, *v.i.,* + *acc.,* to move; cross. П. на но́вую кварти́ру, to move to a new apartment. П. ре́ку на ло́дке, to cross a river in a boat. П. через океа́н, to cross an ocean. П. кого́-нибудь, to run over someone. Пере-е́зд, *n.m.,* passage, transit; removal; crossing. П. из Евро́пы в Аме́рику, the crossing from Europe to America. Железнодоро́жный п., a railroad crossing.

подъ-е́х-ать, *v.p.,* подъ-езж-а́ть, *v.i.,* к + *dat.,* to drive up to; (*fig.*), to coax, flatter. П. к до́му (вокза́лу), to drive up to a house (station). Подъ-е́зд, *n.m.,* entrance. Пара́дный п., main entrance.

по-е́х-ать, *v.p.,* в + *acc.,* to go, set off, depart; slide. П. в го́род, to go to town, to the city. П. верхо́м, to go on horseback. Поезжа́йте! (*imper.*), be off! Ну, пое́хали! Let's go! Let's be off!

по-е́зд-ить, *v.p.,* to travel about, drive for a while. П. по све́ту, to travel all over the world. По-е́зд-ка, *n.f.,* trip, journey, voyage. Двухдне́вная п., a two-day trip. По́-езд, *n.m.,* train. Пассажи́рский п., passenger train. П. прихо́дит в 8 утра́, the train is due at 8 a.m.

при-е́х-ать, *v.p.,* при-езж-а́ть, *v.i.,* to come, arrive. П. домо́й, to come home. При-е́зд, *n.m.,* arrival, coming. При-езж-а́ющий, *adj. part. act. pres.,* a new-comer, visitor. При-е́зж-ий, *adj.,* a non-resident, new-comer, visitor. Гости́ница для прие́зжих, a hotel for transients. Там бы́ло не́сколько приéзжих актёров, there were several visiting actors.

про-е́х-ать, *v.p.,* про-езж-а́ть, *v.i.,* + *acc.,* to pass; drive, ride through, by, past. Как туда́ п.,? how does one get there? Мы то́лько что прое́хали ста́нцию, we have just passed the station. Про-е́х-ать-ся, *v.p.r.,* про-езж-а́ть-ся, *v.i.r.,* (*colloq.*), to take a ride, drive. Не прое́хаться ли нам за́ го́род? Why don't we take a drive out of the city? П. на чей-либо счёт, (*fig.*), to be witty at someone's expense. Про-е́зж-ий, *adj.,* public; *used as n.,* traveler, passerby. П-ая доро́га, a public road. Про-е́зд, *n.m.,* passage, thoroughfare. П. воспреща́ется! No thoroughfare!

про-е́зд-ить, *v.p.,* + *acc.,* to drive, ride for a limited time. Я прое́здил два часа́, оты́скивая доро́гу, I drove around for two hours looking for the road. Я прое́здил 100 рубле́й, (*fig.*), I spent 100 rubles. Про-е́зд-ить-ся, *v.p.r.,* to spend all one's money travelling. Проездио́й, *adj.,* traveling. П-ая пла́та, fare. П. биле́т, a railroad, train ticket. Про-е́зд-ом, *adv.,* in passing. while passing through.

разъ-езж-а́ть, *v.i.,* to drive, ride about. Р. по дела́м слу́жбы, to travel on business. Разъ-езж-а́ть-ся, *v.i.r.,* разъ-е́х-ать-ся, *v.p.r,* to break up, separate; pass one another. Улица так узка́, что тру́дно бы́ло двум автомоби́лям разъе́хаться, the street is so narrow, two cars would find it difficult to pass. Го́сти давно́ разъе́хались, the guests left long ago. Супру́ги разъе́хались, husband and wife have separated. Разъ-е́зд, *n.m.,* departure; separation; mounted patrol. Железнодоро́жный р., railroad siding Разъ-ездно́й, *adj.,* pertaining to travel. Р-ы́е де́ньги, traveling expenses.

съ-е́х-ать, *v.p.,* съ-езж-а́ть, *v.i.,* с + *gen.,* на + *acc.,* to drive off, down; move. С. с горы́, to drive downhill. С. с горы́ на са́нках, to coast down hill on a sled. С. с кварти́ры, to move out of an apartment. У меня́ шля́па съе́хала на́бок, my hat was all awry. Съ-е́х-ать-ся, *v.p.r.,* съ-езж-а́ть-ся, *v.i.r.,* to meet, assemble, gather. Друзья́ съе́хались потанцева́ть, the friends got together for a dance. Съ-езд, *n.m.,* congress, convention, conference, meeting, reunion. С. учёных, a convention of scientists.

съ-е́зд-ить, *v.p.,* в + *acc.,* to go and return. С. в магази́н, в го́род, to go to a store, the city and return home.

у-е́х-ать, *v.p.,* у-езж-а́ть, *v.i.,* в + *acc.,*

to leave, depart. Он уезжа́ет в Аме́рику в апре́ле, he is leaving for America in April.

у-е́зд, *n.m.,* (*obs.*), district. У-е́зд-ный, *adj.,* (*obs.*), pertaining to a district, county, district seat. У. го́род, county, district seat.

у-е́зд-ить, *v.p.,* + *acc.,* (*colloq.*), to smooth, level. У. коня́, to ride a horse till it has become tired. У-е́зд-ить-ся, *v.p.r.,* to be smoothed (*as* a road); to become fatigued, quieted. Был конь, да уе́здился, (*saying*) he is not the dashing young man he used to be.

ЕД-, ЕСТ-, ЯД-, ЯСТ-, EATING, FOOD; POISON

ед-а́, *n.f.,* meal, food. Обѝльная (вку́сная), еда́, abundant (tasty) food. Еда́ ей не впрок, (*colloq.*), food does her no good. Вре́мя еды́, mealtime.

е́д-кий, *adj.,* corrosive, caustic. Е. дым (газ), pungent, acrid smoke (gas). Е. за́пах, penetrating odor. Е-ая жи́дкость, acid liquid. Е-ое замеча́ние, a sarcastic remark. Ед-кость, *n.f.,* corrosiveness, causticity; bitterness. Ед-ко, *adv.,* bitterly. Ед-о́к, *n.m.,* eater, consumer; gulper. Хоро́ший е., a hearty eater.

ест-ь, *v.i.,* съ-ест-ь, *v.p.,* + *acc.,* to eat. Е. кусо́к хле́ба, to eat a piece of bread. Е. жа́дно, to eat greedily. Е. ма́ло, to eat sparingly. Дым ест глаза́, smoke makes one's eyes smart.

въ-ед-а́ть-ся, *v.i.r.,* въ-ест-ь-ся, *v.p.r.,* в + *acc.,* (*colloq.*), to corrode, eat into a surface. Хими́ческая кра́ска въеда́ется в мате́рию, chemical dye eats into material.

взъ-ед-а́ть-ся, *v.i.r.,* взъ-е́ст-ь-ся, *v.p.r.,* на + *acc.,* (*colloq.*,), to become angry, furious. Хозя́йка взъе́лась на жильца́, the landlady has taken a dislike to the tenant.

вы-ед-а́ть, *v.i.,* вы́-ест-ь, *v.p.,* + *acc.,* to eat up, consume. В. мя́киш из бу́лки, to eat the crumb, the soft part of a loaf. Это вы́еденного яйца́ не сто́ит, (*saying*), it's not worth a thing (literally: it isn't worth an empty egg shell).

до-ед-а́ть, *v.i.,* до-е́ст-ь, *v.p.,* + *acc.,* to finish eating. Д. бу́лку, to finish a whole loaf of bread.

за-ед-а́ть, *v.i.,* за-е́ст-ь, *v.p.,* + *acc.,* to eat after a drink; worry. З. чужо́й век, (*fig.*), to spoil another's life. Меня́ зае́ли комары́, I've been eaten up by mosquitoes. За-я́д-лый, *adj.,* inveterate. З. картёжник, an inveterate gambler.

изъ-ед-а́ть, *v.i.,* изъ-е́сть, *v.p.,* + *acc.,* to consume; cover with bites;; corrode. Моль изъе́ла мех, moths have eaten the fur.

на-ед-а́ть-ся, *v.i.,* на-е́сть-ся, *v.p.,* + *gen.,* + *instr.,* (*colloq.*), to eat one's fill, gorge. Н. хле́ба (хле́бом), to gorge oneself with bread.

объ-ед-а́ть, *v.i.,* объ-е́сть, *v.p.,* + *acc.,* to crop (*e.g.,* grass); gnaw round; (*fig.*), be a burden, eat more than one's share, eat someone out of house and home. О. кость, to gnaw a bone clean. Объ-ед-а́ть-ся, *v.i.r.,* объ-е́сть-ся, *v.p.r.,* + *gen.,* + *instr.,* to overeat, gorge, gormandize. Он объе́лся ви́шнями (ви́шен), he gorged himself with cherries. Объе́дки, *n.pl.,* scraps, remnants of food.

объ-яд-е́ние, *n.n.,* gluttony, greediness; treat, dainty dish. Пиро́жки вку́сные - пря́мо о., tasty patties are a real treat.

отъ-ед-а́ть, *v.i.,* отъ-е́сть, *v.p.,* + *acc.,* to eat, gnaw off; finish eating. О. кусо́к, to eat a piece off. Ржа́вчина отъе́ла винты́, rust has corroded the screws. Отъ-ед-а́ть-ся, *v.i.r.,* отъ-е́сть-ся, *v.p.r.,* to become fat; to build oneself up after a period of starvation, fasting. Ну, и отъе́лся он на чужи́х хлеба́х, (*colloq.*), he certainly fattened himself up by sponging.

пере-ед-а́ть, *v.i.,* пере-е́сть, *v.p.,* + *gen.,* to overeat; corrode. Ребёнок перее́л ка́ши, the child ate too much porridge. Ржа́вчина перееда́ет желе́зо, rust corrodes iron.

подъ-ед-а́ть, *v.i.,* подъ-е́сть, *v.p.,* + *acc.,* (*colloq.*), to consume. Мураве́й подъеда́ет ко́рни расте́ния, an ant eats the roots of a plant.

по-ед-а́ть, *v.i.,* по-е́сть, *v.p.,* + *acc.,* + *gen.,* to consume, devour; have a meal. Ко́шка пое́ла всё мя́со, the cat ate all the meat. П. мя́са, to have some meat. По-ед-о́м, *adv.,* (*colloq.*), *used in the expressions*: Есть кого́-нибудь п., to make life miserable for some one; nag. Она́ е́ла его́ поедо́м, she made life miserable for him.

при-ед-а́ть-ся, *v.i.r.,* при-е́сть-ся, *v.p.r.,* + *dat.,* to have one's fill of something; take a dislike to; become insipid. Мне прие́лось э́то ку́шанье, I'm fed up with this food. Все развлече́ния прие́лись, I've become bored by all diversions.

про-ед-а́ть, *v.i.,* про-е́сть, *v.p.,* + *acc.,* to corrode; consume. Моль прое́ла сукно́, moths have eaten through the cloth. П. своё жа́лование, to spend one's whole salary on food.

разъ-ед-а́ть, *v.i.*, разъ-е́сть, *v.p.,* + *acc.,* to corrode. Ржа́вчина разъе́ла желе́зо, rust has corroded the iron. Разъ-ед-а́ть-ся, *v.i.r.,* разъ-е́сть-ся, *v.p.r.,* to eat heartily, to become fat from good food, from eating a lot.

съ-ед-а́ть, *v.i.,* съ-е́сть, *v.p.,* + acc., to eat up, devour. Он съеда́ет фунт мя́са в день, he eats a pound of meat a day. Съесть соба́ку на чём-либо, (*fig.*), to be a past master at something. Съ-ед-о́бный, *adj.,* edible, eatable. С-ые грибы́, edible mushrooms. Съ-ест-но́й, *adj.,* edible. С-ы́е припа́сы, foodstuff, provisions, victuals.

об-е́д-ать, *v.i.,* по-об-е́д-ать, *v.p.,* to dine, have dinner. Обе́дать не до́ма, to dine out. Об-е́д, *n.m.,* dinner. Мясно́й о., a meat dinner. Зва́ный о., dinner party. Семе́йный о., family dinner. Об-е́д-енный, *adj.,* pertaining to dinner. О. переры́в, dinner recess. О-ое вре́мя, dinner time. Об-е́д-ня, *n.f.,* the Holy Eucharist; Mass.

яд, *n.m.,* poison, venom. Яд-ови́тость, *n.f.,* virulence; (*fig.*), malice, bitterness. Яд-ови́тый, *adj.,* poisonous, venomous, virulent. Я-ый газ, poison gas. Я-ая змея, venomous snake. Я-ое замеча́ние, (*fig.*), malicious remark, observation. Яд-ови́то, *adv.,* maliciously, cuttingly.

траво-я́д-ный, *adj.,* herbivorous. Мясо-я́д-ный, *adj.,* carnivorous. Все-я́д-ный, *adj.,* omnivorous. Всея́дное живо́тное, an omnivorous animal.

яс-л-и, *n.pl.,* crib, manger; creche. Я. для дете́й, nursery.

яст-в-а, *n.pl.,* (*obs.*), viands. На столе́ вку́сные я., there are choice foods on the table.

ЕЛ-(Ь), ЕЛ-, SPRUCE, FIR TREE

ел-ь, ёл-ка, *n.f.,* fir, fir tree, spruce tree. Бе́лая америка́нская ель, white American spruce, fir. Рожде́ственская ёлка, Christmas tree. Устро́ить ёлку для дете́й, to have a Christmas tree for children. Ёл-очка, *n.f.,* (*dim.*), small fir tree. Вышива́ть ёлочкой, to embroider a spruce tree design. Ел-ь-ник, *n.m.,* spruce grove; fir branches, twigs. Ел-о́вый, *adj.,* of or pertaining to a fir, spruce. Е. лес, spruce forest. Е-ая игла́, spruce needle. Е-ая ши́шка, spruce cone. Ёл-очный, *adj.,* pertaining to a spruce, Christmas tree. Блестя́щие ёлочные украше́ния, brilliant Christmas tree decorations.

ЕСТ-Ь, EXISTENCE, BEING

ест-ь, *3d pers. sing. pres. of the verb* быть, to be; *used only as 3rd pers. sing. and pl.,* is, are. Что есть и́стина? What is truth? Есть-ли у вас де́ньги? Do you have any money? У меня́ есть 5 рубле́й, I have 5 rubles. Из вся́кого положе́ния есть вы́ход, there is a way out of every situation. Кри́кнуть, что есть си́лы, to shout with all one's might. Ты ду́маешь обо мне ху́же, чем я есть, you think worse of me than I am. *Idioms:* Что ни на есть, (*colloq.*), whatever there is. Как есть, as is; such as it is. Взял всё, как есть, (*colloq.*), he made a clean sweep of it. Есть тако́е де́ло, (*colloq.*), all right, I agree, let it be so.

ест-е́ств-ен-н-ик, *n.m.,* ест-е́ственница, *n.f.,* naturalist; student of natural science. Ест-е́ственность, *n.f.,* naturalness. Е. по́зы, naturalness of a pose. Ест-е́ственный, *adj.,* natural, unartificial. Е. отбо́р, natural selection. Е. ход веще́й, the natural course of events. Е-ая жизнь, natural life. Е-ые бога́тства, natural resources. Е-ые цветы́, natural flowers. Есте́ственным о́бразом, in a natural way. Ест-е́ственно, *adv.,* naturally, of course; *used impers.,* it is natural. Ему́ да́ли непоси́льную рабо́ту; есте́ственно, он её не испо́лнил, they gave him an assignment beyond his strength; naturally, he did not complete it. Ест-е́ственно-нау́чный Институ́т, Institute of Natural Sciences. Ест-еств-о́, *n.n.,* nature; substance; innate character. Естество-ве́дение, естество-зна́ние, *n.n.,* the natural sciences. Естество-ве́д, *n.m.,* natural scientist. Естество-испыта́тель, *n.m.,* naturalist. Сверхъ-ест-е́ственность, *n.f.,* supernaturalness; miraculousness. Сверхъ-ест-е́ственный, *adj.,* supernatural; miraculous; unearthly. С-ое явле́ние (существо́), a supernatural phenomenon, creature. Распространя́ться с с-ой быстрото́й, to spread like wildfire. Сверхъ-ест-е́ственно, *adv.,* supernaturally; miraculously.

Ж

ЖАД-, ЖАЖД-, GREED THIRST

жа́д-н-ич-ать, *v.i.,* по-жа́д-ничать, *v.p.,* to be greedy, be tempted by greed. Жа́д-ничание, *n.n.,* greediness. Жа́дность, *n.f.,* greed, avidity, covetousness, cupidity. Он взял большо́й кусо́к из жа́дности, he took a large piece out of greediness. Жа́д-ный, *adj.,* greedy, avid, covetous, gluttonous. Ж. челове́к, a greedy man, glutton. Жа́д-но, *adv.*, greedily. Ж. глота́ть, пить, to gulp, guzzle. Ж. есть, to eat greedily.

жа́жд-а, *n.f.*, thirst; craving, appetite. Я чу́вствую жа́жду, I feel thirsty. Томи́ться от жа́жды, to suffer from thirst. Утоля́ть жа́жду, to quench a thirst. Ж. зо́лота, lust for gold. Ж. зна́ний, thirst for knowledge.

жа́жд-ать, *v.i.,* + *gen.,* to thirst for, be thirsty; crave, hunger for. Ж. сла́вы, to thirst for glory. Ж. приключе́ний, to crave adventure. Жа́жд-ущий, *adj. part. act. pres.,* thirsty, hungry; one who craves. Алчущие и жа́ждущие пра́вды, (*Bib.*), "those who hunger and thirst for righteousness".

ЖАЛ-, REGRET, SYMPATHY, PITY, LAMENT, COMPLAINT

жал-е́-ть, *v.i.,* по-жал-е́ть, *v.p.,* о + *prep.,* + *acc.,* to regret, be sorry; spare. Ж. о поте́рянном вре́мени, to regret lost time. Ж. о свои́х оши́бках, to be sorry for one's mistakes. Ж. сироту́, to pity an orphan. Не ж. де́нег, not to begrudge money. Не ж. сил, to spare no pains. Жал-ь, *impers.,* it's a pity; pity. Ж. мне её, I'm sorry for her. Как жаль! What a pity! Для вас мне ничего́ не жаль, there is nothing I won't do for you. Жа́л-кий, *adj.,* pitiful, pitiable, miserable, sad. Ж. трус, a miserable coward. Ж-ое существова́ние, a miserable existence. Жа́л-ко, *adv.,* pitifully. Мне вас ж., I'm sorry for you. Как жа́лко! What a pity!

со-жал-е́ть, *v.i.,* о + *prep.,* to regret, deplore; repent, be sorry for, have pity for. С. о своём посту́пке, to regret one's behavior, action. Со-жал-е́ние, *n.n.,* repentance, regret; pity, compassion. Вы́сказать с., to express regret. Досто́йный сожале́ния, worthy of, deserving pity; deplorable. К сожале́нию, unfortunately.

жа́л-об-а, *n.f.,* complaint, grievance; grumbling. Пода́ть жа́лобу в бюро́ жа́лоб, to file a complaint in a complaint office. Жа́л-общик, *n.m.,* plaintiff. Жа́л-обность, *n.f.,* plaintiveness. Жа́л-обный, *adj.,* mournful, sad, plaintive. Ж-ая пе́сня, plaintive song. Ж-ая кни́га, (*colloq.*), complaint-book. Ж. крик, plaintive cry. Жа́л-обно, *adv.,* mournfully, sadly, plaintively. "Жа́лобно сто́нет ве́тер осе́нний", (*song*), "the autumn wind moans plaintively".

раз-жа́л-об-ить, *v.p.,* + *acc.,* to move to pity. Она́ разжа́лобила меня́ свои́ми слеза́ми, her tears aroused my pity.

Раз-жа́л-обить-ся, *v.p.r.,* to be overwhelmed with pity, compassion.

с-жа́л-ить-ся, *v.p.r.,* над + *instr.,* to take pity. С. над несча́стным челове́ком, to take pity on an unfortunate person. Сжа́льтесь на́до мной! Have pity on me! Жа́л-остливый, *adj.,* (*colloq.*), pitiful, compassionate. Ж-ая стару́ха, a pitiful old woman. Жа́л-остливо, *adv.,* piteously. Жа́л-остливость, *n.f.,* pitifulness. Жа́л-остный, *adj.,* (*colloq.*), piteous, woeful, lamentable, sorrowful, sad. Ж-ое выраже́ние лица́, a rueful expression. Жа́л-остно, *adv.,* piteously, woefully, lamentably, sorrowfully, sadly. Он ж. стона́л, he was moaning sorrowfully. Жа́л-ость, *n.f.,* pity, compassion, mercy. Ж. к самому́ себе́, self-pity. Из жа́лости, for pity's sake.

жа́л-овать, *v.i.,* по-жа́л-овать, *v.p.,* + *instr.,* к + *dat.,* (*obs.*), to give, grant, bestow. Ж. о́рденом, to award a decoration. Ж. гра́мотой, grant a charter. Он ре́дко к нам жа́лует, (*obs.*), he seldom comes to visit us. Добро́ пожа́ловать! Welcome! Пожа́луйте ку́шать! (*obs.*), Dinner is served! (*announced by a servant*). По-жа́л-ование, *n.n.,* granting, reward, conferment. По-жа́луй, *parenthetical word,* I dare say; maybe; perhaps; if you like; I don't mind. Я, пожа́луй, пойду́ гуля́ть, I think I'll go for a walk. Что-ж, начнём, пожа́луй, well, let's start. По-жа́луйста, please, be so kind; I shall be much obliged. Жа́л-ование, *n.n.,* salary, wages. Ме́сячное ж., monthly salary. Жа́л-ованный, *adj. part. pass. past,* granted, given, bestowed, presented. Ж-ая гра́мота, charter.

жа́л-овать-ся, *v.i.r.,* по-жа́л-овать-ся, *v.p.r.,* to complain. Пострада́вший пожа́ловался в суд, the victim filed a complaint in court.

об-жа́л-овать, *v.p.,* + *acc.,* to appeal a case. О. пригово́р суда́, to appeal a court decision. Об-жа́л-ование, *n.n.,* the action of appealing a case

раз-жа́л-овать, *v.p.,* + *acc.,* to degrade, demote, reduce in rank. Раз-жа́л-ование, *n.n.,* degradation, demotion. Раз-жа́л-ованный, *adj. part. pass. past,* degraded, demoted. Офице́р, р. в солда́ты, an officer demoted to the ranks.

ЖАЛ-, STING

жа́л-о, *n.n.,* sting; organ for piercing, stinging. У пчелы́ о́строе ж., the bee has a sharp sting.
жа́л-ить, *v.i.,* у-жа́л-ить, *v.p.,* + *acc.,* +

instr., to sting. Пчела́ ре́дко жа́лит пчелово́да, a bee seldom bites the apiarist. У-жа́л-енный, *adj. part. pass. past*, stung. Он вскочи́л как у., he jumped as if he had been stung. Жа́л-истый, *adj.*, having a sting. Жал-о-подо́бный, *adj.*, resembling a sting. Жал-о-обра́зный, *adj.*, shaped like a sting.

ЖАР-, HEAT

жар, *n.m.*, heat, glow, fever, temperature; animation, ardor. Выгреба́ть ж. из пе́чки, to take embers out of a stove. Горе́ть, как ж., (*poet.*), to glitter like gold. У ребёнка ж., the child has a fever. Чужи́ми рука́ми жар загреба́ть, (*saying*), to profit by the labor of others. Жар-а́, *n.f.*, heat, hot weather. Ле́тняя ж., summer heat. Жа́р-кий, *adj.*, hot, torrid; ardent. Ж. день, a hot day. Жа́р-ко, *adv.*, hotly, torridly. Жа́рко! It's hot! Жар-о-понижа́ющий, *adj.*, febrifugal. Ж-ее сре́дство, febrifuge. Жар-пти́ца, (*poet., folklore*), the fire-bird.

жа́р-и-ть, *v.i.*, + *acc.*, to roast, fry, broil, grill. Ж. говя́дину, to roast beef. Со́лнце жа́рит, the sun is scorching. Жа́р-ить-ся, *v.i.r.*, to be roasted, fried, broiled, grilled. Бара́нина жа́рится на костре́, mutton is roasted on an open fire. Ж. на со́лнце, to bask in the sun. Жа́р-енье, *n.n.*, roasting, frying, toasting. Жа́р-еный, *adj., part. pass. past*, roasted, fried, broiled. Жар-ко́е, *n.n.*, roast of meat; meat course, dish. Жар-о́вня, *n.f.*, brazier.

до-жа́р-ить, *v.p.*, до-жа́р-ивать, *v.i.*, + *acc.*, to fry, roast, sufficiently; to finish roasting, frying. До-жа́р-енный, *adj. part. pass. past*, well-done. Не-до-жа́р-енный, *adj. part. pass. past*, rare. Н-ое мя́со, rare meat; insufficiently roasted, fried meat.

за-жа́р-ить, *v.p.*, за-жа́р-ивать, *v.i.*, + *acc.*, see жа́рить.

из-жа́р-ить, *v.p.*, + *acc.*, see жа́рить.

на-жа́р-ить, *v.p.*, на-жа́р-ивать, *v.i.*, + *acc.*, to roast in quantity; heat to excess. Н. блю́до котле́т, to fry a whole dish of cutlets.

об-жа́р-ить, *v.p.*, об-жа́р-ивать, *v.i.*, + *acc.*, to fry, brown, sear.

пере-жа́р-ить, *v.p.*, пере-жа́р-ивать, *v.i.*, + *acc.*, to overroast, over-heat. П. ко́фе, to overroast coffee. Е́сли пере-жа́ришь мя́со, оно́ бу́дет сли́шком сухо́е, if you roast meat too long, it will be too dry. Пере-жа́р-енный, *adj. part. pass. past*, overdone, well-done.

П-ая ку́рица, an overdone fowl, chicken.

под-жа́р-ить, *v.p.*, под-жа́р-ивать, *v.i.*, + *acc.*, to roast, fry, toast lightly. П. карто́шку, to fry, brown potatoes. П. хлеб, to make toast. Под-жа́р-ить-ся, *v.p.r.*, под-жа́р-ивать-ся, *v.i.r.*, to be roasted, fried, toasted lightly. Котле́ты поджа́риваются на сковоро́дке, cutlets are fried in a frying pan. Под-жа́р-ивание, *n.n.*, light roasting, frying, toasting. Под-жа́р-енный, *adj. part. pass. past*, roasted, toasted, fried. П. карто́фель, fried potatoes. Под-жа́р-ый, *adj.*, (*colloq.*), lean; meagre, thin. П-ая скакова́я ло́шадь, a lean race horse.

про-жа́р-ить, *v.p.*, про-жа́р-ивать, *v.i.*, + *acc.*, to roast, fry, toast thoroughly. Хорошо́ прожа́ренный бифште́кс, well-done steak.

с-жа́р-ить, *v.p.*, + *acc.*, (*colloq.*), to roast, fry; *used instead of* изжа́рить.

у-жа́р-ить, *v.p.*, у-жа́р-ивать, *v.i.*, + *acc.*, to reduce by roasting; to roast to a given degree. У-жа́р-ить-ся, *v.p.r.*, у-жа́р-ивать-ся, *v.i.r*, to be reduced by roasting; to be thoroughly roasted. Мя́со не ужа́рилось, the meat is underdone, too rare.

по-жа́р, *n.m.*, fire, conflagration. В. до́ме п., the house is on fire, in flames. Пожа́ром уничто́жило полови́ну го́рода, half the town was destroyed by fire. По-жа́р-ище, *n.n.*, site of a conflagration. По-жа́р-ный, *adj.*, pertaining to fire; *used as n.*, fireman. П. сигна́л, fire alarm. П-ая кома́нда, fire brigade, department. П-ые маши́ны, fire engines. Пожа́рные потуши́ли пожа́р, the firemen extinguished the fire.

ЖАТ(Ь)-, ЖМ-, ЖИМ-, SQUEEZING

жат-ь, **жм-у**, *v.i.*, + *acc.*, to squeeze, press, strain; wring out; oppress. Ж. ру́ку, to shake hands (in greeting). Башма́к жмёт, the shoe is pinching. Ж. подчинённых, to oppress one's subordinates. Жа́ть-ся, *v.i.r.*, to huddle. Ж. от хо́лода, to huddle together from cold.

вы́-жать, *v.p.*, вы-жим-а́ть, *v.i.*, + *acc.*, to squeeze, press, wring out. В. сок из апельси́на, to squeeze orange juice. В. бельё, to wring out clothing. Вы́-жат-ый, *adj. part. pass. past*, squeezed; wrung out. В. лимо́н, a squeezed lemon. Вы-жим-а́ние, *n.n.*, squeezing, wringing. Вы́-жим-ки, *n.pl.*, residue; husks.

до-жа́ть, *v.p.*, до-жим-а́ть, *v.i.*, + *acc.*,

to press, squeeze, wring out thoroughly.
за-жа́ть, *v.p.,* за-жим-а́ть, *v.i.,* + *acc.,* to press, grip, clamp; gag. З. желе́зо в тиски́, to clamp iron in a vice. З. рот кому́-нибудь, (*fig.*), to gag someone. З. нос от ды́ма, to hold one's nose against smoke. З. в руке́ моне́ту, to grip a coin in one's hand. За-жа́ть-ся, *v.p.r.,* за-жим-а́ть-ся, *v.i.r.,* + *instr.,* в + *acc.,* to be clamped; (*fig.*), suppressed. За-жи́м, *n.m.,* (*tech.*), clamp, clutch; (*fig.*), suppression, oppression. З. самокри́тики, (*recent*), suppression of self-criticism.

на-жа́ть, *v.p.,* на-жим-а́ть, *v.i.,* + *acc.,* to press down, upon; *perf. only,* to squeeze in quantity. Н. кно́пку звонка́, to ring a bell, press a bell button. Нажа́ть стака́н лимо́нного сока, to squeeze a glass of lemon juice. Нажи́м, *n.m.,* pressure. Н. на избира́телей, pressure exerted on voters. На-жим-а́ть-ся, *v.i.r.,* + *instr.,* to be pressed. Рыча́г нажима́ется руко́й, the lever is pressed by hand.

об-жа́ть, *v.p.,* об-жим-а́ть, *v.i.,* + *acc.,* to squeeze, press, wring out thoroughly. О. мо́крую оде́жду, to wring out wet clothes thoroughly. Об-жа́ть-ся, *v.p.r.,* об-жим-а́ть-ся, *v.i.r.,* to be wrung out thoroughly.

от-жа́ть, *v.p.,* от-жим-а́ть, *v.i.,* + *acc.,* to wring out; twist and strain. От-жа́ть-ся, *v.p.r.,* от-жим-а́ть-ся, *v.i.r.,* to be pressed, wrung out thoroughly.

под-жа́ть, *v.p.,* под-жим-а́ть, *v.i.,* + *acc.,* to draw in, fold under. П. гу́бы, to purse one's lips. Под-жа́т-ый, *adj. part. pass. past,* drawn in, folded under. Соба́ка с поджа́тым хвосто́м, a dog with its tail between its legs.

по-жа́ть, *v.p.,* по-жим-а́ть, *v.i.,* + *instr.,* to press, squeeze a little. П. плеча́ми, to shrug one's shoulders. П. кому́-нибудь ру́ку, to shake hands with some one. При-жим-а́ние, *n.n.,* pressing, squeezing. При-жа́ть-ся, *v.p.r.,* при-жим-а́ть-ся, *v.i.r.,* to press oneself against; nestle, cuddle.

при-жа́ть, *v.p.,* при-жим-а́ть, *v.i.,* + *acc.,* к + *dat.,* to press close; press to oneself. П. ребёнка к груди́, to press a child to one's bosom. П. к стене́, (*fig.*), to nail, press up against a wall. П. кно́пку на пла́тье, to fasten a snap on a dress.

раз-жа́ть, *v.p.,* раз-жим-а́ть, *v.i.,* + *acc.,* to unclasp, unfasten, open. Р. кула́к, to open one's fist. Она́ не разжа́ла рта, she didn't once open her mouth. Раз-жим-а́ние, *n.n.,* unclasping, opening, unfastening. Раз-жа́ть-ся, *v.p.r.,*

раз-жим-а́ть-ся, *v.i.r.,* to be unclasped, unfastened, opened.

с-жать, *v.p.,* с-жим-а́ть, *v.i.,* + *acc.,* to press together, squeeze, contract, condense. С. зу́бы, to clench one's teeth. С-жа́ть-ся, *v.p.r.,* с-жим-а́ть-ся, *v.i.r.,* to be condensed, contracted; shrink. С-жа́т-ие, *n.n.,* condensation, compression, shrinkage. С-жа́т-ый, *adj. part. pass. past,* condensed, clenched, compressed. С. кула́к, a clenched fist. С-ые гу́бы, pressed-together lips. С. во́здух, compressed air. Рассказа́ть в сжа́том ви́де, to relate in condensed form. С-жим-а́ние, *n.n., see* сжа́тие. С-жим-а́емость, *n.f.,* compressibility, contractibility.

у-жи́м-ка, *n.f.,* grimace. Обезья́ньие ужи́мки, monkeyish grimaces.

ЖАТ(Ь)-, ЖН-, ЖИН-, REAPING, HARVEST

жат-ь, жн-у, *v.i.,* с-жать, *v.p.,* + *acc.,* to creep, harvest. Ж. рожь, to reap rye. Жа́т-ва, *n.f.,* harvest, reaping; crop. Вре́мя жа́твы, harvest time. Жа́т-вен-ный, *adj.,* pertaining to reaping, harvesting. Ж-ая маши́на, *see* жне́йка, жа́тка. Жн-е́йка, *n.f.,* harvester, reaping machine. Жн-ец, *n.m.,* Жн-и́ца, *n.f.,* reaper, harvester (a person). Жн-и́во, *n.n.,* stubble. Покры́тый жни́вом, stubbled.

вы́-жать, *v.p.,* вы-жин-а́ть, *v.i.,* + *acc.,* to reap. В. по́ле, to reap a field clean.
на-жа́ть, *v.p.,* на-жин-а́ть, *v.i.,* + *acc.,* to reap, harvest in quantity. Н. со́тню снопо́в, to reap a hundred sheaves.
по-жа́ть, *v.p.,* по-жин-а́ть, *v.i.,* + *acc.,* to reap. П. пшени́цу, to reap wheat. Что посе́ешь, то и пожнёшь, (*Bib.*), as thou sowest, so shalt thou reap. П. ла́вры, (*fig.*), to reap laurels. П. полы свои́х трудо́в, to reap the fruit of one's labor.
с-жать, *v.p.,* to finish reaping; *see* жать.
у́-жин-ать, *v.i.,* по-у́-жин-ать, *v.p.,* to eat supper. У́-жин, *n.m.,* supper. Ру́сские обы́чно у́жинают в 8 часо́в ве́чера, Russians usually eat supper at eight o'clock in the evening.

ЖГ-, ЖЖ-, ЖЕЧ-, ЖИГ-, ЖЕГ-, ЖОГ-, BURNING

жеч-ь, жг-у, *v.i.,* с-жечь, *v.p.,* + *acc.,* to burn. Ж. дрова́, to burn wood. Крапи́ва жжёт, a nettle stings, smarts. Жéчь-ся, *v.p.r.,* to be burned. Жг-у́честь, *n.f.,* causticity; (*fig.*), glow, burning. Ж. взгля́да, the glow of an expression. Жг-у́чий, *adj.,* burning, hot; caustic. Ж-ая боль, a smarting pain. Ж-ее со́лнце, broiling sun. Ж-ие глаза́, (*fig.*), fiery eyes. Ж-ие вопро́сы, vital questions, issues.

жж-е́ние, *п.п.,* burning, consuming. Жж-ёнка, *n.f.,* hot punch. Жж-ёный *adj. part. pass. past,* roasted, burnt. Ж. ко́фе, roasted coffee. Ж. са́хар, burnt sugar.

воз-же́ч-ь, *v.р,* воз-жиг-ать, *v.i.,* + *acc.,* to burn; (*obs.*), light; (*fig.*), provoke. В. фимиа́м, to burn incense. Воз-жиг-а́ние, *п.п.,* (*obs.*), lighting, burning.

вы́-жеч-ь, *v.р.,* вы-жиг-а́ть, *v.i.,* + *acc.,* to burn out; sear, cauterize. В. лес, to burn down a forest. В. клеймо́, to brand. В. по де́реву, to burn in wood. Вы́-жж-енный, *adj. part. pass. past,* burnt, scorched (*e.g.,* grass). Вы-жиг-а́ние, *п.п.,* burning out; cauterizing. В. по де́реву, pyrography. Вы́-жиг-а, *n.m.,* and *n.f.,* (*colloq.*), a cunning, crafty man; rogue.

за-же́ч-ь, *v.р.,* за-жиг-а́ть, *v.i.,* + *acc.,* to set a fire, light. *see* поджига́ть. З. свет, to light a light. З. фона́рь, to light a lantern. З. спи́чку, to light a match. З. страсть, to kindle a passion. За-же́ч-ь-ся, *v.р.г.,* за-жиг-а́ть-ся, *v.i.r.,* to begin to burn, flare up. За-жиг-а́лка, *n.f.,* cigarette lighter. За-жиг-а́тельный, *adj.,* fiery, inflammatory, incendiary. З-ая бо́мба, incendiary bomb. З-ая речь, (*fig.*), inflammatory speech. Из-жо́г-а, *n.f.,* heart-burn, stomach acidity.

об-же́ч-ь, *v.р.,* об-жиг-а́ть, *v.i.,* + *acc.,* to burn, scorch; bake; kiln; calcine. О. ру́ку, to burn one's hand. О. кирпи́ч, to bake bricks. Об-же́ч-ся, *v.р.г.,* об-жиг-а́ть-ся, *v.i.r.,* + *instr.,* to burn, scald oneself. Обожжёшься на молоке́, ду́ешь на́ воду, (*prov.*), once bitten, twice shy. О́б-жиг, *n.m.,* kilning, glazing. О. гли́няных горшко́в, kilning of pottery. Об-жиг-а́ние, *п.п.,* burning, scorching, glazing. Об-жиг-а́тельный, *adj.,* burning, glazing. О-ая печь, furnace, glazing oven, kiln. О-же́ч(ь)-ся, see обже́чься. О-жиг-а́ть, *see* обжига́ть. О-жо́г, *n.m.,* a burn; scald; baking (*e.g.,* of bricks, pottery).

от-же́ч-ь, *v.р.,* от-жиг-а́ть, *v.i.,* + *acc.,* to temper (*as* steel); burn off. О. коне́ц па́лки, to burn off the end of a stick. От-жиг, *n.m.,* (*tech.*), tempering (*as* steel).

от-жиг-а́тельный, *adj.,* tempering. О-ая печь, tempering furnace.

пере-же́ч-ь, *v.р.,* пере-жиг-а́ть, *v.i.,* + *acc.,* to burn again, through; *see* жечь. П. про́вод, to burn a wire through. Пере-жо́г, *n.m.,* overheating; excessive consumption of fuel. Пере-же́чь-ся,

v.р.г., пере-жиг-а́ть-ся, *v.i.r.,* to be burnt, overroasted. Ко́фе пережига́ется на си́льном огне́, coffee becomes burnt on too hot a flame.

под-же́ч-ь, *v.р.,* под-жиг-а́ть, *v.i.,* + *acc.,* to set afire, kindle; (*fig.*), excite, provoke. П. дрова́, to start a wood fire. П. дом, to set fire to a house. П. пиро́г, to burn a pie. Под-же́чь-ся, *v.р.г.,* под-жиг-а́ть-ся, *v.i.r.,* + *instr.,* to be set afire. Под-жиг-а́тель, *n.m.,* arsonist, incendiary. Под-жиг-а́тели войны́, (*recent*), war-mongers. Под-жиг-а́тельство, *п.п.,* incendiarism. Под-жиг-а́ющий, *adj. part. act. pres.,* incendiary. П. снаря́д, (*mil.*), incendiary shell.

при-же́ч-ь, *v.р.,* при-жиг-а́ть, *v.i.,* + *acc.,* to sear; cauterize. П. ра́нку йо́дом, to cauterize a wound with iodine. При-жиг-а́ние, *п.п.,* searing, cauterizing. При-же́чь-ся, *v.р.г.,* при-жиг-а́ть-ся, *v.i.r.,* + *instr.,* to be cauterized.

раз-же́ч-ь, *v.р.,* раз-жиг-а́ть, *v.i.,* + *acc.,* to kindle; (*fig.*), inflame, excite, stimulate. Р. костёр, to kindle, lay a campfire. Р. национа́льную рознь, to provoke national enmity. Раз-же́чь(ь)-ся, *v.р.г.,* раз-жиг-а́ть-ся, *v.i.r.,* to become inflamed.

с-же́ч-ь, *v.р.,* с-жиг-а́ть, *v.i.,* + *acc.,* to burn up, down, out; incinerate; cremate. С. до тла, to burn to ashes. С. свой корабли́, (*fig.*), to burn one's boats. С-же́чь-ся, *v.р.г.,* с-жиг-а́ть-ся, *v.i.r.,* to be burned up, down, out; be incinerated; cremated. Сор сжига́ется во дворе́, rubbish is burned in the yard. С-жиг-а́ние, *п.п.,* burning; incineration; cremation.

ЖД- ЖИД-, EXPECTATION, WAITING

жд-а-ть, *v.i.,* + *acc.,* + *gen.,* to wait, wait for, expect, await. Ж. письма́, to expect a letter. Он заста́вил меня́ ж., he kept me waiting. Мы жда́ли её час, we waited an hour for her.

вы-жд-а́ть, *v.р.г.,* вы-жид-а́ть, *v.i.r.,* + *gen.,* to await; bide one's time. В. удо́бного слу́чая, to wait for an opportunity. Вы-жид-а́ние, *п.п.,* expectancy; waiting. Вы-жид-а́тельный, *adj.,* expectant. В-ая поли́тика, a policy of waiting for the development of events. Вы-жид-а́ть-ся, *v.i.r.,* used only in 3d pers. Выжида́ется по́вод к нача́лу вое́нных де́йствий, they are biding their time, waiting for a pretext to start hostilities.

до-жд-а́ть-ся, *v.р.г.,* до-жид-а́ть-ся, *v.i.r.,* + *gen.,* to wait sufficiently long. Я дожда́лся письма́, I waited until I finally received a letter. Я жду - не дождусь вашего ответа, I am waiting impatiently for your answer. Д. конца занятий, to wait impatiently for the end of classes.

обо-жд-ать, *v.p.,* + *acc.,* (*colloq.*), to wait, await. О. грозу, to wait until a storm has passed. Обождите! Wait a little!

о-жид-ать, *v.i.,* + *gen.,* to expect. О. гостей, to expect guests. Я не ожидал этого, I didn't expect this. О-жид-аться, *v.i.r., used only in 3d pers.,* to be expected. Сегодня к чаю ожидаются гости, guests are expected today for tea. О-жид-ание, *п.п.,* expectation, waiting, anticipation. Обмануть о., to disappoint. Зал ожидания, waiting room. Пассажиры сидели в зале ожидания, the passengers were sitting in the waiting room. Сверх ожидания, beyond expectation. Не-жд-анный, *adj.,* unexpected. Не-о-жид-анность, *n.f.,* suddenness, surprise. Не-о-жид-анный, *adj.,* surprising, sudden. Н-ое нападение, an unexpected attack. Н-ое счастье, a windfall. Не-о-жид-анно, *adv.,* suddenly, unexpectedly. Пришли, н. гости, guests arrived unexpectedly. Долго-жд-анный, *adj. part. pass. past,* long-awaited, expected.

пере-жд-ать, *v.p.,* пере-жид-ать, *v.i.,* + *acc.,* to wait until something has come to an end. П. грозу, to wait until a storm has passed.

подо-жд-ать, *v.p.,* + *acc.,* to wait a short while. Подождёмте её, она сейчас придёт, let's wait for her, she'll be here soon. Подождите немного! Wait a while! Have a little patience!

под-жид-ать, *v.i.,* + *gen.,* + *acc.,* (*colloq.*), to wait for, expect; lie in wait. П. поезд, to wait for a train. П. друзей, to expect friends. Под-жид-ание, *п.п.,* waiting, expectation.

про-жд-ать, *v.p.,* + *acc.,* + *gen.,* to wait a certain period of time. Я прождал его целый день, I waited for him a whole day.

ЖЕЛ-, DESIRE

жел-а-ть, *v.i.,* по-жел-ать, *v.p.,* + *dat.,* + *gen.,* to wish, want, desire, be willing, anxious. Ж. добра, to wish well. Ж. невозможного, to cry for the moon. (*literally:* to wish for the impossible.) Сильно ж. чего-нибудь, to long for something. Желаю вам счастья, I wish you happiness. Желал-бы я знать, кто написал это, I should like to know who wrote this. Жел-ающий, *adj. part. act. pres., used as n.,* one who wishes, de-

sires, longs for. Жел-ание, *п.п.,* wish, desire; hunger. Ж. учиться, a desire to study. Удовлетворить чьи-либо желания, to satisfy someone's wishes. Гореть желанием, to burn with desire. Желанный, *adj.,* desirable, desired. Желательность, *n.f.,* desirability. Желательный, *adj.,* desirable. Жел-ательно, *adv.,* desirably, advisably. Ж. было-бы пойти. (*colloq.*), it would be pleasant to go. По-жел-ание, *п.п.,* wish. Высказать п., to express one's wishes. Шлю вам лучшие пожелания, I send you my best wishes. Благо-жел-атель, *п.т.,* благо-жел-ательница, *n.f.,* well-wisher. Благо-жел-ательный, *adj.,* well-wishing, well-disposed, benevolent. Б. приём, a friendly welcome. Б-ая рецензия, a favorable review. Благо-жел-ательно, *adv.,* benevolently. Добро-жел-атель, *п.т.,* добро-жел-ательница, *n.f.,* well-wisher. Добро-жел-ательность, *n.f.,* goodwill; kindness. Добро-жел-ательный, *adj.* well-wishing, friendly, benevolent, kindly disposed. Д-ое отношение, friendly, kindly attitude.

ЖЕЛЕЗ-, (ЖЕЛѢЗ-), IRON

желез-о, *п.п.,* iron. Железо-, a combining form meaning iron. Железо-бетон, iron-reinforced concrete. Железо-делательный завод, ironworks. Железо-плавильная печь, iron-smelting furnace. Желез-истый, *adj.,* ferruginous; of or pertaining to iron. Железный, *adj.,* ferric, ferrous, iron. Ж. век, (*hist.*), the Iron Age. Ж. лист, iron plate. Ж-ая руда, iron ore. Ж-ая дорога, railroad, railway. Воздушная ж-ая дорога, cable railway. Подземная ж-ая дорога, subway; underground railroad. Ехать по железной дороге, to travel by railroad. Железн-о-дорожник, *п.т.,* railwayman. Железн-о-дорожный, pertaining to a railroad, railway. Ж. путь, railroad track. Железн-як, *п.т.,* iron clay, iron ore. Бурый ж., brown hematite, limonite. Красный ж., blood-stone, hematite.

ЖЁЛТ-, ЖЕЛЧ-, YELLOWNESS

желт-е-ть, *v.i.,* по-желт-еть, *v.p.,* to yellow, turn yellow. Осенью листья желтеют, the leaves turn yellow in the fall. По-желт-ение, *п.п.,* yellowing, turning yellow. По-желт-евший, *adj. part. act. past,* that which has turned yellow. П-ая бумага, yellowed paper.

за-желт-е́ть, *v.p.,* to turn yellow, ripen. Рожь зажелте́ла, the rye has ripened.

желт-й-ть, *v.i.,* по-желт-и́ть, *v.p.,* вы́-желт-ить, *v.p.,* + *acc.,* to paint, dye, color yellow. П. пасха́льные яи́чки, to paint Easter eggs yellow. В. кусо́к мате́рии, to dye a piece of cloth yellow. Желт-изна́, *n.f.,* yellowness. Желт-ова́тость, *n.f.,* yellowishness; sallowness. Желт-ова́тый, *adj.,* yellowish, nankeen-colored; sallow. Желт-о́к, *n.m.,* yolk of an egg. Желт-у́ха, *n.f.,* (*med.*), jaundice, icterus. Желт-у́шный, *adj.,* icteric.

под-желт-и́ть, *v.p.,* + *acc.,* to yellow slightly. П. кружева́, to dye lace yellow. Жёлт-ый, *adj.,* yellow. Ж. цвет, yellow color. Ж-ая - лихора́дка, yellow fever.

жёлч-ь, *n.f.,* gall, bile. Разли́тие жёлчи, (*med.*), jaundice. Он по́лон жёлчи, (*fig.*), he is full of bitterness. Жёлч-ный, *adj.,* bilious. Ж. ка́мень, gall stone. Ж. пузы́рь, gall-bladder. Ж. челове́к, choleric person. Жёлч-ность, *n.f.,* jaundice, biliousness. Ж. хара́ктера, an embittered disposition.

ЖЕН-, WOMAN; MARRIAGE

жен-и́-ть, *v.i.* and *v.p.,* + *acc.,* на + *prep.,* to marry. Оте́ц жени́л сы́на, the father married off his son. Без меня́ меня́ жени́ли, (*saying, iron.*), they married me against my will. Жен-а́тый, *adj.,* married. Жен-и́ть-ся, *v.p.r.* and *v.i.r.,* to get married, marry, take a wife. Ж. уда́чно, to make a good match, marry well. Ж. по любви́, to marry for love. Никола́й жени́лся на Мари́и, Nicholas married Mary.

пере-жен-и́ть, *v.p.,* see жени́ть. Он пережени́л всех свои́х сынове́й, (*colloq.*), he married off all his' sons. Пере-жен-и́ть-ся, *v.p.r.,* see жени́ться. Все его́ бра́тья пережени́лись, (*colloq.*), all of his brothers have married.

по-жен-и́ть, *v.p.,* + *acc.,* (*colloq.*), to marry. Они́ лю́бят друг дру́га; на́до их п., they love each other; we must get them married. По-жен-и́ть-ся, *v.p. r.,* to marry. Они́ уж давно́ пожени́лись, they married a long time ago.

жен-и́тьба, *n.f.,* marriage, matrimony. Жен-и́х, *n.m.,* fiancé, bridegroom, betrothed.

жен-а́, *n.f.,* wife. Быть под башмако́м у свое́й жены́, (*iron.*), to be henpecked, be under one's wife's thumb. Жён-ка, *n.f.,* (*folk*), wife. Жён-ушка, *n.f.,* (*affectionate, colloq.*), wife.

жён-щина, *n.f.,* woman, female. Заму́жняя ж., married woman. Передова́я ж., progressive woman. Жен-о-лю́бие, *n.n.,*. philogyny. Жен-о-люби́вый, *adj.,* philogynous. Жен-о-ненави́стник, *n.m.,* woman hater, misogynist. Жен-организа́тор, *n.m.,* (*recent*), organizer of women's activities. Жен-отде́л, *n.m.,* (*recent*), division of an organization for women's social and political activities. Жён-ский, *adj.,* female, feminine, womanly. Ж. пол, the female sex. Ж-ая нату́ра, feminine nature. Жён-ственность, *n.f.,* femininity. Жён-ственный, *adj.,* womanly, effeminate, feminine.

ЖЕРТ-, ЖР-, ЖИР-, SACRIFICE, VICTIM

жёрт-в-ова-ть, *v.i.,* по-жёрт-вовать, *v.p.,* + *acc.,* + *instr.,* to give, contribute. Ж. де́ньги на бе́дных, to contribute for the poor. Ж. собо́й, to sacrifice oneself. Ж. жи́знью, to sacrifice one's life. Жёрт-ва, *n.f.,* sacrifice; victim; offering, immolation. Ж. войны́, war victim. Приноси́ть в же́ртву, to bring in sacrifice. Стать же́ртвой, to become a victim, fall prey to. Жёрт-венник, *n.m.,* (*eccl.*) credence. Жёрт-венный, *adj.,* sacrificial. Жёрт-вование, *n.n.,* offering, donation. По-жёрт-вование, *n.n.,* gift, contribution. Жёрт-вователь, *n.m.,* donor, giver. Жерт-во-приноше́ние, *n.n.,* oblation, offering, sacrifice. Жрец, *n.m.,* druid; heathen priest. Жрецы́ нау́ки, (*fig.*), high priests of science. Жр-е́ческий, *adj.,* sacerdotal, druidical. Жр-е́чество, *n.n.,* pagan, heathen priesthood. Жр-и́ца, *n.f.,* priestess.

жр-а-ть, *v.i.,* со-жр-а́ть, *v.p.,* + *acc.,* (*colloq.*), to guzzle, gorge, devour. Он жрёт, как свинья́, (*colloq.*), he gobbles like a pig. Жр-анье́, *n.n.,* (*vulgar*), guzzling, gorging, gormandizing. Жр-атва́, *n.f.,* (*vulgar*), chow, На-жр-а́ть-ся, *v.p.r.,* обо-жр-а́ть-ся, *v.i.r.,* + *gen.,* + *instr.,* (*vulgar*), to gorge.

по-жр-а́ть, *v.p.,* + *acc.,* to devour. По-жир-а́ть, *v.i.,* + *acc.,* + *instr.,* to devour. П. свою́ же́ртву, to devour a victim (animal). Ого́нь пожира́ет леса́, the fire is destroying the forests. П. глаза́ми, (*fig.*), to devour with one's eyes; gloat.

со-жр-а́ть, *v.p.,* с-жир-а́ть, *v.i.,* + *acc.,* to devour, gorge. С. обе́д, (*vulgar, colloq.*), to gobble a dinner. Зверь сожра́л всё мя́со, the beast devoured all the meat. Хи́щные зве́ри сжира́ют ме́лких живо́тных, wild beasts devour small animals.

жир, *n.m.,* fat, grease. Гуси́ный ж., goose fat. Бара́ний ж., mutton fat. Ры́бий ж., fish oil, cod liver oil. Заплы́ть жи́ром, to grow fat. С жи́ру бе́сится, (*saying*), one becomes hard to please from a too easy life. Жир-ови́к, *n.n.,* (*med.*), fatty tumor, lipoma. Жи́р-ный, *adj.,* fat, greasy, rich. Ж. кусо́к мя́са, fat piece of meat. Ж. шрифт, boldface type.

жир-е́-ть, *v.i.,* о-жир-е́ть, *v.p.,* to grow fat. От кукуру́зы сви́ньи жире́ют, pigs fatten on corn. О-жир-е́ние, *n.n.,* obesity, adiposity. О. се́рдца, (*med.*), an adipose heart. О-жир-е́вший, *adj. part. act. past,* one who has become fat; obese. О. челове́к, obese person.

по-жир-е́ть, *v.p.,* to grow fatter. Скот пожире́л к о́сени, the cattle became fatter toward autumn. По-жир-е́ние, *n.n.,* the process of becoming fatter.

раз-жир-е́ть, *v.p.,* to have become fatter, very fat. Купчи́ха разжире́ла на пиро́га́х и бу́лках, the merchant's wife grew very fat on a diet of pies and buns.

ЖЕСТ-, ЖЁСТ-, HARDNESS, RIGIDNESS, STIFFNESS

жест-ь, *n.f.,* tin, tin plate. Кро́вельная ж., sheet lead. Оцинко́ванная ж., white metal. Покры́ть жёстью, to cover with zinc. Жест-я́ник, *n.m.,* tinsmith, whitesmith. Жест-я́нка, *n.f.,* tin can. Жест-яно́й, *adj.,* of or pertaining to tin. Ж-а́я посу́да, tinware.

жёст-к-ий, *adj.,* hard, stiff, rigid; tough. Ж. ваго́н, (*recent*), railway carriage with wooden seats (formerly 3rd class). Ж-ая во́да, hard water. Ж-ое мя́со, tough meat. Ж-ие пра́вила, rigid rules. Де́лать жёстким, to harden, stiffen. Де́латься жёстким, to become hard, stiff, rigid. Жёст-кость, *n.f.,* hardness, stiffness. Жёст-ко, *adv.,* rigidly, in a harsh manner. Мя́гко сте́лет, да жёстко спать, (*saying*), an iron hand in a velvet glove. Жест-кова́тый, *adj.,* quite hard, stiff.

жест-о́кий, *adj.,* cruel, heartless, brutal; savage. Ж. челове́к, cruel, brutal person. Ж. моро́з, sharp, hard frost. Ж-ие нра́вы, savage, brutal mores, ways of living. Жест-о́кость, *n.f.,* cruelty, brutality, ferocity, savagery, heartlessness. Име́ть ж. сказа́ть, to have the cruelty to say. Ж-ое се́рдце, a cruel heart. Жест-ок-о-се́рдие, *n.n.,* hard-heartedness, cruelty. Жест-ок-о-се́рдный, *adj.,* pitiless, merciless, hard-hearted. Жест-

ок-о-се́рдно, *adv.,* mercilessly, pitilessly, cruelly.

о-жест-о-чи́ть, *v.p.,* о-жест-оча́ть, *v.i.,* to harden; (*fig.*), embitter. О-жест-очи́ть-ся, *v.p.r.,* о-жест-оча́ть-ся, *v.i.r.,* to become cruel, fierce. О-жест-оче́ние, *n.n.,* harshness, bitterness, fierceness; violence. О-жест-оче́нный, *adj. part. pass. past,* violent, fierce. О-ое сраже́ние, a fierce battle.

ЖИ-, ЖИТ(Ь)-, ЖИВ-, ЖИЗН(Ь), LIFE

жи-ть, жив-у́, *v.i.,* в + *prep.,* + *instr.,* to live, be alive. Ж. мно́го лет, to live many years. Ж. в своём до́ме, to live in one's own house. Ж. в доста́тке, to live in abundance. Ж. бе́дно, to live in poverty. Жил-был..., (*obs.*), there was..., there once was... Жил-был стари́к со свое́ю старухою, there once was an old man who lived with his old wife. Век живи́, век учи́сь, (*prov.*), the longer you live, the more you learn. Жить-ё, *n.n.,* (*colloq.*), life, existence. Плохо́е ж., a wretched life. Пра́здное ж., a festive life; idle life. Жи-т-ие́, *n.n.,* hagiography. Жития́ святы́х, lives of the saints. Жи-т-е́йский, *adj.,* worldly. Ж-ие забо́ты, the concerns of everyday life. Ж-ое мо́ре, (*fig.*), a sea of troubles. Жи́т-ель, *n.m.,* жи́-т-ельница, *n.f.,* inhabitant, dweller, resident. Городско́й ж., city dweller. Дереве́нский ж., country dweller; a rustic. Жи́т-ели, *n.m.pl.,* population, inhabitants. Жи́т-ельство, *n.n.,* habitation, abode. Вид на ж., (*obs.*), temporary residence permit. Перемени́ть ж., to move, change residence. Жи́т-ельствовать, *v.i.,* (*obs.*), to reside, dwell, live, inhabit. Жи́т-о, *n.n.,* grain, rye (*in Southern Russia*). Жи́т-ница, *n.f.,* granary; barn. Жи́т-ный, *adj.,* grain, rye.

вы́-жить, *v.p.,* вы-жи-ва́ть, *v.i.,* + *acc.,* to drive out; to survive. Больно́й вы́жил, the patient survived, recovered. В. из до́му неспоко́йного жильца́, to drive a troublesome lodger out of a house. В. из ума́, to become feebleminded. Она́ не вы́живет до ле́та, she won't live until summer.

до-жи́ть, *v.p.,* до-жи-ва́ть, *v.i.,* до + *gen.,* to attain, reach. Д. до глубо́кой ста́рости, to reach a ripe old age. До чего́ мы дожи́ли! What have we come to! Д. до побе́ды, to live to see a victory.

за-жи́-ть, *v.p.,* за-жи-ва́ть, *v.i.,* to heal; begin to live. Ра́на зажива́ет, the wound is healing. До сва́дьбы заживёт, (*saying*), it will heal by the time you marry. З. семьёй, to begin to lead a family life З. честной, трудовой жизнью, to begin to live an honest, hard-working life. За-жит-очность,, *n.f.,* the state of being well off. За-житочный, *adj.,* well-to-do; wealthy.

из-жить, *v.p.,* из-жи-вать, *v.i.,* + *acc.,* to rid oneself of; overcome. И. недостатки, to overcome one's faults, shortcomings.

на-жить, *v.p.,* на-жи-вать, *v.i.,* + *acc.,* to gain, profit; acquire. Н. состояние, to make a fortune. Н. болезнь, to contract a disease. Н. врагов, to make enemies. На-жи-той, *adj. part. pass. past,* acquired. Н-ое состояние, an acquired fortune. На-жить-ся, *v.p.r.,* на-живать-ся, *v.i.r.,* to become rich, make a fortune. На-жи-ва, *n.f.,* gain, profit. На-жи-вной, *adj.,* lucrative, profitable; acquired, gained. Деньги - вещь наживная, (*saying*), money is a thing acquired.

о-жить, *v.p.,* о-жи-вать, *v.i.,* to revive, resuscitate; (*fig.*), cheer up.

от-жить, *v.p.,* от-жи-вать, *v.i.,* + *acc.,* to become obsolete, die out; be out of date (*as* laws, customs, manners). О. свой век, to have had one's day; to be living on borrowed time. От-жи-вающий, *adj. part. act. pres.,* becoming obsolete, dying out. О. обычай, a dying custom. От-жи-вший, *adj. part. act. past,* which has become obsolete, has died out.

об-жить-ся, *v.p.r.,* об-жи-вать-ся, *v.i.r.,* to become acclimated, become accustomed to one's new surroundings. О. на новом месте, to become used to a new place.

пере-жить, *v.p.,* пере-жи-вать, *v.i.,* + *acc.,* to outlive, outlast; experience, relive; endure, suffer. Он пережил своих детей, he outlived his children. Жизнь пережить — не поле перейти, (*prov.*), life is not a bowl of cherries (*literally*: to live a life is not like crossing a field). П. что-либо тяжело, to take something to heart. Пере-жи-вание, *n.n.,* experience. Радостные переживания, happy experiences.

по-жить, *v.p.,* + *acc.,* to live a while; (*fig.*), *see* life, have a good time. П. год на юге, to live a year in the South. Поживём - увидим, (*saying*), time will tell. (*literally*: we'll live a little and see). По-жи-лой, *adj.,* elderly. П. господин, an elderly gentleman. П-ая дама, an elderly lady. По-житки, *n.m.pl.,* goods, chattels, things, belongings. Со всеми пожитками, (*colloq.*), bag and baggage. Выбросили его из квартиры со всеми его пожит-

ками, they turned him out of the apartment with all his belongings.

по-жи-вать, *v.i.,* to live along; feel. П. хорошо (плохо), to feel well, (unwell). Как поживаете? How are you? ... стали жить - поживать, да добра наживать..., (*saying, often the closing sentence of Russian fairy tales*), and they lived happily ever after, enjoying good health and acquiring riches.

при-жи-ть, *v.p.,* при-жи-вать, *v.i.,* + *acc.,* (*folk*), to beget. П. детей, to have children. При-жи-ть-ся, *v.p.r.,* при-живать-ся, *v.i.r.,* to become accustomed, become acclimatized. П. к местности, to become used to a location, place. П. к людям, to become accustomed to people. При-жи-валка, *n.f,* при-живальщик, *n.m.,* (*obs.*), toady, sponger.

про-жить, *v.p.,* про-жи-вать, *v.i.,* + *acc.,* to live, reside; spend. Мы два года прожили в Киеве, we lived two whole years in Kiev. Они прожили своё состояние, they squandered their fortune. Он проживает в Еропе, he resides in Europe. Про-жить-ся, *v.p.r.,* про-живать-ся, *v.i.r.,* to spend all one's money. Он совсем прожился; остался без копейки, he has spent all he had; now he is penniless. Про-жит-ие, *n.n.,* living, livelihood. Зарабатывать на п., to earn a living. Про-жит-очный, *adj.,* pertaining to living, livelihood. П. минимум, (*recent*), a living wage.

раз-жить-ся, *v.p.r.,* раз-жи-вать-ся, *v.i.r.,* to make a profit, grow rich; get, obtain, acquire. Фабрикант разжился после войны, the manufacturer became prosperous after the war.

с-жить, *v.p.,* с-жи-вать, *v.i.,* + *acc.,* to get rid of; (*colloq.*), shake off; misuse, abuse. С. кого-либо со свету, to cause someone's death. С-жить-ся, *v.p.r.,* с-жи-вать-ся, *v.i.r.,* с + *instr.,* to become accustomed. С. с работой, to get used to one's work. С. с кем-либо, to get used to living with someone. Со-жит-ель, *n.m.,* со-жит-ельница, *n.f.,* companion, roommate; (*folk, obs.*), lover, mistress. Со-жит-ельство, *n.n.,* cohabitation; state of living together in one room. Со-жит-ельствовать, *v.p.,* to maintain a household together.

у-жить-ся, *v.p.r.,* у-жи-вать-ся, *v.i.r.,* с + *instr.,* to agree, live in harmony.

жив, *adj. pred.,* alive, living. Жив и здоров, alive and healthy, safe and sound. Ни жив, ни мёртв, (*idiom.*), in mortal fright; not daring to breathe. От страха он был ни жив, ни мёртв, he was so frightened, he didn't dare to breathe. Ж. ребёнок, a lively child. Ж. ум, a lively wit. Ж-ая улика, eyewitness, living evidence. Всё живо́е, all that is alive. Ж-ы́е цве́ты, natural flowers. Жи́в-ость, *n.f.*, animation, vivacity, liveliness, verve. Жи́в-о, *adv.*, promptly, quickly. Живе́й! Hurry! Faster! Писа́тель жи́во описа́л э́то происше́ствие, the author described this event vividly. Жив-о-пи́сец, *n.m.*, artist, painter. Жив-о-пи́сность, *n.f.*, picturesqueness. Жив-о-пи́сный, *adj.*, picturesque. Ж-ое местоположе́ние, a picturesque site. Жи́в-о-пись, *n.f.*, pictorial art, painting. Жив-о́т, *n.m.*, stomach, abdomen; (*colloq.*), belly; (*obs.*), life. Резь (спа́змы) в животе́, colic (cramps) in the stomach. Спаса́ть свой живо́т, (*obs.*), to save one's life. Жив-о́тик, *n.m.*, (*dim.*), tummy, Со́ сме́ху живо́тики надорва́ли, (*colloq.*), we laughed so hard, our tummies ached. Жив-о́тное, *adj. used as n.n.*, animal; beast, brute. Четвероно́гое ж., quadruped. Живо́тные, *n.n.pl.*, animals. Жив-о́тный, *adj.*, animal; bestial, brutal. Ж. жир, animal fat. Ж-ое ца́рство, the animal kingdom. Жив-о-тво́рный, *adj.*, жив-о-творя́щий, *adj. part. act. pres.*, life-giving. Ж. во́здух, vivifying air. Жив-о-трепе́шущий, *adj., part. act. pres.*, palpitating, exciting, thrilling, stirring. Ж-ая но́вость, thrilling news. Ж-ие собы́тия, stirring events. Жив-у́щий, *adj. part. act. pres.*, living. Всё живу́щее, every living creature. Жив-у́честь, *n.f.*, viability, tenacity to life. Жив-у́чий, *adj.*, viable. Живу́ч, как ко́шка, (*saying*), he has nine lives. Жи́в-чик, *n.m.*, a lively creature; small fish used for bait; (*biol.*), spermatozoon. Ж. в глазу́, a twitch in the eye. Жив-(ь)-ём, *adv.*, alive. Охо́тники взя́ли зве́ря живьём, the hunters took the animal alive.

жив-и́ть, *v.i.*, о-жив-и́ть, *v.p.*, + *acc.*, to vivify, animate. Жив-и́тельный, *adj.*, revivifying, restorative; bracing. Ж. во́здух, crisp air. Ж-ая вла́га, (*colloq.*), intoxicating liquor. Жи́в-ность, *n.f.*, fowl, poultry.
за-жив-и́ть, *v.p.*, за-жив-ля́ть, *v.i.*, + *acc.*, to heal. З. ра́ну, to heal a wound. За-жив-ле́ние, *n.n.*, за-жив-а́ние, *n.n.*, healing. За́-жив-о, *adv.*, while still alive; during one's life. З. погребён-ный, buried alive.
о-жив-и́ть, *v.p.*, о-жив-ля́ть, *v.i.*, + *acc.*, + *instr.*, to revive, enliven. О. умира́ющего, to revive a dying person. О. о́бщество, to enliven a party. О. торго́влю, to revive trade. О. карти́ну я́ркими кра́сками, to brighten a picture with bright colors. О-жив-ле́ние, *n.n.*, revival. О-жив-лённый, *adj. part. pass.*

past, lively, animated; revived. О-жив-и́ть-ся, *v.p.r.*, о-жив-ля́ть-ся, *v.i.r.*, to become lively, animated.
по-жив-и́ть-ся, *v.p.r.*, по-жив-ля́ть-ся, *v.i.r.*, + *instr.*, to profit; feather one's nest. Здесь не́чем п., there is nothing here one can profit by. По-жи́в-а, *n.f.*, (*colloq.*), gain, profit.
жи-зн-ь, *n.f.*, life, existence, living. Моя́ ж. висе́ла на волоске́, my life hung by a thread. Борьба́ за ж., the struggle for life. Вопро́с жи́зни и сме́рти, a matter of life and death. О́браз жи́зни, a way of life. Жи́зн-енность, *n.f.*, vitality, life. Жи́зн-енный, *adj.*, vital. Ж. вопро́с, a vital question. Ж. путь, the path of life. Жи́зн-енно, *adv.*, vitally. Жизн-е-, *a combining form meaning* life. Жизн-е-описа́ние, *n.n.*, biography. Жизн-е-описа́тельный, *adj.*, biographical. Жизн-е-ра́достность, *n.f.*, joy of living; cheerfulness. Жизн-е-ра́достный, *adj.*, joyous, cheerful. Жизн-е-ра́достно, *adv.*, joyously. Жизн-е-спосо́бность, *n.f.*, vitality; ability to live, to adapt oneself to life. Жизн-е-спосо́бный, *adj.*, viable.
жи-л-е́ц, *n.m.*, жи-л-и́ца, *n.f.*, lodger. Сдать ко́мнату жильцу́, to rent a room to a tenant. Он не ж. на э́том све́те, (*express.*), he's not long for this world. Жил-и́ще, *n.n.*, abode, dwelling, residence. Жил-и́щный, *adj.*, pertaining to dwelling, housing. Ж. вопро́с, housing problem. Ж-ая поли́тика, (*recent*), housing policy. Ж-ое строи́тельство, house construction. Жил-ьё, *n.n.*, abode, dwelling, habitation, domicile, lodging. Жи́лкооп, (*recent*), *abbr. of* жили́щный кооперати́в, housing cooperative.

3

ЗВ-, ЗОВ-, ЗЫВ-, CALL, NAME; INVITATION, SUMMONING

зв-а́ть, зов-у́, *v.i.*, по-зв-а́ть, *v.p.*, + *acc.*, to call, invite, bid, summon. Вас зову́т к телефо́ну, you are wanted on the telephone. Позови́те до́ктора, call the doctor, please. З. госте́й, to invite guests. Его́ позва́ли в конто́ру, he was summoned to the office. Зв-ать, *v.i.*, на-зв-а́ть, *v.p.*, + *acc.*, to name. Как вас зову́т? (Как вас звать?), What is your name? Меня́ зову́т Мари́я (Мари́ей), my name is Maria. Мы назва́ли дочь Еле́ной, а сы́на назовём Петро́м, we named our daughter Helen, and shall name our son Peter. Зв-а́ть-ся, *v.i.r.*, to be named, called. Её сестра́ звала́сь Татья́ной, her sister's name was Tatiana. Зв-а́ние, *n.n.*, calling; dignity, social standing, condition, rank. З. профе́ссора, professorial rank. З. чле́на како́го-либо о́бщества, membership of a society, company. Зв-а́ный, *adj.*, invited summoned, called. З. ве́чер, party. З. обе́д, dinner party. З-ые го́сти, invited guests. Не-зв-а́ный, *adj.*, uninvited, unasked; self-invited. Н. гость, an uninvited guest. Зв-а́тельный паде́ж, (*gram.*), vocative case. Зов, *n.m.*, call, summons, invitation. ...Вы на зов мой не пришли́, (*song*), you did not answer my call.

воз-зв-а́ть, *v.p.*, в-зыв-а́ть, *v.i.*, о + *prep.*, k + *dat.*, to appeal, invoke, call. В. к Бо́гу, to invoke God. В. о справедли́вости, to invoke justice. Воз-зв-а́ние, *n.n.*, proclamation, appeal. В. к населе́нию, an appeal to the people (inhabitants). В-зыв-а́ние, *n.n.*, invocation, appeal. В. о спасе́нии, an appeal for salvation.

вы́-зв-ать, *v.p.*, вы-зыв-а́ть, *v.i.*, + *acc.*, to provoke, stimulate, call forth, rouse; call, send for; summon; cause, evoke. В. ученика́, to summon a pupil. В. аппети́т, to stimulate one's appetite. В. воспомина́ния о чём-либо, to evoke memories of something. В. кого́-либо в суд, to summon someone to court. В. сомне́ние (сострада́ние), to evoke doubt (compassion). Вы́-зов, *n.m.*, provocation, summons, challenge. В. ско́рой по́мощи, a call for help, for an ambulance. В. по телефо́ну, a telephone call. Броса́ть в., to defy, challenge. Вы́-зв-ать-ся, *v.p.r.*, вы-зыв-а́ть-ся, *v.i.r.*, to be summoned, called; offer. Он вы́звался сде́лать э́то, he offered to do it. Он вызыва́лся по э́тому де́лу, he was summoned in connection with this matter. Вы-зыв-а́ющий, *adj. part. act. pres.*, defiant, provocative. В. вид, provocative, challenging, look, air. Вы-зыв-а́юще, *adv.*, defiantly, provocatively. Смотре́ть в., to look defiantly, provocatively.

до-зв-а́ть-ся, *v.p.r.*, to call and be heard. Я не мог д. его́, I called him, but failed to reach him. Её не дозове́шься, it is impossible to reach her. Я, наконе́ц, дозва́лся его́, I called him until finally he answered.

за-зв-а́ть, *v.p.*, за-зыв-а́ть, *v.i.*, + *acc.*, to invite, call in. Торго́вцы зазыва́ли в свои́ ла́вки, the merchants were inviting (customers) into their shops. Она́ зазвала́ нас в свой дом, she asked us to come into her house. За-зыв-а́ние, *n.n.*, inviting, calling in.

на-зв-а́ть, *v.p.*, на-зыв-а́ть, *v.i.*, + *acc.*, + *instr.*, to call, name, term, designate,

qualify as. Учени́к назва́л гла́вные города́ Аме́рики, the pupil named the chief cities in America. Н. госте́й, to invite many guests to one's house. Н. ве́щи свои́ми имена́ми, to call a spade a spade. На-зв-а́ть-ся, *v.p.r.*, на-зыв-а́ть-ся, *v.i.r.*, to be called, named, termed, designated. Как называ́ется э́то село́? What is the name of this village? Назва́лся грузде́м, полеза́й в ку́зов, (*saying*), one has to live up to one's promise, or act the part. На-зв-а́ние, *n.n.*, name, denomination, designation, title. Н. кни́ги, a title of a book. На-зв-а́ный, *adj.*, adopted, sworn (as a brother). Н. сын, adopted son. Н-ые бра́тья, sworn brothers. На́-зв-анный, *adj. part. pass. past*, mentioned, said. Н-ые ли́ца, the said persons.

обо-зв-а́ть, *v.p.*, об-зыв-а́ть, *v.i.*, + *acc.*, + *instr.*, to call names. О. кого́-нибудь оби́дным про́звищем, to offend by giving an insulting nickname. Об-зыв-а́ть-ся, *v.i.r.*, + *instr.* (*colloq.*), to be called names. Он ча́сто обзыва́лся тру́сом, he was often called a coward.

ото-зв-а́ть, *v.p.*, от-зыв-а́ть, *v.i.*, + *acc.*, to cancel, call off, recall. О. посла́, to recall an ambassador. О́т-зыв, *n.m.*, testimonial; reference; recall. Ото-зв-а́ть-ся, *v.p.r.*, от-зыв-а́ть-ся, *v.i.r.*, о + *prep.*, to respond, sympathize. О. ду́рно о ко́м-нибудь, to speak ill of a person. О. на чужо́е го́ре, to sympathize with someone in grief. От-зыв-но́й, *adj.*, pertaining to recall. О-ые гра́моты, letters of recall. От-зы́в-чивость, *n.f.*, responsiveness; sympathy. От-зы́в-чивый, *adj.*, responsive; sympathetic. О. челове́к, a sensitive person. О-ая душа́, a sensitive soul. Ото-зв-а́ние, *n.n.*, recall. О. войск, withdrawal of troops.

по-зв-а́ть, *v.p.*, see звать. По-зы́в, *n.n.*, urge, desire, inclination. П. к рво́те, feeling of nausea. По-зыв-но́й, *adj.*, of a call. П. сигна́л, call signal.

подо-зв-а́ть, *v.p.*, под-зыв-а́ть, *v.i.*, + *acc.*, to beckon, summon.

при-зв-а́ть, *v.p.*, при-зыв-а́ть, *v.i.*, + *acc.*, to call up, summon. П. на вое́нную слу́жбу, to call up for military service. При-зв-а́ть-ся, *v.i.r.*, to be drafted. При-зы́в, *n.m.*, call, appeal; draft. При-зв-а́ние, *n.m.*, calling, vocation. П. к му́зыке (к нау́ке), to have a calling for music (science). У него́ есть призва́ние к медици́не, he has a calling for medicine. При-зыв-ни́к, *n.m.*, a young man of military age. При-зыв-но́й, *adj.*, subject to draft.

П. во́зраст, draft age. При-зы́в-ный, *adj.*, beckoning, alluring. П. крик, a call for help. П. сигна́л, beckoning signal.

про-зв-а́ть, *v.p.,* про-зыв-а́ть, *v.i.,* + *acc.,* to name, nickname. За ма́лый рост мы прозва́ли его́ кро́шкой, because of his short stature, we nicknamed him Tiny. Про-зв-а́ть-ся, *v.p.r.,* про-зыв-а́ть-ся, *v.i.r.,* to be nicknamed. По прозва́нию (по про́звищу), surnamed, nicknamed. Крестья́нин по про́звищу Хорь, a peasant nicknamed Khor.

со-зв-а́ть, *v.p.,* со-зыв-а́ть, *v.i.,* + *acc.,* to summon, call, convoke. С. парла́мент, to convoke parliament. С. конси́лиум враче́й, to call doctors for a consultation. Со-зыв-а́ть-ся, *v.i.r.,* to be convoked, called, summoned. Со-зы́в, *n.m.,* convocation. С. конфере́нции (собра́ния), convocation of a conference (meeting). С. Верхо́вного Сове́та СССР, (*recent*), convocation of the Supreme Soviet of the USSR.

ЗВЕЗД-, ЗВЁЗД-, STAR

звезд-а́, *n.f.,* star. Вече́рняя з., evening star. Па́дающая з., shooting, falling star. Поля́рная З., North Star, Polar Star. У́тренняя з., morning star. Морска́я з., (*zool.*), starfish. Его́ з. восхо́дит, (*fig.*), his star is rising. Орден Кра́сной Звезды́, (*recent*), Order of the Red Star. Роди́ться под счастли́вой звездо́й, to be born under a lucky star. Он звёзд с не́ба не хвата́ет, (*fig.*), he is not gifted. Усе́янный звёздами, star-studded, star-spangled. Звёзд-очка, *n.f.,* (*dim.*), little star; asterisk. Отмеча́ть звёздочкой, to mark with an asterisk. Звёзд-ный, adj., starry, starlit, star-studded. З-ое не́бо, starlit sky. З-ая ка́рта, celestial map. З-ая ночь, starlit night. Звезд-о-обра́зный, *adj.,* star-shaped. Звезд-о-чёт, *n.m.,* (*obs.*), astrologer. Звезд-о-чётство, *n.n.,* (*obs.*), astrology. Звёздчатый, *adj.,* starry. З. флаг, star-spangled flag. Над-звёзд-ный, *adj.,* above the stars. Н-ые края́, (*fig.*), the world above. Со-звёзд-ие, *n.n.,* (*astr.*), constellation. С. Большо́й Медве́дицы, (*astr.*), Ursa Major, the Big Dipper.

вы́-звезд-ить, *v.p.,* *impers.,* to become studded, covered with stars. Не́бо вы́звездило, the sky has become star-studded.

ЗВЕР-, BEAST, ANIMAL LIFE

звер-ь, *n.m.,* wild beast. Пушно́й з., fur-bearing animal. Хи́щный з., beast of prey; (*fig.*), brute. Звер-и́нец, *n.m.,* menagerie; zoo. Звер-и́ный, *adj.,* pertaining to wild beasts. З. про́мысел, chase; hunting. Звер-о-ло́в, *n.m.,* trapper, hunter. Звер-о-ло́вство, *n.n.,* trapping, hunting. Звер-о-подо́бие, *n.n.,* bestiality. Звер-о-подо́бный, *adj.,* bestial, brutal, cruel. Зве́р-ский, *adj.,* brutal, ferocious, cruel. З. посту́пок, brutal act. З. аппети́т, (*colloq.*), ferocious appetite. Звéр-ство, *n.n.,* brutality, ferocity, cruelty; atrocity.

звер-ьё, *n.n.,* wild (savage) beasts.

звéр-ств-ова-ть, *v.i.,* to behave brutally; commit atrocities.

звер-е́ть, *v.p.,* о-звер-е́ть, *v.i.,* to become bestial, brutal; brutalize. От гне́ва он звере́л, he used to become brutal when he was angry. О-звер-е́лый, *adj.,* become like a beast. О-ая, толпа́ бро́силась на него́, the crowd, turned into wild animals, rushed at him.

ЗВОН-, ЗВЕН-, ЗВАН-, ЗВУК-, ЗВУЧ-, RINGING, SOUND

звон, *n.m.,* peal, ringing. З. колоколо́в, ringing of bells. Пасха́льный з., Easter bells. З. в уша́х, a ringing in one's ears. Звон-а́рь, *n.m.,* bell-ringer. Звоно́к, *n.m.,* bell. Дать з., to ring. Зво́нкий, *adj.,* resounding, sonorous, clear; (*phon.*), voiced, sonant. З. го́лос, a sonorous voice. З-ие согла́сные, voiced consonants.

звон-и́ть, *v.i.,* по-звон-и́ть, *v.p.,* в + *acc.,* по + *dat.,* у + *gen.,* to ring, chime. З. в колокола́, to ring bells. З. по телефо́ну, to telephone. З. у входно́й две́ри, to ring at an entrance.

до-звон-и́ть-ся, *v.p.r.,* to ring till one is heard. Я не мог к вам дозвони́ться, I couldn't reach you by telephone.

за-звон-и́ть, *v.p.,* to begin to ring; *see* звони́ть. Зазвони́л ко́локол, the bell began to ring.

от-звон-и́ть, *v.p.,* to stop, finish ringing; (*fig.*), rattle off; *see* звони́ть. Уже́ отзвони́ли к вече́рне, they have finished ringing for vespers.

по-звон-и́ть, *v.p.,* звони́ть, *v.i.,* to ring. П. по телефо́ну, to telephone.

про-звон-и́ть, *v.p.,* to ring through, sound. Прозвони́л звоно́к и ученики́ вы́бежали из шко́лы, the bell sounded and the pupils ran out of school.

пере-звон-и́ть, *v.p.,* *see* звони́ть. П. во все колокола́, to ring all the bells, one after the other.

пере-зва́н-ивать-ся, *v.i.r.,* to chime, peal. Пере-зво́н, *n.m.,* chime, peal. П. церко́вных колоколо́в, the peal of church bells.

со-звон-и́ть-ся, *v.p.r.,* (*colloq.*), only in expression: С. по телефо́ну, to call, talk over the telephone (with), get in touch by telephone.

тре-зво́н-ить, *v.i.,* за-тре-зво́н-ить, *v.p.,* to ring all the bells, ring a full peal. На Па́сху трезво́нят во всех церква́х, at Easter they ring a full peal from all the churches. Уже́ затрезво́нили в Иса́киевском Собо́ре, they have already started to ring a full peal in St. Isaac's Cathedral. Тре-зво́н, *n.m.,* full peal of church bells; (*fig.*), loud and persistent ringing. Пасха́льный т., Easter peal of bells. Пошёл т. по всему́ го́роду, (*colloq.*), rumors and gossip spread all over the city.

рас-тре-зво́н-и-ть, *v.p.,* тре-зво́н-ить, *v.i.,* (*fig.*), to spread rumors. Р. но́вость по всему́ го́роду, to spread news all over town.

звен-е́-ть, *v.i.,* + *instr.,* to ring, jingle, tinkle, clank. Де́ньги звеня́т в кошельке́, the money is jingling in the purse. З. шпо́рами, to jingle spurs. У меня́ в уша́х звени́т, I have a ringing in my ears.

за-звен-е́ть, *v.p.,* see звене́ть. Стекло́ зазвене́ло от далёкого взры́ва, the glass rattled from the distant explosion.

про-звен-е́ть, *v.p.,* to ring through. Прозвене́ли де́тские голоса́, как колоко́льчики, the children's voices resounded like little bells.

звук, *n.m.,* sound, tone. З. го́лоса, the sound of a voice. Гла́сный звук, vowel. Фоне́тика есть уче́ние о зву́ках ре́чи, phonetics is the science of speech sounds. Звук-ово́й, *adj.,* pertaining to a sound. З-ая волна́, sound wave. З-о́е кино́, sound film. Звуч-а́ние, *n.n.,* sounding, phonation; vibration. Зву́чность, *n.f.,* sonorousness, sonority. Зву́ч-ный, *adj.,* sonorous, loud, resonant. З. го́лос, deep-toned, resonant voice.

звуч-а́ть, *v.i.,* про-звуч-а́ть, *v.p.,* to sound. З. гро́мко (ти́хо), to sound loud (soft). З. и́скренно (фальши́во), to ring true (false). Его́ слова́ звуча́ли и́скренно, his words sounded sincere. Его́ го́лос звучи́т у меня́ в уша́х, his voice still rings in my ears.

за-звуч-а́ть, *v.p.,* to resound, begin to resound. Где́-то зазвуча́л роя́ль, somewhere a piano could be heard.

от-звуч-а́ть, *v.p.,* to cease sounding. Отзвуча́ли после́дние ре́чи, the echo of the last speeches has ceased. О́т-звук, *n.m.,* echo.

про-звуч-а́ть, *v.p.,* to be heard; echo, resound.

благо-зву́ч-ие, *n.n.,* благо-зву́ч-ность, *n.f.,* euphony. Благо-зву́ч-ный, *adj.,* euphonious, harmonious, melodious. Благо-зву́ч-но, *adv.,* euphonically. Одно-зву́ч-ный, *adj.,* monotonous. Одно-зву́ч-но, *adv.,* monotonously.

со-зву́ч-ие, *n.n.,* consonance, accord, harmony. Со-зву́ч-ный, *adj.,* consonant, harmonious. С. эпо́хе, in harmony with the times.

ЗВЕН-, ЗВОН-, LINK

звен-о́, *n.n.,* звён-ья, *pl.,* link (*e.g.,* of a chain); unit, group, squad. З. цепи́, link of a chain. Пулемётное (стрелко́вое) з., (*mil.*), machine gun, rifle unit. Вы́сшие звенья сове́тского аппара́та, (*recent*), the highest units of the Soviet government. Звен-ово́й, звен-ь-ево́й, *adj.,* pertaining to a link; used as *n.,* unit leader. З. пионе́рского отря́да, (*recent*), unit leader of a Pioneer detachment. Звен-о́рг, *n.m.,* (*recent*), unit organization. З. колхо́за, (*recent*), unit organization of a collective farm. Звен-ь-ево́й, *adj.,* (*recent*), pertaining to a unit, unit leader. З-а́я сде́льщина, (*recent*), piecework performed by a unit, section. З-а́я систе́ма пионе́рского отря́да, (*recent*), unit system of a Pioneer detachment.

по-звон-о́к, *n.m.,* (*anat.*), vertebra. Ше́йный п., (*anat.*), cervical vertebra. Позвон-о́чный, *adj.,* vertebral. П-ое живо́тное, (*zool.*), vertebrate. Млекопита́ющие принадлежа́ют к позвоно́чным живо́тным, mammals belong to the order of vertebrates. По-звон-о́чник, *n.m.,* vertebral column; spine, backbone. П. ина́че называ́ется "спинно́й хребе́т", the vertebral column is also called the spine. Он слома́л себе́ п., he broke his back.

ЗД-, ЗИД-, ЗИЖД-, ЗОД-, BUILDING, CONSTRUCTION, CREATION

зд-а́ние, *n.n.,* building, edifice. Зижди́тель, *n.m.,* (*Ch.-Sl.*), creator, author, founder. Бог — Зижди́тель ми́ра, God is the creator of the world. Зижди́тельный, *adj.,* (*obs.*), creative. З-ая си́ла приро́ды, the creative forces of nature. Зи́жд-ить-ся, *v.i.r.,* на + *prep.,* (*obs.*), to be based on, founded on. Зако́н зи́ждется на справедли́вости, law is founded on a principle of justice.

зо́д-чий, *n.m.,* (*obs.*), architect. Зо́дчество, *n.n.,* architecture.

со-зд-а́ть, *v.p.,* со-зд-ава́ть, *v.i.,* + *acc.,* to create, make; form; build. С. роль, to create a role, part. Со́зд-ан(ный), *adj. part. pass. past*, created. Она не создана для мира, (*poet.*), she was not made for this world. Со-зд-а́ние, *п.п.*, creature, creation. Со-зд-ава́ние, *п.п.*, creation, elaboration. В проце́ссе создава́ния, in the making. Со-зд-а́ть-ся, *v.p.r.*, со-зд-ава́ть-ся, *v.i.r.*, to be created. Культу́ра создаётся века́ми, it takes centuries to create a culture. Со-зд-а́тель, *п.т.*, creator, maker, originator, founder.

со-зид-а́ть, *v.i.* + *acc.*, to create, build. Созида́ть трудне́е, чем разруша́ть, it is more difficult to create than to destroy. Со-зид-а́ние, *п.п.*, erection, construction, building, creation. Со-зид-а́тель, *п.т.*, builder, founder.

пере-со-зд-а́ть, *v.p.*, пере-со-зд-ава́ть, *v.i.* + *acc.*, to recreate. Цель революции - п. госуда́рственный строй, the aim of the revolution is to recreate the structure of the state. Пере-со-зд-ава́ть-ся, *v.i.r.*, to be recreated. Эконо́мика страны́ пересоздаётся бы́стрым развитием промы́шленности, the economy of the country is recreated by the quick development of industry.

ЗДОРОВ-, ЗДРАВ-, ЗДОРАВ-, HEALTH

здоро́в-ье, *п.п.*, health. Как ва́ше з.? How is your health? Пью за ва́ше з.! I drink to your health! Не-здоро́в-ье, *п.п.*, indisposition, ill health. Здоро́вый, *adj.*, healthy, strong; sane, sound. З. челове́к, healthy man. Не-здоро́в-ый, *adj.*, sick, indisposed, unhealthy, ill; unwholesome. Н. вид, sickly look. Н-ые лёгкие, unsound lungs. Н-ые настрое́ния, unhealthy tendencies. Здоров-е́нный, *adj.*, (*colloq.*), robust, hearty, strong, muscular. З. па́рень, a strapping young fellow. Здоров-я́к, *п.т.*, a healthy, robust fellow.

здоро́в-ать-ся, *v.i.r.*, по-здоро́в-ать-ся, *v.p.r.*, с + *instr.*, to greet, bid good day. При встре́че лю́ди здоро́ваются, on meeting people greet each other. Здоро́в-о!, (*folk*), Good day! Good morning! Здо́ров-о, *adv.*, (*colloq.*), splendidly, fine; well done, capital. Они́ здо́рово рабо́тали, they worked splendidly.

здоров-е́-ть, *v.i.*, по-здоров-е́ть, *v.p.*, to become strong, healthy, become stronger, healthier. Де́ти поздорове́ли за́ лето, the children became stronger during the summer. Не-здоро́в-ит-ся, *v.i.*, *impers.*, + *dat.*, used only in expression: to feel unwell. Мне нездоро́вится сего́дня, I don't feel well today. По-здоро́в-ит-ся, *v.p.*, *impers.*, +

dat., used only in express.: Ему́ от э́того не поздоро́вится, he'll have to pay for this, he won't be any better off for this.

вы́-здоров-еть, *v.p.*, вы-здора́в-ливать, *v.i.*, to recover, convalesce, grow well, improve in health. Она́ вы́здоровела оконча́тельно, she has definitely recovered. Больно́й ме́дленно выздора́вливал, the sick man was slowly recovering. Вы-здора́в-ливающий, *adj. part. act. pres.*, convalescent. Вы-здоров-ле́ние, *п.п.*, recovery, convalescence.

о-здоров-и́ть, *v.p.*, о-здора́в-ливать, *v.i.*, + *acc.*, to improve sanitary conditions. О. ме́стность путём осу́шки боло́т, to improve a location by draining swamps. О. дете́й с по́мощью спо́рта, to improve the health of children through athletics. О. шко́лу, (*fig.*), to improve conditions in a school. О. настрое́ние, to boost morale. О-здоров-ле́ние, *п.п.*, sanitation; improvement of sanitary conditions. О. бы́та, improvement of one's way of life. О. ме́стности, improvement of sanitary conditions.

здра́в-ница, *n.f.*, (*recent*), sanatorium, nursing-home. В Крыму́ мно́го здра́вниц, there are many sanatoria in the Crimea. Здра́в-ый, *adj.*, sound. Здрав и невреди́м, (*idiom*), safe and sound. Здра́вый смысл, common sense. Быть в здра́вом уме́, to be of sound mind. Подписа́ть завеща́ние в здра́вом уме́ и твёрдой па́мяти, to sign a will in sound mind and memory. Здра́в-о, *adv.*, soundly, sanely, healthily. Суди́ть о чём-либо з., to form a sound judgment. Здрав-о-мы́слие, *п.п.*, common sense, sensibleness. Здрав-о-мы́слящий, *adj.*, *part. act. pres.*, sensible, sane; *used as n.*, sensible man. Здрав-о-охране́ние, *п.п.*, health department. Здрав-отде́л, (*recent*), *abbr. of* Отдел Здравоохране́ния, Department of Health.

здра́в-ств-ова-ть, *v.i.*, to be well, prosper. Как здра́вствуете? How are you? Да здра́вствует а́рмия! Long live the army! Здра́вствуй, здра́вствуйте, hello; good morning, afternoon, evening; greetings.

ЗЕЛ-, ЗЕЛ(ЕН)-, GREENNESS

зе́л-ен-ь, *n.f.*, verdure, greens, herbage, vegetables. Весе́нняя з. са́да, the spring verdure of a garden. В овощно́й ла́вке продаю́т вся́кую зе́лень, they sell all kinds of greens in the vegetable store. Зе́л-ье, *п.п.*, (*obs.*), potion. Любо́вное з., (*folklore*), love potion. Зел-ёный, *adj.*, green. З-ые насажде́ния, plantations. З-ая трава́, green grass. Зел-енова́тый, *adj.*, greenish. У него́ нездоро́вый, з. цвет лица́, he has an unhealthy, greenish complexion. Зеленно́й, *adj.*, pertaining to vegetables. З. ряд на ры́нке, row of vegetable stalls at a market. З-а́я ла́вка, green-grocer's shop, vegetable market. Зеленщи́к, *n.m.*, green-grocer; vegetable vendor.

зел-ен-е́-ть, *v.i.*, по-зел-ене́ть, *v.p.*, to become green; appear green. Весно́й трава́ зелене́ет, in spring the grass grows green. Медь от вре́мени позелене́ла, the copper became green with time. Зел-ене́ющий, *adj. part. act. pres.*, turning, growing green. З-ие поля́, green fields; fields in the process of becoming green. Зел-ене́ть-ся, *v.i.r.*, to show green. За реко́й зелене́ются луга́, the fields show green beyond the river.

за-зел-ен-е́ть, *v.p.*, to turn, become green; to begin to turn green. Дере́вья зазелене́ли, the trees have begun to turn green. За-зел-ене́ть-ся, *v.p.*, to turn green, break into leaf.

зел-ен-й-ть, *v.p.*, по-зел-ени́ть, *v.i.*, + *acc.*, to paint green. По-зел-енённый, *adj. part. pass. past*, painted green. Неда́вно п-ые садо́вые скаме́йки, garden benches recently painted green.

о-зел-ен-и́ть, *v.p.*, о-зел-еня́ть, *v.i.*, + *acc.*, to plant trees, shrubbery, gardens. О. го́род сада́ми, to plant trees and gardens in a city. О-зел-ене́ние, *n.n.*, planting of trees and gardens. О-зел-енённый, *adj. part. pass. past*, planted with trees and gardens. О-зел-ени́тельный, *adj.*, pertaining to the planting of of trees and gardens. О-ые рабо́ты, tree-planting. О-зел-ени́ть-ся, *v.p.r.*, о-зел-еня́ть-ся, *v.i.r.*, to become covered with trees and gardens.

под-зел-ен-и́ть, *v.p.*, под-зел-ен-я́ть, *v.i.*, + *acc.*, to give green hue. П. во́ду, to color water green.

пере-зел-ен-и́ть, *v.p.*, + *acc.*, to dye too green. П. мате́рию, to dye a material too green.

ЗЕМ-, ЗЕМЛ-, EARTH

зем-л-я́, *n.f.*, earth; ground, soil, land, country; globe. Плодоро́дная з., fertile land. Взры́хленная з., turned up, loosened earth. Пограни́чная з., borderland. Кусо́к земли́, plot of land. Зем-л-я́к, *n.m.*, fellow countryman, compatriot. Мы с ним земляки́, о́ба с

Во́лги, we are fellow countrymen, we both come from the Volga Region. Зем-л-я́чество, *n.n.*, community, society; fellow countrymen. Зем-л-яни́ка, *n.f.*, strawberry. Зем-л-я́нка, *n.f.*, mud hut, dugout. Зем-л-яно́й, *adj.*, earthy. З-а́я гру́ша, root vegetable; kind of artichoke. З-ые рабо́ты, excavation. Зем-л-и́стый, *adj.*, sallow. З. цвет лица́, sallow complexion.

зем-е́ль-ный, *adj.*, land, agrarian. З. уча́сток, lot, plot of land. З-ая со́бственность, land property, real estate. Зем-л-е, *a combining form meaning* earth. Зем-л-е-веде́ние, *n.n.*, *syn.*, геогра́фия, geography. Зем-л-е-владе́лец, *n.m.*, landowner. Зем-л-е-владе́ние, *n.n.*, agriculture. Зем-л-е-де́лец, *n.m.*, farmer, tiller of the soil. Зем-л-е-де́льческий, *adj.*, agricultural. Зем-л-е-ко́п, *n.m.*, one who digs. Зем-л-е-ме́р, *n.m.*, surveyor. Зем-л-е-ме́рный, *adj.*, surveying. Зем-л-е-па́шец, *n.m.*, (*obs.*), ploughman. Зем-л-е-трясе́ние, *n.n.*, earthquake.

зе́м-ств-о, *n.n.*, (*pre-Rev.*), elective district council in pre-revolutionary Russia. Зе́м-ец, *n.m.*, (*pre-Rev.*), member of a *zemstvo*. Зе́м-ский, *adj.*, pertaining to a *zemstvo*.

за-зем-л-я́ть, *v.i.*, за-зем-л-и́ть, *v.p.*, + *acc.*, to ground. З. электри́ческий про́вод, to ground an electric wire. За-зем-л-е́ние, *n.n.*, grounding, ground connection.

на́-зем-ь, *adv.*, on the ground. Опусти́ть что́-нибудь н., to let something down on the ground. На-зём, *n.m.*, manure.

о́-зем-ь, *adv.*, (*folk*), down, against the ground. Гря́нуться о., to fall on the ground.

зем-но́й, *adj.*, terrestrial, earthly. З. магнети́зм, terrestrial magnetism. З-а́я жизнь, earthly life. На-зе́м-ный, *adj.*, terrestrial, surface. Н-ые войска́, land forces, ground troops. Над-зе́м-ный, *adj.*, elevated. Н-ая желе́зная доро́га, elevated railroad. Под-зе́м-ный, *adj.*, subterranean, underground. П. толчо́к, shock of an earthquake. П-ая желе́зная доро́га, underground railroad, subway. Под-зем-е́ль-е, *n.n.*, cave, vault, catacomb.

при-зём-истый, *adj.*, thickset, squatty, stocky. П-ая фигу́ра, squat figure.

при-зем-л-и́ть-ся, *v.p.r.*, при-зем-л-я́ть-ся, *v.i.r.*, (*recent*), to land. Самолёт пла́вно приземли́лся, the plane landed smoothly. При-зем-л-е́ние, *n.n.*, landing (*e.g.*, of a plane).

ту-зём-ец, *n.m.*, native, aborigine. Ино-зём-ец, *n.m.*, foreigner, stranger. Тузе́м-ный, *adj.*, native, indigenous; aboriginal. Т-ое населе́ние, native population. Ино-зе́м-ный, *adj.*, foreign.

черно-зём, *n.m.*, black fertile soil. Черно-зём-ный, *adj.*, pertaining to black fertile soil. Ч-ая полоса́, black earth belt.

красно-зём, *n.m.*, loess, loam.

ЗИ- ЗЕ-, ЗЕВ-, ЗЕЙ-, GAPING, STARING; YAWNING

зи-я́-ть, *v.i.*, to gape. Зи-я́ющий, *adj.*, gaping. З-ая бе́здна, gaping abyss. Зи-я́ние, *n.n.*, gaping; (*gram.*), hiatus.

зев-, *n.m.*, (*med.*), pharynx. Воспале́ние зе́ва, pharyngitis.

зев-а́-ть, *v.i.*, зев-ну́ть, *v.p.smf.*, to yawn. Не зева́й! Look sharp! З. от ску́ки, to yawn from boredom. Зев-о́та, *n.f.*, yawning, fit of yawning. На меня́ напа́ла з., a fit of yawning has come over me. Я подави́л зево́ту, I stifled a yawn. Зев-а́ка, *n.m.*, idler, gaper. По-зёв-ывать, *v.i.iter.*, to yawn repeatedly, continuously.

про-зев-а́ть, *v.p.*, + *acc.*, to yawn; to miss, let slip. П. весь ве́чер, to keep yawning all evening. П. по́езд, to miss one's train. П. удо́бный слу́чай, to let an opportunity slip by.

за-зев-а́ть-ся, *v.p.r.*, to gape, stand gaping. Переходя́ у́лицу, смотри́ не зазева́йся, а то попадёшь под автомоби́ль, when you cross the street, watch you don't stand gaping or you'll find yourself under a car.

ра-зев-а́ть, *v.i.*, ра-зи́-нуть, *v.p.*, + *acc.*, to open wide. Рази́нув рот, agape. На чужо́й карава́й, рот не разева́й, (*saying*), do not covet things which are not yours. Ра-зи́-ня, *n.m.*, simpleton, gawk. Не будь рази́ней! Don't be a gawk!

раз-зев-а́ть-ся, *v.p.r.*, to begin to yawn, indulge in yawning. Р. вовсю́, (*colloq.*), to indulge in yawning.

рото-зе́й, *n.m.*, (*colloq.*), loafer, rubberneck. Рото-зе́й-ство, *n.n.*, gaping, loafing.

рото-зе́й-ничать, *v.i.*, to gape, loaf.

ЗЛ-, ЗОЛ-, EVIL, WICKEDNESS; ANGER

зл-и-ть, *v.i.*, + *acc.*, to irritate, vex, tease, provoke. З. кого́-нибудь, to anger someone. З. соба́ку, to tease a dog. Это меня́ злит, this makes me mad. Зл-и́ть-ся, *v.i.r.*, на + *acc.*, to be irritated, vexed, become angry.

обо-зл-и́ть, *v.p.*, + *acc.*, to anger. О. соба́ку, to anger a dog. Обо-зл-и́ть-ся, *v.p.r.*, to become angry. О. на кого́-

нибудь, to become angry at someone.

по-зл-и́ть, *v.p.*, + *acc.*, to irritate, tease a little. По-зл-и́ть-ся, *v.p.r.*, to be angry for a short while. Он позли́тся и переста́нет, he'll be a little angry and then he'll get over it.

разо-зл-и́ть, *v.p.*, + *acc.*, to enrage, make angry, infuriate. Разо-зл-и́ть-ся, *v.p.r.*, to become angry, enraged, infuriated.

зл-о, *n.n.*, evil, wrong, ill; harm. По́мнить з., to bear a grudge. Не де́лай зла други́м, do not wrong others. Плати́ть добро́м за зло, to repay evil with good. Исто́чник зла, the root of evil. Из двух зол, выбира́й ме́ньшее, (*saying*), choose the lesser of two evils. Зл-о, *adv.*, wickedly, mischievously, spitefully. З. посмея́ться, to laugh spitefully. На-зл-о́, *adv.*, out of spite, contemptuously. Он сде́лал э́то н., he did it purposely, out of spite. Зл-о́б-а, *n.f.*, wickedness, spite, malice, bitterness, fury. З. дня, the latest news of the day. Зл-о́бный, *adj.*, malicious, wicked, evil-minded, evil-natured. З. челове́к, ill-tempered, malicious person. Зл-о́бно, *adv.*, maliciously, wickedly. Зл-о́бно смотре́ть, to look daggers. Зл-об-о-дне́вный вопро́с, a burning question.

зл-о́б-ств-ова-ть, *v.i.*, to bear malice.

зл-ой, *adj.*, wicked, malicious, spiteful. З. челове́к, wicked person. З-о́е лицо́, wicked face. Зла́я улы́бка, wicked, mean smile. З. рок, evil fate. Зл-о-вре́дный, *adj.*, pernicious, mischievous. Зл-о-ка́чественный, *adj.*, malignant. З-ая о́пухоль, malignant growth, tumor.

зл-о-де́йствовать, *v.i.*, to act villainously. Зл-о-де́й, *n.m.*, evildoer, miscreant, rascal, scoundrel, villain; criminal. Зл-о-дея́ние, *n.n.*, crime, misdeed, evil deed. Зл-о-де́йство, *n.n.*, villainy. Зл-о-де́йский, *adj.*, villainous, wicked, evil. Зл-о-па́мятный, *adj.*, spiteful, resentful. Зл-о-па́мятность, *n.f.*, spitefulness, rancor, resentment.

зл-о-ра́дствовать, *v.i.*, to rejoice in another's misfortune. Зл-о-ра́дство, *n.n.*, malicious joy, gloating at another's misfortune. Зл-о-ра́дный, *adj.*, gloating, maliciously joyful.

зл-о-сло́вить, *v.i.*, to repeat gossip, create scandal, slander. Зл-о-сло́вие, *n.n.*, malicious gossip, scandal. Зл-ость, *n.f.*, anger, maliciousness, malice. Зл-о́стный, *adj.*, malicious, fraudulent. З. прогу́льщик, (*recent*), malingerer, absentee. З-ые наме́рения, wicked intentions.

зл-о-умышля́ть, *v.i.*, to plot (against). Зл-о-умы́шленник, *n.m.*, malefactor.

Зл-о-умы́шленный, *adj.*, ill-meaning, ill-disposed, ill-intentioned.

зл-о-употребля́ть, *v.i.*, + *instr.*, to abuse. З. доброду́шием, to take advantage of someone's good nature. З. дове́рием, to abuse someone's confidence. Зл-о-употребле́ние, *n.n.*, abuse, misuse. З. вла́стью, abuse of power, authority. Зл-ю́к-а, зл-ю́ч-ка, *n.m.*, and *n.f.*, malicious creature, shrew. Зл-ю́щий, *adj.*, furious, very angry.

о-зл-о́б-ить, *v.p.*, о-зл-об-ля́ть, *v.i.*, + *acc.*, to anger, provoke, irritate. О-зл-о́б-ить-ся, *v.p.r.*, о-зл-об-ля́ть-ся, *v.i.r.*, to become angry, provoked, irritated, embittered. О-зл-об-ле́ние, *n.n.*, anger, wrath. О-зл-о́б-ленный, *adj. part. pass. past*, angry, angered, infuriated.

ЗНА-, KNOWLEDGE

зна-ть, *v.i.*, to know, have a knowledge of, be aware of, be informed, be acquainted with. З. уро́к, to know one's lesson. На́до з. свои́х враго́в, one must know one's enemies. Дать з., to inform. Отку́да мне знать? How should I know? Я её в глава́ не зна́ю, (*express.*), I have never set eyes on her.

зна-ва́ть, *v.i.iter.*, *see* знать. Я знава́л их семью́ мно́го лет наза́д, I used to know their family many years ago. Зна́-ть-ся, *v.i.r.*, с + *instr.*, to keep company, associate with. Не хочу́ с тобо́й з., I don't want to have anything to do with you. Зна́-ющий, *adj. part. act. pres.*, expert, competent, knowing. З. челове́к, an expert. З. врач, competent physician. Зна́-ние, *n.n.*, knowledge, learning, science, scholarship; skill. Глубо́кое з. чего́-либо, a profound knowledge of something. По-ве́рхностное з., superficial knowledge. Не-зна́-ние, *n.n.*, ignorance, lack of knowledge. Зна-то́к, *n.m.*, connoisseur, judge, expert. З. карти́н, a connoisseur of art. З. му́зыки (поэ́зии), a good judge of music (poetry).

до-зна́-ть-ся, *v.p.r.*, до-зна-ва́ть-ся, *v.i.r.*, (*colloq.*), to inquire about, investigate, find out. Д. пра́вды, to learn the truth. До-зна́-ние, *n.n.*, inquest, judicial inquiry.

за-зна́-ть-ся, *v.p.r.*, за-зна-ва́ть-ся, *v.i.r.*, to give oneself airs, be conceited. За-зна-ю́щийся, *adj. part. act. pres.*, conceited.

обо-зна́-ть-ся, *v.p.r.*, обо-зна-ва́ть-ся, *v.i.r.*, to mistake somebody for somebody else.

опо-зна́-ть, *v.p.*, опо-зна-ва́ть, *v.i.*, + *acc.*, to identify, recognize. О. труп, to identify a corpse. Опо-зна́-ние, *n.n.*, identification.

по-зна́-ть, *v.p.*, по-зна-ва́ть, *v.i.*, + *acc.*, to know, perceive. П. жизнь, to know life. Позна́й самого́ себя́! Know thyself! По-зна-ва́ть-ся, *v.i.r.*, to know each other. Друзья́ познаю́тся в беде́, a friend in need is a friend indeed. По-зна́-ние, *n.n.*, knowledge, notion, perception. У э́того студе́нта больши́е позна́ния в матема́тике, this student has a thorough knowledge of mathematics.

при-зна́-ть, *v.p.*, при-зна-ва́ть, *v.i.*, + *acc.*, to acknowledge, recognize, admit. П. незави́симость страны́, to recognize the independence of a country. При́-зна-н(ный), *adj. part. pass. past*, recognized, deemed. Обвиня́емый был при́знан вино́вным, the defendant was declared guilty. При-зна́-ть-ся, *v.p.r.*, при-зна-ва́ть-ся, *v.i.r.*, to admit, confess. На́до призна́ться, что..., the truth is that..., one must confess, admit that... П. в свои́х оши́бках, to admit one's mistakes. П. сказа́ть, (*colloq.*), to tell the truth. При-зна́-ние, *n.n.*, acknowledgement, recognition; confession, avowal. П. в любви́, to declare one's love. При-зна-н-ный, *adj.*, acknowledged. П. факт, an acknowledged fact. При-зна́-тельность, *n.f.*, gratitude, thankfulness. При-зна́-тель-ный, *adj.*, grateful, thankful. При-зна́-тельно, *adv.*, gratefully, thankfully.

раз-у-зна́-ть, *v.p.*, раз-у-зна-ва́ть, *v.i.*, + *acc.*, to inquire, investigate, spy. Р. чьи́-либо наме́рения, to sound out someone's intentions. Раз-у-зна-ва́ние, *n.n.*, inquiry, investigation.

рас-по-зна́-ть, *v.p.*, рас-по-зна-ва́ть, *v.i.*, + *acc.*, to distinguish, discern, discriminate. Он не распознаёт чёрного от бе́лого, (*fig.*), he does not know black from white. Рас-по-зна-ва́ние, *n.n.*, discernment, discrimination. Рас-по-зна-ю́щий, *adj. part. act. pres.*, discriminating, discerning.

со-зна́-ть, *v.p.*, со-зна-ва́ть, *v.i.*, + *acc.*, to acknowledge, recognize, feel, be conscious of. С. свои́ оши́бки, to recognize, acknowledge one's mistakes. С. своё превосхо́дство, to be conscious of one's superiority. Со-зна́-ть-ся, *v.p.r.*, со-зна-ва́ть-ся, *v.i.r.*, to confess, admit. С. в свое́й неправоте́, to admit one is wrong. Престу́пник во всём созна́лся, the criminal confessed everything. Со-зна́-ние, *n.n.*, consciousness, sense; acknowledgement, avowal, confession. С. опа́сности, awareness of danger. Потеря́ть с., to lose consciousness.

Притти в с., to regain consciousness. Со-зна́-тельность, *n.f.*, consciousness, awareness. Со-зна́-тельный, *adj.*, conscious. Бес-со-зна́-тельный, *adj.*, unconscious. Со-зна́-тель-но, *adv.*, consciously, wittingly. Бес-со-зна́-тельно, *adv.*, unconsciously, unwittingly.

у-зна́-ть, *v.p.*, у-зна-ва́ть, *v.i.*, + *acc.*, to recognize, know, identify, learn, find out. У. ста́рого знако́мого, to recognize an old friend. У. свою́ вещь, to recognize something of one's. У. нужду́, to know want. У-зна-ва́ние, *n.n.*, recognition, learning, discovery.

зна-ть, *parenthetical word, (colloq.)*, used as *adv.*, it seems, seemingly, evidently. З. и ты мно́го го́ря виде́л, you must have had your share of bitterness.

зна-ть, *n.f.*, gentry, nobility, aristocracy. Ста́рая Моско́вская з., old Muscovite aristocracy. Зна́-т-ность, *n.f.*, nobility, birth, rank, notability, eminence. Зна́-т-ный, *adj.*, noble, of high rank, distinguished. З-ая осо́ба, a person of eminence. З-ые лю́ди, distinguished people.

зна-ко́м-ить, *v.i.*, по-зна-ко́м-ить, *v.p.*, + *acc.*, с + *instr.*, to acquaint. З. студе́нтов с литерату́рой, to acquaint students with literature. З. кого́-нибудь с ке́м-либо, to introduce one person to another. Познако́мьте меня́ с ва́шей сестро́й, introduce me to your sister. Зна-ко́м-ить-ся, *v.i.r.*, по-зна-ко́м-ить-ся, *v.p.r.*, с + *instr.*, to become acquainted with. З. с ке́м-либо, to make someone's acquaintance. З. с литерату́рой, to study, become acquainted with literature. Зна-ко́м-ый, *adj.*, acquainted; *used as n.*, an acquaintance. Зна-ко́мо, *adj. pred.*, familiarly, known; *in expression*: Это мне з., this is familiar to me. Знако́мство, *n.n.*, acquaintance.

о-зна-ко́м-ить, *v.p.*, о-зна-ком-ля́ть, *v.i.*, + *acc.*, с + *instr.*, to acquaint thoroughly. О. прие́зжих с расположе́нием го́рода, to acquaint newcomers with the layout of a city. О-зна-ко́м-ить-ся, *v.p.r.*, о-зна-ка́м-ливать-ся, *v.i.r.*, с + *instr.*, to become acquainted. familiar with. О. с дела́ми, to become familiar, acquainted with business matters. О. с окре́стностями го́рода, to become acquainted with the environs of a city. О-зна-комле́ние, *n.n.*, acquaintance, knowledge.

раз-зна-ко́м-ить-ся, *v.p.r.*, с + *instr.*, to sever relations. Р. со все́ми, to sever relations with everybody.

зна́-м-я, *n.n.*, banner, ensign, standard. З. полка́, regimental standard. Боевы́е

знамёна, battle standards. Зна-м-е-но́сец, зна-ме́нщик, *n.m.*, standard bearer. Зна́-м-ение, *n.n.*, sign, token, phenomenon. З. вре́мени, sign of the times. Пред-зна-м-енова́ние, *n.n.*, omen, foreboding.

зна-м-ен-ова́ть, *v.i.*, о-зна-менова́ть, *v.p.*, + *acc.*, to mark, celebrate. Ознаменова́ть годовщи́ну, to celebrate an anniversary. О-зна-м-енова́ние, *n.n.*, sign, token. В о. чего́-либо, in token of something. Зна-м-ена́тель, *n.m.*, (*math.*), denominator. Приводи́ть дро́би к одному́ знамена́телю, to reduce fractions to a common denominator. Зна-м-ена́тельный , *adj.*, significant, noteworthy, important. З-ое собы́тие, a significant event. Зна-м-ени́тость, *n.f.*, celebrity; renown, fame. Эта певи́ца-знамени́тость, this singer is a celebrity. Зна-мени́тый, *adj.*, famous, eminent, great, known. Зна́-харь, *n.m.*, зна́-хар-ка, *n.f.*, (*obs.*), village doctor, quack, sorcerer, sorceress.

пред-зна-менова́ть *v.i.*, + *acc.*, to augur. Пред-зна-м-енова́ние *n.n.*, omen, presage. Это хоро́шее (плохо́е) п., this is a good (bad) omen.

ЗНАК-, ЗНАЧ-, SIGN, SIGNAL, SYMBOL

знак, *n.m.*, sign, symbol, mark, token; indication, omen. Дать з., to signal. З. отли́чия, insignia. Твёрдый (мя́гкий) знак, (*gram.*), hard (soft) sign. З. умноже́ния, multiplication sign. В знак дру́жбы, in token of friendship. При́-знак, *n.m.*, sign, indication, token, symptom. При́знаки жи́зни, signs of life.

знач-о́к, *n.m.*, sign, emblem, badge.

зна́ч-ить, *v.i.*, + *acc.*, to mean, signify. Что э́то зна́чит? What is the meaning of this? What does this mean? Зна́ч-ить-ся, *v.i.r.*, to be mentioned. З. в спи́ске, to be on a list. Знач-е́ние, *n.n.*, meaning, sense, importance, significance. З. промы́шленности, the importance of industry. Име́ть большо́е (ма́лое) з., to have great (little) importance. Придава́ть большо́е з., to attach great importance. Одно-зна́чный, *adj.*, (*math.*), simple. Много-зна́ч-ный, *adj.*, (*math.*), multiciphered. Знач-и́тельность, *n.f.*, importance, gravity, significance. Невозмо́жно переоцени́ть з. э́того явле́ния, the importance of this event cannot be overestimated. Знач-и́тельный, *adj.*, important, significant. Он был и́збран значи́тельным большинство́м голосо́в, he was elected by an overwhelming majority of votes. В з-ой сте́пени, to a great extent. Знач-и́тельно, *adv.*, considerably, significantly. Не-знач-и́тельно, *adv.*, insignificantly.

на-зна́ч-ить, *v.p.*, на-знач-а́ть, *v.i.*, + *acc.*, to appoint, name, assign. Н. вре́мя, to set a time. Н. свида́ние, to arrange an interview. Н. лече́ние, to prescribe a treatment. На-знач-е́ние, *n.n.*, appointment. До́лжность по назначе́нию, an office by appointment.

обо-зна́ч-ить, *v.p.*, обо-знач-а́ть, *v.i.*, + *acc.*, to mark, denote. Что э́то обозна́чает? What does this mean? О. тропи́нку на ка́рте, to mark a trail on a map. Обо-знач-е́ние, *n.n.*, designation, sign, symbol.

о-зна́ч-ить, *v.p.*, о-знач-а́ть, *v.i.*, (*obs.*), *see* зна́чить. О-зна́ч-енный, *adj. part. pass. past,* foregoing. Вы́ше-о-зна́ч-енный, *adj. part. pass. past,* aforesaid, aforementioned.

пред-на-зна́ч-ить, *v.p.*, пред-на-знач-а́ть, *v.i.*, + *acc.*, to intend, reserve; destine. Для кого́ э́то предназна́чено? Whom is this for? Whom is this intended for? Предна-знач-е́ние, *n.n.*, destination, predestination. Пред-назнач-а́ть-ся, *v.i.r.*, to be intended for. Это помеще́ние предназнача́ется для шко́лы, these premises are intended for a school.

ЗОЛОТ-, ЗЛАТ-, ЗОЛОЧ-, GOLD

зо́лот-о, *n.n.*, зла́т-о, (*obs.*), gold. Зо́лото - драгоце́нный мета́лл, gold is a precious metal. Черво́нное з., pure gold. Не всё то зо́лото, что блести́т, (*saying*), all that glitters is not gold. Про́ба зо́лота, standard of gold. Зо́лот-ко, *n.n.*, (*colloq.*), expression of endearment. Зо́лотко моё ненагля́дное, my precious little one. Золот-о́й, (злат-о́й), *adj.*, of gold, golden; *used as n.*, a gold piece. В кошельке́ бы́ло два золоты́х, there were two gold coins in the purse. З. брасле́т, gold bracelet. З-а́я ры́бка, goldfish. З. век, the Golden Age. З-а́я валю́та, gold currency. "У лукомо́рья дуб зелёный, Злата́я цепь на ду́бе том",... (*Pushkin*), "by a sea strand an oak tree green, upon that oak a chain of gold." Это золото́й челове́к, (*fig.*), he's worth his weight in gold. Золоты́х дел ма́стер, goldsmith, jeweller. Золоты́е при́иски, gold fields. Золот-ни́к, *n.m.*, (*obs.*), a 96th part of a Russian pound. Мал з. да до́рог, (*saying*), it is not quantity but quality that matters. Золот-о-иска́тель, *n.m.*, gold prospector. Золот-о-промы́шленник, *n.m.*,

gold mine owner. Золот-о-но́сный, *adj.*, gold bearing. Золот-о-ку́дрый, *adj.*, having golden locks. Золот-о-гла́вый, *adj.*, golden-domed, having golden cupolas. З. храм, gold-domed church.

золот-и́ть, *v.i.*, по-золот-и́ть, вы́-золот-ить, *v.p.*, + *acc.*, to gild. П. пилю́лю, (*fig.*), to sugar-coat a pill. Золот-и́ть-ся, *v.i.r.*, to be gilded. Золот-и́льщик, *n.m.*, gilder. По-золо́т-а, *n.f.*, gilding, gold-leaf. Покры́ть позоло́той, to gild. Золот-и́льный, *adj.*, used in gilding. З. пресс, gilding press. Золот-и́стый, *adj.*, gold-like, golden in color. З. цвет воло́с, golden color of hair.

золоч-е́ние, *n.n.*, gilding. Золоч-ёный, *adj.*, gilded. По-золо́ч-енный, *adj. part. pass. past,* gilded. П-ое серебро́, gold plated silver.

по-злат-и́ть, *v.p.*, по-злащ-а́ть, *v.i.*, + *acc.*, (*Ch.-Sl.*), to gild. По-злащ-ённый, *adj. part. pass. past,* gilded. П-ое стре́мя, (*poet.*), gilt stirrup.

ЗР-, ЗАР-, ЗИР-, ЗОР-, SIGHT, VISION

зр-е́ть, у-зр-ю́, *v.i.*, у-зр-е́ть, *v.p.*, (*obs.*), to see, behold, catch sight of. Зр-е́ние, *n.n.*, eyesight. У неё сла́бое з., her eyesight is weak. Глаз - о́рган зре́ния, the eye is an organ of sight. Обма́н зре́ния, optical illusion. Мира́ж - э́то обма́н зре́ния, a mirage is an optical illusion. То́чка зре́ния, point of view. Зр-е́лище, *n.n.*, spectacle, show. Како́е прия́тное з., what a pleasant sight. Зр-и́тель, *n.m.*, spectator. Быть зри́телем, to be a spectator; to look on. Толпа́ зри́телей, a crowd of spectators. Зр-и́тельный, *adj.*, visual, optical, pertaining to sight. З. зал, auditorium. З-ая па́мять, visual memory. Зр-и́мый, *adj. part. pass. pres.,* (*obs.*), visible. Не-зр-и́мый, *adj.*, invisible. Не-зр-и́мость, *n.f.*, invisibility. Зр-ак, *n.m.*, (*obs.*), *see* взор. Зр-ачо́к, *n.m.*, pupil of the eye. Зр-я́чий, *adj.*, one who sees. Зр-я, *adv.*, (*colloq.*), carelessly, purposelessly. Не трать де́нег зря, don't squander money. Не-в-зр-а́чность, *n.f.*, plainness, homeliness. Не-в-зр-а́чный, *adj.*, plain, insignificant. Н. молодо́й челове́к, an insignificant young man. При́зр-ак, *n.m.*, ghost, phantom, apparition, shadow. При́зраки про́шлого, shadows of the past. Боро́ться с при́зраками, (*fig.*), to fight ghosts, phantoms, shadows. При-зр-а́чность, *n.f.*, unreality, illusion. При-зр-а́чный, *adj.*, unreal, illusory. Про-зр-а́чность, *n.f.*, transparence, limpidity. П. воз-

духа, limpidity of the air. Про-зр-
а́чный, *adj.*, transparant, limpid. П.
вода́, limpid water. П. намёк, hint.
П-ая ткань, transparent material.
Де́латься прозра́чным, to become
clear, transparent. Про-зр-а́чно, *adv.*,
transparently.

воз-зр-е́ть, *v.p.*, в-зир-а́ть, *v.i.*, на +
acc., (*obs.*), to look at. Богомо́льцы
с умиле́нием взира́ли на о́браз, the
pilgrims were looking with veneration
at the icon. Не взира́я на, in spite of,
disregarding. Не взира́я на ли́ца, disregarding personalities. Воз-зр-е́ние,
п.п., view, opinion, outlook. Воз-зр-
и́ть-ся, *v.p.r.*, (*obs.*), на + *acc.*, to
fix one's eyes upon. В-зор, *п.т.*, look,
glance, gaze. Поту́пить взор, to lower
one's eyes.

обо-зр-е́ть, *v.p.*, обо-зр-ева́ть, *v.i.*, +
acc., to survey, review, inspect. С
высоты́ о. окре́стности, to scan the
environs from an elevation. Обо-зр-
е́ние, *п.п.*, survey, review. Обо-зр-
ева́тель, *п.т.*, reviewer. Об-зо́р, *п.т.*,
survey, review. О. печа́ти, press
review.

подо-зр-ева́ть, *v.i.*, + *acc.*, to suspect,
doubt, distrust, have doubts, suspicions.
П. кого́-нибудь в изме́не, to suspect
someone of treason. Подо-зр-е́ние,
п.т., suspicion, distrust. Подо-зр-
и́тельность, *п.f.*, suspiciousness. Подо-
зр-и́тельный, *adj.*, suspicious. П. чело-
ве́к, a suspicious-looking person. У
него́ п. вид, he has a suspicious
look. Подо-зр-и́тельно, *adv.*, sus-
piciously.

за-подо́-зр-ить, *v.p.*, за-подо́-зр-ивать,
v.i., + *acc.*, to suspect. З. сосе́да в
кра́же, to suspect a neighbor of theft.

пре-зр-е́ть, *v.p.*, (*obs.*), пре-зи-ра́ть, *v.i.*,
+ *acc.*, to despise, scorn, disdain. П.
тру́сов, to despise cowards. П. опа́с-
ность, to scorn danger. Пре-зр-е́ние,
п.п., contempt, scorn, disdain. Пре-зр-
е́нный, *adj.*, contemptible, despicable.
П. мета́лл, (*hum.*), filthy lucre. Пре-зр-
и́тельность, *п.f.*, contemptuousness.
Пре-зр-и́тельный, *adj.*, contemptuous,
scornful, disdainful. Пре-зр-и́тельно,
adv., contemptuously.

при-зр-е́ть, *v.p.*, при-зр-ева́ть, *v.i.*, +
acc., to protect, take care of, support.
При-зр-е́ние, *п.п.*, protection, care,
charity. При-зр-ева́емый, *adj. part.*
pass. pres., person supported by
charity. При-зо́р, *п.т.*, *in expression*:
Без призо́ра, without care. По́сле
сме́рти ма́тери, ребёнок оста́лся без
призо́ра, after the mother's death, the
child was uncared for. Бес-при-зо́р-

ный, *adj.*, uncared for; *used as n.*,
waif.

про-зр-е́ть, *v.p.*, про-зр-ева́ть, *v.i.*, to
recover one's sight. Слепо́й прозре́л,
the blind man recovered his sight.
Про-зр-е́ние, *п.п.*, recovery of sight.
Про-зор-ли́вый, *adj.*, perspicacious, penetrating. П. ум, perspicacious mind.
Про-зор-ли́вость, *п.f.*, perspicacity, sagacity, penetration, clairvoyance. Про-
зор-ли́вец, *п.т.*, про-зор-ли́вица, *п.f.*,
(*obs.*), clairvoyant, perspicacious person.

зар-ни́ц-а, *п.f.*, summer lightning; heat
lightning.

зар-я́, *п.f.*, glow, redness; dawn, daybreak, sunrise; sunset, afterglow; re-
veille, retreat. Что ты встал ни свет
ни з.? Why did you get up at this
unearthly hour?

зор-ьк-а, зо́р-енька, *п.f.*, (*dim*)., *see*
заря́. Зо́р-кий, *adj.*, sharp-sighted,
far-sighted. Зо́р-ко, *adv.*, with eyes
wide open. З. смотре́ть, to watch
keenly. Следи́ за ним з., to keep a
sharp eye on him. Дально-зо́р-кий,
adj., far-sighted. Дально-зо́р-кость,
п.f., far-sightedness. Круг-о-зо́р, *п.т.*,
scope, horizon, outlook.

о-зар-и́ть, *v.p.*, о-зар-я́ть, *v.i.*, + *acc.*, to
illuminate, irradiate, light up; (*fig.*),
flash, dawn upon. Луч со́лнца озари́л
верху́шки дере́вьев, a ray of sunlight
lighted up the treetops. Её лицо́
озари́лось улы́бкой, her face brightened into a smile. Луч-е-за́р-ность,
п.f., radiance, effulgence. Луч-е-за́р-
ный, *adj.*, radiant, beaming, effulgent.
Л-ое со́лнце, radiant sun. Л-ые
наде́жды, radiant hopes. Луч-е-за́р-но,
adv., radiantly.

зе́р-к-ал-о, *п.п.*, mirror, looking-glass.
Ручно́е з., hand mirror. Криво́е з.,
distorting mirror. Зер-ка́льный, *adj.*,
mirror-like. З-ая пове́рхность реки́,
the glassy surface of a river. З-ое
окно́, plate glass window.

со-зер-ца́ть, *v.i.*, + *acc.*, (*obs.*), to
contemplate. С. су́щность явле́ния, to
contemplate the essence of a phenomenon. Со-зер-ца́ние, *п.п.*, contemplation. С. приро́ды, contemplation
of nature. Со-зер-ца́тель, *п.т.*, (*obs.*),
contemplator. Со-зер-ца́тельный, *adj.*,
contemplative.

над-зир-а́ть, *v.i.*, за + *instr.*, to over-
see, control, supervise. Н. за рабо́-
тами, to supervise work. Над-зир-
а́тель, *п.т.*, над-зир-а́тельница, *п.f.*,
overseer, inspector, supervisor. Тюре́м-
ный н., jailer. Тюре́мная н-ца, ma-
tron (in a jail). Над-зир-а́тельство,
п.п., inspecting, overseeing duties.

Над-зо́р, *п.т.,* inspection, control, supervision. Техни́ческий н., technical inspection. Быть под надзо́ром, to be under surveillance. Без-над-зо́р-ный, *adj.,* without supervision, surveillance. Под-над-зо́р-ный, *adj.,* under surveillance.

о-зир-а́ть, *v.i., (obs.),* to look around. О-зир-а́ть-ся, *v.i.r.,* to look around, about. Идти́ озира́ясь, to proceed while gazing around. О. вокру́г себя́, to look around.

до-зо́р, *п.т.,* patrol, round. Ночно́й д., nightwatch. Ходи́ть дозо́ром, to patrol. До-зо́р-ный, *adj.,* pertaining to patrolling; patrol; *used as n.,* scout. Подзо́рная труба́, telescope.

за-зо́р, *п.т., (folk),* shame, disgrace. За-зо́р-ный, *adj.,* dishonorable, shameful. За-зо́р-но, *adv.,* dishonorably, shamefully. За-зр-е́ние, *п.п., (obs.),* blame, reproach, *used only in expression:* без зазре́ния со́вести, without scruples, misgivings. Он лгал без зазре́ния со́вести, he lied unscrupulously.

о-зор-нича́ть, *v.i.,* to be insolent, impudent. О-зор-ни́к, *п.т.,* impudent, mischievous person. О-зор-ство́, *п.п.,* mischief, wanton trickery.

по-зо́р-ить, *v.i.,* о-по-зо́р-ить, *v.p.,* + *acc.,* to defame, shame, dishonor, disgrace. П. до́брое и́мя, to disgrace, dishonor a good name. О. роди́телей свои́ми посту́пками, to disgrace one's parents by one's actions. По-зо́р-ить-ся, *v.i.r.,* о-по-зо́р-ить-ся, *v.p.r.,* to disgrace, discredit oneself. По-зор, *п.т.,* shame, infamy, ignominy, disgrace, dishonor. Заклейми́ть позо́ром, to brand with shame. По-зо́р-ище, *п.п.,* disgraceful spectacle. По-зо́р-ность, *n.f.,* shamefulness, disgrace. По-зо́р-ный, *adj.,* shameful, infamous, disgraceful, scandalous. Веду́щий позо́рную жизнь, one leading a shameful life.

у-зо́р, *п.т.,* pattern, design, figure. У. для вышива́ния, a design for embroidery. У-зо́р-ный, у-зо́р-чатый, *adj.,* ornamented, figured, inwrought. Узо́рная ткань, damask cloth.

ЗРЕ-, RIPENING, MATURATION

зре-ть, зре́-ю, *v.i.,* to ripen. Ви́шни зре́ют на со́лнце, cherries ripen in the sun. Зр-е́ющий, *adj. part. act. pres.,* ripening. Зре́-лость, *n.f.,* ripeness, maturity. Аттеста́т зре́лости, certificate of matriculation. Зре́-лый, *adj.,* ripe, mature. З. во́зраст, mature age. З-ые сужде́ния, mature judgments. З-ые фру́кты, ripe fruit.

вы́-зре-ть, *v.p.,* вы-зре-ва́ть, *v.i.,* to ripen,
become ripe. Кукуру́за не мо́жет вы́зреть в холо́дном кли́мате, corn cannot ripen in a cold climate. Вы-зре-ва́ние, *п.п.,* ripening process.

до-зре́-ть, *v.p.,* до-зре-ва́ть, *v.i.,* to ripen, become ripe. Виногра́д дозрева́ет в октябре́, grapes ripen in October. До-зре-ва́ние, *п.п.,* ripening.

на-зре́-ть, *v.p.,* на-зре-ва́ть, *v.i.,* to be preparing, to be about to happen. По́чки назре́ли, the buds are about to open. На-зре-ва́ющий, *adj. part. act. pres.,* gathering, coming to a head. Н-ее восста́ние, a simmering revolt.

пере-зре́-ть, *v.p.,* пере-зре-ва́ть, *v.i.,* to overripen, be past maturity. Эти гру́ши уже́ перезре́ли, these pears are overripe. Пере-зре́-лый, *adj.,* overripe. П. арбу́з, overripe watermelon.

со-зре́-ть, *v.p.,* со-зре-ва́ть, *v.i.,* to ripen, mature, gather, come to a head. Фру́кты созре́ли, the fruit has ripened. Тала́нт э́того музыка́нта созре́л, *(fig.),* this musician's talent has matured. Со-зре-ва́ние, *п.п.,* ripening, ripening process.

И

ИГР-, ИГОР-, ЫГР-, GAME, PLAY

игр-а́ть, *v.i.,* + *acc.,* в + *acc.,* на + *prep.,* + *instr.,* to play, play a game; act, perform. И. роль, to play a part, role; act. И. на роя́ле, to play a piano. И. цепо́чкой, to play with a chain. И. в ка́рты, to play cards. И. в те́ннис, to play tennis. Игр-а́, *n.f.;* game; sport. И. актёра, an actor's performance. И. приро́ды, freak of nature. И. в футбо́л (в те́ннис), football (tennis) game, match. Иго́р-ный, *adj.,* pertaining to gaming, playing. И. дом, gambling house. И. стол, gambling table. Игр-а́льный, *adj.,* playing. И-ые ка́рты, playing cards. Игр-и́вый, *adj.,* playful, frolicsome. И-ое настрое́ние, playful mood. Игр-и́вость, *n.f.,* playfulness, frolicsomeness. Игр-и́во, *adv.,* playfully. Игр-и́стый, *adj.,* sparkling. И-ое вино́, sparkling wine. Игр-о́к, *п.т.,* player. Аза́ртный и., gambler. Игр-у́шка, *n.f.,* plaything, toy. Де́тская и., child's toy. Игр-у́шечка, *n.f., (dim.),* toy. Игр-у́шечный, *adj.,* pertaining to a toy.

вз-ыгр-а́ть, *v.p., (poet., obs.),* to leap for joy, rejoice. Душа́ взыгра́ла от ра́дости, *(fig.),* my soul rejoiced.

вы́-игр-ать, *v.p.,* вы-и́гр-ывать, *v.i.,* + *acc.,* to win, gain. В. де́ньги, to win money. В. сраже́ние, to win a battle, contest. В. вре́мя, to gain time. Вы́-игр-ыш, *n.m.*, winning, victory; gain, prize. Быть в вы́игрыше, to have won, gained. Вы́-игр-ышный, *adj.*, pertaining to winning, to a lottery. В. биле́т, lottery ticket. В. заём, lottery-loan. В-ая роль, strong, effective, advantageous role.

до-игр-а́ть, *v.p.,* до-и́гр-ывать, *v.i.,* + *acc.,* to finish a game, play out. До-игр-а́ть-ся, *v.p.r.,* (*colloq.*), to play, take risks (until); merit unpleasantness. Он доигра́лся до того́, что его́ уво́лили со слу́жбы, he went so far they finally dismissed him.

за-игр-а́ть, *v.p., see* игра́ть. Орке́стр заигра́л вальс, the orchestra began to play a waltz. За-и́гр-ывать, *v.i.,* с + *instr.,* to flirt, make advances. З. с ком-ли́бо, to flirt with someone. За-игр-а́ть-ся, *v.p.r.,* за-и́гр-ывать-ся, *v.i.r.,* to play too long. З. в ка́рты, до по́лночи, to play cards until midnight.

на-игр-а́ть, *v.p.,* на-и́гр-ывать, *v.i.,* + *acc.,* to play. Н. мело́дию, to play a melody. Н. пласти́нку, to make a record. На-игр-а́ть-ся, *v.p.r.,* to play to one's heart's content.

об-ыгр-а́ть, *v.p.,* об-ы́гр-ывать, *v.i.,* + *acc.,* to beat, defeat, win. О. кого-нибу́дь в ка́рты (в те́ннис), to beat someone at cards (tennis). Об-ы́гр-анный, *adj. part. pass. past,* beaten, defeated, trounced. О. инструме́нт, (*fig.*), an instrument mellowed by use. О. игро́к, loser in a card game.

от-ыгр-а́ть, *v.p.,* от-ы́гр-ывать, *v.i.,* + *acc.,* to regain, win back. О. свой де́ньги, to win back one's money. От-ыгр-а́ть-ся, *v.p.r.,* от-ы́гр-ывать-ся, *v.i.r.,* + *acc.,* to recoup one's losses. От-ыгр-ыш, *n.m.,* recouped losses.

пере-игр-а́ть, *v.p.,* пере-и́гр-ывать, *v.i.,* + *acc.,* to play over, again. П. па́ртию в ша́хматы, to replay a game of chess. Актёр в э́той ро́ли переигра́л, the actor overplayed his role. Пере-и́гр-ывать-ся, *v.i.r.,* to be replayed. Пье́са бу́дет п., the play will be performed again.

по-игр-а́ть, *v.p.,* по-и́гр-ывать, (*colloq.*), *v.i.,* + *instr.,* с + *instr.,* в + *acc.,* на + *prep.,* to play now and then, play for a short while. П. с ребёнком, to play with a child. П. на роя́ле, to play a piano. Пои́грывать и́зредка в ка́рты, to play cards occasionally.

под-ыгр-а́ть, *v.p.,* под-ы́гр-ывать, *v.i.,* + *dat.,* to play up to, play into somebody's hands. Под-ыгр-а́ть-ся, *v.p.r.,* под-ы́гр-ывать-ся, *v.i.r.,* (*colloq.*), to court, court favor. Он поды́грывается к нача́льнику, he is trying to get into

the good graces of his chief. Ро́з-ыгр-ыш, *n.m.,* draw, drawn game. Р. лоте-ре́и, drawing of a lottery.

с-ыгр-а́ть, *v.p.,* + *acc.,* на + *prep.,* to play (*e.g.,* an instrument), perform. С. вальс, to play a waltz. С. роль, to perform a role. С. шу́тку, to play a trick. С. сва́дьбу, (*colloq.*), to celebrate a wedding. С. на людски́х сла́бостях, to take advantage of human weaknesses. С-ыгр-а́ть-ся, *v.p.r.,* с-ы́гр-ывать-ся, *v.i.r.,* to rehearse, practice together; achieve. Актёры хорошо́ сыгра́лись, the cast played together well.

ИМ-, ЙМ-, ЕМ-, ЫМ-, ЯТ-, TAKING

йм-а-ть, *v.i.,* ят-ь, *v.p.,* (*obs.*), to take. Ём-кость, *n.f.,* holding capacity, cubic content, volume. Ё. резервуа́ра, tankage, capacity of a reservoir. Ме́ра ёмкости, measure of capacity, cubic measure. Ём-кий, *adj.,* capacious. Ё. котёл, capacious boiler. Вод-о-ём, *n.m.,* tank, reservoir.

вз-им-а́ть, *v.i.,* + *acc.,* to collect, levy taxes. В. дань, (*hist.*), to impose tribute. Тата́ры взима́ли дань с ру́сских, the Tatars imposed tribute on the Russians. В. нало́ги, to levy taxes. В. по́шлину, to collect duty. В. штраф, to impose a fine; fine. Вз-им-а́ние, *n.n.,* levying of taxes, collecting of taxes. В. нало́гов с населе́-ния, collection of taxes from a populace. Вз-им-а́ть-ся, *v.i.r.,* to be levied, collected. За иностра́нные това́ры взима́ется по́шлина, customs duties are levied on foreign goods.

вз-ят-ь, *v.p.,* + *acc.,* to take; invade, seize, arrest; *see* брать, взима́ть. В. кни́гу из библиоте́ки, to take a book from a library. В. де́ньги у прия́теля, to borrow money from a friend. В. во́жжи в ру́ки, to take the reins into one's hands. В. под стра́жу, to place under arrest. Поли́ция взяла́ его́ но́чью, the police arrested him in the night. В. кре́пость, to take a fortress. С чего́ вы э́то взя́ли? (*colloq.*), Where did you hear this? where did you get this? В. верх, to take the upper hand. В. своё, to take one's due. В. наза́д (обра́тно), to take back. В. си́лой, to take by force. В. в свиде́тели, to take as a witness. В. в долг, to borrow. В. себя́ в ру́ки, to control oneself, take oneself in hand. В. де́ло в ру́ки, to take charge of a matter. Его́ взял страх, (*colloq.*), he was seized with fright. Ни дать, ни взять, (*colloq.*), just so; exactly. Чья возьмёт? На́ша взяла́, (colloq.), Who will win? We have won! С него́ не́чего в., (fig.), he has nothing to give. В. под ого́нь самокри́тики, (recent), to subject to self-criticism. Чорт возьми́! the devil take it! Вз-я́т-ь-ся, v.p.r., to take up, undertake. В. за рабо́ту, to set to work. В. за ору́жие, to take up arms. В. за уче́ние, to begin to study. В. за ум, to become sensible, stop acting foolishly. В. за́ руки, to join hands. Он взя́лся доста́ть биле́т, he took it upon himself to obtain a ticket. Отку́да ни возьми́сь, (idiom), suddenly. Вз-я́т-ие, n.n., taking. В. кре́пости, the taking of a fortress. Вз-я́т-ка, n.f., bribe, trick. Дава́ть взя́тку, to give a bribe; bribe. Брать взя́тки, to take bribes. После́дняя взя́тка реша́ет исхо́д игры́, the last trick decides the game. С него́ взя́тки гла́дки, (saying), you cannot get anything out of him. Вз-я́т-очничество, n.n., corruption, graft. Борьба́ со взя́точничеством, the fight against corruption. Вз-я́т-очник, n.m., one who accepts graft, bribes. За-вз-я́т-ый, adj., (colloq.), inveterate. З карте́жник, an inveterate gambler, card player. З. кури́льщик, an inveterate smoker. З. плут, shrewd crook. Пред-вз-я́т-ый, adj., prejudiced, preconceived. П-ое мне́ние, preconceived notion, opinion. У вас п-ое мне́ние о нём, you have a preconceived opinion of him. П-ое сужде́ние, prejudiced opinion.

в-н-им-а́-ть, v.i., в-н-ят-ь, v.p., + dat., (obs., poet.), to listen, hear. В. го́лосу рассу́дка, to listen to the voice of reason. В. певцу́, to listen to a singer. В. мольба́м, to listen to entreaties. Я тот, кото́рому внима́ла ты в полуно́чной тишине́, (Lermontov), I am the one to whom you listened in the midnight silence. Он не внял мои́м про́сьбам, he did not listen to my entreaties. В-н-им-а́я, adj. part. act. pres., listening. Внима́я у́жасам войны́, (Nekrasov), listening to the horrors of war... В-н-им-а́ние, n.n., attention, notice, regard. Обрати́те в., pay attention. Обраща́ть чьё-ли́бо в. на, + acc., to draw some one's attention to. Ока́зывать в. кому́-ли́бо, to pay attention to someone. Привлека́ть в., to attract attention. Принима́я во в., considering; taking into consideration. В-н-им-а́тельность, n.f., attentiveness. В-н-им-а́тельный, adj., attentive, considerate. В. учени́к, attentive pupil. В. по отноше́нию к други́м, thoughtful, considerate towards others. В-н-им-а́тельно, adv., attentively. Слу́шать в.,

to listen attentively. В-н-я́т-ный, adj., distinct. Не-в-н-я́т-ный, adj., indistinct. Н-ая речь, indistinct speech. Н-ое произноше́ние, indistinct pronunciation. В-н-я́т-но, adv., distinctly. Не-в-н-я́т-но, adv., indistinctly.

вы-н-им-а́ть, v.i., вы́-н-ут-ь, v.p., + acc., из + gen., to take, draw out. В. часы́ из карма́на, to take a watch out of a pocket. В. де́ньги из ба́нка, to draw money from a bank. В. пу́лю из ра́ны, to extract a bullet from a wound. Вы́-н-ут-ый, adj. part. pass. past, taken, drawn out. Карти́на, в-ая из ра́мы, a picture taken out of a frame. Вы-н-им-а́ть-ся, v.i.r., (colloq.), to be taken out. Ключ легко́ вынима́ется из замка́, the key comes out of the lock easily. Вы-н-им-а́ние, n.n., extraction. В. зано́зы, extraction of a splinter. Вы́-ем-ка, n.f., hollow. В. в земле́, hollow in the ground. В. в доске́, groove in a board. Земляна́я в., excavation. В. докуме́нтов, seizure of documents. В. пи́сем из почто́вого я́щика, collection of letters from a mailbox.

до-н-им-а́ть, v.i., до-н-я́т-ь, v.p., + acc., + instr., to worry; wear out; annoy, plague. Д. тре́бованиями, to annoy with demands. Д. рабо́той, to overwork. Д. в коне́ц, (colloq.), to plague, annoy to death. Он до́нял меня́ рабо́той в коне́ц, he worked me to death. Ма́льчик донима́л всех свои́ми прока́зами, the boy annoyed everyone with his pranks.

за-и́м-ств-ова-ть, v.i., по-за-и́м-ство-вать, v.p., + acc., у, из + gen., to borrow, adopt. З. иде́и (иностра́нные слова́, чужи́е обы́чаи), to borrow, adopt ideas, (foreign words, foreign customs). Пу́шкин заи́мствовал "Бори́са Годуно́ва" из ру́сской исто́рии, Pushkin drew the subject of *Boris Godunov* from Russian history. За-и́м-ствование, n.n., borrowing. За-и́м-ствованный, adj. part. pass. past, borrowed, adopted. В ру́сском языке́ нема́ло заи́мствованных слов, there are many borrowed words in the Russian language.

в-за-и́м-н-ость, n.f., reciprocity. Люби́ть без взаи́мности, to love without reciprocation. В-за-и́м-ный, adj., mutual, reciprocal. В. глаго́л, (gram.), reciprocal verb. В-ая по́мощь, mutual aid. В-за-им-о-по́мощь, n.f., mutual aid, assistance. Ка́сса взаимопо́мощи, mutual aid fund. В-за-и́м-но, adv., mutually, reciprocally.

за-н-им-а́ть, v.i., за-н-я́т-ь, v.p., + acc., to borrow, lend; occupy; interest, entertain. З. де́ньги у кого́-либо, to borrow money from someone. З. де́ньги кому́-либо, to lend someone money. Я за́нял у дру́га 20 рубле́й, I borrowed 20 rubles from my friend. Займи́те мне, пожа́луйста, 100 рубле́й, please lend me 100 rubles. З. го́род, to occupy a city. Войска́ проти́вника за́няли но́вые пози́ции, enemy troops occupied new positions. З. кварти́ру (дом), to rent, occupy a new apartment (house). З. высо́кое положе́ние, to occupy an important position. З. вре́мя, to occupy, take up time. Рабо́та занима́ет всё моё вре́мя, work takes up all my time. З. ме́сто в теа́тре, to occupy a seat in a theater. З. ме́сто по слу́жбе, to fill a post. З. госте́й в гости́ной, to entertain guests in the living room. Его́ судьба́ меня́ ма́ло занима́ет, I am not interested in his fate. За-ём, *n.m.*, loan. Госуда́рственный (вы́игрышный) з., government (lottery) loan. Де́лать з., to raise a loan. За-ём-ный, *adj.*, pertaining to a loan. З-ое письмо́, acknowledgement of a debt. За-ём-щик, *n.m.*, debtor. За-им-о-да́вец, за-им-о-да́тель, *n.m.*, creditor, money lender. За-им-о-обра́зно, *adv.*, in the form of a loan. Дать кому́-либо де́ньги з., to lend someone money, give money in the form of a loan. В-за-йм-ы́, *adv.*, as a loan. Брать в., to borrow. Дава́ть в., to lend. Служащий взял в. 25 рубле́й до сле́дующей зарпла́ты, the employee took 25 rubles as an advance on his salary.

за-н-им-а́ть-ся, *v.i.r.*, за-н-я́ть-ся, *v.p.r.*, + *instr.*, to occupy oneself, work at; study. Я занима́юсь ру́сским языко́м, I am studying the Russian language. Она́ мно́го занима́ется собо́й, she is absorbed in, preoccupied with herself. Занима́ется заря́, it is dawning. Заняла́сь кры́ша, the roof is on fire. За-н-им-а́тельность, *n.f.*, interest, engrossing, absorbing qualities. Эта кни́га меня́ привлекла́ свое́й занима́тельностью, this book attracted me by its entertaining qualities. За-н-им-а́тельный, *adj.*, interesting, entertaining, absorbing. З. расска́з, interesting, absorbing story. За-н-им-а́тельно, *adv.*, in an absorbing, interesting manner. За-н-я́т-ный, *adj.*, (*colloq.*), entertaining, amusing. З. анекдо́т, entertaining anecdote. За-н-я́т-ие, *n.n.*, occupation, job; (*mil.*), capture. Заня́тия в городски́х учрежде́ниях начина́ются в 8 часо́в утра́, work in city offices begins at 8 o'clock in the morning. Како́й род заня́тий

вы избра́ли? What kind of occupation did you choose? За́-н-ят, *adj. pred.*, busy, occupied. Он з., he is occupied, busy. За́нято, *adj. pred.*, taken, busy. Это ме́сто за́нято, this seat is taken. За-н-ят-о́й, *adj.*, busy. Он з. челове́к, he is a busy man. За́-н-ят-ый, *adj. part. pass. past*, occupied, captured. Террито́рия, за́нятая неприя́телем, the territory occupied by the enemy. За́нятые де́ньги на́до возвраща́ть в срок, the borrowed money must be returned when due.

изъ-я́т-ь, *v.p.*, изъ-ым-а́ть, *v.i.*, + *acc.*, to withdraw, remove from; confiscate. И. из обраще́ния ста́рые де́ньги, to withdraw obsolete currency from circulation. Изъ-я́т-ие, *n.m.*, removal. И. церко́вных це́нностей, confiscation of church valuables. Изъ-я́т-ый, *adj. part. pass. past*, withdrawn, removed, confiscated. И-ая кни́га, confiscated book; book withdrawn from school circulation.

на-н-им-а́ть, *v.i.*, на-н-я́ть, *v.p.*, + *acc.*, to hire, engage, rent. Н. прислу́гу, to engage a servant. Н. дом, to rent a house. На-н-им-а́ть-ся, *v.i.r.*, на-н-я́ть-ся, *v.p.r.*, to be hired, engaged, rented. Н. в куха́рки, to apply for a cook's position. На-ём, *n.m.*, hire, rent. Н. рабо́чих, the hiring of workers, workmen. Взять в н., to rent. Сдава́ть в наём, to let. Дом сдаётся в наём, this house is for rent. На-ём-ник, *n.m.*, (*obs.*), hireling. На-ём-ный, *adj.*, hired, rented; rentable. Н. труд, hired labor. Н-ая пла́та, rent. На-ём-щик, на-н-им-а́тель, *n.m.*, employer, one who hires; tenant, lessee. На́-н-ят-ый, *adj. part. pass. past*, hired, rented. Н-ые рабо́чие, hired workmen.

об-н-им-а́ть, *v.i.*, об-н-я́ть, *v.p.*, + *acc.*, (*obs., poet.*), to embrace, clasp in one's arms; encompass, comprehend. Он обня́л и поцелова́л жену́, he embraced and kissed his wife. Во́лга с прито́ками обнима́ет большо́е простра́нство, the Volga with tributaries encompasses a large territory. Об-н-им-а́ть-ся, *v.i.r.*, об-н-я́ть-ся, *v.p.r.*, to embrace each other. Брат с сестро́й обняли́сь, the brother and sister embraced. Объ-я́т-ия, *n.n.*, embrace. Бро́ситься в объя́тия, to fling oneself into someone's embrace. Объ-я́т-ый, *adj. part. pass. past*, + *instr.*, embraced; overwhelmed. О. стра́хом, overwhelmed by fear. О. пла́менем, enveloped in flames. Не-объ-я́т-ность, *n.f.*, immensity, vastness, boundlessness. Н. не́ба, vastness of the sky. Не-объ-я́т-ный, *adj.*, immense, vast, boundless. Н. мир, vast, wide world. Объ-ём, *n.m.*, size, bulk, volume. О. тéла, (*phys.*), volume of a body. О. знáний, extent of knowledge. Кубúческий о., cubic volume. Увелúчиваться в объёме, to expand. Объ-ём-ный, *adj.*, pertaining to volume. О. вес, bulk, weight. Объ-ём-истый, *adj.*, bulky, voluminous, large. О. кусóк свинúны, a large piece of pork.

от-н-им-áть, *v.i.*, от-н-ят-ь, *v.p.*, + *acc.*, у, от + *gen.*, to deprive, take away; subtract; (*med.*), amputate; wean; bereave. О. дéньги у когó-нибудь, to deprive someone of money. От десятú отнять пять, to subtract five from ten. О. нóгу, to amputate a leg. О. ребёнка от грудú, to wean a child. О. надéжду, to deprive someone of hope. От-н-ят-ый, *adj. part. pass. past,* taken away; deprived; subtracted; amputated. Ó-ая рукá, amputated hand. От-н-ят-ие, *n.n.*, taking away; subtraction; amputation. От-н-им-áть-ся, *v.i.r.*, от-н-ят-ь-ся, *v.p.r.*, to be taken away; deprived. Подáренное не отнимáется назáд, gifts are not taken back. У негó язык отнялся, he has become speechless. Не-отъ-ём-лемость, *n.f.*, inalienability, imprescriptibility. Не-отъ-ём-лемый, *adj. part. pass. pres.*, inalienable. Н-ое прáво, an inalienable right.

пере-н-им-áть, *v.i.*, пере-н-ят-ь, *v.p.*, + *acc.*, to imitate; intercept; catch by surprise. П. обычаи, to adopt customs (manners). Коль п. чужóе, так нáдобно с умóм, (*Krylov*), if you imitate something foreign, do so with intelligence. П. вóра, to catch a thief. П. вóду плотúной, to dam up water. Перé-н-ят-ый, *adj. part. pass. past,* imitated; adopted; intercepted. Пере-н-яв-ший, *adj. part. act. past,* having acquired, adopted. Пере-н-им-áть-ся, *v.i.r.*, to be imitated, adopted. Дурные привычки легкó перенимáются, bad habits are easily adopted, imitated.

под-н-им-áть, под-ым-áть, *v.i.*, под-н-ят-ь, *v.p.*, + *acc.*, to raise, lift. П. бумáгу с пóла, to pick up paper from the floor. П. тяжесть, to lift a weight. П. глазá, to raise one's eyes. П. зáнавес, to raise a curtain. П. воротнúк, to turn up one's collar. П. вопрóс, to raise a question. П. орýжие, to take up arms. П. тревóгу, to sound an alarm. П. когó-нибудь нá-смех, to ridicule someone, subject to ridicule. П. рýку на когó-нибудь, to raise a hand against someone. П. нос, to assume airs; be conceited. П. цéну, to raise a price. П. якорь, to weigh anchor. П. произ-

водúтельность трудá, to raise the productivity of labor. Под-н-им-áть-ся, под-ым-áть-ся, *v.i.r.*, под-н-ят-ь-ся, *v.p.r.*, (*colloq.*), to be lifted, raised; rise, climb, ascend, gain altitude. П. нá гору, to climb, ascend a mountain. П. на лéстницу, to climb a ladder, go upstairs. П. с мéста, to rise from one's seat. П. на цыпочки, to stand on tiptoe. П. на дыбы, to rear (*as* a horse). Поднимáется вéтер, the wind is rising. Сóлнце поднимáлось, the sun was rising. Тéсто поднимáется, the dough is rising. Больнóй ужé поднялся, the patient is already up and about (has recovered). Пóд-н-ят-ый, *adj. part. pass. past,* picked up, lifted, raised. П. флаг, raised, hoisted flag. П-ая целинá, freshly plowed soil. Под-н-им-áние, *n.n.*, lifting, raising. П. грýза на парохóд, hoisting of freight, cargo, aboard a ship. Под-н-ят-ие, *n.n.*, lift, lifting, rise, rising. П. рук при голосовáнии, the raising of hands during a vote. П. кáчества, improvement of quality. Подъ-ят-ь, *v.p.*, + *acc.*, (*Ch.-Sl., obs.*). to raise. Подъ-я-вший, *adj. part. act. past, also used as n.*, raised, one who has raised. Подъ-ём, *n.m.*, lift, ascent, rise; instep; (*fig.*), enthusiasm. П. произвóдства, increase of industrial output. П. ногú, (*anat.*), instep. Лёгок на п., (*idiom*), alert; on one's toes. Тяжёл на п., sluggish, hard to raise. Подъ-ём-ник, *n.m.*, elevator. Подъ-ём-ный, *adj.*, pertaining to lifting. П. кран, crane, derrick. П-ая машúна, elevator. П-ые дéньги, moving expenses.

при-под-н-им-áть, (при-под-ым-áть, *colloq.*), *v.i.*, при-под-н-ят-ь, *v.p.*, + *acc.*, to raise, lift slightly. П. крышку сундукá, to lift the lid of a trunk. П. окóнную занавéску, to raise a window curtain slightly. П. шляпу в знак привéтствия, to lift one's hat in greeting. При-под-н-им-áть-ся, при-под-ым-áть-ся, *v.i.r.*, при-под-н-ят-ь-ся, *v.p.r.*, to raise oneself a little. П. со стýла, to rise slightly from a chair. При-пóд-н-ят-ый, *adj. part. pass. past,* slightly lifted, raised; (*fig.*), enthusiastic. П. зáнавес, a curtain slightly lifted. П-ое настроéние, enthusiastic mood, atmosphere. При-под-н-им-áние, *n.n.*, slight lifting. П. языкá при произношéнии звýков "д" и "т", slight raising of the tongue in pronouncing the sounds "d" and "t".

по-йм-á-ть, *v.p.*, + *acc.*, to capture, catch, seize. *see* ловúть, П. птúцу (рыбу, вóра), to catch a bird (a fish, a thief). П. в сéти, to catch in a net; (*fig.*), to ensnare. П. на ýдочку, to

catch on a hook; (*fig.*), ensnare. П. с
поли́чным, to catch in the act, catch
redhanded. Сло́во не воробе́й,
вы́летит - не пойма́ешь, (*prov.*), a
word once spoken cannot be recalled.
По-йма́ть-ся, *v.p.r.*, to be caught. Ры́ба
пойма́лась на у́дочку, the fish was
caught on a hook. Я пойма́лся на
у́дочку, (*fig.*), I became ensnared.
Судья́ пойма́лся на взя́тках, the judge
was caught accepting bribes. Учени́к
спи́сывал отве́ты и пойма́лся, the
pupil was caught cribbing. По́-йм-ан,
adj. pred., part. pass. past, caught.
Граби́тели по́йманы поли́цией, the
burglars were caught by the police. По́-
йм-анный, *adj. part. pass. past,* caught.
В сетя́х би́лась по́йманная ры́ба, a
fish was struggling in the net. По-йм-
ка, *n.f.,* apprehension, capture. П. пле́н-
ного (престу́пника) capture of a prisoner (criminal). По-йм-щик, *n.m.,*
(*recent*), captor.

по-н-им-а́ть, *v.i.,* по-н-я́т-ь, *v.p.,* + *acc.,*
to understand, conceive, comprehend. П.
су́щность фа́кта, to comprehend the
essence of a fact. Непра́вильно п.
смысл ска́занного, to mistake, misinterpret the meaning of what was said.
Понима́ю, I see; I understand. По-н-
им-а́ть-ся, *v.i.r.,* to be understood.
Филосо́фские тео́рии не все́ми пони-
ма́ются, philosophical theories are not
understood by everyone. По-н-им-а́ние,
n.n., understanding, comprehension. Это
вы́ше моего́ понима́ния, this is beyond
me. По-н-я́т-ие, *n.n.,* conception, notion, idea. Высо́кое п. о че́сти, a high
sense of honor. Я поня́тия не име́л,
что он придёт, I had no idea he would
come. По-н-я́т-ливость, *n.f.,* understanding, comprehension. По-н-я́т-
ливый, *adj.,* intelligent, bright, quick-
witted; comprehending. П. ма́льчик,
an intelligent, bright, boy. По-н-я́т-
ность, *n.f.,* clarity, intelligibility. П.
ре́чи, intelligibility of a speech. П.
объясне́ния, comprehensibility of an
explanation. По-н-я́т-ный, *adj.,* under-
standable, intelligible, clear, comprehensible. По-н-я́т-но, *adv.,* under-
standably, clearly, plainly; naturally,
of course. Не-по-н-им-а́ние, *n.n.,* in-
comprehension, lack of understanding.
Не-по-н-я́т-ливость, *n.f.,* slow in comprehending. Не-по-н-я́т-ливый, *adj.,*
lacking in comprehension, slow-witted.
Тру́дно учи́ть непоня́тливого учени-
ка́, it is difficult to teach a slow-witted
pupil. Не-по-н-я́т-ный, *adj.,* incomprehensible, obscure. Н. язы́к, an incomprehensible language. Н-ая кни́га,
an incomprehensible book. Не-по́-н-я́т-

ый, *adj.,* misunderstood, misinter-
preted. Н. поэ́т, misunderstood, unap-
preciated poet. Н-ое объясне́ние, an
explanation that has been misunderstood. По-я́т-ь, *v.p.,* (*obs.*), *see* взять.
По-я́т-ь в жёны, (*hist.*), to take as a
wife. По-н-ят-о́й (*from* по-я́т-ый),
adj., used as n., witness at an inquest.
Взять в п-ы́е, to summon as a witness.
При о́быске прису́тствовали поня́тые,
witnesses were present during the
search. По-ём-ный, *adj.,* under water.
П-ые луга́, meadows rendered fertile by
spring floods. Пре-я́т-ь, *v.p.,* + *acc.,*
(*Ch.-Sl., obs.*), to assume authority by
appointment, inheritance. П. ца́рский
вене́ц, (*hist.*), to accept the crown.
Пре-ём-ник, *n.m.,* successor, heir.
Прее́мником Ба́йрона в ру́сской лите-
рату́ре был Ле́рмонтов, Byron's heir
in Russian literature was Lermontov.
Быть чьи́м-либо прее́мником, to succeed someone. Пре-ём-ственность, *n.f.,*
succession. П. вла́сти, succession to
authority, power. Пре-ём-ство, *n.n.,*
heritage. Культу́рное п., cultural
heritage.

при-я́т-ь, *v.p.,* to receive; *see* при-н-я́т-ь,
П. му́ченический вене́ц, (*Ch.-Sl.*), to
receive a martyr's crown. При-я́т-ель,
n.m., при-я́т-ельница, *n.f.,* friend.
"Оне́гин, до́брый мой прия́тель,
роди́лся на брега́х Невы́," (*Pushkin*),
Onegin, a good friend of mine, was
born on the shores of the Neva. При-
я́т-ельский, *adj.,* friendly, amicable. П-
ые отноше́ния, friendly relations. При-
я́т-ность, *n.f.,* agreeableness, pleasant-
ness. При-я́т-ный, *adj.,* agreeable,
pleasant, pleasing. П. на вкус (на вид),
pleasing to the taste (pleasant to look
at). П-ая но́вость, welcome news. При-
я́т-но, *adv.,* agreeably, pleasantly. П.
слы́шать э́то, it is pleasant to hear
this. Не-при-я́т-ель, *n.m.,* enemy, adversary. Не-при-я́т-ель-ский, *adj.,*
enemy, hostile. Н. самолёт, enemy
plane. Не-при-я́т-ность, *n.f.,* unpleasantness, nuisance. Не-при-я́т-ный,
adj., unpleasant, disagreeable. Н.
за́пах, unpleasant odor. Н-ое поло-
же́ние, unpleasant situation. Благо-
при-я́т-ствовать, *v.i.,* + *dat.,* to show
favor towards; favor. Пого́да благо-
прия́тствовала путеше́ствию, the weather was favorable for the journey.
Благо-при-я́т-ность, *n.f.,* propitiousness. Благо-при-я́т-ный, *adj.,* propitious, favorable. Б. ве́тер, a favorable
wind. Б. слу́чай помо́г мне, a lucky
chance helped me. Благо-при-я́т-но,
adv., favorably. Всё сложи́лось б.,
everything worked out favorably. При-

я́-знь, *n.f.*, friendliness. Не-при-я́-знь, *n.f.*, enmity, hostility. Не-при-я́-знен-ный, *adj.*, hostile, unfriendly. Н-ые отноше́ния, unfriendly relations.

лице-при-я́т-ствовать, *v.i.,* + *dat.*, to act with partiality, show favoritism, favor. Лице-при-я́т-ие, *n.п.*, partiality, favoritism. На слу́жбе не должно́ быть лицеприя́тия, there should be no partiality (favoritism) on the job. Лице-при-я́т-ный, *adj.*, partial.

меро-при-я́т-ие, *n.п.*, action, measure, legislative enactment; activity. Стро́ить шко́лы - э́то культу́рное м., building schools is a cultural activity. М. по оборо́не страны́, measure taken for the defense of a country.

при-н-им-а́ть, *v.i.,* при-н-я́т-ь, *v.p.,* + *acc.,* to take, receive, accept; admit; assume, adopt. П. учени́ка в шко́лу, to admit a pupil to school. П. вы́зов, to accept a challenge. П. уча́стие, to take part; participate. П. приглаше́ние, to accept an invitation. Врач сего́дня не принима́ет, the doctor is not receiving patients today. При-ём, *n.m.*, reception; dose; method; way, mode. П. госте́й, reception of guests. Раду́шный п., cordial reception, welcome. В оди́н п., at one time, at one fell swoop. Часы́ прие́ма, office hours, receiving hours. Часы́ прие́ма у врача́ от двена́дцати до трёх, the doctor's receiving hours are from twelve to three o'clock in the afternoon. При-ём-ка, *n.f.*, (*colloq.*), acceptance, receiving. П. това́ров (зака́зов), receiving of merchandise (orders). При-ём-лемость, *n.f.*, acceptability. Обсуди́ть п. предложе́ния, to discuss the acceptability of an offer. Не-при-ём-лемость, *n.f.*, inacceptability. Н. э́того предложе́ния очеви́дна, the inacceptability of this offer is obvious. При-ём-лемый, *adj.*, acceptable. Не-при-ём-лемый, *adj. part. pass. pres.*, inacceptable. При-ём-ник, *n.m.*, (*tech.*), receiver. Ра́дио-при-ём-ник, *n.m.*, radio receiver. При-ём-ный, *adj.*, receiving. П. день, receiving day, reception day. П. поко́й, emergency ward, receiving ward. П. экза́мен, entrance examination. П-ая (ко́мната), reception, waiting room. П-ая коми́ссия, reception committee; board of inspectors. П. оте́ц, foster father. П. сын, foster son, adopted son. При-ём-щик, *n.m.*, receiving agent. При-ёмыш, *n.m.*, adopted child. Э́та де́вочка - приёмыш на́ших сосе́дей, this girl is an adopted child of our neighbors. Взять в приёмыши, to adopt a child.

вос-при-н-им-а́ть, *v.i.,* вос-при-н-я́т-ь,

v.p., (вос-при-я́т-ь, *v.p.*, + *acc., obs.*), to take; perceive, grasp; interpret. В. ребёнка, to stand godfather (godmother) to a child. Вос-при-я́т-ие, *n.п.*, perception. Вос-при-ём-ник, *n.m.*, вос-при-ём-ница, *n.f.*, godfather, godmother. Вос-при-и́м-чивость, *n.f.*, receptivity, susceptibility. Вос-при-и́м-чивый, *adj.*, susceptible, receptive.

пред-при-н-им-а́ть, *v.i.,* пред-при-н-я́т-ь, *v.p.,* + *acc.,* to undertake. П. путеше́ствие, to undertake a journey. Пред-при-и́м-чивость, *n.f.*, enterprise. Пред-при-и́м-чивый, *adj.*, enterprising. Пред-прии́мчивые морепла́ватели открыва́ли но́вые зе́мли, enterprising navigators discovered new lands. Не-пред-при-и́м-чивый, *adj.*, unenterprising. Пред-при-и́м-чиво, *adv.*, enterprisingly. Пред-при-н-им-а́тель, *n.m.*, owner of an enterprise. Пред-при-я́т-ие, *n.п.*, undertaking, enterprise, business. Торго́вое п., commercial enterprise. Риско́ванное п., a risky enterprise.

про-н-им-а́ть, *v.i.,* про-н-я́т-ь, *v.p.,* + *acc.,* + *instr.,* to penetrate, pierce. Како́й моро́з! Меня́ пронима́ет хо́лод, How cold it is! I'm chilled to the bone. Его́ ниче́м на проймёшь, he is absolutely unyielding. Про-н-им-а́ющий, *adj. part. act. pres.*, penetrating, piercing. Про-н-им-а́вший, *adj. part. act. past*, which pierced, penetrated. Про-н-я́-вший, *adj. part. act. past*, which had pierced, penetrated.

раз-н-им-а́ть, *v.i.,* раз-н-я́т-ь, *v.p.,* + *acc.,* to take apart, separate; disentangle. Р. дра́ку, to stop a brawl, fight. Р. сжа́тые ру́ки, to unclasp one's hands.

с-н-им-а́ть, *v.i.,* с-н-я́т-ь, *v.p.,* + *acc.,* to take off, down; draw off; rent. С. пла́тье, to take off a dress. С. перча́тки, to take off gloves. С. кры́шу, to take the roof off a house. С. таре́лку с по́лки, to take a plate from a shelf. С. ме́рку, to measure. С. сли́вки, to skim milk, take cream off milk. С. допро́с, to interrogate, examine. С. кого́-нибудь с рабо́ты, (*recent*), to discharge, dismiss, lay off. С. отве́тственность с кого́-нибудь, to release from responsibility. С. фотогра́фию, to take a photograph. С. урожа́й, to harvest. С. кварти́ру, to rent an apartment. С-н-я́т-ие, *n.m.*, taking down, off. С. запреще́ния, (*law*), replevin. С-н-я́т- о́й, *adj.*, skimmed. С-о́е молоко́, skimmed milk. С-н-я́т-ый, *adj. part. pass. past*, taken off; photographed; rented. Фотогра́фия, сня́тая год тому́ наза́д, a photograph taken a year ago. С-ая

кварти́ра, a rented apartment. С-н-им-
а́ть-ся, *v.i.r.*, с-н-я́ть-ся, *v.p.r.*, to be
photographed; taken off. С. у фото́-
графа, to have one's picture taken by a
photographer. С. с мели́, to be re-
floated. С. с я́коря, to weigh anchor.
Я́блоки снима́ются с де́рева о́сенью,
apples are picked in the fall. С-н-и́м-ок,
п.т., photograph, print. Рентге́новский
с., X-ray. С. с докуме́нта, photostat of a
document. Фотографи́ческий с., photograph. Съ-ём-ка, *n.f.*, surveying plan;
filming. С. берего́в, coastal survey.
Геодези́ческая (топографи́ческая) с.,
geodetic (topographic) survey. Фото-с.,
n.f., photografic survey. Кино-с., filming, shooting film Съ-ём-щик, *п.т.*,
surveyor, tenant. С. кварти́ры, tenant.
за-с-н-я́т-ь, *v.p.,* + *асс.,* (*recent, colloq.*),
to photograph. З. краси́вый вид, to
photograph a beautiful view. З. фильм,
to make a film, shoot a film. За-с-н-
я́т-о, filmed, photographed.
пере-с-н-им-а́ть, *v.i.,* пере-с-н-я́т-ь, *v.p.,*
+ *асс.,* to re-photograph. П. ко́пии с
докуме́нтов, to make photostats of
documents. П. фотогра́фию, to take
another photograph.
по-с-н-им-а́ть, *v.p.,* to take off, down.
see снима́ть. П. все кни́ги с по́лки, to
take all the books down from a shelf.
у-н-им-а́ть, *v.i.,* у-н-я́т-ь, *v.p.,* + *асс.,* to
calm, quiet, soothe. У. боль, to soothe,
alleviate pain. У. буя́на, to repress
a ruffian. У. ребёнка, to quiet a child.
У-н-им-а́ть-ся, *v.i.r.,* у-н-я́т-ь-ся,
v.p.r., to become quiet; subside. Боль
унима́ется, the pain is dying down.
Гроза́ уняла́сь, the storm has abated.

ИМ-, ЫМ-, POSSESSION

им-е́-ть, *v.i.,* + *асс.,* to have, possess. И.
де́ньги, to have money. И. дете́й, to
have children. Не и. ни друзе́й, ни
родны́х, to have neither kith nor kin.
И. возмо́жность, to have the opportunity of, be in a position to. И. зна-
че́ние, to be of importance, matter.
Это име́ет большо́е значе́ние, this is
of great importance. Это не име́ет
значе́ния, this is of no importance. И.
си́лу, to be valid (*e.g.,* a visa, permit);
come into force. Про́пуск име́ет си́лу
с 12-ого по 15-ое ноября́, the pass is
valid from Nov. 12 to Nov. 15. И.
ме́сто, to take place; occur, happen.
Ивано́в ещё безрабо́тный? — Нет,
он уже́ име́ет ме́сто в конто́ре, Ivanov
still without a job? — No, he has a position in an office. Когда́ э́то проис-
ше́ствие име́ло ме́сто? (*obs.*), When

did this event take place? И. в виду́,
to bear in mind. Я не име́л в виду́
обижа́ть вас, I did not intend to offend
you. И. го́лову на плеча́х, (*fig.*), to
know what's what; have a head on
one's shoulders. Им-е́ть-ся, *v.i.r.,* *used
only in 3d pers. sing. and pl.,* there is,
there are. Здесь име́ется хоро́ший
теа́тр, there is a good theater here.
У меня́ име́ется его́ распи́ска, I have
a receipt from him. Не им-е́ть-ся, not
to be had; there isn't, there are not.
В селе́ не име́ется ни больни́цы, ни
апте́ки, in the village there is neither
a hospital nor a pharmacy. Им-е́ющий,
adj. part. act. pres., *also used as n.,*
having, possessing; one having, possessing. Челове́к, име́ющий де́ньги,
мо́жет купи́ть себе́ дом, a man who
has money can buy himself a house.
"Име́ющий у́ши, да слы́шит!" (*Bib.*),
"He that hath ears, let him hear!" Им-
е́ние, *п.п.,* estate, domain. Родово́е и.,
ancestral estate. Лев Толсто́й жил в
своём родово́м име́нии "Я́сная Поля́-
на," Leo Tolstoy lived on his ancestral
estate, Yasnaya Polyana. Им-у́щество,
п.п., property, belongings, stock. Госу-
да́рственное и., state property. Ча́ст-
ное и., private (personal) property.
Дви́жимое и., movable property, goods.
Недви́жимое и. immovable property;
real estate. О́пись иму́щества, inventory. Им-у́щественный, *adj.,* pertaining
to property. И. ценз, property qualification (*e.g.,* for voting). И-ое по-
ложе́ние, wealth in terms of property.
По-им-у́щественное обложе́ние, estate
duty, property taxation. Им-у́щий, *adj.,*
also used as n., well off, wealthy;
wealthy man. Не-им-у́щий, *adj.,* poor.
Иму́щие и неиму́щие кла́ссы насе-
ле́ния, the wealthy and the poor classes
of the population. Пре-им-у́щество,
п.п., advantage, preference. Получи́ть
п. над ке́м-либо, to gain the advantage
over someone. Права́ и преиму́щества,
rights and privileges. Уда́рники име́ют
социа́льные преиму́щества, (*recent*),
the shock workers have social privileges. Пре-им-у́щественно, *adv.,* pre-
ferably, for the most part, chiefly. На
Кавка́за п. занима́ются скотово́д-
ством, in the Caucasus cattle raising is
the chief occupation. По преиму́щест-
ву, *adv.,* see преиму́щественно. Пре-
им-у́щественный, *adj.,* preferential.
П-ое пра́во, preferential treatment.
П-ое снабже́ние стаха́новцев, (*recent*),
preferential supply to Stakhanovites.
воз-ым-е́ть, *v.p.,* + *асс.,* (*obs.*), to conceive. В. жела́ние, + *inf.,* to set one's

mind, heart. В. жела́ние просла́виться, to conceive a desire to become famous. В. зло́бу про́тив кого́-нибудь, to conceive animosity toward someone. В. не́нависть к кому́-нибудь, to begin to hate someone. В. страсть к кому́-нибудь, to conceive a passion for someone. Воз-ым-е́вший, *adj. part. act. past,* conceived.

ИМ- (Я, -ЕН-), NAME

и́м-я, *n.n.,* name; proper, Christian name. Моё и́мя - Пётр, my name is Peter. Как ва́ше и́мя? What is your name? Во и́мя, in the name of. Во и́мя Отца́ и Сы́на и Свято́го Ду́ха, in the name of the Father, and the Son, and the Holy Ghost. Называ́ть ве́щи свои́ми имена́ми, (*fig.*), to call things by their names. Говори́ть от и́мени кого́-нибудь, to speak in behalf of someone. Адвока́т говори́л от и́мени своего́ клие́нта, the lawyer spoke in behalf of his client. И. существи́тельное, (*gram.*), noun. И. прилага́тельное, (*gram.*), adjective. И. числи́тельное, (*gram.*), numeral. Име́ть и́мя в иску́сстве, to be famous in art. Просла́вить своё и., to become famous, make one's name known. Мара́ть своё и., to ruin one's reputation. Учёный с больши́м и́менем, an eminent, well-known scientist. Имени́ны, nameday. 24-ого ноября́ - имени́ны всех Екатери́н, Nov. 24 is the nameday of all Catherines. Им-ен-и́нник, *n.m.,* им-ен-и́нница, *n.f.,* one whose name day it is. Я имени́нник 23 апре́ля, в день Гео́ргия-Победоно́сца, My saint's day is on April 23, St. George's Day. Имен-и́нный, *adj.,* pertaining to a saint's day. И. пиро́г, saint's day cake. Им-ен-и́тельный, *adj.,* nominative; pertaining to a name. И. паде́ж, (*gram.*), nominative case. Имен-и́тость, *n.f.,* (*obs.*), eminence, notability. Им-ен-и́тый, *adj.,* notable, eminent, reputable. И. купе́ц, (*obs.*), wealthy merchant. И. граждани́н, (*obs.*), respected citizen. Им-ен-но, *adv.,* just, exactly. А и́менно, namely. Вот и́менно, just so. Я об э́том, и́менно, и говорю́, this is exactly what I say. Им-ен-но́й, *adj.,* nominal. И. чек, personal check. И-ое кольцо́, ring engraved with one's personal name.

им-ен-ова́-ть, *v.i.,* на-им-ен-ова́ть, *v.p.,* + *acc.,* to name, call, address. Им-ен-ова́ть-ся, *v.i.r.,* на-им-ен-ова́ть-ся, *v.p.r.,* to be called, named. Таки́е просту́пки имену́ются обы́чно преступле́нием, such actions are usually called crimes. Им-ен-ова́ние, *n.n.,* (*obs.*), name, nomination. На-им-ен-ова́ние, *n.n.,* denomination, name. Привести́ к одному́ наименова́нию, (*math.*), to reduce to a common denominator. Им-ен-о́ванный, *adj. part. pass. past,* called, named. И-ое число́, (*math.*), concrete number. Им-ен-у́емый, *adj. part. pass. pres.,* (*obs.*), called. Царь Ива́н, имену́емый Гро́зным, Tsar Ivan, called the Terrible.

пере-им-ен-ова́ть, *v.p.,* пере-им-ен-о́вывать, *v.i.,* + *acc.,* to rename, give a new name. В 1924 г. Петрогра́д переименова́н в Ленингра́д, in 1924 Petrograd was renamed Leningrad. Пере-им-ен-ова́ние, *n.n.,* change of name.

по-им-ен-ова́ть, *v.p.,* + *acc.,* to enumerate each person, article. По-им-ённый, *adj.,* listing names, by name. П. спи́сок, list of names. По-им-ённо, *adv.,* by name. Вызыва́ть п., to call the roll. По-им-ен-о́ванный, *adj. part. pass. past,* whose name has been called. П-ые ли́ца должны́ яви́ться, the persons mentioned above must appear.

ИН-, DIFFERENCE, DISSIMILARITY, CONTRARIETY

ин-а́че, *adv.,* otherwise, differently, else. Беги́те, ина́че вы опозда́ете, run, or else you'll be late. Она́ ду́мает так, а отвеча́ет ина́че, she thinks one way, and answers another. Ин-ако-мы́слящий, *adj.,* heterodox. Спо́рить с инакомы́слящими, to argue with those who think otherwise.

ин-о́й, *pron.,* other, some. И. раз, some other time, sometimes. Никто́ ино́й, как он, none but he; no one else but he. Это ино́е де́ло, this is another matter. По-ин-о́му, *adv.,* otherwise.. Он ду́мает не так, как все, а по-ино́му, he does not think like anyone else, but in his own way. Ин-о-, *a compound form meaning* other. Ин-о-ве́рие, *n.n.,* heterodoxy. Ин-о-ве́рец, *n.m.,* one of a different religion. Ин-о-ве́рный, *adj.,* also used as n., of a different religion. Ин-о-ве́рческий, *adj., used only as an adj.,* see инове́рный. Ин-о-горо́дний, *adj.,* of another town. Ин-о-зе́мец, *n.m.,* (*obs.*), foreigner, stranger. Ин-о-зе́мный, *adj.,* foreign, of another land. Ин-о-сказа́тельный, *adj.,* allegorical, parabolical. Ин-о-стра́нец, *n.m.,* foreigner, alien. Ин-о-стра́нный, *adj.,* foreign, alien. Ин-о-язы́чный, *adj.,* of another tongue, speaking another tongue. Ин-о-хо́дец, *n.m.,* ambler, pacer (of a horse). Ин-о-хо́дь, *n.f.*, pace.

ин-о-гда́, *adv.*, sometimes, occasionally, now and then, at times.

пере-ин-а́ч-ить, *v.p.*, пере-ин-а́чивать, *v.i.,* + *acc.*, to alter, modify; misinterpret. П. фра́зу, to modify a sentence. П. фасо́н пла́тья, to alter the cut of a dress.

ИСК-, ИЩ-, ЫСК-, ЫЩ-, SEARCH, INQUIRY

иск-а́-ть, ищ-у́, *v.i.,* + *acc.,* + *gen.,* to search, look for. И. потеря́нное, to search for something lost. И. кварти́ру, to look for an apartment. И. по́мощи, to seek help. И. рабо́ты, to seek work. И. утеше́ния, to seek consolation. Иска́ние, *n.n.*, search, searching, quest. Иск-а́тель, *n.m.*, searcher, seeker; one who aspires. И. же́мчуга, pearl diver. И. приключе́ний, adventurer, one who seeks adventure. Золото-иска́тель, gold prospector. Иск-а́тельный, *adj.*, prospecting, searching; humble, lowly. Золото-иска́тельные рабо́ты, gold prospecting. Иск-а́тельство, *n.n.*, (*obs.*), suit, solicitation; prospecting. Бог-о-иска́тельство, search for faith.

иск, *n.m.*, suit, action, claim. Иск по де́лу о клеве́те, a libel suit. Предъявля́ть иск, to sue. Отказа́ть в и́ске, to reject an action, suit.

ист-е́ц, *n.m.*, plaintiff, petitioner. И. по́дал жа́лобу в суд, the plaintiff filed suit in court.

ищ-е́йка, *n.f.*, police dog, bloodhound. Соба́ка-ище́йка нашла́ во́ра, the police dog located the thief.

вз-ыск-а́ть, *v.p.*, вз-ы́ск-ивать, *v.i.,* + *acc.,* to demand, claim; prosecute. В. долг, to exact the payment of a debt. В. изде́ржки судо́м, to recover damages. Вз-ыск-а́ние, *n.n.*, exaction; penalty. Наложи́ть стро́гое в., to punish severely. Подве́ргнуться взыска́нию, to suffer a penalty. Вз-ыск-а́тельность, *n.f.*, exigence, severity. Вз-ыск-а́тельный, *adj.*, exigent, exacting, strict. Взыска́тельному покупа́телю тру́дно угоди́ть, it is hard to please an exacting customer. Не-вз-ыск-а́тельный, *adj.*, unexacting; unassuming.

вы́-иск-ать, *v.p.*, вы-и́ск-ивать, *v.i.,* to ferret out; search, seek. В. удо́бный слу́чай, to look for an opportunity.

до-иск-а́ть-ся, *v.p.r.,* до-и́ск-ивать-ся, *v.i.r.,* + *gen.,* to find out, discover, hunt out. Он всё дои́скивается пра́вды, he is trying hard to find out the truth.

за-и́ск-ива-ть, *v.i.*, пе́ред + *instr.,* to ingratiate oneself; flatter, court. З. пе́ред нача́льством, to ingratiate oneself with one's superiors. За-и́ск-ива-ние, *n.n.,* flattery, obsequiousness. За-и́ск-ивающий, *adj. part. act. pres.,* sycophant. З. челове́к, ingratiating person, sycophant. За-и́ск-ивающе, *adv.,* ingratiatingly.

из-ыск-а́ть, *v.p.*, из-ы́ск-ивать, *v.i.,* + *acc.,* to seek out, investigate, search for. И. но́вые пути́, to discover new ways. И. сре́дства, to seek new means. Из-ы́ск-ание, *n.n.,* investigation, search. Геологи́ческие изыска́ния, prospecting; geological surveys. Из-ы́ск-анность, *n.f.,* refinement; daintiness. И. вку́са (наря́да), refinement in taste (dress). Из-ы́ск-анный, *adj.,* refined, dainty. И-ые мане́ры, refined manners.

об-ыск-а́ть, об-ыщ-у́, *v.p.*, об-ы́ск-ивать, *v.i.,* + *acc.,* to search, visit, rummage, ransack. О. ко́мнату, to search a room. О. престу́пника, to search a criminal. О́б-ыск, *n.m.,* search. Производи́ть о., to conduct a search.

от-ыск-а́ть, от-ыщ-у́, *v.p.*, от-ы́ск-ивать, *v.i.,* + *acc.,* to find. Он всегда́ стара́ется о. недоста́тки в други́х, he always tries to find fault with others. От-ыск-а́ть-ся, *v.p.r.,* от-ы́ск-ивать-ся, *v.i.r.,* to be found. Потеря́нная вещь отыска́лась, the lost object was found.

пере-иск-а́ть, *v.p.*, пере-и́ск-ивать, *v.i.,* + *acc.,* to look for again, look through again. Переиска́л всё всю́ду, но не нашёл, I looked through everything but did not find it.

по-иск-а́ть, *v.p.,* + *acc.,* to seek, look for, for a short time. Поищи́те мои́ очки́, look for my glasses. По́-иск-и, *n.pl.,* search, hunt, quest, pursuit. П. рабо́ты, search for employment.

под-ыск-а́ть, *v.p.*, под-ы́ск-ивать, *v.i.,* + *acc.,* to try to find; find. П. подходя́щие слова́, to find appropriate words.

при-иск-а́ть, *v.p.*, при-и́ск-ивать, *v.i.,* + *acc.,* to find, seek successfully. П. хоро́шую кварти́ру, to find a fine apartment. При́-иск, *n.m.,* mine. Золоты́е при́иски, gold mine; gold fields.

про́-иск-и, *n.pl.,* intrigues, machinations, underhand plotting. П. врага́, enemy intrigues.

раз-ыск-а́ть, *v.p.*, раз-ы́ск-ивать, *v.i.,* + *acc.,* to look and find, discover; look, hunt for. Р. пропа́вшую вещь, to find a lost thing. Р. граби́телей, to find thieves. Раз-ыск-а́ть-ся, *v.p.r,* раз-ы́ск-ивать-ся, *v.i.r.,* to be found, sought. Раз-ыск-а́ние, *n.n.,* research, investigation. Раз-ы́ск-ивание, *п.п.,* searching, hunt. Раз-ы́ск-иваемый, *adj. part. pass. pres.,* wanted, hunted. Р. полицией, wanted by the police. **ро́з-ыск,** *п.т.,* search, inquest, inquiry. Р. пропа́вших де́нег, search for lost money. Уголо́вный р., (угро́зыск, *recent*), criminal investigation.

сн-иск-а́ть, *v.p.,* сн-йск-ивать, *v.i.,* + *acc.,* (*obs.*), to ingratiate oneself, seek the favor of. С. дове́рие, to secure someone's confidence. С. уваже́ние, to earn someone's respect.

с-ыск-а́ть, *v.p.,* с-ы́ск-ивать, *v.i.,* + *acc.,* to find, discover. С-ыск, *п.т.,* (*obs.*), search, perquistion. Полити́ческий с., (*recent*), investigation by political police. С-ыск-но́й, *adj.,* (*obs.*), detective. Аге́нт с. поли́ции, detective, police agent. С-о́е отделе́ние, (*obs.*), detective department. С-ы́щ-ик, *п.т.,* detective.

ИСТ-, TRUTH, VERITY, VERACITY

йст-ин-а, *п.f.,* truth. Это свята́я и., this is the holy truth. В э́том есть до́ля и́стины, there is a grain of truth in this. Соотве́тствовать и́стине, to be in accordance with the truth. Это сообще́ние соотве́тствует и́стине, this announcement is in accord with the truth. Показа́ния подсуди́мого не соотве́тствовали и́стине, the testimony of the accused is not in accordance with the truth. Во-и́стину, *adv.,* (*relig.*), verily so. В. Воскре́се! Christ is truly risen! (*response to Easter greeting:* Христо́с Воскре́се! Christ is risen!) Ист-инно, *adv.,* truly. Ньюто́н был и. вели́кий учёный, Newton was a truly great scientist. Сострада́ние - э́то и́стинно челове́ческое чу́вство, compassion is a truly human feeling. Ист-инный, *adj.,* true. И. расска́з, true narrative, story. И-ая быль, true fact. И. геро́й, a real hero.

йст-ов-ый, *adj.,* (*obs.*), dignified, earnest. И. челове́к, respectable, dignified person. И-ая речь, dignified speech. Ист-ово, *adv.,* fervently, earnestly. Моля́щиеся и. крести́лись, the people praying were fervently crossing themselves.

не-йст-ов-ствова-ть, *v.i.,* to rage, rave, storm. Лю́ди в зло́бе нейсто́вствуют, people in their anger are frantically violent. Бу́ря нейсто́вствовала, the storm raged. Не-йст-вующий, *adj. part. act. pres.,* raving, frantic. Н-ие язы́чники истяза́ли христиа́н, the frantic pagans tortured the Christians.

Не-йст-овство, *п.п.,* violence, rage. Не-йст-овый, *adj.,* violent, furious, raving. Н. крик, frantic scream. Кто́-то крича́л нейстовым го́лосом, someone was screaming frantically. Н-ые вы́ходки взбешённого челове́ка, the frantic actions of a raving man.

К

КАЗ-, КАЖ-, APPEARANCE, SEMBLANCE, EXPRESSION

каз-а́ть, *v.i.,* (*colloq.*), *used in expression:* Она́ ко мне́ глаз не ка́жет, she avoids me, never comes to see me.

каз-а́ть-ся, *v.i.r.,* по-каз-а́ть-ся, *v.p.r.,* to seem, appear. Ка́ж-ет-ся (кажи́сь, *colloq.*), it seems, it appears. Ка́жется, бу́дет гроза́, it looks as if there'll be a thunderstorm. Во́здух х. холо́дным, the air feels cold. Каза́лось-бы, it would seem. Не-каз-и́стый, *adj.,* plain, insignificant looking. Н-ая нару́жность, plain looks. Ка́ж-ущийся, *adj., part. act. pres.,* seeming, apparent. К-ееся сопротивле́ние, apparent resistance.

вы́-каз-ать, *v.p.,* вы-ка́з-ывать, *v.i.,* + *acc.,* to show, display, manifest. В. большо́е внима́ние, to pay much attention to. В. му́жество, to display courage. В. ра́дость (печа́ль), to manifest joy (sorrow). В. ум, to display wit.

до-каз-а́ть, *v.p.,* до-ка́з-ывать, *v.i.,* + *acc.,* to demonstrate, prove. Д. теоре́му, to demonstrate a theorem. Д. свою́ пре́данность, to prove one's devotion. Что и тре́бовалось доказа́ть, Q.E.D., which was to be proved. Принима́ть как дока́занное, to take for granted. Это дока́зывает, что он умён, it proves him to be clever. До-каз-у́емый, *adj. part. pass. pres.,* demonstrable, provable. До-каз-а́тельный, *adj.,* demonstrative, convincing, conclusive. До-каз-а́тельство, *п.п.,* argument, demonstration, proof, evidence. В д. чего́-либо, in witness, evidence of. Служи́ть доказа́тельством, to serve as evidence. Приводи́ть доказа́тельства, to show proof, evidence.

за-каз-а́ть, *v.p.,* за-ка́з-ывать, *v.i.,* + *acc.,* to order. З. костю́м (пла́тье), to order a suit (dress). З. обе́д (за́втрак), to order dinner (breakfast). За-ка́з-ывать-ся, *v.i.r.,* to be ordered. Костю́м зака́зывается у лу́чшего портно́го, the suit is being ordered at the best tailor's. За-ка́з, *п.т.,* order, command. Де́лать на з., to make to order. За-каз-но́й, *adj.,* ordered. З-о́е письмо́, registered letter. За-ка́з-чик, *п.т.,* за-ка́з-чица, *n.f.*, client, customer, one who orders.

на-каз-а́ть, *v.p.*, на-ка́з-ывать, *v.i.*, + *acc.*, to punish, chastise; charge, command. Н. вино́вного, to punish a culprit. Н. самого́ себя́, to punish oneself. Н. сы́ну быть че́стным, to exhort a son to be honest. На-ка́з, *n.m.*, (*obs.*), order, direction, mandate. На-каз-а́ние, *n.n.*, punishment, penalty, chastisement. Теле́сное н., corporal punishment. На-каз-у́емость, *n.f.*, (*obs.*), punishability. На-каз-у́емый, *adj. part. pass. pres.*, (*obs.*), punishable; penal. На-каз-анный, *adj. part. pass. past*, punished, penalized, chastised. Без-на-ка́з-анность, *n.f.*, impunity. Без-на-ка́з-анный, *adj.*, unpunished. Без-на-ка́з-анно, *adv.*, with impunity.

о-каз-а́ть, *v.p.*, о-ка́з-ывать, *v.i.*, + *acc.*, to render, show, pay. О. услу́гу, to render one a service. О. внима́ние, to show attention. О. влия́ние, to influence. О. сопротивле́ние, to resist. О-каз-а́ть-ся, *v.p.r.*, о-ка́з-ывать-ся, *v.i.r.*, to show oneself, appear, find oneself, prove. О. в тру́дном положе́нии, to find oneself in a difficult situation. Ока́зывается, что я был прав, it turns out I was right. О-каз-а́ние, *n.n.*, showing, rendering. О. по́мощи, rendering, extending of help.

от-каз-а́ть, *v.p.*, от-ка́з-ывать, *v.i.*, + *dat.*, от + *gen.*, to refuse, deny; renounce. О. жениху́, to refuse; break an engagement. О. от до́ма, to forbid the house (to someone). О. от слу́жбы, to dismiss, discharge (from a job). О. себе́ в чём-либо, to deprive oneself of something. От-каз-а́ть-ся, *v.p.r.*, от-ка́з-ывать-ся, *v.i.r.*, от + *gen.*, to give up, renounce, deprive oneself. О. от до́лжности, to resign, retire. О. от престо́ла, to abdicate. О. от упла́ты до́лга, to repudiate a debt. О. от вина́, to refuse, give up, wine. О. от своего́ сло́ва, to repudiate one's promise. От-ка́з, *n.m.*, refusal, denial, rejection. Получи́ть о., to be refused, rejected. По́лный до отка́за, (*colloq.*), replete. Маши́на рабо́тает без отка́за, (*tech.*), the machine runs smoothly, without a hitch.

по-каз-а́ть, *v.p.*, по-ка́з-ывать, *v.i.*, + *acc.*, + *dat.*, to show, indicate, display, exhibit; depose; testify; bear witness. П. го́род (музе́й), to show someone around a city (a museum). П. дру́жбу, to express friendship. П. пятки, (*fig.*), to show ones' heels. Да́йте ей показа́ть себя́, give her a chance to show what she can do. По-каз-а́ть-ся,

v.p.r., по-ка́з-ывать-ся, *v.i.r.*, to show oneself, appear, figure. Мне показа́лось, it seemed to me; I thought. Со́лнце показа́лось, the sun appeared. Они́ показа́лись в дали́, they came into sight in the distance. По-ка́з, *n.m.*, show. На-по-ка́з, *adv.*, for show, showing. Она́ лю́бит всё де́лать н., she is fond of showing off. По-каз-а́ние, *n.n.*, deposition, testimony, evidence. Дава́ть п., to depose, bear witness. По-каз-а́тель, *n.m.*, exponent, index. Ка́чественный п., qualitative index. Показа́тели соцсоревнова́ния, (*recent*), indexes of socialist competition. По-каз-а́тельный, *adj.*, significant, model. П. проце́сс, test case, trial. П. уро́к, model lesson. По-каз-а́тельно, *adv.*, it is significant; significantly. По-каз-но́й, *adj.*, for show. П-а́я ро́скошь, pretentious luxury. По-ка́з-ывание, *n.n.*, showing, exhibition.

при-каз-а́ть, *v.p.*, при-ка́з-ывать, *v.i.*, + *dat.*, to order, command, enjoin, bid, charge. Команди́р приказа́л вы́ступить с рассве́том, the commanding officer ordered his men to start out at dawn. Приказа́л до́лго жить, (*colloq.*), he died. Как прика́жете, as you command. При-ка́з, *n.m.*, order, command, injunction. П. о выступле́нии, (*mil.*), marching orders. При-каз-а́ние, *n.n.*, order, command. Отда́ть п., to give a command, order. При-ка́з-чик, *n.m.*, (*obs.*) salesman, clerk, steward. При-ка́з-ный, *adj.*, used as n., (*hist.*), clerk, scrivener. Душе-при-ка́з-чик, *n.m.*, executor of a will.

с-каз-а́ть, *v.p.*, говори́ть, *v.i.*, + *acc.*, to say, tell, speak. С. пра́вду пря́мо в лицо́, to tell the truth directly, straight to one's face. С. в шу́тку ,to say in jest. Так сказа́ть, so to speak. Скажи́те ва́шу це́ну, name your price. Что ска́жут? What will people say? Ска́зано - сде́лано, (*saying*), no sooner said than done. С-каз-а́ть-ся, *v.p.r.*, + *instr.*, to pretend. Она́ сказа́лась больно́й, she alleged she was ill. С-ка́з-ывать-ся, *v.i.r.*, с-каз-а́ть-ся, *v.p.r.*, to tell, show. Боле́знь ска́зывается на челове́ке, an illness shows on one. С-каз, *n.m.*, tale. Вот тебе́ и весь с., (*colloq.*), and that's the whole story. С-каз-а́ние, *n.n.*, legend, story. С. о гра́де Ки́теже, the legend of the city of Kitezh. С-ка́з-ка, *n.f.*, tale, story; (*fig.*), fib. Волше́бная с., fairy tale. Де́тская с., nursery tale. Рас-сказа́ть ска́зку, to tell a fairy tale. С-ка́з-очник, *n.m.*, teller of fairy tales. С-ка́з-очный, *adj.*, fantastic, fabulous.

С-ая страна́, fairyland. С-каз-и́тель, *п.т.*, с-каз-и́тельница, *n.f.*, (*obs.*), narrator, reciter. С-каз-у́емое, (*gram.*), predicate. Ино-с-каз-а́ние, *п.п.*, allegory. Ино-с-каз-а́тельный, *adj.*, allegorical.

вы́-с-каз-ать, *v.p.*, вы-с-ка́з-ывать, *v.i.*, + *acc.*, to express, come out with. В. мне́ние, to advance an opinion. В. предложе́ние, to surmise. Вы́-с-каз-ать-ся, *v.p.r.*, вы-с-ка́з-ывать-ся, *v.i.r.*, за + *acc.*, про́тив, + *gen.*, о + *prep.*, to speak out, speak one's mind, declare for. В. за (про́тив), to declare oneself for (against).

до-с-каз-а́ть, *v.p.*, до-с-ка́з-ывать, *v.i.*, + *acc.*, to tell to the end. Д. расска́з до конца́, to tell a story to the very end.

пере-с-каз-а́ть, *v.p.*, пере-с-ка́з-ывать, *v.i.*, + *acc.*, to tell over again, retell, relate; give the contents; gossip. П. содержа́ние ле́кции, to list the contents of a lecture. Лу́чше не досказа́ть, чем пересказа́ть, (*prov.*), it is better to tell too little than too much. Пере-с-ка́з, *п.т.*, rendering of a story. Написа́ть п. прочи́танного, to write a summary of what has been read.

под-с-каз-а́ть, *v.p.*, под-с-ка́з-ывать, *v.i.*, + *acc.*, + *dat.*, to prompt. П. уро́к това́рищу, to prompt a classmate. Под-с-ка́з-ывание, *п.п.*, prompting. Под-с-ка́з-ка, *n.f.*, (*colloq.*), prompting in class. Под-с-ка́з-чик, *п.т.*, a pupil who prompts.

рас-с-каз-а́ть, *v.p.*, рас-с-ка́з-ывать, *v.i.*, + *acc.*, о + *prep.*, to relate, narrate, tell, recount. Р. ска́зку, to tell a fairy tale. Р. о своём приключе́нии, to tell of one's adventure. Рас-с-ка́з, *п.т.*, story, tale, narrative. Р. Че́хова, a story by Chekhov. Р. очеви́дца, story of an eyewitness. Рас-с-ка́з-чик, *п.т.*, storyteller, narrator. Весёлый р., humorist. Ро́с-с-каз-ни, *n.pl.*, (*colloq.*), idle tales.

у-каз-а́ть, *v.p.*, у-ка́з-ывать, *v.i.*, + *acc.*, + *instr.*, to indicate, point out, show, denote. У. доро́гу, to show the way. У. па́льцем на кого́-либо, to point at someone. У-ка́з-ывать-ся, *v.i.r.*, to be indicated, pointed out. У-ка́з, *п.т.*, (*obs.*), ukase, order; decree. У-каз-а́ние, *п.п.*, indication, direction; instruction. У-каз-а́тель, *п.т.*, sign, indication; guide, indicator. У-каз-а́тельный, *adj.*, indicating, indicative; (*gram.*), demonstrative. У. па́лец, forefinger, index finger. У-ая стре́лка, pointer; needle, hand of a dial. Он мне не ука́зчик, (*colloq.*), he can't lay

down the law to me. У-ка́з-ка, *n.f.*, pointer. Ука́зкой пока́зывают города́ на ка́рте, cities are indicated on a map with a pointer. Де́лать всё по ука́зке, (*idiom.*), to follow someone's instructions stupidly.

КАЗ-, КАЖ-, SPOLIATION, MUTILATION

ис-каз-и́ть, **ис-каж-у́**, *v.p.*, ис-каж-а́ть, *v.i.*, + *acc.*, to distort, misrepresent, spoil; pervert. И. слова́, to distort words. Страх искази́л его́ лицо́, terror distorted his face. Ис-каз-и́ть-ся, *v.p.r.*, ис-каж-а́ть-ся, *v.i.r.*, + *instr.*, to be distorted, disfigured; disfigure oneself. Лицо́ искази́лось су́дорогой, the face was distorted by convulsions. Ис-каж-е́ние, *п.п.*, distortion; misrepresentation. И. и́стины, distortion of truth. Ис-каж-ённый, *adj. part. pass. past*, disfigured, distorted. И. смысл фра́зы, to distort the sense of a phrase, sentence. Ис-каз-и́тель, *п.т.*, one who distorts, disfigures. И. пра́вды, one who distorts the truth.

про-ка́з-ить, *v.i.*, на-про-ка́з-ить, *v.p.*, to frolic, play pranks, be up to mischief. Де́ти опя́ть напрока́зили, the children have again played pranks.

про-ка́з-нич-ать, *v.i.*, на-про-ка́з-ничать, *v.p.*, to play pranks, be up to mischief. Шко́льники всегда́ прока́зничают, pupils always play pranks. Напрока́зничали и разбежа́лись, they played a prank and then ran away. Про-ка́з-ник, *п.т.*, про-ка́з-ница, *n.f.*, prankish, mischievous person, child. Прока́зница-марты́шка, mischievous monkey. Про-ка́з-ливый, *adj.*, prankish, mischievous. П. мальчи́шка, mischievous, prankish boy.

с-про-ка́з-ить, *v.p.*, с-про-ка́з-ничать, *v.i.*, (*colloq.*), to play pranks. Скажи́, кто э́то спрока́зил? Tell me, who played this prank?

про-ка́з-а, *n.f.*, про-ка́з-ы, *n.pl.*, (*generally used in pl.*), prank, trick, mischief. Де́тские прока́зы, childish pranks, tricks. Что ни шаг, то п., he cannot take a step without playing a prank. Про-ка́з-а, *n.f.*, (*med.*), leprosy. Прока́за - неизлечи́мая боле́знь, leprosy is an incurable disease. Заболе́ть прока́зой, to contract leprosy. Про-каж-ённый, *adj.*, *also used as n.*, leprous; leper. П. больно́й, a person inflicted with leprosy. П-ые содержатся в лепрозо́риях, lepers are kept in leprosariums.

КАЗН(Ь)-, PUNISHMENT

казн-ь, *n.f.,* execution; capital punishment. Приговори́ть к сме́ртной ка́зни, to sentence to death. Ме́сто ка́зни, place of execution. Ка́зни Еги́петские, (*Bib.*), the Plagues of Egypt.
казн-и́-ть, *v.p.* and *v.i., + acc.,* to execute, put to death. Престу́пника казни́ли, they executed the criminal (the criminal was executed). Казни́ть поро́ки (неве́жество), (*fig.*), to fulminate against vices (ignorance). Казни́ть-ся, *v.i.r.,* to accuse oneself; repent. За грехи́ свое́й мо́лодости он казни́лся всю жизнь, he repented the sins of his youth all his life. Казн-ённый, *adj. part. pass. past,* executed. Тру́пы казнённых, bodies of the executed. Казн-я́щий, *adj. part. act. pres.,* executing. Пала́ч, к. престу́пника, the executioner (hangman) who is executing the criminal.

КАМ-(ЕН)-, STONE, ROCK

ка́м-ен-ь, *n.m.,* (ка́м-ни, кам-е́н-ь-я, *pl.*), stone, rock. Драгоце́нный ка́мень, precious stone, gem. Подво́дный к., submerged (underwater) rock. К. преткнове́ния, stumbling block. Не оста́вить ка́мня на ка́мне, (*fig.*), to raze to the ground. Броса́ть ка́мни в чужо́й огоро́д, (*fig.*), to slander. Ка́м-ушек, *n.m.,* small stone; pebble. Ка́м-енный, *adj.,* of or pertaining to stone. К. век, the Stone Age. К. у́голь, coal. К-ая кла́дка, masonry; stone work. К-ая соль, rock salt. Кам-ен-о-, *a combining form meaning* rock, stone. Кам-ен-о-ло́мня, *n.f.,* quarry, stone-pit. Кам-ен-о-ло́м, *n.m.,* quarryman. Кам-ен-о-тёс, *n.m.,* stone-cutter. Ка́м-енщик, *n.m.,* mason. Кам-ен-и́стый, *adj.,* stony, rocky. К. бе́рег, rocky shore. К-ое дно, rocky bottom (*as of a river, lake*). К-ая по́чва, rocky soil.
кам-ен-е́-ть, *v.i.,* о-кам-ен-е́ть, *v.p.,* to petrify, harden, turn to stone. От несча́стья се́рдце камене́ет, through misfortune the heart turns to stone. О-кам-ен-е́лость, *n.f.,* fossil. О-камене́ние, *n.n.,* petrification. О-камен-е́лый, *adj.,* petrified; pertaining to a fossil. О. о́стов живо́тного, petrified skeleton of an animal. О-ое де́рево, petrified tree.

КАТ-, КАЧ-, MOVEMENT ON WHEELS, WHEELING, ROLLING; RIDING

кат-а́-ть, *v.i.indet.,* to roll, wheel; mangle; take for a drive. К. бельё, to mangle clothes. К. те́сто, to roll pastry. К. ребёнка в коля́ске, to push a child in a perambulator. Кат-а́ть-ся, *v.i.r.,* to roll, ride. К. верхо́м, to ride horseback. К. в экипа́же, to drive in a carriage. К. на конька́х, to skate. К. на ло́дке, to boat. К. со́ сме́ху, (*colloq.*), to roll around with laughter. Кат-а́ние, *n.n.,* rolling, wheeling, driving, riding, boating, skating. К. с горы́, sliding down a hill on a sled; coasting. Кат-а́льщик, *n.m.,* mangler, roller, wheeler. Кат-ышо́к, *n.m.,* pellet.
в-кат-а́ть, *v.p.,* в-ка́т-ывать, *v.i., + acc.,* (*obs.*), to roll, wheel in. В. изю́м в те́сто, to roll raisins into dough.
вы́-кат-ать, *v.p.,* вы-ка́т-ывать, *v.i., + acc.,* to mangle. В. бельё, to mangle clothes. В. кого́-нибудь в снегу́, to roll someone in the snow.
за-кат-а́ть, *v.p.,* за-ка́т-ывать, *v.i., + acc.,* roll up. З. ковёр, to roll up a carpet. З. в тюрьму́, (*colloq.*), to send someone to jail; convict.
на-кат-а́ть, *v.p.,* на-ка́т-ывать, *v.i., + acc.,* to roll. Н. доро́гу, to roll a road. Н. письмо́, (*slang*), to write a letter hurriedly. На-кат-а́ть-ся, *v.p.r.,* to have one's fill of riding. Н. вдо́воль, to ride to one's heart's content. На-ка́т, *n.m.,* (*tech.*), a counter floor, subflooring.
об-кат-а́ть, *v.p.,* об-ка́т-ывать, *v.i., + acc.,* to roll. О. котле́ту в муке́, to roll a cutlet in flour.
пере-кат-а́ть, *v.p.,* пере-ка́т-ывать, *v.i., + acc.,* to mangle, wring. П. все бельё, to mangle, wring all the clothes. П. всех дете́й, to give all the children a ride (*as in a sleigh*). Пере-ка́т, *n.m.,* sandbank. П. на реке́, sandbank in a river.
по-кат-а́ть, *v.p., + acc.,* to take for a drive. П. кого́-нибудь в автомоби́ле, to take someone for a drive in a car. По-кат-а́ть-ся, *v.p.r.,* to take a drive. П. на велосипе́де, to take a ride on a bicycle.
про-кат-а́ть, *v.p.,* про-ка́т-ывать, *v.i., + acc.,* to roll, spread, flatten with a roller; take for a drive. П. листы́ желе́за, to flatten sheets of iron with a roller. Дава́ть на прока́т, to rent out. Взять на прока́т, to rent. Про-ка́т-ка, *n.f.,* (*tech.*), rolling. Про-ка́т-ный, *adj.,* rolled. П. заво́д, rolling mill. П-ое желе́зо, rolled iron. Про-кат-а́ть-ся, *v.p.r.,* про-ка́т-ывать-ся, *v.i.r,* to go for a drive. П. весь день, to drive around all day, spend a whole day riding.
рас-кат-а́ть, *v.p.,* рас-ка́т-ывать, *v.i., + acc.,* to roll; unroll; drive around. Р.

тéсто на пирóг, to roll dough for a pie. Рас-кат-áть-ся, *v.p.r.,* рас-кáт-ывать-ся, *v.i.r.,* to be rolled.

с-кат-áть, *v.p.,* с-кáт-ывать, *v.i.,* + *acc.,* to roll up. С. шинéль, to roll a military greatcoat. С. бинт, to roll a bandage. С. диктóвку, (*school slang*), to crib during dictation. С-кáт-ывать-ся, *v.i.r.,* с + *gen.,* to roll down, off; be rolled. С-кáт-ка, *n.f.,* rolling up; (*mil.*), rolled greatcoat.

у-кат-áть, *v.p.,* у-кáт-ывать, *v.i.,* + *acc.,* to roll, smooth out. У. дорóгу, to roll a road. У-кат-áть-ся, *v.p.r.,* у-кáт-ывать-ся, *v.i.r.,* to be smoothed. Укатáли сúвку крýтые гóрки, (*saying*), life has been too hard.

кат-úть, кач-ý, *v.i.det.,* + *acc.,* to roll, wheel, trundle. Кат-úть-ся, *v.i.r.,* to roll, trundle. К. с горы́, to slide down a hill. Слёзы кáтятся из глаз, tears are rolling from his eyes. Кат-óк, *n.m.,* skating rink; mangle for clothes; roller, rolling press. Кат-ýшка, *n.f.,* reel, spool, bobbin. К. нúток, spool of thread. Индукциóнная к., induction coil.

в-кат-úть, *v.p.,* в-кáт-ывать, *v.i.,* + *acc.,* to roll, wheel in. В. крéсло, to wheel in an armchair. В-кат-úть-ся, *v.p.r.,* в-кáт-ывать-ся, *v.i.r.,* to roll in. Мяч вкатúлся в кóмнату, the ball rolled into the room.

вы́-кат-ить, *v.p.,* вы-кáт-ывать, *v.i.,* + *acc.,* to roll, wheel out. В. бóчки из подвáла, to roll casks out of a cellar. Он вы́катил глазá, (*colloq.*), his eyes popped out. На-вы́-кат, *adv.,* bulging. Глазá н., bulging eyes. Вы́-кат-ить-ся, *v.p.r.,* вы-кáт-ывать-ся, *v.i.r.,* to wheel, roll out. Яблоки вы́катились из корзúны, the apples rolled out of the basket. Вы-кáт-ывание, *n.n.,* rolling out; mangling.

до-кат-úть, *v.p.,* до-кáт-ывать, *v.i.,* + *acc.,* to roll up to. Д. бóчку до сарáя, to roll a barrel up to a shed. Д. в два дня до Москвы́, to reach Moscow in two days.

за-кат-úть, *v.p.,* за-кáт-ывать, *v.i.,* + *acc.,* to roll behind, beyond. З. мяч под дивáн, to roll a ball under a sofa. З. большýю дóзу лекáрства, (*colloq.*), to give a big dose of medicine. З. истéрику, (*colloq.*), to go into hysterics. За-кат-úть-ся, *v.p.r.,* за-кáт-ывать-ся, *v.i.r.,* to disappear (behind something). Сóлнце закатúлось, the sun has set. Моя звездá закатúлась, (*fig.*), star has set. За-кáт, *n.m.,* setting, decline. З. сóлнца, sunset. З. жúзни, the last years of life.

об-кат-úть, о-кат-úть, *v.p.,* о-кáч-ивать, *v.i.,* + *instr.,* drench. О. водóй, to douse, drench with water. О-кат-úть-ся, *v.p.r.,* о-кáч-ивать-ся, *v.i.r.,* to drench with water. О. холóдной водóй, to drench, douse oneself with cold water; take a shower.

от-кат-úть, *v.p.,* от-кáт-ывать, *v.i.,* + *acc.,* to roll, wheel off. О. телéгу, to roll a cart away. О. бревнó, to roll a log away, off. От-кат-úть-ся, *v.p.r.,* от-кáт-ывать-ся, *v.i.r.,* to roll away. Неприя́тель откатúлся, (*mil., colloq.*), the enemy retreated. От-кáт-ывание, *n.n.,* rolling off; wheeling off.

под-кат-úть, *v.p.,* под-кáт-ывать, *v.i.,* под + *acc.,* к + *dat.,* to roll up to, under. П. под чтó-либо, to roll, drive under. Подкатúло под гóрло, I felt a lump in my throat. Извóзчик лúхо подкатúл к подъéзду, the cabman drove up smartly to the entrance. Под-кат-úть-ся, *v.p.r.,* под-кáт-ывать-ся, *v.i.r.,* to roll under. Шáрик подкатúлся под кровáть, the ball rolled under the bed.

по-кат-úть, *v.p.,* + *acc.,* to drive off; set out; roll, begin rolling. П. шар (мяч), to roll a ball. По-кат-úть-ся, *v.p.r.,* to roll, start rolling, roll down. П. с горы́, to roll downhill. П. сó смеху, to rock with laughter. По-кáт-ость, *n.f.,* slope, decline, declivity. По-кáт-ый, *adj.,* sloping. П. лоб, sloping forehead. По-кáт-о, *adv.,* aslope.

пере-кат-úть, *v.p.,* пере-кáт-ывать, *v.i.,* to roll from one place to another. *see* катúть. Перекатú-пóле, eryngium, a steppe plant; (*fig.*), rolling stone (of a person).

при-кат-úть, *v.p.,* при-кáт-ывать, *v.i.,* to roll; (*colloq.*), come, arrive. П. бóчку, to roll a barrel, cask. "Чéрез два часá прикатúл слéдователь", (*Chekhov*), two hours later the investigating magistrate arrived.

про-кат-úть, *v.p.,* про-кáт-ывать, *v.i.,* + *acc.,* to take for a ride, drive. П. на автомобúль, to take for a drive in a car. П. когó-нибудь на воронóых, (*fig.*), to blackball. Про-кат-úть-ся, *v.p.r.,* про-кáт-ывать-ся, *v.i.r.,* to go for a drive. П. верхóм, to go for a ride (horseback). П. на парохóде, to take a pleasure cruise via steamer. По толпé прокатúлся рóпот, a murmur ran through the crowd.

рас-кат-úть, *v.p.,* рас-кáт-ывать, *v.i.,* + *acc.,* to set rolling, give a forward motion to. Р. колесó, to push, roll a wheel, start rolling. Рас-кат-úть-ся, *v.p.r.,* рас-кáт-ывать-ся, *v.i.r.,* to roll down, begin rolling. Салáзки раскатились с горы́, the sled glided down the hill. Рас-ка́т, *n.m.*, roll, peal; slide. Раска́ты гро́ма, peals of thunder. Рас-ка́т-истый, *adj.*, rolling, rumbling. Р. смех, peal of laughter.

с-кат-и́ть, *v.p.*, с-ка́т-ывать, *v.i.*, + *acc.*, to roll down, off. С. бо́чку в по́греб, to roll a cask into a cellar. С-кат-и́ть-ся, *v.p.r.*, с-ка́т-ывать-ся, *v.i.r.*, to roll off. С. с горы́ на сала́зках, to slide downhill on a toboggan. Ка́пля скати́лась с листа́, a drop of water rolled off the leaf.

у-кат-и́ть, *v.p.*, у-ка́т-ывать, *v.i.*, + *acc.*, to roll away, drive away. У. колесо́ (шар), to roll away a wheel (ball). Она́ давно́ укати́ла в Москву́, (*colloq.*), she went off to Moscow quite a long time ago. У-кат-и́ть-ся, *v.p.r.*, у-ка́т-ывать-ся, *v.i.r.*, to roll away, under. Мяч укати́лся под стол, the ball rolled away under the table.

КАЧ-, ROCKING, SWINGING

кач-а́-ть, *v.i.*, + *acc.*, + *instr.*, to rock, swing, sway, shake; pump. К. ребёнка на рука́х, to rock a child in one's arms. Во́лны кача́ют ло́дку, the waves are rocking the boat. К. голово́й, to shake one's head. Кач-а́ть-ся, *v.i.r.*, to oscillate, rock, swing, sway, reel. К. на каче́лях, to swing on a swing. Кач-е́ли, *n.pl.*, swing, seesaw. Ка́ч-ка, *n.f.*, tossing, rocking. Боковая и килевая к., rolling and pitching (of a ship). Водо-ка́ч-ка, *n.f.*, water-tower. Кач-ну́-ть, *v.p. smf.*, to cause to totter, jolt. *see* кача́ть. Парохо́д качну́ло налете́вшим ве́тром, a gust of wind caused the ship to roll. Кач-ну́ть-ся, *v.p.r.*, to rock, swing; reel, stagger. Ло́дка качну́лась, the boat rocked.

в-кач-а́ть, *v.p.*, в-ка́ч-ивать, *v.i.*, + *acc.*, to pump in. В бак вкача́ли со́рок вёдер воды́, they pumped forty buckets of water into the tank.

вы́-кач-ать, *v.p.*, вы-ка́ч-ивать, *v.i.*, + *acc.*, to pump out. В. во́ду из корабля́, to pump water out of a ship. В. во́здух из ши́ны, to deflate a tire. Вы-ка́ч-ивание, *n.n.*, pumping out.

за-кач-а́ть, *v.p.*, за-ка́ч-ивать, *v.i.*, to start swinging, rocking. Его́ закача́ло, he became seasick. Си́льный ве́тер закача́л дере́вья, a strong wind began to sway the trees. За-кач-а́ть-ся, *v.p.r.*, за-ка́ч-ивать-ся, *v.i.r.*, to reel, begin to rock; to become seasick. Он закача́лся и упа́л, he reeled and fell.

на-кач-а́ть, *v.p.*, на-ка́ч-ивать, *v.i.*, + *acc.*, + *gen.*, to pump up. Н. ши́ну,

to inflate a tire. Н. воды́ в резервуа́р, to pump water into a tank.

от-кач-а́ть, *v.p.*, от-ка́ч-ивать, *v.i.*, + *acc.*, to pump away. О. во́ду, to pump off water. О. уто́пленника, to revive a drowned man. От-ка́ч-ивать-ся, *v.i.r.*, от-ка́ч-ну́ть-ся, *v.p.r.*, to swing off, away, aside.

пере-кач-а́ть, *v.p.*, пере-ка́ч-ивать, *v.i.*, + *acc.*, to pump over. П. нефть из нали́вной ба́ржи в цисте́рну, to pump oil from a barge into a tank. Пере-ка́ч-ивание, *n.n.*, transferring of liquid from one container into another by means of a pump.

по-кач-а́ть, *v.p.*, + *acc.*, *see* кача́ть. П. на каче́лях (в лю́льке), to swing, rock in a swing (cradle). П. во́ду, to pump some water. П. голово́й, to shake one's head slightly. По-ка́ч-ивать, *v.i.*, + *acc.*, + *instr.*, to keep swinging lightly. По-кач-а́ть-ся, *v.p.r.*, по-ка́ч-ивать-ся, *v.i.r.*, to totter, walk unsteadily. Он шёл пока́чиваясь, he walked unsteadily. По-кач-ну́-ть, *v.p. smf.*, + *acc.*, to shake, unsettle. По-кач-ну́ть-ся, *v.p.r.*, to be shaken; totter suddenly. Он покачну́лся и упа́л на ступе́ни, he reeled and fell on the steps. Его́ дела́ покачну́лись, his business has taken a turn for the worse.

под-кач-а́ть, *v.p.*, под-ка́ч-ивать, *v.i.*, + *acc.*, to pump some more. П. воды́ в бак, to pump some more water into a tank. Не подкача́й! (*slang*), Don't spoil the game!

рас-кач-а́ть, *v.p.*, рас-ка́ч-ивать, *v.i.*, + *acc.*, to swing, set swinging; shake. Р. ма́ятник (каче́ли), to set a pendulum (swing) in motion. Его́ не раскача́ешь, (*colloq.*), you can't get him started. Рас-кач-а́ть-ся, *v.p.r.*, рас-ка́ч-ивать-ся, *v.i.r.*, to swing, sway, oscillate. Когда́ ещё он раскача́ется! (*fig.*, *colloq.*), he is in no hurry.

у-кач-а́ть, *v.p.*, у-ка́ч-ивать, *v.i.*, + *acc.*, to cause seasickness; rock to sleep. Её укача́ло на парохо́де, she became seasick on board ship. У. ребёнка, to rock a child to sleep. У-ка́ч-ивание, *n.n.*, rocking to sleep.

КИД-, КИ-, TOSSING, THROWING

кид-а́-ть, *v.i.*, ки́-ну-ть, *v.p.smf.*, + *acc.*, (*colloq.*), to throw, fling, cast, toss; abandon. К. дрова́ в по́греб, to throw wood into a cellar. К. полки́ в ата́ку, to throw troops into an attack. Кид-а́ть-ся, *v.i.r.*, ки́-нуть-ся, *v.p.r.*, to throw oneself, rush, bounce. Соба́ки кида́ются на прохо́жих, the dogs are attacking passers-by. Кинуться в объятия, to fling onself into someone's arms. Кид-а́ние, *n.n.*, throwing.

в-ки́-ну-ть, *v.p.smf.*, в-ки́д-ывать, *v.i.*, to throw in, into. В. мяч в окно́, to throw a ball into a window.

вы-ки́д-ывать, *v.i.*, вы́-ки-нуть, *v.p.smf.*, + *acc.*, to throw out, eject; exclude; miscarry. В. му́сор to throw out trash. В. флаг, to hoist (unfurl) a flag. В. шту́ку, to play a trick, prank. Вы-ки́д-ывать-ся, *v.i.r.*, вы́-ки-нуть-ся, *v.p.r.*, to be thrown out. Во вре́мя пожа́ра ве́щи выки́дываются из кварти́ры, during a fire things are thrown out of an apartment. В. бреду́ больно́й вы́кинулся из окна́, in his delirium, the patient threw himself out of the window. Вы́-кид-ыш, *n.m.*, miscarriage, abortion.

до-ки́д-ывать, *v.i.*, до-ки́-нуть, *v.p.smf.*, + *acc.*, to throw, fling as far as. Д. ка́мень до противополо́жного бе́рега, to throw a stone over to the opposite bank of a river.

за-ки́д-ывать, *v.i.*, за-ки́-нуть, *v.p.smf.*, + *acc.*, to throw beyond, behind. Де́ти закину́ли мяч за забо́р, the children threw the ball over the fence. З. мешо́к за́ спину, to throw a bag over one's shoulder. З. у́дочку, to cast a line; also, (*fig.*), З. слове́чко за кого́-либо (*idiom.*), to put in a good word for someone. За-ки́д-ывать-ся, *v.i.r.*, за-ки́-нуть-ся, *v.p.r.*, to fall back, to be thrown aside.

за-ки-да́ть, *v.p.*, за-ки́д-ывать, *v.i.* + *instr.*, to throw, shower upon. З. камня́ми, to stone; also, (*fig.*), З. я́му землёй, to fill a hole with earth. З. вопро́сами, to shower with questions.

за-про-ки́д-ывать, *v.i.*, за-про-ки́-нуть, *v.p.smf.*, + *acc.*, to throw back. З. го́лову, to toss, throw back one's head. За-про-ки́д-ывать-ся, *v.i.r.*, за-про-ки́-нуть-ся, *v.p.r.*, to be thrown back.

на-ки́д-ывать, *v.i.*, на-ки́-нуть, *v.p.smf.*, + *acc.*, to throw, fling on, upon. Н. плато́к на пле́чи, to throw a shawl over one's shoulders. Н. це́ну, to raise a price. На-ки́д-ываться, *v.i.r.*, на-ки́-нуть-ся, *v.p.r.*, to throw oneself on; fall on; attack. Он с интере́сом наки́нулся на кни́гу, he fell to reading the book with great interest. Н. на врага́, to attack an enemy. На-ки́д-ка, *n.f.*, cape; pillow cover. Наде́ть пальто́ в наки́дку, to throw one's coat over one's shoulders.

на-ки-да́ть, *v.p.*, на-ки́д-ывать, *v.i.*, + *gen.*, + *acc.*, to throw about, in quantity. Н. бума́ги на полу́, to litter

the floor with paper. Н. дров в пе́чку, to throw wood into a stove.

о-ки́д-ывать, *v.i.*, о-ки́-нуть, *v.p.smf.*, + *acc.*, to fling around; encircle. О. взгля́дом, to cast a glance. О. кого́-либо презри́тельным взгля́дом, to measure someone with a scornful eye.

о-про-ки́д-ывать, *v.i.*, о-про-ки́-нуть, *v.p.smf.*, + *acc.*, to upset; overthrow, overturn. О. ло́дку, to capsize a boat. О. ведро́, to tip over a pail. О-про-ки́д-ывать-ся, *v.i.r.*, о-про-ки́-нуть-ся, *v.p.r.*, to upset, overturn, keel over; capsize. Ча́йник опроки́нулся, the teapot overturned.

от-ки́д-ывать, *v.i.*, от-ки́-нуть, *v.p.smf.*, + *acc.*, to throw, fling off; reject, dismiss. О. ка́мни с доро́ги, to throw, remove stones from a road. О. одея́ло, to throw off a blanket. О. мы́сли, to dismiss thoughts. От-ки́д-ывать-ся, *v.i.r.*, от-ки́-нуть-ся, *v.p.r.*, to lean back. От-ки́д-ной, *adj.*, reversible. О-а́я кры́шка стола́, the top of a tilt-top table.

пере-ки́д-ывать, *v.i.*, + *acc.*, to fling over. Пере-ки-да́ть, *v.p.*, to fling down many objects. Пере-ки́-нуть, *v.p.smf.*, to throw, fling over, across, too far. П. мост че́рез реку́, to throw a bridge across a river. Пере-ки́д-ывать-ся, *v.i.r.*, пере-ки́-нуть-ся, *v.p.r.*, + *instr.*, to throw back and forth. П. взгля́дом, to exchange glances. П. слова́ми, to exchange words.

под-ки́д-ывать, *v.i.*, под-ки́-нуть, *v.p.smf.*, to throw under, in, up. П. дров в пе́чку, to add wood to a fire in a stove. П. мяч вверх, to throw a ball in the air. П. ребёнка, to leave a child on someone's doorstep. Под-ки́д-ыш, *n.f.*, foundling.

по-ки-да́ть, *v.i.*, по-ки́-нуть, *v.p.*, + *acc.*, to forsake, abandon, desert, leave. П. кого́-либо, в тру́дную мину́ту, to forsake someone at a difficult moment. П. ро́дину, to leave one's country. Му́жество поки́нуло его́, his courage deserted him. По-ки́-нутый, *adj. part. pass. past*, forsaken, forlorn. П. дом, an abandoned house.

при-ки́д-ывать, *v.i.*, при-ки́-нуть, *v.p.smf.*, + *acc.*, (*colloq.*), to throw in; add, reckon, estimate, approximate. П. це́ну-то add to a price. П. в уме́, to estimate mentally. При-ки́д-ывать-ся, *v.i.r.*, при-ки́-нуть-ся, *v.p.r.*, to be thrown in; feign, pretend. П. больны́м, to feign illness.

рас-ки́д-ывать, *v.i.*, рас-ки́-нуть, *v.p.smf.*, + *acc.*, to pitch; scatter, throw about, around. Р. се́ти, to cast nets; also,

(*fig.*), Р. умом, (*colloq.*), to consider.
рас-кид-а́ть, *v.p.,* раски́дывать, *v.i.,* to throw around, about. Р. кни́ги по всему́ столу́, to spread books all over a table. Рас-ки́д-ывать-ся, *v.i.r.,* раски́-нуть-ся, *v.p.r.,* to stretch, extend, spread. Р. на дива́не, to stretch oneself out on a sofa. Рас-ки́д-ывание, *n.n.,* spreading, scattering, unfolding. Рас-кид-ной, *adj.,* extensible, folding (*as* a chair, table).

с-ки́д-ывать, *v.i.,* с-ки́-нуть, *v.p.smf.,* (*colloq.*), to throw off. С. пальто́, to throw off one's coat. С. с цены́, to reduce the price, abate, deduct. С. снег с кры́ши, to shovel snow off a roof. С-ки́д-ка, *n.f.,* abatement, reduction. С. с цены́, reduction in price. Де́лать ски́дку, to make a reduction, give a discount.

с-кид-а́ть, *v.p.,* + *acc.,* to throw together into a pile. С. песо́к в ку́чу, to throw together a pile of sand.

КИП-, BOILING

кип-е́-ть, *v.i.,* + *instr.,* to boil; (*fig.*), bubble. Вода́ кипи́т ключо́м, the water is boiling over. К. гне́вом, to boil with rage. Рабо́та кипи́т, the work is in full swing. Кип-е́ние, *n.n.,* boiling, bubbling, effervescence. Температу́ра кипе́ния, boiling temperature. То́чка кипе́ния, boiling point. Кип-у́честь, *n.f.,* intensity, fervor. К. хара́ктера, fervor of temperament. Кип-у́чий, *adj.,* intense, fervent, effervescent. К-ая де́ятельность, intense activity. Кип-я́щий, *adj. part. act. pres.,* boiling. К-ая вода́, boiling water.

вс-кип-е́ть, *v.p.,* вс-кип-а́ть, *v.i.,* to come to a boiling point; boil up; fly into a rage; boil with indignation. Молоко́ вскипе́ло, the milk has come to a boil. Вс-кип-а́ние, *n.n.,* the action of coming to a boiling point.

вы́-кип-еть, *v.p.,* вы-кип-а́ть, *v.i.,* to boil down, away. Вода́ на си́льном огне́ ско́ро выкипа́ет, water boils away quickly over a hot flame. Вы́-кип-а́ние, *n.n.,* action of boiling away.

за-кип-е́ть, *v.p.,* за-кип-а́ть, *v.i.,* to begin to boil, bubble. Вода́ закипа́ет, the water is beginning to boil. Де́ло закипе́ло, the work was in full swing.

на-кип-е́ть, *v.p.,* на-кип-а́ть, *v.i.,* to form a scum, scale. Накипа́ет пе́на, scum is forming. В нём накипе́ла зло́ба, he built up a feeling of resentment. На́-кип-ь, *n.f.,* scum (on liquid); scale on boiler, kettle. Очи́стить котёл от на́кипи, to scour a boiler, kettle.

пере-кип-е́ть, *v.p.,* пере-кип-а́ть, *v.i.,* to overboil. Суп перекипе́л, the soup has boiled too long.

по-кип-е́ть, *v.p.* to boil for a while. Пусть суп покипи́т ещё немно́го, let the soup boil for a while.

про-кип-е́ть, *v.p.,* про-кип-а́ть, *v.i.,* to boil thoroughly.

у-кип-е́ть, *v.p.,* у-кип-а́ть, *v.i.,* to reduce by boiling. В ча́йнике укипа́ет вода́ наполови́ну, the water in the tea kettle is being reduced by half through boiling. Мя́со хорошо́ укипе́ло, the meat is well cooked.

кип-ят-и́ть, *v.i.,* вс-кип-яти́ть, *v.p.,* + *acc.,* to boil; bring to boiling point. К. во́ду (молоко́), to boil water (milk). Кип-яти́ть-ся, *v.i.r.,* to be boiled; (*fig.*), to be excited, angry. Вс-кип-яти́ть-ся, *v.p.r.,* (*colloq.*), to get excited. Кип-ято́к, *n.m.,* boiling water. Кип-яти́ль-ник, *n.m.,* boiler. Кип-яче́ние, *n.n.,* boiling. Кип-ячёный, *adj.,* boiled. К-ая вода́, boiling water.

вс-кип-яти́ть, *v.p.,* + *acc.,* (*colloq.*), to bring to a boil. В. молоко́, to bring milk to a boil.

по-кип-яти́ть, *v.p.,* + *acc.,* to boil for a while. П. молоко́ подо́льше, to boil milk for a while longer.

про-кип-яти́ть, *v.p.,* + *acc.,* to boil thoroughly, through. П. как сле́дует во́ду (суп), to boil water (soup) thoroughly.

рас-кип-е́ть-ся, *v.p.r.,* (*colloq.*), to reach a full boil. Ча́йник раскипе́лся на плите́, the kettle reached a full boil on the range.

рас-кип-яти́ть-ся, *v.p.,* *see* раскипе́ться, Он раскипе́лся (раскипяти́лся) и на всех накрича́л, he boiled with rage and scolded everybody.

с-кип-е́ть-ся, *v.p.r.,* с-кип-а́ть-ся, *v.i.r.,* to curdle. Молоко́ скипе́лось, the milk has curdled.

КИС- (КИС-Л-), КВАС-, КВАШ-, ACID, ACIDITY, SOURING

кис-л-ота́, *n.f.,* acid. Лимо́нная к., citric (lemon) acid. Азо́тная к., nitric acid. Се́рная к., sulphuric acid. Ки́с-лый, *adj.,* sour, acid. К-ая капу́ста, sauerkraut. К-ая улы́бка, sour smile. К. вид, (*fig.*), sour, long face. Кис-л-ова́тость, *n.f.,* acidulousness. Кис-л-ова́тый, *adj.,* acidulous, somewhat acid. Кис-л-о́тность, *n.f.,* acidity. Кис-л-о́тный, *adj.,* acid. Кис-л-о-ро́д, *n.m.,* oxygen. Кис-л-о-ро́дный, *adj.,* oxygenous. Кис-л-о-сла́дкий, *adj.,* sweet-sour. Кис-л-я́й, *n.m.,* (*colloq.*), moping fellow.

Кис-л-я́тина, *n.f.*, anything very sour.
ки́с-ну-ть, *v.i.*, to turn sour; (*fig.*), mope.
за-ки́с-нуть, *v.p.*, за-кис-а́ть, *v.i.*, to turn sour; (*fig.*), grow rusty. Те́сто заки́сло, the dough has turned sour. Он совсе́м заки́с в э́той глуши́, he has grown stale in this remote place. За́кис-ь, *n.f.*, (*chem.*), oxide. З. желе́за, iron oxide.

о-ки́с-нуть, *v.p.*, о-кис-а́ть, *v.i.*, to sour, turn sour, tarnish, oxidize. О-кис-а́ние, *n.n.*, souring, oxidization. О́-кис-ь, *n.f.*, oxide. О. ка́льция, calcium oxide. О. углеро́да, carbon oxide.

о-ки́с-л-и́ть, *v.p.*, о-кис-л-я́ть, *v.i.*, + *acc.*, to oxidize, sour. О-кис-л-е́ние, *n.n.*, souring, oxidization. О-кис-л-ённый, *adj. part. pass. past,* soured, oxidized.

пере-ки́с-нуть, *v.p.*, пере-кис-а́ть, *v.i.*, to become exceedingly sour. Пере-кис-л-и́ть, *v.p.*, пере-кис-л-я́ть, *v.i.*, to acidify to excess. П. щи, to make soup too sour. Пе́ре-кис-ь, *n.f.*, peroxide. П. водоро́да, hydrogen peroxide.

про-ки́с-нуть, *v.p.*, про-кис-а́ть, *v.i.*, to turn completely sour, clabber, curdle. Про-ки́с-лый, *adj.*, rank, completely sour. Про-ки́с-ший, *adj. part. act. past,* rank. П-ее молоко́, clabber.

рас-ки́с-нуть, *v.p.*, рас-кис-а́ть, *v.i.*, (*fig.*), to be depressed. Совсе́м раски́с от жары́, he has lost all his energy because of the heat.

рас-кис-л-и́ть, *v.p.*, рас-кис-л-я́ть, *v.i.*, to deoxidize.

с-ки́с-нуть, *v.p.*, с-кис-а́ть, *v.i.*, to turn sour, curdle. Молоко́ ски́сло, the milk has turned sour.

кис-е́ль, *n.m.*, jelly-like dish made of farina, fruit-juice and sugar. Клю́квенный к., cranberry jelly. Страна́ с моло́чными ре́ками и кисе́льными берега́ми, (*fig.*), a land flowing with milk and honey. Она́ мне деся́тая вода́ на кисе́ле, (*colloq.*), she is a very remote relative of mine.

квас, *n.m.*, kvas (a type of fermented drink). Квас-ни́к, *n.m.*, kvas-brewer; kvas vendor. Квас-но́й, *adj.*, pertaining to kvas. Квас-цы́, *n.pl.*, alum. Квасцо́вый, *adj.*, aluminous. К. заво́д, alum works.

ква́с-ить, ква́ш-у, *v.i.*, + *acc.*, to make sour; leaven. К. капу́сту, to make sauerkraut. К. молоко́, to curdle milk. Ква́с-ить-ся, *v.i.r.*, to ferment. Ква́ш-а, *n.f.*, leavening; leavened dough. Ква́ш-ение, *n.n.*, leavening. Кваш-ня́, *n.f.*, a dough trough, kneading trough. Ква́ш-еный, *adj.*, sour, fermented, leavened. К-ая капу́ста, sauerkraut.

за-ква́с-ить, *v.p.*, за-кваш-ивать, *v.i.*, + *acc.*, to leaven; add yeast. За-ква́с-ка, *n.f.*, leavening; yeast; (*fig.*), disposition, inclination. Видна́ хоро́шая з., (*fig., colloq.*), innate good qualities are evident. За-кваш-енный, *adj. part. pass. past,* leavened, raised.

пере-ква́с-ить, *v.p.*, пере-кваш-ивать, *v.i.*, + *acc.*, to use an excess of yeast.

рас-ква́с-ить, *v.p.*, рас-кваш-ивать, *v.i.*, + *acc.*, (*colloq.*), to squash, make into a pulp. Р. себе́ нос, to smash one's nose.

КЛАД-, КЛАС-, КЛАЖ-, PLACEMENT, CONCEALMENT

клад, *n.m.*, treasure. Найти́ к. зо́лота, to find gold treasure. Это не челове́к, а клад, this man is a treasure. Кла́д-бище, *n.m.*, cemetery, burial ground, graveyard, churchyard. Клад-би́щенский, *adj.*, pertaining to a cemetery. Кла́д-ка, *n.f.*, laying. Ка́менная к., masonry. Кирпи́чная к., brickwork. Клад-ова́я, *n.f.*, pantry, larder, storeroom. Клад-овщи́к, *n.m.*, store-keeper. Кла́д-чик, *n.m.*, workman who piles up logs, boards, rails, etc. Кла́д-ь, *n.f.*, load.

клас-ть, *v.i.*, по-лож-и́ть, *v.p.*, + *acc.*, to lay, deposit, put, place, set: *see* лог-. К. де́ньги в банк, to deposit money in a bank. К. в карма́н, to put in a pocket. К. но́гу на́ ногу, to cross one's legs. К. фунда́мент, to lay a foundation. Кла́с-ть-ся, *v.i.r.*, *used in 3d pers only,* to be laid, placed, put. Де́ньги кладу́тся в банк под проце́нты, money is deposited in a bank to gather interest.

в-клад, *n.m.*, deposit, investment. В. в банк, bank deposit. Це́нный в. в нау́ку, valuable contribution to science. В-клад-ка, *n.f.*, insertion, inserted page. В-клад-но́й, *adj.*, pertaining to inserting, depositing. В. лист, inserted page. В-кла́д-чик, *n.m.*, investor, depositor. В-кла́д-ывание, *n.n.*, inserting, laying in, placing in, enclosing. В-кла́д-ыш, *n.n.*, (*tech.*), bush.

в-кла́д-ывать, *v.i.*, в-лож-и́ть, *v.p.*, + *acc.*, to put in, into; enclose; invest. В-кла́д-ывать-ся, *v.i.r.*, to be put in, inserted, invested, deposited.

вы-кла́д-ывать, *v.i.*, вы́-лож-ить, *v.p.*, + *acc.*, to lay out, take out. В. гря́дку дёрном, to edge a flower-bed with turf. В. кирпичо́м, to face with brick. В. ве́щи на стол, to lay things out on a table. Вы́-клад-ка, *n.f.*, (*math.*), calculation, computation.

до-кла́д-ывать, *v.i.,* до-лож-и́ть, *v.p.,* + *dat.,* о + *prep.,* to report, announce, add. Проси́ть доложи́ть о себе́, to send in one's name. До-кла́д, *n.m.,* report, paper. Без докла́да не входи́ть, visitors are requested not to enter without being announced. До-клад-на́я запи́ска, memorandum, report. До-кла́д-чик, *n.m.,* lecturer, speaker.

за-кла́д-ывать, *v.i.,* за-лож-и́ть, *v.p.,* + *acc.,* to lay a foundation; to pawn, mortgage; to harness (horses); to feel stuffed up; to put a marker in a book. З. дом, to mortgage a house. З. зда́ние, to lay a foundation for a house. З. лошаде́й в экипа́ж, to harness horses to a carriage. У меня́ у́ши заложи́ло, my ears are stuffed up. За-кла́д-ывать-ся, *v.i.,* to be pawned; harnessed. За-кла́д, *n.m.,* mortgage, pawn; bet, wager, stake. Би́ться об з., to wager, bet. За-кла́д-ка, *n.f.,* see за-кла́д, bookmark; harnessing. З. фунда́мента, laying of foundations. За-клад-на́я, *n.f.,* mortgage (the document). За-кла́д-чик, *n.m.,* mortgager.

на-кла́д-ывать, *v.i.,* на-лож-и́ть, *v.p.,* + *acc.,* to lay, put on. Н. воз, to load a cart. Н. швы на ра́ну, to suture a wound. На-кла́д-ывать-ся, *v.i.r.,* to be applied, loaded. На-кла́д-ка, *n.f.,* (*tech.*), lap. Чай в накла́дку, (*colloq.*), tea with sugar in it. На-клад-на́я, *n.f.,* invoice. Н-ы́е расхо́ды, overhead expenses. На-кла́д-но, *adv.,* (*colloq.*), costly. На-кла́д-ывание, *n.n.,* laying on, placing on, loading. Остава́ться в накла́де, (*colloq.*), to be the loser.

об-кла́д-ывать, *v.i.,* об-лож-и́ть, *v.p.,* + *acc.,* + *instr.,* to lay something around, cover with. О. печку кирпичо́м, to face a stove with brick. Об-кла́д-ывать-ся, *v.i.r,* to be faced, covered with; taxed. Населе́ние обкла́дывается подохо́дным нало́гом, income tax is levied from the population.

о-кла́д, *n.m.,* tax; salary; frame. О. лица́, contour of a face. Его́ ме́сячный о.— 400 рубле́й, his monthly salary is 400 rubles. Окла́ды ико́н, icon frames. О-клад-но́й, *adj.,* pertaining to taxes, salaries. О-кла́д-истый, *adj., used in expression:* О-ая борода́, large, thick beard.

от-кла́д-ывать, *v.i.,* от-лок-и́ть, *v.p.,* + *acc.,* to lay aside, put away; delay; postpone; save. О. отъе́зд, to postpone a departure. О. на чёрный день, to lay aside for an emergency, against a rainy day (*as* money). О. в до́лгий я́щик, (*idiom., fig.*), to postpone in-

definitely. От-кла́д-ывать-ся, *v.i.r.,* to be postponed. Мой отъе́зд откла́дывается на неде́лю, my departure has been postponed a week. От-кла́д-ывание, *n.n.,* putting off, postponement, laying aside; delaying.

пере-кла́д-ывать, *v.i.,* пере-лож-и́ть, *v.p.,* + *acc.,* to interlay; change from one location to another. П. печь, to reset a stove. Пере-кла́д-ывать-ся, *v.i.r.,* + *instr.,* to be interlaid; be changed from one place to another. Пере-кла́д-ина, *n.f.,* cross-beam. Ехать на перекладны́х, (*obs.*), to travel by postchaise.

по-клад-а́-ть, *v.i., only in expression:* Рабо́тать не покладая рук, to work like a Trojan. По-клад-истый, *adj.,* compliant, yielding, easy-going. П. хара́ктер (челове́к), agreeable disposition, person.

по-кла́ж-а, *n.f.,* load, luggage.

под-кла́д-ывать, *v.i.,* под-лож-и́ть, *v.p.,* + *acc.,* + *gen.,* to lay under; pad. П. ва́ту в пальто́, to interline a coat. П. то́плива, to add fuel. Под-кла́д-ывать-ся, *v.i.r.,* to be padded; be added. В зимнее пальто́ подкла́дывается ва́та, a winter coat is padded (interlined) with cotton. Под-кла́дка, *n.f.,* lining. Де́лать пиджа́к на подла́дке, to make a jacket with a lining. Кака́я тут подкла́дка? What is behind this? Под-кла́д-очный, *adj.,* pertaining to lining, padding. П. материа́л, padding, lining. Под-кла́д-ывание, *n.n.,* padding, lining. Под-клад-но́й, *adj.,* pertaining to lining. П-о́е су́дно, bedpan.

при-кла́д-ывать, *v.i.,* при-лож-и́ть, *v.p.,* + *acc.,* к + *dat.,* to add; apply; enclose. П. печа́ть, to apply a seal. П. ру́ку, to set one's hand. При-кла́д-ывать-ся, *v.i.r.,* к + *dat.,* to be applied; take aim; kiss. При-кла́д-ывание, *n.n.,* application. При-кла́д, *n.m.,* butt (of a rifle); trimmings (sewing). П. для пла́тья, accessories, trimmings for a dress. При-клад-но́й, *adj.,* applied. П-ая нау́ка, applied sciences.

про-кла́д-ывать, *v.i.,* про-лож-и́ть, *v.p.,* + *acc.,* to lay railway tracks, roads; interlay. П. кни́гу бе́лыми ли́стами, to interleave a book. П. желе́зную доро́гу, to build a railway. П. себе́ доро́гу, to work one's way. Про-кла́д-ывать-ся, *v.i.r.,* to be laid, padded, interleaved. Про-кла́д-ка, *n.f.,* packing, stuffing, padding; laying. П. ка́беля, laying of a cable. П. труб, laying of pipes.

рас-кла́д-ывать, *v.i.,* раз-лож-и́ть, *v.p.,* + *acc.,* to spread, lay out; unpack. Р.

огóнь, to build a fire. Р. кáрты, to lay out cards. Рас-клáд-ывать-ся, *v.i.r.*, рас-лож-йть-ся, *v.p.r.*, to be unpacked, laid out. Рас-клáд-ка, *n.f.*, distribution, apportionment, allotment. Р. податéй, assessment of taxes.

с-клáд-ывать, *v.i.*, с-лож-йть, *v.p.*, + *acc.*, to put, lay together; fold; add, sum up. С. дровá в сарáй, to pile up wood in a shed. С. матéрию, to fold material, cloth. С. пéсни, to compose songs. С-клáд-ывать-ся, *v.i.r.*, to be folded, stacked; composed. С-клад, *n.m.*, (с-клáд-ы, *pl.*), warehouse, storage, storeroom; turn; habit. На склáде, in storage, in stock. Сдать в с. на хранéние, to put in storage. Склад умá, habit of mind; mentality. Ни склáду, ни лáду, (*saying*) neither rhyme, nor reason. С-клáд-ка, *n.f.*, tuck, fold, crease, pleat. Дéлать склáдки, to make tucks, folds, creases, pleats. Юбка в склáдках, pleated skirt. С-клад-нóй, *adj.*, folding, portable. С. стол (стул), folding table (chair). С-áя кровáть, folding cot, campbed. С-клáд-ность, *n.f.*, harmony, coherence. С. рéчи, coherence of a speech. С-клáд-ный, *adj.*, harmonious, coherent. Несклáдно стрóен, да крéпко сшит, (*saying*), not a handsome figure, but sturdily built. С-клáдочный, *adj.*, pertaining to storage. С-ое мéсто, storage place. С-клáд-чина, *n.f.*, collection. Дéлать чтó-либо в склáдчину, to chip in. С-клад-ы, *n.pl.*, syllables. Читáть по складáм, to read by syllables; syllabize.

у-клáд-ывать, *v.i.*, у-лож-йть, *v.p.*, + *acc.*, to pack, pack up, stow. У. ребёнка в постéль, to put a child to bed. У. железнодорóжный путь, to lay rails. У-клáд-ывать-ся, *v.i.r.*, у-лож-йть-ся, *v.p.r.*, to lie down, go to bed; be packed, stowed; pack up. Это не уклáдывается в моём сознáнии, I can hardly believe it. Я уже уложúлась, I have already packed my things. У-клад, *n.m.*, usage, trend of life. У-клáд-ка, *n.f.*, packing, laying. У-клáд-ывание, *n.n.*, packing. У-клáд-чик, *n.m.*, у-клáд-чица, *n.f.*, packer.

КЛЕВ-, КЛЮ-, КЛЮВ-, BEAK, PECKING

клев-á-ть, клю-ю, *v.i.*, + *acc.*, + *instr.*, to peck, pick, bite, nibble; *see* клюнуть. Петýх клюёт зёрна, the rooster is pecking at the grain. Сегóдня рыба не клюёт, the fish are not biting today. К. нóсом, (*fig.*), to nod, be sleepy. Клёв, *n.m.*, biting, nibbling. Хорóший к., good fishing.

вы-клев-ать, *v.p.*, вы-клёв-ывать, *v.i.*, + *acc.*, to peck out. Птицы выклевали весь овёс, the birds have pecked out and eaten all the oats.

за-клев-áть, *v.p.*, за-клёв-ывать, *v.i.*, + *acc.*, to bite, peck at, pick. Ворóны заклевáли гóлубя, the crows have pecked the pigeon to death.

ис-клев-áть, *v.p.*, ис-клёв-ывать, *v.i.*, + *acc.*, to eat completely by pecking. Кýры исклевáли всё зернó, the chickens have eaten all the grain.

на-клёв-ывать-ся, *v.i.*, (*colloq.*), used in 3d pers. only, to bite, appear, turn up. Ничегó не наклёвывается, (*fig.*), nothing seems to be turning up.

об-клев-áть, *v.p.*, об-клёв-ывать, *v.i.*, to peck all over; *see* клевáть.

по-клев-áть, *v.p.*, по-клёв-ывать, *v.i.*, + *acc.*, to peck at slightly. Воробьй поклевáли все вишни, the sparrows have pecked at all the cherries.

рас-клев-áть, *v.p.*, рас-клёв-ывать, *v.i.*, + *acc.*, to peck open; open by pecking. Кýрица расклевáла подсóлнух, the hen has pecked open the sunflower.

с-клев-áть, *v.p.* с-клёв-ывать, *v.i.*, + *acc.*, to peck off. Рыба склевáла червякá с крючкá, the fish bit the worm off the hook.

клюв, *n.m.*, beak, bill. У орлá óстрый к., the eagle has a sharp beak. Клюв-о-обрáзный, *adj.*, beaklike.

клю-ну-ть, *v.p.smf.*, *see* клевáть.

КЛЕВЕТ-, КЛЕВЕЩ-, CALUMNY

клевет-á-ть, клевещ-ý, *v.i.*, на-клеветáть, *v.p.*, на + *acc.*, to calumniate, slander, defame. Не клевещй на невúнного, do not slander an innocent man. Клевет-á, *n.f.*, calumny, slander, defamation. За клеветý привлекáют к судý, for slander one can be taken to court. Взвестú клеветý на когó-нибудь, to slander someone. Клеветнúк, *n.m.*, calumniator, slanderer. Клевет-нúческий, *adj.*, slanderous, calumnious; injurious, libelous. К-ая кампáния, campaign of calumny.

о-клевет-áть, *v.p.*, + *acc.*, to slander, calumniate, defame. *see* клеветáть.

КЛИК-, КЛИЧ-, КЛИЩ-, КРИК-, CALLING, CALL, SCREAM

клик, *n.m.*, (*poet.*), call. Рáдостный к., a joyous call.

клик-á-ть, клúч-у, *v.i.*, + *acc.*, (*colloq.*), to call. Хозяйка клúчет кур, the housewife is calling the hens.

клúк-ну-ть, *v.p.*, to call. К. клич, to

rouse a community to action; send out a call. Клич, *n.m.*, call, cry, shout. Боевóй к., war cry. Клич-ка, *n.f.*, name, nickname. Собáка с клúчкой Барбóс, a dog with the name Barboss.

вос-клúк-нуть, *v.p.smf.,* вос-клиц-áть, *v.i.,* to exclaim, cry. Вос-клиц-áние, *n.n.,* exclamation, ejaculation. Раздалúсь рáдостные восклицáния, joyous exclamations could be heard. Восклиц-áтельный, *adj.,* exclamatory. В. знак, (*gram.*), exclamation mark.

вы́-клик-нуть, *v.p.smf.,* вы-клик-áть, *v.i.,* + *acc.,* to shout out, call by name. В. по спúску, to call the roll.

на-клúк-ать, *v.p.,* на-клик-áть, *v.i.,* + *acc.,* to call down upon oneself. Н. на себя́ бедý, (*colloq*), to invite misfortune.

о-клúк-нуть, *v.p.,* о-клик-áть, *v.i.,* + *acc.,* to call by name; hail. О. прохóжего, to hail a passerby. Ó-клик, *n.m.,* call, hail.

от-клúк-нуть-ся, *v.p.r.smf.,* от-клик-áть-ся, *v.i.r.,* на + *acc.,* to respond, answer. О. на призы́в, to respond to a call, an appeal. Óт-клик, *n.m.,* response, echo. Óтклики в печáти, press comments.

пере-клúк-нуть, *v.p.,* пере-клик-áть, *v.i.,* + *acc.,* to call over; call the roll. П. присýтствующих, to call out the names of those present. Пере-клúк-нуть-ся, *v.p.r.,* пере-клик-áть-ся, *v.i.r.,* to call back and forth. П. в лесý, to shout to one another in the woods. Пере-клúч-ка, *n.f.,* rollcall. Дéлать переклúчку, to call the roll.

с-клик-áть, *v.i.,* + *acc.,* to call together, convoke. Кóлокол скликáл прихожáн, the bell called the parishioners together. С-клик-áть-ся, *v.i.r.,* to be called together, convoked. Нарóд скликáется на плóщадь, the people are being summoned to the square.

крик, *n.m.,* shout, cry, call, scream, shriek. К. отчáяния, scream of despair. Крúки о пóмощи, call for help. Послéдний к. мóды, the latest fashion. Крик-лúвость, *n.f.,* vociferousness. Крик-лúвый, *adj.,* vociferous, clamorous, loud-voiced, noisy. К. гóлос, a loud voice. Крик-лúво, *adv.,* noisily, loudly. К. одевáться, to dress ostentatiously, pretentiously, loudly. Крик-ýн, *n.m.,* крик-ýнья, *n.f.,* noisy person.

крúк-ну-ть, *v.p.smf.,* крич-áть, *v.i.,* to shout, cry out, call, scream.

вс-крúк-нуть, *v.p.smf.,* вс-крúк-ивать, *v.i.,* to cry out, utter a cry. С испýгу онá вскрúкнула, she screamed with fright. Вс-крúк-ивание, *n.n.,* shrieking, screaming, crying out.

вы́-крик-нуть, *v.p.smf.,* вы-крúк-ивать, *v.i.,* + *acc.,* to cry out, yell. Вы́крикнули пя́тый нóмер, number five was called out. Вы́-крик, *n.m.,* cry, yell. Вы-крúк-ивание, *n.n.,* crying out, shouting. Вы́-крич-ать-ся, *v.p.r.,* вы-крúк-ивать-ся, *v.i.r.,* (*colloq.*), shout to cry oneself out. Ребёнок вы́кричался и утúх, the child has shouted himself out and has quieted down. Отдéльные словá выкрúкивались орáторами, the speakers were shouting out certain of their words.

о-крúк-ивать, *v.p.,* о-крúк-ивать, *v.i.,* + *acc.,* to call, shout, cry. О. знакóмого на ýлице, to call a friend in the street. Ó-крик, *n.m.,* shout, cry. Грýбый о., harsh shout; rude cry.

по-крúк-ивать, *v.i.,* (*colloq.*), на + *acc.,* to shout at someone; scold. П. на когó-либо, to shout at someone. Отéц иногдá покрúкивал на детéй, from time to time the father scolded the children.

при-крúк-ивать, *v.i.,* при-крúк-нуть, *v.p.,* на + *acc.,* to raise one's voice. П. на шалунá, to scold a mischievous boy.

крич-á-ть, *v.i.,* + *acc.,* на + *acc.,* о + *prep.,* to shout, cry out, call out, scream, roar, clamor. Пронзúтельно к., to scream piercingly. К. на когó-либо, to scold someone. Газéты кричáт о войнé, the newspapers are warmongering. Крич-áщий, *adj. part. act. pres.,* (*fig.*), loud, gaudy, flashy. К. гáлстук, a loud tie.

вс-крич-áть, *v.p.,* (*obs.*), to shriek. Вс-крик, *n.m.,* shriek, sudden scream. Вс-крúк-ивание, *n.n.,* shrieking, screaming, crying out.

до-крич-áть-ся, *v.p.r.,* (*colloq.*), + *gen.,* to shout until. Д. до хрипоты́, to shout oneself hoarse.

за-крич-áть, *v.p.,* от + *gen.,* to cry out.

на-крич-áть, *v.p.,* на + *acc.,* to scold violently. Мать накричáла на ребёнка, the mother scolded the child violently. На-крич-áть-ся, *v.p.r.,* (*colloq.*), to be tired out from shouting.

пере-крич-áть, *v.p.,* пере-крúк-ивать, *v.i.,* + *acc.,* to outvoice, outshout, talk down. П. спóрящих, to shout down those who are arguing.

про-крич-áть, *v.p.,* + *acc.,* to cry out, wear out one's voice. Гдé-то прокричáл петýх, somewhere a cock crowed. П. гóлос, to lose one's voice from shouting. П. ýши, (*fig.*), to wear out by praising, advertising.

рас-крич-áть-ся, *v.p.r.,* на + *acc.,* to shout, scold, abuse, bellow at. Что вы на меня раскричались? Why are you shouting at me so?

КЛОН-, КЛАН-, INCLINE, BEND, BOW

клон-и́-ть, *v.i.,* + *acc.,* to lean, incline; bend. Ве́тер кло́нит верху́шки дере́вьев, the wind is bending the tops of the trees. Меня́ кло́нит ко сну, I am sleepy. Куда́ он кло́нит? What is he driving at? Клон-и́ть-ся, *v.i.r.,* к + *dat.,* to incline, verge, bend, slope. День кло́нится к ве́черу, the day is drawing toward evening. Со́лнце кло́нится к за́паду, the sun is setting.

на-клон-и́-ть, *v.p.,* на-клон-я́ть, *v.i.,* + *acc.,* to incline, lean. Н. го́лову, to bend one's head. На-клон-и́ть-ся, *v.p.r.,* на-клон-я́ть-ся, *v.i.r.,* to incline, lean, stoop. И́вы наклоня́лись над водо́й, the willows were bending over the water. На-кло́н, *n.m.,* slope, declivity, inclination. Бревно́ скати́лось по накло́ну, the log rolled down the slope. На-клон-е́ние, *n.n.,* inclination; (*gram.*), mood. Повели́тельное н., (*gram.*), imperative mood. На-кло́н-ность, *n.f.,* inclination, proclivity, leaning, tendency, bent. Проявля́ть н. к уедине́нию, to show a tendency towards solitude. Ду́рные накло́нности, bad inclinations. На-кло́н-ный, *adj.,* inclined, sloping. Н-ая пло́скость, inclined plane. На-кло́н-но, *adv.,* sideways, slopingly.

от-клон-и́ть, *v.p.,* от-клон-я́ть, *v.i.,* + *acc.,* to decline, avert, deviate. Измене́ние пого́ды отклони́ло стре́лку баро́метра, a change in the weather caused the needle of the barometer to deviate. О. предложе́ние, refusal of an offer. От-клон-и́ть-ся, *v.p.r.,* от-клон-я́ть-ся, *v.i.r.,* to digress, deviate, depart from. О. от те́мы разгово́ра, to depart from the subject of a conversation. От-клон-е́ние, *n.n.,* act of deviating; digression, deviation.

по-клон-и́ть-ся, *v.p.r.,* + *dat., see* кла́няться. П. кому́-либо, to greet, bow, salute. Поклони́тесь ва́шей сестре́, please remember me to your sister. По-кло́н, *n.m.,* bow, greeting, salute. Переда́йте п. ва́шей ма́тери, my compliments to your mother. Посыла́ть п., to send one's greetings. По-клон-я́ть-ся, *v.i.r.,* + *dat.,* to worship, idolize, adore, admire. П. ге́нию Толсто́го, to admire Tolstoy's genius. По-клон-е́ние, *n.n.,* worship, adoration. По-кло́н-ник, *n.m.,* admirer, fan.

пре-клон-и́ть, *v.p.,* пре-клон-я́ть, *v.i.,* + *acc.,* to bend down, bow. П. го́лову, to bend one's head. П. коле́ни, to kneel. Пре-клон-и́ть-ся, *v.p.r.,* пре-клон-я́ть-

ся, *v.i.r.,* перед + *instr.,* to admire; submit; worship; П. пе́ред тала́нтом, to admire talent. Пре-клон-е́ние, *n.n.,* admiration, worship. Пре-кло́н-ный, *adj., in expression*: П. во́зраст, прекло́нные лета́, extreme old age. Не-пре-кло́н-ность, *n.f.,* inflexibility, rigidity. Не-пре-кло́н-ный, *adj.,* inflexible, rigid, unbending. Н. хара́ктер, rigid disposition. Н-ая во́ля, unbending will.

при-клон-и́ть, *v.p.,* при-клон-я́ть, *v.i.,* + *acc.,* to bend down. П. ве́тви де́рева к земле́, to bend the branches of a tree toward the ground. Не́где го́лову приклони́ть, (*express.*), nowhere to lay one's head.

с-клон-и́ть, *v.p.,* с-клон-я́ть, *v.i.,* на + *acc.,* to incline, bend; (*gram.*), decline. С. кого́-нибудь на свою́ сто́рону, to win someone over to one's side. Склоня́ть и́мя существи́тельное, to decline a noun. С-клон-и́ть-ся, *v.p.r.,* с-клон-я́ть-ся, *v.i.r.,* to be disposed, inclined, declined. День склоня́ется к ве́черу, the day is coming to an end. Мать склони́лась над ребёнком, the mother bent over her child. С-клон, *n.m.,* slope, side (*as* of mountain). Отло́гий с., gentle slope. На скло́не лет, in his declining years. С-клон-е́ние, *n.n.,* (*gram.*), declension. С. существи́тельных, declension of nouns. С-кло́н-ность, *n.f.,* inclination, propensity, bent, leaning; taste, penchant. С. к заболева́нию, susceptibility to illness. Име́ть с. к му́зыке, to have a bent for music. С-кло́н-ный, *adj.,* inclined, disposed, given to. С. к полноте́, inclined to corpulence. Я скло́нен приня́ть его́ реше́ние, I am inclined to accept his decision. С-клон-я́емость, *n.f.,* (*gram.*), declineability. С-клон-я́емый, *adj. part. pass. pres.,* declineable. С-ые ча́сти ре́чи, declineable parts of speech.

благо-с-кло́н-ность, *n.f.,* favor, benevolence. Заслужи́ть чью-либо б., to earn someone's favor. По́льзоваться чьей-либо благоскло́нностью, to be in someone's good graces. Благо-с-кло́н-ный, *adj.,* favorable, benevolent. Благо-с-кло́н-но, *adv.,* favorably, benevolently. Относи́ться б., to favor. Смотре́ть на что́-либо б., to view something with favor.

у-клон-и́ть-ся, *v.p.,* у-клон-я́ть-ся, *v.i.,* от + *gen.,* to evade, avoid, shirk, shun; deviate. У. от до́лга, to evade one's duty. У. от отве́та, to evade a question. У. от те́мы, to digress. У-кло́н, *n.m.,* declivity, slope; gradient, deviation. У-клон-е́ние, *n.n.,* deviation, aberration, evasion, avoiding; digression. У. от генера́льной ли́нии па́ртии, deviation from the general party line. У-клон-и́зм, *n.m.*, (*recent*), deviationism. У-клон-и́ст, *n.m.*, (*recent*), deviationist. У-кло́н-чивость, *n.f.*, evasiveness. У-кло́н-чивый, *adj.*, evasive. У. отве́т, evasive answer. У-кло́н-чиво, *adv.*, evasively. Не-у-кло́н-ный, *adj.*, steady, steadfast. Н-ая реши́мость, steady determination. Не-у-кло́н-но, *adv.*, steadily. Н. стреми́ться к чему́-либо, to strive steadily toward something.

кла́н-ять-ся, *v.i.r.*, по-клон-и́ть-ся, *v.p.r.*, + *dat.*, to bow, greet; send one's compliments; to humiliate oneself. Кла́няйтесь от меня́ друзья́м, remember me kindly to your friends. Переста́ть к. (не к.), to refuse to recognize, snub, ignore.

от-кла́н-ять-ся, *v.p.r.*, от-кла́н-ивать-ся, *v.i.r.*, to take one's leave. Го́сти откла́нялись и уе́хали, the guests took their leave and departed.

КЛЮЧ-, KEY, SPRING

ключ, *n.m.*, key; spring, fountain; (*mus.*), key, clef. К. к замку́, key to a lock. Подзе́мные ключи́, underground springs. Бить ключо́м, (*fig.*), spout, eject forcibly. Кипе́ть ключо́м, (*fig.*), boil over. Ключ-ево́й, *adj.*, pertaining to a spring. К-а́я вода́, spring water. Ключ-а́рь, (*eccl.*), sacristan. Ключ-ник, *n.m.*, клю́ч-ница, *n.f.*, steward, stewardess; housekeeper. Клю́ч-ик, *n.m.*, a little key. К. от часо́в, watch key. Ключ-и́ца, *n.f.*, (*anat.*), clavicle, collar-bone. Ключ-и́чный, *adj.*, (*anat.*), clavicular. У-клю́ч-ина, *n.f.*, rowlock, thole, tholepin.

в-клю́ч-и́-ть, *v.p.*, в-ключ-а́ть, *v.i.*, + *acc.*, to include. В. ток, to switch on power, make contact. В. мото́р (газ), to switch on a motor (turn on the gas). В. что́-либо в програ́мму, to include something in a program. В. в усло́вия догово́ра, to include in the terms of a treaty. В-ключ-и́ть-ся, *v.p.r.*, в-ключ-а́ть-ся, *v.i.r.*, to be included, get into contact, be switched. В. в соцсоревнова́ние, (*recent*), to enter into socialist competition. В-ключ-а́я, including. Зри́телей, включа́я дете́й, бы́ло до 100 челове́к, there were 100 spectators, including the children. В-ключ-е́ние, *n.n.*, inclusion, insertion. Со включе́нием по́шлин, customs duties included. В-ключ-и́тельно, *adv.*, inclusively. С 1-ого по 10-ое ию́ня в., from June 1st to the 10th inclusively.

вы́-клю́ч-ить, *v.p.*, вы-ключ-а́ть, *v.i.*, + *acc.*, to turn, switch off. В. газ, to turn off the gas. В. мото́р, to switch, turn off a motor. В. ток, to switch off a current. Вы́-клю́ч-ить-ся, *v.p.r.*, вы-ключ-а́ть-ся, *v.i.r.*, to be turned, switched off. Вы-ключ-а́тель, *n.m.*, switch. Вы-ключ-е́ние, *n.n.*, switching off.

за-ключ-и́ть, *v.p.*, за-ключ-а́ть, *v.i.*, + *acc.*, to confine, shut in; come to a conclusion, conclude, deduce, infer. З-а́ть в себе́, to comprise. З. в ско́бки, to put in brackets. З. в тюрьму́, to imprison. З. догово́р, to conclude a treaty. З. пакт о ненападе́нии, to conclude a non-agression pact. З. речь, to conclude a speech. З. из слов кого́-либо, to deduce from someone's words. За-ключ-а́ть-ся, *v.i.r.*, to be concluded; be imprisoned. Су́щность заключа́ется в сле́дующем, the gist of the matter consists in the following. Тру́дность заключа́ется в..., the difficulty lies in. За-ключ-е́ние, *n.n.*, epilogue; imprisonment. З. догово́ра, conclusion of a treaty. З. ми́ра, conclusion of a peace. З. под стра́жу, commitment; placement under guard. Тюре́мное з., imprisonment. За-ключ-ённый, *adj. part. pass. past,* imprisoned; *used as n.,* prisoner. Пожи́зненно з., imprisoned for life. Во́ры заключа́ются в тюрьму́, thieves are imprisoned. За-ключ-и́тельный, *adj.*, final, conclusive. З. акко́рд, final chord. З-ое сло́во, final word; concluding remarks.

ис-ключ-и́ть, *v.p.*, ис-ключ-а́ть, *v.i.*, + *acc.*, to exclude, except; expel. И. кого́-нибудь из спи́ска, to strike someone off a list. И. ученика́ из шко́лы, to expel a pupil from school. Ис-ключ-а́ть-ся, *v.i.r.*, to be excluded, expelled. Ис-ключ-а́я, excluding; *in expression:* И. прису́тствующих, present company excepted. Не и. дете́й, not excluding the children. Ис-ключ-е́ние, *n.n.*, exception, expulsion. И. из шко́лы, expulsion from school. И. из па́ртии, (*recent*), expulsion from the party. Сде́лать и., to make an exception. За исключе́нием, with the exception of. Нет пра́вил без исключе́ния, (*saying*) there are no rules without exceptions. Ис-ключ-и́тельный, *adj.*, exceptional, exclusive. И-ое пра́во, monopoly; exclusive right. И. музыка́нт, exceptional musician. Ис-ключ-и́тельно, *adv.*, exclusively, exceptionally; only, solely.

пере-ключ-и́ть, *v.p.*, пере-ключ-а́ть, *v.i.*, + *acc.*, to switch to another circuit, switch over. П. внима́ние, to turn one's attention to something else. Пере-ключ-е́ние, *n.n.*, switching over. Пере-ключ-и́ть-ся, *v.p.r.*, пере-ключ-а́ть-ся, *v.i.r.*, на + *acc.*, to switch over. П. на другу́ю рабо́ту, to switch to other work. Пере-ключ-а́тель, *n.m.*, switch.

при-ключ-и́-ть, *v.p.,* при-ключ-а́ть, *v.i.,* + *acc.,* to switch to, connect with. П. про́вод к се́ти, to connect a wire to a network. При-ключ-и́ть-ся, *v.p.r.,* при-ключ-а́ть-ся, *v.i.r.,* с + *instr.,* to happen, occur. Кака́я беда́ приключи́-лась с ним? What misfortune befell him? При-ключ-е́ние, *n.n.,* adventure. Иска́тель приключе́ний, adventurer. При-ключ-е́нческий, (*recent*), *adj.,* pertaining to adventure. П. рома́н, novel of adventure.

КЛЯ-(Н), КЛИН-, OATH, AVOWAL; MALEDICTION, SWEARING

кля-сть, клян-у́, *v.i.,* + *acc.,* to curse. Кля-сть-ся, *v.i.r.,* по-кля-сть-ся, *v.p.r.,* + *dat.,* в + *prep.,* to swear, vow, take an oath. К. в ве́рности, to take an oath of loyalty. К. кому́-либо в любви́, to pledge one's love. К. отомсти́ть, to swear vengeance. Кля́-тва, *n.f.,* oath. Торже́ственная к., solemn oath. Брать кля́тву с кого́-нибудь, to take someone's oath. Дава́ть кля́тву, to take an oath. Кля́-твенный, *adj.,* pertaining to an oath; sworn. Кля́-твенное обеща́ние, a sworn promise. Кля-тво-престу́пник, *n.m.,* perjurer; one who breaks an oath. Кля-тво-престу́пни-чество, *n.n.,* perjury, Кля-тво-престу́п-ный, *adj.,* perjured. За-кля́-тие, *n.n.,* (*obs.*), see заклина́ние.

за-клин-а́ть, *v.i.,* за-кля́-сть, *v.p.,* + *acc.,* to conjure, exorcise, charm, invoke. З. клад, to cast a spell on a treasure. За-клин-а́ние, *n.n.,* invocation, conjuration. З. ду́хов, exorcism. За-клин-а́тель, *n.m.,* conjurer, exorciser. З. змей, snake charmer. За-кля́-тый, *adj.,* part. pass. past, sworn. З. враг, sworn enemy.

про-клин-а́ть, *v.i.,* про-кля́-сть, *v.p.,* + *acc.,* to curse, damn. П. тот час, когда́... to curse the hour when... Про-клин-а́ть-ся, *v.i.r.,* to be cursed. Про-клин-а́ющий, *adj. part. act. pres.,* cursing. Про-кля́-тие, *n.n.,* curse, malediction. Преда́ть кого́-нибудь про-кля́тию, to curse someone. Осы́пать прокля́тиями, to hurl curses. Про-кля́-тый, *adj.,* cursed, damned. П. вопро́с, accursed question. Про́-кля́-тый, *adj. part. pass. past,* cursed, damned. П. отцо́м, cursed by one's father. Будь оно́ про́клято! Damn it!

КНИГ-, КНИЖ-, BOOK

кни́г-а, *n.f.,* book, volume. Уче́бная к.,

textbook. Прихо́до-расхо́дная к., account book. Вам и кни́ги в ру́ки, (*saying*), you know best. Кни́г-о-, *a combining form meaning* book, volume. Кни́г-о-изда́тельство, *n.n.,* book publisher, publishing. Кни́г-о-но́ша, *n.m.,* peddler of books. Кни́г-о-печа́тание, *n.n.,* printing of books. Кни́г-о-тор-го́вля, *n.f.,* book trade, book-seller's shop. Кни́г-о-торго́вец, *n.m.,* bookseller. Кни́г-о-храни́лище, *n.n.,* library, depository for books.

кни́ж-ка, *n.f.,* (*dim.*), little book. Кни́ж-ечка, *n.f.,* booklet. Кни́жка с карти́н-ками, picture book. Записна́я к., notebook. Сберега́тельная к., Savings Bank book. Кни́ж-ный, *adj.,* pertaining to books. К. магази́н, bookstore. К. шкаф, bookcase. К-ая торго́вля, book shop, trade. Кни́ж-ник, *n.m.,* bookman. Кни́жники и фарисе́и, (*bib.*), the scribes and the Pharisees. Черно-кни́жник, *n.m.,* (*obs.*), magician.

КОВ-, КУ-, КУЗ-, CONFINEMENT; FORGING

ков-а́-ть, ку-ю́, *v.i.,* + *acc.,* to forge, work, beat, hammer; shoe. К. желе́зо, to forge iron, hammer iron. Куй желе́зо, пока́ горячо́, (*saying*), strike while the iron is hot. Ко́в-аный, *adj.,* forged, wrought. К-ое желе́зо, wrought iron. Ко́в-ка, *n.f.,* forging, shoeing. Ко́в-кий, *adj.,* (*tech.*), malleable, flexible. Ко́в-кость, *n.f.,* malleability, flexibility, ductility.

вы́-ков-ать, *v.p.,* вы-ко́в-ывать, *v.i.,* + *acc.,* to forge, hammer. В. подко́ву, to make a horseshoe. Вы́-ков анный, *adj. part. pass. past,* wrought, forged. В. из желе́за, wrought in iron.

за-ков-а́ть, *v.p.,* за-ко́в-ывать, *v.i.,* + *acc.,* to put in irons. З. ареста́нта в кандалы́, to shackle a convict.

на-ков-а́ть, *v.p.,* + *acc.,* to forge. Н. топо́р, to make an axe. На-ков-а́льня, *n.f.,* anvil.

о-ков-а́ть, *v.p.,* о-ко́в-ывать, *v.i.,* + *acc.,* + *instr.,* to iron, bind with iron. О. сунду́к желе́зом, to bind a trunk with iron. О-ков-а́ть-ся, *v.p.r.,* о-ко́в-ывать-ся, *v.i.r.,* to be bound in, with iron. О-ко́в-анный, *adj. part. pass. past,* bound with iron. О-ко́в-ка, *n.f.,* binding, iron-work. О-ко́в-ы, *n.f.pl.,* fetters, irons, shackles.

пере-ков-а́ть, *v.p.,* пере-ко́в-ывать, *v.i.,* + *acc.,* to forge well, to reforge. П. коня́, to shoe a horse again. Труд пере-кова́л мно́гих бы́вших престу́пни-ков, (*fig.*), work has rehabilitated many former criminals. Пере-ко́в-ка,

n.f., (*recent*, *fig.*), *see* перевоспита́-
ние.
под-ков-а́ть, *v.p.r.*, под-ко́в-ывать, *v.i.r.*,
to shoe. П. пере́дние копы́та ло́шади,
to shoe the front hooves of a horse.
Под-ков-а́ть-ся, *v.p.r.*, под-ко́в-ывать-
ся, *v.i.r.*, + *acc.*, to be shod. П. на все
четы́ре ноги́, (*fig.*), to get well prepared, prepare oneself well. Под-ко́в-
анный, *adj. part. pass. past.*, shod.
Быть подко́ванным, (*fig.*), to be well
versed in a subject. Под-ко́в-а, *n.f.*,
horseshoe. Под-ко́в-ка, *n.f.*, a bread
roll in the shape of a horseshoe. Под-
ков-о-обра́зный, *adj.*, in the shape of
a horseshoe.
при-ков-а́ть, *v.p.*, при-ко́в-ывать, *v.i.*,
+ *acc.*, to chain, rivet; (*fig.*), arrest.
П. це́пью к столбу́, to chain to a
pillar. П. себе́ внима́ние, to draw attention to oneself. При-ко́в-анный,
adj. part. pass. past, riveted; (*fig.*),
t'ed to. П. к посте́ли, to be bedridden.
рас-ков-а́ть, *v.p.*, рас-ко́в-ывать, *v.i.*,
+ *acc.*, to unchain, unfetter, unshoe.
Р. коня́, to unshoe a horse. Рас-ков-
а́ть-ся, *v.p.r.*, рас-ко́в-ывать-ся, *v.i.r.*,
to become unshod, lose a shoe.
с-ков-а́ть, *v.p.*, с-ко́в-ывать, *v.i.*, + *acc.*,
to weld together, forge; put in irons,
fetters. Лёд скова́л ре́ку, the river is
ice-bound. С-ко́в-ка, *n.f.*, welding. С-
ко́в-ывание, *n.n.*, chaining, fettering.
С-ков-о-рода́, *n.f.*, frying pan.
куз-не́ц, *n.m.*, blacksmith, hammersmith.
К. куёт желе́зо, the blacksmith is
forging iron.
ку́з-ница, ку́з-ня, *n.f.*, smithy, forge. Куз-
не́ц рабо́тает в ку́знице, a blacksmith
works in a blacksmith's shop. Куз-
не́чный, *adj.*, pertaining to a blacksmith. К-ое ремесло́, the blacksmith's
trade.
куз-не́чик, *n.m.*, (*zool.*), grasshopper.

КОЖ-, SKIN, HIDE, LEATHER

ко́ж-а, *n.f.*, skin, hide, leather. Бара́нья
к., sheepskin. Гуси́ная к., gooseflesh.
Сапо́жная к., shoe-leather. У боль-
но́го оста́лись то́лько ко́жа да ко́сти,
the patient is nothing but skin and
bones. Из ко́жи лезть, (*fig.*), to try
hard. Ко́ж-аный, *adj.*, of leather. К-ые
рукави́цы, leather mittens. Ко́ж-ица,
n.f., pellicle, film, thin skin; husk.
Снима́ть ко́жицу с фру́ктов, to peel
fruit; pare. Кож-ура́, *n.f.*, rind, skin,
peel, husk, pod. Ко́ж-ный, *adj.*, (*med.*),
cutaneous.
на-ко́ж-ный, *adj.*, *see* ко́жный. Врач по
нако́жным боле́зням, (*med.*) dermato-
logist, skin specialist.

под-ко́ж-ный, *adj.* subcutaneous, hypodermic. П-ая клетча́тка, hypodermic
tissue. П-ое впры́скивание, hypodermic injection.
кож-е́вник, *n.m.*, currier, tanner, one who
dresses leather. Кож-е́вня, *n.f.*, tan-
yard, currier's shop. Кож-е́венный,
adj., pertaining to tanning. К. заво́д,
tannery. К. ма́стер, tanner. Ко́ж-анка,
n.f., (*colloq.*, *recent*), leather jacket.
Кож-у́х, *n.m.*, leather coat. Кож-ушо́к,
n.m., (*dim.*), short leather coat.

КОЗ-, КОС(Л)-, GOAT

коз-а́ *n.f.*, ко́з-ы, *pl.*, goat. Коза́ -
дома́шнее живо́тное, the goat is a
domestic animal.
коз-ёл, *n.m.*, коз-л-ы́, *pl.*, bucks, buck.
К. идёт впереди́ ста́да, a buck is leading the flock. К. отпуще́ния, (*fig.*),
scapegoat. Коз-лёнок, ко́з-лик, *n.m.*,
kid. Коз-у́ля, *n.f.*, (*zool.*), roe, roe-
buck, roedeer. Ко́з-ий, *adj.*, caprine; of
or pertaining to goats. К-ье молоко́,
goat's milk. Коз-ли́ный, *adj.*, goatish.
К-ая боро́дка, (*colloq.*), goatee. К.
го́лос, reedy voice. Коз-лето́н, (*colloq.*), one who sings out of key.
Коз-ло́вый, *adj.*, goat skin. Коз-л-и́ть,
v.i., to kick; bleat. Он не поёт, а коз-
ли́т, he doesn't sing, he bleats. Коз-
л-я́тина, *n.f.*, goat meat. Ко́з-л-ы, box,
coach box, trestle, saw-buck. Ста́вить
винто́вки в к., to stack arms.

КОЛ-, КАЛ-, КЛ-, POINT, PRICK

кол, *n.m.*, ко́л-ь-я, *pl.*, stake, picket
paling. Вбива́ть к. в зе́млю, to pound
stakes into the ground. Нет ни кола́
ни двора́, (*saying*), neither house, nor
home. Обноси́ть ко́льями, to fence in.
Ко́л-ышек, *n.m.*, (*dim.*), peg, picket.
Часто-ко́л, *n.m.*, paling, picket fence.
Обнести́ частоко́лом, to surround with
palings.
кол-о́-ть, *v.i.*, + *acc.*, to thrust, stab,
prick; cleave, split. К. дрова́, to split
wood. У меня́ ко́лет в боку́, I have a
stitch in my side. Кол-о́ть-ся, *v.i.r.*, to
be pricked, stabbed. Кол-отьё, *n.n.*,
colic, stitch, gripes. Ко́л-ка, *n.f.*, splitting, cleaving. К. дров, splitting of
wood. Ко́л-ющая боль, shooting pain.
Кол-ю́честь, *n.f.*, prickliness. Кол-
ю́чий, *adj.*, prickly, spiny, thorny. К-ая
про́волока, barbed wire. Кол-ю́чка,
n.f., prickle, thorn, spine.
в-кол-о́ть, *v.p.*, в-ка́л-ывать, *v.i.*, + *acc.*,
to stick in. В. була́вку, to stick a pin
into. В-кол-о́ть-ся, *v.p.r.*, в-ка́л-ывать-
ся, *v.i.r.*, to be pinned.

вы́-кол-оть. *v.p.,* вы-ка́л-ывать, *v.i.,* + *acc.,* to gouge; prick out. В. глаза́, to gouge out someone's eyes.

за-кол-о́ть, *v.p.,* за-ка́л-ывать, *v.i.,* + *acc.,* to stab; slaughter; pin. З. кабана́, to slaughter a boar. З. пла́тье була́вками, to pin up a dress. За-кол-о́ть-ся, *v.p.r.,* за-ка́л-ывать-ся, *v.i.r.,* to stab oneself. За-кла́-ние, *п.п.,* (*obs.*), offering in sacrifice.

ис-кол-о́ть, *v.p.,* ис-ка́л-ывать, *v.i.,* + *acc.,* to prick, stab repeatedly. И. весь па́лец иго́лкой, to prick one's finger all over with a needle. Ис-кол-о́ть-ся, *v.p.r.,* ис-ка́л-ывать-ся, *v.i.r.,* to be pricked all over. Он весь исколо́лся шипо́вником, he was all scratched up by wild roses.

над-кол-о́ть, *v.p.,* над-ка́л-ывать, *v.i.,* + *acc.,* to split slightly; pierce, prick, slightly. Н. абрико́сы для варе́нья, to pierce apricots (to obtain more juice) in jam-making.

на-кол-о́ть, *v.p.,* на-ка́л-ывать, *v.i.,* + *acc.,* + *gen.,* to split, break. Н. дров, to split a pile of wood. Н. ба́бочку на була́вку, to affix a butterfly with a pin. На-кол-о́ть-ся, *v.p.r.,* на-ка́л-ывать-ся, *v.i.r.,* to prick oneself. На-ко́л-ка, *n.f.,* head dress.

об-кол-о́ть, *v.p.,* об-ка́л-ывать, *v.i.,* + *acc.,* to chop off; prick around. О. лёд, to chop off ice. О. па́льцы шипо́вником, to prick one's fingers with wild roses.

от-кол-о́ть, *v.p.,* от-ка́л-ывать, *v.i.,* + *acc.,* to chop off, break off; unpin. О. бант, to unpin a bow. О. шу́тку, (*fig.*), to play a prank, trick. От-кол-о́ть-ся, *v.p.r.,* от-ка́л-ывать-ся, *v.i.r.,* от + *gen.,* to be chipped off, chopped off. О. от па́ртии, (*recent*), to secede, break away from the party.

пере-кол-о́ть, *v.p.,* пере-ка́л-ывать, *v.i.,* + *acc.,* to re-pin. П. рука́в на приме́рке, to re-pin a sleeve at a fitting.

под-кол-о́ть, *v.p.,* под-ка́л-ывать, *v.i.,* + *acc.,* to split, cleave slightly; pin up. П. подо́л пла́тья, to pin up the hem of a dress. П. проше́ние к де́лу, to attach, clip an application to a file.

по-кол-о́ть, *v.p.,* + *acc., see* коло́ть. П. дрова́, to split wood. По-ка́л-ывать, *see* коло́ть. У меня́ пока́лывает в боку́, I feel an occasional pain in my side.

при-ка́л-ывать, *v.i.,* при-кол-о́ть, *v.p.,* to pin, fasten with a pin. П. цвето́к, to pin on a flower. П. ра́неного зве́ря, to finish off a wounded animal.

про-кол-о́ть, *v.p.,* про-ка́л-ывать, *v.i.,* + *acc.,* to pierce, prick through; run through. Про-ко́л, *n.m.,* puncture. Про-

кол-о́ть-ся, *v.p.r.,* про-ка́л-ывать-ся, *v.i.r.,* to be punctured, run through.

рас-кол-о́ть, *v.p.,* рас-ка́л-ывать, *v.i.,* + *acc.,* to cleave, split, chop, crack. Р. оре́х, to crack a nut. Р. голоса́ на вы́борах, to split a vote. Рас-кол-о́ть-ся, *v.p.r.,* рас-ка́л-ывать-ся, *v.i.r.,* to be split, cracked. Рас-ко́л, *n.m.,* (*fig.*), split, cleavage; (*relig.*), dissension. Р. в па́ртии, (*recent*), party split. Рас-ко́л-ь-ник, *n.m.,* рас-ко́л-ь-ница, *n.f.,* member of a sect of dissenters from the Russian Orthodox Church in the seventeenth century, called the "Old Believers". Рас-ко́л-ь-нический, рас-ко́л-ь-ничий, *adj.,* pertaining to "Old Believers". Рас-ко́л-ь-ничество, *n.n.,* (*hist.*), secession of "Old Believers". Рас-ко́л-ка, *n.f.,* chopping, splitting.

с-кол-о́ть, *v.p.,* с-ка́л-ывать, *v.i.,* + *acc.,* + *instr.,* to cleave, chop off; pin together. С. лёд с поро́га, to chop ice from a threshold. С. була́вками, to pin with pins. С-ка́л-ывание, *n.n.,* cleaving. С-ко́л-ок, *n.m.,* pricked pattern, copy, picture. Соверше́нный с. с него́, the very image of him.

у-кол-о́ть, *v.p.,* у-ка́л-ывать, *v.i.,* + *acc.,* + *instr.,* to prick. У. па́лец була́вкой, to prick one's finger with a pin. У-кол-о́ть-ся, *v.p.r.,* у-ка́л-ывать-ся, *v.i.r.,* to prick oneself. У-ко́л, *n.m.,* prick, sting; (*fig.*), pin-prick. У. шпри́цем, hypodermic injection. У. самолю́бию, a pin-prick to one's pride.

КОЛ-, КОЛ(ЕС)-, КОЛ-ЬЦ-, WHEEL, CIRCLE, RING

кол-ес-о́, *n.n.,* wheel. К. теле́ги, cart wheel. К. на рези́новом ходу́, rubber-tired wheel. К. форту́ны, (*fig.*), wheel of fortune.

кол-ес-ова́-ть, *v.i.,* and *v.p.,* (*hist.*), + *acc.,* to break on a wheel. Кол-ёсико, *n.n.,* small wheel; caster.

кол-ес-и́ть, *v.i.,* ис-кол-еси́ть, *v.p.,* + *acc.,* to travel all over (a region, country). К. по всему́ све́ту, to travel all over the world; roam. За год исколеси́л всю о́бласть, in a year, I travelled all over the province. Кол-е́сник, *n.m.,* wheelwright. Кол-ёсный, *adj.,* wheel; wheeled. К-ая мазь, cart grease. Кол-есни́ца, *n.f.,* (*obs.*), chariot.

кол-ьц-о́, *n.n.,* ring. Золото́е к., gold ring. К. ды́ма, wreath of smoke. Обруча́льное к., wedding ring, band. Согну́ться кольцо́м, to be bent into a ring. Кол-е́чко, *n.n.,* (*dim.*), small ring.

кол-ьц-ева́-ть, *v.i.,* о-кол-ьц-ева́ть, *v.p.,* + *acc.,* to ring, girdle; put a ring upon a bird's leg. Кольц-ево́й, *adj.,* annular.

Кольц-е-обра́зный, *adj.*, annular, ring-shaped.

кол-ьч-у́га, *n.f.*, (*hist.*), coat of mail; chain armor. Оде́тый в кольчу́гу, clad in a coat of mail. Ко́л-ьч-атый, *adj.*, annulated. К-ая змея́, (*zool.*), ringed snake.

кол-ея́, *n.f.*, rut, track. Железнодоро́жная к., railroad track. Вы́битый из коле́й, (*fig.*), one whose routine has been disturbed. Изре́занный коле́ями, rutted. Кол-е́йный, *adj.*, pertaining to tracks. Узко-кол-е́йная желе́зная доро́га, narrow-gauge railroad. Широ-ко́-кол-е́йная желе́зная доро́га, broad-gauge railroad.

о́-коло, *prep.*, + *gen.*, near, towards; around, about, by, hereabouts. О. Москвы́, near Moscow. О. тридцати́ лет, about thirty years of age. Говори́ть вокру́г, да о́коло, (*idiom*), to speak in a roundabout way. О-ко́л-ьный, *adj.*, roundabout. О. путь, roundabout way. О-кол-ёсица, о-кол-ёсная, *n.f.*, nonsense, rubbish. Нести́ околёсицу, (*colloq.*), to talk nonsense. О-ко́лица, *n.f.*, roundabout way, circuitous road; boundary of a village. О-кол-о́ток, *n.m.*, (*obs.*), environs; township; (*mil.*), infirmary. О-к-ол-о́точный, *adj.*, constabulary. О. надзира́тель, (*obs.*), police-officer; petty constable.

о-ко́л-ыш, *n.m.*, cap band. Фура́жка с кра́сным око́лышем, a military cap with a red band.

КОЛЕБ-, КОЛЫБ-, КОЛЫХ-, КОЛЫШ-, ROCKING, SWAYING, WAVERING, TOSSING, SHAKING

кол-еб-а́ть, *v.i.*, по-кол-еба́ть, *v.p.*, + *acc.*, to shake, waver. Ве́тер колеба́л ве́тви дере́вьев, the wind was rocking the branches of the trees. К. осно́вы госуда́рства, to shake the foundations of a State. Колеб-а́ть-ся, *v.i.r.*, по-колеб-а́ть-ся, *v.p.r.*, to oscillate, vibrate, sway; hesitate, waver, falter. Вода́ в о́зере колеба́лась, the water in the lake rippled. Его́ авторите́т поколеба́лся, his authority has wavered. К. в своём реше́нии, to falter in one's decision. Колеб-а́ние, *n.n.*, vacillation, wavering, hesitation; fluctuation. К. по́чвы, tremor, earthquake. Колеб-а́тельный, *adj.*, oscillatory. Колеб-лющийся, *adj. part. act. pres.*, unsteady, shaky, wavering. К. челове́к, one who wavers. К. го́лос, tremulous voice.

за-колеб-а́ть, *v.p.*, + *acc.*, to ruffle, agitate. Ве́тер заколеба́л тростни́к, the wind ruffled the reeds. За-колеб-

а́ть-ся, *v.p.r.*, to begin to sway, waver. Ве́тви заколеба́лись, the branches of the trees began to sway. Су́дьи заколеба́лись по́сле ре́чи защи́тника, the judges began to waver after the defending lawyer's speech.

колыб-е́ль, *n.f.*, cradle. К. ребёнка, child's cradle. От колыбе́ли до моги́лы, from the cradle to the grave. Колыб-е́льная пе́сня, cradle song, lullaby.

колых-а́-ть, колы́ш-у, *v.i.*, колых-ну́ть, *v.p.*, + *acc.*, to sway, swing, toss, shake. Ве́тер колы́шет дере́вья, the wind is causing the trees to sway. Колых-а́ть-ся, *v.i.r.*, колых-ну́ть-ся, *v.p.r.*, to sway, swing, toss, shake, waver, quiver. Трава́ колы́шется, the grass is swaying. Колых-а́ние, *n.n.*, rocking, swinging, swaying.

вс-колых-а́ть, *v.p.*, вс-колых-ну́ть, *v.p. smf.*, + *acc.*, to stir up, rouse. Вс-колых-ну́ть-ся, *v.p.r.*, to start rocking, set in motion. Колыб-е́ль всколыхну́лась и ребёнок просну́лся, the cradle began to rock and the baby woke up.

КОН-Ь-, HORSE

кон-ь, *n.m.*, horse; (*poet.*), steed; (*chess*), knight. Боево́й к., charger. По ко́ням! To horse! Ход конём, a movement of the knight (*in chess*). Кон-е-во́дство, кон-но-заво́дство, *n.n.*, horse breeding. Кон-е-во́д, *n.m.*, horse breeder. Кон-ёк, *n.m.*, (*dim.*) fad, hobby. Кон-ь-ки́, *n.m.pl.*, skates. Ката́ться на конька́х, to skate. Кон-ь-ко-бе́жец, *n.m.*, skater. Кон-ь-ко-бе́жный, *adj.*, pertaining to skating. К. спорт, skating as a sport. К-ые состяза́ния, skating matches. Кон-и́на, *n.f.*, horse flesh, meat. Ко́н-ка, *n.f.*, horse-drawn street-car. Ко́н-ница, *n.f.*, cavalry; mounted troops. Ко́н-ный, *adj.*, mounted; pertaining to a horse. К. завод, horse breeding farm. К-ая артилле́рия, horse artillery. К-ая я́рмарка, horse fair. Ко́н-ский, *adj.*, pertaining to a horse. К-ая гри́ва, horse's mane. Кон-о-ва́л, *n.m.*, farrier. Ко́н-о-вязь, *n.f.*, tether; picket rope. Кон-о-кра́д, *n.m.*, horse thief. Кон-о-кра́дство, *n.n.*, horse stealing. Ко́н-юх, *n.m.*, groom; stable boy. Кон-ю́шня, *n.f.*, stable. Ко́н-юший, *adj.*, used as n., (*hist.*), equerry. Кон-ю́шенный, *adj.*, pertaining to a stable. К. двор, stable yard.

КОН-, КАН- END, TERMINATION

кон-е́ц, *n.m.*, end, termination, close; (*colloq.*), distance, journey's end. К. па́лки, the end of a stick, cane. К.

доро́ги, end of a road, journey. По-ложи́ть к., to put an end. В оди́н коне́ц, one way only. Биле́т в о́ба конца́, round-trip ticket. Под к., in the end, towards the end. Коне́ц - де́лу вене́ц, the end crowns the work. В конце́ концо́в, after all; in the end. Своди́ть концы́ с конца́ми, (*fig.*), to make ends meet. Вкон-е́ц, *adv.*, entirely, totally, wholly. Маши́на испо́рти-лась в., (*colloq.*), the machine is completely ruined. На-коне́ц, *adv.*, at last, at length, finally. Н., вы пришли́, you came finally. Ко́н-чик, *n.m.*, (*dim.*), tip, point, end. На ко́нчике языка́, on the tip of one's tongue.

кон-е́ч-но, *adv.*, certainly, of course, naturally, surely. К. да! of course! К. нет! certainly not!

кон-е́ч-ность, *n.f.*, finiteness; (*anat.*), extremity. Коне́чности (ру́ки, но́ги), extremities (hands, feet). Онеме́ние коне́чностей, numbness of the extremities. Кон-е́чный, *adj.*, final, terminal, ultimate. К-ая ста́нция, terminal station. К-ая цель, final, ultimate goal. Бес-кон-е́чность, *n.f.*, infinity, endlessness, eternity. Бес-кон-е́чный, *adj.*, infinite, endless. Б-ое простра́нство, infinite space. Бес-кон-е́чно, *adv.*, infinitely, endlessly.

ко́н-ч-ить, *v.p.*, кон-ча́ть, *v.i.*, + *acc.*, + *instr.*, to finish, end, terminate, bring to an end. К. университе́т, to graduate from a university. К. рабо́ту, to finish a job. К. самоуби́йством, to end by suicide. Ко́н-чить-ся, *v.p.r.*, кон-ча́ть-ся, *v.i.r*, to end; сконча́ться, *v.p.r.*, to die, expire.Э́то ко́нчится несча́стием, this will end in a misfortune. Запа́сы конча́ются, the supplies are running low. Он ко́нчился, (сконча́лся) he is dead. Ко́н-чено, *adv.*, enough; that's that, it's all over. Ко́н-ченный, *adj. part. pass. past,* finished. К. челове́к, (*fig.*), a man who is finished. Кон-чи́на, *n.f.*, death. Безвре́менная к., untimely death.

до-ко́н-чить, *v.p.*, до-ка́н-чивать, *v.i.*, + *acc.*, to finish, end, complete. Д. на́чатый вчера́ рису́нок, to complete a sketch started yesterday.

до-кон-а́ть, *v.p.*, + *acc.*, (*colloq.*), to finish, break. Го́ре её докона́ло, her grief was too much for her; it finished her.

за-ко́н-чить, *v.p.*, за-ка́н-чивать, *v.i.*, + *acc.*, to finish, end, complete, conclude; (*fig.*), crown. З. речь, to conclude a speech. З. разгово́р, to finish a conversation. За-ко́н-чить-ся, *v.p.r.*, за-ка́н-чивать-ся, *v.i.r.*, + *instr.*, to be finished, ended, completed, concluded.

Как зака́нчивается рома́н "Евге́ний Оне́гин?" How does the novel *Eugene Onegin* end? За-ко́н-ченный, *adj. part. pass. past,* finished, completed, ended, concluded. З. худо́жник, a consummate artist. Не-за-ко́н-ченный, *adj. part. pass. past,* incomplete, unfinished. Н-ое сочине́ние, unfinished work.

за-ко́н, *n.m.*, law. Госуда́рственный з., public law. З. насле́дственности, the law of heredity. З. приро́ды, law of nature. Наруша́ть з., to break a law. Объяви́ть вне зако́на, to outlaw. За-ко́н-ник, *n.m.*, legal expert. За-ко́н-ность, *n.f.*, legality, lawfulness; validity. З. тре́бования, legality of a demand. За-ко́н-ный, *adj.*, legal, lawful, rightful; valid. З. брак, legal marriage. За-ко́н-но, *adv.*, legally, lawfully, rightfully. Закон-о-, *a combining form meaning* law. Закон-о-да́тель, *n.m.*, legislator, lawmaker. За-кон-о-да́тель-ный, *adj.*, legislative. З-ое собра́ние, legislative assembly. За-кон-о-да́тель-ство, *n.n.*, legislation. За-кон-о-ме́р-ность, *n.f.*, conformity to an established law. За-кон-о-ме́рный, *adj.*, conforming to a law.

у-за-ко́н-ить, *v.p.*, у-за-кон-я́ть, *v.i.*, + *acc.*, to legalize. У-за-кон-е́ние, *n.n.*, legalization. Де́йствующее у., operative law.

о-ко́н-чить, *v.p.*, о-ка́н-чивать, *v.i.*, + *acc.*, to finish, end; *see* ко́нчить. О-ко́н-чить-ся, *v.p.r.*, о-ка́н-чивать-ся, *v.i.r.*, + *instr.*, to be finished, ended. О-кон-ча́ние, *n.n.*, ending, completion, finishing, termination, conclusion; (*gram.*), ending. О. рома́на, ending of a novel. О. сле́дует, the conclusion follows. О-кон-ча́тельный, *adj.*, final, definitive. О-ая отде́лка, finishing touch. О-ое реше́ние, final decision. О-кон-ча́тельно, *adv.*, finally, definitely.

по-ко́н-чить, *v.p.*, + *acc.*, + *instr.*, to bring to an end, finish off; conclude. П. де́ло ми́ром, to make peace. П. с собо́й, to commit suicide. П. с э́тим, to be done with something.

при-ко́н-чить, *v.p.*, при-ка́н-чивать, *v.i.*, + *acc.*, (*colloq.*), to finish off, kill. Пле́нных прико́нчили, (*colloq.*), the prisoners were killed.

ис-кон-и́, *adv.*, испо-ко́н ве́ка, from time immemorial, since primordial, primeval times. Э́ти поря́дки существова́ли иско́нь, these customs have existed from time immemorial. Ис-ко́н-ный, *adj.*, primordial, primeval.Но́вгород - иско́н-ный ру́сский го́род, Novgorod is a primeval Russian city.

КОП-, КАП-, DIGGING

коп-á-ть, *v.i.,* + *acc.,* to dig, excavate. К. канáвы (траншéи), to dig ditches (trenches). К. картóфель, to dig up potatoes. Коп-áть-ся, *v.i.r.,* to be dug; rummage; work sluggishly, dawdle. К. в чужúх вещáх, to rummage in someone else's things. К. в душé, (*fig.*), to indulge in soul searching.

коп-нý-ть, *v.p., smf.,* + *acc., see* копáть. Коп-ýн, *n.m.,* коп-ýнья, *n.f.,* (*colloq.*), slow poke, sluggard.

коп-ь, *n.f.,* mine. Угóльная к., coal mine. Разрабáтывать каменноугóльные кóпи, to work coal mines.

вс-коп-áть, *v.p.,* вс-кáп-ывать, *v.i.,* + *acc.,* to dig up, grub up, trench. В. грýдки в огорóде, to dig beds in a vegetable garden. Вс-кáп-ывание, *n.n.,* digging. Вс-кóп-анный, *adj. part. pass. past,* furrowed. Вс-кáп-ывать-ся, *v.i.r.,* + *instr.,* to be dug up. Земля вскáпывается, earth is dug up.

вы́-коп-ать, *v.p.,* вы-кáп-ывать, *v.i.,* + *acc.,* to dig out, excavate, unearth. Вы́копать колодéц, to dig a well. Вы-кáп-ывание, *n.n.,* digging; exhumation.

до-коп-áть-ся, *v.p.r.,* до-кáп-ывать-ся, *v.i.r.,* + *acc.,* to find out, discover. Копáли зéмлю и докопáлись до воды́, they dug until they struck water. Д. до сýти дéла, (*fig.*), to get to the bottom of a case.

ис-коп-áть, *v.p.,* ис-кáп-ывать, *v.i.,* + *acc.,* to dig in; bury. З. я́му, to fill in a pit. За-коп-áть-ся, *v.p.r.,* за-кáп-ывать-ся, *v.i.r.,* to be buried.

на-коп-áть, *v.p.,* на-кáп-ывать, *v.i.,* + *acc.,* to dig up. Ископáли всё пóле, they dug up the whole field. Ис-коп-áемый, *adj. part. pass. pres.,* pertaining to a fossil. И. растéния, fossil plants. И-ые живóтные, animal fossils. Ис-коп-áемое, *n.n.,* mineral; fossil. Полéзные ископáемые, useful minerals.

на-коп-áть, *v.p.,* на-кáп-ывать, *v.i.,* + *gen.,* to dig a given quantity. Н. мешóк картóшки, to dig a sack of potatoes.

об-коп-áть, *v.p.,* об-кáп-ывать, *v.i.,* + *acc.,* to dig round. О. я́блоню, to dig up the earth around an apple tree.

о-коп-áть, *v.p.,* о-кáп-ывать, *v.i.,* + *acc.,* to dig in. О-коп-áть-ся, *v.p.r.,* о-кáп-ывать-ся, *v.i.r.,* (*mil.*), to entrench oneself; dig in. О-кóп, *n.m.,* trench. Окружáть окóпами, (*mil.*), to surround with trenches. О-кóп-ный, *adj.,* pertaining to trenches. О-ая мортúра, (*mil.*), trench mortar.

от-коп-áть, *v.p.,* от-кáп-ывать, *v.i.,* to dig up, disinter, exhume, unearth. О.

кóрни, to dig up roots. О. засы́панных гóрным обвáлом, to dig out people buried by a mountain landslide. Я откопáл рéдкую кнúгу, (*colloq. fig.*), I have dug up (found) a rare book.

пере-коп-áть, *v.p.,* пере-кáп-ывать, *v.i.,* + *acc.,* to dig across, dig again. П. дорóгу, to dig a trench, furrow, across a road. П. весь огорóд, to dig up, fork over, the whole vegetable garden. Пере-кóп, *n.m.,* canal, ditch.

под-коп-áть, *v.p.,* под-кáп-ывать, *v.i.,* + *acc.,* to dig under, undermine, sap. П. укреплéния протúвника, to dig under an enemy's fortifications. Под-коп-áть-ся, *v.p.r.,* под-кáп-ывать-ся, *v.i.r.,* to dig under, sap, undermine. Под негó не подкопáешься, (*idiom*), you can't undermine him; there is no tripping him up. Под-кóп, *n.m.,* mine, undermining; (*fig.*), plot, machinations. Под-кóп-ный, *adj.,* pertaining to undermining.

про-коп-áть, *v.p.,* про-кáп-ывать, *v.i.,* to dig through; tunnel. П. канáву, (подзéмный ход), to dig a ditch (underground passage). Про-коп-áть-ся, *v.p.r.,* с + *instr.,* (*colloq.*), to dawdle. Онá прокопáлась с э́той задáчей цéлый час, she dawdled for a whole hour over this problem.

рас-коп-áть, *v.p.,* рас-кáп-ывать, *v.i.,* + *acc.,* to dig out, excavate. Р. кургáн в степú, to dig a funeral mound in the steppe. Где э́то вы раскопáли? (*fig.*), Where did you dig that up? Рас-кóп-ка, *n.f.,* digging, excavation. Рас-кóп-ки, (*archeol.*), excavations. Р. в Афúнах, excavations in Athens. Рас-кóп-анный, *adj. part. pass. past,* excavated. Р. скúфский могúльник, an excavated Scythian funeral mound.

КОП-, КОП-Л-, КАП-Л-, КУП-, КУЧ-, ACCUMULATION, AMASSMENT

коп-éйка, *n.f.,* kopek. Копéйка - сáмая мéлкая монéта, the kopek is the smallest Russian coin. К. рубль бережёт, (*prov.*), a penny saved is a penny earned. Я без копéйки дéнег, I am penniless. Коп-é-ечка, *n.f.,* (*dim.*), kopek. Это встáнет емý в копéйку, (*idiom*), it will cost him a pretty penny. Коп-éечный, *adj.,* pertaining to a kopek, to the value of a kopek. К-ые расхóды, small expenses. К-ая дýша, (*fig.*), petty person.

коп-ú-ть, коп-л-ю́, *v.i.,* с-коп-úть, *v.p.,* + *acc.,* to save, store up, put away. К. дéньги, to save money. К. злóбу, to store up anger. Коп-нá, *n.f.,* shock (*as* of hair); rick, stack. К. волóс, shock of hair. Снопы́ сло́жены в ко́пны, sheaves piled in stacks.

на-коп-и́ть, *v.p.,* на-ка́п-ливать, *v.i.,* на-коп-л-я́ть, *v.i.,* + *acc.,* to amass, accumulate, heap up. Н. состоя́ние, to amass a fortune. На-коп-и́ть-ся, *v.p.r.,* на-коп-л-я́ть-ся, *v.i.r.,* to be amassed, accumulated. На-коп-л-е́ние, *n.n.,* accumulation. Н. капита́ла, accumulation of capital. Н. воды́, accumulation of water.

при-коп-и́ть, *v.p.,* при-ка́п-л-ивать, *v.i.,* + *acc.,* + *gen.,* to save, save up. П. де́нег на поку́пку до́ма, to save money for the purchase of a house.

с-коп-и́ть, *v.p.,* с-ка́п-л-ивать, *v.i.,* + *acc.,* to collect, hoard, treasure. С. больши́е запа́сы проду́ктов, to hoard large stocks of food. С-коп-и́ть-ся, *v.p.r.,* с-ка́п-л-ивать-ся, *v.i.r.,* to be collected, hoarded, accumulated. Скопи́лось мно́го това́ров, much merchandise has piled up. С-ко́п-ище, *n.n.,* (*obs.*), horde, mob, crowd. С-коп-л-е́ние, *n.n.,* heap, multitude, accumulation. С. пу́блики у ка́ссы теа́тра, a crowd of people at a ticket office. С-ко́п-ом, *adv.,* (*obs.*), all together. Пойти́ ско́пом куда́-нибудь, to go somewhere in a crowd.

ку́п-а, *n.f.,* cluster, group. К. дере́вьев, cluster of trees. Со-во-ку́п-ность, *n.f.,* sum total, aggregate, totality, combination. С. обстоя́тельств (ули́к), combination of circumstances (evidence). Со-во-ку́п-ный, *adj.,* combined, joint. С-ые уси́лия, combined efforts. Со-во-ку́п-но, *adv.,* jointly, in common. Де́йствовать с., to act jointly. Со-во-куп-и́ть, *v.i.,* + *acc.,* (*obs.*), to merge, fuse, unite. С. разноро́дные поня́тия, to merge heterogeneous ideas. При-со-во-куп-и́ть, *v.p.,* + *acc.,* к + *dat.,* to attach, add. П. бума́гу к де́лу, to attach a document to a dossier.

ку́ч-а (*from* ку́п-ча), *n.f.,* heap, mass, pile. К. дете́й, swarm of children. Муравьи́ная к., anthill. У меня́ ку́ча неприя́тностей, I have a heap of troubles. Ку́-ч-ка, *n.f.,* *dim. of* ку́ча. К. люде́й, small group of people. Ку-чево́й, *adj.,* cumulative, cumulous. К-о́е о́блако, cumulous cloud.

о-ку́ч-ить, *v.p.,* о-ку́ч-ивать, *v.i.,* + *acc.,* to dig up (in earth). О. карто́фель, to dig potatoes. О-ку́ч-ивание, *n.n.,* digging up (in earth).

с-ку́ч-ить-ся, *v.p.r.,* с-ку́ч-ивать-ся, *v.i.r.,* to huddle together. С-ку́ч-енность, *n.f.,* density. С. населе́ния, density of population. С-ку́ч-енный, *adj.,* dense, piled up. С-ку́ч-енно, *adv.,* densely. Бед-

няки́ жи́ли с., the poor people lived crowded together.

КОР-, REPROACH, SUBMISSION

кор-и́ть, *v.i.,* + *acc.,* to reproach, upbraid. К. кого́-нибудь за невнима́тельность, to reproach someone for inattentiveness.

у-кор-и́ть, *v.p.,* у-кор-я́ть, *v.i.,* + *acc.,* *see* кори́ть. У. кого́-нибудь во лжи, to accuse someone of lying. У-ко́р, *n.m.,* reproach, blame. У-ко́р-ы со́вести, pangs of conscience. У-кор-и́зна, *n.f.,* reproach, blame. У-кор-и́зненный, *adj.,* reproachful. У. взгляд, reproachful look. У-кор-и́зненно, *adv.,* reproachfully. Без-у-кор-и́зненность, *n.f.,* irreproachability, blamelessness. Без-у-кор-и́зненный, *adj.,* irreproachable, blameless. Б-ая че́стность, unimpeachable honesty Б-ое поведе́ние, irreproachable conduct. Без-у-кор-и́зненно, *adv.,* irreproachably.

по-кор-и́ть, *v.p.,* по-кор-я́ть, *v.i.,* + *acc.,* to subdue, subjugate, conquer, vanquish. П. чужу́ю страну́, to conquer a foreign country. Изобрете́нием авиа́ции челове́к покори́л во́здух, through the invention of aviation man conquered the air. П. се́рдце, to conquer someone's heart. По-кор-и́ть-ся, *v.p.r.,* по-кор-я́ть-ся, *v.i.r.,* to submit, yield; become resigned. П. судьбе́, to become resigned to one's fate. По-кор-е́ние, *n.n.,* subjugation, conquest. П. Каза́ни Ива́ном Гро́зным, the conquest of Kazan by Ivan the Terrible. По-кор-и́тель, *n.m.,* subjugator, conqueror. Ерма́к - п. Сиби́ри, Yermak, the conqueror of Siberia.

по-ко́р-ность, *n.f.,* submission, obedience, resignation. По-ко́р-ный, *adj.,* submissive, obedient. Ваш п. слуга́, (*obs.*), your obedient servant (*in letter writing*). П. судьбе́, resigned to one's fate. Быть поко́рным, to be submissive, obedient. Поко́рнейшая про́сьба, (*obs.*), a most humble request. Проси́ть поко́рнейше, (*obs.*), to beg most humbly. По-ко́р-но, *adv.,* submissively. П. благодарю́, (*obs.*), thank you humbly, my humble thanks.

пере-кор-я́ть-ся, *v.i.r.,* (*colloq.*), to squabble. В э́той семье́ ча́сто перекоря́ются и браня́тся, in this family they often squabble and abuse each other. Пере-ко́р-ы, *n.pl. only,* squabbles. Ме́жду ни́ми иду́т переко́ры и спо́ры, they squabble and argue. На-пере-ко́р, *adv.,* despite; in opposition to. Идти́ н. инстру́кциям, to run counter to instructions. Н. судьбе, to fly in the face of fate.

КОР-, КОР(ЕН)-, BARK, ROOT, RIND

кор-á, *n.f.*, bark, rind, cortex. Древе́сная к., tree bark. Земна́я к., crust of the earth. Покры́тый коро́й, covered with bark. Ко́р-ка, *n.f.*, crust, peel, rind. Очища́ть ко́рку, to peel, pare. Разруга́ть на все ко́рки, (*colloq.*), to berate. Ко́р-очка, *n.f.*, (*dim.*), peel, rind. Кор-и́ца, *n.f.*, cinnamon. Кори́чневый, *adj.*, brown, cinnamon in color. К-ое пла́тье, brown dress.

ко́р-ень, *n.m.*, root; (*math.*), root, radical. К. де́рева, the root of a tree. К. зла, the root of all evil. К. зу́ба, root of a tooth. К. квадра́тный, (*math.*), square root. Извлека́ть к., to extract the root. Хлеб на корню́, wheat on the stalk, not yet reaped. Вырыва́ть с ко́рнем, to root out, eradicate. Пуска́ть ко́рни, to put out roots, take root. Корешо́к, *n.m.*, (*dim.*), small root; (*bot.*). stalk. К. расте́ния, stalk of a plant. К. кни́ги, spine of a book. Кор-е́нья, *n.m.pl.*, root vegetables. Суп с коре́ньями, soup with root vegetables. Коренни́к, *n.m.*, shaft-horse, wheeler. Коренно́й, *adj.*, radical; fundamental, thorough. К. жи́тель, native. К. зуб, molar tooth. Произвести́ к-о́е преобразова́ние, to reform root and branch. Кор-н-е-пло́ды, *n.m.pl.*, root vegetables. Кор-н-е-сло́в, *n.m.*, a dictionary of word roots. Кор-ена́стый, *adj.*, having strong, deep roots (*e.g.* a tree); thick-set, stocky. К. мужчи́на, thick-set man.

Кор-ен-и́ть-ся, *v.i.r.*, у-кор-ен-и́ть-ся, *v.p.r.*, в + *prep.*, to root, be founded on.

в-кор-ени́ть, *v.p.*, в-кор-еня́ть, *v.i.*, + *acc.*, to implant; inculcate. В-кор-ени́ть-ся, *v.p.r.*, в-кор-еня́ть-ся, *v.i.r.*, to become implanted, inculcated. Это́ уже́ вкорени́лось, this has already taken root.

За-кор-ене́лость, *n.f.*, inveterateness. З. привы́чек, inveterateness of habits. За-кор-ене́лый, *adj.*, inveterate.

ис-кор-ени́ть, *v.p.*, ис-кор-еня́ть, *v.i.*, + *acc.*, to eradicate, extirpate, uproot. И. зло, to eradicate evil. Ис-кор-ени́ть-ся, *v.p.r.*, ис-кор-еня́ть-ся, *v.i.r.*, to be uprooted, eradicated. Этот предрассу́док уже́ искорени́лся, this prejudice has been eradicated. Ис-кор-ене́ние, *n.n.*, eradication.

у-кор-ени́ть, *v.p.*, у-кор-еня́ть, *v.i.*, + *acc.*, to implant, take root, inculcate. У. в де́тях созна́тельное отноше́ние к уче́нию, to inculcate in children a responsible attitude toward study. У-кор-ени́ть-ся, *v.p.r.*, у-кор-еня́ть-ся, *v.i.r.*, to take root, become implanted. У-кор-ени́вшийся, *adj. part. pass. past*, rooted, inveterate. У. обы́чай, a deep-rooted custom.

кор-ен-изи́ровать, *v.i.*, + *acc.*, (*recent*), to organize Soviet national regions for management by natives in their own language. Кор-ениза́ция, *n.f.*, process of such organization.

КОРМ-, КОРМ(Л)-, КАРМ-, FOOD, FEEDING

корм, *n.m.*, food, forage, fodder. К. для коро́в, fodder for cows. Задава́ть корм, to feed. На подно́жном корму́, out at pasture. Корм-а́, *n.m.pl.*, (*colloq.*), fodder. В э́том году́ корма́ для скота́ плохи́е, this year the fodder is poor. Корм-ёжка, *n.f.*, (*colloq.*), feeding. Кормово́й, *adj.*, of fodder. К-а́ятрава́, fodder grass. К-ы́е культу́ры, fodder crops. Корм-у́шка, *n.f.*, trough, rack.

корм-и́ть, *v.i.*, to feed, nourish; board, provide for, keep. К. голо́дных, to feed the hungry. К. коро́в, to feed cows. К. обеща́ниями, (*fig.*), to feed with promises. Корм-и́ть-ся, *v.i.r.*, + *instr.*, to nourish oneself, subsist, live on. К. каки́м-либо заня́тием, (*colloq.*), to subsist by means of an occupation. К. хле́бом и водо́й, to live on bread and water. Корм-л-е́ние, *n.n.*, feeding, nourishing. К. гру́дью, nursing, breast feeding; (*med.*), lactation. Корм-и́лица, *n.f.*, wet nurse. Корм-и́лец, *n.m.*, bread-winner; (*obs.*), benefactor.

вс-корм́ить, *v.p.*, вс-ка́рм-л-ивать, *v.i.*, + *acc.*, to rear, bring up. В. гру́дью, to nurse, suckle. В. иску́ственно, to feed artificially. Вс-ко́рм-л-енный, *adj. part. pass. past*, raised, reared. В. гру́дью, breast fed. В. иску́ственно, artificially (bottle) fed.

вы́-корм-ить, *v.p.*, вы-ка́рм-л-ивать, *v.i.*, + *acc.*, to rear, bring up. В. поросёнка, to fatten a suckling pig.

за-корм́ить, *v.p.*, за-ка́рм-л-ивать, *v.i.*, + *acc.*, to overfeed, fatten. Хлебосо́льные хозя́ева совсе́м закорми́ли госте́й, the hospitable hosts overfed their guests. За-ка́рм-л-ивание, *n.n.*, feeding, fattening, overfeeding. На-корм-и́ть, *v.p.*, to feed.

об-корм́ить, *v.p.*, об-ка́рм-л-ивать, *v.i.*, + *acc.*, to overfeed. О. ребёнка, to overfeed a child.

от-корм́ить, *v.p.*, от-ка́рм-л-ивать, *v.i.*, + *acc.*, to feed, fatten. О. инде́йку к пра́днику, to fatten a turkey for a holiday. От-ко́рм, *n.m.*, fattening. От-ко́рм-л-енный, *adj. part. pass. past,* fattened, well fed. О-ые сви́ньи, fattened pigs.

пере-корм-и́ть, *v.p.,* пере-ка́рм-л-ивать, *v.i.,* + *acc.,* to overfeed. П. чéм-либо, to feed with an excess of something. П. ребёнка, to overfeed a child. Пере-ко́рм-л-енный, *adj. part. pass. past,* overfed; gross.

под-корм-и́ть, *v.p.,* под-ка́рм-л-ивать, *v.i.,* + *acc.,* to feed, fatten up. П. скот, to fatten up cattle. На́до его́ п. по́сле болéзни, he needs fattening up after his illness. Под-корм-и́ть-ся, *v.p.r.,* под-ка́рм-л-ивать-ся, *v.i.r., (colloq.),* to be fed, fattened up. Он подкорми́лся в селé у ро́дственников, he ate well and put on weight while staying with his relatives in the village.

при-корм-и́ть, *v.p.,* при-ка́рм-л-ивать, *v.i.,* + *acc.,* to feed; lure. П. голубéй, to tame pigeons by feeding them. При-ко́рм, *n.m.,* extra rations; lure, bait.

про-корм-и́ть, *v.p.,* про-ка́рм-л-ивать, *v.i.,* + *acc.,* to maintain, keep, provide for. П. семью́, to provide for a family. Про-корм-и́ть-ся, *v.p.r.,* про-ка́рм-л-ивать-ся, *v.i.r.,* + *instr.,* to subsist, live on. Про-ко́рм, *n.m.,* nourishment, sustenance. Про-корм-л-éние, *n.n.,* nourishment, sustenance. Зарабáтывать себé на проко́рм, *(colloq.),* to earn one's daily bread.

рас-корм-и́ть, *v.p.,* рас-ка́рм-л-ивать, *v.i.,* + *acc.,* to make fat, fatten. Р. бо́рова на убо́й, to fatten a hog for slaughter. Рас-корм-и́ть-ся, *v.p.r.,* рас-ка́рм-л-иваться, *v.i.r.,* на + *prep.,* to fatten oneself, grow fat. Рас-ка́рм-л-ивание, *n.n., (colloq.),* fattening.

с-корм-и́ть, *v.p.,* с-ка́рм-л-ивать, *v.i.,* + *acc., (colloq.),* to feed a definite amount of fodder.

КОС-, КОШ-, КАШ-, SCYTHE; MOWING.

кос-á, *n.f.,* scythe; plait, tress, projecting sandbank. Сéно кóсят косо́й, hay is mown with a scythe. Нашлá косá на кáмень, *(saying)* when the scythe hits a rock, neither yields. Морскáя косá, headland.

кос-и́-ть, кош-у́, *v.i.,* с-кос-и́ть, *v.p.,* + *acc.,* to mow, cut. К. травý (сéно), to mow grass (hay). Эпидéмия ти́фа коси́ла населéние, *(fig.),* a typhoid epidemic was mowing down the population. Коси́ косá покá росá, *(saying)* mow while there is dew.

кос-ь-бá, *n.f.,* mowing. Кос-áрь, косéц,

n.m., mower. Кос-и́лка, *n.f.,* mower, mowing machine.

кос-и́ть, *v.i.,* + *instr.,* to squint. К. глáзом, to squint. Онá коси́т, she is cross-eyed. Кос-и́ть-ся, *v.i.r.,* на + *acc.,* to look askance, sidelong; squint. Начáльство давно́ коси́лось на него́, *(colloq.),* his superiors have been looking askance at him for a long time. Кос-о́й, *adj., also used as n.,* one-sided; squint-eyed; slanting, oblique, sloping. К-ы́е глазá, squint eyes. Для косы́х нужны́ осо́бенные очки́, cross-eyed people need special glasses. Кóс-о, *adv.,* obliquely, slantwise, sidelong. Кос-о-, *a combining form meaning* oblique. Кос-о-воро́тка, *n.f.,* a Russian shirt. Кос-о-глáзие, *n.n.,* squinting, state of being walleyed. Кос-о-глáзый, *adj.,* walleyed. Кос-о-гóр, *n.m.,* slope of a hill. Кос-о-лáпый, *adj.,* pigeon-toed; *(fig.),* awkward, clumsy. Кос-о-уго́льный, *adj.,* oblique-angled. Ко(а)с-áтка, *n.f.,* darling; *(zool.),* swallow-tail. Кос-ы́нка, *n.f.,* three-cornered kerchief. Кос-я́к, *n.m.,* jamb. К. ры́бы, shoal of fish. К. лошадéй, herd of horses. Кóс-венный, *adj.,* oblique. К-ые падежи́, *(gram.),* oblique cases. Кóс-венно, *adv.,* obliquely, indirectly. Этот прикáз к. отно́сится и к нам, this order concerns us indirectly.

вы́-кос-ить, *v.p.,* вы-кáш-ивать, *v.i.,* + *acc.,* to mow clean, completely. В. луг, to mow an entire field, meadow.

ис-кос-и́ть, *v.p.,* ис-кáш-ивать, *v.i.,* + *acc.,* to mow thoroughly; wear out a scythe. Ис-кос-а, *adv.,* askance. Взгляд и., sidelong glance. На-ис-кос-о́к, нá-ис-кос-ь, *adv.,* aslant, slantwise, obliquely. Крóйть н., to cut on the bias.

на-кос-и́ть, *v.p.,* на-кáш-ивать, *v.i.,* + *gen.,* to mow a certain quantity. Н. травы́, to mow a quantity of grass.

от-ко́с, *n.n.,* slant, slope, declivity. О. холмá, hillside. Вагóн свали́лся под о., the raildroad car rolled down the slope. Пускáть под о., to derail.

пере-кос-и́ть, *v.p.,* пере-кáш-ивать, *v.i.,* + *acc.,* to mow again; warp; distort. П. все лугá, to mow all the meadows again. Злóба перекоси́ла всё его́ лицо́, anger distorted his face. П. дверь, the door has become warped. Пере-кос-и́ть-ся, *v.p.r.,* пере-кáш-ивать-ся, *v.i.r.,* от + *gen.,* to be warped, distorted. От сы́рости рáмы перекоси́лись, the frames became warped from dampness. От óпухоли у негó перекоси́лось лицо́, his face became distorted from the swelling. Пере-ко́с, *n.m.,* curving, bending.

под-кос-и́ть, *v.p.,* под-ка́ш-ивать, *v.i.,* + *acc.,* to trim with a scythe, mow under; (*fig.*), sink under. На́до п. траву́ о́коло забо́ра, it is necessary to trim the grass near a fence. Это несча́стие подкоси́ло его́, this misfortune was the last straw for him. Под-кос-и́ть-ся, *v.p.r.,* под-ка́ш-иваться, *v.i.r.,* to be mowed under, be trimmed with a scythe; (*fig.*), to go under, sink. У него́ подкоси́лись но́ги, his knees buckled under him.

по-кос-и́ть, *v.p.,* + *acc.,* to mow for a short while; to become crooked, cause to become crooked. По-кос-и́ть-ся, *v.p.r.,* to become awry, ramshackle; look askance. Две́ри покоси́лись, the doors have become warped. Он покоси́лся на меня́, he looked askance at me. По-ко́с, сено-ко́с, *n.m.,* meadowland; haymaking. Второ́й п., aftergrass. По-ко́с-ный, *adj.,* of or pertaining to hay. П-ые луга́, hay fields.

про-кос-и́ть, *v.p.,* про-ка́ш-ивать, *v.i.,* + *acc.,* to mow a given length of time; mow through a strip. Про-ко́с, *n.m.,* a mowed strip of hay, as wide as the swing of a scythe.

рас-кос-и́ть, *v.p.,* рас-ка́ш-ивать, *v.i.,* + *acc.,* to reinforce with braces; look cross-eyed; squint. Рас-ко́с, *n.m.,* (*tech.*), strutting. Рас-ко́с-ость, *n.f.,* squinting, squint. Рас-ко́с-ый, *adj.,* squint-eyed.

с-кос-и́ть, *v.p.,* с-ка́ш-ивать, *v.i.,* + *acc.,* to cut aslant; slope; squint. С. всю траву́ на лужа́йке, to mow the grass of a lawn. С. глаза́, to squint one's eyes. С-ка́ш-ивание, - *n.n.,* sloping, slanting. С-кос, *n.m.,* (*tech.*), level, splay. Сено-ко́с, *n.m.,* haymaking, hay mowing.

у-ко́с, *n.m.,* hay harvest. Пе́рвый у., first harvest.

КОС-, ЧЕС-, ЧЕТ-, COMBING

коса́, *n.f.,* braid. Де́вичья к., maiden's braid. Заплести́ ко́су, to braid a braid.

кос-м-а́т-ить, *v.i.,* вс-кос-ма́тить, *v.p.,* + *acc.,* (*colloq.*), to tousle, dishevel. Кос-ма́тый, *adj.,* shaggy, hairy. К. пёс, shaggy dog. Ко́с-мы, *n.pl.,* matted hair; dishevelled locks.

чес-а́-ть, *v.i.,* + *acc.,* to scratch; comb; hackle, card. Ч. го́лову (во́лосы) to comb one's hair. Ч. лён (пенькý, хло́пок), to card flax (hemp, cotton). Ч. языко́м, (*colloq.*), to chatter. Чес-а́ть-ся, *v.i.r.,* по-чес-а́ть-ся, *v.p.r.,* to itch, scratch oneself. У него́ ру́ки че́шутся сде́лать э́то, (*colloq.*), his fingers are itching to do it. Чес-а́лка, *n.f.,* hemp comb, flax comb;

carding machine. Чес-а́льщик, *n.m.,* чес-а́льщица, *n.f.,* wool-comber, carder. Чёс-ка, *n.f.,* combing, scratching. Чес-о́тка, *n.f.,* itch, scab, mange. Чес-о́точный, *adj.,* scabby, mangy. Ч. клещ, wood tick.

вы́-чес-ать, *v.p.,* вы-чёс-ывать, *v.i.,* + *acc.,* to comb out, comb. В. пе́рхоть из воло́с, to comb dandruff out of one's hair. Вы́-чес-ки, *n.pl.,* (*tech.*), combings. Вы́-чес-ка, *n.f.,* (*tech.*), carding.

за-чес-а́ть, *v.p.,* за-чёс-ывать, *v.i.,* + *acc.,* to comb, brush back. З. гла́дко во́лосы, to comb hair back smoothly. За-чес-а́ть-ся, *v.p.r.,* за-чёс-ывать-ся, *v.i.r.,* to begin to itch; comb one's hair back.

на-чес-а́ть, *v.p.,* на-чёс-ывать, *v.i.,* + *acc.,* + *gen.,* to comb, hackle, card. Н. во́лосы на виски́, to comb the hair over one's temples. Н. льну, to hackle (dress) flax.

о-чес-а́ть, об-чес-а́ть, *v.p.,* о-чёс-ывать, об-чёс-ывать, *v.i.,* to comb thoroughly; card flax, hemp, wool, cotton. О-чёс-ки, *n.pl.,* flocks, combings.

пере-чес-а́ть, *v.p.,* пере-чёс-ывать, *v.i.,* + *acc.,* to do one's hair over again. Пере-чес-а́ть-ся, *v.p.r.,* пере-чёс-ывать-ся, *v.i.r.,* to dress one's hair again.

по-чес-а́ть, *v.p., see* чеса́ть. по-чёс-ывать, *v.i.iter.,* to scratch a little. По-чёс-ывать-ся, *v.i.r.,* по-чес-а́ть-ся, *v.p.r.,* to scratch oneself a little.

при-чес-а́ть, *v.p.,* при-чёс-ывать, *v.i.,* + *acc.,* to dress, brush, comb one's hair. П. ребёнка, to comb a child's hair. П. под одну́ гребёнку, (*fig.*), to treat everyone alike. При-чес-а́ть-ся, *v.p.r.,* при-чёс-ывать-ся, *v.i.r.,* to dress, brush, comb one's hair. П. по мо́де, to have the latest hair-do. П. у парихма́хера, to have one's hair set by a hairdresser. При-чёс-ка, *n.f.,* head-dress, coiffure. При-чёс-ывание, *n.n.,* the act of dressing one's hair.

про-чес-а́ть, *v.p.,* про-чёс-ывать, *v.i.,* + *acc.,* to comb thoroughly. П лён, to card flax thoroughly. П. лес, (*mil. recent*), to comb a forest with artillery fire.

рас-чес-а́ть, *v.p.,* рас-чёс-ывать, *v.i.,* + *acc.,* to comb, card thoroughly; scratch. Р. во́лосы на пробо́р, to part one's hair. Рас-чёс-анный, *adj. part. pass. past,* combed sleekly. Рас-чёс-анные во́лосы, sleek hair. Рас-чёс-ка, *n.f.,* (*colloq.*), comb.

с-чес-а́ть, *v.p.,* с-чёс-ывать, *v.i.,* + *acc.,* to comb off; card off; scratch off (*e.g.,* a scab). С-чес-а́ть-ся, *v.p.r.,* с-чёс-ывать-ся, *v.i.r.*, to be combed, carded off

КОСТ-, КОЩ-, КОС-, BONE

кост-ь, *n.f.,* bone. Кóсти скелéта, bones of a skeleton. Игрáльные кóсти, dice. Слонóвая к., ivory. Вправлять к., to set a bone. Промóкнуть до костéй, to be soaked to the bone. До мóзга костéй, (*fig.*), down to the marrow. Игрáть в кóсти, to play dice. Кóсточка, *n.f.,* small bone; stone, seed. Вынимáть кóсточки, to pit fruit. Перемывáть кóсточки, (*fig.*), to gossip. Кост-як, *n.m.,* skeleton. К. здáния, framework of a building. Основнóй к., fundamental structure. Кост-яшка, *n.f.,* die. Костяшки на счётах, counters of an abacus. Кост-янóй, *adj.,* of or pertaining to a bone. К-áя мукá для удобрéния, bone meal for fertilizing. Кост-истый, *adj.,* bony, having bones. К-ая рыба, bony fish. Кост-л-явый, *adj.,* bony, fleshless. К-ые рýки, bony hands. Кóст-ный, *adj.,* osseous. К. мозг, bone marrow. Над-кóст-ница, *n.f.,* periosteum. Воспалéние надкóстницы, (*med.*), periostitis. Над-кóст-ный, *adj.,* pertaining to the periosteum. Кост-о-éда, *n.f.,* (*med.*), caries. Кост-о-прáв, *n.m.,* (*colloq.*), bone-setter, osteopath.

кост-ен-éть, *v.i.,* от + *gen.,* to ossify, stiffen, become rigid. К. от хóлода, to become stiff with cold. Трýпы костенéют, corpses become rigid.

за-кост-енéть, *v.p.,* за-кост-еневáть, *v.i.,* to become stiff, rigid. Пáльцы закостенéли, the fingers became stiff.

о-кост-енéть, *v.p.,* о-кост-еневáть, *v.i.,* от + *gen.,* to ossify, harden. Рýки окостенéли от морóза, the hands became stiff from cold. О-кост-енéлость, *n.f.,* ossification, numbness, stiffness. О-кост-енéлый, *adj.,* ossified, hardened, stiff. О-кост-енéние, *n.n.,* ossification.

кост-й-ть, кощ-ý, *v.i.,* + *acc.,* (*colloq.*), to scold, berate. Бывáло хозяин костит рабóтников, (*colloq., obs.*), the employer used to berate his workers.

кос-нéть (*from* кост-нéть), *v.i.,* в + *prep.,* to stagnate. К. в невéжестве, to remain in ignorance. К. в порóках, to sink in vice. Кос-нéющий, *adj. part. act. pres.,* stiffening. Кóс-ность, *n.f.,* inertness, lack of progress; sloth. Кóс-ный, *adj.,* inert, stagnant, unprogressive. К. ум, inert brain, mind. К. óбраз жизни, stagnant way of life. Кос-но-язычие, *n.n.,* speech defect. Кос-но-язычный, *adj.,* tongue-tied. Не-у-кос-нительный, *adj.,* (*obs.*), strict, unfailing. Не-у-кос-нительно, *adv.,* (*obs.*), strictly; without fail.

за-кос-нéть (*from* за-кост-нéть), *v.p.,* за-кос-невáть, *v.i.,* to become hardened; be obdurate. З в своих грехáх, to be steeped in sin. За-кос-нéлость, *n.f.,* obduracy. За-кос-нéлый, *adj.,* obdurate. З. в предрассýдках, steeped in prejudice. З. злодéй, hardened criminal.

кост-ыль, *n.m.,* crutch; (*tech.*), spike. Рáненый хóдит на костылях, the wounded man is walking on crutches. В стéну забили костыль, they drove a spike into the wall.

кост-ылять, *v.i.,* на-кост-ылять, *v.p.,* + *acc.,* + *dat.,* (*slang*), to cudgel, thrash. Н. шéю комý-либо, (*vulgar*), to thrash someone.

кощ-éй, *proper n.,* Кощéй Бессмéртный, Koschey the Deathless, *in folklore,* a bony old man who knows the secret of eternal life; *by analogy,* emaciated old man; (*colloq.*), miser.

КРАС-, КРАШ-, BEAUTY; REDNESS; COLOR

крас-á, *n.f.,* (*obs.*), beauty; ornament. Дéвица-красá (*folklore*), beautiful maiden. Во всей красé, in all its beauty. Для красы, for the sake of beauty; for ornamentation. Крас-á-вец, *n.m.,* handsome man. Крас-á-вчик, *n.m.,* beautiful youth; (*fig.*), dandy. Крас-á-вица, *n.f.,* beautiful woman; beauty. Рас-крас-á-вица, *n.f.,* (*folklore*), perfect beauty. Крас-ивость, *n.f.,* mere prettiness. Поэзия должнá стремиться к красотé, но избегáть красивости, poetry must strive toward beauty, but avoid embellishments. Крас-ивый, *adj.,* fine, handsome, good looking, pretty. Крас-иво, *adv.,* handsomely, beautifully; well. Не-крас-ивость, *n.f.,* plainess, ugliness. Не-крас-ивый, *adj.,* ugly, plain. Не-крас-иво, *adv.,* in an ugly way; poorly.

крас-ов-áть-ся, *v.i.r.,* to show off, be seen. Вдали красовáлось нóвое здáние теáтра, the new theatre appeared in all its beauty in the distance. По-крас-овáть-ся, *v.p.r.,* to display oneself. Всáдник покрасовáлся пéред гуляющими и ускакáл, the rider showed off before the strollers and galloped away.

крас-от-á, *n.f.,* beauty. К. сéверных лесóв, the beauty of northern forests. К. рисýнка, beauty of design. Во всей красотé, in all its beauty. Онá отличáется исключительной красотóй, she stands out by her unique beauty. Крас-óтка, *n.f.,* pretty woman.

Кра́с-очный, *adj.*, picturesque, vivid; colorful. К. язы́к Го́голя, Gogol's vivid style. Кра́с-очность, *n.f.*, vividness, picturesqueness. К. ви́да, picturesque view.

кра́с-н-ый, *adj.*, red; bright; fine. К. как кровь, red as blood. К. уголо́к, (*recent*), reading corner in any Soviet building. К-ое со́лнышко, the bright sun. К-ые дни, fine days, days of prosperity. Не красна́ изба́ угла́ми, а красна́ пирога́ми, (*saying*), a house is judged by its hospitality, not by its furnishings. К-ая де́вица, beautiful maiden. К-ая ры́ба, cartilaginous fish. К-ая цена́, (*colloq.*), fair price. К-ая строка́, new paragraph. Кра́сная пло́щадь в Москве́, Red Square in Moscow. Кра́сный Крест, the Red Cross. Кра́сное зна́мя (*recent*), the Red Banner. Кра́сная а́рмия, (*recent*), the Red Army. Крас-но-арме́ец, *n.m.*, a Red Army soldier. Кра́сный флот, (*recent*), the Red fleet, navy. Крас-но-фло́тец, *n.m.*, Red navyman. Крас-нота́, *n.f.*, redness. Крас-ну́ха, *n.f.*, (*med.*), German measles. Крас-н-о-ба́й, *n.m.*, (*derog.*), a fine speaker. Крас-но-ва́тый, *adj.*, reddish. Крас-но-ко́жий, *adj.*, red-skinned; Indian. Крас-но-ли́цый, *adj.*, red-faced. Крас-но-ре́чие, *n.f.*, eloquence. Крас-но-речи́вый, *adj.*, eloquent. Крас-но-ле́сье, *n.n.*, coniferous forest. Крас-но-щёкий, *adj.*, red-cheeked. Пре-кра́с-ный, *adj.*, beautiful, fine, excellent. П. челове́к, a fine person. П. пол, (*joc.*), the fair sex. В оди́н п. день, one fine day. Пре-кра́с-ное, *adj.*, *used as n.*, the beautiful. П. должно́ быть велича́во, the beautiful must have majesty. Пре-кра́с-но, *adv.*, beautifully, excellently, very well. Он п. зна́ет, что я име́ю в виду́, he knows perfectly well what I mean.

крас-н-е́ть, *v.i.*, по-крас-не́ть, *v.p.*, от + *gen.*, to redden, blush, flush. При нагрева́нии желе́зо красне́ет, iron becomes red when heated. К. от стыда́, to blush with shame. Не заставля́йте её к., spare her blushes. До́-крас-на́, *adv.*, until red. Д. раскалённый, *adj.*, red-hot. Крас-не́ть-ся, *v.i.r.*, to shine red.

рас-крас-не́ть-ся, *v.p.r.*, to grow hot, become flushed. Р. от бы́строго движе́ния, to become flushed from rapid movement. Рас-крас-не́вшийся, *adj. part. pass. past*, flushed.

крас-и-ть, кра́ш-у, *v.i.*, + *acc.*, to color, paint, adorn, be an ornament. К. гу́бы, to paint one's lips. К. забо́р зелёной кра́ской, to paint a fence green. Не ме́сто кра́сит челове́ка, а челове́к ме́сто, (*saying*), it's the man who makes the job, not the job the man. Кра́с-ить-ся, *v.i.r.*, to color, be colored; make up, paint one's face. Она́ си́льно к., she is heavily made up. Кра́с-ящий, *adj. part. act. pres.*, dyeing, coloring. К-ие вещества́, dyeing materials. Кра́с-ка, *n.f.*, paint, dye, color. Ма́сляная (акваре́льная) к., oil (water) colors. Я́ркие кра́ски зака́та, the vivid colors of sunset. К. стыда́, blushing from shame. Сгусти́ть кра́ски, (*fig.*), to exaggerate. Писа́ть кра́сками, to paint with oils. Я́щик с кра́сками, paint box. Крас-и́льня, *n.f.*, dyer's shop, establishment. Крас-и́льный, *adj.*, pertaining to dyeing. К. заво́д, dye works. Крас-и́льщик, *n.m.*, dyer.

вы́-крас-и-ть, *v.p.*, вы-кра́ш-ивать, *v.i.* + *acc.*, to paint, dye, color. В. дом в зелёный цвет, to paint a house green.

за-кра́с-и-ть, *v.p.*, за-кра́ш-ивать, *v.i.* + *acc.*, to paint over, cover with paint. З. вы́веску, to paint over a sign.

о-кра́с-и-ть, *v.p.*, о-кра́ш-ивать, *v.i.*, + *acc.*, to dye, stain, paint. О. пол (кры́шу), to paint an entire floor (roof). О-кра́с-ка, *n.f.*, hue, color, tint, shade. О-кра́ш-ивание, *n.n.*, dying, painting, staining. О-кра́с-ить-ся, *v.p.r.*, о-кра́ш-ивать-ся, *v.i.r.*, в + *acc.*, to be tinted, colored, stained. Облака́ окра́сились в ро́зовый цвет, the clouds were tinted pink.

пере-кра́с-ить, *v.p.*, пере-кра́ш-ивать, *v.i.*, + *acc.*, to recolor, repaint, dye again. П. мате́рию, to redye material, cloth. Пере-кра́с-ить-ся, *v.p.r.*, пере-кра́ш-ивать-ся, *v.i.r.*, to be dyed over; (*fig.*), to become a turncoat. По́сле Октя́брьской револю́ции не́которые меньшевики́ перекра́сились, after the October Revolution certain Mensheviks changed their colors, became turncoats.

под-кра́с-ить, *v.p.*, под-кра́ш-ивать, *v.i.*, + *acc.*, to tint, touch up with paint, color. П. меха́, to dye furs. Под-кра́с-ить-ся, *v.p.r.*, под-кра́ш-ивать-ся, *v.i.r.*, to be tinted; make up, primp.

при-кра́с-ить, *v.p.*, при-кра́ш-ивать, *v.i.*, + *acc.*, + *instr.*, to embellish, adorn, beautify. Он люби́л п. свой расска́з, he liked to embellish his story. При-кра́с-а, *n.f.*, embellishment. Изобража́ть что́-либо без прикра́с, to describe something without embellishments. При-кра́ш-ивание, *n.n.*, *see* прикра́са. При-кра́ш-енный, *adj. part. pass. past*, embellished. П. портре́т, a flattering likeness.

про-кра́с-и-ть, *v.p.*, про-кра́ш-ивать, *v.i.*,

+ *acc.*, to paint thoroughly. П. вторично крышу, to repaint a roof.

рас-крас́-ить, *v.p.*, рас-краш́-ивать, *v.i.*, + *acc.*, + *instr.*, to paint, color, grain. Р. картинки, to color pictures. Раскрас́-ка, *n.f.*, coloration. Рас-краш́-ивание, *n.n.*, painting, coloring. Раскрас́-ить-ся, *v.p.r.*, рас-краш́-ивать-ся, *v.i.r.*, + *instr.*, to be colored, painted in various colors. Рисунки в детских книгах ярко раскрашиваются, pictures in children's books are painted in vivid (bright) colors.

с-крас́-ить, *v.p.*, с-краш́-ивать, *v.i.*, + *acc.*, to gloss over, smooth. С. жизнь, to make life pleasanter. С. недостаток, to conceal a defect, shortcoming. Скрас́-ить-ся, *v.p.r.*, с-краш́-ивать-ся, *v.i.r.*, + *instr.*, to be concealed, glossed over. Жизнь семьи скрасилась рождением сына, the life of the family was made happier by the birth of a son.

у-крас́-ить, *v.p.*, у-краш́-ать, *v.i.*, + *acc.*, to adorn, decorate, ornament, embellish, beautify, trim. У. платье кружевами, to trim a dress with lace. У. голову цветами, to wear flowers in one's hair. У-крас́-ить-ся, *v.p.r.*, у-краш́-ать-ся, *v.i.r.*, + *instr.*, to be adorned. Дом украсился флагами, the house was decorated with flags. У-краш́-ение, *n.n.*, ornament, decoration. Драгоценные украшения, precious ornaments. Елочные украшения, Christmas tree trimmings.

из-у-крас́-ить, *v.p.*, из-у-краш́-ивать, *v.i.*, (*obs.*), + *acc.*, + *instr.*, to bedeck. И. комнату цветами, to adorn a room with flowers.

раз-у-крас́-ить, *v.p.*, раз-у-краш́-ивать, *v.i.*, + *acc.*, + *instr.*, to decorate, adorn. Раз-у-краш́-енный, *adj. part. pass. past,* lavishly adorned. Р. флагами, decorated lavishly with flags. Раз-у-крас́-ить-ся, *v.p.r.*, раз-у-краш́-ивать-ся, *v.i.r.*, + *instr.*, to be decorated, adorned lavishly.

КРАД-, КРАЖ-, КРАС(-ТЬ), STEALING, THIEVERY

крас-ть, крад-у́, *v.i.*, у-крас́-ть, *v.p.*, + *acc.*, to steal, filch, make off with. У. деньги, to steal money. Крас́-ть-ся, *v.i.r.*, к + *dat.*, to creep; sneak, move furtively. Кошка крадётся к воробьям, the cat is stalking the sparrows. Крад-у-чись, *adv. part. pres.*, stealthily, by stealth. Он шёл, к., на цыпочках, he was advancing stealthily on tiptoes.

краж́-а, *n.f.*, theft, larceny. К. со взломом, burglary. Мелкая к., petty larceny. Крад́-еное, *adj., used as n.*, stolen goods. К. добро впрок не идёт, (*prov.*), ill gotten gains profit no one. У-крад́-кой, *adv.*, by stealth, furtively, stealthily. Взглянуть у., to cast a furtive glance.

вы́-крас-ть, *v.p.*, вы-крад́-ывать, *v.i.*, + *acc.*, to steal. У меня выкрали документы из кармана, my papers were stolen from my pocket. Вы-крад́-ывать-ся, *v.i.r.*, из + *gen.*, to be stolen.

обо-крас́-ть, *v.p.*, об-крад́-ывать, *v.i.*, + *acc.*, to rob. О. кассу (квартиру), to rob a cash register (an apartment). Об-крад́-ывать-ся, *v.i.r.*, to be robbed.

по-крас́-ть, *v.p.*, + *acc.*, to steal, plunder. Вор покрал всё, что мог, the thief stole everything he could. По-краж́-а, *n.f.*, theft.

рас-крас́-ть, *v.p.*, рас-крад́-ывать, *v.i.*, + *acc.*, to steal, pilfer, sneak, filch. Р. всё до конца, to steal everything. Рас-крад́-ывание, *n.n.*, stealing, thievery.

с-крас́-ть, *v.p.*, с-крад́-ывать, *v.i.*, + *acc.*, to conceal, hide; tone down. Плохое освещение скрадывало неприглядность комнаты, poor lighting concealed the unsightliness of the room. С-крас́-ть-ся, *v.p.r.*, с-крад́-ывать-ся, *v.i.r.*, to be concealed. Его недостатки скрадывались его любезностью, his shortcomings were concealed by his amiability.

в-крас́-ть-ся, *v.p.r.*, в-крад́-ывать-ся, *v.i.r.*, в + *acc.*, to steal into; insinuate oneself. В. в чьё-либо доверие, to work oneself into a person's confidence. Тут вкралась опечатка, a misprint has slipped in. В-крад́-чивость, *n.f.*, wheedling, insinuating character. Вкрад́-чивый, *adj.*, smooth-spoken, insinuating. В. голос (человек), ingratiating voice (person). В-крад́-чиво, *adv.*, ingratiatingly, insinuatingly. В. говорить, to speak ingratiatingly.

за-крас́-ть-ся, *v.p.r.*, за-крад́-ывать-ся, *v.i.r.*, to steal into; creep in. В душу закралось сомнение, doubt crept into my heart.

под-крас́-ть-ся, *v.p.*, под-крад́-ывать-ся, *v.i*, to steal up, creep up, sneak up. Незаметно подкралась зима, winter has crept up on us imperceptibly.

про-крас́-ть-ся, *v.p.r.*, про-крад́-ываться, *v.i.r.*, to steal in; (*colloq.*), embezzle. Кассир прокрался, the cashier embezzled funds. Мальчики прокрались на чердак, the boys crept stealthily up into the attic. П. в доверие кому-нибудь, to worm one's way into someone's confidence.

КРАТ- КОРОТ-, КРАЩ-, КОРОЧ-, КОРАЧ-, BREVITY, BRIEFNESS, SHORTNESS

крáт-к-ий, *adj.*, short, brief, concise, summary. К. глáсный, (*phon.*), short vowel. К-ое прилагáтельное, (*gram.*), short adjective. К-ое изложéние, summary. Крáт-кость, *n.f.*, shortness, brevity. Для крáткости, for short. Знак крáткости, (*philol.*), symbol designating shortness (*as* of a vowel). Крáт-ко, *adv.*, briefly, concisely. Крат-ко-врéменность, *n.f.*, short duration, transitoriness. Крат-ко-врéменный, *adj.*, transitory, short, of short duration. Крат-ко-врéменно, *adv.*, transitorily. Крат-ко-днéвный, *adj.*, of short duration. Кратко-срóчный, *adj.*, short-term. В-крáт-це, *adv.*, briefly, in a few words, in short. Рассказáть чтó-нибудь в., to tell something briefly.

пре-крат-й-ть, *v.p.*, пре-кращ-áть, *v.i.*, + *acc.*, to discontinue, cease, stop, leave off, end. П. войнý, to put an end to a war. П. знакóмство, to break off an acquaintance, friendschip. П. платежú, to suspend payments. П. разговóр, to end a conversation. Пре-крат-йть-ся, *v.p.r.*, пре-кращ-áть-ся, *v.i.r.*, to cease, end, be stopped. Головнáя боль прекратúлась, my head stopped aching. Прекращ-éние, *n.n.*, cessation, ceasing, stopping. П. воéнных дéйствий, cessation of hostilities.

со-крат-úть, *v.p.*, со-кращ-áть, *v.i.*, + *acc.*, с + *gen.*, to abbreviate. С. расхóды, to cut down expenses. С. роль, to cut a part. С. со слýжбы, to dismiss, lay off. Со-крат-úть-ся, *v.p.r.*, со-кращ-áть-ся, *v.i.r.*, to shorten itself, contract; close in. Дни сократúлись, the days became shorter. Со-кращ-éние, *n.n.*, abbreviation, reduction, contraction. С. мýскула, contraction of a muscle. С. жáлованúя, wage cut. С. вúвоза, decline in exports. Со-кращ-ённость, *n.f.*, brevity, conciseness. Со-кращ-ённый, *adj. part. pass. past*, abridged, abbreviated. С. курс фúзики, short course in physics. С-ое слóво, abbreviated word. Со-кращ-ённо, *adv.*, briefly, shortly, in short. Написáть чтó-либо с., to write, compose an outline; give an abstract.

корóт-к-ий, *adj.*, short, brief; intimate. К. срок, short time, short term. К. путь, short cut. К-ая пáмять, (*fig.*), short memory. Быть с кéм-либо на корóткой ногé, (*idiom.*), to be on intimate terms with someone. К-ое замыкáние, (*elec.*), short circuit. К-ие вóлосы, short hair. Рýки кóротки, (*saying*),

out of reach. Корóт-кость, *n.f.*, shortness; intimacy. К. отношéний, intimacy; friendliness of relations. Кóрот-ко, *adv.*, briefly; intimately. К. и ясно, briefly and clearly. Корóч-е, *adv. comp.*, shorter. К. говоря, in a word; briefly speaking. Говорúте к., be brief. Коротко-нóгий, *adj.*, short-legged. Коротко-хвóстый, *adj.*, short-tailed. Коротко-вóлновый, *adj.*, (*tech.*), short-wave. Корот-ыш, корот-ышка, *n.m. and n.f.*, (*colloq.*), short, stocky person.

корот-áть, *v.i.*, с-корот-áть, *v.p.*, + *acc.*, to shorten, while away; *in expression*: К. врéмя, к. свой век, to while away the time, one's life.

у-корот-úть, у-короч-ý, *v.p.*, у-корáч-ивать, *v.i.*, to shorten. У. рукавá, to shorten sleeves. У-корот-úть-ся, *v.p.r.*, у-корáч-ивать-ся, *v.i.r.*, to be shortened. Верёвка укоротúлась, the rope became shorter. У-короч-éние, *n.n.*, shortening. У. ногú пóсле перелóма, shortening of a leg due to a fracture.

КРЕП-, КРЕП(Л)-, STRENGTH, VIGOR, FIRMNESS

крéп-к-ий, *adj.*, strong, solid, firm, hard, tough, robust, vigorous. К. сон, sound sleep. К-ая матéрия, strong cloth. К-ое здорóвье, robust health; strong constitution. К-ое словцó, (*colloq.*), strong language. Он крéпок на ногáх, he has sturdy legs; (*fig.*), he is far from old. Крéп-ко, *adv.*, strongly, solidly, firmly, robustly, vigorously. К. задýматься, (*colloq.*), to fall into deep thought. К. поцеловáть, to kiss soundly. Держúтесь к., hold tight. Крéпко-нáкрепко, *adv.*, firmly, fast, tightly. К. забúть, to nail tightly.

крéп-ну-ть, *v.i.*, о-крéп-нуть, *v.p.*, to become stronger, firmer. Больнóй выздоровел и окрéп, the sick man recovered and became stronger.

крéп-ость, *n.f.*, strength, solidity, firmness, fastness, toughness; fortress. К. раствóра, strength of a solution. Осáда крéпости, siege of a fortress. Кýпчая к., (*obs.*), deed of purchase. Крепостнúчество, *n.n.*, (*obs.*), form of feudalism, serfdom. Креп-остнúческий, *adj.*, (*hist.*), pertaining to ownership of serfs. Креп-остнúк, *n.m.*, (*obs.*), one who owns serfs. Креп-остнóй, *adj.*, *used as n.*, (*obs.*), serf. К-óе прáво, (*hist.*), serfdom. К-áя артиллéрия, fortress artillery.

креп-ч-á-ть, *v.i.*, (*colloq.*), to grow stronger, more intense. Морóз крепчáет, the frost is becoming more intense. Креп-ы́ш, *п.т.*, (*colloq.*), robust boy.

креп-и́-ть, креп-л-ю́, *v.i.*, + *acc.*, to strengthen, fortify; constipate. К. оборо́ну, (*recent*), to strengthen military defenses. Креп-и́ть-ся, *v.i.r.*, to restrain oneself; take courage. Крепи́тесь, по́мощь ско́ро придёт, stand fast, help will come soon. Креп-л-е́ние, *п.п.*, strengthening, fastening.

за-креп-и́ть, *v.p.*, за-креп-л-я́ть, *v.i.*, + *acc.*, to fasten; ratify; consolidate. З. верёвку, to fasten a rope. З. сни́мок, to fix a photographic negative. З. крепостно́й вал, to strengthen a rampart. З. достиже́ния, to achieve; attain successes. За-креп-л-е́ние, *п.п.*, securing, attaching; binding. Мы хлопо́чем о закрепле́нии за на́ми э́того до́ма, we are trying to secure this house. За-крёп-а, *n.f.*, за-крёп-ка, *n.f.*, (*dim.*), (*tech.*), split pin.

за-креп-ости́ть, *v.p.*, за-креп-о-ща́ть, *v.i.*, + *acc.*, to impose serfdom on. За-креп-още́ние, *п.п.*, imposition of serfdom.

рас-креп-ост-и́ть, *v.p.*, рас-креп-о-ща́ть, *v.i.*, + *acc.*, to liberate from serfdom. Рас-креп-още́ние, *п.п.*, liberation, emancipation from serfdom. Р. крестья́н произошло́ в 1861 г., the emancipation of the peasants took place in 1861.

от-креп-и́ть, *v.p.*, от-креп-л-я́ть, *v.i.*, + *acc.* to unfasten, detach. От-креп-и́ть-ся, *v.p.r.*, от-креп-л-я́ть-ся, *v.i.r.*, to be detached, unfastened.

под-креп-и́-ть, *v.p.*, под-креп-л-я́ть, *v.i.*, + *acc.*, + *instr.*, to strengthen. П. забо́р подпо́рками, to prop up a fence. П. больно́го вино́м, to fortify a sick man with wine. П. своё мне́ние ве́скими до́водами, to bolster one's opinion with weighty arguments. Под-креп-и́ть-ся, *v.p.r*, под-креп-л-я́ть-ся, *v.i.r.*, to fortify oneself, be fortified. П. пе́ред доро́гой, to eat before setting out on a journey. Под-креп-л-е́ние, *п.п.*, (*mil.*), reinforcement, relief; corroboration, confirmation. Отпра́вить подкрепле́ния на фронт, to send reinforcements to the front. Под-креп-л-я́ющий, *adj. part. act. pres.*, strengthening, fortifying, supporting, reinforcing. П. напи́ток, fortifying, bracing drink. П. во́здух, bracing air.

при-креп-и́ть, *v.p.*, при-креп-л-я́ть, *v.i.*, + *acc.*, + *dat.*, to fasten, attach, affix. П. к земле́, (*hist.*), to attach to the land. П. бума́гу кно́пкой, to tack down a piece of paper. При-креп-и́ть-ся, *v.p.r.*, при-креп-л-я́ть-ся, *v.i.r.*, to be fastened, attached, affixed. П. к мест-ко́му, (*recent*), to register at a local

Trade Union committee. При-креп-л-е́ние, *п.п.*, fastening, attachment. При-креп-л-ённый, *adj. part. pass. past*, attached. П. к земле́, (*hist.*), attached to the land.

с-креп-и́ть, *v.p.*, с-креп-л-я́ть, *v.i.*, + *acc.*, + *instr.*, to strengthen, consolidate, tie, clamp. С. болта́ми, to bolt. С. по́дписью, to countersign. С. печа́тью, to seal. С. догово́р по́дписями, to ratify. С-креп-л-е́ние, *п.п.*, fastening, tightening; countersignature. С. бума́г, countersigning of papers, documents. С. рельс га́йками, action of pinning rails to ties. С-крёп-ка, *n.f.*, (*tech.*), split-pin; clamp. С-креп-я́, *adv.*, *in expression*: С. се́рдце, unwillingly, reluctantly, grudgingly.

у-креп-и́ть, *v.p.*, у-креп-л-я́ть, *v.i.*, + *acc.*, to strengthen, fortify, brace, consolidate, reinforce. У. здоро́вье, to improve one's health. У. го́род, to fortify a city. У. обороноспосо́бность, to strengthen the defensive capacities of a country. У-креп-и́ть-ся, *v.p.r.*, у-креп-л-я́ть-ся, *v.i.r.*, to be strengthened, fortified. У. на за́нятых пози́циях, to fortify occupied positions. У-креп-л-е́ние, *п.п.*, strengthening, fortifying; fortification, fort. У-креп-л-е́ния, ramparts, fortifications. У. берего́в, protection of a coast, shoreline. У-креп-л-я́ющий, *adj. part. act. pres.*, bracing, invigorating. У-ее сре́дство, tonic.

КРЕСТ-, КРЕЩ-, CROSS

крест, *п.т.*, cross. Крёст-ик, *п.т.*, (*dim.*), little cross. Нате́льный к., baptismal cross. Ю́жный Крест, (*astr.*), the Southern Cross. Кра́сный Крест, Red Cross. Крест-на́-крест, crosswise. Крест-ь-я́нин, *п.т.*, peasant. Крест-ь-я́нство, *п.п.*, peasantry. Крест-ь-я́нский, *adj.*, peasant. Крест-о-но́сец, *adj.*, (*hist.*), pertaining to the Crusades. Кресто́вые похо́ды, the Crusades. Крест-о-ви́дный, *adj.*, cruciferous. Крест-о-обра́зный, *adj.*, shaped like a cross. Крест-е́ц, *п.т.*, (*anat.*), sacrum. Крест-о-сло́вица, crossword puzzle.

крест-и́-ть, крещ-у́, *v.i.*, о-крест-и́ть, *v.p.*, to baptize, christen; (*fig.*), name. К. ребёнка, to baptize (christen) a child. Крест-и́ть-ся, *v.i.r.*, to be baptized.; cross oneself. И́стово к., to make a sign of the cross with fervor. К. в правосла́вную ве́ру, to be baptized in the Greek Orthodox faith. Крест-и́тель, *п.т.*, used only for: Иоанн Крести́тель, St. John the Baptist. Крест-и́ны, *п.pl.*, baptism, christening. Крёст-ник, *n.m.,* godson. Крёст-ница, *n.f.,* goddaughter. Крёст-ный, *adj., used as n.,* godfather. К-ая мать, godmother. Крёстная дочь, goddaughter. Крест-йльный, *adj.,* baptismal. К. крест, baptismal cross. Крещ-ёние, *n.n.,* baptism; christening. Крещёние, Epiphany. Боевое к., baptism of fire. Крещ-ёный, *adj.,* baptized, christened. К. ребёнок, baptized, christened child. Крещ-ёнский, *adj.,* pertaining to the time of the Epiphany. Вы-крест, *n.m.,* (*obs.*), one who is converted to Christianity.

вы-крест-ить, *v.p.,* + *acc.,* to convert to Christianity.

о-крест-йть, *v.p.,* + *acc.,* (*obs.*), to give a name in baptism; (*derog.*), to nickname. О-крёст, *prep.,* around. О. ни один не мерцает маяк, all around, not a lighthouse flashes. О-крёст-ность, *n.f.,* neighborhood, vicinity, environs, suburb. Живопйсные окрёстности, picturesque environs. О-крёст-ный, *adj.,* neighboring. О-ые жйтели, neighboring inhabitants.

от-крест-йть-ся, *v.p.r.,* от-крёщ-ивать-ся, *v.i.r.,* от + *gen.,* to rid oneself of someone by making the sign of the cross; disavow, deny. Ленйвый всегда открёщивается от работы, a lazy man always shirks work.

пере-крест-йть, *v.p.,* крест-йть, *v.i.,* *acc.,* to give one's blessing by making the sign of the cross over someone. Прощаясь, мать перекрестйла сына, saying farewell, the mother made the sign of the cross over her son. П. две балки, to cross two beams. Пере-крест-йть-ся, *v.p.r.,* to make the sign of the cross; cross oneself. Пере-крёщ-ивать-ся, *v.i.r.,* to be crossed; cross. Пере-крёст-ок, *n.m.,* crossing, intersection. Толпы народа стояли на перекрёстке, crowds of people stood at the crossing (intersection). Пере-крёст-ный, *adj.,* cross. П. допрос, cross examination. П. огонь, (*mil.*), crossfire.

с-крест-йть, *v.p.,* с-крёщ-ивать, *v.i.,* + *acc.,* to cross; (*biol.*), crossbreed, hybridize. С. руки на груди, to cross one's hands on one's chest. С. шпаги на поедйнке, to cross swords in a duel.

КРЕС-, КРЕШ-, RESURRECTION

вос-крёс-нуть, *v.p.smf.,* вос-крес-ать, *v.i.,* to rise again; rise from the dead; become resurrected. Христос Воскрёсе! Christ is risen! Вос-крес-ёние, *n.n.,* Resurrection. Святое Христово Воскресёние, Resurrection of Christ.

Вос-крес-ёнье, *n.n.,* Sunday. Вос-крёс-ник, *n.m.,* (*recent*), a Sunday devoted to voluntary work for the community. Вос-крёс-ный, *adj.,* Sunday. В. отдых, Sunday rest. В. день, Sunday.

вос-крес-йть, *v.p.,* вос-креш-ать, *v.i.,* + *acc.,* to resurrect; resuscitate, revive. Южный клймат воскресйл меня, the southern climate has revived me. В. старый обычай, to revive an old custom. Вос-креш-ёние, *n.n.,* resurrection, resurrecting. В. Лазаря, (*Bib.*), the Resurrection of Lazarus.

КРОВ(Ь)-, BLOOD

кров-ь, *n.f.,* blood. Проливать к. за отёчество, to shed blood for one's country. Разбйть нос в кровь, to make someone's nose bleed. Жаждать крови, to thirst for blood. Истекать кровью, to bleed. Она кровь с молоком, (*fig.*), she is brimming with health. Кров-авый, *adj.,* bloody, blood-stained. Рубйн кровавого цвёта, blood-red ruby. Кров-йнка, *n.f.,* particle of blood. Ни кровйнки, not a drop, trace of blood. Ни кровйнки в лицё, the face is bloodless, pale. Кров-е-носный, *adj.,* blood-carrying. К. сосуд, blood vessel. Кров-яной, *adj.,* blood. К-ое давлёние, blood pressure. Кров-о, *a combining form meaning* blood. Кров-о-жадность, *n.f.,* blood-thirstiness. Кров-о-жадный, *adj.,* blood-thirsty. Кров-о-излияние, *n.n.,* hemorrhage. Кров-о-обращёние, *n.n.,* blood circulation. Кров-о-пийца, *n.n.,* blood-sucker. Кров-о-пролйтие, *n.n.,* bloodshed, slaughter. Кров-о-пролйтный, *adj.,* bloody. Кров-о-течё-ние, *n.n.,* hemorrhage, blood-letting.

кров-о-точйть, *v.i.,* to bleed. Рана сйльно кровоточйт, the wound is bleeding heavily. Кров-о-точащий, *adj.,* bleeding. К-ая рана, bleeding wound. Кров-о-точйвость, *n.f.,* bleeding.

кров-ный, *adj.,* consanguineous. К-ое родство, blood relationship. К-ая лошадь, thoroughbred. Чистокровная лошадь, thoroughbred. К-ые дёньги, money earned through hard labor.

о-кров-ав-ить, *v.p.,* о-кров-авливать, *v.i.,* + *acc.,* to stain with blood. О. себё лицо и руки при падёнии, to bloody one's hands and face in a fall. О-кров-авленный, *adj.,* blood-stained.

бело-кров-ие, *n.n.,* (*med.*), leukemia.

мало-кров-ие, *n.n.,* anaemia. Мало-кров-ный, *adj.,* anaemic.

полно-кров-ие, *n.n.,* (*med.*), plethora, full-bloodedness. Полно-кров-ный, *adj.,* full-blooded; (*fig.*), healthy, joyful, full of vitality.

КРОТ-, КРОЩ-, MILDNESS, MEEKNESS, GENTLENESS

крóт-к-ий, *adj.,* mild, gentle, meek. К. нрав, gentle disposition. К. взгляд, meek look. Крóт-ость, *n.f.,* meekness, gentleness, mildness. Крóт-ко, *adv.,* mildly, meekly, gently.

у-крот-и́ть, *v.p.,* у-крощ-áть, *v.i.,* + *acc.,* to tame, subdue, break, curb, pacify, appease, calm. У. ди́кого звéря, to tame a wild animal. У. шалунá, to subdue an unruly child. У-крот-и́ть-ся, *v.p.r.,* у-крощ-áть-ся, *v.i.r,* to be tamed, subdued. Гнев укроти́лся, his anger subsided. Я́рость волн укроти́лась, the fury of the waves subsided. У-крощ-ённый, *adj. part. pass. past,* tamed, subdued. У. лев, a tame lion. У-крот-и́тель, *n.m.,* у-крот-и́тельница, *n.f.,* tamer of wild animals. У. зверéй, *n.n.,* taming. "Укрощéние стропти́вой," (*Shakespeare*), The Taming of the Shrew.

КРОХ-, КРОШ-, SMALL QUANTITY, FRAGMENT

крóх-а, *n.f.,* crumb; крóх-и, *n.f.pl.,* remains, remnants. Пита́ться крóхами, to feed on crumbs; (*fig.*), to be destitute.

крóх-от-ка, *n.f.,* tiny bit. Крóх-отный, *adj.,* tiny. К. котёнок, tiny kitten.

крóш-ка, *n.f.,* crumb; (*fig.*), a small child, baby. Крóш-ечка, *n.f.,* crumb, little bit, grain. Ни крóшки во рту с утрá нé было, I haven't had a bite since morning. Крóш-ечный, *adj.,* tiny, little. К-ая дéвочка, a tiny little girl. Ни крóшечки, not even a crumb.

крош-и́ть, *v.i.,* по-крош-и́ть, *v.p.,* + *acc.,* to crumble, mince. К. хлеб кýрам, to crumble bread for hens. Крош-и́ть-ся, *v.i.r.,* to crumble, break, shred, be reduced to fragments. Крóш-ево, *n.n.,* minced eatables. О-крóш-ка, *n.f.,* a Russian cold soup.

ис-крош-и́ть, *v.p.,* + *acc.,* to crumble completely. Ис-крош-и́ть-ся, *v.i.r.,* to be reduced to fragments.

на-крош-и́ть, *v.p.,* + *acc.,* to crumble, mince. Н. на столé, to scatter crumbs on a table.

рас-крош-и́ть, *v.p.,* + *acc.,* to crumble, break into fragments, shred. Р. хлеб (табáк), to crumble bread (shred tobacco). Рас-крош-и́ть-ся, *v.p.r.,* to be crumbled, shredded. Кирпичи́ совсéм раскроши́лись, the bricks have crumbled.

КРУГ-, КРУГ(Л)-, КРУЖ-, ROTUNDITY, CIRCULARITY, ROUNDNESS, SPHERITY

круг, *n.m.,* circle, ring. Начерти́ть к., to trace a circle. К. вокрýг сóлнца, halo. К. знáний, range of knowledge. К. знакóмых, circle of acquaintances. Литератýрные (полити́ческие) круги́, literary (political) circles.

крýг-л-ый, *adj.,* round, circular, globular. К. стол, round table. К-ая шля́па, round hat. К. год, the year round. К-ые сýтки, around the clock. К. дурáк, (*colloq.*), perfect, complete fool. К. сиротá, orphan (having lost both parents). Крýг-л-енький, *adj.,* (*dim.*), round, circular.

круг-л-éть, *v.i.,* по-круг-л-éть, *v.p.,* to become round. Крýг-л-ость, *n.f.,* roundness, rotundity. Круг-л-ы́ш, круг-л-я́к, *n.m.,* round stone. Круг-л-овáтый, *adj.,* somewhat round. Крýг-л-о, *adv.,* roundly. Кругло-голóвый, *adj.,* round-headed. Кругло-ли́цый, *adj.,* round-faced.

круг-л-и́ть, *v.i.,* + *acc.,* to make round. Круг-л-и́ть-ся, *v.i.r.,* to assume a round shape.

за-круг-л-и́ть, *v.p.,* за-круг-л-я́ть, *v.i.,* + *acc.,* to round off, make round. З. фрáзу, to round off a sentence. За-круг-л-éние, *n.n.,* rounding, curve.

о-круг-л-и́ть, *v.p.,* о-круг-л-я́ть, *v.i.,* + *acc.,* to round off, round out. О. счёт, to round off an account. О. капитáл, to increase capital. О-круг-л-éние, *n.n.,* rounding. О-круг-л-ённость, *n.f.,* roundness, rotundity. О-крýг-л-ость, *n.f.,* circle, round. О-крýг-л-ый, *adj.,* rounded, curved; plump.

ó-круг, *n.m.,* district, circuit. Кáрта óкруга, district map. Воéнный о., military district. О-круж-нóй, *adj.,* district, circuit. О. суд, district court. О-круж-кóм, (*recent*), *abbr. of* окружнóй комитéт, District Committee.

круг-овóй, *adj.,* circular, round. К-ая игрá, game played in a circle. К-ая порýка, common responsibility. Круг-о-ворóт, *n.m.,* circular motion; rotation. Круг-о-зóр, *n.m.,* mental outlook; range of vision. Круг-о-свéтный, *adj.,* circumnavigatory; round-the-world. К-ое путешéствие, a trip around the world. Круг-óм, *adv.,* round, around, about; (*fig.*), entirely. Направó к., right about turn. Вы кругóм винова́ты, you are entirely to blame. Круг-óм, *adv.,* in a ring, in a circle. У меня́ головá идёт к., my head is in a whirl. Во-крýг, *adv. and prep.,* around. В. свéта, around the world.

крýж-ево, *n.n.,* lace. Отдéлывать крúжевом, to trim with lace. Круж-евни́ца, *n.f.,* lacemaker. Круж-евно́й, *adj.,* of lace. К. шарф, lace scarf.

круж-о́к, *n.m.,* (*dim.*), circle; club, society, association. Деревя́нный к., wooden disc. Физкульту́рный к., physical culture club. Круж-ко́вый, *adj.,* pertaining to a club, society. К-ые заня́тия, club activities.

круж-и́ть, *v.i.,* + *acc.,* to turn, whirl, twirl, spin. Я́стреб кружи́т над ку́рами, a hawk is circling above the hens. К. кому́-либо го́лову, (*fig.*), to turn someone's head. Круж-и́ть-ся, *v.i.r.,* to whirl, wheel, spin. У меня́ кру́жится голова́, I am dizzy. Круж-е́ние, *n.n.,* whirling, turning, spinning, wheeling. Голово-круж-е́ние, *n.n.,* giddiness, dizziness. Г. от успе́хов, giddiness from success. Голово-круж-и́тельный, *adj.,* causing dizziness. С г-ой быстрото́й, at dizzying speed. Кру́ж-ный, *adj.,* (*colloq.*), circuitous. Кру́жным путём, (*colloq.*), in a roundabout way.

вс-круж-и́ть, *v.p.,* + *acc., used only in expression:* В. кому́-нибудь го́лову, to turn someone's head, infatuate. Успе́х вскружи́л ему́ го́лову, his success went to his head. Вс-круж-и́ть-ся, *v.p.r., see* за-кружи́ться. Пофило-со́фствуй - ум вскру́жится, philosophize and your head will begin to whirl.

за-круж-и́ть, *v.p.,* + *acc., see* кружи́ть. За-круж-и́ть-ся, *v.p.r.,* to begin to whirl. З. волчко́м, to turn, spin like a top. Ли́стья закружи́лись, the leaves spun round and round.

о-круж-и́ть, *v.p.,* о-круж-а́ть, *v.i.,* to surround, encircle, enclose, envelop. Его́ окружа́ло всео́бщее уваже́ние, he was generally respected, surrounded by respect. О-круж-е́ние, *n.n.,* encircling, enclosing. Литерату́рное о. Пу́шкина, Pushkin's literary milieu. Капиталисти́ческое о., (*recent*), capitalistic encirclement. О. проти́вника, encirclement of an enemy. В окруже́нии, in the surroundings, environs of. О-кру́ж-ность, *n.f.,* circumference. Я́ма десяти́ ме́тров в окру́жности, a pit 10 meters in circumference. О-круж-ённый, *adj. part. pass. past,* surrounded, encircled. О. льдо́м, ice-bound. О. ла́ской и забо́той, surrounded by affection and solicitude.

КРЫ-, КРО-, КРОВ-, SHELTER, COVER

кры-ть, кро́-ю, *v.i.,* to cover; (*in cards*), take with a higher card, trump; (*slang*), swear. К. дом желе́зом, to roof a house with sheet iron. К. соло́-мой, to thatch. К. черепи́цей, to tile. В его́ слова́х кро́ется угро́за, there is a veiled threat in his words. Здесь что́-то кро́ется, there is something behind this. Кры́-тый ры́нок, covered market place. Кры́-ша, *n.f.,* roof. Кры́шка, *n.f.,* cover, lid, top; (*slang*), failure.

вс-кры́-ть, *v.p.,* вс-кры-ва́ть, *v.i.,* + *acc.,* to open, dissect, uncover. В. конве́рт (посы́лку), to open a letter (a parcel). В. нары́в, to lance an abscess. Вс-кры́-ть-ся, *v.p.r.,* вс-кры-ва́ть-ся, *v.i.r.,* to be opened. Река́ вскры́лась, the ice in the river has broken up. Вс-кры-ва́ние, *n.n.,* opening, disclosure. Вс-кры́-тие, *n.n.,* (*anat.*), post mortem examination; dissection. В. тру́па, dissection of a corpse; post mortem examination.

за-кры́-ть, *v.p.,* за-кры-ва́ть, *v.i.,* + *acc.,* to shut, close. З. дверь (окно́), to shut a door (a window). З. глаза́ на что́-нибудь, to shut one's eyes to something. З. кран, to turn off a faucet. З. се́ссию, to close a session, meeting. Откры́ть и з. кавы́чки, to enclose in quotation marks. З. грани́цу, to close a border, a frontier. За-кры́-ть-ся, *v.p.r.,* за-кры-ва́ть-ся, *v.i.r.,* to shut, close, cover oneself. З. простынёй, to cover oneself with a sheet. Воро́та закры́лись, the gates closed. За-кры́-тие, *n.n.,* closing, shutting. Вре́мя для закры́тия магази́на, closing time of a store. З. сезо́на, closing of a season. За-кры́-тый, *adj. part. pass. past,* closed, shut, covered. З. просмо́тр, private showing. З. распредели́тель, (*recent*) co-operative stores closed to non-members. З-ое письмо́, sealed letter.

на-кры́-ть, *v.p.,* на-кры-ва́ть, *v.i.,* + *acc.,* + *instr.,* to cover. Н. стол ска́тертью, to lay a cloth on a table. Н. на стол, to set a table. Н. на ме́сте преступле́ния, to catch in the act. Н. на пять рубле́й, (*colloq.*) to do someone out of 5 rubles. На-кры́-ть-ся, *v.p.r.,* на-кры-ва́ть-ся, *v.i.r.,* + *instr.,* to cover oneself, be covered. Н. плащо́м, to cover oneself with a cloak, raincoat. На-кры-ва́ние, *n.n.,* covering.

от-кры́-ть, *v.p.,* от-кры-ва́ть, *v.i.,* + *acc.,* to open, reveal, disclose, discover. О. я́щик, to open a drawer. О. ста́вни, to open shutters. О. де́ло (ла́вку, ми́тинг, счёт), to open a business (a shop, a meeting, an account). О. ка́рты, (*fig.*), to show one's hand. От-кры́-ть-ся, *v.p.r.,* от-кры-ва́ть-ся, *v.i.r.,* to be opened. Магази́ны открыва́ются в

9 часо́в утра́, the shops open at 9 a.m. Та́йна откры́лась, the secret has been disclosed. От-кры-ва́ние, *n.n.*, opening. О. две́ри, opening of a door. От-кры́-тие, *n.n.*, discovery, opening; unveiling. Сде́лать о., to make a discovery. Нау́чное о., scientific discovery. От-кры́-т-ка, *n.f.*, postcard. От-кры́-тый, *adj. part. pass. past,* open, straightforward, outspoken. О. я́щик, open box. О. гла́сный, (*phon.*), open vowel. О. сканда́л, open scandal. С о-о́й душо́й, open-heartedly. В о-о́м мо́ре, on the open sea. О-ые вражде́бные де́йствия, open hostilities. От-кры́-то, *adv.*, openly, publicly, manifestly; honestly.

пере-кры́-ть, *v.p.,* пере-кры-ва́ть, *v.i.,* + *acc., see* кры́ть. П. кры́шу желе́зом, to cover a roof with sheet iron. Лётчик перекры́л пре́жний реко́рд, (*recent*), the pilot has surpassed the previous record. Пере-кры́-тие, *n.n.*, overlapping. Бето́нное п., concrete floor.

по-кры́-ть, *v.p.,* по-кры-ва́ть, *v.i.,* + *acc.,* + *instr.,* to cover, veil, spread over; pay off; roof. П. что́-либо желе́зом, to iron, cover with iron. П. ла́ком, to varnish. П. артиллери́йским огнём простра́нство, to cover an area with artillery fire. Он покры́л себя́ сла́вой, he covered himself with glory. П. расхо́ды (долги́), to pay off one's expenses (debts). По-кры́-ть-ся, *v.p.r.,* по-кры-ва́ть-ся, *v.i.r.,* to cover oneself, be covered. П. одея́лом, to be covered with a blanket. П. румя́нцем, to blush. По-кры-ва́ло, *n.n.,* veil; bedspread; coverlet. По-кры-ва́льце, *n.n.,* (*bot.*), involucre. По-кры-ва́ние, *n.n.,* covering; incrustation. По-кры́-тие, *n.n.,* covering; payment; discharge. По-кры́-шка, *n.f.,* cover, lid; tire-tread. По-кры́-тый, *adj. part. pass. past,* covered. П. ко́ркой, crusted. П. листво́й, verdant.

при-кры́-ть, *v.p.,* при-кры-ва́ть, *v.i.,* + *acc.,* + *instr.,* to cover, screen, shelter, protect. П. кастрю́лю кры́шкой, to cover a pot with a lid. П. отступле́ние, to cover a retreat. П. от ве́тра, to shelter from the wind. При-кры́-ть-ся, *v.p.r.,* при-кры-ва́ть-ся, *v.i.r.,* to be covered, cover oneself. Он прикрыва́ется свои́м незна́нием, he hides behind his ignorance. При-кры́-тие, *n.n.,* covering; escort, convoy, shelter. Под при-кры́-тый, *adj. part. pass. past,* covered.

рас-кры́-ть, *v.p.,* рас-кры-ва́ть, *v.i.,* + *acc.,* to uncover, bare, reveal, disclose. Р. кни́гу (рот, дверь), to open a book (one's mouth, the door). Он не раскры́л рта, (*colloq.*), he never

opened his mouth. Р. объя́тия, to open one's arms (*as* in welcome). Рас-кры́-ть-ся, *v.p.r.,* рас-кры-ва́ть-ся, *v.i.r.,* to be opened, revealed, disclosed. Лепестки́ цветка́ раскры́лись, the petals of the flower have opened. Рас-кры́-тие, *n.n.,* opening, uncovering, disclosure. Р. преступле́ния, disclosure of a crime. Рас-кры́-тый, *adj. part. pass. past,* open, disclosed, exposed, revealed. С широко́ раскры́тыми глаза́ми, wide-eyed. Та́йна раскры́та, the secret is out. Я сиде́л у раскры́того окна́, I sat at the open window.

с-кры́-ть, *v.p.,* с-кры-ва́ть, *v.i.,* + *acc.,* to conceal, hide, secrete, draw a curtain over. С. своё про́шлое, to conceal one's past. С. свою́ ра́дость, to hide one's joy. С. престу́пника, to conceal a criminal. С-кры́-ть-ся, *v.p.r.,* с-кры-ва́ть-ся, *v.i.r.,* to disappear, vanish. С. неизве́стно куда́, to disappear no one knows where. Со́лнце скры́лось за ту́чи, the sun disappeared behind the clouds. С-кры́-тие, *n.n.,* concealment, hiding. С-кры-ва́ние, *n.n.,* secretiveness. С-кры́-тый, *adj. part. pass. past,* hidden, concealed, secret; latent. С. смысл слов, hidden meaning of words. С-ое наме́рение, hidden intention.

с-кры́-т-нич-ать, *v.i.,* (*colloq.*), to be furtive, secretive. С-кры́-т-ность, *n.f.,* lack of candor, secretiveness, furtiveness, stealth. С. хара́ктера, secretive disposition. С-кры́-т-ный, *adj.,* secretive. С. челове́к, secretive person.

у-кры́-ть, *v.p.,* у-кры-ва́ть, *v.i.,* + *acc.,* to cover, conceal, shelter. На́до у. ребёнка одея́лом, it is necessary to cover the child with a blanket. У. кра́деное, to conceal stolen goods. У-кры́-ть-ся, *v.p.r.,* у-кры-ва́ть-ся, *v.i.r.,* to cover, shelter oneself. У. от неприя́теля, to take cover from the enemy. От вас ничто́ не укро́ется, nothing escapes you. У-кры́-ва́ние, *n.n.,* concealment. У-кры-ва́тель, *n.m.,* one who conceals. У. кра́деного, receiver of stolen goods. У-кры-ва́тельство, *n.n.,* concealment. У-кры́-тие, *n.n.,* shelter. У. от руже́йного огня́, shelter from rifle fire.

кров, *n.m.,* shelter; roof; home. Лишённый кро́ва, homeless. Кро́в-ля, *n.f.,* roof, roofing, covering. Кро́в-ельщик, *n.m.,* roofer. Кро́в-ельный, *adj.,* roofing. К. материа́л, roofing material. К-ое желе́зо, sheet iron.

по-кро́в, *n.m.,* cover, veil; (*fig.*), pall, shroud; Покро́в, (*relig.*), feast of the Intercession of the Holy Virgin. Ко́жный п., *n.m.,* (*anat.*), integument. Под покро́вом но́чи, under cover of night. Под покро́вом та́йны, under a cloak of secrecy. По-кро́в-ный, *adj.*, covering. П-ые тка́ни, (*anat.*), protective tissues.

по-кров-и́тельствовать, *v.i.*, + *dat.*, to act as a patron, a sponsor.

по-кров-и́тель, *n.m.*, patron, protector. По-кров-и́тельница, *n.f.*, patroness, protectress. По-кров-и́тельство, *n.n.*, patronage. О́бщество покрови́тельства живо́тным, Society for the Prevention of Cruelty to Animals. По-кров-и́тельственный, *adj.*, condescending, patronizing. П-ая систе́ма, (*econ.*), protectonism. По-кров-и́тельственно, *adv.*, condescendingly, patronizingly.

от-кров-е́ние, *n.n.*, revelation. Боже́ственное Открове́ние, Divine Revelation Это бы́ло о-ем для всех нас, this was a revelation to all of us. От-кров-е́нность, *n.f.*, frankness. От-кров-е́нный, *adj.*, frank, candid. Быть открове́нным, to be frank, candid, open. От-кров-е́нно, *adv.*, frankly, openly, candidly. О. вы́сказать кому́-либо неприя́тную и́стину, to tell someone the plain truth.

со-кров-е́н-ность, *n.f.*, secrecy, mystery; occultness. Со-кров-е́нный, *adj.*, secret, mysterious, clandestine. С-ые чу́вства, innermost feelings. С-ые мы́сли, intimate thoughts.

со-кро́в-ище, *n.n.*, treasure. Бере́чь, как с., to treasure. Ни за каки́е сокро́вища, (*colloq.*), not at any price. Со-кро́в-ищница, *n.f.*, treasure-house, depository. С. зна́ний, storehouse of information.

кры-ло́, *n.n.*, wing; sail; vane. К. пти́цы, wing of a bird. К. самолёта, wing of a plane. Подреза́ть кому́-нибудь кры́лья, (*fig.*), to clip someone's wings. Кры́-лышко, *n.n.*, (*dim.*), little wing. Взять под своё к., (*fig.*), to take under one's wing. Кры-ла́тый, *adj.*, winged. К-ое сло́во, famous dictum. К-ый конь, (*fig.*), winged horse. Дву-кры́лый, *adj.*, two-winged.

о-кры-л-и́ть, *v.p.*, о-кры-ля́ть, *v.i.*, + *acc.*, to give wings to; (*fig.*), encourage, inspire, give hope. О. наде́ждой, to inspire with hope.

кры-л-ьц-о́, *n.n.*, flight of steps; porch. Кры-л-е́чко, *n.n.*, (*dim.*); *see* крыльцо́.

КУП-, BATHING

куп-а́-ть, *v.i.*, вы́-куп-ать, *v.p.*, + *acc.*, to bathe. К. ребёнка, to bathe a child. Куп-а́ть-ся, *v.i.r.*, вы́-куп-ать-ся, *v.p.r.*, to bathe oneself; go swimming. К. в реке́, to bathe, swim, in a river. К. в зо́лоте, (*fig.*), to swim in gold. Куп-

а́ние, *n.n.*, bathing, swimming. Морско́е к., sea bathing. Куп-а́льня, *n.f.*, bathhouse. Куп-а́льщик, *n.m.*, куп-а́льщица, *n.f.*, bath attendant. Куп-а́льный, *adj.*, bathing. К. сезо́н, bathing season. К. костю́м, bathing suit. Куп-е́ль, *n.f.*, (*rel.*), baptismal font.

ис-куп-а́ть, *v.p.*, (*colloq.*); *see* вы́-куп-ать. Ис-куп-а́ть-ся, *v.p.r.*, to bathe, swim; take a bath. И. в реке́ (о́зере), to bathe, swim, in a river (lake).

на-куп-а́ть-ся, *v.p.r.*, (*colloq.*), to have one's fill of bathing, swimming. За ле́то я накупа́лся в мо́ре, during the summer I had my fill of bathing in the sea.

по-куп-а́ть, *v.p.*, + *acc.*, (*colloq.*); *see* купа́ть. П. ребёнка в ва́нне, to bathe a child in a tub. По-куп-а́ть-ся, *v.p.r.*, to bathe, take a swim. П. в мо́ре, to go bathing in the sea.

КУП-, КУП(Л)-, PURCHASE, PURCHASING

куп-и́-ть, куп-л-ю́, *v.i.*, по-куп-а́ть, *v.p.*, + *acc.*, to buy, purchase. Я не в состоя́нии к. э́то, I cannot afford it, I am not in a position to buy it. Здоро́вья за де́ньги не ку́пишь, (*saying*), one cannot buy health with money. Ку́п-ля, *n.f.*, buying. К. и прода́жа, buying and selling. Куп-е́ц, *n.m*, shopkeeper, tradesman, merchant. Куп-чи́ха, *n.f.*, merchant's wife. Куп-е́чество, *n.n.*, merchant class. Куп-е́ческий, *adj.*, mercantile. К-ое сосло́вие, merchant class. Ку́п-чая, *adj.*, used as n., К-ая кре́пость, *n.f.*, title-deed.

вы́-куп-ить, *v.p.*, вы-куп-а́ть, *v.i.*, + *acc.*, to buy back, redeem. В. ве́щи из ломба́рда, to redeem things in a pawn shop. В. пле́нных, to ransom prisoners. Вы́-куп, *n.m.*, ransom, redeeming. Тре́бовать вы́купа, to hold for ransom. Вы́-куп-л-енный, *adj. part. pass. past*, redeemed, taken out of pawn.

до-куп-и́ть, *v.p.*, до-куп-а́ть, *v.i.*, + *acc.*, to buy in addition. Д. метр сукна́, to buy an additional meter of cloth.

за-куп-и́ть, *v.p.*, за-куп-а́ть, *v.i.*, + *acc.*, to buy in quantity. З. дров на́ зиму, to buy wood for the winter. За-ку́п-ка, *n.f.*, purchase; goods purchased. Де́лать заку́пки, to shop. За-ку́п-щик, *n.m.*, buyer, purchaser. За-куп-а́ть-ся, *v.i.r.*, used only in 3d pers., to be bought in quantity. Прови́зия закупа́ется на це́лую неде́лю, provisions are bought for the whole week.

ис-куп-и́ть, *v.p.*, ис-куп-а́ть, *v.i.*, + *acc.*, to expiate, atone, redeem. И. вину́ раска́янием, to atone one's fault through repentance. Ис-куп-и́тель, *n.m.*, redeemer; savior. Ис-куп-л-е́ние, *n.n.*, expiation, atonement, redemption. Ис-куп-а́ть-ся, *v.i.r.*, + *instr.*, to be redeemed.

на-куп-и́ть, *v.p.*, на-куп-а́ть, *v.i.*, + *acc.*, + *gen.*, to buy up, amass through purchases. Н. це́лый во́рох книг, to buy a stack of books.

о-куп-и́ть, *v.p.*, о-куп-а́ть, *v.i.*, + *acc.*, to compensate, repay. О-куп-и́ть-ся, *v.p.r.*, о-куп-а́ть-ся, *v.i.r.*, to be compensated, repaid, justified.

от-куп-и́ть, *v.p.*, от-куп-а́ть, *v.i.*, + *acc.*, to take on lease; pay off; redeem. О. зе́млю, to redeem land. От-куп-и́ть-ся, *v.p.r.*, от-куп-а́ть-ся, *v.i.r.*, от + *gen.*, to pay off, ransom oneself, be ransomed. О́т-куп, *n.m.*, (*obs.*), lease. От-ку́пщи́к, *n.m.*, (*hist.*), tax-farmer.

пере-куп-и́ть, *v.p.*, пере-куп-а́ть, *v.i.*, + *acc.*, to buy used goods; outbid. Он перекупи́л у меня́ дом, he outbid me for the house. Пере-ку́п-щик, *n.m.*, second-hand dealer. Пере-куп-но́й, *adj.*, second-hand. П. това́р, second-hand goods.

под-куп-и́ть, *v.p.*, под-куп-а́ть, *v.i.*, to bribe. П. свиде́теля, to bribe a witness. П. кого́-нибудь свое́й доброто́й, to win over through kindness. По́д-куп, *n.m.*, bribe, bribery. Под-куп-но́й, *adj.*, venal. Под-ку́п-л-енный, *adj. part. pass. past,* bribed.

по-куп-а́ть, *v.i.*, *see* купи́ть. П. в креди́т, to buy on credit. П. за нали́чный расчёт, to buy for cash. П. в рассро́чку, to buy on the instalment plan. По-ку́п-ка, *n.f.*, buying, purchasing, purchase. Вы́годная п., bargain. Де́лать поку́пки, to shop a little, do some shopping. По-куп-а́тель, *n.m.*, purchaser, customer. Тре́бовательный п., a particular customer. По-куп-а́тель-ный, *adj.*, purchasing. П-ая спосо́бность, purchasing power. По-куп-но́й, *adj.*, purchasable; purchase. П-а́я цена́, purchase price.

при-куп-и́ть, *v.p.*, при-куп-а́ть, *v.i.*, + *acc.*, + *gen.*, to buy additionally. П. мате́рии на пла́тье, to buy additional material for a dress. При-ку́п-ка, *n.f.*, additional purchase. При-куп-но́й, *adj.*, bought additionally.

рас-куп-и́ть, *v.p.*, рас-куп-а́ть, *v.i.*, + *acc.*, to buy up. Рас-куп-а́ть-ся, *v.i.r.*, *used only in 3d pers.*, to be sold out, bought up. Кни́га хорошо́ раскупа́ется, this book is having good sales. Рас-ку́п-л-енный, *adj. part. pass. past,* sold out, bought up. Газе́та была́ раску́плена в два-три часа́, the paper was sold out in two, three hours.

с-куп-и́ть, *v.p.*, с-куп-а́ть, *v.i.*, + *acc.*, to buy up. С. карти́ны изве́стных худо́жников, to buy up the paintings of famous artists. С-ку́п-ка, *n.f.*, buying up. С. това́ров, the buying up of merchandise. С-ку́п-щик, *n.m.*, one who buys up; (*colloq.*), fence.

с-куп-и́ть-ся, *v.i.*, по-с-куп-и́ть-ся, *v.p.*, на + *acc.*, to stint, grudge. С. на похвалы́, to be sparing in praise. С. на де́ньги, to be stingy with money, be parsimonious. С-ку́п-ость, *n.f.*, avarice, miserliness, parsimony, stinginess. С-куп-е́ц, *n.m.*, miser, niggard, hoarder, skinflint. С-куп-ердя́й, *n.m.*, (*slang*); see скупо́й. С-куп-о́й, *adj.*, *also used as n.*, avaricious, miserly, stingy. С. челове́к, a miserly person. "Скупо́й," Молье́ра, Molière's "The Miser." С-куп-ова́тый, *adj.*, somewhat miserly.

КУР-, SMOKE, STEAM

кур-и́ть, кур-ю́, *v.i.*, по-кур-и́ть, *v.p.*, + *acc.*, + *instr.*, из + *gen.*, to smoke; fumigate; distill. К. таба́к, to smoke tobacco. К. фимиа́м, (*fig.*), to flatter. Кури́ть воспреща́ется, no smoking; smoking is forbidden. Она́ ку́рит папиро́сы, she smokes cigarettes. В це́ркви кури́ли ла́даном, they were burning incense in the church. Спирт куря́т из карто́феля, alcohol is distilled from potatoes. Кур-и́ть-ся, *v.i.r.*, to smoulder; steam; emit smoke, steam. Сыро́й таба́к пло́хо ку́рится, damp tobacco does not burn well. Дрова́ ку́рятся, the wood is smouldering. Река́ кури́лась, the river was steaming. Вино-ку́р-енный заво́д, distillery. Вино-ку́р, *n.m.*, distiller.

кур-е́нь, *n.m.*, hut, shanty, hovel; (*hist.*), Cossack cottage, homestead. В Донски́х стани́цах дома́ называ́ются куреня́ми, houses in the Don region are called *kurens*. Кур-енно́й, *adj.*, pertaining to a *kuren*. К. атама́н, (*hist.*), commander of a Cossack military detachment. Кур-но́й, *adj.*, smoky. К-а́я изба́, a hut without a chimney.

кур-ну́ть, *v.p.smf.*, (*colloq.*); *see* кури́ть. Дай к. разо́к, give me a puff from your cigarette. Ку́р-ево, *n.n.*, (*colloq.*), tobacco, cigarettes. Кур-е́ние, *n.n.*, smoking; fumigation. К. о́пиума, opium smoking. За́пах благово́нных куре́ний, the scent of incense. Кур-и́льная, *adj.*, *used as n.*, smoking room. К-ая ко́мната, smoking room. Кур-и́льня, *n.f.*, smoking den. К. о́пиума, opium den. Кур-и́льница, *n.f.*, (*obs.*), incense burner. Кур-и́льщик, *n.m.*, smoker. Кур-и́лка, *n.f.*, (*colloq.*), smoking room; (*fig.*), inveterate smoker. Кури́тельный, *adj.*, smoking. К. таба́к, smoking tobacco. К-ая тру́бка, pipe.

вы́-кур-ить, *v.p.*, вы-ку́р-ивать, *v.i.*, + *acc.*, to smoke; distill alcohol. В. сига́ру, to smoke a cigar. Ка́ждый день я выку́риваю деся́ток папиро́с, every day I smoke a pack of ten cigarettes. В. лису́ из норы́, to smoke a fox out of its hole. В. неприя́тного челове́ка из своего́ до́ма, (*fig.*), to force an unpleasant person to leave one's home. Е́ле вы́курили э́того незва́ного го́стя, they barely got rid of the uninvited guest.

до-кур-и́ть, *v.p.*, до-ку́р-ивать, *v.i.*, to smoke to the end. Д. папиро́су, to finish a cigarette.

за-кур-и́ть, *v.p.*, за-ку́р-ивать, *v.i.*, + *acc.*, to light; fill with smoke. Он взял спи́чку и закури́л папиро́су, he took a match and lighted a cigarette.

на-кур-и́ть, *v.p.*, на-ку́р-ивать, *v.i.*, to fill with smoke. В ко́мнате си́льно наку́рено, the room is filled with smoke.

о-кур-и́ть, *v.p.*, о-ку́р-ивать, *v.i.*, + *acc.*, to envelope in smoke, fragrance, perfume; fumigate; disinfect. О-ку́р-ок, *n.m.*, cigarette butt.

пере-кур-и́ть, *v.p.*, пере-ку́р-ивать, *v.i.*, to smoke to excess. Он перекури́л и у него боли́т голова́, he has smoked too much and has a headache. Пере-ку́рка, *n.f.*, (*colloq.*), a short smoke. Солда́ты останови́лись на перекýрку, the soldiers stopped for a smoke.

по-кур-и́ть, *v.p.*, по-ку́р-ивать, *v.i.*, + *acc.*, to have a smoke; smoke repeatedly. Он покури́л и ушёл на рабо́ту, he had a smoke and went to work.

под-кур-и́ть, *v.p.*, под-ку́р-ивать, *v.i.*, to smoke out. П. пчёл, to smoke out bees.

при-кур-и́ть, *v.p.*, при-ку́р-ивать, *v.i.*, + *acc.*, to light one's cigarette from another cigarette. Позво́льте п., May I light my cigarette from yours?

рас-кур-и́ть, *v.p.*, рас-ку́р-ивать, *v.i.*, + *acc.*, to light up. Р. тру́бку ми́ра, (*fig.*), to smoke a peace pipe. Рас-ку́р-ивание, *n.n.*, lighting up.

КУС-, КУШ-, BITING, TASTING

кус-а́-ть, *v.i.*, + *acc.*, to bite, sting, nibble. Соба́ка куса́ет прохо́жих, the dog bites passersby. К. гу́бы, to bite one's lips. Кус-а́ть-ся, *v.i.r.*, to bite, sting; snap; (*fig.*), be expensive. Соба́ки куса́ются, dogs bite. Веща́ца хороша́,

да не ку́пишь - куса́ется, it's a nice thing, but you can't buy it—it's too expensive. Попа́лся, кото́рый куса́лся, (*saying*), he got a dose of his own medicine. Кус-о́к, *n.m.*, morsel, bit, piece. К. хле́ба, a piece of bread; livelihood. К. сы́ра, a piece of cheese. Зараба́тывать кусо́к хле́ба, to earn a living. Кус-о́чек, *n.m.*, (*dim.*), piece, bit, morsel. Ла́комый к., dainty morsel. Кус-и́ще, *n.n.*, huge piece. Кус-ково́й, *adj.*, piece, lump. К. са́хар, lump sugar. Кус-а́ние, *n.n.*, biting. Кус-а́ка, *n.m.*, (*colloq.*), one who bites, one given to biting.

ку́ш-ать, *v.i.*, с-ку́ш-ать, *v.p.*, + *acc.*, to eat, drink, consume food. Ку́шайте, пожа́луйста, please eat. Пожа́луйте к., the food is served.

в-кус-и́ть, *v.p.*, в-куш-а́ть, *v.i.*, + *acc.*, (*poet.*), to taste, partake of. В. спо-ко́йствие, to enjoy rest. В. любо́вь, to experience love. В. блаже́нства, to enjoy bliss. В-кус, *n.m.*, taste, flavor, savor. Конфе́ты потеря́ли в., the candies have lost their flavor. Придава́ть чему́-нибудь в., to flavor. Прия́тный в., pleasant flavor, tastiness. У неё плохо́й, в., she has bad taste. На в. и цвет, това́рищей нет, (*saying*) there is no accounting for taste. В-ку́с-ный, *adj.*, tasty, delicious, savory. В-ая пи́ща, palatable food. В-ое пече́нье, delicious cake. В-ку́с-но, *adv.*, tastily, with taste, palatably. Это замеча́тельно в., this is delicious. В-кус-ово́й, *adj.*, pertaining to taste. В-ы́е ощуще́ния, sensations of taste. При́-в-кус, *n.m.*, smack, flavor, touch, dash, tang. Со́ус с неприя́тным при́вкусом, sauce with a disagreeable flavor.

вы́-кус-ить, *v.p.*, вы-ку́с-ывать, *v.i.*, + *acc.*, to bite out. В. мя́киш из ло́мтика хле́ба, to bite out the center of a piece of bread.

за-кус-и́ть, *v.p.*, за-ку́с-ывать, *v.i.*, + *acc.*, to bite. З. удила́, to take the bit between one's teeth. Я кое-чём, закуси́л, I've had a snack. За-ку́с-ка, *n.f.*, snack, hors d'oeuvre. За-ку́с-очная, *adj.*, used as n., snack bar.

ис-кус-а́ть, *v.p.*, ис-ку́с-ывать, *v.i.*, + *acc.*, to cover with bites. Соба́ки искуса́ли прохо́жего, the passerby was badly bitten by dogs.

ис-кус-и́ть, *v.p.*, ис-куш-а́ть, *v.i.*, + *acc.*, (*obs.*), to tempt, try. И. свою́ судьбу́, to tempt Providence, Fate. Ис-ку́с, *n.m.*, ordeal; temptation; trial. Ис-ку́с-итель, *n.m.*, tempter, seducer. Ис-куш-е́ние, *n.n.*, temptation. Вводи́ть кого́-либо в и., to seduce, lead into temptation. Ис-ку́с-ник, *n.m.*, (*colloq.*), skillful, clever. Ис-ку́с-ный, *adj.*, expert. И. портно́й, master tailor. И-ая рабо́та, skillful workmanship. Ис-ку́сно, *adv.*, cleverly, dexterously, artistically, skillfully. Ис-ку́с-ство, *n.n.*, art; skill, craft, proficiency. Изя́щные (изобрази́тельные) искусства, fine arts. Вое́нное и., military art. Ис-кус-ство-ве́дение, *n.n.*, study of art. Иску́сственность, *n.f.*, artificiality. Иску́сственный, *adj.*, artificial, false. И. жёмчуг, imitation pearls. Ис-ку́с-ственно, *adv.*, artificially. И. пита́емый ребёнок, bottle-fed baby.

над-кус-и́ть, *v.p.*, над-ку́с-ывать, *v.i.*, + *acc.*, to nip. Н. я́блоко, to take a bite out of an apple.

об-кус-а́ть, *v.p.*, об-ку́с-ывать, *v.i.*, + *acc.*, to bite, gnaw, nibble. О. я́блоко, to bite around an apple.

от-кус-и́ть, *v.p.*, от-ку́с-ывать, *v.i.*, + *acc.*, to bite, snap off. О. пол я́блока сра́зу, to bite off half an apple at once. О. хле́ба, to bite off some bread. От-ку́с-ывание, *n.n.*, biting, snapping off.

от-ку́ш-ать, *v.p.*, (*obs.*), to finish a meal. Они́ уже́ отку́шали, they have already eaten. Отку́шайте на́шего хле́ба-со́ли, enjoy our hospitality; stay for dinner.

пере-кус-а́ть, *v.p.*, + *acc.*, to bite. Бе́шеная соба́ка перекуса́ла всех во дворе́, the mad dog bit every one in the yard.

пере-кус-и́ть, *v.p.*, пере-ку́с-ывать, *v.i.*, + *acc.*, to bite through, bite in two. П. ни́тку, to break a thread with one's teeth. П. пе́ред отъе́здом, to have a snack before leaving.

по-кус-а́ть, *v.p.*, + *acc.*; *see* куса́ть. Меня́ си́льно покуса́ли комары́, I was badly bitten by mosquitoes.

по-ку́с-ывать, *v.i.*, (*colloq.*), to nibble; *see* куса́ть,. Комары́ поку́сывают, the mosquitoes are beginning to bite.

по-ку́ш-ать, *v.p.*, *see* ку́шать. Поку́шайте, пото́м пойдём, have something to eat first and then let's go. Она́ лю́бит поку́шать, she likes to regale herself.

по-куш-а́ть-ся, *v.i.r.*, по-кус-и́ть-ся, *v.p.r.*, на + *acc.*, to attempt. П. на самоуби́йство, to attempt suicide. Покуш-е́ние, *n.n.*, attempt. П. на чью-либо жизнь, attempt on someone's life. П. с него́дными сре́дствами, attempt to do something with inadequate means.

при-кус-и́ть, *v.p.*, при-ку́с-ывать, *v.i.*, + *acc.*, to take small bites. П. язы́к, to hold one's tongue. Пить чай в при-

ку́ску, to drink one's tea unsweetened, taking small bites of sugar between sips.

про-кус-и́ть, *v.p.*, про-ку́с-ывать, *v.i.*, + *acc.*, to bite through. Соба́ка проку-си́ла мне сапо́г, the dog bit through my boot.

рас-кус-и́ть, *v.p.*, рас-ку́с-ывать, *v.i.*, + *acc.*, + *instr.*, to crack with the aid of one's teeth, crack in two; understand, grasp. Р. оре́х, to crack a nut. Его́ тру́дно раскуси́ть, he is a hard nut to crack.

у-кус-и́ть, *v.p.*, + *acc.*, to bite, sting. Пчела́ укуси́ла меня́, a bee stung me. Кака́я му́ха тебя́ укуси́ла? (*fig.*), What's bitten you? what possesses you? У-ку́с, *n.m.*, bite, sting. Уку́с пчелы́ (комара́), sting of a bee (mosquito). У-ку́ш-енный, *adj. part. pass. past*, bitten, stung.

КУТ-, WRAP, MUFFLE; CORNER

ку́т-а-ть, *v.i.*, to wrap, muffle. Вы сли́шком ку́таете ва́шего ребёнка, you keep your child too heavily dressed. Ку́т-ать-ся, *v.i.r.*, to wrap oneself. Она́ лю́бит к., she likes to smother herself in wraps. Ку́т-анье, *n.n.*, muffling, wrapping.

за-ку́т-ать, *v.p.*, за-ку́т-ывать, *v.i.*, + *acc.*, to muffle, wrap. З. дымово́й заве́сой, to camouflage with a smoke screen. За-ку́т-ать-ся, *v.p.r.*, за-ку́т-ывать-ся, *v.i.r.*, в + *acc.*, to wrap oneself, be wrapped. За-ку́т-ок, *n.m.*, (*colloq.*), small closet, corner in a cottage. За-ку́т-а, *n.f.*, pigsty, sheep-cot.

о-ку́т-ать, *v.p.*, о-ку́т-ывать, *v.i.*, + *acc.*, + *instr.*, to wrap up, envelop. О. но́ги одея́лом, to wrap one's feet in a blanket. О. та́йной, to enshroud in mystery. О-ку́т-ать-ся, *v.p.r.*, о-ку́т-ывать-ся, *v.i.r.*, to wrap oneself, be wrapped. Доли́на оку́талась тума́ном, the valley is enveloped in fog.

рас-ку́т-ать, *v.p.*, рас-ку́т-ывать, *v.i.*, + *acc.*, to unwrap, uncover. Р. ребёнка, to unwrap a child. Рас-ку́т-ать-ся, *v.p.r.*, рас-ку́т-ывать-ся, *v.i.r.*, to unwrap oneself, be unwrapped. Ребёнок раску́тался, the child has become unwrapped.

у-ку́т-ать, *v.p.*, у-ку́т-ывать, *v.i.*, to wrap closely, snugly. У. дете́й, to muffle up children. У. де́рево соло́мой, to wrap a tree with straw. У-ку́т-ать-ся, *v.p.r.*, у-ку́т-ывать-ся, *v.i.r.*, + *instr.*, to be wrapped up. У. ша́рфом, to wrap oneself in a scarf. У-ку́т-ывание, *n.n.*, wrapping up, muffling up.

Л

ЛАД-, ЛАЖ-, HARMONY

лад, *n.m.,* harmony, concord. Дéло не идёт на лад, things are in a bad way. Дéло пошлó на лад, things went well. Запéть на другóй лад, (*fig.*), to sing another tune. Петь в лад (не в лад), to sing in tune (out of tune). Жить в ладý, to live in harmony. Быть в ладáх, to be in concord. Ни склáду, ни ладу, (*saying*), neither order, nor harmony. Лáд-ный, *adj.,* harmonious. Лáд-но, *adv.,* well, in tune, in concord; very well, agreed, all right.

лáд-и-ть, лáж-у, *v.i.,* с + *instr.,* to be on good terms, agree, live in accord. Л. с обéими сторонáми, to straddle. Они не лáдят мéжду собóй, they are at odds. Лáд-ить-ся,*v.i.r.,* to go well, succeed. Бесéда у нас кáк-то не лáдилась, our conversation somehow did not go smoothly.

за-лáд-ить, *v.p.,* + *acc.,* (*colloq.*), to harp, repeat. З. однó и тó же, to harp on one thing.

на-лáд-ить, *v.p.,* на-лáж-ивать, *v.i.,* + *acc.,* to organize, put right, mend, repair. Н. нóвое произвóдство, to organize a new industry. Н. рабóту, to set the work going. На-лáд-ить-ся, *v.p.r.,* на-лáж-ивать-ся, *v.i.r.,* to be organized, run smoothly. Жизнь налáживается, life is becoming organized. Рабóта в клýбе налáживается, club activities are beginning to run smoothly.

по-лáд-ить, *v.p.,* с + *instr.,* to arrange, come to an understanding, agree. *see* лáдить. Мы с ним полáдим, we'll get along with him.

под-лáд-ить, *v.p.,* под-лáж-ивать, *v.i.,* + *acc.,* to fit, suit; adapt. П. ось к телéге, to fit an axle to a cart. П. балалáйку, to tune a balalaika. Под-лáд-ить-ся, *v.p.r.,* под-лáж-ивать-ся, *v.i.r.,* к + *dat.,* to adapt oneself; humor, suit. П. к привычкам, to adapt oneself to habits. П. к начáльству, (*derog.*), to humor superiors.

при-лáд-ить, *v.p.,* при-лáж-ивать, *v.i.,* + *acc.,* к + *dat.,* to fit, adjust. П. пружину к двéри, to adjust a spring to a door. При-лáж-ивание, *n.n.,* fitting, adjusting, adjustment.

раз-лáд-ить, *v.p.,* раз-лáж-ивать, *v.i.,* + *acc.,* to put out of tune, break off, disagree. Они друг с дрýгом разлáдили, they have severed their friendship. Раз-лáд-ить-ся, *v.p.r.,* раз-лáж-ивать-ся, *v.i.r.,* to take a bad turn, go wrong. Дéло разладилось, (*colloq.*),

the deal was called off. Раз-лáд, *n.m.,* dissonance, discord, dissension. Вносить в семью́ р., to sow seeds of discord in a family.

с-лáд-ить, *v.p.,* с-лáж-ивать, *v.i.,* с + *instr.,* to arrange, put together. Ему́ э́тим не слáдить, he can't cope with it. С детьми́ нé бы́ло слáду, (*colloq.*), the children were unmanageable.

у-лáд-ить, *v.p.,* у-лáж-ивать, *v.i.,* + *acc.,* to settle, arrange; reconcile, make up. У. спóрный вопрóс, to settle a controversial question. У. дéло, to settle a matter. У-лáд-ить-ся, *v.p.r.,* у-лáж-ивать-ся, *v.i.r.,* to be settled, arranged. Дéло улáдилось, the matter was settled. У-лáж-ивание, *n.n.,* settling, arranging, reconciliation. У. отношéний, settlement of relations.

ЛАСК-, ЛАСТ-, ЛАЩ-, CARESS

лáск-а, *n.f.,* caress; endearment; kindness. Матери́нская л., motherly caress. Согрéть дýшу лáской, to comfort with affection, warm the heart. Лáск-овость, *n.f.,* tenderness, sweetness. Лáск-овый, *adj.,* caressing, tender, sweet. Л. ребёнок, affectionate child. Л-ое обращéние, kindness; loving treatment. Лáск-ово, *adv.,* caressingly. Ласк-áтельный, *adj.,* caressing, cajoling. Л. тон, caressing tone. Л-ое и́мя, pet name.

ласк-áть, *v.i.,* по-ласк-áть, *v.p.,* + *acc.,* to caress, fondle, pet. Л. ребёнка, to fondle a child. Ласк-áть-ся, *v.i.r.,* to be affectionate, caressing. Она ласкáться не умéла к отцý ни к мáтери своéй, (*Pushkin*), she did not know how to be affectionate to her mother or father. Ласк-áющий, *adj., part. act. pres.,* caressing. Напéв, л. слух, a tune sweet to the ear (*i.e.,* melodious, pleasant to hear).

лáст-ить-ся, лáщ-усь, *v.i.r.,* при-лáст-ить-ся, *v.p.r.,* to fawn upon, lean upon, cling to. Лáщусь к мáтери, I cling to my mother. Щенóк нáчал визжáть и лáститься к своемý хозя́ину, the puppy began to whine and to rub up against his master. Лáст-очка, *n.f.,* swallow. Однá л. весны́ не дéлает, (*saying*), one swallow does not make a spring.

об-ласк-áть, *v.p.,* об-лáск-ивать, *v.i.,* + *acc.,* to be kind, affectionate. О. гóстя, to welcome a guest heartily. О. бедняка, to be kind to a poor man.

при-ласк-áть, *v.p.,* + *acc.,* to caress, stroke, pet. П. сиротý, to treat an orphan affectionately. При-ласк-áть-ся, *v.p.r.*, к + *dat.*, to show affection, snuggle up.

ЛГ-, ЛОЖ-, ЛЖ-, ЛЫГ-, DECEPTION, PREVARICATION

лг-а́-ть, *v.i.,* со-лг-а́ть, *v.p.,* + *dat.*, to lie, deceive. Л. в глаза́, to lie brazenly. Не лги никому́, don't lie to anyone. Лг-ун, *n.m.,* лг-у́нья, *n.f.,* liar. Презре́нный, л., despicable liar.

изо-лг-а́ть-ся, *v.p.r.,* to become an incorrigible liar. И. в коне́ц, (*colloq.*), to become entangled in one's own lies. Изо-лг-а́вшийся, *adj., part. pass. past,* lost in one's own lies. И. челове́к, an inveterate, incorrigible liar.

на-лг-а́ть, *v.p.,* на + *acc.*, to tell lie after lie, calumniate, slander. Ты налга́л на меня́, you've slandered me.

обо-лг-а́ть, *v.p.,* + *acc.*, to cover with calumny, slander; lie about. О. неви́нного, to slander an innocent person.

лож-ь, *n.f.,* lie, falsehood, untruth. На́глая л., outrageous lie. Изоблича́ть во лжи, to expose as a liar. Ло́ж-ность, *n.f.,* falseness, falsity. Л. све́дений, erroneousness of information. Ло́ж-ный, *adj.,* false, untrue; feigned. Л. стыд, false shame. Л. шаг, false step. Л-ая ата́ка, feigned attack. Л-ая трево́га, false alarm. Ло́ж-но, *adv.,* falsely.

лж-ец, *n.m.,* liar. Л. и клеветни́к, a liar and a slanderer. Лж-и́вость, *n.f.,* falsity, mendacity, pretence. Л. показа́ний, falseness of testimony. Лж-и́вый, *adj.,* lying, false, deceitful, mendacious, faking. Лж-е-, *a combining form meaning* false, mock. Лже-прися́га, *n.f.,* perjury. Лже-проро́к, *n.m.,* false prophet. Лже-свиде́тель, *n.m.,* perjurer, false witness. Лже-уда́рник, *n.m.,* (*recent*), a supposed shock-worker.

при-лыг-а́ть, *v.i.,* (*obs.*), to lie occasionally. И к пра́вде небыли́цы прилыга́л, (*Krylov*), and he used to add fibs even to the truth.

ЛЕГ-, ЛЁГ-, ЛЬГ-, ЛЕЗ-, ЛЬЗ-, FACILITY, EASE, LIGHTNESS

лёг-к-ий, *adj.,* light, slight, easy, simple. Л. ветеро́к, gentle breeze. Л. как паути́на, light as gossamer. Л. слу́чай (боле́зни), mild case (of an illness). Л. уро́к, easy lesson. Л-ая кавале́рия, light cavalry. С лёгким се́рдцем, with a light heart. Име́ть лёгкую ру́ку, to have a light hand (nimble fingers). Лёгок на поми́не, (*saying*), talk of the devil, and he is sure to appear. Легкова́тый, *adj.,* somewhat light, easy. Л. кошелёк, light pocketbook (i.e.,

containing little money). Нелёгкая, *adj., used as n. in expression:* Н. куда́ его́ понесла́? Where the devil has he gone?

лёг-кость, *n.f.,* lightness, easiness. Л. зада́чи, easiness of an problem. Л. по́ступи, light tread. Лег-ко́, *adv.,* lightly, easily, readily. Л. косну́ться, to touch lightly. Это ему́ даётся легко́, he does it with ease. Легко-ве́рие, *n.n.,* credulity. Легко-ве́рный, *adj.,* credulous. Легко-мы́сленность, *n.f.,* thoughtlessness, lightness. Легко-мы́сленный, *adj.,* thoughtless, irresponsible. Легко-мы́сленно, *adv.,* thoughtlessly, irresponsibly. Легко-мы́слие, *n.n.,* thoughtlessness, irresponsibility. Лёг-кое, *n.n.,* lung. Воспале́ние лёгких, pneumonia.

лёг-оч-ный, *adj.,* pulmonary. Л. больно́й, lung case. Лёг-онький, *adj.,* very light. Лег-о́нько, *adv.,* gently, softly, slightly.

лег-ч-а́ть, *v.i.,* по-лег-ча́ть, *v.p.,* (*colloq.*), to lighten, grow lighter. Больно́му с утра́ полегча́ло, (*colloq.*), the patient is better this morning.

лег-ч-е, *adv., comp.,* lighter, easier; more lightly, easily, readily. Мне л. писа́ть, чем говори́ть, it is easier for me to write than to speak. Ле́гче лёгкого, easy does it; easy is as easy does. Мне от э́того не ле́гче, I am none the better for it. Ле́гче! Gently! Take care! Поднима́йте больно́го, как мо́жно ле́гче, lift the patient as gently as possible. На-лег-ке́, *adv.,* without luggage. Путеше́ствовать н., to travel light. По-лег-че, *adv. comp.,* somewhat easier, better, lighter. По-лег-о́ньку, *adv.,* in an easy manner. С-лег-ка́, *adv.,* slightly. Она́ слегка́ взволно́вана, she is somewhat excited. С. оби́жен, somewhat offended.

об-лег-ча́ть, *v.i.,* об-лег-чи́ть, *v.p.,* + *acc.*, to relieve, facilitate, lighten. О. рабо́ту, to lighten work. О. се́рдце, (*fig.*), to unburden oneself. Об-лег-че́ние, *n.n.,* relief. В це́лях облегче́ния, in order to facilitate, relieve, lighten. Вздохну́ть с облегче́нием, to sigh with relief. Об-лег-чённый, *adj., part. pass. past,* relieved, lightened. С облегчённым се́рдцем, with a sense of relief. Об-лег-ча́ть-ся, *v.i.r.,* об-лег-чи́ть-ся, *v.p.r.,* to be relieved, relieve oneself.

льг-о́та, *n.f.,* privilege, immunity, exemption, advantage. Экспо́ртные льго́ты, export privileges. Льг-о́тный, *adj.,* favorable, reduced. Л. биле́т, reduced ticket. На льго́тных усло́виях, at a reduced price; on favorable terms. Во-льг-о́тный, *adj.,* (*folk*), free. В-ое

житьё, (*idiom folk*), the life of Riley.
не-льз-я́, *adv.,* it is impossible; it is prohibited; forbidden. Н. входи́ть, no entrance; entrance forbidden. Н. кури́ть, no smoking; smoking forbidden.

по-ле́з-ность, *n.f.,* usefulness, utility, wholesomeness. П. мероприя́тия, usefulness of a measure. По-ле́з-ный, *adj.,* useful, profitable, beneficial, helpful. П. челове́к, useful, helpful man. П-ая де́ятельность, useful activities. Быть поле́зным, to be useful. Не могу́-ли я быть вам поле́зным? May I be of some service to you? По-ле́з-но, *adv.,* usefully, profitably, beneficially, helpfully.

по́-льз-а, *n.f.,* use, good, profit, benefit. Кака́я от э́того по́льза? What is the good of that? Извлека́ть по́льзу из чего́-либо, to make use of something. Ра́ди о́бщей по́льзы, for the common good. Он говори́л в его́ по́льзу, he spoke in his favor. По́-льз-ование, *n.n.,* use; treatment, care. Места́ о́бщего по́льзования, public places. Пра́во по́льзования, right of use.

по́-льз-овать, *v.i.,* + *acc.,* (*obs.*), to attend, treat, doctor. Больно́го по́льзовал изве́стный врач, the patient was attended by a well known physician. По́-льз-овать-ся, *v.i.r.,* + *instr.,* to make use of, take advantage of, enjoy. П. дове́рием, to enjoy someone's confidence. П. креди́том, to have credit. П. лу́чшим учебником, to use the best textbook. П. слу́чаем, to take advantage of an opportunity, occasion. П. у врача́, (*obs.*), to be treated by a physician.

ис-по́-льз-овать, *v.p.,* and *v.i.,* + *acc.,* to use, make use of; consume, profit. И. слу́жащих по их специа́льностям, to use employees according to their specialties. И. во всю, (*colloq.*), to make the most of. Пра́вильно и. си́лы на произво́дстве, (*recent, slogan*), to use manpower efficiently in industry. Ис-по́-льз-овать-ся, *v.p.r.* and *v.i.r,* to be used, utilized. Произво́дственные возмо́жности далеко́ не испо́льзуются, production possibilities are far from being fully utilized. Ис-по́-льз-ование, *n.n.,* utilization. Ис-по́-льз-ованный, *adj., part. pass. past,* used; consumed. Ис-по́-льз-уемый, *adj., part. pass. pres.,* being utilized, useable. Сре́дства, испо́льзуемые для достиже́ния це́ли, the means utilized to attain a goal, the means to an end.

вос-по́-льз-овать-ся, *v.p.r.,* + *instr.,* to profit; take advantage of, make use. В. возмо́жностью, to avail oneself of an opportunity. Мы не могли́ в.

ва́шим приглаше́нием, we were not able to accept your invitation.

ЛЕЖ-, ЛЁЖ-, ЛЕГ-, ЛЁГ-, ЛЕЧ-, ЛАГ-, ЛЯГ-, ЛЯЖ-, ЛОГ-, ЛОЖ-, RECLINATION, RECUMBENCY

леж-а́-ть, *v.i.,* to lie, recline, repose. Л. в посте́ли, to remain in bed. У него́ лежа́т де́ньги в ба́нке, he has money in the bank. Го́род лежи́т на холме́, the town is situated on a hill. Эта обя́занность лежи́т на вас, it is your duty. Леж-а́ние, *n.n.,* lying. Леж-а́нка, *n.f.,* low stove for lying on. Леж-а́лый, *adj.,* not fresh. Л. хлеб, stale bread. Л-ая мука́, stale flour. Леж-а́чий, *adj.,* used as n., one who is lying. Лежа́чего не бьют, (*saying*) one doesn't beat a dead dog; one doesn't beat a man when he's down. Леж-а́щий, *adj., part. act. pres.,* lying. Л. ничко́м, prone. Леж-е-бо́к, *n.m.,* loafer, idler. Лёж-ень, *n.m.,* (*tech.*), foundation beam. Леж-мя́, *adv.,* (*colloq.*), prone, supine. Лежмя́ лежа́ть (*folk*), to stay fast in bed. В-лёж-ку, *adv.,* lying. Лежа́ть в., (*colloq.*), to remain in bed.

воз-леж-а́ть, *v.i.,* воз-ле́чь, *v.p.,* (*obs.*), to recline.

вы́-леж-ать, *v.p.,* вы-лёж-ивать, *v.i.,* to lie, keep to one's bed for a certain length of time. Врач предписа́л больно́му вы́лежать три неде́ли, the doctor ordered the patient to stay in bed for three weeks.

до-леж-а́ть-ся, *v.p.r.,* до-лёж-ивать-ся, *v.i.r.,* до + *gen.,* to remain in bed up to a given time. Д. до полу́дня, to remain in bed till noon.

за-леж-а́ть-ся, *v.p.r.,* за-лёж-ивать-ся, *v.i.r.,* to lie a long time; remain in bed too long. За́-леж-ь, *n.f.,* stale, shopworn goods; layer, stratum, bed. З. то́рфа, deposit of peat. За-леж-а́лый, *adj.,* stale. З. това́р, stale goods, merchandise.

на-леж-а́ть, *v.p.,* + *acc.,* (*colloq.*), to have one's fill of lying. Н. про́лежень, to get a bedsore. На-леж-а́ть-ся, *v.p.r.,* to be tired of lying in bed.

над-леж-а́ть, *v.i.,* (*obs.*), to be necessary. Надлежи́т э́то сде́лать, it must be done. Над-леж-а́щий, *adj., part. act. pres.,* fitting, proper, suitable. Надлежа́щим о́бразом, properly, fittingly, duly.

от-леж-а́ть, *v.p.,* от-лёж-ивать, *v.i.,* + *acc.,* to lie in bed a long time. Я отлежа́ла себе́ но́гу, my leg has become numb from lying. От-леж-а́ть-ся, *v.p.r.,* от-лёж-ивать-ся, *v.i.r.,* to recover by lying in bed Он отлёживается после тяжёлой работы, he is lying down after hard work.

пере-леж-а́ть, *v.p.,* пере-лёж-ивать, *v.i.,* to lie too long. Я перележа́л на со́лнце и обжёг спи́ну, I lay too long in the sun and burned my back.

под-леж-а́ть, *v.i.,* to be subject to; be under the jurisdiction of. Это не подлежи́т ни мале́йшему сомне́ию, this is beyond the slightest doubt. Под-лежа́щий, *adj., part. act. pres.,* subject to. П. суде́бному пресле́дованию, (*jurid.*), indictable. Под-леж-а́щее, *n.n.,* (*gram.*), subject.

по-леж-а́ть, *v.p.,* (*colloq.*), to lie for a while. Я́блоки полежа́ли не́сколько дней в кладово́й, the apples were kept for a while in the storeroom. Ему́ сле́дует не́сколько дней п., he ought to stay in bed for a few days.

по-лёж-ивать, *v.i.,* (*colloq.*), to lie in bed. Он все полёживает, по́сле боле́зни, he spends most of his time in bed since his illness.

при-над-леж-а́ть, *v.i.,* + *dat.,* to belong, pertain, relate, concern. Кни́га принадлежи́т библиоте́ке, this book belongs to the library. При-над-ле́ж-ность, *n.f.,* appliance, implement. П. туале́та, toilet article. П. к па́ртии, party membership. Пи́сьменные принадле́жности, writing implements, materials. Возврати́ть де́ньги по принадле́жности, to restore money to its rightful owner.

про-леж-а́ть, *v.p.,* про-лёж-ивать, *v.i.,* + *acc.,* to spend a certain time in bed. Я пролежа́ла три неде́ли в посте́ли, I stayed in bed three weeks. Про́-леж-ень, *n.m.,* bedsore. При хоро́шем ухо́де у больно́го не должно́ быть про́лежней, under good care a patient should not get bedsores.

с-леж-а́ть-ся, *v.p.r.,* с-лёж-ивать-ся, *v.i.r.,* to deteriorate in storage. Зерно́ слежа́лось в скла́де, the grain has spoiled in storage.

леч-ь, ляг-у, (*from* лег-ть), *v.p.,* to lie down. Л. спать, to go to bed. Л. костьми́, (*fig.*), to die, lay down one's life. Ляг, ляг-отдохни́! Lie down and rest! Ночле́г *n.m,* night's lodging.

воз-ле́ч-ь, *v.p.,* воз-леж-а́ть, *v.i.,* (*obs.*), to recline.

за-ле́ч-ь, *v.p.,* за-лег-а́ть, *v.i.,* to lie down, take to one's bed. Зале́чь спать, to lie down to sleep. Медве́дь залега́ет на́ зиму в берло́гу, the bear takes to his den for the winter to hibernate. За-лег-а́ние, *n.n.,* bed, vein, seam. Райо́н залега́ния у́гля, a region of coal-fields.

на-ле́ч-ь, *v.p.,* на-лег-а́ть, *v.i.,* на + *acc.,* to set oneself to something; make an effort. Н. на рабо́ту, to work with

might and main. Н. на еду́, to eat heartily.

об-ле́ч-ь, *v.p.,* об-лег-а́ть, *v.i.,* to drape with vestments; surround. Ту́чи облега́ли горизо́нт, clouds have covered the horizon.

от-ле́ч-ь, от-ля́г-у, *v.p.,* от-лег-а́ть, *v.i.,* (*used mainly in 3d pers.,*) to be better, feel relieved. У него́ отлегло́ от се́рдца, he felt relieved.

пере-ле́ч-ь, пере-ля́г-у, *v.p.,* to move to another place and lie down, lie down somewhere else. П. с дива́на на крова́ть, to move from the sofa to the bed. П. с одного́ бо́ка на друго́й, to turn from one side to the other.

по-ле́ч-ь, *v.p.* (see лечь). В боя́х полегло́ мно́го наро́ду, many people were killed in the battles. Овёс полёг, the oats have been flattened.

при-лег-а́ть, *v.i.,* к + *dat.,* to lie or be situated near; to be adjacent to, to adjoin. Пла́тье хорошо́ прилега́ло к та́лии, the dress fitted neatly at the waist. Сад прилега́ет к реке́, the garden is near the river. При-лег-а́ющий, *adj. part. act. pres.,* adjacent, contiguous, adjoining.

при-ле́ч-ь, *v.p.,* to lie down for a short while. П. отдохну́ть на часо́к, to lie down for a short hour.

при-на-ле́ч-ь, *v.p.,* на + *acc.,* (*colloq.*), to make an effort, strain, apply oneself. П. на учёбу, (*colloq.*), to apply oneself to one's studies. П. на вёсла, to lay to one's oars. При-леж-а́ние, *n.n.,* diligence, industry, application, assiduousness, studiousness. При-ле́ж-ный, *adj.,* diligent, assiduous, industrious. П. учени́к, diligent pupil.

про-лег-а́ть, *v.i.,* to, go, run through. Доро́га пролега́ет в гора́х, the road runs through the mountains.

раз-ле́ч-ь-ся, *v.p.r.,* to stretch oneself out, lie down to sleep; sprawl. Р. на дива́не (на траве́), to sprawl on a sofa, (on the grass).

с-ле́ч-ь, *v.p.,* to take to one's bed; fall ill. Она́ слегла́ от огорче́ния, she became ill from grief.

у-ле́ч-ь-ся, *v.p.r.,* у-кла́д-ывать-ся, *v.i.r.,* to lie down, go to bed; become quiet, composed; subside, abate. У. в посте́ль, to go to bed. Дать возбужде́нию уле́чься, to let the excitement subside. Бу́ря улегла́сь, the storm has abated.

лож-и́ть-ся, *v.i.r.,* to lie down. Я ложу́сь спать в де́сять часо́в ве́чера, I go to bed at ten p.m. Лож-би́на, *n.f.,* hollow. Ло́ж-е, *n.n.,* (*obs.*), couch, bed; river bed, channel.

в-лож-и́ть, *v.p.,* в-кла́д-ывать, *v.i.,* + *acc.,* to put in, into; enclose; invest. В.

са́блю в ножны́, to put a sword into a scabbard. В. всю ду́шу в рабо́ту, to put one's heart and soul into one's work. В-лож-е́ние, *n.n.*, insertion. В. средств, investment of capital. Письмо́ со вложе́нием де́нег, letter containing money.

воз-лож-и́ть, *v.p.*, воз-лаг-а́ть, *v.i.,* + *acc.,* на + *acc.,* to lay on; charge; rest on. В. вено́к на моги́лу, to lay a wreath on a grave. В. наде́жды, to pin one's hopes on. В. отве́тственность на кого́-либо, to lay the responsibility on someone. Воз-лаг-а́ть-ся, *v.i.r.,* to be laid upon. Это возлага́ется на вас, this is incumbent on you. Воз-лож-е́ние, *n.n.,* laying (*as* of a wreath).

вы́-лож-ить, *v.p.,* вы-кла́д-ывать, *v.i.,* + *acc.,* to lay out, take out. В. бельё из сундука́, to take linen out of a trunk. В. кирпичём, to face with brick.

до-лож-и́ть, *v.p.,* до-кла́д-ывать, *v.i.,* + *gen.,* to add; о + *prep.,* (*colloq.*), report, announce. Д. варе́нья в ба́нку, to fill a jar with jam. Д. на заседа́нии о результа́тах свои́х иссле́дований, to report on the results of one's research.

за-лож-и́ть, *v.p.,* за-кла́д-ывать, *v.i.,* + *acc.,* to pawn, mortgage; lay a foundation, cornerstone; harness. З. шу́бу в ломба́рд, to pawn a fur coat. З. фунда́мент зда́ния, to lay the foundation of a building. З. тро́йку, to harness three horses in a team. За-ло́г, *n.m.,* deposit, pledge, pawn, mortgage; (*gram.*), voice. З. успе́ха, promise of success. Дать (оста́вить), з., to leave a deposit. Действи́тельный з., (*gram.*), active voice. Страда́тельный з., (*gram.*), passive voice. За-ло́ж-ник, *n.m.,* hostage.

из-лож-и́ть, *v.p.,* из-лаг-а́ть, *v.i.,* + *acc.,* to state, expound, give an account. И. пи́сьменно, своё мне́ние (свою про́сьбу), to write one's opinion; put one's request in writing. Бе́гло и. свои мы́сли, to present one's thoughts fluently. Из-лож-е́ние, *n.n.,* account, statement, exposition. Кра́ткое и., summary. Из-лаг-а́емый, *adj., part. pass. pres.,* which is being stated, presented, expounded. Из-ло́ж-енный, *adj., part. pass. past,* stated, written, expounded, presented.

на-лож-и́ть, *v.p.,* на-лаг-а́ть, на-кла́д-ывать, *v.i.,* на + *acc.,* to lay, put; impose. Н. печа́ть, to affix a seal. Н. по́шлину, to impose a duty, Н. на себя́ ру́ки, (*idiom*), to commit suicide. Налага́ть взыска́ние, to impose, set a punishment. На-ло́г, *n.m.,* tax, assessment. Н. на насле́дство, inheritance tax. Подохо́дный н., income tax. На-ло́г-овый, *adj.,* pertaining to taxes,

taxation. На-лог-о-плате́льщик, *n.m.,* taxpayer. На-лож-е́ние, *n.n.,* laying, imposing. На-ло́ж-енный, *adj. part. pass. past,* laid on, *used in the expression*: На-ло́ж-енным платежо́м, cash on delivery.

низ-лож-и́ть, *v.p.,* низ-лаг-а́ть, *v.i.,* + *acc.,* to depose, dethrone. Н. царя́, to depose the Tsar. Низ-лож-е́ние, *n.n.,* deposition, dethronement.

об-лож-и́ть, *v.p.,* об-лаг-а́ть, об-кла́д-ывать, *v.i.,* + *acc.,* + *instr.,* (*obs.*), to cover; blockade; invest; surround. О. штра́фом, to impose a fine. О. нало́гом, to levy a tax. Об-лож-и́ть-ся, *v.p.r.,* об-кла́д-ывать-ся, об-лаг-а́ть-ся, *v.i.r.,* to surround oneself, be subject to. Иноземные това́ры облага́ются высо́кими по́шлинами, foreign goods are subject to high tariffs. Об-лож-е́ние, *n.n.,* taxation, imposition; surrounding. О. кре́пости, siege of a fortress. Об-ло́ж-енный, *adj., part. pass. past,* surrounded. О. язы́к, coated tongue. Не́бо обло́жено ту́чами, the sky is clouded over. Об-ло́ж-ка, *n.f.,* cover. Кни́га в наря́дной обло́жке, a book in an attractive cover. Об-лож-но́й, *adj., used in the expression*: Обложно́й дождь, rain from all directions.

от-лож-и́ть, *v.p.,* от-кла́д-ывать, *v.i.,* to lay aside, save; defer, postpone. О. отъе́зд, to postpone one's departure. О. на чёрный день, (*idiom*), to save for a rainy day. О. воротни́к, to turn down a collar. От-лож-и́ть-ся, *v.p.r.,* to fall away, secede. Коло́нии отложи́лись от метропо́лии, the colonies seceded from the mother country. От-лож-е́ние, *n.n.,* defection; accumulation of deposit. О. зубно́го ка́мня, accumulation of deposit on the teeth. От-лож-е́ния, *n.n.pl.,* sediment, deposit. О. го́рных поро́д, deposits of minerals. От-лож-но́й, *adj.,* turned down. О. воротни́к, turned-down collar. От-ло́г-ость, *n.f.,* slope, declivity. От-ло́г-ий, *adj.,* sloping. О. бе́рег реки́, sloping river bank. От-ло́г-о, *adv.,* slopingly.

пере-лож-и́ть, *v.p.,* пере-лаг-а́ть, пере-кла́д-ывать, *v.i.,* + *acc.,* to transpose, move from one place to another; set to music. Переложи́ть кни́ги из шка́фа на по́лку, to transfer books from a bookcase to shelves. П. собра́ние на сле́дующий день, to postpone a meeting to the next day. Пере-лож-е́ние, *n.n.,* transposition. П. про́зы в стихи́, transposition of prose into verse. П. стихи́ на про́зу, transposition of verse into prose.

под-лож-и́ть, *v.p.,* под-кла́д-ывать, *v.i.,*

+ *acc.*, + *gen.*, to lay under. На́до п. что́-нибудь под стол - он шата́ется, the table is unsteady, it needs a wedge under one of its legs. Под-ло́ж-ность, *n.f.*, falseness, spuriousness. Под-ло́ж-ный, *adj.*, false, counterfeit. П. ве́ксель, forged note. П-ая по́дпись, forged signature. Под-ло́г, *n.m.*, forgery.

по-лож-и́ть, *v.p.*, to put, lay, place. П. кни́гу на стол, to put a book on the table. П. на о́бе лопа́тки, to pin, (wrestling). П. нача́ло, to initiate. П. слова́ на му́зыку, to write words for music. Как Бог на́ душу поло́жит, (*saying*), as one pleases. Э́тот судья́ реша́ет не по зако́нам, а как Бог на́ душу поло́жит, this judge does not follow the law, but judges as he pleases. По-лож-е́ние, *n.n.*, position, situation, place, П. дел, condition of affairs. П. без переме́н, situation unchanged. Вое́нное п., martial law. Высо́кое обще́ственное п., high public position, rank. Оса́дное п., state of siege. По-лож-и́тельность, *n.f.*, positiveness. По-ложи́тельный, *adj.*, positive, reliable; steady. П. знак, positive sign. П. отве́т, positive, affirmative reply. П-ая сте́пень, (*gram.*), positive degree. По-лож-и́тельно, *adv.*, positively, decidedly.

по-лаг-а́ть, *v.i.*, to think, deem, reckon, suppose, assume П. свои́м до́лгом, to deem it one's duty. Полага́ю, что..., I take it that..., I suppose that.

по-лаг-а́ть-ся, *v.i.r.*, по-лож-и́ть-ся, *v.p.r.*, to rely on, confide in, depend on. П. то́лько на себя́, to rely solely on oneself. Полага́ется, it is the custom. Здесь не полага́ется кури́ть, you are not supposed to smoke here. По-лаг-а́ющийся, *adj.*, *part. act. pres.*, due, supposed to be. Не п., not due, not supposed to be. По-ло́г-лй, *adj.*, slanting, sloping. По-ло́г-ость, *n.f.*, slope, declivity.

пред-лож-и́ть, *v.p.*, пред-лаг-а́ть, *v.i.*, + *acc.*, to offer. П. по́мощь, to proffer help, assistance. П. ру́ку, to offer one's hand. П. ру́ку и се́рдце, to propose marriage. Пред-ло́г, *n.m.*, (*gram.*), preposition; pretext, pretence. Под предло́гом, under the pretext. Пред-лож-е́ние, *n.n.*, offer, proposal, overture; proposition, suggestion, (*gram.*), sentence. Вво́дное п., (*gram.*), parenthesis. Гла́вное (прида́точное) п., (*gram.*), principal (subordinate) clause. Спрос и п., supply and demand. Ми́рные предложе́ния, overtures to peace. Предло́ж-ный паде́ж, (*gram.*), prepositional case.

пред-по-лаг-а́ть, *v.i.*, пред-по-лож-и́ть, *v.p.*, + *acc.*, to suppose, surmise, conjecture. Что вы предполага́ете де́лать за́втра? What do you intend to do tomorrow? Предположи́м, let us suppose. Пред-по-лож-е́ние, *n.n.*, supposition, surmise, conjecture, assumption. Пред-по-лож-и́тельный, *adj.*, conjectural, hypothetical. Пред-по-лож-и́тельно, *adv.*, supposedly.

при-лож-и́ть, *v.p.*, при-лаг-а́ть, *v.i.*, to attach; make a particular effort. П. стара́ния, to do one's best. При сём прилага́ю, (*obs.*), I enclose herewith. Ума́ не приложу́, (*idiom*), I cannot understand. При-лож-и́ть-ся, *v.p.r.*, при-кла́д-ывать-ся, *v.i.r.*, к + *dat.*, to aim (*e.g.*, a gun); (*rel.*), to kiss an icon, religious relics. П. к кресту́, to kiss a cross. При-лож-е́ние, *n.n.*, supplement При-ло́ж-енный, *adj.*, *part. pass. past*, attached. При-лож-и́вший, *adj.*, *part. act. past*, who had attached, applied. Учёный, приложи́вший все уси́лия к откры́тию но́вых средств лече́ния ра́ка, не про́жил да́ром, the scientist, who has applied all his efforts to discovering a means of curing cancer, has not lived in vain. При-лаг-а́тельное, и́мя прилага́тельное, *n.n.*, (*gram.*), adjective. При-лаг-а́емый, *adj.*, *part. pres. pass.*, being attached; attached, attachable. По прилаг-а́емому спи́ску, according to the attached list.

про-лож-и́ть, *v.p.*, про-кла́д-ывать, *v.i.*, + *acc.*, to lay, build a road. П. доро́гу, to lay out a road.

раз-лож-и́ть, *v.p.*, раз-лаг-а́ть, рас-кла́д-ывать, *v.i.*, + *acc.*, to divide into parts; decompose. Раскла́дывать ка́рты, to lay out cards. Разложи́ть сло́во на приста́вку, ко́рень, су́ффикс, to divide a word into its prefix, root, and suffix. Разлож-е́ние, *n.n.*, putrefaction, decomposition. Р. о́бщества, demoralization of society. Раз-лож-и́вшийся, *adj. part. act. past*, corrupt, putrefied. Р. труп, decayed corpse.

рас-по-лож-и́ть, *v.p.*, рас-по-лаг-а́ть, *v.i.*, + *acc.*, + *instr.*, to dispose, place; intend, purport. Р. ме́бель в ко́мнате, to place furniture in a room. Р. в свою́ по́льзу, to win someone's favor. Р. вре́менем, to have time. (only располага́ть). Он располага́ет больши́ми сре́дствами, he has large means at his disposal. Рас-по-лаг-а́ть-ся, *v.i.r.*, рас-по-лож-и́ть-ся, *v.p.r.*, to be stationed, encamp. Р. на житьё, to take up quarters, to settle down for a long stay. Рас-пол-о́женный, *adj.*, *part. pass. past*, situated. Го́род располо́жен на холме́, the town is situated on a hill. Рас-по-лож-е́ние, *n.n.*, disposition;

situation; distribution; order. Р. ду́ха, frame of mind; mood. Заслужи́ть чьё-ли́бо р., to win someone's favor. Удо́бное р. ко́мнат, convenient arrangement of rooms. Рас-по-ло́ж-ен(ный), *adj., part. pass.*, situated; well disposed towards. Нача́льник располо́жен ко мне, my boss is well-disposed towards me.

пред-рас-по-лож-и́ть, *v.p.,* пред-рас-по-лаг-а́ть, *v.i.,* to predispose, make susceptible. Пред-рас-по-лож-е́ние, *п.п.,* predisposition, propensity. П. к чахо́тке, susceptibility to tuberculosis.

с-лож-и́ть, *v.p.,* с-кла́д-ывать, *v.i.,* + *acc.,* to put together, join, clasp; sum up; compose. С. ве́щи, to put things together. С-лаг-а́ть, *v.i.,* to resign, to put together, take off. С. бре́мя, to shed one's burden, responsibilities. С. зва́ние, to resign. С. ору́жие, to lay down arms. С. стихи́, to versify. С-лаг-а́ть-ся, *v.i.r.,* to be added, summed up. С-лаг-а́емое, *п.п.,* additament, item. С-лож-е́ние, *п.п.,* (*math.*), addition; figure, build, physique; constitution. Кре́пкое с., sound constitution. С. с себя́ до́лжности, resignation from an office. С-ло́ж-енный, *adj., part. pass. past,* folded, built. Стена́, сло́женная из кирпича́, a wall built of bricks. С-лож-ённый, *adj., in expression*: Пло́хо сложённый, ungainly, gawky. Хорошо́ с., well built, well knit. С-ло́ж-ность, *n.f.,* complication, complexity. В о́бщей сло́жности, on the whole; after all. С-ло́ж-ный, *adj.,* complicated, complex, compound. С-ая ситуа́ция, complicated situation. С-ло́ж-но, *adv.,* complicatedly. С-лож-а́, *adv., in expression*: Сиде́ть сложа́ ру́ки, (*fig.*), to twiddle one's thumbs, sit idly. С-лож-и́ть-ся, *v.p.r.,* с-кла́д-ывать-ся, *v.i.r.,* to pool. Бра́тья сложи́лись и купи́ли автомоби́ль, the brothers pooled their money and bought a car.

о-с-лож-ни́ть, *v.p.,* о-с-лож-ня́ть, *v.i.,* + *acc.,* to complicate. Это о́чень осложня́ет положе́ние, this complicates the situation. О-с-лож-ни́ть-ся, *v.p.r.,* о-с-лож-ня́ть-ся, *v.i.r.,* + *instr.,* to be complicated. Просту́да осложни́лась воспале́нием в лёгких, the cold was complicated by pneumonia. О-с-лож-не́ние, *п.п.,* complication. О. по́сле гри́ппа, complications after an attack of influenza. О. отноше́ний, complication of relations.

у-лож-и́ть, *v.p.,* у-кла́д-ывать, *v.i.,* + *acc.,* to lay down; pack; kill. У. ребёнка спать, to put a child to bed. У. ве́щи в чемода́н, to pack things in a trunk. У-лож-и́ть-ся *v.p.r.,* у-кла́д-

ывать-ся *v.i.r.,* to pack up. У-лож-е́ние, *п.п.,* (*hist.*), legal code.

лог, *n.m.,* wide ravine; fallow land. Ло́говище, ло́г-о, *п.п.,* lair, den. Зверь лежи́т в своём ло́говище, the animal is lying in its lair.

ЛЕЗ-, ЛАЗ-, ЛАЖ-, ЛЗ-, ЛОЗ-, ЛЕС(Т)-, ASCENT, ASCENSION, CLIMBING, SCALING

лез-ть, *v.i.det.,* на, в + *acc.,* to climb, scale; intrude; come out. Ма́льчик ле́зет на кры́шу, the boy is climbing on the roof. Колесо́ не ле́зет на ось, the wheel does not fit the axle. Сапоги́ мне не ле́зут на но́ги, I cannot put these boots on. Пёс ле́зет в дра́ку, the dog is spoiling for a fight. Л. из ко́жи, (*fig., idiom.*), to try hard. Л. на́ стену, (*fig.*), to be in a rage.

вз-лез-ть, *v.p.,* вз-лез-а́ть, *v.i.,* на + *acc.,* (*colloq.*), to climb in; get in, find one's way in. В. на де́рево, to climb a tree.

в-лез-ть, *v.p.,* в-лез-а́ть, *v.i.,* на, в + *acc.,* to climb in, get in. В. в окно́, to climb in through a window. В. в дове́рие, (*colloq.*), to insinuate oneself into someone's confidence.

вы-лез-ть, *v.p.,* вы-лез-а́ть, *v.i.,* из + *gen.,* to climb out. В. из окна́, to climb out of a window.

до-ле́з-ть, *v.p.,* до-лез-а́ть, *v.i.,* до + *gen.,* to reach. Д. до поро́га, to reach the threshold.

за-ле́з-ть, *v.p.,* за-лез-а́ть, *v.i.* на, в + *acc.,* to climb on; creep in. З. на́ гору, to climb a hill. З. в долги́, to run into debt. З. в чужо́й карма́н, to steal.

на-ле́з-ть, *v.p.,* на-лез-а́ть, *v.i.,* на + *acc.,* to crawl, climb over. На я́блоню нале́зли муравьи́, ants crawled all over the apple tree. Башма́к не налеза́ет мне на́ ногу, the shoe does not fit me.

об-ле́з-ть, *v.p.,* об-лез-а́ть, *v.i.,* to peel, come off; become bare; wear out. Мех облеза́ет, the fur is wearing out. Кра́ска облезла, the paint peeled off. Во́лосы обле́зли, the hair has fallen out. Об-ле́з-лый, *adj.,* shabby, bare, motheaten. О. пёс, mangy dog.

от-ле́з-ть, *v.p.,* от-лез-а́ть, *v.i.,* от + *gen.,* to withdraw creeping. О. от стены́ на два фу́та, to withdraw from the wall two feet.

пере-ле́з-ть, *v.p.,* пере-лез-а́ть, *v.i.,* че́рез + *acc.,* to climb over. П. че́рез забо́р, to climb over a fence.

под-ле́з-ть, *v.p.,* под-лез-а́ть, *v.i.,* to creep, crawl under, thrust oneself under. Ребёнок подлёз под стол, to child crawled under the table.

по-лéз-ть, *v.p.,* to start climbing. Мáльчик полéз на дéрево, the boy climbed the tree. П. в кармáн, to put one's hand into a pocket. По-лез-áй, climb in; crawl in. Назвáлся груздём — полезáй в кýзов, (*prov.*), you've made your bed, you must lie in it.

при-лéз-ть, *v.p.,* при-лез-áть, *v.i.,* to crawl up to, in. В шалáш прилéзли муравьи́, ants crawled into the hut.

про-лéз-ть, *v.p.,* про-лез-áть, *v.i.,* to creep, crawl through. П. незамéтно, to get in by stealth.

раз-лéз-ть-ся, *v.p.r.,* раз-лез-áть-ся, *v.i. r.,* to tear, unravel. Муравьи́ разлéзлись в рáзные стóроны, the ants crawled away in all directions. Р. по швам, to give at the seams. Мои́ сапоги́ разлéзлись, my boots are gaping.

с-лез-ть, *v.p.,* с-лез-áть, *v.i.,* с + *gen.,* to descend, come down; dismount, alight. С. с дéрева, to climb down from a tree. С. с лóшади, to dismount. Нóготь слез, the nail came off. Кóжа слéзла, the skin peeled off.

лáз-ить, *v.i. indet.,* to climb, clamber. Лáзанье (*colloq.*); лáз-енье, *n.n.,* climbing. Лаз, *n.m.,* gap. Лаз-éйка, *n.f.,* (*dim.*), small gap, hole. Хи́трый всегдá лазéйку найдёт, a crafty, cunning man will always find a loophole. Лаз-ýтчик, *n.m.,* spy, scout. Вод-о-лáз, *n.m.,* diver; Newfoundland dog.

вы-лáз-ить, *v.i.,* (*colloq.*), *syn.* вы-лез-áть, to climb out. Вы́-лаз-ить, *v.p.,* + *acc.,* (*colloq.*), to search around, *syn.* об-лáз-ить. Вы́-лаз-ка, *n.f.,* sally, sortie. Дéлать вы́лазку, to sally forth.

из-лáз-ить, *v.p.,* + *acc.,* to climb all over. И. все гóры, to climb all over the mountains.

об-лáз-ить, *v.p.,* + *acc.,* (*colloq.*), to search around. О. все закоýлки, to search every nook and cranny.

пере-лáз-ить, пере-лáж-у, *v.p.,* + *acc.,* *syn.* излáзить всё, to make a thorough search. Пере-лáз-ить, *v.i.,* (*colloq.*), to climb over, *syn.* перелезáть. П. чéрез забóр, to climb over a fence. Перелáз, *n.m.,* a gap, break, through which one can climb. Шёл вдоль плетня́ и дошёл до перелáза, I was walking along beside the fence and reached a spot where I could climb over.

по-лáз-ить, по-лáж-у, *v.p.,* to do some climbing. Полáзить по углáм (по дерéвьям), to look around, to climb trees.

Про-лáз-ить, *v.p.,* to climb for a long time. П. по горáм весь день, to climb in the mountains for a whole day.

Пролáза, *n.m.,* (*colloq.*), sly, pushing person.

пó-лз-ать, пó-лз-аю, *v.i. indet.,* по-лз-ти́, по-лз-ý, *v.i. det.,* to creep, crawl. По-лз-ýщий, пó-лз-ающий, *adj. part. act. pres.,* the one who is crawling, crawls. Пó-лз-ший, пó-лз-авший, *adj. part. act. past,* the one who used to crawl, was crawling. П. в грязи́, one who grovelled in dirt. Матéрия ползёт, (*fig.*), this material is coming apart. Над рекóй ползёт тумáн, fog is creeping in over the river. Пó-лз-ание, *n.n.,* creeping, crawling. По-лз-óк, *n.m.,* distance covered by crawling. В два ползкá я добрáлся до кустá, in two moves I reached the bush. По-лз-ýн, *n.m.,* по-лз-ýнья, *n.f.,* one who crawls. По-лз-ýчий, *adj.,* serpentine. П-ие растéния, creepers. По-лз-кóм, *adv.,* on all fours. Прибли́зился ползкóм, he crept up on all fours. Пó-лоз, *n.m.,* по-лóз-ья, *n.pl.,* runners on a sled. Сáни на полóзьях, a sleigh on runners.

в-по-лз-áть, в-по-лз-áю, *v.i.,* в-по-лз-ти́, в-по-лз-ý, *v.p.,* на, в + *acc.,* to crawl on, in. Гýсеницы вползáли на черёмуху, caterpillars crawled all over the birdcherry tree.

вы-по-лз-áть, *v.i.,* вы́-по-лз-ти, *v.p.,* to crawl out. Из норы́ выползáла змея́, a snake crawled out of the hole.

до-по-лз-áть, *v.i.,* до-по-лз-ти́, *v.p.,* до + *gen.,* to reach by creeping, crawling. Червя́к допóлз до цветкá, the worm crawled up to the flower.

за-по-лз-áть, *v.i.,* за-по-лз-ти́, *v.p.,* за + *gen.,* to creep, crawl into. Букáшка заползлá за вóрот, the bug crawled into the collar.

ис-пó-лз-ать, *v.p.,* + *acc.,* (*colloq.*), to creep all over. Ребёнок испóлзал весь пол, the child crept all over the floor.

на-пó-лз-ать-ся, *v.p.r.,* (*colloq.*), to creep, crawl as much as one desires.

о-по-лз-áть, *v.i.,* о-по-лз-ти́, *v.p.,* to crawl around; slide. Бéрег си́льно опóлз, the river bank caved in. О-по-лз-ень, *n.m.,* landslide.

от-по-лз-áть, *v.i.,* от-по-лз-ти́, *v.p.,* to crawl, creep away; drag oneself away.

пере-по-лз-áть, *v.i.,* пере-по-лз-ти́, *v.p.,* to crawl over, creep over. П. чéрез кóмнату, to crawl across a room.

под-по-лз-áть, *v.i.,* под-по-лз-ти́, *v.p.,* к + *dat.,* под + *acc.,* to creep up, under. П. к кустý, to creep up to a bush. Ребёнок подпóлз под кровáть, the child crawled under the bed.

по-пó-лз-ать, *v.p.,* to crawl for a short time.

по-по-лз-ти́, *v.p.,* to start crawling. Черепáха поползлá на бéрег, the turtle began to crawl up the bank. По-по-лз-нове́ние, *п.п.,* faint inclination, longing, wish. У него́ бы́ло п. уе́хать, не сказа́в никому́ ни сло́ва, he was inclined to depart without telling anyone.

при-по-лз-а́ть, *v.i.,* при-по-лз-ти́, *v.p.,* to creep, crawl up.

про-по-лз-а́ть, *v.i.,* про-по-лз-ти́, *v.p.,* to creep, crawl past, through. П. под мосто́м, to crawl under a bridge. П. де́сять ме́тров, to crawl a distance of 10 meters. Про-по́-лз-ать, *v.p.,* to pass a definite time in crawling, creeping. Ребёнок всё у́тро пропо́лзал, the child spent the whole morning crawling about.

рас-по-лз-а́ть-ся, *v.i.r.,* рас-по-лз-ти́-сь, *v.p.r.,* to crawl about, sprawl; tear; unravel, fall to pieces. Я́щерицы расползли́сь по но́рам, the lizards crawled into their respective holes. Пла́тье расползло́сь, the dress tore. Рас-по-лз-а́ние, *п.п.,* sprawling; tearing; falling to pieces.

с-по-лз-а́ть, *v.i.,* с-по-лз-ти́, *v.p.,* to creep off, down. С. вниз, to slip down. Шу́ба сползла́ с его́ плеч, the furcoat slipped off his shoulders. С-по-лз-а́ние, *п.п.,* slipping off.

у-по-лз-а́ть, *v.i.,* у-по-лз-ти́, *v.p.,* to creep, crawl away. Змея́ уползла́, the snake crawled away.

ле́ст-ниц-а, *n.f.,* staircase, stairs, ladder.

ле́с-енка, *n.f.,* (*dim.*), stairs, ladder. Пожа́рная л., fire-escape. Верёвочная л., rope ladder. Складна́я, л., folding ladder. Идти́ вверх (вниз) по ле́стнице, to go up the stairs (down the stairs). Ле́ст-нич-ный, *adj.,* pertaining to stairs. Ле́стничные пери́ла, banisters.

ЛЕК-, ЛЕЧ-, TREATMENT, HEALING, CURE

лек-а́р-ств-о, *п.п.,* medicine, drug, medicament. Дава́ть л., to give medicine. Приготовля́ть л., to prepare medicine. Ле́к-арь, *n.m.* (*obs.*), physician, doctor. Лек-по́м, (*recent*), *abbr.* of ле́карский помо́щник, physician's assistant. Лека́р-ственный, *adj.,* medicinal. Л-ые снадо́бья, (*colloq.*), drugs. Л-ые расте́ния, medicinal herbs, plants.

леч-и́-ть, *v.i.,* + *acc.,* to doctor, treat. Л. больно́го от ка́шля, to treat a patient for a cough. Леч-и́ть-ся, *v.i.r.,* to take a cure, undergo treatment. Л. у изве́стного врача́, to be treated by a well-known doctor. Леч-е́ние, *п.п.,* treatment. Л. больни́чное (до-ма́шнее), hospital (home) treatment. Л.

хирурги́ческое, surgical treatment. Леч-е́б-ник, *п.m.,* handbook of medical advice. Леч-е́бница, *n.f.,* hospital. Леч-е́бный, *adj.,* medical, medicinal; pertaining to treatment. Л. персона́л, medical staff.

вы́-леч-ить, *v.p.,* вы-ле́ч-ивать, *v.i.,* + *acc.,* to cure, heal. Вы́-леч-ить-ся, *v.p.r.,* вы-ле́ч-ивать-ся, *v.i.r.,* to be cured, healed. Больно́й оконча́тельно вы́лечился, the patient has completely recovered.

до-леч-и́ть, *v.p.,* до-ле́ч-ивать, *v.i.,* + *acc.,* to cure completely.

за-леч-и́ть, *v.p.,* за-ле́ч-ивать, *v.i.,* + *acc.,* to heal. З. ра́ну, to heal a wound. За-ле́ч-ивать-ся, *v.i.r.,* за-леч-и́ть-ся, *v.p.r.,* to heal, be healed.

из-леч-и́ть, *v.p.,* из-ле́ч-ивать, *v.i.,* + *acc.,* to cure, heal thoroughly. Из-леч-и́ть-ся, *v.p.r.,* из-ле́ч-ивать-ся, *v.i.r.,* to recover, be cured, healed. Мно́гие боле́зни излечи́ваются дие́той, many diseases are cured through diet. Из-леч-е́ние, *п.п.,* cure, healing, recovery. Отпра́вить в го́спиталь на и., to send to a hospital for treatment. Из-леч-и́мый, *adj.,* curable. И-ая (не-из-лечи́мая) боле́знь, curable (incurable) disease.

по-леч-и́ть, *v.p.,* + *acc.,* to give medical care for a short while. По-леч-и́ть-ся, *v.p.r.,* to be treated. Вам необходи́мо п., you need some medical treatment.

под-леч-и́ть, *v.p.,* под-ле́ч-ивать, *v.i.,* + *acc.,* to treat, heal, improve health. П. ста́рую ра́ну, to heal up an old wound. Под-леч-и́ть-ся, *v.p.r.,* под-ле́ч-ивать-ся, *v.i.r.,* to receive treatment, cure oneself.

про-леч-и́ть, *v.p.,* про-ле́ч-ивать, *v.i.,* + *acc.,* (*colloq.*), to treat a certain length of time. П. после́дние де́ньги, to spend all one's money for treatment. Про-леч-и́ть-ся, *v.p.r.,* to take prolonged treatment. П. не́сколько лет, to be treated for several years.

ЛЕС-, ЛЕШ-, TIMBER, FOREST, WOOD

лес, *n.m.,* forest, wood; timber. Хво́йный (ли́ственный) лес, coniferous (deciduous) forest. Строево́й лес, building lumber. Пусти́ть под лес, to let an area become a forest. Вы́рубить лес, to cut down a forest. Лес-о́к, *n.m.,* (*dim.*), small wood, grove. Лес-а́, *n.m.pl.,* woodlands, forests; scaffolding. Лес-и́стость, *n.f.,* woodiness. Лес-и́стый, *adj.,* wooded, woody, timbered, (*poet.*), silvan. Л-ая ме́стность, woody area.

лес-ни́к, *n.m.,* woodsman. Лес-ни́чий, *n.m.,* forester. Лес-но́й, *adj.,* pertaining to woods; silvan. Л. материа́л, timber, lumber. Л. пейза́ж, woodland scenery. Л. склад, lumber yard. Л-ые бога́тства, timber resources. Лес-о, *a combining form meaning* wood. Лес-о-во́д, *n.m.*, forester. Лес-о-во́дство, *n.n.*, forestry.

лес-о-загото́вка, *n.f.*, logging, lumbering, timber cutting. Лес-о-насажде́ние, *n.n.*, forest planting. Лес-о-охране́ние, *n.n.*, forest conservation. Лес-о-пи́лка, *n.f.*, saw-mill. Лес-о-промы́шленник, *n.n.*, lumber merchant. Лес-о-разрабо́тки, *n.pl.*, forest exploitation. Лес-о-ру́б, *n.m.*, woodcutter, lumberjack. Лес-о-се́ка, *n.f.*, cutting area. Лес-о-спла́в, *n.m.*, timber rafting.

ле́ш-ий, *n.m.*, (*folk.*), wood-goblin. Куда́ тебя́ л. занёс? Where in the world have you been?

об-лес-е́ние, *n.n.*, reforestation. О. сте́пей, the planting of forests in the steppes.

по-ле́с-ье, *n.n.*, low forest area. Белору́сское Поле́сье, a forest region in White Russia, known as Polesie.

по-леш-а́не, *n.pl.*, inhabitants of Polesie.

пере-ле́с-ье, *n.n.*, glade. Пере-ле́с-ок, *n.m.*, copse.

под-ле́с-ок, *n.m.*, underbrush, undergrowth, underwood.

ЛЕТ-, ЛЁТ-, ЛЕЧ-, FLIGHT

лет, *n.m.*, flight, flying. На лету́, in the air, in flight. Пойма́ть мяч на лету́, to catch a ball on the fly. Лёт-ный, *adj.*, pertaining to flying. Л. сезо́н, flying season. Л-ое иску́сство, flying skill. Лет-а́ние, *n.n.*, flying. Лет-а́тельный, *adj.*, flying.

лет-а́-ть, *v.i.*, *indet.*, to fly. Пти́цы лета́ют, birds fly. Над го́родом лета́ли аэропла́ны, planes flew over the city. Па́льцы его́ лета́ли по кла́вишам, (*fig.*), his fingers flew over the keys.

лет-е́ть, леч-у́, *v.i.*, *det.* to fly; hasten, hurry. За́втра я лечу́ в Крым, tomorrow I am flying to the Crimea. Пти́цы летя́т на юг, the birds are flying south. Самолёт лете́л в Москву́, a plane flew to Moscow. Тро́йка лети́т, the troika is going at full speed. Лете́ть сломя́ го́лову, (*idiom.*) to go at breakneck speed. Дни летя́т за дня́ми, days are flying by. Лет-у́н, *n.m.*, (*recent*), flyer; (*fig.*), rolling stone. Лет-у́честь, *n.f.*, (*chem.*), volatility. Камфора́ изве́стна свое́й летучестью, camphor is known for its volatility Лет-у́чий, *adj.*, volatile. Л. ми́тинг, (*recent*), short meeting. Л. ревмати́зм, shifting rheumatism. Л-ая мышь, (*zool.*), bat. Лет-

у́чка, *n.f.*, leaflet, pamphlet. Лёт-чик, *n.m.*, airman, aviator, flier, pilot.

вз-лет-е́ть, вз-леч-у́, *v.p.*, вз-лет-а́ть, *v.i.*, to fly, take wing, take to the air. В. в во́здух, to be blown up. Пти́ца взлете́ла на верши́ну ду́ба, the bird flew to the top of the oak tree. Вз-лёт, *n.m.*, flying up, takeoff.

в-лет-е́ть, *v.p.*, в-лет-а́ть, *v.i.*, to fly into. Ла́сточка влете́ла в откры́тое окно́, the swallow flew in through the open window.

вы́-лет-еть, *v.p.*, вы-лет-а́ть, *v.i.*, to fly out, rush out; escape. Самолёты вы́летят при хоро́шей лётной пого́де, the planes will take off, provided the weather is good. Вы́лететь из кле́тки, to fly out of a cage. В. в трубу́, (*fig.*), to be penniless. В. со слу́жбы, (*colloq.*), to be dismissed. Вы́-лет, *n.m.*, flying out; departure. На вы́лет, through. Быть ра́неным на в., to be wounded through.

до-лет-е́ть, *v.p.*, до-лет-а́ть, *v.i.*, + *acc.*, до + *gen.*, to reach, fly as far as. Снаря́д не долете́л до око́пов, the shell did not reach the trenches.

за-лет-е́ть, *v.p.*, за-лет-а́ть, *v.i.*, to fly into, beyond, away. В око́шко залете́ла пти́ца, a bird flew into the window. Самолёт залете́л за поля́рный круг, the plane flew beyond the Arctic Circle.

из-лет-а́ть, *v.i.*, + *acc.*, (*colloq.*), to fly, run around. Он излета́л на самолёте всю Евро́пу, he flew all over Europe. Из-лёт, *n.m.*, take-off, *in expression:* Пу́ля на изле́те, a spent bullet.

на-лет-е́ть, *v.p.*, на-лет-а́ть, *v.i.*, на + *acc.*, to swoop down; fly, rush at; collide. Автомоби́ль налете́л на столб, the car smashed into a pole. На балко́н налете́ли сухи́е ли́стья, dry leaves blew in onto the porch. Налете́л урага́н, a tornado blew in. На-лёт, *n.m.*, raid, inroad, incursion. Н. грабителей, burglar's raid. Н. в го́рле, patch, spot. Н. авиа́ции, air raid. С нале́ту, with a swoop. На-лёт-чик, *n.m.*, burglar, robber.

об-лет-е́ть, *v.p.*, об-лет-а́ть, *v.i.*, to fly around, by-pass in flight; circle. Изве́стие облете́ло весь мир, the news went around the world. Ли́стья облете́ли, the leaves have fallen off.

от-лет-е́ть, *v.p.*, от-лет-а́ть, *v.i.*, to fly away, off. Мяч отлете́л от стены́, the ball bounced away from the wall. Подмётка отлете́ла, (*colloq.*), the sole has come off. От-лёт, *n.m.*, flying away. О. у́ток, duck flight. Он уже́ на отлёте, he is about to leave.

пере-лет-е́ть, *v.p.,* пере-лет-а́ть, *v.i.,* + *acc.,* to fly over, across. П. океа́н, to fly across an ocean. Пере-лёт, *n.m.,* flight, passage; migration. Безостано́вочный п., non-stop flight. Соверша́ть п., to migrate; make a flight. Ору́дие дало́ не́сколько перелётов, the gun sent several shots over the target. Не-до-лёт, *n.m.,* a flight short of a target. Пере-лёт-ная пти́ца, bird of passage, migratory bird.

под-лет-е́ть, *v.p.,* под-лет-а́ть, *v.i.,* к + *dat.,* to fly up; (*fig.*), run, run up. Го́лубь подлете́л к окну́, a pigeon flew up to the window. Он подлете́л ко мне, he rushed up to me.

по-лет-е́ть, *v.p.,* to take wing, take off; (*fig.*), to fall headlong. Самолёт полете́л в Аме́рику, the plane took off for America. Я поскользну́лся и полете́л, (*colloq.*), I slipped and fell headlong.

по-лет-а́ть, *v.p.,* лета́ть, *v.i.,* to fly a little. Хо́чется п. на самолёте, I would like to take a short flight. По-лёт, *n.m.,* flight, fly. Беспоса́дочный п., non-stop flight. Да́льность полёта, distance of flight. П. фанта́зии, flight of fancy. С пти́чьего полёта, bird's-eye view.

при-лет-е́ть, *v.p.,* при-лет-а́ть, *v.i.,* to come, arrive, fly in. Прилете́ли ла́сточки, the swallows have flown back. Прилёт, *n.m.,* arrival, coming. П. самолёта ожида́ется за́втра, the arrival of the plane is expected tomorrow.

про-лет-е́ть, *v.p.,* про-лет-а́ть, *v.i.,* to fly past, across, over; pass rapidly. П. ты́сячу киломе́тров, to fly one thousand kilometers. Самолёт пролете́л над го́родом, a plane flew over the city. Незаме́тно пролете́ло ле́то, the summer flew by. Про-лёт, *n.m.,* span, stair well; flight. Про-лёт-ка, *n.f.,* (*obs.*), cab, gig.

раз-лет-е́ть-ся, *v.p.r.,* раз-лет-а́ть-ся, *v.i.r.,* to fly away, off; billow; rush up; be dispersed. Пти́цы разлете́лись, the birds dispersed. Раз-лет-а́йка, *n.f.,* (*colloq.*), a cape-like coat.

с-лет-е́ть, *v.p.,* с-лет-а́ть, *v.i.,* с + *gen.,* to fly down, off; fall from. С него́ слете́ла шля́па, his hat blew off. С. с до́лжности, (*fig., colloq.*), to be dismissed, fired. С-лет-а́ть, *v.i.,* (*colloq.*), to go and return. Я слета́л в оди́н миг на по́чту, I went to the post office and returned in no time. С-лет-е́ть-ся, *v.p.r.,* с-лет-а́ть-ся, *v.i.r,* to fly together; (*fig.*), gather. На ме́сто происше́ствия слете́лось мно́го пу́блики, many people rushed to the scene of the accident. С-лёт, *n.m.,* assembly, gathering. С. уда́рников, (*recent*), assembly

of shock-workers. Сам-о-лёт, *n.m.,* plane. Сам-о-истреби́тель, *n.m.,* fighter plane. Эскадри́лья самолётов, squadron of planes. Ковёр-самолёт, *n.m.,* magic carpet.

у-лет-е́ть, *v.p.,* у-лет-а́ть, *v.i.,* to fly away, take to flight; elapse. Бума́жка улете́ла со стола́, the piece of paper blew off the table. Самолёт улете́л на се́вер, the plane flew north. У. в бу́дущее, (*fig.*), to dream of the future.

у-лет-у́ч-ить-ся, *v.p.r.,* у-лет-у́ч-иваться, *v.i.r.,* to evaporate; (*fig.*), disappear. Камфора́ улету́чилась, the camphor has evaporated. Наде́жды улету́чились, (*fig.*), all hope has vanished. У-лет-у́чивание, *n.n.,* volatilization, evaporation. У. духо́в, evaporation of perfume.

ЛИ-, ЛЬ-, ЛЕЙ-, FLUENCE, FLOW, STREAM, POURING

ли-ть, ль-ю, *v.i.,* + *acc.,* to pour; shed; spill. Дождь льёт, как из ведра́, it is raining cats and dogs. Пот льёт с него́ гра́дом, he is dripping with sweat. Ли-ть-ся, *v.i.r.,* to flow, pour, stream. Кровь лила́сь реко́й, (*fig.*), the blood was gushing out; it was a massacre. Вино́ лило́сь реко́й, (*fig.*), wine flowed like a stream. Слёзы лью́тся ручьём по её щека́м, tears are streaming down her cheeks. Пу́шки лили́сь из ме́ди, cannons were cast in copper. Ли-тьё, *n.n.,* founding, casting, molding.Чугу́нное л., iron casting. Ли-те́йная, *n.f.,* foundry. Ли-те́йный, *adj.,* casting. Ли-те́йщик, *n.m.,* founder; one who casts metals. Ли-то́й, *adj.,* cast. Л. чугу́н, cast iron. "В ша́пке зо́лота лито́го ста́рый ру́сский велика́н...," (*Lermontov*), "in a cap of pure gold an old Russian giant..."

лей-ка, *n.f.,* watering can, pot. Садо́вая л., garden watering can. Кероси́новая л., kerosene can.

в-ли-ть, *v.p.,* в-ли-ва́ть, *v.i.,* + *acc.,* to pour into; infuse. В. лека́рство в стака́н, to pour medicine into a glass. В. мета́лл в фо́рму, to pour metal into a mold. В-ли-ть-ся, *v.p.r.,* в-ли-ва́ть-ся, *v.i.r.,* to be poured in; fall in. Река́ влива́ется в мо́ре, the river flows into the sea. В. ряды́ а́рмии влива́ются но́вые си́лы, fresh forces are joining the army. В-ли-ва́ние, *n.n.,* pouring in, infusion. В. кро́ви, blood transfusion.

в-ли-я́ть, *v.i.,* по-в-ли-я́ть, *v.p.,* на + *acc.,* to influence. В-ли-я́ние, *n.n.,* influence, mastery, prestige, authority. Мора́льное в., moral influence, authority. Находи́ться под влия́нием, to be under an influence. Име́ть в., to have influence. В-ли-я́тельный, *adj.*, influential, authoritative. В-ое лицо́, an influential person. В-ые круги́, influential circles. Воз-ли-я́ние, *п.п.*, (*obs.*), libation.

вы́-ли-ть, *v.р.*, вы-ли-ва́ть, *v.i.*, + *acc.*, to pour out; throw out; spill, cast out, mold. В. во́ду за окно́, to throw water out of a window. В. в фо́рму, to cast a mold. Вы́-ли-ть-ся, *v.р.r.*, вы-ли-ва́ть-ся, *v.i.r.*, to run out, flow out; materialize, develop. В. че́рез край, to overflow, run over the edge. Неизве́стно, во что вы́льются э́ти собы́тия, one cannot tell how events will develop.

до-ли́-ть, *v.р.*, до-ли-ва́ть, *v.i.*, + *acc.*, + *gen.*, to pour, fill to the top. Д. ко́фе молоко́м, to add milk to coffee. Д. воды́ в буты́лку, to fill up a bottle with water.

за-ли́-ть, *v.р.*, за-ли-ва́ть, *v.i.*, + *acc.*, to pour over, wash over; overflow; drown. Река́ весно́й залила́ луга́, in the spring the river flooded the meadows. З. кало́ши, to repair rubbers; rubberize. З. го́ре вино́м, (*fig.*), to drown one's sorrow in wine. З. ого́нь, to extinguish a fire with water. За-ли́-ть-ся, *v.р.r.*, за-ли-ва́ть-ся, *v.i.r.*, + *instr.*, to be poured over; break into. З. ла́ем, to bark furiously. З. пе́снями, to burst into song. З. слеза́ми, to break into tears. З. соловьём, to sing like a nightingale. За-ли́-вка, *п.f.*, repairing, rubberizing. З. кало́ш, rubberizing of galoshes. За-ли́-в, *п.т.*, bay, gulf, cove, creek. За-ли-вно́е, *adj.*, *used as n.*, jelly, gelatine, aspic. З. из ры́бы, fish aspic. За-ли-вно́й луг, water meadow.

из-ли́-ть, *v.р.*, из-ли-ва́ть, *v.i.*, + *acc.*, (*obs.*, *poet.*), to pour out; (*fig.*), express, give vent to. И. гнев, to give vent to one's anger. И. своё го́ре, to pour out one's grief. Из-ли-я́ние, *п.п.*, effusion, outpouring. Серде́чные изли́яния, outpourings of a soul.

на-ли́-ть, *v.р.*, на-ли-ва́ть, *v.i.*, + *acc.*, + *gen.*, to pour on, upon; fill up; cast, mold. Н. стака́н ча́ю, to pour a cup of tea. Н. воды́, to pour some water. Нали́-ть-ся, *v.р.r.*, на-ли-ва́ть-ся, *v.i.r.*, to be poured; ripen. Вода́ налила́сь в ло́дку, the boat filled with water. Гру́ши налили́сь, the pears ripened. На-ли́в, *п.т.*, pouring in; ripening. Н. коло́сьев, the ripening of ears of corn. На-ли́-вка, *п.f.*, fruit liqueur. На-ливно́й, *adj.*, juicy, ripe. Н-о́е я́блоко, juicy apple. Н-о́е су́дно, tanker. На-ли́вший(ся), *adj.*, *part. act. past*, filled,

suffused Нали́вшиеся кро́вью глаза́, bloodshot eyes.

об-ли́-ть, *v.р.*, об-ли-ва́ть, *v.i.*, + *acc.*, + *gen.*, to pour around, wet, drench. О. го́лову холо́дной водо́й, to pour cold water over one's head. Об-ли́-ть-ся, *v.р.r.*, об-ли-ва́ть-ся, *v.i.r.*, to take a shower, drench oneself. О. холо́дной водо́й, to shower in cold water. О. по́том, to be drenched in perspiration. Се́рдце кро́вью облива́ется, (*fig.*), my heart is bleeding, bleeds for you. Об-ли-ва́ние, *п.п.*, pouring over, suffusion. Лечи́ться облива́ниями, to undergo hydrotherapeutic treatment.

от-ли́-ть, *v.р.*, от-ли-ва́ть, *v.i.*, + *acc.*, + *instr.*, + *gen.*, to pour off, decant. О. ста́тую, to cast a statue. О. вина́ в стака́н, to pour a glass of wine. Отлива́ть все́ми цвета́ми ра́дуги, to radiate with all the colors of the rainbow. От-ли́-в, *п.т.*, ebb, low tide, low water. Отли́в и прили́в, ebb and flow. Пунцо́вый с золоты́м отли́вом, crimson shot with gold. От-ли́-вка, *п.f.*, casting, molding, founding. От-ли-вно́й, *adj.*, cast, molded. О. насо́с, pump.

пере-ли́-ть, *v.р.*, пере-ли-ва́ть, *v.i.*, + *acc.*, to pour over, transfuse, decant. П. во́дку из буты́лки в графи́н, to pour vodka from a bottle into a decanter. Перелива́ть из пусто́го в поро́жнее, (*fig.*), to talk nonsense. Пере-ли́-ть-ся, *v.р.r.*, пере-ли-ва́ть-ся, *v.i.r.*, to overflow, run over; modulate. Вода́ перелива́ется че́рез край, the water is spilling over the edge. Колокола́ перелива́лись на пу́шки, bells were recast into cannons. Пере-ли́-в, *п.т.*, modulation; warbling; irridescence, tint, tinge. Переливы и тре́ли соловья́, the modulations and trills of a nightingale. Пере-ли-ва́ние, *п.п.*, transfusion, decanting. Де́лать п. кро́ви, to perform a blood transfusion. Пере-лива́ющий, *adj. part. act. pres.*, pouring over, transfusing. Пере-ли́-вка, *п.f.*, melting, recasting. П. ко́локола, recasting of a bell. Пере-ли́-вчатый, *adj.*, iridescent.

под-ли́-ть, *v.р.*, под-ли-ва́ть, *v.i.*, + *acc.*, + *gen.*, to pour a little, fill up. П. су́па в таре́лку, to fill a plate with soup. П. ма́сла в ого́нь, (*fig.*), to make matters worse. Под-ли́-вка, *п.f.*, sauce, gravy. Под-ли-ва́ние, *п.п.*, adding to a liquid.

по-ли́-ть, *v.р.*, по-ли-ва́ть, *v.i.*, + *acc.*, + *instr.*, to pour on, water. П. цветы́, to water flowers. П. со́усом, to pour gravy on. По-ли́-вка, *п.f.*, watering. П. у́лиц, watering of streets.

при-ли́-ть, *v.р.*, при-ли-ва́ть, *v.i.*, к +

dat., to flow, rush. Кровь прилива́ет к щека́м, blood rushes to one's cheeks. При-ли́-в, *п.т.*, influx, flood, flow, tide. П. иностра́нного капита́ла, influx of foreign capital. П. кро́ви, blood congestion. П. рабо́чих, influx of workers. Волна́ прили́ва, tidal wave.

про-ли́-ть, *v.p.*, про-ли-ва́ть, *v.i.*, + *acc.*, to shed (*as* blood, tears); spill. П. во́ду, to spill water. П. свет на что́-нибудь, to shed light on something. Про-ли́-ть-ся, *v.p.r.*, про-ли-ва́ть-ся, *v.i.r.*, to be shed, spilled. Вино́ проли-ло́сь на ска́терть, the wine was spilled on the tablecloth. Про-ли́-тие, *п.п.*, shedding, spilling. П. кро́ви, bloodshed. Про-ли-вно́й, *adj.*, pouring, spilling. П. дождь, pouring rain. Про-ли́-в, *п.т.*, (*geog.*), straight, sound. Гибралта́рский Проли́в, the Strait of Gibraltar.

раз-ли́-ть, *v.p.*, раз-ли-ва́ть, *v.i.*, + *acc.*, to pour out; bottle; spill; distribute. Р. молоко́ на столе́, to spill milk on a table. Река́ разлила́ свой во́ды, the river overflowed. Р. суп по таре́лкам, to serve out the soup. Раз-ли́-ть-ся, *v.p.r.*, раз-ли-ва́-ть-ся, *v.i.r.*, to overflow. Весно́й ре́ки разлива́ются, in spring the rivers overflow. Раз-ли́-в, *п.т.*, overflow, inundation, flood. Р. реки́, flooding of a river. Раз-ли́-вка, *п.f.*, bottling. Раз-ли-вно́й, *adj.*, in bottles; bottled. Р. квас, bottled kvas. Р-о́е пи́во, bottled beer. Раз-ли́-тие, *п.п.*, overflow, inundation, flood. Р. жёлчи, bilious attack.

с-ли́-ть, *v.p.*, с-ли-ва́ть, *v.i.*, + *acc.*, to pour off; mix, melt. С. сли́вки с молока́, to pour the cream off milk. С. о́лово со свинцо́м, to make an alloy of tin and lead. С. два поня́тия в одно́, to merge two concepts into one. С-ли́-ть-ся, *v.p.r.*, с-ли-ва́ть-ся, *v.i.r.*, to unite, fuse, combine; form into a unit. Два ручья́ слили́сь в ре́чку, two streams joined to form a small river. С. душо́й с ке́м-нибудь, to establish communion of souls with someone. С. с ма́ссами, (*recent*), to merge with the masses. С-ли-в, *п.т.*, spillway. С-ли́-вки, *п.т.pl.*, cream. Сби́тые с., whipped cream. С-ли́-вочный, *adj.*, cream. С-ое ма́сло, sweet butter; cream butter. С-ое моро́женое, ice cream. С-ли-я́ние, *п.п.*, confluence, fusion, union, blend, blending. С. рек, confluence of rivers. С. па́ртий, merging of parties. С-ли́-тность, *п.f.*, fusion, confluence, blend, merging. С. це́лей, unification of aims, goals. С-ли́-тный, *adj.*, merged, fused. С-ое предложе́ние, (*gram.*), contracted sentence. С-ли́-ток, *п.т.*, ingot.

у-ли́-тка, *п.f.*, snail. Съедо́бная у., edible snail Ра́ковина ули́тки, snail-shell. У-ли-тко-обра́зный, snail-like, spiral.
ли́-в-ень, *п.т.*, heavy rain, shower, downpour. Ли́-в-мя, *adv.*, in torrents. Дождь ли́вмя льёт, (*colloq.*), the rain is pouring down in torrents.

ЛИК-, ЛИЦ-, ЛИЧ-, FACE, VISAGE, COUNTENANCE

лик, *п.т.*, (*Ch.-Sl.*), face, image; choir. Л. Богоро́дицы, image of the Holy Virgin. Л. а́нгелов, choir of angels. Л. святы́х, communion of saints. Хоро́ш ли́ком, но душа́ приши́та лы́ком, (*saying*), he is handsome, but he has no soul. О́б-лик, *п.т.*, face, countenance, figure; look; features. Благообра́зный о., noble features. Дву-ли́к-ий, *adj.*, two-faced. Д. Янус, two-faced Janus.

ли́ч-ность, *п.f.*, personality; individual, person, character. Что э́то за л.? Who is that individual? Это кру́пная л., that is a famous person. Перейти́ на ли́чности, to become personal. Ли́ч-ный, *adj.*, personal; individual; private; particular. Л. соста́в, personnel. Л-ая охра́на, personal bodyguard. Л-ая отве́тственность, personal, individual responsibility. Л-ое местоиме́ние, (*gram.*), personal pronoun. Л-ое мне́ние, personal opinion. Ли́ч-но, *adv.*, personally, in person; individually. Л. от себя́, at one's own expense. На-ли́ч-ность, *п.f.*, cash, ready money. Н. преступле́ния, evidence of a committed crime. В нали́чности у меня́ то́лько сто рубле́й, I have only one hundred rubles on hand. На-ли́ч-ный, *adj.*, ready cash, on hand. Н. расчёт, payment on the spot; cash down. Н-ые де́ньги, cash. Н. соста́в во́йска, effective force of an army. Дву-ли́ч-ие, *п.п.*, duplicity, double-dealing. Дву-ли́ч-ность, *п.f.*, duplicity. Д. э́той осо́бы возмуща́ет окружа́ю-щих, the duplicity of this individual outrages everyone around him. Дву-ли́ч-ный, *adj.*, two-faced, hypocritical. Д. челове́к, hypocritical person; hypocrite. По-ли́ч-ное, *п.п.*, corpus delicti, the body of the crime, *in expression*: Быть по́йманным с поли́чным, to be caught in an act. Вор был по́йман с п., the thief was seized in the act, with the goods.

об-лич-а́ть, *v.i.*, об-лич-и́ть, *v.p.*, + *acc.*, в + *prep.*, to accuse, indict, unmask, expose, reveal. О. во лжи, to give the lie to. Об-лич-а́ть-ся, *v.i.r.*, to be indicted, exposed. Об-лич-е́ние, *п.п.*, indictment, exposure. Об-лич-и́тель, *n.m.*, one who indicts, accuses. Об-лич-и́тельный, *adj.*, accusatory, indicting.

из-об-лич-а́ть, *v.i.,* из-об-лич-и́ть, *v.p.,* + *acc.,* в + *prep.,* to show, demonstrate. И. обвинённого в преступле́нии, to expose the accused in a crime. Из-об-лич-е́ние, *n.n.,* proof of guilt. Из-об-лич-и́тель, *n.m.,* accuser. Из-об-лич-и́тельный, *adj.,* pertaining to evidence of guilt.

от-лич-а́ть, *v.i.,* от-лич-и́ть, *v.p.,* + *acc.,* to distinguish, discriminate, discern. О. одно́ от друго́го, to distinguish one from another. О. фальши́вую моне́ту от настоя́щей, to distinguish a counterfeit coin from a real coin. От-лич-а́ть-ся, *v.i.r.,* от-лич-и́ть-ся, *v.p.r.,* to be distinguished, stand out, differ from; distinguish oneself. Этот студе́нт отлича́ется свои́м прилежа́нием, this student is outstanding for his diligence. Ве́жливостью они́ не отлича́ются, they are not noted for politeness. О. на состяза́ниях, to be top-notch in competition. О. на войне́, to distinguish oneself in war. От-ли́ч-ие, *n.n.,* distinction, difference. Зна́ки отли́чия, insignia. От-ли́ч-ный, *adj.,* distinct, distinguished, excellent, perfect. О. учени́к, excellent pupil. О-ая пого́да, perfect weather. От-ли́ч-но, *adv.,* excellently, perfectly, differently, distinctly. Вы о. зна́ете, что я име́ю в виду́, you know perfectly well what I have in mind. От-лич-и́тельный, *adj.,* distinctive, characteristic. О-ые черты́ хара́ктера, distinguishing traits. О-ые при́знаки, distinguishing features.

раз-лич-а́ть, *v.i.,* раз-лич-и́ть, *v.p.,* + *acc.,* to distinguish, discern, discriminate, make a distinction. Я с трудо́м различа́ю э́тих двух близнецо́в, I can hardly tell the twins apart. Он не мо́жет различи́ть, кто там, he cannot make out who is there. Раз-лич-а́ть-ся, *v.i.r.,* to differ, be unlike, be different. Раз-ли́ч-ие, *n.n.,* distinction, difference. То́нкое слове́сное, р., word-splitting. Не де́лать разли́чия, to make no distinction. Р. взгля́дов (мне́ний), difference of opinion. Раз-ли́ч-ный, *adj.,* different, various, diverse, distinct. Р. по существу́, basically different. По разли́чным соображе́ниям, for various reasons. Раз-ли́ч-но, *adv.,* differently. Без-раз-ли́ч-ие, *n.n.,* indifference. Без-раз-ли́ч-ный, *adj.,* indifferent. Без-раз-ли́ч-но, *adv.,* indifferently.

раз-ли́ч-еств-ова-ть, *v.i.,* (*obs.*), *syn.* различа́ться, to differ, be unlike, be different. Р. по во́зрасту, to differ in age. Раз-лич-е́ние, *n.n.,* distinction,

discrimination, discernment. Раз-лич-и́тельный, *adj.,* distinctive.

с-лич-а́ть, *v.i.,* с-лич-и́ть, *v.p.,* + *acc.,* с + *instr.,* to compare; collate. С. по́длинник с ко́пией, to compare the original with the copy. С-лич-а́ть-ся, *v.i.r.,* to be compared. С-лич-е́ние, *n.n.,* comparing.

у-лич-а́ть, *v.i.,* у-лич-и́ть, *v.p.,* + *acc.,* to detect, catch in the act. У. кого́-нибудь в преступле́нии, to catch someone in the act of committing a crime. У. во лжи, to expose someone as a liar. У-лич-и́ть-ся, *v.p.r,* to be detected, exposed, caught in the act. У-лич-е́ние, *n.n.,* detection. У-лич-и́тель, *n.m.,* detector. У-лич-ённый, *adj., part. pass. past,* caught in the act. У-ли́к-а, *n.f.,* evidence, convincing proof. Служи́тьули́кой, to serve as evidence. Все ули́ки преступле́ния налицо́, all the evidence of the crime is at hand.

при-ли́ч-еств-ова-ть, *v.i.,* (*obs.*), to be becoming; be fitting, proper. П. его́ высо́кому зва́нию, appropriate to his high station, position. При-ли́ч-ие, *n.n.,* decency, decorum, propriety, seemliness. Соблюда́ть пра́вила прили́чия, to observe the rules of propriety. Из прили́чия, for propriety's sake. Ра́ди прили́чия, for propriety's sake. При-ли́ч-ный, *adj.,* decent, proper, becoming, seemly. П-ые мане́ры, proper manners. П-ая оде́жда, decent clothes. При-ли́ч-но, *adv.,* decently. Веди́те себя́ п., behave yourself! Не-при-ли́ч-ие, *n.n.,* не-при-ли́ч-ность, *n.f.,* indecency, unseemliness. Не-при-ли́ч-ный, *adj.,* inappropriate, indecent, improper. Н. анекдо́т, indecent anecdote. Не-при-ли́ч-но, *adv.,* indecently.

лиц-о́, *n.n.,* face, countenance, visage; person; (*gram.*), person. Прия́тное л., a nice face. Я зна́ю его́ то́лько в л., I know him only by sight. Измени́ться в лице́, to undergo a facial change. Он не лю́бит но́вых лиц, he does not like new faces. Исче́знуть с лица́ земли́, (*idiom.*), to disappear from the face of the earth. Я сказа́л ей э́то в лицо́, I said it to her face. Э́то пла́тье вам не к лицу́, this dress does not become you. Он не уда́рит лицо́м в грязь, (*idiom.*), he will not disgrace himself. Кри́тика, не взира́я на ли́ца, impartial criticism. Глаго́л во второ́м лице́, (*gram.*), a verb in the second person. Лиц-ево́й, *adj.,* facial; pertaining to a face. Л-а́я сторона́ карт, face side of a playing card. Л-а́я сторона́ до́ма, front of a house. Ли́ч-ико, *n.n.,* (*dim.*), little face. Хоро́шенькое л., a pretty little face. Лиц-но́й, *adj.,* facial. Лич-ны́е мускулы, muscles of the face. Лич-и́на, *n.f.*, mask, visor. Под личи́ною благоче́стия, under a mask of piety. Личи́нка, *n.f.*, larva, pupa.

об-лиц-ева́ть, *v.p.*, об-лиц-о́вывать, *v.i.*, + *acc.*, to face with stone, tile, etc. Об-лиц-о́вка, *n.f.*, facing; (*arch.*), revetment. Об-лиц-о́ванный, *adj.*, *part. pass. past,* faced, covered.

пере-лиц-ева́ть, *v.p.*, пере-лиц-о́вывать, *v.i.*, + *acc.*, to reverse, touch up, repair. П. пальто́, to reverse a coat.

лиц-е-де́йствовать, *v.i.*, (*obs.*), to act, perform. Лиц-е-де́й, *n.m.*, actor. Лиц-е-де́йствие, *n.n.*, (*obs.*), spectacle, play.

лиц-е-зре́ть, *v.i.*, у-лиц-е-зре́ть, *v.p.*, + *acc.*, (*obs.*), to contemplate; see face to face. Лиц-е-зре́ние, *n.n.*, contemplation, intuitive sight.

лиц-е-ме́рить, *v.i.*, to be hypocritical. Лиц-е-ме́рие, *n.n.*, hypocrisy, imposture, simulation, dissimulation, Лиц-е-ме́р, *n.m.*, hypocrite, dissembler. Лиц-е-ме́рный, *adj.*, hypocritical. Л-ые уве-ре́ния, lip service; hypocritical assertions. Лиц-е-ме́рно, *adv.*, hypocritically.

лиц-е-прия́тствовать, *v.i.*, (*obs.*), to behave with partiality. Лиц-е-прия́тие, *n.n.*, partiality, favoritism. Лиц-е-прия́тный, *adj.*, partial. Лиц-е-прия́тно, *adv.*, partially.

о-лиц-е-творя́ть, *v.i.*, о-лиц-е-твори́ть, *v.p.*, + *acc.*, to personify, embody. О. неви́нность (доброде́тель), to personify innocence, virtue. О-лиц-е-творя́ться, *v.i.r.*, to be personified, embodied. О-лиц-е-твор-е́ние, *n.n.*, personification, embodiment. О. зла, personification of evil.

ЛИХ-, ЛИШ-, EVIL, DEPRIVATION, OVERABUNDANCE, SUPERFLUOUSNESS

лих-о́й, *adj.*, spirited, dashing, bold; evil. Л. нае́здник, dashing horseman. Л. челове́к, (*folk*), wicked person. Л-а́я езда́, fast, skillful, daring riding. Ли́хость, *n.f.*, boldness, recklessness. Лих-а́ч, *n.m.*, fast driver, cabman.

лих-ва́, *n.f.*, (*obs.*), usury, interest, profit. Отплати́ть с лихво́й, to pay back with interest, lavishly.

ли́х-о, *n.n.*, evil; *adv.*, dashingly, boldly; badly. О ли́хо нам! (*obs.*) Woe to us! Помина́ть ли́хом, to bear one a grudge. Не помина́йте меня́ ли́хом, remember me kindly. Он ли́хо промча́лся, he drove by dashingly. Лих-о-де́й, *n.m.*, лих-о-де́йка, *n.f.*, (*obs.*) malefactor, wicked person, villain. Лих-о-де́йство, *n.n.*, malefaction, evil deed. Лих-о-и́мец, *n.m.*, (*obs.*), usurer, extortioner. Лих-

о-и́мный, *adj.*, usurious. Лих-о-и́мство, *n.n.*, usury, extortion.

лих-о-ра́дить, *v.i.*, to have a fever, have chills, be feverish. Больно́го лихора́дит, the sick man is running a fever. Лих-о-ра́дка, *n.f.*, chills, fever. Боло́тная л., malaria. Сенна́я л., hay-fever. При́ступ лихора́дки, attack of fever. Лих-о-ра́дочность, *n.f.*, feverishness. Лих-о-ра́дочный, *adj.*, feverish. Л-ое состоя́ние, feverishness. Лих-о-ра́дочно, *adv.*, feverishly.

лиш-а́ть, *v.i.*, лиш-и́ть, *v.p.*, + *acc.*, + *gen.*, to deprive, bereave, strip, rob, defraud. Л. кро́ва, to dispossess. Л. насле́дства, to disinherit. Л. го́лоса, to deprive of a vote. Л. прав, to deprive of rights. Лиш-а́ть-ся, *v.i.r.*, лиш-и́ть-ся, *v.p.r.*, to lose, be deprived of, forfeit. Л. сы́на, to lose a son. Л. чувств, to swoon, faint, lose consciousness.

лиш-ён-ец, *n.m.*, лиш-ёнка, *n.f.*, (*recent*), disfranchised person. Лиш-е́ние, *n.n.*, deprivation, loss, forfeiture. Л. иму́щества, confiscation of property. Л. свобо́ды, loss of liberty. Л. прав, disfranchisement. Терпе́ть лише́ния, to suffer privations. Лиш-ённый, *adj.*, *part. pass. past,* deprived, devoid, destitute. Л. избира́тельных прав, deprived of voting rights. Ума-лиш-ённый, *adj.*, *used as n.,* madman, insane person, lunatic. Дом у-ых, mad house, insane asylum.

ли́ш-ний, *adj.*, superfluous, unnecessary; extra, spare. Л-ие разгово́ры, useless conversations. Лу́чше взять ли́шнюю ши́ну, it is better to take a spare tire. Л. раз, once more. Он здесь л., he is superfluous here. Л-ие лю́ди, superfluous people; unwanted people. Геро́и произведе́ний Турге́нева - ли́шние лю́ди. Turgenev's heroes are superfluous people. Л-ее об э́том говори́ть, it is needless to speak of it. Шесть ты́сяч с ли́шним, six thousand odd. Ли́ш-ек, *n.m.*, (*colloq.*), surplus. 20 фу́нтов с ли́шком, twenty odd pounds. Из-ли́ш-ек, *n.m.*, surplus, excess, surfeit. И. жилпло́щади, (*recent*), extra floorspace. Из-ли́ш-ество, *n.n.*, superfluity, excess; intemperance; overindulgence. И. в пи́ще, overindulgence in eating. Из-ли́ш-ний, *adj.*, superfluous, unnecessary. И-яя ро́скошь, superfluous luxury. И-яя поспе́шность, too great a hurry. Из-ли́ш-не, *adv.*, unnecessarily. И. об э́том упомина́ть, needless to say. С-ли́ш-ком, *adv.*, too much, too many, in excess. С. больши́е ру́ки, overlarge hands. С. ма́ло, too little, not enough. С. мно́го, too much, too many. Он с. мно́го себе́

позволя́ет, he takes too many liberties.
лиш-ь- *adv.*, only, just. Л. бы то́лько,
if only, provided. Нехвата́ет лишь
одного́ рубля́, only one ruble is missing. Ли́шь бы то́лько дождь не
испо́ртил на́шей ирогу́лки. If only the
rain does not spoil our stroll. Лиш-ь
то́лько, hardly, as soon as.

ЛОВ-, ЛОВ(Л)-, ЛАВ-, ЛАВ(Л)-, PURSUIT, QUEST, HUNT

лов, *п.т.*, ло́в-ля, *n.f.*, catching, hunting,
fishing. Ло́в-ля птиц, bird catching.
Ры́бная ло́в-ля, fishing. Лов-е́ц, *п.т.*,
(*obs.*), hunter. На ловца́ и зверь
бежи́т, (*prov.*), a crook always finds
a victim. Ло́в-чий, *adj.*, (*obs.*), huntsman.
лов-и́-ть, лов-л-ю́, *v.i.,* $+$ *acc.*, to catch,
hunt. Л. ры́бу, to fish. Л. ры́бу в
му́тной воде́, (*fig.*), to fish in troubled
waters. Л. ка́ждое сло́во, to catch
every word. Л. моме́нт, to seize the
right moment. Л. на сло́ве, to take one
at one's word. Лов-у́шка, *n.f.*, snare,
trap; pitfall. Пойма́ть в лову́шку, to
ensnare, trap. Об-ла́в-а, *n.f.*, raid, encirclement.
вы́-лов-ить, *v.p.*, вы-ла́в-л-ивать, *v.i.,* $+$
acc., to catch, draw out, fish out. В.
всю ры́бу в реке́, to catch all the fish
in a stream. В. бревно́ из воды́, to
drag a log out of water.
из-лов-и́ть, *v.p.*, из-ла́в-л-ивать, (*obs.*),
v.i., $+$ *acc.*, to catch, draw out, fish
out.
на-лов-и́ть, *v.p.*, на-ла́в-л-ивать, *v.i.,* $+$
acc., $+$ *gen.*, to fish, catch in quantity.
пере-лов-и́ть, *v.p.*, пере-ла́в-л-ивать,
(*obs.*), *v.i.,* $+$ *acc.*, to catch, seize, lay
hold of, take over. Поли́ция перело-
ви́ла всю ша́йку, the police caught the
whole gang.
про-лов-и́ть, *v.p.*, to have fished. П.
це́лый день, to have spent the whole
day fishing. Лови́ли во́ра, да про-
лови́ли, (*saying*), to have missed apprehending a thief.
у-лов-и́ть, *v.p.*, у-ла́в-л-ивать, *v.i.,* $+$
acc., to catch; detect; discern. У. смысл
шу́тки, to get the sense of a joke. У.
схо́дство, to catch a likeness. У.
удо́бный слу́чай, to seize an opportunity. У-ла́в-л-ивать-ся, *v.i.r.*, to be
caught. У-ло́в, *п.т.*, catch, take,
amount caught, taken. Рыбаки́ взя́ли
неплохо́й уло́в, the fishermen made a
pretty good catch. У-лов-и́мый, *adj.*,
perceptible. Не-у-лов-и́мый, *adj.*, imperceptible, elusive; subtle. Н-ые
зву́ки, imperceptible sounds. Н-ое
движе́ние, imperceptible motion. Н.

вор, elusive thief. У-ло́в-ка, *n.f.*, trick,
ruse, stratagem, shift, dodge. Отступ-
ле́ние врага́ то́лько уло́вка, the
enemy's retreat is only a stratagem.
ло́в-к-ий, *adj.*, adroit, clever, dexterous,
skillful, shrewd, cunning. Л. ход,
master stroke. Л. челове́к, shrewd
man. Л-ая проде́лка, trick. Ло́в-кость,
n.f., adroitness, dexterity, cleverness,
skill. Л. уда́ра, skill of a blow. Л. рук,
dexterity of hands. Обнару́жить л. в
дипломати́ческих перегово́рах, to
manifest adroitness in diplomatic negotiations. Ло́в-ко, *adv.*, adroitly, cleverly. Ло́вко отби́ть уда́р, to parry a
blow dexterously. Лов-ка́ч, *п.т.*, (*colloq., derog.*), dodger. Не-ло́в-кость,
n.f., awkwardness, blundering, uneasiness. Не-ло́в-кий, *adj.*, awkward,
clumsy, maladroit. Он чу́вствовал
себя́ нело́вко, he felt ill at ease.
лов-ч-и́ть-ся, *v.p.r.*, (*slang*), to dodge,
shrink. Он ловчи́лся, чтоб не попа́сть
в а́рмию, he dodged in every possible
way in order to avoid the draft.
из-лов-ч-и́ть-ся, *v.p.r.*, to manage, succeed. И. попа́сть в цель, he managed
to hit the target.
на-лов-ч-и́ть-ся, *v.p.r.*, to become dexterous, skillful. Он бы́стро наловчи́лся
управля́ть тра́ктором, he quickly became skilled in operating the tractor.

ЛОМ-, ЛОМ(Л)-, ЛАМ-, DISJUNCTION, BREAK, FRACTURE, BREACH

лом, *п.т.*, scrap, fragment; crow bar.
Желе́зный лом, scrap iron. Лёд
разби́ли ло́мом, they broke the ice
with a crow bar. Лом-ови́к, *п.т.*,
carter, teamster. Лом-ово́й, *п.т.*, carter, teamster. Л-а́я ло́шадь, draft-
horse. Л-а́я подво́да, cart, wagon,
dray.
лом-а́-ть, *v.i.*, с-лом-а́ть, *v.p.,* $+$ *acc.*, to
break, demolish. Ве́тер лома́ет де́рево,
the wind is breaking the tree. Л. ка́-
мень, to quarry, break stone. Л. себе́
го́лову, (*fig.*), to rack one's brains.
Лом-а́ть-ся, *v.i.r.*, с-лом-а́ть-ся, *v.p.r.*,
to break, become fractured, broken,
smashed; only "лома́ться", grimace,
pose, give oneself airs. Сухи́е су́чья
легко́ лома́ются, dry boughs break
easily. Мы её проси́ли спеть, а она́
всё лома́ется, we asked her to sing,
but she assumed a haughty air and
refused. Лом-а́нье, *n.n.*, affected manner. Лом-а́ка, *n.f.*, (*colloq., derog.*),
mincing, simpering woman, girl. Ло́м-
аный, *adj.*, broken, fractured. Л.
англи́йский язы́к, broken English.
Ло́м-ка, *n.f.*, breaking, demolishing;

razing. Л. старого быта, breaking up of the old ways of life. Лом-кий, *adj.*, fragile, breakable, brittle. Л. лёд, thin ice. Л-ая посуда, fragile dishes, china. Лом-кость, *n.f.*, brittleness, fragility. Лом-оть, *n.m.*, hunk, chunk, thick lump. Л. хлеба, chunk of bread. Лом-тик, *n.m.*, (*dim.*), slice.

лом-и́ть, лом-л-ю́, *v.i.,* + *acc.,* to break. Л. напролом, to break through, force a way through. У меня ломят кости, my bones ache. Лом-и́ть-ся, *v.i.r.,* to be bursting, breaking. Л. в дверь, to force a door. У него сундуки ломятся от золота, (*fig.*), he has trunks bursting with gold. Ломота, *n.f.,* rheumatic pain.

вз-лом-а́ть, *v.p.,* вз-ла́м-ывать, *v.i.,* + *acc.,* to break open, force. В. замок, to break a lock. Вз-ла́м-ывать-ся, *v.p.r.,* to be broken, forced. Вз-ла́м-ывание, *n.n.,* breaking open. Вз-лом, *n.m.,* breaking in, open. Кража со взломом, burglary. Вз-лом-щик, *n.m.,* burglar, house-breaker.

в-лом-и́ть-ся, *v.p.r.,* в-ла́м-ывать-ся, *v.i.r.,* to break in, enter by force. Громилы вломились в магазин, burglars broke into the store. В. в амбицию, (*colloq.*), to take offense, umbrage.

вы́-лом-ать, вы́-лом-ить, (*colloq.*), *v.p.,* вы-ла́м-ывать, *v.i.,* + *acc.,* to break open, off. В. дверь, to break down a door. В. зуб, to break a tooth.

до-лом-а́ть, *v.p.,* до-ла́м-ывать, *v.i.,* + *acc.,* to complete the breakage. До-лом-ать-ся, *v.p.r.,* до-ла́м-ывать-ся, *v.i.r.,* to be completely broken.

за-лом-и́ть, *v.p.,* за-ла́м-ывать, *v.i.,* + *acc.,* to overcharge, overrate. З. цену, to overcharge. Купец заломил такую цену, что я отказался от покупки дома, the merchant asked so high a price, I refused to buy the house. З. шапку, to put one's cap at a jaunty angle. З. берёзу, (*folk*), to partly break a birch tree.

из-лом-а́ть, *v.p.,* из-ла́м-ывать, *v.i.,* + *acc.,* to break completely, break into fragments. И. палку, to break a cane into pieces. Лихорадка изломала его, the fever has exhausted him. Из-лом, *n.m.,* fracture, break; bend. И. реки, sharp bend in a river. Из-лом-анный, *adj., part. pass. past,* broken, bent. Из-лом-ать-ся, *v.p.r.,* из-ла́м-ывать-ся, *v.i.r.,* to be broken into pieces.

на-лом-а́ть, *v.p.,* на-ла́м-ывать, *v.i.,* + *acc.,* to break extensively. Н. сухих веток для печки, to break dry branches for a stove.

об-лом-а́ть, *v.p.,* об-ла́м-ывать, *v.i.,* + *acc.,* to break, chip off. О. ветки, to break off some branches. О. кого-нибудь, (*colloq.*), to persuade someone. Об-лом-и́ть, *v.p.,* to break off. Сел на сук и обломил его, he sat on the branch and broke it. Об-лом-ок, *n.m.,* piece of wreckage. Об-лом-а́ть-ся, об-лом-и́ть-ся, *v.p.r,* об-ла́м-ывать-ся, *v.i.r.,* to be broken; become manageable.

от-лом-а́ть, от-лом-и́ть, *v.p.,* от-ла́м-ывать, *v.i.,* + *acc.,* to break off. От-лом-и́ть кусок хлеба, to break off a piece of bread. От-лом-а́ть ножку стола, to break a leg off a table. От-лом-а́ть-ся, от-лом-и́ть-ся, *v.p.r.,* от-ла́м-ывать-ся, *v.i.r.,* to be broken off.

пере-лом-а́ть, *v.p.,* пере-ла́м-ывать, *v.i.,* + *acc.,* to break into pieces, crush; fracture; overcome. П. кости, to give a sound thrashing. Пере-лом-и́ть, *v.p.,* + *acc.,* to break in two, to fracture; to overcome. П. палку, to break a cane in two. П. себя, (*fig.*), to control one's feelings. Пере-лом, *n.m.,* climax, turning point; (*med.*), fracture; (*fig.*), crisis, sudden change. П. кости, bone fracture. П. в ходе болезни, a change in the course of an illness. Год великого перелома, the year of the great climax. Пере-лом-а́ть-ся, пере-лом-и́ть-ся, *v.p.r.,* пере-ла́м-ывать-ся, *v.i.r.,* to break in two.

по-лом-а́ть, *v.p.,* + *acc.,* to smash; *see* сломать. По-лом-ка, *n.f.,* breaking. По-лом-а́ть-ся, *v.p.r.,* to be broken, smashed.

под-лом-а́ть, *v.p.,* под-ла́м-ывать, *v.i.,* + *acc.,* to break, crack under; split. П. пол снизу, to break up a floor from underneath. Под-лом-и́ть, *v.p.,* to break partly. П. ветку на дереве, to partly break off, to crack the branch of a tree. Под-лом-и́ть-ся, *v.p.r.,* под-ла́м-ывать-ся, *v.i.r.,* to break, give way. Лёд подломился под ним, the ice broke under him. Ноги подломились, (*fig.*), his legs gave way.

пре-лом-и́ть, *v.p.,* пре-лом-л-я́ть, *v.i.,* *acc.,* to break; refract. Призма преломила солнечный луч, the prism refracted the sun's rays. Пре-лом-и́ть-ся, *v.p.r.,* пре-лом-л-я́ть-ся, *v.i.r.,* to be deflected, refracted. Всё это по иному преломилось в его сознании, all this was transformed into something quite different in his mind. Пре-лом-л-е́ние, *n.n.,* deflection, refraction. П. света, refraction of light. Пре-лом-л-ённый, *adj., part. pass. past,* refracted.

про-лом-а́ть, про-лом-и́ть, *v.p.,* про-ла́м-ывать, *v.i.,* + *acc.,* to break through, in; cut open. П. отверстие (дыру), to make an opening, a hole. Про-лом-и́ть-ся, *v.p.r.,* про-ла́м-ывать-ся, *v.i.r.,* to break through. Не ходи туда — там лёд тонкий, проломится, don't go there, the ice is thin, it will break through. Про-лом, *n.m.*, breach, gap, split. П. черепа, skull fracture. На-про-лом, *adv.*, *in expression*: Идти н., to smash through.

раз-лом-а́ть, раз-лом-и́ть, *v.p.*, раз-ла́м-ывать, *v.i.*, + *acc.*, to break to pieces, smash; pull down, demolish. Раз-лом-а́ть забо́р, to pull down a fence. Раз-лом-и́ть хлеб, to break bread. Раз-лом-а́ть-ся, раз-лом-и́ть-ся, *v.p.r.*, раз-ла́м-ывать-ся, *v.i.r.*, to break up, be broken up into pieces. Шкаф совсе́м разлома́лся, the wardrobe is falling apart. Раз-ла́м-ывание, *n.n.*, breaking, fracture.

с-лом-а́ть, с-лом-и́ть, *v.p.*, с-ла́м-ывать, *v.i.*, + *acc.*, to break up; *see* лома́ть. С-лом-а́ть забо́р, to break a fence. С-лом-и́ть сопротивле́ние врага́, to break the enemy's resistance. С. себе́ ше́ю, (*fig.*), to break one's neck. Сломя́ го́лову, (*colloq.*), headlong; in violent haste; recklessly. С-лом-и́ть-ся, с-лом-а́ть-ся, *v.p.r.*, с-ла́м-ывать-ся, *v.i.r.*, to be destroyed, broken. Де́рево от ве́тра мо́жет сломи́ться, the wind can break a tree. С-лом, *n.m.*, breaking, demolition, scrapping, razing. Продава́ть (покупа́ть) что́-нибудь на слом, to sell (buy) scrap.

у-лом-а́ть, *v.p.*, у-ла́м-ывать, *v.i.*, (*colloq.*), to persuade, induce, prevail upon. Я не мог его улома́ть, I couldn't persuade him. Мне удало́сь улома́ть нача́льника - он согласи́лся дать мне о́тпуск, I succeeded in persuading my chief-he agreed to give me a vacation.

ЛУГ-, ЛУЖ-, ЛУЗ-, MEADOW

луг-, *n.m.*, meadow. Заливно́й луг, water meadow. Зелёные луга́, green meadows. Луг-ови́на, *n.f.*, (*colloq.*), see лужа́йка. Луг-ово́дство, *n.n.*, cultivation of meadows. Луг-ово́й, *adj.*, meadow. Л-о́е се́но, meadow hay. Л-ы́е цветы́, meadow field flowers. Л-а́я сторона́ реки́, the meadow, low bank of a river.

луж-а́йка, *n.f.*, lawn, grass-plot. Лесна́я л., wood clearing. Луж-о́к, *n.m.*, small meadow.

лу́ж-а, *n.f.*, puddle. Лу́жи по́сле дождя́, rain puddles. Попа́сть в лу́жу, to fall into a puddle. Сесть в лу́жу, (*slang*), to come to grief.

во-луз-я́х, (*folk*), in the meadows. "Во зелёных во лузя́х," (*folksong*), "In the green meadows."

ЛУК-, ЛУЧ-, CURVATURE, BENDING

лук, *n.m.*, bow. Стреля́ть из лу́ка, to shoot an arrow from a bow.

лук-а́, *n.f.*, river bend; pommel; *see* из-лу́ч-ина. Сама́рская лука́ на Во́лге, the Samara Bend in the Volga. Из-лу́ч-ина, *n.f.*, curve, bend; winding. Вса́дник держа́лся за луку́ седла́, the rider held on to the pommel. Река́ в э́том ме́сте де́лает не́сколько излу́чин, in this spot the river makes several bends. Из-лу́ч-истый, *adj.*, bending, winding. И-ая река́, winding river. Об-луч-о́к, *n.m.*, box. Ямщи́к сиди́т на облучке́, (*Pushkin*), the coachman is sitting on the box. "У лукомо́рья дуб зелёный," (*Pushkin*), "A green oak by a sea cove."

лук-а́вить, *v.i.*, с-лук-а́вить, *v.p.*, to act in a sly, crafty manner. Я вас люблю́, к чему́ лука́вить, (*Pushkin*) I love you, there's no denying it. Лук-а́вство, *n.n.*, slyness, archness, craftiness. Л. посту́пка, slyness of manner. Лук-а́вый, *adj.*, sly, crafty, cunning; *used as n.*, devil, evil one. Л. взгляд, sly glance. А всё про́чее от лука́вого, (*saying*), all the rest is inspired by the devil himself. Лук-а́во, *adv.*, slyly. *Note*: лук, *n.m.*, onion, *from German Lauch*, does not belong to this root.

ЛУЧ-, RAY, LIGHT

луч, *n.m.*, ray, beam, shaft. Лучи́ восходя́щего со́лнца, the rays of the rising sun. Луч наде́жды, a ray of hope. Рентге́новские лучи́, X-rays. Испуска́ть лучи́, to radiate. Сноп луче́й сквозь ту́чи, a shaft of light piercing the clouds. Луч-ево́й, *adj.*, radial. Л-а́я эне́ргия, solar energy. Л-а́я кость, (*anat.*), radius. Луч-е-, *a combining form meaning* ray. Луч-е-за́рность, *n.f.*, radiance, effulgence. Луч-е-за́рный, *adj.*, radiant, effulgent, beaming. Луч-е-за́рно, *adv.*, radiantly, effulgently. Луч-е-испуска́ние, *n.n.*, radiation. Луч-е-преломле́ние, *n.n.*, refraction of rays. Луч-и́стый, *adj.*, radiant, radial, beaming. Л-ые глаза́, luminous eyes. Л-ый свет ме́сяца, luminosity of the moon, moonlight. Л-ая теплота́, radiant heat. Л-ая эне́ргия, solar energy, heat.

луч-и́на, *n.f.*, splinter, match-wood. Щепа́ть лучи́ну, (*obs.*), to splinter wood, make splinters.

луч-и́-ть, *v.i.*, + *acc.*, to catch fish by torchlight. Луч-е́ние, *n.n.*, fishing by torching. Луч-и́ть-ся, *v.i.r.*, to emit light. Глаза́ луча́тся, the eyes are shining. Ры́ба лучи́лась в ти́хие тёмные но́чи, fish were caught by torch-light on calm, dark nights.

из-луч-и́ть, *v.p.,* из-луч-а́ть, *v.i.,* + *acc.,* to radiate, irradiate. Со́лнце излуча́ет тепло́, the sun radiates heat. Её глаза́ излуча́ют ти́хую ра́дость, her eyes radiate calm joy. Из-луч-е́ние, *п.п.,* radiation, emanation. Из-луч-и́ть-ся, *v.p.r.,* из-луч-а́ть-ся, *v.i.r.,* to emanate, radiate. Из его́ глаз излуча́лась доб-рота́, kindness radiated from his eyes.

ЛУЧ-, ЛУК-, UNIFICATION, SEPARA-TION AND RECEIVING

за-луч-и́ть, *v.p.,* за-луч-а́ть, *v.i.,* (*colloq.*), to entice, lure. З. кого́-нибудь в го́сти, to entice someone into a visit. З. за́йца в тенёта, to trap a hare.

от-луч-и́ть, *v.p.,* от-луч-а́ть, *v.i.,* + *acc.,* от + *gen.,* to separate; excommunicate. О. ребёнка от груди́, to wean an infant. О. от це́ркви, to excommunicate. О. здоро́вый скот от больно́го, to separate healthy cattle from sick cattle. От-луч-и́ть-ся, *v.p.r.,* от-луч-а́ть-ся, *v.i.r.,* to be absent, separate oneself. О. со слу́жбы, to be absent from one's job. От-луч-е́ние, *п.п.,* excommunication. От-лу́ч-ка, *n.f.,* (*colloq.*), absence. Самово́льная о., (*mil.*), absence without authorized leave. Быть в отлу́чке, to be absent.

по-луч-и́ть, *v.p.,* по-луч-а́ть, *v.i.,* + *acc.,* to receive, obtain, get; succeed. П. насле́дство, to inherit. П. образова́ние, to obtain an education. П. жа́лование, to draw pay. П. замеча́ние, to be reprimanded. П. учёную сте́пень, to receive a scientific degree. По-луч-и́ть-ся, *v.p.r.,* по-луч-а́ть-ся, *v.i.r,* to be received. П. в результа́те, to result, ensue. Пи́сьма получа́ются в 8 часо́в утра́, letters are delivered at eight o'clock in the morning. По-луч-е́ние, *п.п.,* receipt. П. письма́ (де́нег) receipt of a letter (money). По-лу́ч-ка, *n.f.,* (*colloq.*), receipt; pay-day. Благо-по-лу́ч-ие, *п.п.,* well-being. Благо-по-лу́ч-но, *adv.,* happily, safely. Б. дое́хать, to arrive safely.

раз-луч-и́ть, *v.p.,* раз-луч-а́ть, *v.i.,* + *acc.,* с + *instr.,* to part, separate, sever. Обстоя́тельства разлучи́ли нас, circumstances separated us. Раз-луч-и́ть-ся, *v.p.r.,* раз-луч-а́ть-ся, *v.i.r.,* to be parted, separated. Раз-лу́к-а, *n.f.,* separation, parting. Раз-лу́ч-е́ние, *п.п.,* severance, parting. Раз-лу́ч-ник, *n.m.,* (*colloq.*), successful rival.

с-луч-и́ть, *v.p.,* с-луч-а́ть, *v.i.,* + *acc.,* с + *instr.,* to couple, pair, mate. С. живо́тных, to mate animals. С-лу́ч-ка,

n.f., coupling, mating. С-луч-но́й, *adj.,* mating. С. пункт, horse-breeding stable.

с-луч-и́ть-ся, *v.p.r.,* с-луч-а́ть-ся, *v.i.r.,* to be mated; happen, chance, befall, occur, take place. Но так не случа́ется в жи́зни, but things do not work out that way in life. Случи́лась больша́я неприя́тность, a very unpleasant thing happened. Что случи́лось? What happened? С-лу́ч-ай, *n.m.,* case, occurrence, circumstance, chance, happening. Непредви́денный с., an unforeseen occurrence. Несча́стный с., accident. Удо́бный с., chance, opportunity. На вся́кий с., in case of need. Закры́то по слу́чаю ремо́нта, closed for repairs. Во вся́ком слу́чае, at any rate, in any case. С-луч-а́йность, *n.f.,* chance, occurrence, accident. По несча́стной случа́йности, as ill luck would have it. По счастли́вой случа́йности, by good fortune. С-луч-а́йности войны́, hazards of war. С-луч-а́йный, *adj.,* accidental. С-ая встре́ча, chance meeting. С-ое обстоя́тельство, accidental circumstances. С-луч-а́йно, *adv.,* by chance. Найти́ с., to happen upon; find an opportunity. Она́ с. оказа́лась там, she happened to be there.

у-луч-и́ть, *v.p.,* у-луч-а́ть, *v.i.,* + *acc.,* to find time; seize. У. вре́мя (мину́ту), to find time (a minute). У. пря́мо в цель, to hit the bull's eye.

ЛЮБ-, ЛЮБ(Л)-, LOVE

люб-о́вь, *n.f.,* love, affection, fondness. Матери́нская л., motherly love. Брак по любви́, a love match. Мне недо́рог твой пода́рок, дорога́ твоя́ любо́вь, (*saying*), it is not the gift that counts, but the thought behind it. Любви́ все во́зрасты поко́рны (*Pushkin*), all ages are susceptible to love. Люб-о́вник, *n.m.,* lover. Люб-о́вница, *n.f.,* mistress. Люб-о́вный, *adj.,* amorous, affectionate. Л. напи́ток, love potion. Л-ая исто́рия, love affair, romance. Л-ая связь, amour, intrigue, illicit love affair. Л-ое письмо́, love letter. Люб-о́вно, *adv.,* lovingly. Люб-о, *adv.,* agreeably, pleasantly. Любо-до́рого смотре́ть, (*idiom.*), a pleasure to behold. Люб-в-е-оби́льный, *adj.,* loving. Л-ое се́рдце, a heart full of love.

люб-ова́ть-ся, *v.i.r.,* по-люб-ова́ть-ся, *v.p.r.,* + *instr.,* на + *acc.,* to look with pleasure, admire. Л. приро́дой, to admire nature. Л. на восхо́д со́лнца, to admire a sunrise.

за-люб-ова́ть-ся, *v.p.r.,* + *instr.,* to lose oneself in admiration, find pleasure in looking, be enraptured by. З. краси́ вым ви́дом, to be enraptured by a beautiful view.

на-люб-ова́ть-ся, *v.p.r.,* + *instr.,* на + *acc.,* to admire fully. Дай мне тобо́й н., let me admire you to my heart's content.

об-люб-ова́ть, *v.p.,* + *acc.,* to choose, favor. О. себе́ дом, to choose a pleasant home.

люб-и́ть, люб-л-ю́, *v.i.,* + *acc.,* to love, be fond of, like. Де́ти лю́бят свои́х роди́телей, children love their parents. Л. ро́дину, to love one's native country. Л. нау́ку (иску́сство), to love science (art). Мы не люби́ли друг дру́га, we did not love each other; there was no love lost between us. Это расте́ние лю́бит ухо́д, this plant requires care. Его́ не люби́ли, he was unliked, unpopular Лю́бишь ката́ться, люби́ и са́ночки вози́ть, (*prov.*), if you like to coast down the hill, you must also like to climb it. Люб-и́мец, *n.m.,* люби́мица, *n.f.,* pet, favorite, darling. Люб-и́мый, *adj., part. pass. pres.,* beloved, darling, favorite. Л. сын, beloved son. Л. го́род, beloved city. Л. писа́тель, favorite writer. Л. цвет, favorite color. Л-ая соба́ка, pet dog. Люб-я́щий, *adj., part. act., pres.,* loving, fond, affectionate. Л. оте́ц, loving father. Л-ая мать, loving mother. Л-ий Вас, yours affectionately (*in letters*). Из-люб-л-енный, *adj., part. pass. pres.,* favorite. И-ое ме́сто, favorite haunt. Люб-и́тель, *n.m.,* люб-и́тельница, *n.f.,* amateur, dabbler, dilettante. Она́ больша́я люби́тельница му́зыки, she is very fond of music. Люб-и́тельство, *n.n.,* dilettantism, dabbling. Люб-и́тельский, *adj.,* amateurish. Л. спекта́кль, amateur performance. Л-ие фотогра́фии, amateur photographs.

воз-люб-и́ть, *v.p.,* + *acc.,* (*obs.*), to love. Воз-люб-л-енный, *adj., part. pass. past., used as n.,* beloved; lover. Воз-люб-л-енная, *n.f.,* sweetheart, lady-love, mistress. Не-вз-люб-и́ть, *v.p.,* + *acc.,* to come to dislike, hate. Ма́чеха не взлюби́ла свою́ па́дчерицу, stepmother developed a dislike for her stepdaughter.

в-люб-и́-ть, *v.p.,* в-люб-л-я́ть, *v.i.,* в + *acc.,* to captivate, enamor, charm. В. в себя́ молоду́ю де́вушку, to captivate a young girl. В-люб-и́ть-ся, *v.p.r.,* в-люб-л-я́ть-ся, *v.i.r.,* в + *acc.,* to fall in love, lose one's heart. В. в краса́вицу, to fall in love with a beautiful woman. В Крыму́ я влюби́лся в мо́ре, in the Crimea, I lost my heart to the sea. В-люб-л-ённый, *adj.,* in love, amorous; lover, sweetheart. Броса́ть в-ые взгля́ды, to cast amorous glances. Быть по́ уши в-ым, (*fig.*), to be head over heels in love. В-люб-чивость, *n.f.,* amorousness. В-люб-чивый, *adj.,* of an amorous disposition.

не-до-люб-л-ивать, *v.i.,* + *acc.,* to dislike.

по-люб-и́ть, *v.p.,* + *acc.,* to grow fond, take a fancy to, fall in love. П. на всю жизнь, to fall in love for keeps. Полюби́те нас чёрненькими, а бе́ленькими нас вся́кий полю́бит, (*saying*), take us as you find us. Раз-люб-и́ть, *v.p.,* to cease to love. По-люб-и́ть-ся, *v.p.r.,* (*obs.*), to win someone's heart. Она́ ему́ полюби́лась с пе́рвого взгля́да, he fell in love with her at first sight. По-люб-о́вный, *adj.,* amicable. П-ая сде́лка, amicable settlement. По-люб-о́вно, *adv.,* amicably. Реши́ть де́ло п., to settle a matter amicably. Разойти́сь п., to part amicably.

раз-люб-и́ть, *v.p.,* раз-люб-л-я́ть, *v.i.,* + *acc.,* to cease to love, grow tired of. "Ка́бы мы люби́ли, да не разлюбля́ли," (*poet.*), "If only love were permanent."

с-люб-и́ть-ся, *v.p.r.,* с-люб-л-я́ть-ся, *v.i.r.,* (*colloq.*), to grow fond of one another. Сте́рпится - слю́бится, (*saying*), if you are patient enough, you'll end up liking it.

люб-е́зн-ича-ть, *v.i.,* с + *instr.,* to pay compliments; court. Л. с же́нщинами, to court women. Люб-е́зность, *n.f.,* politeness, civility, courtesy, kindness. Люб-е́зный, *adj.,* polite, civil, courteous, kind. Любе́зный! (*obs.*), My man! Л. чита́тель, gentle reader. Люб-е́зно, *adv.,* politely, courteously, kindly. Он л. пригласи́л меня́ войти́, he politely asked me to enter.

люб-о-зна́тельность, *n.f.,* intellectual curiosity, thirst for knowledge. Люб-о-зна́тельный, *adj.,* curious, inquiring. Быть л-ым, to be eager to learn.

люб-о-пы́тствовать, *v.i.,* (*obs.*), по-люб-о-пы́тствовать, *v.p.,* to be curious, inquisitive. Люб-о-пы́тство, *n.n.,* curiosity, inquisitiveness. Люб-о-пы́тный, *adj.,* curious, inquisitive. Крыло́в написа́л ба́сню "Любопы́тный", Krylow wrote a fable "The Inquisitive Man." Люб-о-пы́тно, *adv.,* curiously, inquisitively.

люб-о́й, *adj.,* whichever one likes best. Л. цено́й, at any price. Лю́б-о, *adv.,* (*obs.*), *in express.:* лю́бо смотре́ть на + *acc.,* it is pleasant to look at; лю́бо-до́рого, it is a real pleasure.

пре-люб-о-де́йствовать, *v.i.,* (*obs.*), to

commit adultery. Пере-люб-о-деяние, *п.п.*, adultery. Пре-люб-о-действо, *п.п.*, adultery. Пре-люб-о-дей, *п.т.*, adulterer. Пре-люб-о-дейный, *adj.*, adulterous.

ЛЮД-, MANKIND, HUMANITY, PEOPLE

люд, *п.т.*, people. Рабочий л., working people, workers. Чиновный л., (*obs.*), bureaucrats, officials, civil servants.

люд-и, *п.pl.*, men, people, human beings. Русские л., Russian people. Молодые л., young people. Выйти в л., to make one's way, fortune. Быть на людях, to be with people. Люд-ность, *п.f.*, population, populousness. Люд-ный, *adj.*, crowded, populous. Л. город, populous, thickly-populated city. Л-ая улица, crowded street. Люд-но, *adv.*, densely; dense, crowded. На этом перекрёстке очень людно, it is very crowded at this intersection. Людской, *adj.*, human. Людская молва, что морская волна, (*prov.*), people's opinions are as changeable as the waves of the sea. Люд-о-ед, *п.т.*, cannibal, man-eater. Люд-о-едство, *п.п.*, cannibalism.

много-люд-ность, *п.f.*, populousness. Много-люд-ство, *п.п.*, multitude of people. Много-люд-ный, *adj.*, populous, crowded. М-ое собрание, a crowded meeting.

не-люд-им, *п.т.*, не-люд-имка, *п.f.*, unsociable person; recluse. Наш сосед нелюдим, our neighbor is unsociable. Не-люд-имость, *п.f.*, unsociability, shyness. Не-люд-имый, *adj.*, *part. act. pres.*, unsociable, shy, remote. Нелюдимо наше море, (*poet.*), unfriendly is our sea.

просто-люд-ин, *п.т.*, (*obs.*), peasant, workman, humble folk. Люд-неть, *v.i.*, по-люд-неть, *v.p.*, (*colloq.*), to grow in population, become more crowded. К вечеру улицы полюднели, towards evening the streets became more crowded.

о-без-люд-еть, *v.p.*, + *acc.*, to become deserted, cause to become deserted. После войны этот край обезлюдел, after the war this region became deserted. О-без-люд-ение, *п.п.*, exodus of population, depopulation.

о-без-люд-ить, *v.p.*, + *acc.*, to cause a place to become deserted. Война обезлюдила этот край, the war depopulated this region.

М

МАЗ-, МАЖ-, МАС-, LUBRICATION, GREASE, OIL

маз-а-ть, маж-у, *v.i.*, + *acc.*, to daub, smear, rub; soil; grease. М. хлеб маслом, to butter bread. М. хату, to whitewash a cottage. М. кого-либо по губам, (*fig.*), to tantalize; raise one's hopes. Маз-ать-ся, *v.i.r.*, to smear oneself, paint, rouge. Маз-анка, *п.f.*, mud-walled hut. Маз-илка, *п.f.*, (*derog.*), inferior painter.

маз-ну-ть, *v.p.smf.*, *see* мазать. Маз-ня, *п.f.*, daub. Маз-ок, *п.т.*, brush stroke, touch. Маз-ь, *п.f.*, ointment, grease. Дело на мази, (*fig.*), the wheels have been greased.

в-маз-ать, *v.p.*, в-маз-ывать, *v.i.*, + *acc.*, to cement, putty in. В. кирпич в стену, to cement a brick into a wall. В-маз-ывание, *п.п.*, cementing.

вы-маз-ать, *v.p.*, вы-маз-ывать, *v.i.*, + *acc.*, to soil, smear, besmear. В. дёгтем (смолой), to tar. Вы-маз-ать-ся, *v.p.r.*, вы-маз-ывать-ся, *v.i.r.*, + *instr.*, to become covered with dirt, mud, paint. Вы-маз-анный, *adj.*, *part. pass. past*, smeared with dirt; dirty.

за-маз-ать, *v.p.*, за-маз-ывать, *v.i.*, + *acc.*, to cement, plaster; soil, smear over, cover over with, daub; (*fig.*), soft pedal. З. окно известью, to cover the window over with whitewash, lime. З. пальто краской, to soil an overcoat with paint. З. недостатки, (*colloq.*), to slur over defects. З. окна, to putty windows. За-маз-ка, *п.f.*, putty.

из-маз-ать, *v.p.*, из-маз-ывать, *v.i.*, + *acc.*, to smear dirt all over, soil, dirty; use up, consume all the paint. И. стол чернилами, to dirty a table with ink. Из-маз-ать-ся, *v.p.r.*, из-маз-ывать-ся, *v.i.r.*, to smear oneself, get dirty. И. в краске, to become smeared with paint.

на-маз-ать, *v.p.*, на-маз-ывать, *v.i.*, + *acc.*, + *instr.*, to smear, daub, spread. Н. хлеб маслом, to spread butter on bread. Н. губы, (*colloq.*), to paint one's lips. На-маз-ать-ся, *v.p.r.*, на-маз-ывать-ся, *v.i.r.*, (*colloq.*), to apply cosmetics thickly.

об-маз-ать, *v.p.*, об-маз-ывать, *v.i.*, + *acc.*, to lay on a coat, coating; to grease, putty, besmear, soil all around, thoroughly, entirely. О. печку глиной, to cover a stove with clay. Об-маз-ка, *п.f.*, coating; putty. Об-маз-ывание, *п.п.*, coating, puttying. Об-маз-ать-ся, *v.p.r.*, об-маз-ывать-ся, *v.i.r.*, + *instr.*, to besmear oneself.

пере-маз-ать, *v.p.*, пере-маз-ывать, *v.i.*,

+ *acc.*, to besmear, cover with mud. П. маслом все пирожки, to smear all the patties with butter. Пере-маз-ать-ся, *v.p.r.*, пере-маз-ывать-ся, *v.i.r.*, + *instr.*, to besmear, soil oneself.

по-маз-ать, *v.p.*, + *acc.*, to oil, grease; anoint. П. на царство, (*hist.*), to anoint (a king). П. рану иодом, to paint a wound with iodine. По-маз-ать-ся, *v.p.r.*, to be anointed. По-маз-ание, *n.n.*, anointing. По-маз-анник, *n.f.*, (*rel.*), the Lord's Anointed. Миро-по-маз-ание, *n.n.*, (*rel.*), chrismation. По-маз-ок, *n.m.*, little brush; shaving brush.

под-маз-ать, *v.p.*, под-маз-ывать, *v.i.*, + *acc.*, to grease, oil, paint. П. колёса, to oil the wheels. Под-маз-ать-ся, *v.p.r.*, под-маз-ывать-ся, *v.i.r.*, к + *dat.*, to paint, make up; fawn upon. П. к кому-либо, (*colloq.*), to get into someone's good graces.

при-маз-ать, *v.p.*, при-маз-ывать, *v.i.*, + *acc.*, to smooth down. with the aid of grease, oil. П. волосы помадой, to smooth down one's hair with pomade. При-маз-ать-ся, *v.p.r.*, при-маз-ывать-ся, *v.i.r.*, к + *dat.*, to stick to, hang on. П. к партии, (*recent*), to worm one's way into the Party.

про-маз-ать, *v.p.*, про-маз-ывать, *v.i.*, + *acc.*, to coat, oil; miss a stroke, fail to hit. П. окно замазкой, to putty a window.

раз-маз-ать, *v.p.*, раз-маз-ывать, *v.i.*, + *acc.*, to spread; (*colloq.*), pad. Р. грязь по всему лицу, to smear mud all over one's face. Он размазал свой доклад, (*colloq.*), he padded his report. Раз-маз-ать-ся, *v.p.r.*, раз-маз-ывать-ся, *v.i.r.*, to spread, smear, blur. Грязь размазалась по всей стене, the mud spread all over the wall. Раз-маз-ня, *n.f.*, thin gruel; (*colloq.*), listless person.

с-маз-ать, *v.p.*, с-маз-ывать, *v.i.*, + *acc.*, + *instr.*, to grease, oil, lubricate; bribe, pay graft. С. жиром, to grease. С. маслом, to oil. С. машину, to lubricate a machine. С. порез иодом, to paint a cut with iodine. С-маз-ка, *n.f.*, greasing, oiling, lubrication. С. лыж, waxing of skis. Вещество для смазки, grease, lubricant. С-маз-чик, *n.m.*, greaser, lubricator. С-маз-ывание, *n.n.*, painting, greasing, oiling, daubing. С-маз-очный, *adj.*, lubricating. С-ое масло, lubricating oil. С. материал, lubricant. С-маз-ной, *adj.*, smeared with tar, grease. С-ые сапоги, boots smeared with tar, grease. С-маз-ливый, *adj.* comely.

мас-л-ить, *v.i.*, по-мас-лить, *v.p.*, + *acc.*, to butter, oil. М. кашу, to add butter, oil to porridge. Мас-ло, *n.n.*, butter, oil. Сливочное м., butter. Растительное м., vegetable oil. Всё идёт, как по маслу, (*colloq.*), things are going smoothly. Писать картины маслом, to paint in oils. Мас-л-еница, *n.f.*, Мас-л-еная, *adj.*, Shrovetide, carnival. Мас-л-еничный, *adj.*, carnival. Мас-л-ёнка, *n.f.*, butter dish, oil can. Мас-л-ёнок, *n.m.*, edible mushroom. Мас-л-ина, *n.f.*, olive tree; olive. Мас-л-ичный, *adj.*, olive. Мас-л-о-делие, *n.n.*, butter, oil production. Мас-л-янистость, *n.f.*, oiliness. Мас-л-янистый, *adj.*, oily. Мас-л-яный, *adj.*, oil, butter. М-ое пятно, oil stain. М-ые краски, oil colors.

МАЛ-, SMALLNESS, LITTLENESS, INSIGNIFICANCE

мал-еньк-ий, *adj.*, little, small; undersized, diminutive; young; *used as n.*, the baby, child, little one. М. мальчик, little boy. Играть по маленькой, to play for small stakes. М-ие люди, humble folk. М. человек, narrow-minded man. Мал-ёнько, *adv.*, (*colloq.*), a little, a bit. Мал-ец, *n.m.*, (*folk*), lad, stripling. Мал-о, *adv.*, little, few, not enough. В этой школе мало книг, there are few books in this school. М. народу, few people. М. сахару, little sugar. Мало того, moreover. М. ли что, (*colloq.*), What then? Мал-оват, *adj.*, (*colloq.*), rather too small, not quite the right size. Мал-овато, *adv.*, not quite enough. Мал-о-, *a combining form meaning* little, small. Мал-о-вероятный, *adj.*, hardly probable, unlikely. Мал-о-водный, *adj.*, shallow. Мал-о-грамотный, *adj.*, almost illiterate; (*fig.*), raw, unskilled. Мал-о-душный, *adj.*, cowardly, faint-hearted. М. человек, coward, faint-hearted man. Мал-о-душие, *n.n.*, faint-heartedness, cowardice. Мал-о-душествовать, *v.i.*, to play the coward. Мал-о-заметный, *adj.*, slight, unobtrusive, hardly noticeable. Мал-о-кровие, *n.n.*, anemia. Мал-о-кровный, *adj.*, anemic. Мал-о-летний, *adj.*, young, under age; *used as n.*, infant, juvenile. Мал-о-сольный, *adj.*, slightly salted. М-ые огурцы, freshly salted cucumbers.

мал-о-мал-ь-ски, *adv.*, in the slightest degree. М. грамотный человек, a man in the slightest degree literate.

мал-о-по-мал-у, *adv.*, gradually, little by little, bit by bit. М. ребёнок научился ходить, gradually the child learned to walk. Мал-ость, *n.f.*, (*colloq.*), trifle.

Са́мая м. оста́лась, there is just a little left.

ма́л-ый, *adj.,* мал, *adj. pred.,* small; *used as n.,* fellow, boy, lad. Мал ро́стом, мала́ ро́стом, short. Зна́ния его́ сли́шком малы́, his knowledge is insignificant. Теа́тр ма́лых форм, (*recent*), variety theatre. М-ая ско́рость, low speed. Мал золотни́к, да доро́г, (*saying*), it is not quantity, but quality that counts. С ма́лых лет, from childhood. Сла́вный ма́лый, a fine fellow. Са́мое ма́лое, the least. Мал-ы́ш, *n.m.,* small child, tot; (*colloq.*), little man. Мал-ю́сенький, *adj.,* (*colloq.*), tiny, wee. Мал-ю́тка, *n.f.,* baby; my little one.

ма́л-ь-чик, *n.m.,* boy, lad. М. с па́льчик, Tom Thumb. Беспризо́рный м., homeless boy, waif. Мал-ь-чи́шеский, *adj.,* boyish, puerile. М-ие вы́ходки, boyish pranks. Мал-ь-чи́шество, *n.n.,* childishness, puerility. Мал-ь-чи́шка, *n.m.,* urchin, boy. Уличный м., street urchin. Вести́ себя́ как м., to behave like a teen-ager. Мал-ь-чи́шник, *n.m.,* a stag reception for a bridegroom on the eve of his wedding. Мал-ь-чуга́н, *n.m.,* (*colloq.*), little boy, laddie.

у-ма́л-ить, *v.p.,* у-мал-я́ть, *v.i.,* + *acc.,* to belittle. У. чьи-либо заслу́ги, to belittle someone's services, achievements. У-ма́л-ить-ся, *v.p.r.,* у-мал-я́ть-ся, *v.i.r.,* to be diminished. У-мал-е́ние, *n.n.,* lessening, diminution, decrease. У. досто́инства, to belittle one's dignity. У. заслу́г, belittling of one's services, achievements.

МАХ-, МАШ-, WAVING

мах-а́-ть, маш-у́, *v.i.,* мах-ну́ть, *v.p.smf.,* + *instr.,* to wave; take off, depart. М. руко́й, to wave one's hand. М. хвосто́м, to wag one's tail. М. кры́льями, to flap one's wings. Он махну́л домо́й, (*colloq.*), he took off for home. М. руко́й на что́-либо, (*fig.*), to give something up for lost. Мах, *n.m.,* (*colloq.*), stroke, *in expressions*: Одни́м ма́хом, at one stroke. Дать ма́ху, to miss a chance; blunder. С ма́ху, rashly. Мах-а́льный, *adj.,* used as n., (*colloq.*), signalman. Мах-а́ние, *n.n.,* waving. Мах-ово́й, *adj.,* (*tech.*), fly. М-о́е колесо́, fly-wheel, *syn.,* мах-ови́к, *n.m.*

вз-мах-ну́-ть, *v.p.,* smf., вз-ма́х-ивать, *v.i.,* + *instr.,* to wave, flourish, swing, flap. Пти́ца взмахну́ла кры́льями, the bird flapped its wings. Вз-мах, *n.m.,* stroke, sweep. Одни́м взма́хом, at one stroke.

за-мах-а́ть, *v.p.,* + *instr.* to start to wave, flap. Оте́ц замаха́л рука́ми, подзыва́я ма́льчика, the father waved his hands, calling the boy. За-ма́х-ну́ть-ся, *v.p.r.,* за-ма́х-ивать-ся, *v.i.r.,* на + *acc.,* to threaten someone. З. руко́й на кого́-либо, to raise one's hand against someone. З. па́лкой на кого́-либо, to raise a cane, threaten with a cane. За-ма́ш-ки, *n.pl.,* (*colloq.*), ways, manners. Ба́рские за-ма́ш-ки, (*iron.*), lordly ways.

об-мах-ну́-ть, *v.p.,* об-ма́х-ивать, *v.i.,* + *acc.,* + *instr.,* to dust, brush away; fan. О. лицо́ ве́ером, to fan one's face. Об-мах-ну́т-э-ся, *v.p.r.,* об-ма́х-ивать-ся, *v.i.r.,* + *instr.,* to fan oneself. О. платко́м, to fan oneself with a handkerchief.

от-мах-а́ть, от-мах-ну́ть, *v.p.,* от-ма́х-ивать, *v.i.,* + *acc.,* to cover distance; wave away. Он отмаха́л 5 киломе́тров (*colloq.*), he covered five kilometers. От-мах-ну́ть-ся, *v.p.r.,* от-ма́х-ивать-ся, *v.i.r.,* от + *gen.,* to wave away, brush aside. О. от му́хи, to brush aside a fly. О. от тру́дного вопро́са, to dodge a difficult question.

пере-мах-ну́ть, *v.p.smf.,* пере-ма́х-ивать, *v.i.,* + *acc.,* (*colloq.*), to jump over; overshoot. П. че́рез забо́р, to jump over a garden wall.

по-мах-а́ть, *v.p.,* по-ма́х-ивать, *v.i.,* to wave for a short time; wave, whisk, swing. П. руко́й, to wave one's hand. Он шёл, пома́хивая тро́сточкой, he walked, whisking his cane. Соба́ка пома́хивает хвосто́м, the dog is wagging its tail.

под-мах-ну́ть, *v.p.smf.,* под-ма́х-ивать, *v.i.,* + *acc.,* (*colloq.*), to sign hurriedly. Он подмахну́л бума́ги и уе́хал, he signed the papers hurriedly and departed.

про-мах-ну́ть-ся, *v.p.r.smf.,* про-ма́х-ивать-ся, *v.i.r.,* to miss; fail to hit. Он вы́стрелил, но промахну́лся, he fired, but missed. Про́-мах, *n.m.,* miss; (*fig.*), slip, blunder. Он ма́лый не про́мах, (*colloq.*), he is a bright lad.

раз-мах-ну́ть, *v.p.smf.,* раз-ма́х-ивать, *v.i.,* + *instr.,* to brandish; swing. Разма́хивать рука́ми, to swing one's arms, gesticulate. Раз-мах-ну́ть-ся, *v.p.r.,* раз-ма́х-ивать-ся, *v.i.r.,* to swing one's arms, hands. Размахну́ться и уда́рить, to swing and to strike. Раз-ма́х, *n.m.,* range; swing, sweep. Уда́рить с разма́ху, to strike with all one's might. Р. кры́льев, wing-spread. Р. жи́зни, living in a grand style. Раз-ма́ш-истый, *adj.,* bold; loose; sweeping. Р. по́черк, sprawling handwriting. Р-ые

движéния, swinging motion. Раз-мáш-исто, *adv.*, boldly, sweepingly. Р. грестú, to row with sweeping strokes.
с-мах-нýть, *v.p.smf.,* с-мáх-ивать, *v.i.,* + *acc.,* to whisk away; flap away; brush off. С. пыль со столá, to dust off a table. С. слезý, to brush away a tear. С-мáх-ивать, *v.p.,* на + *acc.,* (*colloq.*), to look alike, resemble. Он смáхивает на отцá, (*colloq.*), he slightly resembles his father. С-мáх-у, *adv.,* (*colloq.*), offhand. Удáрить с, to swing back and hit.
на-óт-маш-ь, *adv., in expression*: Удáрить наóтмашь, to strike with the back of one's hand.

МГ-, МИГ-, TWINKLE, WINK, BLINK, FLICKER, FLASH

мг-н-овéние, *n.n.,* instant, moment, flash. В м. óка, (*poet.*), in the twinkling of an eye. "Я пóмню чýдное мгновéнье...," (*Pushkin*), "I recall an entrancing moment." Мг-новéнный, *adj.,* instantaneous, momentary. Мг-новéнно, *adv.,* instantly.
мг-л-á, *n.f.,* mist, haze. М. застилáет даль, a mist covers the distance. Мглúстый, *adj.,* nebulous, misty. М. вóздух, misty air.
миг, *n.m.,* moment, instant. В одúн миг, in a flash. Ни на миг, not for a moment. Мúг-ом, *adv.,* (*colloq.*), in a flash, in a jiffy.
миг-áть, *v.i.,* миг-нýть, *v.p.smf.,* + *dat.,* + *instr.,* to blink, flicker. Миг-áние, *n.n.,* blinking, flickering. Миг-áтельный, *adj.,* pertaining to blinking, flickering. М-ая перепóнка, (*med.*), nictating membrane.
за-миг-áть, *v.p.,* to begin to wink. З. глазáми, to begin blinking one's eyes. Электрúчество замигáло, the electric light began to flicker.
под-миг-нý-ть, *v.p.smf.,* под-мúг-ивать, *v.i.,* + *dat.,* + *instr.,* to wink. Он мне подмигнýл глáзом, he winked at me. Под-мúг-ивание, *n.n.,* winking.
пере-миг-нýть-ся, *v.p.r.,* пере-мúг-ивать-ся, *v.i.r.,* (*colloq.*), to wink at one another.

МЕЖ-, МЕЖД-, INTERJACENCE, BOUNDARY

меж-á, *n.f.,* boundary. М. мéжду полями, the boundary between fields. Меж-евáние, *n.n.,* land surveying.
меж-евá-ть, *v.i.,* + *acc.,* to survey; set, fix boundaries. М. поля (лугá), to survey fields (meadows). Меж-евóй, *adj.,* pertaining to surveying. М. знак,

boundary mark. М-áя цепь, measuring chain.
от-меж-евá-ть, *v.p.,* от-меж-ёвывать, *v.i.,* + *acc.,* to survey, mark off, draw a boundary. О. себé нéсколько учáстков, to mark off several lots for oneself. От-меж-евá-ть-ся, *v.p.r.,* от-меж-ёвывать-ся, *v.i.r.,* от + *gen.,* to draw a boundary, to separate one's property from; (*fig.*), to renounce, disavow. О. от врéдной теóрии, to renounce a nefarious theory.
пере-меж-евá-ть, *v.p.,* пере-меж-ёвывать, *v.i.,* + *acc.,* to survey again. Пере-меж-евá-ть-ся, *v.p.r.,* пер-меж-ёвывать-ся, *v.i.r.,* to be surveyed, fixed anew.
пере-меж-á-ть-ся, *v.p.,* to be intermittent. Пере-меж-áющийся, *adj., part. act. pres.,* intermittent. П-аяся лихорáдка, (*med.*), intermittent fever.
рез-меж-евá-ть, *v.p.,* раз-меж-ёвывать, *v.i.,* + *acc.,* to mark boundaries. Р. лес, to mark the boundaries of a wood. Р. сфéры влияния, to delimit spheres of influence. Раз-меж-евáние, *n.n.,* delimitation, demarcation. Раз-меж-евá-ть-ся, *v.p.r.,* раз-меж-ёвывать-ся, *v.i.r.,* to fix common boundaries, delimit functions, activities, spheres of action.
с-меж-úть, *v.p.,* с-меж-áть, *v.i.,* + *acc.,* to close together; to make contiguous. С. глазá, to close one's eyes. С-мéжность, *n.f.,* contiguity. Ассоциáция по смéжности, association by contiguity. С-мéж-ный, *adj.,* adjacent, contiguous. С. ýгол, adjacent angle. С-ые госудáрства, contiguous nations, states.
меж, *prep.,* (*obs.*), between; among, amongst; *see* мéжду.
мéж-ду, *prep.,* + *instr.,* between. М. двéрью и окнóм, between the door and the window. М. двумя и тремя (часáми), between two and three o'clock. Войнá мéжду нарóдами, a war between nations. Меж, between, *in expression*: меж двух огнéй, (*fig.*), between two fires. Мéжду, between. М. нáми, between the two of us, between us (*secret*). Пусть э́то остáнется мéжду нáми, Let us keep it between ourselves, confidential. Мéж(ду) тем, meanwhile. Мéжду прóчим, by the way, incidentally. Читáть мéж-(ду) строк, to read between the lines.
межд-у-вéдомственный, *adj.,* interdepartmental. М-ая комúссия, joint commission. Межд-у-горóдний, *adj.,* interurban, inter-city. М. телефóн, trunk line; inter-city telephone. Межд-у-нарóдный, *adj.,* international. М-ое прáво, international law. М-ые отношéния, international relations. Межд-о-мéтие, *n.n.,* (*gram.*), interjection.

Межд-у-ца́рствие, *п.п.*, (*hist.*), interregnum. Межд-о-усо́бие, *п.п.*, civil war. Межд-о-усо́бица, *п.f.*, civil war. Кня́жеские междоусо́бицы в дре́вней Руси́, (*hist.*), the wars between reigning princes in Medieval Russia. Меж-плане́тный, *adj.*, interplanetary. Меж-рёберный, *adj.*, (*anat.*), intercostal.

про-ме́ж, *prep.*, + *gen.* (or + *instr.*), (*folk*), among; between. П. себя́, between us, ourselves, among themselves.

про-ме́ж-ность, *n.f.*, (*anat.*), perineum.

про-меж-у́т-ок, *n.m.*, interval, space, span. П. вре́мени, period of time, space of time. Про-меж-у́точный, *adj.*, intermediate, intervening. П-ая ста́нция, way station.

МЕК-, МЁК-, HINT, ALLUSION, IMPLICATION

на-мёк, *n.m.*, hint, allusion, implication. То́нкий н. delicate hint. Говори́ть пря́мо, без намёков, to speak frankly, without innuendo.

на-мек-а́ть, *v.i.*, на-мек-ну́ть, *v.p.*, на + *acc.*, to hint at, allude to, insinuate. На что вы намека́ете? What are you driving, hinting at? Не-в-до-мёк, *adv.*, *in expression*: Ему́ невдомёк, (*idiom.*), it never occurred to him.

с-мек-а́ть, *v.i.*, с-мек-ну́ть, *v.p.*, (*colloq.*), to grasp the meaning. Он в э́том де́ле смека́ет, he understands this business. С-мек-а́лка, *n.f.*, sharpness, keenness of wit. Челове́к со смека́лкой, clever, smart man. С-мек-а́листый, *adj.*, (*colloq.*), clever, smart. С. па́рень, clever young man.

МЕЧТ-, DREAMING, DREAM

мечт-а́ть, *v.i.*, о + *prep.*, to dream. М. о сла́ве, to dream of glory, fame. М. о путеше́ствии, to dream of a journey. Мечт-а́ть-ся, *v.i.r.*, (*obs.*), to feel like dreaming. Мечт-а́, *n.f.*, dream, daydream; (*fig.*), castles in the air. Несбы́точная м., vain dream. Мечты́, мечты́, где ва́ша сла́дость, (*poet.*), Oh dreams, oh dreams, where is your sweetness? Завоева́ние Аркти́ки переста́ло быть мечто́й, the conquest of the Arctic is no longer a dream. Мечт-а́ние, *n.n.*, dreaming. Предава́ться мечта́ниям, to become lost in reverie. Мечт-а́тель, *n.m.*, dreamer. Меч-та́тельность, *n.f.*, dreaminess. Мечт-а́тельный, *adj.*, dreamy, moony.

воз-мечт-а́ть, *v.p.*, (*obs.*), to conceive, dream up. В. о себе́, to conceive a high opinion of oneself.

за-мечт-а́ть-ся, *v.p.r.*, to become lost in dreams. З. над увлека́тельным рома́ном, to become lost in a fascinating novel.

по-мечт-а́ть, *v.p.*, see мечта́ть. П. при луне́, to dream for a while in the moonlight.

раз-мечт-а́ть-ся, *v.p.r.*, (*colloq.*), to become lost in dreams.

МЕЛЬК-, FLASH, FLICKER

мельк-а́-ть, *v.i.*, мельк-ну́-ть, *v.p.smf.*, to flash, flicker, gleam, appear for a moment. Вдали́ мелька́ла мо́лния, lightning flashed in the distance. У него́ мелькну́ла мысль, an idea flashed through his mind. Свет мелькну́л и пога́с, a light flickered and went out. Мельк-а́ние, *n.n.*, flash, flicker, gleam. М. фонаря́, маяка́, flicker of a lantern, beacon. Ме́льком, *adv.*, in passing. Взгляну́ть м., to cast a cursory glance. Ви́деть м., to catch a glimpse of. Мельк-а́ющий, *adj.*, *part. act. pres.*, flickering. Мельк-ну́вший, *adj.*, *part. act. past*, flashed, appeared for a moment. М. вдали́ огонёк, a light which flickered in the distance.

за-мельк-а́ть, *v.i.*, to begin to flash, flicker, gleam. Замелька́ли огни́ го́рода, the lights of the city gleamed in the distance.

при-мельк-а́ть-ся, *v.p.r.*, to become familiar. Его́ лицо́ мне примелька́лось, his face became familiar to me.

про-мельк-ну́ть, *v.p.*, to flash by, fly by, pass swiftly. Про-мельк-ну́ли две неде́ли, two weeks flew by. В его́ слова́х промелькну́ла иро́ния, there was a shade of irony in his words. В газе́тах проме́лькнуло сообще́ние об э́том изобрете́нии, this invention was mentioned incidentally in the newspapers. Луч наде́жды промелькну́л, (*fig.*), a ray of hope flashed.

МЕН-, (МѢН-), TRANSFORMATION, CHANGE, EXCHANGE

мен-я́-ть, *v.i.*, + *acc.*, to change, shift, vary; exchange, barter, truck, trade. М. де́ньги, to change money. М. своё мне́ние, to change one's opinion. М. положе́ние, to shift position. Мен-я́ть-ся, *v.i.r.*, + *instr.*, to change, shift, vary. М. ко́мнатами, to exchange rooms. М. в лице́, to change countenance. М. роля́ми, to exchange parts, roles. Ме́н-а, *n.f.*, exchange, barter. Мен-ово́й, *adj.*, barter, М-а́я торго́вля, barter trade. Мен-я́ла, *n.m.*, money changer. Мен-я́льный, *adj.*, money changing.

в-мен-я́ть, *v.i.,* в-мен-и́ть, *v.p.,* + *acc.,* + *dat.,* во(в) + *acc.,* to lay on, upon; reckon; impose on. В. что́-либо в вину́ кому́-нибудь, to charge someone with something. В. что́-либо в заслу́гу кому́-нибудь, to credit someone with something. В. что́-либо в обя́занность кому́-нибудь, to require someone to do something. В-мен-я́емость, *n.f., (law),* responsibility; sanity. Суд призна́л по́лную в. престу́пника, the tribunal found the criminal sane. Не-в-мен-я́емость, *n.f.,* irresponsibility; insanity. Быть в состоя́нии невменя́емости, to be insane; to be not responsible for one's actions. В-мен-я́емый, *adj., part. pres. pass., (law),* responsible, of sound mind. Не-в-мен-я́емый, *adj., part. pass. pres.,* irresponsible. Н-ое состоя́ние, mental derangement.

вы́-мен-ять, *v.p.,* вы-ме́н-ивать, *v.i.,* + *acc.,* to barter, exchange. В. ло́шадь на коро́ву, to exchange a horse for a cow.

за-мен-и́ть, *v.p.,* за-мен-я́ть, *v.i.,* + *acc.,* + *instr.,* to substitute; compensate, replace. З. ма́сло маргари́ном, to use margarine instead of butter. З. одно́ сло́во други́м, to substitute one word for another. Она́ замени́ла мать осиро́те́вшему ребёнку, she was a mother to the orphaned child. Не́кому меня́ з., there is none to replace me. За-ме́н-а, *n.f.,* substitution, replacement; substitute. З. поте́рянной кни́ги но́вой, the replacement of a lost book by a new one. З. сме́ртной ка́зни тюре́мным заключе́нием, commutation of a death sentence to imprisonment. За-мен-и́мый, *adj.,* replaceable. Не-за-мен-и́мый, *adj.,* irreplaceable. Н. рабо́тник, irreplaceable worker. В-за-ме́н, *adv.,* instead of, in exchange for.

из-мен-и́ть, *v.p.,* из-мен-я́ть, *v.i.,* + *acc.,* + *dat.,* to alter, change, modify; betray, be false. И. фасо́н пла́тья, to alter the style of a dress. И. законопрое́кт, to amend a law, bill. И. му́жу, жене́, to be unfaithful to one's husband, wife. И. своему́ до́лгу, to fail in one's duty. Из-мен-и́ть-ся, *v.p.r.,* из-мен-я́ть-ся, *v.i.r.,* to change. И. к лу́чшему, to change for the better. Из-ме́н-а, *n.f.,* treason; infidelity; betrayal. Госуда́рственная и., high treason. Из-ме́н-ник, *n.m.,* из-ме́н-ница, *n.f.,* traitor. Из-ме́н-нический, *adj.,* treacherous. Из-мен-е́ние, *n.n.,* alteration, change. Вноси́ть измене́ния, to make alterations, changes. Из-ме́н-чивый, *adj.,* changeable, unsteady. И-ая

пого́да, changeable weather. И. хара́ктер, unsteady disposition. Не-из-ме́н-ный, *adj.,* invariable, immutable, unalterable. Не-из-ме́н-ность, *n.f.,* immutability.

на-мен-я́ть, *v.p.,* на-ме́н-ивать, *v.i.,* + *acc.,* + *gen.,* to exchange, barter. Н. ме́лочи, to secure a quantity of small change.

об-мен-я́ть, об-мен-и́ть, *v.p.,* об-ме́н-ивать, *v.i.,* + *acc.,* to exchange, barter. О-я́ть кни́гу в библиоте́ке, to exchange a book in the library. Обмени́ть пальто́ на чужо́е, to take someone else's overcoat by mistake, instead of one's own. Об-мен-и́ть-ся, об-мен-я́ть-ся, *v.p.r.,* об-ме́н-ивать-ся, *v.i.r.,* to exchange, barter, swap; interchange. Обменя́ться гало́шами, to take rubbers in mistake for one's own. Обменя́ться мне́ниями (взгля́дами), to exchange opinions. Об-ме́н, *n.m.,* exchange. Взаи́мный, о., interchange. Торго́вый о., barter, trade. О. о́пытом, exchange of experiences. О. мне́ний, exchange of opinions. О. веще́ств, *(biol.),* metabolism. Об-ме́н-ный, *adj.,* exchangeable.

от-мен-и́ть, *v.p.,* от-мен-я́ть, *v.i.,* + *acc.,* to repeal, abrogate, revoke. О. прика́за́ние, to cancel an order. О. реше́ние, to cancel a decision. О. пригово́р, to rescind a sentence. От-ме́н-а, *n.f.,* abolition, revocation, abrogation, repeal. О. ча́стной со́бственности, abolition of private property. О. пригово́ра, reprieve. От-ме́н-ный, *adj.,* excellent.

пере-мен-и́ть, *v.p.,* пере-мен-я́ть, *v.i.,* + *acc., (colloq.),* to change over. П. разгово́р, to change the subject (*e.g.* in a conversation). П. кварти́ру, to change apartments. Пере-мен-и́ть-ся, *v.p.r.,* пере-мен-я́ть-ся, *v.i.r.,* to be changed. Времена́ перемени́лись, times have changed. Перемени́ться к кому́-либо, to change towards someone. Же́нится-перемени́тся, *(saying),* a youth will settle down when he marries. Пере-ме́н-а, *n.f.,* change; recess. Больша́я п., long school recess. П. белья́, change of underwear. Пере-ме́н-ный, *adj.,* variable. П. ток, alternating current. Пере-ме́н-чивость, *n.f.,* changeability; volatility. Пере-ме́н-чивый, *adj.,* changeable. П-ая пого́да, changeable, variable weather.

под-мен-и́ть, *v.p.,* под-ме́н-ивать, под-мен-я́ть, *v.i.,* + *acc.,* to substitute. Кто́-то подмени́л мне гало́ши, someone has taken my rubbers for his. Под-ме́н-а, *n.f.,* substitution. Под-ме́н-ный, *adj.,* substituted.

по-мен-я́ть, *v.p., see* меня́ть. По-мен-я́ть-ся, *v.p.r.,* to exchange; *see* меня́ться.

при-мен-и́ть, *v.p.,* при-мен-я́ть, *v.i.,* to apply, adapt, put into practice. П. свои́ зна́ния на пра́ктике, to put one's knowledge into practice. При-мен-и́ть-ся, *v.p.r.,* при-мен-я́ть-ся, *v.i.r.,* к + *dat.,* to adapt oneself. П. к ме́стности, to adapt oneself to a locality. П. к обстоя́тельствам, to adapt oneself to circumstances. При-мен-е́ние, *n.n.,* adaptation, application. При-мен-и́мый, *adj.,* applicable, adaptable, suitable. Не-при-мен-и́мый, *adj.,* inapplicable, inadaptable. При-мен-и́тельно, *adv.,* applicably.

про-мен-я́ть, *v.p.,* про-мéн-ивать, *v.i.,* + *acc.,* to exchange, barter. П. куку́шку на я́стреба, (*saying*), to exchange a cuckoo for a hawk; a fool's bargain.

раз-мен-я́ть, *v.p.,* раз-мéн-ивать, *v.i.,* + *acc.,* to exchange, give change. Р. кру́пные де́ньги на мéлкие, to change money of larger denominations for smaller. Раз-мен-я́ть-ся, *v.p.r.,* раз-мéн-ивать-ся, *v.i.r.,* to be exchanged; (*fig.*), cheapen. Р. на мéлочи, (*fig.*), to squander one's gifts, talents. Раз-мéн, *n.m.,* exchange. Р. де́нег, money exchange. Раз-мéн-ный, *adj.,* exchangeable. Р-ая монéта, small change.

с-мен-и́ть, *v.p.,* с-мен-я́ть, *v.i.,* + *acc.,* to relieve; replace. С. лошадéй, to change horses. С. карау́л, to change the guard. На э́той ста́нции на́до смени́ть лошадéй, (*obs.*), at this station the horses must be changed. Прика́зано сменя́ть карау́л три ра́за в день, it has been ordered that the guard be changed three times a day. Смени́ть гнев на ми́лость, (*idiom.*), to change from anger to mercy. С-мен-и́ть-ся, *v.p.r.,* с-мен-я́ть-ся, *v.i.r.,* to take turns, change. Испу́г смени́лся ра́достью, fright changed into joy. Дневно́й зной смени́лся прохла́дой, the day's heat gave way to coolness. Румя́нец сменя́лся блéдностью, когда́ она́ пуга́лась, when she was frightened, pallor replaced the color in her cheeks. С-мéн-а, *n.f.,* shift, replacement. С. впечатлéний, change of impressions. На смéну кому́-либо, to replace someone. Утрéнняя (дневна́я, вечéрняя) смéна, morning (noon, night) shift. Рабóчий рабóтал на дневнóй смéне, the worker worked the day shift. На завóде рабóтают в три смéны, they work in three shifts at the plant. С. белья́, change of linen, underwear. С-мéн-ный, *adj.,* pertaining to change, shift. С-ое колесó, spare wheel. С-мен-я́емость, *n.f.,* removability. С-мен-я́емый, *adj.,* removable. С-ые ча́сти, removable, changeable parts. Бес-с-мéн-ный, *adj.,* permanent, continuous. Бес-с-мéн-но, *adv.,* continuously; without relief. Б. прослужи́ть пять лет в однóм учреждéнии, to serve five years in a row in one place. По-с-мéн-но, *adv.,* in shifts. Рабóтать п., to work in shifts.

МЕР-, (МѢР-), MEASURE

мéр-а, *n.f.,* measure. М. длины́, measure of length. М. наказа́ния, degree of punishment. Приня́ть реши́тельные мéры, to take drastic measures. По мéре тогó, to the degree. По кра́йней мéре, at least.

мéр-и-ть, *v.i.,* с-мéр-ить, *v.p.,* + *acc.,* to measure, М. кóмнату, to measure a room. С. взгля́дом, to survey, measure with one's eye. М. на свой арши́н, (*idiom., colloq.*), to judge others by oneself. Мéр-ить-ся, *v.i.r.,* по-мéр-ить-ся, *v.p.r.,* + *instr.,* to be measured. М. си́лами с кéм-либо, to measure one's strength with someone. Мéр-ка, *n.f.,* measure. Снять мéрку с когó-либо, to take somebody's measure. По мéрке, according to measurement. Мéр-ность, *n.f.,* regularity; rhythm. Мéр-ный, *adj.,* measured, slow, regular. М-ые шаги́, measured steps. Мер-о-прия́тие, *n.n.,* arrangement, measure. Законода́тельное м., legislative enactment.

вы́-мер-ить, *v.p.,* вы́-мéр-ивать, вы-мер-я́ть, *v.i.,* to measure out.

до-мéр-ить, *v.p.,* до-мéр-ивать, *v.i.,* + *acc.,* to measure completely; to measure out more.

из-мéр-ить, *v.p.,* из-мер-я́ть, *v.i.,* to measure. И. глубину́ мóря, to measure the depth of a sea. И. больнóму температу́ру, to take a patient's temperature. Из-мер-éние, *n.n.,* measuring, survey; sounding, fathoming; (*math.*), dimension. И. углóв, measurement of angles. Из-мер-и́тель, *n.m.,* measuring instrument. Из-мер-и́тельный, *adj.,* pertaining to measuring. И. прибóр, measuring instrument. Из-мер-и́мость, *n.f.,* measurability. Из-мер-и́мый, *adj.,* measurable, fathomable. Не-из-мер-и́мость, *n.f.,* immeasurability; immensity. Не-из-мер-и́мый, *adj.,* immeasurable, immense. Н-ое прострáнство, immeasurable space. Н-ое мнóжество, countless multitude.

на-мер-евáть-ся, *v.i.r.,* to intend, purport, mean. Я намеревáюсь поéхать в Москву́, I intend to go to Moscow. Я намéрен отказа́ться, I intend to refuse. Что вы намѐрены дѐлать? What do you intend to do? На-мѐр-ение, *п.п.*, intention, purpose. Дóбрые намѐрения, good intentions. На-мѐр-енный, *adj.*, intentional, deliberate; premeditated. На-мѐр-енно, *adv.*, intentionally, deliberately; premeditatedly. Пред-на-мѐр-енно, *adv.*, by design.

на-мѐр-ить, *v.p.*, на-мѐр-ивать, *v.i.*, + *acc.*, + *gen.*, to measure out in quantity. Намѐрить, 20 мѐтров сукнá, to measure out twenty meters of cloth.

об-мѐр-ить, *v.p.*, об-мер-ѝть, об-мѐр-ивать, *v.i.*, + *acc.*, to measure; cheat in measuring. О. земѐльный учáсток, to measure, survey a lot. Об-мѐр-ить-ся, *v.p.r.*, to make a mistake in measuring. Обмѐр, *п.т.*, measurement; short measure.

от-мѐр-ить, *v.p.*, от-мер-ѝть, от-мѐр-ивать, *v.i.*, + *acc.*, to measure off. О. 10 мѐтров матѐрии, to measure off ten meters of material. Семь раз отмѐрь, а одѝн раз отрѐжь, (*prov.*), measure seven times before you cut.

пере-мѐр-ить, *v.p.*, пере-мѐр-ивать, *v.i.*, to measure anew, try on. П. мнóго плáтьев, to try on many dresses. П. штýку матѐрии, to measure anew a bolt of material.

по-мѐр-ить, *v.p.*, + *acc.* (*colloq.*); see мѐрить.

при-мѐр-ить, *v.p.*, при-мер-ѝть, при-мѐр-ивать, *v.i.*, + *acc.*, to try, fit. При-мѐр-ка, *п.f.*, fitting. При-мѐр, *п.т.*, instance, example. Привѐсти п., to give an example. Постáвить хорóшего ученикá в п., to cite a good pupil as an example. К примѐру, (*colloq.*), by way of illustration. На-при-мѐр, for instance, for example. При-мѐр-ный, *adj.*, exemplary; approximate. П. студѐнт, exemplary student. П. подсчѐт расхóдов и дохóдов, approximate count of expenses and income.

про-мѐр-ить, *v.p.*, про-мѐр-ивать, *v.i.*, + *acc.*, to measure; sound; gauge. Промѐр, *п.т.*, measurement; error in measurement.

раз-мѐр-ить, *v.p.*, раз-мер-ѝть, *v.i.*, + *acc.*, to measure off; divide; estimate dimensions. Р. мѐсто для постро́йки, to measure off a lot for building. Р. сѝлу удáра, to gauge the force of a blow. Раз-мѐр, *п.т.*, dimension, proportion, size; amount. Р. óбуви (воротничкá), size of shoes (collar). Это не мой р., it is not my size. Р. стихá, metre (in poetry). Музыкáльный р., measure in music. Раз-мѐр-енный, *adj.*, measured. Р-ая похóдка, measured steps.

с-мѐр-ить, *v.p.*, + *acc.*; see мѐрить.

у-мѐр-ить, *v.p.*, у-мер-ять, *v.i.*, + *acc.*, to moderate, temper. У. тѝгнуть... tighten one's belt. У. трѐбования, to lower one's demand. У-мѐр-ить-ся, *v.p.r.*, у-мер-ять-ся, *v.i.r.*, to become moderate, temperate. У-мѐр-енность, *n.f.*, moderation, temperance. У-мѐр-енный, *adj.*, moderate, temperate, abstemious. У. клѝмат, temperate climate. У-ая скóрость, moderate speed. У-ая ценá, reasonable price. У-мѐр-енно, *adv.*, moderately, temperately. Жить у., to live moderately.

МЕР-, МЕР(Т)-, МИР-, МРАК-, МРАЧ-, МР-, МОРОК-, МОРОЧ-, МЕРК-, МЕРЦ-, МОР-, МАР-, DARKNESS, DEATH

мер-ѐ-ть, мр-у, *v.i.*, (*colloq., obs.*), to die: see умирáть. Лю́ди мрут от гóлода, people are dying from hunger. Душá мрѐт от стрáха, the soul is scared to death.

мѐр-т-вый, *adj.*, dead. Мѐр-т-в, *m.*, мер-т-вá, *f.*, мер-т-вó, *neut.*, *adj. pred.* М-ый человѐк, dead man. М-ый капитáл, dead stock. Латѝнь - мѐртвый язык, Latin is a dead language. М-ая зыбь, swell, ripples. М-ая тишинá, dead silence. Спать мѐртвым сном, (*fig.*), to be fast asleep. Ни жив, ни мѐртв, (*idiom.*), more dead than alive. Мѐр-т-вѐц, *п.т.*, corpse, dead man. Мѐр-т-вѐцкая, *п.f.*, mortuary, morgue. Мѐр-т-вѐцки, *adv.*, as if dead. М. пьян, (*colloq.*), dead drunk. Мѐр-т-вечѝна, *п.f.*, carrion, dead flesh.

мер-т-вѐть, *v.i.*, о-мер-т-вѐть, *v.p.*, to grow numb. Рýки мертвѐют от хóлода, my hands are becoming numb from the cold. Мѐр-твенный, *adj.*, deathly pale. М. цвет лицá, deathly paleness of a face. Мѐр-твенно, *adv.*, deathly. М. блѐдный, deathly pale. Мер-тв-о-рождѐнный, *adj.*, still-born. О-мер-твлѐние, *п.п.*, numbness. О-мер-твѐлость, *n.f.*, numbness. О-мер-твѐлый, *adj.*, numb, deadened.

по-мер-т-вѐть, *v.p.*, to become stiff, rigid. П. от ýжаса (гóря), to grow stiff with fright (grief).

мер-т-вѝть, *v.i.*, to deaden. Мер-твó, *adv.*, lifelessly, dully. Зá-мер-тво, *adv.*, (left) for dead, as if dead.

у-мер-т-вѝть, *v.p.*, у-мер-щ-влять, *v.i.*, + *acc.*, to put to death, kill, slay. У. нерв больнóго зýба, to destroy, kill the nerve of a bad tooth. У-мер-щ-влѐние, *п.п.*, killing, putting to death.

с-мер-ть, *n.f.*, death. Голóдная смерть, death from starvation. Он ýмер смéртью герóя, he died the death of a hero. Быть при смéрти, to be at death's door, near death. Двум смертя́м не бывáть, однóй не миновáть, (*prov.*), a man can die but once. С-мéр-тник, *n.m.*, prisoner sentenced to death. С-мéр-тность, *n.f.*, mortality. Дéтская с., infant mortality. С-мéртный, *adj.*, mortal; *also used as n.* С-мéр-тен, *adj. pred.* Человéк смéртен, man is mortal. Смéртный час, hour of death. С. приговóр, death sentence. Бес-с-мéр-тие, *n.n.*, immortality. Бес-с-мéр-тный, *adj.*, immortal. С-мертéльный, *adj.*, deadly, fatal. С-ая рáна, fatal wound. С. яд,, deadly poison. С-мер-тéльно, *adv.*, fatally. С. рáненный, fatally wounded. С. ненавидеть когó-либо, to have a deadly hatred for someone. С. скучáть, (*fig.*), to be bored to death; miss someone.

у-мер-éть, у-мр-ý, *v.p.*, у-мир-áть, *v.i.*, to die, pass away, be dead. У. от воспалéния лёгких, to die of pneumonia. У. от гóлода, to die of starvation, hunger. У. за рóдину, to die for one's country. У. от скýки, (*fig.*), to die of boredom. У-мéр-ший, *adj., part. act. past,* dead, deceased. У-мéр-шие, the dead, the deceased.

вы́-мер-еть, *v.r.*, вы-мир-áть, *v.i.*, to die out, become extinct, desolate. Гóрод вы́мер во врéмя эпидéмии, the city became desolate during the epidemic. Вы́-мор-очный, *adj.*, escheated. В-ое имéние, escheated property. Передавáть в кáчестве вы́морочного имýщества, to transmit as escheated property.

за-мер-éть, *v.r.*, за-мир-áть, *v.i.*, to stand still; sink; stop beating. Он так и зáмер от ýжаса, he froze with terror. За-мир-áние, *n.n.*, death-like immobility. С замирáнием сéрдца, with a sinking heart.

об-мер-éть, *v.r.*, об-мир-áть, *v.i.*, (*colloq.*), to faint, fall into a swoon. О от стрáха, to be paralyzed with fear. У меня́ óбмерло сéрдце, my heart sank.

от-мер-éть, *v.r.*, от-мир-áть, *v.i.*, to die off; disappear; atrophy. Óтмерли мнóгие стáрые обы́чаи, many old customs have died out. От-мир-áние, *n.n.*, dying off; disappearance; atrophy.

пере-мер-éть, *v.r.*, пере-мир-áть, *v.i.*, to die out. Цéлые дерéвни перемёрли от эпидéмии, whole villages died out from the epidemic.

по-мер-éть, *v.r.*, по-мир-áть, *v.i.*, с + *gen.*, (*colloq.*), to die. Он уж óчень стар, порá емý помирáть, he's very old, it's time for him to die. П. со

смéху, to die from laughter; split, burst one's sides from laughter.

мор, *n.m.*, pestilence, plague.

мор-и́-ть, *v.i.*, + *acc.*, + *instr.*, exterminate; exhaust. М. крыс (мышéй), to exterminate rats (mice). М. гóлодом, to starve out.

вы́-мор-ить, *v.p.*, вы-мáр-ивать, *v.i.*, + *acc.*, + *instr.*, to exterminate, destroy. В. таракáнов, to exterminate roaches. В. гóлодом осаждённых, to starve out the besieged.

за-мор-и́ть, *v.p.*, за-мáр-ивать, *v.i.*, + *acc.*, + *instr.*, to work to death; overwork; underfeed. З. гóлодом, to starve. З. рабóтой, to overwork. З. лóшадь, to overwork a horse. З. червячкá, (*fig.*), to have a snack. За-мóр-ыш, *n.m.*, (*colloq.*), starveling. За-мóр-енный, *adj., part. pass. past,* (*colloq.*), emaciated. З. вид, starved appearance, look. Из-мóр, *n.m.*, starvation. Взять гóрод измóром, to overcome a city through starvation.

по-мор-и́ть, про-мор-и́ть, *v.p.,* see морить. Я егó немнóжко помори́л, (*colloq.*), I've tried his patience a little. П. гóлодом, to starve for a while.

раз-мор-и́ть, *v.p.*, раз-мáр-ивать, *v.i.*, + *acc., used only in 3d pers.* Жáра меня́ размори́ла, the heat has exhausted me.

у-мор-и́ть, *v.p.*, + *acc.*, (*colloq.*), to kill, starve to death; exhaust. Онá егó умори́т своéй скýпостью, (*fig.*), she will be the death of him with her stinginess. У. со смéху, (*fig.*), to kill with laughter. У-мор-и́ть-ся, *v.p.r.*, (*colloq.*), to be dead tired. У-мóр-а, *n.f.*, (*colloq.*), very amusing item, incident, etc. Это прóсто умóра, it makes one split with laughter. У-мор-и́тельный, *adj.*, laughable, extremely funny. У-мор-и́тельно, *adv.*, laughably, in an extremely funny manner.

мрак, *n.m.*, gloom, darkness, blackness. Во мрáке нóчи, under cover of night, dark. М. невéжества, abysmal ignorance. Мрак-о-бéсие, *n.n.*, obscurantism.

мрач-н-éть, *v.i.*, по-мрач-нéть, *v.p.*, to grow gloomy, dark; darken. Мрáчность, *n.f.*, sombreness, gloom, darkness. Мрáч-ный, *adj.*, sombre, gloomy, dark; dreary, grim. Мрáч-ное настроéние, sombre mood.

о-мрач-и́-ть, *v.p.*, о-мрач-áть, *v.i.*, + *acc.*, to darken, becloud. Гóре и белá омрачи́ли егó дéтство, grief and misery darkened his childhood. О-мрачи́ть-ся, *v.p.r.*, о-мрач-áть-ся, *v.i.r.*, to become darkened, beclouded. О-мрачённый, *adj., part. pass. past,* darkened. "Над омрачённым Петрогрáдом дышáл ноя́брь осéнним хла́дом," (*Push-kin*), "o'er darkened Petrograd there rolled November's breath of autumn cold."

по-мрач-и́ть, *v.p.*, по-мрач-а́ть, *v.i.*, to darken; obscure. По-мрач-и́ть-ся, *v.p.r.*, по-мрач-а́ть-ся, *v.i.r.*, to become darkened, obscured, confused. По-мрач-éние, *n.n.*, obscuring. П. рассу́дка, confusion of mind. Ум-о-по-мрач-éние, *n.n.*, temporary insanity. Ум-о-по-мрач-ённый, *adj.*, insane. Ум-о-по-мрач-и́тельный, *adj.*, astounding. У. успéх, astounding success.

мо́рок, *n.m.*, (*obs.*), *see* мрак; used in the words: Моро́к-а, *n.f.*, something confused, incomprehensible. Вот моро́ка! What confusion! Об-моро́к, *n.m.*, swoon, fainting spell, coma. Па́дать в о́., to faint. Об-мор-о́чный, *adj.*, fainting. О́-ое состоя́ние, coma, fainting spell.

мороч-ить, *v.i.*, об-моро́ч-ить, *v.p.*, + *acc.*, (*colloq.*), to hoax, fool, mystify. М. го́лову кому́-либо, to fool, confuse someone. Моро́ч-ение, *n.n.*, mystification, deception, fooling.

мéрк-ну-ть, *v.i.*, по-мéрк-нуть, *v.p.*, to grow dark, dim; fade. Звёзды мéркнут и га́снут, the stars are growing dim and fading. У меня́ в глаза́х помéркло, I blacked out.

с-мерк-á-ть-ся, *v.i.r.*, с-мéрк-нуть-ся, *v.p.r.*, to become dark. С-мéрк-áется, it is getting dark; night is falling. Су́-мерк-и, *n.pl.*, twilight. В су́мерках, at twilight.

су́-мер-нич-ать, *v.i.*, (*colloq.*), take one's rest, sit in the twilight. Су́-мер-ечный, *adj.*, twilight, dusk.

мерц-á-ть, *v.i.*, по-мерц-а́ть, *v.i.*, twinkle, shimmer, glimmer. Звёзды мерца́ют во тьме, the stars are twinkling in the dark. Огонёк померца́л и потух, the light twinkled and faded out. Мерц-а́ние, *n.n.*, twinkling, shimmering; scintillation.

МЕРЗ-, МОРОЗ-, МОРОЖ-, COLD, FROST

мёрз-ну-ть, *v.i.*, to freeze; shiver. Мерз-л-ота́, *n.f.*, frozen ground. Вéчная м., permafrost. Мёрз-л-ый, *adj.*, frozen, congealed. Мерз-л-я́к, *n.m.*, (*colloq.*), a person sensitive to cold.

вы́-мерз-нуть, *v.p.*, вы-мерз-а́ть, *v.i.*, to be destroyed by frost; freeze. В холо́дные зи́мы мéлкие рéки вымерза́ют до дна, during cold winters shallow rivers freeze to the bottom.

за-мёрз-нуть, *v.p.*, за-мерз-а́ть, *v.i.*, to freeze, congeal; die of cold. Цветы́ замёрзли, the flowers were frostbitten. Река́ замёрзла, the river is frozen fast. За-мерз-а́ние, *n.n.*, freezing, congelation. То́чка замерза́ния, freezing point.

на-мёрз-нуть, *v.p.*, на-мерз-а́ть, *v.i.*, freeze; cover with frost. Лёд намёрз на о́кнах, the windows became covered with frost.

об-мёрз-нуть, *v.p.*, об-мерз-а́ть, *v.i.*, to become thoroughly covered with frost. Борода́ обмёрзла, the beard became covered with frost. Ру́ки обмёрзли, the hands froze.

от-мёрз-нуть, *v.p.*, от-мерз-а́ть, *v.i.*, + *instr.*, to become chilled; freeze; У него́ отмёрзли ру́ки (но́ги), his hands (feet) are frozen.

пере-мёрз-нуть, *v.p.*, пере-мерз-а́ть, *v.i.*, to become chilled; freeze. Все цветы́ перемёрзли, all the flowers were nipped by frost. Я уста́л и перемёрз, I was tired and frozen.

под-мёрз-нуть, *v.p.*, под-мерз-а́ть, *v.i.*, to freeze slightly. Лу́жи подмёрзли, the puddles were frozen over.

по-мёрз-нуть, *v.p.*, (*colloq.*), to be frostbitten; *see* вымерза́ть. Все я́блони помёрзли, all the apple trees were frostbiten.

с-мёрз-нуть, *v.p.*, с-мерз-а́ть, *v.i.*, (*colloq.*), to be cold, chilly. Ру́ки и но́ги у меня́ совсéм смёрзли, my hands and feet are chilled. С-мёрз-нуть-ся, *v.p.r.*, с-мерз-а́ть-ся, *v.i.r.*, to become frozen together. Кутки́ льда смёрзлись, the pieces of ice were frozen together.

моро́з-и-ть, *v.i.*, to freeze, congeal. Моро́зит, it is freezing. Моро́з, *n.m.*, frost; freezing weather. Си́льный м., hard, bitter frost. Трескучий м., biting cold. М. подира́ет по ко́же, (*fig.*), to have one's flesh creep. Дед-моро́з, *n.m.*, Santa Claus. Моро́з-ный, *adj.*, frosty. М-ое у́тро, cold, frosty morning. Моро́з-но, *adv.*, *impers.*, it is freezing. Моро́ж-ен-ое, *n.n.*, ice cream. Моро́ж-енщик, *n.m.*, ice cream vendor. Моро́ж-еница, *n.f.*, freezer, ice cream mold. Моро́ж-еный, *adj.*, frozen. М. карто́фель, frozen potatoes. М-ое мя́со, chilled, frozen meat.

вы́-мороз-ить, *v.p.*, вы-мора́ж-ивать, *v.i.*, + *acc.*, to freeze out. В. ко́мнату, to chill a room; disinfect by chilling. В. бельё, to freeze the laundry, wash. Вы-мора́ж-ивание, *n.n.*, freezing; extermination, disinfection by freezing.

за-моро́з-ить, *v.p.*, за-мора́ж-ивать, *v.i.*, + *acc.*, to freeze, congeal, ice. З. мя́со, to freeze meat. З. шампа́нское, to chill champagne. За́-мороз-ки, *n.pl.*, first autumn frosts. Ночны́е з., night frosts. За-мора́ж-ивание, *n.n.*, freezing, congelation. За-морóж-ен-ный, *adj. part. pass. past*, frozen, congealed. З-ое мя́со, refrigerated meat. З-ые фру́кты, frozen fruit.

об-морóз-ить, *v.p.,* об-морáж-ивать, *v.i.,* + *acc.,* to suffer frostbite. Он обморóзил себе́ ру́ки (нóги, у́ши, нос), his hands (feet, ears, nose), became frostbitten. Об-морóж-енный, *adj. part. pass. past*, frostbitten.

от-морóз-ить, *v.p.,* от-морáж-ивáть, *v.i.,* + *acc.,* to become frostbitten, freeze. От-морóж-енный, *adj. part. pass. part*, frostbitten. О-ое ме́сто, frostbitten part.

пере-морóз-ить, *v.p.,* пере-морáж-ивать, *v.i.,* + *acc., (colloq.),* to overexpose to cold, to freeze to excess.

под-морóз-ить, *v.p.,* под-морáж-ивать, *v.i.,* to freeze slightly. Подморáживает, it is beginning to freeze; the weather is slightly cold.

про-морóз-ить, *v.p.,* про-морáж-ивать, *v.i., see* морóзить. П. ры́бу, to freeze fish.

мéрз-к-ий, *adj.,* vile, loathsome, abominable, detestable. М. человéк, loathsome man. М-ая вещь, loathsome thing. Мéрз-ость, *n.f.,* abomination. М. запустéния, *(fig.),* a fearful desolation. Мерз-áвец, *n.m.,* (swear word), villain, scoundrel.

о-мерз-éние, *n.n.,* loathing. Внушáть о., to inspire with loathing. Испы́тывать о., to loathe. О-мерз-и́тельный, *adj.,* loathsome, sickening.

мраз-ь, *n.f., (colloq.),* nasty wretch, trash.

МЕС-, (МѢС), МЕШ-, (МЯШ), МЕХ-, (МЯХ), KNEADING; DISTURBANCE, CONFUSION, MIXING

мес-и́-ть, меш-у́, *v.i.,* с-мес-и́ть, *v.p.,* + *acc.,* to knead. М. тéсто, to knead dough. М. грязь, *(fig.),* to walk in mud. Мéс-иво, *n.n.,* mash. Мес-и́льщик, *n.m.,* kneader.

вы́-мес-ить, *v.p.,* вы-мéш-ивать, *v.i.,* + *acc.,* to knead. В. тéсто, to knead dough.

до-мес-и́ть, *v.p.,* до-мéш-ивать, *v.i.,* + *acc.,* to finish kneading. Д. гли́ну, to finish mixing clay.

за-мес-и́ть, *v.p.,* за-мéш-ивать, *v.i.,* + *acc.,* to mix.

на-мес-и́ть, *v.p.,* + *acc.,* to knead in quantity. Н. тéста, to knead a quantity of dough. Н. гли́ны, to mix a quantity of clay.

про-мес-и́ть, *v.p.,* про-мéш-ивать, *v.i.,* + *acc.,* to mix, knead well, properly. П. корм, to mix feed. Про-мес-и́ть-ся,

v.p.r., про-мéш-ивать-ся, *v.i.r.,* to be kneaded, mixed. Тéсто должнó хорошó промеси́ться, dough must be kneaded thoroughly.

раз-мес-и́ть, *v.p.,* раз-мéш-ивать, *v.i.,* + *acc.,* to knead out; mix thoroughly.

с-мес-и́ть, *v.p., see* меси́ть. С-мес-и́тель, *n.m., (tech.),* mixer. С-мес-ь, *n.f.,* mixture; medley.

меш-áть, *v.p.,* по-меш-áть, *v.i.,* + *dat.,* + *acc.,* to prevent, hinder, disturb; stir, agitate, confound. Мне здесь никтó не мешáет, nobody disturbs me here. Не мешáет (не мешáло-бы), *(colloq.),* it would be advisable. М. жар в пéчке, to stir a fire in a stove. М. песóк с гли́ной, to mix sand with clay. Меш-áть-ся, *v.i.r.,* to meddle, interfere. М. не в свои́ делá, to meddle in other people's matters. Меш-ани́на, *n.f., (colloq.),* medley, jumble.

в-меш-áть, *v.p.,* в-мéш-ивать, *v.i.,* + *acc.,* to mix in. В. песóк в гли́ну, to mix sand into clay. В-меш-áть-ся, *v.p.r.,* в-мéш-ивать-ся, *v.i.r.,* to interfere with, meddle in. В. в чужи́е делá, to meddle in other people's affairs. В. в разговóр, to intrude into a conversation. Суд вмешáлся, the law stepped in. В-меш-áтельство, *n.n.,* interference, meddling, intervention.

до-меш-áть, *v.p.,* до-мéш-ивать, *v.i.,* + *acc.,* to finish mixing.

за-меш-áть, *v.p.,* за-мéш-ивать, *v.i.,* to mix up; involve; entangle. За-меш-áть-ся, *v.p.r.,* за-мéш-ивать-ся, *v.i.r.,* to be mixed with. З. в толпу́, to lose oneself in a crowd, mix with a crowd. За-меш-áтельство, *n.n.,* confusion, embarrassment. Вноси́ть з. в ряды́ проти́вника, to disorganize the ranks of an enemy. Привести́ в з., to confuse, embarrass. Прийти́ в з., to become confused, embarrassed.

на-меш-áть, *v.p.,* на-мéш-ивать, *v.i.,* + *acc.,* + *gen.,* to add, admix. Н. муки́ в молокó, to add milk to flour and mix them.

пере-меш-áть, *v.p.,* пере-мéш-ивать, *v.i.,* + *acc.,* to intermingle; shuffle. П. у́гли в пéчке, to poke the coals in a stove. П. кáрты в колóде, to mix, shuffle a deck of playing cards. Пере-меш-áть-ся, *v.p.r.,* пере-мéш-ивать-ся, *v.i.r.,* *(colloq.),* to be mixed, shuffled.

под-меш-áть, *v.p.,* под-мéш-ивать, *v.i.,* + *acc.,* + *gen.,* to mix into. П. песку́ в цемéнт, to add and mix sand into cement. Под-мéш-анный, *adj., part. pass. past,* mixed, not pure.

по-меш-áть, *v.p., see* мешáть, П. пéчку, to poke a fire in a stove. П. чай, to stir tea. П. чему́-нибу́дь, to prevent, hamper, impede. Я вам не помешал? Did I disturb you? По-меш-а́ть-ся, *v.p.r.*, to become insane. П. на му́зыке, (*colloq.*), to go mad about music. По-ме́шаный, *adj.*, lunatic, madman, maniac. По-меш-а́тельство, *n.n.*, madness, lunacy, infatuation. Ум-о-поме-ша́тельство, *n.n.*, mental derangement, insanity. По-мех-а, *n.f.*, hindrance, impediment, obstacle. Служи́ть п-ой, to obstruct, be in the way.

при-меш-а́ть, *v.p.*, при-ме́ш-ивать, *v.i.*, + *acc.*, + *gen.*, to add, admix. П. воды́ в вино́, to add water to wine.

про-меш-а́ть, *v.p.*, про-ме́ш-ивать, *v.i.*, + *acc.*, to stir well.

раз-меш-а́ть, *v.p.*, раз-ме́ш-ивать, *v.i.*, to stir, knead thoroughly. Р. са́хар в ча́е, to stir sugar in tea. Р. муку́ в воде́, to stir flour in water. Раз-меш-а́ть-ся, *v.p.r.*, раз-ме́ш-ивать-ся, *v.i.r.*, to be stirred; kneaded. Раз-ме́ш-ивание, *n.n.*, stirring; kneading.

с-меш-а́ть, *v.p.*, с-ме́ш-ивать, *v.i.*, + *acc.*, to mix, compound, mingle, combine; put out of order. С. в ку́чу, to lump together. Я сме́шиваю э́ти два цве́та, I mix these two colors. С. кого́-либо с гря́зью, (*fig.*), to sully, besmirch someone's name, to sling mud at someone. С-меш-а́ть-ся, *v.p.r.*, с-ме́ш-ивать-ся, *v.i.r.*, to be mixed, blended; be confused. Смеша́ться от стыда́, to be confused from shame. С. с толпо́й, to mingle with a crowd, disappear in a crowd. С-ме́ш-ивание, *n.n.*, mixing; blending. С-меш-е́ние, *n.n.*, confusion; blend, merging. С. поня́тий, confusion of notions. С. поро́д, cross-breeding. С-ме́ш-анный, *adj.*, *part. pass. past*, mixed, hybrid. С-ое число́, (*math.*), mixed number. С-ое чу́вство гру́сти и ра́дости, mixed feelings of sorrow and joy.

МЕСТ-, (МѢСТ), МЕЩ-, (МѢЩ), PLACE, LOCATION

ме́ст-о, *n.n.*, place, spot, location, site, locality. М. рожде́ния, birthplace. Уступа́ть м. кому́-либо, to give up one's place. Хоро́шее м. для до́ма, a good site for a house. По места́м! To your places, seats Быть без ме́ста, to be unemployed. Больно́е м., tender, sore spot. Заста́ть на ме́сте преступле́ния, to catch on the scene of a crime. Сла́бое м., weak spot. Мест-е́чко, *n.n.*, (*dim.*), place; borough, small town. Тёплое м., (*fig., derog.*), snug berth. Ме́ст-ность, *n.f.*, locality. Да́чная м., country place. Ме́ст-ный, *adj.*, local. М. жи́тель, local inhabitant. М. го́вор,

local dialect. М. нало́г, local tax. М-ое вре́мя, local time. М. комите́т, local committee. Ме́ст-ничество, *n.n.*, (*hist.*), order of precedence; seniority. Ме́ст-о-, *a combining form meaning* place. Мест-о-жи́тельство, *n.n.*, residence. Мест-о-име́ние, *n.n.*, (*gram.*), pronoun. Мест-о-положе́ние, *n.n.*, position, location, site. Мест-о-пребыва́ние, *n.n.*, abode, residence. На-ме́ст-ник, *n.m.*, deputy viceroy, vice-regent. На-ме́ст-ничество, *n.n.*, vice-regency, region ruled by a viceroy.

в-мест-и́ть, *v.p.*, в-мещ-а́ть, *v.i.*, + *acc.*, to contain, hold; accomodate. В-мест-и́ть-ся, *v.p.r.*, в-мещ-а́ть-ся, *v.i.r.*, to fit in, fill. В кувщи́н вмеща́ется три ли́тра, a jug contains, holds three liters. В шкаф вмеща́ется 50 книг, fifty books fit into this bookcase. В-мест-и́тельность, *n.f.*, capacity. В-мест-и́мый, *adj.*, *part. pass. pres.*, capable of containing, accomodating. В-мест-и́лище, *n.n.*, receptacle. В-мест-и́мость, *n.f.*, capacity. Ме́ры вмести́мости, measures of capacity. В-ме́ст-е, *adv.*, together. Вме́сте с тем, at the same time. Всё вме́сте взя́тое, taken together. В-ме́ст-о, *adv.*, in lieu of, instead of, in place of. В. мое́й сестры́, instead of my sister, in my sister's place.

воз-мест-и́ть, *v.p.*, воз-мещ-а́ть, *v.i.*, + *acc.*, + *dat.*, to make up for, compensate. В. кому́-либо расхо́ды (убы́тки), to reimburse someone for expenses, losses. Воз-мещ-е́ние, *n.n.*, compensation, damages.

за-мест-и́ть, *v.p.*, за-мещ-а́ть, *v.i.*, + *acc.*, + *instr.*, to act for someone, replace, substitute for. Сестра́ замеща́ет мне мать, my sister is like a mother to me. За-мест-и́тель, *n.m.*, substitute; proxy; deputy. З. дире́ктора, (замдире́ктора, *recent*), assistant director. З. председа́теля, vice-chairman. За-мещ-е́ние, *n.n.*, substitution. Для замеще́ния, for the purpose of filling, substituting. Для з. до́лжности, for the purpose of filling a post, office.

пере-мест-и́ть, *v.p.*, пере-мещ-а́ть, *v.i.*, + *acc.*, to move, transfer. П. ме́бель с одного́ ме́ста на друго́е, to move furniture from one place to another. Пере-мест-и́ть-ся, *v.p.r.*, пере-мещ-а́ть-ся, *v.i.r.*, to be moved, transferred, shifted. Пере-мещ-е́ние, *n.n.*, transfer, shift; displacement; dislocation; travel. Пере-мещ-ённый, *adj.*, *part. pass. past*, moved, transferred, shifted. П-ые ли́ца, displaced persons.

по-мест-и́ть, *v.p.*, по-мещ-а́ть, *v.i.*, + *acc.*, to place, locate. П. капита́л, to invest capital. П. объявле́ние, to advertise. П. статью́ в журна́л, to publish an article in a magazine. По-мест-и́ть-ся, *v.p.r.*, по-мещ-а́ть-ся, *v.i.r.*, to be situated; placed; be invested. В э́том до́ме помеща́ется 200 челове́к, this house will accommodate 200 people. По-мест-и́тельность, *n.f.*, roominess, spaciousness; capacity. По-мест-и́тельный, *adj.*, roomy, spacious. По-ме́ст-ный, *adj.*, *in expression*: П-ое дворя́нство, landed gentry. По-ме́ст-ье, *n.n.*, estate; patrimony. Пред-ме́ст-ье, *n.n.*, suburb. По-мещ-е́ние, *n.n.*, location, lodging, apartment, room; investment. Здесь большо́е п., there is plenty of room here, these are large premises. По-ме́щ-ик, *n.m.*, по-ме́щ-ица, *n.f.*, (*pre-Rev.*), landlord, landowner. По-ме́щ-ичий, *adj.*, pertaining to a landlord.

раз-мест-и́ть, *v.p.*, раз-мещ-а́ть, *v.i.*, + *acc.*, to place; distribute; (*mil.*), billet. Р. заём, to place a loan. Р. войска́, to billet troops. Раз-мест-и́ть-ся, *v.p.r.*, раз-мещ-а́ть-ся, *v.i.r.*, to be distributed; be accommodated. В гости́нице мо́гут размести́ться 300 челове́к, 300 hundred persons can be accommodated in the hotel. Раз-мещ-е́ние, *n.n.*, placing. Р. займа́, placing of a loan. Р. гру́за, arrangement of freight.

с-мест-и́ть, *v.p.*, с-мещ-а́ть, *v.i.*, + *acc.*, to displace, remove. С. заве́дующего, to remove, dismiss a manager. С-мест-и́ть-ся, *v.p.r.*, с-мещ-а́ть-ся, *v.i.r.*, to be displaced, dismissed. С-мещ-е́ние, *n.n.*, displacement, dislodgement, removal, dislocation.

со-в-мест-и́ть, *v.p.*, со-в-мещ-а́ть, *v.i.*, + *acc.*, to combine, join. Рахма́нинов совмеща́л в себе́ замеча́тельного компози́тора и пиани́ста, Rachmaninoff combined the talents of a remarkable composer and pianist. С. рабо́ту машини́стки и секретаря́, to work as a typist and a secretary; combine the duties of a typist and secretary. Со-в-мещ-е́ние, *n.n.*, combination. С. должносте́й, combining of jobs, holding of more than one office, plurality of offices. Со-в-ме́ст-ный, *adj.*, joint, common. С-ая рабо́та, team work. С-ые де́йствия, joint action. В тече́ние их совме́стной жи́зни, during their life together. Шко́ла совме́стного обуче́ния, co-educational school.

со-в-мест-и́тель-ствовать, *v.i.*, to hold more than one office, position; combine the duties of more than one position. Со-в-мест-и́тельство, *n.n.*, pluralism in holding jobs. Рабо́тать по с-у, (*recent*), to hold more than one office,

position. Со-в-мест-и́тель, *n.m.*, holder of more than one office. Со-в-мест-и́мость, *n.f.*, compatibility. Со-в-мест-и́мый, *adj.*, compatible. Не-со-в-мест-и́мость, *n.f.*, incompatibility. Не-со-в-мест-и́мый, *adj.*, incompatible.

у-мест-и́ть, *v.p.*, у-мещ-а́ть, *v.i.*, + *acc.*, to find room; put in. У. все ве́щи в чемода́н, to fit all one's things into a suitcase. У-мест-и́ть-ся, *v.p.r.*, у-мещ-а́ть-ся, *v.i.r.*, to have room for; seat. Все го́сти умести́лись за столо́м, the guests all took seats around the table. У-ме́ст-ность, *n.f.*, suitability, propriety. У-ме́ст-ный, *adj.*, appropriate; in its place; to the point. Эта статья́ здесь вполне́ у-а, this article is most suitable, appropriate, to the point, here. Это у-ое замеча́ние, this is a timely remark. Не-у-ме́ст-ный, *adj.*, inappropriate, out of place, unsuitable, untimely. У-ме́ст-но, *adv.*, appropriately. Не-у-ме́ст-но, *adv.*, inappropriately. Здесь э́то не уме́стно, it is out of place here.

мещ-ани́н, *n.m.*, мещ-а́нка, *n.f.*, (мещ-а́не, *pl.*), (*hist.*), lower middle-class citizen; (*fig.*), bourgeois; Philistine. Мещ-а́нство, *n.n.*, lower middle class; townsfolk: petty bourgeoisie. Мещ-а́нский, *adj.*, pertaining to the lower middle class, the bourgeoisie; vulgar; narrow-minded. М-ая мора́ль, Philistine morality.

МЕСТ-, МСТ-, МЩ-, МЕЩ-, VENGEANCE, REVENGE

мест-ь, *n.f.*, vengeance, revenge. Кро́вная м., blood feud. Жа́жда ме́сти, thirst for vengeance.

мст-и-ть, мщ-у, *v.i.*, ото-мст-и́ть, *v.p.*, + *dat.*, за + *acc.*, to revenge oneself, avenge. М. врагу́, to take vengeance on one's enemy. Отомсти́ть за дру́га, to avenge a friend. Мст-и́тель, *n.m.*, avenger. Мст-и́тельность, *n.f.*, vindictiveness, vengefulness. Мст-и́тельный, *adj.*, vindictive, revengeful. М. хара́ктер, vindictive disposition. Мщ-е́ние, *n.n.*, vengeance, revenge. От-мщ-е́ние, *n.n.*, (*obs.*), vengeance, revenge. От-ме́стка, *n.f.*, revenge. В отме́стку, in revenge.

вы́-мест-ить, *v.p.*, вы-мещ-а́ть, *v.i.*, на + *prep.*, to vent, wreak. В. зло́бу, доса́ду на ко́м-либо, to vent one's anger, vexation on someone.

МЗД-, МЕЗД-, RECOMPENSE

мзд-а- *n.f.*, (*obs.*), recompense; bribe. М. вели́кая на небесе́х, (*Ch-Sl.*), a great reward in heaven. За соответствующую мзду, (satir.), for an appropriate bribe. Мзд-о-и́мец, n.m., (obs.), venal person. Мзд-о-и́мство, n.n. (obs.), venality, corruption.

воз-ме́зд-ие, n.n., retribution, punishment. Получи́ть заслу́женное в., to receive a well-deserved retribution.

без-воз-ме́зд-ный, adj., gratuitous, free. Б-ая услу́га, favor, gratuitous service. Без-воз-ме́зд-но, adv., gratis, free of charge, complimentary. Получи́ть что́-либо б., to receive something free of charge.

МЕТ-, (МѢТ), МЕЧ-, (МѢЧ), MARK

ме́т-и-ть, v.i., + acc., to mark; aim at. М. бельё, to mark linen. Ме́тил в воро́ну, попа́л в коро́ву, (saying), he aimed at the crow, but hit the cow. М. в генера́лы, (colloq.), to aspire to a general's rank. Ме́т-ить-ся, v.i.r., to be marked, aimed at. М. в цель, to be aimed at a target. Ме́т-ка, n.f., marking; mark, sign. М. носовы́х платко́в, handkerchief monogram. М. на бельё, linen monogram. Ме́т-кий, adj., well-aimed; (fig.), neat. М. стрело́к, good shot. М. глаз, keen eye. М-ое замеча́ние, pointed remark. Ме́т-кость, n.f., accuracy; marksmanship; (fig.), neatness. М. гла́за, keen sight, a sharp eye. М. вы́стрела, marksmanship.

за-ме́т-ить, v.p., за-меч-а́ть, v.i., + acc., to notice, remark, observe. За-меч-а́ть-ся, v.i.r., to be noticed. Среди́ молодёжи замеча́ется интере́с к нау́ке, there is a noticeable interest in science among young people. За-ме́т-ка, n.f., notice, note. З. в газе́те, mention, a notice in the newspaper. Путевы́е заме́тки, travel notes. Брать на заме́т-ку, (recent), to note. Заме́тки на поля́х, marginal notes. Де́лать заме́т-ки, to take notes. За-ме́т-ный, adj., noticeable; visible; remarkable, outstanding. З-ая ра́зница, marked difference. З-ая величина́, outstanding quantity, value. За-ме́т-но, adv., noticeably. Он заме́тно постаре́л, he has aged noticeably. За-меч-а́ние, n.n., remark, observation; rebuke, reprimand. Сде́лать з., to rebuke. За-меч-а́тельный, adj., remarkable, wonderful, outstanding. З. писа́тель, outstanding writer. З-ое вино́, wonderful wine. За-меч-а́тельно, adv., remarkably, wonderfully; it is wonderful.

на-ме́т-ить, v.p., на-меч-а́ть, v.i., + acc., to plan, project, outline; Н. направле́ние, to mark a direction; select; make a mark. Н. направле́ние доро́ги на пла́не, to mark the direction of a road on a map. Н. кандида́та в парла́мент, to nominate a candidate for parliament. Н. платки́ гла́дью, to embroider handkerchiefs with satin stitch initials. На-ме́т-ить-ся, v.p.r., на-меч-а́ть-ся, v.i.r., to be outlined, begin to show.

от-ме́т-ить, v.p., от-меч-а́ть, v.i., + acc., to mark, note, check; mention; register. О. глаго́л пти́чкой, to check, mark a verb. О. по́двиги, to record feats. От-ме́т-ить-ся, v.p.r., от-меч-а́ть-ся, v.i.r., to register; be checked, marked. О. в мили́ции, (recent), to register with the police. От-ме́т-ка, n.f., note, mark. О. на поля́х кни́ги, marginal notes in a book. Получи́ть удовлетвори́тельную отме́тку, to receive a satisfactory grade. От-ме́т-ина, n.f., (colloq.), mark. О. на лбу у живо́тного, a star marking on the forehead of an animal. От-ме́т-чик, n.m., marker.

пере-ме́т-ить, v.p., пере-меч-а́ть, v.i., + acc., to mark again; change a mark. П. все бельё, to mark all the laundry.

под-ме́т-ить, v.p., под-меч-а́ть, v.i., + acc., to notice, observe.

по-ме́т-ить, v.p., по-меч-а́ть, v.i., + acc., to mark; date; check. Она́ поме́тила письмо́ 12-м декабря́, she dated the letter the 12th of December. По-ме́т-ка, n.f., mark.

при-ме́т-ить, v.p., при-меч-а́ть, v.i., + acc., (colloq.), to notice. "Слона́-то я и не приме́тил," (Krylov), "I could not see the elephant before my eyes". При-ме́т-а, n.f., sign, token; mark, symptom. Име́ть на приме́те, to have in mind. При-ме́т-ы, n.pl., distinctive marks. При-ме́т-ливость, n.f., power of observation. При-ме́т-ливый, adj., observant. При-ме́т-ный, adj., (colloq.), perceptible, visible, conspicuous. При-меч-а́ние, n.n., note, comment, footnote, annotation. Снабди́ть примеча́ниями, to provide with footnotes; annotate. При-меч-а́тельность, n.f., notability, noteworthiness. При-меч-а́тельный, adj., notable, noteworthy, remarkable.

раз-ме́т-ить, v.p., раз-меч-а́ть, раз-ме́ч-ивать, v.i., + acc., to distribute. Р. кре́стиками про́пуски, to check omissions. Раз-ме́т-ка, n.f., marking.

с-ме́т-а, n.f., estimate. Составля́ть сме́ту, to make an estimate. Превы́сить сме́ту расхо́дов, to exceed the estimate of expenses. С-ме́т-ный, adj., estimate. С-ые ассигнова́ния, budget allowances.

с-ме́т-ливость, n.f., shrewdness, cleverness. Обнару́жить большу́ю с., to display shrewdness. С-ме́т-ливый, adj., sharp, keen-witted. С. ма́льчик, clever boy.

с-мёт-ка, *n.f.,* (*colloq.*), shrewdness, sagacity. У него́ приро́дная смётка, he is naturally shrewd.

МЕТ-, МЁТ-, МЕЧ-, МЕС-, THROWING, CASTING, FLINGING

мет-а́-ть, меч-у́, *v.i.,* мет-ну́ть, *v.p.smf.,* помета́ть, *v.p.,* + *acc.,* to throw, cast, fling. М. копьё, to throw a javelin. М. бо́мбы, to throw bombs. М. банк (ка́рты), to keep the bank (*in cards*). М. икру́, to spawn. Ры́бы ме́чут икру́, fish spawn. Рвать и мета́ть, (*fig.*), to be in a rage. М. гром и мо́лнии, (*fig.*), to be in a rage. М. би́сер пе́ред свинья́ми, (*fig.*), to cast pearls before swine. Мет-а́ние, *n.n.,* throwing, casting, flinging. М. жре́бия, casting lots. М. икры́, spawning. Мет-а́тель-ный, *adj.,* missile. М-ое ору́жие, missile weapon. Мет-а́ть-ся, *v.i.r.,* to rush around aimlessly. М. по ко́мнате, to rush around a room. По-мёт, *n.m.,* dung, excrement, droppings; litter. Пти́чий п., bird droppings. Свино́й п., litter of pigs.

мета́ть, мета́ю, *v.i.,* об-мет-а́ть, по-мет-а́ть, *v.p.,* *acc.,* to baste. М. пе́тли, to make buttonholes.

вз-мет-а́ть, *v.p.,* вз-мёт-ывать, *v.i.,* вз-мет-ну́ть, *v.p.smf.,* + *instr.,* to throw up, fling up. Взметну́ть кры́льями, to flap one's wings. Взметну́ть рука́ми, to throw up one's hands. Вз-мет-ну́ть-ся, *v.p.r.,* (*colloq.*), to spring up, jump up.

вы́-мет-ать, *v.p.,* вы-мёт-ывать, *v.i.,* + *acc.,* to edge, buttonhole. В. пе́тли, to sew, make buttonholes.

за-мет-а́ть, *v.p.,* за-мёт-ывать, *v.i.,* + *acc.,* to baste, sew up. З. скла́дки на пла́тье, to baste pleats in a dress.

на-мет-а́ть, *v.p.,* see мета́ть. На-мёт-ывать, *v.i.,* + *acc.* to baste. Н. руба́шку, to baste a shirt. Н. ру́ку, (*fig.*), to acquire skill. Н. глаз, (*fig.*), to acquire an eye for. На-мёт-ка, *n.f.,* basting, tacking. Н. рукаво́в, basting of sleeves. Н. пятиле́тнего пла́на, (*recent*), preliminary outline of a five-year plan.

об-мет-а́ть, *v.p.,* об-мёт-ывать, *v.i.,* + *acc.,* to make buttonhole stitches; whipstitch; overcast. О. пе́тли, to sew buttonholes. От лихора́дки обмета́ло гу́бы, (*impers.*), lips are sore from fever.

пере-мет-а́ть, *v.p.,* пере-мёт-ывать, *v.i.,* + *acc.,* to baste again. П. пла́тье, to baste a dress again.

пере-мет-ну́ть, *v.p.,* + *acc.,* (*colloq.*), to throw over. П. ка́мень че́рез забо́р, to throw a stone over a fence. Пере-мет-ну́ть-ся, *v.p.r.,* (*colloq.*), to desert. П. на сто́рону врага́, to desert to the enemy; defect. Пере-мёт-ный, *adj.,* used as n., a person who changes sides easily, repeatedly. П-ая сума́, (*obs., folk*), saddle-bag; (*also fig. of a person*), weathercock.

под-мет-а́ть, *v.p.,* под-мёт-ывать, *v.i.,* + *acc.,* to baste, tack. П. подо́л пла́тья, to baste the hem of a dress. Под-мёт-ка, *n.f.,* sole. Под-бива́ть подмётки, to have one's shoes soled. Он ей и в подмётки не годи́тся. (*colloq.*), he cannot hold a candle to her.

под-мет-ну́ть, *v.p.,* под-мёт-ывать, *v.i.,* + *acc.,* (*obs.*), to throw under, put under. П. пи́сьма, to send anonymous letters. Под-мёт-ный, *adj.,* (*obs.*), anonymous. П-ое письмо́, anonymous letter.

пред-мет, *n.m.,* object, article; subject, topic, theme. П-ы пе́рвой необходи́мости, bare necessities of life. П. нау́чного иссле́дования, subject of scientific research. П. спо́ра, point at issue. П. в преподава́нии, subject in school program, curriculum. Пред-мет-ный, *adj.,* object. П. указа́тель, subject index.

при-мет-а́ть, *v.p.,* при-мёт-ывать, *v.i.,* + *acc.,* to baste. П. рукава́ к пла́тью, to baste sleeves to a dress.

про-мет-а́ть, *v.p.,* see мета́ть. П. пе́тли шёлковыми ни́тками, to make buttonholes with silk thread. О-про-мёт-чивый, *adj.,* rash, hasty. О. посту́пок, rash, precipitate act. О-про-мёт-чиво, *adv.,* rashly, too hastily. Де́йствуй обду́манно, а не опроме́тчиво, act cautiously, not rashly. О́-про-мет-ью, *adv.,* (*colloq.*), headlong. Он вбежа́л о́., he rushed in headlong.

раз-мет-а́ть, *v.p.,* раз-мёт-ывать, *v.i.,* + *acc.,* to disperse, scatter, spread. Р. се́но для просу́шки, to spread hay for drying. Ве́тер размета́л соло́му, the wind scattered the straw. Р. враго́в. to disperse the enemy. Раз-мет-а́ть-ся, *v.p.r.,* to toss about. Ребёнок размета́лся на посте́ли, the child tossed about on the bed.

с-мет-а́ть, *v.p.,* с-мёт-ывать, *v.i.,* to baste, stitch together. С. ю́бку, to baste a skirt.

мес-ти́, мет-у́, *v.i.,* + *acc.,* to sweep. М. сор , to sweep dirt. М. ко́мнату, to sweep a room. Метёт, (*impers.*), there is a snowstorm. Ве́тер метёт ли́стья по доро́ге, the wind is blowing leaves over the road. Мет-е́ль, *n.f.*, snowstorm. Мет-е́лица, *n.f.*, snowstorm; a Russian folkdance. И ста́рые, и ма́лые пля́шут мете́лицу, (*folk.*), both old and young are dancing the metelitsa. Как по у́лице мете́лица мете́т, (*folksong*), as the snow sweeps down the street. Мет-ла́, *n.f.*, broom. Но́вая метла́ чи́сто мете́т, (*prov.*), a new broom sweeps clean. Мет-ёлка, *n.f.*, whisk broom; (*bot.*), panicle. Сбить я́йца мете́лкой, to whip eggs with an egg-beater. Мете́лки камыша́, про́са, panicles of reed, millet. Мет-е́льщик, *n.m.*, sweeper.

вы́-мес-ти, *v.p.*, вы-мет-а́ть, *v.i.*, + *acc.*, to sweep out. В. сор из ко́мнаты, to sweep the dirt out of a room.

до-мес-ти́, *v.p.*, до-мет-а́ть, *v.i.*, + *acc.*, to finish sweeping. Д. у́лицу до угла́, to sweep a street up to the corner.

за-мес-ти́, *v.p.*, за-мет-а́ть, *v.i.*, + *acc.*, to sweep; (*impers.*), be covered. Доро́гу замело́ сне́гом, the road has become covered with snow. З. следы́ преступле́ния, (*fig.*), to cover up the traces of a crime.

на-мес-ти́, *v.p.*, на-мет-а́ть, *v.i.*, + *acc.*, *gen.*, to sweep in quantity. Н. ку́чу со́ра, to sweep up a heap of dirt. Сне́гу намело́ це́лые сугро́бы, much snow has drifted.

об-мес-ти́, *v.p.*, об-мет-а́ть, *v.i.*, + *acc.*, to sweep, dust. О. потоло́к, to dust the ceiling.

от-мес-ти́, *v.p.*, от-мет-а́ть, *v.i.*, + *acc.*, to sweep away. О. ли́стья со скаме́йки, to sweep leaves off a bench.

под-мес-ти́, *v.p.*, под-мет-а́ть, *v.i.*, + *acc.*, to sweep. П. пол, to sweep a floor. По-ме-ло́, *n.n.*, broom.

раз-мес-ти́, *v.p.*, раз-мет-а́ть, *v.i.*, to sweep clear. Р. доро́жку, to clear a path. Р. снег, to sweep something clear of snow.

с-мес-ти́, *v.p.*, с-мет-а́ть, *v.i.*, + *acc.*, to dust off, flick off. С. пыль со стола́, to dust a table, wipe the dust off a table. С. сор в ку́чу, to sweep dust into a heap. С. с лица́ земли́, (*fig.*), to wipe off the face of the earth. С-мет-а́на, *n.f.*, sour cream. С-мет-а́нный, *adj.*, sour cream.

МЁД-, МЕД-, HONEY

мёд, *n.m.*, honey, mead. Ли́повый м., linden blossom honey. Сла́дкий, как мёд, sweet as honey. Вари́ть мёд, to brew mead. Ва́шими уста́ми да мёд пить, (*saying*), if only it were true. Мед-о́вый, *adj.*, honey, mellifluous. М. пря́ник, honey cake. М-ые ре́чи, (*fig.*),

honeyed words. М. ме́сяц, honeymoon. Мед-о́к, *n.m.*, (*dim.*), honey. Мед-о-но́сный, *adj.*, producing honey. Мед-о-точи́вый, *adj.*, mellifluous. Мед-ве́дь, *n.m.*, bear. Мед-ве́д-ица, *n.f.*, she-bear. Больша́я Медве́дица, (*astr.*), Ursa Major. Мед-вежо́нок, *n.m.*, bear cub. Мед-ве́жий, *adj.*, bear. М. у́гол, (*fig.*), far away place. М-жья охо́та, bear hunting. М-жья услу́га, disservice.

МОТ-, МАТ-, EXTRAVAGANCE, WASTE; WINDING

мот, *n.m.*, (*colloq.*), prodigal, spendthrift, squanderer. Отъя́вленный мот, inveterate spendthrift. Мот-о́вка, *n.f.*, (*colloq.*), extravagant woman. Мот-овство́, *n.n.*, prodigality; extravagance. Мот-овско́й, *adj.*, wasteful, extravagant. М. о́браз жи́зни, extravagant way of life.

мот-а́-ть, *v.i.*, + *acc.*, to wind, reel; (*colloq.*), shake; squander, waste. М. ни́тки (шёлк), to wind thread (silk). М. голово́й, to shake one's head. М. что́-либо на ус, (*fig.*), to take good note of something; observe silently. Сын мота́ет отцо́вский капита́л, the son is squandering his father's fortune. Мот-о́к, *n.m.*, skein. М. ни́ток (пря́жи), a skein of thread (yarn). Мот-а́льный, *adj.*, winding. М-ая маши́на, winding machine.

мот-ну́-ть, *v.p.smf.*, (*colloq.*), see мота́ть. М. голово́й, to shake one's head. Мот-а́ть-ся, *v.i.r.*, to dangle; hang loose. Верёвка мота́ется от ве́тра, the rope is swinging in the wind. М. по све́ту, (*colloq.*), to knock about the world.

мот-ыл-ёк, *n.m.*, moth, butterfly. Ночно́й м., night moth. Мот-ылько́вый, *adj.*, butterfly.

вы́-мот-ать, *v.p.*, вы-ма́т-ывать, *v.i.*, + *acc.*, (*colloq.*), to drain, exhaust. В. все си́лы у кого́-либо, to drain someone of all his strength. В. всю ду́шу кому́-либо, to exhaust someone. Вы́-мот-ать-ся, *v.p.r.*, вы-ма́т-ывать-ся, *v.i.r*, (*colloq.*), to be exhausted.

за-мот-а́ть, *v.p.*, за-ма́т-ывать, *v.i.*, + *acc.*, to roll, fold up; begin to shake. З. у́дочку, to draw in a fishing line. Де́ти совсе́м замота́ли меня́, (*colloq.*), the children have exhausted me. Замота́ть голово́й, to begin to shake one's head. Замота́ть хвосто́м, to begin to wag one's tail. За-мот-а́ть-ся, *v.p.r.*, за-ма́т-ывать-ся, *v.i.r.*, to wind round; be overworked.

из-мот-а́ть, *v.p.*, из-ма́т-ывать, *v.i.*, + *acc.*, to exhaust, wear down. И. не́рвы, to overstrain one's nerves. Из-мот-а́ть-ся, *v.p.r.*, из-ма́т-ывать-ся, *v.i.r.*, + *acc.*, to exhaust, be exhausted. Я совсе́м измота́лся за э́ти 2-3 дня, I exhausted myself during those two, three days.

на-мот-а́ть, *v.p.*, на-ма́т-ывать, *v.i.*, + *acc.*, to wind in quantity. Н. ни́тки на кату́шку, to wind thread on a spool. Намота́й себе́ на ус, (*fig.*), take good note of this; put that in your pipe and smoke it. На-ма́т-ывание, *n.n.*, winding, reeling. На-мо́т-ка, *n.f.*, winding, reeling.

об-мот-а́ть, *v.p.*, об-ма́т-ывать, *v.i.*, + *acc.*, + *instr.*, to wind around. О. го́лову полоте́нцем, to wind a towel around one's head. Об-мот-а́ть-ся, *v.p.r.*, об-ма́т-ывать-ся, *v.i.r.*, + *instr.*, to wrap oneself in. О. ша́рфом, to wind a scarf around one's neck. Об-мо́т-ка, *n.f.*, winding, coiling. О. кату́шек, winding on reels. Об-мо́т-ки, *n.pl.*, puttees.

от-мот-а́ть, *v.p.*, от-ма́т-ывать, *v.i.*, + *acc.*, + *gen.*, to unwind. О. немно́го ше́рсти, to unwind some wool.

пере-мот-а́ть, *v.p.*, пере-ма́т-ывать, *v.i.*, + *acc.*, to re-wind. П. ни́тки с кату́шки на шпу́льку, to wind a bobbin from a spool, Пере-ма́т-ывание, *n.n.*, rewinding.

по-мот-а́ть, *v.p.*, see мота́ть. П. голово́й, to shake one's head a little.

про-мот-а́ть, *v.p.*, про-ма́т-ывать, *v.i.*, + *acc.*, to waste. П. состоя́ние, to run through a fortune. П. де́ньги, to squander money. Про-мот-а́ть-ся, *v.p.r.*, про-ма́т-ывать-ся, *v.i.r.*, to ruin oneself.

раз-мот-а́ть, *v.p.*, раз-ма́т-ывать, *v.i.*, + *acc.*, to unwind, uncoil; unreel. Р. шёлк (повя́зку), to unwind silk (a bandage). Раз-мот-а́ть-ся, *v.p.r.*, раз-ма́т-ывать-ся, *v.i.r.*, to become unwrapped, unwound, unrolled. Клубо́к размота́лся, the ball became unwound.

с-мот-а́ть, *v.p.*, с-ма́т-ывать, *v.i.*, + *acc.*, to wind, make into a ball. С. шерсть в клубо́к, to wind yarn into a ball. С. у́дочки, (*slang*), to take to one's heels.

МЕХ-, (МѢХ-), МЕШ-, (МѢШ-), FUR

мех, *n.m.*, fur. мех-а́, *n.pl.*, furriery. Ли́сий мех, fox fur. На меху́, (подби́тый ме́хом), fur lined. Кузне́чный мех, bellow. Кузне́чные мехи́, bellows. Мехи́ для вина́, wine flasks. Мехо́вщи́к, *n.m.*, furrier. Мех-ово́й, *adj.*, of or pertaining to fur. М-о́е пальто́, fur coat. М-о́й воротни́к, fur collar. М-а́я торго́вля, furriery.

меш-о́к, *n.m.*, sack, bag. М. с муко́й, bag of flour. М. карто́шки, bag of potatoes. Вещево́й м., kit bag. Огнево́й м., (*mil.*), fire-pocket. Мешки́ под глаза́ми, bags under the eyes. Костю́м сиди́т на нём мешко́м, his suit fits like a bag. Меш-о́чек, *n.m.*, (*dim.*), bag. Свари́ть яйцо́ в мешо́чек, to cook a soft boiled egg. Меш-о́чник, *n.m.*, (*recent*), bagger; during famine, one who travels to the villages to barter something for food. Меш-кова́тый, *adj.*, awkward, clumsy; baggy.

меш-к-а́ть, *v.i.*, с + *instr.*, (*colloq.*), to loiter, linger, tarry, delay. Она́ ме́шкала с отъе́здом, she tarried and delayed before her departure. Меш-ко́тный, *adj.*, (*colloq.*), sluggish, slow. М. рабо́тник, slow worker. Меш-ко́тно, *adv.*, (*colloq.*), sluggishly, slowly. Рабо́тать м., to work slowly.

за-ме́ш-кать-ся, *v.p.r.*, (*colloq.*), to linger, tarry, be late. З. в доро́ге, to tarry on the way. Он заме́шкался у свои́х прия́телей, he overstayed at his friends' house.

МИЛ-, KINDNESS, CHARITY, TENDERNESS

ми́л-ый, *adj.*, nice, sweet; dear (*in addressing someone*); used as *n.*, sweetheart, darling. Ми́л-енький, *adj.*, (*dim.*). М-ое ли́чико, comely little face. "Не по-хорошу́ мил, а по́-милу хоро́ш," (*saying*), it's dear to you because you like it, not for its value. Ми́л-очка, *n.f.*, dear, darling. Ми́л-о, *adv.*, nicely, politely, gently, kindly. Это о́чень ми́ло с ва́шей стороны́, that is very kind of you. Мил-о-ви́дность, *n.f.*, comeliness. Мил-о-ви́дный, *adj.*, comely.

мил-ова́ть, мил-у́ю, *v.i.*, to caress, fondle. Целова́ла, милова́ла, называ́ла "ми́лый мой," (*folksong*), she kissed me, caressed me, called me "My loved one."

ми́л-ова-ть, *v.i.*, + *acc.*, to show mercy; pardon; reprieve, remit. М. престу́пников, to pardon, reprieve criminals.

по-ми́л-овать, *v.p.*, + *acc.*, to pardon, forgive. По-ми́л-ованный, *adj.*, *part. pass. past*, pardoned, reprieved. Быть п-ым, to be pardoned, reprieved, forgiven; obtain mercy. По-ми́л-ование, *n.n.*, reprieve, pardon. По-ми́л-уй, по-ми́л-уйте, (*colloq.*), For goodness sake! Го́споди поми́луй! Lord, have mercy upon us! С-ми́л-овать-ся, *v.p.*, над + *instr.*, (*obs.*), to become merciful. С. над осуждёнными, to be merciful to the condemned.

ми́л-ость, *n.f.*, favor, grace; mercy, charity. Втере́ться в м. кому́-либо, (*colloq.*), to get into someone's favor. ...Я... ми́лость к па́дшим призыва́л, (*Pushkin*), ...I... begged for mercy toward those cast down. (trans. by B. Deutsch). Сда́ться на м. победи́теля, to throw oneself upon the mercy of the conqueror. Из ми́лости, out of charity. Ва́ша ми́лость, (*obs.*), your worship. Ми́лости про́сим, (*obs.*), you are welcome, please do. Ми́л-остивый, *adj.*, gracious, kind. М. госуда́рь, (*obs.*), Dear Sir, Gracious Sir. М-ая госуда́рыня, (*obs.*), Dear Madam.

ми́л-ост-ын-я, *n.f.*, alms, charity. Проси́ть ми́лостыни, to beg. Пода́ть ми́лостыню, to give alms.

мил-о-се́рд-ие, *n.n.*, mercy, charity, clemency. Сестра́ милосе́рдия, sister of charity; mercy; nurse. Мил-о-се́рдный, *adj.*, merciful, charitable.

мил-о-се́рдствовать, *v.i.*, по-мил-о-се́рдствовать, *v.p.*, (*obs.*), to take pity upon, have mercy upon. Помилосе́рдствуйте, пощади́те меня́! Have mercy, spare me!

у-мил-я́ть, *v.i.*, у-мил-и́ть, *v.p.*, + *acc.*, + *instr.*, to touch; move. Он умили́л меня́ свое́й не́жностью, he touched me with his tenderness. У-мил-я́ть-ся, *v.i.r.*, у-мил-и́ть-ся, *v.p.r.*, + *instr.*, to be touched. У-мил-е́ние, *n.n.*, tender emotion. Привести́ кого́-либо в у., to move someone deeply. У-мил-ённый, *adj. part. pass. past*, touched, moved. У-мил-и́тельный, *adj.*, touching, moving. У-ми́л-ь-ность, *n.f.*, touching quality; sweetness. У-ми́л-ь-ный, *adj.*, touching, sweet. У. го́лос, sweet voice. У-ая улы́бка, sweet smile, sugary smile.

МИР-, (МІР), UNIVERSE

мир, *n.m.*, universe, world; (*hist.*), village, community. Сотворе́ние ми́ра, (*Bib.*), the creation of the world. Звёздный мир, the world of stars. Мир расте́ний (живо́тных), flora (fauna). Христиа́нский мир, the Christian world. Мир пореши́л, (*folk, pre-rev.*), the village community decided. Она́ не от ми́ра сего́, she is not of this world. На миру́ и смерть красна́, (*prov.*), two in distress lessen sorrow. С ми́ру по ни́тке, го́лому руба́шка, (*prov.*), if everyone gives a thread, the beggar will have a shirt; large oaks from little acorns grow. Ходи́ть по́ миру, to live by begging. Мир-ово́й, *adj.*, worldly, universal. М-а́я война́, world war. М-а́я сла́ва, world fame. М-о́е хозя́йство, world economy. В мирово́м масшта́бе, on a

world-wide scale. Мир-о-воззре́ние, мир-о-понима́ние, *n.n.*, world outlook. Лю́ди ра́зных мировоззре́ний, people of different outlooks, philosophies. Мир-о-зда́ние, *n.n.*, Creation, the universe. Исто́рия мирозда́ния, the history of the creation of the world. Мир-я́нин, *n.m.*, layman, secular. Мир-я́не, *n.pl.* the laity, laymen. Мир-ско́й, *adj.*, secular, lay, mundane, temporal. В монасты́рь не проника́ла мирска́я жизнь, secular life did not penetrate into the monastery. Мирска́я молва́, что морска́я волна́, (*saying*), public opinion is as inconstant as the waves of the sea. М-а́я суета́, vanity of worldly life.

мир-о-е́д, *n.m.*, village usurer. Кула́к-мироед, (*obs.*), arch kulak usurer.

МИР-, PEACE

мир, *n.m.*, peace. Душе́вный мир, peace of mind. Заключи́ть мир, to conclude a peace treaty. Угро́за де́лу ми́ра, (*recent*), menace to peace. Худо́й мир лу́чше до́брой ссо́ры, (*prov.*), better a lean peace than a fat victory. Ми́рный, *adj.*, peaceful. М. догово́р, peace treaty. М-ая поли́тика, peace policy. Ми́р-ные перегово́ры, peace negotiations. Ми́р-но, *adv.*, peacefully, quietly. мир-ов-а́я, *n.f.*, (*obs.*), peace-making. Заключа́ть м-у́ю, to make peace. Пойти́ на м-у́ю, to settle peacefully. Мир-ово́й, *adj.*, peace. М. посре́дник, (*pre-Rev.*), conciliator, arbitrator. М. судья́, justice of the peace. М-а́я сде́лка, peaceful settlement. Мир-о-люби́вость, *n.f.*, conciliation; love of peace. Мир-о-лю́бие, *n.n.*, love of peace. Мир-о-люби́вый, *adj.*, peace-loving.

мир-и́ть, *v.i.*, по-мир-и́ть, *v.p.*, + *acc.*, reconcile. М. враго́в, to make peace between enemies. Мир-и́ть-ся, *v.i.r.*, по-мир-и́ть-ся, *v.p.r.*, с + *instr.*, to be reconciled. М. со свои́м положе́нием, to become resigned to one's situation.

пере-мир-и́ть, *v.p.*, + *acc.*, see помири́ть. Пере-мир-ие, *n.n.*, armistice, truce. Заключа́ть п., conclude a truce, armistice.

при-мир-и́ть, *v.p.*, при-мир-я́ть, *v.i.*, + *acc.*, to reconcile. При-мир-и́ть-ся, *v.i.r.*, to become reconciled. П. со свое́й уча́стью, to reconcile oneself to one's lot. При-мир-и́тельный, *adj.*, conciliatory. П-ая ка́мера, (*recent*), court of conciliation. При-мир-е́ние, *n.n.*, reconciliation. При-мир-и́мый, *adj.*, reconcilable. При-мир-и́тель, *n.m.*, reconciler, peace-maker. При-мир-я́ющий, *adj.*, *part. act. pres.*, recon-

ciling. При-мир-я́юще, *adv.*, in a conciliating way. При-мир-е́нчество, *n.n.*, (*recent, polit.*), spirit of compromise. При-мир-е́нческий, *adj.*, compromising.
с-мир-и́ть, *v.p.*, с-мир-я́ть, *v.i.*, + *acc.*, to subdue, restrain; abase. С. го́рдость, to humble. С. непоко́рных, to subdue recalcitrants. С. свои́ стра́сти, to control one's passions. С-мир-и́ть-ся, *v.p.r.*, с-мир-я́ть-ся, *v.i.r.*, to submit; humble oneself. С-мир-е́ние, *n.n.*, humility, meekness. С-мир-е́нничать, *v.i.*, (*obs.*), to pretend to be humble. С-мир-е́нность, *n.f.*, humility. С-мир-е́нный, *adj.*, humble, meek; submissive. С. вид (нрав), humble appearance (disposition). С-мир-е́нник, *n.m.*, (*obs.*), a meek person. С-ми́р-ный, *adj.*, quiet, mild. С. челове́к, quiet, unobtrusive man. С-мир-и́тельная руба́шка, strait-jacket. С-ми́р-но, *adv.*, quietly. Вести́ себя́ с., to be quiet, behave quietly. Сиде́ть с., to sit still. Сми́рно! (*mil.*), Attention!
у-мир-о-твори́ть, *v.p.*, у-мир-о-творя́ть, *v.i.*, + *acc.*, to pacify, appease. У. вражду́ющих, to appease enemies. У-мир-отвори́ть-ся, *v.p.r.*, у-мир-о-творя́ть-ся, *v.i.r.*, to be, become appeased. У-мир-о-творе́ние, *n.n.*, pacification. У-мир-о-твори́тель, *n.m.*, peace-maker, appeaser, pacifier. Мир-о-тво́рец, *n.m.*, (*obs.*), peace-maker.

МЛАД-, МОЛОД-, МОЛОЖ-, МОЛАЖ-, YOUTH

млад-е́н-ец, *n.m.*, baby, infant. Грудно́й м., infant in arms. Млад-е́нчество, *n.n.*, infancy; babyhood. Охра́на матери́нства и младе́нчества, maternity and child protection. Млад-е́нческий, *adj.*, infantile. Мла́д-ость, *n.f.*, (*poet.*), youth. Млад-о́й, *adj.*, (*poet.*), young, youthful. Мла́д-ший, *adj. comp. and superl.*, younger, youngest, junior. М. компаньо́н, junior partner, companion. М. кома́ндный соста́в, noncommissioned officers.
молод-о́й, *adj.*, young, youthful; new; *used as n.*, bridegroom. М. ме́сяц, new moon. М-ое вино́, new wine. М. челове́к, young man. М-а́я, *adj. used as n.*, bride. Молод-о-жёны, *n.pl.*, newlyweds. Моло́д-енький, *adj.*, (*dim.*), young. Мо́лод-ость, *n.f.*, youth. Втора́я м., (*fig.*), rejuvenation. Не пе́рвой мо́лодости, (*colloq.*), middle-aged. Мо́лод-о, *adv.*, youthfully. Мо́лодо-зе́лено, (*fig.*), unripe, green. М. вы́глядеть, to look young. С-мо́лод-у, *adv.*, from one's youth.
моло́ж-е, *adj. comp.*, younger. Брат моло́же меня́ на 5 лет, my brother is five years younger than I. Она́ вы́глядит моло́же свои́х лет, she looks younger than her years.
молод-е́-ть, *v.i.*, по-молод-е́ть, *v.p.*, to grow, become young.
молод-и́-ть, *v.i.*, + *acc.*, to make young, rejuvenate. Эта шля́па вас молоди́т, this hat makes you look younger. Молод-и́ть-ся, *v.i.r.*, to try to appear younger than one's years. Молод-ёжь, *n.f.*, youth, young people. Уча́щаяся м., students. Молод-ёжный, *adj.*, (*recent*), pertaining to youth. М. клуб, (*recent*), young people's club. М-ое собра́ние, (*recent*), young people's meeting.
о-молод-и́ть, *v.p.*, о-мола́ж-ивать, *v.i.*, + *acc.*, to rejuvenate. О-молод-и́ть-ся, *v.p.r.*, о-мола́ж-ивать-ся, *v.i.r.*, to be rejuvenated. О-моло́ж-ение, *n.n.*, rejuvenation. Молож-а́вость, *n.f.*, youthful appearance. Молож-а́вый, *adj.*, youthful, young looking. Име́ть м. вид, to look young for one's age.
под-молод-и́ть, *v.p.*, под-мола́ж-ивать, *v.i.*, + *acc.*, to make look younger. Под-молод-и́ть-ся, *v.p.r.*, под-мола́ж-ивать-ся, *v.i.r.*, to make oneself look younger.
молод-е́ц, *n.m.*, lad, young fellow; fine fellow. Вести́ себя́ молодцо́м, (*colloq.*), to behave well. Молоде́ц! Good boy! Well done! Молод-е́цкий, *adj.*, valiant; mettlesome. Уда́ль молоде́цкая, valor. Молод-е́чество, *n.n.*, display of courage, bravado. Молод-цева́тость, *n.f.*, sprightliness, dashing appearance. Молод-цева́тый, *adj.*, dashing, sprightly. Молод-чик, *n.m.*, (*colloq.*), young fellow. Молод-чи́на, *n.f.*, (*colloq.*), good fellow. Молод-ня́к, *n.m.*, (*colloq., recent*), youth; young cattle, horses; young forest.

МЛЕК-, МЛЕЧ-, МОЛОК-, МОЛОЧ-, MILK

мле́к-о, *n.n.*, (*Ch.-Sl.*), milk. Млек-о-пита́ющее, *adj. used as n.*, mammal. Мле́ч-ный, *adj.*, lactic, lacteal. Мле́чный Путь, (*astr.*), Milky Way. М-ые же́лезы, lactic glands.
молок-о́, *n.n.*, milk. Сгущённое м., condensed milk. У него́ молоко́ на губа́х не обсо́хло, (*saying*), the milk is not yet dry on his lips. Кровь с молоко́м, (*fig.*), blooming health. Обожжёшься на молоке́, ста́нешь дуть и на́ воду, (*prov.*), a burned child dreads fire. Молок-о-со́с, *n.m.*, (*colloq.*), greenhorn, unfledged youth.
моло́ч-ный, *adj.*, milky, lactic. М. режи́м,

(м-ая дие́та), milk diet. М-ое хозя́йст-, во, dairy farm. М-ые проду́кты, dairy products. Моло́ч-ная, *adj., used as n.f.,* creamery, dairy; milk shop. Моло́ч-ник, *n.m.,* milk jug. Моло́ч-ник, *n.m.,* milkman, dairyman. Моло́ч-ница, *n.f.,* milkmaid, dairymaid.

молоч-а́й, *n.m.,* (*bot.*) spurge.

молок-а́не, *n.pl.,* members of a sect denying Greek Orthodox rituals, war, living near Molochnaya River in Tauris Province, Russia.

МН-, МИН-, МЯТ-, МЯ-, IMAGINA-TION, MEMORY, OPINION

мн-е́ние, *n.n.,* opinion. Обще́ственное м., public opinion. Быть хоро́шего (пло-хо́го) мне́ния о ко́м-нибудь, to have a high (low) opinion of someone. По моему́ мне́нию, in my opinion.

мн-и-ть, *v.i.,* + *acc.,* о + *prep.,* (*obs.*), to think, imagine. Сли́шком мно́го м. о себе́, to think too highly of oneself. Мн-и́мый, *adj.,* imaginary; sham. М. больно́й, pretendedly sick person; hypochondriac. М-ая величина́, imaginary value. Мн-и́мо, *adv.,* seemingly, pretendedly. Мни́мо-уме́рший, *adj.,* seemingly dead. Мн-и́тельность, *n.f.,* hypochondria; apprehensiveness. Мн-и́тельный, *adj.,* hypochondriac; appre-hensive. М. хара́ктер, hypochondriac disposition. М. челове́к, hypochondriac.

возо-мн-и́ть, *v.p.,* о + *prep. used in expression*: В. о себе́, to become con-ceited.

по́-мн-ить, *v.i.,* + *acc.,* о + *prep.,* to remember, keep in mind. П сво́е де́тство, to remember one's child-hood. Она́ всё вре́мя по́мнит об э́том, she thinks of nothing else. Не п., себя́ от гне́ва, to be beside oneself with anger. По́-мн-ить-ся, *v.i.r.,* + *dat.,* *used in 3d pers.,* to remember. Ему́ (ей) по́мнится, he (she) remembers, recalls. Ему́ (ей) хорошо́ по́мнились э́ти стро́ки, he (she) remembered, recalled these lines very well. Наско́лько мне по́мнится, as far as I remember, recall. По́мнится, I remember.

вс-по́-мн-ить, *v.p.,* вс-по-мин-а́ть, *v.i.,* + *acc.,* о + *prep.,* to remember, recall, recollect. Вспо́мните хороше́нько! Think well! Вс-по́-мн-ить-ся, *v.p.r.,* вс-по-мин-а́ть-ся, *v.i.r.,* be remembered, recalled, recollected. Ему́ (им) вспо-мина́ется, he (they) remember(s), recall(s). Вос-по-мин-а́ние, *n.n.,* re-collection, memory, reminiscence. Вос-помина́ния, *n.pl.,* reminiscences, me-moirs. Оста́лось одно́ воспомина́ние, only a reminiscence, memory, remains.

за-по́-мн-ить, *v.p.,* за-по-мин-а́ть, *v.i.,* + *acc.,* to memorize; remember. З. стихи́ наизу́сть, to memorize ·verses. За-по́-мн-ить-ся, *v.p.r.,* за-по-мин-а́ть-ся, *v.i.r.,* to be remembered, retained in memory. Мне запо́мнилось одно́ ме́сто из рома́на, I remember one passage in the novel. За-по-мин-а́ние, *n.n.,* me-morizing.

на-по́-мн-ить, *v.p.,* на-по-мин-а́ть, *v.i.,* + *acc.,* + *dat.,* о + *prep.,* to remind. Сын напомина́ет своего́ отца́, the son resembles his father. Напо́мним, что..., I would remind you that... "Здесь всё напомина́ет мне было́е," (*Pushkin*), Everything here reminds me of the past." На-по-мин-а́ние, *n.n.,* reminder, reminding. Письмо́ с напомина́нием о сро́ке платежа́, a letter reminding of a payment date.

о-по́-мн-ить-ся, *v.p.r.,* to come to one's senses, collect oneself. "Она́ опомни-лась, но сно́ва закры́ла о́чи," (*Push-kin*), "She recovered consciousness, but then again closed her eyes."

по-по́-мн-ить, *v.p.,* + *acc.,* + *dat.,* (*col-loq.*), to remember, bearing a grudge. Я тебе́ э́то попо́мню, I'll repay you; I'll take my revenge some day. Попо́м-ните моё сло́во, mark my words.

при-по́-мн-ить, *v.p.,* при-по-мин-а́ть, *v.i.,* + *acc.,* to remember, recollect, recall. Наско́лько припомина́ю, as far as I remember. Припо́мнил, I remember it now. Она́ вам э́то припо́мнит, she'll pay you back some day.

у-по-мин-а́ть, *v.p.,* у-по-мя-ну́ть, *v.p.,* о + *prep.,* to mention, refer to. У. вскользь (случа́йно), to mention in passing. У-по-мин-а́ние, *n.n.,* mention. При упомина́нии, at the mention of. У-по-мя́-нутый, *adj., part. pass. past,* mentioned. Вы́ше-упомя́нутый, the above mentioned. Ни́же-упомя́нутый, mentioned below.

со-мн-е́ние, *n.n.,* doubt. С. в чём-нибудь, doubt as to something. В э́том нет сомне́ния, there is no doubt about that. Без сомне́ния, without doubt, beyond doubt . Не-со-мн-е́нно, *adv.,* un-doubtedly.

со-мн-ева́ть-ся, *v.i.r.,* в + *prep.,* to doubt. Я не сомнева́юсь в ва́ших спосо́б-ностях, I have no doubts as to your abilities. Мо́жете не с., you may rely on. Сомнева́юсь в его́ и́скренности, I doubt his sincerity. Со-мн-и́тель-ность, *n.f.,* doubtfulness. С. результа́-та, doubtful result. С. репута́ции, doubtful reputation. Со-мн-и́тельный, *adj.,* doubtful, questionable, dubious, shady. С. комплиме́нт, equivocal com-pliment. С-ое преиму́щество, questionable advantage. Челове́к с-ой че́стности, man of dubious honesty. Со-мни́тельно, *adv.*, doubtfully; it is doubtful. **у-со-мн-и́ть-ся,** *v.p.r.,* в + *prep.,* to doubt. У. в пра́вильности показа́ний, to doubt the evidence. У. в дру́ге, to doubt a friend.

па́-мят-ь, *n.f.,* memory; recollection, remembrance. Зри́тельная п., visual memory. Плоха́я (хоро́шая) п., poor (good) memory. Подари́ть на п., to give as a keepsake. Оста́вить по себе́ до́брую п., to leave fond memories of oneself. Ве́чная п., eternal memory; hymn at end of requiem. Быть без па́мяти, to be without memory; to be unconscious. Быть без па́мяти от кого́-либо, (*colloq.*), to be head over heels in love with someone. Учи́ть на п., to memorize, learn by heart, Па́-мят-ка, *n.f.,* leaflet; booklet; memorandum; instruction; written rules of behavior. Па́-мят-ливость, *n.f.,* retentiveness. Па́-мят-ливый, *adj.,* retentive, having a retentive memory. П. челове́к, one with a retentive memory. Па́-мят-ник, *n.m.,* monument, memorial, tombstone. Литерату́рный п., literary monument. Ста́вить кому́-либо п., to erect a monument to someone. Па́-мят-ный, *adj.,* memorable. П. день, memorable day. П-ое собы́тие, memorable event. П-ая кни́жка, memorandum book; notebook. П-ая доска́, memorial plate. Бес-па́-мят-ность, *n.f.,* forgetfulness. Бес-па́-мят-ный, *adj.,* forgetful. Бес-па́-мят-ство, *n.n.,* unconsciousness. Лежа́ть в беспа́мятстве, to lie unconscious. Впасть в б-о, to lose consciousness; lapse into a coma.

за-па́-мят-овать, *v.p.,* + *acc.,* (*obs.*), to forget. Я запа́мятовал ва́ше и́мя, I have completely forgotten your name.

о-бес-па́-мят-еть, *v.p.,* to lose one's memory; lose consciousness; faint. О. от испу́га (го́ря), to faint from fear (grief).

по-мя-ну́-ть, *v.p.,* по-мин-а́ть, *v.i.,* + *acc.,* to mention. П. хоро́шим сло́вом, (*colloq.*), to speak well of. Помяни́те моё сло́во, (*colloq.*), take my word. Не помина́йте ли́хом, (*idiom.*), think kindly of me. Помина́й, как зва́ли, (*colloq.*), disappeared, forgotten, gone (of a person). Не́чего помина́ть ста́рое, (*idiom.*), let bygones be bygones.

по-ми́н, *n.m.,* (*colloq.*), mention. Лёгок на поми́не, (*idiom. fig.*), talk of the devil. Об э́том и поми́ну не́ было, there was no mention of it. По-ми́н-ки, *n.pl.,* funeral repast; feast commemorating the dead. По-мин-а́нье, *n.n.,*

a prayer for the dead. П. о здра́вии (за упоко́й), to pray for someone's health (peace).

МНОГ-, МНОЖ-, QUANTITY

мно́г-ие, *adj.,* many; *used as n.,* many. Во мно́гих отноше́ниях, in many respects. Во мно́гих слу́чаях, in many cases. Мно́гие так ду́мают, there are many who think so. М. из них мне знако́мы, I know many of them. Мно́г-о, *adv.,* much, plenty. М. рабо́ты, much work. М. наро́ду, many people, multitude of people. М. раз, many times, frequently. М. знать, to know much. Не-мно́г-ие, not many. Не-мно́г-о, *adv.,* a little, some. Н. воды́, a little water. Н. люде́й, a few people. По-не-мно́г-у, *adv.,* little by little. По-не-мно́ж-ку, *adv.,* little by little. Не́бо понемно́гу проясня́лось, little by little, the sky cleared. Много-, *a combining form meaning* much, many, (poly-, multi-). Много-бра́чие, *n.n.,* polygamy. Много-во́дие, *n.n.,* abundance of water. Многово́дный, *adj.,* brimming with water. Много-значи́тельность, *n.f.,* significance. Многозначи́тельный, *adj.,* significant. Многозначи́тельно, *adv.,* significantly. Много-то́чие, *n.n.,* ellipsis; suspension. Много-уважа́емый, *adj.,* highly respected: Dear Sir (*in letters*). Много-чи́сленный, *adj.,* numerous, multiple.

мно́ж-ество, *n.n.,* great number, multitude, numbers, lots. М. рабо́чих, a lot of workers. М. хлопо́т, a great deal of trouble. Мно́ж-ественность, *n.f.,* plurality. Мно́ж-ественный, *adj.,* plural. М-ое число́, (*gram.*), plural number.

мно́ж-и-ть, *v.i.,* у-мно́ж-ить, по-мно́ж-ить, *v.p.,* + *acc.,* to multiply; increase. М. пять на два, to multiply 5 by 2. Мно́ж-ить-ся, *v.i.r.,* (*math.*), to increase, be multiplied. Мно́ж-имое, *adj.,* used as n., (*math.*), multiplicand. Мно́ж-итель, *n.m.,* (*math.*), multiplier, factor.

пере-мно́ж-ить, *v.p.,* пере-множ-а́ть, *v.i.,* + *acc.,* (*math.*), to multiply. П. пять чи́сел, to multiply five figures.

по-мно́ж-ить, *v.p.,* множ-ить, по-множ-а́ть, *v.i.,* to multiply. П. два на пять, to multiply 2 by 5. По-мно́ж-енный, *adj., part. pass. past,* multiplied. Два, помно́женное на пять, равня́ется десяти́, two times five equals ten.

раз-мно́ж-ить, *v.p.,* раз-множ-а́ть, *v.i.,* + *acc.,* (*math.*), to multiply; propagate; manifold; mimeograph. Размно́жить ру́копись в ста экземпля́рах, to make one hundred copies of a manuscript. Р-а́ть расте́ния, to raise plants, in quantity. Раз-мно́ж-ить-ся, *v.p.r.*, раз-множа́ть-ся, *v.i.r.*, to be multiplied, propagated, reproduced. Кро́лики размножа́ются о́чень бы́стро, rabbits multiply very rapidly. Размнож-е́ние, *n.n.*, propagation, reproduction in quantity.

у-мно́ж-ить, *v.p.,* у-множ-а́ть, *v.i.,* + *acc.,* to increase, augment, multiply. У. дохо́ды, to increase the income. У. на́ два (три, четы́ре), to multiply by 2 (three, four). У-мно́ж-ить-ся, *v.p.r.,* у-множ-а́ть-ся, *v.i.r.,* to be increased, multiplied. У-множ-е́ние, *n.n.,* increase, augmentation, multiplication. Табли́ца умноже́ния, multiplication table.

МОГ-, МОЖ-, МОЖД-, МОЧ-, МОЩ-, POWER, MIGHT

мог-у́чий, *adj.,* powerful, mighty. М-ая страна́, powerful nation, country. Могу́честь, *n.f.,* strength, might, power. Мог-ота́, *n.f., (colloq.), only in expression:* Не в моготу́, beyond endurance.

мог-у́щ-еств-енный, *adj.,* potent, powerful, mighty. Мог-у́щественность, *n.f.,* power, might. Мог-у́щество, *n.n.,* power, might.

мо́ж-но, *adv., used as pred.,* it is possible, one can, one may. Это мо́жно прочёсть, one can read it. Здесь м. кури́ть, one may smoke here. М. мне войти́? May I come in? Как мо́жно скоре́е, as soon as possible. Как м. лу́чше, as best one can. Мо́жет быть, perhaps, maybe, possibly. М. быть, э́то пра́вда, it may be true.

воз-мо́ж-но, *adv.,* it is possible, it may be; possibly, perhaps. В. скоре́е, as soon, quickly as possible. Воз-мо́ж-ность, *n.f.,* possibility, opportunity, chance. Дава́ть кому́-нибудь в., to give someone a chance. Материа́льные возмо́жности, material means. Воз-мо́ж-ный, *adj.,* possible. Сде́лать всё возмо́жное, to do one's best; to do all that is possible.

не-воз-мо́ж-но, *adv.,* impossible. Не-возмо́ж-ное, *adj., used as n.,* the impossible. Не-воз-мо́ж-ность, *n.f.,* impossibility. В слу́чае невозмо́жности, in case it is impossible. Не-воз-мо́ж-ный, *adj.,* impossible.

моч-ь, мог-у́, *v.i.,* to be able; *n.f., (colloq.),* power, might. Она́ мо́жет, she can, she is able. Мо́жет-ли он пойти́ туда́? May he go there? Могу́-ли я попроси́ть вас? May I ask you? Мо́жет быть, maybe, perhaps. Мо́жет

быть, я пойду́, I may go. Это мо́жет быть пра́вда, that may be true. Изо всей мо́чи, with all one's might. Что есть мо́чи, with all one's might. Мо́чи нет, at the end of one's tether.

не́-моч-ь, *n.f., (colloq.),* sickness, illness, infirmity. Бле́дная н., leukemia, anaemia. Не́-мощ-ь, *n.f.,* infirmity, feebleness. Не́-мощ-и, *pl.,* illnesses. Не́мощи одоле́ли…, illnesses have overwhelmed (me). Не́-мощ-ный, *adj.,* infirm, sick, feeble. Н. стари́к, feeble old man.

по-мо́ч-ь, по-мог-у́, *v.p.,* to help, assist, aid, support; relieve. П. кому́-либо око́нчить рабо́ту, to help someone finish a job. Это де́лу не помо́жет, this will not help matters. Вс-по-мог-а́тельный, *adj.,* auxiliary. В. глаго́л, *(gram.),* auxiliary verb.

за-не-мо́ч-ь, *v.p.,* за-не-мог-а́ть, *v.i., (obs.),* to fall ill; become, be taken sick.

из-не-мо́ч-ь, *v.p.,* из-не-мог-а́ть, *v.i.,* to be exhausted, break down. Я изнемога́ю от жары́, I'm exhausted from the heat. Она́ изнемога́ет от уста́лости, she is dead tired. Из-не-мож-е́ние, *n.n.,* breakdown, exhaustion. Рабо́тать до изнеможе́ния, to work to exhaustion. Из-можд-ённый, *adj.,* emaciated, exhausted. И. вид, emaciated appearance. И-ое лицо́, emaciated face.

пре-воз-мо́ч-ь, *v.p.,* пре-воз-мог-а́ть, *v.i.,* + *acc.,* to overcome, master. Я не в си́лах превозмо́чь дремо́ту (уста́лость, отвраще́ние), I cannot overcome drowsiness (exhaustion, repugnance).

вы-мог-а́ть, *v.i.,* + *acc.,* to extort. В. де́ньги у кого́-либо, to extort money from someone. В. обеща́ние, to extort a promise. Вы-мог-а́тель, *n.m.,* extortioner. Вы-мог-а́тельство, *n.n.,* extortion; blackmail. Вы-мог-а́тельский, *adj.,* extortionate.

до-мог-а́ть-ся, *v.i.r.,* + *gen.,* to solicit. Д. чьей-либо любви́, to woo someone. До-мог-а́тельство, *n.n.,* solicitation.

не-до-мог-а́ть, *v.i., (colloq.),* to be unwell. Не-до-мог-а́ние, *n.n.,* indisposition. Чу́вствовать н., to be indisposed, feel unwell.

пере-мог-а́ть, *v.i.,* пере-мо́ч-ь, *v.p.,* + *acc.,* to overcome. Встал, с трудо́м перемога́я боль в ноге́, he rose, trying with difficulty to overcome the pain in his leg. Пере-мог-а́ть-ся, *v.i.,* пере-мо́ч-ь-ся, *v.p.,* + *acc., (colloq.),* to force oneself to work while sick.

мощ-ь, *n.f.,* power, might. Хозя́йственная м., economic power. Полити́ческая м., political power. Вое́нная м., military power. Мо́щ-ность, *n.f.,* power. Мо́щ-ный, *adj.,* powerful, mighty, strong.

Мо́щи, *n.pl.*, (*rel.*), relics (of a saint). Живы́е м., (*fig.*), living mummy.

по́-мощ-ь, *n.f.*, help, assistance, aid, relief. Пода́ть ру́ку по́мощи, to give a helping hand. На по́мощь! Help! Медици́нская п., medical aid. Ско́рая п., emergency, first aid. По-мо́щ-ник, *n.m.*, по-мо́щ-ница, *n.f.*, assistant, helper. Вс-по-мощ-ествова́ние, *n.n.*, (*obs.*), relief, aid, assistance.

МОК-, МОЧ-, МАК-, МАЧ-, MOISTURE

мо́к-ну-ть, *v.i.*, to become wet, soak. М. под дождём, to be out in the rain. Мок-рота́, *n.f.*, humidity, wetness. Мок-ро́та, *n.f.*, (*med.*), phlegm. Отха́ркивать м-у, to clear the phlegm in one's throat. Мок-ри́ца, *n.f.*, (*zool.*), wood louse. Мо́к-рый, *adj.*, wet, moist, soggy. М. до ни́тки, wet to the skin, soaked through. М-ая ку́рица, (*fig.*), a wet rag. У неё глаза́ на мо́кром ме́сте, (*fig.*), she is easily moved to tears. Мок-рова́тый, *adj.*, moist, rather wet.

вы́-мок-нуть, *v.p.*, вы́-мок-а́ть, *v.i.*, to be steeped, drenched, soaked. В. до ни́тки, (*colloq.*), to be drenched, soaked to the skin.

из-мо́к-нуть, *v.p.*, из-мок-а́ть, *v.i.*, to get drenched, soaked. Я весь измо́к на дожде́, I was thoroughly drenched.

на-мо́к-нуть, *v.p.*, на-мок-а́ть, *v.i.*, to become wet. Плащ не намока́ет на дожде́, a raincoat is waterproof.

от-мо́к-нуть, *v.p.*, от-мок-а́ть, *v.i.*, to become wet; come off as a result of moisture. Накле́йка отмока́ет в сы́рости, moisture causes the label to loosen.

пере-мо́к-нуть, *v.p.*, пере-мок-а́ть, *v.i.*, to soak through, get drenched. П. под дождём, to get drenched in the rain.

под-мо́к-нуть, *v.p.*, под-мок-а́ть, *v.i.*, to become slightly wet, damp. Мука́ подмо́кла, the flour has become damp.

по-мо́к-нуть, *v.p.*, see, мо́кнуть. Пусть горо́х помо́кнет в воде́, let the peas soak a little in the water.

про-мо́к-нуть, *v.p.*, про-мок-а́ть, *v.i.*, to become wet, soaked; be soaking; let water through. П. до косте́й, (*colloq.*), to get drenched. Вся оде́жда на нём промо́кла, his clothes were soaked through. Этот плащ промока́ет, this raincoat lets water through. Про-мо́к-ший, *adj.*, *part. pass. past*, soaked through, drenched. П насквозь, dripping wet.

раз-мо́к-нуть, *v.p.*, раз-мок-а́ть, *v.i.*, to get soaked, saturated, sodden. Сухари́ размо́кли в воде́, the rusks were thoroughly soaked.

моч-и́-ть, *v.p.*, + *acc.*, to wet, soak. М. во́лосы одеколо́ном, to wet the hair with eau de cologne. М. селёдку, to soak herring. Моч-ёный, *adj.*, soaked. Моч-и́ть-ся, *v.i.r.*, по-моч-и́ть-ся, *v.p.r.*, to urinate, pass water. Моч-а́, *n.f.*, urine, water. Ана́лиз мочи́, urinalysis. Моч-ево́й, *adj.*, urinary. М. пузы́рь, bladder. Моч-е-го́нный, *adj.*, diuretic. М-ое сре́дство, diuretic medicine. Мо́ч-ка, *n.f.*, soaking, macerating; lobe of the ear. Лён был до́лго в мо́чке, the flax soaked for a long time.

вы́-моч-ить, *v.p.*, вы-ма́ч-ивать, *v.i.*, + *acc.*, to soak, steep; drench. В. до ни́тки, to drench to the skin.

за-моч-и́ть, *v.p.*, за-ма́ч-ивать, *v.i.*, + *acc.*, to wet. З. но́ги, to wet one's feet. З. лён, to soak flax. З. край ю́бки, to wet the hem of a skirt.

на-моч-и́ть, *v.p.*, на-ма́ч-ивать, *v.i.*, + *acc.*, to wet, moisten, soak; spill water. Н. бельё, to soak the laundry.

об-моч-и́ть, *v.p.*, об-ма́ч-ивать, *v.i.*, + *acc.*, to wet. Дождь обмочи́л меня́, I got soaked in the rain. Об-моч-и́ть-ся, *v.p.r.*, об-ма́ч-ивать-ся, *v.i.r.*, to wet oneself. Ребёнок обмочи́лся, the baby is wet.

от-моч-и́ть, *v.p.*, от-ма́ч-ивать, *v.i.*, + *acc.*, to loosen, unglue by wetting.

под-моч-и́ть, *v.p.*, под-ма́ч-ивать, *v.i.*, + *acc.*, to wet slightly; dampen. П. тюки́ с табако́м, to damage bales of tobacco with moisture. Под-мо́ч-енный, *adj.*, *part. pass. past*, wet, dampened; damaged. П-ая репута́ция, (*colloq.*), reputation.

по-моч-и́ть, *v.p.*, + *acc.*, to moisten slightly. П. себе́ го́лову, to moisten one's head. По-моч-и́ть-ся, *v.p.r.*, see мочи́ться.

при-моч-и́ть, *v.p.*, при-ма́ч-ивать, *v.i.*, + *acc.*, + *instr.*, to moisten, wet; bathe; apply a compress. П. уши́б холо́дной водо́й, to apply cold water to a bruise. При-мо́ч-ка, *n.f.*, bathing lotion. Свинцо́вая п., (*med.*), goulard. Де́лать примо́чки, to apply a lotion.

про-моч-и́ть, *v.p.*, про-ма́ч-ивать, *v.i.*, + *acc.*, to wet thoroughly. П. но́ги, to wet one's feet. П. го́рло, (*colloq.*), to have a drop of liquid, liquor; wet one's throat.

раз-моч-и́ть, *v.p.*, раз-ма́ч-ивать, *v.i.*, + *acc.*, to soak, steep. Дождь размочи́л гли́нистую зе́млю, rain soaked the clay. Раз-моч-и́ть-ся, *v.p.r.*, раз-ма́ч-ивать-ся, *v.i.r.*, to be soaked, steeped.

с-моч-и́ть, *v.p.*, с-ма́ч-ивать, *v.i.*, + *acc.*, to moisten, wet. С. тря́пку, to wet a rag. С-ма́ч-ивание, *п.п.*, moistening, wetting.

мак-а́ть, *v.i.*, to dip, sop, soak.

об-мак-ну́ть, *v.p.*, об-ма́к-ивать, *v.i.*, + *acc.*, to dip. О. перо́ в черни́льницу, to dip a pen in an inkwell. Об-ма́к-ивание, *п.п.*, dipping.

про-мак-ну́ть, *v.p.*, про-мак-а́ть, *v.i.*, + *acc.*, to blot. П. напи́санное, to blot writing. Про-мак-а́тельный, *adj.*, pertaining to, capable of, blotting. П-ая бума́га, (*recent*), blotting paper, blotter. Про-мак-а́шка, про-мок-а́шка, *п.f.*, (*colloq.*), blotter.

МОК-, МОЧ-, МК-, МЫК-, МЫЧ-, LOCK, CASTLE, LIVING WRETCHEDLY, CRAWLING

за́-мок, *п.т.*, castle; за́-мк-и, *п.т.pl.*, castles. Виндзо́рский з. в А́нглии, Windsor Castle in England. Возду́шные за́мки, castles in the air; daydreams. За́-мк-овый, *adj.*, of or pertaining to a castle. З-ая стена́, castle wall.

за-мо́к, *п.т.*, lock; (*arch.*), keystone; за-мк-и́, *п.т.pl.*, locks. Вися́чий з., padlock. Под замко́м, under lock and key. За семью́ замка́ми, (*fig.*), well-locked.

за-мо́ч-ек, *п.т.*, (*dim.*), *see* замо́к. За-мо́ч-ный, *adj.*, pertaining to a lock. З-ая сква́жина, keyhole.

за-мк-ну́ть, *v.p.*, за-мык-а́ть, *v.i.*, + *acc.*, to lock, close. З. цепь, to close a circuit. З. ше́ствие (коло́нну), to bring up the rear. За-мк-ну́ть-ся, *v.p.r.*, за-мык-а́ть-ся, *v.i.r.*, to be locked, become locked. З. в круг, to form a circle. З. в себя́, (*fig.*), to shrink into oneself. За-мык-а́ние, *п.п.*, closing, locking. З. то́ка, short circuit. Коро́ткое з., short circuit. За-мык-а́ющий, *adj.*, *part. act. pres.*, closing, locking. За́-мк-нутость, *п.f.*, reticence, reserve. За́-мк-нутый, *adj.*, reserved, closed, buttoned up. З. хара́ктер, reserved, reticent personality. За́-мк-нуто, *adv.*, in a secluded way. Жить з., to lead a secluded life.

мы́к-а-ть, *v.i.*, *used mostly in expression*: Го́ре мы́кать, (*folk, poet.*), to live in misery. Го́ре-мы́к-а, *п.т.*, (*colloq.*), poor wretch. Го́ре-мы́ч-ный, *adj.*, *also used as a noun*, wretched, miserable. Мы́к-ать-ся, *v.i.r.*, to knock about. М. по́ свету, (*colloq.*), to knock about the world, lead a wretched life.

от-мык-а́ть, *v.i.*, ото-мк-ну́ть, *v.p.*, + *acc.*, to unlock, unbolt. О. дверь (замо́к), to unlock a door (open a lock). От-мык-а́ть-ся, *v.i.r.*, ото-мк-

ну́ть-ся, *v.p.r.*, to become unlocked. Дверь отомкну́лась, the door opened, became unlocked. От-мы́ч-ка, *п.f.*, master-key; skeleton key.

по-мык-а́ть, *v.i.*, to dominate. П. ке́м-либо, to dominate someone.

пере-мык-а́ть, *v.i.*, пере-мк-ну́ть, *v.p.*, + *acc.*, to connect with a crosspiece. Пе-ре-мы́ч-ка, *п.f.*, straight arch; bulkhead; cross-piece. Соедини́ть перемы́ч-кой, to connect with a cross-piece.

при-мык-а́ть, *v.i.*, при-мк-ну́ть, *v.p.*, к + *dat.*, + *acc*, to join; fix; adjoin, border. П. штыки́, (*mil.*), to fix bayonets. Кана́да примыка́ет к Соединён-ным Шта́там, Canada borders on the United States.

раз-мык-а́ть, *v.i.*, разо-мк-ну́ть, *v.p.*, + *acc.*, to break, open. Р. ток, to disconnect an electric current. Р. строй, to open ranks. Раз-мык-а́ние, *п.п.*, breaking, disconnecting.

раз-мы́к-ать, *v.p.*, + *acc.*, (*folk.*), to shake off. Р. го́ре, (*idiom.*), to shake off one's grief.

с-мык-а́ть, *v.i.*, со-мк-ну́ть, *v.p.*, *smf.*, + *acc.*, to close. С. глаза́, to close one's eyes. Не с. глаз, not to sleep a wink. С. ряды́ (*mil.*), to close ranks. С-мык-а́ть-ся, *v.i.r.*, со-мк-ну́ть-ся, *v.p.r.*, to close, be closed. Глаза́ смыка́ются от уста́лости, my eyes are closing from fatigue.

с-мы́ч-ка, *п.f.*, clamp; union. С. го́рода с дере́вней, (*recent*), union between town and country. С-мы́ч-ный, *adj.*, (*gram.*), occlusive. С-мыч-о́к, *п.т.*, bow. С-мыч-ко́вый, *adj.*, bow. С-ые инструме́нты, bowed instruments.

пре-с-мык-а́ть-ся, *v.i.r.*, перед + *instr.*, to creep, crawl; (*fig.*), grovel. П. перед властя́ми, бога́тством, to grovel before the authorities, money. Пре-с-мык-а́тельство, *п.п.*, (*derog.*), groveling. Пре-с-мык-а́ющийся, *adj. part. act. pres.*, creeping, crawling, groveling. П-ющееся, *used as п.п.*, reptile.

у-мык-а́ть, *v.i.*, + *acc.*, (*obs.*), to abduct (a bride). У. неве́сту, (*hist.*), to abduct a bride. У-мык-а́ние, *п.п.*, abduction.

МОЛ-, МАЛ-, PRAYER

мол-и́ть, *v.i.*, + *acc.*, о + *prep.*, to pray; entreat, implore. М. о пощя́де, to cry for mercy. Мол-и́ть-ся, *v.i.r.*, по-мол-и́ть-ся, вз-мол-и́ть-ся, *v.p.r.*, *dat.*, о + *prep.*, to pray, offer prayers; adore. Мол-и́тва, *п.f.*, prayer. Мол-и́твенник, *п.f.*, prayer book. Мол-и́твенный, *adj.*, prayerful, devout.

вы́-мол-ить, *v.p.*, вы-ма́л-ивать, *v.i.*, +

acc., to get, obtain by entreaties, prayer. В. прощение, to obtain forgiveness through prayer.

за-мол-и́ть, *v.p.,* за-ма́л-ивать, *v.i.,* + *acc.,* to atone through prayer. З. грехи́, to atone for one's sins through prayer.

у-мол-и́ть, *v.p.,* + *acc.,* to obtain by entreaties. У. жесто́кого челове́ка, to obtain something from a cruel person by imploring, pleading. У-мол-я́ть, *v.i.,* to entreat, beseech, implore. У. о по́мощи, to plead for help. У-мол-я́ющий, *adj., part. act. pres.,* pleading, supplicatory. У. взгляд (го́лос), pleading look (voice).

мол-ьб-а́, *n.f.,* entreaty, supplication. М. о спасе́нии, a plea for salvation.

мол-е́бен, *n.m.,* мол-е́бствие, *n.n., (relig.),* short religious service. Отслужи́ть благода́рственный м., to hold a thanksgiving service. Мол-е́бствовать, *v.i.,* to sing a short church service.

мол-е́ль-ня, *n.f.,* meeting house for prayer; chapel in the home of Greek Orthodox Christians. Мол-е́ние, *n.n.,* praying, supplication. М. о ча́ше, *(Bib.),* Christ's prayer in Gethsemane.

МОЛК-, МАЛК-, МОЛЧ-, МАЛЧ-, SILENCE

мо́лк-ну-ть, *v.i.,* to grow still, silent.

за-мо́лк-нуть, *v.p.,* за-молк-а́ть, *v.i.,* to become silent, cease speaking, singing, etc. Разгово́р замо́лк, the conversation ceased.

при-мо́лк-нуть, *v.p.,* при-молк-а́ть, *v.i.,* to fall silent.

с-мо́лк-нуть, *v.p.smf.,* с-молк-а́ть, *v.i.,* to grow silent, become silent. Дневно́й шум смолк, the noises of the day died down. Выступа́вший растеря́лся и смолк, the speaker became confused and lapsed into silence.

у-мо́лк-нуть, *v.p.,* у-молк-а́ть, *v.i.,* to become silent. Она́ умо́лкла, she became silent. Гром умо́лк, the thunder stopped. У́-молк, *in expression:* Без у́молку, ceaselessly, without stopping. Без у́молку тверди́ть одно́ и то́ же, to repeat something over and over again. Без-у-мо́лч-ный, *adj.,* unceasing. Б. шум мо́ря, unceasing noise of the sea.

молч-а́-ть, *v.i.,* to keep silent. Упо́рно м., to refuse to utter a word. Вся приро́да молчи́т, all nature is silent. Молч-а́ние, *n.n.,* silence. Наруша́ть м., to break the silence. Обойти́ что́-нибудь молча́нием, to pass over silently. Молча́ние - знак согла́сия, silence is a sign of consent. Мол-ч-а́нка, *n.f., in expression:* Игра́ть в молча́нку, to play a game in which the first player to break

the silence pays a fine. Молч-али́вость, *n.f.,* taciturnity, reticence. Молч-али́вый, *adj.,* taciturn, silent. М-ое согла́сие, tacit consent. Мо́лч-а, *ger. pres., also used as adv.,* silently, tacitly. Молч-ко́м, *adv., (colloq.),* silently, in silence. Молч-о́к! Not a word!

за-молч-а́ть, *v.p.,* за-молк-а́ть, *v.i., see* за-мо́лк-нуть, *v.p.smf.,* to become silent. Ребёнок замолча́л, the child became silent. Заста́вить з. неприя́тельскую батаре́ю, to silence the enemy's battery.

за-ма́лч-ивать, *v.i.,* + *acc., (colloq.),* to ignore; keep silent about. Кри́тика зама́лчивала но́вый рома́н, the critics ignored the new novel. За-ма́лч-иваться, *v.i.r.,* to be ignored. Этот вопро́с стара́тельно зама́лчивается, this question is carefully ignored.

от-молч-а́ться, *v.p.r.,* от-ма́лч-иваться, *v.i.r.,* to keep silent, keep mum, keep something to oneself. Его́ спроси́ли, а он отмолча́лся, they asked him but he kept silent.

по-молч-а́ть, *v.p.,* to be silent for a while. По-молч-и́те, be silent. По-ма́лк-ивать, *v.i.,* to lapse into occasional silence. По-ма́лк-ивай, *(colloq.),* keep silent at least from time to time.

про-молч-а́ть, *v.p., see* молча́ть. Они́ промолча́ли весь ве́чер, they kept silent all evening.

с-мол-ча́ть, *v.p., (colloq.),* to hold one's tongue. Он уме́ет во́-время с., he knows when to hold his tongue.

у-молч-а́ть, *v.p.,* у-ма́лч-ивать, *v.i.,* о + *prep.,* to pass over in silence. Газе́ты умолча́ли об э́том, the newspapers ignored this event. У-ма́лч-ивать-ся, *v.i.r.,* о + *prep.,* to be held back, be hushed up. Об э́том ума́лчивается, this is not mentioned. У-ма́лч-ивание, *n.n.,* ignoring. У-молч-а́ние, *n.n.,* passing over in silence; failure to mention.

в-тих-о-мо́лк-у, *adv.,* on the quiet; surreptitiously.

МОЛ-, МАЛ-, МЕЛ-, GRINDING, MILLING

мол-о́-ть, *v.i.,* с-мол-о́ть, *v.p.,* + *acc.,* to grind, mill. М. зерно́, to grind grain. М. ко́фе, to grind coffee. М. вздор, *(colloq.),* to talk nonsense.

до-мол-о́ть, *v.p.,* до-ма́л-ывать, *v.i.,* + *acc.,* to finish grinding. Д. всё зерно́, to finish grinding all the grain.

из-мол-о́ть, *v.p.,* из-ма́л-ывать, *v.i.,* + *acc.,* to grind through.

на-мол-о́ть, *v.p.,* на-ма́л-ывать, *v.i.,* + *acc.,* + *gen.,* to grind, mill a given quantity. Н. мешо́к зерна́, to grind a bag of grain.

пере-мол-о́ть, *v.p.*, пере-ма́л-ывать, *v.i.*, + *acc.*, to grind, mill anew, thoroughly. П. всё ко́фе, to grind all the coffee. Переме́лется - мука́ бу́дет, (*saying*), things will turn out all right.

по-мол-о́ть, *v.p.*, + *acc.*, to grind for a while. По-мо́л, *n.m.*, grinding. Мука́ ме́лкого помо́ла, finely ground flour.

про-мол-о́ть, *v.p.*, про-ма́л-ывать, *v.i.*, + *acc.*, to grind everything to the end.

раз-мол-о́ть, *v.p.*, раз-ма́л-ывать, *v.i.*, + *acc.*, to grind thoroughly. Раз-мо́л, *n.m.*, grind, grist. Кру́пный р., coarse grind. Ме́лкий р., fine grind. Коли́чество размо́ла, amount of grist.

ме́л-ь-ниц-а, *n.f.*, mill. Ручна́я м., handmill. Ветряна́я м., windmill. Лить во́ду на чью-либо ме́льницу, (*saying*), to serve somebody's cause. Ме́л-ь-ник, *n.m.*, miller. Ме́л-ь-ничиха, *n.f.*, miller's wife. Ме́л-ь-ничный, *adj.*, mill. М-ая плоти́на, mill dam.

МЕЛК-, МЕЛЬЧ-, МЕЛОЧ-, МЕЛ(Ь), SMALL, SHALLOW

ме́лк-ий, *adj.*, shallow, small (fine), trifling, insignificant, petty. М-ое зерно́, small grain. М. дождь, fine rain, drizzle. М-ое хозя́йство, farming on a small scale. М-ой ры́сью, at a gentle trot. М. ручей, shallow stream. М-ая таре́лка, flat dinner plate. М. челове́к, petty person. Ме́лк-о, *adv.*, fine, in small particles. М. моло́ть, grind finely. М. писа́ть, to write in a small, delicate hand. Ме́льч-е, *adj.*, *comp.*, shallower, finer. Мельч-а́йший, *adj.* *superl.*, smallest, finest. М. узо́р, fine design. Мелк-о-зерни́стый, *adj.*, small grained. М-ая рожь, small grain rye. Мелк-ота́, *n.f.*, smallness, pettiness, meanness; (*colloq.*), small fry. Мел-юзга́, *n.f.*, (*colloq.*), small fry.

ме́лоч-ь, *n.f.*, small change; trifle, insignificant point. Кру́пные де́ньги я истра́тил, оста́лась то́лько м., I spent the large notes, only small change remains. Ме́лочи жи́зни, the trifles of life. Разме́ниваться на ме́лочи, (*fig.*), to waste time, energy on trifles. Ме́лочность, *n.f.*, meanness, pettiness, triviality. Ме́лоч-ный, *adj.*, small-minded, petty, mean-spirited. М. челове́к, petty person. Мелоч-но́й, *adj.*, in retail, of small wares, goods. М. торго́вец, retailer, dealer in groceries, small wares. М-а́я торго́вля, selling of small wares, goods in retail, groceries.

мельч-а́ть, *v.i.*, из-мельч-а́ть, *v.p.*, to become small, shallow; degenerate. Из-

мельч-а́ние, *n.n.*, action of becoming shallow; degeneration, lowering of moral standards.

мельч-и́ть, *v.i.*, + *acc.*, to grind finely, reduce to fragments. Из-мельч-и́ть, *v.p.* + *acc.*, to reduce to fragments. И. ще́бень, to crush stone into gravel. Из-мельч-е́ние, *n.n.*, reduction to fragments.

раз-мельч-и́ть, *v.p.*, раз-мельч-а́ть, *v.i.* + *acc.*, to crush into bits, pulverize. Раз-мельч-е́ние, *n.n.*, pulverization.

мел-ь, *n.f.*, shoal. Подво́дная м., bank, bar. Снять су́дно с ме́ли, to set a ship afloat. От-мел-ь, *n.f.*, bank, shallow, shoal.

мел-е́ть, *v.i.*, об-мел-е́ть, *v.p.*, to become shallow. Река́ обмеле́ла, the river became shallow. Об-мел-е́ние, *n.n.*, shallowing.

МОЛОТ-, МЛАТ-, МОЛОЧ-, МОЛАЧ-, HAMMER; THRESHING

мо́лот, *n.m.*, hammer. Кузне́чный мо́лот, sledge hammer. Паро́вой м., steam hammer. Молот-о́к, *n.m.*, (*dim.*), little hammer. Столя́рный м., carpenter's hammer. Молот-о-бо́ец, *n.m.*, hammer man, blacksmith's striker. Прода́ть с молотка́ (с аукцио́на), to auction off.

млат, *n.m.*, (*Ch.-Sl.*), hammer; *see* мо́лот. Так тя́жкий млат, дробя́ стекло́, куёт була́т, (*Pushkin*), thus the heavy hammer can crush glass and also forge steel.

молот-и́ть, молоч-у́, *v.i.*, с-молот-и́ть, *v.p.*, + *acc.*, to thresh. М. хлеб (пшени́цу), to thresh grain (wheat). Молот-и́ть-ся, *v.i.r.*, + *instr.*, to be threshed. Хлеб моло́тится молоти́лкой, grain is threshed with a threshing machine. Молот-и́льщик, *n.m.*, thresher. Молот-ь-ба́, *n.f.*, threshing. М. хле́ба, threshing of grain. Молоч-е́ние, *n.n.*, (*recent*), threshing. Молочёный, *adj.*, threshed. На гумне́ лежи́т м-ая рожь, threshed rye lies on the threshing floor. Молот-и́лка, *n.f.*, threshing machine. Молот-и́льный, *adj.*, pertaining to threshing. М-ая маши́на, threshing machine.

на-молот-и́ть, *v.p.*, на-мола́ч-ивать, *v.i.* + *acc.*, to thresh a quantity. На-мола́ч-ивать-ся, *v.i.r.*, to be threshed in quantity. На-моло́ч-енный, *adj.*, *part. pass. past*, threshed.

об-молот-и́ть, *v.p.*, об-мола́ч-ивать, *v.i.* + *acc.*, to thresh thoroughly. Об-мола́ч-ивать-ся, *v.i.r.*, об-молот-и́ть-ся, *v.p.r.*, + *instr.*, to be thoroughly threshed. Зерно́ пло́хо обмола́чивается при сыро́й пого́де, grain is poorly threshed in damp weather. Об-молóт, *n.m.*, threshing; yield of grain in threshing. Хорóший о., good yield. Порá обмолóта, threshing season. Об-молóч-енный, *adj., part. pass. past*, threshed.

с-молот-и́ть, *v.p.,* с-молáч-ивать, *v.i.,* + *acc., see* молоти́ть. С. овёс, to thresh oats. С-молáч-ивать-ся, *v.i.r.,* to be threshed.

у-молóт, *n.m.,* yield of grain after threshing. Хорóший у., good, large yield. Большóй у., large yield. У-мо-лóт-ный, *adj.,* pertaining to yield of grain.

МУ́Ж-, MAN, MASCULINITY

муж, *n.m.,* husband; man; муж-ья́, *pl.,* husbands. Му́ж-и, *(obs.),* warriors in medieval Russia. Муж-енёк, *n.m., (colloq.),* my dear husband.

муж-á-ть, *v.i., (obs.),* to reach manhood. Муж-áть-ся, *v.i.r., used in imper.,* to take heart, courage. Мужáйтесь, друзья́, Courage, friends! Му́ж-ество, *n.n.,* courage, fortitude. Проявить м., to show courage. Имéть м. говори́ть пра́вду, to have the courage to speak the truth. Му́ж-ественность, *n.f.,* manliness, virility, manhood. Му́ж-ествен-ный, *adj.,* manly, manful. М. хара́ктер, virile, strong character.

муж-чи́на, *n.m.,* man, male. Муж-скóй, *adj.,* masculine, male. Мужскóй род, *(gram.),* masculine gender. Мужскóе пла́тье, men's clothes. Муж-скóй пол, male sex. М. портнóй, gentlemen's tailor. Муж-е-подóбный *(adj.),* man-like, mannish, masculine. М-ая же́нщи-на, masculine-looking woman.

муж-и́к, *n.m., (obs.),* Russian peasant; *(colloq.),* fellow; man, husband; *(derog.),* boor. Муж-и́чка, *n.f., (obs.),* coarse, vulgar woman. Муж-икова́тый, *adj.,* rustic; boorish. Муж-и́цкий, *adj.,* rustic, boorish; peasant.

воз-муж-áть, *v.p.,* to grow up, grow into manhood, reach manhood; *see* мужáть. За послéдний год он си́льно возмужáл, during this past year he has become more manly. Воз-муж-áлость, *n.f.,* maturity, virility. Воз-муж-áлый, *adj.,* mature, virile, grown up. Вы́гля-деть возмужáлым, to look virile, manly.

зá-муж, *adv., in expression:* Вы́йти за когó-либо з., to marry *(of a woman).* Вы́дать когó-либо з., to give someone in marriage *(of a woman).* Зá-муж-ем, married. Быть з. за кéм-либо, to be married. За-муж-ество, *n.n.,* married state, married life. За-муж-няя, *n.f.,*

married woman. З. же́нщина, married woman.

МУК-, МУЧ-, FLOUR

мук-á, *n.f.,* flour, meal. Ржана́я м., rye flour. Пшени́чная м., wheat flour. Перемéлется - мукá бýдет, *(saying),* in the end everything will turn out all right.

мук-о-мóл, *n.m.,* miller. Мук-о-мóльный, *adj.,* pertaining to flour grinding. М. завóд, flour mill. Мук-о-мóльня, *n.f.,* flour mill.

муч-ни́к, *n.m.,* dealer in meal, flour. Муч-нóй, *adj.,* meal, flour, tarch. М. мешóк, flour sack. М-áя ла́вка, flour shop. М-áя пи́ща, starchy food. Муч-нóе, *adj.,* used as *n.,* farinaceous, starchy food. Не есть мучнóго, to be on a non-starch diet. Мучни́стый, *adj.,* farinaceous. М-ы́е óвощи, starchy vegetables.

МУ́К-, МУЧ-, TORTURE, TORMENT

му́к-а, *n.f.,* torment, torture. Му́ки болéзни, suffering caused by an illness. Му́ки рéвности, pangs of jealousy. Му́ки тво́рчества, throes of creation. Му́ка мне с тобóй, *(colloq.),* the trouble you give me. Хождéние по му́кам, *(fig.),* life, road full of suffering.

муч-éние, *n.n.,* torture, torment. Му́ч-еник, *n.m.,* му́ч-еница, *n.f.,* martyr. Му́ч-еничество, *n.n.,* martyrdom. Му́ч-енический, *adj.,* martyr. М-ая смéрть, a martyr's death.

муч-и-ть, *v.i.,* + *acc.,* to torment, harass, worry. Её му́чит ка́шель, a cough is causing her great suffering. Это мýчит мою́ сóвесть, it lies heavy on my conscience. Му́ч-ить-ся, *v.i.r.,* to worry, suffer. М. над зада́чей, to take a lot of trouble over a problem. Муч-и́тель, *n.m.,* tormentor, torturer. Муч-и́тель-ный, *adj.,* painful, agonizing; unbearable. М-ая болéзнь, painful illness.

вы́-муч-ить, *v.p.,* вы-му́ч-ивать, *v.i.,* + *acc.,* to extort; *(colloq.),* squeeze out. В. из себя́ мысль, to squeeze out an idea. Вы́-муч-енный, *adj. part. pass. past,* extorted, forced. В-ое призна́ние, an extorted confession.

за-му́ч-ить, *v.p.,* за-му́ч-ивать, *v.i.,* + *acc.,* to torture, wear out, tire out. З. до смéрти, to torture to death.

из-му́ч-ить, *v.p.,* из-му́ч-ивать, *v.i.,* + *acc.,* to exhaust. Непоси́льная рабóта изму́чила меня́, work beyond my strength has exhausted me. Из-му́ч-ить-ся, *v.p.r.,* из-му́ч-ивать-ся, *v.i.r.,* to exhaust oneself. Из-му́ч-енный, *adj.*, *part. pass. past,* exhausted, worn out. И. боле́знью, exhausted by illness.

на-му́ч-ить-ся, *v.p.r.,* to be troubled, have much trouble with. Он тяжёлый челове́к, с ним наму́чишься, (*colloq.*), he's a difficult man, you'll have trouble with him.

пере-му́ч-ить-ся, *v.p.r.,* (*colloq.*), to suffer much. Но́чью мы си́льно перему́чились от хо́лода, during the night we suffered very much from the cold.

по-му́ч-ить, *v.p.,* + *acc.,* to torment a while. По-му́ч-ить-ся, *v.p.r.,* to suffer a little, take pains. Я помучился над реше́нием зада́чи, I took pains over the solution of this problem.

про-му́ч-ить, *v.p.,* + *acc.,* + *instr.,* to torment for a while. П. го́лодом це́лый день, to torment by starving all day. Про-му́ч-ить-ся, *v.p.r.,* to torment oneself, suffer. П. над чём-либо, to worry over something.

МУТ-, МУЧ-, МУЩ-, МЯТ-, DISTURBANCE, MUTINY

мут-и́ть, муч-у́, *v.i.,* за-мут-и́ть, по-мут-и́ть, *v.p.,* + *acc.,* to disturb, stir up. М. во́ду, to make water cloudy. Мути́ть наро́д, (*fig.*), to stir up the people. Меня́ мути́т, I feel sick. Мут-и́ть-ся, *v.i.r.,* за-мут-и́ть-ся, по-мут-и́ть-ся, *v.p.r.,* to become turbid, dull, blurred. Вода́ замути́лась, the water became turbid. Ра́зумом помути́ться, to go mad.

мут-не́-ть, *v.i.,* по-мут-не́ть, *v.p.,* to grow turbid, muddy, dim. Му́т-ность, *n.f.,* turbidity, dullness. М. воды́, turbidity of water. Му́т-ный, *adj.,* turbid, dull, cloudy, muddy. М-ое стекло́, frosted, opaque, translucent glass. М-ое созна́ние, cloudy, confused consciousness. В му́тной во́де ры́бу лови́ть, (*saying*), to fish in troubled waters. Мут-ь, *n.f.,* turbidity, muddiness. О́-мут, *n.m.,* eddy, deep spot (in water). В ти́хом о́муте че́рти во́дятся, (*saying*) still waters run deep. По-мут-не́ние, *n.n.,* blurring; action of becoming cloudy, dull, turbid. П. зре́ния, blurring of vision.

воз-мут-и́ть, *v.p.,* воз-мущ-а́ть, *v.i.,* + *acc.,* to perturb; incite to revolt; arouse indignation. Его́ дурно́й посту́пок возмути́л меня́, his bad action aroused my indignation. Воз-му́т-ить-ся, *v.p.r.,* воз-мущ-а́ть-ся, *v.i.r.,* + *instr.,* to be filled with indignation, be exasperated; rebel. Все возмуща́лись его́ слова́ми, everyone was indignant at his words. Воз-мущ-е́ние, *n.n.,* in-

dignation; rebellion. Воз-мущ-ённый, *adj., part. pass. past,* outraged, indignant. В. го́лос (жест), indignant voice (gesture). Воз-мут-и́тельный, *adj.,* outrageous, revolting, disgraceful, shocking. В. посту́пок, disgraceful action. Воз-мут-и́тельно, *adv.,* outrageously, disgracefully, shockingly.

на-мут-и́ть, *v.p.,* (*colloq.*), to make muddy; trouble, disturb very much. Он во всём до́ме намути́л, he disturbed the whole house.

пере-мут-и́ть, *v.p.,* + *acc.,* to set at variance; upset. Эта же́нщина всю дере́вню перемути́ла, this woman upset the whole village.

с-мут-и́ть, *v.p.,* с-мущ-а́ть, *v.i.,* + *acc.,* to confuse; embarrass. С. душе́вный поко́й, to disturb one's peace of mind. С. кого́-либо похвало́й, to embarrass someone through praise. С-мут-и́ть-ся, *v.p.r.,* с-мущ-а́ть-ся, *v.i.r.,* to become confused, embarrassed. С-мущ-е́ние, *n.n.,* confusion, diffidence, embarrassment. Красне́ть от смуще́ния, to blush from embarrassment. С-мущ-ённый, *adj., part. pass. past,* confused, embarrassed. С. взор, confused look. С-му́т-а, *n.f.,* disturbance; sedition; disorder. Се́ять сму́ту, to sow disorder, rebellion. С-му́т-ный, *adj.,* vague, dim. С-ое представле́ние, dim, vague idea. С-ые воспомина́ния, dim memories. Сму́тное Вре́мя, (*hist.*), period in Russian history known as *The Time of Troubles* (1605-1613). С-му́т-но, *adv.,* vaguely, dimly. С-мут-ь-я́н, *n.m.,* (*colloq.*), troublemaker; seditionary.

мят-е́ж, *n.m.,* rebellion, insurrection, mutiny, revolt. Мят-е́жник, *n.m.,* rebel, insurgent, mutineer. Мят-е́жный, *adj.,* rebellious, mutinous; restless. М-ая душа́, restless soul. М-ые войска́, rebel troops. Без-мят-е́жность, *n.f.,* serenity, tranquility. Без-мят-е́жный, *adj.,* serene, tranquil. Мят-е́ль, *n.f.,* see мете́ль, snowstorm.

с-мят-е́ние, *n.n.,* confusion, disturbance, alarm. Приводи́ть в с., to perturb.

су-мя́т-ица, *n.f.,* bustler.

МЫ-, МО-, МОЙ-, WASHING

мы́-л-о, *n.n.,* soap. Жи́дкое м., soft soap, liquid soap. Туале́тное м., toilet soap. Мыл-о-ва́р, *n.m.,* soap boiler. Мыл-о-варе́ние, *n.n.,* process of boiling soap. Мыл-о-ва́ренный, *adj.,* pertaining to the manufacture of soap. Мы́-ль-ница, *n.f.,* soap dish. Мы́-ль-ный, *adj.,* soapy, soap. М-ая пе́на, lather, soap suds. М. пузы́рь, soap bubble. Пуска́ть м-ые пузыри́, to blow soap bubbles.

Мы́-л-кий, *adj.,* lathery, soapy. Об-мы́-лок, *n.m.,* remnant of soap.

мы́-л-ить, *v.i.,* на-мы́-лить, *v.p.,* + *acc.,* to soap, lather. М. ру́ки, to soap one's hands. Н. го́лову кому́-либо, (*fig.*), to scold someone. Мы́-лить-ся, *v.i.,* на-мы́-лить-ся, *v.p.,* to soap, lather oneself.

из-мы́-л-ить, *v.p.,* из-мы́-ливать, *v.i.,* + *acc.,* to use up, consume soap. И. всё мы́ло, to use up all the soap.

на-мы́-л-ить, *v.p., see* мы́лить. На-мы́-ливать, *v.i.,* + *acc.,* to rub, cover with soap. Н. ру́ки (го́лову), to lather one's hands (head, hair).

мы́-ть, мо́-ю, *v.i.,* по-мы́-ть, *v.p.,* + *acc.,* + *instr.,* to wash. М. посу́ду, to wash dishes. М. щёткой, to scrub. М. гу́бкой, to sponge. Мы́-ть-ся, *v.i.r.,* по-мы́-ть-ся, *v.p.r.,* to wash oneself. Мы-тьё, *n.n.,* washing. Не мытьём - так ката́ньем, (*saying*), by hook, or by crook. Мо́й-ка, *n.f.,* washing. Голов-о-мо́й-ка, *n.f.,* (*colloq.*), scolding. Зада́ть кому́-либо г-у, to scold someone. Пол-о-мо́й-ка, *n.f.,* scrubwoman, charwoman. По-мо́и, *n.pl.,* slops. По-мо́й-ка, *n.f.,* slop, garbage pit. По-мо́й-ный, *adj.,* pertaining to refuse, garbage. П-ое ведро́, garbage pail. П-ая я́ма, garbage pit. Суд-о-мо́й-ка, *n.f.,* kitchen maid.

вы́-мы-ть, *v.p.,* вы-мы-ва́ть, *v.i.,* + *acc.,* to wash, wash away. В. ру́ки, to wash one's hands. В. ребёнка в ва́нне, to wash a child in a bathtub. Вы́-мы-ть-ся, *v.p.r.,* вы-мы-ва́ть-ся, *v.i.r.,* to wash oneself, be washed.

до-мы́-ть, *v.p.,* до-мы-ва́ть, *v.i.,* to finish washing. Д. пол, to finish washing the floor.

за-мы́-ть, *v.p.,* за-мы-ва́ть, *v.i.,* + *acc.,* (*colloq.*), to wash off, wash away. З. пятно́ на ска́терти, to wash out a spot on a tablecloth.

из-мы-ва́ть-ся, *v.p.r.,* + *instr.,* (*colloq.*), to treat cruelly.

на-мы́-ть, *v.p.,* на-мы-ва́ть, *v.i.,* + *acc.,* + *gen.,* to wash a quantity. Н. золото́го песку́, to pan a quantity of gold dust.

об-мы́-ть, *v.p.,* об-мы-ва́ть, *v.i.,* + *acc.,* to bathe, wash completely. О. ра́ну, to wash a wound, bathe a wound. Об-мы́-ть-ся, *v.p.r.,* об-мы-ва́ть-ся, *v.i.r.,* to have a complete bath. Об-мы-ва́ние, *n.n.,* bathing, washing.

о-мы́-ть, *v.p.,* о-мы-ва́ть, *v.i.,* + *acc.,* to wash. Áфрику омыва́ют два океа́на, Africa's shores are washed by two oceans. О-мы́-тый, *adj., part. pass. past,* washed. О-мы́-тый дождём, washed by rain. О-мов-éние, *n.n.,*

ablution. О. рук, (*rel.*), washing of hands.

от-мы́-ть, *v.p.,* от-мы-ва́ть, *v.i.,* + *acc.,* to wash away, out, off. О. гли́ну (са́жу), to wash away clay (soot). От-мы́-ть-ся, *v.p.r.,* от-мы-ва́ть-ся, *v.i.r.,* to wash oneself, be washed off. Черни́ла не отмы́лись, the ink did not wash off.

пере-мы́-ть, *v.p.,* пере-мы-ва́ть, *v.i.,* + *acc.,* to wash anew; wash completely. П. всю посу́ду, to wash all the dishes. Перемыва́ть кому́-либо ко́сточки, (*colloq.*), to gossip about someone. На́до пол перемы́ть, the floor has to be washed.

под-мы́-ть, *v.p.,* под-мы-ва́ть, *v.i.,* + *acc.,* to undermine with water. Река́ подмы́ла берега́, the river has undermined the banks. Меня́ так и подмыва́ет, (*fig.*), I feel an irresistible longing. Под-мы́-ть-ся, *v.p.r.,* под-мы-ва́ть-ся, *v.i.r.,* to be washed away. Под-мы-ва́ние, *n.n.,* washing. Под-мы́в, *n.m.,* erosion, washing away.

про-мы́-ть, *v.p.,* про-мы-ва́ть, *v.i.,* + *acc.,* to wash thoroughly. В жёсткой воде́ нельзя́ п. во́лосы, you cannot wash your hair properly in hard water. П. и перевяза́ть ра́ну, to wash and bandage a wound. Вода́ промы́ла плоти́ну, the river has washed out the dam. Про-мы-ва́ние, *n.n.,* (*med.*), irrigation. П. желу́дка, lavage of the stomach. Про-мы́-вка, *n.f.,* washing through. Про-мы-ва́тельный, *adj.,* (*med.*), pertaining to an irrigation.

раз-мы́-ть, *v.p.,* раз-мы-ва́ть, *v.i.,* + *acc.,* to wash away; erode. Река́ размы́ла бе́рег, the river eroded the banks. Раз-мы́в, *n.m.,* erosion. Р. плоти́ны, bursting of a dike. Раз-мы-ва́ние, *n.n.,* washing out, away.

с-мыть, *v.p.,* с-мы-ва́ть, *v.i.,* + *acc.,* to wash off, wash overboard. Волна́ смы́ла матро́са за борт, a wave washed the sailor overboard. С. оби́ду, to wipe out an insult. С-мы́-ть-ся, *v.p.r.,* с-мы-ва́ть-ся, *v.i.r.,* to wash, come off; (*slang*), disappear, slip away. Он в миг смы́лся с рабо́ты, he left his work in a twinkling.

у-мы́-ть, *v.p.,* у-мы-ва́ть, *v.i.,* + *acc.,* to wash. У. лицо́, to wash one's face. У. ру́ки, to wash one's hands (of something), deny any responsibility. У-мы́-ть-ся, *v.p.r.,* у-мы-ва́ть-ся, *v.i.r.,* to wash oneself, be washed. У-мы-ва́ние, *n.n.,* washing. Для умыва́ния, for washing oneself. У-мы-ва́льная, *adj., used as n.,* washroom. У-мы-ва́льник, *n.m.,* washstand. У-мы-ва́льный, *adj.,* washing, wash. У. таз, wash basin.

МЫСЛ-, МЫСЕЛ-, МЫШЛ-, THOUGHT

мысл-ь, *n.f.,* thought, reflection; conception, idea. Внеза́пная м., sudden thought. Основна́я м., basic idea, conception. Образ мы́слей, views, opinions. Не допуска́ть да́же мы́сли о чём-либо, even not to dare think of something. Мы́сл-енный, *adj.,* mental. М. о́браз, mental image. Мы́сл-енно, *adv.,* mentally.

мы́сл-и-ть, *v.i.,* + *acc.,* to think, conceive. М. логи́чески, to think logically. Мышл-е́ние, *n.n.,* thinking, thought. Мысл-и́тель, *n.m.,* thinker. Мысл-и́тельный, *adj.,* thinking; pertaining to thought. М-ые спосо́бности, understanding; intellectual capacities. Мы́слящий, *adj., part. act. pres.,* thinking. Мы́сл-имый, *adj.,* conceivable, thinkable. М-ое-ли э́то де́ло? (*colloq.*), Is it possible? Не-мы́сл-имый, *adj.,* inconceivable, unthinkable. Э́то немы́слимо, it is impossible, inconceivable. Мысл-е́те, *n.n.,* Church Slavonic name for the letter М.

вы́-мысл-ить, *v.p.,* вы-мышл-я́ть, *v.i.,* (*obs.*), invent, conceive. Вы́-мысел, *n.m.,* invention; falsehood, lie (*poet.*), fancy. Э́то сплошно́й в., it is pure invention. Вы́-мышл-енный, *adj., part. pass. past,* invented, imaginary, fictitious. До́-мысел, *n.m.,* conjecture, fantasy. Не-до-мы́сл-ие, *n.n.,* stupidity, thoughtlessness.

за-мы́сл-ить, *v.p.,* за-мышл-я́ть, *v.i.,* + *acc.,* to plan, intend. Что вы замышля́ете? What are you plotting? За́-мысел, *n.m.,* project, plan, intention; scheme, conception. З. худо́жественного произведе́ния, the conception of a work of art. З. нау́чного иссле́дования, scientific research project. За-мысл-ова́тость, *n.f.,* intricacy. За-мысл-ова́тый, *adj.,* intricate, complicated. З-ая крестосло́вица, intricate crossword puzzle.

из-мы́сл-ить, *v.p.,* из-мышл-я́ть, *v.i.,* + *acc.,* to contrive, fabricate. Из-мышл-е́ние, *n.n.,* fabrication; prevarication.

по-мы́сл-ить, *v.p.,* по-мышл-я́ть, *v.i.,* о + *prep.* (*colloq.*), to think about, dream of. О жени́тьбе пока́ и не помышля́йте, don't even think of marriage for the time being.

про-мы́сл-ить, *v.p.,* про-мышл-я́ть, *v.i.,* + *acc.,* + *instr.,* (*obs.*), to get, obtain, procure; earn one's living. Промышля́ть охо́той, to earn one's living by hunting. Про-мы́шл-енность, *n.f.,* industry. Тяжёлая п., heavy industry. Лёгкая п., light industry. Основны́е о́трасли п-ости, main branches of industry. Промы́шл-енный, *adj.,* industrial. П. капита́л, industrial capital. П. переворо́т в Англии, (*hist.*), the Industrial Revolution in England. П-ые запа́сы, industrial reserves. Про-мы́шл-енник, *n.m.,* industrialist, manufacturer. Про́мысел, *n.m.,* trade, business. Куста́рный п., domestic industry. Ры́бные про́мыслы, fishery. Бо́г-промысел, *n.m.* Providence. Бо́жественный П., Divine Providence. Про-мысл-о́вый, *adj.,* trade. П-ая коопера́ция, trade cooperation. П-ое свиде́тельство, trade license.

раз-мы́сл-ить, *v.p.,* раз-мышл-я́ть, *v.i.,* о + *prep.,* to reflect; meditate, ponder, muse. Р. о прочи́танном, to meditate on material read. Раз-мышл-е́ние, *n.n.,* reflection, meditation. Пять мину́т на р., five minutes for meditation, for thinking something over. Э́то наво́дит на р-ия, it makes one wonder. Погрузи́ться в р-ия, to be lost in thought, in meditation.

с-мы́сл-ить, *v.p.,* с-мышл-я́ть, *v.i.,* (*colloq.*) to understand. Она́ ничего́ в э́том не смы́слит, she is incapable of understanding it. С-мысл, *n.m.,* sense, meaning. Прямо́й (перено́сный) смысл, literal (figurative) meaning. Здра́вый с., sound common sense. Нет никако́го смы́сла, there is no meaning to this. С-мысл-ово́й, *adj.,* meaning. С-ы́е отте́нки, shades of meaning. Бес-смы́сл-ица, *n.f.,* nonsense, absurdity. Бес-смы́сл-енность, *n.f.,* senselessness, foolishness. Бес-смы́сл-енный, *adj.,* senseless, foolish, silly, Б. посту́пок, senseless action. Б. взгляд, vacant, insipid look. Бес-смы́сл-енно, *adv.,* senselessly, foolishly. Б. улыбну́ться, to smile inanely. Э́то б., it is silly, foolish. С-мышл-ённость, *n.f.,* cleverness, smartness. С-мышл-ёный, *adj.,* clever, bright. С. па́рень, (*colloq.*), clever young man.

о-с-мы́сл-ить, *v.p.,* о-с-мысл-я́ть, о-с-мы́сл-ивать, *v.i.,* + *acc.,* to comprehend, interpret. На́до по но́вому осмы́слить происходя́щие собы́тия, it is necessary to interpret present events from a new approach. О-с-мысл-я́ть-ся, *v.i.r.,* о-с-мы́сл-ить-ся, *v.p.r.,* to be comprehended. О-с-мысл-е́ние, *n.n.,* comprehension. О. истори́ческих фа́ктов, (*recent*), understanding, comprehension of historical facts. О-с-мы́сл-енность, *n.f.,* comprehension. О-с-мы́сл-енный, *adj.,* intelligent, meaningful, comprehensible. О-ая речь, sensible speech. О-с-мы́сл-енно, *adv.,* comprehensibly, sensibly. Ребёнок смо́-

трит уже о., the child already shows some comprehension.

у-мы́сл-ить, *v.p.,* у-мышл-я́ть, *v.i.,* + *acc., (obs.),* to design; plot. У́-мысел, *n.m.,* design, intention, intent. Злой у., evil intent. Зло-у-мы́шл-енник, *n.m.,* malefactor. Зло-у-мы́шл-енный, *adj.,* ill-intentioned. У-мы́шленность, *n.f.,* premeditation. У-мы́шленный, *adj., part. pass. past,* designed, intentional, ill-intentioned. У-мы́шл-енность, *n.f.,* murder. У-мы́шл-енно, *adv.,* intentionally, deliberately, on purpose.

МЯГ-, МЯК-, SOFTNESS

мя́г-к-ий, *adj.,* soft; gentle, mild. М. хлеб, fresh bread. М-ое кре́сло, easy-chair. М-ая посте́ль, soft bed. М. хара́ктер, mild, gentle disposition. М-ое се́рдце, soft heart. М. кли́мат, mild climate. Мя́г-онький, *adj.,* very soft. Мя́г-кость, *n.f.,* softness; gentleness, mildness. Мя́г-ко, *adv.,* softly; gently, mildly. М. выража́ясь, to put it mildly. Мяг-к-о-серде́чие, *n.n.,* soft-heartedness. Мяг-к-о-серде́чный, *adj.,* softhearted. Мяг-к-о-те́лость, *n.f.,* limpness, flabbiness. Мяг-к-о-те́лый, *adj.,* nerveless; weak.

мяг-ч-и́-ть, *v.i.,* + *acc.,* to soften. Мягчи́тельный, *adj.,* softening. М-ые сре́дства, *(med.),* soothing medicines.

раз-мяг-ч-и́ть, *v.p.,* раз-мяг-ча́ть, *v.i.,* to soften, make soft. Р. ко́жу, to soften leather. Р. се́рдце, to touch one's heart. Раз-мяг-чи́ть-ся, *v.p.r.,* раз-мяг-ча́ть-ся, *v.i.r.,* to grow, become soft. Раз-мяг-че́ние, *n.n.,* softening. Р. мо́зга, *(med.),* softening of the brain.

с-мяг-ч-и́ть, *v.p.,* с-мяг-ча́ть, *v.i.,* + *acc.,* to soften, mollify; *(gram.),* palatalize. С. кра́ски, to tone down colors. С. гнев, to mollify one's anger. С. наказа́ние, to mitigate a punishment. С-мяг-чи́ть-ся, *v.p.r.,* с-мяг-ча́ть-ся, *v.i.r.,* to become softer; *(fig.),* kinder. С-мяг-че́ние, *n.n.,* softening; mollification; mitigation. С-мяг-ча́ющий, *adj., part. act. pres.,* mitigating, softening. С-ие вину́ обстоя́тельства, extenuating circumstances.

у-мяг-чи́ть, *v.p.,* у-мяг-ча́ть, *v.i.,* + *acc.,* to soften, make soft; mollify.

мяк-и́на, *n.f.,* chaff. Ста́рого воробья́ на мяки́не не проведёшь, *(prov.),* you cannot fool an experienced person. Мя́к-иш, *n.m.,* crumb; soft inner part of bread. Мя́к-оть, *n.f.,* flesh; pulp.

мя́к-ну-ть, *v.i.,* раз-мя́к-нуть, *v.p., (colloq.),* to soften, become pulpy, flabby. Суха́рь мя́кнет в молоке́, the cracker is becoming soft in the milk.

об-мяк-ну́-ть, *v.p.,* об-мяк-а́ть, *v.i.,* to become thoroughly soft, moist, flabby. Гли́на под дождём обмя́кла, clay became soft and moist in the rain.

от-мяк-нуть, *v.p.,* от-мяк-а́ть, *v.i.,* to grow soft, soften. Сухари́ отмя́кли, the crackers have become soft.

Н

НЕБ-, НЁБ-, FIRMAMENT, SKY, HEAVENS; PALATE

не́б-о, *n.n.,* sky, heaven. неб-еса́, *n.pl.,* the heavens. Под откры́тым не́бом, under the open sky. Быть на седьмо́м не́бе, *(fig.),* to be in seventh heaven. Превозноси́ть до небе́с, to praise, exalt to the skies. Копти́ть не́бо, *(colloq.),* to lead a useless existence. Это так далеко́, как не́бо от земли́, that is as far as heaven from earth. Неб-е́сный, *adj.,* celestial, heavenly, pertaining to the sky; divine. Н. свод, firmament. Н-ые свети́ла, the heavenly bodies. Жить, как пти́цы н-ые, to live a carefree life. Неб-о-сво́д, *n.m.,* firmament, sky; arch. Неб-о-скло́н, *n.m.,* horizon. Неб-о-скрёб, *n.m.,* skyscraper.

нёб-о, *n.n.,* palate. Твёрдое н., the hard palate. Мя́гкое н., the soft palate. Нёбный, *adj., (anat.),* pertaining to the palate; *(gram., phon.),* palatal. Н-ая занаве́ска, the uvula. Н-ые согла́сные, palatal consonants.

под-неб-е́сь-е, *n.n.,* the skies, heavens. Под-неб-е́сный, *adj. (poet.),* earthly. Под-неб-е́сная, *adj. used as n.,* sublunary sphere; universe.

НЕГ-, НЕЖ-, LANGUOR, LUXURY, TENDERNESS

не́г-а, *n.f.,* voluptuousness; languor; care, comfort. Жизнь в не́ге, a life of luxury.

не́ж-и-ть, *v.i.,* + *acc.,* to indulge, pamper, coddle. Н. дете́й, to pamper children. Н. те́ло, to pamper one's body. Не́ж-ить-ся, *v.i.r.,* to indulge in luxury. Н. на со́лнце, to bask in the sun. Н. в посте́ли, to loll in bed. Не́ж-енка, *n.f. and n.m., (colloq.),* softy, sissy.

не́ж-н-ич-ать, *v.i., (colloq.),* to indulge in endearments. Не́ж-ность, *n.f.,* neж-ности, *n.pl.,* kind words, endearments; tenderness, delicacy. Н. го́лоса, tenderness of voice. Н. души́, delicateness of a soul. Не́ж-ный, *adj.,* tender, delicate; loving, fond. Не́ж-ное здоро́вье, delicate health. Н-ый сын, loving son. Н-ый во́зраст, tender age. Раз-не́ж-нич-ать-ся, *v.p.r., (colloq.),* to grow soft.

из-не́ж-ить, *v.p.,* из-не́ж-ивать, *v.i.,* + *acc.,* to coddle; render effeminate. **◄И.** ребёнка, to spoil a child. Из-не́ж-ить-ся, *v.p.r.,* из-не́ж-ивать-ся, *v.i.r.,* to become soft, effeminate. Он изне́жился от жи́зни в ро́скоши, he became soft from a life of luxury. Из-не́ж-енность, *n.f.,* delicacy; susceptibility; effeminacy. Из-не́ж-енный, *adj.,* delicate, soft. **И.** ребёнок, delicate child.

по-не́ж-ить, *v.p.,* see не́жить, По-не́ж-ить-ся, *v.p.r.,* to luxuriate. Он лю́бит у́тром поне́житься в посте́ли, he likes to loll in bed in the morning.

раз-не́ж-ить-ся, *v.p.r.,* раз-не́ж-ивать-ся, *v.i.r.,* to soften, become soft, lazy; relax.

НЕМ-, NUMBNESS, MUTENESS

нем-е́-ть, о-нем-е-ва́ть, *v.i.,* о-нем-е́ть, *v.p.,* to become numb. Н. от восто́рга, *(fig.),* to become speechless, numb with delight. Н. от у́жаса, *(fig.),* to become numb with terror. О. от конту́зии, to lose the capacity for speech from a concussion. Нем-о́й, *adj.,* dumb, mute; *used as n.,* dumb mute. Н. призы́в, mute appeal. Н-о́е обожа́ние, mute adoration. Немо́й объясня́ется зна́ками, a mute person talks in sign language. Н-а́я ка́рта, skeleton map. Нем-ота́, *n.f.,* dumbness, muteness. О-нем-е́лость, *n.f.,* numbness. О-нем-е́лый, *adj.,* numb. О-ые ру́ки, numb hands. О-нем-е́ние, *n.n.,* numbness; paralysis.

нем-ец, *n.m.,* не́м-ка, *n.f.,* не́м-цы, *pl.,* German. Не́мцы пово́лжья, the Volga Germans. Нем-е́цкий, *adj.,* German. Н. язы́к, the German language. Говори́ть по-неме́цки, to speak German.

о-нем-е́ч-и-ть, *v.p.,* о-нем-е́чивать, *v.i.,* + *acc.,* to Teutonize, Germanize. Герма́нский наци́зм стреми́лся онеме́чить други́е цивилиза́ции, German Nazism strove to Germanize other civilizations. О-нем-е́чивание, *n.n.,* Germanization.

НЕС-, НЁС-, НОС-, НОШ-, НАШ-, CONVEYANCE, CARRYING

нес-ти́, *v.i.det.,* + *acc.,* to carry, bring; lay. Н. ребёнка к врачу́, to carry a child to the doctor's. Н. убы́тки (наказа́ние, отве́тственность), to bear a loss (penalty, responsibility). Н. обя́занности, to perform duties. Н. дежу́рство, to be on duty. От окна́ несёт хо́лодом, there is a cold draft from the window. От него́ несёт табако́м (во́дкой), *(colloq.),* he reeks of tobacco (vodka). Н. вздор, to talk nonsense. Куда́ его́ несёт?

(colloq.), Where is he going? Where is he headed? Ку́рица несёт я́йца, a hen lays eggs. Нес-ти́-сь, *v.i.r.,* to rush; fly; drift; lay *(as eggs).* Н. во весь опо́р, to ride at top speed. Э́та ку́рица хорошо́ несётся, this hen is a good layer. Нес-е́ние, *n.n.,* carrying, bearing, wearing, laying. Н. обя́занностей, performance of duties.

нос-и́-ть, нош-у́, *v.i. indet.,* to carry; wear. Н. чемода́н (кни́ги), to carry a trunk (books). Учени́к ка́ждый день но́сит кни́ги в шко́лу, the pupil carries his books to school every day. Н. пальто́ (шля́пу, сапоги́, ко́льца), to wear a coat (a hat, boots, a ring). Н. на руках́ кого́-либо, *(fig.),* to make much of someone. Куда́ их но́сит? *(colloq.),* Where are they going? Нос-и́ть-ся, *v.i.r.,* нес-ти́-сь, *v.p.r.,* to rush about, gallop; fly about; to be worn *(impf. only).* Конькобе́жец несётся по льду́, the skater is skimming over the ice. Он но́сится по степи́ на коне́, he is galloping over the steppe. Она́ но́сится со свое́й до́черью, *(colloq.),* she fusses over her daughter. Н. с мы́слью, *(fig.),* to cherish, nurse a thought, idea. Э́та мате́рия бу́дет хорошо́ носи́ться, this material will wear well. Но́с-ка, *n.f.,* wearing; carrying; bearing; laying. Но́с-кий, *adj.,* strong, durable. Нос-и́лки, *n.pl.,* stretcher; litter. Нос-и́льный, *adj., only in expression:* Н-ое бельё, underclothing, underwear. Нос-и́льщик, *n.m.,* porter, carrier. Нос-и́тель, *n.m.,* носи́тельница, *n.f.,* bearer. Н. но́вой иде́и, one who bears new ideas.

в-нес-ти́, *v.p.,* в-нос-и́ть, *v.i.,* + *acc.,* to bring in, carry in, introduce; pay. В. ве́щи в дом, to carry things into a house. В. измене́ния, (попра́вки), to introduce, insert changes (amendments). В. в спи́сок, to enter on a list. В. законопрое́кт, to introduce a bill. В-нес-е́ние, *n.n.,* introduction, insertion; carrying in; deposit. В. в спи́сок, enlisting, entry. В. законопрое́кта, introduction of a bill.

вз-нес-ти́, *v.p.,* вз-нос-и́ть, *v.i.,* + *acc.,* to pay, deposit. В. чле́нские взно́сы, to pay membership dues. Вз-нос, *n.m.,* payment, fee; deposit. Вступи́тельный в., entrance fee. Чле́нский в., membership dues.

вы́-нес-ти, *v.p.,* вы-нос-и́ть, *v.i.,* + *acc.,* to carry out, bear out; take away, remove; stand, endure, bear. В. ме́бель из ко́мнаты to take furniture out of a room. В. тяжёлые испыта́ния, to undergo severe trials. В. прия́тное (тяжёлое) впечатле́ние, to be pleasantly (painfully) impressed. В. на поля (книги), to make a marginal note. Не выносить сóра из избы, (*saying*), not to wash one's dirty linen in public. Онá егó не выносит, she cannot stand him. Вы-нес-ти-сь, *v.p.r.*, вы-нос-ить-ся, *v.i.r.*, to dart out, fly out. Трóйка вынеслась из ворóт, the troika dashed out through the gates. Вы-нос, *n.m.*, carrying, bearing out. В. покóйника, carrying out of a body. На в., (*obs.*), for consumption off the premises. Вы-нос-ка, *n.f.*, removal, taking out, carrying out; note, footnote, marginal note. Вы-нóс-ливость, *n.f.*, endurance, stamina. Вы-нóс-ливый, *adj.*, hardy, enduring. Он óчень вынослив, he is capable of great endurance. Не-вы-нос-имый, *adj.*, intolerable, unbearable, insufferable. Н-ая боль, excruciating pain. Не-вы-нос-имо, *adv.*, intolerably, unbearably, insufferably. Это н. скучно, it is insufferably dull. Вы-нос-ить, *v.p.*, вы-нáш-ивать, *v.i.*, + *acc.*, to bear; mature. В. ребёнка, to be with child.

воз-нос-и́ть, *v.i.*, воз-нес-ти́, *v.p.*, + *acc.*, to raise, lift up. "... то вознесёт егó высóко, то в бéздну брóсит без следá," (*song*), "... will raise him high, then throw him into an abyss without trace." Воз-нос-и́ть-ся, *v.i.r.*, воз-нес-ти́-сь, *v.p.r.*, to rise, tower; (*colloq.*), to become conceited. Воз-нес-éние, *n.n.*, Ascension Day.

пре-воз-нос-и́ть, *v.i.*, пре-воз-нес-ти́, *v.p.*, + *acc.*, to praise highly. П. писáтеля (чéй-нибудь талáнт), to praise a writer (someone's talent). П. до небéс, (*fig.*), to praise to the skies. Пре-воз-нош-éние, *n.n.*, inordinate praise.

до-нес-ти́, *v.p.*, до-нос-и́ть, *v.i.*, + *acc.*, о + *prep.*, to carry to, bring to; inform, inform against, denounce. Д. багáж до вагóна, to carry luggage to a car. Д. начáльству, to report to the authorities. До-нес-ти́-сь, *v.p.r.*, до-нос-и́ть-ся, *v.i.r.*, to reach one's ears; be reported, denounced. Звуки роя́ля доноси́лись из сосéдней кóмнаты, the sounds of a piano reached the next room. До-нес-éние, *n.n.*, report, dispatch. До-нóс, *n.m.*, denunciation. До-нóс-чик, *n.m.*, informer, denunciator; sneak.

до-нос-и́ть, *v.p.*, до-нáш-ивать, *v.i.*, + *acc.*, to wear out. Д. ребёнка, to carry a child until normal birth. Д. пальтó, to wear a coat out completely. До-нос-и́ть-ся, *v.p.r.*, до-нáш-ивать-ся, *v.i.r*, to get, become worn out. Не-до-нóс-ок, *n.m.*, (*derog.*) prematurely born child. Не-до-нóш-енный, *adj.*, part.

pass. past, premature. Н. ребёнок, premature baby.

за-нес-ти́, *v.p.*, за-нос-и́ть, *v.i.*, + *acc.*, to carry, beyond, away; to leave in passing; register; fill up. З. зарáзу, to bring infection. З. в спи́сок (в указáтель), to register (index). Всю дорóгу занеслó снéгом, the road has been covered with snowdrifts. Каки́м вéтром вам сюдá занеслó (*fig.*), What wind brings you here? За-нес-ти́-сь, *v.p.r.*, за-нос-и́ть-ся, *v.i.r.*, (*colloq.*), to put on airs; be carried off, away. За-нóс-чивость, *n.f.*, arrogance, insolence; presumption. З. повéдения (рéчи), arrogance of behavior (of speech). За-нóс-чивый, *adj.*, arrogant, insolent. З. человéк, arrogant man. За-нóс-ы, *n.m.*, *pl.*, drifts, *used only in*: снéжные з., snowdrifts. За-нóс-ный, *adj.*, foreign, strange. З-ая мóда, foreign fashion.

за-нос-и́ть, *v.p.*, за-нáш-ивать, *v.i.*, + *acc.*, to wear out; wear without changing. З. пальтó (плáтье), to wear out a coat (dress).

из-нос-и́ть, *v.p.*, из-нáш-ивать, *v.i.*, + *acc.*, to wear out. В год износи́л две пáры сапóг, I wore out two pairs of boots in a year. Из-нос-и́ть-ся, *v.p.r.*, из-нáш-ивать-ся, *v.i.r.*, (*colloq.*), to be used up, worn out, played out. Шуба износи́лась до дыр, the furcoat was worn to tatters. К тридцати́ годáм он износи́лся совершéнно, (*colloq.*), at about the age of thirty he was completely dissipated. Из-нáш-ивание, *n.n.*, wearing out. И. оборýдования, wear and tear of equipment. Из-нóш-енный, *adj.*, part. pass. past, threadbare, shabby. Из-нóс, *n.m.*, (*colloq.*), wear; (*tech.*), wear and tear. Этому пальтó нет изнóса, this coat will never wear out.

на-нес-ти́, *v.p.*, на-нос-и́ть, *v.i.*, + *acc.*, на + *acc.*, + *gen.*, to cast up; drift; inflict; heap up. Лóдку нанеслó на мель, the boat was washed up onto a shoal. Н. рáну, to inflict a wound. Н. удáр, to strike. Н. оскорблéние, to offend, insult. Н. пораже́ние, to inflict a defeat. Н. визи́т, to pay a visit. Н. подáрков, to bring loads of presents. На-нес-éние, *n.n.*, drawing, plotting, marking. Н. озёр на кáрту, the marking of lakes on a map. Н. крáсок на полотнó, the placing, spreading of paint on a canvas. Н. ущéрба, damaging.

на-нос-и́ть, *v.p.*, на-нáш-ивать, *v.i.*, + *acc.*, + *gen.*, to bring in quantity. Н. бóчку воды́, to bring enough water to fill a cask. На-нóс, *n.m.*, alluvium, deposit. Дюны явля́ются песчáными нанóсами, dunes are sand deposits. На-нóс-ный, *adj.*, alluvial; borrowed; superficial. На-нóс-ные мнéния, foreign, superficial opinions.

об-нес-тú, *v.p.,* об-нос-úть, *v.i.,* + *acc.,* + *instr.,* to enclose; pass around a table, serve around. О. стенóй (úзго-рóдью), to enclose with a wall (a fence). Гостéй обносúли жаркúм, the guests were served a roast. Об-нос-úть-ся, *v.p.r.,* об-нáш-ивать-ся, *v.i.r.,* to lack clothing. Об-нóс-ки, *n.m.pl.,* cast-off clothing.

от-нес-тú, *v.p.,* от-нос-úть, *v.i.,* + *acc.,* к + *dat.,* to take to; carry away; attribute. О. чтó-либо на мéсто, to put something in its place. О. письмó, to carry a letter, deliver a letter. От-нес-тú-сь, *v.p.r.,* от-нос-úть-ся, *v.i.r.,* к + *dat.,* to treat, regard, relate oneself to. Хорошó (плóхо) о. к комý-либо, treat someone kindly (badly), to like (dislike) someone. Это к дéлу не отнóсится, this is beside the point. Это здáние отнóсится к четырнáдца-тому вéку, this building dates back to the fourteenth century. От-нос-úтельность, *n.f.,* relativity. Теóрия относúтельности, Theory of Relativity. От-нос-úтельный, *adj.,* relative. О-ое местоимéние, (*gram.*), relative pronoun. От-нос-úтельно, *adv.,* relatively; *prep.,* concerning, about. О. этого плáна, concerning this plan. От-нош-éние, *n.n.,* attitude, relation; letter, memorandum. Бéрежное (небрéжное) о. к комý-либо, careful (careless) treatment of someone. Имéть о. к чемý-либо, to have a relation to something. В этом отношéнии, in this respect. Натянутые отношéния, strained relations. Быть в хорóших (плохúх) отношéниях с кéм-либо, to be on good (bad) terms with someone.

пере-нес-тú, *v.p.,* пере-нос-úть, *v.i.,* + *acc.,* to carry, transport, remove; transfer; endure, bear, stand. П. мéбель с одногó мéста на другóе, to transfer furniture from one place to another. П. болéзнь, to go through an illness. Он этого не перенóсит, he cannot endure it. Пере-нес-тú-сь, *v.p.r.,* пере-нос-úть-ся, *v.i.r.,* to be carried, transferred. П. мысленно, to cast one's mind, reflect. Пере-нес-éние, *n.n.,* transfer, transportation. П. дéла в суд, to take a case to court. Пере-нóс, *n.m.,* transfer, transport, carrying over. П. чáсти слóва, division of syllables, carrying over of a word. Пере-нос-úмый, *adj., part. pass. pres.,* bearable, endurable. Эта боль легкó переносúма, this pain is easily bearable. Не-пере-

нос-úмый, *adj.,* unbearable, intolerable. Н-ые страдáния, unbearable suffering. Пере-нóс-ка, *n.f.,* carrying over. Пере-нóс-ный, *adj.,* portable, figurative. В перенóсном смысле, figuratively; in a figurative sense. Пере-нóс-чик, *n.m.,* пере-нóс-чица, *n.f.,* carrier. П. слýхов (новостéй) rumor monger; gossip.

под-нес-тú, *v.p.,* под-нос-úть, *v.i.,* + *acc.,* to bring to, take to; hold up; treat. П. подáрок, to make a present; present a gift. П. рюмку вóдки комý-нибудь, to offer someone a glass of vodka. Под-нес-éние, *n.n.,* presentation. Под-нóс, *n.m.,* tray. Серéбряный п. silver tray. Чáйный п., tea tray. Под-нóс-ка, *n.f.,* bringing up. Под-нóс-чик, *n.m.,* carrier. Под-нош-éние, *n.n.,* present, gift.; presentation of a gift.

по-нес-тú, *v.p.,* + *acc., see* нестú. Мать понеслá ребёнка домóй, the mother carried the child home. Лóшади понеслú, the horses bolted. По-нóс, *n.m.,* (*med.*), diarrhea. Кровáвый п., (*med.*), dysentery.

по-нос-úть, *v.i.,* + *acc.,* to defame, abuse, slander. П. когó-нибудь грýбыми словáми, to abuse someone with rude words. По-нóс-ный, *adj.,* (*obs.*), defamatory, abusive. П-ые словá, (*obs.*), abusive words. По-нош-éние, *n.n.,* defamation, abuse.

по-нос-úть, *v.p.,* + *acc.,* to carry for a while, wear for a while. По-нóш-енный, *adj., part. pass. past,* worn, frayed, shabby, threadbare. П. костюм, shabby suit. П. вид, haggard look, appearance.

пре-под-нес-тú, *v.p.,* пре-под-нос-úть, *v.i.,* + *acc.,* + *dat.,* to present with a gift. П. подáрок, to present a gift. П. áдрес юбиляру, to present a complimentary scroll to one honored. Пре-под-нош-éние, *n.n.,* presentation of a gift.

при-нес-тú, *v.p.,* при-нос-úть, *v.i.,* + *acc.,* + *dat.,* to bring. П. письмó, to bring, deliver a letter. П. чтó-нибудь обрáтно, to bring back something (to a store). Учéние принеслó емý пóльзу, learning was of benefit to him. П. в жéртву, to bring in sacrifice. Я приношý вам глубóкую благодáрность, I want to express my deep gratitude to you. При-нес-тú-сь, *v.p.r.,* при-нос-úть-ся, *v.i.r.,* to be brought; come running at full speed. При-нош-éние, *n.n.,* offering.

про-нес-тú, *v.p.,* про-нос-úть, *v.i.,* + *acc.,* to carry by, past, through. По улице пронеслú плакáты с лóзунгами, posters with slogans were carried through the streets.

про-нос-и́ть, *v.p.,* + *acc.,* (*colloq.*), to wear for a time; carry about. Она́ пpoноси́ла э́то па́льто три го́да, she wore the coat for three years. Он весь день проноси́л э́ту кни́гу, he carried the book about all day. Про-нес-ти́-сь, *v.p.r.,* про-носи́ть-ся, *v.i.r.,* to shoot past; spread; rush, sweep past. Пронесла́сь ста́я птиц, a swarm of birds flew by. Пронёсся слух, что... there was a rumor that...

про-из-нес-ти́, *v.p.,* про-из-нос-и́ть, *v.i.,* + *acc.,* to pronounce; utter; deliver. П. речь, to deliver a speech. П. пригово́р, to pronounce sentence. Пра́вильно п. иностра́нное сло́во, to pronounce a foreign word correctly. Про-из-нос-и́ть-ся, *v.i.r.,* to be pronounced, articulated. В сло́ве "че́стный" бу́ква "т" не произно́сится, the letter "t" is not pronounced in the word че́стный. Про-из-нес-е́ние, *n.n.,* pronouncing, utterance, delivery. Про-из-нос-и́тельный, *adj.,* (*phon.*), articulatory. П. аппара́т, articulatory apparatus. П-ые о́рганы, organs of speech. Про-из-нош-е́ние, *n.n.,* pronunciation; articulation. Карта́вое п., burr. Хоро́шее п., good pronunciation. Англи́йское, ру́сское п., English, Russian pronunciation.

раз-нес-ти́, *v.p.,* раз-нос-и́ть, *v.i.,* + *acc.,* to distribute, disperse, deliver. Р. газе́ты и пи́сьма, to deliver newspapers and letters. Р. счета́ по кни́гам, to make entries in an account book. Ве́тер разнёс ту́чи, the wind dispersed the clouds. Его́ разнесло́, (*colloq.*), he has grown fat. Разноси́ть в пух и прах, (*idiom.*), to pick to pieces. Нача́льник разнёс своего́ подчинённого, the boss reprimanded his subordinate. Раз-нес-ти́-сь, *v.p.r.,* раз-нос-и́ть-ся, *v.i.r.,* to become spread, distributed, dispersed. Но́вость о войне́ разнесла́сь по всему́ го́роду, the news of the war spread all over the city. Пе́ние соловья́ разноси́лось в саду́, the singing of a nightingale resounded in the garden. Раз-но́с, *n.m.,* раз-но́с-ка, *n.f.,* (*colloq.*), rating; dressing. Торгова́ть в р., to peddle, hawk. Р. пи́сем, mail delivery. Раз-но́с-ный, *adj.,* pertaining to delivery. Р-ая торго́вля, street hawking. Раз-но́с-чик, *n.m.,* peddler, hawker.

раз-нос-и́ть, *v.p.,* раз-на́ш-ивать, *v.i.,* + *acc.,* to make wider by wearing. Р. ту́фли (башмаки́, сапоги́), to widen, enlarge slippers (shoes, boots). Раз-нос-и́ть-ся, *v.p.r.,* раз-на́ш-ивать-ся,

v.i.r., to become loose. Башмаки́ разноси́лись, the shoes became loose.

с-нес-ти́, *v.p.,* с-нос-и́ть, *v.i.,* + *acc.,* to take, carry off; bring together; to blow off, carry away; to demolish, take down, pull down; endure, bear, suffer; discard. С. мешо́к в подва́л, to carry a bag down into a cellar. Бу́ря снесла́ кры́шу, the storm blew the roof off the house. С. зда́ние, to tear down a building. С. мо́лча оби́ду, to suffer an offense silently. С. с лица́ земли́, to level with the ground, to raze from the face of the earth, to the ground. Ему́ не сноси́ть головы́, (*idiom*), it will cost him his head. С-нес-ти́-сь, *v.p.r.,* с-нос-и́ть-ся, *v.i.r.,* с + *instr.,* (*colloq.*), to communicate with. С. друг с дру́гом по телефо́ну, to communicate with one another by telephone. С. друг с дру́гом по по́чте, to communicate with one another by mail. Дом сно́сится, the house is being torn down. С-нос, *n.m.,* drift; demolition. С. ве́тром, wind drift. С. тече́нием, drift. Дом про́дан на снос, the house has been sold to be demolished. Э́тому сно́су нет, you cannot wear it out. С-но́с-ка, *n.f.,* footnote. С-но́с-ный, *adj.,* bearable, tolerable; fairly good. С-ые результа́ты игры́, fairly good results of a game. С-но́с-но, *adv.,* tolerably; (*colloq.*), so-so, pretty well. Не-с-но́с-ный, *adj.,* intolerable, unbearable, insufferable. Н. челове́к, unbearable man. Не-с-но́с-но, *adv.,* intolerably, unbearably, insufferably. С-нош-е́ние, *n.n., used mostly in pl.,* intercourse, dealings. Диплома́тические с-ия, diplomatic relations. Прерыва́ть с-ия с ке́м-либо, to sever relations with someone.

у-нес-ти́, *v.p.,* у-нос-и́ть, *v.i.,* to carry off, take away. У. с собо́й ключи́, to take the keys away with one. Во́ры унесли́ бельё с чердака́, the thieves carried off the linen from the attic. Воображе́ние унесло́ его́ далеко́, his fancy carried him far away. У-нес-ти́-сь, *v.p.r.,* у-нос-и́ть-ся, *v.i.r.,* to be taken, carried away. Ту́чи унесли́сь на се́вер, the clouds were swept off to the north.

НЗ-, НОЗ-, НИЗ-, НИЖ-, НЖ-, НОЖ-, PENETRATION, PIERCING

во-нз-и́-ть, во-нж-у́, *v.p.,* во-нз-а́ть, *v.i.,* + *acc.,* to stick, thrust, plunge. В. книжа́л в грудь, to plunge a dagger into the chest. Во-нз-и́ть-ся, *v.p.r.,* во-нз-а́ть-ся, *v.i.r.,* to be plunged, thrust. Зано́за глубоко́ вонзи́лась в па́лец, the splinter sank deep into the finger.

за-ноз-и́ть, *v.p.,* + *acc.,* to get a splinter. Она́ занози́ла себе́ ру́ку (но́гу), she got a splinter in her hand (foot). За-но́з-а, *n.f.,* splinter; (*colloq.*), squabbler. Она́ така́я з.! (*colloq.*), she is such a squabbler! За-но́з-истый, *adj.,* (*fig.*), meddlesome, quarrelsome. З. челове́к, a quarrelsome man.

про-ноз-и́ть, *v.p.,* про-нз-а́ть, *v.i.,* + *acc.,* + *instr.,* to pierce, run through; transfix. П. копьём, to spear, pierce with a spear. П. взгля́дом, to pierce with a look. Про-нз-ённый, *adj., past. pass. past,* pierced. Про-нз-и́тельный, *adj.,* shrill, sharp, piercing, strident. П. крик, piercing shriek. П. взгляд, piercing look. Пронзи́тельным го́лосом, in a shrill voice, stridently.

низ-а́-ть, ниж-у́, *v.p.,* + *acc.,* to string, thread. Н. же́мчуг, to string pearls.

до-низ-а́ть, *v.p.,* до-низ-ывать, *v.i.,* + *acc.,* to complete stringing. Д. би́сер до конца́, to string the beads to the end. Низ-а́ть-ся, *v.i.r.,* to be strung, threaded.

на-низ-а́ть, *v.p.,* на-ни́з-ывать, *v.i.,* + *acc.,* to restring. На-ни́з-ывание, *n.n.,* stringing, threading.

пере-низ-а́ть, *v.p.,* пере-ни́з-ывать, *v.i.,* + *acc.,* to restring. П. бу́сы, to restring beads.

про-низ-а́ть, *v.p.,* про-ни́з-ывать, *v.i.,* to pierce, penetrate. Хо́лод пронза́л всё те́ло, the cold penetrated my whole body. Про-ни́з-ывающий, *adj., part. act. pres.,* piercing. П. хо́лод, piercing cold.

у-низ-а́ть, *v.p.,* у-ни́з-ывать, *v.i.,* + *acc.,* to cover; stud. У. кокошник же́мчугом, to stud a kokoshnik (headdress) with pearls.

нож, *n.m.,* knife. Столо́вый н., table knife. Кухо́нный н., kitchen knife. Быть на ножа́х, (*fig.*), to be at daggers' points. Но́ж-ик, *n.m.,* knife. Перо́чинный н., penknife. Но́ж-ичек, *n.m.,* (*dim.*), little knife. Но́ж-ницы, scissors. Садо́вые н., pruning shears. Н. для ре́зки про́волоки, wire-cutter. Нож-ны́, *n.pl.,* scabbard, sheathe. Вынима́ть из ноже́н, to unsheathe. Нож-о́вка, *n.f.,* (*tech.*), hacksaw. По-нож-о́вщина, *n.f.,* throat-cutting.

НИЗ-, НИЖ-, НИС-, LOWNESS

низ, *n.m.,* bottom, lower part. С ве́рху до́ низу, from top to bottom. Низ-и́на, *n.f.,* lowland, low place. Ни́з-кий, *adj.,* low; base, mean. Н. го́лос, low, deep voice. Ни́зкого ро́ста, of short stature; undersized. Н-ое ка́чество, inferior quality. Ни́з-ко, *adv.,* low; basely, meanly, despicably. Низ-ко-покло́нник, *n.m.,* groveller, toady. Низ-ко-покло́нничать, *v.i.,* пе́ред + *instr.,* to cringe. Низ-ко-покло́нство, *n.n.,* servility. Низ-ко-ро́слый, *adj.,* undersized, shortish. Ни́з-менность, *n.f.,* lowland. Голла́ндия располо́жена на ни́зменности. Holland is located on the lowlands. Ни́з-менный, *adj.,* lying low; base, vile. Н-ое побужде́ние, vile motive. Н-ый инсти́нкт, animal instinct. Низ-ость, *n.f.,* baseness, meanness. Низ-о́вье, *n.n.,* lower reaches of a river. Низо́вья Во́лги, the Lower Volga. Низ-ово́й, *adj.,* lower; local. Н-а́я организа́ция, (*recent*), local party organization. Ни́з-ший, *adj., superl.,* lowest. Н-ее образова́ние, elementary, primary education. Н-ая то́чка, the lowest point. Низ-ы́, *n.pl.,* lower strata. Н. населе́ния, (*obs.*), the lower classes. Ни́жние но́ты, (*mus.*), low, bass notes. В-низ, *adv.,* down, downward. Гляде́ть в., to look down. В. по тече́нию, down stream. В-низ-у́, *adv.,* below, downstairs; at the bottom.

ни́ж-е, *adj. comp. and adv. comp.,* lower; *prep.,* below; *combining form meaning* below. Спуска́ться н., to descend. Смотри́ ни́же, see below. Н. го́рода, (о́строва) по тече́нию ре́ки, down stream from a town (island). Н. вся́кой кри́тики, beneath criticism. Ниже-изло́женный, *adj., part. pass. past,* set forth below. Ниж-е-озна́ченный, *adj., part. pass. past,* mentioned below. Ниж-е-подписа́вшийся, *adj., part. pass. past,* the undersigned. Ниж-е-сле́дующий, *adj., part. pass. past,* the following. Ни́ж-ний, *adj.,* lower. Н. эта́ж, ground floor. Н-ее бельё, underclothing. Н-ее тече́ние реки́, the lower reaches of a river. Н-яя пала́та, the lower chamber (*as of Parliament*). Ниж-а́йший, *adj., superl.,* the lowest.

по-ни́з-ить, по-ни́ж-у, *v.p.,* по-ниж-а́ть, *v.i.,* + *acc.,* to lower, reduce; drop. П. це́ны, to lower, cut prices. П. по слу́жбе, to demote. П. го́лос, to lower, drop one's voice. По-ни́з-ить-ся, *v.p.r.,* по-ниж-а́ть-ся, *v.i.r.,* to fall, go down; become lower, sink. Температу́ра у больно́го пони́зилась, the patient's temperature has gone down, dropped. По-ниж-е́ние, *n.n.,* fall, lowering; drop; reduction. Наблюда́ется п. цен, there is a noticeable drop in prices. П. давле́ния, lowering of pressure. По-ни́ж-е, *adv., comp.,* lower, shorter. По-низ-о́вье, *n.n.,* lower reaches of a river. По́-низ-у, *adv.,* low, along the ground. Дым сме́лется п., the smoke hangs low.

при-ни́з-ить, *v.p.,* при-ниж-а́ть, *v.i.,* + *acc.,* to humble; humiliate, belittle, depreciate. П. значе́ние чего́-нибудь, to belittle the significance of something. При-ни́ж-енность, *n.f.,* humility. При-ни́ж-енный, *adj.,* humbled, humiliated.

с-ни́з-ить, *v.p.,* с-ниж-а́ть, *v.i.,* + *acc.,* to bring down, lower; reduce, cut, abate. С. тре́бования, to reduce one's demands. С. по слу́жбе, to degrade, demote. С. тон, to lower one's tone. С-ни́з-ить-ся, *v.p.r.,* с-ниж-а́ть-ся, *v.i.r.,* to lower, descend, lose height; be reduced, sink, fall. Самолёт сни́зился, the plane came down. Це́ны сни́зились, the prices have been reduced. С-ниж-е́ние, *n.n.,* lowering, sinking, abatement, reduction. С. себесто́имости, lowering of costs of production. С-ни́з-у, *adv.,* also used as *prep.,* from below. Посмотре́ть с., to look from below. Пя́тая строка́ с., the fifth line from the bottom. С. вверх, upward.

у-ни́з-ить, *v.p.,* у-ниж-а́ть, *v.i.,* + *acc.,* to humble; humiliate, abase. У. себя́, to humiliate, abase oneself. У-ни́з-ить-ся, *v.p.r.,* у-ниж-а́ть-ся, *v.i.r.,* to abase oneself, be abased. У. до лжи, to stoop to lying. У-ниж-е́ние, *n.n.,* humiliation, abasement. Терпе́ть униже́ния, to bear humiliation. У-ни́ж-енность, *n.f.,* humility, humbleness.

низ-ве́ргнуть, *v.p.,* низ-верга́ть, *v.i.,* + *acc.,* to overthrow, precipitate. Н. прави́тельство, to overthrow a government. Низ-верже́ние, *n.n.,* overthrow. Н. диктату́ры, the overthrow of a dictatorship. Низ-ве́ргнутый, *adj., part. pass. past,* overthrown.

низ-вести́, *v.p.,* низ-води́ть, *v.i.,* + *acc.,* to bring down. Н. мни́мого геро́я с пьедеста́ла, to knock a fake hero off his pedestal.

низ-о-йти́, *v.p.,* нис-ходи́ть, *v.i.,* + *acc.,* to come over. "... на та́бор кочево́й нисхо́дит со́нное молча́ние," (*Pushkin*), "a sleepy silence descends on the nomads' camp." Нис-ходя́щий, *adj., part. pres. act.,* descending, decreasing. Н-ее поколе́ние, the following, next generation.

с-низ-о-йти́, *v.p.,* с-нис-ходи́ть, *v.i.,* к + *dat.,* to condescend. С. к нужда́м проси́телей, to acquiesce to the needs of the petitioners. С. на про́сьбы подчинённых, to acquiesce to the requests of subordinates. С-низ-хож-де́ние, *n.n.,* condescension, indulgence.

нис-па́сть, *v.p.,* нис-пада́ть, *v.i.,* на + *acc.,* (*obs.*), to fall, drop. Ку́дри ниспада́ли на пле́чи, the locks fell down over the shoulders.

нис-посла́ть, *v.p.,* нис-посыла́ть, *v.i.,* + *acc.,* (*rel., Ch.-Sl.*), to grant. Бог ниспосла́л благода́ть, God granted grace.

нис-прове́ргнуть, *v.p.smf.,* нис-провергáть, *v.i.,* + *acc.,* to overthrow.

НИК-, НИЧ-, НИЦ-, BEND, INCLINE

ни́к-ну-ть, *v.i.,* по-ни́к-нуть, *v.p.,* to droop. П. голово́й, to hang one's head. Нич-ко́м, *adv.,* prone. Лежа́ть н., to lie prone, face downwards. Лежа́щий н., lying prone. Ниц, *adv.,* (*obs.*), prone. Пасть ниц, (*obs.*), to fall on one's face.

в-ни́к-ну-ть, *v.p.,* в-ник-а́ть, *v.i.,* в + *acc.,* to try to grasp, understand; investigate, probe into. В. в де́ло, to examine a matter thoroughly. В-ник-а́ние, *n.n.,* investigation, probing, probe.

воз-ни́к-ну-ть, *v.p.,* воз-ник-а́ть, *v.i.,* to arise, spring up; appear. У него́ возни́кло чу́вство сострада́ния, a feeling of compassion arose in him. Но́вые города́ возника́ют по всей стране́, new cities are springing up all over the country. Воз-ник-нове́ние, *n.n.,* origin, beginning, rise. Леге́нда о возникнове́нии Ри́ма, the legend about the origin of Rome.

по-ни́к-ну-ть, *v.p.,* по-ник-а́ть, *v.i.,* see ни́кнуть. П. голово́ю, to hang one's head. Ко́лос пони́к, the ear of wheat drooped.

при-ни́к-ну-ть, *v.i.,* при-ник-а́ть, *v.i.,* в + *acc.,* to nestle; lean against, toward; incline. П. у́хом к земле́ (*fig.*), to put one's ear to the ground.

про-ни́к-ну-ть, *v.p.,* про-ник-а́ть, *v.i.,* в + *acc.,* to penetrate; go, pass through. Вода́ прони́кла в трюм, the water penetrated into the hold. П. в чьи́-либо наме́рения, to fathom someone's intentions. Пу́ля прони́кла до са́мой кости́, the bullet penetrated as far as the bone. Про-ни́к-нуть-ся, *v.p.r.,* про-ник-а́ть-ся, *v.i.r,* to be imbued with. П. созна́нием своего́ до́лга, to be imbued with the sense of one's duties. П. любо́вью (уваже́нием), to be inspired with love (respect). Про-ник-нове́ние, *n.n.,* penetration. Про-ник-нове́нность, *n.f.,* emotion, feeling. Про-ник-нов-е́нный, *adj.,* penetrating; pathetic, moving. П. го́лос, взгляд, penetrating voice (glance). Про-ни́к-нутый, *adj., part. pass. past,* imbued, inspired.

про-ниц-а́-ть, *v.i.,* (*obs.*), see проника́ть. Про-ниц-а́емость, *n.f.,* permeability, penetrability, permeation. Магни́тная п., magnetic permeance. Про-ниц-áемый, *adj.*, penetrating. П. для свéта, translucent. Не-про-ниц-áемый, *ădj.*, impenetrable. Про-ниц-áтельность, *n.f.*, perspicacity, insight. Про-ниц-áтель-ный, *adj.*, perspicacious, acute, shrewd. П. взор, searching, piercing look. П. ум, penetrating mind; shrewd, astute mind.

НОВ-, NEWNESS, NOVELTY

нов-ь, *n.f.*, (*agric.*), virgin soil. Подни-мáть новь, to plow virgin lands.
нов-из-нá, *n.f.*, novelty. Н. дéла, novelty of an action, work. Нов-úнка, *n.f.*, novelty. Нов-ичóк, *n.m.*, novice; greenhorn. Нов-инá, *n.f.*, (*folk*), virgin soil; *see* новь.
нóв-ый, *adj.*, new; modern. Нóвый Год, New Year. Н. Свет, the New World. Н-ые языкú, modern languages. Н-ая мóда, new fashion. Он н. человéк в этом дéле, he is a new hand at this. Что нóвого? what's new? Вводúть н-ые словá, to introduce new words. Н-ая экономúческая полúтика (НЭП), (*recent*), New Economic Policy. Нóв-енький, *adj.*, (*dim.*), brand new; *used as n.*, novice. Нов-éйший, *adj. superl.*, newest, latest. Н-ие достижéния тéх-ники (науки), latest achievements in technology (science). Нов-о-, *combining form meaning* new. Нов-о-брáнец, *n.m.*, recruit. Нов-о-брáчная, *n.f.*, bride. Нов-о-брáчный, bridegroom. Нов-о-брáчные, newlyweds. Нов-о-введéние, *n.n.*, innovation. Нов-о-гóдний, *adj.*, pertaining to the New Year. Н-яя ёлка, New Year's tree. Н-ие поздравлéния, New Year's greetings. Нов-о-прибы́в-ший, *adj.*, *used as n.*, newly-arrived, new-comer. Нов-о-рождённый, *adj.*, *used as n.*, new-born child. Н-ая идéя, new idea. Нов-о-стрóйка, *n.f.*, (*recent*), new project; erection of a new building.
нóв-ш-ество, *n.n.*, innovation, novelty. Нóв-ость, *n.f.*, news. Какúе сегóдня нóвости? What news today?
в-нов-ь, *adv.*, newly, recently; anew, again, once more. В. прибы́вший, newly arrived.
зá-нов-о, *adv.*, anew. Эта статья́ не годúтся, придётся написáть зáново, this article won't do, it must be re-written.
с-нóв-а, *adv.*, anew, afresh, again. Начинáть с., to begin again, from the beginning. Друзья́ с. с нáми, our friends are with us again. С. рассказы́-вать, to retell.
по-нóв-ому, *adv.*, according to a new

fashion. Начáть жить п., to begin a new life.
об-нов-úть, *v.p.*, об-нов-л-я́ть, *v.i.*, + *acc.*, to renovate, refresh; repair, make as good as new; put clothes on for the first time. О. кры́шу, to renovate a roof. О. плáтье, to renovate a dress. Наступúла веснá, лес обновúл свою́ листву́, spring came, and the forest renewed its foliage. Об-нов-úть-ся, *v.p.r.*, об-нов-ля́ть-ся, *v.i.r.*, to be renewed, revived. Странá обновúлась, the country has revived. Об-нóв-а, об-нóв-ка, *n.f.*, new acquisition. Обнóв-ки к прáзднику, new clothes for a holiday. Об-нов-лéние, *n.n.*, renovation. Морáльное о., moral rebirth. Об-нов-лённый, *adj.*, *part. pass. past*, renovated, reborn.
воз-об-нов-úть, *v.p.*, воз-об-нов-л-я́ть, *v.i.*, + *acc.*, to renew, revive; resume. В. подпúску (договóр), to renew a subscription (an agreement). В. заня́-тия, to resume lessons. Воз-об-нов-úть-ся, *v.p.r.*, воз-об-нов-л-я́ть-ся, *v.i.r.*, to be resumed. Воз-об-нов-л-éние, *n.n.*, resumption, renewal. В. заня́тий, resumption of studies, classes. В. знакóмства, renewal of acquaint-ance.
под-нов-úть, *v.p.*, под-нов-л-я́ть, *v.i.*, + *acc.*, to refurbish, renew, renovate slightly. П. костю́м, to freshen, renovate a suit. П. крáски на картúне, to retouch a painting. Под-нов-úть-ся, *v.p.r.*, под-нов-л-я́ть-ся, *v.i.r.*, to be renewed, renovated. Здáния пóсле ремóнта подновúлись, the buildings looked new after renovation.

НОГ-, НОЖ-, FOOT, LEG

ног-á, *n.f.*, foot, leg. Прáвая (лéвая) н., right (left) leg. У человéка две ногú, a man has two legs (feet). Положúть нóгу нá ногу, to cross one's legs. Идтú в нóгу, to keep in step. Быть без ног от устáлости, (*fig.*), to walk one's legs off. С головы́ до ног, from head to foot. Встать с лéвой ногú, (*fig.*), to get out of bed on the wrong side. Едвá нóги нóсят, (*idiom.*), his legs will hardly carry him. Жить на широ́-кую нóгу, to live in grand style. Стать нá ноги, to become independent, stand on one's own feet. Стоя́ть на своúх ногáх, to be independent. Стоя́ть вверх ногáми, to stand on one's head. Бос-о-нóг-ий, *adj.*, barefooted. Длинно-нóг-ий, *adj.*, long-legged. Коротко-нóг-ий, *adj.*, short-legged. Криво-нóг-ий, *adj.*, bow-legged.
нóж-ка, *n.f.*, (*dim.*), leg, foot; leg, stem.

Пры́гать на одно́й но́жке, to hop, jump on one leg. Н. стола́ (сту́ла), leg of a table (of a chair). Подста́вить кому́-нибудь но́жку, (*fig.*), to trip someone up. Ко́зья но́жка, (*colloq.*), hand-rolled cigarette. Босо-но́ж-ка, *n.f.*, barefoot dancer. Босо-но́ж-ки, *n.pl.*, (*recent*), sandals. Но́ж-еньк-а, *n.f.*, (*dim.*), little foot. Нож-но́й, *adj.*, leg, foot. Н-а́я ва́нна, foot bath. Н-а́я швейная маши́на, treadle sewing machine.

под-но́ж-ие, *n.n.*, foot, pedestal. До́мики расположи́лись у подно́жия горы́, small houses stood at the foot of the hill. Ста́туя на гранитном подно́жии, a statue on a granite pedestal.

под-но́ж-ка, *n.f.*, step, footboard. Стоя́ть на подно́жке трамва́я воспреща́ется, standing on the steps of the streetcar is prohibited. Под-но́ж-ный, *adj.*, underfoot. П. корм, pasture, grass. Пуска́ть на п. корм, to put out to pasture.

тре-но́ж-н-ик, *n.m.*, тре-но́г-а, *n.f.*, tripod. Тре-но́ж-ный, *adj.*, tripodal. Трено́г-ий, *adj.*, tripodal. Трено́гий стол, a three-legged table.

тре-но́ж-и-ть, *v.i.*, с-тре-но́ж-ить, *v.p.*, + *acc.*, to fetter, hobble. Т. коне́й, to hobble horses.

НОРОВ-, НОРАВ-, НРАВ-, TEMPER, HABIT, DISPOSITION, CUSTOM

но́ров, *n.m.*, (*obs.*), habit, custom; obstinacy; temperament. Что ни го́род, то свой но́ров, (*saying*), every city has its own customs. С но́ровом, obstinate, capricious. Ло́шадь с но́ровом, balky horse. Норов-и́стый, *adj.*, restive, balky. Н-ая ло́шадь, balky horse.

норов-и́-ть, *v.i.*, + *inf.*, (*colloq.*), to aim, try, endeavor. Он норови́т пообе́дать на чужо́й счёт, he always tries to dine at someone else's expense.

при-норов-и́ть, *v.p.*, при-нора́в-ливать, *v.i.*, + *acc.*, to fit, adapt, adjust; time. П. свой отъе́зд к концу́ ме́сяца, to time one's departure for the end of the month. При-норов-и́ть-ся, *v.p.*, при-нора́в-ливать-ся, *v.i.*, к + *dat.*, to adapt oneself, accomodate oneself. П. к обы́чаям страны́, to adapt oneself to the customs of a country. П. к совреме́нным поня́тиям, to adapt oneself to contemporary ideas.

с-норов-и́ть, *v.p.*, to hit the mark; *see* угоди́ть, попа́сть. На вся́кого не снорови́шь, (*saying*), you can't satisfy everyone. С-норо́в-ка, *n.f.*, skill, knack. Име́ть сноро́вку в чём-либо, to be skilled in something.

нрав, *n.m.*, temper, disposition. У него́ весёлый н., he is of a cheerful disposition. Кро́ткий (бу́йный) н., modest (tempestuous) disposition. Это ему́ не по нра́ву, he does not like it; it is not to his liking. Нра́в-ы, *n.pl.*, customs, morals, manners, mores. Другие времена́ - другие нра́вы, other times, other ways. Нрав-о-описа́ние, *n.n.*, description of mores. Нрав-о-описа́тельный, *adj.*, describing mores. Н. рома́н, *roman de moeurs.* Нрав-о-уче́-ние, *n.n.*, lecture, moral, admonition. Н. в ба́сне, moral of a fable. Чита́ть нравоуче́ния кому́-нибудь, to lecture someone. Нрав-о-учи́тельный, *adj.*, moralizing. Н. расска́з, story with a moral. Благо-нра́в-ие, *n.n.*, good, conduct, behavior. Благо-нра́вный, *adj.*, well-behaved. Б. учени́к, well-behaved pupil. Добр-о-нра́в-ие, *n.n.*, good character; good behavior, morals. Добро-нра́в-ный, *adj.*, of good disposition, good morals, good character. Зло-нра́в-ие, *n.n.*, immorality. Зло-нра́в-ный, *adj.*, of wicked, mean disposition; immoral. Свое-нра́в-ие, *n.n.*, willfulness. Свое-нра́вность, *n.f.*, willfulness. Свое-нра́в-ный, *adj.*, willful, self-willed, capricious.

нра́в-ить-ся, *v.i.r.*, по-нра́в-ить-ся, *v.p.r.*, + *dat.*, to please, be pleasing. Нра́вится-ли вам э́та кни́га? Do you like this book? Ему́ н. е́здить верхо́м, he likes to ride. Разо-нра́в-ить-ся, *v.p.r.*, to displease, be displeasing. Снача́ла она́ ему́ понра́вилась, а пото́м разонра́вилась, at first he liked her, then she began to displease him.

нра́в-ств-ен-н-ость, *n.f.*, morals. Нра́вственный, *adj.*, moral. Н. челове́к, moral man. Без-нра́в-ственность, *n.f.*, immorality; dissoluteness. Искореня́ть б., to stamp out immorality. Без-нра́в-ственный, *adj.*, immoral, dissolute. Б. о́браз жи́зни, immoral way of life.

НОС-, NOSE

нос, *n.m.*, nose; bow, head, prow. Нос прямо́й (вздёрнутый, с горби́нкой), straight (hooked, Roman) nose. У него́ кровь идёт и́з носу, his nose is bleeding. Показа́ть нос, (*fig., colloq.*), to thumb one's nose. Оста́ться с но́сом, (*fig.*), to be duped. Пове́сить н., to be discouraged. Води́ть за́ н. кого-либо, to lead someone by the nose. Не ви́деть да́льше своего́ но́са, not to see beyond one's nose. Клева́ть но́сом, to be drowsy. Н. ло́дки, prow of a boat. Корабе́льный н., ship's prow. Но́с-ик, *n.m.*, (*dim.*), little nose. Н. ча́йника, spout of a teapot. Долго-но́с-ик, weevil. Нос-а́тый, *adj.*, large-nosed. Без-но́с-ый, *adj.*, spoutless, noseless. Б. ча́йник, spoutless teapot. Кур-но́с-ый, *adj.*, pug-nosed. Нос-ово́й, *adj.*, nose, nasal. Н. плато́к, handkerchief. Н. согла́сный, nasal consonant. Н-а́я часть корабля́, ship's bow. Н-а́я ка́чка, pitching of a ship. Нос-о-, *combining form meaning* nose. Нос-о-гло́тка, *n.f.*, (*anat.*), nasopharynx. Нос-о-гло́точный, *adj.*, (*anat.*), nasopharynxal. Нос-о́к, *n.m.*, toe, sock. Боти́нки с у́зкими носка́ми, shoes with narrow toes. Шерстяны́е носки́, woolen socks. Нос-о-ро́г, *n.m.*, rhinoceros.

пере-но́с-ье, *n.n.*, пере-но́с-ица, *n.f.*, bridge of the nose.

НОЧ-Ь-, NIGHT

ноч-ь, *n.f.*, night. Всю ночь, all night. Глуха́я н., the dead of night. Н. на дворе́, it is dark outside. По ноча́м, by night; nights. Споко́йной но́чи, good night. Но́чью, *adv.*, at night, by night. Днём и н., day and night. Ночни́к, *n.m.*, night lamp. Ноч-но́й, *adj.*, nightly. Н-о́е вре́мя, night time. Н-о́й сто́лик, bedside table. Н-а́я руба́шка, night shirt, nightgown. Н-а́я сме́на, night shift. Ноч-но́е, *adj.*, used as *n.*, nightwatch.

ноч-ева́-ть, *v.i.*, and *v.p.*, to pass, spend a night; to sleep. Н. в гостя́х, to visit overnight. Днева́ть и н., (*colloq.*), to stay day and night. Ноч-ёвка, *n.f.*, (*colloq.*), spending, passing a night. Оста́ться на ночёвку у кого́-либо, to spend a night at someone's house. Ноч-лёг, *n.m.*, lodging for the night. Останови́ться на́ н., to stay overnight. Пла́та за н., payment for a night's lodging. Ноч-лёжка, *n.f.*, (*colloq.*), ноч-лёжный дом, flop house. Ноч-лёжник, *n.m.*, destitute person who spends the night in a flophouse.

за-ноч-ева́ть, *v.p.*, to stay overnight, spend the night. З. у знако́мых, to stay overnight with friends.

пере-ноч-ева́ть, *v.p.*, see ночева́ть, заночева́ть. П. в гости́нице, to spend the night in a hotel.

по́л-ночь, *n.f.*, midnight; (*poet.*), north, septentrion. Часы́ бьют по́лночь, the clock is striking midnight. „По не́бу полу́ночи а́нгел лете́л," (*Lermontov*), An angel flew across the midnight sky. Снега́ угрю́мой полуно́чи, (*poet.*), the snows of the gloomy North. Пол-но́чный (полно́щный), *adj.*, midnight. П. час, midnight, hour of midnight. П-ые стра́ны, northern countries, countries of the midnight sun. … Полно́щных

стран краса́ и ди́во, (*Pushkin*), the glory and beauty of the northern countries.

полу-но́ч-нич-ать, *v.i.*, (*colloq.*), to stay up after midnight. Дово́льно тебе́ полуно́чничать за кни́гой, иди́ спать! You have stayed up late enough, reading, go to bed! Полу-но́ч-ник, *n.m.*, (*colloq.*), night owl, nightbird; latecomer (especially after card-playing). Эти полуно́чники спать никому́ в до́ме не даю́т, these nightbirds prevent everyone in the house from sleeping.

НУД-, НУЖД-, НУЖ-, NEED, NECESSITY

нуд-и́-ть, нуж-у́, *v.i.*, (*obs.*), see принужда́ть. Я тебя́ не нужу́, (*colloq.*), I am not forcing you. Бе́дность нуди́т побира́ться, poverty compels one to beg, to live by begging. Ну́д-ность, *n.f.*, tedium. Ну́д-ный, *adj.*, tedious, tiresome; irksome. Н. челове́к, bore. Како́й он н.! What a bore he is!

нужд-а́, *n.f.*, need; straits, indigence, destitution. Н. в деньга́х, need of money. Испы́тывать нужду́, to be in need. В слу́чае нужды́, in case of need. Быть в нужде́, to live in poverty, be in need. Нужды́ нет, (*idiom*), never mind; there's no need. Нужда́ ска́чет, нужда́ пля́шет, нужда́ пе́сенки поёт, (*saying*), poverty forces people to do things they dislike. Нужд-а́емость, *n.f.*, destitution, need. Определи́ть н. населе́ния в жилпло́щади, (*recent*), to determine the need for housing of a population.

нужд-а́ть-ся, *v.i.r.*, в + *prep.*, to need, want, require, be hard up. Больно́й нужда́ется в све́жем во́здухе, the sick man needs fresh air. Нужд-а́ющийся, *adj.*, *part. act. pres.*, needy, indigent.

ну́жн-о, *impers.* it is necessary, one should, one must. Н. пое́хать туда́, it is necessary to go there. Это н. сде́лать, it must be done, it has to be done. Н. быть осторо́жным, one must be careful. Вам н. отдохну́ть, you need a rest. Им н. молока́, they need milk. Очень н.! (*colloq.*), What do I care! Ну́ж-ный, *adj.*, (ну́ж-ен, нуж-на́, *adj. pred.*), necessary. Это ну́жная кни́га, this is a much needed book. Сон ну́жен для здоро́вья, sleep is necessary for good health. Эта кни́га бу́дет нужна́ ей сего́дня, she will need this book today. Что ему́ ну́жно? What does he want? What is he driving at?

вы́-нуд-ить, *v.p.*, вы-нужд-а́ть, *v.i.*, + *acc.*, to force, compel. В. согла́сие (призна́ние), to force assent (admission). Вы́-нужд-енный, *adj., part. pass. past,* forced, compelled. В-ая поса́дка, forced landing. В-ое призна́ние, a forced confession. Он вы́нужден пойти́, сде́лать..., he is forced, compelled to go, do...

по-ну́д-ить, *v.p.,* по-нужд-а́ть, *v.i.,* + *acc.,* к + *dat.,* to force, compel. П. кого́-либо к опроделённому реше́нию, to force someone to make a definite decision. По-нуд-и́тельный, *adj.,* enforced, pressing. П-ые ме́ры, enforced measures. По-нужд-е́ние, *n.n.,* compulsion.

при-ну́д-ить, *v.p.,* при-нужд-а́ть, *v.i.,* + *acc.,* к + *dat.,* to compel, force; coerce. П. кого́-либо к молча́нию, to force someone to be silent. При-нужд-а́ться, *v.i.r.,* to be forced, compelled; coerced. При-нужд-е́ние, *n.n.,* compulsion, constraint, coercion. По принужде́нию, under compulsion, constraint. Без принужде́ния, without constraint, without compulsion. При-нужд-ённость, *n.f.,* constraint; stiffness. П. в обраще́нии (в разгово́ре), constraint in relations (in conversation). При-нужд-ённый, *adj., part. pass. past,* constrained, forced. П-ая улы́бка, forced smile. П. смех, forced laughter. Не-при-нужд-ённость, *n.f.,* ease; lack of embarrassment. Не-при-нужд-ённый, *adj., part. pass. past,* natural, unconstrained, nonchalant. Н-ая поза, easy, natural attitude, pose. Не-при-нужд-ённо, *adv.,* without embarrassment, nonchalantly. Чу́вствовать себя́ н., to feel at ease. Вести́ себя́ н., to be unconstrained, nonchalant.

НЮХ-, НЮШ-, УХ-, SCENT, SMELL

нюх, *n.m.,* scent; (*fig.*), flair, scent. У соба́ки хоро́ший н., a dog has a good sense of smell.

ню́хать, *v.i.,* по-ню́х-ать, *v.p.,* + *acc.,* to smell. Н таба́к, to take snuff. Н. духи́, to smell perfume. Он по́роху и не ню́хал, (*fig.*), he did not even smell gunpowder, never went to war, was never in action. Нюх-а́льщик, нюх-а́тель, *n.m.,* snuffer. Н. табака́, one who uses snuff. Нюх-а́тельный, *adj.,* pertaining to snuff. Н. таба́к, snuff.

нюх-ну́-ть, *v.p.smf.,* (*colloq.*), to smell, get a whiff of, sniff at. Он нюхну́л пе́рцу и чихну́л, he sniffed at the pepper and sneezed.

вы́-нюх-ать, *v.p.,* вы-ню́х-ивать, *v.i.,* + *acc.,* (*colloq.*), to sniff, snuff; nose out, smell out. Он вы́нюхал всё, что

там говори́лось, he nosed out everything that was said there.

об-ню́х-ать, *v.p.,* об-ню́х-ивать, *v.i.,* + *acc.,* to sniff over. Соба́ка обнюхала оде́жду, the dog sniffed over the clothes.

пере-ню́х-ать, *v.p.,* пере-ню́х-ивать, *v.i.,* + *acc.,* (*colloq.*), to smell one after another. П. все цветы́, to smell all the flowers, one after another.

по-ню́х-ать, *v.p., see* нюхать. Не дать и понюхать, (*colloq.*), not to give a whiff of. По-ню́ш-ка, *n.f.,* (*colloq.*), pinch. П. табаку́, a pinch of snuff, of tobacco.

при-ню́х-ать-ся, *v.p.r.,* при-ню́х-иваться, *v.i.r.,* к + *dat.,* (*colloq.*), to sniff; become accustomed to a smell. П. к таба́чному ды́му, to become used to the smell of tobacco smoke.

про-ню́х-ать, *v.p.,* про-ню́х-ивать, *v.i.,* + *acc.,* (*colloq.*), to smell, nose out. П. но́вость, to find out the news.

раз-ню́х-ать, *v.p.,* рах-ню́х-ивать, *v.i.,* + *acc.,* (*colloq.*), to smell about, smell out, nose out. Соба́ка разню́хала, где спря́тали мя́со, the dog smelled out the hidden meat. Я э́то разнюха́ю, (*slang*), I'll smell it out.

благо-ух-а́ть, *v.i.,* to give off a fragrance. Цветы́ благоуха́ют, flowers give off a fragrance. Благо-ух-а́ние, *n.n.,* fragrance. Благо-ух-а́ющий, *adj., part. act. pres.,* fragrant. Б. куст сире́ни, fragrant lilac bush.

НЯН-Я-, NURSE

ня́н-я, *n.f.,* nurse, nursemaid; (*colloq.*), nursie, nannie. Н. у колыбе́ли ребёнка, a nursemaid at a child's cradle. Ня́н-ь-ка, *n.f.,* (*dim.*), nurse, nursemaid. У семи́ ня́нек дитя́ без гла́зу, (*prov.*), too many cooks spoil the broth. Ня́н-ечка, ня́н-юшка, *n.f., in addressing,* nannie, nurse.

ня́н-чи-ть, *v.i.,* + *acc.,* to nurse; take care of children. Ня́нчить-ся, *v.i.r.,* с + *instr.,* to nurse, dandle. Н. с детьми́, to nurse children; (*fig.*), fuss over children. Она́ век свой ня́нчится с ма́лыми ребя́тами, she devotes her life to taking care of children.

вы́-нян-чить, *v.p.,* вы-ня́н-чивать, *v.i.,* + *acc.,* (*colloq.*), to bring up, rear. Ста́рая ня́ня вы́нянчила всех дете́й в на́шей семье́, the old nurse raised all the children in our family.

по-ня́н-чить, *v.p.,* + *acc.,* (*colloq.*), to nurse for a while. Поня́нчи ребёнка, пока́ я в ла́вку сбе́гаю, take care of the baby while I run to the store.

про-ня́н-чить, *v.p.,* + *acc.,* to nurse through. Про-ня́н-чить-ся, *v.p.r.,* с + *instr.,* to nurse. П. с ребёнком весь день, to take care of a (capricious) child for the whole day.

О

ОБИД-, ОБИЖ-, OFFENSE, INSULT

оби́д-а, *n.f.,* offense; injury; wrong; resentment. Нанести́ оби́ду, to offend. Го́рькая о., deep mortification. Кро́вная о., mortal deep offense. Не дать себя́ в оби́ду, to stand up for oneself. В тесноте́, да не в оби́де, (*saying*), uncomfortable, but not neglected.

оби́д-е-ть, *v.p.,* обиж-а́ть, *v.i.,* + *acc.,* to offend, hurt, hurt one's feelings. Он меня́ оби́дел, he offended me. Оби́д-еть-ся, *v.p.r.,* обиж-а́ть-ся, *v.i.r.,* to be offended. Не обижа́йтесь на меня́, don't be offended; I don't mean to offend you. Оби́ж-енный, *adj., part. pass. past,* offended. Оби́д-чивость, *n.f.,* touchiness. Оби́д-чик, *n.m.,* оби́д-чица, *n.f.,* offender. Оби́д-чивый, *adj.,* touchy, easily offended. О. челове́к, an easily-offended man. Оби́д-ный, *adj.,* vexing offensive. О-ое замеча́ние, an offensive remark. О-ое сравне́ние, offensive comparison. Оби́д-но, *adv.,* offensively; it is a pity. Оби́дно, что вы опозда́ли на интере́сную ле́кцию, it is a pity you came late for this interesting lecture. Мне о., I am hurt, offended.

раз-оби́д-еть, *v.p.,* раз-обиж-а́ть, *v.i.,* + *acc.,* (*colloq.*), to offend deeply. Раз-оби́д-еть-ся, *v.p.r.,* (*colloq.*), to become deeply offended. Гость разоби́делся на хозя́ина, the guest was offended by the host. Раз-обиж-енный, *adj., part. pass. past,* deeply offended.

ОБИЛ-, ABUNDANCE

оби́л-ие, *n.m.,* abundance, plenty. В Крыму́ о. фру́ктов, there is an abundance of fruit in the Crimea. „Ты зна́ешь край, где всё оби́льем ды́шит," (*A. Tolstoy*), You know the land, which breathes abundance. Оби́л-ь-ный, *adj.,* abundant, plentiful, copious, ample, profuse. О. урожа́й, abundant harvest. О. дождь, abundant rain. О-ая еда́, abundant food. Оби́л-ь-но, *adv.,* abundantly, plentifully, amply. Дождь о. ороси́л поля́, the rain soaked the fields. Любв-е-оби́лье, *n.n.,* lovingness. Любв-е-оби́льный, *adj.,* loving, full of love. Л-ое се́рдце, loving heart.

оби́л-ова-ть, *v.i.,* + *instr.,* to abound in, be rich in. Ура́льские го́ры оби́луют желе́зной рудо́й, iron ore is abundant in the Urals.

из-оби́л-ова-ть, *v.i.,* + *instr.,* to abound in, teem with. Чёрное мо́ре изоби́лует ры́бой, the Black Sea abounds in fish. Из-оби́л-ующий, *adj., part. act. pres.,* abounding in. На се́вере нахо́дятся леса́, изоби́лующие пушны́м зве́рем, in the north there are forests that abound in furbearing animals. Из-оби́л-ование, *n.n.,* abundance. Из-оби́л-ие, *n.n.,* superabundance, plenty, profusion, luxuriance. И. плодо́в земны́х, (*fig.*), an abundance of the fruits of the earth. И. цвето́в на луга́х, a profusion of flowers in the meadows. В изоби́лии, in plenty. В бога́том до́ме всего́ в изоби́лии, in a rich home there is plenty of everything. Рог изоби́лия, (*fig.*), horn of plenty. На него́ посы́пались де́ньги, как из ро́га изоби́лия, (*fig.*), money rained down on him, as if from a horn of plenty. Из-оби́л-ь-ный, *adj.,* plentiful, copious, luxurious, teeming. Гостя́м по́дали вино́ в изоби́льном коли́честве, the guests were served wine in abundance.

ОБИТ-, HABITATION, HABITAT

обит-а́-ть, *v.i.,* (*obs.*), to inhabit, dwell, reside. В стра́нах с уме́ренным кли́матом люде́й обита́ет бо́льше, чем в холо́дных или жа́рких стра́нах, more people live in temperate climates than in the hot or cold countries. Обит-а́ние, *n.n.,* habitation, dwelling, residing. Обит-а́емость, *n.f.,* (*obs.*), habitableness. Обит-а́емый, *adj., part. pass. pres.,* habitable inhabitable. Земля́-обита́емая плане́та, the earth is a habitable planet. Не-обит-а́емый, *adj., part. pass. pres.,* uninhabitable Н. о́стров, uninhabitable island. Обит-а́лище, *n.n.,* habitation, dwelling, dwelling place, abode. Этот подва́л-обита́лище беспризо́рных, this cellar is a refuge for waifs. Обит-а́тель, *n.m.,* обит-а́тельница, *n.f.,* inhabitant. Обит-а́тели, *pl.,* residents; population; inmates. Я ста́рый обита́тель э́того го́рода, I am an old resident of this town. Кто обита́тели э́того до́ма? Who are the occupants of this house? Обит-ель, *n.m.,* cloister, convent, monastery. Солове́цкая оби́тель нахо́дится на о́строве на Бе́лом мо́ре, the monastery of Solovets is on an island in the White Sea. Ти́хая о., peaceful, secluded place; haven.

ОБЩ-, COMMUNITY, SOCIETY

óбщ-еств-о, *n.n.,* society; company. Первобы́тное о., primitive society. Избра́нное о., select society. О. страхова́ния, insurance company. Обще́ство-ве́дение, *n.n.,* social science, sociology. Общ-е-досту́пный, *adj.,* popular priced. О. спекта́кль, performance at popular prices. О-ые це́ны, popular prices. Общ-е-жи́тие, *n.n.,* dormitory. Студе́нческое о., student dormitory. Общ-е́ние, *n.n.,* communication. Ли́чное о., personal contact. Общ-е́ственность, *n.f.,* community, public. Общ-е́ственник, *n.m.,* обще́ственница, *n.f.,* public, social worker. Общ-е́ственный, *adj.,* public, social. О-ая со́бственность, community property. О-ое мне́ние, public opinion. О-ые нау́ки, social sciences. О-ый строй, social order.

óбщ-ий, *adj.,* general; common. О. враг, common enemy. О. наибо́льший дели́тель, *(math.),* greatest common divisor, denominator. О-ее собра́ние, general meeting. О-ая су́мма, sum total. В о́бщих черта́х, in general outline. В о́бщем, *adv.,* in general. В. о́бщем, всё идёт норма́льно, in general, everything is going along normally. Не име́ть ничего́ о́бщего, to have nothing in common. Найти́ о́бщий язы́к, to find a common language. О́бщ-ина, *n.f.,* community, commune. О. сестёр милосе́рдия, *(pre-Rev.),* community of nurses. Крестья́нская о., *(pre-Rev.),* village, peasant community. Общ-и́нный, *adj.,* communal. О-ое землевладе́ние, *(pre-Rev.),* community land-ownership. Общ-ность, *n.f.,* community. О. владе́ния, community ownership.

общ-а́ть-ся, *v.i.r.,* с + *instr.,* to associate with. Нельзя́ обща́ться с зара́зными больны́ми, one must not associate with patients who have contagious diseases.

общ-и́тель-ность, *n.f.,* communicativeness. Общ-и́тельный, *adj.,* communicative, talkative, unreserved.

об-общ-а́ть, *v.i.,* об-общ-и́ть, *v.p.,* + *acc.,* to generalize. О. ча́стный слу́чай, to generalize from a single case. О. едини́чное явле́ние, to generalize from a single phenomenon. Об-общ-е́ние, *n.n.,* generalization, general conclusion.

об-общ-еств-л-я́ть, *v.i.,* об-общ-ествить, *v.p.,* + *acc.,* to socialize. О. произво́дство, (труд), *(recent),* to socialize industry (labor). Об-общ-ествле́ние, *n.n.,* socialization. О. средств произво́дства, *(recent),* socialization of the means of production. Об-общ-ествлён-

ный, *adj., part. pass. past,* socialized. О. се́ктор се́льского хозя́йства, *(recent),* collectivized sector of agriculture.

при-общ-а́ть, *v.i.,* при-общ-и́ть, *v.p.,* + *acc.,* к + *dat.,* to join; administer the holy Sacrament. П. к де́лу, to file. При-общ-а́ть-ся, *v.i.r.,* при-общ-и́ть-ся, *v.p.r.,* to join, unite; communicate. П. св. Тайн, to take, receive communion. При-общ-е́ние, *n.n.,* uniting, junction.

раз-общ-а́ть, *v.i.,* раз-общ-и́ть, *v.p.,* + *acc.,* to separate, disunite, estrange; *(tech.),* disconnect, uncouple. Обстоя́тельства нас разобщи́ли, circumstances separated us. Р. провода́, to disconnect wires. Раз-общ-а́ть-ся, *v.i.r.,* раз-общ-и́ть-ся, *v.p.r.,* to be disconnected. Раз-общ-и́тель, *n.m.,* disconnector.

со-общ-а́ть, *v.i.,* со-общ-и́ть, *v.p.,* + *acc.,* о + *prep.,* to report, let know, communicate, impart. С. по ра́дио, to inform by radio. С. ра́достную но́вость, to communicate joyful news. Со-общ-а́ть-ся, *v.i.r., used only in imprf. aspect,* to communicate with one another; be communicated, imparted, informed. Как сообща́лось в газе́тах, as announced, as reported in the papers. Со-общ-а́ющийся, *adj., part. pass. pres.,* being communicated, reported. С-иеся сосу́ды, communicating vessels. Со-общ-е́ние, *n.n.,* report, information, communication. Прави́тельственное с., communiqué. Пути́ с-ия, means of communication. Железнодоро́жное с., railway communication. Возду́шное с., air service, communication.

со-о́бщ-ество, *n.n.,* association. В сообще́стве, in cooperation with, together with. Со-о́бщ-ник, *n.m.,* со-о́бщ-ница, *n.f.,* accomplice. Со-о́бщ-ничество, *n.n.,* complicity. Та́йное с., secret complicity.

со-общ-а́, *adv.,* all together, jointly.

во-общ-е́, *adv.,* in general, generally, on the whole; always; at all. В о́бщем, in general. Он в. тако́й, he is usually like this. Он в. не придёт, he will not come at all.

ОВ-, SHEEP

ов-ц-а́, *n.f.,* sheep. Парши́вая овца́ всё ста́до по́ртит, *(prov.),* one mangy sheep spoils the whole flock. Ов-ц-е-во́д, *n.m.,* sheep-breeder. Ов-ц-е-во́дство, *n.n.,* sheep-breeding. Ове́чка, *n.f.,* *(dim.),* little sheep, lamb. Она́ тиха́, как о., *(fig.),* she's as quiet as a lamb. Ов-е́чий, *adj.,* ovine, of or pertaining to a sheep. О. сыр, çheese made of ewe's milk. Волк в овéчьей шкýре, (fig.), a wolf in sheep's clothing.

ов-ч-áр, n.m., sheep-breeder, sheep-farmer. Ов-чáрка, n.f., sheep dog. Неméцкая овчáрка, German shepherd. Ов-чáрня, n.f., sheepfold, pen.

ов-ч-ѝн-а, n.f., sheepskin. Ов-чѝнка, n.f., (dim.), sheepskin. Овчѝнка выделки не стóит, (prov.), the game is not worth the candle. Мне нéбо с овчѝнку показáлось, I was frightened out of my wits. Ов-чѝнный, adj., pertaining to a sheepskin. О. тулýп, sheepskin coat.

ОГН-, ОГОН-, FIRE

огóн-ь, n.m., fire. Развестѝ (погасѝть) о., to start (extinguish) a fire. Заградѝтельный о., (mil.), defensive fire. Перекрёстный о., (mil.), cross-fire. Антóнов о., (folk), gangrene. Говорѝть с огнём, (fig.), to speak with fervor. Из огня да в пóлымя, (saying), out of the frying pan into the fire. Нет дыма без огня, (prov.), there is no smoke without a fire (where there is smoke, there is fire). Огон-ёк, n.m., (dim.), small light. Блуждáющий о., will-o'-the-wisp. Огн-евóй, adj., pertaining to firearms. О-áя завéса, (mil.), firescreen. О-áя тóчка, (mil.), weapon emplacement. О-ые рéчи, fiery speeches. óгн-енный, adj., fiery, burning; ignited; (fig), ardent. Сóлнце - óгненный шар, the sun is a fiery orb. О. взор, (fig.), fiery glance.

огн-ь, n.m., (obs.), fire. Огн-е-, a combining form meaning fire. Огне-вѝдный, adj., firelike. Огн-е-опáсный, adj., inflammable. Огн-е-поклóнник, n.m., fire-worshipper. Огн-е-стрéльный, adj., pertaining to firearms. О-ое орýжие, firearms. Огн-е-упóрный, adj., fireproof. О-ая глѝна, fire-resistant clay. Огн-евѝк, n.m., firestone, flint; (med.), carbuncle. Огн-евѝца, n.f., (bot.), Spanish camomile. Огн-е-мёт, n.m., (mil.), flame thrower. Огн-е-тушѝтель, n.m., fire extinguisher.

óгн-ив-о, n.n., flint; (mil.), hammer, lock. Вздуть óгниво, (colloq., obs.), to start a fire.

ОК-, ОЧ-, EYE

óк-о, n.n., (obs.), eye. Во мгновéние óка, in the twinkling of an eye. Óко за óко, и зуб зá зуб, (Bib.), an eye for an eye, a tooth for a tooth.

ок-н-ó, n.n., window; (tech.), opening, slot. Слуховóе о., dormer window.

Без óкон, windowless. Ок-óнный, adj., window. О-ая рáма, window frame, casement. О-ое стеклó, window pane.

оч-к-ѝ, n.pl., spectacles, glasses, goggles. О. для дальнозóрких (близорýких), glasses for farsighted (nearsighted) people. Смотрéть на жизнь сквозь рóзовые очкѝ, (fig.), to look at things through rose-colored glasses; be optimistic. Втирáть очкѝ, (fig.), to throw dust in one's eyes.

оч-к-ó, n.n., pip, point, hole. Дать нéсколько очкóв вперёд, (colloq.), (in a game) to give points, a handicap. Смотровóе о., peep-hole. Оч-к-о-втирáтельство, n.n., humbug. Оч-к-о-втирáтель, n.m., deceiver.

óч-н-ый, adj., visual. Ó-ая стáвка, (law), confrontation. Дать óчную стáвку, to confront. За-óч-ный, adj., out of sight. З-ое обучéние, instruction by correspondence. З-ое решéние судá, judgment by default, in absentia. За-óч-но, adv., without seeing. За-óч-ник, n.n., (recent), student of a correspondence course.

оч-е-вѝдец, n.m., eyewitness. Оч-е-вѝдно, adv., obviously, apparently. Вы, очевѝдно, дýмаете, что..., You apparently think that. Оч-е-вѝдный, adj., obvious, evident, manifest, patent. О-ое доказáтельство, obvious proof.

во-óч-ию, adv., (obs.), with one's own eyes, personally. Убедѝться в чём-либо воóчию, to see something with one's own eyes.

ОРЁЛ-, ОРЛ-, EAGLE

орёл, n.m., eagle. Орлы, n. pl., eagles. Орл-ѝца, n.f., eagle. Орёл - царь птиц, the eagle is the king of birds. Орлы летáли над вершѝнами гор, eagles were soaring over the mountain tops. Геральдѝческий орёд, (heraldry), spread eagle. Двуглáвый орёл - герб Россѝйской Импéрии, (hist.), the two-headed eagle (was) the coat-of-arms of the Russian Empire. Орёл (fig.), brave soldier. Орл-ёнок, n.m., (dim.), eaglet, young eagle. Орл-ята, n.pl., eaglets, young eagles. Орлёнок пытáется летáть, the eaglet is trying to fly. Орлѝца кóрмит орлят, the mother eagle is feeding her eaglets. Орл-ёнок, (fig.), young hero; hero's son. Орёл и рéшка, toss penny. Орёл или рéшка? Heads or tails? Орл-янка, (obs.), toss penny. Орл-ѝный, adj., eagle. О-ое гнездó, eagle's nest. О. взгляд, eagle-eyed look. Человéк с орлѝным нóсом, an acquiline-nosed man.

орл-и́-ть, *v.i.*, (*hist.*), to stamp with an eagle.

орл-и́ть, *v.i.*, вз-орл-и́ть, *v.p.*, (*fig., poet.*), to soar like an eagle.

ОРЕХ-, ОРЕШ-, NUT

оре́х, *n.m.*, nut; nut tree; walnut (*wood*). Лесно́й о., hazelnut. Гре́цкий о., walnut. Ему́ доста́лось на оре́хи, (*colloq.*), he got it hot; he caught hell. Отде́лать или разде́лать под оре́х, (*fig., colloq.*), to scold soundly. Отде́лать ме́бель под оре́х, to give furniture a walnut finish. Оре́х-овка, *n.f.*, (*zool.*), nut-cracker bird. Оре́х-овый, *adj.*, nut. О-ое де́рево, walnut tree. О-ого цве́та, nut brown. О-ое моро́женое, nut-flavored ice cream. О-ое ма́сло, nut oil. О-ая скорлупа́, nutshell.

оре́ш-ек, *n.m.*, (*dim.*), орех. Молодо́й о., young nut tree. Оре́ш-ник, *n.m.*, nut grove.

ОСЕН-Ь-, AUTUMN

о́сен-ь, *n.f.*, autumn, fall. Глубо́кая о., late fall. Дождли́вая о., rainy autumn. Цыпля́т по о́сени счита́ют, (*saying*), don't count your chickens before they're hatched. О́сен-ью, *adv.*, in autumn. О́сенью быва́ет дождли́во и сы́ро, in the fall it is often rainy and damp. Осе́н-ний, *adj.*, autumnal. О. день, an autumn day. О-ие полевы́е рабо́ты, autumn work in the fields. Не осе́нний ме́лкий до́ждичек бры́зжет, бры́зжет сквозь тума́н... (*folksong*), it is not the autumn rain falling, dripping through the fog... Люблю́ осе́ннее приро́ды увяда́нье, (*Pushkin*), I love the fading of nature in autumn.

ОСТР-, ОСТЁР-, ОЩР-, SHARPNESS, ACUTENESS, KEENNESS

о́стр-ый, *adj.*, sharp, acute, keen. О. нож, sharp knife. О-ая боль, sharp pain. О-ое замеча́ние, sharp remark. О-ое положе́ние, critical situation.

остёр, *adj., pred., m.*, sharp. Он о. на язы́к, he has a sharp tongue. Остр-а́, *adj. pred. f.*, sharp. Са́бля о., the sabre is sharp. Остр-иё, *n.n.*, point, spike, edge. О. иглы́, point of a needle. Остр-ота́, *n.f.*, sharpness, acuteness, keenness. О. зре́ния (слу́ха, вку́са), keenness of seeing (hearing, taste). О-о́та, witticism, joke. Уда́чная о., good joke. Зла́я о., sarcasm. Остр-о́, *adv.*, sharply, acutely, keenly. Остр-о-, *a combining form meaning* sharp, keen,

acute. Остр-о-гла́зый, *adj.*, (*colloq.*), keen-sighted. Остр-о-гу́бцы, *n.pl.*, cutting pliers. Остр-о-коне́чный, *adj.*, sharp-pointed. Остр-о-ли́ст, (*bot.*), holly. Остр-о-но́сый, *adj.*, sharp-nosed. Остр-о-у́мие, *n.n.*, wit. Блиста́ть остр-о-у́мием, to sparkle with wit, be witty. Остр-о-у́мный, *adj.*, witty. Остр-я́к, *n.m.*, wit.

остр-и́-ть, *v.i.*, + *acc.*, to sharpen, whet. О. ножи́, to sharpen knives. Нужда́ ум остри́т, (*saying*), poverty (necessity) sharpens one's wits. Остр-и́ть, *v.i.*, с-остр-и́ть, *v.p.*, (*fig.*), to be witty, make jokes. О. на чужо́й счёт, to provoke laughter at someone else's expense.

за-остр-и́ть, *v.p.*, за-остр-я́ть, *v.i.*, + *acc.*, to sharpen; (*fig.*), to stress, emphasize. З. каранда́ш, to sharpen a pencil. З. внима́ние, to direct one's attention. За-остр-и́ть-ся, *v.p.r.*, за-остр-я́ть-ся, *v.i.r.*, to become sharp, be sharpened. У больно́го заостри́лся нос, the sick man's nose became peaked. За-остр-ённость, *n.f.*, pointedness, sharpness, acuteness. Полити́ческая з., political acuteness. За-остр-ённый, *adj., part. pass. past*, pointed, sharpened. З. но́сик у де́вочки, the girl's little pointed nose.

на-остр-и́ть, (на-в-остр-и́ть, *colloq.*), *v.p.*, + *acc.*, to sharpen. Навостри́ть у́ши, to prick up one's ears. Навостри́ть лы́жи, (*fig.*), to run away, flee. На-в-остр-и́ть-ся, *v.p.r.*, в + *prep.*, (*colloq.*), to acquire proficiency in something. Н. стреля́ть, to become a good shot.

об-остр-и́ть, *v.p.*, об-остр-я́ть, *v.i.*, + *acc.*, to intensify, sharpen; aggravate. О. отноше́ния, to strain relations. Об-остр-и́ть-ся, *v.p.r.*, об-остр-я́ть-ся, *v.i.r.*, to become sharp, strained, intensified. Положе́ние обостри́лось, the situation has become aggravated. Боле́знь обостри́лась, the illness became acute, worse, more serious. Об-остр-е́ние, *n.n.*, aggravation, О. боле́зни, acute condition. Об-остр-ённый, *adj., part. pass. past*, sharp, oversensitive. О-ое чутьё, sharp sense of smell. О. интере́с, keen interest.

остр-о́г, *n.m.*, (*obs.*), jail; (*hist.*), fortress. Поста́вить вокру́г го́рода о., to build a stockade around a city. Посади́ть в остро́г, to jail. Остро́ж-ник, *n.m.*, prisoner Остр-о́жный, *adj.*, pertaining to a rampart, fortress; jail. О. вал, fortress, rampart. Го́род Остро́г, the city of Ostrog.

остр-ог-а́, *n.f.*, harpoon, spear. Бить острого́й, to harpoon. Остро́-жить, *v.p.*, + *acc.*, to harpoon. О. рыбу, to spear a fish.

из-ощр-я́-ть, (*from*, из-остр-и́ть), *v.p.*, из-ощр-я́ть, *v.i.*, + *acc.*, to cultivate; refine; perfect. И. ум (па́мять), to sharpen, cultivate one's mind (memory). Из-ощр-и́ть-ся, *v.p.r.*, из-ощр-я́ть-ся, *v.i.r.*, в + *prep.*, to become cultivated, refined. нз-ощр-я́ться в остроу́мии, to cultivate wit. Из-ощр-е́ние, *n.n*, perfecting, refinement, cultivation. И. хи́трости, cultivation of deceitfulness. И. вку́са, refinement of taste. Из-ощр-ённый, *adj.*, *part. pass. past,* keen, sensitive, refined. И. ум, keen intellect.

по-ощр-и́ть, *v.p.*, по-ощр-я́ть, *v.i.*, + *acc.*, to encourage; countenance. Оте́ц поощря́л заня́тия сы́на жи́вописью, the father encouraged the son's study of painting. По-ощр-е́ние, *n.n.*, encouragement. По-ощр-и́тельный, *adj.*, encouraging. П. тон, encouraging tone. П-ая награ́да, honorable mention.

ОТЕЦ-, ОТЦ-, ОТЕЧ-, ОТЧ-, FATHER

оте́ц, *n.m.*, father. Крёстный о., godfather. Приёмный, о., foster-father. Посаженый о., one who gives away the bride in marriage. Отцы́ Це́ркви (Святы́е Отцы́), Church Fathers. Оте́ческий, *adj.*, fatherly, paternal. О-ая любо́вь, paternal love. О-ое наставле́ние, fatherly advice. Оте́ч-ески (по-оте́чески), *adv.*, in a fatherly way, manner. Относи́ться к кому́-нибудь по-оте́чески, to be paternal to someone in a fatherly way. Отц-о́вский, *adj.*, pertaining to one's father; paternal. О-ое насле́дие, patrimony. Отц-о́вство, *n.n.*, paternity. Отц-е, *a combining form meaning* father. Отц-е-уби́йство, *n.n.*, patricide. Отц-е-уби́йца, *n.m.*, patricide.

оте́ч-еств-о, *n.n.*, native land, fatherland. На́ше вели́кое о., our great fatherland. Второ́е о., second country, one's adopted country. Оте́ч-ественный, *adj.*, native, home. Вели́кая Оте́чественная Война́, the Great Patriotic War of 1812. О-ая промы́шленность, home industry.

о́тч-еств-о, *n.n.*, patronymic. Как ва́ше о., What is your patronymic?

отч-и́зн-а, *n.f.*, (*poet.*), native, mother country. "Для берего́в отчи́зны да́льней..." (*Pushkin*), "For the faraway shores of your fatherland..." О́тч-ий, *adj.*, (*obs., poet.*), paternal. О. дом, paternal house. О́тч-им, *n.m.*, stepfather.

в-о́тч-ин-а, *n.f.*, (*hist.*), ancestral lands, patrimonial estate. Кня́жеская в., (*hist.*), a prince's patrimonial domain. В-о́тч-инник, *n.m.*, (*obs.*), owner of ancestral lands; large landowner. В-о́тч-инный, *adj.*, patrimonial. В-ое землевладе́ние, patrimonial landownership.

П

ПАД-, ПАС-, ПА-, FALLING

па́д-а-ть, *v.i.*, у-па́с-ть (пас-ть), *v.p.*, to fall, drop, sink. П. на́взничь, to fall on one's back. Свет па́дает на кни́гу, the light is falling on the book. Отве́тственность за э́то па́дает на вас, the responsibility for this falls on you. Ударе́ние па́дает на пе́рвый слог, the accent falls on the first syllable. П. в о́бморок, to faint. Пасть на по́ле бра́ни, (*idiom.*), to be killed, fall in action. Па́-вший, *adj.*, *part. act. past,* fallen, killed. П-ие в бою́, killed in action. Па́д-аль, *n.f.*, carrion. Пад-ёж (скота́) *n.m*, epidemic. Пад-е́ж, *n.m.*, (*gram.*), case. Пад-е́ние, *n.n.*, fall, drop, sinking; downfall; incidence. П. температу́ры, drop in temperature. П. напряже́ния, drop in voltage. Па́д-ающий, *adj.*, *part. act. pres.*, incident; falling. П-ие звё́зды, shooting stars. Па́д-кий, *adj.*, having a weakness for, fond of. П. на лесть, susceptible to flattery. П. на де́ньги, mercenary; venal. Па́д-ший, *adj.*, *part. act. past,* fallen, morally debased. П. челове́к, fallen man. П-ая же́нщина, fallen woman. Пад-у́чая, *adj.*, used as *n.*, epilepsy. Пас-ть, *n.f.*, mouth of an animal; jaws; (*colloq.*), trap. Вод-о-па́д, *n.m.*, waterfall, falls, cascade. Снег-о-па́д, *n.m.*, snowfall.

в-пад-а́ть, *v.i.*, в-пас-ть, *v.p.*, в + *acc.*, to fall, flow into; lapse, sink. Во́лга впада́ет в Каспи́йское мо́ре, the Volga flows into the Caspian Sea. В. в отча́яние, to give way to despair. В. в неми́лость, to fall into disfavor. В. в де́тство, to sink into senility, dotage. В-пад-е́ние, *n.n.*, confluence. Го́род Го́рький стои́т при впаде́нии Оки́ в Во́лгу, the city of Gorki is located at the confluence of the Oka and the Volga rivers. В-па́д-ина, *n.f.*, hollow, cavity, depression. Глазна́я в., eye-socket. В-па́л-ый, *adj.*, hollow, sunken. В-ые щёки, sunken cheeks.

вы-пад-а́ть, *v.i.*, вы́-пас-ть, *v.p.*, to fall out, come out, slip out. Кни́га вы́пала у меня́ из рук, the book fell out of my hands. Мно́го дождя́ (сне́гу) вы́пало э́той зимо́й, there has been a heavy rainfall (snowfall), this winter. Ему́ вы́пал жре́бий, the lot fell to him. Ей вы́пало сча́стье, happiness has fallen to her lot. Вы-пад-е́ние, *n.n.*, fall. В. воло́с (зубо́в), falling out of hair (teeth). Вы́-пад, *n.m.*, lunge, thrust; attack. Ре́зкие вы́пады ора́тора, sharp attacks of the speaker.

за-пад-а́ть, *v.i.*, за-па́с-ть, *v.p.*, to fall back, sink deeply. Кла́виша запада́ет, (*mus.*), the key does not rise. Слова́ его́ запа́ли мне глубоко́ в ду́шу, his words were deeply imprinted in my mind. За-пад-ня́, *n.f.*, trap, pitfall. Поста́вить кому́-нибудь западню́, to set a trap for someone. Попа́сть в западню́, to be caught in a trap.

за-па́д-ать, *v.p.*, to begin to fall. Ка́пли дождя́ запа́дали одна́ за друго́й, drops of rain began to fall one after the other.

за́-пад, *n.m.*, west, West. На з., к з-у, to the West. С за́пада, from the west. Ве́тер ду́ет с за́пада, the wind is blowing from the west. За́-пад-ник, *n.m.*, (*hist.*), Westernizer. За́-пад-ничество, *n.n.*, (*hist.*), Westernism. За́-пад-ный, *adj.*, west, western, Occidental. З. ве́тер, western wind. З-ая Евро́па, Western Europe. Западноевропе́йский, *adj.*, Western European.

на-пад-а́ть, *v.i.*, на-па́с-ть, *v.p.*, на + *acc.*, to attack, assault, fall on. Н. врасплóх, to make a surprise attack. На меня́ напа́ла тоска́, a sadness (melancholy) came over me. На-пад-е́ние, *n.n.*, attack, assault, aggression. Внеза́пное н., surprise attack. Хими́ческое н., gas attack. На-па́д-ки, *n.pl.*, attacks. Кни́га подве́рглась напа́дкам кри́тиков (рецензе́нта), the book was subjected to the critics' (reviewer's) attacks.

на-па́с-ть, *n.f.*, (*colloq.*), misfortune. Что за напа́сть! How unfortunate! What a misfortune!

на-па́д-ать, *v.p.*, + *gen.*, to fall in quantity. За ночь напа́дало сне́гу, much snow fell during the night.

о-пад-а́ть, *v.i.*, о-па́с-ть, *v.p.*, to fall off, fall away; sag, subside. Ли́стья опа́ли, the leaves have fallen. Опу́холь опа́ла, the swelling has gone down. О-пад-е́ние, *n.n.*, dropping off. О. ли́стьев, defoliation; falling of leaves.

от-пад-а́ть, *v.i.*, от-па́с-ть, *v.p.*, to fall off, fall away; pass; abjure, renounce. Карни́з отпа́л, the molding fell off. У меня́ отпа́ла охо́та к э́тому, my desire to do it has passed. Вопро́с отпада́ет, the question no longer arises. От-пад-е́ние, *n.n.*, falling away; defection. О. приве́рженцев, defection of followers.

пере-пад-а́ть, *v.i.*, пере-па́с-ть, *v.p.*, to fall occasionally; *impers.*, to fall to one's lot. Перепада́ют дожди́, it rains now and then. Снег лишь перепада́ет в э́той ме́стности, it snows but seldom in these parts. П. на чью́-либо до́лю, to fall to one's lot. Из добы́чи ему́ ма́ло перепа́ло, few spoils fell to his lot. Перепа́д, *n.m.*, (*tech.*), overfall.

под-пад-а́ть, *v.i.*, под-па́с-ть, *v.p.*, под, + *acc.*, to fall under. П. под чьё-либо влия́ние, to fall under someone's influence.

по-пад-а́ть, *v.i.*, по-па́с-ть, *v.p.*, в + *acc.*, to fall in, into; get into; find oneself. П. в цель, to hit the mark. П. на по́езд (авто́бус), to catch a train (an autobus). Письмо́ попа́ло не по а́дресу, the letter was delivered to the wrong address. П. под суд, to be brought to trial. Пу́ля попа́ла ему́ в но́гу, the bullet struck his leg. П. в беду́, to get into a scrape. П. впроса́к, (*colloq.*), to make a blunder. Ему́ попа́ло, (*colloq.*), he caught hell; he was scolded. Как попа́ло, (*colloq.*), carelessly. По-пад-а́ть-ся, *v.i.r.*, по-па́с-ть-ся, *v.p.r.*, to be caught, be found out. П. на у́дочку, to take the bait. Ры́ба попа́лась на у́дочку, the fish took the bait. Я попа́лся на у́дочку, (*fig.*), I was taken. П. кому́-либо на глаза́, (*colloq.*), to catch someone's eye. П. в ру́ки, to fall into the hands of. На экза́мене ему́ попа́лся тру́дный биле́т, at the examination he drew a difficult question. Пе́рвый попа́вшийся, the first comer; anybody. Сесть в пе́рвый попа́вшийся авто́бус, to take the first bus that comes along. Спроси́ть на у́лице пе́рвого попа́вшегося, to ask the first person you encounter on the street. По-пад-а́ние, *n.n.*, hit. Прямо́е п. в цель, (*mil.*), direct hit. В-по-па́д, *adv.*, (*colloq.*), a propos, to the point. Невпопа́д, *adv.*, inopportunely. Он сказа́л э́то н., he said that inopportunely.

при-пад-а́ть, *v.i.*, при-па́с-ть, *v.p.*, к + *dat.*, to fall down to; press oneself to. П. к груди́ кого́-либо, to fall on someone's bosom. Припада́ть на пра́вую (ле́вую) но́гу, to be lame in the right (the left) leg. При-па́д-ок, *n.m.*, attack; fit. П. бе́шенства, paroxysm of rage. При-па́д-очный, *adj.*, also used as *n.*, epileptic. П-ые явле́ния, epileptic fits.

про-пад-а́ть, *v.i.*, про-па́с-ть, *v.p.*, to be missing, be lost; disappear, vanish, die, pass away. Кни́га пропа́ла, the book was lost. Пропа́ла охо́та, my desire disappeared. П. от ску́ки, to be bored to death. Про-па́в-ший, *adj.*, lost. П. бе́з вести, missing. Пиши́ пропа́ло, (*idiom., colloq.*), it is as good as lost. Про-па́ж-а, *n.f.*, loss. Все пропа́жи нашли́сь, all the lost things have been found. Про́-пас-ть, *n.f.*, precipice, abyss; (*fig.*), gulf. Быть на краю про́пасти, to be on the verge of disaster, ruin. До про́пасти мно́го, (*colloq.*), there is so much one could fill a pit. Про-па́-щий, *adj.*, (*colloq.*), *in expression*: Он п. челове́к, he is a hopeless case. Это пропа́щее де́ло, it's a bad job; nothing will come of it. На-про-па-лу́ю, *adv.*, recklessly, headlong, desperately.

рас-пад-а́ть-ся, *v.i.r.,* рас-па́с-ть-ся, *v.p.r.,* на + *acc.,* to disintegrate; fall to pieces; break down; collapse. Моле́кула распа́лась на а́томы, the molecule was broken down into atoms. О́бщество распа́лось на не́сколько групп, the company broke up into several groups. Рас-па́д, *n.m.,* disintegration; collapse, decay. Р. кле́ток, disintegration of cells.

с-пад-а́ть, *v.i.,* с-пас-ть, *v.p.,* с + *gen.,* to fall down from; abate. Шине́ль спа́ла с плеч, the cloak slipped off his shoulders. Вода́ в реке́ спа́ла, the waters of the river have subsided. Жара́ спа́ла, the heat abated. С-пад, *n.m.,* abatement. С-пад-е́ние, *n.n.,* abatement. С-пад-а́ть-ся, *v.i.r.,* to collapse, be collapsed. Лёгкое спада́ется, a lung is collapsed.

сов-пад-а́ть, *v.i.,* сов-па́с-ть, *v.p.,* с + *instr.,* to coincide with. Не с., to not coincide with. Свиде́тельские показа́ния не совпада́ют, the evidence is conflicting. Сов-пад-е́ние, *n.n.,* coincidence. С. обстоя́тельств, coincidence of circumstances.

у-па́с-ть, *v.p.,* *see* па́дать. Упа́сть (пасть) ду́хом, to become discouraged. У-па́д-ок, *n.m.,* decline, fall, decay, decadence. Приходи́ть в у., to decay, fall into decay. У. сил, breakdown, collapse. У. ду́ха, depression, low spirits. У-па́д-ничество, *n.n.,* decadence. У-па́д-нический, *adj.,* decadent. У-па́д-очный, *adj.,* depressive. У-ое настрое́ние, low spirits. У-ое состоя́ние, depression. У-ая литерату́ра, decadent literature. У-ое иску́сство, decadent art. У-па́д, *n.m.,* *in expression*: До упа́ду, till one falls. Смея́ться до упа́ду, to roll with laughter. Танцова́ть ло упа́ду, to dance till one drops.

ПАЛ-, FINGER, STICK

па́л-ец, *n.m.,* finger, toe; (*tech.*), pin. Большо́й п. руки́ (ноги́), thumb (big toe). Указа́тельный п., forefinger,

index finger. Ему́ па́льца в рот не клади́, (*fig.*), he is not to be trusted. Смотре́ть сквозь па́льцы на что́-либо, (*fig.*), to look at something through one's fingers. Знать что́-либо, как свои́ пять па́льцев, (*saying*), to have something at one's finger tips. Па́л-ь-чик, *n.m.,* (*dim.*), *see* па́лец. Ма́льчик с па́льчик, Tom Thumb. Па́л-ь-чатый, пал-ь-ц-е-обра́зный, пал-ь-ц-е-ви́дный, *adj.,* finger-shaped. Бес-па́л-ый, *adj.,* toeless. Б-ые живо́тные, toeless animals.

па́л-иц-а, *n.f.,* (*hist.*), club, cudgel.

па́л-ка, *n.f.,* stick. П. для прогу́лки, walking stick, cane. П. метлы́, broomstick. Бить па́лкой, to cane. Рабо́тать (учи́ться) из-под па́лки, (*colloq.*), to study under duress. П. о двух конца́х, (*lit.*), the stick has two ends; it may boomerang. Па́л-очка, *n.f.,* (*dim.*), little stick. Бараба́нная п., drumstick. Дирижёрская п., conductor's baton. Па́лочки Ко́ха, (*med.*), tuberculosis bacilli. Па́л-очный, *adj.,* pertaining to a cane. П-ые уда́ры, blows from a cane. П-ая дисципли́на, discipline with a cane.

ПАЛ-, ПЛАМ-, ПЕЛ-, FLAME

пал-и́ть, *v.i.,* с-пал-и́ть, о-пал-и́ть, *v.p.,* + *acc.,* to burn, scorch, singe, fire. П. соло́му, to burn straw. П. гу́ся, to singe a goose. Со́лнце пали́т, the sun burns, is hot. Пали́! (пли!) (*mil.*), Fire! Пал-ь-ба́, *n.f.,* firing. Пу́шечная п., cannonade.

вос-пал-и́ть, *v.p.,* вос-пал-я́ть, *v.i.,* + *acc.,* to inflame. Вос-пал-и́ть-ся, *v.p.r.,* вос-пал-я́ть-ся, *v.i.r.,* + *instr.,* to become inflamed. В. гне́вом, (*fig.*), to be aroused to anger. Рука́ си́льно воспаля́ется, the hand becomes inflamed. Вос-пал-е́ние, *n.n.,* inflammation. В. лёгких, pneumonia, inflammation of the lungs. Вос-пал-ённый, *adj.,* *part. pass. past,* inflamed. В. глаз, inflamed eye. В. взор, feverish look, countenance. Вос-пал-и́тельный, *adj.,* inflammatory. В. проце́сс, inflammatory process.

за-пал-и́ть, *v.p.,* за-па́л-ивать, *v.i.,* + *acc.,* (*colloq.*), to set fire to; kindle. З. соло́му, to set fire to straw. З. ло́шадь, to break the wind of a horse. За-па́л, *n.m.,* heaves, fuse. Ло́шадь с запа́лом, a horse with heaves. Автомати́ческий п., automatic ignition device. За-па́л-ь-ный, *adj.,* ignition. З-ая свеча́, spark-plug. За-па́л-ь-чивость, *n.f.,* quick temper, vehemence. З. хара́ктера (рече́й) vehemence of disposition, (of speeches). За-па́л-ь-чивый, *adj.*, quick-tempered, vehement. З. челове́к, quick-tempered man. За-па́л-ь-чиво, *adv.*, passionately.

о-пал-и́ть, *v.p.,* о-па́л-ивать, пал-и́ть, *v.i.,* + *acc.,* to singe, burn. О. цыплёнка, to singe a chicken. О. со́лнцем лицо́ (спи́ну), to sunburn one's face (back). О-пал-и́ть-ся, *v.p.r.,* о-па́л-ивать-ся, *v.i.r.,* to be singed, burn oneself. О. на со́лнце, (to become) sunburned. О. на пожа́ре, to be burned in a fire. О-па́л-а, *n.f.,* (*obs.*), disfavor. Быть в опа́ле, to fall into disfavor. О-па́л-ь-ный, *adj.,* fallen into disfavor. О. боя́рин, (*hist.*), a boyar who has fallen into the Tsar's disfavor.

под-пал-и́ть, *v.p.,* под-па́л-ивать, *v.i.,* + *acc.,* (*colloq.*), to singe, scorch, set fire to. П. дом, to set fire to a house. П. лес, to set fire to a forest.

рас-пал-и́ть, *v.p.,* рас-пал-я́ть, *v.i.,* + *acc.,* to make burning hot, inflame; excite. Рас-пал-и́ть-ся, *v.p.r.,* рас-пал-я́ть-ся, *v.i.r.,* + *instr.,* to become burning hot, be incensed, inflamed; be excited. Р. гне́вом, (*fig.*), to become infuriated. Распали́лся и наговори́л мно́го ли́шнего, he was infuriated and said too much.

с-пал-и́ть, *v.p., see* пали́ть. С. лес, to burn a forest. С. во́лосы, to singe one's hair. С. спи́ну на со́лнце, to sunburn one's back.

пере-па́л-ка, *n.f.,* (*colloq.*), skirmish.

пла́м-я, *n.n.,* flame, flare; blaze. Вспы́хнуть пла́менем, to burst into flames; flare up. По́лым-я, *n.n.,* (*folk*), *see* пла́мя. Из огня́ да в по́лымя (*saying*), out of the frying pan into the fire.

плам-ен-е́-ть, *v.p.,* to flame, blaze; (*fig.*), + *instr.,* to burn with. Зака́т пламене́ет, the sunset sky is aflame. П. стра́стью, to burn with passion. Пла́м-енность, *n.f.,* ardor. П. воображе́ния, fieriness of imagination. Пла́м-енный, *adj.,* flaming, fiery; (*fig.*), ardent, flaming. П. патриоти́зм, ardent patriotism.

вос-плам-ен-и́ть, *v.p.,* вос-плам-еня́ть, *v.i.,* + *acc.,* to set afire, ignite, inflame with enthusiasm. Слова́ команди́ра воспламени́ли бойцо́в, the commanding officer's words inflamed the soldiers with enthusiasm. Вос-плам-ени́ться, *v.p.r.,* вос-плам-еня́ть-ся, *v.i.r,* to catch fire, become ignited, blaze up, become inflamed; become enthusiastic. Соло́ма легко́ воспламеня́ется, straw is highly inflammable. Вос-плам-ене́-ние, *n.n.,* ignition. Вос-плам-еня́емость, *n.f.,* inflammability. По́рох облада́ет

хоро́шей воспламеня́емостью, gunpowder is easily ignited. Вос-пламеня́емый, *adj., part. pres. pass.,* inflammable.

пе́-пел, *n.m.,* ashes. Обраща́ть в п., to incinerate. Пе́-пел-ище, *n.n.,* site of a burned house; (*fig.*), home, hearth. Дом сгоре́л, оста́лось то́лько п., the house burned, only ashes remained. Верну́ться на ста́рое п., to return to one's homestead, ancestral home. Пе́-пел-ь-ница, *n.f.,* ashtray. Пе́-пел-ь-ный, *adj.,* ashy. П. цвет воло́с, ash-blond hair.

ис-пе́-пел-ить, *v.p.,* ис-пе-пел-я́ть, *v.i.,* + *acc.,* to incinerate, reduce to ashes. Война́ испепели́ла мно́жество цвету́щих селе́ний, war has reduced to ashes many a flourishing village.

ПАР-, STEAM

пар, *n.m.,* steam; exhalation. Водяно́й п., water steam. Отрабо́танный (насы́-щенный) п., exhaust (saturated) steam. Преврати́ться в пар, to evaporate. От ло́шади идёт п., the horse is steaming. Быть под пара́ми, to be under steam, be ready to start (*as a locomotive*). На всех пара́х, at full speed. Пар косте́й не ло́мит, (*saying*), warmth (heat) cannot hurt. Пар, *n.m.,* (*agric.*), fallow land. Земля́ под па́ром, this land is fallow. Пар-ови́к, *n.m.,* boiler; (*colloq.*), steam engine. Пар-о-во́з, *n.m.,* locomotive. Пар-о-во́зный, *adj.,* locomotive. П-ое депо́, engine shed. Пар-о-воз-о-строи́тельный заво́д, locomotive works. Пар-ово́й, *adj.,* steam; (*agric.*), fallow. П. котёл, steam boiler. П-а́я маши́на, steam engine. П-а́я ме́льница, steam mill. П-ое отопле́ние, steam heat, central heating. П-ое по́ле, fallow field. Пар-о-хо́д, *n.m.,* steamer, steamship, liner. Пар-о-хо́дный, *adj.,* steamship. П-ое сообще́ние, steamship communication, transportation. Пар-о-хо́дство, *n.n.,* steam navigation.

па́р-ить, *v.i.,* вы́-пар-ить, *v.p.,* + *acc.,* to steam, stew. П. ре́пу, to steam turnips. П. бельё, to steam laundry. Па́рит, (*impers.*), it is sultry. Па́р-ить-ся, *v.i.r.,* to steam oneself, be steamed. Ре́па па́рится в котле́, turnip is steamed in a cauldron. Па́р-еный, *adj.,* steamed, stewed. Дешёвле па́реной ре́пы, (*idiom.*), dirt cheap. Пар-ни́к, *n.m.,* hotbed, seed-bed. В парнике́, under glass, in a seed-bed. Пар-нико́-вый, *adj.,* hotbed, hothouse. П-ые расте́ния (огурцы́), hothouse plants (cucumbers). Пар-но́й, *adj.,* fresh.

П-о́е молоко́, milk fresh from the cow.

вы́-пар-ить, *v.p.,* па́р-ить, *v.i.,* вы-па́р-ива-ть, *v.i.,* + *acc.,* to cause to evaporate, steam out; clean, disinfect by steam. В. бельё, to steam laundry. Вы́-пар-ить-ся, *v.p.r.,* вы-па́р-ивать-ся, *v.i.r.,* to be steamed out, evaporated, disinfected by steam. Вся вода́ в ча́йнике вы́парилась, all the water has evaporated from the kettle. Вы́-пар-ивание, *n.n.,* (chem.), evaporation.

за-па́р-ить, *v.p.,* за-па́р-ивать, *v.i.,* + *acc.,* to start steaming, stewing. З. корм скоту́, to prepare mash for cattle. За-па́р-ить-ся, *v.p.r.,* за-па́р-ивать-ся, *v.i.r.,* (*colloq.*), to be exhausted from too prolonged a steam bath; (*fig.*), to be fatigued, tired from work, activity, etc. Запа́рился чуть не до́ смерти, (*colloq.*), to feel dead from overwork.

ис-пар-и́ть, *v.p.,* ис-пар-я́ть, *v.i.,* + *acc.,* to evaporate; exhale; turn into vapor, vaporize. Не́которые расте́ния испаря́ют неприя́тные для обоня́ния вещества́, some plants exhale substances with a disagreeable odor. Ис-пар-и́ть-ся, *v.p.r.,* ис-пар-я́ть-ся, *v.i.r.,* to evaporate; be exhaled, vaporized; (*colloq.*), to disappear, vanish. Он то́тчас же испари́лся, когда́ уви́дел, что его́ мо́гут притяну́ть к отве́ту, (*colloq.*), he vanished as soon as he saw that he might be held responsible. Ис-паре́ние, *n.n.,* evaporation, exhalation; fumes. И. жи́дкости, evaporation of a liquid. Вре́дные испаре́ния, harmful vapors. Ис-па́р-ина, *n.f.,* perspiration, sweat. У больно́го си́льная и., the patient is covered with sweat. Ис-пар-и́тель, *n.m.,* evaporator, vaporizer.

о-па́р-а, *n.f.,* leavened dough. Вздулся как те́сто на опа́ре, (*saying*), he puffed up with conceit.

от-па́р-ить, *v.p.,* от-па́р-ивать, *v.i.,* + *acc.,* to press with steam; remove with steam. О. ба́рхатное пла́тье, to steam a velvet dress. О. присо́хшую повя́зку, to remove a bandage by steaming.

по-па́р-ить-ся, *v.p.r.,* па́р-ить-ся, *v.i.r.,* to take a steam bath. П. в ба́не, to steam oneself in a steam bath.

пере-па́р-ить, *v.p.,* пере-па́р-ивать, *v.i.,* + *acc.,* to overstew, oversteep. П. чай, to steep tea too long. Пере-па́р-ить-ся, *v.p.r.,* пере-па́р-ивать-ся, *v.i.r.,* to be oversteamed, steam oneself too long. П. в ба́не, to steam oneself too long in a Russian bath. Ре́па пере-па́рилась, the urnips were oversteamed.

при-па́р-ить, *v.p.,* при-па́р-ивать, *v.i.,* +

acc., to apply a poultice; steam. П. нары́в насто́ем, to draw out an abcess by steaming. П. кипятко́м, to steam with boiling water. При-па́р-ка, *n.f.,* poultice. Класть припа́рки, to apply a poultice.

рас-па́р-ить, *v.p.,* рас-па́р-ивать, *v.i.,* + *acc.,* to steam thoroughly. Р. ко́жу (о́вощи), to steam one's skin (vegetables). Рас-па́р-ить-ся, *v.p.r.,* рас-па́р-ивать-ся, *v.i.r.,* to be steamed thoroughly. Ло́шади распа́рились, the horses are steaming.

у-па́р-ить, *v.p.,* у-па́р-ивать, *v.i.,* + *acc.,* to soften by steaming. У. свину́ю ко́жу, to soften pigskin by steaming. У-па́р-ить-ся, *v.p.r.,* у-па́р-ивать-ся, *v.i.r.,* (*colloq.*), to be in a sweat. У. на рабо́те, (*colloq.*), to perspire from work.

ПАС-, PASTURE, HERD, TENDING

пас-ти́, *v.i.,* + *acc.,* to graze, shepherd, pasture. П. скот, to graze cattle; tend grazing cattle. Пас-ти́-сь, *v.i.r.,* to graze, pasture; browse. В по́ле пасу́тся коро́вы, cows are grazing in the open field. Па́с-тбище, *n.n.,* вы́-пас, *n.m.,* (*colloq.*), pasture. Ове́чье п., sheeprun. Па́с-тбищный, *adj.,* pasturable. Пастьба́, *n.f.,* pasturage. Па́с-тва, *n.f.,* (*rel.*), flock, congregation. Пас-ту́х, *n.m.,* herdsman, shepherd. Пас-ту́шка, *n.f.,* shepherdess. Пас-тушо́к, *n.m.,* (*dim.*), see пасту́х. Под-па́с-ок, *n.m.,* young shepherd. Пас-ту́шеский, пасту́ший, *adj.,* shepherd's. П. по́сох, shepherd's crook. Па́с-тырь, *n.m.,* pastor; shepherd. Па́с-тырский, *adj.,* pastoral. П-ое благослове́ние, pastoral blessing.

за-пас-ти́, *v.p.,* за-пас-а́ть, *v.i.,* + *acc.,* + *gen.,* to stock, store. З. ча́ю (вина́, муки́), to stock tea (wine, flour). За-пас-ти́-сь, *v.p.r.,* за-пас-а́ть-ся, *v.i.r.,* + *instr.,* to provide for oneself. З. дрова́ми на́ зиму, to lay in firewood for the winter. З. терпе́нием, to cultivate patience. За-па́с, *n.m.,* stock, supply, reserve. З. това́ров, stock in trade. З. зна́ний, fund of knowledge, erudition. З. слов, vocabulary. З. боеприпа́сов, ammunition supply, reserve. Отложи́ть про з., to lay aside; reserve Уво́лить в з., (*mil.*), to transfer to a reserve. За-па́с-ливость, *n.f.,* thriftiness; reserving for a future. За-па́с-ливый, *adj.,* thrifty, provident. За-пас-но́й, *adj.,* spare, reserve. З-а́я ши́на, spare tire. За-па́с-ный, *adj.,* extra, additional. З. вы́ход, emergency exit. З. путь, side track, siding. За-паснóй, *adj., used as n.*, (mil.), reservist. З. красноармéец, Red Army reservist.

о-пас-áть-ся, *v.i.*, + *gen.*, to apprehend; fear; avoid. О. врагóв, to fear enemies. Врач предписáл о. жúрной пúщи, the doctor prescribed that fat foods be avoided. О-пас-éние, *n.n.*, fear, misgiving, apprehension. Вызывáть о., to excite apprehension, provoke fear. О-пáс-ка, *n.f.*, (*colloq.*), caution. С опáской, (*colloq.*), with caution, cautiously, apprehensively. О-пáс-ливый, *adj.*, cautious, apprehensive. Ступáть по льду опáсливыми шагáми, to walk on ice cautiously. О-пáс-ность, *n.f.*, danger, peril. Быть в опáсности, to be in danger. С опáсностью для жúзни, in peril of one's life. О-пáс-ный, *adj.*, dangerous, perilous. О. слýчай, perilous case. О-пáс-но, *adv.*, dangerously, perilously. Здесь о., it is dangerous here, it is dangerous to be here.

при-пас-тú, *v.p.*, при-пас-áть, *v.i.*, + *acc.*, to store, stock, provide; prepare. П. семенá к сéву, to store seed for planting. При-пáс-ы, *n.pl.*, stores, supplies, provisions. Съестнýе п., provisions, food supplies. Боевýе п., ammunition.

про-пас-тú, *v.p.*, до + *gen.*, to pasture. П. стáдо до сáмых зáморозков, to pasture a flock until the frosts set in. Про-пас-тú-сь, *v.p.r.*, to be pastured for a definite period of time. Óвцы пропаслúсь в степú до глубóкой óсени, the sheep were pastured in the steppe until late autumn.

с-пас-тú, *v.p.*, с-пас-áть, *v.i.*, + *acc.*, to save, rescue. С. утопáющего, to rescue a drowning man. С. положéние, to save a situation. С-пас-тú-сь, *v.p.r.*, с-пас-áть-ся, *v.i.r.*, + *instr.*, to save oneself, escape. С. бéгством, to flee for one's life. С-пас-éние, *n.n.*, rescuing, saving, rescue, escape; (*fig.*), salvation. Это нáше едúнтсвенное с., this is our only salvation. С-пас-áтель-ный, *adj.*, lifesaving. С. пóяс, lifesaver. С-ая шлюпка, lifeboat. С-пас-úбо (*from* спасú Бог), thanks; thank you. Большóе с., many thanks. С-пас-úтель, *n.m.*, rescuer; Saviour, Redeemer. С-пас-úтельный, *adj.*, salutary. С-пас-úтельное срéдство, saving remedy.

у-пас-тú, *v.i.*, (*colloq.*), *used only in expression*: Упасú Бóже! Lord preserve us! Упасú от бедý! Preserve us from misfortune!

ПАХ-, ПАШ-, PLOW

пах-áть, паш-ý, *v.i.*, + *acc.*, to plow, till. П. под пар, to plow fallow land. Пáх-

арь, *n.m.*, plowsman. Пáх-ота, *n.f.*, tillage, plowing. Пáх-отный, *adj.*, arable, tillable. П-ая земля, *n.f.*, arable, tillable land. Пáш-ня, *n.f.*, plowed land, field.

вс-пах-áть, *v.p.*, вс-пáх-ивать, *v.i.*, + *acc.*, to plow up. Вс-пáш-ка, *n.f.*, plowing, tillage.

вý-пах-ать, *v.p.*, вы-пáх-ивать, *v.i.*, + *acc.*, see пахáть. В. пóлосы, to plow strips.

за-пах-áть, *v.p.*, за-пáх-ивать, *v.i.*, + *acc.*, to plow down. За-пáх-ивать-ся, *v.i.r.*, to be plowed down. За-пáш-ка, *n.f.*, tillage.

ис-пах-áть, *v.p.*, ис-пáх-ивать, *v.i.*, + *acc.*, to plow in entirety. И. всё пóле, to plow a whole field.

о-пах-áть, *v.p.*, о-пáх-ивать, *v.i.*, + *acc.*, to plow around.

от-пах-áть, *v.p.*, + *acc.*, to finish plowing. О. свой учáсток, to plow one's lot.

пере-пах-áть, *v.p.*, пере-пáх-ивать, *v.i.*, + *acc.*, to plow again, anew. П. пáшню, to plow a field again.

при-пах-áть, *v.p.*, при-пáх-ивать, *v.i.*, + *acc.*, to encroach on land by plowing.

про-пах-áть, *v.p.*, про-пáх-ивать, *v.i.*, + *acc.*, to plow, cultivate; to plow for a certain length of time. П. грáды, to plow furrows. Он пропахáл всё ýтро, he plowed the whole morning. Про-пáш-ка, *n.f.*, cultivation. Про-пáш-ник, *n.m.*, cultivator.

рас-пах-áть, *v.p.*, рас-пáх-ивать, *v.i.*, + *acc.*, to plow thoroughly. Р. новь, to plow virgin soil. Рас-пáш-ка, *n.f.*, thorough plowing.

ПАХ-, ПАШ-, SMELLING, EMITTING FRAGRANCE; PUFFING

пáх-ну-ть, пáх-ну, *v.i.*, + *instr.*, to smell, reek, savor. Рóзы приятно пáхнут, roses smell good; roses have a pleasant smell. Понимáете-ли вы, чем это пáхнет? (*fig.*), Do you realize what this implies? Пáхнет пóрохом, this means war. В вóздухе пáхнет грозóй, there's a storm in the air. Пах-ýчесть, *n.f.*, redolence, fragrance. Пах-ýчий, *adj.*, redolent, fragrant. П-ее мýло, fragrant soap. П-úе трáвы, fragrant herbs.

за-пáх-ну-ть, *v.p.*, + *instr.*, to begin to smell, emit a smell. За-пáх-ло жáреным мясом, it started to smell of fried meat. Зá-пах, *n.m.*, odor, smell, scent. Приятный зáпах рóзы, pleasant smell of a rose. Слýшать (чýвствовать) з., to notice a smell. За-паш-óк, *n.m.*, (*colloq.*), unpleasant odor. Рýба с запашкóм, spoiled, putrid fish.

по-пáх-ива-ть, *v.i.*, + *instr.*, (*colloq.*), to

emit a slight odor. Здесь попа́хивает ды́мом, there is a smell of smoke here.

пах-ну́-ть, *v.p.smf.*, to puff, sweep, blow. Из печи́ пахну́ло ды́мом, smoke puffed out of the stove. Пахну́л ве́тер, there was a gust of wind.

за-пах-ну́-ть, *v.p.*, за-па́х-ивать, *v.i.*, + *acc.*, to wrap; draw tighter, closer; close. З. шу́бу, to wrap a furcoat round oneself. За-пах-ну́ть-ся, *v.p.r.*, за-па́х-ивать-ся, *v.i.r.*, в + *acc.*, to wrap oneself in something. З. в хала́т, to wrap oneself in a bathrobe.

о-пах-ну́-ть, о-пах-а́ть, *v.p.*, о-па́х-ивать *v.i.*, + *acc.*, to fan. О. лицо́ ве́ером, to fan one's face. О-пах-а́ло, *п.п.*, (*obs.*), large fan.

от-пах-ну́-ть, *v.p.*, от-па́х-ивать, *v.i.*, + *acc.*, to brush aside, fling aside. От-пах-ну́ть-ся, *v.p.r.*, от-па́х-ивать-ся, *v.i.r.*, to be brushed aside, flung aside. Две́рца автомоби́ля отпахну́лась, the car door was thrown open.

рас-пах-ну́-ть, *v.p.*, рас-па́х-ивать, *v.i.*, + *acc.*, to throw, fling, thrust open. Р. пальто́, to throw open one's coat. Р. окно́, to open a window. Рас-пах-ну́ть-ся, *v.p.r.*, рас-па́х-ивать-ся, *v.i.r.*, to fly, swing, sweep open. Две́ри распахну́лись от ве́тра, the doors were flung open by the wind. Рас-паш-о́нка, *n.f.*, infant's first garment. На-рас-па́ш-ку, *adv.*, unbuttoned; (*fig.*), sincerely. Он но́сит шу́бу н., he wears his fur coat open. Душа́ н., open-hearted soul; extrovert.

ПАЧК-, SOIL, SOILAGE

па́чк-а-ть, *v.i.*, + *acc.*, to soil, dirty, stain. П. лицо́, to dirty one's face. П. чью́-либо репута́цию, to sully someone's reputation. Па́чк-ать-ся, *v.i.r.*, to soil oneself, make oneself dirty. Пачк-отня́, *n.f.*, (*colloq.*), daubing. Пачк-у́н, *n.m.*, пачк-у́нья, *n.f.*, sloven, dauber; inferior painter.

вы́-пачк-ать, *v.p.*, + *acc.*, в + *prep.*, to soil, dirty thoroughly. В. ру́ки в гли́не, to soil one's hands in clay. Вы́-пачк-ать-ся, *v.p.r.*, to get thoroughly dirty, soiled. В. черни́лами, to become soiled with ink.

за-па́чк-ать, *v.p.*, + *acc.*, + *instr.*, see пачкать, З. пла́тье, to soil a dress. З. свое́ и́мя, to dishonor one's name. За-па́чк-ать-ся, *v.p.r.*, + *instr.*, see па́чкаться. Я запа́чкался ме́лом, I became soiled with chalk.

ис-па́чк-ать, *v.p.*, + *acc.*, + *instr.*, to soil completely, thoroughly. И. оде́жду, to soil one's clothes thoroughly. Ис-па́чк-ать-ся, *v.p.r.*, + *instr.*, see па́ч-

каться. И. черни́лами, to become soiled with ink.

на-па́чк-ать, *v.p.*, (*colloq.*), to soil, dirty in quantity. Ой, ско́лько посу́ды напа́чкали! The dishes you have dirtied!

пере-па́чк-ать, *v.p.*, + *acc.*, to besmear, soil badly. П. ру́ки в са́же, to soil one's hands with soot. Пере-па́чк-ать-ся, *v.p.r.*, to become soiled. П. в кра́сках, to be covered with paint.

ПЕК-, ПЕЧ-, KILN, OVEN, BAKING; GUARDIANSHIP, TRUSTEESHIP, TUTELAGE

пе́к-арь, *n.m.*, baker. Пек-а́рня, *n.f.*, bakery. Пе́к-арский, *adj.*, baker's, baking. П-ие дро́жжи, baking yeast. Пе́к-ло, *n.n.*, (*colloq.*), scorching heat; (*fig.*), hell. Сиде́ть на са́мом пе́кле, to sit where the sun is hottest. Попа́сть в са́мое пе́кло, to fall into the worst of a fray.

печ-ь, *n.f.*, stove, oven, kiln. Желе́зная п., iron stove. Духова́я п., oven. Электри́ческая п., electric stove. Доме́нная п., blast furnace. Пе́ч-ка, *n.f.*, (*colloq.*), stove. Истопи́ть пе́чку, to heat a stove. Танцова́ть от пе́чки, (*fig.*), to begin from the very beginning. Печ-у́рка, *n.f.*, small stove. Печ-ни́к, *n.m.*, stove-setter, stove maker. Печ-но́й, *adj.*, pertaining to a stove. П-а́я труба́, stovepipe, chimney. П-о́е отопле́ние, heating by stove.

печ-ь (*from* пек-ти́), пек-у́, *v.i.*, ис-пе́ч-ь, с-пе́ч-ь, *v.p.*, + *acc.*, to bake. П. пироги́ (хлеб), to bake pies (bread). Со́лнце печёт, the sun is hot. Пе́ч-ь-ся, *v.i.r.*, to bake, broil; о + *prep.*, to take care of. Пиро́г печётся, the pie is baking. До́брая же́нщина печётся о сиро́тах, the good woman is taking care of the orphans. Печ-е́ние, *n.n.*, baking; pastry. Сухо́е п., biscuits, crackers. Печ-ёный, *adj.*, baked.

вы́-печ-ь, *v.p.*, вы-пек-а́ть, *v.i.*, + *acc.*, to bake through. Пека́рня вы́пекла за день 100 килогра́ммов хле́ба, the bakery baked 100 kilograms of bread in a day. Вы́-печ-ь-ся, *v.p.r.*, вы-пек-а́ть-ся, *v.i.r.*, to be baked; be done, be ready. Хлеб ещё не вы́пекся, the bread is not baked yet. Вы́-печ-ка, *n.f.*, baking; batch of bread. Плоха́я в., something poorly baked.

до-пе́ч-ь, *v.p.*, до-пек-а́ть, *v.i.*, + *acc.*, to bake completely, finish baking. Д. хле́бы, to finish baking bread loaves. Допека́ет он меня́, (*fig.*), he annoys me. До-пе́ч-ь-ся, *v.p.r.*, до-пек-а́ть-ся, *v.i.r.*, to be baked, be baked well. Пирог допёкся, the pie was baked exactly right.

за-пе́ч-ь, *v.p.,* за-пек-а́ть, *v.i.,* + *acc.,* to bake. З. о́корок ветчины́, to bake a ham. За-пе́ч-ь-ся, *v.p.r.,* за-пек-а́ть-ся, *v.i.r.,* to be baked; clot, coagulate. Карто́шка запекла́сь, the potatoes are baked through. За-пёк-шийся, *adj., part. act. past,* baked; clotted. З-иеся гу́бы, parched lips. З-аяся кровь, clotted blood. За-пек-а́нка, *n.f.,* baked pudding; spiced brandy.

ис-пе́ч-ь, *v.p.,* + *acc.,* to bake through; *see* печь. Ис-пе́ч-ь-ся, *v.p.r., see* пе́чь-ся. Ис-печ-ённый, *adj., part. pass. past,* baked through, Све́же-и. хлеб, freshly baked bread. Вновь и. студе́нт (*colloq.*), new student.

на-пе́ч-ь, *v.p.,* на-пек-а́ть, *v.i.,* + *acc.,* + *gen.,* to bake in quantity. Она́ напекла́ дю́жину пирого́в, she baked a dozen pies.

по-пе́ч-ь, *v.p.,* + *acc.,* to do some baking, bake a little.

пере-пе́ч-ь, *v.p.,* пере-пек-а́ть, *v.i.,* + *acc.,* to overbake.

при-пе́чь, *v.p.,* при-пек-а́ть, *v.i.* + *acc.,* to scorch in baking; to be very hot in the sun. Пиро́г с ни́зу си́льно припечён, the pie is burned on the bottom. Со́лнце припека́ет сего́дня, the sun is very hot today. При-пёк, *n.m.,* excess in weight of bread over flour used. Эта мука́ даёт большо́й п., this flour gives a good increase in weight after baking. На припёке, (*idiom.*), in the hottest place in the sun. Солнцепёк, a place where the sun is hottest. На солнцепёке, in the full sun.

про-пе́ч-ь, *v.p.,* про-пек-а́ть, *v.i.,* + *acc.,* to bake thoroughly. П. хлеб, to bake a loaf of bread thoroughly. П. спи́ну на со́лнце, to bask, warm one's back in the sun.

рас-пе́ч-ь, *v.p.,* рас-пек-а́ть, *v.i.,* + *acc.,* (*colloq.*), to scold soundly. Нача́льник всех распёк, the chief scolded everybody.

с-пе́ч-ь, *v.p.,* (*colloq.*), *see* печь, испе́чь. С-пе́ч-ь-ся, *v.p.r.,* с-пек-а́ть-ся, *v.i.r.,* to be baked; coagulate, curdle; coke. С-пек-а́ющийся, *adj., part. act. pres.,* coagulating; coking. С. ка́менный у́голь, coking coal.

у-пе́ч-ь, *v.p.,* у-пек-а́ть, *v.i.,* + *acc.,* (*colloq.*), to bake; imprison. Пиро́г не упечён, the pie is not thoroughly baked yet. У. под суд, (*colloq.*), to bring to trial. У. в тюрьму́, to send to prison, imprison. У-пе́ч-ь-ся, *v.p.r.,* у-пек-а́ть-ся, *v.i.r.,* to be baked thoroughly; shrink in baking. Хлеб хорошо́ упёкся,

the bread is well baked. У-пёк, *n.m.,* shrinkage in baking.

о-пек-а́ть, *v.i.,* + *acc.,* to be a guardian; tend, take care of a minor. О. малоле́тнего, to be a guardian to a minor. О. име́ние сестры́, to act as guardian to one's sister's estate. О-пёк-а, *n.f.,* guardianship. Быть под опе́кой кого́-либо, to be under someone's guardianship. Вы́йти из-под опе́ки, to become of age. Междунаро́дная О., International Trusteeship. О-пек-а́емый, *adj., part. pass. pres., also used as n.,* pertaining to a guardian; ward. О-пек-у́н, *n.m.,* о-пек-у́нша, *n.f.,* guardian. О-пек-у́нство, *n.n.,* guardianship. О-пек-у́нский, *adj.,* guardian.

по-печ-и́тель-ств-ова-ть, *v.i.,* to be a trustee. По-печ-е́ние, *n.n.,* care. Име́ть п., to take care of, tend. Име́ть на попече́нии, to have in one's charge. Име́ть на попече́нии двух сиро́т, to be guardian to two orphans. Быть на попече́нии, to be in charge of. По-печ-и́тель, *n.m.,* по-печ-и́тельница, *n.f.,* trustee. По-печ-и́тельство, *n.n.,* trusteeship.

о-бес-пе́ч-ить, *v.p.,* о-бес-пе́ч-ивать, *v.i.,* + *acc.,* + *instr.,* to provide; ensure, assure, protect, safeguard. О. успе́х, to ensure, success. О. а́рмию боеприпа́сами, to provide an army with supplies. О-беспе́ч-ение, *n.n.,* guaranty, security. Социа́льное о., social security. О-беспе́ч-енность, *n.f.,* security. Материя́льная о., material security. О-бес-пе́ч-енный, *adj., part. pass. past,* well-to-do, provided for. О. челове́к, a man well provided for. О-ая жизнь, financial security. Бес-пе́ч-ность, *n.f.,* freedom from; unconcern from care; security. Бес-пе́ч-ный, *adj.,* carefree; lighthearted. Б-ая жизнь, carefree life. Бес-пе́ч-но, *adv.,* in a carefree way, lightheartedly, with complete lack of concern.

печ-а́л-ь, *n.f.,* grief, sorrow. Глубо́кая п., deep sorrow. Не твоя́ п., (*colloq.*), it is of no concern to you. "Ве́тер осе́нний наво́дит печа́ль." (*Nekrasov*), "The autumn wind fills one with sadness." Печ-а́льный, *adj.,* sad, mournful. П-ые результа́ты, unfortunate results. П. коне́ц, dismal end. П-ая песнь, sad song.

печ-а́л-ить, *v.i.,* о-печ-а́лить, *v.p.,* + *acc.,* to grieve, sadden, Она́ меня́ опеча́лила свои́м го́рестным сообще́нием, she saddened me with her sad news. Печ-а́лить-ся, *v.i.r.,* о-печ-а́лить-ся, *v.p.r.,* to grieve, be sad. Не сто́ит п. ра́ньше вре́мени, there is no sense worrying beforehand.

пе́ч-ен-ь, *n.f.,* (*anat.*), liver. П. нахо́дит-ся в брюшно́й по́лости, the liver is located in the abdominal cavity. Печ-ёнка, *n.f.,* (*dim., colloq.*), liver. (*food*). Пиро́г с печёнкой, liver pie. Печ-ёноч-ный, *adj.,* liver. П-ая колбаса́, liver sausage.

ПЕЧА́Т-, SEALING, PRINTING, STAMP-ING

печа́т-ь, *n.f.,* seal, stamp; press; print, type. Госуда́рственная п., state seal. Наложи́ть п. (на), to stamp, set a seal. Носи́ть п., bear a seal. П. молча́ния, (*fig.*), sealed lips. Ме́стная п., local press. Свобо́да печа́ти, freedom of the press. Ме́лкая (кру́пная) п., small (large) print. Печа́т-ание, *n.n.,* printing. Печа́т-ка, *n.f.,* signet. Печа́т-ник, *n.m.,* printer. Печа́т-ный, *adj.,* printed. Чи-та́ть по печа́тному, to read in print. Писа́ть печа́тными бу́квами, to print, write in print. П. стано́к, printing press. П-ое де́ло, typography, printing.
печа́т-а-ть, *v.i.,* на-печа́т-ать, *v.p.,* + *acc.,* to print, type. П. кни́ги (газе́ты, но́ты), to print books (papers, music). П. на маши́нке, to type. Печа́т-ать-ся, *v.i.r.,* to be printed, published. Пу́шкин на́чал печа́таться пятнадцатиле́тним ю́ношей, Pushkin began to be pub-lished when he was fifteen years old. Газе́ты печа́таются, newspapers are printed.
в-печат-л-е́ние, *n.n.,* impression; sensa-tion. Производи́ть в., to make an im-pression. Находи́ться под впечатле́-нием, to be under an impression. В-печат-л-и́тельность, *n.f.,* sensitive-ness, impressionability. В-печат-л-и́тельный, *adj.,* impressionable, sensi-tive.
до-печа́т-ать, *v.p.,* до-печа́т-ывать, *v.i.,* + *acc.,* to complete printing, typing. Д. страни́цу до конца́, to finish typing a page. До-печа́т-ка, *n.f.,* (*colloq.*), supplement, supplementary edition.
за-печа́т-ать, *v.p.,* за-печа́т-ывать, *v.i.,* + *acc.,* to seal. З. письмо́, to seal a letter.
за-печат-л-е́ть, *v.p.,* за-печат-л-ева́ть, *v.i.,* + *acc.,* to impress, imprint on one's mind, memory. З. что́-либо в па́мяти, to stamp something on someone's mem-ory. За-печат-ле́ть-ся, *v.p.r.,* за-печат-лева́ть-ся, *v.i.r.,* to be imprinted, stamped, impress itself; imprint itself. З. у кого́-либо в па́мяти, to be im-pressed on someone's memory.
о-печа́т-ать, *v.p.,* о-печа́т-ывать, *v.i.,* + *acc.,* to seal, apply a seal. О. кварти́ру, to seal an apartment. О-печа́т-

ка, *n.f.,* misprint, typographical error. В текст вкра́лась доса́дная о., an un-fortunate error slipped into the text.
от-печа́т-ать, *v.p.,* от-печа́т-ывать, пе-ча́т-ать, *v.i.,* + *acc.,* to type, print, im-print. О. кни́гу в ме́стной типогра́-фии, to print a book in a local print-ing shop. От-печа́т-ать-ся, *v.p.r.,* от-печа́т-ывать-ся, *v.i.r.,* to be printed, imprinted; leave an impression. Следы́ босы́х ног отпеча́тались на песке́, traces of bare feet were imprinted in the sand. От-печа́т-ывание, *n.n.,* im-print, impression. От-печа́т-ок, *n.m.,* impression, imprint. О. па́льцев, finger-prints.
пере-печа́т-ать, *v.p.,* пере-печа́т-ывать, *v.i.,* + *acc.,* to reprint, retype. Газе́ты перепеча́тали изве́стие из столи́чной пре́ссы, the newspapers reprinted the news from the press of the capital. Пере-печа́тка, *n.f.,* reprinting. П. вос-преща́ется, reprinting (reproduction) forbidden; copyright reserved.
при-печа́т-ать, *v.p.,* при-печа́т-ывать, *v.i.,* + *acc.,* (*colloq.*), to seal, affix a seal; print in addition. П. оглавле́ние, to append an index.
про-печа́т-ать, *v.p.,* про-печа́т-ывать, *v.i.,* + *acc.,* (*colloq.*), to attack in print. П. кого́-нибудь в газе́те, to attack someone in the press.
рас-печа́т-ать, *v.p.,* рас-печа́т-ывать, *v.i.,* + *acc.,* to unseal, take off a seal; open a letter. Р. конве́рт (письмо́, помеще́-ние), to unseal an envelope (open a letter, open premises). Рас-печа́т-ать-ся, *v.p.r.,* рас-печа́т-ывать-ся, *v.i.r.,* to be unsealed, opened. Рас-печа́т-ывание, *n.n.,* unsealing, opening.

ПЕН- (ПѢН-), FOAM

пе́н-а, *n.f.,* foam, scum, froth. Мы́льная п., soapsuds, lather. Снима́ть пе́ну, to remove scum. Говори́ть с пе́ной у рта, (*fig.*), to foam at the mouth. Пе́н-ка, *n.f.,* scum. Снима́ть пе́нки, to skim milk.
пе́н-и-ть, *v.i.,* + *acc.,* to cause to foam. Пе́н-ить-ся, *v.i.r.,* to foam, froth. Шам-па́нское пе́нилось в бока́лах, the champagne foamed in the glasses. Пе́н-ящийся, *adj., part. act. pres.,* foaming, frothing. Пе́н-истый, *adj.,* foamy, frothy. П-ое вино́, sparkling wine.
вс-пе́н-ить, *v.p.,* вс-пе́н-ивать, *v.i.,* + *acc.,* to cause to foam, froth; lather. В. коня́, to ride a horse hard. Ве́тер вспе́нил реку́, the wind has stirred up the river. Вс-пе́н-ить-ся, *v.p.r.,* вс-пе́н-ивать-ся, *v.i.r.,* to froth, foam. Пи́во вспе́нилось, the beer foamed up.

за-пён-ить-ся, *v.p.r.,* to begin to foam, froth. Вино запёнилось в бокале, the wine foamed in the glass.

на-пён-ить, *v.p.,* + *gen.,* to make froth, lather, in quantity. Н. мыла для бритья, to make lather for shaving.

ПЕРВ-, PRECEDENCE, PRECESSION, FIRST

пёрв-ый, *пит., ord.,* first. П-ое число месяца, the first of the month. Первого января, on the first of January. П-ые плоды, early harvest, first fruits. П-ый этаж, ground floor. П-ый ученик, leading, best pupil. П-ое время, at first. Половина пёрвого, half past twelve, twelve-thirty. Не пёрвой молодости, not in one's first youth. Пёрвым делом, (*colloq.*), in the first place, first of all. В пёрвую очередь, in the first place. П-ая скрипка, first violin. Играть пёрвую скрипку, to play the first violin; (*fig.*), to be first, most important, play the leading role. П. шаг труден, the first step is always difficult. П. блин комом, (*saying*), a bad beginning.

пер-вёйший, *adj., superl.,* the first, best; (*colloq.*), first-rate. П-его сорта, of the best quality.

пёрв-ен-ец, *п.п.,* first-born. Королёвский престол передаётся пёрвенцу, the royal throne is inherited by the first-born son. Пёрв-енство, *п.п.,* primogeniture; superiority. Завоевать п., to win a contest, attain first place.

пёрв-ен-ств-овать, *v.i.,* над + *instr.,* среди + *gen.,* to take precedence, priority over something, have rights of primogeniture, bear the bell. П. над товарищами, to take precedence over, be a leader among one's classmates (colleagues). Пёрв-енствующий, *adj., part. act. pres.,* most important. П-ее значёние, utmost significance. Выборы правительства имёют пёрвенствующее значёние для страны, the government elections are of primary importance to the country. Пёрв-енствовавший, *adj., part. act. past,* leading.

перв-ич-н-ый, *adj.,* primary, initial. П. ток, primary current. П-ые породы, primary rocks. П-ые выборы, primary elections.

перв-о-бытность, *n.f.,* primitiveness, primitive state. П. народа, primitiveness of a people, nation. Перв-о-бытный, *adj.,* primitive. П. образ жизни, primitive way of life.

перв-о-источник, *п.т.,* origin, primary source. Чёрпать свёдения из первои-сточника, to gather information from primary sources.

перв-о-классник, *п.т.,* перв-о-классница, *n.f.,* pupil in the first class, grade Перв-о-классный, *adj.,* first-class, first-rate. П. актер, superior actor.

перв-о-курсник, *п.т.,* перв-о-курсница, *n.f.,* first-year student. Этот студёнт - первокурсник медицинского факультёта, this student is in his first year of studies in the faculty of medicine.

Перв-о-май, *п.т.,* (*recent*), the First of May, May-day. Перв-о-майский, pertaining to the first of May. П-ая демонстрация, demonstration, parade held on the first of May.

перв-о-начальный, *adj.,* primary. П-ые свёдения по грамматике, the rudiments of grammar. П-ые числа, (*math.*), prime numbers. Перв-о-начально, *adv.,* originally, at first.

перв-о-престольный, *adj.,* pertaining to the first capital. Москва - первопрестольный город, Moscow, the ancient (first) capital.

перв-о-родство, *п.п.,* primogeniture. Права первородства, rights of primogeniture. Перв-о-родный, *adj.,* original. П. грех, original sin. Адам и Ёва совершили п. грех, Adam and Eve committed the original sin. Перв-о-рождённый, *adj.,* first-born.

перв-о-степённый, *adj.,* paramount. Факт первостепённой важности, a fact of paramount importance.

перв-о-цвёт, *п.т.,* primrose.

в-перв-ые, *adv.,* first, for the first time. В девятом вёке Русь в. узнала о христианстве, in the ninth century Russia heard of Christianity for the first time.

во-пёрв-ых, *adv. expression,* first of all, in the first place. Чтобы хорошо учиться, надо, во-пёрвых, имёть способности, а во-вторых, прилежание, to study well it is necessary, first, to have ability; secondly - diligence.

с-перв-а, *adv.,* at first, firstly. С. подумай, а потом говори, (*saying*), think first, then speak.

ПЕРЕД-, ПЕРЁД-, ПРЕД-, ПРЕЖД-, ПРЕЖ-, PRECEDENCE, ANTECEDENCE

перед, перед-о, (пред-о), + *instr.,* before, in front of, in the presence of. Она остановилась п. столом (двёрью), she stopped in front of the table (door). Стул стоит п. столом, the chair is standing in front of the table. Не останавливаться п. трудностями, to not stop in the face of difficulties. П. нача́лом заня́тий, before the beginning of the lessons. Извини́ться п. кем-нибудь, to apologize to someone. Перёд, *n.т.*, front; forepart. П. пла́тья испа́чкан, the front of the dress is soiled. Перёд до́ма, the front (facade) of a house. Перёд-ний, *adj.*, frontal, first. П-яя часть, forepart. П. план, foreground. П-ие зу́бы, front teeth. В-перёд, *adv.*, forward; in the future, henceforth. Идти́ в., to advance. Ни взад, ни в., (*idiom.*), neither backward nor forward. Плати́ть в., to pay in advance. В., к побе́де, forward, onward to victory.

в-перед-и́, *adv.*, in front of, before, ahead. Идти́ в. всех, to walk in front of everyone, precede. У ю́ноши ещё це́лая жизнь впереди́, a youth has his whole life before him. В-перед-ь, *adv.*, in the future, henceforth. В. до, pending, until. В. до его́ приéзда, until his arrival, up to his arrival. В. не поступа́й так легкомы́сленно и будь рассуди́тельней, in the future do not act so foolishly, be more sensible. Он соде́ржится под аре́стом в. до выясне́ния ли́чности, he is being kept under arrest until he is identified.

перед-н-ик, *n.т.*, apron, pinafore. Си́тцевый п., cotton apron. Де́тский п., child's apron, pinafore.

перед-н-яя, *n.f.*, anteroom, hall. Го́рничная откры́ла две́ри, и гость вошёл в пере́днюю, the maid opened the door and the guest stepped into the hall.

перед-ов-о́й, *adj.*, headmost, forward, advance; progressive. П-ы́е взгля́ды, progressive views. П-ы́е пози́ции, advanced lines. П-а́я статья́, editorial. Перед-ови́к, *n.т.*, (*recent*), one who is foremost in something. Передовики́ се́льского хозя́йства, foremost people in agriculture. Перед-ови́ца, *n.f.*, (*colloq.*), lead article, editorial.

перед-о́к, *n.т.*, detachable front of a vehicle; upper part of a plow; boot vamp. П. плу́га, forepart of a plow. Снять пу́шки с передко́в, to detach cannons from their carriages. Передки́ сапо́г, boot vamps.

о-перед-и́ть, о-переж-у́, *v.р.*, о-пережа́ть, *v.i.*, + *acc.*, to outstrip; leave behind; pass. О. кого́-нибудь на ска́чках (го́нках), to pass someone in a race. О. кого́-нибудь в разви́тии, to outstrip someone in development. Автомоби́ль опереди́л по́езд, the car passed ahead of the train.

пре́д-ок, *n.т.*, ancestor, forefather.

"На́ши пре́дки Рим спасли́," ... (Krylov), "our ancestors saved Rome."

пред, *prep.*, *also a combining form meaning ante,* before. Пред-ви́деть, *v.i.*, + *acc.*, to foresee. Пред-сказа́ть, *v.р.*, + *acc.*, to foretell. Пред-чу́вствовать, *v.i.*, to have a feeling of foreboding. Пред-ше́ствовать, *v.i.*, to precede.

пред-у-пред-и́ть, *v.р.*, пред-у-прежда́ть, *v.i.*, + *acc.*, о + *prep.*, to let know beforehand, warn; forestall, prevent. П. пожа́р (несча́стный слу́чай), to prevent a fire (an accident). Я хоте́л э́то сде́лать для вас, но он предупреди́л меня́, I wanted to do it for you, but he forestalled me. Пред-у-прежд-е́ние, *n.n.*, notice, warning, prevention. Вы́говор с предупрежде́нием, a reprimand with a warning. Пред-у-пред-и́тельность, *n.f.*, obligingness, attention, courtesy. Прояви́ть кра́йнюю предупреди́тельность, to display extreme courtesy. Пред-у-пред-и́тельный, *adj.*, preventative, precautionary, obliging, attentive. П-ые ме́ры, preventative measures. П. ремо́нт, precautionary repairs. П. челове́к, obliging man.

пре́жд-е, *adv.*, before, beforehand; in former times; *also used as prep.*, Надо бы́ло ду́мать об э́том п., you should have thought of it earlier. Он пришёл сюда́ пре́жде всех, he came here before anyone else. Пре́жде всего́, first of all. Пре́жде всего́, на́до найти́ рабо́ту, first of all you must find work. Прежд-е-вре́менно, *adv.*, prematurely. Сконча́ться п., to die prematurely. Прежд-е-вре́менность, *n.f.*, prematureness. Прежд-е-вре́менный, *adj.*, premature, untimely. П. прихо́д по́езда, arrival of a train before time. П-ое разви́тие, premature development. П-ая смерть, untimely death.

пре́ж-ний, *adj.*, previous, former, В п-ее вре́мя, in the old days, in former times. По-пре́ж-нему, *adv.*, as before. Жить п., to live as one once used to.

ПЕРЕК-, ПЕРЁК-, ПЕРЕЧ-, ПРЕК-, ПРЁК-, TRANSVERSION

переч-и-ть, *v.i.*, по-переч-ить, *v.р.*, + *dat.*, to contradict. Никогда́ сра́зу не согласи́тся, лю́бит п., he never agrees at once, he likes to contradict. По-переч-ник, *n.т.*, diameter. Пять ме́тров в попере́чнике, five meters in diameter. По-переч-ина, *n.f.*, cross-beam, cross-piece. По-пере́ч-ный, *adj.*, diametrical, transverse. П. разре́з, cross section. П-ое сече́ние, cross-section. П-ая ба́лка, cross-beam.

по-перёк, *adv., also used as prep.,* across. Перерéзать чтó-либо п., to cut something crosswise. П. ýлицы, across the street. Стоя́ть у когó-либо п. дорóги, (*fig.*), to be in someone's way.

во-прек-й, *prep.,* in spite of, despite, regardless. В. всем прáвилам, despite all the rules. В. чьемý-либо желáнию, regardless of someone's wish. "Рассýдку в., наперекóр стихи́ям..." (*Griboyedov*), "disregarding reason, against the elements of nature....."

на-перек-óр, *adv.,* in defiance, of, in spite of. Идти́ н., to disregard.

прек-о-слóвить, *v.i.,* + *dat.,* (*obs.*), to contradict, cross. П. стáршим (роди́телям), to contradict one's elders (one's parents). Прек-о-слóвие, *n.n.,* (*obs.*), contradiction. Без прекослóвия, (*obs.*), without contradiction. Бес-прек-о-слóвно, *adv.,* implicitly, unquestioningly. Подчиня́ться б. распоряжéнию начáльника, to submit implicitly to the orders of one's superior. Бес-прек-о-слóвный, *adj.,* absolute, implicit, unquestioning.

по-прек-á-ть, *v.i.,* по-прек-нýть, *v.p.,* + *acc.,* + *instr.,* за + *acc.,* to reproach. П. кускóм хлéба, (*idiom*), to grudge a piece of bread. По-прёк, *n.m.,* reproach.

у-прек-áть, *v.i.,* у-прек-нýть, *v.p.smf.,* + *acc.,* в + *prep.,* to reproach, upbraid. У. себя́, to reproach oneself. У. когó-нибудь в скýпости, to reproach someone for stinginess. У-прёк, *n.m.,* reproach, reproof, rebuke. С упрёком, *n.m.,* reproachfully, reprovingly.

без-у-прéч-ность, *n.f.,* irreproachability, blamelessness. Б. поведéния, irreproachability of conduct. Без-у-прéчный, *adj.,* irreproachable, blameless. Человéк б-ой чéстности, a man of irreproachable honesty. Без-у-прéчно, *adv.,* irreproachably.

ПЕР-, ПР-, ПИР-, ПОР-, ПАР-, PROPULSION, PUSH

пер-é-ть, пр-у, *v.i.,* (*slang*), to push, press. Пер-éть-ся, *v.i.r.,* (*slang*), to be pushing, pressing. Пер-и́ла, *n.pl.,* handrail, banister.

в-пер-éть, во-пр-ý, (*slang*), *v.p.,* в-пир-áть, в-пир-áю, *v.i.,* + *acc.,* в + *acc.,* to push in, thrust. Еле впёр вéщи в вагóн, I barely managed to push the baggage into the car. В-пер-éть-ся, *v.p.r.,* в-пир-áть-ся, *v.i.r.,* в + *acc.,* to force one's way in. Пья́ный впёрся в дом, the drunkard pushed his way into the house.

в-пер-и́ть, *v.p.,* в-пер-я́ть, *v.i.,* + *acc.,* в + *acc.,* to fix. В. взор (взгляд) в когó-либо, to fix one's gaze on someone.

вы́-пер-еть, *v.p.,* вы-пир-áть, *v.i.,* + *acc.,* (*colloq.*), to bulge, stick out; (*fig.*), to be too prominent, too obvious. Егó выпирáют со слýжбы, they are easing him out of his job. Вы́-переть-ся, *v.p.r.,* вы-пир-áть-ся, *v.i.r.,* to be pushed out, stick out. Из толпы́ вы́перся оди́н человéк, (*slang*), one man pushed himself out of the crowd. Онá такáя худáя, что у неё кóсти выпирáются, she is so thin that her bones are sticking out.

за-пер-éть, *v.p.,* за-пир-áть, *v.i.,* + *acc.,* на + *acc.,* to lock; bar, block up. З. на засóв, to bolt. З. дверь на замóк, to lock a door. За-пер-éть-ся, *v.p.r.,* запир-áть-ся, *v.i.r.,* to lock oneself up, be locked up. Я́щик запирáется автомати́чески, the box locks itself. В-запер-ти́, *adv.,* locked up, under lock and key. Сидéть в., to be locked up. Жить в., to live in seclusion.

за-пóр, *n.m.,* bolt, lock; (*med.*), constipation. Дверь на запóре, the door is bolted.

на-пер-éть, *v.p.,* на-пир-áть, *v.i.,* на + *acc.,* to press, emphasize, stress. Напирáть на слóво, to place emphasis on a word. Он напёр на двéри так, что вы́ломал их, he pushed so hard against the door that it broke. Напóр, *n.m.,* pressure. Н. воды́ (пáра), water (steam) pressure. Дéйствовать с напóром, to apply pressure. На-пóристость, *n.f.,* energy; impetuosity; assertiveness. Н. харáктера, impetuosity of disposition. На-пóр-истый, *adj.,* energetic, hustling, assertive. Н. человéк, assertive person. На-пóр-ный, *adj.,* pertaining to pressure. Н. бак, pressure tank.

о-пер-éть-ся, *v.p.,* о-пир-áть-ся, *v.i.,* на + *acc.,* to lean upon, against; rely upon. О. на трость, to lean on a cane. О. на провéренные дáнные, to rely on verified facts. О-пóр, *n.m.,* full speed (*as* of a horse). Во весь опóр, at full speed. Лóшади несли́сь во весь опóр, two horses were rushing at full speed. О-пóр-а, *n.f.,* support, bearing. О. мостá, support of a bridge. Тóчка опóры, fulcrum.

от-пер-éть, *v.p.,* от-пир-áть, *v.i.,* + *acc.,* to unlock, open. О. двéри (ворóта), to open doors (a gate). От-пер-éть-ся, *v.p.r.,* от-пир-áть-ся, *v.i.r.,* to unlock oneself, be unlocked; deny. Дверь отпирáется, the door unlocks itself. "Вы мне писáли, не отпирáйтесь...",

(*Pushkin*), "you wrote to me, do not deny it." От-пир-а́тельство, *n.n.*, disavowal, denial. От-по́р, *n.m.*, rebuff, repulse. Дать о., to repulse. Встре́тить о., to meet with a rebuff.

по-пир-а́ть, *v.i.*, по-пр-а́ть, *v.p.*, + *acc.*, (*obs.*), to trample under foot; scorn, defy. П. вра́жескую зе́млю, to trample over the enemy's territory. П. чьи́-нибудь права́, to violate someone's rights.

под-пер-е́ть, *v.p.*, под-пир-а́ть, *v.i.*, + *acc.*, to prop, support. П. сте́ны, to underpin walls. Под-по́р-ка, *n.f.*, prop, support.

пре-пир-а́ть-ся, *v.i.r.*, с + *instr.*, to dispute, altercate. Пре-пир-а́тельство, *n.n.*, altercation, dispute. Ра́с-пр-я, *n.f.*, discord, strife.

при-пер-е́ть, *v.p.*, при-пир-а́ть, *v.i.*, + *acc.*, + *instr.*, (*colloq.*), to press shut. П. чём-либо дверь, to place something heavy against a door. П. кого́-либо к стене́, (*fig.*), to drive someone into a corner.

рас-пер-е́ть, *v.p.*, рас-пир-а́ть, *v.i.*, + *acc.*, + *instr.*, *usually impers.*, to push, drive, thrust asunder; expand; project. От сы́той жи́зни его́ распёрло, (*slang*), he became fat from a life of luxury.

с-пер-е́ть, *v.p.*, с-пир-а́ть, *v.i.*, + *acc.*, (*colloq.*), to take stealthily; have one's breath taken away. У меня́ дыха́ние спёрло, it took my breath away. У меня́ спёрли чемода́н, (*slang*), my suitcase was stolen.

у-пер-е́ть, *v.p.*, у-пир-а́ть, *v.i.*, + *acc.*, в + *acc.*, to rest, set against; (*colloq.*), pilfer, filch; lay stress on something. У. ру́ку в бок, to place one's hands on one's hip. У. глаза́ в кого́-либо, to stare at someone. Упёрли у меня́ часы́ на база́ре, (*slang*), my watch was stolen at the market. Упира́ть на какой-нибудь вопро́с, to emphasize a question. У-пер-е́ть-ся, *v.p.r.*, у-пир-а́ть-ся, *v.i.r.*, + *instr.*, в + *acc.*, to rest, set against; persist; resist. У. нога́ми в зе́млю, to plant one's feet firmly on the ground; take a firm stand. У. глаза́ми в кого́-либо, to stare at someone. У-по́р, *n.m.*, rest; (*tech.*), stop, lug. Стреля́ть в у., to fire point-blank. Смотре́ть в у. на кого́-либо, to stare at someone. У-по́р-ный, *adj.*, persistent; stubborn. У. челове́к, persistent person. У. ка́шель, stubborn cough. У-ая борьба́, stubborn struggle. У-по́р-ство, *n.n.*, persistence, stubbornness, obstinacy.

у-по́р-ств-ова-ть, *v.i.*, в + *prep.*, to persist, be stubborn, obstinate. Враг упо́рствует и не сдаётся, the enemy is obstinate and is not surrendering.

с-по́р-ить, *v.i.*, по-с-по́р-ить, *v.p.*, с + *instr.*, о + *prep.*, to argue about, against; dispute. С. о слова́х, to quibble over words; debate, discuss, bet, wager. О вку́сах не спо́рят, tastes differ; there is no accounting for taste. С-пор, *n.m.*, argument, controversy, dispute. Горя́чий, с., heated discussion. Спо́ру нет, it goes without saying. С-по́р-ность, *n.f.*, disputability. С-по́р-ный, *adj.*, disputable, debatable. С. вопро́с, debatable question. Бес-с-по́р-ный, *adj.*, indisputable. Б-ая и́стина, indisputable truth. С-по́р-щик, *n.m.*, с-по́р-щица, *n.f.*, debater; squabbler. Ло́вкий спо́рщик, skillful debater. С-по́р-но, *adv.*, disputably. Бес-с-по́р-но, *adv.*, indisputably.

со-пе́р-нич-ать, *v.i.*, с + *instr.*, to rival, emulate; vie, compete. Он уха́живает за э́той де́вушкой, но с ним сопе́рничает его́ прия́тель, he is courting this girl, but his friend is competing with him. Со-пе́р-ник, *n.m.*, rival, competitor; antagonist, opponent. Это мой сопе́рник на получе́ние пе́рвого приза, this is my opponent in competition for the first prize. Со-пе́р-ничество, *n.n.*, rivalry, competition. Ме́жду ни́ми идёт с., there is a rivalry between them.

о-спо́р-ить, *v.p.*, о-спа́р-ивать, *v.i.*, + *acc.*, to dispute, call in question. О. завеща́ние, to contest a will.

ПЕРЕЦ-, ПЕРЦ-, ПЕРЧ-, ПЕРЕЧ-, PEPPER

пе́рец, *n.m.*, pepper, Кра́сный п., red pepper. Стручко́вый п., capsicum. Зада́ть пе́рцу кому́-либо, (*fig.*), to make it hot for someone. Фарширо́ванный п.- вку́сное блю́до, stuffed peppers are a tasty dish.

перц-о́в-ка, *n.f.*, vodka flavored with pepper. Перц-о́вый, *adj.*, pepper.

перч-и́ть, *v.i.*, по-перч-и́ть, *v.p.*, + *acc.*, to pepper. П. суп, to pepper soup, season soup with pepper. Перч-и́нка, *n.f.*, peppercorn. Я. ка́щляю, оттого́ что в го́рло попа́ла п., I am coughing because a particle of pepper got into my throat.

пере-перч-и́ть, *v.p.*, пере-пе́рч-ивать, *v.i.*, + *acc.*, to pepper too much. П. помидо́р, to put too much pepper into tomatoes. Со́ус так переперчен, что есть нельзя́, the sauce has so much pepper in it, it is impossible to eat.

пе́реч-ница, *n.f.,* pepperbox, pepper shaker. Пе́рец насы́пали в пе́речницу, they poured pepper into the pepper shaker. Пе́реч-ный, *adj.,* peppery. П. за́пах, pepper smell.

ПЕР-, ПЁР-, FEATHER, PEN, QUILL

пер-о́, *n.n.,* feather, plume; pen, writing pen. Пти́чье п., bird feather. Стра́усовое п., ostrich feather. Пи́счее п., writing pen. Ве́чное п., fountain pen. Взя́ться за п., to put pen to paper. Владе́ть о́стрым перо́м, *(fig.),* to wield a formidable pen. Ни пу́ха, ни пера́, *(saying),* Good luck! Про́ба пера́ *(fig.),* a test of one's writing ability. Пер-о-чи́нный, *adj., in expression:* П. но́жик, penknife. Пе́р-истый, *adj.,* pinnate. П-ое о́блако, cirrus cloud. Пер-исто-ли́стый, *adj.,* feather-leaved. П-ая па́льма, feather-leaved palm.

пё́р-ышко, *n.n.,* *(dim.),* plumelet; small feather. Лёгкий, как п., feathery, light; light as a feather.

пер-на́т-ый, *adj.,* feathery, feathered. П-ое ца́рство, birds, kingdom of birds. "Перна́тый царь лесны́х певцо́в," *(Pushkin),* "the feathered tsar of the forest singers."

пер-и́н-а, *n.f.,* feather bed. Пухо́вая п., down-quilt.

о-пер-и́ть-ся, *v.p.r.,* о-пер-я́ть-ся, *v.i.r.,* to become full-fledged; become independent. В ию́не галча́та опери́лись, in June the fledgeling crows grew wings. Да́йте молодо́му челове́ку опери́ться, give the young man a chance to get on his feet. О-пер-е́ние, *n.n.,* feathering; plumage. Павли́н отлича́ется бога́тством и пестрото́й опере́ния, the peacock is noted for his rich and multicolored plumage. Хвосто́вое опере́ние, tail unit of an aircraft *(aviation).*

ПЕРСТ-, ПЕ́РСТ-, ПЕРЧ-, FINGER, GLOVE

перст, *n.m.,* *(obs.),* finger. Оди́н, как перст, *(fig.),* quite alone; completely alone. Пе́рст-ень, *n.m.,* finger ring; seal ring; signet ring. На па́льце у неё блесте́л п. с бриллиа́нтом, a diamond ring was shining on her finger. Перст-ено́к, перст-ене́чек, *n.m.,* *(dim.),* *see* пе́рстень. "Дам тебе́ я на проща́нье перстене́чек золото́й," *(song),* "I will give you a little golden ring as a farewell gift." Перст-н-е-ви́дный, *adj.,* shaped like a ring.

на-пёрст-ок, *n.m.,* thimble. Величино́й с н., *(fig.),* as small as a thimble; very small, tiny.

на-перст-я́нка, *n.f.,* *(bot.),* foxglove.

перч-а́т-ка, *n.f.,* glove, mitten, gauntlet. Ла́йковая п., kid glove. Боксёрская п., boxing glove. В бе́лых перча́тках, white-gloved, in white gloves. Броса́ть перча́тку, *(fig.),* to challenge to a duel. Поднима́ть перча́тку, *(fig.),* to accept a challenge. Перч-а́точник, *n.m.,* перч-а́точница, *n.f.,* glover. Перч-а́точный, *adj.,* glove. П-ое произво́дство, glove industry.

ПЕ-, (ПѢ-), ПО-, ПЕС-, (ПѢС-), ПЕВ-, (ПѢВ-), ПЕТ-, (ПѢТ-), SONG, SINGING

пе-ть, по-ю́, *v.i.,* + *acc.,* to sing, chant, intone; hum, warble, pipe, crow. П. ве́рно (фальши́во), to sing in tune (out of tune). Ве́тер поёт, *(poet.),* the wind is singing. П. сла́ву, to sing someone's praises. Пе-ва́ть, *v.i.iter.,* *(poet., obs.),* to sing. В мо́лодости не раз пева́л я э́ти пе́сни, in my youth I used to sing these songs.

вос-пе́-ть, *v.p.,* вос-пе-ва́ть, *v.i.,* + *acc.,* to sing, glorify in song. В. по́двиги в стиха́х, to sing the deeds in verses.

до-пе́-ть, *v.p.,* до-пе-ва́ть, *v.i.,* + *acc.,* to sing to the end, finish singing, crowing. Д. пе́сню до конца́, to sing a song to the end.

за-пе́-ть, *v.p.,* за-пе-ва́ть, *v.i.,* to break into song, begin to sing, start singing, crowing; set a tune, intone. З. бу́ду я, а вы подтя́гивайте, I shall set the tune and you will join in. За-пе-ва́ла, *n.m.,* leader of a choir. Петь запева́лой, to lead a tune, lead the singing of a choir. За-пе́в, *n.m.,* introductory verse in song.

на-пе́-ть, *v.p.,* на-пе-ва́ть, *v.i.,* + *acc.,* to hum. Н. знако́мую мело́дию, to hum a familiar tune. Н. пласти́нку, to have one's voice recorded. Н. кому́-либо в у́ши, *(fig.),* to flatter; slander. На-пе́в, *n.m.,* tune, melody. Гру́стный (жа́лостный) н., sad (pitiful) tune.

от-пе́-ть, *v.p.,* от-пе-ва́ть, *v.i.,* + *acc.,* to perform a funeral service. О. поко́йника, to perform a funeral ceremony for a deceased person. От-пе-ва́ние, *n.n.,* funeral service, ceremony. От-пе́тый, *adj., part. pass. past, (colloq.),* inveterate. О. дура́к (пья́ница), inveterate fool (drunkard).

пере-пе́-ть, *v.p.,* пере-пе-ва́ть, *v.i.,* + *acc.,* to sing again, anew. П. все пе́сни, to sing all the songs again.

под-пе́-ть, *v.p.,* под-пе-ва́ть, *v.i.,* + *dat.,* to sing with, accompany. П. второ́й, to accompany, sing an accompaniment. Под-пе-ва́ла, *n.m.*, one who sings in tune with, accompanies.

по-пе́-ть, *v.p.*, to sing, crow for a short time. Ве́чером он попе́л и поигра́л, in the evening he sang and played for a while.

при-пе-ва́ть, *v.i.*, (*colloq.*), to accompany in song. При-пе́в, *n.m.*, refrain. Жить припева́ючи, (*fig.*), to live in clover.

про-пе́-ть, *v.p.*, to sing through; (*colloq.*), lose one's voice by singing. Они́ пропе́ли всё у́тро, they sang the whole morning through. Давно́ пропе́ли петухи́, the cocks crowed a long time ago. Пропо́йте стари́нную пе́сню, sing an old song.

рас-пе-ва́ть, *v.i.*, + *acc.*, to sing heartily. Р. пе́сни, to sing songs heartily. Рас-пе́-ть-ся, *v.p.r.*, рас-пе-ва́ть-ся, *v.i.r.*, to be sung; sing for joy, sing heartily; crow lustily. Она́ ещё не распе́лась, she hasn't warmed up yet. На-рас-пе́в, *adv.*, in a singing voice. Говори́ть н., to speak in a singing, melodious voice.

с-пе́-ть, *v.p.*, + *acc.*, to sing through. С-пе́-ть-ся, *v.p.r.*, с-пе-ва́ть-ся, *v.i.r.*, to rehearse a chorus, part; set one's voice in accord; (*colloq.*), come to an agreement. С-пе́в-ка, *n.f.*, chorus rehearsal.

пев-е́ц, *n.m.*, пев-и́ца, *n.f.*, singer, artist. О́перный певе́ц, о́перная певи́ца, opera singer. Ка́мерный певе́ц, ка́мерная певи́ца, lieder singer. Пев-и́чка, *n.f.*, (*dim., colloq.*), music-hall singer, popular singer. Пев-у́н, *n.m.*, пев-у́нья, *n.f.*, (*colloq.*), songster, songstress. Пев-у́честь, *n.f.*, melodiousness. Пев-у́чий, *adj.*, melodious. П. го́лос (стих), melodious voice (verse). Пе́в-чий, *adj.*, used as *n.*, chorister, choir boy. П-ая пти́ца, singing bird.

пес-ня, *n.f.*, пес-нь, *n.f.*, song, air, melody. Песнь Пе́сней, Canticles, the Song of Songs, the Song of Solomon. Наро́дная пе́сня, folk song. Лебеди́ная п., swan song. Э́то ста́рая п., (*fig.*), it's the same old story; it's the old story. Пе́с-енка, *n.f.*, (*dim.*), song, ditty. Его́ п. спе́та, (*colloq., fig.*), he's done for; he's finished; his goose is cooked. Пе́с-енник, *n.m.*, songbook; (*obs.*), chorus singer. Пе́с-енный, *adj.*, song.

пет-у́х, *n.m.*, cock, rooster. Инде́йский п., turkey cock. Встава́ть с петуха́ми, (*colloq.*), to rise with the hens. Пусти́ть кра́сного петуха́, (*fig.*), to set afire. Пет-ушо́к, *n.m.*, cockerel; weathercock. Пет-уши́ный, пет-у́ший, *adj.*, pertaining to a rooster. Петуши́ный бой, cockfight. Петуши́ный гребешо́к, coxcomb.

пет-уш-и́ть-ся, *v.i.r.*, (*colloq.*), to ride the high horse; fume.

вс-пет-уш-и́ть-ся, *v.p.r.*, *see* петуши́ться

рас-пет-уш-и́ть-ся, *v.p.r.*, (*colloq.*), to become huffy.

ПЕС-, ПЁС-, ПС-, DOG

пёс, *n.m.*, dog, male dog; cur, despicable person. Пс-ы, *n.pl.*, dogs. Злой п., angry, mad dog. Не слы́шно ла́я псов сторожевы́х the barking of the watchdogs cannot be heard. Ах ты, ста́рый пёс! (*colloq.*), You old goat! Созве́здие Большо́го Пса, (*astron.*), Great Dog, *Canis Major.* Созве́здие Ма́лого Пса, (*astron.*), *Canis Minor.* Пёс-ик, *n.m.*, little dog, doggie. Пёс-ий, *adj.*, of or pertaining to a dog. П. нос, dog's nose. Пёс-ь-я мо́рда, dog's muzzle. Пес-е́ц, *n.m.*, polar fox; polar fox fur. Голубо́й (бе́лый) п., blue (white) fox. Пес-цо́вый, *adj.*, pertaining to a polar fox. П. мех, polar fox fur.

пс-ар-ь, *n.m.*, huntsman, whip, whipper-in. П. со сво́рой го́нчих соба́к, a whipper-in with a pack of hounds. Жа́лует царь, да не ми́лует псарь, (*saying*), the chief is gracious to me, but his subordinates are antagonistic. Пс-а́рня, *n.f.*, kennel. Пс-а́рный, *adj.*, pertaining to a kennel.

пс-и́н-а, *n.f.*, dog's flesh. Па́хнет пси́ной, it smells of dog. Пс-и́ный, *adj.*, (*colloq.*), of a dog. П. за́пах, smell, scent of a dog.

ПЕШ-, (ПѢШ-), ПЕХ-, (ПѢХ-), LOCOMOTION ON FOOT

пеш-ий, *adj.*, used as *n.*, pedestrian; (*mil.*), unmounted. П. ко́нному не това́рищ, (*prov.*), a man on foot is no companion to one on horseback, (*fig.*), a poor man is no companion to a rich man). В пе́шем строю́, (*mil.*), dismounted formation (*of cavalry*). Пеш-е-, *a combining form meaning* foot, locomotion on foot. Пеш-е-хо́д, *n.m.*, pedestrian. Пеш-е-хо́дный, *adj.*, pedestrian. П-ая тропа́, footpath. П. мост, footbridge. Пеш-ко́м, *adv.*, on foot, afoot. Идти́ п., to go on foot. Пе́ш-ка, *n.f.*, pawn; (*also used fig.*).

пех-о́т-а, *n.f.*, infantry. Отря́д пехо́ты, (*mil.*), infantry detachment. Пех-оти́нец, *n.m.*, foot soldier, infantryman. Пех-о́тный, *adj.*, infantry. П. полк, infantry regiment. П. бой, infantry combat. Пех-туро́й, *adv.*, (*slang*), on shank's mare. Пришёл п., на свои́х, на двои́х, (*slang*), I came on foot.

с-пе́ш-и-ть, *v.p.,* с-пе́ш-ивать, *v.i.,* + *acc.,* to dismount. С. кавале́рию, to employ cavalry in dismounted formation. С-пе́ш-ить-ся, *v.p.r.,* с-пе́ш-ивать-ся, *v.i.r.,* to dismount, alight from a horse. С-пе́ш-ивание, *n.n.,* dismounting. С-пе́ш-енный, *adj., part. pass. past,* dismounted. С-ая кавале́рия, dismounted cavalry.

ПИ- (ПИТ-), ПЬ-, ПИВ-, ПО-, ПОИ-, ПА-, DRINKING

пи-ть, пь-ю, *v.i.,* + *acc.,* to drink, sip. П. чай, to drink tea. П. за чьё-нибудь здоро́вье, to drink to someone's health. П. го́рькую (мёртвую), (*colloq.*), to drink hard, drink like a fish. Пи-тьё, *n.n.,* drinking; drink, beverage. Пи-тьево́й, *adj.,* drinkable. П-а́я вода́, drinking water. Пи-те́йный, *adj.,* (*obs.*), pertaining to drinking. П. дом (п-ое заведе́ние), pub, saloon.

вы́-пить, *v.p.,* вы-пи-ва́ть, *v.i.,* + *acc.,* + *gen.,* to drink. В. ча́шку ча́ю, to drink a cup of tea. В. воды́, to have a drink of water, drink some water. Он выпива́ет, he likes his liquor; he gets drunk occasionally. Вы́-пив-ка, *n.f.,* (*colloq.*), carousal; drinking bout; spree. Вы́пивки и заку́ски, strong drinks and hors d'oeuvres.

в-пить, *v.p.,* в-пи-ва́ть, *v.i.,* + *acc.,* to drink in, to suck in, up; absorb, imbibe. Впива́ть арома́т цвето́в, to drink in the fragrance of flowers. Гу́бка впила́ в себя́ во́ду, the sponge absorbed the water. В-пить-ся, *v.p.r.,* в-пи-ва́ть-ся, *v.i.r.,* + *instr.,* в + *acc.,* to stick into, pierce, bite into. В. глаза́ми, (*fig.*), to fix one's glance on. В. зуба́ми (ногтя́ми) во что́-либо, to dig one's teeth (claws) into something.

до-пить, *v.p.,* до-пи-ва́ть, *v.i.,* + *acc.,* to drink up, drink the remainder, finish drinking. Д. вино́, to drain a cup of wine. До-пи́ть-ся, *v.p.r.,* до-пи-ва́ть-ся, *v.i.r.,* до + *gen.,* to drink to a given point. Д. до бе́лой горя́чки, (*colloq.*), to drink to the point of delirium tremens.

за-пи́ть, *v.p.,* за-пи-ва́ть, *v.i.,* на + *acc.,* + *instr.,* to drink; to take to drink; to take a drink of a liquid to remove a disagreeable taste. З. на це́лую неде́лю, to drink for a whole week. З. лека́рство водо́й, to take a medicine with water.

за-по́-й, *n.m.,* hard drinking; drinking bout. Страда́ть запоем, to be an alcoholic. Рабо́тать запоем, (*fig.*), to work excessively. Чита́ть запоем, to read avidly. За-по́й-ный, *adj.,* per-

taining to immoderate drinking. З. пья́ница, heavy drinker, drunkard.

ис-пи́ть, изо-пь-ю́, *v.p.,* ис-пи-ва́ть, *v.i.,* + *acc.,* + *gen.,* (*poet., obs.*), to drink up, off. И. го́рькую ча́шу страда́ний (униже́ний), (*poet.*), to drain the cup of sorrow (humiliation). Ис-пи-то́й, *adj.,* (*colloq.*), wasted, sallow; hollow-cheeked. И-о́е лицо́, wasted, sallow face.

на-пи́ть-ся, *v.p.r.,* на-пи-ва́ть-ся, *v.i.r.,* to drink one's fill, quench one's thirst; get drunk. Да́йте мне воды́ н., give me a drink of water. Он напи́лся и не пришёл на рабо́ту, he got drunk and failed to come to work. На-пи́т-ок, *n.m.,* drink, beverage. Спиртны́е напи́тки, liquor, alcoholic beverages. Кре́пкие напи́тки, strong liquors. Прохлади́тельные напи́тки, cold drinks.

о-пи́ть, *v.p.,* о-пи-ва́ть, *v.i.,* + *acc.,* (*colloq., obs.*), to drink at someone else's expense. Опива́ть и объеда́ть кого́-нибудь, (*colloq.*), to drink and eat at someone else's expense. О-пи́ть-ся, *v.p.r.,* о-пи-ва́ть-ся, *v.i.r.,* + *instr.,* to drink too much. О-пи́в-ки, *n.pl.,* excess, leftover liquid.

от-пи́ть, *v.p.,* от-пи-ва́ть, *v.i.,* + *acc.,* + *gen.,* to sip, take a sip. О. глото́к воды́, to take a sip of water.

пере-пи́ть, *v.p.,* пере-пи-ва́ть, *v.i.,* + *gen.,* (*colloq.*), to drink to excess; outdrink others. Он всех мо́жет перепи́ть, he can outdrink anyone. Пере-пи́ть-ся, *v.p.r.,* пере-пи-ва́ть-ся, *v.i.r.,* to drink to excess, Они́ все перепи́лись, they all got drunk.

по-пи́ть, *v.p.,* + *gen.,* to drink a little, sip. Дай п., let me have a drink, a sip. По-пи-ва́ть, *v.i.,* (*colloq.*), to get drunk occasionally.

под-пи́ть, *v.p.,* (*colloq.*), to tipple.

про-пи́ть, *v.p.,* про-пи-ва́ть, *v.i.,* + *acc.,* to squander money on drink. П. де́сять рубле́й, to squander ten rubles on drink. П. го́лос, to ruin one's voice through drinking. Про-пи́ть-ся, *v.p.r.,* про-пи-ва́ть-ся, *v.i.r.,* to ruin oneself through drinking. Про-по́й-ца, *n.m.,* (*colloq.*), drunkard.

рас-пи́ть, *v.p.,* рас-пи-ва́ть, *v.i.,* + *acc.,* + *instr.,* to drink in company, drink with. Р. буты́лку вина́ с ке́м-либо, to share a bottle of wine with someone. Рас-пи́в-очный, *adj.,* on tap; *used as n.,* tavern. Р-ая прода́жа вина́ (пи́ва), wine (beer) sold for consumption on the premises.

с-пи́ть-ся, *v.p.r.,* с-пи-ва́ть-ся, *v.i.r.,* to become an inveterate drunkard.

у-пи́ть-ся, *v.p.r.,* у-пи-ва́ть-ся, *v.i.r.,* + *instr.,* to become intoxicated. У. вино́м, to become intoxicated on wine. У. му́зыкой, (*fig.*), to be enraptured by music.

у-по-е́ние, *n.n.,* rapture, ecstasy. Быть в упое́нии, to be in rapture. У. успе́ха, flush of success. У-по-и́тельный, *adj.,* ravishing, entrancing. У-ая му́зыка, entrancing music. У-по-ённый, *adj., part. pass. past,* entranced, ravished. У. сла́вой, drunk with glory.

по-и́ть, *v.r.,* на-по-и́ть, *v.i.,* + *acc.,* + *instr.,* to water, give to drink. Н. скот, to water cattle. П. ча́ем, to treat to tea. По́й-ло, *n.n.,* swill, hogwash. Вод-о-по́й, *n.m.,* watering; watering place. Пере-по́й, *n.m.,* excessive drinking. С перепо́ю, from drinking to excess. По-по́й-ка, *n.f.,* spree; *see* вы́пивка.

вс-по-и́ть, *v.p.,* + *acc.,* + *instr.,* (*colloq.*), to rear, bring up. В. телёнка молоко́м, to rear a calf on milk. Вспои́л и вы́кормил сиро́т, (*idiom. folk.*), he brought up orphans.

на-по-и́ть, *v.r.,* на-па́-ивать, *v.i.,* + *acc.,* + *instr., see* пойть. Н. во́дкой допьяна́, to make someone drunk on vodka. Напои́ть гостя́ ча́ем, to offer a guest tea. На-по-ён(ный), *adj., part. pass. past,* intoxicated, drunk; watered (animals). Во́здух напоён за́пахом сире́ни, the air is filled (permeated) with the fragrance of lilacs.

о-по-и́ть, *v.r.,* о-па́-ивать, *v.i.,* + *acc.,* + *instr.,* to poison. О. ло́щадь водо́й, to founder a horse.

под-по-и́ть, *v.r.,* под-па́-ивать, *v.i.,* + *acc.,* to make drunk with a purpose. Чтобы он согласи́лся, на́до его́ подпои́ть, in order to impel him to agree, you must make him drunk.

с-по-и́ть, *v.r.,* с-па́-ивать, *v.i.,* + *acc.,* to accustom to drinking.

пь-ян-е́-ть, *v.i.,* о-пь-яне́ть, *v.r.,* от + *gen.,* to become drunk. П. от во́дки, to become drunk from vodka. П. от успе́ха, to be intoxicated with success.

пь-ян-и́-ть, *v.i.,* о-пь-яни́ть, *v.p.,* + *acc.,* to make drunk. Вино́ пьяни́т, wine intoxicates. Успе́хи пьяня́т, success goes to the head. Пь-яня́щий, *adj., part. act. pres.,* intoxicating. П. арома́т, intoxicating fragrance. П. во́здух, bracing air.

пь-ян-ство-ва-ть, *v.i,* to drink hard; carouse. Пь-я́ный, *adj.,* drunk, tipsy, intoxicated; *used as n.m.,* drunkard. П-ая похо́дка, tipsy gait. Пь-я́нство, *n.n.,* drunkenness, hard drinking, excessive drinking. Пь-я́ница, *n.m.,* drunkard, alcoholic. Го́рький п., inveterate drunkard, hard drinker. Быть пья́ницей, to be a drunkard. Пь-янчу́га,

пь-янчу́жка, *n.m.* (*colloq.*), sot. Пь-я́нка, *n.f.,* (*colloq.*), drinking bout, spree, binge. До́-пь-зна, *adv.,* (*colloq.*), until drunk. Напи́ться д., to drink until one becomes drunk. С-пь-я́на, с-пь-я́ну, *adv.,* (*colloq.*), in a state of drunkenness. Это тебе́ померё́щилось спья́ну, you thought you saw it when you were drunk.

пи́в-о, *n.n.,* beer. Све́тлое (тёмное) п., light (dark) beer. Пив-но́й, *adj.,* of or pertaining to beer. Пив-на́я, *adj., used as n.f.,* beer house, beer tavern. П-ы́е дро́жжи, brewer's yeast. П-а́я кру́жка, stein, beer mug. Пив-о-ва́р, *n.m.,* brewer. Пив-о-варе́ние, *n.n.,* brewing. Пив-о-ва́ренный, *adj.,* brewing. П. заво́д, brewery. П-ая промы́шленность, brewing industry.

пи-я́вк-а, пья́вка, *n.f.,* leech. Медици́нские пия́вки, (*med.*), leeches. Ста́вить пия́вки, (*med.*), to apply leeches. Прилипа́ть как пья́вка, (*colloq.*), to stick like a leech.

ПИЛ-, SAW, SAWING

пил-а́, *n.f.,* saw. Ручна́я п., handsaw. Механи́ческая п., mechanical, automatic saw. Пила́-ры́ба, sword-fish. Пи́л-ка, *n.f.,* sawing; nail file. П. дров, sawing of wood. Пил-ёный, *adj.,* sawed, filed. П. са́хар, lump, cut sugar. П. лес, cut lumber; timber. Пил-о-обра́зный, *adj.,* saw-like.

пил-и́ть, *v.i.,* + *acc.,* to saw; (*fig.*), to nag, pester. П. дрова́, to saw firewood. П. му́жа (жену́), (*fig. colloq.*), to nag a husband (wife). Пи́л-ь-щик, *n.m.,* sawer, wood-cutter. Лес-о-пи́л-ь-ня, *n.f.,* sawmill.

вы́-пил-ить, *v.r.,* вы-пи́л-ивать, *v.i.,* + *acc.,* to saw out, cut out. В. украше́ние (ра́мку), to make fretwork.

над-пил-и́ть. *v.r.,* над-пи́л-ивать, *v.i.,* + *acc.,* to make an incision with a saw.

на-пил-и́ть, *v.r.,* на-пи́л-ивать, *v.i.,* + *acc.,* + *gen.,* to saw a quantity of. Н. дров на́ зиму, to saw firewood for the winter. На-пи́л-ок, на-пи́л-ь-ник, *n.m.,* file.

о-пил-и́ть, *v.r.,* о-пи́л-ивать, *v.i.,* + *acc.,* to saw around. О-пи́л-ок, *n.m.,* sawdust. Металли́ческие опи́лки, filings. О-пило́вка, *n.f.,* filing around.

от-пил-и́ть, *v.r.,* от-пи́л-ивать, *v.i.,* + *acc.,* to saw off. О. сук, to saw off a branch.

пере-пил-и́ть, *v.r.,* пере-пи́л-ивать, *v.i.,* + *acc.,* to saw through. П. все дрова́, to saw all the firewood.

под-пил-и́ть, *v.r.,* под-пи́л-ивать, *v.i.,* + *acc.,* to saw under. П. но́жки у стола́, (стула), to shorten the legs of a table (a chair). Под-пи́л-ок, *n.m.*, file.

про-пил-и́ть, *v.p.,* про-пи́л-ивать, *v.i.,* + *acc.,* + *instr.,* to saw through. П. око́шечко в две́ри, to cut a window in a door. Пропи́л, *n.m.,* (*tech.*), slit; sawkerf.

рас-пил-и́ть, *v.p.,* рас-пи́л-ивать, *v.i.,* + *acc.,* to saw up; cut into lengths. Р. на до́ски (на ба́лки), to cut up into boards (into beams). Рас-пи́л-ка, рас-пило́вка, *n.f.,* sawing, cutting.

с-пил-и́ть, *v.p.,* с-пи́л-ивать, *v.i.,* + *acc.,* to saw off. С. верху́шку де́рева, to saw off the top of a tree.

ПИН-, ПН-, ПОН-, ПЯТ-, KICKING, PUSHING WITH FOOT; STRETCHING, TENSION, MOTION

пин-о́к, *n.m.,* (*colloq.*), kick. Дава́ть пинка́, to kick.

пин-а́ть, *v.i.,* пн-у́ть, *v.p. smf.,* + *acc.* (*obs.*), to kick; spurn.

за-пин-а́ть-ся, *v.i.r.,* за-пн-у́ть-ся, *v.p.r.,* to hesitate; halt; stumble, stammer, falter; stop short. З. на сло́ве, to stumble over a word. За-пи́н-ка, *n.f.,* hesitation; stumble, stammer, stutter. За́-пон-ка, *n.f.,* stud, link, collar-button. За-пят-а́я, *n.f.,* (*gram.*), comma. Поста́вить запяту́ю, to insert a comma.

на-пин-у́ть-ся, *v.p.r.,* на + *acc.,* to run against, stumble on. Н. на пень, to stumble on a tree trunk.

по-по́н-а, *n.f.,* horse blanket.

препина́ния, *n.n.,* punctuation. Зна́ки препина́ния, (*gram.*), punctuation marks. Расставля́ть зна́ки препина́ния, to punctuate.

пре-по́н-а, *n.f.,* (*obs.*), obstacle. Перепо́н-ка, *n.f.,* membrane. Бараба́нная п., eardrum. Пере-по́н-чатый, *adj.,* webbed, membranous.

рас-пя́т-ь, *v.p.,* рас-пин-а́ть, *v.i.,* + *acc.,* to crucify. Распни́ его́! Crucify him! Рас-пи́н-ый, *adj., part. pass. past,* crucified. Рас-пин-а́ть-ся, *v.i.r.,* за + *acc.,* to put oneself out, oblige, please. Рас-пя́т-ие, *n.n.,* crucifixion; cross, crucifix.

ПИР-, FEAST, FEASTING

пир *n.m.* (*obs.*) feast, banquet. Бога́тый п., sumptuous feast. В чужо́м пиру́ похме́лье, (*saying*), to bear another's troubles. П. на весь мир, пир горо́й, (*idiom.*), sumptuous feast. Пир-у́шка, *n.f.,* (*dim.*), carousal, convivial meeting.

пир-ова́-ть, *v.i.,* to feast, revel, carouse. П. сва́дьбу, to celebrate a wedding. „Пиру́ет с дружи́ною ве́щий Оле́г"

(*Pushkin*), "The wise Oleg is feasting with his warriors."

пи́р-шеств-ова-ть, *v.i.* (*obs.*), to feast, revel, celebrate. Пи́р-шество, *n.n.,* feast, banquet.

за-пир-ова́-ть, *v.p.,* see пирова́ть. "И запиру́ем на просто́ре..." (*Pushkin*), "and we shall feast freely."

по-пир-ова́-ть, *v.p.,* to feast a little. П. на ра́достях, to be joyful over something.

ПИРОГ-, ПИРОЖ-, PIE, TART

пиро́г, *n.m.,* pie, tart. П. с я́блоками, apple pie. Возду́шный п., soufflé. Сва́дебный п., wedding cake. Бе́лый п., (*folk*), white wheat bread. Ешь п. с гриба́ми, а язы́к держи́ за зуба́ми, (*saying*), keep your breath to cool your porridge. Не красна́ изба́ угла́ми, а красна́ пирога́ми, (*saying*), a fine cage does not fill a bird's belly.

пиро́ж-ник, *n.m.,* пиро́ж-ница *n.f.,* (*obs.*), pastry cook, baker. "Беда́ коль пироги́ начнёт печи́ сапо́жник, а сапоги́ тача́ть пиро́жник," (*Krylov*), great is the misfortune when pastry is baked by cobblers and boots are made by bakers. Пиро́ж-ное, *n.n.,* pastry, cake. Пирож-о́к, *n.m.,* patty. Суп с пирожка́ми, soup and patties.

ПИС-, ПИШ-, WRITING

пис-а́-ть, пиш-у́, *v.i.,* на-пис-а́ть, *v.p.,* + *acc.,* to write. П. кру́пно (ме́лко, разбо́рчиво), to write in large (small, plain) handwriting. П. перо́м (каранда́шо́м), to write with a pen (pencil). П. про́зой (стиха́ми), to write prose (verse). П. карти́ны (портре́ты), to paint pictures (portraits). Пиши́ пропа́ло! Consider it lost! Пис-а́ть-ся, *v.i.r.,* to be spelled, written. Как пи́шется э́то сло́во? How do you spell this word? How is this word spelled? Пис-а́ка, *n.m.,* (*sarc.*), scribbler. Пис-а́ние, *n.n.,* writing. Свяще́нное Писа́ние, Holy Scriptures. Пи́с-аный, *adj.,* written, painted. П-ая краса́вица, picture of beauty. Говори́ть, как по пи́саному, (*fig.*), to talk like a book. Пи́с-анка, *n.f.,* decorated Easter egg, traditional folk designs on Easter eggs. Пис-а́рь, *n.m.,* clerk. Пис-а́тель, *n.m.,* пис-а́тельница, *n.f.,* author, writer. Пис-а́тельский, *adj.,* pertaining to a writer. П. тала́нт (труд), literary talent (work). Пис-е́ц, *n.m.,* clerk; scribe. Пис-цо́вый, *adj.,* (*hist.*), cadastral. П-ые кни́ги, (*hist.*), cadasters; registers of taxable property. Пи́с-чий, *adj.,* writing. П-ая бума́га, writing paper, stationery. Пис-че-бума́жный, *adj.*, stationery. П-ое произво́дство, paper industry. П-ый магази́н, stationery store. П-ые принадле́жности, stationery supplies. Пис-ь-мена́, *n.pl.*, (*obs.*), characters, letters. Пи́с-ь-менно, *adv.*, in written form. Изложи́ть что́-либо п., to put something in writing. Пи́с-ь-менность, *n.f.*, written language; literature. Пи́с-ь-менный, *adj.*, writing, written. П. стол, writing table, desk. П-ые принадле́жности, writing materials, implements; stationery. П. прибо́р, desk set. П. о́тзыв, written reference. В пи́сьменной фо́рме, in written from, in writing. П. знак, letter (*of the alphabet*). Пис-ь-мо́, *n.n.*, letter, epistle; writing. Заказно́е п., registered letter. Делово́е п., business letter. Пись-мо́, *a combining form meaning* letter, writing. Письм-о-води́тель, *n.m.*, clerk. Письм-о-но́сец, (*recent*), *n.m.*, mailman, postman. Пи́ш-ущий, *adj., part. act. pres.*, writing. П-ая маши́нка, typewriter. П-ая бра́тия, (*coll.*), authors, writers.

в-пис-а́ть, *v.p.*, в-пи́с-ывать, *v.i.*, + *acc.*, to enter, insert, inscribe, write in. В. пропу́щенное сло́во, to insert an omitted word. В. в спи́сок своё и́мя, to enter one's name. В-пис-а́ть-ся, *v.p.r.*, в-пи́с-ывать-ся, *v.i.r.*, to join, subscribe. В-пи́с-ка, *n.f.*, (*colloq.*), entry, insertion.

вы́-пис-а́ть, *v.p.*, вы-пи́с-ывать, *v.i.*, + *acc.*, из + *gen.*, to extract, write out; order, subscribe; send for; strike off a list, delete. В. не́сколько цита́т из кни́ги, to copy a few quotations from a book. В. кни́гу (журна́л), to order a book (subscribe to a magazine). В. бра́та из Евро́пы, to send for one's brother from Europe. В. из больни́цы, to discharge from a hospital. Вы́-пис-ать-ся, *v.p.r.*, вы-пи́с-ывать-ся, *v.i.r.*, to be discharged. Он уже́ вы́писался из больни́цы, he has already been discharged from the hospital. Вы́-пис-ка, *n.f.*, excerpts, copying, writing out; ordering, subscription. В. газе́т (журна́лов), subscription to newspapers, magazines. Больно́й предназна́чен к вы́писке, the patient is to be discharged. Вы́-пис-ь, *n.f.*, see вы́писка. Метри́ческая в., birth certificate.

до-пис-а́ть, *v.p.*, до-пи́с-ывать, *v.i.*, + *acc.*, to finish writing, painting. Д. страни́цу, to complete a page, finish writing a page. Д. карти́ну, to finish a painting.

за-пис-а́ть, *v.p.*, за-пи́с-ывать, *v.i.*, + *acc.*, в + *acc.*, to write down, jot down, put down, take down, note, record; enter. З. ле́кцию, to take down a lecture. З. в расхо́д (прихо́д), to enter the expenditures (income). З. в протоко́л, to enter in a police record. За-пис-а́ть-ся, *v.p.r.*, за-пи́с-ывать-ся, *v.i.r.*, в + *acc.*, + *instr.*, to register, enter one's name. З. доброво́льцем, в а́рмию, to enlist as a volunteer in the army. З. к врачу́, to make an appointment with a doctor. З. в библиоте́ку, to subscribe to a library. За-пи́с-ка, *n.f.*, note, notes, memoirs. Дипломати́ческая (делова́я) з., diplomatic (business) memorandum. Докладна́я з., report. Любо́вная з., love letter. Путевы́е запи́ски, travel notes. За-пис-но́й, *adj.*, pertaining to writing. З-а́я кни́жка, notebook. З-о́й игро́к, inveterate player. За́-пис-ь, *n.f.*, entry; record; notation. З. на приём, record of an appointment. З. а́ктов гражда́нского состоя́ния, (*recent*), registry office; office of registry of births, deaths, etc.

ис-пис-а́ть, *v.p.*, ис-пи́с-ывать, *v.i.*, + *acc.*, + *instr.*, to fill with writing, cover with writing. И. каранда́ш (бума́гу), to use up an entire pencil (all the paper). И. тетра́дь ме́лким по́черком, to fill a notebook with fine writing. Ис-пис-а́ть-ся, *v.p.r.*, ис-пи́с-ывать-ся, *v.i.r.*, to be exhausted, tired, from writing; be written out. Каранда́ш исписа́лся, the pencil is all used up, worn out. Писа́тель исписа́лся, the writer has written himself out.

на-пис-а́ть, *v.p.*, see писа́ть. На-писа́ние, *n.n.*, written symbol. Бу́ква "д" име́ет в ру́сском письме́ двоя́кое н., хвосто́м вверх и́ли вниз, the letter "d" is represented by two symbols in the Russian language: with the tail up, or with the tail down.

над-пис-а́ть, *v.p.*, над-пи́с-ывать, *v.i.*, + *acc.*, to superscribe, inscribe; make an inscription. Н. ве́ксель, to endorse a bill, a note. Н. конве́рт, to address an envelope. На́д-пис-ь, *n.f.*, inscription. Н. на кни́ге (на ка́мне), an inscription on a book (on a stone).

о-пис-а́ть, *v.p.*, о-пи́с-ывать, *v.i.*, + *acc.*, to describe, portray, depict; inventory. Э́то невозмо́жно о., this is beyond description. О. иму́щество, to inventory. О. за долги́, to distrain for debts. О. окру́жность, (*math.*), to describe a circle; circumscribe. О-пис-а́ние, *n.n.*, description, account. Э́то не поддаётся описа́нию, this defies description. О-пи́с-анный, *adj., part. pass. past,* circumscribed, described. О. у́гол, (*math.*), circumscribed angle. О-пис-а́тельный, *adj.*, descriptive. О-пи́с-ка, *n.f.,* slip of a pen. Ошибок нет, но описок мно́го, there are no mistakes in spelling but there are many misprints. О-пис-ь, *n.f.,* inventory; schedule. О. иму́щества, distraint.

от-пис-а́ть, *v.p.,* от-пи́с-ывать, *v.i.,* + *acc.,* + *dat.,* (*obs.*), to bequeath. О. всё иму́щество кому́-нибудь, to bequeath all one's property to someone. От-пис-а́ть-ся, *v.p.r.,* от-пи́с-ывать-ся, *v.i.r.,* to write back evasively as a bureaucratic formality. От-пи́с-ка, *n.f.,* formal reply. Канцеля́рская о., formal business reply, evasive reply, characteristic of bureaucratic organizations.

пере-пис-а́ть, *v.p.,* пере-пи́с-ывать, *v.i.,* + *acc.,* to copy, transcribe. П. текст на пи́шущей маши́нке, to transcribe a text on a typewriter; retype. П. на́бело, to make a clean copy. П. всех, to register, enter everyone's name. Пере-пи́с-ывать-ся, *v.i.r.,* с + *instr.,* to correspond, be in correspondence with. Пере-пи́с-ка, *n.f.,* copying, typing; correspondence. Пере-пи́с-чик, *n.m.,* пере-пи́с-чица, *n.f.,* copyist, typist. Пере-пи́с-ывание, *n.n.,* copying, typing. Пе́ре-пис-ь, *n.f.,* census; inventory. Пе́репись населе́ния, census of a population.

под-пис-а́ть, *v.p.,* под-пи́с-ывать, *v.i.,* + *acc.,* to sign; subscribe. П. кого́-либо на газе́ту, to subscribe to a newspaper for someone. П. докуме́нт (догово́р), to sign a document (a treaty). Под-пис-а́ть-ся, *v.p.r.,* под-пи́с-ывать-ся, *v.i.r.,* на + *acc.,* to sign. П. на письме́, to sign a letter. П. на заём, to subscribe to a loan. Под-пи́с-ывание, *n.n.,* signing. П. бума́г, signing of papers. Под-пи́с-ка, *n.f.,* subscription; written promise. П. на газе́ту (журна́л), to subscribe to a paper (a magazine). Дать подпи́ску, to make a signed statement, give a written promise. Под-пи́с-чик, *n.m.,* под-пи́счица, *n.f.,* subscriber. Под-пис-но́й, *adj.,* subscription. П. лист, subscription list. П-а́я цена́, subscription price. Под-пис-а́вшийся, *adj., part. act. past,* signed, having signed. Ниже-под-пис-а́вшийся, the undersigned.

по-пи́с-ывать, *v.i.,* + *acc.,* (*colloq.*), to write occasionally; scribble. Писа́тель попи́сывает, а чита́тель почи́тывает, (*derog.*), the writer scribbles, and the readers read it.

пред-пис-а́ть, *v.p.,* пред-пи́с-ывать, *v.i.,* + *dat.,* + *acc.,* to order; prescribe; direct. Врач предписа́л больно́му лече́ние, the doctor prescribed a treatment for the sick man. Предписа́но приня́ть стро́гие ме́ры, strict measures have been prescribed. Предпис-а́ние, *n.n.,* directions, instructions; order. Секре́тное п., secret order. Согла́сно предписа́нию, in accordance with orders.

при-пис-а́ть, *v.p.,* при-пи́с-ывать, *v.i.,* + *acc.,* + *dat.,* to add, attach; register; ascribe, attribute. П. в письме́ не́сколько строк, to add a few lines to a letter. Чему́ вы мо́жете п. его успе́х? To what do you attribute his success? Приписа́ть-ся, *v.p.r.,* при-пи́с-ывать-ся, *v.i.r.,* к + *dat.,* to be registered. П. к призывно́му уча́стку, to be registered for conscription in a district. При-пи́с-ка, *n.f.,* addition; postscript; registration. При-пи́с-ывание, *n.n.,* imputing, adding, attributing.

про-пис-а́ть, *v.p.,* про-пи́с-ывать, *v.i.,* + *acc.,* to prescribe; register. П. лече́ние, to prescribe a treatment, cure. П. па́спорт, to register a passport. Пропис-а́ть-ся, *v.p.r.,* про-пи́с-ывать-ся, *v.i.r.,* to be registered; register. П. в. домо́вой кни́ге (*recent*), to register one's name in a house record book. Пропи́с-ка, *n.f.,* visa; registration. Пропис-но́й, *adj.,* capital. П-а́я бу́ква, capital letter. Про́-пис-ь, *n.f.,* samples of writing, of script. Писа́ть ци́фры про́писью, to write out figures.

рас-пис-а́ть, *v.p.,* рас-пи́с-ывать, *v.i.,* + *acc.,* to paint; assign; describe. Р. сте́ны (потоло́к), to paint murals on walls (the ceiling). Р. счета́ по кни́гам, to enter bills in an account book. Он так расписа́л свой успе́х, что все удиви́лись, he drew such a picture of his success, that everyone was surprised. Рас-пис-а́ть-ся, *v.p.r.,* рас-пи́с-ывать-ся, *v.i.r.,* в + *prep.,* to sign for; be married in a registry office; get into a writing mood. Прочти́те э́ту бума́гу и распиши́тесь, read this paper and sign it. Распиши́тесь в получе́нии жа́лования, sign for your salary. Он расписа́лся в со́бственном неве́жестве (в со́бственной глу́пости), he showed off his own ignorance (stupidity). Они́ расписа́лись в За́гсе, (*recent*), they registered their marriage in the registry office. Он так расписа́лся, что за два ме́сяца написа́л це́лый рома́н, he was in such a writing mood that he wrote a novel in two months. Рас-пис-а́ние, *n.n.,* time-table; schedule. Р. поездо́в, train schedule. Р. ле́кций, lecture schedule. Рас-пи́с-ка, *n.f.,* receipt; painting. Р. в получе́нии, acknowledgement of receipt. Письмо́ с обра́тной распи́ской, letter accompanied by a return receipt. Рас-пис-но́й, *adj.,* decorated with designs. Р.

потолóк, decorated ceiling. Р. чáйник, decorated teapot.

с-пис-áть, *v.p.,* с-пи́с-ывать, *v.i.,* + *acc.,* с + *gen.,* у + *gen.,* to copy, crib. С. со счёта, to write off. С. стихотворéние для пáмяти, to copy a poem in order to assist one's memory. С. услóвия задáчи с доскú, to copy a problem from a blackboard. С-пис-áть-ся, *v.p.r.,* с-пи́с-ывать-ся, *v.i.r.,* с + *instr.,* to exchange letters; settle by letter. Я с ним списáлся и он согласúля продáть дом, I exchanged letters with him and he agreed to sell his house. С-пи́с-ок, *n.m.,* list. С. избирáтелей, list of voters; poll. Трудовóй с., service record.

у-пис-áть, *v.p.,* у-пи́с-ывать, *v.i.,* + *acc.,* (*colloq.*), to write in; eat heartily. У. письмó на однóй страни́чке, to crowd a letter on one page. Уписáл весь пирóг, (*colloq.*), he gobbled up the whole pie. У-пис-áть-ся, *v.p.r.,* у-пи́с-ывать-ся, *v.i.r.,* на + *prep.,* (*colloq.*), to be closely written. Запúска уписáлась на мáленьком клочкé бумáги, the note was closely written on a scrap of paper.

живо-пис-ь, *n.f.,* painting. Ж. мáсляными крáсками, oil painting; painting in oils. Батáльная ж., battle painting. Живо-пи́с-ец, *n.m.,* painter, artist. Живо-пи́с-ный, *adj.,* picturesque, pictorial. Ж-ая мéстность, picturesque site.

лéто-пис-ь, *n.f.,* chronicle, annal. Лето-пи́с-ец, *n.m.,* (*hist.*), chronicler. Кúевский монáх Нéстор был пéрвый рýсский летопúсец, Nestor, a Kiev monk, was the first Russian chronicler. Лето-пи́с-ный, *adj.,* chronicle.

рýко-пис-ь, *n.f.,* manuscript. Дрéвняя р., ancient manuscript. Рукó-пис-ный, *adj.,* handwritten. Р. журнáл, handwritten magazine. Р. отдéл библиóтеки, division of manuscripts in a library.

ПИСК-, ПИЩ-, SQUEAK

писк, *n.m.,* peep, chirp, cheep, squeak. Жáлобный п., whine. П. птенцá (ребёнка), peep of a fledgling (whine of a child). Писк-лúвый, *adj.,* squeaky. П. гóлос, squeaky voice.

пи́ск-ну-ть, *v.p.smf.,* (*colloq.*), to give, make a squeak. Писк-отня́, *n.f.,* (*colloq.*), squeaking, peeping. Писк-ýн, *n.m.,* писк-ýнья, *n.f.,* one who squeaks.

пищ-áть, *v.i.,* to squeak, chirp, peep; squeal, whine. Цыплёнок пищи́т, the chick is peeping. Ребёнок пищи́т, the child is whining. Пищ-áль, *n.f.,* (*obs.*), harquebus. Пищ-áлка, *n.f.,* children's small whistle, pipe. Пи́щ-ик, *n.m.,* small pipe for luring birds.

за-пищ-áть, *v.p.,* to begin to squeak, squeal. Запищáли комарь́, the mosquitoes began to buzz.

про-пищ-áть, *v.p.,* to squeal. Жáлобно пропищáла пти́чка, a little bird squealed pitifully.

ПИТ-, ПИЩ-, FOOD, FEEDING, NOURISHMENT

пит-á-ть, *v.i.,* + *acc.,* to nourish, feed. П. больнóго, to feed a patient. П. чýвство, (*fig.*), to harbor a feeling. П. надéжду (симпáтию), to cherish a hope (feel a sympathy for). Пит-áть-ся, *v.i.r.,* + *instr.,* to feed, live on. Хорошó (плóхо) п., to receive good (bad) nourishment. Они́ питáлись рыбóй, they lived on fish. Пит-áние, *n.n.,* nourishment; nutrition. Усúленное п., high caloric diet. Недостáточное п., undernourishment. Искýсственное п., artificial feeding. Пит-áтельность, *n.f.,* nutritiousness. Пит-áтельный, *adj.,* nourishing, feeding. П. пункт, soup kitchen,, feeding station. П-ая пúща, nourishing food. Пит-óмник, *n.m.,* nursery, seed-plot. Пит-óмец, *n.m.,* пит-óмица, *n.f.,* nursling, fosterling, foster child. Гóголь - питóмец Нéжинского лицéя, Gogol is an alumnus of the Nezhin Lycée.

вос-пит-áть, *v.p.,* + *acc.,* to educate, bring up, train, cultivate, foster. В. детéй в любви́ и уважéнии к трудý, to raise children to have love and respect for work. Вос-пит-áть-ся, *v.p.r.,* вос-пи́т-ывать-ся, *v.i.r.,* в + *prep.,* to be raised, educated, trained. Вос-питáние, *n.n.,* training, upbringing, education. В. масс, education of the masses. Физи́ческое в., physical training. Юноша без воспитáния, ill-bred youth. Воспи́т-анник, *n.m.,* вос-пи́т-анница, *n.f.,* pupil, student; ward. Воспи́танник гимнáзии назывáлся гимнази́стом, (*pre-Rev.*), a pupil in a classical high school was called a "gymnasist." Воспи́т-анность, *n.f.,* breeding; good manners. Вос-пи́т-анный, *adj.,* well-bred. Благо-вос-пи́т-анный, *adj.,* courteous, genteel. Дурно-вос-пи́т-анный, *adj.,* ill-bred, rude. Не-вос-пи́т-анный, *adj.,* ill-bred. Вос-пит-áтель, *n.m.,* вос-пит-áтельница, *n.f.,* teacher, master (mistress), tutor, educator. Он хорóший в., he is a good educator. Вос-пит-áтельный, *adj.,* educational, educative. В-ые мéтоды, educational methods. Вос-пит-áтельский, *adj.,* educative. В-ая рабóта, educational work.

в-пит-áть, *v.p.,* в-пи́т-ывать, *v.i.,* +

acc., to absorb, drink in; (*fig.*), imbibe. Земля́ бы́стро впита́ла всю вла́гу, the soil quickly absorbed all the moisture. В-пит-а́ть-ся, *v.p.r.*, в-пи́т-ывать-ся, *v.i.r.*, в + *acc.*, to soak into; be absorbed. Вла́га впита́лась в зе́млю, the moisture was absorbed by the soil.

на-пит-а́ть, *v.p.*, + *acc.*, + *instr.*, to saturate; *see* пита́ть. Н. гу́бку водо́й, to saturate a sponge with water. Н. голо́дных, to feed the hungry. На-пит-а́ть-ся, *v.p.r.*, на-пи́т-ывать-ся, *v.i.r.*, + *instr.*, to become saturated, become filled. Гу́бка напита́лась водо́й, the sponge was saturated with water.

про-пит-а́ть, *v.p.*, про-пи́т-ывать, *v.i.*, + *acc.*, + *instr.*, to saturate, soak, steep; feed until grown up. П. малоле́тних сиро́т, to feed small orphans till they are grown. П. тря́пку ма́слом, to saturate a rag with oil. Про-пит-а́ть-ся, *v.p.r.*, про-пи́т-ывать-ся, *v.i.r.*, + *instr.*, to be saturated, soaked. Про-пит-а́ние, *n.n.*, subsistence. Зараба́тывать себе́ на п., to earn one's daily bread, earn one's living. Про-пи́т-ка, *n.f.*, thorough saturation. П. древеси́ны, saturation of wood (*as* with chemicals).

у-пит-а́ть, *v.p.*, у-пи́т-ывать, *v.i.*, + *acc.*, to fatten. У. телёнка, to fatten a calf. У-пи́т-анность, *n.f.*, fatness; condition of being well-fed. Скот сре́дней упи́танности, cattle of average fatness. У-пи́т-анный, *adj.*, well-fed. У. ребёнок, well-nourished child.

пи́щ-а, *n.f.*, food; pabulum. Горя́чая п., hot food. П. для ума́, food for thought. Духо́вная п., spiritual food. Дава́ть пи́щу кому́-нибудь, to feed, nourish, nurture someone. Пищ-е-, *a combining form meaning* food, nourishment. Пищ-е-варе́ние, *n.n.*, digestion. Расстро́йство пищеваре́ния, indigestion. Пищ-е-вари́тельный, *adj.*, digestive. П. проце́сс, digestive process. Пищ-е-во́д, *n.m.*, esophagus. Пищ-е-во́й, *adj.*, food. П-ы́е проду́кты, foodstuffs, victuals. П-а́я промы́шленность, food industry. Пищ-еви́к, *n.m.*, (*recent*), worker in the food industry. Профсою́з пищевико́в, (*recent*), union of food industry workers.

ПЛАВ-, ПЛОВ-, ПЛЫ-, ПЛЫВ-, ПЛАВ(Л)-, SWIMMING, FLOATING

пла́в-а-ть, *v.i.indet.*, to swim, float, drift; sail, navigate. П. на я́хте, to sail a yacht, in a yacht. П. вдоль побере́жья, to sail along a shore. Он хорошо́ пла́вает, he swims well. Ле́том он пла́вает ка́ждый день, in summer he swims

every day. Пла́в-ание, *n.n.*, swimming; navigation, sailing; voyage, cruise. Шко́ла пла́вания, swimming school. Да́льнее п., long voyage. Кругосве́тное п., world cruise; circumnavigation of the world. Большо́му кораблю́ большо́е пла́вание, (*saying*), large ships require deep waters. Пла́в-ательный, *adj.*, swimming. П-ая перепо́нка, web. Пла́в-ки, *n.pl.*, swimming trunks. Плавни́к, *n.m.*, fin, flipper. Плав-но́й, *adj.*, drifting. П-а́я сеть, drifting net. Пла́вный, *adj.*, smooth; (*phon.*), liquid. П-ая похо́дка, easy, light step, gait. П-ая речь, fluent speech. Плав-у́н, *n.m.*, (*geol.*), quicksand. Плав-унёц, *n.m.*, (*zool.*), water-tiger. В-плав-ь, *adv.*, swimming. Бро́ситься в., to jump into water and swim. Перепра́виться че́рез ре́ку в., to swim across a river.

по-пла́в-ать, *v.p.*, to swim for a short while. П. немно́го, to swim a little. По-плав-о́к, *n.m.*, float; (*colloq.*), floating restaurant, bar. Поплавки́ на рыба́чьей се́ти, floats on a fishing net. Мы поза́втракали на поплавке́, we had lunch on a floating restaurant. По-плав-ко́вый, *adj.*, having floats. П. гидросамолёт, hydroplane, seaplane.

про-пла́в-ать, *v.p.*, to swim; pass time swimming. Он проплава́л два часа́, he swam for two hours. Кора́бль проплава́л два дня, the ship sailed two days.

плов-е́ц, *n.m.*, swimmer. Плов-у́чий, *adj.*, floating. П. мая́к, lightship. П. мост, floating bridge. П-ая льди́на, ice floe.

плы-ть, *v.i.*, *det.*, по-плы́-ть, *v.p.*, swim, float, sail; swim in one direction. Пла́в-ать, *v.i. indet.*, to swim in various directions, to know how to swim. Легко́ плыть по тече́нию, it is easy to swim with the current. Плы-вя́, *adv.*, *part. pres.*, while swimming. Пловéц уста́л, плывя́ про́тив тече́ния, the swimmer tired while swimming against the current.

в-плы-ть, *v.p.*, в-плыв-а́ть, *v.i.*, в + *acc.*, to swim into, sail into; steam in, float in.

вс-плы-ть, *v.p.*, вс-плыв-а́ть, *v.i.*, на + *acc.*, to come to the surface; come to light, reveal oneself, arise. Труп уто́пленника всплыл на пове́рхность, the body of the drowned man rose to the surface. Этот вопро́с всплывёт сего́дня, this question will arise today.

вы́-плы-ть, *v.p.*, вы-плы-ва́ть, *v.i.*, в + *acc.*, из + *gen.*, to swim out, come to the surface, emerge; crop up. В. в откры́тое мо́ре, to swim, sail out into the open sea. Луна́ вы́плыла из-за туч, the moon sailed out of the clouds.

до-плы́-ть, *v.p.*, до-плыв-а́ть, *v.i.*, до + *gen.*, to swim, sail to a given point; reach by sailing, swimming. Д. до бе́рега, to reach the shore. Д. до середи́ны реки́, to reach the middle of the river.

за-плы́-ть, *v.p.*, за-плыв-а́ть, *v.i.*, to swim far beyond, sail in, float, to be swollen with fat. З. далеко́ за мол, to swim very far beyond the breakwater. Он весь заплы́л жи́ром, (*colloq.*), he was bulging with fat. Све́чка заплыла́, the candle melted down. За-плы́-в, *n.m.*, (*sport*), round, lap.

на-плы́-ть, *v.p.*, на-плы-ва́ть, *v.i.*, на + *acc.*, to swim, sail onto. Н. на ка́мень (на льди́ну), to hit a rock (an iceberg). На-плы́-в, *n.m.*, influx; abundance. Н. посети́телей, an influx of visitors. На-плыв-но́й, *adj.*, alluvial. Н-а́я земля́, alluvium.

о-плы́-ть, *v.p.*, о-плыв-а́ть, *v.i.*, + *acc.*, to swim around, sail around. О. о́стров, to swim, sail around an island.

от-плы́-ть, *v.p.*, от-плыв-а́ть, *v.i.*, от + *gen.*, to swim off, away, sail off, away. О. от бе́рега, to swim, sail away from the shore. Кора́бль отплыва́ет но́чью, the ship sails at midnight. От-плы́-тие, *n.n.*, sailing, departure. Гото́вый к отплы́тию, ready to sail.

пере-плы́-ть, *v.p.*, пере-плыв-а́ть, *v.i.*, + *acc.*, to swim across, sail across. П. ре́ку, to cross a river. П. океа́н на парохо́де, to cross an ocean by steamship.

по-плы́-ть, *v.p.*, to strike out, start swimming. Ло́дка поплыла́, the boat sailed out. Всё поплыло́ пе́ред глаза́ми, everything began to swim before my eyes. Он поплы́л к бе́регу и вы́лез на песо́к, he swam ashore and came out on the sand.

под-плы́-ть, *v.p.*, под-плы-ва́ть, *v.i.*, к + *dat.*, to sail up, swim up; approach by sailing, swimming. П. к бе́регу, to swim to a shore, reach the shore.

при-плы́-ть, *v.p.*, при-плы-ва́ть, *v.i.*, to swim to, sail to. Ры́ба приплыла́ к бе́регу, the fish swam up to the shore. П. на ло́дке, to arrive by boat.

про-плы́-ть, *v.p.*, про-плы-ва́ть, *v.i.*, ми́мо +*gen.*, че́рез + *acc.*, to swim, sail by, past, through. Он проплы́л два киломе́тра, he covered two kilometres swimming. Пе́ред глаза́ми проплы́ли карти́ны далёкого де́тства, scenes from my distant childhood passed before my eyes.

рас-плы́-ть-ся, *v.p.r.*, рас-плы-ва́ть-ся, *v.i.r.*, to run, spread (*as* a liquid); (*colloq.*), grow obese. Черни́ла расплыва́ются на э́той бума́ге, ink runs

on this paper. Р. в улы́бку, to break into a smile. Рас-плы́в-чатость, *n.f.*, diffuseness, dimness. Р. выраже́ний, prolixity. Рас-плы́в-чатый, *adj.*, diffuse, dim. Р-ые очерта́ния, dim outlines. Р. стиль, diffuse style.

с-плы́-ть, *v.p.*, с-плы-ва́ть, *v.i.*, to be carried away by water. Бы́ло, да сплы́ло, (*fig.*), it's all gone.

у-плы́-ть, *v.p.*, у-плы-ва́ть, *v.i.*, to swim away, sail away, float away. Ры́ба уплыла́, the fish swam away. Де́ньги уплы́ли в оди́н день, (*fig.*), the money was spent in one day. Не ма́ло вре́мени уплыло́ с тех пор, much time has passed since then.

пла́в-и-ть, пла́в-л-ю, *v.i.*, + *acc.*, to melt, smelt; fuse. П. лес, to float wood. П. мета́лл (стекло́, руду́), to smelt metal (glass, ore). Пла́в-ить-ся, *v.i.r.*, to be melted, fused. Пла́в-ка, *n.f.*, smelting, melting, fusion; floating. Пла́в-кость, *n.f.*, fusibility. Пла́в-кий, *adj.*, fusible. Плав-ле́ние, *n.n.*, smelting, melting, fusion. То́чка плавле́ния, melting point. Пла́в-ленный, *adj.*, *part. pass. past*, melted, smelted; processed. Пла́в-леный, *adj.*, *used in expression*. П. сыр, processed cheese. Плав-и́льный, *adj.*, melting, smelting. П-ая печь, smelting furnace. Пла́в-и́льня, *n.f.*, foundry. Плав-и́льщик, *n.m.*, founder, smelter.

в-пла́в-ить, *v.p.*, в-плав-ля́ть, *v.i.*, в + *acc.*, to fuse in, into.

вы́-плав-ить, *v.p.*, вы-плав-л-я́ть, *v.i.*, + *acc.*, to smelt. В. мета́лл, to smelt metal. Вы́-плав-ка, *n.f.*, smelting; smelted metal. В. чугуна́ из желе́зной руды́, smelting of pig iron out of iron ore.

пере-пла́в-ить, *v.p.*, пере-плав-л-я́ть, *v.i.*, + *acc.*, на + *acc.*, to smelt into; smelt everything. П. церко́вный ко́локол на медь, to melt down a church bell into copper.

рас-пла́в-ить, *v.p.*, рас-плав-л-я́ть, *v.i.*, + *acc.*, to smelt down, melt. Р. мета́лл (чугу́н), to melt a metal (pig iron). Рас-пла́в-ить-ся, *v.p.r.*, рас-плав-ля́ть-ся, *v.i.r.*, to be melted, smelted, fused. Рас-пла́в-ливание, *n.n.*, melting, smelting, fusion.

с-пла́в-ить, *v.p.*, с-плав-ля́ть, *v.i.*, + *acc.*, + *instr.*, с + *instr.*, to float; alloy, fuse together; (*colloq.*), get rid of. С. лес плота́ми, to float timber. С. свине́ц с о́ловом, to alloy lead with tin. С. плохо́го рабо́тника куда́-нибудь, (*colloq.*), to discharge an unsatisfactory worker and assign him to another job. С-плав, *n.m.*, alloy; floating timber. С-плав-но́й, *adj.*, floatable. С. лес, floatable lumber. С-а́я река́, river ap-

propriate for floating lumber. С-плáв-
щик, *n.m.*, raftsman; logroller.

ПЛАК-, ПЛАЧ-, WEEPING, MOURN-ING, LAMENT

плáк-а-ть, плáч-у, *v.i.,* по-плáк-ать, *v.p.,*
о + *prep.,* от + *gen.,* to weep, cry,
mourn. Гóрько п., to weep bitterly; cry
one's heart out. П. навзрыд, to sob.
Хоть плачь! It is enough to make one
cry. Плáк-ать-ся, *v.i.r.,* по-плáк-ать-
ся, *v.p.r.,* + *dat.,* на + *acc.,* to complain; lament. П. на свою судьбý, to
lament one's fate. Плáк-áльщик, *n.m.,*
плáк-áльщица, *n.f.,* weeper, mourner.
Причитáния плáкáльщиц, (*obs.*), wailing songs of professional wailers, weep-
ers. Плáк-са, *n.f.,* (*colloq.*), weeper;
cry-baby. Плак-сивость, *n.f.,* tearful-
ness. Плак-сивый, *adj.,* whining. П.
ребёнок, cry-baby. Плаксивым гóло-
сом, in a whining voice. Плак-ýн
травá, *n.f.,* willow herb, a magic
plant mentioned in fairy tales. Плак-
ýчий, *adj.,* weeping. Плак-ýчая ива,
weeping willow. П-ая берёза, weeping
birch.

плач, *n.m.,* weeping, crying. Дéтский, п.,
crying of a child. Плáчем гóрю не
помóжешь, (*saying*), no use crying
over spilt milk. Плач-éвность, *n.f.,*
deplorableness. П. положéния, deplorableness of a situation. Плач-éвный,
adj., lamentable, deplorable, mournful,
sad. П. вид, sad sight. П. исхóд, deplorable result. Плач-éвно, *adv.,* lamentably, deplorably, mournfully, sadly. Плáчущий, *adj., part. act., pres.,*
crying, tearful.

вс-плак-нý-ть, *v.p.,* о + *prep.,* (*colloq.*),
to shed a few tears; have a little cry.
Всплакнýла о прóшлом, she shed a
few tears over the past. Вс-плак-
нýть-ся, *v.p.r., used only in 3d person,*
+ *dat.,* to weep a little. Ей всплакнý-
лось, сегóдня, she wept a little today.

вы́-плак-ать, *v.p.,* вы-плáк-ивать, *v.i.,* +
acc., to weep, sob. В. гóре, to sob out
one's grief. В. глазá, to cry one's eyes
out. Вы́-плак-ать-ся, *v.p.r.,* вы-плáк-
ивать-ся, *v.i.r.,* to have a good cry.
Ребёнок вы́плакался и успокóился,
the child had a good cry and quieted
down.

за-плáк-ать, *v.p.,* to begin to cry, burst
into tears. Не говорите печáльного, я
заплáчу, don't say sad things, or else
I'll burst into tears. За-плáк-анный,
adj., tear-stained. З-ые глазá, eyes red
from weeping.

на-плáк-ать, *v.p.,* to have a good cry.
Как кот наплáкал, (*fig.*), nothing to

speak of; practically nothing. На-плáк-
ать-ся, *v.p.r.,* to have had a good cry.
Он ещё наплáчется, he'll be sorry.

о-плáк-ать, *v.p.,* о-плáк-ивать, *v.i.,* +
acc., to mourn, bemoan. О. смерть
брáта, to mourn the death of one's
brother.

по-плáк-ать, *v.p.,* to cry, weep for a
while; shed a few tears; *see* плáкать.

про-плáк-ать, *v.p.,* + *acc.,* to weep
through. П. всю ночь, to weep all
night. П. все глазá, to cry one's eyes
out.

рас-плáк-ать-ся, *v.p.r.,* to burst into
tears.

ПЛАТ-, ПЛАЧ-, PAYMENT

плáт-а, *n.f.,* pay, fee. П. за проéзд, fare.
П. за прáво учéния, tuition. Квартир-
ная п., rent. Зáработная п., *n.f.,* wages.
Зар-плáта, (*recent*), wages. Входнáя
п., entrance, admission fee. Сдéльная
плáта, piecework, payment.

плат-и́-ть, плач-ý, *v.i.,* + *acc.,* + *instr.,*
за + *acc.,* + *dat.,* to pay. П. налич-
ными, to pay in cash. П. по счёту, to
settle an account. П. комý-нибудь той
же монéтой, (*fig.*), to pay someone in
his own coin. П. налóги, to pay taxes.
П. услýгой за услýгу, to pay back.
П. комý-нибудь взаимностью, to return someone's love. Плат-и́ть-ся, *v.i.r.,*
по-плат-и́ть-ся, *v.p.r.,* + *instr.,* за +
acc., to be paid. П. здорóвьем, to
impair one's health; pay with one's
health. Плáт-ный, *adj.,* requiring payment; paying paid. П-ая рабóта, paid
work. Бес-плáт-ный, *adj.,* free of
charge; free, gratuitous. Бес-плáт-но,
adv., free of charge.

плат-ёж, *n.m.,* payment. Прекрати́ть
платежи́, to suspend payment. Налóженным платежóм, cash on delivery.
Присла́ть кни́гу налóженным платежóм, to send a book c.o.d. Плат-еж-
е-спосóбность, *n.f.,* solvency; ability to
make payments. Плат-еж-е-спосóбный,
adj., solvent. Плат-ёжный, *adj.,* pay.
П. день, payday. П-ая вéдомость,
payroll. Плат-éльщик, *n.m.,* плат-
éльщица, *n.f.,* payer. П. налóгов,
taxpayer.

вы́-плат-ить, *v.p.,* вы-плáч-ивать, *v.i.,* +
acc., to pay, pay off, pay in full. В.
долг, to pay off, liquidate a debt. В. в
рассрóчку, to pay by instalments. Вы́-
плат-а, *n.f.,* payment. В. зарплáты
(*recent*), payment of salary.

до-плат-и́ть, *v.p.,* до-плáч-ивать, *v.i.,* +
acc., to pay the balance, in addition.
Вы не всё заплати́ли; вам придётся
д., You haven't paid in full, you will

have to pay the balance. До-плáт-а, *n.f.*, (*colloq.*), additional payment. Письмó с доплáтой. (доплáтное письмó), a letter with postage due.

за-плат-и́ть, *v.p.*, + *acc.*, + *dat.*, + *instr.*, to make a payment. З. по счёту, to settle an account. З. жи́знью за любóвь к рóдине, to give one's life for one's country.

о-плат-и́ть, *v.p.*, о-плáч-ивать, *v.i.*, + *acc.*, to pay, repay; return. О. убы́тки, to pay damages. О. расхóды, to meet expenses. О-плáт-а, *n.f.*, payment, remuneration. Подённая о. трудá, payment by the day for labor. Сдéльная о., payment for piecework. О-плáч-енный, *adj.*, *part. pass. past*, paid. Телегрáмма с оплáченным отвéтом, telegram with prepaid reply.

от-плат-и́ть, *v.p.*, от-плáч-ивать, *v.i.*, + *acc.*, + *instr.*, to pay back, repay; requite. О. комý-либо за услýгу, to repay someone for a service. О. комý-либо той же монéтой, (*fig.*), to pay someone in his own coin. От-плáт-а, *n.f.*, repayment.

пере-плат-и́ть, *v.p.*, пере-плáч-ивать, *v.i.*, + *acc.*, + *dat.*, to overpay. П. букини́сту за кни́гу, to overpay a bookdealer. П. дéсять рублéй, to pay ten rubles too much. Пере-плáт-а, *n.f.*, overpayment.

при-плат-и́ть, *v.p.*, при-плáч-ивать, *v.i.*, + *acc.*, to pay extra. При-плáт-а, extra payment; *n.f.*, *see* доплáта.

рас-плат-и́ть-ся, *v.p.r.*, рас-плáч-ивать-ся, *v.i.r.*, с + *instr.*, to pay off. Р. с долгáми, to pay off one's debts. Р. за оши́бку, to pay for one's mistake. Рас-плáт-а, *n.f.*, payment; atonement.

у-плат-и́ть, *v.p.*, у-плáч-ивать, *v.i.*, + *acc.*, to pay. У. долг, to pay a debt. У. за кварти́ру, to pay rent for an apartment. У-плáт-а, *n.f.*, payment, paying. У. по вéкселю, payment on a note. В уплáту, on account. Остаётся к уплáте пять рублéй, the balance due is five rubles.

ПЛАТ-, ПЛАЩ-, ПОЛОТ-, CLOTHING, CLOTH, VESTMENT, LINEN

плáт-ь-е, *n.n.*, clothes, clothing; dress, gown, frock. Си́тцевое п., cotton dress. Штáтское п., plain clothes, civilian clothing. Готóвое п., ready-made clothing. Шкаф для плáтья, wardrobe; clothes closet. Вéрхнее п., overcoat, coat, outer clothing. Вечéрнее п., evening dress. Плáт-ь-ице, *n.n.*, (*dim.*), child's dress, nice little dress. Дéтское п., children's clothing. Плáт-ь-и́шко,

n.n. (*derog.*), threadbare, shabby dress. Понóшенное п., shabby dress. Платяно́й, *adj.*, of or pertaining to clothes, clothing. П. шкаф, wardrobe. П-áя щётка, clothesbrush.

плат-óк, *n.m.*, плат, *n.m.*, (*poet.*, *obs.*), shawl, kerchief. Носово́й платóк, handkerchief. Плат-óчек, *n.m.* (*dim.*), small kerchief.

плат-á-ть, *v.i.*, за-плат-áть, *v.p.*, + *acc.*, to patch, mend. З. штаны́, to patch trousers. За-плáт-а, *n.f.*, за-плáт-ка, *n.f.*, patch, piece. Наложи́ть з-у на рукáв, to patch a sleeve. За-плáт-анный, *adj.*, *part. pass. past*, patched, mended. З. пиджáк, patched coat.

плащ, *n.m.*, cloak, mantle. П. с капюшóном, hooded cloak. Непромокáемый п., raincoat. Плащ-а-ни́ца, *n.f.*, (*rel.*), shroud of Christ; representation of Christ in the grave.

полот-нó, *n.n.*, linen. Льняно́е п., flax, linen. Небелёное п., unbleached linen. Железнодорóжное п., railroad bed. П. пилы́, web of a saw. П. худóжника, painting, artist's canvas. Блéдный, как п., as white as a sheet. Полотня́ный, *adj.*, linen. П-ое бельё, linen underwear. Полóт-нище, *n.n.*, a width of a cloth. П. знáмени, (*mil.*), colors. П. палáтки, tent section. Юбка из двух полóтнищ, a skirt consisting of two gores. Полот-éнце, *n.n.*, towel. Личнóе п., face towel. Посýдное п., kitchen towel. Мохнáтое п., Turkish towel.

ПЛЕВ-, ПЛЁВ-, ПЛЮ-, SPIT

плев-á-ть, плю-ю́, *v.i.*, плю́-ну-ть, *v.p. smf.*, на + *acc.*, to spit, expectorate; (*colloq.*), spit upon. Плевáть воспрещáется, spitting is forbidden. Емý плевáть на всё, (*colloq.*), he doesn't care a bit. Не плюй в колóдец: приго́дится воды́ напи́ться, (*prov.*), do not foul the well, you may need its waters. Плев-áть-ся, *v.i.r.*, (*colloq.*), to spit. Плев-áтельница, *n.f.*, spittoon. Плев-óк, *n.m.*, spit, sputum. Плёв-ый, *adj.*, (*slang*), trifling. П-ое дéло, (*slang*), trifling matter; child's play.

вы́-плю-ну-ть, *v.p.*, вы-плёв-ывать, *v.i.*, + *acc.*, to spit out. Вы-плёв-ывать-ся, *v.i.r.*, to spit out.

за-плев-áть, *v.p.*, за-плёв-ывать, *v.i.*, + *acc.*, to cover with spit; begin to spit. За-плёв-анный, *adj.*, *part. pass. past*, bespattered; (*fig.*), foul, dirty. З. пол, splattered floor.

на-плев-áть, *v.p.*, (*colloq.*), to dirty, soil; not to care. Н. и насори́ть, to dirty. На-плев-áтельский, *adj.*, (*colloq.*),

contemptuous; careless. Н-ое отноше́-
ние, к + *dat.*, careless, contemptuous
attitude. На-плев-а́тельски, *adv.*, with
negligence, contempt. Относи́ться к
де́лу н., to be careless, negligent
toward the matter.

о-плев-а́ть, *v.p.*, о-плёв-ывать, *v.i.*, +
acc., to cover with spit; abuse, humiliate, debase, besmirch. О. че́стного
челове́ка, (*fig.*), to slander, besmirch
an honest man.

от-плю́-ну-ть, *v.p.smf.*, от-плёв-ывать,
v.i., + *acc.*, to expectorate, spit aside.
От-плю́-нуть-ся, *v.p.r.*, от-плёв-
ывать-ся, *v.i.r.*, to spit with disgust,
spit away, express repugnance. Он
отплёвывался, слы́ша брань, hearing
all the abuse, he spat in disgust.

по-плев-а́ть, *v.p.*, по-плёв-ывать, *v.i.*, на
+ *acc.*, (*colloq.*), Поплева́л на́ руки
и взя́лся за рабо́ту, he spat on his
hands and started to work.

пере-плю́-ну-ть, *v.p.*, пере-плёв-ывать,
v.i., че́рез + *acc.*, + *acc.*, to spit over;
(*colloq.*), surpass. П. че́рез забо́р, to
jump lightly, swiftly over a fence. Этот
физкульту́рник далеко́ переплю́нул
ста́рые реко́рды, (*recent*), this athlete
has beaten the old records by far.

с-плю́-нуть, *v.p.smf.*, с-плёв-ывать, *v.i.*,
+ *acc.*, to spit out. С. че́рез плечо́,
(*colloq.*), to spit over one's back, make
a gesture of disgust.

ПЛЕМ-,   TRIBE,   RACE,   FAMILY,
GENERATION

пле́м-я, *n.n.*, tribe. Кочу́ющее п., no-
madic tribe. Славя́нские племена́,
Slavic tribes. Плем-енно́й, *adj.*, pedigreed. П. скот, pedigreed cattle. Плем-
я́нник, *n.m.*, nephew. Плем-я́ннница, *n.n.*,
niece. Ино-плем-е́нник, *n.n.*, one of
another nationality. Ино-плем-е́нный,
adj., foreign, alien. И-ое во́йско,
(*obs.*), foreign troops. Одно-плем-
е́нный, *adj.*, homogeneous, of the same
nationality. Разно-плем-е́нный, *adj.*,
heterogeneous, of different nationalities.
Р-ое населе́ние Росси́и, the heterogeneous population of Russia. Со-плем-
е́нник, *n.m.*, tribesman, kinsman. Со-
плем-е́нный, *adj.*, (*poet.*), of the same
tribe. "Ка́к-то раз пе́ред толпо́ю
соплеме́нных гор, у Казбе́ка с Шат-
горо́ю был вели́кий спор…", (*Lermontov*), "Once before a tribal meeting
of the mountain throng Mount Kaz-
bek   and   Shat-mountain   wrangled
loud and long…" Чуж-е-плем-е́нник,
n.m., (*obs.*), foreigner. Чуж-е-плем-
е́нный, *adj.*, of foreign nationality.
Ч-ые наро́ды, foreign nations, peoples.

ПЛЕН- (ПЛѢН-), ПОЛОН-, CAPTIVITY

плен, *n.m.*, captivity. Быть в плену́, to
be in captivity. Попа́сть в п. to be
taken prisoner, captive. Плен-ник,
n.m., плен-ница, *n.f.*, prisoner, captive.
Пле́н-ный, *adj.*, captive; used as *n.*,
prisoner of war, captive.

плен-и́-ть, *v.p.*, плен-я́ть, *v.i.*, + *acc.*, +
instr., (*poet.*), to captivate, fascinate.
П. кого́-нибудь свое́й красото́й, to
fascinate with beauty. Плен-ённый,
adj., *part. pass. past*, captivated. Плен-
и́ть-ся, *v.p.r.*, плен-я́ть-ся, *v.i.r.*, +
instr., to be fascinated, captivated. П.
остроу́мием собесе́дника, to be captivated by the wit of one with whom
one is conversing. Плен-и́вшийся, *adj.*,
part. act. past, fascinated. Плен-и́тель-
ность, *n.f.*, fascination. П. о́браза, the
charm of an image. Плен-и́тельный,
adj., captivating, charming, fascinating.
П-ая красота́, fascinating beauty.

поло́н, *n.m.*, (*obs.*), see плен. Взять в п.,
to take prisoner.

полон-и́-ть, *v.i.*, + *acc.*, (*obs.*), to take
prisoner (in war); see плени́ть. Полон-
ённый, *adj.*, *part. pass. past*, captured, taken prisoner; (*fig.*), captivated.
П. во́ин, captive warrior. Полон-я́нин,
n.m., полон-я́нка, *n.f.* (*hist.*), prisoner.
See "пле́нник".

за-полон-и́-ть, *v.p.*, за-полон-я́ть, *v.i.*, +
acc. to captivate, enthrall. З. всю
ду́шу, to enthrall the soul.

**ПЛЕСК-, ПЛЁСК-, ПЛЕЩ-, ПЛЕС-,
ПЛЁС-, ПОЛОС-, ПОЛОСК-, ПОЛАСК,
ПОЛОЩ-**, SPLASH, SPLASHING

плеск, *n.m.*, splash, lapping. П. волны́,
splashing of waves. Плеска́ние, *n.n.*,
splashing.

плёс, *n.m.*, reach, pool of river.

плеск-а́-ть, **плещ-у́**, *v.i.*, плес-ну́-ть, *v.p.*
smf., to splash. "Ничего́ не сказа́ла
ры́бка, лишь хвосто́м по воде́ плес-
ну́ла.", (*Pushkin*), "the little fish was
silent, it only splashed with its tail."
Плеск-а́ть-ся, *v.i.r.*, to splash. Во́лны
пле́щутся о бе́рег, the waves are
splashing against the shore. Ребёнок
плеска́ется в ва́нне, the child is splashing itself in the tub.

вс-плеск-ива-ть, *v.i.*, вс-плес-ну́ть, *v.p.*
smf., + *acc.*, + *instr.*, to splash up,
ripple up. Ве́тер всплёскивает во́ду,
the wind ripples up the water. Всплес-
ну́ть рука́ми, to clap one's hands.
Она́ в у́жасе всплесну́ла рука́ми, she
clasped her hands in dismay. Вс-плеск,
вс-плёск, *n.m.*, splash. Ти́хие вспле́ски
воды́, gentle splashes of water.

вы-плёск-ивать, *v.i.,* **вы́-плес-нуть,** *v.p.,* *smf.,* + *acc.,* из + *gen.,* to splash out. В. всю во́ду из уша́та, to splash all the water out of a tub. Вы-плёск-ивать-ся, *v.i.r.,* вы́-плес-нуть-ся, *v.p.r.,* из + *gen.,* to be splashed out.

рас-плёск-ивать, *v.i.,* **рас-плеск-а́ть,** *v.p.,* + *acc.,* to spill around. Всю во́ду из ведра́ расплеска́ла, she splashed out all the water from the pail. Рас-плёск-ну́ть, *v.p., see* расплеска́ть. Рас-плёск-ивать-ся, *v.i.r.,* рас-плеск-а́ть-ся, *v.p.r.,* to be spilled, splashed all over.

руко-плеск-а́ть, *v.i.,* + *dat.,* to applaud, clap. Весь зал рукоплеска́л певцу́, the whole house applauded the singer. Руко-плеск-а́ние, *n.n.,* applause, clapping.

полоск-а́-ть, полощ-у́, *v.i.,* + *acc.,* to rinse, gargle. П. бельё, to rinse laundry. П. себе́ го́рло, to gargle. Полоск-а́ть-ся, *v.i.r.,* to paddle, dabble in shallow water; be rinsed. Де́ти полоска́лись в воде́, the children were splashing around in the water. Поло́щутся паруса́, the sails are flapping, luffing. Полоск-а́ние, *n.n.,* rinse, rinsing; gargling. Полоск-а́тельница, *n.f.,* slop basin; finger bowl. Полоск-а́тельный, *adj.,* pertaining to rinsing. П-ая ча́шка, *see* полоска́тельница.

вс-полос-ну́ть, *v.p.,* вс-пола́ск-ивать, *v.i.,* + *acc.* (*colloq.*), to rinse out lightly. В. ча́шку, to rinse a cup.

вы́-полоск-ать, *v.p.,* вы-пола́ск-ивать, *v.i.,* + *acc.,* to rinse out thoroughly. В. рот, to rinse one's mouth. В. го́рло, to gargle.

о-полос-ну́ть, *v.p.,* о-пола́ск-ивать, *v.i.,* + *acc.,* to rinse thoroughly.

пере-полоск-а́ть, *v.p.,* пере-пола́ск-ивать, *v.i.,* + *acc.,* to rinse again, rinse out. П. простыню́, to rinse a sheet. П. всё бельё, to rinse all the washing, all the laundry.

по-полоск-а́ть, *v.p.,* + *acc.,* to rinse, gargle for a short time. П. бельё, to rinse the laundry lightly. П. себе́ го́рло бо́рной кислото́й, to gargle with a solution of boric acid.

про-полоск-а́ть, *v.p.,* про-пола́ск-ивать, *v.i.,* + *acc.,* to rinse through. П. себе́ рот, to rinse one's mouth. Про-полоск-а́ть-ся, *v.p.r.,* про-пола́ск-ивать-ся, *v.i.r.,* to be rinsed; splash. Бельё про-пола́скивается в холо́дной воде́, the laundry is rinsed in cold water.

с-полос-ну́-ть, *v.p.,* с-пола́ск-ивать, *v.i.,* + *acc.,* to rinse lightly. С. кастрю́лю, to rinse a pot.

ПЛОД-, ПЛОЖ-, HARVEST, FRUIT

плод, *n.m.,* fruit. Приноси́ть плоды́, to bear fruit. Это де́рево прино́сит плоды́ ка́ждый год, this tree bears fruit every year. П. многоле́тнего труда́, (*fig.*), the fruits of many years of labor. Пожина́ть плоды́ свои́х трудо́в, to reap the fruits of one's labor. Запре́тный плод сла́док, (*fig.*), forbidden fruit is sweet. Ко́рень уче́ния го́рек, а плоды́ его́ сла́дки, (*prov.*), the root of learning is bitter but its fruits are sweet.

плод-и́-ть, плож-у́, *v.i.,* + *acc.,* to procreate, produce, engender. Это де́рево плоди́т мно́го ви́шен, this tree produces a lot of cherries. Живо́тные плодя́т детёнышей, animals give birth to offspring. Плоди́ть одну́ статью́ за друго́й, to write one article after another. Плод-и́ть-ся, *v.i.r.,* to propagate. Кро́лики плодя́тся о́чень бы́стро, rabbits propagate very rapidly. От безде́лья плодя́тся спле́тни и раздо́ры, idleness engenders gossip and quarrels. Плод-ови́тость, *n.f.,* fruitfulness, fertility, fecundity. Плод-ови́тый, *adj.,* fruitful, fertile, fecund, prolific. П. писа́тель, prolific writer. П-ые ку́ры, productive, prolific hens. Плод-о-во́дство, *n.n.,* fruit-growing. Плод-о-во́дческий, *adj.,* pertaining to the growing of fruit. Плод-о́вый, *adj.,* fruit. П. сад, orchard. П-ое де́рево, fruit tree. Плод-о-но́сный, *adj.,* fruit bearing. П-ая по́чва, fertile soil. Плод-о-ро́дие, *n.n.,* fertility, fecundity. Плод-о-ро́дность, *n.f.,* fertility, fecundity. Плод-о-ро́дный, *adj.,* fertile, fecund. П. край, fertile country. П-ая по́чва, fertile soil. Плод-о-тво́рность, *n.f.,* fruitfulness. П. иде́й, creative ideas. Плод-о-тво́рный, *adj.,* fruitful. П-ая рабо́та, fruitful work. Плод-о-суши́лка, *n.f.,* fruit kiln.

о-плод-о-твори́ть, *v.p.,* о-плод-о-творя́ть, *v.i.,* + *acc.,* to fecundate, impregnate, fertilize, engender. Дожди́ оплодотвори́ли зе́млю, the rains made the soil fertile. О-плод-о-твори́ть-ся, *v.p.r.,* оплод-о-творя́ть-ся, *v.i.r.,* to be fertilized, inseminated. О-плод-о-творе́ние, *n.n.,* fertilization, insemination. Иску́сственное о., artificial fertilization. О-плод-о-творённый, *adj., part. pass. past,* fertilized. О-ое яйцо́, fertilized egg.

на-плод-и́ть, *v.p.,* + *acc.,* (*colloq.*), to bear in quantity, be prolific. Ко́шка наплоди́ла котя́т, the cat bore very many kittens. На-плод-и́ть-ся, *v.p.r., used in 3d person only,* to be bred in quantity. От гря́зи наплоди́лось мно́го таракáнов, because of the dirt the cockroaches multiplied.

рас-плод-и́ть, *v.p.,* рас-плож-áть, *v.i.,* to breed in large quantities. Р. кур, to breed hens. Р. племеннóй скот, to breed pedigreed cattle. Рас-плод-и́ть-ся, *v.p.r.,* рас-плож-áть-ся, *v.i.r.,* to be bred in large quantities, prolifically. Скóт расплоди́лся, the cattle multiplied. Зáйцы распложáются óчень бы́стро, hares multiply prolifically.

ПЛЕТ-, ПЛЁТ-, ПЛЕС-, ПЛЕ-, PLAITING, BRAIDING, WEAVING

плет-éн-ь, *n.m.,* wattle fence; (*mil.*), hurdle. Плет-ёнка, *n.f.,* wicker basket. Плет-ёный, *adj.,* wattled, wicker. П. стул, wicker chair. Плеть, плёт-ка, *n.f.,* lash; branch of creeping plant. Накáзывать плéтью, to lash, give a lashing.

плес-ти́, плет-ý, *v.i.,* с-плес-ти́, *v.p.,* + *acc.,* to braid, plait, weave, wattle. П. сéти, to weave nets. П. паути́ну, to weave a cobweb. П. венóк, to twine a wreath. Рыбáк плетёт сеть, the fisherman is weaving a net.

плес-ти́-сь, *v.i.r.,* по-плес-ти́-сь, *v.p.r.,* to lag behind, drag along; be woven. П. в хвостé, (*fig.*), to lag; drag behind. Кружевá плетýтся из ни́ток, lace is made with thread. Стари́к вы́шел на ýлицу и ти́хо поплёлся, the old man went out into the street and plodded slowly along. Плет-éние, *n.n.,* weaving, braiding, netting. Плет-éльщик, *n.m.,* плет-éльщица, *n.f.,* plaiter, one who weaves.

в-плес-ти́, *v.p.,* в-плет-áть, *v.i.,* + *acc.,* в + *acc.,* to intertwine, interlace, plait into; intersperse. В. лéнту в кóсу, to weave a ribbon into braided hair. Зачéм ты вплёл меня в э́то дéло? (*colloq.*), Why did you involve me in this matter?

вы́-плес-ти, *v.p.,* вы-плет-áть, *v.i.,* + *acc.,* to make designs by weaving. Кружевни́ца выплетáет рáзные узóры, the lacemaker weaves various designs. В. лéнту из косы́, to remove a ribbon from a braid of hair.

до-плес-ти́, *v.p.,* до-плет-áть, *v.i.,* + *acc.,* to complete weaving. Рыбáк доплетáл сеть, the fisherman was completing the net.

до-плес-ти́-сь, *v.p.r.,* до-плет-áть-ся, *v.i.r.,* до + *gen.,* (*colloq.*), to drag oneself; reach. Он éле доплёлся дó дому, he barely dragged himself home.

за-плес-ти́, *v.p.,* за-плет-áть, *v.i.,* + *acc.,*

to braid, plait. З. кóсу, to plait one's hair. З. венóк, to weave a wreath. За-плес-ти́-сь, *v.p.r.,* за-плет-áть-ся, *v.i.r.,* to be intertwined, interlaced. У негó язы́к заплетáлся, his speech became thick. У пья́ницы нóги заплетáются, the drunkard is stumbling over his own feet. Хмель заплёлся вокрýг столбá, hops crept around the pole.

на-плес-ти́, *v.p.,* на + *acc.,* (*colloq.*), + *acc.,* + *gen.,* to slander; make a quantity by weaving. Н. крýжев, to weave a quantity of lace. Н. вздóру, to talk nonsense. Он всё наплёл о своём успéхе, he lied about his success.

о-плес-ти́, *v.p.,* о-плет-áть, *v.i.,* + *acc.,* + *instr.,* to entwine, braid; cheat, swindle. О. прóволочными заграждéниями, to protect with barbed wire.

пере-плес-ти́, *v.p.,* пере-плет-áть, *v.i.,* + *acc.,* + *instr.,* to interlace, interknit, plait, braid anew; bind. П. кóсы лéнтами, to weave ribbons into hair braids. П. кни́гу, to bind a book. П. зáново, to rebind a book. Пере-плес-ти́-сь, *v.p.r.,* пере-плет-áть-ся, *v.i.r.,* с + *instr.,* to be interlaced, interwoven, interknit; be bound; (*fig.*), become entangled. Плющ переплёлся с хмéлем, the ivy became intertwined with the hops. Собы́тия переплетáлись, things became confused. Пере-плёт, *n.m.,* binding, bookcover. Кни́ги в сафья́новом переплёте, books bound ın morocco leather. Окóнный п., transom, window-sash. Попáсть в п., (*fig., colloq.*), to get into trouble. Пере-плет-éние, *n.n.,* interlacing, interweaving. Пере-плёт-ный, *adj.*; П-ая, мастерскáя, bindery. Пере-плёт-чик, *n.m.,* bookbinder.

при-плес-ти́, *v.p.,* при-плет-áть, *v.i.,* + *acc.,* в + *acc.,* to weave in; (*colloq.*), implicate. П. ещё кусóк крýжева, to weave on an additional piece of lace. П. (впýтать) когó-нибудь во чтó-нибудь, to implicate someone in something. При-плес-ти́-сь, *v.p.r.,* при-плет-áть-ся, *v.i.r.,* (*colloq.*), to drag oneself along. Еле приплёлся домóй, I barely dragged myself home.

рас-плес-ти́, *v.p.,* рас-плет-áть, *v.i.,* + *acc.,* to untwine, untwist. Р. кóсу, to undo a braid. Р. верёвку, to untwist a rope. Рас-плес-ти́-сь, *v.p.r.,* рас-плет-áть-ся, *v.i.r,* to become untwined, untwisted. Верёвки расплели́сь, the ropes became undone. Рас-плет-áние, *n.n.,* untwining, undoing.

с-плес-ти́, *v.p.,* с-плет-áть, *v.i.,* + *acc.,* to interlace; weave, plait. С. корзи́ну, to weave a basket. С. венóк, to make a wreath. С-плес-ти́-сь, *v.p.r.*, с-плет-а́ть-ся, *v.i.r.*, to be interlaced. Дере́вья сплели́сь ве́тками, the branches of the trees were intertwined. С-плет-е́ние, *п.п.*, interlacing, interweaving. С. обстоя́тельств, complications. С. лжи, tissue of lies. Со́лнечное с., (*anat.*), solar plexus.

с-плёт-нич-ать, *v.i.*, на-с-плёт-ничать, *v.p.*, to gossip, spread tales, create scandals.

с-плёт-ник, *п.т.*, с-плёт-ница, *п.f.*, gossip, gossiper. Зло́стный с., scandal monger. С-плёт-ня, *п.f.*, gossip, scandal.

у-плес-ти́, *v.p.*, у-плет-а́ть, *v.i.*, + *acc.*, + *instr.*, (*colloq.*), to intertwine, interweave; (*colloq.*), to eat heartily, greedily. Он уплета́ет за о́бе щёки, (*fig.*), he is gobbling up all the food.

ПЛОСК-, ПЛОЩ-, ПЛАШ-, ПЛОШ-, ПЛЮС(К)-, ПЛЮЩ-, FLATNESS

пло́ск-ий, *adj.*, flat, plane; trivial. П-ая пове́рхность, plane surface. П-ая стопа́, flatfoot. П-ая шу́тка, flat, stupid joke. П-ое замеча́ние, platitude; commonplace remark. Пло́ск-ость, *п.f.*, level surface, plane. Накло́нная п., inclined plane. Кати́ться по накло́нной пло́скости, (*fig.*), to deteriorate. Плоск-о-го́рье, *п.п.*, plateau, tableland. Плоск-о-гу́бцы, *п.pl.*, pliers. Плоск-о-до́нка, *п.f.*, flatboat. Плоск-о-до́нный, *adj.*, flat-bottomed. П-ая ло́дка, flat-bottomed boat. Пло́ск-о, *adv.*, flatly. Пло́с-че, пло́щ-е, *adj.*, and *adv. comp.*, flatter.

пло́щ-адь, *п.f.*, area; square; place. Жила́я п., жилпло́щадь, *п.f.*, (*recent*), living space. Городска́я п., square. База́рная п., market place. Кра́сная П. в Москве́, Red Square in Moscow. Площ-а́дка, *п.f.*, ground; landing; platform. Спорти́вная п., athletic ground, field. Те́нннисная п., tennis court. Де́тская п., open-air kindergarden. Поса́дочная п., (*aviation*), landing field. Площ-адно́й, *adj.*, vulgar, language of the street, *used in expression*: П-а́я брань, vulgar abuse.

пло́ш-ка, *п.f.*, earthen saucer. Нет ни ло́жки, ни пло́шки, (*saying*), there is neither spoon, nor saucer (there is nothing with which to begin housekeeping). Пло́ш-ечный, *adj.*, pertaining to an earthen cup.

пла́ш-мя, *adv.*, flat, prone. Упа́сть п., to fall prone. Уда́рить са́блей п., to strike with the flat of a sword.

плющ-и-ть, *v.i.*, с-плющ-ить, *v.p.*, с-плющ-ивать, *v.i.*, + *acc.*, to flatten, compress; laminate; roll. П. желе́зо, to roll, flatten iron. Плющ-ить-ся, *v.i.r.*, с-плющ-ить-ся, *v.p.r.*, с-плющ-ивать-ся, *v.i.r.*, + *instr.*, to be flattened, laminated, rolled. Металли́ческие тру́бы сплющиваются мо́лотом, metal pipes are flattened with a sledge hammer. Плющ-и́льный, *adj.*, rolling, flattening. П. стано́к, flattening, rolling mill. С-плющ-енный, *adj.*, *part. pass. past*, flattened. С-ые гу́бы, flat lips.

с-плюс-нуть, *v.p.*, с-плющ-ить, *v.p.*, to flatten, compress, collapse. С-плюс-нуть-ся, *v.p.r.*, с-плющ-ить-ся, *v.p.r.*, to become flattened, laminated. С-плюс-нутый, *adj.*, *part. pass. past*, flattened; *see* сплющенный.

при-плюс-нуть, *v.p.*, при-плюск-ивать, *v.i.*, to flatten by pressure. П. гвоздь молотко́м, to flatten a nail with a hammer. При-плюс-нутый, *adj.*, *part. pass. past*, flattened. П. нос, flat nose. Плюс-на́, *п.f.*, (*anat.*), metatarsus.

ПЛОТ-, ПЛАЧ-, ПЛОЧ-, RAFT

плот, *п.т.*, raft. Сплавля́ть лес в плота́х, to float rafts of lumber. Плот-и́на, *п.f.*, dam, dike. Водосли́вная п., overflow dam. Плот-о́вщи́к, *п.т.*, raftsman.

пло́т-нич-а-ть, *v.i.*, to carpenter. Пло́т-нич-ество, *п.п.*, carpentry. Пло́т-ничий, *adj.*, of or pertaining to a carpenter. П. инструме́нт, carpenter's tools. Пло́т-ник, *п.т.*, carpenter.

пло́т-ный, *adj.*, compact, dense, close, thick. П. материа́л, solid, strong material. П-ое населе́ние, dense population. П. за́втрак, a heavy breakfast. П. челове́к, thick-set man. Пло́т-ность, *п.f.*, compactness, density, solidity. П. населе́ния, density of population. Пло́т-но, *adv.*, close, tightly, densely, compactly. П. заколоти́ть дверь, to board, nail up a door. П. облега́ть, to fit close, tightly. П. позавтракать (пообе́дать, пое́сть), to have a heavy breakfast, (dinner, a square meal).

в-пло́т-ь, *adv.*, up to. В. до са́мого утра́ (ве́чера), to morning (to evening). В-плот-ну́ю, *adv.*, closely. В. оди́н к друго́му, close to each other. Сиде́ть в., to sit close together.

о-пло́т, *п.т.*, stronghold; bulwark. Армия-оплот госуда́рства, the army is the bulwark of the state.

с-плот-и́-ть, *v.p.*, с-плач-ивать, *v.i.*, + *acc.*, to join; make into a raft; unite, rally. С. брёвна (до́ски), to join logs, (boards). С. ряды́, to close ranks.

С-плот-и́ть-ся, *v.p.r.*, с-пла́ч-ивать-ся, *v.i.r.*, to become united, rallied. С. про́тив о́бщего врага́, to unite against a common enemy.

с-плоч-е́ние, *n.n.*, rallying; unity. С. единомы́шленников, unity of partisans, adherents. С-плоч-ённость, *n.f.*, solidarity, unity, cohesion. С. бойцо́в, solidarity of combatants. С-плоч-ённый, *adj.*, *part. pass. past*, united, solid. С-ые ряды́, serried ranks.

у-плот-ни́ть, *v.p.*, у-плот-ня́ть, *v.i.*, + *acc.*, + *instr.*, to crowd. Наш дом бу́дут уплотня́ть но́выми жильца́ми, (*recent*), they will crowd new tenants into our house. У-плот-ни́ть-ся, *v.p.r.*, у-плот-ня́ть-ся, *v.i.r.*, to be crowded in living quarters. Вам придётся у., (*recent*), you will have to crowd together. У-плот-нённый, *adj.*, *part. pass. past*, overcrowded. Пассажи́р е́ле влез в ваго́н, уплотнённый до отка́зу, (*colloq.*), the passenger barely climbed into the overcrowded car.

ПЛОТ-, ПЛОЩ-, FLESH

плот-ь, *n.f.*, flesh, body. Дух силён, а п. не́мощна, (*saying*), the spirit is strong, but the flesh is weak. Аскети́зм - э́то умерщвле́ние пло́ти, asceticism is the mortification of the flesh. А́нгел во пло́ти, (*fig.*), personification of an angel. Пло́т-ский, *adj.*, flesh, carnal. П-ие наслажде́ния, pleasures of the flesh. Плот-о-уго́дие, *n.n.*, sensuality, voluptuousness. Плот-о-уго́дник, *n.m.*, sensualist. Плот-о-уго́дный, *adj.*, sensual, voluptuous. Плот-о-я́дие, *n.n.*, carnivorousness. Плот-о-я́дный, *adj.*, carnivorous. Хи́щные зве́ри плотоя́дные живо́тные, beasts of prey are carnivorous animals. Посмотре́ть плотоя́дным взгля́дом, (*fig.*), to cast a sensual glance. Бес-пло́т-ный, *adj.*, incorporeal; angelic; immaterial. Б. дух, angelic spirit.

во-плот-и́ть, *v.p.*, во-площ-а́ть, *v.i.*, + *acc.*, to incarnate. Пу́шкин в "Скупо́м Ры́царе" воплоти́л о́браз ску́пости, in the "Covetous Knight" Pushkin personified miserliness. Во-плот-и́ть-ся, *v.p.r.*, во-площ-а́ть-ся, *v.i.r.*, в + *acc.*, to be incarnated, personified. В. наро́дных пе́снях воплоща́ется дух наро́да, the spirit of a people is personified in folk songs. Во-площ-е́ние, *n.n.*, incarnation, personification, embodiment. Этот челове́к - в. благоро́дства, this man is the personification of honor. В. идеа́лов в жизнь, realization of ideals in life. Во-площ-ённый, *adj.*, *part.*

pass. past, incarnated, personified, embodied.

пере-во-плот-и́ть, *v.p..*, пере-во-площ-а́ть, *v.i.*, + *acc.*, в + *acc.*, reincarnate, transform. П. старика́ в молодо́го, to transform an old man into a young one. П. сельскохозя́йственную страну́ в индустриа́льную, (*recent*), to transform an agricultural country into an industrial one. Пере-во-плот-и́ть-ся, *v.p.r.*, пере-во-площ-а́ть-ся, *v.i.r.*, в + *acc.*, to be reincarnated, transformed. Актёр на сце́не перевоплоща́ется, on the stage the actor transforms himself. Пере-во-площ-е́ние, *n.n.*, transformation, reincarnation. Пере-во-площ-ённый, *adj.*, *part. pass. past*, transformed, reincarnated.

ПЛОХ-, ПЛОШ-, BAD

плох-о́й, *adj.*, bad, mediocre. П-а́я пого́да, bad, wretched, nasty weather. П-о́е настрое́ние, low spirits. Получи́ть п-у́ю отме́тку, to receive a low grade (in school). Больно́й о́чень плох, the patient is low, poorly (in health). С ним шу́тки пло́хи, he is not one to be trifled with. Пло́х-онький, *adj.*, rather bad. Плох-ова́тый, *adj.*, rather bad. Пло́-хо, *adv.*, badly. П. себя́ чу́вствовать, to feel bad, unwell. Это пло́хо па́хнет, it smells bad. П. себя́ вести́, to behave badly. П. лежи́т, (*fig.*), it lies in temptation's way. Конча́ть п., to come to a bad end. Получи́ть "п.", to receive "poor" as a grade. Учени́ца получи́ла п. по геогра́фии, the student was graded "poor" in geography.

плош-а́-ть, *v.i.*, с-плош-а́ть, *v.p.*, (*colloq.*), to fail; become worse. Смотри́, не плоша́й! (*colloq.*), Look out, don't fail! Его́ здоро́вье плоша́ет, (*colloq.*), his health is getting worse. На Бо́га наде́йся, а сам не плоша́й, (*prov.*), Hope in God, but stand firm yourself.

о-плош-а́ть, *v.p.*, + *instr.*, (*colloq.*), to take a false step. Оплоша́л я отве́том, сра́зу не нашёлся, I answered badly, I wasn't at my best. О-пло́ш-ность, *n.f.*, inadvertence; negligence. Сде́лать о., to take a false step. Воспо́льзоваться опло́шностью врага́, to take advantage of the enemy's negligence. О-пло́ш-ный, *adj.*, negligent, careless. О. посту́пок, careless action. О-пло́ш-но, *adv.*, negligently, carelessly. Поступи́ть о., to act carelessly.

с-плох-ова́ть, с-плош-а́ть, *v.p.*, (*colloq.*), to fail; become worse; *see* плоша́ть. Что́-то моё здоро́вье сплохова́ло, my health has somehow become worse.

ПЛУТ-, CHEATING, FRAUD

плут, *n.m.,* cheat, swindler; knave. Плут-о́вка, *n.f.,* swindler. Плут-и́шка, *n.m.,* swindler. Плу́т-ни, *n.pl.,* swindle; trickery. Плут-овство́, *n.n.,* trickery, imposture; knavery. Плут-овско́й, *adj.,* knavish. П. приём, knavish trick. П-а́я улы́бка, mischievous smile.

плут-ова́ть, плут-у́-ю, *v.i.,* с-плут-ова́ть, *v.p.,* (*colloq.*), to cheat, defraud, swindle. П. при игре́ в ка́рты, to cheat at cards.

плут-а́-ть, плут-а́-ю, *v.i.,* (*colloq.*), to stray, wander. Плута́л два часа́, пока́ вы́брался на доро́гу, I wandered about for two hours until I found the road.

за-плут-а́ть-ся, *v.p.r.,* (*colloq.*), to lose one's way. Заплута́лся в лесу́, I got lost in the forest.

ПЛЯС-, ПЛЯШ-, DANCING

пляс, *n.m.,* (*colloq.*), dance. Пусти́ться в п., to begin to dance. Пля́с-ка, *n.f.,* folk dance, folk dancing. Наро́дные пля́ски, folk dances. П. Св. Ви́тта, (*med.*), chorea, St. Vitus' dance. Пляс-ова́я, *adj., used as n.,* dance tune. Пляс-ово́й, *adj.,* dancing. П-а́я пе́сня, dance melody. Пляс-у́н, *n.m.,* пляс-у́нья, *n.f.,* dancer. Кана́тный п., rope dancer.

пляс-а́-ть, пляш-у́, *v.i.,* (*colloq.*), to dance. П. ру́сскую, to dance a Russian folk dance. П. под чью́-нибудь ду́дку, (*fig.*), to dance to someone's tune.

вы-пля́с-ыва-ть, *v.i.,* + *acc.,* + *gen.,* (*colloq.*), to dance. В. гопака́, to dance the Ukrainian hopak. В. ру́сскую, to dance a Russian folk dance.

за-пляс-а́ть, *v.p.,* (*colloq.*), to begin to dance.

на-пляс-а́ть-ся, *v.p.r.,* (*colloq.*), to dance one's fill. Н. вдо́воль, to have one's fill of dancing.

от-пляс-а́ть, *v.p.,* от-пля́с-ывать, *v.i.,* + *acc.,* to dance with zest, with vigor. О. казачка́, to dance the Cossack dance. О. все но́ги, to dance one's feet off.

под-пля́с-ывать, *v.i.,* to join in a dance; dance to someone's music. Она́ шла, подпля́сывая от ра́дости, she walked along, dancing with joy.

по-пляс-а́ть, *v.p.,* (*colloq.*), to dance a little; *see* пляса́ть. Он у меня́ попля́шет, (*fig.*), he will get it hot from me.

при-пля́с-ыва-ть, *v.i.,* to dance; skip. Шли, ве́село припля́сывая, they skipped along gayly. В припля́ску, *adv.,* in a dance step.

рас-пляс-а́ть-ся, *v.p.r.,* (*colloq.*), to dance wildly, exultantly.

с-пляс-а́ть, *v.p.,* + *acc.,* to dance an entire folk dance. С. кама́ринскую, to dance the Kamarinskaya.

ПОЗД-, ПАЗД-, ПОЗЖ-, LATENESS

по́зд-но, *adv.,* late. П. но́чью, late at night. Лу́чше п., чем никогда́, (*saying*), better late than never. **по́зж-е,** *adv. comp.,* later. Они́ займу́тся э́тим п., they will attend to this later. По́зд-ний, *adj.,* late, tardy. Чита́ть до по́здней но́чи, to read late into the night. П. гость, late arrival, late guest. П-яя о́сень, late autumn. Позд-не́е, *adv., comp.,* (*colloq.*), later. *See* по́зже. Я приду́ п., I'll come later. Позд-не́нько, *adv.,* rather late. Позд-не́хонь-ко, *adv.,* very late. П. но́чью, very late in the night. Позд-нова́то, *adv.,* rather late.

за-позд-а́-ть, *v.p.,* за-па́зд-ывать, *v.i.,* to be late. З. с упла́той, to be late with a payment. За-па́зд-ывание, *n.n.,* delay; action of being late. За-позд-а́ние, *n.n.,* state of being late; delay. За-позд-а́лый, *adj.,* belated, delayed; backward. З. платёж, delayed payment. З-ое разви́тие, late development; backwardness. З. гость, late arrival, guest.

о-позд-а́ть, *v.p.,* о-па́зд-ывать, *v.i.,* to be late, be overdue. По́езд опозда́л на пять мину́т, the train was five minutes late. Часы́ опа́здывают на четы́ре мину́ты, this watch is four minutes slow. О-позд-а́ние, *n.n.,* delay, lateness. Без опозда́ния, on time, without delay. С опозда́нием на час, an hour late. О-позд-а́вший, *adj., part. act. past,* late.

ПОКОЙ-, ПОКО-, ПОЧ-, TRANQUILITY, PEACE

поко́й, *n.m.,* rest, peace; (*obs.*), room, chamber. Не знать поко́я, to have no peace. Не дава́ть поко́я, to give no rest. Оста́вить в поко́е, to leave in peace. Ве́чный п., eternal peace. В госпо́дских поко́ях жил ста́рый ба́рин, (*obs.*), in the master's rooms there lived an old gentleman. Поко́й-ный, *adj.,* quiet, calm, restful; the late, deceased, defunct. П-ое кре́сло, comfortable armchair. П. ребёнок, quiet child. П-ой но́чи! Good night! *See* споко́йной но́чи! Поко́й-но, *adv.,* quietly, calmly. Чу́вствовать себя́ п., to be comfortable.

поко́-и-ть, *v.i.,* + *acc.,* (*obs.*), to procure rest; take care. П. роди́телей в ста́рости, to take care of one's parents in their old age. Поко́-ить-ся, *v.i.r.,* на + *prep.,* to rest upon; repose; rest in peace. Это сооружéние покóится на кáменном фундáменте, this building rests on a stone foundation. Здесь покóится прах, here lies the body (of). Покóй-ник, *п.т.*, покóй-ница, *п.f.*, dead man, woman; the deceased. Покóй-ницкая, *adj.*, *used as n.f.*, morgue, mortuary.

бес-покó-ить, *v.i.*, о-бес-покó-ить, по-бес-покó-ить, *v.p.*, + *acc.*, to worry, cause anxiety, disturb, trouble, inconvenience. Её отсýтствие беспокóило нас, her absence worried us. Шум беспокóит больнóго, the noise is disturbing the sick man. Бес-покó-ить-ся, *v.i.r.*, о-бес-покó-ить-ся, *v.p.r.*, по-бес-покó-ить-ся, о + *prep.*, to worry, be anxious about; (*colloq.*), trouble, bother. Не беспокóйтесь обо мне! Don't worry about me! Не беспокóйтесь! Don't trouble! Не беспокóйтесь! Don't bother! Бес-покó-йство, *п.п.*, anxiety, uneasiness, nervousness, agitation. Простúте за беспокóйство, I am sorry to have troubled you. Никакóго беспокóйства, no trouble at all. Бес-покó-й-ный, *adj.*, uneasy, anxious, restless. Б. ребёнок, restless child. Б. взгляд, troubled look. Б-ое мóре, choppy, turbulent sea.

поч-й-ть, *v.p.*, поч-ивáть, *v.i.*, (*obs.*), to sleep; die, pass away. П. от дел, to rest after work. П. на лáврах, (*fig.*), to rest on one's laurels. П. в могúле, to lie in a grave. Поч-úвший, *adj.*, *part. act. past, also used as n.*, deceased. Поч-ивáльня, *п.f.*, (*obs.*), bedroom. О-поч-ивáльня, *п.f.*, (*hist.*), state bedroom, bedroom of the tsar.

о-поч-йть, *v.p.*, (*obs.*), о-поч-ивáть, *v.i.*, to retire, rest, repose; pass away, die. Он опочúл, (*poet.*), he died. Он опочивáет пóсле обéда, he is resting after dinner.

ПОЛ-, HALF; SEX; FLOOR

пол, *п.т.*, пóл-ы, *pl.*, sex. Обóего пóла, of both sexes. Жéнский (мужскóй), пол, female (male) sex. Жéнского (мужскóго) пóла, of the female (of the male) sex. Прекрáсный (нéжный) пол, the fair sex (*jokingly*). Сúльный п., the strong sex. Пол-овóй, *adj.*, sexual, sex. П-ы́е óрганы, genitals, sex organs. П-óе влечéние, sexual attraction.

пол, *п.т.*, пол-овúна, *п.f.*, half. Пол-часá, half hour, half an hour. Пол-кóмнаты, half of a room. Пол-вéка, half a century. Пол-гóда, half a year. Пóл-день, пол-ý-день, *п.т.*, noon, midday. Пóсле полýдня, in the afternoon. Пол-ý-денный, *adj.*, midday.

П. зной, midday heat. Пол-днéвный, *adj.*, noon. "В пол-днéвный жар, в долúне Дагестáна...", (*Lermontov*), "In the midday heat, in the valley of Dagestan..." Пóл-дник, *п.т.*, (*obs.*), noon meal. Пóл-дничать, *v.i.*, (*obs.*), to eat a meal at noon. Пóл-ночь, *п.f.*, midnight. Пол-нóчи, *п.f.*, midnight. Пол-нóчный, пол-нóщный, *adj.*, midnight. Пол-у-нóчник, *п.т.*, пол-у-нóчница, *п.f.*, (*colloq.*), nightbird, nightowl. Пол-у-нóчничать, *v.i.*, to burn the midnight oil. Пол-торá, *num. card.*, one and a half. Пол-ý-торный, *adj.*, pertaining to one and a half. В пол-ý-торном размéре, increased by one and a half. Пол-тúнник, *п.т.*, пол-тúна, *п.f.*, (*colloq.*), coin of fifty kopeks, half a ruble. С рубля́ мне дáли полтúнник сдáчи, they gave me fifty kopeks in change from a ruble. Пол-бутылки пúва, (винá), half a bottle of wine (beer). Пол-у-, *a combining form meaning* half. Пол-у-óстров, *п.т.*, peninsula (*literally*: half an island). Пол-у-мрáк, *п.т.*, semi-obscurity. Пол-у-свéт, *п.т.*, feeble light; twilight; demimonde. Пол-у-ботúнки, *п.т.pl.*, low shoes, oxfords. Пол-у-шубóк, *п.т.*, knee-length sheepskin coat. Пол-у-глáсный, *adj.*, *also used as n.*, semivowel. По-пол-áм, *adv.*, in two halves. Разделúть п., to divide into two parts. Пол-овúна, *п.f.*, half, middle. П. трéтьего, half past two, two-thirty. Приéхать в половúне пя́того, to arrive at four-thirty, half past four. В половúне ию́ля, in the middle of July. Пол-овúнка, *п.f.*, (*dim.*), half, middle. Пол-овúнный, *adj.*, half. В половúнном размéре, (состáве), in half size, with half of a contingent (personnel). Пол-овúнчатость, *п.f.*, halfway policy. Пол-овúнчатый, *adj.*, undecided; half and half. Пол-éно, *п.п.*, log. Пол-ýшка, *п.f.*, (*obs.*), one quarter of a kopek. Не имéть ни полýшки, (*idiom.*), to be penniless.

пол-á, *п.f.*, skirt; flap of a coat. Прáвая (лéвая) п., right (left) flap. П. шýбы (палáтки), flap of a furcoat (of a tent). Откúнуть полý палáтки, to throw open the flap of a tent. Из-под полы, (*colloq.*), on the sly. Торговáть из-под полы, (*colloq.*), to sell illicitly, on the black market.

пол, *п.т.*, пол-ы́, *pl.*, floor. Деревя́нный (паркéтный) п., wooden, (inlaid) floor. Настилáть полы, to floor. Пол-овúк, *п.т.*, пол-овичóк, *п.т.*, (*dim.*), rug, door mat. Пол-овúца, *п.f.*, floor board. Пол-овóй, *adj.*, *used as n.*, (*obs.*), waiter. П. в трактúре, (*obs.*), waiter in a tavern. Пол-овой, *adj.*, of or pertaining to the floor. П-áя трáпка (щётка), floor mop (brush). Пол-омóйка, *n.f.*, charwoman, janitress. Пришлá п. мыть полы́, the charwoman came to wash the floor. Пол-о-тёр, *n.m.*, floor polisher. Полотёры натирáют полы́, floor polishers wax and polish floors. Пóл-ка, *n.f.*, shelf, rack. Книжная п., bookshelf. Пóл-ок (в бáне), sweating bench in a steam bath. Полéзу на пóлок попáриться, I shall climb on the bench to steam myself. под-пóл-ь-е, *n.n.*, cellar; (*fig.*), underground. Óвощи слóжены в подпóлье, the vegetables are stored in the cellar. Рабóтать в подпóлье, (*fig.*), to work in the underground. Под-пóл-ь-ный, *adj.*, underground. П-ая организáция, underground organization. Под-пóл-ь-щик, *n.m.*, one associated with an underground organization.

ПОЛ-, FIELD, GROUND

пóл-е, *n.n.*, field, ground; margin; brim. Крестьáне сéют рожь в пóле, the peasants are sowing rye in the field. Пóле би́твы (сражéния), battlefield, field of battle. Сдéлать замéтки на поля́х кни́ги, to make notes on the margin of a book. На ней былá шля́па с широ́кими поля́ми, she wore a hat with a wide brim. Пóле зрéния, field of vision. Перекати́-пóле, *n.n.*, eryngium (*botany*); (*fig.*), rolling stone. Пол-евóй, *adj.*, field. П-ы́е рабóты начинáются рáнней вéсной, work in the fields begins early in the spring. П-ы́е цветы́, field flowers. П-áя мышь, field mouse. П. гóспиталь, field hospital. П. бинóкль, field glasses, binoculars. П. суд, court martial. П-áя су́мка, (*mil.*), dispatch case. П-áя артиллéрия, field artillery. пол-я́на, *n.f.*, glade. Леснáя п., forest glade. Пол-я́нка, *n.f.*, small glade. пол-я́н-е, (*hist.*), Pólians (people of the plains); Slavic tribe, living along the Dnieper. пол-я́к, *n.m.*, Pole. Пол-я́ки, the Poles, the Polish nation. Пóл-ь-ка, *n.f.*, a Pole; polka (*dance*). Танцовáть пóльку, to dance a polka. Пóл-ь-ша, *n.f.*, Poland. Пóл-ь-ский, *adj.*, Polish. П. язы́к, the Polish language. П-ая литератýра (му́зыка, истóрия), Polish literature (music, history).

ПОЛК-, ПОЛЧ-, REGIMENT

полк, *n.m.*, regiment. Пехóтный (кавалери́йский) п., infantry (cavalry) regiment. Полк-óвник, *n.m.*, colonel. Полк-о-вóдец, *n.m.*, commander, great general; leader of an army. Вели́кие полковóдцы дрéвних времён, the great commanders of ancient times. Полк-овóй, *adj.*, regimental. Полковóй команди́р, commander of a regiment. П-áя канцеля́рия, office, headquarters. пóлч-ищ-е, *n.n.* (*obs.*), horde; (*fig.*), mass. Татáрские пóлчища, the Tatar hordes. Нарóду шли цéлые пóлчища, hordes of people were going. о-полч-и́-ть-ся, *v.p.r.*, о-полч-áть-ся, *v.i.r.*, на + *acc.*, to take up arms against. Нижегорóдцы ополчи́лись в 1613 году́ прóтив поля́ков, the people of Nizhnii Novgorod rose in arms against the Poles in 1613. О-полч-éнец, *n.m.*, (*hist.*), member of the national reserve. О-полч-éние, *n.n.*, home guard; national reserve. Одно-полч-áнин, *n.m.*, fellow, brother soldier, officer; comrade-in-arms.

ПОЛН-, ПОЛОН-, FULLNESS

полн-é-ть, *v.i.*, по-полн-éть, *v.p.*, to grow stout, put on weight. Зá лето он пополнéл, during the summer he put on weight. Полн-отá, *n.f.*, plenitude, completeness; corpulence, stoutness. От полноты́ сéрдца (души́), in the fullness of one's heart. П. влáсти, plenary authority.

пóл-ный, *adj.*, пóлон, *m.* полн-á, *f.*, полн-ó, *neut. pred.*, full; packed; complete, total; absolute, perfect; stout, plump, obese. Пóлон до краёв, full to the brim. П-ая тарéлка, full plate. П-ое собрáние сочинéний, complete works. П. комплéкт, set. П-ое затмéние, total eclipse. П. покóй, absolute rest. П-ое невéжество, absolute ignorance. П-ая лунá, full moon. У них дом пóлная чáша, they live in plenty. В кóмнате (в трамвáе) пóлным полнó, the room (the streetcar) is overcrowded with people. Полн-éйший, *adj. superl.*, sheer, utter. Полн-ó, *adv.*, full; enough. Сли́шком п. , too full. Полн-о-, *a combining form meaning* full. Полн-о-влáстие, *n.n.*, sovereignty. Полн-о-влáстный, *adj.*, sovereign. Полн-о-вóдье, *n.n.*, high water. Полн-о-вóдный, *adj.*, deep, abundant in water. П-ая рекá, river abundant in water. Полн-о-звýчный, *adj.*, sonorous. Полн-о-крóвие, *n.n.*, (*med.*), plethora. Полн-о-крóвный, *adj.*, full-blooded, sanguineous. Полн-о-лýние, *n.n.*, full moon. Полн-о-мóчие, *n.n.*, power, plenary power; authority. Полн-о-прáвие, *n.n.*, competency; full civil rights. Полн-о-пра́вный, *adj.*, enjoying full rights. П. граждани́н, citizen enjoying full rights. По́лн-остью, *adv.*, fully, in full, completely, utterly. Всё сде́лано п., everything has been completed, done. В-полн-е́, *adv.*, quite, fully. Это его́ в. успоко́ило, this gave him full assurance, it reassured him completely. В. образо́ванный, well educated.

полн-и́-ть, *v.i.*, + *acc.*, to make look stout. Это пла́тье меня́ полни́т, this dress makes me look stout.

вос-по́лн-ить, *v.p.*, вос-полн-я́ть, *v.i.*, + *acc.*, to fill; supply. В. пробе́лы, to make up deficiencies.

вы́-полн-ить, *v.p.*, вы-полн-я́ть, *v.i.*, + *acc.*, to carry out, implement, execute, fulfill, accomplish. В. свой долг, to do one's duty, carry out one's obligations. В. чьи́-либо жела́ния, to fulfill someone's wishes. В. приказа́ние, to obey; carry out an order. Вы-полн-е́ние, *n.n.*, execution, fulfillment, carrying out. В. обеща́ния, fulfillment of a promise. В. пла́на, accomplishment, realization of a plan. Вы-полн-и́мый, *adj.*, *part. pass. pres.*, feasible. В-ое зада́ние, feasible task.

до-по́лн-ить, *v.p.*, до-полн-я́ть, *v.i.*, + *acc.*, + *instr.*, to supplement, fill up. Он дополнил свой расска́з но́выми подро́бностями, he supplemented his story with new details. Дополня́ть друг дру́га, to make a pair, to supplement each other. До-полн-е́ние, *n.n.*, supplement, addition; (*gram.*), object. В дополне́ние, in addition, to supplement. Прямо́е (ко́свенное) д., direct (indirect) object. До-полн-и́тельный, *adj.*, additional, supplementary. Д-ая подпи́ска, supplementary subscription. Д-ое придаточное предложе́ние, (*gram.*), object clause. До-полн-и́тельно, *adv.*, in addition.

за-по́лн-ить, *v.p.*, за-полн-я́ть, *v.i.*, + *acc.*, to fill in. З. анке́ту, to fill out a questionnaire. З. вре́мя, to occupy time. За-по́лн-ить-ся, *v.p.r.*, за-полн-я́ть-ся, *v.i.r.*, + *instr.*, to fill up, be filled up. Вся пло́щадь запо́лнилась наро́дом, the entire square was filled with people.

ис-по́лн-ить, *v.p.*, ис-полн-я́ть, *v.i.*, + *acc.*, to carry out, execute, perform; *see* вы́-полнить. И. обя́занности, to fulfill one's duties; be in charge. И. рабо́ту, to complete work. Ис-по́лн-ить-ся, *v.p.r.*, ис-полн-я́ть-ся, *v.i.r.*, to be fulfilled, become fulfilled. Моё жела́ние испо́лнилось, my wish has been granted. Ему́ испо́лнилось 20 лет, he is twenty years of age. Моё се́рдце

испо́лнилось жа́лостью, (*obs.*), my heart filled with pity. Ис-полн-е́ние, *n.n.*, fulfillment, execution. Приступи́ть к исполне́нию свои́х обя́занностей, to enter upon one's duties. Приводи́ть пригово́р в и., to carry out a sentence, verdict. Симфо́ния Чайко́вского в исполне́нии орке́стра, Tschaikovsky's symphony performed by an orchestra. Ис-по́лн-енный, *adj.*, *part. pass. past*, performed; full. И-ая певцо́м а́рия, an aria performed by a singer. Взгляд испо́лненный тоски́, a look full of grief. Ис-полн-и́мый, *adj.*, *part. pass. pres.*, feasible. Ва́ше жела́ние вполне́ и-мо, your wish can easily be granted. Ис-полн-и́тель, *n.m.*, ис-полн-и́тельница, *n.f.*, executor, performer. Изве́стная исполни́тельница ру́сских пе́сен, famous singer of Russian songs. Суде́бный и., bailiff. Ис-полн-и́тельный, *adj.*, executive; industrious; careful. И. комите́т, executive committee. Исполко́м, (*recent*), *abbr. of* исполни́тельный комите́т. И-ая власть, executive power. И. рабо́тник, industrious worker. И. лист, writ.

на-по́лн-ить, *v.p.*, на-полн-я́ть, *v.i.*, + *acc.*, to fill. Н. га́зом, to inflate with gas. Н. арома́том, to fill with fragrance. На-по́лн-ить-ся, *v.p.r.*, на-полн-я́ть-ся, *v.i.r.*, + *instr.*, to be filled. Ко́мната напо́лнилась ды́мом, the room was filled with smoke. На-полн-е́ние, *n.n.*, filling, inflation. Пульс хоро́шего наполне́ния, (*med.*), strong pulse.

пере-по́лн-ить, *v.p.*, пере-полн-я́ть, *v.i.*, + *acc.*, + *instr.*, to cause to overflow, overcrowd. П. сосу́д водо́й, to let a vessel overflow. Ча́ша моего́ терпе́ния перепо́лнена, my patience is at an end. Пере-по́лн-ить-ся, *v.p.r.*, пере-полн-я́ть-ся, *v.i.r.*, + *instr.*, Моё се́рдце перепо́лнилось ра́достью, my heart overflowed with joy. Пере-полн-е́ние, *n.n.*, overcrowding, repletion.

по-по́лн-ить, *v.p.*, по-полн-я́ть, *v.i.*, + *acc.*, to replenish, fill up, enrich; widen. П. соста́в слу́жащих, to increase a staff to capacity. П. поте́ри, (*mil.*), to replace casualties. По-полн-е́ние, *n.n.*, replenishment. П. боеприпа́сами, replenishment of ammunition stock. П. библиоте́ки, addition of books to a library.

пре-ис-по́лн-ить, *v.p.*, пре-ис-полн-я́ть, *v.i.*, + *acc.*, + *instr.*, (*obs.*), to fill with. Пре-ис-по́лн-ить-ся, *v.p.r.*, пре-ис-полн-я́ть-ся, *v.i.r.*, to be filled with. П. реши́мости, to be firmly resolved. Пре-ис-по́лн-енный, *adj.*, *part. pass.*

past, full, filled with. П. опáсности, fraught with danger.

полн-о-мóчие, *n.n.,* power, plenary powers, proxy. Давáть п., to empower. Полн-о-мóчный, *adj.,* plenipotentiary. П. минúстр, minister plenipotentiary. П. посóл, ambassador. П. представúтель, plenipotentiary.

у-полн-о-мóчить, *v.p.,* у-полн-о-мóчивать, *v.i.,* + *acc.,* to authorize, empower. Правúтельство уполномóчило послá на подписáние торгóвого договóра, the government authorized the ambassador to sign the trade treaty. У-полн-о-мóчие, *n.n.,* authorization, power of attorney, proxy. По у-ю, upon authorization. У-полн-о-мóченный, *adj., part. pass. past, used as n.m.,* commissioner, authorized agent, representative.

ПОЛОС-, STRIPE

полос-á, *n.f.,* stripe, strip, band; period; region, zone. П. желéза, iron band. П. землú, strip of land. Чернозёмная п., black earth belt. П. реáкции, period of reaction. П. хорóшей погóды, spell of fine weather. Полóс-ка, *n.f., (dim.),* stripe, strip, band. Сúтец в полóску, striped cotton material. Полос-áтый, *adj.,* striped. П-ая матéрия, striped material, cloth.

полос-нý-ть, *v.p.,* + *acc.,* + *instr., (colloq.),* to slash. П. ножóм по спинé, to knife someone in the back.

полос-овáть, *v.i.,* + *acc.,* to make into bars. П. желéзо, to make iron into bars. Полос-овóй, *adj.,* bar. П-óе желéзо, iron bars.

ис-полос-овáть, *v.p.,* + *acc., (colloq.),* to cut into strips; flay. И. матéрию, to cut cloth into strips. Исполосовáть комý-нибудь всю спúну, *(colloq.),* to flay someone's back.

чрес-полóс-иц-а, *n.f., (hist.),* strip plowing. Чрес-полóс-ный, *adj.,* pertaining to strip farming.

ПОРОК-, ПОРОЧ-, VICE, SHAME, FLAW, DEFECT

порóк, *n.m.,* vice; defect; flaw. П. рéчи, speech defect. П. сéрдца, heart defect. Душéвные п-и, moral vices. Бéдность - не порóк, *(saying),* poverty is no vice.

порóч-и-ть, *v.i.,* о-порóч-ить, *v.p.,* + *acc.,* to libel, cover with shame, discredit. П. показáния свидéтелей, to discredit the witnesses' testimony. П. чéстное úмя, to libel someone. Порóчность, *n.f.,* depravity, viciousness. П.

харáктера, viciousness of character. Порóч-ный, *adj.,* depraved, vicious. П. человéк, depraved person. Беспорóчный, *adj.,* pure, noble. Непорóч-ный, *adj.,* immaculate. Н-ая Дéва Марúя, the Immaculate Virgin Mary.

о-порóч-ить, *v.p.,* о-порóч-ивать, *v.i.,* + *acc.,* to defame, libel. О-порóч-енный, *adj., part. pass. past,* defamed, libeled, covered with shame. У негó о-ое úмя, his name is covered with shame. О-порóч-ить-ся, *v.p.r.,* о-порóч-ивать-ся, *v.i.r.,* to become covered with shame.

ПОР-, ПАР-, RIPPING, UNDOING, THRASHING, FLOGGING

пор-ó-ть, *v.i.,* вы-пор-оть, *v.p.,* + *acc.,* to flog, thrash, whip; рас-пор-óть, *v.p.,* + *acc.,* to undo, rip, unstitch, unpick. П. горячку, *(colloq.),* to hurry, hustle. Нéчего п. горячку, there is no need to hurry, to make such a bustle. Порóть-ся, *v.i.r.,* рас-пор-óть-ся, *v.p.r.,* to be undone, ripped; be unstitched. Рукáв пóрется потомý, что нúтки тóнки, the sleeve is ripping because the thread is too fine. Пóр-ка, *n.f., (colloq.),* thrashing, whipping; ripping, unstitching. О-пóр-ки, *n.pl.,* ragged, wornout footwear.

вс-пор-óть, *v.p.,* вс-пáр-ывать, *v.i.,* + *acc.,* + *dat., (colloq.),* to rip, open up; disembowel. В. брюхо быкý, to disembowel a steer.

вы-пор-оть, *v.p.,* вы-пáр-ывать, *v.i.,* + *acc., (colloq.),* to rip open, out. В. подклáдку из пальтó, to rip the lining out of a coat.

за-пор-óть, *v.p.,* за-пáр-ывать, *v.i.,* + *acc., (obs.),* to flog to death. З. когó-нибудь дó смерти, to flog someone to death.

над-пор-óть, *v.p.,* над-пáр-ывать, *v.i.,* + *acc.,* to rip out, take out a few stitches, rip slightly. Н. рукáв, to rip a sleeve slightly. Над-пор-óть-ся, *v.p.r.,* над-пáр-ывать-ся, *v.i.r.,* + *acc.,* to be ripped out, off. Мешóк надпорóлся и зернó вýсыпалось, the bag was slightly ripped and grain leaked out.

от-пор-óть, *v.p.,* от-пáр-ывать, *v.i.,* + *acc.,* to rip out, rip off. О. рукáв, to rip out a sleeve. О. кружевá, to rip off lace.

пере-пор-óть, *v.p.,* пере-пáр-ывать, *v.i.,* + *acc.,* to rip again; *(colloq.),* to whip everyone. П. все швы, to rip all the seams again. Перепорóть всех до однóго, to whip everyone one after the other.

под-пор-óть, *v.p.,* под-пáр-ывать, *v.i.,* +

acc., to rip slightly. П. подкла́дку, to rip a lining slightly. Под-пор-о́ть-ся, *v.p.r.*, под-па́р-ывать-ся, *v.i.r.*, to be ripped, become unstitched. Подкла́дка у рукава́ подпоро́лась, the lining of the sleeve has become ripped.

рас-пор-о́ть, *v.p.*, рас-па́р-ывать, *v.i.*, + *acc.*, to rip open entirely, rip apart. Р. пла́тье, to rip a dress apart. Рас-пор-о́ть-ся, *v.p.r.*, рас-па́р-ывать-ся, *v.i.r.*, to become unstitched, ripped apart. На спине́ распоро́лись швы, the seams on the back became unstitched. Рас-па́р-ывание, *n.n.*, ripping up, unstitching.

с-пор-о́ть, *v.p.*, с-па́р-ывать, *v.i.*, + *acc.*, to rip off, unsew. С. пу́говицу с пиджака́, to rip the buttons off a coat. С. наши́вку, (*mil.*), to rip off a chevron, stripe. С-по́р-ок, *n.m.*, cloth cut for garment, unsewn.

ПОРОХ-, ПОРОШ-, ПРАХ-, ПРАШ-, ПОРХ-, ПЕРХ-, ПАРХ-, ПОРШ-, ПЕРШ-, POWDER, DUST, WHIRL

по́рох, *n.m.*, powder. Чёрный п., gunpowder. Безды́мный п., smokeless powder. Па́хнет по́рохом, (*fig.*), there is war in the air. У него́ по́роха нехвата́ет, (*fig.*), it is beyond him. Держа́ть по́рох сухи́м, (*fig.*), to keep powder dry (be prepared for war). Порох-овни́ца, *n.f.*, powder flask. Порох-ово́й, *adj.*, gunpowder. П. заво́д, gunpowder works. П. по́греб, powder magazine.

поро́ш-а, *n.f.*, first snow of the season; newly fallen snow. Порош-и́нка, *n.f.*, snowflake.

порош-и́ть, *v.i.*, на-порош-и́ть, *v.p.*, to snow lightly. Пороши́т, (снег пороши́т), it is snowing lightly. Порош-о́к, *n.m.*, powder. Зубно́й п., tooth powder. Посы́пать порошко́м, to powder. Порош-к-о-обра́зный, *adj.*, powder-like, powdery. Порошкообра́зное вещество́, powdery substance.

за-порош-и́ть, *v.p.*, + *acc.*, + *instr.*, to powder, dust. Доро́гу запороши́ло сне́гом, the road has become covered with snow. Запороши́ло глаза́ пы́лью, to be blinded by dust.

прах, *n.m.*, (*obs.*), earth, ashes; corpse. Здесь поко́ится прах, here lies the body (of). Отряхну́ть п. с ног, (*fig.*), to shake the dust off one's feet. Обрати́ть в п., to reduce to dust, to ashes. Разнести́ в пух и прах, (*idiom.*), to scold soundly; (*mil.*), to rout.

верто-пра́х, *n.m.*, (*colloq.*), superficial, flighty person.

верто-пра́ш-нич-а-ть, *v.i.*, to be fickle, flighty. Он то́лько вертопра́шничает и де́ньги прожива́ет, he only flutters around and squanders money.

порх-а́-ть, *v.i.*, порх-ну́ть, *v.p.smf.*, to flutter. Танцу́ющие порха́ли по за́лу, the dancing couples whirled around the hall. Пти́чка порха́ла вокру́г гнезда́, the bird fluttered about his nest.

вс-порх-ну́-ть, *v.p.smf.*, вс-па́рх-ивать, *v.i.*, to fly up, take wing, take off. Ла́сточка вспорхну́ла и улете́ла, the swallow rose and flew off.

у-порх-а́ть, *v.i.*, у-порх-ну́ть, *v.p.*, to fly off, fly away. Пти́цы ста́ей упорхну́ли от охо́тника, the flock of birds flew away from the hunter.

по́рш-ен-ь, *n.m.*, piston. По́ршень в насо́се необходи́м, the piston is a necessary part of a pump. П. в дви́гателях, piston of an engine. По́рш-невый, *adj.*, piston. П-ое кольцо́, piston ring.

перш-и́ть, *v.i.*, за-перш-и́ть, *v.p.*, *impers.*, to produce a tickling sensation. У меня́ перши́т в го́рле. I have a tickling in my throat. Пе́рх-оть, *n.f.*, dandruff.

ПОРТ-, ПОРЧ-, DETERIORATION, SPOILING

по́рт-и-ть, по́рч-у, *v.i.*, ис-по́рт-ить, *v.p.*, + *acc.*, to spoil; (*fig.*), mar, corrupt. П. аппети́т, to spoil one's appetite. П. себе́ не́рвы, (*colloq.*), to irritate oneself. По́рт-ить-ся, *v.i.r.*, ис-по́рт-ить-ся, *v.p.r.*, to deteriorate, go bad, become worse; decay, rot. Часы́ по́ртятся от неуме́лого обраще́ния, watches are damaged by unskilled handling. Не по́ртиться от жары́ (сы́рости), to resist heat (moisture); be heatproof (moistureproof). У него́ по́ртится настрое́ние, he is losing his good spirits. По́рч-а, *n.f.*, damage, deterioration, spoiling. П. инструме́нтов, damage to instruments. П. зре́ния, damage to eyesight. Ис-по́рч-енность, *n.f.*, depravity. Ис-по́рч-енный, *adj.*, spoiled, depraved; rotten. И. ребёнок, vicious child. И. вкус, perverted taste.

на-по́рт-ить, *v.p.*, (*colloq.*), to spoil, wreck someone's plans. Ребёнок напо́ртил мно́го игру́шек, the child ruined many toys.

пере-по́рт-ить, *v.p.*, to ruin, spoil, damage. П. ку́шанье, to spoil food. Пере-по́рт-ить-ся, *v.p.r.*, (*colloq.*), to become spoiled, ruined.

по-по́рт-ить, *v.p.*, (*colloq.*), *see* по́ртить, испо́ртить.

ПОРТ-, CLOTH, MATERIAL

порт-к-й, порт-ы, *n.pl.,* (*obs.*), trousers. Крестья́нин вы́шел в порта́х и си́ней руба́хе, the peasant came out in a blue shirt and trousers. Порт-я́нка, *n.f.,* footcloth, used in place of socks. Солда́т обмота́л но́ги портя́нками и пото́м наде́л сапоги́, the soldier wrapped his feet in cloth and put on his boots.

порт-но́й, *n.m.,* tailor. Да́мский (мужско́й), п., ladies' (gentlemen's) tailor. Порт-ни́ха, *n.f.,* dressmaker. Портно́вский, *adj.,* tailor's. П-ие но́жницы, tailoring scissors. П-ая мастерска́я, tailor's workshop.

порт-н-я́ж-и-ть, *v.i.,* порт-н-я́ж-нич-ать, *v.i.,* to tailor. Э́тот портно́й п. весь свой век, this man has been a tailor all his life. Порт-ня́жничество, *n.n.,* tailoring. Порт-ня́жный, *adj.,* sartorial. П-ое мастерство́, tailor's skill, craftsmanship. Порт-ня́жная, *adj., used as n.,* tailor's workshop.

ПОТ-, PERSPIRATION

пот, *n.m.,* perspiration, sweat. Холо́дный п., cold sweat. Облива́ться по́том, to be running with sweat. Труди́ться в по́те лица́, (*fig.*), to work in the sweat of one's brow. По́том и кро́вью, (*fig., idiom.*), in blood and sweat.

пот-е́-ть, *v.i.,* вс-пот-е́ть, *v.p.,* to perspire, sweat. П. (всп.) от жары́, to break into a sweat from heat. П. над зада́чей, to toil, grind at a problem. Пот-е́ние, *n.n.,* perspiration, sweating. Пот-ли́вость, *n.f.,* tendency to perspire. Пот-ли́вый, *adj.,* tending to perspire. Пот-ни́к, *n.m.,* sweat-cloth; saddle pad. По́т-ный, *adj.,* damp with perspiration. П-ые ру́ки, perspiring hands, clammy hands. Пот-ово́й, *adj.,* (*anat.*), sudoriferous, sudorific. П-ые же́лезы, sudoriferous glands. Пот-о-го́нный, sudorific. Пот-о-го́нное, *adj., used as n.,* sudorific. П-ое лека́рство, sudorific medicine. П-ая систе́ма, sudorific system.

за-пот-е́ть, *v.p.,* за-пот-ева́ть, *v.i.,* to become, grow dim. Окно́ запоте́ло, the window has become damp, steamed.

от-пот-е́ть, *v.p.,* от-пот-ева́ть, *v.i.,* to moisten; become moist, damp; *see* запоте́ть.

по-пот-е́ть, *v.p.,* to sweat, perspire a little; (*fig.*), to give oneself much trouble. Больно́й но́чью немно́го попоте́л и ему́ полегча́ло, the sick man perspired slightly in the night and his condition is better. П. над зада́чей, (*colloq.*), to sweat, labor over a problem.

про-пот-е́ть, *v.p.,* to perspire freely; be soaked in perspiration. П. в ба́не, to sweat in a steam bath. Оде́жда пропоте́ла, the clothing has become soaked with perspiration.

ПРАВ-, (ПРАВ-Д-), ПРАВ(Л)-, RIGHT, TRUTH; GOVERNING; STEERING

пра́в-д-а, *n.f.,* truth, justice; *used as adv.,* true, indeed, really. Э́то п., it is the truth. Иска́ть пра́вды, to seek justice. Пострада́ть за пра́вду, to suffer in the name of justice. Пра́вда, он не тако́й плохо́й рабо́тник... Пра́вда, я с ва́ми не согла́сен, но..., though I do not agree with you, still... Пра́вда? Indeed? Really? Прав-д-и́вость, *n.f.,* truthfulness, veracity. Прав-ди́вый, *adj.,* truthful, upright, true. П. челове́к, truthful, upright man. П-ое изве́стие, true tidings. Прав-д-о-подо́бие, *n.n.,* likelihood, probability. Прав-д-о-подо́бный, *adj.,* likely, probable. Пра́в-ед-ник, *n.m.,* пра́в-ед-ница, *n.f.,* just man (woman), righteous man (woman). Пра́в-едный, *adj.,* just, righteous; pious, religious. П. судья́, fair judge.

о-прав-д-а́ть, *v.i.,* о-прав-д-ывать, *v.p.,* + *acc.,* to justify; warrant; acquit; excuse. О. подсуди́мого, to acquit a defendant. О. расхо́ды, to justify expenses. О. наде́жду, to justify hopes. О-правда́ть-ся, *v.p.r.,* о-пра́в-дывать-ся, *v.i.r.,* пе́ред + *instr.,* to justify oneself; come true. Обвиня́емый опра́вдывался пе́ред судьёй, the accused was trying to justify himself in the eyes of the judge. О-прав-да́ние, *n.n.,* justification; acquittal; discharge excuse. Э́то не оправда́ние! That is no excuse! О-правда́тельный, *adj.,* exculpating. О. пригово́р, verdict of not guilty. О. докуме́нт, voucher.

с-прав-ед-ли́в-ост-ь, *n.f.,* justice, equity, fairness. По справедли́вости, in justice. С. судьи́, fairness, impartiality of a judge. С-прав-едли́вый, *adj.,* just. С. пригово́р, just sentence, verdict. С-ые тре́бования, just demands.

прав-е́-ть, *v.i.,* по-прав-е́ть, *v.p.,* to become more conservative. Пра́в-ый, *adj., used as n.,* right-wing, conservative, reactionary. П. укло́н, (*recent*), deviation to the right. П-ая па́ртия, right-wing party.

пра́в-ил-о, *n.n.,* rule, maxim, principle. Пра́вила вну́треннего распоря́дка, interior regulations. Пра́вила вожде́ния, driving regulations. Пра́вила арифме́тики, arithmetical principles.

Соблюдáть прáвила, to observe regulations. По прáвилам, according to rules, to regulations. Взять за п., to make it a rule. Человéк без прáвил, a man without principles. Прáв-ильно, *adv.*, rightly, correctly. Часы идýт п., the watch is right. Прáв-ильность, *n.f.*, rightness, correctness, regularity. П. отвéта, correctness of an answer. Прáв-ильный, *adj.*, right, correct; regular. П-ое решéние, correct, sound decision. П-ое соотношéние, *n.n.*, just proportion. П-ая дробь, proper fraction. П-ые черты лицá, regular features of a face.

прáв-и-ть, прáв-л-ю, *v.i.*, + *instr.*, to govern, rule; drive, steer; (*tech.*), true up, correct. П. странóй, to govern a country. П. лошадьмú, to drive horses. П. автомобúлем, to drive an automobile. П. брúтвы, to strop, set razors. Прáв-ка, *n.f.*, trueing up, correcting; stropping. Прав-úтель, *n.m.*, ruler; regent. Прав-úтельство, *n.n.*, government. Прав-лéние, *n.n.*, government; administration; rule. Образ правлéния, form of government, rule. Состоять члéном правлéния, to be a member of an administrative board. Бразды правлéния, (*fig.*), the reins of government. Прáв-ящий, *adj., part. act. pres.*, ruling. П-ие клáссы, the ruling classes.

в-прáв-ить, *v.p.*, в-прав-л-ять, *v.i.*, + *acc.*, to set; reduce. В. вывихнутую рýку, to set an arm. В-прáв-ка, *n.f.*, setting; reduction.

вы́-прав-ить, *v.p.*, вы-прав-л-я́ть, *v.i.*, + *acc.*, to straighten, rectify, correct; get, obtain. В. погнýвшуюся лóжку, to straighten a bent spoon. В. рýкопись, to correct a manuscript. Вы́-прав-ить-ся, *v.p.r.*, вы-прав-л-я́ть-ся, *v.i.r.*, to become straight, straighten oneself; improve. Растéние постепéнно вы́правилось, the plant straightened itself out gradually. Мáльчик вы́правился, the boy improved. Вы́-прав-ка, *n.f.*, correction; carriage, bearing. В. ошú-бок, (*colloq.*), correction of errors (*as* in a dictation). Воéнная в., military bearing. У негó настоящая воéнная в., he has real military bearing.

за-прáв-ить, *v.p.*, за-прав-л-я́ть, *v.i.*, + *acc.*, + *instr.*, to set; season; trim, adjust; tuck in. З. суп сметáной, to season a soup with sour cream. З. лáмпу, to adjust a lamp. З. горючим, to refuel, fuel. Солдáт заправил брюки в сапогú, the soldier stuck his trousers into his boots. За-прáв-ить-ся, *v.p.r.*, за-прав-л-я́ть-ся, *v.i.r.*, to refresh oneself, be refueled. За-прáв-

ка, *n.f.*, seasoning; refuelling. Заправ-úла, *n.m.*, (*colloq.*), boss. Он у нас з., все егó слýшают, he is our boss, everyone listens to him. За-прáвский, *adj.*, (*colloq.*), true, real; regular. З. картёжник, regular gambler.

ис-прáв-ить, *v.p.*, ис-прав-л-я́ть, *v.i.*, + *acc.*, to correct, repair, reform; redress; atone. И. ошúбку, to make up for a mistake. Горбáтого однá могúла испрáвит, (*saying*), a hunchback can be cured only by the grave; a leopard does not change its spots. Ис-прáв-ить-ся, *v.p.r.*, ис-прав-л-я́ть-ся, *v.i.r.*, to be corrected, repaired; improve, reform. Он совсéм исправился и перестáл пить, he reformed completely and stopped drinking. Ис-прав-л-éние, *n.n.*, correction, correcting; repairing. И. тéкста, correction, emendation of a text. И. корректýры, correcting of proof sheets. Ис-прав-úтельный, *adj.*, correctional. И. дом (исправдóм), reformatory. Ис-прáв-ник, *n.m.*, (*preRev.*), district police officer. Ис-прáвность, *n.f.*, good condition; exactness, punctuality. Инструмéнты в пóлной исправности, the instruments are in good working order. И. в служéбных делáх, reliability, exactness in matters of service. Ис-прáв-ный, *adj.*, in good repair; careful; industrious; punctual. И. ученúк, industrious student.

на-прáв-ить, *v.p.*, на-прав-л-я́ть, *v.i.*, + *acc.*, to direct, turn. Н. внимáние, to direct attention. Н. сúлы, to direct one's energies. Н. шагú, to direct one's steps. Н. заявлéние, to file an application, a statement. На-прáв-ить-ся, *v.p.r.*, на-прав-л-я́ть-ся, *v.i.r.*, на + *acc.*, to make one's way, direct one's steps. Н. на юг, to take a southerly direction. На-прав-лéние, *n.n.*, direction, trend; order; permit. Н. полёта, course of flight. Н. наступлéния, line of advance. Во всех направлéниях, in all directions. По направлéнию к, towards, in the direction of. Литератýрное н., literary school, trend. На-прáв-л-енность, *n.f.*, direction, trend, tendency. Социáльная н. ромáна, social tendency of a novel.. Н. удáра, direction of a blow. На-прав-л-я́ющий, *adj., part. act. pres.*, directing. Н. рóлик, guide roller. На-прав-л-я́ющая, *adj.*, *used as n.*, (*tech.*), guide.

о-прáв-ить, *v.p.*, о-прав-л-я́ть, *v.i.*, + *acc.*, to set right, put in order; mount. О. плáтье (причёску), to tidy one's dress (hair). О. драгоцéнный кáмень, to set, mount a precious stone. О-прáв-ить-ся, *v.p.r.*, о-прав-л-я́ть-ся, *v.i.r.*, to recover, recoup, put in order. Он совсём опра́вился по́сле ти́фа, he recovered completely after an attack of typhus. О. от испу́га (от волне́ния), to recover from fright (anxiety). О. пе́ред зе́ркалом, to put one's clothing in order in front of a mirror. О-пра́в-а, *n.f.*, setting, mounting, casing, rim. Очки́ без опра́вы, rimless glasses. Вста́вить в опра́ву, to set, mount.

от-пра́в-ить, *v.p.*, от-прав-л-я́ть, *v.i.*, + *acc.*, to ship, forward, dispatch; perform, exercise. О. письмо́, to send a letter. О. на тот свет, (*colloq.*), to send to a better world. Отправля́ть обя́занности, to perform one's duties. От-пра́в-ить-ся, *v.p.r.*, от-прав-л-я́ть-ся, *v.i.r.*, to set off, out; start, leave, go. По́езд отправля́ется в 5 часо́в, the train leaves at five o'clock. От-пра́в-ка, *n.f.*, send-off, forwarding, dispatch. О. това́ров, shipping of goods. О. поездо́в, expedition of trains. О. пи́сем, posting of letters. От-прав-л-е́ние, *n.n.*, sending, departure, dispatching. О. обя́занностей, exercising of one's duties. О. органи́зма, function of the body. От-прав-и́тель, *n.m.*, от-прав-и́тельница, *n.f.*, sender. От-прав-но́й, *n.f.*, starting. О. пункт, starting point, point of departure.

пере-пра́в-ить, *v.p.*, пере-прав-л-я́ть, *v.i.*, + *acc.*, to convey, forward; (*colloq.*), correct. П. на паро́ме, to ferry. П. кого́-нибудь че́рез грани́цу, to take someone over a frontier. П. пло́хо напи́санную бу́кву, to correct a badly written letter. Пере-пра́в-ить-ся, *v.p.r.*, пере-прав-л-я́ть-ся, *v.i.r.*, to swim, sail, ferry across. Они́ перепра́вились че́рез ре́ку на паро́ме, they ferried across the river. Пере-пра́в-а, *n.f.*, passage, crossing; ford. П. че́рез ре́ку, river crossing.

под-пра́в-ить, *v.p.*, под-прав-л-я́ть, *v.i.*, + *acc.*, to retouch, retouch. П. рису́нок, to retouch a drawing. Под-пра́в-ка, *n.f.*, touching up.

по-пра́в-ить, *v.p.*, по-прав-л-я́ть, *v.i.*, + *acc.*, to repair, correct, set right, readjust. П. забо́р (мостову́ю), to repair a fence (roadway). П. здоро́вье, to recover one's health. П. причёску, to smooth one's hair. П. де́нежные дела́, to better one's financial position. По-пра́в-ить-ся, *v.p.r.*, по-прав-л-я́ть-ся, *v.i.r.*, to recover, get well, correct oneself, improve. Вы хорошо́ попра́вились, you have improved. Уме́л оши́бться, уме́й и попра́виться, (*prov.*), if you know how to make mistakes, you must know how to correct them. По-пра́в-ка, *n.f.*, recovery, repairing,

mending, correction, amendment. Внести́ попра́вку в резолю́цию, to amend a resolution. По-прав-л-е́ние, *n.n.*, recovery; correction. Он пое́хал в дере́вню для поправле́ния здоро́вья, he went to the country to improve his health. По-пра́в-имый, *adj.*, reparable, remediable. Эта беда́ ещё попра́вима, this misfortune can be remedied. По-пра́в-очный, *adj.*, correction, correcting. П. коэфицие́нт, (*math.*), correction factor.

при-пра́в-ить, *v.p.*, при-прав-л-я́ть, *v.i.*, + *acc.*, + *instr.*, to season, dress, flavor, spice; to make ready for printing. П. со́ус, to season a sauce. При-пра́в-а, *n.f.*, seasoning, relish, flavoring. С припра́вой, seasoned (with). Без припра́вы, unseasoned. При-пра́в-ка, *n.f.*, printing make-ready.

рас-пра́в-ить, *v.p.*, рас-прав-л-я́ть, *v.i.*, + *acc.*, to straighten, smooth out. Р. скла́дки, to smooth out creases. Р. морщи́ны на лбу, to smooth out wrinkles on one's forehead. Р. кры́лья, to spread, open one's wings. Рас-пра́в-ить-ся, *v.p.r.*, рас-прав-л-я́ть-ся, *v.i.r.*, с + *instr.*, to be smoothed out, straightened out; make short work of. Р. без суда́, to take the law into one's own hands. Рас-пра́в-а, *n.f.*, chastisement, punishment (*often by taking the law into one's own hands*). Чини́ть суд и распра́ву, (*idiom.*), to administer justice and mete out punishment. У меня́ с ним р. коротка́, (*colloq.*), I'll deal with him summarily. Крова́вая р., slaughter; lynching.

с-пра́в-ить, *v.p.*, с-прав-л-я́ть, *v.i.*, + *acc.*, (*colloq.*), to celebrate. С. день рожде́ния, to celebrate one's birthday. С. сва́дьбу, to celebrate a wedding. С-пра́в-ить-ся, *v.p.r.*, с-прав-л-я́ть-ся, *v.i.r.*, о + *prep.*, to inquire, ask about, make inquiries about; с + *instr.*, to manage, master, get the better of. С. в словаре́, to consult a dictionary. С. о здоро́вье, to inquire about someone's health С. со свое́й зада́чей, to cope with one's problem, task. С ним нелегко́ с., it is had to cope with him. С-пра́в-ка, *n.f.*, information; reference; certificate. Наводи́ть спра́вки о ком-нибудь, to make inquiries about someone. С. с ме́ста рабо́ты, employment reference. С-пра́в-очник, *n.m.*, reference book; guide. Железнодоро́жный с., railway guide. С-пра́вочный, *adj.*, inquiring. С-ое бюро́, information bureau. С-ая кни́га, guide, reference book.

у-прав-л-я́ть, *v.p.*, + *instr.*, to govern,

control, rule; operate, drive; (*gram.*), govern. У. госуда́рством, to govern a state, a country. У. автомоби́лем, to drive a car. У. орке́стром, to conduct an orchestra. У. дела́ми, to manage business, affairs. Перехо́дные глаго́лы управля́ют вини́тельным падежо́м, transitive verbs govern the accusative case. У-пра́в-ить-ся, *v.p.r.*, у-прав-ля́ть-ся, *v.i.r.*, + *instr.*, to manage; be governed, ruled. Одному́ со все́ми дела́ми не у-иться, one cannot manage everything alone. Госуда́рство управля́ется прави́тельством, the state is ruled by its government. У-пра́в-а, *n.f.*, justice; board. Иска́ть упра́вы, to seek justice. Городска́я у., (*obs.*), town, city council. Управдо́м, *abbr. of* управля́ющий до́мом, (*recent*), house manager, superintendent. У-прав-и́тель, *n.m.*, (*obs.*), steward; estate manager. У-прав-ле́ние, *n.n.*, management; government control; direction; office, administration, board. У. на расстоя́нии, distant, absentee control. Гла́вное у. гражда́нского возду́шного фло́та, central governing board of civil air fleet. Симфо́нию испо́лнит орке́стр под управле́нием компози́тора, the symphony will be conducted by its composer. У-прав-ле́нческий, *adj.*, administrative. У-ие расхо́ды, management expenses. У-прав-ля́емый, *adj.*, *part. pass. pres.*, administered, governed, managed, directed. У-прав-ля́ющий, *adj.*, *part. act. pres.*, managing; *used as n.*, manager. У. дела́ми, business manager.

пра́в-о, *n.n.*, right; license; law. П. ве́то, right of veto. П. го́лоса, right of vote, voting. П-а гражда́нства, right of citizenship. Води́тельские права́, (*recent*), driver's license. Гражда́нское п., civil law. Междунаро́дное п., international law. Уголо́вное п., penal code. Пра́в-о, *used as adv.*, really, truly, indeed. Пра́во, уже́ по́здно, it is really late. Пра́в-о-, *a combining form meaning* law, rule. Прав-о-ве́д, *n.m.*, lawyer, jurist; (*pre-Rev.*), graduate student of school of jurisprudence. Прав-о-ве́дение, *n.n.*, jurisprudence; science of law. Прав-о-писа́ние, *n.n.*, spelling, orthography. Прав-о-сла́вие, *n.n.*, Greek orthodoxy. Прав-о-сла́вный, *adj.*, Greek orthodox. П-ая це́рковь, Greek Orthodox Church. Правота́, *n.f.*, rightness; innocence. Пра́вый, *adj.*, right. П-ая сторона́, the right side. Вы пра́вы, you are right. В-пра́в-о, *adv.*, to the right. Находи́ть-ся в. от чего́-нибудь, to be on the right side of something. На-пра́в-о,

adv., to the right. Напра́во и нале́во, right and left. Напра́во! (*mil.*), Right turn! С-пра́в-а, *adv.*, to the right of. С. от него́, on his right, on his right side.

ПРАЗД-, ПОРОЖ-, ПОРАЖ-, IDLENESS

пра́зд-ник, *n.m.*, holiday, feast. Бу́дет и на на́шей у́лице п., (*saying*), our day will come. С пра́здником! Best wishes of the season. Пра́зд-нество, *n.f.*, festival, solemnity. Пра́зд-ничность, *n.f.*, festiveness. П. настрое́ния, festive mood. Пра́зд-ничный, *adj.*, festive. П. наря́д, festive dress.

пра́зд-нич-а-ть, *v.i.*, to feast, celebrate; loaf. Он то́лько пра́здничает и ничего́ не де́лает, he just celebrates, he doesn't do any work.

пра́зд-н-ова-ть, *v.i.*, от-пра́зд-новать, *v.p.*, + *acc.*, to celebrate. П. Па́сху, to celebrate Easter. П. успе́шное оконча́ние рабо́ты, to celebrate the successful completion of a task. Пра́зднование, *n.n.*, celebration, celebrating.

пра́зд-н-ость, *n.f.*, idleness, inactivity, uselessness. П. разгово́ра, idleness of talk. П. мать всех поро́ков, (*prov.*), idleness is the mother of all vices. Пра́зд-ный, *adj.*, idle; useless, unnecessary. П-ые слова́, idle, empty words. П-ые попы́тки, idle attempts. Вести́ пра́здную жизнь, to lead an idle life. Пра́зд-но, *adv.*, idly. Сиде́ть п., to sit idly. Празд-н-о-шата́ющийся, *adj.*, *part. act. pres.*, *used as n.*, loafer. Празд-н-о-сло́вие, *n.n.*, idle talk.

поро́ж-ний, *adj.*, (*colloq.*), empty. Перелива́ть из пусто́го в поро́жнее, (*saying*), to mill the wind. Порож-ня́к, *n.m.*, (*colloq.*), empty container. Порож-няко́м, *adv.*, empty, without a load. Изво́зчик возвраща́лся домо́й порожняко́м, the cabman drove home without a passenger.

о-порож-ни́ть, *v.p.*, о-пора́ж-нивать, о-порож-ня́ть, *v.i.*, + *acc.*, to empty. О. буты́лки (стака́н), to drink up a bottle (a glass). О. кише́чник, to evacuate the intestinal tract. О-поро́ж-ненный, *adj.*, *part. pass. past*, emptied.

ПРЕТ-, ПРЕЩ-, ПРОТ(ИВ)-, FORBIDDANCE

прет-и́-ть, *v.i.*, + *dat.*, to sicken; be forbidding. По́стное ма́сло мне прети́т, vegetable oil sickens me.

вос-прет-и́ть, *v.p.*, вос-прещ-а́ть, *v.i.*, + *acc.*, + *dat.*, to prohibit, forbid. В. кому́-нибудь что́-нибудь де́лать, to

forbid someone to do something. Вос-•прещ-а́ть-ся, *v.i.r.*, *impers.*, to be prohibited. Кури́ть воспреща́ется, smoking is forbidden; no smoking. Вход воспреща́ется no admittance. Воспрещ-е́ние, *n.n.*, prohibition.
за-прет-и́ть, *v.p.*, за-прещ-а́ть, *v.i.*, + *acc.*, + *dat.*, to forbid, prohibit. З. газе́ту, to suppress a paper. За-прещ-а́ть-ся, *v.i.r.*, *impers.* to be prohibited, be forbidden. Кури́ть запреща́ется, smoking is forbidden; no smoking. За-пре́т, *n.m.*, interdiction. Наложи́ть з., to veto. Под запре́том, prohibited. За-прет-и́тельный, *adj.*, prohibitive, prohibitory. З. зако́н, prohibitory law. З. тари́ф, prohibitive tax, tariff. За-пре́т-ный, *adj.*, forbidden, restricted. З. плод, (*fig.*), forbidden fruit. З-ая зо́на, restricted area. За-прещ-е́ние, *n.n.*, prohibition. Суде́бное з., injunction. За-прещ-ённый, *adj.*, *part. pass. past*, forbidden. З-ая пье́са, banned play.
про́т-ив, *prep.*, against, opposite, contrary. Боро́ться п. врага́, to fight against the enemy. Плыть п. тече́ния, to swim against the current. Вы ничего́ не име́ете п. того́, что я курю́? Do you mind my smoking? Do you have anything against my smoking? Де́рево п. до́ма, the tree opposite the house. П. его́ ожида́ний всё сошло́ хорошо́, contrary to his expectations, all went well. Рост проду́кции п. про́шлого го́да, an increase in output over last year. Про́тив-о-, *a combining form meaning* anti-. Про́тив-о-ве́с, *n.m.*, counterpoise, counterweight. В противове́с ему́ я вы́двинул своё предложе́ние, to counterbalance his offer I made mine. Про́тив-о-возду́шная, anti-aircraft artillery. Про́тив-о-га́з, *n.m.*, gas mask. Про́тив-о-я́дие, *n.n.*, (*med.*), antidote. Про́тив-о-есте́ственный, *adj.*, unnatural. Про́тив-о-зако́нный, *adj.*, illegal, contrary to law. Он соверши́л п. посту́пок, he committed an illegal action. На-про́тив, *adv.*, on the contrary; *prep.*, opposite. Соверше́нно н., just the opposite. Н. на́шего до́ма, opposite our house.
прот-и́в-ить-ся, *v.i.r.*, вос-прот-и́в-ить-ся, *v.p.r.*, + *dat.*, to oppose, object, resist, stand up against. Одна́ полити́ческая па́ртия проти́вилась друго́й, one political party opposed the other. Вос-против-ля́ть-ся, *v.i.r.*, + *dat.*, to raise objections, stand up against. Оте́ц воспроти́вился жени́тьбе сы́на, the father objected to his son's marriage. Проти́в-ник, *n.m.*, проти́в-ница, *n.f.*, opponent; antagonist, adversary,

enemy. Вы́бить проти́вника из око́пов, to dislodge the enemy from its trenches. Против-ле́ние, *n.n.*, (*obs.*), resistance. Не-против-ле́ние, *n.n.*, non-resistance. Н. злу, non-resistance to evil. Лев Толсто́й учи́л непротивле́нию злу, Tolstoy taught non-resistance to evil. Проти́в-и́тельный, *adj.*, adversative. П. сою́з, (*gram.*), adversative conjunction. "Не" - противи́тельный сою́з, "but" is an adversative conjunction.
проти́в-н-ый, *adj.*, opposite, contrary; adverse; offensive. П. ве́тер, contrary wind. П-ая сторона́, opposite side, party. В проти́вном слу́чае, otherwise. П. за́пах, offensive odor. П. челове́к, repulsive man. Проти́в-ное, *adj.*, *also used as n.*, opposite; repulsive. Доказа́тельство от проти́вного, the rule of opposites. Проти́в-но, *adv.*, in a disgusting way; *prep.*, against. П. па́хнуть, to smell offensively. П. смотре́ть на э́ту гря́зную оде́жду, it is unpleasant to look at these dirty clothes. Де́йствовать п. указа́ниям, to act against instructions.
о-проти́в-еть, *v.p.*, + *dat.*, to become loathsome, repugnant, repulsive. Мне опроти́вела э́та пи́ща, I am sick of this food. О-проти́в-евший, *adj.*, *part. act. past*, loathsome. Я поки́нул о-мне го́род, I left the city which had become loathsome to me.
против-о-бо́рствовать, *v.i.*, + *dat.*, (*obs.*), to oppose, resist, fight against. Добро́ противобо́рствует злу, good opposes, resists evil. Против-о-обо́рство, *n.n.* (*obs.*), opposition; antagonism; combat. Враги́ вступи́ли в п., the enemies became locked in combat.
против-о-де́йствовать, *v.i.*, + *dat.*, to oppose, counteract. П. про́искам врага́, to counteract the machinations of the enemy. Против-о-де́йствие, *n.n.*, opposition, counteraction. Против-о-де́йствующий, *adj.*, *part. act. pres.*, resisting, opposing. П-ие си́лы, resisting, opposing forces.
против-о-полага́ть, *v.i.*, порт-ив-о-положи́ть, *v.p.*, + *acc.*, + *dat.*, to oppose; set against. Он противоположи́л свой доказа́тельства оппоне́нту, he set his evidence against his opponent's. Против-о-положе́ние, *n.n.*, opposition; antithesis. Против-о-поло́жность, *n.f.*, opposition; contrast, difference. П. взгля́дов, difference of opinions. Прот-ив-о-поло́жный, *adj.*, opposite, contrary. Село́ лежи́т на противополо́жном берегу́ реки́, the village is located on the opposite bank of the river.

против-о-поста́вить, *v.p.,* против-о-поставля́ть, *v.i.,* + *acc.,* + *dat.,* to contrast, set off, oppose. П. поро́к доброде́тели, to oppose vice with virtue.

против-о-ре́чить, *v.i.,* + *dat.,* to contradict; gainsay. Его́ слова́ противоре́чили его́ де́йствиям, his actions belied his words. Против-о-ре́чие, *n.n.,* contradiction. Дух противоре́чия, spirit of contradiction. Против-о-ре́чивый, *adj.,* contradictory. П-ые тре́бования, conflicting demands.

против-о-стоя́ть, *v.i.,* против-о-ста́ть, *v.p.,* + *dat.,* to confront; resist; oppose someone; stand against.

со-против-л-я́ть-ся, *v.i.r.,* + *dat.,* to resist, fight against. С. проти́внику, to stand up to the enemy. С. боле́зни, to resist, fight, disease. Со-против-ле́ние, *n.n.,* resistance, struggle. С. вла́сти, resistance to authority. С. во́здуха, air resistance. С. мета́ллов, resistance of metals. Идти́ по ли́нии наиме́ньшего сопротивле́ния, to follow the line of least resistance. Со-против-ля́емость, *n.f.,* capacity to resist.

ПРОК-, ПРОЧ-, BENEFIT, STRONG

прок, *n.m.,* (*colloq.*), use, benefit. Из э́того не бу́дет про́ку, nothing good will come of this. Что в э́том про́ку, what is the use of it. В-прок, *adv., in expressions:* Заготовля́ть в., to lay in, store. Ему́ всё идёт в., he profits by anything and everything.

про́ч-ий, *adj.,* other. И про́чее, and so on, etc. Ме́жду про́чим, by the way. В-про́ч-ем, *conj.,* however, though; nevertheless. Проч-ь, *adv.,* Away! Off! Убра́ть п., to take away, clear away. Поди́ п.! Go away! Be off! Прочь с мои́х глаз! Get out of my sight! Я не п. пойти́ в теа́тр, I'll be glad to go to the theatre. Прочь отсю́да! Get out of here! Ру́ки прочь! Hands off!

про́ч-ный, *adj.,* firm, durable, strong, solid. П. фунда́мент, stable foundation. П-ая мате́рия, durable material. П. мир, durable, lasting peace. Про́чность, *n.f.,* durability, solidity. П. о́буви, durability of shoes. Про́ч-но, *adv.,* firmly, solidly. Мост сде́лан п., the bridge is solidly built.

про́ч-и-ть, *v.i.,* + *acc.,* в + *acc.,* to designate. Его́ про́чат в председа́тели, they are running, supporting him for chairman.

у-про́ч-ить, *v.p.,* у-про́ч-ивать, *v.i.,* + *acc.,* to strenghen, consolidate. Он упро́чил своё положе́ние, he has improved his position. У-про́ч-ить-ся, *v.p.r.,* у-про́ч-ивать-ся, *v.i.r.,* to

strengthen, gain strength, become consolidated. За ним упро́чилась сла́ва выдаю́щегося учёного, he gained the reputation of an outstanding scholar. У-проч-е́ние, *n.n.,* strengthening, consolidation.

ПРОС-, ПРОШ-, ПРАШ-, REQUEST, BEGGARY

прос-и́-ть, прош-у́, *v.i.,* по-прос-и́ть, *v.p.,* + *acc.,* + *gen.,* о + *prep.,* to ask, request. Она́ проси́ла кни́гу, she asked for a book. П. ми́лостыню, to beg. П. одолже́ния, to ask a favor. П. к столу́, to call to dinner, a meal. Про́сят не кури́ть, it is requested not to smoke. Прос-и́ть-ся, *v.i.r.,* по-прос-и́ть-ся, *v.p.r.,* to ask for permission. П. в о́тпуск, to request leave. Про́сится с языка́, it is on the tip of one's tongue. Пейза́ж так и про́сится на карти́ну, this landscape begs to be painted. Прос-и́тель, *n.m.,* прос-и́тельница, *n.f.,* applicant, petitioner. Прос-и́тельный, *adj.,* petitionary. Про́с-ь-ба, *n.f.,* request; application; petition. У меня́ к вам про́сьба, I have a favor to ask of you. П. не шуме́ть, silence, please. П. о поми́ловании, to appeal for a reprieve. Прош-е́ние, *n.n.,* application, petition. Пода́ть п., to file an application, forward a petition.

во-прос-и́ть, *v.p.,* во-прош-а́ть, *v.i.,* + *acc.,* (*obs.*), to inquire, question. Во-прош-а́ющий, *adj., part. act. pres.,* questioning. В. взгляд, questioning look. Во-про́с, *n.m.,* question; matter; issue. Зада́ть вопро́с, to ask a question. Спо́рный в., moot question. Что за в.! What a question! (*in the meaning of* of course). В. чести, point of honor. В. жи́зни и сме́рти, matter of life and death. Во-прос-и́тельный, *adj.,* interrogative, inquiring, questioning. В. знак, (*gram.*), question mark. В-ое предложе́ние, (*gram.*), interrogative sentence. Во-про́с-ник, *n.m.,* questionnaire.

вы́-прос-ить, *v.p.,* вы-пра́ш-ивать, *v.i.,* + *acc.,* у + *gen.,* (*colloq.*), to wheedle, solicit, try to obtain; ask.

до-прос-и́ть, *v.p.,* до-пра́ш-ивать, *v.i.,* + *acc.,* to interrogate, question; examine. Д. свиде́телей (обвиня́емого), to question witnesses (the defendant). До-прос-и́ть-ся, *v.p.r.,* до-пра́ш-ивать-ся, *v.i.r.,* у + *gen.,* to obtain by requesting, asking, questioning. У него́ ничего́ не допро́сишься, one cannot get anything out of him. До-про́с, *n.m.,* inquest, examination. Переκрёстный д., cross-examination. Подвергáть допрóсу, to question, cross-examine.

за-прос-и́ть, *v.p.*, за-прáш-ивать, *v.i.*, + *acc.*, о + *prep.*, to ask for information. З. в пи́сьменной фóрме, to write for information, ask in writing З. высóкую цéну, to charge too much, ask exorbitant prices. За-прóс, *n.m.*, inquiry; overcharging; Сдéлать з. правúтельству, to make an inquiry of the government, ask for information, question the government (in parliament). Цéны без запрóса, fixed prices. За-прóс-ы, *n.pl.*, spiritual interests, intellectual needs.

ис-прос-и́ть, *v.p.*, ис-прáш-ивать, *v.i.*, + *acc.*, у + *gen.*, to solicit, beg; obtain. И. креди́ты, to obtain credits. И. разрешéние, to secure permission.

на-прос-и́ть, *v.p.*, на-прáш-ивать, *v.i.*, + *acc.*, *in expression*: Н. гостéй, (*colloq.*), to invite a large number of guests. На-прос-и́ть-ся, *v.p.r.*, напрáш-ивать-ся, *v.i.r.*, на + *acc.*, to obtrude oneself, invite oneself, intrude; *v.i.r. only*, to suggest itself. Н. на обéд, to invite oneself to dinner. Н. на комплимéнты, to fish for compliments. Напрáшивается сравнéние, a comparison suggests itself.

о-прос-и́ть, *v.p.*, о-прáш-ивать, *v.i.*, + *acc.*, to interrogate, examine. О. свидéтеля, to cross-examine a witness. О-прóс, *n.m.*, interrogation, inquest. О. военноплéнных, interrogation of war prisoners. О-прóс-ный, *adj.*, questioning. О. лист, questionnaire.

от-прос-и́ть-ся, *v.p.r.*, от-прáш-ивать-ся, *v.i.r.*, у + *gen.*, to ask, obtain leave; beg off.

пере-с-прос-и́ть, *v.p.*, пере-с-прáш-ивать, *v.i.*, + *acc.*, to ask again; to question one after another. Нáдо п. всех ученикóв, it is necessary to question all the students. Стари́к глухóй и потомý переспроси́л, скóлько стóит сáхар, the old man is deaf, that is why he again asked for the price of the sugar.

по-прос-и́ть, *v.p.*, *see* проси́ть.

по-прош-áй-нич-ать, *v.i.*, (*colloq.*), to beg, cadge. По-прош-áй-ничество, *n.n.*, (*colloq.*), begging, cadging. По-прош-áйка, *n.m.*, *also n.f.*, (*colloq.*), beggar, cadger.

рас-с-прос-и́ть, *v.p.*, рас-с-прáш-ивать, *v.i.*, + *acc.*, о + *prep.*, to ask about, make inquiries. Р. когó-нибудь о чём-нибудь, to ask someone about something. Врач расспроси́л больнóго о егó болéзни, the doctor questioned the patient about his illness. Рас-с-прóс-ы, *n.m.pl.*, extensive questioning.

Надоедáть с расспрóсами, to annoy, pester with questions.

с-прос-и́ть, *v.p.*, с-прáш-ивать, *v.i.*, + *acc.*, о + *prep.*, у + *gen.*, to ask, demand, inquire. С. у кондýктора, когдá отхóдит пóезд, to ask a conductor when the train leaves. С вас бýдут спрáшивать за э́то, you will be responsible for this. Спрáшивают врачá, they are asking for a doctor. С-прос-и́ть-ся, *v.p.r.*, с-прáш-ивать-ся, *v.i.r.*, у + *gen.*, to ask someone's permission; to be asked for, demanded. Нáдо спроси́ться у учи́теля, чтóбы вы́йти из клáсса, you must ask the teacher's permission to leave class. Билéты спрáшиваются у вхóда, tickets are demanded at the entrance. Спрáшивается, the question is. Спрáшивается, как вы́йти из э́того положéния, the question is how to get out of this predicament. С-прос, *n.m.*, demand. С. и предложéние, demand and supply. Без спрóса, without permission. Уходи́ть без спрóса, to leave without permission.

у-прос-и́ть *v.p.*, у-прáш-ивать, *v.i.*, + *acc.*, to entreat, obtain by entreaty. Наси́лу егó упроси́ли остáться, with great effort, he was prevailed upon to stay. У-прáш-ивание, *n.n.*, begging, entreaty.

ПРОСТ-, ПРОЩ-, SIMPLICITY, FORGIVENESS, CONDONATION

прост-óй, *adj.*, simple, easy; common, plain, ordinary. П. óбраз жи́зни, plain living. П-ы́е лю́ди, plain, homely, unpretentious people. П-óе числó, (*math.*), prime number. П-óе письмó, non-registered letter. П-óе любопы́тство, mere curiosity. Прост-áк, *n.m.*, simpleton. Игрáть роль простакá, to play the role of a simpleton. Прост-я́к, *n.m.*, simpleton. Прост-отá, *n.f.*, simplicity. Прост-овáтость, *n.f.*, simplicity, simple-mindedness, plainness. Простофи́ля, *n.m.*, *and n.f.*, duffer, ninny, dunce. Прост-éйший, *adj.*, *super.*, the simplest. Прóст-енький, *adj.*, (*colloq.*), quite simple, plain, unpretentious. Прост-и́тельный, *adj.*, pardonable, justifiable, excusable. Э́то вполнé прости́тельно, this is quite excusable. Не-прост-и́тельный, *adj.*, unpardonable, inexcusable. Н. постýпок, an unforgivable action. Прóст-о, *adv.*, simply. Э́то óчень п., this is quite simple. Онá п. ничегó не знáет, she knows nothing, she simply doesn't know anything. А лáрчик п. открывáлся, (*saying*), the solution was quite simple.

П. на́просто, (*idiom.*), simply. За́-просто, *adv.*, (*colloq.*), informally, without ceremony. Быва́ть у кого́-нибудь з., to pay informal calls on someone. По́-просту, *adv.*, simply, without ceremony. П. говоря́, bluntly speaking. С-прос-та́, *adv.*, without thinking, thoughtlessly. Не-с-прос-та́, *adv.*, not without purpose, with some hidden design. Он приходи́л к нам н., he must have come to us with a purpose. Прост-о-, *a combining form meaning* simple, unadorned. Прост-о-воло́сый, *adj.*, (*colloq.*), bareheaded, hatless. Прост-о-ду́шие, *n.n.*, openheartedness, simple-mindedness. Прост-о-ду́шный, *adj.*, openhearted, simpleminded. Прост-о-ква́ша, *n.f.*, sour milk. Прост-о-ре́чие, *n.n.*, (*ling.*), popular, common language; vernacular.

прост-и́-ть, прощ-у́, *v.p.*, прощ-а́ть, *v.i.*, + *acc.*, + *dat.*, to pardon, excuse; remit a debt. Прости́те меня́! I beg your pardon! Прост-и́ть-ся, *v.p.r.*, прощ-а́ть-ся, *v.i.r.*, по-прощ-а́ть-ся, *v.p.r.*, с + *instr.*, to say good-bye, bid farewell. Они́ до́лго проща́лись, they were a long time saying good-bye. Прощ-а́й, прощ-а́йте, good-bye, farewell, adieu. Проща́ние, *n.n.*, farewell, parting. Помаха́ть руко́й на п., to wave good-bye. Прощ-а́льный, *adj.*, parting, farewell. П-ые слова́, parting words. П. спекта́кль, farewell performance.

о-прост-и́ть, *v.p.*, о-прощ-а́ть, *v.i.*, + *acc.*, to simplify, make simple. О-прост-и́ть-ся, *v.p.r.*, о-прощ-а́ть-ся, *v.i.r.*, to ignore the outward convention-alities of life. О-прощ-е́ние, *n.n.*, simplification. Толсто́вская про́поведь опроще́ния, Tolstoy's preaching on simplifying life. О-прост-о-воло́сить-ся, *v.p.r.*, (*colloq.*), to make a fool of oneself. В учёном разгово́ре он опростоволо́сился, in a scholarly conversation he made a fool of himself. О-прост-а́ть, *v.p.*, + *acc.*, (*folk*), to empty. *See* "опорожни́ть".

рас-прост-и́-ть-ся, *v.p.r.*, рас-прощ-а́ть-ся, *v.i.r.*, с + *instr.*, to take final leave of. Р. с друзья́ми пе́ред отъе́здом, to bid friends a final farewell before departing.

у-прост-и́ть, *v.p.*, у-прощ-а́ть, *v.i.*, + *acc.*, to simplify, diminish. У. зада́чу, to simplify a problem. У. орфогра́фию, to simplify the spelling. У. смысл собы́тий, to belittle the meaning of events. У-прост-и́ть-ся, *v.p.r.*, у-прощ-а́ть-ся, *v.i.r.*, + *instr.*, to become simplified. Зада́ча упроща́ется для мла́дших ученико́в, the problem is simplified for the junior students. У-прощ-е́ние, *n.n.*, simplification. У-прощ-ённый, *adj.*, *part. pass. past*, simplified. У. спо́соб обуче́ния, simplified method of teaching. У-прощ-е́нец, *n.m.*, (*recent*), simplifier. У-прощ-е́нство, *n.n.*, (*recent*), vulgar simplification. У-прощ-е́нчество, *n.n.*, (*recent*), vulgarization.

ПРУГ-, ПРУЖ-, ПРЯГ-, ПРЯЖ-, ПРЯЧ-, ELASTICITY, SPRING; HARNESS

у-пру́г-ий, *adj.*, elastic, resilient. У-ая пружи́на, resilient spring. У-ие рессо́ры, resilient springs (*as of a vehicle*). У-пру́г-ость, *n.f.*, elasticity, resiliency. У. мышц, resilience of muscles. Под-пру́г-а, *n.f.*, girth.

у-пру́ж-и-ть, *v.i.*, + *acc.*, to make resilient. У. сталь, to make steel resilient.

пруж-и́н-а, *n.f.*, spring. Гла́вная п., mainspring. Явля́ться гла́вной пружи́ной чего́-нибудь, (*fig.*), to be the mainspring of something. Пруж-и́нка, *n.f.*, small spring, hairspring. Пруж-и́нистость, *n.f.*, elasticity, springiness. Пруж-и́нистый, *adj.*, elastic, springy. Пруж-и́нный, *adj.*, spring. П. матра́ц, spring mattress. П-ая крова́ть, bedstead with a spring mattress.

пруж-и́нить, *v.i.*, *used only in 3d pers.*, to be elastic, resilient. Рессо́ры хорошо́ пружи́нят, the springs have good resiliency. Пруж-и́нить-ся, *v.i.r.*, to be elastic, resilient. На-пру́ж-ить-ся, *v.p.r.*, на-пру́ж-ивать-ся, *v.i.r.*, (*colloq.*), to strain, become tense, taut. Му́скулы напру́жились, the muscles became strained.

су-пру́г, *n.m.*, су-пру́г-а, *n.f.*, spouse. Су-пру́г-и, *n.pl.*, husband and wife. *See* "сопряга́ть". Су-пру́ж-ество, *n.n.*, matrimony, marriage. Су-пру́ж-еский, *adj.*, conjugal, marital. С-ая жизнь, conjugal life.

пря́ж-ка, *n.f.*, clasp, buckle. П. от куша́-ка́, belt buckle.

в-пряг-а́-ть, *v.i.*, **в-пряч-ь,** *v.p.*, + *acc.*, в + *acc.*, to harness. В. лошаде́й в са́ни, to harness horses to a sleigh. В-пряг-а́ть-ся, *v.i.r.*, в-пряч-ь-ся, *v.p.r.*, в + *acc.*, to harness oneself, become harnessed.

вы-пряг-а́ть, *v.i.*, **вы́-пряч-ь,** *v.p.*, + *acc.*, to unharness. В. лошаде́й из теле́ги, unhitch horses from a cart. Вы-пряг-а́ть-ся, *v.i.r.*, вы́-пряч-ь-ся, *v.p.r.*, to be unharnessed.

за-пряг-а́ть, *v.i.*, **за-пря́ч-ь,** *v.p.*, + *acc.*, в + *acc.*, to harness, yoke. З. воло́в, to yoke oxen. З. кого-либо в работу, (*colloq.*), to set someone to work. За-пряг-а́ть-ся, *v.i.r.*, за-пря́ч-ь-ся, *v.p.r.*, to harness oneself, be harnessed, buckle down, settle down. За-пря́ж-ка, *n.f.*, team; harnessing.

на-пряг-а́ть, *v.i.*, **на-пря́ч-ь**, *v.p.*, + *acc.*, to strain. Н. все силы, to strain every nerve, every muscle. Н. слух (зрение), to strain one's ears (eyes). На-пряг-а́ть-ся, *v.i.r.*, на-пря́ч-ь-ся, *v.p.r.*, to strain oneself, exert oneself. Чрезмерно напряга́ться вредно, it is harmful to overexert oneself. На-пряж-е́ние, *n.n.*, effort, tension, strain. Слушать с напряжением, to listen with strained attention. Ток высокого напряжения, high tension current. На-пряж-ённость, *n.f.*, intensity, tenseness. Н. в работе, tension, tenseness in work. На-пряж-ённый, *adj.*, *part. pass. past*, strained, tense. Н-ые нервы, tense, strained nerves. Н-ое ожидание, tense expectation.

от-пряг-а́ть, *v.i.*, **от-пря́ч-ь**, *v.p.*, + *acc.*, to unharness, unhitch, take out of the shafts. О. лошадей, to unhitch horses. От-пряг-а́ть-ся, *v.i.r.*, от-пря́ч-ь-ся, *v.p.r.*, to be unharnessed. Пристяжная в дороге отпрягла́сь, the side horse became unhitched on the way.

пере-пряг-а́ть, *v.i.*, **пере-пря́ч-ь**, *v.p.*, + *acc.*, to reharness; change horses. Пере-пря́ж-ка, *n.f.*, changing of horses.

при-пряг-а́ть, *v.i.*, **при-пря́ч-ь**, *v.p.*, + *acc.*, to harness additional horses. П. третью лошадь к кибитке, to harness a third horse to a covered sleigh. При-пря́ж-ка, *n.f.*, harnessing.

рас-пряг-а́ть, *v.i.*, **рас-пря́ч-ь**, *v.p.*, + *acc.*, to unharness. Р. лошадей, to unharness horses. Рас-пряг-а́ть-ся, *v.i.r.*, рас-пря́ч-ь-ся, *v.p.r.*, to become unharnessed. Рас-пря́ж-ка, *n.f.*, unhitching, unharnessing.

с-пряг-а́ть, *v.i.*, **про-с-пряг-а́ть**, *v.p.*, + *acc.*, (*gram.*), to conjugate; yoke. П. глаго́л, to conjugate a verb. С-пряг-а́ть-ся, *v.i.r.*, (*gram.*), to be conjugated. С-пряж-е́ние, *n.n.*, (*gram.*), conjugation. В русском языке - два спряжения, Russian has two conjugations.

со-пряг-а́ть, *v.i.*, со-пря́ч-ь, *v.p.*, + *acc.*, to join in matrimony. *See* "супруги". Со-пряж-ён (ный), *adj.*, *part. pass. past*, invited, joined. Путь с. с опасностью, a journey fraught with danger.

у-пря́ж-ка, *n.f.*, team. У-пряж-ь, *n.f.*, harness, gear. У-пряж-ной, *adj.*, pertaining to harnessing. У-ная лошадь, draft horse, carriage horse.

ПРУД-, ПРУЖ-, POND, DAM

пруд, *n.m.*, pond. Выпустить пруд, to drain a pond. Пруд-овой, *adj.*, of or pertaining to a pond. П-а́я рыба, pond fish.

пруд-и́ть, пруж-у́, *v.i.*, + *acc.*, to dam. Их там хоть пруд пруди́, (*idiom.*), there is an abundance of them.

за-пруд-и́ть, *v.p.*, **за-пру́ж-ивать**, *v.i.*, + *acc.*, to dam, dike. З. реку плотиной, to dam a river. Толпа запруди́ла улицу, the crowd blocked the whole street. За-пру́д-а, *n.f.*, dam, weir, millpond.

пере-пруд-и́ть, *v.p.*, **пере-пру́ж-ивать**, *v.i.*, + *acc.*, to dam. П. реку, to dam a river.

ПРЫГ-, ПРЫЖ-, LEAP, JUMP, SPRING

пры́г-ну-ть, *v.p.*, пры́г-ать, *v.i.*, to jump, leap, spring. П. на одной ноге, to hop. Пры́г-ание, *n.n.*, jumping, leaping, skipping. Пры́г-алка, *n.f.*, skipping rope. Прыг-у́н, *n.m.*, jumper, hopper, leaper, skipper.

прыж-о́к, *n.m.*, jump; caper. П. с парашютом, parachute jump. П. в воду, dive into water.

в-пры́г-ну-ть, *v.p.*, *smf.*, в-пры́г-ивать, *v.i.*, в, на + *acc.*, to jump onto, into. В. в лодку, to jump into a boat.

вы́-пры́г-ну-ть, *v.p.smf.*, вы-пры́г-ивать, *v.i.*, на + *acc.*, to jump up, on, onto. В. на лошадь (на стол), to jump on a horse (on a table).

вы́-пры́г-ну-ть, *v.p.smf*, вы-пры́г-ивать, *v.i.*, из + *gen.*, to jump out. В. из окна, to jump out of a window.

до-пры́г-ну-ть, *v.p.*, до-пры́г-ивать, *v.i.*, до + *gen.*, to jump as far as, up to. Яблоки висят высоко, не допры́гнешь, the apples are hanging high, one cannot reach them by jumping. До-пры́г-ать-ся, *v.p.r.*, до-пры́г-ивать-ся, *v.i.r.*, до + *gen.*, to jump too far, in excess. Д. до изнеможения, to exhaust oneself by jumping. Д. до беды, (*fig.*), to get into trouble. Ну, что, допры́гался? (*colloq.*), Well, you've gotten in too deep.

за-пры́г-ать, *v.p.*, to begin to jump. З. от радости, to start jumping with joy.

от-пры́г-нуть, *v.p.*, *smf.*, от-пры́г-ивать, *v.i.*, от + *gen.*, to jump, spring, leap back. Мяч отпры́гнул от стены, the ball bounced back from the wall.

пере-пры́г-ну-ть, *v.p. smf.*, пере-пры́г-ивать, *v.i.*, + *acc.*, через + *acc.*, to jump over, leap over. П. ров, to jump over a ditch. П. через ручей, to jump over a stream. П. че́рез забо́р, to jump over a fence.

под-пры́г-ну-ть, *v.p., smf.,* под-пры́г-ивать, *v.i.,* to jump up, bob up and down. Он шёл, подпры́гивая, he was skipping along.

по-пры́г-ать, *v.p.,* to jump, hop about for a while. Ма́льчик попры́гал и убежа́л, the boy jumped around for a while and then ran off. По-пры́г-у́н, *n.m.,* по-пры́г-у́нья, *n.f.,* (*colloq.*), hopper.

при-пры́г-ива-ть, *v.i.,* (*colloq.*), to hop, skip. В-при-пры́ж-ку, *adv.,* skipping, hopping. Бежа́ть в., to skip along.

рас-пры́г-ать-ся, *v.p.r.,* to jump, leap, skip with zest.

с-пры́г-ну-ть, *v.p. smf.,* с-пры́г-ивать, *v.i.,* с + *gen.,* to jump, spring off, down. С. с кры́ши, to jump from a roof. С-пры́г-ивание, *n.n.,* jumping, springing off, down.

ПРЯМ-, STRAIGHTNESS, ERECTNESS

прям-о́й, *adj.,* straight, upright, erect; through; direct; frank, sincere; real. П-а́я у́лица, straight street. П-о́й у́гол, right angle. По́езд прямо́го сообще́ния, through train. Прямы́м путём, directly. П-ы́е вы́боры, direct elections. П. вопро́с (отве́т), direct question (answer). В прямо́м смы́сле э́того сло́ва, in the true sense of the word. П-а́я речь, (*gram.*), direct speech. П-о́е дополне́ние, (*gram.*), direct object. П. челове́к, sincere person. П. убы́ток, sheer loss. П. пробо́р, part in the middle of the hair. Прям-а́я, *adj., used as n.,* straight line. Провести́ прямы́ю, to draw, project a straight line. Расстоя́ние по прямо́й, in a straight line as the crow flies. Прям-ёхонько, *adv.,* straight, directly. Прям-ико́м, *adv.,* (*colloq.*), cross country. На-прям-и́к, *adj.,* straight, by the shortest route; (*fig.*), point blank. В-прям-ь, *adv.,* (*colloq.*), really, indeed, to be sure. Прям-изна́, *n.f.,* straightness. П. доро́ги, straightness of of a road.

прям-и́-ть, *v.i.,* + *acc.,* to straighten out, keep straight. П. про́волоку, to straighten a wire. Прям-ота́, *n.f.,* straightforwardness, rectitude; uprightness; straightness. П. хара́ктера, uprightness of character. Пря́м-о, *adv.,* straight, frankly, openly, exactly. Держа́ться, п., to keep oneself upright, erect. Идти́ п. к це́ли, to go straight to the goal. Попа́сть п. в цель, to hit the mark. Смотре́ть п. в глаза́ кому́-либо, to look someone straight in the

eye. Прям-о-ду́шие, *n.n.,* straightforwardness, frankness, sincerity. Прям-о-ду́шный, *adj.,* straightforward, frank, sincere. Прям-о-лине́йность, *n.f.,* straightness; straightforwardness. Прям-о-лине́йный, *adj.,* rectilinear; (*fig.*), straightforward. П. отве́т, straightforwardness of an answer. П-ое направле́ние, straight direction. П. челове́к, straightforward person. Прям-о-уго́льник, *n.m.,* (*math.*), rectangle. Прям-о-уго́льный, *adj.,* rectangular.

вы́-прям-ить, *v.p.,* вы-прям-ля́ть, *v.i.,* + *acc.,* to straighten out, rectify. В. ли́нию, to straighten a line. В. ток, to rectify a current. Вы́-прям-ить-ся, *v.p.r.,* вы-прям-ля́ть-ся, *v.i.r.,* to be straightened out, become straight; stand erect, draw oneself up. Вы-прям-и́тель, *n.m.,* rectifier.

у-прям-ить-ся, *v.i.r.,* to be obstinate, persist. У-пря́м-ец, *n.m.,* у-пря́м-ица, *n.f.,* obstinate child. У-пря́м-ство, *n.n.,* obstinacy. У-пря́м-ый, *adj.,* obstinate, stubborn. У. ребёнок, obstinate child. У-пря́м-о, *adv.,* obstinately.

за-у-пря́м-ить-ся, *v.p.r., see* упря́миться.

ПРЯТ-, ПРЯЧ-, CONCEALMENT, TIDINESS

пря́т-а-ть, пря́ч-у, *v.i.,* с-пря́т-ать, *v.p.,* + *acc.,* в + *acc.,* to hide, conceal. П. де́ньги, to hide money. П. концы́ в во́ду, (*fig.*), to conceal something successfully. Пря́т-ать-ся, *v.i.r.,* с-пря́т-ать-ся, *v.p.r.,* to hide, conceal oneself; be hidden, concealed. Пря́т-ки, *n.pl.,* hide-and-seek. Игра́ть в п., to play hide-and-seek.

за-пря́т-ать, *v.p.,* за-пря́т-ывать, *v.i.,* + *acc.,* to hide, conceal. З. что́-нибудь так, что не найти́, to conceal something so well that it cannot be found. За-пря́т-ать-ся, *v.p.r.,* за-пря́т-ывать-ся, *v.i.r.,* to hide oneself. Де́вочка запря́талась под крова́ть, the little girl hid under the bed.

пере-пря́т-ать, *v.p.,* пере-пря́т-ывать, *v.i.,* + *acc.,* to hide, conceal again. П. де́ньги в друго́е ме́сто, to transfer money to another hiding place.

при-пря́т-ать, *v.p.,* при-пря́т-ывать, *v.i.,* + *acc.,* to hide, cache; lay up, store up, put aside. П. что́-нибудь от дете́й, to hide something from children.

с-пря́т-ать, *v.p., see* пря́тать.

у-пря́т-ать, *v.p.,* у-пря́т-ывать, *v.i.,* + *acc.,* (*colloq.*), to hide, put away. У. кого́-нибудь в тюрьму́, (*colloq.*), to put someone into prison. У-пря́т-ать-ся, *v.p.r.,* у-пря́т-ывать-ся, *v.i.r.,*

to hide oneself. Котёнок упря́тался за занаве́ской, the kitten hid behind the curtain.
о-пря́т-н-ость, *n.f.,* tidiness, cleanness. О. костю́ма, tidiness of clothing. О-пря́т-ный, *adj.,* tidy, clean, orderly. О. челове́к, tidy person. О-ая ко́мната, tidy room. О-пря́т-но, *adv.,* neatly, tidily.

ПТ- BIRD

пт-и́ца, *n.f.,* bird. Пе́вчая п., singing bird. Перелётная п., migrating bird. Дома́шняя п., poultry. Пт-ице-во́д, *n.m.,* poultry farmer, breeder. Пт-ице-во́дство, *n.n.,* poultry breeding, farming. Пт-ице-ло́в, *n.m.,* fowler. Пт-ице-ло́вство, *n.n.,* fowling. Пт-ице-фе́рма, poultry farm. Пт-а́ха, *n.f.,* (*obs.*), bird. Пт-а́шка, *n.f.,* birdie. Пт-ене́ц, *n.m.,* nestling, fledgling; (*fig.*), young pupil. В гнезде́ пища́ли птенцы́, fledglings were chirping in the nest. Пт-и́чка, *n.f.,* (*dim.*), *see* пти́ца; tick. Ста́вить пти́чки в тетра́ди ученика́, (*fig., colloq.*), to make checks in a student's notebook. Пт-и́чий, *adj.,* bird, poultry. П. двор, poultry yard. С пти́чьего полёта, from a bird's-eye view. Го́род сфотографи́рован с пти́чьего полёта, this is a bird's-eye view of the city. Пт-и́чник, *n.m.,* poultry yard; aviary. Пт-и́чница, *n.f.,* poultry maid.

ПУГ-, FRIGHT

пуг-а́-ть, *v.i.,* ис-пуг-а́-ть, *v.p.,* + *acc.,* + *instr.,* to frighten, scare; intimidate, threaten. П. дете́й, to frighten children. Пуг-а́ть-ся, *v.i.r.,* ис-пуг-а́ть-ся, *v.p.r.,* to be frightened, scared, startled. Пуг-а́ние, *n.n.,* act of frightening, scaring. Пу́г-аный, *adj.,* scared, frightened. Пу́ганая воро́на куста́ бои́тся, (*saying*), once bit, twice shy; the burned child dreads fire. Пу́г-ало, *n.n.,* scarecrow, bugbear. На огоро́де поста́вили пу́гало для птиц, they put a scarecrow in the vegetable garden. Она́ вы́рядилась пу́галом, (*colloq.*), she made a fright of herself. Пуг-а́ч, *n.m.,* toy pistol; screech owl. Пуг-ли́вость, *n.f.,* fearfulness, timidity. Лань отлича́ется необыкнове́нной пугли́востью, the doe is usually timid. Пуг-ли́вый, *adj.,* fearful, easily frightened, shy, timid. П-ая ло́шадь, shy horse. Ис-пу́г, *n.m.,* fright, scare; shock. С испу́гу, from fright. Ис-пу́г-анный, *adj., part. pass. past,* frightened, scared, startled. И. взгляд, frightened look.

пуг-ну́-ть, *v.p. smf.,* пуг-а́ть, с-пуг-ивать, *v.i.,* + *acc.,* to frighten off, scare off. П. воро́ну, to scare away a crow. С. ко́шку, to scare away a cat.
вс-пуг-ну́-ть, *v.p. smf.,* вс-пуг-ивать, *v.i.,* + *acc.,* to frighten off, away. Соба́ка вспугну́ла вы́водок ди́ких у́ток, the dog scared off a covey of ducks.
вы́-пуг-ну-ть, *v.p.,* вы-пу́г-ивать, *v.i.,* + *acc.,* to scare out. В. медве́дя из берло́ги, to scare a bear out of its den.
за-пуг-а́ть, *v.p.,* за-пу́г-ивать, *v.i.,* + *acc.,* + *instr.,* to intimidate, cow. З. ребёнка, to intimidate a child. За-пу́г-анный, *adj., part. pass. past,* intimidated. З. ребёнок, intimidated, frightened child. За-пу́г-ивание, *n.n.,* intimidation.
ис-пуг-а́ть, *v.p., see* пуга́ть.
на-пуг-а́ть, *v.p.,* + *acc.,* + *instr.,* to frighten out of one's wits. Н. до сме́рти, to frighten to death. На-пуг-а́ть-ся, *v.p.r.,* to be frightened, become frightened. На-пу́г-анный, *adj., part. pass. past,* frightened, scared. Н. вид, frightened, scared look.
от-пуг-ну́-ть, *v.p.,* от-пу́г-ивать, *v.i.,* + *acc.,* + *instr.,* + *gen.,* to frighten, scare away. О. птиц от огоро́да, to drive birds away from a garden. Отпу́гивать всех свои́м мра́чным ви́дом, to drive people away with one's gloominess.
пере-пуг-а́ть, *v.p.,* + *acc.,* + *instr.,* to frighten, scare badly. Пере-пуг-а́ть-ся, *v.p.r.,* to become very frightened. Перепуга́лся не на шу́тку, he became seriously frightened. Пере-пу́г, *n.m., used in expressions:* С перепу́гу, от перепу́гу, in one's fright, from fright.
по-пуг-а́ть, *v.p.,* по-пу́г-ивать, *v.i.,* + *acc.,* + *instr.,* to frighten, scare lightly. Люби́л попуга́ть мра́чными расска́зами, he liked to startle people with his sombre stories.
при-пуг-ну́-ть, *v.p.,* при-пу́г-ивать, *v.i.,* + *acc.,* + *instr.,* (*colloq.*), to frighten, threaten. Ма́льчика припугну́ли наказа́нием, the boy was threatened with punishment.
рас-пуг-а́ть, *v.p.,* рас-пу́г-ивать, *v.i.,* + *acc.,* + *instr.,* to scare, frighten away, off. Волк распуга́л ста́до, the wolf made the flock scatter in fright.
с-пуг-ну́-ть, *v.p. smf.,* с-пу́г-ивать, *v.i.,* + *acc.,* + *instr.,* to frighten, scare off. С. воробьёв, to scare away sparrows.

ПУСК-, ПУСТ-, ПУЩ-, RELEASE

пуск, *n.m.,* starting, setting in motion. П. электроста́нции, setting a power station in motion. П. машины, starting of a machine.

пуск-а́-ть, *v.i.*, пуст-и́ть, *v.p.*, + *acc.*, to let go, allow, permit; set free; set in motion; throw; put forth. П. детей гуля́ть, to let children go for a walk. П. на во́лю, to set free, let out, release. П. во́ду (газ), to turn on water (gas). П. маши́ну, to start an engine, motor. П. ка́мнем в кого́-либо, to throw a stone at someone. П. побе́ги, to shoot, sprout. П. ко́рни, to take root. П. жильцо́в, (*colloq.*), to take in lodgers. Пусти́ть себе́ пу́лю в лоб, to blow one's brains out. Пуск-а́ть-ся, *v.i.r.*, пуст-и́ть-ся, *v.p.r.*, to start something, be launched. П. вдого́нку за ке́м-либо, to take off in pursuit of someone. П. в риско́ванное предприя́тие, to enter a risky undertaking. П. в бе́гство, to take to flight. Пуска́й, пусть, let. Пусть бу́дет так! So be it!

в-пуск-а́ть, *v.i.*, в-пуст-и́ть, *v.p.*, + *acc.*, в + *acc.*, to let in, admit, inject. Не впуска́йте его́! Don't let him in! В. жи́дкость, to inject a liquid. В-пуск, *n.m.*, admittance. В-пуск-но́й, *adj.*, (*tech.*), entrance, inlet. В. кла́пан, inlet valve.

вы-пуск-а́ть, *v.i.*, вы-пуст-ить, *v.p.*, + *acc.*, из + *gen.*, to let out, let go, release; publish; omit. В. во́ду из кра́на, to let water out of a faucet. В. из рук что́-нибудь, to drop something, let fall. В. на свобо́ду, to release, set free. Вы́-пуск, *n.m.*, issue; graduation. В. това́ров на ры́нок, release of goods on the market. В. из печа́ти, publication. В. студе́нтов, graduation of students. Руба́шка на в., a shirt worn outside the trousers. Вы-пуск-а́ние, *n.n.*, evacuation, letting out, discharge. Вы-пуск-ни́к, *n.m.*, graduate. Вы-пуск-но́й, *adj.*, discharging, graduating. В. экза́мен, final examination.

до-пуск-а́ть, *v.i.*, до-пуст-и́ть, *v.p.*, + *acc.*, к + *dat.*, to permit, allow, tolerate; assume, take for granted. Д. оши́бки, to admit, tolerate errors. Д. студе́нта к экза́мену, to admit a student to an examination. Нельзя́ д., it is inadmissible. До-пуск-а́ть-ся, *v.i.r.*, к + *dat.*, to be admitted. К экза́мену допуска́ются то́лько хоро́шие студе́нты, only good students are admitted to the examination. До́-пуск, *n.m.*, admittance; (*tech.*), tolerance, access. Име́ть д. к арестова́нным, to have access to prisoners. До-пущ-е́ние, *n.n.*, assumption. Не-до-пущ-е́ние, *n.n.*, nonadmission. До-пуст-и́мый, *adj.*, admis-

sible, tolerable. Не-до-пуст-и́мый, *adj.*, inadmissible, intolerable.

за-пуск-а́ть, *v.i.*, за-пуст-и́ть, *v.p.*, + *instr.*, в + *acc.*, to fling; neglect. З. ка́мень в окно́, to throw a stone at a window pane. З. хозя́йство, to neglect one's household. За́-пуск, *n.m.*, launching into space. З. "спу́тника" the launching of "Sputnik". За-пу́щ-енность, *n.f.*, neglect; desolation. За-пу́щ-енный, *adj.*, *part. pass. past*, neglected. З. сад, neglected garden. З-ая боле́знь, neglected illness. Бе́гать в за́пуск-и, to chase each other in a game.

ис-пуск-а́ть, *v.i.*, ис-пуст-и́ть, *v.p.*, + *acc.*, to emit, exhale, utter, expire. И. дух, (*fig.*), to expire, breathe one's last breath. Цветы́ испуска́ют прия́тный за́пах, flowers emit a pleasant fragrance.

на-пуск-а́ть, *v.i.*, на-пуст-и́ть, *v.p.*, + *gen.*, на + *acc.*, to fill; let loose. Н. воды́ в ва́нну, to fill a bathtub. Н. соба́ку на кого́-нибудь, to turn a dog on someone. На-пуск-а́ть-ся, *v.i.r.*, на-пуст-и́ть-ся, *v.p.r.*, на + *acc.*, (*colloq.*), to fall on, fly at; reprimand. Н. на кого́-нибудь с бра́нью, to fly out at someone with insults. На́-пуск, *n.m.*, overlapping; full front. Пла́тье с на́пуском, a dress with a full front. На-пуск-но́й, *adj.*, affected, unnatural. Н-а́я весёлость, affected, unnatural gaiety.

о-пуск-а́ть, *v.i.*, о-пуст-и́ть, *v.p.*, + *acc.*, to let down, lower, relax, lose courage. О. письмо́, to drop a letter in the mailbox. О. глаза́, to drop one's eyes, look down. О. ру́ки, (*fig.*), to lose heart. О-пуск-а́ть-ся, *v.i.r.*, о-пуст-и́ть-ся, *v.p.r.*, на + *acc.*, to sink, go down, submerge; become degraded. О. на коле́ни, to sink to one's knees. О. в кре́сло, to sink into an armchair. О. мора́льно, to sink morally. О. по́сле полёта, to alight. О. на дно, to sink to the bottom. О-пуск-но́й, *adj.*, movable. О-а́я дверь, trap door.

от-пуск-а́ть, *v.i.*, от-пуст-и́ть, *v.p.*, + *acc.*, to let out, dismiss; remit; forgive sins; issue (*as* clothing, supplies). О. сре́дства, to issue funds. О. во́лосы, to let one's hair grow. О. грехи́ кому́-либо, to absolve someone from sins. Меня́ отпусти́ли с рабо́ты на два часа́, I was let off from work for two hours. От-пуск-а́ть-ся, *v.i.r.*, to be let off, be dismissed; be absolved. Студе́нты отпуска́ются на кани́кулы, the students are being dismissed for the holidays. О́т-пуск, *n.m.*, leave of absence, holiday, furlough. О. по боле́зни, sick leave. В отпускý, on leave. От-пуск-нѝк, *n.m.* (*recent*), person on leave, on a holiday; vacationer. От-пуск-нóй, *adj.*, *in expression*: notice of furlough. О-бе свидéтельство, notice of furlough. О-ые дéньги, holiday wages. От-пущ-éние, *n.n.*, (*obs.*), remission. Козёл о-я, (*fig.*), scapegoat.

пере-пуск-áть, *v.i.*, пере-пуст-ѝть, *v.p.*, + *acc.*, to allow to go too far; transfer liquids, dry substances from one container into another. П. вóду из однóго прудá в другóй, to drain water from one pond into another.

под-пуск-áть, *v.i.*, под-пуст-ѝть, *v.p.*, + *acc.*, to allow to approach, come near. П. звéря на расстоя́ние вы́-стрела, to permit an animal to come within shooting distance. П. неприя́-теля, to let the enemy approach. П. шпѝльку, (*colloq.*), to make a catty remark. Под-пуск-áть-ся, *v.i.r.*, to be allowed to approach. Дéти не подпус-кáются к колóдцу, children are not allowed to approach the well.

по-пуск-áть, *v.i.*, по-пуст-ѝть, *v.p.*, + *acc.*, *dat.*, (*obs.*), to let pass, allow (through leniency), overlook. "Как же вы попустѝли такóму беззакóнию?" (*Gogol*), "How did you permit such iniquity?"

по-пуст-ѝтель-ство-вать, *v.i.*, to connive, wink at, shut one's eyes to. По-пуст-ѝтельство, *n.n.*, connivance. По-пуст-ѝтель, *n.m.*, conniver.

при-пуск-áть, *v.i.*, при-пуст-ѝть, *v.p.*, + *acc.*, to let out a seam; (*colloq.*), drive faster, speed up. П. плáтье в подóле, to lengthen the dress at the hem. Прѝ-пуск, *n.m.*, (*tech.*), allowance, margin. При-пуск-áть-ся, *v.i.r.*, при-пуст-ѝть-ся, *v.p.r.*, to rush. Он при-пустѝлся бежáть, he broke into a run.

про-пуск-áть, *v.i.*, про-пуст-ѝть, *v.p.*, + *acc.*, to let through, let by; leave out, omit; miss; filter. П. мя́со чéрез мясорýбку, to grind meat. Машинѝст-ка пропустѝла нéсколько слов, the typist omitted several words. Про-пустѝте меня́! Let me pass! П. пóезд, to miss a train. Эта бумáга пропускáет чернѝла, this paper absorbs ink. П. мѝмо ушéй, (*idiom.*), to turn a deaf ear. Про-пуск-áть-ся, *v.i.r.*, to be allowed through, be filtered. Прó-пуск, *n.m.*, absence, non-attendance; lapse, omission; blank, gap; pass, permit, password. П. лéкции, absence from a lecture. Про-пуск-нóй, *adj.*, pertaining to that which allows anything to pass through. П-áя бумáга, blotting paper, blotter. П-áя спосóбность, capacity to accomodate, take care of.

рас-пуск-áть, *v.i.*, рас-пуст-ѝть, *v.p.*, + *acc.*, to dismiss; unfurl, spread; dissolve, undo; circulate; demoralize. Р. парлáмент, to dissolve a parliament. Р. на канѝкулы, to dismiss for the holidays. Р. вóлосы, to let one's hair down. Р. сáхар, to dissolve sugar. Он распустѝл своегó сы́на, he spoiled his son. Рас-пуск-áть-ся, *v.i.r.*, рас-пуст-ѝть-ся, *v.p.r.*, to open, blossom out; become undisciplined; dissolved; become unravelled. Цветы́ распустѝлись, the flowers opened up. Чулóк рас-пустѝлся, the stocking has a run. Рас-пуск-áние, *n.n.*, solution, melting, blooming, blossoming; unknitting, unravelling. Рас-пýщ-енность, *n.f.*, lack of discipline; licentiousness. Р. нрá-вов, licentiousness, laxness of morals. Рас-пýщ-енный, *adj.*, *part. pass. past*, undisciplined, dissolute; (*colloq.*), fast. Рóс-пуск, *n.m.*, breaking up, dismissal, dissolving. Р. áрмии, demobilization.

с-пуск-áть, *v.i.*, с-пуст-ѝть, *v.p.*, + *acc.*, с + *gen.*, to lower, let loose, launch, drop; strike; overlook. С. собáку с цепѝ, to unchain a dog. С. с лéстницы, to knock off a ladder, kick downstairs. Я емý э́того не спущý, I'll not let him get by with this. С. флаг, to haul down a flag. Спустя́ рукавá, (*idiom.*), carelessly, negligently. С-пуск-áть-ся, *v.i.r.*, с-пуст-ѝть-ся, *v.p.r.*, to descend, come down, be lowered, launched. С. по лéстнице, to go downstairs. С. на зéмлю, to land. С. по рекé, to flow with the current of a river. С-пуск, *n.m.*, lowering, hauling down; launching, descent, loss of altitude; slope; trigger. Крутóй с., steep slope. Не давáть ко-мý-либо спýску, to give someone no quarter. С-пуск-нóй, *adj.*, drain. С-пуск-овóй, trigger. С. механѝзм, trigger mechanism. С-пуст-я́, *prep.*, + *acc.*, after, later. С. нéсколько дней, after a few days, a few days later. Немнóго с., not long after.

у-пуск-áть, *v.i.*, у-пуст-ѝть, *v.p.*, + *acc.*, to let escape, let slip; neglect; lose sight of. У. конéц верёвки, to let the end of a rope slip. У. слýчай, to miss an opportunity. У. из вѝду чтó-либо, to lose sight of something. У-пуск-áть-ся, *v.i.r.*, to be neglected, over-looked. Мнóгое вáжное упускáется из вѝду, many important matters are over-looked. У-пущ-éние, *n.n.*, omission, neglect. У. по слýжбе, neglect of one's duties as a civil servant.

ПУСТ-, EMPTINESS, VOID

пуст-óй, *adj.*, empty, hollow; uninhabited,

deserted. П. стака́н, empty glass. П-о́е ме́сто, blank space, vacant seat. На п. желу́док, on an empty stomach. П-а́я болтовня́, idle talk. П-ы́е мечты́, castles in the air. С пусты́ми рука́ми, empty-handed. Перелива́ть из пусто́го в поро́жнее, (colloq.), to talk aimlessly. Пуст-ы́шка, n.f., (colloq.), shallow person.

пуст-ова́-ть, v.i., to be vacant, uninhabited; lie fallow. Помеще́ние пусту́ет, the premises are vacant. Пуст-ова́тый, adj., rather empty. Пу́ст-о, adj., pred., empty. В ко́мнате бы́ло п., the room was empty. Чтоб тебе́ п. бы́ло! (colloq.), I wish you were dead. Пу́ст-о-, a combining form meaning empty. Пуст-о-голо́вый, adj., empty-headed. Пуст-о-зво́н, n.m., idle talker, windbag. Пуст-о-ме́ля, n.m., and n.f., twaddler. Пуст-о-поро́жний, adj., empty, vacant. Пуст-о-сло́вие, n.n., idle talk, twaddle. Пуст-ота́, n.f., emptiness, void; (fig.), futility; frivolousness. Пуст-о-те́лый, adj. (tech.), hollow. П. кирпи́ч, hollow brick. Пуст-о-цве́т, n.m., barren, sterile flower.

пуст-е́-ть, v.i., о-пуст-е́ть, v.p., to become empty, become deserted. С наступле́нием но́чи у́лица опусте́ла, as night fell, the street became deserted. О-пуст-е́лый, adj., deserted, empty. О. дом (сад), deserted house (garden). О-пуст-е́ние, n.n., depopulation.

за-пуст-е́-ть, v.p., (obs.), to grow desolate. За-пуст-е́ние, n.n., neglect, desolation; loneliness. Ме́рзость запусте́ния, (fig., Bib.), abomination of desolation.

пу́ст-ошь, n.f., waste plot of land, waste ground. Пу́щ-а, n.f., dense virgin forest. Белове́жская Пу́ща, State forest in White Russia.

о-пуст-ош-и́-ть, v.p., о-пуст-оша́ть, v.i., + acc., to devastate, ravage, lay waste. Война́ опустоши́ла города́ и селе́ния, the war ravaged the cities and villages. О-пуст-оше́ние, n.n., devastation, ravage. О. городо́в неприя́телем, devastation of cities by an enemy. О-пуст-оше́нный, adj., part. pass. past, devastated, wasted. О. го́род, desolated city. О-пуст-оши́тельный, adj., devastating. О. пожа́р (о-ая война́), devastating fire (war).

пуст-ы́ня, n.f., desert, waste, wilderness. Глас вопию́щего в пусты́не, (Bib.), a voice crying in the wilderness. Пуст-ы́нник, n.m., hermit; anchorite. Пу́ст-ынь, n.f., hermitage. Пуст-ы́нный, adj., desert, uninhabited. Пуст-ы́рь, n.m., vacant land, lot.

пуст-я́к, n.m., trifle, triviality, futility. Пустяки́! Nonsense! Спо́рить из-за пустяко́в, to split hairs; to argue over nonsense. Тра́тить вре́мя по пустяка́м, to waste one's time on trifles. Пуст-яко́вый, adj., trifling, trivial, futile, petty. Пуст-я́чный, adj., trifling, trivial, futile, petty. П-ое де́ло, child's play.

в-пуст-у́ю, adv., for nothing, to no purpose. Оказа́лось, я всё э́то сде́лал впусту́ю, it turned out that I did it all for nothing.

по́-пуст-у, adv., in vain, to no purpose. Не тра́тьте вре́мя по́пусту! don't waste your time!

ПУТ-, ROUTE, ROAD

пут-ь, n.f., way, route, path; journey, passage; means. Далёкий п., long way. Железнодоро́жный п., railway track, railroad. Во́дный п., waterway. Пути́ сообще́ния, means of communications. Сби́ться с пути́, to lose one's way. Мле́чный Путь, (astr.), Milky Way. Счастли́вый путь! Happy journey, Bon voyage. Дыха́тельные пути́, respiratory tract. Ми́рным путём, amicably, peacefully. Соврати́ть с пути́, (idiom.), to lead astray. Пут-ёвка, n.f., (recent), pass. П. в жизнь, (fig.), road to life; new deal. П. в дом о́тдыха, (recent), pass to a rest home. Пут-е-води́тель, n.m., guide, guidebook. Пут-е-во́дный, adj., guiding, leading. П-ая звезда́, guiding star. Пут-ево́й, adj., itinerary, travelling. П-а́я ско́рость, ground speed. П-а́я ка́рта, road map. Не-пут-ёвый, adj., (colloq.), good for nothing, wastrel. Н. челове́к, bad lot. Пут-е́ец, n.m. (colloq.), student of the Institute of Means of Communication; railway engineer. Пут-ём, prep., by means of; adv., properly, at the right time. Узна́ть что́-нибудь путём опро́са населе́ния, to learn something by inquiring of the inhabitants. Он никогда́ путём не пое́ст, he never takes regular meals. Пут-е-ме́р, n.m., adometer, perambulator. Пут-е-прово́д, n.m., railway overpass.

пут-е-ше́ствовать, v.i., to travel. Он лю́бит п., he is fond of travelling. Пут-е-ше́ственник, n.m., пут-е-ше́ственница, n.f., traveler. Пут-е-ше́ствие, n.n., journey, voyage, trip. Кругосве́тное п., voyage around the world. Пу́т-ник, n.m., пу́т-ница, n.f., traveler. По-пу́т-чик, n.m., по-пу́т-чица, n.f., fellow-traveler. По-пу́т-ный, adj., following, passing. П-ое замеча́ние, passing remark. П. ве́тер, favorable wind.

По-пу́т-но, *adv.*, in passing, on one's way, incidentally, at the same time. пере-пу́т-ь-е, рас-пу́т-ь-е, *n.n.*, crossroads. На пере-пу́ть-и, на рас-пу́ть-и, at the crossroads. Он стоя́л на рас-пу́тьи и не знал, куда́ идти́, he stood at the crossroads and did not know where to go. Рас-пу́т-ица, *n.f.*, spring and autumn season of bad roads. Осе́нняя р., bad roads in autumn. на-пу́т-ство-вать, *v.i.*, + *acc.*, to exhort. На-пу́т-ствие, *n.n.*, parting words, exhortation. На-пу́т-ственный, *adj.*, pertaining to parting. Н. моле́бен, service held before starting a journey. Н-ое сло́во, parting word. со-пу́т-ство-вать, *v.i.*, + *dat.*, to accompany, attend. Со-пу́т-ствующий, *adj., part. act. pres.*, used as *n.*, traveling aid, attendant. С-ие обстоя́тельства, accompanying circumstances! С-пу́т-ник, *n.m.*, fellow traveler; (*astron.*), satellite. пу́т-ный, *adj.*, (*colloq.*), sensible, decent; used as *n.*, something sensible. Из него́ ничего́ пу́тного не вы́йдет, you'll never make a man of him. Скажи́ пу́тное сло́во! Say something sensible! бес-пу́т-нич-ать, бес-пу́т-ствовать, *v.i.*, to lead an immoral life. Бес-пу́т-ство, *n.n.*, dissipation, debauchery, libertinage. Бес-пу́т-ник, *n.m.*, debauchee. Бес-пу́т-ный, *adj.*, dissipated, dissolute, licentious. Б. челове́к, immoral person. рас-пу́т-нич-ать, рас-пу́т-ствовать, *v.i.*, to lead a dissolute life. Рас-пу́т-ник, *n.m.*, рас-пу́т-ница, *n.f.*, debauchee, libertine, rake, (*f.*, harlot). Рас-пу́т-ный, *adj.*, dissolute, wanton, rakish. Р-ая жизнь, dissolute life. Рас-пу́т-ство, *n.n.*, dissipation, debauchery, libertinism.

ПУТ-, CONFUSION, ENTANGLEMENT

пу́т-а-ть, *v.i.*, с-пу́т-ать, *v.p.*, + *acc.*, + *instr.*, to tangle, confuse; fetter. П. ни́тки (верёвки), to tangle threads (ropes). Отвеча́я на вопро́сы, он так волнова́лся, что всё пу́тал, while answering he was so excited that he confused everything. Пу́т-ать-ся, *v.i.r*, с-пу́т-ать-ся, *v.p.r.*, to tell a confused story. П. в показа́ниях, to give confused evidence. Не пу́тайся не в своё де́ло! (*colloq.*), Mind your own business! Во́лосы спу́тались, my hair has become snarled. Пу́т-аник, *n.m.*, (*colloq.*), fumbler. Пу́т-аница, *n.f.*, confusion, meddle, tangle. Вноси́ть пу́таницу, to introduce confusion. Пу́т-аный, *adj.*, (*colloq.*), confused, confusing, tangled. П. челове́к, (*colloq.*),

confused person; blunderer. П-ая тео́рия confused theory. Пу́т-ы, *n.pl.*, fetters; (*fig.*), chains. в-пу́т-ать, *v.p.*, в-пу́т-ывать, *v.i.*, + *acc.*, в + *acc.*, to twist in, involve, implicate. В. кого́-либо в неприя́тное де́ло, to implicate someone in a disagreeable affair. В-пу́т-ать-ся, *v.p.r.*, в-пу́т-ывать-ся, *v.i.r.*, в + *acc.*, to become implicated, mixed up in. вы́-пу́т-ать, *v.p.*, вы-пу́т-ывать, *v.i.*, + *acc.*, из + *gen.*, to disentangle, extricate, disengage В. коне́ц верёвки, to disentangle an end of a rope. В. из беды́, to extricate from a predicament. Вы́-пут-ать-ся, *v.p.r.*, вы-пу́т-ывать-ся, *v.i.r.*, из + *gen.*, to be extricated, extricate oneself. В. из долго́в, to get out of debt. за-пу́т-ать, *v.p.*, за-пу́т-ывать, *v.i.*, + *acc.*, to tangle, muddle up; confuse. З. де́ло, to muddle up a business. З. верёвку, to tangle up a rope. За-пу́т-ать-ся, *v.p.r.*, за-пу́т-ывать-ся, *v.i.r.*, в + *prep.*, to be entangled, become embroiled. Бечёвка запу́талась, the string became tangled. З. в долга́х, to be deep in debt. За-пу́т-анность, *n.f.*, intricacy. З. суде́бного де́ла, intricacies of a lawsuit. За-пу́т-анный, *adj.*, *part. pass. past*, tangled, intricate, involved. З. вопро́с, difficult, complex question. З-ое положе́ние, difficult position, situation. на-пу́т-ать, *v.p.*, + *acc.*, + *gen.*, to make a mess; to have it all wrong. Она́ всё напу́тала, she has it all wrong. о-пу́т-ать, *v.p.*, о-пу́т-ывать, *v.i.*, + *acc.*, + *instr.*, to wind around; (*fig.*), to entangle. пере-пу́т-ать, *v.p.*, пере-пу́т-ывать, *v.i.*, + *acc.*, to entangle, confuse, mix up, muddle up. П. ве́щи, to get things mixed. П. имена́ (адреса́), to confuse names (addresses). Пере-пу́т-ать-ся, *v.p.r.*, пере-пу́т-ывать-ся, *v.i.r.*, to be entangled, become confused, mixed up. Ни́тки перепу́тались, the threads became entangled. Всё перепу́талось у меня́ в голове́, everything in my head became confused. по-пу́т-ать, *v.p.*, see пу́тать, спу́тать, перепу́тать. Ви́дно, враг попу́тал меня́ (*folk*), obviously, the devil led me astray. рас-пу́т-ать, *v.p.*, рас-пу́т-ывать, *v.i.*, + *acc.*, to disentangle, unravel, untwine; (*fig.*), to disembroil, puzzle out. Р. у́зел, to unravel a knot. Р. ло́шадь, to unshackle a horse. Р. тёмное де́ло, to unravel an intricate case. Рас-пу́т-ать-ся, *v.p.r.*, рас-пу́т-ывать-ся, *v.i.r.*, to become unraveled, undone, disentangled. Р. с долга́ми, to get out of debt.

с-пу́т-ать, *v.p.,* с-пу́т-ывать, *v.i.,* + *acc.,* to mix up, confuse, entangle; *see* пу́тать. С. ра́зные коло́ды карт, to mix packs of cards. С-пу́т-ать-ся, *v.p.r.,* с-пу́т-ывать-ся, *v.i.r.,* to become entangled, confused; *see* пу́таться. Зря я с ним спу́тался, (*colloq.*), for no good reason I got mixed up with him. С-пу́т-анный, *adj., part. pass. past,* entangled. С-пу́т-анно, *adv.,* confusedly.

ПУХ-, ПУШ-, SWELLING, DOWN

пух, *n.m.,* down. Га́гачий п., eider down. Лебя́жий п., swan's down. Ни пу́ха, ни пера́, (*idiom.*), Good luck! Разоде́ться в пух и прах, (*colloq.*), to don all one's finery. Ры́льце в пуху́, пушку́, (*colloq.*), to be guilty; (*lit.,* of a fox) to have chicken feathers on his muzzle. Пух-ови́к, *n.m.,* feather bed. Пух-о́вка, *n.f.,* powder puff. Пух-о́вый, *adj.,* downy. П-ое одея́ло, comforter.

пу́х-ну-ть, *v.i.,* to swell. Рука́ пу́хнет, the hand is swelling. Пу́х-лый, *adj.,* plump, pudgy. Пу́х-ленький, *adj.,* chubby. П-ие ру́чки ребёнка, plump little hands of a child.

вс-пу́х-ну-ть, *v.p.,* вс-пух-а́ть, *v.i.,* to swell up, become swollen. У меня́ в сыру́ю пого́ду вспуха́ют па́льцы, in damp weather my fingers swell.

за-пу́х-ну-ть, *v.p.,* за-пух-а́ть, *v.i.,* (*colloq.*), to swell all over. У него́ глаза́ запу́хли, his eyes are swollen.

на-пу́х-ну-ть, *v.p.,* на-пух-а́ть, *v.i.,* to swell considerably. Места́ уку́сов на руке́ напу́хли, my hands have swollen where they were bitten. На-пух-а́ние, *n.n.,* swelling.

о-пу́х-ну-ть, *v.p.,* о-пух-а́ть, *v.i.,* to swell all over. Лицо́ отекло́ и опу́хло, the face is all swollen. О-пух-оль, *n.f.,* swelling; tumor. О. пе́чени, swelling of the liver. Вскры́тие о́пухоли, cutting open of a tumor. О-пу́х-ший, (о-пу́х-лый, *colloq.*), swollen. О-ие ру́ки, swollen hands.

при-пу́х-ну-ть, *v.p.,* при-пух-а́ть, *v.i.,* to swell slightly. Щека́ припу́хла от флю́са, the cheek is slightly swollen from a bad tooth. При-пу́х-лость, *n.f.,* slight swelling. П. о́коло но́са (гла́за), slight swelling near the nose (the eyes). При-пу́х-лый, *adj.,* slightly swollen.

рас-пу́х-ну-ть, *v.p.,* рас-пух-а́ть, *v.i.,* от + *gen.,* to swell considerably, bloat. Па́лец распу́х от уши́ба, the finger

swelled from a bruise. Рас-пух-а́ние, *n.n.,* swelling; (*med.*), intumescence.

пуш-о́к, *n.m.,* (*dim., see* пух), fluff, flue; bloom; pubescence. П. чертопо́лоха, thistledown. Пуш-и́нка, *n.f.,* a bit of fluff. Снёжная п., snowflake. В во́здухе выю́тся снёжные пуши́нки, snowflakes are fluttering in the air. Пуш-и́стый, *adj.,* downy, fluffy. П. кот, thick-furred cat. П-ые во́лосы, fluffy hair.

пуш-и́-ть, *v.i.,* рас-пуш-и́ть, *v.p.,* + *acc.,* to make fluffy. П. шерсть, to make wool fluffy. Нача́льник распуши́л свои́х подчинённых, (*fig.*), the chief reprimanded his subordinates. Р. в пух и прах, to smash everything. Рас-пуш-и́ть-ся, *v.p.r.,* to become downy, fluffy.

вы́-пуш-ить, *v.p.,* + *acc.,* + *instr.,* to make piping. Вы́-пуш-ка, *n.f.,* edging, piping, braid.

за-пуш-и́ть, *v.p.,* + *acc.,* to cover slightly with hoarfrost. "Серебри́стый и́ней запуши́л окно́," (*Nikitin*), "silver frost covered the window." За-пуш-и́ть-ся, *v.p.r.,* + *instr.,* to become covered with a fluffy substance. Доро́га запуши́лась сне́гом, there was a light coating of snow on the road.

о-пуш-и́ть, *v.p.,* о-пуш-а́ть, *v.i.,* + *acc.,* + *instr.,* to edge, trim with fur; powder with snow, cover with hoar frost. О. ме́хом, to trim (a coat) with fur. О. сне́гом, to powder with snow. О-пу́ш-ка, *n.f.,* trimming, edging; border, edge of a forest. Пальто́ с ли́сьей опу́шкой, coat trimmed with fox fur. Дом стоя́л на опу́шке ле́са, the house stood on the edge of the forest. О-пуш-ённый, *adj., part. pass. past,* trimmed with, powdered with. О. ме́хом, furtrimmed. О. сне́гом, powdered with snow. О-пуш-и́ть-ся, *v.p.r.,* о-пуш-а́ть-ся, *v.i.r.,* + *instr.,* to grow feathers; to be trimmed, edged. Птенцы́ опуши́лись, the fledglings grew feathers.

пу́ш-ка, *n.f.,* gun, cannon. Зени́тная п., anti-aircraft gun. Стреля́ть из пу́шек по воробья́м, (*saying*), to indulge in futile activity. Пуш-ка́рь, *n.m.* (*hist.*), gunner. Пу́ш-ечный, *adj.,* gun, cannon. П-ая стрельба́, gunfire, gunnery. П-ое мя́со, (*fig.*), cannon fodder.

пуш-ни́на, *n.f.,* furs, fur skins, peltry. Торгова́ть пушни́ной, to trade in furs. Пуш-но́й, *adj.,* pertaining to fur, furs. П. зверь, fur bearing animal. П. това́р, furs. П. про́мысел, fur trade.

ПЧЕЛ-, ПЧЁЛ-, BEE

пчел-а́, *n.f.,* bee, пчёл-ы, *n.pl.,* bees,

Пчела́-рабо́тница, worker bee. Пчёл-ка, пчёл-о́чка, *n.m.*, (*dim.*), bee. Пчёл-ь-ник, *n.m.*, apiary. Пчел-и́ный, *adj.*, of or pertaining to bees. П. воск, bee's wax. П. рой, swarm of bees. П. у́лей, beehive. Пчел-и́стый, *adj.*, rich, abundant in bees. Пчел-о-во́д, *n.n.*, beekeeper, apiarist. Пчел-о-во́дство, *n.n.*, beekeeping, apiculture. Пчел-о-во́дный, *adj.*, pertaining to apiculture.

ПШЕН-, ПШОН-, GRAIN, WHEAT

пшен-о́, *n.n.*, millet. Пшен-и́ца, *n.f.*, wheat. Ярова́я (ози́мая) п., spring (winter) wheat. Пшен-и́чный, *adj.*, of or pertaining to wheat. П. ко́лос, ear of wheat. П. хлеб, wheat bread.
пшо́н-н-ик, *n.m.*, millet pudding. Пшо́н-ный, *adj.*, millet. П-ая крупа́, millet meal. П-ая ка́ша, millet gruel, porridge.

ПЫЛ-(Ь)-, DUST

пыл-ь, *n.f.*, dust. Угольная п., coal dust. Цвето́чная п., pollen. Быть в пыли́, to be covered with dust. Пуска́ть пыль в глаза́, (*colloq.*), to cut a figure, make a splash. Пыл-и́нка, *n.f.*, speck of dust. Пыл-ь-ник, *n.m.*, dust-cloak, dust-coat; (*bot.*), anther. Пыл-ь-ца́, *n.f.*, (*bot.*), pollen. Пыл-ь-ный, *adj.*, dusty. П-ая тря́пка, duster. Пыл-ь-но, *adj.*, *pred.*, *impers.*, it is dusty. Пыл-е-непроница́емый, *adj.*, dustproof. Пыл-е-со́с, *n.m.*, vacuum cleaner.
пыл-и́-ть, *v.i.*, на-пыл-и́ть, *v.p.*, + *instr.*, to raise dust, fill the air with dust. П. метло́й, to raise dust with a broom. Пыл-и́ть-ся, *v.i.r.*, to become dusty. Кни́ги на по́лке пыля́тся, books become dusty on a shelf.
за-пыл-и́ть, *v.p.*, + *acc.*, to cover with dust. З. башмаки́ (пла́тье), to get one's shoes (dress), dusty. За-пыл-и́ть-ся, *v.p.r.*, to become dusty.
о-пыл-и́ть, *v.p.*, о-пыл-я́ть, *v.i.*, + *acc.*, to pollinate. Ве́тер опыли́л цветы́, the wind pollinated flowers. О-пыл-е́ние, *n.n.*, pollination.
рас-пыл-и́ть, *v.p.*, рас-пыл-я́ть, *v.i.*, + *acc.*, to pulverize, atomize; disperse, spray, scatter. Р. нефть, to refine crude oil. Рас-пыл-и́ть-ся, *v.p.r.*, рас-пыл-я́ть-ся, *v.i.r.*, to be dispersed, scattered, pulverized. Рас-пыл-е́ние, *n.n.*, dispersion, atomization, scattering. Рас-пыл-ённость, *n.f.*, dispersion, atomization, scattering. Р. сил, dispersion of forces, of means. Рас-пыл-и́тель, *n.m.*, sprayer, atomizer; pulverizer.

ПЫТ-, ENDEAVOR, ATTEMPT

пыт-а́-ть, *v.i.*, + *acc.*, to torture, torment; (*colloq.*), try, question. П. заключённого, to torture a prisoner. П. кого́-либо жа́ждой, to torture with thirst. Пыт-а́ть-ся, *v.p.r.*, по-пыт-а́ть-ся, *v.i.r.*, to attempt, try, endeavor. П. убеди́ть, to plead with, try to persuade. Пы́т-ка, *n.f.*, torture, torment. Подверга́ть пы́тке, to subject to torture; put to the question. Ору́дие пы́тки, instrument of torture. Пыт-ли́вость, *n.f.*, keenness. П. ума́, keenness of the mind, of intelligence. Пыт-ли́вый, *adj.*, searching, keen. П. ю́ноша, keen-minded youth.
вы́-пыт-ать, *v.p.*, вы-пы́т-ывать, *v.i.*, + *acc.*, у + *gen.*, to elicit something from someone, extort. В. пра́вду, to elicit the truth from someone. В. все та́йны, to extort all the secrets.
до-пыт-а́ть-ся, *v.p.r.*, до-пы́т-ывать-ся, *v.i.r.*, to find out, elicit, try to find out. Я допыта́лся, где они́ бы́ли, I have found out where they were.
ис-пыт-а́ть, *v.p.*, ис-пы́т-ывать, *v.i.*, + *acc.*, to try, test, put to the test; experience, feel. И. де́йствие мото́ра, to test an engine. И. свои́ си́лы, to try one's strength. И. страх (го́лод), to experience fright (hunger). И. удово́льствие, to experience, feel pleasure. Ис-пыт-а́ние, *n.n.*, test, trial; ordeal. Быть на испыта́нии, to be on trial, on probation. Вы́держать и., to pass muster. Пройти́ тя́жкие испыта́ния, to experience severe trials. Приёмные испыта́ния в университе́т, entrance examination into a university. Вступи́тельные испыта́ния, entrance examinations. Вы́держать и., to pass an examination. Ис-пы́т-анный, *adj.*, *part. pass. past,* well tried, tested. И друг, tried friend. И-ое сре́дство, tested remedy. Ис-пыт-а́тель, *n.m.*, tes.er. Лётчик-испыта́тель, test pilot. Ис-пыт-а́тельный, *adj.*, test, trial; probationary. И. полёт, test flight. И-ая ста́нция, experimental station. Ис-пыт-у́емый, *adj.*, *part. pass. pres.*, candidate, applicant; one who is taking an examination. Ис-пыт-у́юще, *adv.*, in a probing way. И. смотре́ть, to look searchingly. Ис-пыт-у́ющий, *adj.*, *part. act. pres.*, searching. И. взгляд, searching look.
по-пыт-а́ть, *v.p.*, + *gen.*, to try, attempt, venture; torture for a short time. П. сча́стья, to try one's luck. По-пыт-а́ть-ся, *v.p.r.*, *see* пыта́ться. По-пы́т-ка, *n.f.*, attempt, endeavor. Отча́янная п., desperate attempt. По-пы́т-ка не пы́тка, и спро́с не беда́, (*saying*), nothing ventured, nothing gained.

ó-пыт, *п.т.,* experiment, test, trial; experience. Производи́ть о́пыты, to experiment, conduct experiments. Жите́йский о., knowledge of life. О. войны́, war experience. Убеди́ться на о́пыте, to learn through experience. О́-пыт-ность, *п.f.,* experience; proficiency. О́-пыт-ный, *adj.,* experienced; experimental. О. преподава́тель (учи́тель), experienced instructor (teacher). О-ая ста́нция, experimental station.

ПЫХ-, ПЫШ-, PANTING, PUFFING

пы́х-ать, *(colloq.),* **пыш-а́ть, пыш-у́,** *v.i.,* **пых-ну́ть,** *v.p. smf.,* to pant; blaze. От пе́чки пы́шет жа́ром, the stove is blazing hot. Пы́ш-уший, *adj., part. act. pres.,* blazing. П. здоро́вьем, brimming with health. П. гне́вом, boiling with rage; raging. Пы́ш-ка, *п.f.,* puff, doughnut, bun; plump person. Пы́шность, *п.f.,* splenaor, magnificence. П. убра́нства, splendor of decorations. Пы́ш-ный, *adj.,* magnificent, splendid, luxuriant; fluffy. П-ые во́лосы, luxuriant hair. П-ый наря́д, magnificent apparel. П. пиро́г, fluffy pie.

пых-ну́-ть, *v.p.smf., (colloq.),* see пы́хать, пыша́ть.

вс-пы́х-ну-ть, *v.p.smf.,* вс-пы́х-ивать, *v.i.,* to blaze up, break out in flames; burst out; flush. Вспы́хнул пожа́р, a fire broke out. Война́ вспы́хнула, war broke out. В. гне́вом (негодова́нием) to flare up with rage (with indignation). Вс-пы́ш-ка, *п.f.,* flash, outbreak, outburst. В. гне́ва, outburst of anger.

за-пых-а́ть-ся, *v.p., (colloq.),* to be short of, out of breath. Взбира́ясь на пя́тый эта́ж, он совсе́м запыха́лся, he became quite breathless while climbing to the fifth floor.

пых-т-é-ть, пых-чу́, *v.i.,* про-пых-те́ть, *v.p.,* to puff, pant. Парово́з пыхти́т, the locomotive is puffing. Второ́й час он пыхти́т над зада́чей, *(colloq.),* he has been slaving over this problem for nearly two hours.

за-пых-т-е́ть, *v.p., (colloq.),* to start puffing. Запыхте́л, как парово́з, he started to puff like an engine.

по-пы́х-ивать, *v.i.,* + *instr., (colloq.),* to puff away. П. сига́рой, to puff away at a cigar. П. из тру́бки, to puff away at a pipe.

ПЯТ-, ПЯЧ-, HEEL

пят-а́, *п.f.,* heel; abutment. Ходи́ть за ке́м-либо по пята́м, to follow on someone's heels. Ахилле́сова п., Achilles' heel. С головы́ до пят, from head to foot. Пя́т-ка, *п.f.,* heel. Двойна́я п. чулка́, double heel of a stocking. У него́ душа́ в пя́тки ушла́, *(fig.),* his heart sank into his boots. Лиза́ть кому́-либо пя́тки, *(fig., derog.),* to lick someone's boots. Удира́ть так, что пя́тки сверка́ют, to run away fast, to show one's heels.

пя́т-и-ть, *v.i.,* по-пя́т-ить, *v.p.,* + *acc.,* to back up, cause to move back. П. ло́шадь, to make a horse back up. Пя́т-ить-ся, *v.i.r.,* по-пя́т-ить-ся, *v.p.r.,* + to move backwards, go back. По-пя́т-ный, *adj., as in expression:* идти́ на п., to go back on one's word. Попя́тное движе́ние, movement in reverse.

вы́-пят-ить, *v.p.,* вы-пя́ч-ивать, *v.i.,* + *acc.,* to stick out, thrust out, protrude; *(fig.),* overemphasize, overstress. В. гу́бы, to stick out one's lips. Вы́-пят-ить-ся, *v.p.r.,* вы-пя́ч-ивать-ся, *v.i.r.,* to bulge out, stick out, protrude. Вы́-пяч-енный, *adj., part. pass. past,* protruding.

с-пя́т-ить, *v.p.,* с + *gen., colloq., in expression:* С. с ума́, to go mad, go out of one's mind.

пре-пя́т-ствовать, *v.i.,* вос-пре-пя́т-ствовать, *v.p.,* + *dat.,* to prevent, hinder. П. чьи́м-нибудь наме́рениям, to frustrate someone's intentions. Пре-пя́т-ствие, *п.п.,* obstacle, impediment, hindrance. Чини́ть препя́тсвия кому́-либо, to put obstacles in someone's path. Ска́чка с препя́тствиями, obstacle race, steeple-chase. Бес-пре-пя́т-ственно, *adv.,* without hindrance.

вс-пят-ь, *adv.,* backwards. Возврати́ть-ся, в., to return, retrace one's steps. Во́лга в. не побежи́т, the Volga will not flow backwards.

о-пя́т-ь, *adv.,* again.

за-пя́т-ки, *п.pl., (obs.),* footboard behind a carriage. Лаке́й на запя́тках каре́ты, a footman on the footboard of the coach.

ПЯТН-, STAIN, BLEMISH

пятн-ó, *п.п.,* spot, blot, stain, blemish. Со́лнечные пя́тна, sun spots. Роди́мое п., birthmark. Пла́тье в пя́тнах, stained dress. Это п. на его́ репута́ции, this is a blemish on his reputation. И на со́лнце есть пя́тна, *(saying),* nothing is perfect. Бе́лое п. на географи́ческой ка́рте - неиссле́дованная ме́стность, a white spot on a map represents unexplored lands. Пятн-ышко, *п.п., (dim.),* see пятно́.

пятн-а́-ть, *v.i.,* за-пят-на́ть, *v.p.,* + *acc.,*

to stain, spot, brand, blemish; put out (in game of tag). З. своё и́мя, to sully one's name, reputation. Пятн-а́ть-ся, *v.i.r.*, за-пятн-а́ть-ся, *v.f.r.*, to soil easily. Эта мате́рия легко́ пятна́ется, this cloth soils easily. Пятн-а́шки, *n.pl.*, tag (children's game). Пятн-и́стый, *adj.*, spotted, dappled, blotched. П. оле́нь, spotted deer. П. тиф, (*med.*), typhus. За-пятн-анный, *adj.*, *part. pass. past*, soiled, sullied. З-ая репута́ция, a sullied reputation.

ПЯТ-, FIVE

пят-ь, *num. card.*, five. Пя́тью пять - два́дцать пять, five times five is twenty-five., Пять-деся́т, *num. card.*, fifty. Пят-ь-со́т, *num. card.*, five hundred.

пят-а́к, *n.m.*, five kopek piece, coin. Пят-ачо́к, *n.m.*, (*dim.*), five kopek coin; snout of a pig. Пят-ёрка, *n.f.*, a five; (*colloq.*), five ruble note. Пят-ёрочник, *n.m.*, пят-ёрочница, *n.f.*, recipient of highest grade in Russian school system, five. Пят-ерня́, *n.f.*, (*colloq.*), five fingers. Пят-и-, *a combining form meaning* five. Пят-и-алты́нный, *adj.*, *used as n.*, (*colloq.*), fifteen kopek coin. Пят-и-гла́вый, *adj.*, five-domed, five-headed. П. собо́р, five-domed cathedral. Пят-и-десятиле́тний, *adj.*, fifty years old, of fifty years. П. юбиле́й, fiftieth anniversary. Пят-и-деся́тый, *num. ord.*, fiftieth. П-ые го́ды, the fifties (1850's). П-ая страни́ца, page fifty. Пят-и-дне́вка, *n.f.*, (*recent*), five-day week. Пят-и-ле́тие, *n.n.*, quinquennial. Пят-и-ле́тка, *n.f.*, (*recent*), five-year plan. Пятиле́тка в четы́ре го́да, (*recent*), completion, fulfillment of a five-year plan in four years. Пят-и-ле́тний, *adj.*, aged five years, of five years. П. план, five-year plan. П. ребёнок, five-year old child. Пят-и-рублёвка, *n.f.*, (*colloq.*), five ruble note. Пят-и-со́тый, *num. ord.*, five-hundredth. Пят-и-то́нка, *n.f.*, (*colloq.*), five ton truck. Пят-и-ты́сячный, *num. ord.*, five-thousandth. Пят-и-эта́жный, *adj.*, five-storied. Пят-на́дцать, *num. card.*, fifteen. Пят-на́дцатый, *num. ord.*, fifteenth. П-ое (число́) января́, the fifteenth of January. Пят-о́к, *n.m.*, five. П. яи́ц (я́блок), five eggs (apples). Пят-ый, *num. ord.*, fifth. П. но́мер, number five. Страни́ца п-ая, page five, the fifth page. П-ая коло́нна, (*polit.*), fifth column. Пят-ница, *n.f.*, Friday. Семь пятниц на неде́ле, (*saying*), referring

to one who is constantly changing his mind.

пят-еро, *num. coll.*, five. У неё п. дете́й, she has five children. Пят-ери́к, *n.m.*, five items. Запряга́ли п. лошаде́й, they harnessed five horses.

в-пят-еро, *adv.*, five times. В. бо́льше, five times as much. Он зарабо́тал впя́теро бо́льше, чем израсхо́довал, he earned five times more than he spent. В-пят-еро́м, *adv.*, five together, in fives. Мы в., five of us. В-пя́т-ых, *adv.*, fifthly, in the fifth place.

у-пят-ер-и́-ть, *v.p.*, у-пят-еря́ть, *v.i.*, + *acc.*, to increase fivefold, quintuple. У-пят-ери́ть-ся, *v.p.r.*, у-пят-еря́ть-ся, *v.i.r.*, to be increased fivefold. Дохо́ды заво́да упятери́лись, the profits of the plant increased fivefold. У-пят-ерённый, *adj.*, *part. pass. past*, increased five times, fivefold.

Р

РАБ- (ОТ-, ОЧ-), SLAVERY, THRALLDOM, BONDAGE, LABOR

раб, *n.m.*, раба́, раб-ы́ня, *n.f.*, slave. Раб-о-, *a combining form meaning* slave. Раб-о-владе́лец, *n.m.*, раб-о-владе́лица, *n.f.*, slave owner. Раб-о-владе́льческий, *adj.*, slave-owning. Р-ое хозя́йство, slave economy. Раб-о-ле́пие, *n.n.*, servility. Раб-о-ле́пный, *adj.*, servile. Р. челове́к, a person who gains favor through flattery. Раб-о-ле́пно, *adv.*, slavishly, in a servile manner. Раб-о-ле́пствовать, *v.i.*, перед + *instr.*, to fawn, cringe, be servile. Р. пе́ред си́льными ми́ра, to fawn upon the mighty. Ра́б-ский, *adj.*, slavish, servile. Р. труд, slave labor. Р-ое подража́ние, slavish imitation. Ра́б-ство, *n.n.*, servitude, slavery. Находи́ться (держа́ть) в ра́бстве, to be held (hold) in servitude. Отме́на ра́бства, abolition of slavery.

раб-о́т-ать, *v.i.*, to labor, work, toil. Р. рука́ми (голово́й), to work with one's hands (one's head). Р. перо́м (ки́стью), to work with the pen (the brush). Р. над чём-либо, to work at something. Р. с ке́м-либо, to work with someone. Р. с чём-либо, to work with something. Р. без о́тдыха, to work without rest. Р. без у́стали, to work untiringly. Р. вдвоём (втроём), to work in two's (in three's). Р. день и ночь, to work day and night. Р. для души́, to work for one's own moral satisfaction. Р. для пропита́ния, to work for one's livelihood. Р. за трои́х, to do the work of three. Р. над карти́ной (ру́кописью), to work on a painting (on a manuscript). Р. непрерывно, to work uninterruptedly. Р. подённо, to work by the day. Р. посменно, to work by shifts. Р. по-ударному, (*recent*), to work in a shock-brigade manner. Р. по-сдельно, to do piecework. Р. с микроскопом, to work with a microscope. Р. спустя рукава, (*idiom*.), to scamp. Р. усердно, to work diligently. Работ-а, *n.f.*, work, labor; task, job. Р. вне дома, outside work. Р. ради денег, to work for money only. Домашняя р., housework. Исследовательская р., research work. Каторжная (адская) р., hard work. Каторжные р-ы, convict labor. Неприятная р., drudgery. Общественная р., community work. Плохая (плохо сделанная) р., bungle, botch. Подённая р., daily work. Разведочная р., prospecting, mining. Ручная р., manual labor, handiwork. Сверхурочная р., overtime work. Сдельная р., piecework. Случайная р., odd job. Совместная р., collaboration, co-operation. Тонкая р., delicate work. Тяжёлая р., hard work, toil, sweat. Ударная р., shock-work. Умственная р., intellectual work. Филигранная р., filigreed work. Быть в работе, to be in process, in operation. Бросать работу, to stop work, to quit a job. Приняться за работу, to set to work. Быть без работы, to be unemployed, jobless. Единица работы, unit of work. Лишать работы, to lay off, discharge, deprive of work. Лишаться работы, to lose one's job. Общественные работы, public works. Работ-о-датель, *n.m.*, employer. Работ-о-способность, *n.f.*, efficiency. Пониженная (повышенная) р., lowered (increased) efficiency. Работ-о-способный, *adj.*, efficient, able-bodied, hard working. Работ-ник, *n.m.*, workman, worker, laborer. Квалифицированный р., skilled, qualified, worker. Научный р., scientific worker. Ответственный, р., responsible worker. Подённый р., day laborer. Подручный р., handyman. Р. прилавка, (*recent*), salesclerk. Р. умственного труда, (*recent*), intellectual worker. Р. искусства, (*recent*), artist. Работ-ница, *n.f.*, workwoman, factory employee; dairymaid. Домашняя р., servant, housemaid. Работ-яга, *n.f.*, *and n.m.*, hard worker. Работ-ящий, *adj.*, hard working.

раб-оч-ий, *adj.*, *also used as n.m.*, worker, workman. Р. металлист, metal worker. Р. подросток, teen age worker. Сельско-хозяйственный р., farm hand. Р. от станка, bench worker. Текстильный р., textile worker. Фабричный р., factory, mill worker.

раб-оч-ий, *adj.*, work, working, labor. Р. вопрос, labor problem. Р. день, working day. 8-часовой р. день, eight hour working day. Р. квартал, district inhabited by workers. Р. класс, working class. Р. план, working (practical) plan. Р-ая артель, worker's association, squad. Р-ая делегация, labor delegation. Р-ая партия, labor party. Британская р-ая партия, British Labor Party. Р-ая сила, manpower. Р-ее время, working hours. Р-ее движение, labor movement. Р-ие руки, hands. Раб-о-, рабоч-, *a combining form meaning*, work, labor, (*recent*). Рабкооп, *abbr.* of рабочий кооператив, workers' and peasants' cooperative. Рабкор, *abbr.* of рабочий корреспондент, labor correspondent. Рабселькор, *abbr. of* рабочий и сельский корреспондент, labor and farm correspondent. Рабсила, *abbr. of* рабочая сила, man power. Рабфак, *abbr. of* рабочий факультет, worker's high school. Рабочком, *abbr. of* рабочий комитет, workers' committee. Рабкрин, *abbr. of* рабоче-крестьянская инспекция, labor and peasant inspection. Рабоче-крестьянский, *adj.*, pertaining to labor and peasantry.

без-работ-н-ый, *adj.*, unemployed. Без-работ-ица, *n.f.*, unemployment. Страхование от безработицы, unemployment insurance.

в-работ-ать-ся, *v.p.r.*, в-работ-ывать-ся, *v.i.r.*, в, во + *acc.*, to become accustomed to, become familiar with (one's work). Рабочий врабо́тался в своё дело, the worker became familiar with his work.

вы-работ-ать, *v.p.*, вы-рабат-ывать, *v.i.*, + *acc.*, to manufacture, produce; work out; earn by working. В. товар, to manufacture, produce. В. план, to work out a plan. В. 100 долларов в неделю, to earn one hundred dollars per week. Вы-работ-ать-ся, *v.p.r.*, вы-рабат-ывать-ся, *v.i.r.*, из + *gen.*, to develop through work. Из него выработался очень хороший работник, he developed into a good worker. Вы-работ-ка, *n.f.*, manufacture, manufacturing, production; produce, amount produced, output. В. стали новым методом, production of steel by a new method. Годичная в. стали, yearly output of steel. В. проекта, working out of a project.

до-работ-ать, *v.p.*, до-рабат-ывать, *v.i.*, + *acc.*, to complete work, finish off, elaborate, finish working. Этот проéкт нáдо ещё доработáть, this project must still be completed. До-рабóт-ать-ся, *v.p.r.*, до-рабáт-ывать-ся, *v.i.r.*, до + *gen.*, to be completed, finished; become exhausted from work.

за-рабóт-ать, *v.p.,* за-рабáт-ывать, *v.i.,* + *acc.*, to earn; start operating (*as* a plant). Завóд заработáл (нáчал рабóтать), the plant began to operate. За-рабóт-ать-ся, *v.p.r.,* за-рабáт-ывать-ся, *v.i.r.,* to work to excess. За-рабóт-анный, *adj., part. pass. past,* earned. З-ые дéньги, earned money. Зарабóтный, *adj., earned.* З-ая плáта, зарплáта (*recent*), salary. Зá-рабóт-ок, *n.m.,* earnings. Лёгкий з., easy money. З. в 100 дóлларов, earnings of one hundred dollars.

на-рабóт-ать, *v.p.,* на-рабáт-ывать, *v.i.,* + *acc.,* (*colloq.*), to accomplish much work. На-рабóт-ать-ся, *v.p.r.,* на-рабáт-ывать-ся, *v.i.r.,* (*colloq.*), to overwork.

об-рабóт-ать, *v.p.,* об-рабáт-ывать, *v.i.,* + *acc.,* to manufacture, cultivate, till, farm, fashion, rework. О. сырьё, to manufacture from raw material. О. зéмлю, to cultivate land. О. когó-нибудь, (*colloq.*), to manage, cultivate, work on someone. О. материáлы, to rework material. Об-рабóт-ка, *n.f.,* об-рабáт-ывание, *n.n.,* cultivation, tillage, farming; adaptation. О. землú, land cultivation. О. книги, adaptation of a book.

от-рабóт-ать, *v.p.,* от-рабáт-ывать, *v.i.,* + *acc.,* to work off, work. О. недéлю, to do a week's work, for a week. О. долг, to work off a debt. От-рабóтанный, *adj., part. pass. past,* worked out, off.

пере-рабóт-ать, *v.p.,* пере-рабáт-ывать, *v.i.,* + *acc.,* to make over, remake, do over again, revise. П. вещь, to remake something. П. план, to revise a plan. П. рýкопись, to revise a manuscript. Пере-рабóт-ать-ся, *v.p.r.,* пере-рабáт-ывать-ся, *v.i.r.,* в + *acc.,* to be remade, revised, made over, to be worked into; to overwork. Чугýн перерабáтывается в сталь, pig iron is made into steel. Я перерабóтался до упáдка сил, I worked to the point of exhaustion. Рýды перерабáтываются в метáллы, ores are worked into metals. Пере-раб-óтка, *n.f.,* пере-рабáтывание, *n.n.,* working over, remaking, revising.

по-рабóт-ать, *v.p.,* to work a little. Он порабóтал два часá, he worked for two hours. Я достáточно порабóтал в своё врéмя, I've worked enough in my time. Она порабóтала и пошлá погулять, she worked for a short while and then went for a stroll.

под-рабóт-ать, *v.p.,* под-рабáт-ывать, *v.i.,* + *acc.,* + *instr.,* to earn additionally. Он подрабáтывал сверхурóчным трудóм, he earned more by working overtime. Онá подрабáтывала 100 рублéй в мéсяц, she earned an additional 100 rubles a month.

при-рабóт-ать, *v.p.,* при-рабáт-ывать, *v.i.,* to earn extra money.

про-рабóт-ать, *v.p.,* про-рабáт-ывать, *v.i.,* to work out, work through. П. вопрóс (законопроéкт), to work out a problem (a bill). П. всю ночь, to work through the night.

раз-рабóт-ать, *v.p.,* раз-рабáт-ывать, *v.i.,* + *acc.,* to exploit, cultivate, elaborate, treat, develop. Р. кóпи, to work, develop a mine. Р. пýстошь, to cultivate a waste plot of land. Р. план, to elaborate on a plan. Р. тéму, to develop a subject, a theme. Раз-рабóт-ка, *n.f.,* treatment, elaboration, exploitation, cultivation.

с-рабóт-ать-ся, *v.p.r.,* to be worn out by work; work as a team, work in harmony. Резéц срабóтался, the chisel is worn out. Эта грýппа рабóтников хорошó срабóталась, this group of workmen achieved good teamwork. С-рабóт-анность, *n.f.,* teamwork; team spirit.

РАВ-, РОВ-, РАВ-Н-, РОВ-Н-, EQUALITY, EVENNESS, LEVEL; SIMILARITY

рав-н-я́-ть, *v.i.,* + *acc.,* to equal, equalize. Рав-н-éние, *n.n.,* equalization. Р. напрáво (налéво), (*mil.*), eyes right, eyes left. Держáть р. на когó-либо, to use someone as a model. Рав-нúна, *n.f.,* plain. Беспредéльная р., limitless plain. Рáв-ный, *adj.,* рáв-ен, *adj. pred.,* equal, alike; similar. Емý нет рáвного, there is no one like him. Рáвным óбразом, equally. На рáвных услóвиях, on equal terms. При прóчих рáвных услóвиях, other things being equal. Рав-н-ó, *adv., also adj., pred.,* equally, alike, the same. Всё равнó, it makes no difference; it comes to the same thing. Мне всё р., it's all the same to me. Двáжды два р. четырём, twice two is four. Рáв-но, *adv.,* to express equality. Равновéсие, *n.n.,* equilibrium. Равноврéменный, *adj.,* equal, uniform in time. Равнодéйствующая сúла, resultant. Равнознáчущий, equivalent, synonymous. Равномéрное движéние, even motion. Равномéрно, *adv.,* uniformly. Равнопрáвие, *n.n.,* equality of rights. Равноце́нность, *n.f.*, equivalent in value. Равноце́нный, *adj.*, equivalent, of equal worth, of equal value.

ро́в-н-ый, *adj.*, even, flat, level, plane, equal. Р-ая пове́рхность, plane surface. Р. кли́мат, even climate. Р. хара́ктер, even temper. Не-ро́в-ный, *adj.*, uneven, unequal. Ро́в-но, *adv.*, just, exactly, equally. Р. в 5 часо́в, at five o'clock sharp. Он р. ничего́ не зна́ет об э́том, he knows exactly nothing about it. Ров-ня́, *n.f.*, equal, person of the same age, same position. Он тебе́ не р., he is not your equal.

ра́в-ен-ство, *n.n.*, equality. Всео́бщее р., general equality. Знак ра́венства, (*math.*), equal sign, sign of equality. Не-ра́в-енство, *n.n.*, inequality. Иму́щественное р., economic equality.

рав-н-я́ть-ся, *v.i.r.*, + *dat.*, с + *instr.*, equalize, be equal; compete with. Два́жды три равня́ется шести́, two times three equals six. Никто́ не мо́жет р. с ним, no one can compete with him. Равня́йся! (*mil.*), Dress!

вы́-ров-н-ять, *v.p.*, вы-ра́в-н-и-вать, *v.i.*, + *acc.*, to straighten, straighten out. Вы-ра́в-нивание, *n.n.*, smoothing, equalization, straightening out. Вы́-ров-нять-ся, *v.p.r.*, вы-ра́в-нивать-ся, *v.i.r.*, to become even, level, smooth. В. с проти́вником в игре́, to improve one's position in a game, to catch up to one's opponent in a game.

за-ров-н-я́ть, *v.p.*, за-ра́в-н-и-вать, *v.i.*, to level. З. вы́рытые я́мы, to fill up and level holes, pits.

по-рав-н-я́ть, *v.p.*, + *acc.*, to equalize. По-рав н-я́ть-ся, *v.p.r.*, to come up to, come alongside. Ло́шадь поравня́лась на бега́х с друго́й ло́шадью, the horse overtook the other horse in the race. По́-ров-н-у, *adj.*, equally, in equal parts, share and share alike. Раздели́ть п., to divide into equal parts.

под-ров-н-я́ть, *v.p.*, под-ра́в-н-ивать, *v.i.*, + *acc.*, to level; make neat, trim; prune. П. газо́н, to clip the grass. П. пла́тье, to even up the hem of a dress. П. дере́вья, to prune trees. Под-ров-н-я́ть-ся, *v.p.r.*, под-ра́в-н-ивать-ся, *v.i.r.*, to be evened off.

при-рав-н-я́ть, *v.p.*, при-ра́в-ивать, *v.i.*, + *acc.*, + *dat.*, to compare, identify with. П. одного́ челове́ка друго́му, to compare one man with another.

раз-ров-н-я́ть, *v.p.*, раз-ра́в-нивать, *v.i.*, + *acc.*, to level, even, smooth.

с-рав-н-и́ть, *v.p.*, с-ра́в-н-ивать, *v.i.*, + *acc.*, + *instr.*, to compare, compare to, with. С. одного́ челове́ка с други́м, to compare two people. С-рав-н-е́ние,

n.n., comparison. Вне сравне́ния, beyond comparison, incomparable. По сравне́нию, compared to, with; in comparison with. С-ра́в-н-ивание, *n.n.*, comparing; levelling, smoothing. С-рав-ни́тельный, *adj.*, comparative. С. ме́тод, comparative method. С-ая грамма́тика, comparative grammar. С-ая сте́пень, (*gram.*), comparative degree. С-рав-ни́тельно, *adv.*, comparatively. Жить с. хорошо́, to live in comparative, relative comfort. Не-с-рав-н-е́нный, *adj.*, *part. pass. past,* incomparable, perfect. Име́ть не-с-рав-н-е́нное преиму́щество, пе́ред ке́м-либо, to have an incomparable advantage over someone. Не-с-равн-и́мый, *adj.*, incomparable. Это две н-ые ве́щи, these two things are incomparable.

с-рав-н-я́ть, *v.p.*, с-ра́в-н-ивать, *v.i.*, + *acc.*, с + *instr.*, to level off, smooth off. С. з землёй, to raze, level with the ground. С-рав-н-я́ть-ся, *v.p.r.*, с-ра́в-н-ивать-ся, *v.i.r.*, с + *instr.*, to equal, be equal, come up to. Никто́ не мо́жет сравня́ться с ним в ло́вкости, no one can touch him for adroitness.

у-рав-н-я́ть, *v.p.*, у-ра́в-н-ивать, *v.i.*, + *acc.*, to level, equalize, even, smooth. У. площа́дку, to level off a playground. У-рав-н-е́ние, *n.n.*, equalization; (*math.*), equation. У. в права́х, equalization of rights. Квадра́тное у., (*math.*), quadratic equation. У-ра́в-н-ивание, *n.n.*, levelling, equalization. У-рав-н-и́ловка *n.f.*, (*recent*), levelling of wages. У-рав-н-и́тельный, *adj.*, levelling У-ая систе́ма, levelling system.

у-рав-н-о-ве́сить, *v.p.*, у-рав-н-о-ве́шивать, *v.i.*, + *acc.*, to balance, counterpoise, counterbalance, put into equilibrium. У. весы́, to balance scales. У. госуда́рственный бюдже́т, to balance the state budget. У-рав-н-о-ве́шенность, *n.f.*, equilibrium. У. хара́ктера, emotional balance. У-рав-н-о-ве́шенный, *adj.*, *part. pass. past,* well balanced; levelheaded, steady. У. груз, balanced load. У. бюдже́т, balanced budget. У. молодо́й челове́к, steady young man. У-рав-н-о-ве́шивание, *n.n.*, balancing, steadying.

РАД-, JOY, GLADNESS, DELIGHT

ра́д-ова-ть, *v.p.*, + *acc.*, to gladden, make happy, give joy. Р. се́рдце, to warm, gladden one's heart. Это меня́ о́чень ра́дует, this delights me. Ра́д-овать-ся, *v.i.r.*, + *dat.*, to rejoice, be glad. Я ра́дуюсь э́тому, I am glad of this. Рад, *adj. pred.*, glad. Я рад э́тому, I am glad of it. Рад, не рад, (*idiom.*), willy-nilly. Очень рад! I'm very glad indeed! Рад-ёшенек, (*folk.*), delighted. Она рада-радёшенька, she is delighted. Рад-ость, *n.f.*, joy, gladness. У него большая р., he has reason to rejoice. Рад-остный, *adj.*, glad, joyful, joyous, cheerful. Получить р-ое известие, to receive glad tidings. Рад-ушие, *n.n.*, cordiality, affability, hospitality. Он проявил много радушия, he showed much cordiality. Рад-ушный, *adj.*, cordial, affable, hospitable. Р. приём, hearty welcome. Р. хозяин, kind host. Рад-ушно, *adv.*, cordially, affably, hospitably. Его приняли р., they gave him a warm welcome.

без-рад-ост-ный, *adj.*, sad, joyless. Б-ые дни, sad days. Без-рад-остно, *adv.*, sadly. Б. смотреть на будущее, to take a gloomy view of the future.

воз-рад-ова-ть-ся, *v.p.r.*, + *dat.*, (*obs.*), to rejoice.

на-рад-ова-ть-ся, *v.p.r.*, на + *acc.*, to rejoice exceedingly. Мать не нарадуется на своего ребёнка, the mother is endlessly delighted in her child.

об-рад-овать, *v.p.*, + *acc.*, to rejoice, give joy. Об-рад-овать-ся, *v.p.r.*, + *dat.*, to rejoice, be glad. Она обрадовалась ему, she was glad to see him.

по-рад-овать, *v.p.*, + *acc.*, + *instr.*, to give joy. Сын порадовал отца своими отметками, the son delighted his father with good grades. Порадуй меня! Make me happy! По-рад-овать-ся, *v.p.r.*, to feel, experience a little joy.

РАЗ-, РАЖ-, ONCE; DEFEAT, STRIKE; IMPRINT, INFLICTION

раз, *n.m.*, *used as adv.*, one, once. В другой раз, another time. Всякий раз, every time. Один раз, once, one time. Ещё раз, once more, again. Как-раз, just. Много раз, many times. Не больше одного раза, not more than once. Раз-ом, at once, at a blow. Все разом, simultaneously, all at once, all together. Ни раз-у, never, not once. Раз-ик, *n.m.*, (*dim.*), *used as adv.*, once. Ещё разик, ещё раз, once more. Раз овый, *adj.*, valid for use only once. Р. билет, ticket for one use.

раз-, рас-, *prefixes meaning* separation, parting from; reversal, undoing, depriving, negation.

Раз-лучить-ся, *v.p.r.*, с + *instr.*, to part, separate. Рас-статься, *v.p.r.*, с + *instr.*, to part, separate.

раз-й-ть, *v.i.*, + *acc.*, + *instr.*, to fell, strike. Св. Георгий разит копьём змея, St. George is striking the dragon with a spear.

раз-й-ть, *v.i.*, *impers.*, to smell, reek, stink. От него разит водкой, he reeks of vodka. Раз-йтельный, *adj.*, impressive, striking. Р-ое сходство, striking likeness.

воз-раз-йть, *v.p.*, воз-раж-ать, *v.i.*, + *dat.*, на + *acc.*, to object, contradict; retort. Вам нечего в. на это, you cannot object to this. Если вы не возражаете, if you have no objections. Воз-раж-ение, *n.n.*, objection. Это вызвало бурю возражений, there was a storm of objections. Закидывать возражениями, to overwhelm with objections.

вы-раз-ить, **вы-раж-у**, *v.p.*, вы-раж-ать, *v.i.*, + *acc.*, + *instr.*, to express, convey. В. неудовольствие, to express dissatisfaction. В. общее мнение, to express a general sentiment. В. словами, to express with words. В. сочувствие, to express sympathy. Вы-раж-енный, *adj.*, pronounced, expressed. Резко в., sharply expressed. Вы-раж-ение, *n.n.*, expression. В. лица, expression of a face. Техническое в., technical term. В простых выражениях, in simple terms, words. Вы-раз-итель, *n.m.*, exponent; one who expresses something. В. демократической идеологии, exponent of a democratic ideology. Вы-раз-ительный, *adj.*, expressive. Вы-раз-ительно, *adv.*, expressively. Вы-раз-ительность, *n.f.*, expressiveness. В. его речи поразила всех, the expressiveness of his speech impressed everyone. Вы-раз-ить-ся, *v.p.r.*, вы-раж-ать-ся, *v.i.r.*, to express oneself. Сильно в., to express oneself bluntly, strongly. Мягко выражаясь, to say the least, put it mildly. Издержки выразились в 5 руб., the expenses came to five rubles.

за-раз, *adv.*, (*folk.*), simultaneously, at the same time. Все з. взялись за эту работу, they all started to work together. Он выпил всю бутылку з., he drank the bottle in one gulp.

за-раз-йть, *v.p.*, за-раж-ать, *v.i.*, + *acc.*, + *instr.*, to infect, contaminate. З. воду, to contaminate, pollute water. За-раж-ение, *n.n.*, contamination, pollution. З. крови, blood poisoning. За-раз-а, *n.f.*, infection, contagion. З. быстро распространилась, the contagion spread rapidly. За-раз-ительный, *adj.*, infectious, contagious. З. смех, contagious laugh, laughter. З-ая болезнь, contagious disease. За-раз-ный, за-раз-ительный, *adj.*, contagious. За-раз-ное отделение больницы, division of contagious diseases in a hospital. За-раз-и́тельно, *adv.*, contagiously. За-раз-и́тельность, *n.f.*, infectiousness, contagiousness. З. ра́ка не дока́зана, the contagiousness of cancer has not been proved. За-раз-и́ть-ся, *v.p.r.*, зараж-а́ть-ся, *v.i.r.*, + *instr.*, to be infected, contaminated.

из-раз-е́ц, *n.m.*, tile. Из-раз-цо́вый, *adj.*, made of tile.

о́б-раз, *n.m.*, shape, form, manner; trend; image, icon. О. де́йствия, procedure, behavior, conduct. О. жи́зни, way, manner of life. О. мы́слей, manner, trend of thought. О. правле́ния, form of rule, form of government. Худо́жественный о., artistic image, type. О. Св. Никола́я, image, icon of St. Nicholas. Гла́вным о́бразом, mainly, in the main. Каки́м о́бразом? In what manner? Надлежа́щим о., properly. Наилу́чшим о., in the best way possible. Нико́им о., by no means. Ра́вным о., equally. Таки́м о., thus, in this way. Об-раз-е́ц, *n.m.*, model, example, sample. Ста́вить кого́-либо в образе́ц други́м, to set somebody up as an example for others. Образцы́ това́ра, samples of merchandise. Об-ра́з-чик, *n.m.*, sample. О. мате́рии, sample of cloth, of material. Об-раз-и́на, *n.f.*, (*derog.*), mug. Об-раз-ный, *adj.*, figurative, picturesque. О. язы́к, picturesque language. Об-раз-ность, *n.f.*, picturesqueness.

без-об-ра́з-ить, *v.i.*, + *acc.*, to disfigure, mutilate. Его́ безобра́зит повреждённый глаз, his injured eye makes him look ugly. Без-об-ра́з-ие, *n.n.*, ugliness, hideousness; outrage. Что за б.! How scandalous! How outrageous! Без-об-ра́з-ный, *adj.*, indecent, hideous, scandalous; featureless, lacking in imagery. Без-об-ра́з-но, *adv.*, scandalously, outrageously, hideously. Без-об-ра́з-ность, *n.f.*, unseemliness, outrageousness. Б. его́ поведе́ния, the outrageousness of his conduct.

без-об-ра́з-нич-ать, *v.i.*, to behave scandalously, outrageously, disgracefully. Без-об-ра́з-ник, *n.m.*, без-об-ра́з-ница, *n.f.*, one who behaves outrageously.

о-без-об-ра́з-ить, *v.p.*, о-без-об-ра́живать, *v.i.*, to disfigure, mutilate, make hideous. О-без-об-ра́ж-енный, *adj.*, *part. pass. past*, disfigured, mutilated. Дом обезобра́жен пристро́йками, the house was made hideous by additions.

об-раз-ова́ть, *v.p.*, об-раз-о́вывать, *v.i.*, + *acc.*, to instruct, educate, form. Он сам себя́ образова́л, he is a self-educated man. В. э́том ме́сте го́ры образу́ют высо́кое плоского́рье, in this place the mountains have formed a

high plateau. Об-раз-ова́ть-ся, *v.p.r.*, об-раз-о́вывать-ся, *v.i.r.*, to be formed. При кипяче́нии воды́ образу́ется пар, when water boils, steam is formed. Образу́ется! (*colloq.*), It will blow over! Об-раз-ова́ние, *n.n.*, education; formation. Профессиона́льное о., vocational training. О. слов, formation of words. Об-раз-о́ванность, *n.f.*, education, culture. Об-раз-ова́тельный, *adj.*, educational. О. ценз, educational qualification. Само-об-раз-ова́ние, *n.n.*, self-education.

от-раз-и́ть, *v.p.*, от-раж-а́ть, *v.i.*, to reflect, parry. От-раз-и́ть-ся, *v.p.r.*, отраж-а́ть-ся, *v.i.r.*, to be reflected; have a repercussion. Это вре́дно отража́ется на здоро́вье, this impairs one's health. От-раж-е́ние, *n.n.*, reflection, repulsion; parrying. О. в зе́ркале, reflection in a mirror. О. кри́зиса, repercussion of a crisis. От-раж-ённый, *adj.*, *part. pass. past*, reflected; repulsed. О. свет, reflected light. О. неприя́тель, repulsed enemy.

по-раз-и́ть, *v.p.*, по-раж-а́ть, *v.i.*, + *acc.*, to strike, rout; surprise, astonish. По-раз-и́ть-ся, *v.p.r.*, по-раж-а́ть-ся, *v.i.r.*, + *instr.*, to be struck, surprised, astonished. П. великоле́пием зда́ния, to be surprised by the grandeur of the building. По-раж-е́ние, *n.n.*, defeat. Неприя́тель понёс п., the enemy was defeated. По-раж-е́нец, *n.m.*, defeatist. По-раж-е́нческий, *adj.*, defeatist. По-раж-е́нчество, *n.n.*, defeatism. По-раз-и́тельный, *adj.*, astonishing. П-ое схо́дство, striking likeness.

раз-раз-и́ть-ся, *v.p.r.*, раз-раж-а́ть-ся, *v.i.r.*, + *instr.*, to burst, explode, give vent to. Р. сме́хом, to burst into laughter.

с-раз-и́ть, *v.p.*, с-раж-а́ть, *v.i.*, + *acc.*, + *instr.*, to throw down, smite, overwhelm. С-раж-ённый, *adj.*, *part. pass. past*, overwhelmed, smitten; see с-раж-ён. Он сражён го́рем, he is overwhelmed with grief. С-раз-и́ть-ся, *v.p.r.*, с-раж-а́ть-ся, *v.i.r.*, с + *instr.*, про́тив + *acc.*, to combat, fight against. С-раж-е́ние, *n.n.*, battle, combat. Вы́играть с., to win a battle.

с-ра́з-у, *adv.*, at once, immediately. С. по́сле э́того, right after this. Они́ с. приступи́ли к рабо́те, they set to work at once.

РАСТ-, РОСТ-, РАС-, РОС-, РАЩ-, РОЩ-, GROWTH

раст-и́, *v.i.*, to grow. Трава́ растёт, grass grows, the grass is growing. Я рос в дере́вне, I grew up in the country.

раст-и́-ть, ращ-у́, *v.i.,* + *acc.,* to grow, raise. Мать забо́тливо расти́т свои́х дете́й, the mother is raising her children carefully. Раст-е́ние, *n.n.,* plant. Вью́щееся р., climber, climbing plant. Ползу́чее р., creeper. Многоле́тнее р., perennial. Раст-и́тельность, *n.f.,* vegetation. Бу́йная р., luxuriant vegetation. Раст-и́тельный, *adj.,* vegetative. Р-ая пи́ща, vegetables, vegetable food. Жить расти́тельной жи́знью, to vegetate.

в-рас-ти́, *v.p.,* в-раст-а́ть, *v.i.,* в + *acc.,* to grow into. В-раст-а́ние, *n.n.,* ingrowing. В-ро́с-ший, *adj., part. act. past,* ingrown.

вз-раст-и́ть, *v.p.,* вз-ра́щ-ивать, *v.i.,* + *acc.,* (*poet.*), to cultivate, bring up, raise, nurture. "Мно́го роз взрасти́л он в нём," (*poet.*), he grew many roses in (his garden). Вз-ро́с-лый, *adj., used as noun,* grownup, adult. В-ая дочь, adult (marriageable) daughter. Шко́ла для взро́слых, school for adults. Вз-ро́слость, *n.f.,* maturity.

во́з-раст, *n.m.,* age. Мы одного́ во́зраста с ним, we are of the same age. Деви́ца на во́зрасте, (*colloq.*), marriageable girl.

воз-раст-й, *v.p.,* воз-раст-а́ть, *v.i.,* to grow up; increase, rise. Воз-раст-а́ющий, *adj., part. act. pres.,* increasing, growing. В-ая ско́рость, accelerated velocity. Воз-раст-а́ние, *n.n.,* growth, increase.

вы́-раст-и, *v.p.,* вы-раст-а́ть, *v.i.,* to grow up, grow out of; increase in growth. В. из оде́жды, to grow out of one's clothing. Вы́-рос-ший, *adj., part. act. past,* grown up. В. в дере́вне, country bred.

на-вы́-рост, *adv.,* large enough to allow for growth. Пла́тье сши́то н., this dress is made to allow for growth.

вы́-раст-ить, *v.p.,* вы-ра́щ-ивать, *v.i.,* + *acc.,* to bring up, rear, raise, cultivate. В. дете́й, to raise children. В. расте́ния, to cultivate plants.

до-раст-й, *v.p.,* до-раст-а́ть, *v.i.,* + *gen.,* to grow up to. Он не доро́с до э́того, he is not mature enough for it.

за-раст-й, *v.p.,* за-раст-а́ть, *v.i.,* + *instr.,* to overgrow. По́ле заросло́ со́рными тра́вами, the field is overgrown with weeds. За-раст-а́ние, *n.n.,* growing over. З. ра́ны, healing of a wound. За́-рос-ль, *n.f.,* brush, thicket. За-раст-а́ть-ся, *v.i.r.,* за-раст-и́ть-ся, *v.p.r.,* to heal. Ра́на зараста́ется, the wound is healing.

на-раст-й, *v.p.,* на-раст-а́ть, *v.i.,* to increase. Нараста́ющая дороговви́зна, inflation, rise in prices. На-раст-а́ние,

n.n., increase, accumulation. Н. революцио́нных настрое́ний, spreading of revolutionary spirit.

на-раст-и́ть, *v.p.,* на-ра́щ-ивать, *v.i.,* + *acc.,* to increase, accumulate. На-ращ-ённый, *adj., part. pass. past,* accumulated. Н. капита́л, accumulated capital. На-ращ-е́ние, *n.n.,* increment. Н. ско́рости, acceleration. На-ро́ст, *n.m.,* excrescence, outgrowth on a tree.

об-раст-й, *v.p.,* об-раст-а́ть, *v.i.,* + *instr.,* to overgrow with. Де́рево обросло́ мхом, the tree was overgrown with moss. Об-раст-а́ние, *n.n.,* overgrowing. Меща́нское о., (*recent*), bourgeois accumulation of property.

от-раст-й, *v.p.,* от-раст-а́ть, *v.i.,* to grow out. У него́ отросли́ во́лосы, his hair has grown out.

от-раст-и́ть, *v.p.,* от-ра́щ-ивать, *v.i.,* + *acc.,* to let grow. Он отрасти́л себе́ бо́роду, he has grown a beard. От-ро́ст-ок, *n.m.,* sprout, shoot, spring. Червеобра́зный о., (*anat.*), appendix. О́т-рас-ль, *n.f.,* branch. О. промы́шленности, branch of industry.

пере-раст-й, *v.p.,* пере-раст-а́ть, *v.i.,* to overgrow, outgrow. Сын переро́с отца́, the son outgrew his father. Пере-раст-а́ние, *n.n.,* overgrowing. Пере-ро́ст-ок, *n.m.,* overgrown youth.

по-раст-й, *v.p.,* по-раст-а́ть, *v.i.,* to grow over. Пшени́ца поросла́ ку́колем, the wheat was overgrown with furrow weed.

под-раст-й, *v.p.,* под-раст-а́ть, *v.i.,* to grow up, be growing up. Под-раст-а́ющий, *adj., part. act. pres.,* growing up, rising by growth. П-ее поколе́ние, the growing generation.

при-раст-й, *v.p.,* при-раст-а́ть, *v.i.,* к + *dat.,* to adhere, grow fast to; increase. П. к ме́сту, to become rooted to a spot. Населе́ние ежего́дно прираста́ет на 5 проце́нтов, the population increases by five percent yearly. При-ро́с-ший, *adj., part. act. past,* grown fast to.

при-раст-и́ть, *v.p.,* при-раст-а́ть, при-ра́щ-ивать, *v.i.,* к + *dat.,* to make something adhere; engraft. При-раст-а́ние, *n.n.,* growing fast. При-ращ-е́ние, *n.n.,* increment, increase. П. ско́рости, acceleration. При-ро́ст, *n.n.,* growth, increase. П. населе́ния, increase in population.

про-раст-й, *v.p.,* про-раст-а́ть, *v.i.,* to germinate, sprout. Про-ро́с-ший, *adj., part. pact. past,* sprouted. П-ее зерно́, germinated, sprouted grain, seed. Про-раст-а́ние, *n.n.,* germination, sprouting.

раз-раст-й-сь, *v.p.,* раз-раст-а́ть-ся, *v.i.,* to expand, widen, develop. Куст разро́сся, the bush spread out (blossomed, sprouted). Дéло разрастáется, business is expanding, growing. Раз-раст-áние, *п.п.*, lushness, luxuriance of growth. Р. семьй, growth, enlargement of a family.

с-раст-úть, *v.p.*, с-рáщ-ивать, *v.i.*, to grow together, join, become joined organically. Нóвый мéтод с. кóсти, new method of grafting bones, of making bones knit.

с-раст-ú-сь, *v.p.r.*, с-раст-áть-ся, с-рáщ-ивать-ся, *v.i.r.*, to knit. Слóманная рукá хорошó срослáсь, the broken arm knitted well. Он срóсся с этим гóро-дом, the city grew on him. С-раст-áние, с-ращ-éние, *п.п.*, growing to-gether, knitting (*as* of bones). Не-прáвильное с. пóсле перелóма, imper-fect knitting after fracture.

рост, *п.m.*, stature, increase, growth; in-terest. Человéк высóкого рóста, a tall man (man of tall stature). Во весь рост, full length. Рост производства, increase of production. Рост дéрева, growth of a tree. Отдавáть дéньги в рост, to advance money at interest. Он рóстом в шесть фýтов, he stands six feet in height. Рóс-лый, *adj.*, tall. Р. мужчúна, tall man. Рост-óвщúк, *п.m.*, usurer. Жáдный р. брал высóкие процéнты со своúх должникóв, the greedy usurer charged his debtors high rates of interest. Рост-óвщúче-ский, *adj.*, usurious. Рост-óвщúчество, *п.п.*, usury. Рост-óк, *п.m.*, sprout, shoot, seedling. Пускáть росткú, to ger-minate, bud.

рóщ-а, *п.f.*, grove. Дубóвая р., oak grove. Рóщ-ица, *п.f.*, (*dim.*), small grove.

РВ-, РЫВ-, TEARING, RENDING

рв-а-ть, *v.i.*, + *acc.*, to tear, rend; vomit. Р. плáтье (письмó, бумáгу), to tear a dress (a letter, paper). Р. цветы, to pick flowers. Р. зýбы, to extract teeth. Р. на себé вóлосы, (*fig.*), to tear one's hair out. Этого ребёнка рвёт в морскýю кáчку, this child becomes seasick in bad weather. Рв-óта, *п.f.*, vomiting. Рв-óтный, *adj.*, emetic. Р-ое лекáрство, an emetic, emetic medicine. Рв-ач, *п.m.*, (*colloq.*), self-seeker. Бесстыдный р., shameless seeker. Рв-áчество, *п.п.*, (*recent*), self-seeking. Рв-áческий, *adj.*, (*recent*), self-seeking. Рв-ань, *п.f.*, рв-аньё, *п.п.*, rags; rab-ble, riff-raff. Снимú с себя эту рвань (это рваньё), take off these rags. Рв-áный, *adj.*, torn Р. рукáв, torn sleeve. Р-ая рáна, lacerated wound. Рв-áть-ся, *v.i.r.*, в + *acc.*, к + *dat.*,

to tear, burst; be torn; rush, long for. Пиджáк рвётся по всем швам, the coat is bursting in all the seams. Где тóнко, там и рвётся, (*prov.*), a chain is as strong as its weakest link. Сéрдце рвётся от гóря, I am heart-broken from grief. Р. в бой (дрáку), (*fig.*), to long for a fight, spoil for a fight. Псы рвýтся вон на дрáку, (*Krylov*), these dogs are spoiling for a fight. Всей душóй я рвусь к друзьям, I am longing to be with my friends. Р. к учéнию (к образовáнию), to long for an education (for learning). Рв-éние, *п.п.*, zeal, fervor. Студéнты с больши́м рвéнием ýчатся рýсскому языкý, the students are learning Rus-sian with great zeal.

рв-а-нý-ть, *v.p.smf.*, to give a jerk; jerk. Ктó-то рванýл меня за рукáв, some-one jerked, tugged at my sleeve. Рв-а-нýть-ся, *v.p.r.*, to rush; get free; jerk. Ребёнок рванýлся к мáтери, но егó увелú, the child rushed to his mother, but they led him away.

взо-рв-áть, *v.p.*, вз-рыв-áть, *v.i.*, + *acc.*, to blow up, dynamite, set off a charge; exasperate. В. скалý, to dynamite a rock. В. крéпость, to blow up a fortress. Взо-рв-áть-ся, *v.p.r.*, вз-рыв-áть-ся, *v.i.r.*, to burst, explode. В. на вóздух, to blow up, explode. Вз-рыв, *п.m.*, explosion, outburst. В. бóмбы, explosion of a bomb. В. негодовáния, outburst of indignation. Вз-рыв-чатый, *adj.*, explosive. В-ые веществá, ex-plosives.

во-рв-áть-ся, *v.p.r.*, в-рыв-áть-ся, *v.i.r.*, в + *acc.*, to burst into, rush into. Насúльно ворвáться в чужóй дом, to break into someone's home. Вз-рв-áвшийся, *adj.*, *part. act. past*, one who has burst in. В-рыв-áющийся, *adj.*, *part. act. pres.*, bursting, breaking in, rushing in.

вы-рв-ать, *v.p.*, вы-рыв-áть, *v.i.*, + *acc.*, из + *gen.*, to tear out, pull out, eradicate, extirpate; extract, wring. В. зуб, to extract a tooth. В. дéрево с кóрнем, to uproot. В. письмó из рук, to snatch a letter out of someone's hands. В. страницу из книги, to tear a page out of a book. В. признáние, to wring a confession. Вы-рв-ать, *v.p.*, рв-ать, *v.i.*, *impers.*, to vomit. Боль-нóго вырвало крóвью, the patient vomited blood. Вы-рв-áть-ся, *v.p.r.*, вы-рыв-áть-ся, *v.i.r.*, to tear oneself away, break away, escape, struggle free, free oneself, break loose. Из тетрáди вырвался лист, a page was torn out of the notebook. Вырваться из объятий, to tear oneself away from the embrace. В. со слу́жбы, to take time off from work. Ого́нь вы́рвался из трубы́, flames burst out of the chimney.

до-рв-а́ть, *v.p.,* до-рыв-а́ть, *v.i.,* + *acc.,* to finish tearing, picking. Д. после́дние цветы́ в саду́, to pick the last flowers in a garden. До-рв-а́ть-ся, *v.p.r.,* до-рыв-а́ть-ся, *v.i.r.,* до + *gen.,* to be completely torn; fall greedily upon. Д. до еды́, to fall greedily upon food. Д. до це́ли, to attain one's goal. Д. до беды́, to get into trouble. Руба́шка, дорыва́ется уже́ до конца́, the shirt is coming completely apart.

за-рв-а́ть-ся, *v.p.r.,* за-рыв-а́ть-ся, *v.i.r.,* (*colloq.*), to go too far, go to extremes, overdo things. З. во лжи, to tell one lie too many. Не зарви́сь в ка́ртах, Don't take too many chances in cards. За-рв-а́вшийся, *adj., part. act. past,* one who has gone too far.

на-рв-а́ть, *v.p.,* на-рыв-а́ть, *v.i.,* + *acc.,* to tear up in quantity, pick fruit, flowers in quantity; come to a head (abscess). Нарва́ть буке́т цвето́в, to pick a bouquet of flowers. Нарва́ть бума́ги, to tear up a lot of paper. Па́лец нарыва́ет, the abscess on my finger is coming to a head. На-рв-а́ть-ся, *v.p.r.,* на-рыв-а́ть-ся, *v.i.r.,* на + *acc.,* (*colloq.*), to run into trouble; run up against, into. Н. на поли́цию, to run into the police. Н. на неприя́тность, to come up against someone's rudeness, experience an unpleasantness. Н. на де́рзость, to run up against rudeness. На-ры́в, *n.m.,* (*med.*), abscess, boil. Н. на десне́, abscess on the gum.

над-о-рв-а́ть, *v.p.,* над-рыв-а́ть, *v.i.,* + *acc.,* to tear slightly, overtax, lacerate. Н. здоро́вье, to overtax one's health. Н. си́лы, to overtax one's strength. Н. го́лос, to strain one's voice. Над-о-рв-а́ть-ся, *v.p.r.,* над-рыв-а́ть-ся, *v.i.r.,* to be slightly torn, overtaxed, impaired. Н. поднима́я тя́жести, to impair one's health by lifting heavy objects. Конве́рт надорва́лся еще́ в пути́, the envelope became slightly torn en route. Над-о́-рв-анный, *adj., part. pass. past,* slightly torn, impaired, overtaxed. Н. лист бума́ги, a torn sheet of paper. Н. го́лос, overstrained voice. Н-ое здоро́вье, impaired health. Над-ры́в, *n.m.,* slight tear, rent; laceration, strain. Душе́вный н., (*fig.*), broken heart.

обо-рв-а́ть, *v.p.,* об-рыв-а́ть, *v.i.,* + *acc.,* to tear off, pluck, pick, gather; break, cut short, break off; snub. О. лепестки́ цветка́, to pluck the petals of a flower.

О. я́годы с куста́, to gather berries from a bush. О. свой расска́з, to cut short one's story. О. пе́сню, to stop singing. Обо-рв-а́ть-ся, *v.p.r.,* об-рыв-а́ть-ся, *v.i.r.,* to be broken off; lose hold; become detached, come to an abrupt end. Ве́шалка у моего́ пальто́ оборва́лась, the tab on my coat has become torn. Этот бедня́к совсе́м оборва́лся, this poor man is in rags. Разгово́р оборва́лся, the conversation came to an abrupt end. О. с отве́сной скалы́, to lose hold and fall from a steep cliff. Об-ры́в, *n.m.,* precipice. Руче́й бежи́т по обры́ву, a brook flows at the bottom of the precipice. Гончаро́в написа́л рома́н "Обры́в," Goncharov wrote the novel entitled "The Precipice." Об-ры́в-истый, *adj.,* steep. О-ые берега́ Во́лги, steep banks of the Volga. Обо́-рв-анный, *adj.,* part torn, ragged. Му́ха с обо́рванным кры́лышком, a fly with a torn wing. О. ни́щий, ragged beggar. Обо-рв-а́нец, *n.m.,* tramp, ragamuffin. Обо́-рв-ыш, *n.m.,* ragged tramp. Ма́ленький о. проси́л де́нег у прохо́жих, the little ragamuffin begged from the passersby.

ото-рв-а́ть, *v.p.,* от-рыв-а́ть, *v.i.,* + *acc.,* от + *gen.,* to tear off. О. пу́говицу от пальто́, to tear a button off a coat. О. листо́к из записно́й кни́жки, to tear a page out of a notebook. Ото-рв-а́ть-ся, *v.p.r.,* от-рыв-а́ть-ся, *v.i.r.,* от + *gen.,* у + *gen.,* to come off, be torn off; take off; lose touch with. Пу́говицы ча́сто отрыва́ются, buttons frequently come off. Не люблю́ отрыва́ться от де́ла, I don't like to get away from my work. Тяжело́ отрыва́ться от родны́х, it is hard to be torn away from one's relatives. Ото́-рв-анность, *n.f.,* isolation, loneliness. Ото́-рв-анный, *adj.,* isolated, lonely. О. от свое́й семьи́, separated from one's family. От-ры́в, *n.m.,* tearing off; alienation; isolation; take-off. Ли́ния отры́ва от квита́нции, perforated line of a receipt. Учи́ться без отры́ва от произво́дства, (*recent*), to study without leaving one's factory job. От-ры́в-ок, *n.m.,* fragment, passage, excerpt. О. из по́вести (о́перы), excerpt from a novel (an opera). От-ры́в-истый, *adj.,* jerky, abrupt. О-ая речь, curt speech. От-ры́в-исто, *adv.,* abruptly, jerkily. Говори́ть о. to speak abruptly.

пере-рв-а́ть, *v.p.,* пере-рыв-а́ть, *v.i.,* + *acc.,* to break off; to tear asunder. П. про́волоку, to break off, a wire.

пре-рв-а́ть, *v.p.,* пре-рыв-а́ть, *v.i.,* + *acc.,* to interrupt, sever, break off. П.

разгово́р, to interrupt a conversation. П. отноше́ния, to discontinue relations. Пере-рв-а́ть-ся, пре-рв-а́ть-ся, *v.p.r.*, пере-рыв-а́ть-ся, пре-рыв-а́ть-ся, *v.i.r.*, to be broken off, interrupted, discontinued. Плато́к перерва́лся попола́м, the handkerchief was torn in two. Разгово́р помину́тно прерыва́лся, the conversation was constantly interrupted. Пере-ры́в, *n.m.*, recess, intermission, break. П. ме́жду уро́ками, recess between classes, between lessons. П. дипломати́ческих отноше́ний, severance of diplomatic relations. Бес-пре-ры́в-ный, *adj*, uninterrupted, continuous. Не-пре-ры́в-ный, *adj.*, constant, uninterrupted. Н-ая рабо́чая неде́ля, continuous work week. Не-пре-ры́в-ность, *n.f.*, continuity. Н. истори́ческого разви́тия, continuity of historical development. Пре-ры́в-истый, *adj.*, broken, interrupted. П-ое дыха́ние больно́го, intermittent breathing of a patient. Пре-ры́в-исто, *adv.*, interruptedly. Он говори́л п., ка́шляя и задыха́ясь, he spoke in a broken voice, coughing and gasping for air.

по-рв-а́ть, *v.p.*, по-рыв-а́ть, *v.i.*, + *acc.*, с +*instr.*, to tear off, break off. П. отноше́ния, to sever relations. Он не раз порыва́л со ста́рыми друзья́ми и сно́ва возвраща́лся к ним, many a time he broke off with his old friends and again came back to them. По-рв-а́ть-ся, *v.p.r.*, по-рыв-а́ть-ся, *v.i.r.*, + *inf.*, to try, endeavor; to be broken off, torn off. Брю́ки порва́лись во мно́гих места́х, the trousers were torn in several places. По-ры́в, *n.m.*, gust; fit, transport, burst, outburst. П. ве́тра, gust of wind. Благоро́дный п., noble outburst. По-ры́в-истый, *adj.*, gusty, violent; impetuous, vehement. П. ве́тер, gusty, violent wind. По-ры́в-истость, *n.f.*, violence, impetuosity. П. в движе́ниях, impetuosity, jerkiness of motions.

подо-рв-а́ть, *v.p.*, под-рыв-а́ть, *v.i.*, + *acc.*, to blow up, blast, undermine. П. зда́ние (мост), to blow up a building. П. здоро́вье (си́лы), to overtax one's health (one's strength). П. дове́рие (ве́ру, наде́жду), to shake one's confidence, (shatter one's faith, one's hope). Подо-рв-а́ть-ся, *v.p.r.*, под-рыв-а́ть-ся, *v.i.r.*, + *instr.*, to be blown up, sapped, undermined, overtaxed. Зда́ния подрыва́ются динами́том, buildings are blown up with dynamite. Под-ры́в, *n.m.*, undermining, dynamiting. П. го́рной поро́ды, dynamiting of rocks. П. авторите́та, undermining of someone's authority. Под-рыв-но́й, *adj.*, blasting, demolition. П.

материа́л, demolition material. Под-ры́в-щик, *n.m.*, one who dynamites, blows up, undermines. Под-ры́в-ник, *n.m.* (*mil.*), demolition man.

про-рв-а́ть, *v.p.*, про-рыв-а́ть, *v.i.*, + *acc.*, to break, tear through. П. рука́в, to tear through a sleeve. П. ды́рку на пла́тье, to tear a hole in a dress. Про-рв-а́ть-ся, *v.p.r.*, про-рыв-а́ть-ся, *v.i.r.*, сквозь, че́рез + *acc.*, к + *dat.*, to burst open; cut, pierce, break one's way through; be pierced, broken, forced through. Со́лнечный луч прорва́лся сквозь ту́чи, a ray of sunlight pierced the clouds. Мои́ карма́ны прорва́лись, my pockets are torn. Нары́в прорва́лся, the abscess burst. Про-ры́в, *n.m.*, breakthrough. П. на фро́нте, breakthrough at the front. П. на заво́де, (*recent*), breakdown in production in a plant.

со-рв-а́ть, *v.p.*, с-рыв-а́ть, *v.i.*, + *acc.*, to tear away, tear off, tear down; pluck, pick; unmask; vent one's temper; frustrate, hamper. С. я́блоки с я́блони, to pick apples from an apple tree. Буре́й сорва́ло кры́шу, the roof was torn off during the storm. С. повя́зку с ра́ны, to tear a bandage off a wound. С. злость на ко́м-нибудь, to vent one's anger on someone. Со-рв-а́ть-ся, *v.p.r.*, с-рыв-а́ть-ся, *v.i.r.*, с + *gen.*, to break loose, become unhinged; fall to the ground; fail, miscarry; be broken off, unchained. Зе́ркало сорвало́сь со стены́, the mirror fell from the wall. Он сорва́лся с ме́ста и вы́бежал на у́лицу, he jumped from his seat and ran out into the street. Де́ло сорвало́сь, the deal failed, fell through. Его́ го́лос сорва́лся от волне́ния, his voice broke from emotion. Бежи́т, как бу́дто с цепи́ сорва́лся, (*idiom.*), he is running like one possessed. Это у него́ сорвало́сь с языка́, it escaped his lips. С-рыв-а́ющийся, *adj., part. act. pres. ref.*, torn off, picked, plucked. Со́-рв-анный, *adj., part. pass. past,* torn off, picked, plucked. С-рыв, *n.m.,* frustration; tearing off, removal. С печа́ти, removal of a seal. С-ры́в-щик, *n.m.* (recent), saboteur. С-рыв-а́ние, *n.n.,* tearing off (*as* of a bandage).

у-рв-а́ть, *v.p.*, у-рыв-а́ть, *v.i.*, + *acc.*, to snatch. У. свобо́дную мину́ту, to snatch a free minute. У-рв-а́ть-ся, *v.p.r.*, у-рыв-а́ть-ся, *v.i.r.*, to tear oneself away, find leisure. Так мно́го рабо́ты до́ма, что не́когда у. к вам и на мину́тку, there is so much work at home that I cannot even get away for a minute to visit you. У-ры́в-ками,

adv., by snatches, by fits and starts.
Приходи́лось учи́ться уры́вками, one
had to study by snatches.

РЕЗ-, РЕЖ-, CUTTING, SCISSION

ре́з-а-ть, ре́ж-у, *v.i.*, + *acc.*, to cut, slice;
slaughter. Р. хлеб, to cut, slice bread.
Р. пра́вду, to speak the truth bluntly.
Р. слух, to grate, offend one's sense
of hearing. Р. по ме́ди, to engrave in
copper. Ре́з-ать-ся, *v.i.r.*, to be cutting.
У ребёнка ре́жутся зу́бы, the baby
is cutting its teeth. Р. в ка́рты, (*colloq.*), to play recklessly at cards.
Рез-а́к, *n.m.*, ploughshare. Рез-е́ц,
n.m., cutter. Р. гравёра (скульптора),
engraver's (sculptor's) chisel. Ре́з-кий,
adj., sharp, cutting, harsh. Р. ве́тер,
sharp wind. Р-ие выраже́ния, sharp
language. Ре́з-ко, *adv.*, sharply. Ре́з-
кость, *n.f.*, sharpness. Рез-но́й, *adj.*,
cut, fretted, ornamented with fretwork.
Р-а́я рабо́та, fretwork. Рез-ня́, *n.f.*,
massacre. Ра́спря ко́нчилась резнёй,
the feud ended in a massacre.
вы́-рез-ать, *v.p.*, вы-ре́з-ывать, вы-рез-
а́ть, *v.i.*, + *acc.*, to cut out. В. ку́клы
из бума́ги, to cut dolls out of paper.
Вы́-рез, *n.m.*, notch, cut. Пла́тье с
ни́зким вы́резом, low-cut dress. Вы́-
рез-ка, *n.f.*, cut (*as* of meat). Газе́тная
в., newspaper clipping.
до-ре́з-ать, *v.p.*, до-рез-а́ть, *v.i.*, + *acc.*,
to cut completely.
за-ре́з-ать, *v.p.*, за-ре́з-ывать, за-рез-
а́ть, *v.i.*, + *acc.*, to butcher, slaughter,
kill, murder. З. ку́рицу на обе́д, to
kill a chicken for dinner. За-ре́з, *n.m.*,
in expression: Это для меня́ з., (*colloq.*), it will be the end of me. Мне
нужны́ де́ньги до заре́зу, I need
money very badly. За-ре́з-ать-ся,
v.p.r., to kill oneself, commit suicide.
из-ре́з-ать, *v.p.*, из-ре́з-ывать, из-рез-
а́ть, *v.i.*, + *acc.*, to cut to pieces,
slash. И. на куски́, to cut to pieces.
на-ре́з-ать, *v.p.*, на-ре́з-ывать, на-рез-
а́ть, *v.i.*, + *acc.*, to cut in quantity.
На-ре́з-ать-ся, *v.p.r.*, на-ре́з-ывать-
ся, на-рез-а́ть-ся, *v.i.r.*, to be cut in
quantity; be rifled; get drunk. Мя́со
наре́зывалось больши́ми куска́ми, the
meat was cut into large pieces. Он
здо́рово наре́зался, (*colloq.*), he got
thoroughly drunk. На-ре́з-ка, *n.f.*, incision, rifling. Н. винта́, thread of a
screw. На-рез-но́й, *adj.*, rifled.
над-ре́з-ать, *v.p.*, над-ре́з-ывать, над-
рез-а́ть, *v.i.*, + *acc.*, to incise, cut in,
notch. Над-ре́з, *n.m.*, cut, incision,
notch. Н. на де́реве, inscription on a
tree.

об-ре́з-ать, *v.p.*, об-ре́з-ывать, *v.i.*, +
acc., to cut, clip, prune; circumcise. Он
обре́зал себе́ па́лец, he cut his finger.
Об-ре́з-ать-ся, *v.p.r.*, об-ре́з-ывать-ся,
v.i.r., to cut oneself: be circumcised.
Но́гти обре́зываются но́жницами,
nails are cut with scissors.
об-ре́з-ать, *v.p.*, об-рез-а́ть, *v.i.*, + *acc.*,
to circumcise according to ritual. Об-
рез-а́ть-ся, *v.p.r.*, to be circumcised.
Об-ре́з, *n.m.*, edge (*as* of a book);
short-barreled rifle. Кни́га с золоты́м
обре́зом, a gilt-edged book. Об-рез-
а́ние, *n.n.*, cutting, pruning. Об-ре́з-
ание, *n.n.*, circumcision. Об-ре́з-ок,
n.m., clipping, shred, scrap. Желе́зные
обре́зки, scraps of iron.
от-ре́з-ать, *v.p.*, от-ре́з-ывать, от-рез-а́ть,
v.i., + *acc.*, to cut off; carve. О. ло́моть
хле́ба, to cut a slice of bread. От-ре́з,
n.m., cut, edge of a cut. О. мате́рии,
length of cloth. От-ре́з-ок, *n.m.*, remnant, piece; (*geom.*), segment. О.
вре́мени, space, period of time. От-
рез-а́ние, *n.n.*, от-ре́з-ывание, *n.n.*,
cutting off, carving.
пере-ре́з-ать, *v.p.*, пере-ре́з-ывать, пере-
рез-а́ть, *v.i.*, + *acc.*, + *instr.*, to
crosscut, intersect; slaughter, kill in
large numbers. П. хлеб попола́м, to
cut a loaf in two. Волк перере́зал
мно́го ове́ц, the wolf has killed many
sheep. Пере-ре́з-ывать-ся, *v.i.r.*, to be
intersected, crosscut. Доро́га пере-
ре́зывается кана́вой, the road is cut
off by a ditch. Пере-ре́з, *n.m.*, cross-
cut. На-пере-ре́з, *adv.*, across one's
path.
по-ре́з-ать, *v.p.*, + *acc.*, to cut. Ты
поре́жешь себе́ па́лец, you will cut
your finger. По-ре́з, *n.m.*, cut, wound.
под-ре́з-ать, *v.p.*, под-ре́з-ывать, под-
рез-а́ть, *v.i.*, + *acc.*, to cut, clip, trim.
П. во́лосы, to trim hair. П. дере́вья,
to clip trees. В ко́рне п., (*fig.*), to nip
in the bud. П. кры́лья, (*fig.*), to clip
one's wings.
при-ре́з-ать, *v.p.*, при-ре́з-ывать, при-
рез-а́ть, *v.i.*, + *acc.*, to add by cutting;
(*colloq.*), kill. К колхо́зу была́ при-
ре́зана земля́, (*recent*), land was added
to the collective farm.
про-ре́з-ать, *v.p.*, про-ре́з-ывать, про-
рез-а́ть, *v.i.*, to slot, trench, cut
through. П. нары́в, to lance an abscess.
П. кана́ву, to cut a ditch through.
Про-ре́з-ать-ся, *v.p.r.*, про-ре́з-ывать-
ся, *v.i.r.*, про-рез-а́ть-ся, *v.i.r.*, to be
cut through. У ребёнка проре́зывается
зуб, the child is cutting a tooth. Он
проре́зался сквозь толпу́, he made
his way through the crowd. Про-ре́з,

n.m., slot, notch. Делать п., to notch, make notches.

раз-ре́з-ать, *v.p.*, раз-ре́з-ывать, раз-рез-а́ть, *v.i.*, + *acc.*, to cut open, carve. Раз-ре́з-ывать-ся, раз-рез-а́ться, *v.i.r.*, to be cut. Гру́ша разреза́ется на две ча́сти, the pear is cut in two. Раз-ре́з, *n.m.*, cut, cross-section, slit. Раз-рез-но́й, *adj.*, pertaining to carving, cutting. Р. нож (для бума́ги), paper knife.

с-ре́з-ать, *v.p.*, с-ре́з-ывать, с-рез-а́ть, *v.i.*, + *acc.*, to cut off, away. С. на экза́мене, (*slang*), to fail a student at an examination. С. верху́шку де́рева, to cut off the top of a tree. С-ре́з-ать-ся, *v.p.r.*, (*colloq.*), to fail. С. на экза́мене, to fail an examination. С-ре́з-ывать-ся, с-рез-а́ть-ся, *v.i.r.*, to be cut off, away. С-рез, *n.m.*, cut. С-рез-а́ние, с-ре́з-ывание, *n.n.*, cutting.

у-ре́з-ать, *v.p.*, у-ре́з-ывать, у-рез-а́ть, *v.i.*, + *acc.*, to cut down, curtail, abridge, reduce. У. сме́ту, to cut down an estimate. У. себя́ во всём, to stint oneself. У-ре́з-ывать-ся, *v.i.r.*, to be curtailed, reduced; be allotted. Жилпло́щадь уре́зывается, (*recent*), living space is allotted by regulation. У-ре́з-ывание, *n.n.*, cutting down, curtailment.

РЕШ-, DECISION, SOLUTION

реш-и́ть, *v.p.*, реш-а́ть, *v.i.*, + *acc.*, to work out, solve, settle, decide. Р. зада́чу, to work out a problem. Р. вопро́с, to settle a question. Он реши́л оста́ться здесь, he decided to remain here. Реш-ённый, *adj., part. pass. past*, decided. Р-ое де́ло, settled matter. Реш-и́ть-ся, *v.p.r.*, реш-а́ть-ся, *v.i.r.*, to decide; be decided, settled, resolved. Он не реши́лся на э́то, he decided against this. Реш-а́ющий, *adj., part. act. pres.*, decisive. Р. фа́ктор, decisive factor. Реш-е́ние, *n.n.*, decision, resolution. Р. вопро́са (зада́чи), solution of a question (a problem). Р. прися́жных, verdict. Выноси́ть р., to pass a resolution. Приня́ть р., to adopt a resolution. Зара́нее при́нятое р., foregone conclusion. Реш-и́мость, *n.f.*, decisiveness, firmness, resoluteness. Реш-и́тельный, *adj.*, resolute, determined, bold. Р. отка́з, categorical refusal. Р. посту́пок, resolute, bold action. Р. тон, resolute tone of voice. Р-ые ме́ры, decisive measures. Реш-и́тельно, *adv.*, resolutely, firmly, decisively. Он р. отрица́л, he flatly denied. Она́ р. про́тив э́того, she is vigorously opposed to this. Он р. ничего́ не

де́лает, he does absolutely nothing. Реш-и́тельность, *n.f.*, resoluteness, firmness. Р. хара́ктера, firmness of character.

от-реш-и́ть, *v.p.*, от-реш-а́ть, *v.i.*, + *acc.* (*obs.*), to dismiss, remove, deprive. От-реш-и́ть-ся, *v.p.r.*, от-реш-а́ть-ся, *v.i.r.*, от + *gen.*, to renounce, give up. О. от ми́ра, to renounce the world. От-реш-е́ние, *n.n.*, dismissal. О. от до́лжности, dismissal from a position.

пере-реш-а́ть, *v.i.*, пере-реш-и́ть, *v.p.*, + *acc.*, to alter one's decision.

по-реш-и́ть, *v.p.*, по-реш-а́ть, *v.i.*, + *acc.*, to kill, do away with; (*colloq.*), decide, agree. Они́ пореши́ли оста́ться, they decided to remain. Всех их безжа́лостно пореши́ли, they killed all of them without pity.

пред-реш-и́ть, *v.p.*, пред-реш-а́ть, *v.i.*, + *acc.*, to predetermine, decide beforehand. Пред-реш-ённый, *adj., part. pass. past*, predetermined. П. отве́т, predetermined answer.

раз-реш-и́ть, *v.p.*, раз-реш-а́ть, *v.i.*, + *acc.*, + *dat.*, to permit; solve, resolve; grant; absolve. Р. зада́чу, to solve a problem. Р. грехи́, (*rel.*), to absolve sins. Разреши́те войти́! May I come in? Раз-реш-и́ть-ся, *v.p.r.*, раз-реш-а́ть-ся, *v.i.r.*, to be permitted; come to a climax. Р. от бре́мени, to be delivered of a child. Сюда́ не разреша́ется! Entrance is forbidden! Раз-реш-е́ние, *n.n.*, permission, permit. Р. на пра́во про́мысла, trade license. Р. вопро́са, solution of a question. Р. печа́тать, imprimatur. Раз-реш-и́мый, *adj.*, solvable. Не-раз-реш-и́мый, *adj.*, insolvable. Раз-реш-и́мость, *n.f.*, solvability (of a question, problem). Не-раз-реш-и́мость, *n.f.*, insolvability.

РОД-, РОЖД-, РОЖ-, BIRTH, TRIBE, NATURE

род, *n.m.*, family, kin, tribe, clan, generation, sort. Мужско́й род, masculine gender. Что́-то в э́том ро́де, something of this sort. Он ро́дом из Москвы́, he was born in Moscow. Без ро́ду, без пле́мени, (*idiom.*), without kith or kin. Пяти́ лет от роду, five years old.

род-и́ть, *v.p.*, рожд-а́ть, *v.i.*, рож-а́ть, *v.i.*, + *acc.*, to give birth. Его́ жена́ родила́ сы́на, his wife gave birth to a son. В чём мать родила́, (*colloq.*), stark naked; as naked as the day he was born, in his birthday suit. Ро́д-ы, *n.pl.*, lying-in, confinement. Преждевре́менные ро́ды, premature delivery.

род-и́ть-ся, *v.p.r.*, рожд-а́ть-ся, рож-а́ть-ся, *v.i.r.*, to be born. Р. слепы́м, to be born blind. Род-и́льница, *n.f.*, woman in confinement. Род-и́льный, *adj.*, lying-in. Р. дом, lying-in hospital. Р-ая горя́чка, puerperal fever. Род-и́мчик, *n.n.*, (*obs.*), child eclampsia, convulsions. Род-и́мый, *adj.*, (*folk.*), my own darling. Р-ое пятно́, birthmark. Ро́д-инка, *n.f.*, mole. Ро́д-ина, *n.f.*, native country, fatherland. Тоска́ по ро́дине, nostalgia, homesickness. Род-и́тель, *n.m.*, род-и́тельница, *n.f.*, (*obs.*), parent. Род-и́тели, *n.pl.*, parents. Род-и́тельный, *adj.*, genitive. Р. паде́ж, (*gram.*), genitive case. Ро́д-ич, *n.m.*, (*colloq.*), relative. Род-ни́к, *n.m.*, source, spring. Род-нико́вый, *adj.*, spring. Р-ая вода́, spring water. Родно́й, *adj.*, native. Р. го́род, native city. Р-а́я страна́, native country. Р. язы́к, native language, tongue. Род-ня́, *n.f.*, *coll.*, relatives, kin, Род-ови́тость, *n.f.*, old lineage. Род-ови́тый, *adj.*, well-born, belonging to an aristocracy. Род-ово́й, *adj.*, ancestral, patrimonial. Р. быт, tribal rule, tribal mode of life. Р-о́е поме́стье, patrimony. Род-о-, *a combining form meaning* birth, tribe, blood relationship. Род-о-нача́льник, *n.m.*, forefather, ancestor. Р. ру́сской поэ́зии, father of Russian poetry. Род-о-сло́вная, *adj.*, *used as n.*, genealogy, pedigree. Род-о-сло́вный, *adj.*, genealogical. Р-ое де́рево, family tree. Ро́д-ственник, *n.m.*, ро́д-ственница, *n.f.*, kinsman, relative. Р. по восходя́щей ли́нии, ascendant. Бли́зкий р., near relation, close relative. Р. по отцу́, relation on the father's side. Р. по ма́тери, relation on the mother's side. Ро́д-ственный, *adj.*, related, akin. Р-ая душа́, kindred soul. Р-ые свя́зи, ties of blood. Род-ство́, *n.n.*, relationship, kindred. Ли́ния родства́, line of parentage. В родстве́, related. Рожд-е́ние, *n.n.*, birth. Поздравля́ю со днём рожде́ния! I congratulate you on your birthday. От рожде́ния, since birth; by nature. Рожд-ённый, *adj.*, *part. pass. past*, born. Р. по́лзать лета́ть не мо́жет, (*Gorky*), one born to creep cannot fly. Ново-рожд-ённый, *adj.*, *used as n.*, newborn child. Рожд-ество́, (Христо́во), *n.n.*, Christmas. До Рождества́ Христо́ва (до Р. Х.), before Christ (B. C.). Рожд-е́ственский, *adj.*, Christmas. Р. пода́рок, Christmas gift.

без-ро́д-ный, *adj.*, without kin.

воз-род-и́ть, *v.р.*, воз-рожд-а́ть, *v.i.*, to regenerate, renew. Воз-рожд-а́ющий, *adj.*, *part. act. pres.*, regenerative. Воз-рожд-ённый, *adj.*, *part. pass. past*, regenerated. Воз-род-и́ть-ся, *v.р.r.*, воз-рожд-а́ть-ся, *v.i.r.*, to be regener-

ated, revived. Воз-рожд-а́ющийся, *adj.*, *part. act. pres.*, renascent, revived. Воз-рожд-е́ние, *n.n.*, regeneration, rebirth, revival. Эпо́ха Воз-рожд-е́ния, the Renaissance.

вы́-род-ить-ся, *v.р.r.*, вы-рожд-а́ть-ся, *v.i.r.*, to degenerate. Вы́-род-ок, *n.m.*, degenerate. Вы-рожд-е́ние, *n.n.*, degeneration.

двою-род-ный брат, first cousin. Трою-род-ный брат, second cousin. Т-ая сестра́, second cousin (female).

за-род-и́ть-ся, *v.р.r.*, за-рожд-а́ть-ся, *v.i.r.*, to be conceived, begotten. За-рожд-а́ющийся, *adj.*, *part. pass. past*, conceived, begotten, nascent. За-ро́д-ыш, *n.m.*, foetus, embryo; (*bot.*), germ. Пресе́чь в заро́дыше, (*idiom.*), to nip in the bud.

из-у-ро́д-овать, *see* уро́довать.

ин-о-ро́д-ный, *adj.*, foreign. Ин-о-ро́д-ец, *n.m.*, of another tribe, not a native.

на-ро́д, *n.m.*, people, nation. Ру́сский н., the Russian people. Челове́к из наро́да, a man of the people. Ули́ца полна́ наро́ду, the street is crowded. Наро́ды Азии, the peoples of Asia. На-ро́д-ник, *n.m.*, (*hist.*), Populist, member of a Russian pre-Rev. party. На-ро́д-ность, *n.f.*, nationality. На-ро́д-ный, *adj.*, national, popular. Н. дохо́д, national income. Н. комисса́р (нарко́м), (*recent*), people's commissar. Н-ая пе́сня, folk song. Н-ое бла́го, common welfare. Наро́д-о-ве́дение, *n.n.*, ethnology. Наро́д-о-вла́стие, *n.n.*, democracy. Наро́д-о-во́лец, *n.m.*, (*hist.*), member of "The People's Will," a Russian pre-Rev. party. Наро́д-о-населе́ние, *n.n.*, population. Наро́д-о-счисле́ние, census.

на-род-и́ть, *v.р.*, на-рожд-а́ть, *v.i.*, to give birth, bring forth in large numbers. На-род-и́ть-ся, *v.р.r.*, на-рожд-а́ть-ся, *v.i.r.*, to be born, arise. На-рожд-е́ние, *n.n.*, birth, spring up. Н. ме́сяца, new moon.

от-ро́д-ье, *n.n.*, (*derog.*), offspring, brat.

пере-род-и́ть, *v.р.*, пере-рожд-а́ть, *v.i.*, + *acc.*, to transform, change completely. Пере-род-и́ть-ся, *v.р.r.*, пере-рожд-а́ть-ся, *v.i.r.*, to reform, be reborn, be regenerated; (*recent*), degenerate. Он совсе́м перероди́лся, he has completely reformed. Пере-род-и́вшийся, *adj.*, *part. act. past*, regenerated; (*recent*) degenerate. П-аяся ткань, degenerated tissue. Пере-рожд-е́ние, *n.n.*, regeneration, transformation; (*biol.*), degeneration. Духо́вное (физи́ческое) п., spiritual (physical) regeneration.

по-ро́д-а, *n.f.*, breed, stock, race; (*geol.*),

stratum. П. овéц, breed of sheep. По-рóд-истый, *adj.*, purebred, pedigreed. П. щенóк, purebred puppy.

по-род-и́ть, *v.p.,* по-рожд-áть, *v.i.,* + *acc.,* to give birth, beget, breed, produce; raise. По-род-и́ть-ся, *v.p.r.,* по-рожд-áть-ся, *v.i.r.,* to be born, begotten, bred, produced; raised. По-рожд-éние, *n.n.,* begetting, producing, product. Это п. фантáзии, this is a product of imagination.

по-род-н-и́ть, *v.p.,* род-н-и́ть, *v.i.,* + *acc.,* to become related. Этот брак породни́л егó с ни́ми, he became related to them through this marriage. По-род-н-и́ть-ся, *v.p.r.,* род-н-и́ть-ся, *v.i.r.,* to become related. Их сéмьи породни́лись, their families became related. Сосéдние племенá родни́лись, the neighboring tribes became related (intermarried).

при-рóд-а, *n.f.,* nature; structure. Закóн прирóды, law of nature. Человéческая п., human nature. П. растéний, nature of plants. По прирóде, by nature. Игрá прирóды, a freak of nature. При-рóд-ный, *adj.,* natural, inborn, innate. П-ые богáтства, natural resources. П-ые даровáния, natural gifts. При-род-о-вéдение, *n.n.,* natural sciences. При-рожд-ённый, *adj.,* innate, inborn, native. П. орáтор, born orator, speaker.

раз-род-и́ть-ся, *v.p.r.,* (*colloq.*), to give birth. Онá разроди́лась двóйней, she gave birth to twins.

с-род-ствó, *n.n.,* relationship, affinity. С. душ, affinity of souls. С-рóд-у, *adv.,* from birth.

с-род-н-и́ть, *v.p.,* + *acc.,* to become related, *see* породни́ть, родни́ть. Это сродни́ло егó с ни́ми, this brought him close to them, made him one of them. С-род-ни́ть-ся, *v.p.r.,* to become close to, become related. С. брáком, to become related by marriage. С. с дéлом, to become familiar with a matter, a business. С-рóд-ный, *adj.,* related, akin. С-рóд-ник, (*obs.*) *n.m.,* relative, relation. С-род-ни́, *adv.,* akin. Он мне сродни́, I am related to him.

у-рóд, *n.m.,* monster, ugly being. Посмотри́те на э́того урóда, look at this monster.

у-рóд-ова-ть, *v.p.,* из-у-рóд-овать, *v.i.,* + *acc.,* to deform, make ugly; mutilate. Оспа урóдует лицó, smallpox disfigures the face. Такóе воспитáние урóдует детéй, such an education demoralizes children. Из-у-рóд-ованный, *adj., part. pass. past,* mutilated, deformed, disfigured. И. труп, mutilated corpse. У-рóд-ование, *n.n.,* mutilation,

defacement. У-рóд-ливый, *adj.,* deformed, ugly. У-рóд-ливость, *n.f.,* deformity, ugliness. У-рóд-ство, *n.n.,* ugliness, defacement, malformation.

у-род-и́ть, *v.p.,* у-рожд-áть, *v.i.,* to yield, bear. Огорóд хорошó уроди́л в э́том годý, the garden produced a good vegetable yield this year. У-рожд-ённый, *adj., part. pass. past,* yielded, produced, born. Петрóва, урождённая Ушакóва, Petrova, born (née) Ushakov. У-род-и́ть-ся, *v.p.r.,* be produced; born; take after. Пшени́ца в э́том годý уроди́лась (*folk.*), there is a good wheat crop this year. Сын уроди́лся в отцá, the son took after his father. У-род-áй, *n.m.,* harvest. В э́том годý хорóший у., the harvest is good this year. У-рож-áйность, *n.f.,* fruitfulness, yielding capacity. У-рож-áйный, *adj.,* fruitful. У. год, year of good harvest. У-рож-éнец, *n.m.,* у-рож-éнка, *n.f.,* native. У. Москвы́, native of Moscow.

ю-рóд-ствовать, *v.i.,* (*obs.*), to be a saintly beggar, be a fool in Christ. Ю-рóд-ство, *n.n.,* state of being a saintly beggar, a fool in Christ. Ю-рóд-ивый, *adj., usually used as n.,* pertaining to a saintly beggar; a fool in Christ.

РОЗН-, РАЗН-, DIFFERENCE, VARIEGATION

розн-ь, *n.f.,* difference; discord. Сéять р., to sow seeds of discord. Рóзн-ица, *n.f.,* retail. Продавáть в рóзницу, to sell retail. Рóзн-ичный, *adj.,* retail. Р-ая продáжа, retail sale. Пó-розн-ь, *adv.,* separately, apart.

рóзн-ить-ся, (*colloq.*), **рáзн-ить-ся,** *v.i.r.,* от + *gen.,* to differ, to be unlike.

рáзн-ица, *n.f.,* difference, distinction. Р. в ценé, difference in price. Какáя мéжду ни́ми р.! What a contrast between them! Рáзн-ость, *n.f.,* variety, difference. Рáзн-ый, *adj.,* different, various. У нас рáзные вкýсы, we have different tastes. Рáзн-о, *adv.,* differently, variantly. Рáзн-о, *a combining form meaning* different, various. Разн-о-вéс, *n.m.,* small weight. Разн-о-ви́дность, *n.f.,* variety, variegation. Разн-о-глáсие, *n.n.,* discord. Разн-о-обрáзие, *n.n.,* diversity, variety. Разн-о-обрáзный, *adj.,* diverse, various. Разн-о-сóлы, *n.pl.,* (*colloq.*), variety of dainty foods. Разн-о-харáктерный, *adj.,* multiplex, of different character.

раз-рóзн-ить, *v.p.,* раз-рóзн-ивать, *v.i.,* to break up (*as* a complete set). Раз-рóзн-енный, *adj., part. pass. past,* odd. Том из разрóзненного собрáния сочинéний, an odd volume from a set of complete works.

РУБ-, РУБ(Л)-, SCISSION, CLEAVAGE

руб-и́-ть, руб-л-ю́, *v.i.*, + *acc.*, to cut, chop, hash. Р. дрова́, to chop wood. Р. дéрево, to fell a tree. Р. са́блей, to hack with a sabre. Р. избу́, (*folk.*), to build a peasant log cabin, peasant hut. Р. нáправо и налéво, (*idiom.*), to hew down right and left, Р. с плечá, (*fig.*), to act rashly. Лес ру́бят, щéпки летя́т, (*saying*), one cannot make an omelet without breaking eggs. Ру́б-л-енный, *adj., part. pass. past,* chopped, minced. Мéлко-р-ая капу́ста, finely chopped cabbage. Ру́б-л-еный, *adj.,* chopped, minced. Р-ое мя́со, hash; minced, chopped meat. Р-ые котлéты, chopped cutlets, hamburger. Руб-а́нок, *n.m.,* plane. Ру́б-ка, *n.f.,* hewing, felling, chopping. Р. лéса, the felling of a forest.

в-руб-и́ть, *v.p.,* в-руб-а́ть, *v.i.,* в + *acc.,* to chop in, cut in. В. бóчку в лёд, to hew a barrel into ice. В-руб-и́ть-ся, *v.p.r.,* в-руб-а́ть-ся, *v.i.r.,* в + *acc.,* to cut into. Дровосéки далекó вру-би́лись в лес, the lumberjacks cut their way deep into the forest. В-руб, *n.m.,* notch, cross-cut. Горнорабóчие про-би́ли вруб в скалé, the miners bored a shaft in the rock. В-ру́б-ка, *n.f.,* cutting, notching (mining). В-рубо-ово́й, *adj.,* pertaining to cutting, channeling (mining). В-ы́е рабóты, channeling, cutting (mining). В-а́я маши́на, cutter, channeling machine (mining).

вы́-руб-ить, *v.p.,* вы-руб-а́ть, *v.i.,* to cut down, fell. В. лес, to fell a forest. Вы́-руб-ить-ся, *v.p.r.,* вы-руб-а́ть-ся, *v.i.r.,* из + *gen.,* to be felled. Исслéдо-ватели вы́рубились из чáщи тропи́-ческого лéса, the explorers cut their way out of the tropical jungle. Вы́-руб-ка, *n.f.,* felling, cutting down, hewing out.

до-руб-и́ть, *v.p.,* до-руб-а́ть, *v.i.,* + *acc.,* to cut completely. Д. дéрево до концá, to cut down a tree.

за-руб-и́ть, *v.p.,* за-руб-а́ть, *v.i.,* + *acc.,* to hew with an axe, hack; cut in, mark. Уби́йца заруби́л топорóм свою́ жéрт-ву, the murderer hacked his victim with an axe. Заруби́ себé на носу́! (*colloq.*), Mark it well, remember it. За-ру́б-ка, *n.f.,* mark, incision, notch. Заруби́ть зару́бку, to notch, make a notch.

из-руб-и́ть, *v.p.,* из-руб-а́ть, *v.i.,* + *acc.,* to cut, mince, chop, hack. Из-ру́б-л-

енный, *adj., part. pass. past,* cut, hashed, hacked.

на-руб-и́ть, *v.p.,* на-руб-а́ть, (*colloq.*), *v.i.,* + *acc.,* + *gen.,* to cut, chop in quantity; hew, notch. Н. дров нá зиму, to chop enough wood for the winter. Н. знáки на дéреве, to make notches in a tree.

над-руб-и́ть, *v.p.,* над-руб-а́ть, *v.i.,* + *acc.,* to cut in, notch. Н. бревнó, to hew part of a log. Над-ру́б-л-енный, *adj., part. pass. past,* hewed, notched. Н-ое дéрево, a notched tree.

об-руб-и́ть, *v.p.,* об-руб-а́ть, *v.i.,* + *acc.,* to trim. О. брёвна, to trim logs. О. хвост собáке, to cut a dog's tail. Об-ру́б-ок, *n.m.,* block, chunk; stump of a dog's tail.

от-руб-и́ть, *v.p.,* от-руб-а́ть, *v.i.,* + *acc.,* to cut off, chop off. О. сук, to cut off a branch. От-руб, *n.m.,* (*pre-Rev.*), small holding, plot of land. От-руб-нóй, *adj.,* pertaining to a small plot of land. О-áя систéма землевладéния, a system of land ownership through small holdings. Óт-руб-и, *n.f.pl.,* bran. Пóйло из от-рубéй, mash.

пере-руб-и́ть, *v.p.,* пере-руб-а́ть, *v.i.,* + *acc.,* to cut in two; to kill with an axe, a sword; massacre. П. дóску пополáм, to chop a board in two.

по-руб-и́ть, *v.p.,* + *acc.,* to cut, fell. Они́ поруби́ли все дерéвья, they felled all the trees. По-ру́б-ка, *n.f.,* illegal cut-ting of timber. По-ру́б-щик, *n.m.,* one who steals wood, one who cuts wood illegally.

под-руб-и́ть, *v.p.,* под-руб-а́ть, *v.i.,* to cut partly. П. дерéвья, to cut trees partly. Под-руб-и́ть, *v.p.,* под-ру́б-ливать, *v.i.,* + *acc.,* to hem. П. плáтье, to hem a dress. Под-ру́б-л-ивание, *n.n.,* hemming.

про-руб-и́ть, *v.p.,* про-руб-а́ть, *v.i.,* + *acc.,* to cut through. П. прóсеку в лесу́, to cut a lane, a path through a forest. Прó-руб-ь, *n.f.,* a hole cut in the ice for washing, for fishing. П. замёрзла, the hole in the ice has frozen over.

раз-руб-и́ть, *v.p.,* раз-руб-а́ть, *v.i.,* + *acc.,* to cut, cleave, slash, split. Р. на чáсти, to slash to pieces. Раз-руб-и́ть-ся, *v.p.r.,* раз-руб-а́ть-ся, *v.i.r.,* to be cut, cleaved, slashed, split. Эта кость для су́па легкó разруба́ется на мéл-кие куски́, this soup bone easily splits into pieces. Раз-ру́б, *n.m.,* cut, section.

с-руб-и́ть, *v.p.,* с-руб-а́ть, *v.i.,* + *acc.,* to cut, hew off. С. дéрево, to fell a tree. С-руб, *n.m.,* shell, felling; frame. С. избы́, frame of a log cabin. Продáть лес на с., to sell wood for felling.

руб-áх-а, руб-áшка, *n.f.,* shirt. Крахмáльная р., starched shirt. Своя рубáшка к тéлу блúже, (*saying*), charity begins at home. Остáться в однóй рубáшке, (*fig.*) to be ruined (*as by fire,* burglary). Родúться в рубáшке, (*fig.*), to be born with a silverspoon in one's mouth. Рýб-ище, *n.m.*, sackcloth, rags. Нúщий, одéтый в р., a beggar dressed in rags.

руб-éж, *n.m.*, border, frontier; limit. На рубежé двух столéтий, at the turn of the century. За рубежóм, beyond the border; abroad. За-руб-éжный, *adj.*, beyond the border; foreign. Зарубéжная Россúя, the Russian people abroad; Russian emigration. По-руб-éжный, *adj.*, frontier; along the border.

руб-éц, *n.m.*, scar, seam, hem; rumen. Всё егó тéло покрыто рубцáми, his whole body is covered with scars. Плáтье подшúто рубцóм, this dress is hemmed. Руб-цы, *n.m.pl.*, tripe. Рýб-цевáтый, *adj.*, scarred, seamed. Рýб-чик, *n.m.*, small seam. Рýб-чатый, *adj.*, ridged, corrugated, ribbed. Рýб-чатое желéзо, corrugated iron.

руб-ц-евáть-ся, *v.i.r.*, to heal, form scar tissue. Рáна рубцýется, the wound is healing. Руб-цевáние, *n.n.*, healing.

за-руб-ц-евáть-ся, *v.r.r.*, за-руб-цёвы-вать-ся, *v.i.r.*, to be cicatrized. Рáна быстро зарубцевáлась, the wound soon healed.

руб-л-ь, *n.m.*, rubble (originally a chopped off piece of silver). Костюм стóит мóлько 500 рублéй, this suit costs only five hundred rubles. Отдáть послéдний рубль, to spend, give away one's last ruble. Руб-л-ёвый, *adj.*, costing one ruble. Руб-л-ёвая матéрия, cloth worth, costing a ruble. Копéйка р. бережёт, (*prov.*), a penny saved is a penny earned; big oaks from little acorns grow. Слóво скáжет, как руб-лём подáрит, (*fig.*), she is very eloquent. Взглянýл, как рублём подарúл, (*fig.*), a glance from him is like a gift of money. Не имéй сто рублéй, а имéй сто друзéй, (*saying*), friends are dearer than money. Не рублём, так дубьём, (*fig.*), to get something by force, if not by persuasion, or graft; to get by hook, or by crook.

РУК-, РУЧ-, HAND

рук-á, *n.f.*, hand; wrist, arm. Прáвая (лéвая) рукá, right (left) hand. Он прáвая рукá минúстра, he is the minister's right-hand man. У негó там рукá, (*fig.*), he has some influence (connections) there. У меня не под-

нялáсь р. э́то сдéлать, I did not have the heart to do it. Игрáть в четыре рукú, to play a duet. Он плут большóй рукú, (*colloq.*), he is a crook of the first order. Просúть чьéй-либо рукú, to ask a woman's hand in marriage. Набúть себé рýку на чём-либо, to acquire skill in something. На скóрую рýку, offhand, in a hurry. Он взял меня пóд руку, he took me by the arm. Под пьяную рýку, under the influence of alcohol. Подáть рýку пóмощи, to lend a helping hand. Пожáть рýку, to shake someone's hand. Приложúть рýку, (*obs.*), to sign. Сон в рýку, a dream-come-true. Это мне нá руку, it suits me. Как рукóй сняло, (*colloq.*), vanished into thin air (of pain). Махáть рукáми, to wave one's arms, hands. Махнýть рукóй на чтó-либо, (*fig.*), to lose interest, give up. Быть под рукóй, to be at hand. Это рукóй подáть, (*colloq.*), it is no distance at all. Рýки вверх! Hands up! Рýки прочь! Hands off! Взять ребёнка нá руки, to take a child in one's arms. Взять себя в рýки, to pull oneself together, take oneself in hand. В сóбственные рýки, to be delivered personally. Мáстер на все рýки, jack-of-all-trades, master of all. Рабóчие рýки, hands, manpower. Наложúть на себя рýки, (*obs.*), to commit suicide. У меня опустúлись рýки, (*fig.*), I feel utterly discouraged. Из пéрвых рук, at first hand. Сбыть с рук, to rid oneself of. Сдéлано из рук вон плóхо, wretchedly done. Это вам не сойдёт с рук, you will have to bear the consequences for this. Рукáм вóли не давáть! Steady with your hands! Прибрáть к рукáм, to take in hand. По рукáм! Agreed! Удáрить по рукáм, to shake hands in agreement. Под рукáми, right at hand. С пустыми рукáми, empty-handed. Чужúми рукáми жар загребáть, to benefit from someone else's effort. Держáть когó-либо в рукáх, to have a person under one's thumb. Без-рýк-ий, *adj.*, armless. Рук-áв, *n.m.*, sleeve. Р. плáтья, sleeve of a dress. Р. рекú, branch of a river. Р. пóрван, the sleeve is torn. Пожáр-ный р., firehose. Относúться к дéлу спустя рукавá, to let things slide. Рук-авúца, *n.f.*, mitten. Рук-áвчик, *n.m.*, cuff. Без-рук-áвка, *n.f.*, sleeveless garment. На-рук-áвник, *n.m.*, oversleeve. Рук-о-, *a combining form meaning* arm, hand.

рук-о-водúть, *v.i.*, рук-о-вóдствовать, *v.i.*, + *instr.*, to guide, direct; *see* водúть. Рук-о-водúтель, *n.m.*, mentor, guide, instructor. Рук-о-во́дство, *п.п.*, manual, handbook; guidance. Р. по меха́нике, handbook of mechanics.

рук-о-де́льничать, *v.i.,* to do needlework. Рук-о-де́лие, *п.п.,* hand embroidery, needlework. Рук-о-де́льница, *n.f.,* needlewoman. Рук-о-мо́йник, *п.т.,* washstand. Рук-о-па́шный, *adj.,* hand to hand, man to man. Р. бой, hand to hand fighting. Вступа́ть в рукопа́шную, to come to blows. Ру́к-о-пись, *n.f.,* manuscript. Рук-о-пи́сный, *adj.,* written by hand; pertaining to a manuscript. Рук-о-плеска́ние, *п.п.,* applause. Рук-о-пожа́тие, *п.п.,* handshake, handshaking.

рук-о-полага́ть, *v.i.,* + *acc.,* to ordain. Рук-о-положе́ние, *п.п.,* ordination, ordaining. Рук-о-тво́рный, *adj., (obs.),* made by hand. Не-рук-о-тво́рный, *adj.,* miraculous, not made by human hands. Н. о́браз, a veronica image of Christ. Рук-о-я́ть, *n.f.,* handle, hilt. Рук-о-я́тка, *n.f., (dim.),* handle, hilt. Р. кинжа́ла, of a dagger-hilt.

ру́ч-ка, *n.f.,* small hand; handle; penholder. Кро́шечная р., tiny hand. Дверна́я р., doorknob. На-ру́ч-ник, *п.т.,* handcuff. Ему́ наде́ли нару́чники, they handcuffed him. По́-руч-ен-ь, *п.т.,* handrail. По́-руч-ни, railings. Руч-и́щ-а, *n.f.,* large, broad hand. Руч-но́й, *adj.,* manual, handmade; domestic; tame. Р. труд, manual labor. Р-а́я пила́, handsaw. Р-а́я рабо́та, handiwork. Р-о́й скворе́ц, tame starling. В-руч-ну́ю, *adv.,* by hand. Де́лать что́-либо в., to make by hand.

руч-а́ть-ся, *v.i.r.,* за + *acc.,* to warrant, guarantee, vouch for. Я за него́ руча́юсь, I'll vouch for him. Р. за пра́вильность ко́пии, to certify a true copy (*as* of a document). Р. за ве́рность све́дений, to guarantee the truth of information. Руча́юсь, что сде́лаю э́то, I guarantee I'll do it. Руч-а́тельство, *п.п.,* guarantee. Лицо́, даю́щее р., one who guarantees. Часы́ с руча́тельством на два го́да, watch guaranteed for two years.

в-руч-и́ть, *v.p.,* в-руч-а́ть, *v.i.,* + *acc.,* + *dat.,* to hand; deliver. В. письмо́ в со́бственные ру́ки, to deliver personally. В. суде́бную пове́стку, to serve a subpoena. В-руч-е́ние, *п.п.,* official presentation.

вы́-руч-ить, *v.p.,* вы-руч-а́ть, *v.i.,* + *acc.,* из + *gen.,* to rescue, relieve; gain. В. из беды́, to rescue. Вы́рученные де́ньги, proceeds. Вы́-руч-ка, *n.f.,* rescue; proceeds, gain. Подоспе́ть на вы́ручку, to rescue in time. Валова́я в..

gross proceeds. Дневна́я в. магази́на, daily intake of a shop.

за-руч-и́ть-ся, *v.p.r.,* за-руч-а́ть-ся, *v.i.r.,* + *instr.,* to secure. З. чье́й-либо по́мощью, to secure somebody's aid. З. согла́сием, to obtain consent. Об-руч, *п.т.,* hoop. Набива́ть о́бручи на бо́чку, to hoop a barrel, a cask.

об-руч-и́ть, *v.p.,* об-руч-а́ть, *v.i.,* + *acc.,* с + *instr.,* to affiance, betroth. Об-руч-а́ть-ся, *v.p.r.,* об-руч-и́ть-ся, *v.i.r.,* с + *instr.,* to become affianced, betrothed. О. с ке́м-либо, to become engaged to someone. Об-руч-а́льный, *adj.,* engagement, betrothal. О-ое кольцо́, engagement ring. Об-руч-е́ние, *п.п.,* betrothal, engagement.

по-ру́к-а, *n.f.,* pledge, bail, guarantee. Кругова́я п., mutual responsibility. Отпусти́ть на пору́ки, to release on bail. Я тому́ пору́кой, I'll guarantee it.

по-руч-и́ть, *v.p.,* по-руч-а́ть, *v.i.,* + *acc.,* + *dat.,* to entrust, charge. Я поруча́ю э́то вам, I am entrusting it to you. По-руч-е́ние, *п.п.,* commission, errand, mission, assignment. Дава́ть кому́-либо п., to give someone a commission, assignment. По поруче́нию, on behalf of. По-руч-а́ть-ся, *v.i.r.,* по-руч-и́ть-ся, *v.p.r.,* за + *acc.,* to warrant, vouch, guarantee. П. за кого́-либо, to vouch for someone. По-ру́ч-ик, *п.т.,* lieutenant. По-руч-и́тель, *п.т.,* по-руч-и́тельница, *n.f.,* sponsor, warrantor. По-руч-и́тельство, *п.п.,* guaranty, bail. Дава́ть де́ньги под чье́-либо п., to lend, advance money on bail.

при-руч-и́ть, *v.p.,* при-руч-а́ть, *v.i.,* + *acc.,* to domesticate, tame. П. зве́ря, to tame a wild animal. При-руч-ённый, *adj., part. pass.,* tamed, domesticated. При-руч-ённый хи́щник всегда́ опа́сен, a tamed wild animal remains dangerous.

РУХ-, РУШ-, РЫХ-, DESTRUCTION, DEMOLITION

ру́х-ну-ть, *v.i.,* to crash, fall, fall into ruin. Все мои́ пла́ны ру́хнули, all my plans have failed, have come to nothing. Зда́ние ру́хнуло, the building crumbled down. Ру́х-нуть-ся, *v.i.r.,* to fall down, fall in, topple. Р. со всего́ разма́ха, to flounder. Ру́х-лядь, *n.f.,* lumber; ramshackle furniture, junk.

ру́ш-ить, *v.i.,* + *acc.,* to break down, demolish, destroy, lay waste, ruin; frustrate. Р. дом, сте́ны, to tear down a house, walls. Р. обы́чай (зако́ны) (*obs.*), to destroy customs (laws). Р. про́со, ячме́нь, to hull millet, barley.

Ру́ш-ить-ся, *v.i.r.*, to topple, crumble, be destroyed. Руш-е́ние, *n.n.*, (*tech.*), hulling.

на-ру́ш-ить, *v.p.*, на-руш-а́ть, *v.i.*, + *acc.*, to break off, infringe, violate, transgress. Н. душе́вное споко́йствие, to disturb, upset one's peace of mind. Н. обще́ственный поря́док, to disturb peace and order. Н. прися́гу, to commit perjury, break one's oath. На-руш-е́ние, *n.n.*, infringement, transgression, violation, breach. Н. пра́вил у́личного движе́ния, violation of a traffic regulation. Н. зако́на, violation of a law. Н. прав, violations of someone's rights. На-руш-и́тель, *n.m.*, violator, disturber, transgressor. Н. обще́ственного поря́дка, a violator of law and order. Наруши́тели постановле́ния бу́дут пресле́доваться зако́ном, trespassers (violators) will be prosecuted. На-ру́ш-ить-ся, *v.p.r.*, на-руш-а́ть-ся, *v.i.r.*, + *instr.*, to be transgressed, violated.

об-ру́ш-ить, *v.p.*, об-руш-а́ть, *v.i.*, + *acc.*, to demolish, destroy; overturn, overthrow. Об-ру́ш-ить-ся, *v.p.r.*, об-ру́ш-ивать-ся, *v.i.r.*, на + *acc.*, to fall in, cave in, collapse; come down upon, beset. Несча́стье обру́шилось на его́ го́лову, misfortunes beset him.

раз-ру́ш-ить, *v.p.*, раз-руш-а́ть, *v.i.*, + *acc.*, to demolish, destroy, ruin, raze to the ground; frustrate. Р. зда́ние, to demolish a building. Р. наде́жды, to blast one's hopes. Р. здоро́вье, to ruin one's health. Раз-ру́ш-ить-ся, *v.p.r.*, раз-руш-а́ть-ся, *v.i.r.*, to go to ruin, sink, fall, decay. Раз-руш-е́ние, *n.n.*, destruction, ruin, collapse, decay. Р. режи́ма, downfall of a regime. По́лное р., complete wreck. Раз-ру́ш-енный, *adj.*, *part. pass. past*, ruined, destroyed, decayed. Р. дом, destroyed house, home. Раз-руш-и́тель, *n.n.*, destroyer. Раз-руш-и́тельный, *adj.*, ruinous, destructive, fatal, consuming. Р-ое де́йствие огня́, destructive effects of fire.

рых-л-е́ть, *v.p.*, по-рых-ле́ть, *v.i.*, to grow soft, become friable, porous. Ры́х-лость, *n.f.*, friability, porousness. Р. по́чвы, porousness of the soil.

ры́х-л-ый, *adj.*, friable, soft, loose, porous. Р. хлеб, spongy, light bread. Р-ая земля́, friable, soft, light soil.

рых-л-и́ть, *v.i.*, + *acc.*, to make friable, soft. Рых-ле́ние, *n.n.*, process of making something friable, soft, porous. Р. карто́феля, loosening of the earth around a potato plant.

вз-рых-ли́ть, *v.p.*, вз-рых-ля́ть, *v.i.*, + *acc.*, to turn up, loosen. В. зе́млю, to loosen, turn up the soil.

раз-рых-ли́ть, *v.p.*, раз-рых-ля́ть, *v.i.*, + *acc.*, to hoe, loosen the earth. Раз-рых-ли́ть-ся, *v.p.r.*, раз-рых-ля́ть-ся, *v.i.r.*, to become friable, loose. Ка́мень разрыхля́ется, stone crumbles, becomes friable.

РЫ-, РО-, EXCAVATION

ры-ть, ро́-ю, *v.i.*, по-ры́ть, *v.p.*, + *acc.*, to dig, hollow, mine, burrow; paw. Р. пруд, to dig a pond. Р. я́му, to dig a pit. Р. самому́ себе́ я́му, (*fig.*), to be one's own undoing. Ры́-ть-ся, *v.i.r.*, по-ры́ть-ся, *v.p.r.*, to burrow, rummage, scrape. Р. в веща́х, to ransack. Ры-ть-ё, *n.n.*, digging. Р. кана́в, ditch digging. Ры́-т-вина, *n.f.*, ravine, rut. Ров, *n.m.*, moat.

вз-ры́-ть, *v.p.*, вз-ры-ва́ть, *v.i.*, + *acc.*, to dig up, turn up. В. зе́млю лопа́той, to turn up the earth with a spade.

вы́-ры-ть, *v.p.*, вы-ры-ва́ть, *v.i.*, + *acc.*, to dig up, exhume. В. клад, to dig up a treasure. В. моги́лу, to dig a grave.

за-ры́-ть, *v.p.*, за-ры-ва́ть, *v.i.*, + *acc.*, to bury, dig, inter. З. зо́лото, to bury gold. З. тала́нт в зе́млю, (*fig.*), to bury one's talents in the ground. За-ры́-ть-ся, *v.p.r.*, за-ры-ва́ть-ся, *v.i.r.*, to bury oneself; dig in. З. в свои́ кни́ги, to bury oneself in books.

из-ры́-ть, *v.p.*, из-ры-ва́ть, *v.i.*, + *acc.*, to dig all around, everywhere. Из-ры́-тый, *adj.*, *part. pass. past*, all dug up. И-ое о́спой лицо́, a face pitted with smallpox.

об-ры́-ть, *v.p.*, + *acc.*, to dig all around.

от-ры́-ть, *v.p.*, от-ры-ва́ть, *v.i.*, + *acc.*, to dig up, out; unearth; excavate. Архео́логи отры́ли дре́вний го́род, the archeologists unearthed an ancient city. От-ры́-тие, *n.n.*, digging up, unearthing.

пере-ры́-ть, *v.i.*, + *acc.*, to dig across; *see* рыть. П. доро́гу (по́ле), to dig across a road, across a field. П. стол (я́щики), to search in a desk, in the drawers.

под-ры́-ть, *v.p.*, под-ры-ва́ть, *v.i.*, + *acc.*, to dig under, sap. П. ко́рни де́рева, to sap the roots of a tree.

про-ры́-ть, *v.p.*, про-ры-ва́ть, *v.i.*, + *acc.*, to dig through. П. кана́л, to dig a canal. П. себе́ ход, to burrow one's way through.

раз-ры́-ть, *v.p.*, раз-ры-ва́ть, *v.i.*, + *acc.*, to dig up, unearth; ransack, rummage. Р. курга́н, to open a barrow.

с-ры́-ть, *v.p.*, с-ры-ва́ть, *v.i.*, + *acc.*, to level off, raze to the ground. С. холм, to level a hillock. С-ры́-тие, *n.n.*, levelling, razing to the ground.

ры-ло, *п.п.*, muzzle, snout. Свинóе р., pig's snout. Ры́-льце, *п.п.*, (*dim.*), muzzle, snout. Ры́льце у негó в пушкý, (*fig.*), he has his fingers in the pie, (*lit.*, of a fox) he has chicken feathers on his muzzle.

РЫБ-, FISH

ры́б-а, *п.f.*, fish. В э́том óзере мнóго ры́бы, there are plenty of fish in this lake. Би́ться, как ры́ба об лёд, (*saying*), to struggle desperately, in vain. Ни ры́ба, ни мя́со, (*idiom.*), neither fish nor fowl. Торгóвец ры́бой, fishmonger. Лови́ть ры́бу, to fish. Ры́бы, (*astron.*), Pisces. Рыб-ёшка, ры́б-ка, *п.f.*, small fry. Золотáя ры́бка, goldfish. Ры́б-ий, *adj.*, fish. Р. жир, cod-liver oil. Ры́бья чешуя́, fish scales. Ры́б-ный, *adj.*, piscine. Р. ры́нок, fish market. Р-ая лóвля, fishing. Р-ое дéло, fishery. Живоры́бный садóк, fish pond. Ры́б-о, *a combining form meaning* fish. Рыбо-вóдство, *п.п.*, pisciculture. Рыб-о-лóв, *п.т.*, angler, fisherman. Рыб-о-промы́шленность, *п.f.*, fishing, fish industry. Рыб-о-раз-ведéние, *п.п.*, fish breeding. Рыб-áк, *п.т.*, fisherman. Р. рыбакá ви́дит издалекá, (*saying*), birds of a feather flock together. Рыб-áчка, *п.f.*, fisherman's wife. Рыб-áчий, *adj.*, pertaining to fishing. Р-ье сýдно, fishing vessel. Рыб-áцкий, *adj.*, fishing. Р. посёлок, fishing village.

рыб-áч-и-ть, *v.i.*, to fish for a livelihood. Рыб-áчение, *п.п.*, fishery. Рыб-áчество, *п.п.*, fishery.

на-рыб-áч-ить, *v.p.*, на-рыб-áчивать, *v.i.*, + *acc.*, to fish in quantity, catch a large quantity of fish. Сегóдня я здóрово нарыбáчил, (*colloq.*), today I caught a lot of fish.

по-рыб-áч-ить, *v.p.*, to fish for a short time.

РЯД-, РЯЖ-, LINE, RANGE, ROW, FILE

ряд, *п.т.*, row, range, file, line. Р. кóмнат, suite, suite of rooms. Р. книг, a row of books. В ряд, in a row. Из ря́да вон выходя́щий, pre-eminent. Торгóвые ряды́, market stalls. Из-ря́д-ный, *adj.*, (*colloq.*), fairly good. И-ое коли́чество, fair quantity. Нáдо быть изря́дным дуракóм, чтóбы э́то слéлать, (*colloq.*), one must be pretty much of a fool to do this. Из-ря́д-но, *adv.*, fairly, tolerably, pretty well. Я и. устáл, I am quite tired. Ряд-овóй, *adj.*, ordinary, rank and file, commonplace; *used as n.*, private, soldier. Р.

человéк, commonplace person. Р. посéв, drill sowing. Р-áя сéялка, grain drill. Ря́дом, *adv.*, alongside, side by side. Сплошь да р., (*idiom.*), very often. Ряд-кóм, *adv.*, side by side. На-ря́д-ý, *adv.*, side by side, equal, on a level with. Н. с э́тим, side by side with his, on a level with this.

ряд-и́-ть, ряж-ý, *v.i.*, + *acc.*, (*obs.*), to hire, engage one's services; dress up, adorn. Суди́ть, да р., (*idiom.*), to gossip. Ряд-и́ть-ся, *v.i.r.*, + *acc.*, to bargain; dress up. Ря́ж-еный, *adj.*, *used as n.*, masker, mummer. Ря́ж-ение, *п.п.*, masquerading, mumming.

вы́-ряд-ить *v.p.*, вы-ряж-áть, *v.i.*, + *acc.*, (*colloq.*), to dress up, bedeck. Вы́-ряд-ить-ся, *v.p.r.*, вы-ря́ж-ивать-ся, *v.i.r.*, to dress up, bedeck oneself. Онá вы́рядилась, как кýкла, she is dressed up like a doll.

за-ряд-и́ть, *v.p.*, за-ряж-áть, *v.i.*, + *acc.*, to load. З. ружьё, to load a gun. За-ря́д, *п.т.*, loading; charge, cartridge. Подрывнóй з., blasting charge. Сýмка для заря́дов, cartridge box. За-ря́д-ка, *п.f.*, charge, charging, loading. Утренняя з., (*mil.*), morning bracing up exercises. Физзаря́дка, *abbr. of.* физкультýрная з., physical training exercises. За-ря́д-ный, *adj.*, powder, ammunition. З. я́щик, powder cart, ammunition wagon.

на-ряд-и́ть, *v.p.*, на-ряж-áть, *v.i.*, + *acc.*, to command, order, appoint; dress, array, adorn. Н. в караýл, to put on guard. Н. слéдствие, (*obs.*), to set up an inquiry. Н. детéй в прáздник, to dress children up for a holiday. Н. невéсту, to adorn a bride. На-ряд-и́ть-ся, *v.p.r.*, на-ряж-áть-ся, *v.i.r.*, to dress, up, overdress. На-ря́д, *п.п.*, order, command; dress, costume, attire, finery. Расписáние наря́дов, (*mil.*), roster. По наря́ду, by order. Прáздничный н., holiday attire, Sunday clothes. Пы́шный н., luxurious apparel. На-ря́д-ность, *п.f.*, elegance. На-ря́д-ный, *adj.*, elegant, smart. Н. костю́м, elegant, smart suit. На-ря́д-но, *adv.*, smartly, elegantly. Одевáться н., to dress smartly.

об-ряд-и́ть, *v.p.*, об-ряж-áть, *v.i.*, + *acc.*, to arrange, attire. Об-ря́д, *п.т.*, ceremony, rite. Свáдебный о., wedding ceremony. Соблюдéние обря́дов, observance of rites. Об-ря́д-ный, *adj.*, ceremonial ritual. Об-ря́д-овый, *adj.*, pertaining to ceremony, ritual. Свáдебные о-ые пéсни, wedding songs.

от-ряд-и́ть, *v.p.*, от-ряж-áть, *v.i.*, + *acc.*, to detach; detail, delegate; tell off. Шестеры́х из нас отряди́ли за тóпливом, six of us were detailed to get fuel. От-ря́д, *п.m.*, detachment, detail. Санита́рный о., medical unit. Разве́дывательный о., reconnoitering detachment.

пере-ряд-и́ть, *v.p.*, пере-ряж-а́ть, *v.i.*, + *acc.*, в + *acc.*, to change clothes; disguise. Пере-ряд-и́ть-ся, *v.p.r.*, переряж-а́ть-ся, *v.i.r.*, to disguise oneself, change clothes. П. в же́нское пла́тье, to disguise oneself as a woman.

под-ряд-и́ть, *v.p.*, под-ряж-а́ть, *v.i.*, + *acc.*, to hire, engage, contract for. П. рабо́чих на постро́йку зда́ния, to hire workers for the building of a building. Под-ряд-и́ть-ся, *v.p.r.*, под-ряж-а́ться, *v.i.r*, to hire out. П. на поста́вку дров, to contract to supply wood. Под-ря́д, *п.m.*, contract; *adv.*, one after another, without interruption. Поставля́ть дрова́ по подря́ду, to supply wood by contract. Не́сколько дней п., several days running. Под-ря́д-чик, *п.m.*, (*pre-Rev.*), contractor.

раз-ряд-и́ть, *v.p.r.*, раз-ряж-а́ть, *v.i.*, + *acc.*, to discharge, unload; overdress, adorn. Р. электри́ческую батаре́ю, to discharge a battery. Р. ружьё, to unload a gun. Раз-ряд-и́ть-ся, *v.p.r.*, раз-ряж-а́ть-ся, *v.i.r.*, to be discharged, unloaded; be discharged, unloaded; overdressed. *see* разряди́ть, разряжа́ть. Р. в пух и прах, (*colloq.*), to overdress. Раз-ря́д, *п.m.*, class, category, division, sort, rank. Пе́рвого разря́да, first-class, first-rate. Второ́го разря́да, second-rate. Раз-ря́д-ка, *п.f.*, discharging, unloading; spacing out (typography). Набира́ть в. разря́дку, to space (typography). Раз-ря́д-ник, *п.m.*, ejector; discharger, spark-gap. Раз-ря́д-ный, *adj.*, pertaining to rank, to classes. Перворазря́дный ма́стер, a first-class craftsman. Раз-ряж-е́ние, *п.n.*, discharge, unloading; adorning. Раз-ряж-енный, *adj., part. pass. past,* overdressed. Раз-ряж-ённый, *adj., part. pass. past,* unloaded (gun).

с-на-ряд-и́ть, *v.p.*, с-на-ряж-а́ть, *v.i.*, + *acc.*, to equip, fit, furnish. С. экспеди́цию, to equip an expedition. С-наряд-и́ть-ся, *v.p.r.*, с-на-ряж-а́ть-ся, *v.i.r.*, to be equipped. С. в путь (доро́гу), to equip oneself for a journey. С-на-ря́д, *п.m.*, shell, missile, projectile. С. со слезоточи́вым га́зом, teargas shell. Раз-рыв-но́й, с., explosive shell. Да́льность полёта снаря́да, range of flight of a shell. С-на-ряж-е́ние, *п.n.*, equipment, outfit. Поставщи́к снаряже́ния, outfitter. С-на-ряж-ённый, *adj., part. pass. past,* equipped, outfitted.

у-ря́д-н-ик, *п.m.*, (*pre-Rev.*), village policeman; Cossack sergeant, noncommissioned officer.

C

САД-, САЖ-, САЖД-, СЕД-, (СѢД-), СЕСТ-, (СѢСТ-), СИД-, СЯД-, SITTING

сад, *п.m.*, garden. Фрукто́вый сад, fruit orchard. Зоологи́ческий сад, zoo; zoological garden. Гуля́ть в саду́, to stroll in a garden. Са́д-ик, *п.m.*, small garden. Сад-о́вник, *п.m.*, gardener. Сад-ово́д, *п.m.*, horticulturalist. Садово́дство, *п.n.*, horticulture. Сад-о́вый, *adj.*, garden. С. нож, garden knife.

сад-и́-ть, саж-у́, *v.i.*, по-сад-и́ть, *v.p.*, to plant. С. де́рево, to plant a tree. Сажа́ть, *v.i.*, по-сад-и́ть, *v.p.*, to seat, set, put, plant. С. ку́рицу на я́йца, to set a hen on eggs. С. на хлеб и на во́ду, to place on bread and water. С. под аре́ст, to put under arrest; imprison. С. те́сто в печь, to put dough into the oven. Саж-а́ть-ся, *v.i.r.*, to be planted, placed. Дере́вья сажа́ются о́сенью, trees are planted in the fall. Сад-о́к, *п.m.*, live fish tank. Живоры́бный садо́к, fishpond. Са́ж-а, *п.f.*, soot, lampblack. Па́чкать са́жей, to soil with soot, with grime. Дела́, как са́жа бела́, (*saying*), business, matters are very poor. Са́ж-енец, *п.m.*, set, seedling. Карто́фель-са́женец, potato seedling.

в-сад-и́ть, *v.p.*, в-са́ж-ивать, *v.i.*, to thrust, stick, plunge, plant; lodge. В. расте́ние в зе́млю, to plant a plant in the earth. В. нож в спи́ну, to stab in the back. В-са́д-ник, *п.m.*, rider, horseman, equestrian.

вы́-сад-ить, *v.p.*, вы-са́ж-ивать, *v.i.*, + *acc.*, из + *gen.*, в + *acc.*, to set out, plant. В. на бе́рег, to set ashore, land, disembark. В. цветы́ из оранжере́и, to transplant flowers from a hothouse into a garden.

до-сад-и́ть, *v.p.*, до-са́ж-ивать, *v.i.*, + *acc.*, to set, plant sufficiently; complete planting. Досади́ли огоро́д то́лько до полови́ны, they planted only half of the garden. Сего́дня доса́живала капу́сту, today I am finishing planting the cabbage. До-са́ж-ивать-ся, *v.i.r.*, to be completely planted. За́втра огоро́д бу́дет д. до конца́, tomorrow we shall finish planting the garden.

до-сад-и́ть, *v.p.*, до-сажд-а́ть, *v.i.*, + *dat.*, to spite, vex, plague, irritate, annoy, provoke. Он де́лает э́то, чтоб досади́ть мне, he does it to spite me. Не досажда́й мне свои́ми глу́пыми расспро́сами, don't annoy me with your stupid questions.

до-са́д-ова-ть, *v.i.,* на + *acc.,* to be displeased, be annoyed, be vexed. Д. на плохи́е времена́, to be annoyed by hard times. До-са́д-а, *n.f.,* vexation, spite. К его́ большо́й доса́де, to his great annoyance. Запла́кать с доса́ды, to weep, cry from disappointment. Доса́д-ный, *adj.,* annoying, vexing, unpleasant. До-са́д-но, *adv.,* vexing, disappointing. Как д.! How annoying! Доса́дно, что опозда́л на по́езд, it's annoying that I was late for the train. До-са́д-ливый, *adj.,* annoyed, irritated. Д. жест, a gesture of annoyance. Доса́д-ливо, *adv.,* in an annoyed manner. Он д. махну́л руко́й, he made a spiteful gesture.

за-са́д-ить, *v.p.,* за-са́ж-ивать, *v.i.,* + *acc.,* to plant. З. сад ро́зами, to plant a garden with roses. З. в тюрьму́, to put in prison. З. за рабо́ту, to set someone to work. За-са́д-а, *n.f.,* ambush. Быть в заса́де, to lie in wait, in ambush. За-са́д-ка, *n.f.,* planting. З. огоро́да овоща́ми, planting of vegetables in a garden.

на-сад-и́ть, *v.p.,* на-са́ж-ивать, *v.i.,* to set, put on, plant in quantity. Н. червяка́ на крючо́к, to put a worm on a hook. На-са́ж-ивать-ся, *v.i.r.,* to be fixed, set, put on. Метла́ наса́живается на па́лку, the broom is fixed to a stick.

на-сад-и́ть, *v.p.,* на-саж-а́ть, *v.i.,* на-са́ж-ивать, *v.i.,* to plant in quantity. Н. овоще́й, to plant vegetables. Н. дете́й в ваго́н, to crowd children into a railway car.

на-сад-и́ть, *v.p.,* на-сажд-а́ть, *v.i.,* + *acc.,* to plant in quantity, spread, propagate (*as* ideas, culture). Н. дере́вьев, to plant trees in quantity. Н. культу́ру, to disseminate culture. На-сажд-а́ть-ся, *v.i.r,* to be planted, spread, propagated, disseminated. За го́родом насажда́ется це́лый парк, they are planting a complete park beyond the city. На-сажд-е́ние, *n.n.,* planting, plantation, propagation, dissemination. Пра́здник древонасажде́ния, a day set aside for planting trees. Фрукто́вое н., planting of fruit trees. Н. вре́дных иде́й, propagation of nefarious ideas.

о-сад-и́ть, *v.p.,* о-са́ж-ивать, *v.i.,* + *acc.,* to press back; rebuke, snub.

о-сад-и́ть, *v.p.,* о-сажд-а́ть, *v.i.,* + *acc.,* to lay siege, besiege; precipitate. О. кре́пость, to besiege a fortress. О. раство́р, to form a sediment in a solution. О-сажд-а́ть-ся, *v.i.r.,* to precipitate, settle. О-са́д-а, *n.f.,* siege. О. кре́пости, siege of a fortress. Вы́держать оса́ду, to withstand a siege. Снять

оса́ду, to raise a siege. О-са́д-ный, *adj.,* siege. О-ое ору́дие, siege gun. О-ое положе́ние, state of siege. О-са́д-ок, *n.m.,* sediment, precipitation, precipitate. Неприя́тный о. на душе́, something unpleasant weighing on one's soul. Атмосфе́рные оса́дки, atmospheric precipitation. О-сажд-е́ние, *n.n.,* precipitation.

об-сад-и́ть, *v.p.,* об-са́ж-ивать, *v.i.,* + *acc.,* to plant around. О. сад живо́й и́згородью, to plant a hedge around a garden. Об-са́д-ка, *n.f.,* hedging in.

от-сад-и́ть, *v.p.,* от-са́ж-ивать, *v.i.,* от + *gen.,* + *acc.,* to transplant, plant by layers. О. земляни́ку, to layer a strawberry plant. О. дете́й от взро́слых, to cause children to sit apart from the adults. От-са́д-ка, *n.f.,* planting by layerage.

пере-сад-и́ть, *v.p.,* пере-са́ж-ивать, *v.i.,* + *acc.,* to transplant. П. цветы́, to transplant flowers. П. ко́жу, to graft skin. П. пассажи́ров из одного́ ваго́на в друго́й, to transfer passengers from one train car into another. Пере-са́д-ка, *n.f.,* transplantation, replanting; transfer. У меня́ п. в Ки́еве, I have to change trains in Kiev.

по-сад-и́ть, *v.p.,* + *acc.,* to plant; seat; compel someone to sit down. П. де́рево, to plant a tree. П. ребёнка, to seat a child. П. за рабо́ту, to put to work. П. на стул, to seat a person. П. су́дно на мель, to strand a boat. П. себе́ на ше́ю, (*fig.*), to hang a millstone round one's neck. П. в ваго́н, to seat in a coach. П. в тюрьму́, to jail. П. на экза́мене, (*slang*), to fail someone in an examination. По-са́ж-енный, *adj., part. pass. past,* planted; imprisoned, jailed. По-са́д, *n.m.,* little town, suburb. По-са́д-ник, *n.m.,* по-са́д-ница *n.f.,* (*hist.*), in ancient Novgorod an elected ruler. По-са́д-ский, *adj.,* (*hist.*), tradesman. П.-ие лю́ди, (*hist.*), trades people. По-са́д-ка, *n.f.,* embarkation; landing; planting. П. дере́вьев, planting of trees. П. самолёта, landing of a plane. По-саж-ёный, *adj., used as n.,* one who blesses a married couple. П. отец, one who gives the bride away. П-ая мать, a stand-in for the mother at a wedding.

под-сад-и́ть, *v.p.,* под-са́ж-ивать, *v.i.,* + *acc.,* to help one to a seat; to seat, mount.

рас-сад-и́ть, *v.p.,* рас-са́ж-ивать, *v.i.,* to transplant. Р. расте́ния, to transplant plants. Р. люде́й, to seat people. Р. ученико́в по кла́ссам, to seat students according to their class. Рас-са́д-а, *n.f.,* seedlings. Сажа́ть расса́ду, to plant seedlings. Рас-са́д-ник, *n.m.*, nursery, seminary, seed plot. Р. просвеще́ния, (*fig.*), seat of learning. Р. зара́зы, center of contagion.

с-сад-и́ть, *v.p.*, с-са́ж-ивать, *v.i.*, + *acc.*, с + *gen.*, to unseat; excoriate. С. с ло́шади, to assist one in alighting from a horse. С. пассажи́ра с по́езда, to eject a passenger from a train. С. себе́ ру́ку, to excoriate one's hand. С-са́д-ина, *n.f.*, cut, abrasion, sore. С. на ноге́, sore on the foot.

у-сад-и́ть, *v.p.*, у-са́ж-ивать, *v.i.*, + *acc.*, to seat, make one sit down, settle, plant. Она́ усади́ла свои́х госте́й, she seated her guests. У-са́ж-ивать-ся, *v.i.r.*, to be seated. У-са́дь-ба, *n.f.*, countryseat, homestead, large farmstead. У-са́д-ебный, *adj.*, pertaining to a countryseat, a farmstead. При-у-са́д-ебный, *adj.*, adjacent to a countryseat, a farmstead.

сад-и́ть-ся, *v.i.r.*, сест-ь, *v.p.*, на + *acc.*, to sit, sit down. С. на ло́шадь, to mount a horse. С. на стул, to sit down, take a chair. С. в ва́нну, to get into a bathtub. С. на зе́млю, to settle on the land, become a farmer. С. на парохо́д, to board a steamer. С. на по́езд, to board a train. С. на мель, to run aground. С. обе́дать, to sit down to dinner. Пыль сади́тся на ме́бель, the dust settles on furniture. Со́лнце сади́тся, the sun is setting, sinking. Зда́ние се́ло, the building settled. Мате́рия се́ла, the cloth shrank.

вы́-сад-ить-ся, *v.p.r.*, вы-са́ж-ивать-ся, *v.i.r.*, на + *acc.*, to alight, get down, descend. В. на бе́рег, to land, disembark. Вы́-сад-ка, *n.f.*, debarkation, disembarkation. В. отря́да, (*mil.*), landing of a detachment. Ме́сто вы́сад-ки, landing place.

от-са́ж-ивать-ся, *v.i.r*, от-се́ст-ь, *v.p.*, от + *gen.*, to move to another seat. Я отсе́л от окна́, I moved away from the window.

пере-са́ж-ивать-ся, *v.i.r.*, пере-се́ст-ь, *v.p.*, из + *gen.*, на, в + *acc.*, to change seats, take another seat, change trains.

под-са́ж-ивать-ся, *v.i.r.*, под-се́ст-ь, *v.p.*, к + *dat.*, to take a seat near, close to. Он подсе́л к ней, he took a seat close to her.

при-са́ж-ивать-ся, *v.i.r.*, при-се́ст-ь, *v.p.*, к + *dat.*, to take a seat, sit down close to. При-се́ст-ь к столу́, to sit, take a seat close to a table. При-се́ст, *n.m.*, (*obs.*), sitting; *used only in expression*: Сде́лать всё в оди́н присе́ст, to do everything at one sitting.

рас-са́ж-ивать, *v.i.*, to seat.

рас-са́ж-ивать-ся, *v.i.r.*, рас-се́ст-ь-ся, *v.p.r.*, по + *dat.*, to sit down, take seats. Лю́ди расса́живались, ряда́ми, the people took seats in rows. Рассе́сть-ся непринуждённо, to sit at ease.

у-са́ж-ивать-ся, *v.i.r.*, у-се́ст-ь-ся, *v.p.r.*, на, в + *acc.*, to seat, settle oneself. У. в кре́сло, to settle in an armchair.

сед-а́л-ище, *n.n.*, (*obs.*), seat. Сед-а́лищный, *adj.*, sciatic. С. нерв, sciatic nerve.

вос-сед-а́ть, *v.i.*, вос-се́ст-ь, *v.p.*, на, в + *prep.*, (*Ch.-Sl.*), to take a seat. Госпо́дь восся́дет на престо́ле во всей сла́ве Свое́й, the Lord shall sit on His throne in all His glory.

за-сед-а́ть, *v.i.*, to take part (*as in conference, meeting, session*). За-сед-а́ние, *n.n.*, conference, meeting, session, sitting. За-сед-а́тель, *n.m.*, assessor. Прися́жный з., (*pre-Rev.*), juryman, member of a jury. Наро́дный з., (*recent*), member of jury.

на-сед-а́ть, *v.i.*, на-се́ст-ь, *v.p.*, на + *acc.*, to settle on, cover; press hard. Н. на врага́, to press the enemy. На-сед-а́ние, *n.n.*, pressing. На-се́д-ка, *n.f.*, brood hen, sitting hen.

о-сед-а́ть, *v.i.*, о-се́ст-ь, *v.p.*, на + *acc.*, to settle down, settle; accumulate on something. Зда́ние оседа́ет, the building is settling. О-сед-а́ние, *n.n.*, settling, settling down. О-се́д-л-ость, *n.f.*, state of settling, being settled. Черта́ осе́длости, prescribed area for a settlement. О-се́д-л-ый, *adj.*, settled. О-ые племена́, settled tribes.

пред-сед-а́тель-ств-овать, *v.i.*, to preside, be chairman. Кто председа́тельствует? Who is the chairman? Who is presiding? Пред-сед-а́тель, *n.m.*, пред-сед-а́тель-ница, *n.f.*, chairman, president. Пред-сед-а́тельствующий, *adj., part. act. pres., used as n.*, chairman. П. собра́ния, chairman of a meeting. П. правле́ния, chairman of a board of directors. Пред-сед-а́тельство, *n.n.*, chairmanship, presidency.

при-сед-а́ть, *v.i.*, при-се́ст-ь, *v.p.*, to squat, curtsy. П. на ко́рточки, to squat. При-сед-а́ние, *n.n.*, squatting, curtsy. Гимна́стика с приседа́ниями, squatting exercises. При-ся́дка, *n.f.*, squatting dance. Пляса́ть в прися́дку, to dance squatting, in a squat.

сед-л-а́ть, *v.i.*, о-сед-л-а́ть, *v.p.*, + *acc.*, to saddle. Сед-ло́, *n.n.*, saddle. Вью́чное с., packsaddle. Да́мское с., sidesaddle. Е́здить верхо́м без седла́, to ride bareback. Ло́шадь под седло́м, saddled horse. Сед-ёлка, *n.f.*, saddle strap. Сед-е́льник, *n.m.*, saddler. Сед-е́льный, *adj.*, saddle. С. вьюк, saddle-bag.

о-сед-л-а́ть, *v.p.*, о-сёд-лывать, *v.i.*, + *acc.*, to saddle. Оседла́ю коня́, I will saddle a horse. О-сёд-ланная ло́шадь, saddled horse.

пере-сед-л-а́ть, *v.i.*, пере-сёд-лывать, *v.p.*, to saddle anew, to change saddles.

рас-сед-л-а́ть, *v.i.*, рас-сёд-лывать, *v.p.*, + *acc.*, to unsaddle.

сест-ь, *v.p.*, в, на + *acc.*, to sit down. С. на стул, to sit down in a chair.

за-сест-ь, *v.p.*, в + *prep.*, to sit firmly, stick, ensconce oneself. З. в заса́де, to lie in ambush. З. за рабо́ту, to sit down to work.

на-сест-ь, *v.p.*, на + *acc.*, press hard, settle, crowd. В ваго́н насе́ло мно́го наро́ду, many people were crowded into the railroad car. На-се́ст, *n.n.*, roost, perch. Ку́ры сиде́ли на насе́сте, hens were sitting on the perch.

о-се́ст-ь, *v.p.*, в + *prep.*, to settle. Населе́ние осе́ло в степя́х, the population settled in the steppes. Песо́к осе́л на дне, the sand settled on the bottom.

об-се́ст-ь, *v.p.*, + *acc.*, to sit around, crowd over. Де́ти обсе́ли ня́ню, the children gathered around the nurse.

пере-се́ст-ь, *v.p.*, в, на + *acc.*, to change seats. П. в друго́й по́езд, to change trains. П. на друго́е ме́сто, to change seats.

под-се́ст-ь, *v.p.*, к + *dat.*, to sit down (near). П. к учи́телю, to sit down near the teacher.

при-се́ст-ь, *v.p.*, to sit down (for a minute). Он присе́л на мину́тку и ско́ро ушёл, he sat down for a minute and soon left.

рас-се́ст-ь-ся, *v.p.r.*, на + *prep.*, по + *dat.*, to take seats, settle. Р. на дива́не, to settle comfortably on a sofa. Р. по свои́м места́м, to take assigned seats.

у-се́ст-ь-ся, *v.p.r.*, на, в + *prep.*, to take seats, settle comfortably. Го́сти усе́лись и на́чали разгова́ривать, the guests sat down and started to talk.

сид-е́-ть, сиж-у́, *v.i.*, сиж-ивать, *v.i., iter.*, на, в + *prep.*, to sit, be seated. С. на сту́ле (в кре́сле), to sit in a chair (in an armchair). С. на ло́шади, to be on horseback. С. до́ма, to sit at home. С. за обе́дом, to dine. С. в тюрьме́, to be in jail. С. сложа́ ру́ки, (*idiom.*), to idle away the time. Он подо́лгу си́живал у них, he used to stay with them for a long time. Сид-и́т-ся, *v.i.r., impers.* Мне не сиди́тся, I feel restless. Сид-е́лец, *n.m.*, (*obs.*), bartender in a tavern. С. в кабаке́, (*obs.*), tapster. Сид-е́лка, *n.f.*, nurse's aide. С. в больни́це, nurse's aid in a hospital.

Сид-е́ние, *n.n.*, sitting. С. по ноча́м у больно́го, to sit up night after night at the bedside of a sick man. Сид-е́ние, *n.n.*, seat. Стул с мя́гким сиде́нием, chair with a soft seat. Сид-я́чий, *adj.*, sedentary. С. о́браз жи́зни, sedentary mode of life. С-ее положе́ние, sitting posture.

вы́-сид-еть, *v.p.*, вы-си́ж-ивать, *v.i.*, to sit out, stay, remain; hatch. В. два го́да в плену́, to spend two years as a prisoner of war. Ку́рица вы́сидела цыпля́т, the hen hatched chicks. Вы-си́ж-ивание, *n.n.*, hatching.

до-сид-е́ть, *v.p.*, до-си́ж-ивать, *v.i.*, до + *gen.*, to sit till, through. Он досиде́л до конца́ конце́рта, he sat through to the end of the concert. Он доси́живал свой срок в тюрьме́, he was completing his jail term. До-сид-е́ть-ся, *v.p.r.*, до-си́ж-ивать-ся, *v.i.r.*, to sit up, remain. Д. до утра́, to remain till morning.

за-сид-е́ть, *v.p.*, за-си́ж-ивать, *v.i.*, + *acc.*, to soil with specks. Му́хи заси́дели зе́ркало, the flies soiled the mirror. Карти́на заси́жена му́хами, the picture is covered with flyspecks. За-сид-е́ть-ся, *v.p.r.*, за-си́ж-ивать-ся, *v.i.r.*, to sit, stay too late; tarry, linger. Я засиде́лся в библиоте́ке, I tarried in the library. По ноча́м я заси́живался за кни́гами, I used to sit up late at night over my books.

на-сид-е́ть-ся, *v.p.r.*, to have one's fill of sitting. Я доста́точно насиде́лся в канцеля́рии, тепе́рь на́до но́ги размя́ть, I've sat long enough in the office, now I have to stretch my legs out.

пере-сид-е́ть, *v.p.*, пере-си́ж-ивать, *v.i.*, + *acc.*, to outsit, outstay, sit up too late, too long. Мы пересиде́ли всех госте́й, we outstayed all the other guests. Хлеб пересиде́л в печи́, the bread was in the oven too long.

по-сид-е́ть, *v.p.*, по-си́ж-ивать, *v.i.*, to sit, stay for a while. Посиди́те ещё не́сколько мину́т, stay a few minutes longer. Быва́ло он ча́сто поси́живал на э́том дива́не, he used to sit frequently on this sofa. Приходи́те вечерко́м посиде́ть с на́ми, come and spend the evening with us. По-сид-е́лки, *n.f. pl.*, (*obs.*), an evening gathering of young villagers during the spinning season. На посиде́лки собира́лись де́вушки и па́рни со всего́ села́, girls and young men from all over the village used to gather in the evening.

под-сид-е́ть, *v.p.*, под-си́ж-ивать, *v.i.*, + *acc.*, (*recent*), to plot, intrigue against someone. Они́ постоя́нно подси́живали его́, they constantly intrigued against him. Под-си́ж-ивание, *п.п.*, (*recent*), plotting, intriguing.

про-сид-е́ть, *v.p.*, про-си́ж-ивать, *v.i.*, + *acc.*, to sit up, sit through. П. всю ночь, to sit up all night. П. в гостя́х, to spend one's time with friends. Про-си́ж-ивание, *п.п.*, sitting up, sitting through. Проси́женный, *adj., part. pass. past,* worn out by sitting. П. дива́н, a worn out sofa.

у-сид-е́ть, *v.p.*, на + *prep.*, to keep one's seat. У. на коне́, to stick to a saddle. Он не усиди́т ни мину́тки, he can't keep still for one moment. У-си́д-чивость, *п.f.*, assiduity, perseverance. У-си́д-чивый, *adj.*, assiduous, persevering student. У. учени́к, persevering, assiduous student.

СВЕТ-, (СВѢТ-), СВЕЧ-, (СВѢЧ-), СВЕЩ-, (СВѢЩ-), LIGHT; WORLD

свет, *п.т.*, light. Дневно́й с., daylight. Я́ркий с., bright, clear light. Свет зари́, light at dawn. Увиде́ть с., to see the light of day, be born. Чем свет; чуть заря́, (*idiom.*), at daybreak. Ни свет, ни заря́ (*idiom.*), at daybreak. Чем свет, крестья́не уже́ рабо́тают в по́ле, at daybreak the peasants are already in the fields working. Он просну́лся чуть свет, he woke up at daybreak. Предста́вить кого́-нибудь в са́мом вы́годном све́те, to present someone in a favorable light. Проли́ть (проли-ва́ть) свет, to shed light on, clarify. Это откры́тие пролива́ет свет на мно́гие зага́дочные явле́ния, this discovery explains many mysterious phenomena. Уче́ние - свет, неуче́ние - тьма, learning (knowledge) is light, ignorance is darkness. Свет-ово́й, *adj.*, lighting. Свет-овы́е сигна́лы, light signals. Свет-о-, *a combining form meaning* light, world. Свет-о-боя́знь, *п.f.*, (*med.*), photophobia. Свет-о-ле-че́бница, *п.f.*, hospital for treatment by light radiation. Свет-о-лече́бный, *adj.*, pertaining to treatment by light radiation. Свет-о-маскиро́вка, *п.f.*, blackout. В го́роде прово́дят светомаскиро́вку, they are organizing a blackout in the city. Све́т-о-пись, *п.f.*, heliotype. Свет-о-представле́ние, *п.п.*, (*obs.*), doomsday. Свет-о-рассе́яние, *п.п.*, dispersal of light. Свет-о-си́ла, *п.f.*, candle power. Свет-о-те́нь, *п.f.*, chiaroscuro. Свет-о-те́ни на карти́не, light and shade on a picture. Свет-о-фо́р, *п.т.*, traffic light. На у́лицах устано́влены светофо́ры для регули́рования у́личного движе́ния, traffic lights are installed on streets to regulate street

traffic. Свет-о-чувстви́тельный, *adj.*, sensitized. Светочувстви́тельная бума́га, sensitized paper. Све́т-оч, *п.т.*, torch. Духо́вный с., spiritual light. С. нау́ки, a luminary in science.

свет, *п.т.*, world. Весь свет, the whole world. Но́вый с., the New World. Четы́ре страны́ све́та, the four cardinal points of the compass. Вы́сший с., the upper classes of society, the elite, high society. Производи́ть на с., to bring into the world. Отре́чься от све́та, to renounce the world. Ни за что на све́те, for nothing in this world, not for anything in this world. Све́т-ский, *adj.*, secular, lay, fashionable. С-ая власть, lay authority. С. челове́к, layman. С-ие мане́ры, worldly manners. Све́т-скость, *п.f.*, worldliness.

свет-а́-ть, *v.i., impers.*, to dawn. Начина́ет с., it is beginning to dawn.

рас-свет-а́ть, *v.i., impers.*, to dawn. Рассвело́, it is dawn. Едва́ рассвело́, он был уже́ на нога́х, it was hardly dawn, he was already up on his feet. Рас-све́т, *п.т.*, dawn, daybreak.

свет-и́-ть, свеч-у́, *v.i.*, to light, twinkle. Свет-и́ло, *п.п.*, star, light, luminary. Небе́сные свети́ла, heavenly bodies. Нау́чное с., luminary in science. Свет-и́льник, *п.т.*, lamp. Свет-и́льный, *adj.*, illuminating, lighting. С. газ, illuminating gas. Свет-и́льня, *п.f.*, candlewick. Свеч-е́ние, *п.п.*, glint, shimmer; luminosity. С. на́ море, phosphorescence in the sea. Свет-и́ть-ся, *v.i.r.*, used in *3d pers.*, to shine, gleam. Вдали́ свети́лся огонёк, a light gleamed in the distance. Свет-я́щийся, *adj., part. act. pres.*, shining. С. мая́к, lighthouse. С-иеся инфузо́рии, phosphorescent infusoria.

за-свет-и́ть, *v.p.*, + *acc.*, to light, strike a light. З. свечу́, to light a candle. За-свет-и́ть-ся, *v.p.r.*, to light up. Засвети́лись звёзды, the stars have appeared.

о-свет-и́ть, *v.p.*, о-свещ-а́ть, *v.i.*, + *acc.*, to light, illuminate. О-свещ-ённый, *adj., part. pass. past*, elucidated, illuminated. Зал был я́рко освещён, the hall was brightly illuminated. О. вопро́с со всех сторо́н, to elucidate a question, an issue.

о-свещ-е́ние, *п.п.*, light, lighting, illumination. Электри́ческое о., electric light. Га́зовое о., gas light. Иску́сственное о., artificial light. В э́том до́ме плохо́е о., the lighting in this house is poor. При со́лнечном освеще́нии, by sunlight. О-свещ-ённый, *adj., part. pass. past*, lighted, illuminated. О. со́лнцем, sunlit. О. луно́й, moonlit. О-свет-и́ть-ся, *v.p.r.*, о-свещ-а́ть-ся, *v.i.r.*, to be lighted, illuminated. Улицы освеща́ются электри́ческими фонаря́ми, streets are lighted by electric streetlamps. Её лицо́ освети́лось ра́достью, her face lighted up with joy.

по-свет-и́ть, *v.p.*, + *dat.*, to give some light, light a little. Посвети́те мне на ле́стнице, Please light the stairs for me.

про-свет-и́ть, про-свеч-у́, *v.p.*, про-све́ч-ивать, *v.i.*, + *acc.*, сквозь + *acc.*, to X-ray, shine through, be translucent, be transparent. До́ктор просве́чивает больно́го рентге́новскими луча́ми, the doctor is X-raying the patient. Со́лнце просве́чивает сквозь облака́, the sun is shining through the clouds. Про-свет-и́ть-ся, *v.p.r.*, про-све́ч-ивать-ся, *v.i.r.*, + *instr.*, сквозь + *acc.*, to be X-rayed. Больно́й просве́чивается рентге́новскими луча́ми, the patient is being X-rayed. Со́лнце просвети́лось сквозь ту́чи и дождь переста́л, the sun shone through the clouds and the rain stopped. Про-све́ч-ивание, *n.n.*, X-raying, radioscopy, making translucent. Больну́ю понесли́ на просве́чивание, they took the patient in for an X-ray. П. то́нкой тка́ни, transparency of thin cloth. Про-све́т, *n.m.*, clear space which admits light; clearing. П. в лесу́, forest clearing. Без просве́та, without a ray of hope. Тяжёлая жизнь без просве́та, hard, hopeless life. Бес-про-све́т-ный, *adj.*, without a glimmer of light, without a gleam of hope. Б-ая тьма, utter darkness. Б-ая тоска́, desperate longing. Б-ая жизнь бедняка́, a beggar's hopeless life.

про-свет-и́ть, про-свещ-у́, *v.p.*, про-свещ-а́ть, *v.i.*, + *acc.*, to enlighten, instruct, teach, enlighten spiritually. Всео́бщее обуче́ние просвети́т наро́д, universal education will enlighten people. Духо́вный свет просвеща́ет люде́й, spiritual light edifies people. Про-свет-и́тель, *n.m.*, one who enlightens, edifies. Святы́е бра́тья Кири́лл и Мефо́дий просвети́ли славя́н, the saints Cyril and Methodius were the spiritual teachers of the Slavs. Про-свет-и́тельный, *adj.*, instructive, enlightening, edifying. П-ое учрежде́ние, educational institution. Про-свещ-е́ние, *n.n.*, enlightenment, instruction, education. Министе́рство Наро́дного Просвеще́ния, Ministry of People's Education. Про-свещ-е́нец, *n.m.*, (*recent*), educator, teacher. Съезд просвеще́нцев, convention of educators. Про-свещ-ённый, *adj.*, *part. pass. past*, educated. П. челове́к,

educated man. П. ум, well informed, enlightened mind. Ва́ше п-ое мне́ние, (*obs., polite*), your enlightened opinion.

свет-л-е́ть, *v.i.*, по-свет-ле́ть, *v.p.*, to lighten, brighten; grow light. Не́бо светле́ет, the sky is clearing up. На дворе́ посветле́ло, it has grown light outside, outdoors. Све́т-лость, *n.f.*, clearness, lucidity; serenity. С. его́ ума́ порази́тельна, the clarity of his mind is amazing. Све́т-лый, *adj.*, light, bright, clear, lucid, light-colored. С. день, bright day. С-ая ко́мната, light room. С-ая ли́чность, person of superior moral character. С-ая Неде́ля, Easter Week. С. Пра́здник, Easter. На ней све́тлое пла́тье, she is wearing a light-colored dress. Свет-ле́йший, *adj. superl.*, the lightest, brightest, clearest. С. князь, (*pre-Rev.*), the highest princely title. Свет-ло́, *adv.*, light, bright. Со́лнце взошло́ и ста́ло совсе́м светло́, the sun has risen and it has become quite light. Свет-ло-, *a combining form meaning* light. Свет-ло-жёлтый, *adj.*, light yellow. Свет-ло-зелёный, *adj.*, light green. Свет-ло-кори́чневый, *adj.*, light brown.

про-свет-л-е́ть, *v.p.*, to clear, clear up, clarify. Ту́чи разошли́сь и не́бо просветле́ло, the clouds have dispersed and the sky has become bright. Созна́ние у больно́го просветле́ло, the sick man regained consciousness.

про-свет-л-и́ть, *v.p.*, про-свет-л-я́ть, *v.i.*, + *acc.*, to clarify. Хими́ческим спо́собом просветли́ть му́тную жи́дкость, chemical clarification of a turbid liquid. Про-свет-ле́ние, *n.n.*, clarifying, clarification. По́сле бре́да у больно́го наступи́ло п., after delirium the sick man's mind became clear again.

свеч-а́, *n.f.*, candle. С. догора́ет, the candle is burning out. Восковы́е све́чи, wax candles, tapers. Электри́ческая ла́мпочка в 100 свече́й, electric bulb of 100 candle power. Све́ч-ка, *n.f.*, (*dim.*), small candle. Свеч-но́й, *adj.*, candle. С. заво́д, candle works, factory. С-ая ла́вка, tallow, candle shop. С.ога́рок, candle end.

СВОБОД-, СВОБОЖ-, СВОБОЖД-, FREEDOM

свобо́д-а, *n.f.*, freedom, liberty. Я даю́ вам по́лную свобо́ду де́йствий, I give you complete freedom of action. С. сло́ва, freedom of speech. Он на свобо́де, he is at large. Вы́пустить на свобо́ду, to set free. Свобо́д-ный, *adj.*, free. С. как ве́тер, as free as the air. День с. от рабо́ты, day off. С-ая ко́мната, spare room, unoccupied room. С-ое вре́мя, free time, leisure. С-ое ме́сто, free place, seat; vacant seat, place. С-ое пла́тье, loose dress. Пра́во с-ого голосова́ния, franchise. С-ые де́ньги, ready money. Свобо́д-но, *adv.*, freely. Он с. говори́т по-ру́сски, he speaks Russian fluently. Свобо́д-о-мы́слие, *n.n.*, free thinking, free thought.

вы́-свобод-ить, вы-свобож-у́, *v.р.,* вы-свобожд-а́ть, *v.i.,* из + *gen.,* + *acc.,* to free, disengage, disentangle, release. Он вы́свободил го́лубя из западни́, he released the pigeon from the trap. Вы́-свобод-ить-ся, *v.р.р.,* вы-свобожд-а́ть-ся, *v.i.r.,* из + *gen.,* to free oneself, become disengaged, disentangled, be released. Он вы́свободился из пле́на, he fled from captivity.

о-свобод-и́ть, *v.р.,* о-свобожд-а́ть, *v.i.,* от + *gen.,* to free, liberate, release. О. арестованного, to discharge a prisoner. Его́ не ско́ро освободя́т, they will not release him soon. О. от вое́нной слу́жбы, to be exempted from military service. О-свобод-и́ть-ся, *v.р.р.,* о-свобожд-а́ть-ся, *v.i.r.,* от + *gen.,* to become free, be released, liberated, discharged. В кото́ром часу́ вы освобожда́етесь? At what time are you free? О. от вое́нной слу́жбы, to be exempted from military service. О-свобожд-е́ние, *n.n.,* deliverance, release, liberation, emancipation. О. рабо́в, liberation, emancipation of slaves. О. крестья́н, emancipation of peasants. О. арестованного, discharge of a prisoner. О-свобод-и́тель, *n.т.,* liberator, rescuer. О-свобод-и́тельный, *adj.,* liberating. О-ое движе́ние, emancipation movement. О-свобожд-ённый, *adj., part. pass. past,* liberated, freed, released, discharged. О-ая страна́, liberated country.

СВЯТ-, СВЯЧ-, СВЯЩ-, HOLINESS, SANCTITY, DEDICATION

свят-и́-ть, свяч-у́, *v.i.,* + *acc.,* to sanctify, consecrate, bless. Вчера́ святи́ли но́вые ико́ны, yesterday they blessed the new icons. Свят-и́ть-ся, *v.i.r.,* to be sanctified, consecrated, blessed. Да святи́тся Имя Твоё, may Thy Name be blessed. Свят-и́тель, *n.т.,* saint. С. Никола́й, Saint Nicholas. Свят-и́тельский, *adj.,* saintly. С. о́блик, saintly face. Свя́т-ки, *n.f.pl.,* Christmas holidays. Гада́ние на свя́тках, fortune telling at Christmas time. Свят-очный, *adj.,* Christmas. С. расска́з, Christmas story. Свят-о́й, *adj.,* saint, saintly,

holy, sacred. Свят-о-та́тство, *n.n.,* sacrilege. Свят-о-та́тственный, *adj.,* sacrilegious. Свят-о́ша, *n.т.,* sanctimonious person; hypocrite. Свят-о́шество, *n.n.,* sanctimoniousness; hypocrisy. Свя́т-цы, *n.т.pl.,* church calendar.

свящ-е́н-ство-вать, *v.i.,* to be a priest. Мой оте́ц свяще́нствовал в э́том селе́, my father was a priest in this village.

свящ-е́н-ник, *n.т.,* priest, clergyman. С. вы́нес распя́тие, the priest brought out the crucifix. Свящ-е́ннический, *adj.,* priestly, sacerdotal. С-ое облаче́ние, priestly vestments.

свящ-енн-о-де́йствовать, *v.i.,* to officiate, do something with solemnity. Свяще́нник свяще́ннодействовал в алтаре́, the priest celebrated the divine service in the apse. Судья́ так серьёзен, то́чно он свяще́ннодействует, the judge is as serious, as if he were officiating. Свящ-енн-о-де́йствие, *n.n.,* celebration of a divine service; solemn performance of an act. Свящ-е́нный, *adj.,* holy, sacred. С. сосу́д, sacred vessel. С-ое Писа́ние, Holy Scripture.

о-свят-и́ть, о-свящ-у́, *v.р.,* о-свящ-а́ть, *v.i.,* + *acc.,* to sanctify, consecrate. О-свят-и́ть-ся, *v.р.р.,* о-свящ-а́ть-ся, *v.i.r.,* to be sanctified, consecrated. О-свящ-ённый, *adj., part. pass. past,* sanctified, consecrated. Обы́чай, о. века́ми, a custom hallowed by the ages. Пре-о-свящ-е́нный, *adj., used as n.,* His Grace, a title used in addressing a bishop. П. митрополи́т, His Grace the Metropolitan.

по-свят-и́ть, *v.р.,* по-свящ-а́ть, *v.i.,* + *acc.,* + *dat.,* to dedicate, devote; sacrifice, ordain, consecrate; dub. П. кни́гу своему́ учи́телю, to dedicate a book to one's teacher. П. у́тро уче́бным заня́тиям, to devote a morning to study. П. жизнь де́тям, to devote one's life to children. П. в сан епи́скопа, to ordain a bishop. П. кого́-либо в та́йну, to confide in someone, let someone in on on a secret. П. в ры́цари, to knight. По-свят-и́ть-ся, *v.р.р.,* по-свящ-а́ть-ся, *v.i.r.,* to be dedicated, devoted, consecrated, ordained. Жизнь ма́тери посвяща́ется де́тям, the mother's life is devoted to her children. Он посвяти́тся в свяще́нники, he will be ordained a priest. По-свящ-е́ние, *n.n.,* dedication, devotion, sacrifice, ordination, knighting. П. в ры́цари, conferring of knighthood. По-свящ-ённый, *adj., part. pass. past,* dedicated, devoted, sacrificed, ordained. Конце́рт, п. па́мяти Чайко́вского, the concert is dedicated to the memory of Tschaikovsky.

СЕК-, (СѢК-), СЕЧ-, (СѢЧ-), AXE, CHOPPING

сек-и́р-а, *n.f.,* (*hist.*), axe, hatchet, battle-axe. С. стари́нное ору́жие, the battle-axe is an ancient weapon.

сеч-ь, сек-у́, *v.i.,* + *acc.,* to whip, thrash, flog; chop, mince. Его́ ча́сто се́кли, he was often flogged. По́вар сек мя́со ножо́м, the cook chopped the meat with a knife. Сеч-ёный, *adj.,* chopped. С-ое мя́со, chopped meat. Сек-у́щий, *adj., part. act. pres.,* chopping. С-ая ли́ния, (*math.*), secant. Сеч-ь, *n.f., used only in expression:* Запоро́жская Сечь, (*hist.*), Cossack Republic of the 16th-18th centuries. Сек-а́ч, *n.m.,* cleaver. Сéч-а, *n.f.,* (*obs.*), carnage, slaughter. Сеч-éние, *n.n.,* whipping, thrashing; (*math.*), section. Ке́сарево с., (*med.*), Caesarean section. Сéч-ка, *nf.,* cleaver; chaff cutter, straw cutter: Скот корми́ли соло́менной сéчкой, the cattle were fed chopped straw. Сéч-ь-ся, *v.i.r.,* to cut, split, break off. Во́лосы секу́тся, hair breaks off. Шёлк сечётся, silk is split, cut.

вы́-сеч-ь, *v.p.,* вы-сек-а́ть, *v.i.,* + *acc.,* to cut, carve, sculpture. В. ого́нь, to strike fire. В. из ка́мня фигу́ру, to carve a figure out of stone. Вы́-сеч-енный, *adj., part. pass., past,* carved, hewn. В. из ка́мня, rock-hewn.

вы́-сеч-ь, *v.p.,* + *acc.,* to whip, flog. Вори́шку вы́секли, the little thief was flogged.

за-сéч-ь, *v.p.,* за-сек-а́ть, *v.i.,* to make a cut. З. на дере́вьях направле́ние, to indicate a direction by making notches in trees. Засеки́ вре́мя, когда́ мы вы́ехали, (*recent, colloq.*), mark the time of our departure.

за-сéч-ь, *v.p.,* + *acc.,* до + *gen.,* to whip, flog. З. до сме́рти, to whip to death. За-сéк-а, *n.f.,* (*mil.*), abatis. Защищённый, засе́кою, protected by an abatis. За-сéч-ка, *n.f.,* gash, notch. На столбе́ оста́лась глубо́кая з., a deep notch remained on the pole.

на-сéч-ь, *v.p.,* на-сек-а́ть, *v.i.,* + *acc.,* to cut in quantity; notch, make incisions. Они́ насекли́ мно́го сухи́х ветве́й, they cut many dry branches. Н. зо́лотом (серебро́м), to damaskeen. На-сеч-ённый, *adj., part. pass. past,* cut, notched. Узо́ры, н-ые на дере́ве, designs cut in wood. На-сек-о́мое, *n.n.,* insect. В саду́ мно́го насеко́мых, there are many insects in the garden. На-сéч-ка, *n.f.,* incision, ridges of a file; damaskeening. Рукоя́тка кинжа́ла с золото́й насе́чкой, a dagger hilt with golden damaskeening. Насе́чки стёр-лись, the ridges (of the file) are worn down.

от-сéч-ь, *v.p.,* от-сек-а́ть, *v.i.,* + *acc.,* + *dat.,* to hew, chop off. От-сеч-éние, *n.n.,* striking, cutting, hewing, chopping off.

пере-сéч-ь, *v.p.,* пере-сек-а́ть, *v.i.,* + *acc.,* to intersect, cut across, traverse. Эта у́лица пересека́ет другу́ю, this street intersects another one. Они́ пересекли́ ему́ доро́гу, they barred his way. Он пересёк ему́ плечо́, he wounded his shoulder. Путеше́ственники пересекли́ плоского́рье, the travelers crossed the plateau. Пере-сеч-éние, *n.n.,* intersection, crossing. То́чка пересече́ния, point of intersection. П. двух доро́г, intersection of two roads. Пере-сéч-ь-ся, *v.p.r.,* пере-сек-а́ть-ся, *v.i.r., only in 3d pers.,* to be intersected. На поворо́те пересекли́сь две доро́ги, two roads crossed at the turn.

пре-сéч-ь, *v.p.,* пре-сек-а́ть, *v.i.,* + *acc.,* to suppress, interrupt, cut short. П. разви́тие боле́зни, to arrest the progress of an illness. П. преступле́ние, to prevent a crime. Пре-сеч-éние, *n.n.,* suppression, interruption, cutting short. Ме́ры пресече́ния за́говора, measures to suppress a conspiracy.

про-сéч-ь, *v.p.,* про-сек-а́ть, *v.i.,* + *acc.,* to hew through, cut through. П. доро́гу в лесу́, to cut a way through a forest. Про́-сек-а, *n.f.,* a clearing through the woods. Они́ вы́шли на широ́кую про́секу, they came out into a wide clearing in the woods.

рас-сéч-ь, *v.p.,* рас-сек-а́ть, *v.i.,* + *acc.,* to cut up, cleave. Кора́бль рассека́л во́лны, the ship cut through the waves. Рас-сеч-éние, *n.n.,* cutting, dissecting.

у-сéч-ь, *v.p.,* у-сек-а́ть, *v.i.,* + *acc.,* to cut away, slash away. У-сеч-ённый, *adj., part. pass. past.,* truncated. У-ая пирами́да, (*geom.*), truncated pyramid. У-сеч-éние, у-сек-нове́ние, *n.n.,* cutting off, truncation. Усекнове́ние главы́ св. Иоа́нна Крести́теля, (*Ch.-Sl.*), the beheading of St. John the Baptist.

СЕМ-, (СѢМ-), СЕ- (СѢ-), SEED, SOWING

сéм-я, *n.n.,* сем-ена́, *n.pl.,* seed, grain; sperm. Огуре́чное се́мя, cucumber seed. Пойти́ в семена́, to go to seed. Семена́ раздо́ра, (*fig.*), seeds of discord. От худо́го се́мени не жди до́брого пле́мени, (*prov.*), ill seed, ill weed. (*literally*: do not expect a superior tribe from inferior seed). Сéм-ечко, *n.n.,* small seed. Сéм-ечки, *n.n.pl.,* (*colloq.*), sunflower seeds.

сем-ен-и́ть-ся, *v.i.r., used in 3d pers. only,* to run to seed. Рожь семени́тся, the rye is going to seed. Сем-енн-и́к, *n.m.,* a plant left to go to seed. Сем-енн-о́й, *adj.,* seminal. С-áя пшени́ца, seed wheat. С-ая коро́бка, seed vessel. С. кана́тик, spermatic cord. Сем-ен-о-во́дческий, *adj.,* pertaining to seed culture.

бес-сем-я́нный, *adj.,* seedless. Бес-сем-я́нка, *n.f.,* seedless fruit. Гру́ша-бес-семя́нка, seedless pear.

об-сем-ен-и́ть, *v.p.,* об-сем-еня́ть, *v.i.,* + *acc.,* to cover with seeds, sow. О. поля́, to sow fields.

се́-я-ть, *v.i.,* + *acc.,* to sow. Крестья́не се́ют пшени́цу, the peasants are sowing wheat. С. ряда́ми, to sow in rows. С. раздо́р, to sow discord. С. зло, to sow evil. Се́йте разу́мное, до́брое, ве́чное, (*Nekrasov*) sow the wise, the good, the eternal. Се́ешь ве́тер, пожнёшь бу́рю, (*saying*), sow the wind and you will reap the storm. Се́-ялка, *n.f.,* sowing, seeder. Рядова́я с., seed drill, seeder. Тра́кторная с., tractor-drawn seeder. Се́янец, *n.m.,* seedling. Лук-с., chive. Се́-ятель, *n.m.,* sower, seeder.

се-в, *n.m.,* sowing. Весе́нний сев, spring sowing.

вы́-се-ять, *v.p.,* вы-се-ва́ть, вы-се́-ивать, *v.i.,* + *acc.,* to sow out; sift. Вы́сеяли ны́нче де́сять мешко́в зерна́, they sowed ten sacks of seed grain today. В. муку́, to sift flour. Вы́-се-вки, *n.f.pl.,* siftings, bran. Ржаны́е в., rye siftings.

за-се́-ять, *v.p.,* за-се-ва́ть, за-се́-ивать, *v.i.,* + *acc.,* + *instr.,* to sow. З. по́ле овсо́м, to sow a field of oats. За-се́-янный, *adj., part. pass. past,* sown. З-ая пло́щадь, sown area. За-се́-в, *n.m.,* sowing. З. поле́й запозда́л, the fields were sown late. За-се́-ять-ся, *v.p.r.,* за-се-ва́ть-ся, за-се́-ивать-ся, *v.i.r.,* to be sown. По́ле само́ засе́ялось со́рными тра́вами, the field was over-grown with self-sown weeds.

на-се́-ять, *v.p.,* на-се-ва́ть, на-се́-ивать, *v.i.,* to sow in quantity. Н. де́сять гекта́ров пшени́цы, to sow ten hectares of wheat. Н. муки́ для пирого́в, to sift flour for pies.

об-се́-ять, *v.p.,* об-се-ва́ть, об-се́-ивать, *v.i.,* + *acc.,* + *instr.,* to sow thorough-ly, sow over a given area. Об-се́-ять-ся, *v.p.r.,* об-се-ва́ть-ся, об-се́-ивать-ся, *v.i.r.,* + *instr.,* to be sown.

от-се́-ять, *v.p.,* от-се-ва́ть, от-се́-ивать, *v.i.,* + *acc.,* to sift, pick out, select. О. муку́, to sift flour. От-се́-в, *n.m.,* sifting, selection. По́сле отсе́ва оста́-лось о́чень ма́ло, little remained after

the sifting. От-се-ва́ние, от-се́-ивание, *n.n.,* sifting, selection.

пере-се́-ять, *v.p.,* пере-се-ва́ть, пере-се́-ивать, *v.i.,* + *acc.,* to sow anew; re-sift. Пришло́сь втори́чно п. э́то по́ле, this field had to be sown again. Мука́ была́ втори́чно пересе́яна, the flour was resifted.

по-се́-ять, *v.p.,* + *acc.,* to sow. П. вражду́, to sow seeds of dissension. Что посе́ешь, то и пожнёшь, (*prov.*), as you sow, so shall you reap. Он где-то посе́ял свой кошелёк, (*colloq.*), he has left his purse somewhere. По-се́-в, *n.m.,* sowing. Ярово́й п., spring sowing. По-се-вно́й, *adj.,* sowing. П. материа́л, sowing material. П-áя пло́щадь, sown area, acreage under crop.

под-се́-ять, *v.p.,* под-се-ва́ть, под-се́-ивать, *v.i.,* + *acc.,* to sow in addition. Реди́ску подсева́ли ка́ждый ме́сяц, radishes were sown each month. Под-се́-в, *n.m.,* additional sowing.

про-се́-ять, *v.p.,* про-се-ва́ть, про-се́-ивать, *v.i.,* + *acc.,* to sift, riddle, screen. П. крупу́ сквозь решето́, to screen groats. Про-се́-ивание, *n.n.,* sifting, riddling, screening.

рас-се́-ять, *v.p.,* рас-се-ва́ть, рас-се́-ивать, *v.i.,* + *acc.,* по + *dat.,* to scatter, disseminate; broadcast; dis-perse. Р. семена́ по́ полю, to scatter seed over a field. Р. сомне́ния, (*fig.*), to dissipate one's doubts. Р. неприя́-теля, to disperse an enemy. Рас-се́-в, method and quality of sowing. Рас-се-ва́ние, *n.n.,* sowing by scattering. Рас-се́-ивание, *n.n.,* dispersal (of a crowd). Рас-се́-яние, *n.n.,* dispersion, diffusion. Р. све́та diffusion of light. Рас-се́-янность, *n.f.,* absent-mindedness, dis-traction. Р. его́ гла́вный недоста́ток, absent-mindedness is his main short-coming. Рас-се́-янный, *adj., part. pass. past,* absent-minded, distracted; dif-fused. Р. взгляд, vacant look. Р. о́браз жи́зни, a life of dissipation. Р. свет, diffused light. Р. челове́к, absent-minded person. Рас-се́-янно, *adv.,* absent-mindedly, distractedly. Рас-се́-ять-ся, *v.p.r.,* рас-се́-ивать-ся, *v.i.r.,* to be dispersed. Толпа́ рассе́ялась, the crowd dispersed. Тума́н рассе́ялся, the fog dispersed. Наде́жды рассе́ялись, как дым, hopes vanished into thin air. Ему́ на́до рассе́яться, he needs a change, diversion.

у-се́-ять, *v.p.,* у-се-ва́ть, у-се́-ивать, *v.i.,* + *acc.,* + *instr.,* to stud, dot. У-се́-янный, *adj. part. pass. past,* studded, dotted. Не́бо, усе́янное звёздами star-studded sky. О по́ле, кто тебя́ усе́ял мёртвыми костя́ми? (*Pushkin*), Oh, field of battle! who has strewn thee with bones of the dead?

СЕРД-, СЕРЖ-, СЕРЕД-, СРЕД-, HEART, MIDDLE

серд-ц-е, *n.п.,* heart. У него́ сла́бое с., he has a weak heart. С. у неё си́льно би́лось, her heart thumped. Ка́менное с., (*fig.*), heart of stone. С. моё! My darling! Защеми́ло с., my heart aches with pity. Име́ть на с., to have at heart. Положа́ ру́ку на с., (*idiom.*), candidly. Скрепя́ с., reluctantly. Чу́ет моё с., I have a premonition. От всего́ се́рдца, wholeheartedly. В сердца́х, in anger. С лёгким се́рдцем, with a light heart. Принима́ть что́-либо к се́рдцу, to take to heart. Серд-е́чко, *n.п.,* (*dim.*), little heart. Её с. затрепета́ло, her heart began to flutter. Серд-е́чный, *adj.,* cordial, hearty; cardiac. С. припа́док, heart attack. С-ая бесе́да, heart-to-heart talk. С-ое спаси́бо, cordial thanks. С. приве́т, cordial greetings. С-ые сре́дства, cardiac medicines. С-ые дела́, affairs of the heart, love affairs. Серд-е́чно, *adv.,* deeply, warmheartedly. С. люби́ть, to all with all one's heart. Серд-е́чность, *n.f.,* warmheartedness. Он прояви́л мно́го серде́чности к нему́, he showed him much warmheartedness. Бес-серд-е́чный, *adj.,* heartless, pitiless. Б-ое обраще́ние с заключёнными, heartless treatment of prisoners. Бес-серд-е́чно, *adv.,* heartlessly. Он б. обману́л её, he heartlessly deceived her. Бес-серд-е́чность, *n.f.,* heartlessness. Серд-о-бо́лие, *n.п.,* pity, compassion, tenderheartedness. Серд-о-бо́льный, *adj.,* pitiful, compassionate, tenderhearted. С-ая вдова́, tenderhearted widow. Серд-ц-е-бие́ние, *n.п.,* palpitation of the heart. Серд-ц-е-ви́дный, *adj.,* heart-shaped. Серд-ц-е-ви́на, *n.f.,* heart, core, pith, heartwood, medulla. С. де́рева сгнила́, the core of the tree has rotted. **серд-и́-ть,** серж-у́, *v.i.,* + *acc.,* to anger, vex, irritate. Он серди́т меня́ свои́м упря́мством, he irritates me with his stubbornness. Серд-и́ть-ся, *v.i.r.,* на + *acc.,* to be angry, fret. Не серди́тесь на меня́, don't be angry with me. Серд-и́тый, *adj.,* angry, cross. С. хара́ктер, cross disposition. У него́ о́чень с. вид, he looks very angry, cross. Серд-и́то, *adv.,* angrily, crossly, sullenly. Он о́чень с. говори́л с ним, he was very sharp with him. Она́ с. посмотре́ла на него́, she threw him an angry look.

рас-серд-и́ть, *v.p.,* + *occ.,* + *instr.,* to anger, make angry, vex. Он рассерди́л меня́ свое́ю ре́чью, he made me angry with his speech. Рас-серд-и́ть-ся, *v.p.r.,* на + *acc.,* to burst into a rage, become angry, lose one's temper. Нача́льник рассерди́лся на слу́жащего за неиспо́лнительность, the chief became angry at his employee for not fulfilling his duties. Рас-се́рж-енный, *adj., part. pass. past,* angry, angered, mad. Р. зверь опа́сен, an angry beast is dangerous.

серед-и́на, сред-и́на, *n.f.,* middle, midst. Мы е́дем на да́чу в середи́не (среди́не) ле́та, we are going to the country in midsummer. Золота́я с., golden means. В са́мой середи́не, in the very middle, midst. Серед-и́нка, *n.f.,* middle. С. я́блока была́ гнила́я, the core of the apple was rotten. Серед-ня́к, *n.т.,* (*recent*), peasant of average means. Сред-и́нный, *adj.,* middle.

сред-а́, *n.f.,* Wednesday; environment, surroundings, medium. Сего́дня среда́, today is Wednesday. Она́ прие́хала в сре́ду, she arrived on Wednesday. Его́ загуби́ла окружа́ющая среда́, his environment ruined him.

сред-и́, **сред-ь,** *prep.,* + *gen.,* among, amid. Среди́ бе́ла дня, in broad daylight. Среди́ у́лицы, in the middle of the street. Среди́-, *a combining form and prefix meaning* among, in the middle. Средизе́мное мо́ре, Mediterranean Sea.

по-сред-и́, *adv.,* in the middle, midst, among. П. реки́ бы́строе тече́ние, the current is strong in the middle of the river. По-сред-и́не, *adv., and prep.,* + *gen.,* in the middle, midst. Ора́тор стоя́л п. толпы́, the orator stood in the midst of the crowd. Он шёл п. у́лицы, he walked in the middle of the street.

сре́д-ний, *adj.,* middle, mean, average, medium. Челове́к сре́дних лет, middle-aged man. С. па́лец, middle finger. Сре́дний род, (*gram.*), neuter gender. С. у́ровень мо́ря, mean sea level. С-ее арифмети́ческое, arithmetical mean. С-ее образова́ние, secondary education. С-ее сосло́вие, middle class. С-яя за́работная пла́та, average wage. Выводи́ть с-ее число́, to average. Вы́ше сре́днего, above average. В сре́днем, on an average. Брать сре́днюю величину́, to take the mean quantity. Сре́дняя то́чка попада́ния снаря́дов, main point of impact. Средне-, *a combining form and prefix meaning* middle. Среднеазиа́тская Область, Central Asia. Средневеко́вый, medieval. Среднево́лжский край, Middle Volga district. Среднеру́сская возвы́шенность, Central Russian uplands.

сред-о-, *a combining form meaning* middle; among. Сред-о-то́чие, *п.п.*, central point; focus. Средото́чием промы́шленности явля́ются города́, cities are the centers of industry.

сре́д-ство, *п.п.*, means; remedy. С. защи́ты, means of defense. Антисепти́ческое с., an antiseptic. Универса́льное с., panacea. Служи́ть сре́дством для, to serve as an instrument for. Сре́дства к существова́нию, means of existence. У них ограни́ченные сре́дства, their means are limited. Жить на свои́ сре́дства, to support oneself. Челове́к со сре́дствами, person with means, of means.

по-сре́д-ство, *п.п.*, means, medium. Че́рез п., through the medium of, by means of. При посре́дстве, by means of. Посре́дством э́того, by means of that; thereby. Посре́дством ча́стого повторе́ния, by dint of repetition.

по-сре́д-ственность, *n.f.*, mediocrity. По-сре́д-ственный, *adj.*, middling, mediocre. П. писа́тель, mediocre writer.

по-сре́д-ничать, *v.i.*, to act as a middleman. По-сре́д-ник, *п.т.*, по-сре́дница, *n.f.*, ме́жду + *instr.*, mediator, negotiator, intermediary, middleman. П. ме́жду двумя́ тя́жущимися сторона́ми, middleman between two litigants. Мирово́й п., conciliator, arbitrator between the peasants and landowners in the reforms of 1861. Торго́вый п., broker. П. по прода́же недви́жимости, real estate agent. Быть посре́дником, to act as a middleman. По-сре́д-нический, *adj.*, intercessory, interceding. Его́ посре́днические де́йствия бы́ли безуспе́шны, his intercession was unsuccessful. По-сре́д-ничество, *п.п.*, mediation. Здесь вся́кое п. изли́шне, any kind of intercession will be useless here.

со-сред-о-то́чить, *v.p.*, со-сред-о-то́чи-вать, *v.i.*, + *acc.*, to concentrate. С. войска́ на за́падной грани́це, to concentrate troops on the western border. Со-сред-о-то́чить-ся, *v.p.r.*, со-сред-о-то́чивать-ся, *v.i.r.*, to concentrate, meditate. Он сосредото́чился над реше́нием зада́чи, he concentrated on the solution of the problem. Шум меша́л ему́ сосредото́читься, the noise prevented him from concentrating. Со-сред-о-то́чение, *п.п.*, concentration. С. войск, concentration of troops. Со-сред-о-то́ченность, *n.f.*, concentration. С. внима́ния, center of attention. Со-

сред-о-то́ченный, *adj.*, centered, concentrated, focussed. С. взгляд, an intent look. Со-сред-о-то́ченно, *adv.*, intently. Он с. гото́вился к экза́мену, he was concentrating on preparing himself for the examination.

СЕТ- (СѢТ-), NET

сет-ь, *n.f.*, net, network, mesh. Рыбо-ло́вная с., dragnet. Железнодоро́жная с., railroad network. Шко́льная с., school system. Электри́ческая с., network of electric wires. Вяза́ть (расставля́ть) се́ти, to weave, set nets. Пойма́ть в се́ти, to ensnare, net. Попа́сться в чьи́-либо се́ти, to become entangled in someone's net. Его́ лицо́ покры́то се́тью морщи́н, his face is covered with a network of wrinkles.

се́т-ка, *n.f.*, (*dim.*), net. Про́волочная с., wire net. С. для воло́с, hairnet. С. в ваго́не для веще́й, rack in a railroad car. Географи́ческая с., graticule, (*on a map*), grid (*radio*). Ба́бочка попа́ла в се́тку, the butterfly was caught in a net.

сет-ча́тка, *n.f.*, (*anat.*), retina. С. его́ гла́за разру́шена, his retina is destroyed. Се́т-чатый, *adj.*, netted, veined, reticulate. С. узо́р, network design. Покрыва́ть се́тчатым узо́ром, to cover with a netlike design.

СКАК-, СКАЧ-, СКОК-, СКОЧ-, LEAP, LEAPING

скак-а́-ть, скак-у́, *v.i.*, скак-ну́-ть, *v.p.*, *smf.* to skip, jump, leap, gallop. Он скакну́л на семь фу́тов, he jumped seven feet. Кто ска́чет на коне́? Who is galloping there? С. на одно́й ноге́, to hop on one foot. Ска́ч-ущий, *adj.*, *part. act. pres.*, galloping, hopping. С. вса́дник, galloping rider. С-ая температу́ра, fluctuating temperature. Скак-а́лка, *n.f.*, skipping rope. Скак-а́ние, *п.п.*, skipping, leaping. Скак-ово́й, *adj.*, racing. С-а́я ло́шадь, race horse. На скаку́, on the gallop. Скак-у́н, *п.т.*, jumper, racing horse. Ска́ч-ка, *n.f.*, race. Бе́шеная с., mad race. Ска́ч-ки, *n.f.pl.*, horse racing С. с перпя́т-ствиями, obstacle race. Уча́ствовать в ска́чках, to participate in a race. Скач-о́к, *п.т.*, jump, leap, skip. Он сде́лал большо́й скачо́к, he made a big leap. Скач-ки́, *n.pl.*, leaps and bounds. Скач-ка́ми, by leaps and bounds.

в-скач-ь, *adv.*, at a gallop.

до-скак-а́ть, *v.p.*, до-ска́к-ивать, *v.i.*, до + *gen.*, to gallop up to, reach by galloping, jumping. На коне́ он бы́стро доскака́л до го́рода, he reached the town at a gallop. До-скак-а́ть-ся, *v.p.r.*, to end up in trouble. Что, брат, доскака́лся, (*colloq.*), it serves you right, you got yourself into trouble.

об-скак-а́ть, *v.p.*, об-ска́к-ивать, *v.i.*, + *acc.*, to gallop round, past. Этот жоке́й обскака́л всех свои́х сопе́рников, this jockey outrode all his competitors. Его́ ло́шадь обскака́ла всех лошаде́й, his horse beat all the other horses. Он обскака́л всю дере́вню и по́днял трево́гу, he rode through the whole village and spread the alarm.

по-скак-а́ть, *v.p.*, to gallop off, away. Не ожида́я никого́, он поскака́л домо́й, he galloped home without waiting for anybody.

под-скак-а́ть, *v.p.*, под-ска́к-ивать, *v.i.*, к + *dat.*, to gallop up, jump to.

при-скак-а́ть, *v.p.*, при-ска́к-ивать, *v.i.*, к + *dat.*, to come galloping. Разве́дчики прискака́ли по́здно но́чью. the scouts arrived at a gallop late at night.

про-скак-а́ть *v.p.*, про-ска́кивать, *v.i.*, + *acc.*, to gallop, rush along, through. Они́ без остано́вки проскака́ли пять киломе́тров, they galloped five kilometers without stopping.

рас-скак-а́ть-ся, *v.p.r.*, to hop, jump, gallop without ceasing.

у-скак-а́ть, *v.p.*, от + *gen.*, to gallop away, skip away. У. от неприя́теля, to gallop away from the enemy.

в-скоч-и́ть, *v.p.*, в-ска́к-ивать, *v.i.*, на + *acc.*, с + *gen.*, to leap up, jump up, spring up. В. на ло́шадь, to jump on one's horse. В. на́ ноги, to leap to one's feet. В. с посте́ли, to jump out of bed. В. в копе́йку, (*colloq.*), it will cost a pretty penny. В-ска́к-ивание, *n.n.*, jumping, leaping, springing up.

вы́-скоч-ить, *v.p.*, вы-ска́к-ивать, *v.i.*, из + *gen.*, to jump out, spring out, dart out, slip out. В. из заса́ды, to attack from ambush. В. вперёд, to push oneself forward. Вы́-скоч-ка, *n.f.*, and *n.m.*, upstart. Я не люблю́ вы́скочек, I do not like upstarts.

за-скоч-и́ть, *v.p.*, за-ска́к-ивать, *v.i.*, to leap behind; catch. З. в тыл неприя́телю, to get behind the enemy's lines. Дверь заскочи́ла и не отворя́ется, the door is caught and does not open. За-ско́к, *n.m.*, (*colloq.*), catch. З. в голове́, quirk.

на-скоч-и́ть, *v.p.*, на-ска́к-ивать, *v.i.*, на + *acc.*, to jump upon, against; run against, smash into, spring upon. Н. на подво́дный ка́мень, to strike a rock. Все наскочи́ли на него́, they all jumped on him. На-ско́к, *n.m.*, swoop,

attack. На-ско́к-ом, *adv.*, with a sudden swoop. Де́йствовать н., to take by surprise.

от-скоч-и́ть, *v.p.*, от-ска́к-ивать, *v.i.*, от + *gen.*, to jump off, back, aside; recoil, rebound. Он отскочи́л от него́ в сто́рону, he jumped aside. Задви́жка отскочи́ла от две́ри, the latch fell off the door.

пере-скоч-и́ть, *v.p.*, пере-ска́к-ивать, *v.i.*, че́рез, + *acc.*, to leap, skip, jump over; clear. Перескочи́ть че́рез забо́р, to jump over a fence. Переска́кивать с предме́та на предме́т, to skip from one subject to another. Бе́лка п. с де́рева на де́рево, the squirrel is jumping from one tree to another. Пере́-ска́к-ивание, *n.n.*, skipping, leaping across. Пере-ско́к, *n.m.*, leap over, across.

под-скоч-и́ть, *v.p.*, под-ска́к-ивать, *v.i.*, к + *dat.*, с + *instr.*, to run, hurry, jump up to. Он подскочи́л к нему́ с кулака́ми, he rushed at him and threatened him with his fists. П. от ра́дости, to jump for joy.

про-скоч-и́ть, *v.p.*, про-ска́к-ивать, *v.i.*, сквозь, в + *acc.*, to spring, slip in, past, through. Ко́шка проскочи́ла сквозь дыру́ в кры́ше, the cat jumped through a hole in the roof. У корре́ктора проскочи́ла опеча́тка, the proofreader overlooked a misprint.

со-скоч-и́ть, *v.p.*, со-ска́к-ивать, *v.i.*, с + *gen.*, to jump from; spring down, off, from. Дверь соска́кивает с пе́тель, the door comes off its hinges. Ко́шка соскочи́ла с де́рева, the cat jumped from the tree.

СЛАВ-, СЛОВ-, СЛЫ-, WORD, FAME, SLAV

сла́в-а, *n.f.*, fame, glory. С. Бо́гу! Glory to God! Дурна́я с., ill fame, disrepute. Дости́чь сла́вы, to win fame. Угости́ть на сла́ву, to treat well, first-rate.

сла́в-ить, сла́в-л-ю, *v.i.*, + *acc.*, to glorify, celebrate, praise. Де́ти сла́вили Христа́, the children were singing carols. Сла́в-ить-ся, *v.i.r.*, to be famous, have a reputation. Этот край сла́вится свои́м кли́матом, this country is famous for its climate, Он сла́вится свое́ю че́стностью, he has a reputation for honesty.

о-сла́в-ить, *v.p.*, о-слав-л-я́ть, *v.i.*, + *acc.*, (*colloq.*), to defame, decry, discredit. О-сла́в-ленный, *adj.*, *part. pass. past*, defamed, discredited.

про-сла́в-ить, *v.p.*, про-слав-л-я́ть, *v.p.*, + *acc.*, to glorify, celebrate. Менде-ле́ева просла́вила его́ периоди́ческая система элементов. Mendeleyev is famous for his periodic system of chemical elements. Про-слáв-ить-ся, *v.p.r.*, про-слав-лять-ся, *v.i.r.*, to become famous, illustrious, be famous. Он прослáвился своúми побéдами, he became famous for his victories. Прослав-лéние, *п.п.*, glorification, celebration, apotheosis. П. мощéй привлеклó мнóго богомóльцев, the glorification of the relics attracted many pilgrims.

рас-слáв-ить, *v.p.*, рас-слав-лять, *v.i.*, + *acc.*, to proclaim the greatness of, glorify. Газéты расслáвили егó как госудáрственного дéятеля, the newspapers proclaimed him a great statesman.

слáв-ный, *adj.*, famous, renowned; nice. С-ое Бородúнское сражéние, the famous battle of Borodino. Ваш отéц с. человéк, your father is a nice man. Он с. мáлый, he's a good fellow. Слáвненький, *adj.*, nice; cunning. С. дóмик, cosy little house.

слав-о-слóвить, *v.i.*, to glorify, sing the praises. С. Гóспода, to praise the Lord. Слав-о-слóвие, *п.п.*, doxology; Gloria in excelsis.

слав-янúн, *п.т.*, (from слов-енúн), (слав-яне, *п.т.pl.*), Slav. Слав-янка, *п.f.*, Slav. Славяне живýт в восточной и центрáльной чáсти Еврóпы, the Slavs live in the eastern and central parts of Europe. Слав-янский, *adj.*, Slav, Slavic. Мы изучáем славянские языкú, we are studying Slavic languages. Слав-янство, *п.п.*, the Slavs. Южное с. живёт на Балкáнах, the Southern Slavs live in the Balkans. Слав-úстика, *п.f.*, Slavistics. Слав-úст, *п.т.*, Slavist. Слав-яно-фúл, *п.т.*, Slavophile. Хомякóв - извéстный славянофúл, Khomyakov was a famous Slavophile. Слав-яно-фúльство, *п.п.*, Slavophilism.

слóв-о, *п.п.*, word; speech. Речь состоúт из слов, speech consists of words. За вáми послéднее с., you've had the last word; you have the last word. Слóво в слóво, word for word. Взять с когó-либо с., to secure a promise. Дать с., to give one's word. Сдержáть с., to keep one's word. Взять назáд с., to break one's word. Пожáлуйста, на два слóва, Please, a word with you. Ни слóва об этом, not a word about this. Это однú словá, these are mere words. Богáтый запáс слов, a rich vocabulary. По егó словáм, according to his story. Другúми словáми, in other words. Сказáть в двух словáх, to say something in a few words. Сдéлать на словáх, to do by word of mouth.

Произнестú вступúтельное (заключúтельное) слóво, to deliver an introductory (a closing) speech. Взять слóво на собрáнии, to take the floor. Слóв-о-, *a combining word meaning* word, letter. Слов-о-лúтня, *п.f.*, letter foundry. Слов-о-лúтчик, *п.т.*, type founder. Слов-о-образовáние, *п.п.*, word formation. Слов-о-охóтливый, *adj.*, talkative, verbose, loquacious. Он слúшком словоохóтлив, he's too talkative. Слов-о-прéние, *п.п.*, argument. Прекратúм излúшние словопрéния, let's put an end to unnecessary arguments. Слов-о-производство, *п.п.*, etymology. Слов-о-сочетáние, *п.п.*, combination, combining of words. Слов-о-твóрчество, *п.п.*, coining of words. Слов-о-употреблéние, *п.п.*, use of words; vocabulary. Слов-цó, *п.п.*, jest, quip. Крáсное с., jest, quip.

слов-áрь, *п.т.*, dictionary, lexicon. Мне нýжен рýсско-англúйский словáрь, I need a Russian-English dictionary.

слов-éс-н-ость, *п.f.*, literature, letters. Устная с., oral literature, folklore. Учúтель словéсности, teacher of literature. Слов-éсник, *п.т.*, man of letters. Слов-éсный, *adj.*, verbal, oral. Словéсная нóта, verbal note. С-ая войнá, war of words; controversy.

бес-слов-éсный, *adj.*, dumb, speechless. Б-ая тварь, (*obs.*), dumb animal.

благо-слов-úть, *v.p.*, благ-о-слов-лять, *v.i.*, + *acc.*, to bless, give one's blessing. Благословúте меня, бáтюшка, (*rel.*) Bless me, father. Благословляю вас, поля роднýе, I bless you, native fields. Мать благословúла сýна икóной, the mother blessed her son with an icon. Благо-слов-éние, *п.п.*, blessing, benediction. Матерúнское б., mother's blessing. Благо-слов-éнный, *adj.*, blessed. Б. край, blessed country.

зло-слóв-ить, *v.p.*, по-зло-слóв-ить, *v.i.*, to calumniate, speak ill, slander; gossip a little. Онá любúла с., she liked to gossip a little. Зло-слóв-ие, *п.п.*, malignant gossip; scandal.

по-слóв-ица, *п.f.*, proverb; saying. Это стáло послóвицей, this has become proverbial. Это вошлó в послóвицу. this has become proverbial.

преди-слóв-ие, *п.п.*, preface, foreword, preamble. Я ужé написáл п. к своéй кнúге, I have already written the preface to my book. П. к договóру, preamble to an agreement. Служúть предислóвием, to preface; be used, serve as a preface.

со-слóв-ие, *п.п.*, estate; social class. Вы кокóго сослóвия? (*obs.*) To what social class do you belong? Трéтье с., the third estate. Со-слóв-ность, *n.f.*, social hierarchy. Совремéнное óбщество отменяет сослóвность, contemporary society does not recognize hierarchies. Со-слóв-ный, *adj.*, class. С-ые предрассýдки, class prejudice.

у-слóв-ие, *n.n.*, condition, stipulation, clause, contract. Услóвия договóра, the terms of a treaty. Стáвить услóвием, to stipulate. С услóвием (при услóвии), что, on condition that. На такúх услóвиях, on such terms, such conditions. Ни при какúх услóвиях, under no circumstances. При дáнных услóвиях, under existing terms. При прóчих рáвных услóвиях, other things being equal.

у-слóв-ить-ся, *v.p.r.,* у-слóв-л-ивать-ся, *v.i.r.,* о + *prep.*, to agree, arrange, make arrangements, settle. Онú зарáнее услóвились о ценé, they agreed upon the price beforehand. У-слóв-л-енный, *adj.*, agreed upon, stipulated. У. срок постáвки товáра, stipulated date for delivery of goods. У-слóв-ный, *adj.*, conditional, provisory; conventional. У-ое наклонéние, (*gram.*), conditional mood. У-ое оправдáние, conditional discharge; release on probation. У-ое наказáние, suspended sentence. У. знак, graphic symbol. Без-у-слóв-ный, *adj.*, absolute, categorical, unconditional. Б-ое трéбование, categorical demand. У-слóв-но, *adv.*, conditionally. Без-у-слóв-но, *adv.*, absolutely, undoubtedly. У-слóв-ность, *n.f.*, convention. В нáшем óбществе мнóго услóвностей, in our society there are many conventions.

об-у-слóв-ить, *v.p.,* об-у-слóв-л-ивать, *v.i.*, to make conditions, stipulate. Егó приéзд обуслóвлен покрытием стóимости егó проéзда, he arrived on condition that his fare be paid. Об-у-слóв-ить-ся, *v.p.r.,* об-у-слóв-л-ивать-ся, *v.i.r.*, to depend on; be stipulated, explained. Клúмат этой мéстности обуслóвливается её примóрским положéнием, the climate of this region depends on its maritime position.

слы-ть, слы-в-ý, *v.i.*, за + *acc.*, to be reputed, considered, looked upon; pass for. Он слывёт за богáтого человéка, he is reputed to be a rich man. С. отшéльником, to be looked upon as a hermit.

про-слы-ть, *v.p.*, + *instr.*, за + *acc.*, to be considered, taken for. П. за дуракá, to be considered a fool. Онá прослылá большóй ýмницей, she has a reputation for cleverness, intelligence.

СЛАД-, СОЛОД-, СЛАСТ-, СЛАЩ-, СЛАЖД-, SWEETNESS

слáд-кий, *adj.*, sweet, sugary, honeyed; dessert. Мёд óчень с., honey is very sweet. Мать готóвит с-ое блюдо, the mother is preparing a dessert. Егó словá были слúшком с-и, his words were too honeyed. Слáд-ко, *adv.*, sweetly; suavely. Он с. спал, he was sleeping soundly. Слад-ковáтый, *adj.*, rather sweet. Слад-ковáто, *adv.*, rather sweetly. Слад-ко-, *a combining form meaning* sweet. Сладко-речúвый (*derog.*), smooth-tongued, fair spoken.

на-слад-úть-ся, *v.p.r.,* на-слажд-áть-ся, *v.i.r.*, + *instr.*, to take delight, pleasure in, enjoy oneself. Он наслаждáлся заслýженным óтдыхом, he enjoyed a well-earned rest. На-слажд-éние, *n.n.*, pleasure, delight, enjoyment. Я получúл большóе н. от вáшего пéния, your singing gave me great pleasure.

у-слад-úть, *v.p.,* у-слажд-áть, *v.i.*, + *acc.*, + *instr.*, to delight, give delight. Он услаждáл нас своéю мýзыкой, he delighted us with his music. У-слáд-а, *n.f.*, (*obs.*), delight, pleasure, joy. Дочь былá егó услáдой, his daughter was his joy. У-слад-úть-ся, *v.p.r.,* у-слажд-áть-ся, *v.i.r.*, + *instr.*, to delight, rejoice. Мы услаждáлись леснóй прогýлкой, we delighted in a stroll in the woods.

слáд-ость, *n.f.*, sweetness, sweetmeat. С. сахарúна выше слáдости сáхара, saccharine is sweeter than sugar. Он óчень любит слáдости, he likes sweets very much. Слáд-остный, *adj.*, suave, delightful, sweet. С. покóй, a delightful peace. Слад-о-стрáстие, *n.n.*, voluptuousness, sensuality. Слад-о-стрáстный, *adj.*, voluptuous, sensual.

сласт-ь, слáст-и, *n.f.pl.*, sweets, sweetmeats. Дéвочка любит слáсти, the little girl likes sweets. Сласт-ёна, *n.m. and n.f.*, sweet-tooth.

в-сласт-ь, *adv.*, to one's heart's content. Он наéлся в., he ate to his heart's content.

сласт-úть, слащ-ý, *v.i.*, + *acc.*, to sweeten.

пере-сласт-úть, *v.p.r.,* пере-слáщ-ивать, *v.i.r.*, + *acc.*, to sweeten, to sweeten to excess, use too much sugar. Вы пересластúли это кýшанье, you have oversweetened this dish.

у-сласт-úть, *v.p.,* у-слащ-áть, *v.i.*, + *acc.*, to sweeten. Он услащáл свой неприятные замечáния изысканной любéзностью, he sweetened his disagreeable remarks with extreme politeness.

слащ-а́вый, *adj.,* sugary. С. го́лос, sugary voice. Он был так слаща́в, he was all sugar and honey. Слащ-а́вость, *n.f.,* sweetness.

сла́щ-е, *adj., and adv. comp.,* sweeter, more sweetly. По-сла́щ-е, *adj., and adv.,* a little sweeter, more sweetly. Сла́ще мёда, sweeter than honey. Нале́йте мне чай посла́ще, make my tea a little sweeter.

со́лод, *n.m.,* malt. Ячме́нный с., barley malt. С. идёт на приготовле́ние пи́ва, malt is used in the preparation of beer.

солод-и́ть, соло́ж-у́, *v.i.,* + *acc.,* to malt. С. ячме́нь, to ferment barley. Солод-ко́вый, *adj.,* malt. С. ко́рень, licorice. Солод-о́вня, *n.f.,* malt house. На пивова́ренном заво́де вы́строена бо́льшая с., a large malt house was built at the brewery. Солод-о́вник, *n.m.,* malt brewer. Солод-о́вый, *adj.,* malt. С. са́хар, malt sugar. Солод-о́венный, *adj.,* pertaining to the making of malt. С. заво́д, malt house. Солож-е́ние, *n.n.,* maltage; conversion into malt. С. ячменя́, conversion of barley into malt.

СЛ-, СОЛ-, СЫЛ-, ШЛ-, SENDING

сл-а-ть, шл-ю, *v.i.,* + *acc.,* to send. С. письмо́ по возду́шной по́чте, to send a letter by air mail. Шлю вам серде́чный приве́т, I am sending you my warmest greetings.

вы́-сл-ать, *v.p.,* вы-сыл-а́ть, *v.i.,* + *acc.,* to send out; deport, banish, exile. В. кни́гу кому́-либо, to send someone a book. Его́ вы́слали из Ленингра́да, he was banished from Leningrad. Вы́-сыл-ка, *n.f.,* sending; shipment; banishment, exile. В. това́ров задержа́лась, the shipment of merchandise was delayed. В. населе́ния из прифронтово́й полосы́, the transfer of the population from the war zone.

до-сл-а́ть, *v.p.,* до-сыл-а́ть, *v.i.,* to send on, send the remainder. Д. недоста́ющие тома́, to send on missing volumes.

за-сл-а́ть, *v.p.,* за-сыл-а́ть, *v.i.,* to send far away, dispatch, exile. По́чта куда́-то засла́ла посы́лку, the post office sent the parcel somewhere else. Аресто́ванных засла́ли в Колыму́, the prisoners were sent to Kolyma. З. за три́девять земе́ль, (*saying*), to exile to land's end.

на-сл-а́ть, *v.p.,* на-сыл-а́ть, *v.i.,* на + *acc.,* to send in quantity; inflict. Бог насла́л на них еги́петские ка́зни, the Lord inflicted on them the plagues of Egypt.

ото-сл-а́ть, *v.p.,* от-сыл-а́ть, *v.i.,* + *acc.,* + *dat.,* to send off. Ото́-сл-анный, *adj., part. pass. past,* dispatched, mailed. Письмо́ бы́ло ото́слано адреса́ту, the letter was forwarded to the addressee. Не-ото́-сл-анный, *adj., part. pass., past,* not sent, not dispatched, unmailed. Н-ые пи́сьма, unmailed letters. Отошли́те де́ньги обра́тно! Send back the money. От-сы́л-ка, *n.f.,* sending off, mailing. О. пи́сем шла норма́льно, the mail was sent out normally.

пере-сл-а́ть, *v.p.,* пере-сыл-а́ть, *v.i.,* + *acc.,* + *dat.,* to forward, remit. Ссы́льные всё вре́мя пересыла́лись с одного́ ме́ста на друго́е, the exiles were constantly moved from one place to another. Пере-сл-а́ть-ся, *v.p.r.,* пере-сыл-а́ть-ся, *v.i.r.,* to be sent, forwarded. Това́ры пересыла́лись по желе́зной доро́ге, the merchandise was transferred by rail. Письмо́ перешлётся на но́вый а́дрес, the letter will be forwarded to the new address. Пере-сы́л-ка, *n.f.,* forwarding, carriage. П. валю́ты запрещена́, remittance of currency is forbidden. Пла́та за пересы́лку, postage, carriage. П. беспла́тно, postage free. Пере-сы́л-ь-ный, *adj.,* pertaining to deportation. П-ая тюрьма́, deportation prison.

по-сл-а́ть, *v.p.,* по-сыл-а́ть, *v.i.,* + *acc.,* to send, dispatch, mail, post. Он посыла́ет нам де́ньги ка́ждый ме́сяц, he sends us money every month. П. за до́ктором, to send for a doctor. П. кого́-либо за че́м-либо, to send someone for something. П. к чо́рту, (*colloq.*), to send to the devil. П. на рабо́ту, to send to work. П. покло́н, to send greetings, compliments. По-сыл-а́ть-ся, *v.i.r.,* to be sent. Това́ры посыла́ются на́ дом, home delivery. По-сла́-нец, *n.m.,* messenger. По-сла́-ние, *n.m.,* message, epistle. П. Апо́стола Па́вла, (*Bib.*), St. Paul's Epistle. По-сл-а́нник, *n.m.,* minister plenipotentiary. По-сл-а́ннический, *adj.,* ministerial. По́-сл-анный, *adj., used as n.m.,* messenger; envoy. П. до сих пор не верну́лся, thus far the messenger has not returned. Посо́л, *n.m.,* ambassador. Англи́йский посо́л прибыл в Вашингто́н, the British ambassador arrived in Washington. По-со́л-ь-ский, *adj.,* ambassador's, ambassadorial. П. прика́з (*hist.*), foreign office. По-со́л-ь-ство, *n.n.,* embassy, legation, mission. Мой брат слу́жит в посо́льстве, my brother is attached to the embassy. По-сы́л-ка, *n.f.,* sending, mailing; premise. Почто́вая п. пропа́ла в пути, the parcel was lost en route. Быть на посылках, to run errands. Большая (малая), п., major (minor) premise. По-сыл-ь-ный, *adj., used as n.m.,* messenger. П. принёс письмо, the messenger brought a letter. По-сыл-ь-ный, *adj.,* pertaining to sending, dispatching. П-ое судно, dispatch vessel.

подо-сл-ать, *v.p.,* под-сыл-ать, *v.i.,* + *acc.,* к + *dat.,* to send secretly. Подо-сл-анный, *adj., part. pass. past,* sent secretly. П. убийца, an assassin, murderer sent secretly.

при-сл-ать, *v.p.,* при-сыл-ать, *v.i.,* + *acc., dat.,* to send (*used by recipient*). Нам прислали билеты на концерт, they sent us tickets for the concert. При-сыл-ать-ся, *v.i.r.,* to be sent. Приложения к газете присылаются бесплатно, the newspaper supplements are sent free of charge. При-сыл-ка, *n.f.,* sending; an item sent.

разо-сл-ать, *v.p.,* рас-сыл-ать, *v.i.,* + *acc.,* to distribute. Р. приглашения, to send out invitations. Повестки разосланы, the summonses, notices have been sent out. Рас-сыл-ка, *n.f.,* distribution. Рас-сыл-ь-ный, *adj., used as n.m.,* errand boy, messenger.

со-сла-ть, *v.p.,* с-сыл-ать, *v.i.,* + *acc.,* to banish, exile, deport. Его сослали без всякой вины, although innocent he was banished. Со-сла-ть-ся, *v.p.r.,* с-сыл-ать-ся, *v.i.r.,* на, в + *acc.,* to be banished, exiled, deported; refer, allude, cite, quote. Осуждённый ссылается в концлагерь на 5 лет, the convicted man is being banished to a concentration camp for five years. Могу-ли я сослаться на вас? May I use your name? Он ссылается на вашу книгу, he refers to your book. С. на болезнь, to plead illness. Со-сл-анный, *adj.,* exiled, banished, deported; *used as n.m.,* exile, deportee. С-ые умирали в лагерях тысячами, the deportees died in camps by the thousands. Особенно страдали сосланные интеллигенты, the banished intellectuals suffered especially.

с-сыл-ка, *n.f.,* banishment, exile, deportation; reference. Отправлять в ссылку, to exile, banish. Подтвердить ссылкой на источник, to document, confirm by quoting a source. С. на поселение, to deport for settlement. С-сыл-ь-ный, *adj.,* convict, exile. Один из ссыльных бежал, one of the convicts escaped.

у-сл-ать, *v.p.,* у-сыл-ать, *v.i.,* + *acc.,* to send away. Куда услал он своего сына? Where has he sent his son?

СЛЕД-, (СЛѢД-), СЛЕЖ-, (СЛѢЖ-), TRAIL, FOLLOWING, INHERITANCE

след, *n.m.,* trace, mark, track, trail. С. пальца, finger mark, fingerprint. С. зверя, scent of an animal. Его и след простыл, no traces of him were left. Идти по горячим следам, to follow a fresh scent. Наконец мы напали на с., at last we have found the track. Ни следа, no sign, no trace. Следом за ним, after him. Следы оспы, pockmarks.

по-след-ний, *adj.,* last, latter. В п. раз, for the last time. Последняя капля терпения, the last straw. Занимать уже п-ее место, to occupy the last place. По последнему слову науки, according to the latest findings of science. По-след, *n.m.,* (*med.*), placenta. По-след-ыш, *n.m.,* the last, the youngest child. На-по-след-ок (на-по-след-ки), *adv.,* (*colloq.*), at last, finally.

след-и-ть, слеж-у, *v.p.,* за + *instr.,* to watch, follow. Я слежу за ним, I keep watch over him. Мы следим за политическими событиями, we follow political events. За мной следят, I am being followed, shadowed.

слеж-ка, *n.f.,* за + *instr.,* trailing, tailing, shadowing. Установить слежку за кем-либо, to dog, shadow, trail, follow someone.

вы-след-ить, *v.p.,* вы-слеж-ивать, *v.i., acc.,* to trace, track down, search out, scent out. Охотник выследил зверя, the hunter tracked down the animal.

на-след-ить, *v.p.,* to leave footprints. Н. грязными ногами на полу, to track mud over the floor.

по-след-ить, *v.p.,* за + *instr.,* to watch for a while. Последите за детьми, look out for the children for a while.

про-след-ить, *v.p.,* про-слеж-ивать, *v.i.,* за + *instr.,* to trace, track, follow, nose. П. за выполнением чего-либо, to see that something is done. Про-слеж-ивать-ся, *v.i.r.,* to be traced. Гражданские войны прослеживаются в истории всех государств, civil wars occur in the history of all nations.

у-след-ить, *v.p.,* за + *instr.,* to follow. За ним не уследить, it is impossible to keep track of him.

след-ова-ть, *v.p.,* за + *instr.,* to follow; *impers.,* it is necessary. Он следует за ней по пятам, he keeps at her heels. Как это следует из сказанного, as it follows from what has been said. Вам следует уйти, you must, ought to go away. Отколотить, как следует, (*colloq.*), to give a sound beating. Сколько с меня следует за это? What is my bill? How much is my bill? Следуемый, *adj., part. pass. pres.,* due. Отдайте, следуемые ему деньги, pay him his due. След-ование, *п.п.,* sequence; imitation. С. событий, sequence of events. След-ователь, *п.т.,* examining magistrate. След-овательно, *conj.,* therefore, consequently, hence. С. он виновен, therefore, he is guilty. Следствие, *п.п.,* consequence, effect, conclusion, deduction; inquest. Причина и следствие, cause and effect. Логическое с., deduction, corollary. Он находится под следствием, he is under investigation. След-ственный, *adj.,* pertaining to investigation. С. материал, evidence. След-ующий, *adj. part. act. pres., also used as n.,* following, next. Вывод с. из этого, the conclusion following from this. С., пожалуйста, next please. С. год, following year. Следующим образом, in the following manner; as follows.

ис-след-овать, *v.i., (also v.p.),* + *acc.,* to investigate, examine, study, explore. Тысячи учёных исследуют происхождение рака, thousands of scientists are studying the origins of cancer. Исслед-ование, *п.п,* investigation, study, research, examination, exploration. Ис-след-ователь, *п.т.,* investigator, researcher, explorer. Ис-след-овательский, *adj.,* pertaining to investigating, research.

на-след-овать, *v.i., (also v.p.),* + *acc.,* от + *gen.,* to inherit; succeed. Он наследует от отца всё его имущество, he is inheriting all his father's goods. На-след-ование, *п.п.,* inheritance, succession. Право наследования, right of succession. На-след-ник, *п.т.,* на-след-ница, *n.f.,* heir, heiress. Сын прямой н. своего отца, the son is his father's legal heir. На-след-ие, *п.п.,* на-след-ство, *п.п.,* inheritance, heritage. Это тяжёлое наследие прошлых веков, this is a heavy heritage of past centuries. Литературное наследство, literary heritage. Получать в наследство, to inherit. Лишать наследства, to disinherit. По наследству, by right of inheritance, by succession. На-след-ственность, *n.f.,* heredity. Учение о наследственности, theory of heredity. На-след-ственный, *adj.,* hereditary.

у-на-след-овать, *v.p.,* + *acc.,* от + *gen.,* to inherit. Он унаследовал свой талант от отца, he has inherited his talent from his father.

об-след-овать, *v.p.,* + *acc.,* to inspect, examine, investigate. Об-след-ование, *п.п.,* inspection, investigation.

по-след-овать, *v.p.,* + *dat.,* to follow. Он последовал его примеру, he followed his example. По-след-ующий, *adj., part. act. pres.,* the following, that which follows. П-ие события доказали, что он был прав, subsequent events proved that he was right. По-след-ование, *п.п.,* following. По-след-ователь, *п.т.,* follower, partisan, adherent. Пламенный п. христианского учения, a devoted follower of Christian teaching. По-след-овательно, *adv.,* in succession, one after another. По-след-овательность, *n.f.,* succession, sequence. П. событий, sequence of events. По-след-овательный, *adj.,* successive, consistent, consecutive. П-ое развитие социальной жизни, successive development of social (community) life. По-след-ствие, *п.п.,* consequence, result. Думали-ли вы о последствиях? Have you thought about the consequences? Чреватый последствиями, eventful.

пре-след-овать, *v.i.,* + *acc.,* to persecute, pursue, chase. П. зверя, to hunt a wild animal. П. врага, to pursue an enemy. Он преследует свои собственные интересы, he pursues his own interest. П. судебным порядком, to prosecute. Пре-след-ование, *п.п.,* persecution, pursuing, pursuit, chase. Мания преследования, persecution mania. П. судебным порядком, prosecution. Пре-след-ователь, *п.т.,* pursuer, persecutor.

про-след-овать, *v.p.,* to pass. Войска проследовали через город, the troops passed through the town.

рас-след-овать, *v.p., (also v.i.),* + *acc.,* to make inquiries, explore, investigate, look into, hold an inquest. Это надо р., this must be looked into. Рас-след-ование, *п.п.,* investigation, inquiry, examination, inquest. Производить р., to hold an inquest.

СЛУГ-, СЛУЖ-, SERVING, SERVANT

слуг-а, *п.т.,* servant. С. отворил дверь, the servant opened the door. Ваш покорный с., your obedient servant (*obs.*), (*in letters*). Служ-ака, *п.т.,* old-timer. Старый с. умер на своём посту, the old-timer died at his post. Служ-анка, *n.f.,* girl, maid, housemaid. Служ-ащий, *adj., part. act. pres.,* used as n., employee, clerk, servant. Рабочие и служащие вели переговоры с хозяевами, the workers and employees were negotiating with their employers. Он хороший с., he is a good employee.

служ-ба, *n.f.,* service, employment, work. С. связи, signal corps; liaison service.

Действительная (военная) с., active service. Быть на службе, to be at work, be in the service. Я иду на службу, I am going to work. С. службой, а дружба дружбой, (saying), friendship does not exempt from duty. Сослужить кому-либо службу, (colloq.), to do someone a favor, a service. Служ-ебный, adj., official; subordinate. С. вагон, service car. С-ые часы, office hours.

служ-ить, v.i., + instr., to serve, work, be employed. Он служит в конторе, he is employed in an office. С. в армии, to serve in the army. С. и нашим и вашим, (derog.), to run with the hare and hunt with the hounds. С. примером, to serve as an example. С. ширмой, to serve as a screen. Служ-ение, n.n., service, ministry. Общественное с., social service. Бог-о-служение, n.n., religious service. Служ-ивый, n.m., (obs.), soldier. Служ-итель, n.m., attendant, servant, orderly. Больничный с., hospital orderly. С. муз, (fig.), poet.

вы-служ-ить, v.p., вы-служ-ивать, v.i., + acc., to have worked for a definite period of time. Он выслужил 30 лет в банке, he has worked for thirty years in the bank. В. пенсию, to obtain a pension after years of service. Вы-служ-ить-ся, v.p.r., вы-служ-ивать-ся, v.i.r., перед + instr., у + gen., to be promoted, raised in rank; curry favor with. В. из рядовых в офицеры, to be promoted from the ranks. В. перед начальством (у начальства), to curry favor with one's superiors. Вы-слуг-а, n.f., years of service. За выслугу, for years of service.

до-служ-ить, v.p., до-служ-ивать, v.i., + acc., to serve one's time, serve a definite length of time. Он дослужил свой срок, he has served out his term of office. До-служ-ить-ся, v.p.r., до-служ-ивать-ся, v.i.r., до + gen., to be promoted after long service. Он дослужился до генерала, he was promoted to a general's rank.

за-служ-ить, v.p., за-служ-ивать, v.i., + acc., + gen., to deserve, merit, earn, be worthy. З. благодарность от кого-либо, to earn someone's gratitude. За-служ-ивающий, adj., worthy of. З. доверия, reliable, trustworthy. За-служ-ённый, adj., part. pass. past, deserved, well-earned. З. отдых, deserved rest. Заслуженный профессор, a highly honored professor. За-слуг-а, n.f., merit. Это его з., this achievement is to his credit. За заслуги перед родиной, for services rendered to one's

country. Он получил по заслугам, (derog.), he got what he deserved.

об-служ-ить, v.p., об-служ-ивать, v.i., + acc., to serve, accommodate. Электрическая станция обслуживает энергией весь город, the plant provides power for the whole city. Об-служ-ивающий, adj., part. act. pres., also used as n., providing, servicing. Об-служ-ивание, n.n., servicing, providing service. Культурно-бытовое о., (recent), providing cultural facilities for a community.

СЛУХ-, СЛУШ-, СЛЫХ-, СЛЫШ-, HEARING, LISTENING, OBEDIENCE

слух, n.m., hearing; ear; rumor. Острый с., keen hearing. Плохой с., bad hearing. Музыкальный с., ear for music. Он весь обратился в с., he was all ears. Ходят слухи о его болезни, there are rumors that he is ill. Пустить слух, to spread a rumor. Не всякому слуху верь, (saying), believe only half of what you hear. Ни слуху, ни духу, (idiom.), neither hide nor hair. Петь по слуху, to sing by ear. По слухам, by hearsay. Слухом земля полнится, (saying), rumors spread quickly. Слух-овой, adj., acoustic, auditory. С. проход, acoustic duct. С-ая трубка, ear trumpet. С-ое окно, dormer window.

в-слух, adv., aloud. Читайте всегда в., always read aloud.

слуш-ать, v.i., + acc., to listen. Ученик слушает учителя со вниманием, the pupil is listening attentively to his teacher. С. радио, to listen to the radio. Слуш-ать-ся, v.i.r., + gen., to obey, follow, listen. Дети слушаются родителей, children obey their parents. Слуш-ание, n.n., listening, hearing. С. лекций обязательно, attendance at lectures is obligatory. С. дела в суде затянулось, the hearing of the case in court has been delayed. Слуш-атель, n.m., слуш-ательница, n.f., listener, auditor, student. С. курсов иностранных языков, auditor of courses in foreign languages. Слушатели вышли из зала, the audience left the hall. Радио-слушатель, radio fan.

вы-слуш-ать, v.p., вы-слуш-ивать, v.i., + acc., to listen through, give ear to; examine by auscultation. В. жалобы, to listen to the complaints. Выслушивать больного, to examine a patient by auscultation. В. просьбу, to listen to a request. Вы-слуш-ивание, n.n., hearing, auscultation. В. лёгких, auscultation of lungs.

до-слуш-ать, v.p., до-слуш-ивать, v.i., +

acc., to hear, hear to the end. Он ушёл, не дослу́шав ле́кции до конца́, he left without hearing the lecture to the end.

за-слу́ш-ать, *v.p.*, за-слу́ш-ивать, *v.i.*, + *acc.*, to hear, listen to. З. протоко́л, (*recent*), to hear the reading of minutes, proceedings. З. резолю́цию, (*recent*), to hear the reading of a resolution. За-слу́ш-ать-ся, *v.p.r.*, за-слу́ш-ивать-ся, *v.i.r.*, + *gen.*, to listen with delight. Певе́ц пел так хорошо́, что все заслу́шались, the singer sang so well we all lost track of time. З. расска́зов, to lose track of time listening to stories.

на-слу́ш-ать-ся, *v.p.r.*, + *gen.*, to hear much; to have heard enough. Ребёнок наслу́шался ба́бушкиных ска́зок, the child heard many of his grandmother's fairy tales.

пере-слу́ш-ать, *v.p.*, пере-слу́ш-ивать, *v.i.*, + *acc.*, to hear over again. Мы переслу́шали все пласти́нки, we have heard all the records over again. Его́ расска́зов не переслу́шаешь, there is no end to his stories. Пласти́нки, напе́тые Шаля́пиным, мы переслу́шивали не́сколько раз, we listened over and over again to Chaliapin's records.

по-слу́ш-ать, *v.p.*, + *acc.*, to listen. По-слу́ш-айте, look here! По-слу́ш-айте меня́, listen to me. По-слу́ш-ать-ся, *v.p.r.*, + *gen.*, to obey. Сын не послу́шался отца́, the son did not obey his father. По-слу́ш-а́ние, *n.n.*, obedience, docility; imposed penance in monastery. Этот ребёнок отлича́лся ре́дким послуша́нием, this child was noted for his obedience. На него́ нало́жено тяжёлое п., a heavy penance has been imposed upon him. По-слу́ш-ник, *n.m.*, novice, lay-brother. По-слу́ш-ница, *n.f.*, novice, lay-sister. Он стал послу́шником в монастыре́, he became a novice in a monastery. По-слу́ш-ность, *n.f.*, obedience. По-слу́ш-ный, *adj.*, obedient, dutiful. Он п. ма́льчик, he is an obedient boy. П. телёнок двух ма́ток сосёт, (*saying*), a flatterer obtains everything he wants; (*lit.*), an obedient calf is able to suck two cows.

под-слу́ш-ать, *v.p.*, под-слу́ш-ивать, *v.i.*, + *acc.*, to eavesdrop, overhear, spy, listen in. П. у двере́й, to listen at a keyhole. Он подслу́шал наш разгово́р, he has overheard our conversation. Он подслу́шивает, he is an eavesdropper. Под-слу́ш-ивание, *n.n.*, eavesdropping, overhearing.

при-слу́ш-ать-ся, *v.p.r.*, при-слу́ш-ивать-ся, *v.i.r.*, к + *dat.*, to listen attentively. Я прислу́шиваюсь к ва́шему произ-

ноше́нию, I am listening closely to your pronunciation. Я уже́ прислу́шался к осо́бенностям его́ ре́чи, I have already accustomed my ear to the peculiarities of his speech.

про-слу́ш-ать, *v.p.*, про-слу́ш-ивать, *v.i.*, + *acc.*, to hear, listen through. П. курс ле́кций, to attend a course of lectures. Винова́т, я прослу́шал, что вы сказа́ли, excuse me, I missed what you said. Я всегда́ прослу́шивал со внима́нием ле́кции э́того профе́ссора, I always listened attentively to this professor's lectures.

слых-а́ть, *v.p.*, + *acc.*, (*colloq.*), to hear. Я слыха́л его́ блестя́щую речь, I heard his brilliant speech. Я давно́ не слыха́л о свои́х ро́дственниках, it is a long time since I heard of my relatives. Чтоб я не слыха́л про э́того моше́нника! Let me hear no more about this crook! Слыха́ть, ты в Москву́ уезжа́ешь, (*colloq.*), they say you are leaving for Moscow. Ничего́ не слыха́ть, (*colloq.*), nothing has been heard. Слы́хан-ное-ли э́то де́ло? Who ever heard of such a thing! Не-слы́х-анный, *adj.*, *part. pass. past*, unheard of. Н-ая де́рзость, an unheard of impertinence.

слы́ш-ать, *v.i.*, + *acc.*, to hear, be told. Я сама́ слы́шала э́то, I heard this myself. Я слы́шал, что его́ здесь нет, I am told that he is not here. Слы́ш-ать-ся, *v.i.r.*, *used only in 3d pers.*, to be heard. Что́-то слы́шится родно́е в его́ пе́сне, there is something native about his song. Слы́шались отдалённые раска́ты гро́ма, one could hear distant peals of thunder. Слы́ш-имость, *n.f.*, high audibility. С. э́того зву́ка о́чень велика́, this sound has a high audibility. Слы́ш-ный, *adj.*, audible. У больно́го е́ле слы́шный го́лос, the patient's voice is hardly audible. Слы́ш-но, *pred. impers.*, *in expression*: С. бы́ло, как му́ха пролети́т, (*fig.*), you might have heard a pin fall. Что слы́шно о нём? What has been heard about him? Не-слы́ш-ный, *adj.*, inaudible. Он подошёл неслы́шными шага́ми, he came up stealthily. Не-слы́ш-но, *adv.*, inaudibly. Зверь подкра́лся н., the animal crept up without being heard.

до-слы́ш-ать, *v.p.*, до-слы́ш-ивать, *v.i.*, *used only in the negative*, to hear enough. Я не дослы́шал после́дних слов, I failed to hear his final words. Стари́к не дослы́шивает, the old man is hard of hearing.

за-слы́ш-ать, *v.p.*, + *acc.*, to start hearing. З. ко́нский то́пот, to hear the trampling of horses.

по-слы́ш-ать-ся, *v.p.r.*, *only in 3d pers.*,

to be heard. Послы́шался стук в дверь, a knock was heard at the door. Мне послы́шалось, it seemed to me that I heard.

рас-слы́ш-ать, *v.p.,* + *acc.,* to hear distinctly. Я о́чень хорошо́ расслы́шал его́ слова́, I heard his words very clearly. Я не расслы́шал ва́шей фами́лии, I did not hear your last name.

у-слых-а́ть, *v.p.,* у-слы́ш-ать, *v.p.,* + *acc.,* to hear. Когда́ я услыха́л (услы́шал) его́ го́лос, when I heard his voice. Осторо́жно, нас услы́шат! Take care, we shall be overheard!

СМЕХ-, (СМѢХ-), СМЕШ-, (СМѢШ-), LAUGH

смех, *n.m.,* laugh, laughter. Весёлый с., gay laughter. Заразительный с., contagious laugh, laughter. Го́рький с., bitter laughter, laugh. С. сквозь слёзы, laughter through tears. Подня́ть на́ с., to ridicule. Это ку́рам на́ с., (*saying*), it's so little it doesn't amount to anything. Ему́ не до сме́ха, he is past laughing. Живо́тики надорва́ть от сме́ха (*colloq.*), to burst one's sides with laughter. Зали́ться сме́хом, to burst out laughing. Пры́снуть со́ смеху, to splutter with laughter. Смех-о-тво́рный, *adj.,* ridiculous.

смеш-о́к, *n.m.,* ripple of laughter. Не́рвный с., nervous laugh. Смешки́, ripples of laughter; giggles. Смеш-ли́вость, *n.f.,* laughability. Смеш-ли́вый, *adj.,* laughable. Смеш-но́й, *adj.,* funny, comical, droll, ludicrous. С-а́я фигу́ра, comic figure. Я не ви́жу в э́том ничего́ смешно́го, I see nothing funny about this. От вели́кого до смешно́го оди́н шаг, from the sublime to the ridiculous is but one step. Выставля́ть кого́-либо в смешно́м ви́де, to ridicule someone. Смеш-но́, *adv.,* funnily, comically. Смешно́! Ridiculous!

сме-я́ть-ся, *v.i.r.,* над + *instr., dat.,* to laugh. Переста́ньте с.! Stop laughing! Вы смеётесь? Surely, you are joking! Он никогда́ не смея́лся над на́ми, he never laughed at us. Не смейся чужо́й беде́, (*saying*), never laugh at the misfortunes of others.

вы́-сме-ять, *v.p.,* вы-сме́-ивать, *v.i.,* + *acc.,* to ridicule, mock, satirize, make fun of.

за-сме-я́ть, *v.p.,* + *acc.,* to ridicule. Весь класс засмея́л ро́бкого новичка́, the whole class made fun of the timid new boy. За-сме-я́ть-ся, *v.p.r.,* to burst out laughing. Он гро́мко засмея́лся, he laughed loudly; he burst into loud laughter.

на-сме-я́ть-ся, *v.p.r.,* над + *instr.,* to mock, insult; have one's fill of laughing. Они́ безжа́лостно насмея́лись над ним, they pitilessly made fun of him. Мы вдо́воль насмея́лись в теа́тре, we had a good laugh at the theatre.

на-смех-а́ть-ся, *v.i.r.,* над + *instr.,* to laugh at, ridicule, mock. Нехорошо́ н. над оши́бкой друго́го, it is not nice to laugh at the mistakes of others.

на-сме́ш-нич-ать, *v.i.,* над + *instr.,* to scoff, sneer. На-сме́ш-ка, *n.f.,* mockery. Это не кни́га, а про́сто н. над здра́вым смы́слом, this is not a book, it is sheer mockery of common sense. На-сме́ш-ливость, *n.f.,* derisiveness. На-сме́ш-ливый, *adj.,* mocking, ironical, sarcastic. Его́ н. тон невыноси́м, his mocking tone is unbearable. На-сме́ш-ливо, *adv.,* mockingly. На-сме́ш-ник, *n.m.,* на-сме́ш-ница, *n.f.,* scoffer. Како́й вы н.! What a scoffer you are!

по-сме-я́ть-ся, *v.p.r.,* над + *instr.,* to laugh, laugh at. Я люблю́ посмея́ться, I like to have a good laugh. Над ним посмея́лись, he was laughed at. По-сме-я́ние, *n.n.,* mockery, derision. Его́ вы́вели на посмея́ние, they exposed him to mockery. По-сме́-ивать-ся, *v.i.r.,* + *instr.,* to laugh up one's sleeve, chuckle. Он всё вре́мя посме́ивается над на́ми, he is always chuckling at us.

рас-сме-я́ть-ся, *v.p.r.,* to burst out laughing. Он гро́мко рассмея́лся, he burst out laughing.

смеш-и́ть, *v.i.,* на-смеш-и́ть, *v.p.,* + *acc.,* to make someone laugh. С. шу́тками, to make laugh with jokes. Ну, и насмеши́ли вы меня́! Well, you certainly gave me a good laugh!

по-смеш-и́ть, *v.p.,* + *acc.,* to make one laugh a little. По-сме́ш-ище, *n.n.,* laughingstock. Он слу́жит о́бщим посме́шищем, he is the general laughingstock.

рас-смеш-и́ть, *v.p.,* + *acc.,* to make one laugh outright. Его́ речь рассмеши́ла весь стол, his speech set the whole company in a roar. Это меня́ рассмеши́ло, it made me laugh.

СОХ-, СОШ-, СУК-, СУЧ-, CROOK, BOUGH

сох-а́, *n.f.,* wooden plow. Паха́ть сохо́й, to plow with a wooden plough. Челове́к от сохи́, (*fig.*), rustic fellow. Сох-а́тый, *adj.,* used as n., elk. Охо́та на соха́того, elk hunting. Соха́тые рога́, the elk's furcated antlers.

сош-ка, *n.f.,* plow share. Мéлкая с., small fry. Сош-нйк, *n.m.,* plowshare, coulter. У негó сломáлся с., he has a broken plowshare.

сук, *n.m.,* (суч-ь-я, *pl.*), branch, bough. Он рýбит сук, на котóром сидйт, (*fig.*), he is sawing the branch on which he is sitting. Сук-овáтый, *adj.,* knobby. С-ая пáлка, knobby cane.

суч-óк, *n.m.,* (*dim.*), small branch, bough. Без сучкá и задóринки, (*idiom.*), not a ripple, not a jar. Суч-ковáтый, *adj.,* knobby. Эти дóски слйшком сучковáты, these boards are too knotty. Суч-ко-рéз, *n.m.,* (*tech.*), clipper for small branches used as fodder. Суч-óч-ек, *n.m.,* (*dim.*), small branch, bough.

СОХ-, СУХ-, СУШ-, СЫХ-, DRYNESS

сóх-нуть, *v.i.,* to dry, parch. Бельё сóхнет на дворé, the laundry is drying outdoors. От лихорáдки сóхнут гýбы, lips become parched from fever. Онá сóхнет от любвй, she is pining away with love.

вы́-сох-нуть, *v.p.,* вы-сых-áть, *v.i.,* to dry up, wither. Бельё ужé вы́сохло, the laundry has already dried. Здесь лéтом высыхáет вся травá, in summer all the grass dries up here. Вы́-сох-ший, *adj., part. act. past,* dried out. В. колодéц, a dry well.

за-сóх-нуть, *v.p.,* за-сых-áть, *v.i.,* to dry up, wither. Цветы́ засóхли, the flowers have withered. За-сóх-ший, *adj., part. act. past,* withered, dried. Засóхший цветóк, dry, withered flower.

об-сóх-нуть, *v.p.,* об-сых-áть, *v.i.,* to dry out, become dry. Мы не успéли обсóхнуть пóсле дождя́, we did not have time to dry off after the rain.

от-сóх-нуть, *v.p.,* от-сых-áть, *v.i.,* to atrophy. У негó отсóхла рукá, his hand became atrophied.

пере-сóх-нуть, *v.p.,* пере-сых-áть, *v.i.,* to dry up, parch. Рекá пересóхла, the river has dried up. Пересóхло во рту, my mouth is parched. Пересóхшие гýбы, parched lips. Пере-сóх-ший, *adj., part. act. past,* parched.

по-сóх-нуть, *v.p.,* to dry up. В садý всё посóхло, everything in the garden has withered.

под-сóх-нуть, *v.p.,* под-сых-áть, *v.i.,* to begin to dry, become dry. Дорóги стáли подсыхáть, the roads began to dry. Под-сых-áние, *n.n.,* drying up. П. рáны шло бы́стро, the wound was healing rapidly.

при-сóх-нуть, *v.p.,* при-сых-áть, *v.i.,* к + *dat.,* to stick fast. Повя́зка присóхла к рáне, the bandage stuck fast to the wound.

ра-с-сóх-нуть-ся, *v.p.r.,* рас-сых-áть-ся, *v.i.r.,* to dry up, parch. Бóчка рассóхлась, the barrel is so dry it has split open. Земля́ рассóхлась от жары́, the earth has cracked. Рас-сóх-ший-ся, *adj., part. act. past,* cracked from heat. Р-ся мéбель, cracked furniture.

с-сóх-нуть-ся, *v.p.r.,* с-сых-áть-ся, *v.i.r.,* to dry off; shrink, contract in drying. Егó лицó ссыхáется и съёживается, his face is becoming dry and shrivelled.

у-сóх-нуть, *v.p.,* у-сых-áть, *v.i.,* to dry away; shrink. Посáженные дерéвья усóхли, the planted trees have dried up. У-сых-áние, *n.n.,* drying, shriveling.

сух-áрь, *n.m.,* rusk, biscuit, cracker, hard tack. Хлеб посушйли на сухарй, they dried the bread to make hard tack. Пить кóфе с сухаря́ми, to drink coffee and crackers. Обваля́ть мя́со в сухаря́х, to roll meat in crumbs. Сух-áрница, *n.f.,* cracker box. Сух-áрный, *adj.,* of or pertaining to rusks. С. квас, a Russian drink made with rye rusks.

сух-óй, *adj.,* dry, arid. С-óе бельё, dry laundry. С-áя мéстность, dry locality. С. пóчва, dry soil. Стоя́ла с-áя óсень, it was a dry autumn. С. кáшель, dry cough. С. отвéт, curt answer. На свою́ прóсьбу он получйл сухóй отвéт, he received a curt reply to his request. С-áя перегóнка дéрева, dry distillation of wood alcohol. Вы́йти сухйм из воды́, (*idiom.*), to emerge from a troublesome situation unscathed. Ехать сухйм путём, to travel by land. Сух-овáтый, *adj.,* dryish, rather dry; curt. Он немнóго суховáт со свойми подчинёнными, he is rather curt with his subordinates. Сух-овáтость, *n.f.,* dryness. Сух-ощáвый, *adj.,* lean, thin. Этот с. человéк óчень силён, this lean man is very strong. Сýх-о, *adv.,* dryly. Он приня́л меня́ с., he was rather curt with me. Сýш-е, *adj. and adv. comp.,* drier, more dryly. Вчерá бы́ло с., it was drier yesterday. Сух-о-цвéт, *n.m.,* immortelle, everlasting flower. Сýх-ость, *n.f.,* dryness, aridity. Эта странá отличáется сýхостью своегó клймата, this country is noted for the dryness of its climate. С. тóна (приёма), dryness of tone (coldness of reception). Сух-óтка, *n.f.,* emaciation; consumption.

дó-сух-а, *adv.,* until dry. Вытирáть д., to rub dry.

зá-сух-а, *n.f.,* drought. Урожáй погйб от зáсухи, the crop was lost as a result of the drought. Засухо-устóйчивое растéние, drought-resisting plant

на́-сух-о, *adv.,* until dry. Вы́тереть сухо-на́сухо, to wipe dry.

по́-сух-у, *adv.,* by land, on land. Путеше́ствовать п.,to travel by land.

су́ш-а, *n.f.,* land. С корабля́ уви́дели су́шу, they saw land from the ship.

суш-и́ть, *v.i.,* + *acc.,* to dry; dessicate. Она́ су́шит во́лосы, she is drying her hair. Сли́вы су́шат на со́лнце, plums are dried in the sun. Суш-и́ть-ся, *v.i.r.,* на + *prep.,* to dry, be dried, dessicated. Бельё суши́лось на дворе́, the laundry was drying outdoors. Суш-е́ние, *n.n.,* drying, dessication. С. фру́ктов, drying of fruit. Суш-ёный, *adj.,* dried. С. горо́х, dried peas. С-ые фру́кты, dried fruit. Суш-и́льный, *adj.,* drying. С-ая печь, kiln, dessicator, drying chamber. Суш-и́лка, суш-и́льня, *n.f.,* dessicator, drying chamber. Суши́льня для фру́ктов, drying chamber for fruit. Су́ш-ка, *n.f.,* ring-shaped cracknel; drying, dessication. Иску́сственная с. де́рева, artificial drying of wood. Он лю́бит су́шки, he likes cracknels. Суш-ь, *n.f.,* dryness, drought. Стра́шная сушь стоя́ла бо́льше ме́сяца, the terrible drought lasted over one month.

вы́-суш-ить, *v.p.,* вы-су́ш-ивать, *v.i.,* + *acc.,* to dry out, drain. Высу́шивают боло́та, they are draining the marshes. Вы-су́ш-ивание, *n.n.,* draining. Вы-суш-ить-ся, *v.p.r.,* вы-су́ш-ивать-ся, *v.i.r.,* to be dried out, drained. В э́том кли́мате всё бы́стре высу́шивается, in this climate everything dries quickly.

до-суш-и́ть, *v.p.,* до-су́ш-ивать, *v.i.,* + *acc.,* to dry thoroughly. Пра́чка не досуши́ла белья́, the laundress failed to dry the linen thoroughly.

за-суш-и́ть, *v.p.,* за-су́ш-ивать, *v.i.,* + *acc.,* to dry up. Я засушу́ э́тот цвето́к, I'll dry this flower. За-су́ш-енный, *adj., part. pass. past,* dried. З. цвето́к, dried flower. За-су́ш-ливый, *adj.,* drying, dry. З. ве́тер, hot dry wind. З. кли́мат, dry climate.

на-суш-и́ть, *v.p.,* на-су́ш-ивать, *v.i.,* to dry in quantity. Она́ насуши́ла я́год и грибо́в на́ зиму, she has dried a lot of berries and mushrooms for the winter. На-суш-и́ть-ся, *v.p.r.,* на-су́ш-ивать-ся, *v.i.r.,* to be dried in quantity, dry. Чего́ то́лько здесь не насу́шивалось! The things (foods) that weren't dried here!

о-суш-и́ть, *v.p.,* о-суш-а́ть, *v.i.,* + *acc.,* to dry, drain. Кана́вами осуши́ли луг, they drained the meadow by making ditches. О. буты́лку во́дки, (*colloq.*), to drink a bottle of vodka. О-суш-е́ние, *n.n.,* drainage. О. боло́т, draining

of marshes. О-су́ш-ка, *n.f.,* drainage, draining.

об-суш-и́ть, *v.p.,* об-су́ш-ивать, *v.i.,* + *acc.,* to dry thoroughly. Они́ бы́ли мо́кры, и мы их обсуши́ли, they were soaked, so we dried their clothes thoroughly. Об-суш-и́ть-ся, *v.p.r.,* об-су́ш-ивать-ся, *v.i.r.,* to be dried thoroughly, dry oneself. Он обсуши́лся у костра́, he dried himself by the campfire.

пере-суш-и́ть, *v.p.,* пере-су́ш-ивать, *v.i.,* to dry to excess, parch. Куха́рка пересуши́ла жарко́е, the cook dried out the roast.

по-суш-и́ть, *v.p.,* + *acc.,* to dry. Посуши́те себе́ но́ги у пе́чки, dry your feet at the stove. По-суш-и́ть-ся, *v.p.r.,* to dry, be dried. Посуши́тесь у огня́, dry yourself a little near the fire.

под-суш-и́ть, *v.p.,* под-су́ш-ивать, *v.i.,* + *acc.,* to dry slightly. Под-суш-и́ть-ся, *v.p.r.,* под-су́ш-ивать-ся, *v.i.r.,* to dry off, be dried slightly. Они́ немно́го подсуши́лись у огня́ и пое́хали да́льше, they dried off a little and then went on.

про-суш-и́ть, *v.p.,* про-су́ш-ивать, *v.i.,* + *acc.,* to dry thoroughly. П. мо́крое бельё, to dry the wet laundry thoroughly. Про-суш-и́ть-ся, *v.p.r.,* про-су́ш-ивать-ся, *v.i.r.,* to be dried thoroughly. Пшени́ца ещё не просуши́-лась, the wheat is not dry yet. П. у огня́, to dry one's clothes near a fire. Про-су́ш-ивание, *n.n.,* про-су́ш-ка, *n.f.,* thorough drying. Просу́шка хле́ба, drying of wheat, grain.

СП-, СП(Л)-, СЫП-, СОН-, СН-, SLEEP

сп-а-ть, сп-л-ю, *v.i.,* to sleep, take a nap. Спи́те-ли вы днём? Do you sleep in the daytime? Он спит, как уби́тый, (*fig.*), he sleeps like a top. С. сла́дким сном, to sleep sweetly. Идти́ с., to go to bed, to sleep. Уложи́ть с., to put to bed. С. ве́чным сном, to sleep eternally; die. Сп-я́щий, *adj., part. act. pres.,* sleeping. С. ребёнок, sleeping child. С-ая краса́вица, sleeping beauty. Сп-а́ть-ся, *v.i.r.,* + *dat., impers.,* used only in 3d pers., one sleeps. На све́жем во́здухе хорошо́ спи́тся, one sleeps well in the open air. Мне не спи́тся, I don't feel like sleeping. Сп-а́льный, *adj.,* sleeping. С. ваго́н, sleeping car, sleeper. Сп-а́льня, *n.f.,* bedroom. В спа́льне две крова́ти, there are two beds in the bedroom. Сп-анье́, *n.n.,* (*colloq.*), sleeping, sleep. Дово́льно спанья́! You've slept long enough! Сп-я́чка, *n.f.,* sleep. Зи́мняя с., hibernation. Спи́те споко́йно, орлы́ боевы́е, (*mil. funeral song*), sleep in peace, oh fighting eagles.

вы́-сп-ать-ся, *v.p.r.*, вы-сып-а́ть-ся, *v.i.r.*, to get enough sleep. Я сего́дня не вы́спался, I haven't slept enough today.

до-сп-а́ть, *v.p.*, до-сып-а́ть, *v.i.*, to sleep sufficiently. Ему́ лу́чше тепе́рь потому́ что он досыпа́ет, he feels better now because he is getting enough sleep. До утра́ он не доспа́л, he did not sleep through the night.

не-до-сп-а́ть, *v.p.*, не-до-сып-а́ть, *v.i.*, to not sleep properly. Сего́дня я недоспа́л, I have not slept enough today. Он всегда́ недосыпа́ет, he never gets enough sleep.

за-сып-а́ть, *v.i.*, за-сн-у́ть, *v.p.*, to fall asleep, go to sleep. Он ча́сто засыпа́ет си́дя, he often falls asleep sitting up. Несмотря́ на шум, де́ти засну́ли, in spite of the noise the children fell asleep.

от-сып-а́ть-ся, *v.i.r.*, ото-сп-а́ть-ся, *v.p.r.*, to catch up on sleep. Он отсыпа́ется по́сле бессо́нной но́чи, he is catching up on his sleep after a sleepless night.

пере-сп-а́ть, *v.p.*, пере-сып-а́ть, *v.i.*, to sleep later than most people; oversleep. Я переспа́л и опозда́л на по́езд, I overslept and missed the train.

по-сп-а́ть, по-сп-л-ю́, *v.p.*, to sleep a little, take a nap. Он лю́бит поспа́ть по́сле обе́да, he likes to take a nap after dinner. Больно́й поспа́л два часа́, the sick man slept for two hours.

про-сп-а́ть, *v.p.*, про-сып-а́ть, *v.i.*, до + *gen.*, to oversleep, sleep until. Пасса́жир проспа́л свою́ ста́нцию, the passenger overslept and missed his station. Больно́й проспа́л до утра́ споко́йно, the patient slept quietly until morning.

про-сып-а́ть-ся, *v.i.r.*, про-сн-у́ть-ся, *v.p.r.* to waken, rouse, awake. Он проснулся ра́но у́тром, he awoke early in the morning. Без про́сыпу, *adv.*, without waking. Спать це́лую ночь без про́сыпу, he slept the whole night without waking.

разо-сп-а́ть-ся, *v.p.r.*, to sleep long and soundly. Ребёнок так разоспа́лся, что его́ разде́ли не будя́, the child slept so soundly that they undressed him without waking him.

у-сып-и́ть, *v.p.*, у-сып-л-я́ть, *v.i.*, + *acc.*, to lull, put to sleep; anesthetize; hypnotize. У. внуше́нием, to hypnotize. У. чте́нием, to read someone to sleep. У. чьё-либо внима́ние, to put one off one's guard. У-сып-и́тельный, *adj.*, soporific. У-ое сре́дство, sleeping po-

tion, soporific. У-сып-а́льница, *n.f.*, tomb, sepulchre, burial vault. В усы-па́льнице те́плились лампа́ды, oil lamps were burning in the tomb. У-сып-ле́ние, *n.n.*, putting to sleep by artificial means. У-сп-е́ние, *n.n.*, (*Ch.-Sl.*), assumption. Пра́здник У-я, Feast of the Assumption. У-сп-е́нский, *adj.*, of the Assumption. У. пост, Fast of the Assumption. У-со́п-ший, *adj.*, (*used as noun*), deceased.

сон, *n.m.*, сн-а, *gen.*, sleep, dream. Сон - лу́чший о́тдых, sleep is the best rest. Меня́ кло́нит ко сну, I am sleepy. Спать непробу́дным сном, to sleep soundly; (*poet.*), be dead. Он ничего́ не разобра́л со сна, he was so sleepy he did not understand anything. Ви́деть во сне, to dream of, see in one's dream. Сон в ру́ку, (*idiom.*), the dream turned out to be a good prophecy. Сон-ли́вость, *n.f.*, somnolence, drowsiness. На него́ напа́ла с, drowsiness overwhelmed him. Сон-ли́вый, *adj.*, sleepy, drowsy. Боле́зненно с, comatose. Со́н-ник, *n.m.*, a book which interprets dreams. Со́н-ный, *adj.*, sleepy. С-ая арте́рия, (*med.*), carrotid. С-ая боле́знь, sleeping sickness. С-ая о́дурь, (*bot.*), belladonna. С-ые ка́пли, sleeping draught, sedative. Со́н-но, *adv.*, sleepily.

бес-со́н-ница, *n.f.*, insomnia. Я страда́ю бессо́нницей, I suffer from insomnia. Во вре́мя бессо́нницы, during his sleepless nights. Бес-со́н-ный, *adj.*, sleepless. Бессо́нная ночь, a sleepless night. Со́н-я, *n.m. and n.f.*, (*colloq.*), sleepy-head; (*zool.*), dormouse. Он был большо́й со́ня, he was a real sleepy-head.

сн-и́ть-ся, *v.i.r.*, to dream. Мне сни́лся чу́дный сон, I had a wonderful dream. И во сне не сни́тся, (*fig.*), undreamed of. Сн-и́вшийся, *adj., part. act. past*, dreamed. Не с. успе́х, an undreamed of success.

при-сн-и́ть-ся, *v.p.r.*, to dream. Мне присни́лся мой оте́ц, I dreamed of my father.

сн-о-виде́ние, *n.n.*, dream. Сон без вся́ких сновиде́ний, dreamless sleep. Сн-о-тво́рный, *adj.*, narcotic, soporific. С-ое сре́дство, sleeping draught, sedative.

за-сн-у́ть, *v.p.*, *see* засыпа́ть.

про-сн-у́ть-ся, *see* про-сып-а́ть-ся.

со-сн-у́ть, *v.p.*, (*obs.*), to take a nap. Он лю́бит сосну́ть часо́к - друго́й, he likes to nap an hour or two.

у-сн-у́ть, *v.p.*, to fall asleep. Он усну́л в по́лночь, he fell asleep at midnight.

СПЕХ-, (СПѢХ-), СПЕШ-, (СПѢШ-), SPEED, HURRY

спех, *n.m.,* hurry, haste (in idiomatic expressions only). Что за с., (*colloq.*), What's the hurry! Это дело не к спеху, there is no hurry for this.

спеш-ка, *n.f.,* haste, hurry, urgency. В спешке растерял вещи, in the bustle I lost my things. Спеш-ность, *n.f.,* haste, hurry. За с. почтового отправления берут добавочную плату, there is an extra charge for special delivery. Спеш-ный, *adj.,* urgent, hasty. С. заказ, pressing order. С-ое письмо, special delivery letter. Спеш-но, *adv.,* hastily, hurriedly, urgently. Врача с. вызвали к больному, the doctor was hurriedly summoned to the sick man.

до-спех-и, *n.m.pl.,* (*hist.*), armor. Рыцарские доспехи, knightly armor.

на-спех, *adv.,* hurriedly. Сделать что-либо наспех, to do something in a hurry.

у-спех, *n.m.,* success. У. вскружил ему голову, success turned his head, went to his head. Пьеса имела у., the play was a success. Книга имеющая большой у., a best seller. Добиться успеха, to win success. Желаю вам успеха, I wish you success. Пользоваться успехом, to be popular, successful. Делать успехи, to make progress, advance. Лекция прошла с успехом, the lecture was successful. У-спеш-ный, *adj.,* successful. У-ая работа, successful work. У-спеш-но, *adv.,* successfully. У.-ли выполнен ваш план, is your plan successful?

без-у-спеш-ность, *n.f.,* unsuccessfulness, failure. Без-у-спеш-ный, *adj.,* unsuccessful, vain, unlucky. Б-ое начинание, *n.n.,* unsuccessful undertaking. Без-у-спеш-но, *adv.,* unsuccessfully, in vain.

не-у-спех, *n.f.,* failure. Н. не обескуражил его, failure did not discourage him. Не-у-спеш-ный, *adj.,* unsuccessful. Н-ая попытка, unsuccessful attempt.

спеш-ить, *v.i.,* to be in a hurry; rush, hasten. Куда вы спешите? Where are you rushing? Часы спешат, the watch is fast.

по-спеш-ить, *v.p.,* по-спеш-ать, *v.i.,* (*obs.*), to hurry, hasten. Поспешишь - людей насмешишь, (*prov.*), haste makes waste. По-спеш-ность, *n.f.,* celerity, hurry, haste. Излишняя п. вредит делу, excessive haste is harmful. По-спеш-ный, *adj.,* prompt, hasty, hurried. Это слишком п-ое заключение, this is too hasty a conclusion. По-спеш-но, *adv.,* hastily, in a hurry, in great haste. П. принятое решение, a hasty decision.

СТА-, СТО-, СТОЙ-, STANDING, BECOMING

ста-ть, *v.p.,* to stand, place oneself; stop, halt; become, begin, start. С. у стола, to place oneself at a table. С. в очередь, to stand in line. С. на ноги, (*fig.*), to become established. Станьте здесь, Stand here. Стань в угол! Stand in the corner! Часы стали, the clock (watch) has stopped. Река стала, the river is icebound. Он стал пить, he began to drink. Его не стало, he has passed away. За чём же дело стало? What is delaying the matter?

ста-ть-ся, *v.p.r.,* с + *instr., impers., used in 3d pers. only,* Всё может статься! Anything can happen! Что сталось с вами? What has happened to you? Ста-ть, *n.f.,* form, shape, stature. Она под стать ему, she is like him in all respects; she is a match for him. С какой стати я буду делать это? Why should I do it?

в-ста-ть, *v.p.,* в-ста-ва-ть, *v.i.,* to get up, rise. В. с места, to rise from one's place. Вставайте, get up. Солнце встало, the sun has risen.

вос-ста-ть, *v.p.,* вос-ста-ва-ть, *v.i.,* из + *gen.,* против + *gen.,* to rise; rebel against. В. из мёртвых, to rise from the dead. Люди восстали с оружием в руках, the people rose in arms. Восста-ние, *n.n.,* rebellion, revolt, insurrection, uprising. В. охватило всю страну, the revolt has spread over the whole country. По-в-ста-нец, *n.m.,* insurgent. По-в-стан-чество, *n.n.,* guerilla activity. По-в-стан-ческий, *adj.,* insurrectional. П. отряд, detachment of rebels.

до-ста-ть, *v.p.,* до-ста-ва-ть, *v.i.,* + *acc.,* to fetch, bring, take out; get, obtain. Д. кастрюлю с полки, to take a pot from a shelf. Д. деньги в долг, to obtain money in loan. Д. платье из шкафа, to take a dress out of a closet. Эту книгу трудно д., this book is difficult to obtain. Он достаёт до потолка, he can reach the ceiling. До-ста-ть-ся, *v.p.r.,* до-ста-ва-ть-ся, *v.i.r.,* to fall to one's lot. Ему досталась хорошая жена, (*colloq.*), he got a good wife. Им досталась львиная доля, they came in for a lion's share. Смотрите, вам достанется за шалость, take care, else you'll pay for this prank.

до-ста-ток, *n.m.,* prosperity, sufficiency. Они живут в достатке, they live in plenty; they are well off. До-ста́-точность, *n.f.*, sufficiency. До-ста́-точный, (до-ста́-точен), *adj.*, sufficient, adequate; prosperous. Его́ дохо́д вполне́ доста́точен, his income is quite sufficient. Приводи́ть д-ые основа́ния, to offer adequate reasons. До-ста́-точно, *adv.*, enough, sufficiently. Чай д. горя́ч, the tea is hot enough. Д. сказа́ть, suffice it to say. Этого д., that will do.

не-до-ста́-ть, *v.p.*, не-до-ста-ва́ть, *v.i.*, + *dat.*, + *gen.*, *used only in 3d pers.*, to be wanting, be insufficient. Недостаёт де́нег на автомоби́ль, there is not enough money for a car. Нам стра́шно недостаёт его́, we miss him badly. Мне недостаёт слов, I lack words. Не-до-ста́-ток, *n.m.*, fault, shortcoming, defect. У него́ мно́го недоста́тков, he has many shortcomings. Не-до-ста́-точный, *adj.*, insufficient. Не-до-ста́-точно, *adv.*, insufficiently. Он н. умён, he is not sufficiently intelligent.

за-ста́-ть, *v.p.*, за-ста-ва́ть, *v.i.*, + *acc.*, to find, catch. З. до́ма, to find at home. З. враспло́х, to catch unawares, catch napping. З. на ме́сте престу́ления, to catch on the scene of a crime.

на-ста́-ть, *v.p.*, на-ста-ва́ть, *v.i.*, *used only in 3d pers.*, to come to pass, come about, happen. Наста́л час распла́ты, the hour of reckoning is here. Наста́нут тяжёлые времена́, hard times will come. Наста́ла ночь, night has fallen, night fell.

о-ста́-ть-ся, *v.p.r.*, о-ста-ва́ть-ся, *v.i.r.*, to remain, stay. О. до́ма, to stay at home. Он оста́лся ве́рен ей, he remained faithful to her. О. в живы́х, to survive, remain alive. Нам не остаётся ничего́ друго́го, как согласи́ться, we cannot but consent. Учени́к оста́лся на второ́й год в том же кла́ссе, the pupil remained in the same class a second year. О-ста́-льно́й, *adj.*, remaining, other. В остально́м же он прав, he is right in other respects. О-ста́-нки, *n.pl.*, remains, relics Сме́рные о, mortal remains. О-ста-ток, *n.m.*, remainder. 100 де́лится на 10 без оста́т-ка, one hundred can be divided by ten without a remainder. О. мате́рии, remnant. Оста́тки сла́дки, (*saying*), the nearer the bone, the sweeter the meat.

от-ста́-ть, *v.p.*, от-ста-ва́ть, *v.i.*, от + *gen.*, to fall, lag behind; be backward. Отста́ть от жи́зни, to fall behind the times. Мой часы́ отстаю́т на 5 мину́т, my watch is five minutes slow. От-ста́-лость, *n.f.*, backwardness. От-ста́-лый, *adj.*, backward. О. учени́к, backward pupil.

пере-ста́-ть, *v.p.*, пере-ста-ва́ть, *v.i.*, to cease, leave off. Дождь переста́л, it has stopped raining. Не переставая, without stopping; unceasingly. Ребё-нок крича́л всю ночь, не переставая, the child cried all night without stopping. Переста́ньте! Stop it!

пре-ста́-вить-ся, *v.p.*, (*Ch.-Sl.*), to die, pass away. Сего́дня преста́вился епи́скоп, the bishop passed away today.

пред-ста́-ть, *v.p.*, перед + *instr.*, to appear before. П. перед лицо́м Го́спода, to appear before God.

пред-ста́-тельствовать, *v.i.*, (*Ch.-Sl.*), за + *gen.*, перед + *instr.*, to intercede, plead for. Святы́е предста́тельствуют за нас перед Бо́гом, the saints inter-cede for us with the Lord. Пред-ста́-тель, *n.m.*, intercessor.

при-ста́-ть, *v.p.*, при-ста-ва́ть, *v.i.*, к + *dat.*, to ply; annoy; stick, adhere; join; put in, come alongside, land, beach; communicate; suit, fit. Грязь пристаёт к сапога́м, mud sticks to the boots. Он всё вре́мя пристаёт к нам, he annoys us all the time. Парохо́д приста́л к бе́регу, the steamer reached the shore. Эта боле́знь легко́ при-стаёт, this sickness communicates itself easily. Это не приста́ло ему́, this does not suit him. При-ста-ю́щий, *adj.*, *part. act. pres.*, adhesive, adhering. При́-стань, *n.f.*, landing, wharf, pier. Парохо́д стои́т у при́стани, the steamer is at the pier, alongside the pier.

рас-ста́-ть-ся, *v.p.r.*, рас-ста-ва́ть-ся, *v.i.r.*, с + *instr.*, to part, leave; give up. Мы навсегда́ расста́лись с ним, he and I have parted for ever. Расста́ться с мы́слью, to put a thought out of one's mind. Рас-ста-ва́-ние, *n.n.*, parting, separation, leave-taking. На́ше р. бы́ло о́чень тя́гостно, our parting was very painful.

у-ста́-ть, *v.p.*, у-ста-ва́ть, *v.i.*, от + *gen.*, to become tired of, tire of, tire. Он устаёт от рабо́ты, he becomes tired from work; work tires him. Мы уста́ли ждать, we got tired of waiting. У-ста́-вший, *adj.*, *part. act. past*, tired. У-ста́-лость, *n.f.*, fatigue, weariness. Он рабо́тал до уста́лости, he worked until he was tired. У-ста́-лый, *adj.*, tired, weary, fatigued. У-ста-ль, *n.f.*, fatigue, *in expression*: Они́ рабо́тали без у́стали, they worked untiringly.

ста́-в-ить, *v.p.*, по-ста́-вить, *v.i.*, + *acc.*, to put, set, place; erect. С. буты́лку на стол, to place a bottle on a table. С. в у́гол, to place in a corner. С. вопро́с, to put a question. С. в тупи́к, to puzzle. С. кого́-либо на своё ме́сто, (*fig.*), to put a person in his place. С. на голосова́ние, to put to a vote. С. себе́ це́лью, to aim at. С. часы́, to regulate a watch. Ни в грош не с., (*idiom.*), to set at naught. С. пье́су на сце́не, to produce a play. С. всё на ка́рту, (*fig.*), to risk everything on one move. Ста́-вить-ся, *v.i.r.*, to be placed, set, put. Графи́н ста́вится на стол, the decanter is being placed on the table. Ста́-вка, *n.f.*, rate (*recent*); headquarters (*mil., pre-Rev.*). С. за́работной пла́ты, (*recent*), wage, rate. С. в игре́, stake. Очная с., confrontation. Ста́-вленник, *n.m.*, puppet, tool, Quisling. Ста́-вень, *n.m.*, ста́-вня, *n.f.*, shutter. Закры́ть ста́вни, to close shutters.

в-ста́-в-ить, *v.p.*, в-ста-вля́ть, *v.i.*, + *acc.*, в + *acc.*, to put in, set in, insert. В. стёкла в окна, to glaze windows. В. карти́ну в ра́му, to frame a picture. В. зу́бы, to put in false teeth. В. слове́чко, to put in a word. В. усло́вие в догово́р, to insert a condition, clause in an agreement. В-ста-вля́ть-ся, *v.i.r.*, в + *acc.*, to be inserted. Драгоце́нные ка́мни вставля́ются в золоты́е опра́вы, gems are set in gold. В-ста́-вка, *n.f.*, insertion, insert. В-ста-вно́й, *adj.*, inserted. В. зуб, false tooth.

вы́-ста-вить, *v.p.*, вы-ста-вля́ть, *v.i.*, + *acc.*, из + *gen.*, на + *acc.*, to push, put, forward; propose; exhibit, display. В. на во́здух, to expose to the air, set out in the open, set outdoors. В. себя́ на пока́з, to make oneself conspicuous, show oneself. В. в смешно́м ви́де, to make a laughing stock of someone. Его́ вы́ставили из ко́мнаты, (*colloq.*), he was put out of the room. Вы́-ста-вить-ся, *v.p.r.*, вы-ста-вля́ть-ся, *v.i.r.*, to be exhibited, shown. Карти́ны Ре́пина выставля́ются на весе́нней вы́ставке, Repin's paintings are exhibited at the spring show. Вы́-ста-вка, *n.f.*, exhibition, show. В. рога́того скота́, cattle show. Эта карти́на ку́плена на вы́ставке, this painting was bought at an exhibition. Всеми́рная в., World's Fair.

до-ста́-вить, *v.p.*, до-ста-вля́ть, *v.i.*, + *acc.*, + *dat.*, to deliver, furnish, supply; cause. Д. това́р, to deliver the merchandise. Она́ доста́вила нам мно́го беспоко́йства, she has caused us a great deal of worry. Д. удово́льствие, to give pleasure. До-ста́-вка, *n.f.*, delivery. Пла́та за доста́вку, payment for delivery. До-ста́-вить-ся, *v.p.r.*, до-ста-вля́ть-ся, *v.i.r.*, to be delivered. Проду́кты доставля́ются на ры́нок, foodstuffs are delivered to the market.

за-ста́-вить, *v.p.*, за-ста-вля́ть, *v.i.*, + *acc.*, to block; compel, force, coerce. З. ко́мнату ме́белью, to fill the room with furniture. З. прохо́д, to block a passage. Нужда́ заста́вила меня́ взять э́ту рабо́ту, poverty forced me take this job. Не заставля́йте меня́ ждать! Don't keep me waiting. За-ста́-вить-ся, *v.p.r.*, за-ста-вля́ть-ся, *v.i.r.*, + *instr.*, to be filled. Вся ко́мната заста́вилась ме́белью, the whole room was filled with furniture. За-ста́-ва, *n.f.*, gate, barrier, outpost. Там неприя́тельская з., there is an enemy outpost there. За-ста́-вка, *n.f.*, illumination. Краси́вая з. в кни́ге, a beautiful illumination in a book.

на-ста́-вить, *v.p.*, на-ста-вля́ть, *v.i.*, + *acc.*, на + *acc.*, to point, direct; teach, place in quantity. Наста́вили буты́лок и рю́мок, they placed many bottles and glasses. Н. револьве́р на кого́-нибудь, to point a gun at someone. Роди́тели наставля́ют дете́й, parents teach children. Наста́вить на ум, на ра́зум, to teach and counsel. Н. нос, (*colloq.*), to fool someone. На-ста-вле́ние, *n.n.*, precept, moral instruction. На-ста-ви́тельный, *adj.*, instructive, edifying, preceptible. На-ста́-вник, *n.m.*, на-ста́-вница, *n.f.*, mentor, tutor, instructor. Кла́ссный н., school tutor.

о-ста́-вить, *v.p.*, о-ста-вля́ть, *v.i.*, + *acc.*, to leave, abandon. О. кни́ги в кла́ссе, to leave one's books in a classroom. О. ключ в замке́, to leave the key in the lock. О. в поко́е, to leave in peace. О. что́-либо за собо́й, to reserve something for oneself. О. у себя́, to keep. Оста́вим э́тот разгово́р, let us drop this subject. Ученика́ оста́вили по́сле уро́ка, the student was detained after class. О-ста-вля́ть-ся, *v.i.r.*, to be left, be abandoned. Лени́вые ученики́ оставля́ются на второ́й год, lazy students are left in the same class for a second year. О-ста-вле́ние, *n.n.*, leaving, forsaking, abandonment. О-ста́-вленный, *adj.*, *part. pass. past*, left, forsaken, abandoned.

об-ста́-вить, *v.p.*, об-ста-вля́ть, *v.i.*, + *acc.*, + *instr.*, to encircle, furnish with, arrange, organize. Он роско́шно обста́вил свою́ кварти́ру, he furnished his apartment luxuriously. О. так конце́рт, что́бы успе́х был обеспе́чен, to arrange a concert in such a way as to ensure success. Об-ста́-вить-ся, *v.p.r.*, об-ста-вля́ть-ся, *v.i.r.*, + *instr.*, to be surrounded, furnished, decorated, arranged, organized. На столе́ графи́нчики во́дки обставля́ются сто́пками, small decanters of vodka on the table are surrounded by small glasses. Об-ста-но́вка, *n.f.*, furniture, furnishings; conditions; situation. Междунаро́дная о., international situation. Купи́ть обстано́вку, to buy some furniture. Об-ста-но́вочный, *adj.*, *in expression*: О-ая пье́са, costume play.

от-ста́-вить, *v.p.*, от-ста-вля́ть, *v.i.*, + *acc.*, от + *gen.*, to set aside, dismiss. Отста́вить! (*mil.*), As you were! Его́ отста́вили, he was dismissed. О. стул от стола́, to set the chairs away from the table. От-ста́-вка, *n.f.*, dismissal, resignation, retirement. Он в отста́вке, he is on the retired list. Вы́йти в отста́вку, to be retired; resign. От-ста-вно́й, *adj.*, retired. О. капита́н, retired captain.

пере-ста́-вить, *v.p.*, пере-ста-вля́ть, *v.i.*, + *acc.*, to transpose, change position, rearrange, shift. П. ме́бель, to rearrange the furniture. П. часы́, to set one's watch. Пере-ста-вля́ть-ся, *v.i.r.*, to be rearranged, shifted. Ме́бель перестав-ля́ется на сце́не по́сле ка́ждого а́кта, the furniture is rearranged on the stage after each act. П. слова́ в фра́зе, to rearrange the words in a sentence.

по-ста́-вить, *v.p.*, + *acc.*, to put, place. П. таре́лки в шкаф, to place plates in a cupboard. П. кни́ги на по́лку, to put books on a shelf. П. вопро́с, to put a question, pose a question. П. отме́тку ученику́, to give a pupil a mark, a grade. П. на ка́рту, (*fig.*), to stake. П. кого́-либо на́ ноги, (*fig.*), to put someone on his feet. П. себе́ за пра́вило, to make it one's rule. П. себе́ це́лью, to set oneself a goal. По-ста́-вить, *v.p.*, по-ста-вля́ть, *v.i.*, + *acc.*, to supply, provide. П. у́голь заво́ду, to supply a plant with coal. П. това́ры на ры́нок, to supply a market with merchandise. По-ста-вля́ть-ся, *v.i.r.*, + *instr.*, to be supplied, provided. Обмун-дирова́ние поставля́ется ра́зными фи́рмами, clothing equipment is supplied by various firms. По-ста́-вка, *n.f.*, supplying. По-ста-вщи́к, *n.m.*, contractor, supplier.

под-ста́-вить, *v.p.*, под-ста-вля́ть, *v.i.*, + *acc.*, под + *acc.*, to place under. Подста́вь ведро́ под водосто́чную трубу́, place a pail under a rain spout. Он подста́вил ему́ но́жку, (*fig.*), he tripped him up. Под-ста-вля́ть-ся, *v.i.r*, to be placed under; be substituted. Блю́дечко подставля́ется под ча́шку, a saucer is placed under a cup. Под-ста-вно́й, *adj.*, (*fig.*), false. П-о́е лицо́, dummy, straw man. Под-ста́-вка, *n.f.*, stand. П. для зонто́в,

umbrella. stand. Под-ста-но́вка, *n.f.*, substitution. П. величи́н, (*math.*), sub-stitution of quantities.

пред-ста́-вить, *v.p.*, пред-ста-вля́ть, *v.i.*, + *acc.*, + *dat.*, to present, introduce, offer. П. что́-либо в воображе́нии, to imagine. П. к награ́де, to recommend for a reward. Предста́вьте меня́ ему́! Introduce me to him. Предста́вьте себе́, он уе́хал! Imagine, he's gone! П. на сце́не, to stage. Это не пред-ставля́ет интере́са для меня́, this has no interest for me. Я представля́л себе́ э́того челове́ка ины́м, I imagined this man to be different. Пред-ста́-вить-ся, *v.p.r.*, пред-ста-вля́ть-ся, *v.i.r.*, + *dat.*, *instr.*, to be presented, introduce oneself; imagine; pretend. Он предста́-вился нача́льству, he presented himself to his superiors. Нам предста́вился слу́чай, the opportunity presented itself to us. П. больны́м, to pretend to be ill, feign illness. Мне представля́лось, что э́то пра́вда, it appeared to me to to be true. Пред-ста-ви́тельство, *n.n.*, representation. Пред-ста-ви́тель, *n.m.*, пред-ста-ви́тельница, *n.f.*, representa-tive. Он был представи́телем наро́да, he was a representative of the people. П. фи́рмы, agent, representative of a company. Пред-ста-ви́тельность, *n.f.*, fine bearing, presence, stateliness. Пред-ста-ви́тельный, *adj.*, stately, im-posing, dignified. Он о́чень представи́-телен, he is very imposing. Пред-ста-вле́ние, *n.n.*, idea, notion; performance; presentation. П. начало́сь в 8 часо́в, the performance began at eight o'clock. Дневно́е п., afternoon performance, matinée. П. чино́вников происходи́ло в большо́м за́ле, the presentation of officials took place in a large hall. Я не име́л представле́ния об э́том, I had no idea of this.

предо-ста́-вить, *v.p.*, предо-ста-вля́ть, *v.i.*, + *acc.*, + *dat.*, to grant, leave, let, allow. П. в чьё-либо распоряже́ние, to place at one's disposal. Предо-ста́-влен, *adj.*, *part. past. pass.*, left, granted, allowed. Он был предос-та́влен самому́ себе́, he was left to get along as best he could. Предо-ста-вля́ть-ся, *v.i.r.*, + *acc.*, + *dat.*, to be granted, offered, allowed. Ему́ предос-тавля́ется возмо́жность уе́хать за-грани́цу, he is being given an oppor-tunity to go abroad. Предо-ста-вле́ние, *n.n.*, granting, allowing. П. свобо́ды, granting of freedom. Он про́дал дом с предоставле́нием ему́ пра́ва по́льзо-ваться одно́й ко́мнатой, he sold his house with the reservation that he could use one room.

при-ста́-вить, *v.p.,* при-ста-вля́ть, *v.i.,* к + *dat.,* to set, put, place; lean against; appoint. П. ле́стницу к стене́, to place a ladder against a wall. П. сто́рожа к са́ду, to appoint a watchman for the garden. При-ста-вля́ть-ся, *v.i.r.,* к + *dat.,* to be placed, set against, appointed to look after. Ле́стница приставля́ется к окну́, the ladder is placed against the window. При́-ста-в, *n.m.,* (*obs.*), police officer. Суде́бный п., (*obs.*), bailiff. Станово́й п., (*obs.*), district police officer. При-ста́-вка, *n.f.,* that which is attached to something; (*gram.*), prefix. "При" явля́ется приста́вкой, "при" is a prefix. При-ста́-вочный, *adj.,* (*gram.*), containing a prefix; prefixed. При-ста-вно́й, *adj.,* added, attached, additional. П. стул в ло́же, a movable chair added in a theater box.

про-ста́-вить, *v.p.,* про-ста-вля́ть, *v.i.,* + *acc.,* to write in, enter in. П. число́, to fill in a number, the date. Про-ста-вля́ть-ся, *v.i.r.,* to be written in, filled in, entered. Фами́лия проставля́ется в опро́сном листе́, the name is entered in the questionnaire.

рас-ста́-вить, *v.p.,* рас-ста-вля́ть, *v.i.,* + *acc.,* to move apart, place apart; arrange, set, put in proper order; distribute by placing. Р. солда́т о́коло зда́ния, to station soldiers near a building. Р. кни́ги на по́лке, to place and arrange books on a shelf. Р. сту́лья в ко́мнате, to arrange the chairs in a room. Рас-ста-вля́ть-ся, *v.i.r.,* to be distributed, placed, stationed, moved apart. Часовы́е расставля́ются вдоль грани́цы, the sentinels are posted along the border.

со-ста́-вить, *v.p.,* сос-та-вля́ть, *v.i.,* + *acc.,* из + *gen.,* to compose, constitute, form; aggregate. С. лека́рство из ра́зных составны́х часте́й, to compose, concoct medicine out of various ingredients. С. фра́зу, to construct a sentence. Э́то соста́вит сто рубле́й, this will come to a hundred rubles. Со-ста́-вить-ся, *v.p.r.,* со-ста-вля́ть-ся, *v.i.r.,* to be formed, constituted. Соста́вилось о́бщество покрови́тельства живо́тным, a society for the protection of animals was formed. Со-ста́-в, *n.m.,* composition, body, staff, contingent. Э́то сло́жный хими́ческий с, this is a complicated chemical compound. Мини́-сте́рство по́дало в отста́вку в по́лном соста́ве, the ministry resigned in a body. Железнодоро́жный подвижно́й с., railroad rolling stock. Со-ста-ви́тель, *n.m.,* со-ста-ви́тельница, *n.f.,* compiler. С. словаря́, compiler of a dictionary. С. поездо́в, railroad cou-

pler. Со-ста-вно́й, *adj.,* compound, composite. С-а́я часть, component.

у-ста́-вить, *v.p.,* у-ста-вля́ть, *v.i.,* + *acc.,* + *instr.,* to stare at, fix one's eyes on; set, fill, cover with. У. по́лки посу́дой, to fill shelves with dishes. У. глаза́ на кого́-либо, to fix one's eyes on someone. Стол был уста́влен цвета́ми, the table was decorated with flowers. У-ста́-вленный, *adj.,* *part. pass. past,* fixed, filled, covered. У-ста́-в, *n.m.,* regulation, statute, rule. У. па́ртии, party statute. Военно-морско́й у., navy regulations. У-ста́-вить-ся, *v.p.r.,* у-ста-вля́ть-ся, *v.i.r.,* + *instr.,* на + *acc.,* to be set, filled with, covered; stare at. Чего́ он уста́вился на нас? Why is he staring at us? Стол уставля́ется буты́лками, the table is set with bottles.

ста-н-ов-и́ть-ся, *v.i.r.,* стат-ь, *v.p.,* + *instr.,* to place oneself, become. С. хоро́шим актёром, to become a good actor. Он стал госуда́рственным де́ятелем, he became a statesman. Он стано́вится недове́рчивым, he is growing distrustful. Стано́вится по́здно, it is growing late. Ста-н, *n.m.,* stature; waist; camp, mill. То́нкий с., slender stature. Вра́жий с., (*obs.*), enemy camp. Прока́тный с., rolling mill. Ста-н-и́ца, *n.f.,* Cossack village. Ста-новле́ние, *n.n.,* settling. В проце́ссе становле́ния, in the process of settling. Ста-ново́й, *adj.,* *also used as n.,* (*pre-Rev.*), district police officer. С. приста́в, (*pre-Rev.*), district police officer. Ста-но́к, *n.m.,* bench, frame, loom. Тка́цкий с., loom. Печа́тный с., printing press. Столя́рный с., joiner's bench. Рабо́чий от станка́, (*recent*), manual laborer, bench worker. То-ка́рный с., lathe worker. Ста-н-ко-строе́ние, *n.n.,* machine tool construction. Ста-н-ко-строи́тельный, *adj.,* pertaining to machine tool construction.

вос-ста-н-ови́ть, *v.p.,* вос-ста-на́вливать, *v.i.,* + *acc.,* to re-establish, reinstate, restore, rehabilitate. В. разру́шенный го́род, to reconstruct a destroyed city. В. в права́х, to restore legal rights. В. здоро́вье, to recover one's health. Вос-ста-нови́тель, *n.m.,* restorer, renovator, renewer. Вос-ста-нови́тельный, *adj.,* restoration. В. пери́од, restoration period. Вос-ста-новле́ние, *n.n.,* restoration, recovery, reconstruction; reduction. В. хозя́йства, reconstruction of the economy. В. промы́шленности, reconstruction of industry. В. в права́х, re-establishment of legal rights. Вос-ста-нови́ть-ся, *v.p.r.,* вос-ста-на́вливать-ся, *v.i.r.,* to be reconstructed, reinstated, restored; recover. Хозя́йство понемно́гу восстана́вливается, the economy is gradually becoming reconstructed. Моё здоро́вье восстанови́лось, I have recovered my health.

о-ста-н-ови́ть, *v.p.,* о-ста-на́вливать, *v.i.,* + *acc.,* to stop, bring to a stand, check. О. ло́шадь, to stop a horse. Он останови́л маши́ну, he stopped a car. О. чьё-либо внима́ние, to attract one's attention. О-ста-нови́ть-ся, *v.p.r.,* о-ста-на́вливать-ся, *v.i.r.,* на, в + *prep.,* пе́ред + *instr.,* to stop, put up, come to a standstill. Все пешехо́ды останови́лись на углу́, all the pedestrians stopped at the corner. Он всегда́ остана́вливается в э́той гости́нице, he always stays at this hotel. Где остана́вливается авто́бус? Where does the bus stop? Он ни пе́ред чем не остана́вливается, he doesn't stop at anything. О-ста-но́вка, *n.f.,* halt, stop. На како́й остано́вке вы выхо́дите? At which stop do you get off? Без остано́вки, without stopping.

по-ста-н-ови́ть, *v.p.,* по-ста-новля́ть, *v.i.,* + *acc.,* to decide; establish, decree. Прави́тельство постанови́ло, the government decreed. По-ста-но́вка, *n.f.,* erection, production. П. о́перы, staging of an opera. П. вопро́са, manner of putting a question. П. го́лоса, voice training, voice placement, По-ста-но́вочный, *adj.,* spectacular. П. пье́са, spectacular play. По-ста-но́вщик, *n.m.,* theatre producer. По-ста-новле́ние, *n.n.,* decision, decree, enactment. Но́вое п. о твёрдых це́нах, a new decree pertaining to price control.

рас-ста-н-ови́ть, *v.p.,* рас-ста́-навливать, *v.i.,* + *acc.,* *(colloq.),* to place, arrange; move apart. Рас-ста-но́вка, *n.f.,* arrangement, order. Р. зна́ков препина́ния, punctuation. Говори́ть с расстано́вкой, to speak, talk haltingly.

у-ста-н-ови́ть, *v.p.,* у-ста-на́вливать, у-ста-новля́ть, *v.i.,* + *acc.,* to set, place; *(tech.),* install; establish, determine, ascertan. У. це́ны на все това́ры, to fix the prices on all goods. У-ста-нови́ть-ся, *v.p.r.,* у-ста-на́вливать-ся, *v.i.r.,* to be settled, established, fixed; *(tech.),* be installed. Пого́да про́чно установи́лась, the weather has become settled. Его́ взгля́ды не установи́лись, his views are unsettled. У-ста-но́вка, *n.f.,* setting, placing, planting; installation; mounting. Силова́я у., power plant. Полити́ческая у., political set-up, political orientation. У-ста-новле́ние, *n.n.,* ascertainment, establishment. У. сро́ка платежа́, establishment of terms of payment. У. нау́чного институ́та, establishment of a scientific institute.

У-ста-но́вленный, *adj., part. pass. past,* established; standard. У. поря́док (факт), established order (fact). У-ого образца́, of a standard pattern. Не-у-ста́-нный, *adj.,* incessant, continual. Н. труд, continual work. Не-у-ста́-нно, *adv.,* incessantly, untiringly.

сто́-и-ть, *v.i.,* + *acc.,* + *gen.,* to cost, come to, be worth. Ско́лько э́то сто́ит? How much does this cost? Это сто́ит оди́н рубль, this costs one ruble. Это сто́ило ему́ больши́х трудо́в, this cost him much labor. Игра́ не сто́ит свеч, *(saying),* the game is not worth the candle. Не сто́ит благода́рности, don't mention it; you're welcome. Сто́-имость, *n.f.,* value, worth. Менова́я с., value in exchange. Потреби́тельная с., utilitarian value. Приба́вочная с., surplus value. Бума́ги про́даны по номина́льной сто́имости, shares (stocks) are sold at par. Сто́-ящий, *adj., part. act. pres.,* costing.

сто-я́-ть, *v.i.,* to stand, stay. Часово́й стои́т на посту́, the sentinel is standing at his post. Все стоя́ли, как вко́панные, they stood as if rooted to the spot. Моро́з стоя́л бо́льше ме́сяца, the frost lasted over a month. С. горо́й за кого́-либо, *(idiom.),* to back someone through thick and thin. С. на своём, to persist. Руга́ть на чём свет стои́т, *(colloq.),* to scold vigorously, curse like a trouper. Стой! Halt! Stop! Сто́йка, *n.f.,* bar, counter; set, point. За сто́йкой стоя́л хозя́ин, the host stood at the counter. Вдруг соба́ка сде́лала сто́йку, suddenly the dog pointed. Сто́й-кий, *adj.,* sturdy, firm, staunch, persevering. У него́ сто́йкий хара́ктер, his is a firm character. Сто́й-ко, *adv.,* staunchly. Сто́й-кость, *n.f.,* staunchness, perseverance. Он прояви́л порази́тельную с., he exhibited amazing perseverance.

вы́-сто-ять, *v.p.,* вы-ста́-ивать, *v.i.,* + *acc.,* to stand a certain length of time. Они́ вы́стояли всю обе́дню, they stood through the whole Mass. Вы́-сто-ять-ся, *v.p.r.,* to have a rest; mature (*of* wine). Ло́шадь вы́стоялась, the horse had a rest.

до-сто-я́ть, *v.p.,* до-ста́-ивать, *v.i.,* до + *gen.,* to remain standing till the end. Они́ достоя́ли до конца́ обе́дни, they remained standing till the end of Mass. До-сто-я́ть-ся, *v.p.r.,* до + *gen.,* to stand until exhausted. До-сто-я́ние, *n.n.,* property, fortune. Это его́ ли́чное д., this is his personal property. Сде́лать что́-либо достоя́нием широ́ких масс, to popularize something among the vast masses.

за-сто-я́ть-ся, *v.p.r.,* за-ста́-ивать-ся, *v.i.r.,* to stand too long; become stale. Вода́ в графи́не застоя́лась, the water in the decanter has become stale. За-сто-я́вшийся, *adj., part. act. past,* restive; stale. 3-ся ло́шадь, restive horse. За-сто́й, *n.m.,* stagnation; depression. Дела́ в засто́е, business is at a standstill. За-сто́-й-ный, *adj.,* stagnant.

на-сто-я́ть, *v.p.,* на-ста́-ивать, *v.i.,* + *acc.,* на + *prep.,* to let draw, infuse; insist, persist; obtain by persistent demands. Н. чай, to let the tea draw. Н. нали́вку на пе́рце, to draw a liqueur with pepper. Н. на приня́тии мер, to insist that measures be taken. Н. на своём, to insist on having one's own way. Подсуди́мый наста́ивает на том, что он невино́вен, the defendant insists that he is innocent. На-сто-я́ть-ся, *v.p.r.,* на-ста́-ивать-ся, *v.i.r., used only in 3d pers.,* to be drawn, infused. Чай настоя́лся, the tea is drawn. На-сто́й, *n.m.,* infusion. На-сто́й-ка, *n.f.,* tincture. Йо́дистая н., tincture of iodine. На-сто́й-чивость, *n.f.,* persistence, insistence. На-сто́й-чивый, *adj.,* persistent. На-сто́й-чиво, *adv.,* persistently. Н. тре́бовать, to demand. На-сто-я́ние, *n.n.,* insistence. Э́то сде́лано по его́ настоя́нию, this was done at his urgent request. На-сто-я́тель, *n.m.,* prior of a monastery. На-сто-я́тельность, *n.f.,* insistence, urgency. Н. про́сьбы, urgency of a request. На-сто-я́тельный, *adj.,* urgent, pressing. На-сто-я́тельно, *adv.,* urgently. Н. прошу́ вас сде́лать э́то, I urge you to do this. На-сто-я́щий, *adj.,* real, genuine. Э́то н. же́мчуг, this is a genuine pearl. Н-ее, *adj., used as n.,* the present. Н-ее вре́мя, *(gram.),* present time.

об-сто-я́ть, *v.i., used only in 3d pers.,* to be, get on. Всё обстои́т благополу́чно, all is well. Как обстоя́т ва́ши дела́? How are you getting on? How are things with you? Об-сто-я́тельство, *n.n.,* case, circumstance. Тут осо́бое стече́ние обстоя́тельств, there is an extraordinary combination of circumstances here. Смотря́ по обстоя́тельствам, depending on circumstances. Семе́йные обстоя́тельства, family circumstances. Находи́ться в затрудни́тельных обстоя́тельствах, to be in difficult circumstances. Об-сто-я́тельность, *n.f.,* thoroughness. Об-сто-я́тельный, *adj.,* thorough. Об-сто-я́тельно, *adv.,* thoroughly, reliably. Об-сто-я́тельственный, *adj., (gram.),* adverbial.

от-сто-я́ть, *v.p.,* от-ста́-ивать, *v.i.,* + *acc.,* to fight, defend; save; last. О. своё мне́ние, to defend one's opinion successfully. Пожа́рной кома́нде удало́сь отстоя́ть дом, the fire brigade succeeded in saving the house. О. на нога́х, to stand on one's feet through something.

от-сто-я́ть, *v.p.,* от + *gen., used only in 3d pers.,* to be distant. Дере́вня отстоя́ла от го́рода на 5 киломе́тров, the village was five kilometers from the town. От-сто-я́ть-ся, *v.p.r.,* от-ста́-ивать-ся, *v.i.r, used only in 3d pers.,* to settle, precipitate. Ко́фе ещё не отстоя́лось, the coffee has not settled yet.

пере-сто-я́ть, *v.p.,* + *acc.,* to stand too long, stand a given length of time. Я перестою́ дождь под э́тим наве́сом, I shall remain under this shed until the rain has stopped. Парохо́д пересто́ит бу́рю в га́вани, the steamer will lie in the harbor until the storm has passed. Пиро́г пересто́ял, the pie was kept in the oven too long. Пере-сто-я́ть-ся, *v.p.r.,* to stand too long, be spoiled by disuse. Рожь в по́ле перестоя́лась и из неё сы́плется зерно́, the rye is overripe and falling over. Пере-сто-я́лый, *adj.,* that which has been kept too long in an oven.

по-сто-я́ть, *v.p.,* to stand for a while. Я постою́ здесь немно́го, I shall stand here for a while. П. за себя́, to hold one's own. По-сто́й! Halt! Wait a minute! П., куда́ идёшь? Wait, where are you going? По-сто́й, *n.m., (mil.),* billeting. Поста́вить на п., to billet. По-сто-я́лец, *n.m.,* lodger, guest. По-сто-я́лый, *adj.,* lodging. П. двор, inn. По-сто-я́нный, *adj.,* constant. По-сто-я́нная величина́, *(math.),* constant. П-ое пребыва́ние, permanent residence. По-сто-я́нно, *adv.,* constantly, always. Он п. без де́нег, he is always without money. По-сто-я́нство, *n.n.,* constancy.

пред-сто-я́ть, *v.i.,* + *dat.,* to be faced with, be forthcoming. Мне предстоя́т больши́е тру́дности, I shall be faced with great difficulties. Ему́ предстои́т да́льний путь, he is in for a long journey. Пред-сто-я́щий, *adj., part. act. pres.,* impending, forthcoming. П-ие вы́боры, forthcoming elections.

про-сто-я́ть, *v.p.,* про-ста́-ивать, *v.i.,* to pass time in standing in a given place; *(mil.),* be quartered; stand idle. Хо́лодная пого́да простои́т недо́лго, the cold weather will not last long. Он простоя́л на у́лице це́лый час, he stood in the street a whole hour. Я проста́ивал часы́ пе́ред карти́нами Ре́пина, I used to stand for hours in front of Repin's paintings. Про-стóй, *п.т.*, standing idle; stoppage. Чáстый п. машúн, frequent idleness of machines.

рас-сто-я́ние, *п.п.*, distance, space. На блúзком расстоя́нии, at no great distance. На расстоя́нии пу́шечного вы́стрела, within gunshot.

со-сто-я́ть, *v.i.*, + *instr.*, из + *gen.*, в + *prep.*, to be, consist of. С. подпúсчиком, to be a subscriber. Квартúра состоúт из 5 кóмнат, the apartment consists of five rooms. Дéло состоя́ло в том, что... the point was that...

со-сто-я́ть-ся, *v.p.r.*, *used only in 3d pers.*, to take place. Концéрт не состоя́лся, the concert did not take place. Со-сто-я́ние, *п.п.*, state, condition, fortune. Егó здорóвье в плохóм состоя́нии, his health is poor. У негó большóе с., he has a great fortune. Я не в состоя́нии сдéлать э́того, I am not in a position to do this. Благосостоя́ние, *п.п.*, well-being, prosperity. Со-сто-я́тельность, *п.f.*, competency, solvency. Не-состоя́тельность, *п.f.*, insolvency, groundlessness. Н. егó аргументáции очевúдна, his arguments are obviously groundless. Со-сто-я́тельный, *adj.* well-to-do, well off. С-ые лю́ди, well-to-do people. Не-состоя́тельный, *adj.*, insolvent, groundless. Н. должнúк, an insolvent debtor. Н-ое обвинéние, a groundless accusation.

у-сто-я́ть, *v.p.*, прóтив + *gen.*, на + *prep.*, to resist, hold out against, manage to stand firm. Ребёнок не устоя́л на ногáх и упáл, the child was unable to stand. Он не устоя́л прóтив искушéния, he could not resist the temptation. У-сто-я́ть-ся, *v.p.r.*, *used only in 3d pers.*, to settle (*as a liquid*). Жúдкость устоя́лась, the liquid has settled. У-стóй, *п.т.*, abutment, basis of a bridge. У-стó-и, *п.т.pl.*, foundations, principles. Нрáвственные устóи, moral principles. У-стóйчивость, *п.f.*, stability, steadiness. У. э́того политúческого строя́ сомнúтельна, the stability of this political system is doubtful. У-стóй-чивый, *adj.*, stable, steady, firm. У-ое правúтельство, stable government. У-ая ценá, stable price. Не-у-стóй-чивый, *adj.*, unstable, unsettled. Н-ая погóда, unsettled weather.

СТЕП-, СТОП-, СТУП-, СТУП(Л)-, STEP

стéп-ен-ь, *п.f.*, degree, grade, class, rate, power. Он получúл с. дóктора, he received a doctor's degree. С. эксплоа-

тáции, degree of utilization. Сравнúтельная с., comparative degree. С. родствá, degree of relationship. Ни в какóй стéпени, in no degree. В рáвной стéпени, in an equal degree. Степéнность, *п.f.*, staidness, sedateness. Степéнный, *adj.*, staid, sedate. С. человéк, staid, sedate person.

стоп-á, *п.f.*, sole of the foot; foot-step; metre (*in verse*); ream, tumbler. Плóская с., flat foot. Кудá напрáвим мы стопы́ свои́? Whither shall we direct our feet? Идтú по егó стопáм, (*fig.*), to tread in his footsteps. Пу́шкин написáл "Евгéния Онéгина", двухслóжной стопóй, Pushkin wrote "Eugene Onegin" in a decasyllabic metre. Огрóмная стопá книг, large pile of books. Стопá бумáги, ream of paper. Стóп-ка, *п.f.*, cup; little roll. Он вы́пил стóпку вóдки, he drank a jigger of vodka.

ступ-áть, *v.i.*, ступ-úть, *v.p.*, to step. Он тяжелó ступáет, he treads heavily, he stomps. Ступáй отсю́да, get away. Сту́п-а (сту́п-ка), *п.f.*, mortar. Толóчь вóду в ступé, (*saying*), to do nothing. Пéстик сту́пки, pestle. Ступ-úца, *п.f.*, nave, hub. Грязь доходúла до ступúцы колёс, the mud reached up to the hub. Ступ-ня́, *п.f.*, foot. Ему́ ампутúровали ступню́, they amputated his foot.

в-ступ-áть, *v.i.*, в-ступ-úть, *v.p.*, в + *acc.*, to enter; step in, into. Войскá вступúли в гóрод, the troops entered the town. Он вступúл в исполнéние свои́х обя́занностей, he assumed his offical duties. В. в профессионáльный сою́з, to become a member of a trade union. В. в разговóр, to join a conversation. В. в правá наслéдства, to inherit legally, obtain rights of inheritance. В. на престóл, to mount a throne. В-ступ-áть-ся, *v.i.r.*, в-ступ-úть-ся, *v.p.r.*, за + *acc.*, to intercede. В. за слáбого, to defend the weaker of two. Он всегдá вступáется за друзéй, he always intercedes for his friends. В-ступ-úтельный, *adj.*, introductory. В. взнос, entrance fee. В-ые словá, introductory words, remarks. В-ступ-лéние, *п.п.*, prelude, introduction, entry, preface. В. к кнúге, the introduction to the book. В. áрмии в гóрод, entrance of army into a town. Это слу́жит вступлéнием, this serves as an introduction, a prelude.

за-ступ-áть, *v.i.*, за-ступ-úть, *v.p.*, (*colloq.*), + *acc.*, to substitute, replace. Вторáя смéна заступáет в 6 часóв, the second shift comes on at 6 o'clock. За-ступ-áть-ся, *v.p.r.*, за-ступ-úть-ся, *v.p.r.,* за + *acc.,* to intercede, plead, defend. Офицéр заступи́лся за своегó солдáта, the officer pleaded for his soldier. За-сту́п-ник, *n.m.,* за-сту́п-ница, *n.f.,* (*obs.*), defender, patron. Бог наш з. и покрови́тель, (*rel.*), God is our defender and protector. Право-застýпник, *n.m.,* (*recent*), advocate. За-сту́п-ничество, *n.n.,* intercession, pleading.

на-ступ-áть, *v.i.,* на-ступ-и́ть, *v.p.,* на + *acc.,* to tread, step on; come; advance. Он наступи́л ногóй на змею́, he stepped on a snake. Наступи́л 1812 год, the year 1812 began. Неприя́тель наступáет, the enemy is advancing, the enemy is on the offensive. Н. нá ногу, to tread on someone's toes. На-ступ-á-ющий, *adj., part. act. pres.,* coming, pending. Н-ая сторонá, assailant. На-ступ-лéние, *n.n.,* advance, approach, offensive. Н. лéта, the coming of summer. Áрмия перешлá в н., the army took the offensive.

о-ступ-áть-ся, *v.i.r.,* о-ступ-и́ть-ся, *v.p.r.,* to stumble. Он оступи́лся и вы́вихнул нóгу, he stumbled and sprained his foot.

об-ступ-áть, *v.i.,* об-ступ-и́ть, *v.p.,* + *acc.,* to surround. Её обступи́ли дéти, she was surrounded by children.

от-ступ-áть, *v.i.,* от-ступ-и́ть, *v.p.,* от + *gen.,* to fall back, recede, retreat. Войскá отступи́ли, the troops retreated. От-ступ-áть-ся, *v.i.r.,* от-ступ-и́ть-ся, *v.p.r.,* от + *gen.,* (*colloq.*), to desist, give up. О. от свои́х слов, to retract one's words. Все отступи́лись от меня́, everyone renounced me. От-ступ-лéние, *n.n.,* retreat, deviation. Им бы́ло отрéзано о., their retreat was cut off. От-сту́п-ник, *n.m.,* apostate, abjurer. Юлиáн Отсту́пник, Julian the Apostate. Отсту́п-ничество, *n.n.,* apostasy, defection. В пáртии началóсь о., defection started in the party. От-ступ-нóе, *adj., used as n.,* bribe, buying off. Дáйте емý отступнóго, give him a bribe, buy him off.

пере-ступ-áть, *v.i.,* пере-ступ-и́ть, *v.p.,* + *acc.,* to cross, step over, transgress. Мы переступи́ли порóг егó дóма, we have crossed the threshold of his house. Лóшадь осторóжно переступáла лýжи, the horse carefully stepped over the puddles. У меня́ едвá переступáют нóги, I can hardly walk.

по-ступ-áть, *v.i.,* по-ступ-и́ть, *v.p.,* to act, treat, behave; enter. Как вам поступи́ть? What are you to do? Он дýрно поступáет, he behaves badly. Он поступи́л на юриди́ческий факультéт, he entered law school. Он поступи́л с ним сурóво, he treated him sternly. Дéло поступи́ло в суд, the case was brought into court. По-ступ-áть-ся, *v.i.r.,* по-ступ-и́ть-ся, *v.p.r.,* + *instr.,* to give up, cede, yield. Он не хóчет ничéм поступи́ться, he does not wish to give up anything. По-ступ-лéние, *n.n.,* entering, return; receipt. П. в шкóлу, entering, entrance into school. П. дохóда, receipt of income. По-сту́пок, *n.m.,* action, step. Это был благорóдный п., that was a generous act. Егó посту́пки мне не нрáвятся, I don't like his conduct, behavior. Пó-ступ-ь, *n.f.,* step, tread. И тя́жкой пóступью своéй, (*poet.*) and with his heavy, firm tread.

под-ступ-áть, *v.i.,* под-ступ-и́ть, *v.p.,* к + *dat.,* to approach. П. к грани́це, (*mil.*), to approach the border. Под-ступ-и́ть-ся, *v.p.r.,* к + *dat.,* (*colloq.*), to come up, step in. Он так серди́т, что к немý нельзя́ п., he is so angry, it is impossible to approach him. Пóд-ступ, *n.m.,* approach. Все пóдступы к крéпости стрóго охраня́лись, all approaches to the fortress were strongly guarded.

пре-ступ-áть, *v.i.,* пре-ступ-и́ть, *v.p.,* + *acc.,* (*obs.*), to transgress, violate, infringe. Они́ преступи́ли все закóны, they have violated all laws. Пре-ступ-л-éние, *n.n.,* crime. П. и наказáние, crime and punishment. Госудáрственное п., a crime against the state. Поймáть на мéсте преступлéния, to catch in the act. Соверши́ть п., to commit a crime. Пре-сту́п-ник, *n.m.,* пре-сту́п-ница, *n.f.,* offender, criminal. Пре-сту́п-ность, *n.f.,* criminality. П. растёт, criminality is increasing. Пре-сту́п-ный, *adj.,* criminal. Пре-сту́п-но, *adv.,* criminally.

при-ступ-áть, *v.i.,* при-ступ-и́ть, *v.p.,* к + *dat.,* to set to, begin. Он приступи́л к рабóте, he has set to work. При-ступ-и́ть-ся, *v.p.r.,* к + *dat.,* (*colloq.*), to approach. Товáры такие дорóгие, что и не присту́пишься, the wares are so expensive that they are beyond our reach. При́-ступ, *n.m.,* assault, storm, fit, attack, paroxysm; approach. Крéпость былá взятá присту́пом, the fortress was taken by storm. П. кáшля (гнéва), fit of coughing (fit of anger). При-сту́п-ка, *n.f.,* step. Не-при-сту́п-ный, *adj.,* impregnable. Этот форт н., this fort is unassailable. Не-при-сту́п-ность, *n.f.,* impregnability, inaccessibility.

про-ступ-ок, *n.m.,* fault, offense. Тяжёлое наказáние за незначи́тельный п., a heavy penalty for a slight offense.

рас-ступ-а́ть-ся, *v.i.r.,* рас-ступ-и́ть-ся, *v.p.r.,* to open, give away, make room. Толпа́ расступи́лась, что́бы пропусти́ть его́, the crowd opened up to let him pass.

у-ступ-а́ть, *v.i.,* у-ступ-и́ть, *v.p.,* + *acc.,* в + *prep.,* to yield, give in, concede. Он уступи́л ей доро́гу, he made way for her. Они́ уступи́ли давле́нию, they yielded to pressure. Я не могу́ у. в э́том вопро́се, I cannot yield in this matter. Он уступи́л мне э́ту вещь за 10 рубле́й, he let me have this thing for ten rubles. У-сту́п-ка, *n.f.,* concession. Взаи́мные усту́пки, mutual concessions. Пойти́ на усту́пки, to make concessions. У-сту́п-чивый, *adj.,* yielding, compliant. У-сту́п-чивость, *n.f.,* compliance. Соглаше́ние дости́гнуто благодаря́ его́ усту́пчивости, the agreement was concluded thanks to his compliance. Не-у-сту́п-чивый, *adj.,* unyielding. Н. хара́ктер, unyielding disposition. Не-у-сту́п-чивость, *n.f.,* noncompliance, obstinacy, unyieldingness.

СТЕРЕЧ-, СТЕРЕГ-, СТЕРЁГ-, СТЕ-РЕЖ-, СТРАЖ-, СТОРОЖ-, СТОРГ-, СТРОЖ-, VIGIL

стере́ч-ь, стерег-у́, *v.i.,* + *acc.,* to watch, guard, take care. С. дом, to watch over a house. Ко́шка мышь стережёт, the cat is watching the mouse.

о-стере́ч-ь, *v.p.,* о-стерег-а́ть, *v.i.,* + *acc.,* to warn. О. от опа́сности, to warn of danger. О-стере́ч-ь-ся, *v.p.r.,* о-стерег-а́ть-ся, *v.i.r.,* + *gen.,* to beware of, be on guard. Остерега́йтесь карма́нщиков! Beware of pickpockets! Остерега́йтесь пить сыру́ю во́ду, take care not to drink unboiled water.

пред-о-стере́ч-ь, *v.p.,* пред-о-стерег-а́ть, *v.i.,* + *acc.,* to warn. Его́ предостерега́ли относи́тельно э́того челове́ка, they warned him against this man. Пред-о-стереж-е́ние, *n.n.,* warning, caution. Несмотря́ на многокра́тное п., in spite of repeated warnings.

по-стере́ч-ь, *v.p.,* + *acc.,* see стере́чь.

под-стере́ч-ь, *v.p.,* под-стерег-а́ть *v.i.,* + *acc.,* to lie in wait, in ambush. Разбо́йники подстерега́ли их на доро́ге, highwaymen were lying in wait for them.

у-стере́ч-ь, *v.p.,* + *acc.,* от + *gen.,* to succeed in guarding against. Мать не устерегла́ ребёнка от зара́зы, the mother did not succeed in guarding the child from contagion.

сторож-и́ть, *v.i.,* + *acc.,* to guard, watch. Соба́ка сторожи́т дом, the dog is guarding the house. Сто́рож, *n.m.,* watchman. С. стои́т у воро́т, the watchman is standing at the gate. На-сторож-е́, on guard. Быть насторо́же, to be on guard. Сторож-ево́й, *adj.,* watch. С-а́я вы́шка, watch tower. Сто́рож-ка, *n.f.,* lodge. С. привра́тника, gate keeper's lodge. О-сторо́ж-ность, *n.f.,* caution; prudence. Де́йствовать с осторо́жностью, to act with caution. О-сторо́ж-ный, *adj.,* careful, prudent. Бу́дьте осторо́жны! Take care! Watch out! О-сторо́ж-но, *adv.,* carefully, with care. Пред-о-сторо́ж-ность, *n.f.,* precaution. Из предосторо́жности, to be on the safe side; out of precaution. Принима́ть ме́ры предосторо́жности, to take precautionary measures.

по-сторож-и́ть, *v.p.,* + *acc.,* to watch. Посторожи́те мои́ ве́щи, пока́ я приду́, keep an eye on my things until I come.

страж, *n.m.,* (*obs.*), see сто́рож. Соба́ка - мой ве́рный с., my dog is my trusty guard. Стра́ж-а, *n.f.,* guard, watch. Стоя́ть на стра́же, to stand on guard. Содержа́ться под стра́жей, to be under arrest. Стра́ж-ник, *n.m.,* mounted policeman in county district.

стро́г-ий (строг), *adj.,* severe, stern, strict. С. учи́тель, strict teacher. Пригово́р суда́ был о́чень строг, the sentence was very severe. Челове́к стро́гого о́браза жи́зни, an austere chaste person. Стро́гие ме́ры, severe measures. Стро́го, *adv.,* severely, strictly. С. запрещено́, strictly prohibited. Стро́г-ость, *n.f.,* severity, rigidity, strictness. С. нра́вов, rigidity of morals. Стро́ж-е, *adj. and adv. comp.,* more severe, more stern, more strict; more severely, more sternly, more strictly. Он отнёсся к нам стро́же обыкнове́нного, he treated us more sternly than usual. Строж-а́йший, *adj., superl.,* severest, sternest, strictest.

СТРАД-, СТРАЖД-, СТРАСТ-, SUFFERING, PASSION

страд-а́ть, *v.i.,* от + *gen.,* to suffer. Я страда́ю от зубно́й бо́ли, I am suffering from a toothache. С. по вине́ кого́-либо, to suffer through somebody's fault. Страд-а́лец, *n.m.,* страд-а́лица, *n.f.,* sufferer, martyr. Страд-а́льческий, *adj.,* of or pertaining to a martyr. С. вид, air of a martyr. Страд-а́ние, *n.n.,* suffering, pain. Боле́знь причини́ла ей мно́го страда́ний, her illness caused her much suffering. Страд-а́тельный, *adj.,* (*gram.*), passive. С. зало́г, (*gram.*), passive voice.

Страд-а́, *n.f.*, harvest time. Стра́д-ный, *adj.*, harvest. Стра́д-ная пора́, harvest time.

вы́-страд-ать, *v.p.*, to suffer through. Он вы́страдал от них мно́го униже́ний, he suffered much humiliation at their hands.

ис-страд-а́ть-ся, *v.p.r.*, to wear oneself out with suffering. Он в коне́ц исстрада́лся, he utterly wore himself out with suffering.

на-страд-а́ть-ся, *v.p.r.*, to suffer very much. Я доста́точно настрада́лся в мое́й жи́зни, I've suffered enough in my life.

от-страд-а́ть, *v.p.*, + *acc.*, to have had one's share of suffering. Она́ отстрада́ла своё, she has had her share of suffering.

по-страд-а́ть, *v.p.*, от + *gen.*, to suffer; sustain injuries. Его́ здоро́вье пострада́ло от недоеда́ния, his health was impaired by hunger. Го́род пострада́л от бомбардиро́вки, the city suffered from bombardments.

про-страд-а́ть, *v.p.*, to suffer over a period of time. Наро́д прострада́л от го́лода це́лый год, the people suffered from famine through a whole year.

со-страд-а́ть, *v.i.*, + *dat.*, (*obs.*), to feel, sympathize. С. слеза́м бли́жнего, to sympathize with the misfortunes of one's fellow man. Со-страд-а́ние, *n.n.*, к + *dat.*, compassion, sympathy. Это несча́стье вы́звало к ним всео́бщее с., this misfortune aroused general sympathy for them. У них нет никако́го сострада́ния, they have no compassion. Со-страд-а́тельный, *adj.*, compassionate.

страст-ь, *n.f.*, passion. С. ослепля́ет люде́й, passion blinds people. Страсть к вину́, passion for drink. Любо́вная с., love, passion. Мне с. как хо́чется, (*colloq.*), I long for. Стра́сти Госпо́дни, Passion of Christ. Стра́ст-ность, *n.f.*, sensuality, passionateness. Стра́ст-ный, *adj.*, passionate; inveterate. С-ая нату́ра, passionate nature, temperament. Страстна́я Неде́ля, Passion Week, Holy Week. Страст-о-те́рпец, (*Ch-Sl.*), *n.m.*, martyr.

при-страст-и́ть-ся, *v.p.r.*, к + *dat.*, to give oneself. П. к вину́, to give oneself to drink. П. к ка́ртам, to become an inveterate card player. При-стра́ст-ие, *n.n.*, passion; partiality. У него́ п. к кни́гам, he has a passion for books. Они́ суди́ли его́ с пристра́стием, they judged him with partiality. При-стра́ст-ность, *n.f.*, partiality. Судья́ проявил большу́ю пристра́стность в приго-во́ре, the judge showed partiality in his

verdict. При-стра́ст-ный, *adj.*, partial, prejudiced. П-ое реше́ние, prejudiced decision. При-стра́ст-но, *adv.*, with partiality. П. суди́ть о чём-либо, to judge something with partiality.

бес-при-стра́ст-ие, *n.n.*, impartiality. Бес-при-стра́ст-ный, *adj.*, impartial. Бес-при-стра́ст-но, *adv.*, impartially, disinterestedly. Обсуди́те э́то б., consider it impartially.

СТРАХ-, СТРАШ-, FEAR, FRIGHT

страх, *n.m.*, fear, fright; risk. С. сме́рти, fear of death. Они́ в смерте́льном стра́хе, they are in mortal fear. Под стра́хом сме́ртной ка́зни, under penalty of death. Взять что́-либо на свой страх, (*idiom.*), to do something at one's own risk. У стра́ха глаза́ велики́, (*saying*), out of fear one makes mountains out of molehills.

страх-ова́-ть, *v.i.*, от + *gen.*, + *acc.*, to insure. Он страху́ет свой дом от огня́, he is insuring his house against fire. Страх-ова́ние, *n.n.*, insurance. С. жи́зни, life insurance. Госуда́рственное с. рабо́чих, social security. Страх-ово́й, *adj.*, insurance. С. по́лис, insurance policy. С-ое о́бщество, insurance company. Страх-о́вщик, страх-ови́к (*recent*), *n.m.*, insurance agent. Страх-ова́ть-ся, *v.i.r.*, to insure oneself. Он страху́ется на вся́кий слу́чай, he is insuring himself against all events.

за-страх-ова́ть, *v.p.*, за-страх-о́вывать, *v.i.*, + *acc.*, от + *gen.*, to insure. З. иму́щество, to insure one's property. За-страхо́ванный, *adj.*, *part. pass. past*, insured. Никто́ не застрахо́ван от оши́бок, no one is insured against mistakes; we all make mistakes. За-страх-ова́ть-ся, *v.p.r.*, за-страх-о́вывать-ся, *v.i.r.*, to insure oneself. Пасса́жир застрахова́лся на слу́чай уве́чья, the passenger insured himself against injuries and maiming.

пере-страх-ова́ть, *v.p.*, пере-страх-о́вывать, *v.i.*, + *acc.*, to reinsure. Он перестрахова́л все свои́ дома́, he reinsured all his houses. Пере-страх-ова́ть-ся, *v.p.r.*, пере-страх-о́вывать-ся, *v.i.r.*, to be insured. П. на слу́чай грабежа́, to reinsure oneself against robbery. Пере-страх-о́вка, *n.n.*, reinsurance. Это о́бщество занима́ется перестрахо́вками, this company is engaged in reinsurance. Пере-страх о́вщик, *n.m.*, (*recent*), overzealous boss, party member.

страш-и́-ть, *v.i.*, + *acc.*, + *instr.*, to frighten. Всех страши́т смерть, death frightens everyone. Страш-и́ть-ся, *v.i.r.,* + *gen.,* to fear. Я страшу́сь предстоя́щих бе́дствий, I fear imminent calamities. Страш-и́лище, *п.п.,* frightening person, object. Он настоя́щее с., he is a regular fright. Стра́ш-ный, *adj.,* frightful, terrible. С. моро́з, terrible frost. День Стра́шного Суда́, Doomsday. С. расска́з, bloodcurdling story. Стра́ш-но, *adv.,* frightfully, terribly. Мне с., I am frightened. Бес-стра́ш-ие, *п.п.,* fearlessness. Бес-стра́ш-ный, *adj.,* fearless. Б. челове́к, fearless man. Бес-стра́ш-но, *adv.,* fearlessly. Солда́т шёл б. в бой, the soldier was going into battle fearlessly.

у-страш-и́ть, *v.p.,* у-страш-а́ть, *v.i.,* + *acc.,* to intimidate. Враги́ меня́ не устраша́ют, enemies do not frighten me. У-страш-а́ющий, *adj., part. act. pres.,* terrifying. У. ого́нь ору́дий, formidable artillery fire. У-страш-е́ние, *п.п.,* intimidation, terror. У. бо́льше не де́йствует, terror has no more effect.

СТРО-, СТРА-, СТРОЙ-, CONSTRUCTION

стро́-и-ть, *v.i.,* + *acc.,* to build, construct. Он стро́ит но́вый дом, he is building a new house. С. фа́брику, to build a factory. С. пла́ны, to plan, make plans. С. ко́зни, to lay snares for someone; scheme. С. фра́зу, to build a sentence. Стро́-ить-ся, *v.i.r.,* to be built, constructed; (*mil.*), fall in. Дом стро́ится, the house is being built. Ро́та стро́ится, (*mil.*), the company falls in. Стро́й-ся! Fall in! Стро-ево́й, *adj.,* (*mil.*), line; timber. С. офице́р, line officer. С. лес, timber, construction lumber. Стро-е́ние, *п.п.,* building, construction; texture. Это са́мое кру́пное с. в го́роде, this is the largest building in town. С. расте́ний, texture of plants. Стро-и́тель, *п.т.,* builder. Инжене́р-строи́тель, construction engineer. Строи́тельный, *adj.,* building, constructional. С. материа́л, building material. Строи́тельство, *п.п.,* construction. Рабо́тать на с-е, to work on a construction project.

строй, *п.т.,* regime, order; (*mil.*), formation. Полити́ческий с., political regime, order. Социа́льный с., social order. Вы́быть из стро́я, become disabled, be a casualty, be out of commission. Стро́й-ка, *п.f.,* construction, building. Шла уси́ленная с., intensive construction was in progress. Стро́й-ный, *adj.,* harmonious, well-shaped, orderly, stately. С-ое пе́ние, harmonious singing. С. челове́к, well-built

man. С-ая систе́ма, orderly system. Стро́й-но, *adv.,* in order, harmoniously.

вы́-стро-ить, *v.p.,* вы-стра́-ивать, *v.i.,* + *acc.,* to build, draw up, erect. Они́ вы́строили це́лый ряд домо́в, they have built a whole row of houses. Вы́строить войска́, to draw up, form troops. Вы́-стро-ить-ся, *v.p.r.,* вы-стра́-ивать-ся, *v.i.r.,* to be built, formed. За про́шлый год вы́строился но́вый кварта́л домо́в, during the last year, a new block of houses has been built.

до-стро́-ить, *v.p.,* до-стра́-ивать, *v.i.,* + *acc.,* to finish building, complete construction. Д. дом, to complete a house.

за-стро́-ить, *v.p.,* за-стра́-ивать, *v.i.,* + *instr.,* to build over, build up, fill with buildings. Пло́щадь была́ застро́ена дома́ми, the square was built up with new houses. За-стро́й-ть-ся, *v.p.r.,* за-стра́-ивать-ся, *v.i.r.,* to be built up. Го́род бы́стро застра́ивался, the town was rapidly building up.

на-стро́-ить, *v.p.,* на-стра́-ивать, *v.i.,* + *acc.,* to build in quantity; tune, incite. Н. мно́го домо́в, to build many houses. Н. роя́ль (*mus.*), to tune a piano. Они́ настра́ивали нас про́тив него́, they incited us against him. На-стро́й-ка, *п.f.,* (*mus.*), tuning. На-стро́й-щик, *п.т.,* tuner. На-стро́-ить-ся, *v.p.r.,* на-стра́-ивать-ся, *v.i.r.,* + *instr.,* to be tuned; to get into the mood, be disposed. Роя́ль настра́ивается настро́йщиком, the piano is being tuned by a tuner. Я настро́ился идти́ в кино́, I made up my mind to go to the movies. На-стро-е́ние, *п.п.,* mood, temper, humor. Она́ сего́дня в хоро́шем н-и, she is in a good humor today.

над-стро́-ить, *v.p.,* над-стра́-ивать, *v.i.,* + *acc.,* to build a superstructure. Н. второ́й эта́ж, to build a second story. Над-стро́й-ка, *п.f.,* superstructure.

об-стро́-ить, *v.p.,* об-стра́-ивать, *v.i.,* + *acc.,* to build, rebuild; build around. О. пло́щадь дома́ми, to build houses around a square. Об-стро́-ить-ся, *v.p.r.,* об-стра́-ивать-ся, *v.i.r.,* + *instr.,* to be built up, around. Го́род обстра́ивается по́сле войны́, the town is being built up after the war.

от-стро́-ить, *v.p.,* от-стра́-ивать, *v.i.,* + *acc.,* to build up, rebuild, complete building, reconstruct. Он за́ново отстро́ил сгоре́вший гара́ж, he rebuilt his burned garage. Он отстро́ил себе́ дом, he built himself a house. От-стро́-енный, *adj., part. pass. past,* built, completed, rebuilt. О-ое зда́ние, a newly completed building.

от-стро́-ить-ся, *v.p.r.,* от-стра́-ивать-ся, *v.i.r.,* to be rebuilt, reconstructed.

Разру́шенный го́род отстра́ивается, the destroyed town is being rebuilt.

пере-стро́-ить, *v.p.,* пере-стра́-ивать, *v.i.,* + *acc.,* to build over, reorganize. П. дом, to rebuild a house. На́до перестро́ить всю рабо́ту, (*fig.*), the whole job must be reorganized. П. гита́ру, to tune a guitar in another key. Пере-стро́-ить-ся, *v.p.r.,* пере-стра́-ивать-ся, *v.i.r.,* to be rebuilt, reorganized, re-oriented; (*mil.*), assume a new formation. Хозя́йство перестра́ивается, the economy is being reorganized. Пере-стро́й-ка, *n.f.,* rebuilding, reorganization; reorientation.

по-стро́-ить, *v.p.,* + *acc., see* стро́ить. П. но́вый дом, to build a new house. По-стро́-ить-ся, *v.p.r.,* to fall in; *see* стро́-ить-ся. По-стро́й-ка, *n.f.,* building, construction, erection. Эта п. непро́чна, this building is flimsy. П. но́вой фа́брики, erection of a new factory.

под-стро́-ить, *v.p.,* под-стра́-ивать, *v.i.,* + *acc.,* под + *acc.,* to build close to, next to; contrive; bring about secretly. П. шу́тку, to play a trick. Он ло́вко подстро́ил э́то всё, he contrived all this very cleverly. П. к до́му гара́ж, to build a garage next to the house. П. скри́пку под роя́ль, to tune a violin to a piano.

при-стро́-ить, *v.p.,* при-стра́-ивать, *v.i.,* + *acc.,* + *dat.,* к + *dat.,* to add, attach to a building; settle, find a place, job; provide for. П. фли́гель к до́му, to add a wing to a house. П. челове́ка к де́лу, to place a man on a job. При-стро́-ить-ся, *v.p.r.,* при-стра́-ивать-ся, *v.i.r.,* к + *dat.,* to be attached to, added to a building; secure a job; be settled. К до́му пристра́ивается крыльцо́, a porch is being added to the house. Он пристро́ился к бога́тым ро́дственникам (*colloq.*), he has settled with rich relatives. Пристро́йка, *n.f.,* addition to a building. П. испо́ртила фаса́д до́ма, the addition has spoiled the facade of the house.

рас-стро́-ить, *v.p.,* рас-стра́-ивать, *v.i.,* + *acc.,* to disconcert, disturb, put out of; derange, upset. Р. состоя́ние, to jeopardize one's finances. Это изве́стие о́чень его́ расстро́ило, this news has upset him very much. Плоха́я пи́ща расстро́ила его́ желу́док, bad food has upset his stomach. Рас-стро́-енный, *adj., part. pass. past,* upset, deranged. Роя́ль расстро́ен, the piano is out of tune. Р-ое воображе́ние, deranged mind. Р-ое состоя́ние, Рас-стро́-ить-ся, *v.p.r.,* рас-стра́-ивать-ся, *v.i.r.,* + *instr.,* от + *gen.,* to be put out, feel

upset, be frustrated. Мои́ пла́ны расстро́ились, my plans were frustrated. Он о́чень расстро́ился, he was very much upset. Не расстра́ивайтесь! Don't be upset! Сва́дьба расстро́илась, the wedding was called off. Рас-стро́й-ство, *n.n.,* disorder, disorganization. Р. хозя́йства, disorganization of economy. Р. желу́дка, indigestion.

у-стро́-ить, *v.p.,* у-стра́-ивать, *v.i.,* + *acc.,* to arrange, organize; place; settle, establish. У. шко́лу, to establish a school. У. вы́ставку, to arrange an exhibition. У. свои́ дела́, to put one's affairs in order. Это меня́ не устра́ивает, (*colloq.*), this does not suit me. Он устро́ил его́ на слу́жбу, he placed him in a job. У-стро́-ить-ся, *v.p.r.,* у-стра́-ивать-ся, *v.i.r.,* to be settled, established. Он хорошо́ устро́ился, he has set himself up very well. У. на но́вой кварти́ре, to settle in a new apartment. Всё устро́илось к лу́чшему, everything turned out for the best. У-стро́-итель, *n.m.,* organizer. У. конце́рта, organizer of a concert. У-стро́й-ство, *n.n.,* arrangement, organization. Удо́бное у. до́ма, comfortable arrangement of a house. У. спекта́кля, organization of a performance.

СТУД-, СТУЖ-, СТЫ-, CHILL, COOL

студ-и́-ть, *v.i.,* + *acc.,* to cool, refrigerate. С. горя́чую во́ду, to cool hot water. Студ-ёный, *adj.,* chilled, cold. С. ключ игра́ет по овра́гу (*poet.*), a cool spring runs through the ravine. Студёность, *n.f.,* coldness, coolness. Сту́день, *n.m.,* jelly, aspic, gelatine. С. из теля́чьих но́жек, calves' foot jelly, aspic. Студ-ени́стый, *adj.,* jellylike. С. клей, jelly-like glue. Сту́ж-а, *n.f.,* cold, frost. На дворе́ с., it is freezing cold outdoors.

вы́-студ-ить, *v.p.,* вы-сту́ж-ивать, *v.i.,* + *acc.,* to cool, make cold. Держа́ окно́ откры́тым, она́ вы́студила ко́мнату, by keeping the window open she cooled the room.

за-студ-и́ть, *v.p.,* за-студ-жа́ть, за-сту́ж-ивать, *v.p.,* + *acc.,* to chill. З. теля́чьи но́жки, to make an aspic out of calves' feet.

на-студ-и́ть, *v.p.,* на-сту́ж-ивать, *v.i.,* + *acc.,* (*colloq.*), to cool in quantity. Он настуди́л мно́го пи́ва, he cooled a quantity of beer.

о-студ-и́ть, *v.p.,* о-студ-жа́ть, *v.i.,* + *acc.,* to chill, cool thoroughly. Остуди́ пре́жде чем есть! Cool thoroughly before eating. О-сту́ж-енный, *adj., part. pass. past,* cooled. Пей, молоко́ уже́

остýжено, drink, the milk has cooled.
про-студ-и́ть, *v.p.,* про-стуж-áть, про-стýж-ивать, *v.i.,* + *acc.,* to permit someone to catch cold. Смотри́те, не простуди́те ребёнка, take care that the child doesn't catch cold. Про-стýж-енный, *adj.,* affected with a cold. Про-студ-и́ть-ся, *v.p.r.,* про-стуж-áть-ся, про-стýж-ивать-ся, *v.i.r.,* to catch cold. Он легко́ про-стýж-ивается, he easily catches cold. Про-стýд-а, *n.f.,* chill, cold. У меня́ си́льная просту́да, I have a bad cold.
сты-ть, стый-н-уть, *v.i.,* to cool, grow cool. Чай сты́нет, the tea is getting cold. Кровь сты́нет от ýжаса, it makes one's blood curdle with horror.
вы́-сты-ть, *v.p.,* вы-сты-ва́ть, *v.i.,* to become cool.
за-сты́-ть, за-сты́-н-уть, *v.p.,* за-сты-ва́ть, *v.i.,* to get cold; jelly. Кровь засты́ла в жи́лах, (*fig.*), the blood curdled in my veins.
о-сты́-ть, о-сты́-н-уть, *v.p.,* о-сты-ва́ть, *v.i.,* to get cold, cool off. У вас чай совсе́м осты́л, your tea is quite cold. Гнев его́ ещё не осты́л, his anger has not cooled yet. О-сты́-вший, *adj.,* *part. act. past,* cooled. О. суп, soup which has cooled!
про-сты́-ть, про-сты́-н-уть, *v.p.,* про-сты-ва́ть, *v.i.,* (*colloq.*), to get, grow cold, be chilled. Обе́д просты́л, the dinner has become cold. Часово́й просты́л на моро́зе, the sentinel froze out in the cold. Любо́вь просты́ла, my love has cooled. След просты́л, there are no traces left.
по-сты́-л-еть, *v.i.,* о-по-сты́-л-еть, *v.p.,* (*folk*), to grow tired of something; begin to dislike, hate. Всё мне опосты́ле-ло здесь, I am sick and tired of everything here. По-сты́-лый, *adj.,* hated, repellent. П. челове́к, hated man. О-по-сты́-левший, *adj., part. act. past,* who has become hated. Она́ бро́сила опосты́левшего мýжа, she left her husband who had become hateful to her.

СТЫД-, СТЫЖ-, SHAME, DISGRACE

стыд, *n.m.,* shame; disgrace. Это про́сто стыд! This is simply a disgrace! Сгоре́ть от стыда́, to burn with shame. Стыд-ли́вый, *adj.,* modest, shy, timid. Стыд-ли́вость, *n.f.,* modesty, shyness, bashfulness. Сты́д-но, *adv.,* shamefully. Это о́чень с., this is shameful. Сты́д-но! Shame! Мне с. за тебя́, I'm ashamed of you. Бес-сты́д-ник, *n.m.,* бес-сты́д-ница, *n.f.,* shameless person.

Ах, ты б.! You shameless creature! Бес-сты́д-ный, *adj.,* shameless. Это б. посту́пок, this is a shameful act. Бес-сты́д-но, *adv.,* shamelessly. Они́ б. лгут наро́ду, they lie shamelessly to the nation. Бес-сты́д-ство, *n.n.,* shamelessness. У них хвати́ло бесстыд-ства, they had the gall to do it.
стыд-и́ть, *v.i.,* по-стыд-и́ть, *v.p.,* + *acc.,* to shame, put to shame. Мать стыди́ла дочь за лень, the mother shamed her daughter for her laziness. Стыд-и́ть-ся, *v.i.,* по-стыд-и́ть-ся, *v.p.,* + *gen.,* to feel, be ashamed. Он стыди́лся показа́ться на глаза́, he was ashamed to appear.
за-стыд-и́ть, *v.p.,* + *acc.,* to confuse. Совсе́м застыди́ли ребёнка, they completely confused the child. За-стыд-и́ть-ся, *v.p.r.,* to blush; become shy, confused. Она́ застыди́лась, she blushed in confusion.
при-стыд-и́ть *v.p.,* при-стыж-а́ть, *v.i.,* + *acc.,* to put to shame. П. его́ за дурно́й посту́пок, he put him to shame for a bad action. При-стыж-енный, *adj., part. pass. past,* ashamed. Он ушёл п., he went out ashamed.
у-стыд-и́ть, *v.p.,* у-стыж-а́ть, *v.i.,* + *acc.,* to put to shame. У. лжеца́, to shame a liar. У-стыд-и́ть-ся, *v.p.r.,* to become ashamed. Он сам устыди́лся того́, что он сде́лал, he himself became ashamed of what he had done.

СТУК-, СТУЧ-, KNOCK, KNOCKING

стук, *n.m.,* knock. Разда́лся стук в дверь, a knock was heard at the door. Без сту́ка не входи́ть! Do not enter without knocking! Сту́к-алка, *n.f.,* a card game; knock-knock. Игра́ете-ли вы в сту́калку? Do you play knock-knock (a child's game)? Стук-отня́, *n.f.,* clatter, knocking, noise. В сосе́дней кварти́ре подняла́сь стукотня́, a clatter was heard in the adjacent apartment.
стýк-ну-ть, *v.p.,* стýк-ать, *v.i.,* to knock, hammer. Стýкнуть кулако́м по столу́, to bang one's fist on the table. Емý стýкнуло со́рок лет (*colloq.*), he is past forty. Стýк-нуть-ся, *v.p.r.,* стýк-ать-ся, *v.i.r.,* + *instr.,* об + *acc.,* to knock against. Он стýкнулся голово́й об сте́ну, he knocked his head against the wall.
вы́-стук-ать, *v.p.,* вы-стýк-ивать, *v.i.,* + *acc.,* to knock; subject to percussion. Ареста́нт вы́стукал це́лую фра́зу, the prisoner tapped out a whole sentence (on the wall). До́ктор выстýкивает ка́ждого больно́го, the doctor taps

each patient on the chest. Вы-стук-ивание, *п.п.*, (*med.*), percussion.

за-сту́к-ать, *v.p.,* + *acc.,* (*colloq.*), to catch in a given place. Его застука́ли на ме́сте преступле́ния, they caught him in the act.

от-сту́к-ать, *v.p.,* от-сту́к-ивать, *v.i.,* + *acc.,* to give a certain number of taps; tick. Телеграфи́ст отсту́кал телегра́мму, the telegraph operator ticked out a telegram.

пере-сту́к-нуть-ся, *v.p.r.,* пере-сту́к-ивать-ся, *v.i.r.,* to knock to each other. Заключённые пересту́кивались ме́жду собо́й, the prisoners tapped out messages to each other.

по-сту́к-ать, *v.p.,* по-сту́к-ивать, *v.i.,* to knock. Я посту́кал не́сколько раз в дверь, но никто́ не отозва́лся, I knocked several times on the door, but no one answered. По-сту́к-ать-ся, *v.i.r.,* to butt. Бара́ны посту́кались лба́ми, the rams butted each other. По-сту́к-ивание, *п.п.,* light knocking, tapping. Раздало́сь лёгкое п., a slight knocking was heard.

про-сту́к-ать, *v.p.,* про-сту́к-ивать, *v.i.,* (*colloq.*), to examine by auscultation. Врач просту́кал больно́му грудь, the doctor examined the patient's chest by auscultation.

при-сту́к-нуть, *v.p.,* при-сту́к-ивать, *v.i.,* to tap dance. П. каблука́ми, to tap with one's heels.

стуч-а́ть, *v.i.,* to knock, hammer. Стучи́т равноме́рно ма́ятник часо́в, the pendulum ticks regularly. В лесу́ стуча́ли дровосе́ки, in the woods could be heard the chopping of the lumberjacks. Стуч-а́ть-ся, *v.i.r.,* to knock. С. в дверь, to knock on a door. До-стуч-а́ть-ся, *v.p.r.,* to knock until one is heard. Наконе́ц, он достуча́лся, he knocked until finally they opened the door.

за-стуч-а́ть, *v.p.,* to start knocking, hammering. Он застуча́л кулака́ми в дверь, he began to pound on the door with his fists.

на-стуч-а́ть, *v.p.,* to make a lot of noise. Вот настуча́л свои́ми сапога́ми - да́же голова́ разболе́лась (*colloq.*), he made so much noise with his boots that my head has begun to ache.

по-стуч-а́ть, *v.p.,* по-стуч-а́ть-ся, *v.p.r.,* to knock. Постучи́ в дверь погро́мче, knock louder. Кто́-то постуча́лся к нам, someone has knocked at our door.

про-стуч-а́ть, *v.p.,* to rumble along through, knock for a period of time. По у́лице простуча́ла теле́га, a cart rumbled through the streets.

СУД-, СУЖ-, СУЖД-, JUDGMENT

суд, *п.m.,* court, justice, trial. Наро́дный суд, (*recent*), people's court. С. прися́жных, jury, trial by jury. Уголо́вный суд, criminal court. Стра́шный Суд, Last Judgment. На него́ по́дали в суд, they took him to court. Без суда́ и сле́дствия, without trial or investigation. На нет и суда́ нет, (*saying*), you can't squeeze blood from a stone. Быть под судо́м, to be on trial. На него́ нет ни суда́, ни распра́вы, (*saying*), there is no way of revenging oneself on him. Иска́ть судо́м, to prosecute. Суд-е́бник, *п.m.,* code of law. Суд-е́бный, *adj.,* legal; pertaining to justice. С. сле́дователь, examining magistrate. С. при́став, (*obs.*), bailiff. Суде́бным поря́дком, in legal form. С-ая оши́бка, judicial error. Суд-и́лище, *п.п.,* (*Ch.-Sl.*), see суд. Суд-и́мость, *n.f.,* conviction. Спра́вка о суди́мости, information about earlier convictions. Суд-о-произво́дство, *п.п.,* law proceedings, legal procedure. Суд-о-устро́йство, *п.п.,* judicial system.

суд-ь-я́, *п.m.,* judge. Мирово́й с., (*pre-Rev.*), justice of the peace. С. его́ оправда́л, the judge acquitted him. Суд-е́йский, *adj.,* judicial. С-ая слу́жба, service as a judge.

суд-ь-б-а́, (суд-ь-би́на, *obs.*), *n.f.,* fate, destiny, lot. Такова́ моя́ с., Such is my fate! От судьбы́ уйдёшь, (*prov.*), you cannot escape your fate. Судьбы́ наро́дов, the fortunes of nations. Каки́ми судьба́ми ты здесь? (*idiom.*), What brings you here?

суд-и́-ть, суж-у́, *v.i.,* + *acc.,* о + *prep.,* to try, judge, criticize, consider. Его́ суди́ли уголо́вным судо́м, he was tried in criminal court. Не суди́те, да не суди́мы бу́дете, (*Bib.*), Judge not that you be not judged. Не суди́те так стро́го, don't judge so severely. Наско́лько я могу́ с., as far as I can see. Суд-и́ть-ся, *v.i.,* с + *instr.,* to be sued; be judged, tried. Он лю́бит суди́ться с ка́ждым, (*colloq.*), he is contentious, litigious. Су́ж-еный, *п.m.,* (*obs.*), fiancé. Су́женого и на коне́ не объе́дешь, (*saying*), you cannot avoid the man you are to marry. Сужд-е́ние, *п.п.,* judgment, opinion; pronouncement. Пра́вильное с., sound reasoning. Выска́зывать с., to pass judgment. Предвзя́тое с., preconceived judgment, opinion.

за-суд-и́ть, *v.p.,* за-су́ж-ивать, *v.i.,* + *acc.,* to condemn, sentence. Его́ засуди́ли на 10 лет тюрьмы́, he has been condemned to prison for ten years.

о-суд-и́ть, *v.p.*, о-сужд-а́ть, *v.i.*, + *acc.*, за + *acc.*, to blame, censure, condemn, sentence. Он осужда́л её за расточи́тельность, he blamed her for her extravagance. О-сужд-е́ние, *n.n.*, blame, censure, conviction.

об-суд-и́ть, *v.p.*, об-сужд-а́ть, *v.i.*, + *acc.*, to consider, discuss. О. ва́жный вопро́с, to discuss an important matter. Об-сужд-е́ние, *n.n.*, discussion. Предлага́ть на о., to open for discussion. Предме́т обсужде́ния, the point discussed, under discussion.

при-суд-и́ть, *v.p.*, при-сужд-а́ть, *v.i.*, + *accus.*, к + *dat.*, to adjudge, award; condemn; sentence. П. пре́мию, to award a prize. П. сте́пень до́ктора, to confer a doctorate upon someone. П-к штра́фу, to sentence to pay a fine. Присужд-е́ние, *n.n.*, adjudgment, awarding. П. Но́белевских пре́мий, awarding of Nobel prizes.

рас-суд-и́ть, *v.p.*, рас-сужд-а́ть, *v.i.*, + *acc.*, о + *prep.*, to judge. Рассуди́те нас, judge between us. Об э́том не́чего мно́го рассужда́ть, there is not much to argue about this. Рас-сужд-е́ние, *n.n.*, reasoning, judgment, consideration; argumentation. Пусти́ться в р., to debate. Без рассужде́ний, without argument. Рас-суд-и́тельный, *adj.*, reasonable, rational, sensible. Рас-су́д-ительность, *n.f.*, sound sense, sagacity, sound judgment. Рас-суд-и́тельно, *adv.*, rationally, reasonably, sensibly. Суди́ть р., to judge sensibly. Рас-су́д-ок, *n.m.*, reason, mind. Потеря́ть р., to lose one's reasoning power, one's reason. Рас-су́д-очный, *adj.*, rational. Р. челове́к, rationalist. Рас-су́д-очность, *n.f.*, rationality. Рас-су́д-очно, *adv.*, rationally.

без-рас-су́д-ный, *adj.*, reckless, rash, irrational. Б. посту́пок, irrational action. Без-рас-су́д-но, *adv.*, rashly recklessly, irrationally. Нельзя́ поступа́ть так б., you must not be so rash. Без-рас-су́д-ство, *n.n.*, recklessness, rashness, irrationality.

СУК-, СУЧ-, SPINNING, TWISTING

сук-но́, *n.n.*, cloth. С. из чи́стой ше́рсти, pure wool cloth. Положи́ть де́ло под с., (*fig.*), to place a case in the inactive file. На по́лках лежа́ли ра́зные су́кна, various cloths lay on the shelves. Сук-о́нка, *n.f.*, piece of cloth; rag. Башмаки́ чи́стят щёткой и суко́нкой, shoes are cleaned with a brush and cloth. Сук-о́нный, *adj.*, of cloth. С. това́р, cloth goods. У него́ с. язы́к, (*fig.*), he has an awkward writing style. Сук-о́нщик,

n.m., cloth weaver, cloth merchant; draper.

суч-и́ть, *v.i.*, + *acc.*, to twist, spin. С. ни́тку, to spin, twist thread. Дитя́ сучи́ло во сне но́жками, the sleeping child twisted its feet. Суч-и́ть-ся, *v.i.r.*, из + *gen.*, to be twisted, spun. Кана́ты суча́тся из пеньки́, ropes are made of twisted hemp. Суч-е́ние, *n.n.*, twisting, spinning. Суч-и́льщик, *n.m.*, twister, spinner. С. верёвок, rope maker.

с-суч-и́ть, *v.p.*, с-су́ч-ивать, *v.i.*, + *acc.*, to twist, spin together. Ссучи́ть все ни́тки, to spin all the threads together. Ссу́чивать шерсть с шёлком, to spin wool with silk. С-суч-и́ть-ся, *v.p.r.*, с-су́ч-ивать-ся, *v.i.r.*, to be spun. Шёлк легко́ ссу́чивается с ше́рстью, silk is easily spun with wool.

рас-суч-и́ть, *v.p.*, рас-су́ч-ивать, *v.i.*, + *acc.*, to untwist, untwine. Р. верёвки, to untwist ropes. Рас-суч-и́ть-ся, *v.p.r.*, рас-су́ч-ивать-ся, *v.i.r.*, to untwine, untwist, be untwined, untwisted. Верёвка рассучи́лась, the rope untwisted, became untwined. Рас-су́ч-ивание, *n.n.*, untwining, untwisting.

за-суч-и́ть, *v.p.*, за-су́ч-ивать, *v.i.*, to begin to twist, twine; roll up, tuck. З. рукава́, to roll up one's sleeves. За-суч-и́ть-ся, *v.p.r.*, за-су́ч-ивать-ся, *v.i.r.*, to roll; tuck in; be twisted. Вот засучу́сь и приму́сь за рабо́ту, I will roll up my sleeves and get to work.

Т

ТА-, ТАЙ-, SECRET

та-и́-ть, *v.i.*, + *acc.*, от + *gen.*, to conceal, hide, secrete. Вы та́йте что́-то от меня́, you are concealing something from me. Он таи́т зло́бу про́тив меня́, he bears a grudge against me. Не́чего греха́ таи́ть, there is no use hiding it. Та-и́ть-ся, *v.i.r.*, от + *gen.*, to hide, conceal oneself. Он таи́тся от всех, he is hiding from everybody. Та-и́нственный, *adj.*, mysterious, secret. Т-ое де́ло, mysterious affair. Та-и́нственность, *n.f.*, secrecy, mysteriousness. Всё полно́ таи́нственности, all this is full of mystery. Та-и́нственно, *adv.*, secretly, mysteriously.

та́й-на, *n.f.*, secret; mystery. Сохрани́ть та́йну, to keep the secret. Де́лать т. из чего́-либо, to make a mystery of something. Та́йны приро́ды, the secrets of nature. Тай-ко́м, *adv.*, secretly, surreptitiously. Тай-ни́к, *n.m.*, secret hiding place; recess. Скры́тые тайники́, the hidden recesses. Та́й-ный, *adj.*, secret, mysterious. И́ми был заключён т. договóр, they concluded a secret treaty. Тáйные прóиски врагóв, underhand dealings of the enemy. Тáй-но, *adv.*, secretly.

за-та-йть, *v.p.,* за-тá-ивать, *v.i.,* + *acc.,* to conceal, hide. Затайть дыхáние, to hold one's breath. За-та-ённый, *adj., part. pass. past,* concealed. З-ое недовóльство, secret resentment. За-тайвший, *adj., part. act. past,* (he) who, (that) which has concealed. Человéк, з. злóбу, опáснее открытого врагá, a man with a secret resentment is more dangerous than an open enemy. За-та-йть-ся, *v.p.r.,* за-тá-ивать-ся, *v.i.r.,* в + *acc.,* to be concealed. Мáльчик затайлся за дивáном, the boy hid behind the sofa. Он глубокó затайлся в сáмом себé, he retreated into himself.

при-та-йть, *v.p.,* + *acc.,* to conceal. П. дыхáние, to hold one's breath. При-та-йть-ся, *v.p.r.,* to hide, conceal oneself; keep quiet, silent. В кустáх притайлась змея, a snake hid in the brush.

у-та-йть, *v.p.,* у-тá-ивать, *v.i.,* + *acc.,* to conceal, hide, keep secret. Он утайл от нас свою болéзнь, he concealed his illness from us. У-та-йть-ся, *v.p.r.,* у-тá-ивать-ся, *v.i.r.,* от + *gen.,* to be concealed, conceal oneself. У-тá-ивание, *n.n.,* concealment, suppression. У-тáй-ка, *n.f.,* concealment, *in expression:* Подсудймый рассказáл всё без утáйки, the accused told everything without concealing anything.

ТАСК-, ТАЩ-, DRAUGHT, TRACTION

таск-áть, *v.i. indet.,* + *acc.,* to pull, draw, pilfer. Т. брёвна из рекй, to drag logs out of the river. Т. для другóго каштáны из огня, (*fig.*), to pull chestnuts out of the fire for somebody else. Он дóлго таскáл у меня дéньги, (*colloq.*), he pilfered money from me for a long time. Таск-áть-ся, *v.i.r.,* to loiter. Где он таскáется по ночáм? (*slang*), Where does he hang out at night? Таск-áние, *n.n.,* dragging, trailing, pulling. Т. из кармáнов, pickpocketing.

тащ-йть, *v.i.det.,* + *acc.,* to carry along, drag. Старйк éле тáщит нóги, the old man can barely drag his feet along. Тащ-йть-ся, *v.i.r.,* (*colloq.*), to lag, drag, crawl. Я éле тащýсь от устáлости, I am so tired I can hardly drag myself.

в-тащ-йть, *v.p.,* в-тáск-ивать, *v.i.,* + *acc.,* to drag in, pull in. Лóшадь с трудóм втащйла телéгу нá гору, the horse pulled the cart up the hill with difficulty. В-тáск-ивать-ся, *v.i.r.,* в-тащ-йть-ся, *v.p.r.,* to trail, drag oneself in. Он éле втащйлся на пятый этáж, he barely dragged himself up to the fifth floor.

вы-тащ-йть, *v.p.,* вы-тáск-ивать, *v.i.,* + *acc.,* из + *gen.,* to draw out, pull out, drag out, extract. В гвоздь, drag out, extract. В. гвоздь из стены, to pull the nail out of the wall.

вы-таск-áть, *v.p.,* + *acc.,* (*colloq.*), to pull out. Он вытаскал егó зá волосы, he pulled him out by the hair.

до-тащ-йть, *v.p.,* до-тáск-ивать, *v.i.,* + *acc.,* до + *gen.,* to pull up to, drag up to. Мне не дотащйть этого мешкá до дóму, I cannot drag this bag home. До-тащ-йть-ся, *v.p.r.,* до-тáск-ивать-ся, *v.i.r.,* до + *gen.,* to drag oneself up to. Рáненый не мог дотащйться до перевязочного пýнкта, the wounded man could not drag himself as far as the dressing station.

за-тащ-йть, *v.p.,* за-тáск-ивать, *v.i.,* + *acc.,* to drag in, pull in. Бандйты затащйли егó в подвáл и убйли, the bandits dragged him into the cellar and murdered him. Мыши затáскивают сыр в нóры, the mice drag cheese into their holes.

за-таск-áть, *v.p.,* + *acc.,* to wear out, bedraggle. За-тáск-анный, *adj., part. pass. past,* bedraggled. Это з-ая фрáза, this is a banal phrase. Костюм был затáскан, the suit was all bedraggled. За-тащ-йть-ся, *v.p.r.,* за-тáск-ивать-ся, *v.i.r.,* (*colloq.*), to disappear. Кудá это он затащйлся с сáмого утрá? (*colloq.*), Where has he been all morning? Объéдки затáскиваются крысами в нóры, the scraps are dragged into holes by the rats. За-таск-áть-ся, *v.p.r.,* to become bedraggled. Моё пальтó совсéм затаскáлось, my overcoat is completely bedraggled.

ис-таск-áть, *v.p.,* ис-тáск-ивать, *v.i.,* + *acc.,* to wear out. Ис-тáск-анный, *adj., part. pass. past,* worn out, dissipated. И-ое лицó, dissipated face. Ис-таск-áть-ся, *v.p.r.,* to wear out; become dissipated. Сапогй истаскáлись за полгóда, the boots wore out in half a year. От пьянства он совершéнно истаскáлся к трйдцати годáм, at thirty he was completely worn out from drinking.

на-тащ-йть, *v.p.,* на-тáск-ивать, *v.i.,* + *gen.,* to bring in, drag in quantity. Он натащйл дров, he brought in a great deal of firewood.

на-таск-áть, *v.p.,* на-тáск-ивать, *v.i.,* + *acc.,* (*colloq.*), to train, coach. Н. ученикá к экзáмену, to coach a pupil for the examination.

от-тащ-и́ть, *v.p.,* от-та́ск-ивать, *v.i.,* + *acc.,* to drag away, pull away, draw away. Они́ с больши́м трудо́м оттащи́ли его́ в сто́рону, they dragged him aside with great difficulty.

от-таск-а́ть, *v.p.,* + *acc.,* (*colloq.*), to pull. О. за́ волосы, to shake (a person) up by the hair.

пере-тащ-и́ть, *v.p.,* пере-та́ск-ивать, *v.i.,* + *acc.,* to drag over, move over. П. ме́бель на но́вую кварти́ру, to move furniture into a new apartment. Переതാск-а́ть, *v.p.,* + *acc.* (*colloq.*), to pilfer.

по-тащ-и́ть, *v.p.,* тащ-и́ть, *v.i.,* + *acc.,* to drag. Его́ потащи́ли в мили́цию, they dragged him to the police station.

по-таск-а́ть, *v.p.,* по-та́ск-ивать, *v.i.,* + *acc.,* to filch, pilfer. Он пота́скивает и подворо́вывает, (*colloq.*), he filches and pilfers. По-тащ-и́ть-ся, *v.p.r.,* (*colloq.*), to drag oneself. Куда́ вы потащи́лись в таку́ю плоху́ю пого́ду? Where are you going in such bad weather?

при-тащ-и́ть, *v.p.,* при-та́ск-ивать, *v.i.,* + *acc.,* to bring in, drag in. Его́ притащи́ли мертве́цки пья́ным, he was brought in dead drunk. При-тащ-и́ть-ся, *v.p.r.,* при-та́ск-ивать-ся *v.i.r.,* to drag oneself. Он едва́ притащи́лся домо́й, he barely dragged himself home.

про-тащ-и́ть, *v.p.,* про-та́ск-ивать, *v.i.,* + *acc.,* через + *acc.,* to drag through, pull through. П. сунду́к сквозь две́ри, to drag a trunk through the door. Прота́скивать свои́х люде́й в чужи́е организа́ции, (*recent*), to infiltrate one's men into other organizations.

рас-тащ-и́ть, *v.p.,* рас-та́ск-ать, *v.p.,* рас-та́ск-ивать, *v.i.,* + *acc.,* to drag apart, pull apart, asunder; separate; steal little by little, pilfer. Пожа́рные растащи́ли горя́щий дом, the firemen tore down the house. Они́ растащи́ли деру́щихся ма́льчиков, they separated the fighting boys. Растащи́ли все дрова́, they pilfered all the firewood. Рас-та́щ-енный *adj., part. pass. past,* pilfered. Все их ве́щи бы́ли раста́щены, all their things were stolen.

с-тащ-и́ть, *v.p.,* с-та́ск-ивать, *v.i.,* + *acc.,* с + *gen.,* to drag, pull together; drag, pull off; steal, pinch. Он ста́скивает всё в одно́ ме́сто, he is dragging everything into one place. Стащи́те с меня́ сапоги́, pull my boots off. У неё кто́-то стащи́л су́мку, (*colloq.*), someone stole her handbag.

у-тащ-и́ть, *v.p.,* у-та́ск-ивать, *v.i.,* + *acc.,* to drag away, carry away; steal. Орёл утащи́л ягнёнка, the eagle snatched, carried off a lamb.

ТВАР-, ТВОР-, CREATION

твар-ь, *n.f.,* creature. Бо́жьи тва́ри, God's creatures.

твор-и́ть, *v.i.,* со-твор-и́ть, *v.p.,* + *acc.,* to create; do, perform. Бог твори́л мир 6 дней, God took six days to create the world. (*Bib.*) Этот до́ктор твори́т чудеса́, this doctor performs wonders. Твор-и́ть-ся, *v.i.r.,* to be created; done; go on. Что там твори́тся? (*colloq.*), What's going on there? What's all this about? В приро́де беспреста́нно твори́тся но́вая жизнь, new life is constantly being created in nature. Творе́ние, *n.n.,* creation, creating; creature; work. Это его́ т., this is his creation. Твор-е́ц, *n.m.,* creator; author. Т. ми́ра, the Creator. Пу́шкин - творе́ц ру́сской национа́льной литерату́ры, Pushkin is the creator of Russian national literature. Твор-и́ло, *n.n.,* lime pit, mortar pit. Твор-и́тельный, *adj.,* (*gram.*), instrumental. Т. паде́ж, instrumental case. Тво́р-ческий, *adj.,* creative. Т. ге́ний Пу́шкина, the creative genius of Pushkin. Твор-чество, *n.n.,* creation, creative work; creative power, genius. Т. и жизнь худо́жника всегда́ тесно свя́заны, the creative work and the life of an artist are always closely connected.

вы-твор-я́ть, *v.i.,* + *acc.,* (*colloq.*), to be up to nonsense. Что вы вытворя́ете, здесь? What are you up to? Он ма́стер вытворя́ть вся́кие шу́тки, he is a past master at tricks.

за-твор-и́ть, *v.p.,* за-твор-я́ть, *v.i.,* + *acc.,* to shut, close. Затвори́те две́ри! Please close the door! Не затворя́йте о́кон! Don't close the windows! За-твор-и́ть-ся, *v.p.r.,* за-твор-я́ть-ся, *v.i.r.,* to be shut, be closed; become a recluse, lock oneself up. От ве́тра окно́ затвори́лось, the windows were slammed shut by the wind. Дверь пло́хо затворя́ется, this door does not close properly. Он затвори́лся в своём до́ме и никуда́ не пока́зывается, he locked himself up in his house and refuses to come out; he has become a recluse. Затвори́ться в монасты́рь, to enter a monastery. За-тво́р, *n.m.,* bolt, bar, lock; seclusion in a monastery. З. у воро́т, gate bolt. З. у ружья́, gun lock, rifle lock. З. у шлю́за, water gate, floodgate. Монасты́рский з., seclusion in a monastery, monastic seclusion. За-тво́р-ник, *n.m.,* за-тво́р-ница, *n.f.,* hermit; anchorite. За-тво́р-ничество, *n.n.,* hermitage; seclusion. За-тво́р-нический, *adj.,* solitary, secluded, hermitic.

на-твор-и́ть, *v.p.,* + *acc.,* to do much damage. Урага́н натвори́л мно́го бед, the hurricane caused much damage. Что ты натвори́л здесь? (*colloq.*), Whatever have you done here?

о-твор-и́ть, *v.p.,* о-твор-я́ть, *v.i.,* + *acc.,* to open. О. дверь, to open a door. О-твор-я́йте воро́та, open the gates. О-твор-и́ть-ся, *v.p.r.,* о-твор-я́ть-ся, *v.i.r.,* to be opened; open. От ве́тра две́ри отвори́лись на́стежь, the doors were blown wide open by the wind. Сунду́к не отворя́ется без ключа́, the trunk does not open without a key.

по-твóр-ств-ова-ть, *v.i.,* + *dat.,* to connive; show too much indulgence towards. П. ша́лостям (ле́ни), to exhibit indulgence towards mischievousness (laziness). По-твóр-ство, *n.n.,* connivance; indulgence. По-твóр-щик, *n.m.,* one who connives.

пре-твор-и́ть, *v.p.,* пре-твор-я́ть, *v.i.,* + *acc.,* to transform. Христо́с претвори́л во́ду в вино́, (*Bib.*), Christ changed the water into wine. Пре-твор-и́ть-ся, *v.p.r.,* пре-твор-я́ть-ся, *v.i.r.,* в + *acc.,* to be transformed. В рука́х ску́льптора гли́на претвори́лась в ста́тую, in the hands of the sculptor the clay became transformed into a statue. Пре-твор-е́ние, *n.n.,* transformation, change.

при-о-твор-и́ть, *v.p.,* при-о-твор-я́ть, *v.i.,* + *acc.,* to open slightly. Приотвори́ окно́, Open the window a little. При-о-твор-и́ть-ся, *v.p.r.,* при-о-твор-я́ть-ся, *v.i.r.,* to open slightly. Дверь приотвори́лась, the door opened slightly.

при-твор-и́ть, *v.p.,* при-твор-я́ть, *v.i.,* + *acc.,* to shut, close a bit (a door or window on hinges). Я притвори́л дверь, I closed the door a bit. Я притвори́л окно́, что́бы не ду́ло, I closed the window a bit, so that there would be no draft. При-твор-и́ть-ся, *v.p.r.,* при-твор-я́ть-ся, *v.i.r,* to be shut, closed; + *instr.,* to feign, pretend, simulate. Дверь пло́тно притворя́ется, the door closes tightly. Он притвори́л-ся больны́м, he feigned illness. При-твóр, *n.m.,* narthex of a church. При-твóр-ность, *n.f.,* hypocrisy, falseness. При-твóр-ный, *adj.,* feigned, pretended, simulated; hypocritical. П-ая улы́бка, hypocritical smile. При-твóр-но, *adv.,* hypocritically, falsely.

при-твóр-ств-ова-ть, *v.i.iter.,* to feign, pretend, simulate. Ты уме́ешь п. в любви́, You know how to feign love. При-твóр-ство, *n.n.,* dissimulation, hypocrisy. Всё э́то не что ино́е, как п.,

this is nothing but pretense. При-твóр-щик, *v.p.,* при-твóр-щица, *n.f.,* hypocrite. Она́ больша́я п., she knows how to pretend.

рас-твор-и́ть, *v.p.,* рас-твор-я́ть, *v.i.,* + *acc.,* в + *prep.,* to dissolve; open wide. Я раствори́л окно́, I opened the window wide. Они́ раствори́ли са́хар в воде́, they dissolved sugar in water. Рас-твор-и́ть-ся, *v.p.r.,* рас-твор-я́ть-ся, *v.i.r.,* в + *prep.,* to be opened wide; be dissolved, dissolve. Две́ри раствори́лись, и он вошёл, the doors opened wide and he came in. Мел не растворя́ется в воде́, chalk does not dissolve in water. Рас-твóр, *n.m.,* solution. 5 % р. соляно́й кислоты́, a five percent solution of hydrochloric acid. Рас-твор-е́ние, *n.n.,* opening; dissolving, diluting. Рас-твор-и́мый, *adj.,* soluble. Рас-твор-и́мость, *n.f.,* solubility. Не-рас-твор-и́мый, *adj.,* insoluble. Не-рас-твор-и́мость, *n.f.,* insolubility.

со-твор-и́ть, *v.p.,* со-твор-я́ть, *v.i.,* + *acc.,* to create, make, do. В шесто́й день Бог сотвори́л челове́ка, (*Bib.*), on the sixth day God created man. Не сотвори́ себе́ куми́ра, (*Bib.*), thou shalt not make unto thee any graven image. Со-твор-е́ние, *n.n.,* creation. С. ми́ра, the creation of the world.

с-твор-и́ть, *v.p.,* с-твор-я́ть, *v.i.,* + *acc.,* to close double doors; place beacons in line. С. два маяка́ в оди́н свет, to place two beacons in line. С-твор-и́ть-ся, *v.p.r.,* с-твор-я́ть-ся, *v.i.r.,* to be closed (*as* double doors); be placed in line (*as* beacons). Створи́лись о́бе полови́ны двере́й, the double doors closed. Створи́лись два огня́ маяка́, the two beacons came into line. С-твор, *n.m.,* с-твóр-ка, *n.f.,* leaf of a folding door. Загреме́ли ство́ры и воро́та откры́лись, the gates clattered and opened. Парохо́ды вхо́дят в порт по ство́ру двух маяко́в, ships enter harbors guided by the leading line of beacons. С-твóр-чатый, *adj.,* folding. С-ые две́ри, folding doors. С-ая ра́ковина, two-valved shell.

твор-óг, *n.m.,* curd(s), cream cheese. Ватру́шки де́лаются с творого́м и са́харом, cheesecake is made with cream cheese and sugar.

твор-óж-ить-ся, *v.p.r.,* с-твор-óж-ить-ся, *v.i.r.,* от + *gen.,* to curdle, clot. От жары́ молоко́ створо́жилось, the milk curdled from the heat. Твор-óж-истый, *adj.,* clotted, clotty. Твор-óж-ник, *n.m.,* curd fritter. Твор-óж-ный, *adj.,* made of curds. Э́то о́чень вку́сное т-ое блю́до, this is a delicious dish of curds.

ТВЕРД-, ТВЕРЖ-, ТВЕРЖД-, HARDNESS

тверд-é-ть, *v.i.,* to harden, become hard. От хо́лода по́чва твердéет, the ground hardens from the cold. Твёрд-ый, *adj.,* hard, firm. Грани́т-т. ка́мень, granite is a hard stone. Т-ая во́ля, firm will. Т-ая цена́, controlled price. Твёрж-е, *adj. and adv. comp.,* firmer; more firmly. Твёрд-о, *adv.,* firmly. Он т. стои́т на своём сло́ве, he stands firmly by his word. Я твёрдо реши́л сде́лать э́то, I have firmly decided to do this. Тверд-о-ло́бый, *adj.,* thick-skulled, thick-witted. Твёрд-ость, *n.f.,* hardness, solidity, firmness. Т. хара́ктера, firmness of character. Тверд-ы́ня, *n.f.,* stronghold, citadel. В старину́ крéпости называ́лись тверды́нями, in olden days fortresses were called citadels. Тверд-ь, *n.f.,* (*Ch.-Sl.*), firmament. Т. небéсная, heavenly firmament.

за-тверд-éть, *v.p.,* за-тверд-ева́ть, *v.i.,* to harden, set. Бето́н бы́стро затвердева́ет, concrete hardens rapidly. За-тверд-éвший, *adj., part. pass. past,* hardened; callous. За-тверд-éлый, *adj.,* hardened, firm. З-ая о́пухоль, (*med.*), hard tumor. За-тверд-éлость, *n.f.,* hardness; callus; callosity. За-тверд-éние, *n.n.,* hardening.

о-тверд-éть, *v.p.,* о-тверд-ева́ть, *v.i.,* to become hard, callous. У него́ от огорчéний отвердéло сéрдце, (*fig.*), sorrows have made him hard-hearted, callous. О-тверд-éлость, *n.f., see* затвердéлость. О-тверд-éние, *n.n.,* see затвердéние.

тверд-и́ть, тверж-у́, *v.i.,* + *acc.,* to repeat over and over again. "Уж ско́лько раз тверди́ли ми́ру," (*Krylov*), "how frequently has it been repeated to the world." Он всё тверди́т наизу́сть, he recites the whole thing from memory.

вы́-тверд-ить, *v.p.,* вы-тве́рж-ивать, *v.i.,* + *acc.,* to memorize. Он ужé вы́твердил уро́к, he has memorized his lesson.

за-тверд-и́ть, *v.p.,* за-тве́рж-ивать, *v.i.,* *acc.,* to learn by heart, by rote. Он затве́рживает уро́ки, как попуга́й, he learns his lessons like a parrot. Он затверди́л одно́ и то́ же, he kept on repeating the same thing.

под-тверд-и́ть, *v.p.,* под-твержд-а́ть, *v.i.,* + *acc.,* to confirm. П. под прися́гой, to affirm under oath. Собы́тия подтвержда́ют на́ши слова́, events have confirmed our contentions. Под-тверд-и́ть-ся, *v.p.r.,* под-твержд-а́ть-ся, *v.i.r.,* to be confirmed. Всё это подтверди́лось фа́ктами, this was all confirmed by the facts. Под-твержд-éние,

n.n., confirmation; corroboration. Да́йте мне пи́сьменное п., give me a written confirmation.

у-тверд-и́ть *v.p.,* у-твержд-а́ть, *v.i.,* + *acc.,* to affirm, maintain, approve, ratify; consolidate. Я утвержда́ю, что э́то так, I maintain that this is so. Нача́льник не утверди́л распоряжéния подчинённого, the director did not endorse the orders of his subordinate. Свои́м умéнием он утверди́л своё положéние, he consolidated his position by his ingenuity. У-тверд-и́ть-ся, *v.p.r.,* у-твержд-а́ть-ся, *v.i.r.,* to be ratified, approved, confirmed; become consolidated. Догово́р утвержда́ется парла́ментом, a treaty is ratified by parliament. У-тверд-и́тельный, *adj.,* affirmative. У. отвéт, affirmative answer. У-тверд-и́тельно, *adv.,* affirmatively. Отвéтить у., to answer in the affirmative. У-твержд-éние, *n.n.,* affirmation, confirmation, approval, ratification. У. догово́ра бы́ло отло́жено, the ratification of the treaty was postponed.

ТЕК-, ТЁК-, ТЕЧ-, ТОК-, ТОЧ-, FLOW, CURRENT

теч-ь, тек-у́, *v.i.,* to flow, run, stream, leak. Из кра́на течёт вода́, water is running from the faucet. Врéмя течёт, time flies. Ло́дка течёт, the boat is leaking. Тек-у́щий, *adj., part. act. pres.,* flowing, running; current. Вода́, теку́щая с гор, water flowing from the mountains. Т-ие дела́, current business. Т. год, the current year. Тек-у́чий, *adj.,* fluid. Распла́вленный мета́лл - теку́чий, molten metal is fluid. Тек-у́честь, *n.f.,* fluidity. Т. рабо́чей си́лы, fluidity of manpower. Теч-éние, *n.n.,* course, flow, stream, current. Т. реки́, river current. Т. воды́, flow of water. Т. дел, course of affairs. ˙Т. со́лнца (звёзд), course of the sun (of the stars). Всё ула́дится с течéнием врéмени, everything will turn out well in the course of time. В течéние ию́ня, during June. В т. недéли, within a week. В т. го́да, in the course of a year. Плыть по течéнию реки́, to sail, swim with the river's current (downstream). Крово-течéние, *n.n.,* bleeding; haemorrhage.

в-теч-ь, *v.p.,* в-тек-а́ть *v.i.,* в + *acc.,* to flow in, into. Во́лга втека́ет в Каспи́йское Мо́ре, the Volga flows into the Caspian Sea. Вода́ втека́ет в бо́чку, water is flowing into the barrel. В-тек-а́ние, *n.n.,* influx.

вы́-теч-ь, *v.p.,* вы-тек-а́ть, *v.i.,* из *gen.,* to flow out. Река́ вытека́ет из óзера, the river flows out of the lake. Из э́того вытека́ет, что он прав, it follows from this that he is right.

за-те́ч-ь, *v.p.*, за-тек-а́ть, *v.i.*, to flow in; become numb. Сюда́ затека́ет холóдное морскóе тече́ние, the cold sea current flows in here. Водá затеклá в пóгреб, water flowed into the cellar. Я так дóлго сиде́ла, что ногá затеклá, I sat so long that my foot became numb.

ис-те́ч-ь, *v.p.*, ис-тек-áть *v.i.*, + *instr.*, to expire, collapse; bleed; derive, proceed, emanate. Срок истёк 20-ого числа исте́кшего ме́сяца, the time limit expired on the 20th of last month. Рáненый истека́ет крóвью, the wounded man is bleeding. Ис-теч-е́ние, *n.n.*, outflow, expiration, discharge. И. срóка приближáется, the deadline is approaching.

на-те́ч-ь *v.p.*, на-тек-áть, *v.i.*, в + *acc.*, to flow in quantity. В лóдку натеклó мнóго водь́, much water flowed into the boat.

о-те́ч-ь, *v.p.*, о-тек-áть, *v.i.* to swell, to become bloated. Нóги сильнó отеклú, the feet were badly swollen. О-тёк, *n.m.*, (*med.*), dropsy, edema. Отёк лёгких, static pneumonia.

от-те́ч-ь *v.p.*, от-тек-áть, *v.i.*, от + *gen.*, to flow away. Водá ме́дленно оттекáла от бе́рега во вре́мя отлúва, the water gradually receded at ebb tide.

пере-те́ч-ь, *v.p.*, пере-тек-áть, *v.i.*, чéрез + *acc.*, to overflow, brim over. Винó перетеклó че́рез край рю́мки, the wine flowed over the brim of the glass. Водá перетекáла че́рез плотúну, the water was flowing over the dam.

по-те́ч-ь, *v.p.*, по + *dat.*, to begin to flow; flow on. Водá потеклá по стене́, the water flowed along the wall. Потёк, *n.m.*, stain caused by dampness. От сы́рости по стенáм шли потёки, the walls were streaked from dampness.

под-те́ч-ь, *v.p.*, под-тек-áть, *v.i.*, to leak under. Водá подтекáет под фундáмент, there is water seeping under the foundation. Под-тёк, *n.m.*, кров-о-под-тёк, *n.m.*, bruise. Егó те́ло бы́ло покры́то кровоподтёками, his body was covered with bruises.

при-те́ч-ь, *v.p.*, при-тек-áть, *v.i.*, к + *dat.*, to flow to. При-тек-áющий, *adj.*, *part. act. pres.*, flowing to. П-ая водá орошáет поля́, water flowing into the fields irrigates them.

про-те́ч-ь, *v.p.*, про-тек-áть, *v.i.*, по + *dat.*, to flow by, leak through, elapse. Рекá протекáет средú лугóв, the river flows through the meadows. Эта кáдка протекáет, this tub leaks. Вре́мя про-

теклó бы́стро, time flew by quickly. Болéзнь протекáет нормáльно, the illness is taking its normal course.

рас-те́ч-ь-ся, *v.p.r.*, рас-тек-áть-ся, *v.i.r.*, по + *dat.*, to spread; run (*as* liquids). Водá растеклáсь по всему́ пóлу, the water spread all over the floor.

с-те́ч-ь, *v.p.*, с-тек-áть, *v.i.*, с + *gen.*, to flow down, from; flow together. Водá стекáет с кры́ши, the water flows down from the roof. С-тек-áть-ся, *v.p.r.*, to flow down, flow into one. Гóрные потóки стекáлись в одну́ ре́ку, the mountain torrents flowed into one. Тудá стекáлось мнóго нарóду, many people crowded together. С-теч-е́ние, *n.n.*, confluence; crowding. Здесь нахóдится с. двух рек, here is the confluence of the two rivers. Неожúданное с. обстоя́тельств, an unexpected concurrence of circumstances.

у-те́ч-ь, *v.p.*, у-тек-áть, *v.i.*, to flow away; (*colloq.*), run away, escape. Вся водá утеклá, all the water has flowed away. Мнóго водь́ утеклó с тех пор, (*fig.*), much water has flowed under the bridge since then. У-тёк, *n.m.*, *used only in expression*: Он пустúлся на утёк, (*colloq.*), he took to his heels. У-те́ч-ка, *n.f.*, leakage; waste caused by leakage. Рассóхшаяся бóчка далá уте́чку винá, the dried out keg caused the wine to leak out. У. тóка (гáза), leakage of electric current (of gas).

ток, *n.m.*, current; stream. Т. вóздуха, stream of air. Электрúческий т., electric current. Включúть (вы́ключить) т., to switch off (switch on) the electricity. Т. высóкого напряже́ния, high tension wire.

вос-тóк, *n.m.*, east; Orient. Мы уезжáем на в., we are going east. Дáльний Востóк, Far East. Жúтель Востóка, an Oriental. Востóк-о-ве́д, *n.m.*, orientalist. Востóк-о-ве́д-ение, *n.n.*, orientology. Востóк-о-ве́д-ческий, *adj.*, pertaining to orientology. В. институ́т, institute of oriental studies. Вос-тóч-ный, *adj.*, Eastern, Oriental. В-ая Úндия, East Indies. В-ые языкú, Oriental languages.

ис-тóк, *n.m.*, efflux, outflow; source, beginning. И. Вóлги мелковóден, the source of the Volga is shallow. Истóки ру́сской истóрии, the beginnings of Russian history. Ис-тóч-ник, *n.m.*, source, spring, origin. Это сáмый ве́рный и., this is the most authoritative source. Нефтянóй и., gusher, oil well. И. болéзни, cause of an illness.

ис-точ-úть, *v.p.*, ис-точ-áть, *v.i.*, to shed, emit; flow from. И. слёзы, to shed tears. И. благоухáние, to emit a fragrance. Кров-о-точ-и́ть, to bleed. Крово-точ-и́вость, *n.f.*, haemophilia. Ра́на кровоточи́т, the wound is bleeding. Крово-точ-и́вый, *adj.*, bleeding.

от-то́к, *n.m.*, flowing away.

по-то́к, *n.m.*, stream, flow, current. Шу́мный го́рный пото́к, roaring mountain torrent. П. слов, flow of words. Лить пото́ки слёз, to shed a flood of tears. По-то́ч-ный, *adj.*, conveying. П-ая систе́ма произво́дства, assembly line system of production.

при-то́к, *n.m.*, tributary; influx. Ка́ма прито́к Во́лги, the Kama is a tributary of the Volga. П. вкла́дов увели́чился, the influx of deposits has increased.

с-то́к, *n.m.*, flow, drip; drainage. Недоста́точный с. воды́ забола́чивает ме́стность, insufficient drainage makes this place marshy, swampy.

ТЕЛ-, (ТѢЛ-), BODY

те́л-о, *n.n.*, body. Он чу́вствует боль во всём те́ле, his whole body aches. Бедня́жку держа́ли в чёрном те́ле (*fig.*), the poor girl was ill-treated. Твёрдые и жи́дкие тела́, solids and liquids. Тел-о-гре́йка, *n.f.*, a warm sleeveless jacket. Тел-о-движе́ние, *n.n.*, motion; gesture. Его́ телодвиже́ния бы́ли углова́ты, his motions were angular. Тел-о-сложе́ние, *n.n.*, frame, build. Он кре́пкого телосложе́ния, he has a strong frame. Тел-о-храни́тель, *n.m.*, bodyguard. Его́ сопровожда́ет т., he is accompanied by a bodyguard. Тел-е́сность, *n.f.*, corporeality. Тел-е́сный, *adj.*, corporeal, bodily; of the flesh. Трико́ т-ого цве́та, flesh-colored tights. Подве́ргнуть теле́сному наказа́нию, to inflict corporal punishment. Тел-е́сно, *adv.*, corporally, bodily. Он т. соверше́нно здоро́в, he is completely sound in body. Бес-тел-е́сность, *n.f.*, absence of corporeality. Бес-тел-е́сный, *adj.*, incorporeal; immaterial; *see* беспло́тный. Те́л-ь-ник, *n.m.*, sweatshirt worn next to the skin. Те́л-ь-це, *n.n.*, little body; corpuscle. Всё её ма́ленькое т. дрожа́ло, her little body was trembling all over. На-те́л-ь-ный, *adj.*, worn next to the body. Н. крест, a cross which is worn next to the body.

ТЕМ-, ТЁМ-, ТМ-, ТЬМ-, DARKNESS

тем-н-е́-ть, *v.i.*, to become dark, darken. Уже́ темне́ет, пора́ домо́й, it's becoming dark, it's time to go home. Темн-и́ть, *v.i.*, + *acc.*, to darken. Худо́жник темни́т све́тлые пя́тна на

карти́не, the painter is darkening the light spots on the painting. Тем-не́ть-ся, *v.i.r.*, used only in 3d pers. only, to loom. Ту́ча темне́ется вдали́, the storm cloud is looming dark in the distance. Тём-ень, *n.f.*, dark, darkness. Кака́я те́мень! How dark it is! Тем-нота́, *n.f.*, darkness. В тако́й темноте́ мо́жно слома́ть но́гу, in this darkness one can break a leg. Тем-ни́ца, *n.f.*, (*obs.*), prison; jail. Тём-ный, *adj.*, dark, shady; obscure. У него́ тёмное про́шлое, he has a shady past. У него́ т-ая вода́ в глазу́, (*med.*), he has amaurosis. Э́то т-ое ме́сто в его́ кни́ге, this is an obscure place in his book. Тем-но́, *adv.*, darkly, obscurely. Т. хоть глаз вы́коли, (*idiom.*), it's pitch dark. Тём-но-, *a combining form and prefix meaning* dark. Тёмно-багро́вый, dark purple. Тёмно-бу́рый, dark brown. Тёмно-воло́сый, darkhaired. Тёмно-кра́сный, dark red. Тёмно-ру́сый, dark blond. Тёмно-си́ний, dark blue, navy blue.

тьм-а, *n.f.*, darkness; (*fig.*), crowd, great multitude; ignorance. Но́чью была́ кроме́шная тьма, at night there was pitch darkness. "Власть тьмы," "The Power of Darkness." Там цари́т тьма неве́жества, the darkness of ignorance reigns there. На у́лицах была́ тьма тьму́щая наро́ду, (*colloq.*), there was a dense crowd in the streets.

по-тем-н-е́ть, *v.p.*, to become dark, dim. У него́ потемне́ло в глаза́х, he blacked out. По-тем-не́ние, *n.n.*, dimness. П. его́ зре́ния вы́звано боле́знью, the dimness of his eyesight is a consequence of an illness. По-тём-ки, *n.m.pl.*, darkness. Они́ шли в потёмках, they advanced in total darkness. В-по-тьм-а́х, *adv.*, in the dark. Мы просиде́ли в. це́лый час, we sat in darkness for a whole hour.

за-тем-н-и́ть, *v.p.*, за-тем-ня́ть, *v.i.*, + *acc.*, to darken, obscure, dim; black out. Во вре́мя войны́ затемня́ли о́кна, during the war windows were darkened. Э́то затемни́т смысл фра́зы, it will obscure the meaning of the phrase. За-тем-ни́ть-ся, *v.p.r.*, за-тем-ня́ть-ся, *v.i.r.*, to be darkened, obscured. За-тем-не́ние, *n.n.*, darkening, blackout. З. бы́ло обяза́тельно во вре́мя войны́, the blackout was compulsory during the war.

за-тм-и́ть, *v.p.*, за-тм-ева́ть, *v.i.*, + *acc.*, to eclipse, overshadow. Он затми́л всех свои́м умо́м, he overshadowed everyone with his intelligence. За-тм-и́ть-ся, *v.p.r.*, за-тм-ева́ть-ся, *v.i.r.*, to be eclipsed, blacked out, overshadowed, tarnished. Сла́ва певца́ затми́лась, the singer's fame has waned. За-тм-е́ние, *n.n.*, eclipse. З. со́лнца, eclipse of the sun.

ТЕП(Л)-, ТЁП(Л)-, ТАП(Л)-, ТОП(Л)-, WARMTH

теп-л-о́, *n.n.*, warmth, heat. Т. стои́т две неде́ли, we've had two weeks of warm weather. Сего́дня 80° тепла́, the temperature is 80 degrees today. Держа́ть ребёнка в тепле́, to keep a child warm. Теп-л-ота́, *n.f.*, warmth, heat. Т. те́ла подде́рживается пи́щей, the heat of the body is maintained by food. Т. его́ письма́ растро́гала меня́, the warmth of his letter touched me. Теп-л-ы́нь, *n.f.*, (*colloq.*), warm weather. Кака́я т. сего́дня! What a warm day it is today! Теп-л-и́ца, *n.f.*, hothouse, greenhouse. Зимо́й в тепли́це цвели́ ро́зы, roses bloomed in winter in the hothouse.

тёп-л-ый, *adj.*, warm. Вчера́ был т. день, yesterday was a warm day. Т. приём, warm, cordial welcome, reception. Т-ые слова́, sympathetic words. Теп-л-ова́тый, *adj.*, tepid. Этот чай то́лько теплова́т, this tea is only tepid. Теп-л-ово́й, *adj.*, thermal, pertaining to heat. Т-а́я эне́ргия, heat energy. Теп-л-о́, *adv.*, warmly. На дворе́ т., it is warm outdoors. Теп-л-о́, *a combining form meaning* warm, heat. Тепло-во́з, *n.m.*, Diesel locomotive. Тепло-ёмкость, *n.f.*, heat capacity. Тепло-кро́вный, *adj.*, warm-blooded. Тепло-ме́р, *n.m.*, thermometer. Тепло-прово́дность, heat conduction. Тепло-прово́дный, *adj.*, diathermic; heat-conveying. Тепло-снабже́ние, *n.n.*, heat supply. Тепло-хо́д, *n.m.*, boat propelled by a Diesel engine. Тёп-л-енький, *adj.*, *dim.*, nice and warm, cosy. Теп-л-у́шка, *n.f.*, railroad freight car with stove.

теп-л-е́ть, *v.i.*, to grow warm. С. ка́ждым днём тепле́ло, with each day it grew warmer.

по-теп-л-е́ть, *v.p.*, to grow warm; warm up. Сего́дня потепле́ло, it warmed up today.

тёп-л-ить, *v.i.*, + *acc.*, to burn faintly; shine. Она́ те́плит свечу́ пе́ред ико́ною, she burns a candle before the icon. Тёп-л-ить-ся, *v.i.r.*, used only in 3d pers., to burn faintly, shine. В углу́ те́плилась лампа́да, a votive candle burned faintly in the corner. Жизнь чуть те́плится в нём, his life is hanging by a thread. Наде́жда ещё те́плилась у нас, we still had a faint glimmer of hope.

за-тё-п-л-ить, *v.p.*, + *acc.*, to light a votive candle. Мать затеплила лампа́ду пе́ред о́бразом, my mother lit a votive lamp before the icon. За-тёп-л-ить-ся, *v.p.r.*, used in 3d pers. only, to glimmer, burn. У всех образо́в затепли́лись лампа́ды, lamps were lit before all the icons.

за-теп-л-и́ть, *v.p.*, за-теп-л-я́ть, *v.i.*, + *acc.*, (*colloq.*), to warm. Они́ затепли́ли ко́мнату, вста́вив двойны́е ра́мы, they installed storm windows and made the room warm.

о-теп-л-и́ть, *v.p.*, о-теп-л-я́ть, *v.i.*, + *acc.*, to warm thoroughly. Они́ отепли́ли дом, поста́вив пе́чи, they warmed the house by installing stoves.

топ-и́-ть, *v.i.*, + *acc.*, to heat. Т. пе́чку, to heat the stove. Т. са́ло, to melt fat. Топ-и́ть-ся, *v.i.r.*, used in 3d pers. only, to be heated, be melted. Печь то́пится, the stove is warming up. Ма́сло легко́ то́пится, butter melts easily. То́п-ка, *n.f.*, furnace, firebox. Т. парово́го котла́, firebox of a steam boiler. Топ-л-е́ние, *n.n.*, heating, melting, scalding. Т. пече́й отнима́ет мно́го вре́мени, it takes time to heat stoves. Т. са́ла не тре́бует высо́кой температу́ры, the melting of fat does not require a high temperature. Топ-л-ёный, *adj.*, melted, scalded. Т-ое молоко́, scalded milk. Т-ое ма́сло, drawn, melted butter. То́п-л-иво, *n.n.*, fuel. У них нет то́плива, they have no fuel.

вы́-топ-ить, *v.p.*, вы-та́п-л-ивать, *v.i.*, + *acc.*, to heat; melt down. Вы́топить печь, to heat the stove. Они́ выта́пливали са́ло, they melted the fat.

за-топ-и́ть, *v.p.*, + *acc.*, to start a fire in a stove. Затопи́те пе́чку! Heat the stove!

ис-топ-и́ть, *v.p.*, + *acc.*, to heat thoroughly. Они́ истопи́ли печь, they heated the stove thoroughly.

на-топ-и́ть, *v.p.*, на-та́п-л-ивать, *v.i.*, + *acc.*, to heat intensely; melt in quantity. На-то́п-л-енный, *adj.*, *part. pass. past*, overheated. Жа́рко н. дом, an overheated house. На свечно́м заво́де бы́ло нато́плено мно́го стеари́на, a large quantity of stearin was melted in the candle works.

о-топ-и́ть, *v.p.*, о-та́п-л-ивать, *v.i.*, + *acc.*, to heat through. Они́ ота́пливают весь дом, they heat the whole house. О-та́п-л-ивать-ся, *v.i.r.*, + *instr.*, to be heated. Дома́ ота́пливаются дрова́ми и́ли ка́менным у́глем, the houses are heated with wood or coal. О-топ-л-е́ние, *n.n.*, heating, heat. В э́том зда́нии центра́льное о., there is central heating in this building.

пере-топ-и́ть, *v.p.,* пере-та́п-л-ивать, *v.i.,* + *acc.,* to heat to excess, remelt. Она́ перета́пливает ма́сло, she is remelting the butter.

под-топ-и́ть, *v.p.,* под-та́п-л-ивать, *v.i.,* + *acc.,* to heat slightly. Подтопи́те немно́го, heat a little.

про-топ-и́ть, *v.p.,* прота́п-л-ивать, *v.i.,* + *acc.,* to heat from time to time. Не забыва́йте прота́пливать дом, do not forget to heat the house from time to time! Про-та́п-л-ивание, *п.п.,* occasionnal heating.

рас-топ-и́ть, *v.p.,* рас-та́п-л-ивать, *v.i.,* + *acc.,* + *instr.,* to light, kindle; melt, fuse, smelt. Он раста́пливает печь ще́пками, he is kindling the fire with chips. Рас-то́п-л-енный, *adj., part. pass. past,* thoroughly kindled. Р-ая печь, well heated stove. Р-ое ма́сло, clarified butter. Р-ый мета́лл, molten metạl. Рас-та́п-л-ивание, *п.п.,* melting, smelting, kindling. Рас-то́п-ка, *п.f.,* kindling. Расто́пкой служи́л хво́рост, dry branches were u⌐ed as kindling.

с-топ-и́ть, *v.p.,* с-та́п-л-ивать, *v.i.,* + *acc.,* to burn up, burn down, burn out. Они́ стопи́ли за́ зиму 5 кубоме́тров дров, they burned up five cubic meters of wood during the winter. Она́ стопи́ла ма́сло, she melted down the butter.

ТЕР-, ТЁР-, ТИР-, ТОР-, ТР-, FRICTION, ABRASION, RUBBING

тер-е́-ть, тр-у, *v.i.,* + *acc.,* to rub, chafe, scrape, grate. Он трёт себе́ ру́ки, he is rubbing his hands. Воротни́к трёт мне ше́ю, the collar is chafing my neck. Она́ трёт сыр, she is grating cheese. Тёр-тый, *adj., part. pass. past,* grated. Т. сыр, grated cheese. Тер-е́ть-ся, *v.i.r.,* о + *prep.,* to rub against, on, over. Ко́шка трётся о её но́гу, the cat is rubbing against her leg. Он всё вре́мя трётся о́коло нас, (*colloq.*), he is always hanging around us. Тёр-ка, *п.f.,* grater. Т. для карто́феля, potato grater. Тр-е́ние, *п.п.,* friction, grating; discord, discordance. Т. заде́рживает движе́ние, friction retards motion. Маши́на рабо́тает без тре́ния, this machine runs smoothly. В па́ртии возни́кли тре́ния, friction has arisen within the party.

в-тер-е́ть, *v.p.,* в-тир-а́ть, *v.i.,* + *acc.,* to rub in. В. мазь, to apply ointment. В. очки́, (*fig.*), to pull the wool over the eyes. В-тер-е́ть-ся, *v.p.r.,* в-тир-а́ть-ся, *v.i.r.,* to be rubbed in. В. в дове́рие, to insinuate oneself into someone's confidence. В-тир-а́ние, *п.п.,* act of rubbing in. В. очко́в, (*fig.*), deception, deceit.

вы́-тер-еть, *v.p.,* вы-тир-а́ть, *v.i.,* + *acc.,* to rub dry, wipe, dry. Она́ вы́терла посу́ду, she dried the dishes.

за-тер-е́ть, *v.p.,* за-тир-а́ть, *v.i.,* + *acc.,* to rub out, eliminate, erase. Она́ затира́ет черни́льные пя́тна, she is rubbing out the ink stains. Парти́йцы затира́ют беспарти́йных, (*recent*), the party members are keeping down the non-party members. Су́дно затёрло льда́ми, the ship became ice-bound. За-то́р, *п.т.,* obstruction, traffic jam.

на-тер-е́ть, *v.p.,* на-тир-а́ть, *v.i.,* + *acc.,* to grate in quantity. Он натёр себе́ но́гу, he rubbed his foot until it became sore. Н. ме́дные ру́чки, to polish copper door knobs. Н. во́ском полы́, to wax the floors. На-тер-е́ть-ся, *v.p.r.,* на-тир-а́ть-ся, *v.i.r.,* + *instr.,* to rub oneself, be rubbed. Он натёрся ма́зью, he rubbed himself with an ointment.

об-тер-е́ть, *v.p.,* об-тир-а́ть, *v.i.,* + *acc.,* to rub off, wipe off, dry. Мать обтёрла ребёнка, the mother wiped the child dry. О. пыль, to dust off. Об-тер-е́ть-ся, *v.p.r.,* об-тир-а́ть-ся, *v.i.r.,* + *instr.,* to dry oneself. Он обтёрся полоте́нцем, he dried himself with a towel. Об-тир-а́ние, *п.п.,* rubdown.

от-тер-е́ть, *v.p.,* от-тир-а́ть, *v.i.,* + *acc.,* to rub; drive back, out. Э́то пятно́ нельзя́ оттере́ть, this stain cannot be removed. Он оттёр своего́ сопе́рника, (*colloq.*), he drove his rival back.

пере-тер-е́ть, *v.p.,* пере-тир-а́ть, *v.i.,* + *acc.,* to rub, dry off again; wear out by rubbing, rub through. Перетере́ть всю посу́ду, to dry all the dishes. Пере-тер-е́ть-ся, *v.p.r.,* пере-тир-а́ть-ся, *v.i.r.,* to be worn through. Верёвка перетёрлась, the rope was worn through. Пере-тир-а́ние, *п.п.,* wearing through, grinding; drying off.

по-тер-е́ть, *v.p.,* по-тир-а́ть, *v.i.,* + *acc.,* to rub. Он потира́ет ру́ки от удово́льствия, he is rubbing his hands with glee. По-тер-е́ть-ся, *v.p.r.,* по-тир-а́ть-ся, *v.i.r.,* + *acc.,* to rub against, rub shoulders with. По-тёр-тый, *adj., part. pass. past,* shabby, threadbare.

под-тер-е́ть, *v.p.,* под-тир-а́ть, *v.i.,* + *acc.,* to mop, wipe, clean. Она́ подтира́ет пол, she is giving the floor a quick mopping. Под-тер-е́ть-ся, *v.p.r.,* под-тир-а́ть-ся, *v.i.r.,* to wipe oneself. Полы́ подтира́ются, the floors are being mopped. Под-ти́р-ка, *п.f.,* quick mopping, wiping up. Под-тир-а́ние, *п.п.,* wiping up, mopping.

при-тер-е́ть, *v.p.,* при-тир-а́ть, *v.i.,* + *acc.,* to rub in slightly; fit (*as valves*);

grind (*as* glass); make up, rouge oneself. При-тёр-тый, *adj., part. pass. past,* ground. Банка с притёртой пробкой, a jar with a ground glass stopper. При-тир-ание, *п.п.,* rubbing, grinding; rouge. Она употребляет разные притирания для лица, she uses various cosmetics for her face. При-тир-ать-ся, *v.i.r.,* to be ground, be slightly rubbed in.

про-тер-éть, *v.p.,* про-тир-ать, *v.i.,* + *acc.,* to rub through, wear through. Она протёрла окна, she cleaned the windows. Про-тёр-тый, *adj., part. pass. past,* frayed, worn through, mashed. Рукава его пиджака протёрты, the sleeves of his coat are worn through. Про-тер-éть-ся, *v.p.r.,* про-тир-ать-ся, *v.i.r.,* to be worn, frayed, mashed. Эта материя скоро протрётся, this cloth will wear out quickly.

рас-тер-éть, *v.p.,* рас-тир-ать, *v.i.,* + *acc.,* to rub, grind thoroughly; massage; chafe; spread. Р. перец, to grind pepper. Растереть себе ногу до крови, to chafe one's foot till it bleeds. Он растирает ему спину, he is rubbing his back. Рас-тер-éть-ся, *v.p.r.,* рас-тер-éть-ся, *v.i.r.,* в + *acc.,* to be ground to powder; rub oneself briskly. Рас-тир-ание, *п.п.,* rubbing, grinding; massage. Р. ему очень помогло, the massage helped him.

с-тер-éть, *v.p.,* с-тир-ать, *v.i.,* + *acc.,* с + *instr.,* to rub off, erase. Она стирает пыль с мебели, she is dusting the furniture. Он стёр это слово, he erased this word. Стереть с лица земли, (*fig.*), to wipe off the face of the earth. С. пот с лица, to mop one's face. С-тер-éть-ся, *v.p.r.,* с-тир-áть-ся, *v.i.r.,* to be rubbed off, erased. Бархат стёрся, the velvet is worn. Сотрите это слово, erase this word. Надпись стёрлась, the inscription has been effaced. Стир-ание, *п.п.,* rubbing, erasure.

с-тир-áть, *v.i.,* + *acc.,* to wash, launder. С. бельё, to do the laundry. С. стиральной машиной, to do the laundry with a washing machine. С-тир-áть-ся, *v.i.r.,* to be washed, be washable. Эта материя хорошо стирается, this material washes well. С-тир-áльный, *adj.,* washing. С-тир-ка, *n.f.,* laundering. По понедельникам у нас с., we do our laundry on Mondays.

вы-с-тир-ать, *v.p.,* вы-с-тир-ывать, *v.i.,* + *acc.,* to do the laundry. Прачка выстирала бельё, the washerwoman has done the laundry.

пере-с-тир-áть, *v.p.,* пере-с-тир-ывать, *v.i.,* + *acc.,* to wash again; relaunder; do all the laundry. Она перестирала

все рубахи, she has washed all the shirts. Ей пришлось перестирывать своё платье, she had to wash her dress again.

по-с-тир-áть, *v.p.,* + *acc.,* (*colloq.*), to wash, launder, do some washing. По-с-тир-áв(ши), *adverbial part. past,* having laundered. Постирав бельё, она приготовила обед, having washed the laundry, she prepared the dinner. По-с-тир-ушка, *n.f.,* small washing.

про-с-тир-áть, *v.p.,* про-с-тир-ывать, *v.i.,* + *acc.,* to do laundering thoroughly. Я простираю вашу рубашку, I'll wash out your shirt. Она простирала всю ночь, she spent the whole night washing.

у-тер-éть, *v.p.,* у-тир-áть, *v.i.,* + *acc.,* to wipe dry, wipe away. У. слёзы, to dry tears. У-тер-éть-ся, *v.p.r.,* у-тир-áть-ся, *v.i.r.,* to be dried, wiped off, dry oneself. Чем ты утираешься? With what do you dry yourself? У-тир-альник, *n.m.,* (*folk*), towel.

ТЕРП-, ТЕРП(Л)-, PATIENCE, SUFFERING

терп-éть, терп-л-ю, *v.p.,* + *acc.,* to suffer, endure, bear, tolerate. Они терпят нужду, they suffer from want. Фирма терпела убытки, the firm bore heavy losses. Я его терпеть не могу, I cannot bear him. Дело не терпит отлагательства, the business is pressing. Время терпит, there is all the time in the world. Терп-éть-ся, *v.i.r., used in 3d pers., only,* to be patient. Ему не терпится увидать вас, (*colloq.*), he is very anxious to see you. Терп-елив(ый), *adj.,* patient. Он терпелив, he is patient. Не-терп-еливый, *adj.,* impatient. Терп-еливо, *adv.,* patiently. Он т. ждёт известий, he is patiently waiting for news. Не-терп-еливо, *adv.,* impatiently. Терп-еливость, *n.f.,* patience, forbearance. Т. отличительная черта его характера, patience is one of his outstanding characteristics. Не-терп-еливость, *n.f.,* impatience. Терп-ение, *п.п.,* patience, endurance. Я потерял т., I've lost my patience. Терпение и труд всё перетрут (*prov.*), patience and work will overcome all. Не-терп-ение, *п.п.,* impatience. Терп-имый, *adj.,* tolerable, sufferable, bearable. Терп-имо, *adj. pred.,* bearable, tolerable. Это ещё терпимо, it is still endurable. Не-терп-имый, *adj.,* intolerant. Терп-имо, *adv.,* tolerantly, bearably. Относиться т. к другим религиям, to be tolerant towards other religions. Не-терп-имо, *adv.,* intolerantly, unbearably. Терпи́мость, *n.f.*, tolerance. Не-терпи́мость, *n.f.*, intolerance. Не-в-терп-ёж, *adv.*, (*colloq.*), unbearably. Мне ста́ло э́то н., I could not bear it any longer.

вы́-терп-еть, *v.p.*, + *acc.*, to endure, bear. Он не вы́терпел их гру́бости. he could not endure their rudeness.

на-терп-е́ть-ся, *v.p.r.*, to have suffered much. Я мно́го натерпе́лся от плохи́х сосе́дей, I have put up with a good deal from disagreeable neighbors.

п(е)ре-терп-е́ть, *v.p.*, п(е)ре-терп-ева́ть, *v.i.*, + *acc.*, to suffer, bear, endure, undergo. П(е)ре-терп-е́вший, *adj.*, *part. act. past, used also as n.*, one who has suffered. Претерпе́вший всё-спасётся, (*Bib.*), "but he that endureth to the end shall be saved."

по-терп-е́ть, *v.p.*, + *acc.*, to suffer; have patience. Потерпи́те немно́го! Have a little patience! По-терп-е́вший, *adj.*, *part. act. past, used as n.*, injured. Потерпе́вшие бы́ли перевезены́ в больни́цу, the injured were transported to a hospital.

с-терп-е́ть, *v.p.*, + *acc.*, to bear, tolerate, endure. Не стерпе́ть оби́ды, not to endure an insult.

у-терп-е́ть, *v.p.*, to forbear, refrain. Я не утерпе́л, чтобы не сказа́ть, пра́вды, I could not refrain from telling the truth.

ТЕС- (ТѢС-), ТИС-, PRESSURE, CROWDING, SQUEEZING; TIGHTNESS

тес-н-и́ть, *v.i.*, + *acc.*, to press, squeeze; drive back. "Тесни́м мы шве́дов рать за ра́тью," (*Pushkin*), "we are driving back the Swedes army after army." Тес-н-и́ть-ся, *v.i.r.*, to be crowded, pressed; stand close. Там тесни́лось мно́го наро́ду, many people crowded there. Тес-ни́на, *n.f.*, (*poet.*), mountain gorge. Т. покры́та мгло́й, the gorge is wrapped in fog. Те́с-ный, *adj.*, narrow; close; intimate. Эти башмаки́ мне те́сны, these shoes are too tight for me. Их свя́зывала те́сная дру́жба, they were bound by a close friendship. Те́с-но, *adv.*, narrowly, closely, tightly. Т. сши́тый пиджа́к, a tight-fitting coat. Здесь т., it is crowded here. Тес-нова́тый, *adj.*, rather tight; crowded. Эта кварти́ра теснова́та для нас, this apartment is rather small for us. Тес-нова́то, *adv.*, rather tight, crowded. Там бы́ло т., it was rather crowded there. Тес-нота́, *n.f.*, tightness, crowded state. В тесноте́, да не в оби́де, (*saying*), there is always room for one more.

вы́-тес-н-ить, *v.p.*, вы-тес-ня́ть, *v.i.*, +

acc., to force out, crowd out. Фа́брика вы́теснила реме́сленника, the factory has forced out the craftsman. Вы́-тес-нить-ся, *v.p.r.*, вы-тес-ня́ть-ся, *v.i.r.*, + *instr.*, to be forced out, crowded out. Ме́лкие предприя́тия вытесня́ются кру́пными, small plants are forced out of business by large ones. Вы-тес-не́ние, *n.n.*, forcing out, dislodging, freezing out.

от-тес-ни́ть, *v.p.*, от-тес-ня́ть, *v.i.*, + *acc.*, to drive back, drive out, drive away. Мы оттесни́ли неприя́теля, we drove the enemy back.

по-тес-ни́ть, *v.p.*, + *acc.*, to press, drive back slightly. П. врага́, to drive the enemy back slightly. По-тес-ни́ть-ся, *v.p.r.*, to make room; press a little; sit closer. Потесни́тесь немно́го, чтобы я мог сесть, move a little, so that I can sit down.

при-тес-ни́ть, *v.p.*, (*rarely*), при-тес-ни́ть, *v.i.*, + *acc.*, to drive against; to oppress, persecute. Не притесня́йте сла́бых, do not oppress the weak. При-тес-не́ние, *n.n.*, oppression, persecution. П. то́лько начина́ется, the persecution is only beginning. При-тес-ни́тель, *n.m.*, oppressor, persecutor.

с-тес-ни́ть, *v.p.*, с-тес-ня́ть, *v.i.*, + *acc.*, to hinder, hamper, press, embarrass. Толпа́ стесни́ла меня́ со всех сторо́н, the crowd pressed me on all sides. Меня́ стесня́ет ва́ша предупреди́тельность, your courtesy embarrasses me. С-тес-нённый, *adj.*, *part. pass. past*, constrained, embarrassed. Он нахо́дится в стеснённых обстоя́тельствах, he is in straitened circumstances. С-тес-ня́ть-ся, *v.i.r.*, + *gen.*, + *inf.*, to feel embarrassed. Он стесня́ется большо́го о́бщества, he feels embarrassed in company. Не стесня́йтесь обраща́ться ко мне, do not hesitate to ask me. Не с. в сре́дствах, to have no scruples. С-тес-не́ние, *n.n.*, embarrassment, constraint. Расскажи́ мне всё без стесне́ния, tell me everything without embarrassment. С-тес-ни́тельность, *n.f.*, embarrassment, shyness; inconvenience. Изли́шняя с. вреди́т челове́ку, needless shyness hampers a person. С-тес-ни́тельный, *adj.*, embarrassing, inconvenient; (*fig.*), shy. С-ое положе́ние, embarrassing position, situation. С-тес-ни́тельно, *adv.*, embarrassingly; inconveniently. Это о́чень с. для меня́, this is very inconvenient for me.

у-тес-ня́ть, *v.i.*, + *acc.*, to press, oppress; *see* притесня́ть.

ти́с-к-а-ть, *v.i.*, + *acc.*, to squeeze, hug, press, cram; be pushed. Меня́ ти́скали в толпе, I was pushed about in the crowd. Тис-кание, *n.n.*, squeezing, pressing. Тис-ки́, *n.m.pl.*, vise, pincers, pliers. Он у него́ в тиска́х, (*fig.*), he is in his clutches.

в-ти́с-кать, *v.p.*, в-ти́с-нуть, *v.p.*, в-ти́с-кивать, *v.i.*, + *acc.*, в + *acc.*, to press, squeeze, cram in. Мо́жно втисну́ть ещё оди́н чемода́н, one more suitcase can be squeezed in. Его́ не вти́снешь в ра́мки повседне́вной жи́зни, you cannot fit him into the mold of everyday life. В-ти́с-кать-ся, *v.p.r.*, в-ти́с-кивать-ся *v.i.r.*, в-ти́с-нуть-ся, *v.p.r.smf.*, в + *acc.*, to be squeezed, crowded, crammed, pressed in. Пассажи́р с трудо́м втисну́лся в ваго́н, the passenger barely managed to squeeze into the car. Вы́-тис-нен(ный), *adj.*, *part pass.* *past*, impressed, imprinted. На перепле́те кни́ги вы́тиснена фами́лия а́втора, the author's name is imprinted on the cover of the book.

за-ти́с-кать, *v.p.*, за-ти́с-нуть, *v.p.*, за-ти́с-кивать, *v.i.*, в + *acc.*, to squeeze into. Они́ затисну́ли его́ в у́гол, they squeezed him into a corner.

на-ти́с-кать, *v.p.*, на-ти́с-нуть, *v.p.*, на-ти́с-кивать, *v.i.*, + *acc.*, to cram into, stuff with. Он сли́шком мно́го натиска́л в свой чемода́н, he has stuffed too many things into his suitcase. На́-тис-к, *n.m.*, rush, attack. Н. неприя́теля осла́бел, the enemy's pressure became weaker.

от-ти́с-нуть, *v.p.*, от-ти́с-кивать, *v.i.*, + *acc.*, to impress, print. Оттисни́те ещё 100 экземпля́ров, print a hundred additional copies. О́т-тис-к, *n.m.*, impression, reprint. О́ттиски па́льцев, fingerprints. Отде́льные о́ттиски статьи́, reprints of an article.

при-ти́с-нуть, *v.p.*, при-ти́с-кивать, *v.i.*, + *acc.*, к + *dat.*, to press close to. Толпа́ притисну́ла его́ к стене́, the crowd pressed him to the wall.

про-ти́с-нуть, *v.p.*, про-ти́с-кивать, *v.i.*, + *acc.*, to press, squeeze, through. Про-ти́с-нуть-ся, *v.p.r.*, про-ти́с-кивать-ся, *v.i.r.*, + сквозь + *acc.*, to press, squeeze through; be pressed, squeezed through. Проти́снуться сквозь толпу́, to elbow one's way through the crowd.

с-ти́с-нуть, *v.p.*, с-ти́с-кивать, *v.i.*, + *acc.*, to squeeze, hug; clench one's teeth. От бо́ли он сти́снул зу́бы, he clenched his teeth with pain.

ТЕХ-, (ТѢХ-), ТЕШ-, (ТѢШ-), AMUSEMENT, PLEASURE

по-те́х-а, *n.f.*, fun, amusement. Вот так п., умру́ со сме́ха! (*saying*), What fun! I'll die laughing. Де́лу - вре́мя, а поте́хе час, (*prov.*), all one's time for work, only an hour for diversion.

у-те́х-а, *n.f.*, pleasure, joy, delight. Ты одна́ моя́ у., you are my single joy. Мне не до уте́х, I have no time for pleasure.

те́ш-и-ть, *v.i.*, + *acc.*, to divert, amuse, entertain. Он те́шит себя́ напра́сной наде́ждой, he deceives himself with a vain hope. Те́ш-ить-ся, *v.i.r.*, + *instr.*, to be amused, diverted. Чём-бы дитя́ ни те́шилось, лишь бы не пла́кало, (*prov.*), do anything for the sake of peace.

на-те́ш-ить-ся, *v.p.r.*, + *instr.*, to take pleasure in, rejoice greatly. Оте́ц не нате́шится свои́м сы́ном, the father cannot rejoice enough over his son.

по-те́ш-ить, *v.p.*, по-теш-а́ть, *v.i.*, + *instr.*, to amuse, divert, laugh at, mock. Кло́уны потеша́ли пу́блику свои́ми шу́тками, the clowns amused the public with their jokes. По-те́ш-ить-ся, *v.p.r.*, по-теш-а́ть-ся, *v.i.r.*, над + *instr.*, to amuse, divert oneself; make fun of, mock. Поте́шился, и дово́льно! That's enough now, you've had your fun! По-те́ш-ный, *adj.*, amusing, funny. У ма́льчика п. вид, the boy looks comical. Поте́шные полки́ Петра́ Вели́кого, (*hist.*), the regiments of boy soldiers under Peter the Great.

у-те́ш-ить, *v.p.*, у-теш-а́ть, *v.i.*, + *acc.*, to console, comfort, solace. Мать утеша́ла дочь, the mother consoled her daughter. У-те́ш-ить-ся, *v.p.r.*, у-теш-а́ть-ся, *v.i.r.*, + *instr.*, to be consoled, be comforted; solace oneself. Она́ о́чень ско́ро уте́шилась, she consoled herself very quickly. У-теш-е́ние, *n.n.*, consolation, comfort, solace. Это плохо́е у. для него́, it is insufficient consolation for him. У-теш-и́тель, *n.m.*, у-теш-и́тельница, *n.f.*, comforter, consoler. Она́ была́ его́ неизме́нной утеши́тельницей, she was his faithful consoler. У-теш-и́тельный, *adj.*, soothing, comforting. Мной полу́чены утеши́тельные изве́стия, I have received comforting news. У-теш-и́тельно, *adv.*, consolingly. Это весьма́ у., this is very comforting. Без-у-те́ш-ный, не-у-те́ш-ный, *adj.*, inconsolable, disconsolate. Б-ая вдова́, disconsolate widow. Без-у-те́ш-но, *adv.*, inconsolably, disconsolately. Ребёнок пла́кал б., the child wept disconsolately. Без-у-те́ш-ность, *n.f.*, disconsolateness. Б. его́ го́ря тро́гала всех его́ друзе́й, the disconsolateness of his grief touched all his friends.

ТИХ-, ТИШ-, TRANQUILITY, QUIES-
CENCE, PEACE

тих-ий, *adj.,* quiet, tranquil, still, calm.
Какáя тихая ночь! What a calm night!
Т. океáн, Pacific Ocean. Т. ýжас
охватил меня, (*colloq.*), horror overwhelmed me. В тихом óмуте чéрти
вóдятся, (*saying*), still waters run
deep. Тих-о, *adv.,* quietly, softly, calmly; slowly. Они живýт т., they live
quietly. Он говорит т., he speaks
softly. Делá идýт т., business is slow.
В-тих-о-мóлку, *adv.,* silently; secretly.
Он в. всё распрóдал, he has secretly
sold all the merchandise. Тих-óнько,
adv., quietly, silently; secretly. Они т.
обвенчáлись, they married secretly.
Тих-óня, *n.m. and n.f.,* demure person.
На вид т., he only appears to be a
demure person.

тиш-е, *adj. and adv. comp.,* quieter; more
quietly. Он говорит т. её, his voice
is softer than hers. Тише! Keep quiet!
Тиш-инá, *n.f.,* тишь, *n.f.,* stillness.
Здесь прохлáда и т., it is cool and
calm here. Тишь да гладь, да Бóжья
благодáть, (*saying*), all is peace and
quiet.

за-тих-áть, *v.i.,* за-тих-нуть, *v.p.,* to grow
calm, still, quiet; fall, subside. Дéти
затихли, the children quieted down.
Ветерóк затих, the breeze let up. За-
тиш-ь-е, *n.n.,* calm, stillness, quiet,
lull. Нá море бы́ло пóлное з., the sea
was quite calm. Это тóлько з. перед
бýрей, it is only a lull before the storm.
Ис-под-тиш-кá, *adv.,* stealthily, on the
sly. У них всё дéлается и., they do
everything on the sly.

при-тих-áть, *v.i.,* при-тих-нуть, *v.p.,* to
quiet down, become silent. Все
притихли, ожидáя решéния, everyone
quieted down, awaiting the decision.

с-тих-áть, *v.i.,* с-тих-нуть, *v.p.,* to calm
down, quiet down; abate, subside.
Вéтер стих, the wind died down. Всё
стихло, all became quiet.

у-тих-áть, *v.i.,* у-тих-нуть, *v.p.,* to fade
away, die away, abate, quiet down,
calm. Бýря утихла, the storm abated.
У-тихáние, *n.n.,* abatement, subsidence,
dying away. У. бóли, subsidence of
pain.

у-тих-о-мирить, *v.p.,* у-тих-о-мирвать,
v.i., + *acc.,* to calm down, appease,
pacify. Утихомирьте вáшу ярость,
control your rage. У-тих-о-мирить-ся,
v.p.r., у-тих-о-мирвать-ся, *v.i.r.,* to
become quiet, become calm. Спóрщики
никáк не хотéли утихомириться, the
quarreling people refused to be quieted.

у-тиш-áть, *v.i.,* у-тиш-ить, *v.p.,* + *acc.,*
to calm, quiet, soothe. Этот порошóк
утишит вáшу боль, this powder will
soothe your pain.

ТК-, ТЫК-, ТЫЧ-, ТОЧ-, WEAVING;
POINTING, THRUST

тк-а-ть, тк-у, to weave. Бáбы ткут
полотнó, the peasant women are
weaving linen. Тк-аньё, *n.n.,* weaving.
Зимóй крестьянки занимáлись тканьём
полотнá, in winter the peasant women
were busy weaving linen. Тк-ань, *n.f.,*
woven fabric, material; web, texture;
(*anat.*), tissue. Это чисто шерстянáя
т., this material is pure wool. Бумáжная
(хлопчáто-бумáжная) т., cotton cloth.
Нéрвная т., (*anat.*), nerve tissue. Тк-
áный, *adj.,* woven. Т-ая скáтерть, woven
tablecloth. Тк-áнный, *adj., part.
pass. past,* handwoven; brocaded; damask.
Это полотнó, ткáнное нáшими
сóбственными рукáми, this linen was
woven by our own hands. Дом-о-тк-
áнный, *adj.,* homespun. Юбка из д-ой
матéрии, skirt of homespun cloth.
Злат-о-тк-áнный, *adj.,* gold brocaded.
На свящéнниках златоткáнные ри́зы,
priests wear gold brocaded vestments.
Тк-áцкий, *adj.,* weaving. На т-ой
фáбрике выдéлывают тóнкие ткáни,
in textile mills, fine fabrics are woven.
Т. станóк, loom. Тк-ач, *n.m.,* тк-ачиха,
n.f., weaver. Ткачи́ рабóтают в три
смéны, weavers work in three shifts.

во-тк-áть, *v.p.,* в + *acc.,* to weave in,
into. Вó-тк-ан(ный), *adj., part. pass.
past,* woven in, into. В матéрию бы́ли
вóтканы золóтые нитки, gold threads
were woven into the cloth.

вы́-тк-ать, *v.p.,* + *acc.,* to weave. Это
полотнó я вы́ткала самá, I have woven
this linen myself.

за-тк-áть, *v.p.,* + *acc.,* to weave in an
allover pattern. Зá-тк-ан(ный), *adj.,
part. pass. past,* woven all over.
Матéрия, з-ая шёлком и зóлотом, a
cloth with an allover pattern of silk
and gold.

на-тк-áть, *v.p.,* + *acc.,* to weave in
quantity. На сегóдня я довóльно наткáла,
I have woven enough for today.

у-тк-áть, *v.p.,* + *acc.,* в + *acc.,* to weave
into a pattern. Онá уткáла рáзные
узóры в ткань, she has woven various
patterns into the cloth.

тк-нуть, *v.p.smf.,* тык-ать, *v.i.,* + *acc.,*
to poke, stick in, prod, thrust. Он
ткнул меня в бок, he poked me in the
ribs. Не ты́кай (тычь) в негó пáльцем!
(*colloq.*), Do not point your finger at
him! Тк-нýть-ся, *v.p.r.,* тык-ать-ся.

v.i.r., в + *acc.*, to nuzzle. Он напрáсно тычется не в свой делá, he should not poke his nose into other people's business. Рыба всё врéмя тыкалась нóсом в стеклó аквáриума, the fish kept nudging the sides of the aquarium.

тыч-и́на, *n.f.*, тыч-ка, *n.f.*, prop, stake. Хмель растёт на высóких тычи́нах (ты́чках), hops grow on high poles. Тыч-и́нка, *n.f.*, (*bot.*), stamen. В махрóвых цветкáх тычи́нки превращены́ в лепестки́, in double-petaled flowers the stamens are transformed into petals. Тыч-и́нковый, *adj.*, staminal. Тыч-óк, *n.m.*, stump; blow, punch. Он сидéл на тычкé, he was sitting on on a stump. Дать тычкá, to punch, land a punch.

во-тк-ну́ть, *v.p. smf.*, в-тык-áть, *v.i.*, в + *acc.*, to thrust in, into; drive in. Уби́йца воткну́л ему́ нож в спи́ну, the murderer stabbed him in the back.

за-тк-ну́ть, *v.p.*, за-тык-áть, *v.i.*, + *acc.*, to stop up, choke up. З. буты́лку прóбкой, to cork a bottle. З. у́ши от шу́ма, to stop up one's ears. Заткни́ глóтку! (*rude*) Hold your tongue!

ис-ты́к-ать, *v.p.*, ис-ты́к-ивать, *v.i.*, + to pierce; make holes. И. дóску гвоздя́ми, to riddle a board with nails.

на-ты́к-ать, *v.p.*, на-тык-áть, *v.i.*, + *acc.*, + *gen.*, to drive in, stick in in quantity (*as* pins, pegs). Они́ наты́кали булáвок, they stuck in many pins.

на-тк-ну́ть, *v.p.*, на-тык-áть, *v.i.*, + *acc.*, на + *acc.*, to pin on, set on. Мáльчик натыкáет бáбочек на булáвки, the boy is piercing the butterflies with pins. На-тк-ну́ть-ся, *v.p.r.*, на-тык-áть-ся, *v.i.r.*, на + *acc.*, to strike; run against; stumble; meet. Наткну́ться на непреодоли́мое препя́тствие, to run up against an insurmountable obstacle.

об-ты́к-ать, *v.p.*, об-тык-áть, *v.i.*, + *acc.*, + *instr.*, to place sticks around; stake. О. гря́дки клубни́ки кóльями, to stake the strawberry beds.

подо-тк-ну́ть, *v.p.*, под-тык-áть, *v.i.*, (*colloq.*), to stick under; tuck. За рабóтой бáбы подтыкáют подóлы, at work the peasant women tuck up their skirts.

при-тк-ну́ть, *v.p.*, при-тык-áть, *v.i.*, + *acc.*, к + *dat.*, to fasten, nail, stick to; lean against. Лéстницу приткну́ли к стенé дóма, (*colloq.*), the ladder was set against the wall of the house. При-тк-ну́ть-ся, *v.p.r.*, к + *dat.*, to stand, sit; find a nook. Мне нéгде п., (*colloq.*), I have nowhere to stand (sit).

про-тк-ну́ть, *v.p.*, про-тык-áть, *v.i.*, +

acc., to pierce, prick. П. штыкóм, to pierce with a bayonet.

рас-ты́к-ать, *v.p.*, рас-тык-áть, *v.i.*, + *acc.*, (*colloq.*), to place in various places. Он расты́кал свой вéщи по всем знакóмым, he left his things with all his friends.

с-тык, *n.m.*, abutment; joint; meeting point.

у-ты́к-ать, *v.p.*, у-тык-áть, у-ты́к-ивать, *v.i.*, (*colloq.*), + *acc.*, + *instr.*, to stick, set in; tuck in.

у-тк-ну́ть, *v.p.*, у-тык-áть, *v.i.*, + *acc.*, в + *acc.*, to shove into; pore over (*as* a book), stick in. Ребёнок уткну́л лицó в поду́шку и заплáкал, the child hid his face in the pillow and began to cry. У-тк-ну́ть-ся, *v.p.r.*, в + *acc.*, to be stopped by; run against; bury oneself in, hide in. У. головóй в поду́шку, to bury one's head in the pillow.

тóч-ка, *n.f.*, (*gram.*), period; point, dot, stop; point of view. Термóметр стои́т вы́ше тóчки замерзáния (нуля́), the thermometer stands above the freezing point. Я не соглáсен с вáшей тóчкой зрéния, I do not agree with your point of view. Дéло сдви́нулось с мёртвой тóчки, the deadlock has been broken. Он попáл в тóчку, (*fig.*), he hit the mark. Стáвить тóчки над i, (*fig.*), to dot the i's.

тóч-ный, *adj.*, precise, exact. Это егó т-ые словá, these are his exact words. Математика т-ая наýка, mathematics is an exact science. Тóч-но, *adv.*, precisely, exactly; as if, like. Это т. такáя матéрия, this is exactly the same cloth. Т. он не знáет, что это запрещенó, as if he did not know that it is forbidden. Он хóдит т. помéшанный, he acts like a madman. Тóч-ность, *n.f.*, preciseness, exactness; accuracy. Он рабóтает с тóчностью механи́зма, he works with mechanical precision. Он сомневáется в тóчности перевóда, he doubts the accuracy of the translation. Не-тóч-ный, *adj.*, inexact, unprecise, inaccurate. Не-тóч-но, *adv.*, inexactly, unprecisely; inaccurately. Не-тóч-ность, *n.f.*, inexactness, inaccuracy. Нетóчный перевóд, inaccurate translation. Нетóчность цитáт роня́ет цéнность кни́ги, the inaccuracy of the quotations decreases the value of the book.

тóч-ь-в-тóч-ь, *adv.*, exactly. Он т. в отцá, he is exactly like his father. Онá переписáла это т., she copied it exactly.

ТОВА́Р-, GOODS, MERCHANDISE; COMPANY, COMPANIONSHIP, COMRADESHIP

това́р, *n.m.*, merchandise, goods. Т. уже́ полу́чен, the merchandise has been received. Хоро́ший т. сам себя́ хва́лит, (*prov.*), good wine needs no bush. Това́р-ность, *n.f.*, marketability. Това́рный, *adj.*, pertaining to freight, goods. Т. по́езд, freight train. Това́р-о-веде́ние, *n.n.*, merchandising. В комме́рческом учи́лище преподаётся т., merchandising is taught in business schools. Това́р-о-обме́н, *n.m.*, barter; trade exchange. Т. ме́жду го́родом и дере́вней, the trade exchange between town and country. Това́р-о-оборо́т, *n.m.*, exchange of commodities. Т. страда́ет от расстро́йства тра́нспорта, the exchange of commodities is suffering from a breakdown in transportation.

това́р-ищ, *n.m.*, comrade; partner; deputy; schoolmate, playmate, classmate. Алёша мой шко́льный т., Alex is my schoolmate. Все они́ на́ши това́рищи по игре́, they are all teammates. В на́шу торго́вую компа́нию вошёл но́вый т., a new partner has joined our company. Т. мини́стра иностра́нных дел замени́л заболе́вшего мини́стра, the under-secretary of state substituted for the secretary, who had fallen ill. Това́р-ищеский, *adj.*, friendly, comradely. С т-им приве́том, with friendly greetings. По-това́р-ищески, *adv.*, as comrades, in comradely fashion, friendlily. Они́ поступи́ли с ним не п., they did not treat him like a comrade. Това́р-ищество, *n.n.*, company, society, association; fellowship, comradeship. Основа́ть т. на пая́х, to found a joint stock company. У студе́нтов си́льное чу́вство това́рищества, the students have a strong feeling of fellowship.

о-това́р-ить, *v.p.*, о-това́р-ивать, *v.i.* + *acc.*, (*recent*), to buy goods allowed by a ration card. О-това́р-ивание проду́ктовых ка́рточек, *n.n.*, (*recent*), purchase of goods allowed by a ration card.

ТОК-, ТОЧ-, ТАЧ-, TURNING, TURNERY, SHARPNESS

то́к-арь, *n.m.*, turner. Т. рабо́тает на тока́рном станке́, the turner is working at the lathe. Ток-а́рня, *n.f.*, turner's workshop. Тока́р-ный, *adj.*, pertaining to a turner, turnery; worked on a lathe. Тока́рная мастерска́я, turner's workshop. Т. стано́к, lathe. Т-ые изде́лья о́чень дёшевы, turned products are very cheap. Т-ое ремесло́, the turner's craft.

точ-и́ть, *v.i.*, + *acc.*, to turn, sharpen, whet, grind; То́карь то́чит но́жки стола́, the turner shapes the legs of a table. Червь то́чит кору́, the worm is eating away the bark. Его́ то́чит го́ре, grief preys on him. Ка́пля то́чит ка́мень, a drop of water wears away a stone. Точ-е́ние, *n.n.*, turning, working on a lathe; sharpening, grinding. Точ-ёный, *adj.*, chiseled. У неё точёные черты́ лица́, she has chiseled features. Точ-и́лка, *n.f.*, точ-и́ло, *n.n.*, whetstone, grindstone, strickle, sharpener. Т. для ноже́й, knife sharpener. Точ-и́льный, *adj.*, pertaining to grinding, sharpening. Т. брусо́к, whetstone. Т. ка́мень, grindstone. Т. реме́нь, razor strop. Т. стано́к, grindstone. Точ-и́льня, *n.f.*, grinding mill. Точ-и́льщик, *n.m.*, knife grinder. Т. то́чит ножи́, the grinder is sharpening knives.

вы́-точ-ить *v.p.*, вы-та́ч-ивать, *v.i.*, из + *gen.*, to turn out; sharpen. То́карь вы́точил но́жки сту́ла, the turner has shaped the legs of the table. Вы-та́ч-ивать-ся, *v.i.r.*, из + *gen.*, to be turned, shaped. Билья́рдные шары́ выта́чиваются из ко́сти, billiard balls are made of bone.

за-точ-и́ть, *v.p.*, за-та́ч-ивать, *v.i.*, + *acc.*, (*colloq.*), to sharpen; imprison, confine. З. в монасты́рь, to confine in a monastery. З. в тюрьму́, to imprison. Заточи́те мне каранда́ш, (*colloq.*), sharpen my pencil. За-точ-е́ние, *n.n.*, confinement, imprisonment. Моё з. дли́лось два го́да, my imprisonment lasted two years.

ис-точ-и́ть, *v.p.*, + *acc.*, to sharpen to excess; reduce by grinding; riddle with holes. Че́рви источи́ли де́рево, the worms have riddled the tree. Исто́ч-енный, *adj.*, *part. pass. past*, gnawed, riddled. Расте́ние источено́ червя́ми, the plant has been eaten by worms.

на-точ-и́ть, *v.p.*, на-та́ч-ивать, *v.i.*, + *acc.*, to turn, sharpen, grind in quantity. На́ши кустари́ ната́чивают ма́ссу ра́зных изде́лий, our craftsmen make quantities of various turned products. Он наточи́л все ножи́, he has ground all the knives.

об-точ-и́ть, *v.p.*, об-та́ч-ивать, *v.i.*, + *acc.*, to turn on a lathe. Ма́стер обта́чивал желе́зную болва́нку, the craftsman was shaping a metal block. Об-то́ч-ка, *n.f.*, об-та́ч-ивание, *n.n.*, turning.

от-точ-и́ть, *v.p.*, от-та́ч-ивать, *v.i.*, to sharpen, whet. От-то́ч-енный, *adj.*, *part. pass. past*, turned; sharpened, whetted. Он бросился на него с отточенным ножом, he attacked him with a sharp knife.

по-точ-и́ть, *v.p.,* + *acc.,* to sharpen a little. Он поточи́л свой охо́тничий нож, he sharpened his hunting knife.

под-точ-и́ть, *v.p.,* под-та́ч-ивать, *v.i.,* + *acc.,* to sharpen a little; gnaw, nibble; undermine. По́вар подточи́л ножи́, the cook sharpened his knives. Под-то́чен(ный), *adj., part. pass. past,* undermined. Его́ здоро́вье бы́ло подто́чено боле́знью, his health was undermined by an illness. Сте́ны бы́ли подто́чены терми́тами, the walls were undermined by termites.

с-точ-и́ть-ся, *v.p.r.,* с-та́ч-ивать-ся, *v.i.r.,* to be worn down by grinding. Я купи́л но́вую косу́, так как ста́рая совсе́м сточи́лась, I bought a new scythe, for my old one is quite worn down.

тач-а́ть, *v.i.,* с-тач-а́ть, *v.p.,* + *acc.,* to stitch through, quilt. Т. сапоги́, to sew boots.

над-тач-а́ть, *v.p.,* над-та́ч-ивать, *v.i.,* + *acc.,* to add by sewing, stitching on. Рукава́ коротки́: на́до надтача́ть, the sleeves are short; it is necessary to add a piece.

при-тач-а́ть, *v.p.,* при-та́ч-ивать, *v.i.,* + *acc.,* to stitch to. Притача́й рукава́ к пиджаку́, sew the sleeves to the coat. Притача́й голени́ща к сапога́м, sew the bootlegs to the boots.

под-тач-а́ть, *v.p.,* под-та́ч-ивать, *v.i.,* + *acc.,* to add by sewing, stitching a piece to the lower part of something. Пла́тье коротко́: на́до сни́зу подтача́ть, the dress is too short; you'll have to add a piece.

с-тач-а́ть, *v.p.,* с-та́ч-ивать, *v.i.,* + *acc.,* to sew, stitch together pieces of material. Стача́йте на маши́не о́бе полови́ны рукава́, sew up the two parts of the sleeve on the machine.

ТОЛК-, ТОЛЧ-, ТАЛК-, ТОЛОК-, ТОЛОЧ-, PUSHING, CRUSHING; EXPLANATION

толк-а́-ть, *v.i.,* толк-ну́ть, *v.p.,* to push, jostle. Я толкну́л его́ ло́ктем, I nudged him with my elbow. Вдруг он толкну́л меня́ в бок, he suddenly poked me in the ribs. Толк-а́ть-ся, *v.i.r.,* толкну́ть-ся, *v.p.r.,* to push, elbow; loaf Не толка́йтесь, Don't push! Он толка́ется без де́ла, (*colloq.*), he loafs about. Он толкну́лся к ней, но её не́ было до́ма, (*colloq.*), he looked her up, but she was not at home. Толк-а́ч, *n.m.,*

expeditor; pusher; pounder; pestle. В. маши́не был винт-толка́ч, the machine had a push screw. Они́ на́ши толкачи́ в э́том де́ле, they are our backers in this matter. Толк-отня́, *n.f.,* crush; crowd; bustle. На ры́нке была́ т., there was a crowd in the market place. Что там за т.? Why is there a crowd? Толк-у́чий, *adj.,* belonging to a second hand market. Т. ры́нок, second hand market. Толк-у́чка, *n.f.,* rag fair; second hand market. На толку́чке прода́ют ста́рые ве́щи, at the rag fair old things are sold.

толч-ея́, *n.f.,* crush, crowd. Толч-о́к, *n.f.,* push, nudge; shock; impulse. Дома́ задрожа́ли от подзе́много толчка́, the houses shook from the earthquake.

в-толк-ну́ть, *v.p., smf.,* в-та́лк-ивать, *v.i.,* + *acc.,* в + *acc.,* to push in, shove in. Они́ втолкну́ли его́ в я́му, they pushed him into a pit.

вы́-толк-ать, вы́-толк-нуть, *v.p.,* вы-та́лк-ивать, *v.i.,* + *acc.,* из + *gen.,* to push out. Его́ вы́толкали из ко́мнаты, they pushed him out of the room. Его́ на́до вы́толкать в ше́ю, he must be thrown out.

за-толк-а́ть, за-толк-ну́ть, *v.p.,* за-та́лк-ивать, *v.i.,* + *acc.,* to push about, jostle; hustle. Нас совсе́м затолка́ли на у́лице, we were badly jostled in the street.

на-толк-а́ть, на-толк-ну́ть, *v.p.,* на-та́лк-ивать, *v.i.,* на + *acc.,* thrust upon. Н. книг в шкаф, to crowd books in a bookcase. Учи́тель натолкну́л нас на э́ту мысль, the teacher urged this idea on us. На-толк-ну́ть-ся, *v.p.r.,* на-та́лк-ивать-ся, *v.i.r.,* на + *acc.,* to run against; stumble upon. Он всегда́ ната́лкивается на одно́ и то́ же препя́тствие, he always runs up against the same obstacle.

от-толк-ну́ть, *v.p.,* от-та́лк-ивать, *v.i.,* + *acc.,* от + *gen.,* to push off, push away; repulse. Он оттолкну́л нас от себя́ свое́й неблагода́рностью, he repulsed us with his ingratitude. От-та́лк-ивающий, *adj.,* repulsive, forbidding. У него́ о. вид, he has a repulsive appearance. От-толк-ну́ть-ся, *v.p.r.,* от-та́лк-ивать-ся, *v.i.r.,* от + *gen.,* to push off, shove off. Ло́дка оттолкну́лась от бе́рега, the boat pushed off from the shore. От-та́лк-ивание, *n.n.,* pushing off; repellence.

под-толк-ну́ть, *v.p.,* под-та́лк-ивать, *v.i.,* + *acc.,* to push, shove under; push up, shove up. Второ́й парово́з подта́лкивал по́езд сза́ди, the second locomotive pushed the train from behind. Под-та́лк-ивание, *n.n.,* nudging, shoving.

про-толк-а́ть, (*colloq.*), про-толк-ну́ть, *v.p.*, про-та́лк-ивать, *v.i.*, + *acc.*, to push through. Протолкну́ть про́бку внутрь буты́лки, to push a cork into a bottle. Про-толк-а́ть-ся, про-толк-ну́ть-ся, *v.p.r.*, про-та́лк-ивать-ся, *v.i.r.*, to shoulder, force one's way. Мы с трудо́м протолка́лись сквозь толпу́, we hardly managed to force our way through the crowd.

рас-толк-а́ть, рас-толк-ну́ть, *v.p.*, рас-та́лк-ивать, *v.i.*, + *acc.*, to push asunder, push in all directions; disperse. Он растолка́л прохо́жих и вы́шел вперёд, he pushed through the passersby and stepped forward. Они́ его́ растолка́ли и он наконе́ц просну́лся, they shook him until he woke up.

с-толк-ну́ть, *v.p.*, с-та́лк-ивать, *v.i.*, + *acc.*, с + *gen.*, в + *acc.*, to push, shove down. С. его́ с кру́чи в про́пасть, to push him over the precipice. С-толк-ну́ть-ся, *v.p.r.*, с-та́лк-ивать-ся, *v.i.r.*, с + *instr.*, to collide; conflict with. Поезда́ столкну́лись, the trains collided. Мне никогда́ не приходи́лось ста́лкиваться с ним, I never met him; (*colloq.*), I never had an argument with him. С-толк-нове́ние, *n.n.*, collision, impact, shock, conflict. Он ча́сто име́л с-ия с поли́цией, he often got into trouble with the police.

толк, *n.m.*, meaning, sense, understanding; doctrine; sect. О чём идёт толк? (*colloq.*), What are they talking about? Он зна́ет т. в му́зыке, he is a competent judge of music. Я ника́к не возьму́ э́того в т. (*colloq.*), I cannot understand it at all. Говори́ть с то́лком, to talk with sense, with meaning. В э́том нет никако́го то́лку, this has no sense whatsoever. Они́ сби́ли меня́ с то́лку, they disconcerted me. К какому старообря́дческому то́лку принадлежа́т они́? To which sect of the Old-Believers do they belong? То́лк-ом, *adv.*, clearly, sensibly. Раскажи́ мне э́то т., Tell me clearly, sensibly.

толк-ова́ть, *v.i.*, + *acc.*, to talk, comment, explain, interpret. Дово́льно т. о пустяка́х, stop talking about trifles. Что тут мно́го т., there's nothing to talk about. Он всё толку́ет в дурну́ю сто́рону, he sees everything in a bad light. Сена́т толку́ет зако́ны, the Senate interprets laws. Он всё толку́ет своё, he is always harping on the same note. Толк-ова́ть-ся, *v.i.r.*, used only in 3d pers., to be interpreted, explained. Как толку́ется э́то ме́сто? How is this passage interpreted? Толк-ова́ние, *n.n.*, interpretation, commentary, explana-tion. Пра́во толкова́ния зако́на принадлежи́т суду́, the right to interpret the laws belongs to the court. Толк-ова́тель, *n.m.*, commentator. Толк-о́вник, *n.m.*, (*obs.*), commentary, explanation. Толк-о́вый, *adj.*, sensible, bright; explanatory. Он т. ма́лый, (*colloq.*), he's a sensible fellow; he has a head on his shoulders. Т. слова́рь ру́сского языка́, explanatory dictionary of the Russian language. Толк-о́во, *adv.*, clearly, sensibly. Он о́чень т. всё объясни́л, he explained everything very clearly. Они́ т. устро́или свои́ дела́, they arranged their business soundly. Бес-толк-о́вый, *adj.*, inefficient; acting without common sense. Он б. челове́к, he is inefficient. Бес-толк-о́во, *adv.*, inefficiently. Он всё де́лает б., he does everything carelessly. Бес-толк-о́вость, *n.f.*, inefficiency. Он отлича́лся ре́дкой бестолко́востью, he was noted for his rare inefficiency (bungling). Бе́с-толк-у, *adv.*, in a haphazard manner. Бес-толк-о́вщина, *n.f.*, disorder, confusion. Бе́с-толоч-ь, *n.f.*, (*colloq.*), disorder, confusion. У них всегда́ невероя́тная б., they live in incredible confusion.

в-толк-ова́ть *v.p.*, в-толк-о́вывать, *v.i.*, + *acc.*, + *dat.*, (*colloq.*), to ram into; inculcate. Втолку́йте ему́, что он до́лжен э́то сде́лать, make him understand that he must do it.

пере-толк-ова́ть, *v.p.*, пере-толк-о́вывать, *v.i.*, + *acc.*, о + *prep.*, to talk about, discuss again; misinterpret. Нам на́до перетолкова́ть об э́том, we must discuss this matter again. Он всегда́ перетолко́вывает мои́ слова́, he always misinterprets my words.

по-толк-ова́ть, *v.p.*, о + *prep.*, to have a talk about. Мы потолкова́ли с ним об э́том де́ле, we had a talk about this matter.

рас-толк-ова́ть, *v.p.*, рас-толк-о́вывать, *v.i.*, + *acc.*, + *dat.*, to interpret, explain. Он до́лжен был растолкова́ть им ка́ждую подро́бность, he was obliged to explain every detail to them.

с-толк-ова́ть-ся, *v.p.r.*, с-толк-о́вывать-ся, *v.i.r.*, с + *instr.*, о + *prep.*, to come to an agreement with, about. Я не мог с ним столкова́ться, I could not agree with him.

толо́ч-ь, толк-у́, *v.i.*, + *acc.*, to crush, pound, powder, pulverize. На ку́хне толкли́ мак в сту́пе, they were crushing poppy seeds in a mortar. Толо́ч-ь-ся, *v.i.r.*, to hang about, loaf; mark time. Мы толчёмся на ме́сте, we are not getting anywhere. Он толчётся без де́ла, he is waiting around with nothing to do. Толо́чь во́ду в сту́пе, (saying), to carry coals to Newcastle. Толо́к-а, n.f., a field manured by pasturing cattle on it. Толо́к-но́, n.n., dry oatmeal. Хле́ба не́ было - е́ли толокно́, there was no bread, they ate dried oatmeal. Толч-е́ние, n.n., crushing, pulverization. Т. камне́й произво́дится маши́нами, stones are crushed in machines. Толч-ёный, adj., powdered, crushed. Она́ пекла́ пиро́жные из толчёного минда́ля, she baked pastry out of crushed almonds.

ис-толо́ч-ь, v.p., + acc., to pound, crush, grind. На́до и. ка́мни, что́бы лить бето́н, it is necessary to crush stones to make concrete.

на-толо́ч-ь, v.p., + acc., to pound, crush in quantity. Они́ натолкли́ мно́го минда́ля, they crushed a lot of almonds.

рас-толо́ч-ь, v.p., толо́ч-ь, v.i., acc., to pound, grind, pulverize. Апте́карь растоло́к в порошо́к лека́рство, the pharmacist pulverized the medicine.

с-толо́ч-ь, v.p., + acc., с + instr., to grind, crush; pound together. Он столо́к са́хар с кори́цей, he pulverized the sugar together with the cinnamon.

ТОЛСТ-, ТОЛЩ-, CORPULENCE, OBESITY, STOUTNESS, THICKNESS

то́лст-ый, adj., thick, stout, fat, corpulent, obese. Ло́дка привя́зана то́лстым кана́том к при́стани, the boat is tied to the wharf with a thick rope. У него́ то́лстое лицо́, he has a fat face. То́лст-енький, толст-ова́тый, adj., rather fat, plump. Он толстова́т и глупова́т, he is rather fat and stupid. То́лст-о, adv., thickly. Т. нама́зан ма́слом, thickly buttered Толст-о-, a combining form meaning fat, stout, thick. Толст-о-брю́хий, adj., (colloq.), big-bellied, fat-bellied. Толст-о-гу́бый, adj., thick-lipped. Толст-о-ко́жий, adj., thick-skinned. Толст-о-но́гий, adj., thick-legged. Толст-о-но́сый, adj., bottle-nosed. Толст-о-су́м, n.m., (obs.), moneybag. Толст-о-та́, n.f., thickness, stoutness. Толст-у́ха, толст-у́шка, n.f., (colloq.), buxom girl, woman. Толст-я́к, n.m., stout, corpulent man. Толсту́ха и толстя́к представля́ли смешну́ю па́ру, the buxom woman and the fat man made a comical couple.

толст-е́ть, v.i., от + gen., to grow stout, fatten. Лю́ди толсте́ют от мучно́й пи́щи, people grow fat from starchy foods.

толст-и́-ть, v.i., + acc., to make look stout. Э́то пла́тье толсти́т её, this dress makes her look stout.

то́лщ-а, n.f., thickness; thick mass; lump. Иде́я переворо́та зре́ет в наро́дной то́лще, the idea of a coup d'état is growing among the masses. То́лщ-е, adj., and adv., comp., thicker; more thickly. Лёд на о́зере то́лще, чем на реке́, the ice on the lake is thicker than on the river. Толщ-ина́, n.f., thickness, stoutness, obesity. Т. чернозёмного сло́я превыша́ет полме́тра, the layer of black earth is more than half a meter thick.

у-толщ-а́ть, v.i., у-толст-и́ть, v.p., to thicken. У-толщ-а́ть-ся, v.i.r., у-толст-и́ть-ся, v.p.r., to become thicker. В э́том ме́сте труба́ утолща́ется, the pipe becomes thicker in this place. У-толщ-е́ние, n.n., thickening; thicker part, section. Здесь у вас я́вное утолще́ние кости́, here you have an obvious thickening of the bone.

ТОНК-, ТОНЧ-, ТОН-, THINNESS

то́нк-ий, adj., thin, fine, delicate. У него́ т. го́лос, he has a thin voice. Для возду́шной по́чты употребля́ется то́нкая бума́га, thin paper is used for air mail. То́нкие ни́тки, fine thread. Т-ая рабо́та, delicate work. Он т. цени́тель иску́сства, a subtle judge of art. То́н-енький, adj., very thin, very fine. Де́вочка пе́ла то́неньким го́лосом, the girl sang in a thin little voice. То́нк-о, adv., thinly. Там был т. постро́енный план, there was a subtly devised plan. То́н-ь-ше, adj., and adv. comp., thinner; more thinly. Тонч-а́йший, adj., superl., extremely thin, thinnest. То́нк-о-, a combining form meaning thin, fine. Тонк-о-ко́жий, adj., thin-skinned. Тонк-о-но́гий, adj., spindle-legged. Тонк-о-но́сый, adj., tenuirostral (of birds). Тонк-о-ру́нный, pertaining to sheep having a fine fleece. Разведе́ние тонкору́нных ове́ц бы́ло вы́годно, the raising of sheep with a fine fleece was profitable. То́нк-ость, n.f., thinness, fineness, delicacy; sharpness. Т. шёлка, the fineness of the silk. Т. его́ сужде́ния была́ порази́тельна, the subtlety of his reasoning was amazing.

у-тонч-и́ть, v.p., у-тонч-а́ть, v.i., + acc., to thin, make thinner; refine. Но́вые тексти́льные маши́ны утончи́ли ни́ти и тка́ни, new textile machines are producing thinner threads and materials. У-тонч-а́ть-ся, v.i.r., у-тонч-и́ть-ся, v.p.r., to become thinner, more refined; taper off. Ма́чта утонча́ется к ве́рху, the mast tapers off towards the top. У-тонч-е́ние, n.n., thinning, refining; tapering. У. культу́ры способствовало развитию искусств, the refinement of culture contributed to the development of the arts. У-тонч-ённость, *n.f.*, refinement, subtlety. Он превосходит других утончённостью своего вкуса, he surpasses others through the refinement of his taste. У-тонч-ённый, *adj., part. pass. past,* refined, subtle. У-ая жестокость, refined cruelty.

ТОН-, ТОП-, ТОП(Л)-, ТАП(Л)-, DROWNING, SINKING

тон-у́-ть, *v.i.,* по-тон-у́ть, *v.p.,* to drown; sink. Помогите, человек тонет! Help, a man is drowning!

за-тон-у́ть, *v.p.,* to sink, be submerged. Корабль затонул возле берега, the ship sank near the shore. За-тонувший, *adj., part. act. past,* sunk, submerged. З. корабль лежал на дне, the sunken ship lay at the bottom.

по-тон-у́ть, *v.p.,* тон-уть, *v.i.,* to be drowned; drown; sink. По-тон-увший, *adj., part. act. past,* sunken. П. град Китеж, (*folklore*), the sunken city of Kitezh.

у-тон-у́ть, *v.p.,* у-топ-а́ть, тон-у́ть, *v.i.,* to be drowned; founder, sink. Мальчик утонул, купаясь в реке, the little boy drowned while swimming in the river. Комната утопала в цветах, the room was filled with flowers. У-топ-а́я, *v. adv.,* sinking; wallowing; disappearing. Она исчезла, утопая в сияньи голубого дня, (*poet.*), she disappeared into the blue of day.

топ-и́-ть, топ-л-ю, *v.i.,* + *acc.,* to drown, sink. Мина топила суда, the torpedo sank ships. Топ-и́ть-ся, *v.i.,* to drown oneself. С горя он побежал топиться, he ran to drown himself from grief. Топ-кий, *adj.,* swampy, muddy, marshy. Здесь т-ое место, there is a swampy place here. Топ-кость, *n.f.,* swampiness. Т. поляны грозила опасностью для охотников, the swampiness of the clearing was dangerous for hunters.

за-топ-и́ть, *v.p.,* за-топ-л-я́ть, *v.i.,* to flood, inundate, sink. Разлившаяся река затопила луга, the overflowing river flooded the meadows. Они сами затопили свои суда, they scuttled their ships.

пере-топ-и́ть, *v.p.,* + *acc.,* to sink in quantity. Подводные лодки перетопили много кораблей, submarines have sunk many ships.

по-топ-и́ть, по-топ-л-ю, *v.p.,* по-топ-ля́ть, *v.i.,* + *acc.,* to sink, drown. Буря потопила много пароходов, the hurricane sank many ships. По-топ, *n.m.,*

flood, deluge. Всемирный потоп, (*Bib.*), the Great Deluge. После меня хоть потоп, (*saying*), after me the deluge. По-топ-ле́ние, *n.n.,* sinking. Опасность потопления подводными лодками увеличилась, the danger of ships being sunk by submarines has increased.

у-топ-и́ть, *v.p.,* топ-и́ть, *v.i.,* + *acc.,* to drown, sink. Убийца утопил свою жертву, the killer drowned his victim. Он утопил своё горе в вине, (*fig.*), he drowned his sorrow in wine. У-топ-а́ющий, *adj., part. act. pres.,* drowning. Медаль за спасение утопающего, medal for saving a drowning man. У-топ-и́ть-ся, *v.p.r,* to be drowned, drown. Он утопился в этом озере, he drowned in this lake. У-топ-ле́ние, *n.n.,* drowning. У-топ-ленник, *n.m.,* у-топ-ленница, *n.f.,* one who has drowned. Волна выбросила утопленника на берег, the wave washed ashore the body of a drowned man.

ТОРГ-, ТОРЖ-, TRADE; TRIUMPH

торг, *n.m.,* bargain, bargaining; auction. Мы продаём без торгу, we sell without bargaining. Имение продали с торгов, the estate was sold at auction. Торг-а́ш, *n.m.,* one who haggles, who bargains; peddler, small dealer. На ярмарку приезжало много мелких торгашей, many peddlers came to the fair. Торг-а́шеский, *adj.,* mercenary. У него т-ая душа, he has a mercenary soul. Торг-а́шествовать, *v.i.,* to haggle. Всё село торгашествовало, the village consisted of small dealers. Торг-а́шество, *n.n.,* peddling, petty bargaining. Т. было их главным занятием, peddling was their main occupation. Торг-пред, *abbr.* торговый представитель, (*recent*), trade representative. Т. был отозван в Москву, the trade representative was recalled to Moscow. Торг-предство, *abbr. of* торговое представительство, (*recent*), trade mission, trade delegation.

торг-ова́ть, *v.i.,* + *instr.,* to trade, deal, sell. Чем вы торгуете? What do you trade in? Он торгует без запроса, he is selling at fixed prices. Т. в разнос, to peddle. Т. оптом, to deal in wholesale. Т. в розницу, to deal in retail. Торг-ова́ть-ся, *v.i.r.,* to bargain, haggle. Он торгуется из-за каждого гроша, he haggles over every penny. Торг-овец, *n.m.,* tradesman, merchant. Он крупный т. вином, he is a big wine merchant. Т. галантереей, haberdasher. Т. железом и скобяным товаром, ironmonger; hardware merchant. Т. хлебом (хлеботоргóвец), grain merchant. Торг-óвцы, tradespeople. Торг-óвка, *n.f.*, market woman. На базáре сидéли торгóвки овощáми и фрýктами, in the market place sat women selling fruit and vegetables. Торг-óвля, *n.f.*, commerce; trade. Внéшняя т., foreign trade. Внýтренняя, т., domestic trade. Колхóзная т., collective farm trade. Молóчная т., general store. Меновáя т., barter. Оптóвая т., wholesale trade. Рóзничная т., retail trade. Торг-óвый, *adj.*, trading, commercial. mercantile. Заключúть мéжду собóй торгóвый договóр, to conclude a trade agreement. Т. дом брáтьев Орлóвых, the trading firm of Orlov Brothers. Т. оборóт, trade turnover. Т. флот, merchant fleet. Т-ая палáта, chamber of commerce. Т-ое сýдно, merchant ship, freighter. Т-ые кнúги, accounting books. Торг-ов-о-промýшленный,◄ *adj.*, pertaining to commerce and industry.

вы́-торг-овать, *v.p.,* вы-торгóвывать, *v.i.,* + *acc.,* to gain by trading, by bargaining. Он вы́торговал себé 10-процéнтную скúдку, by bargaining he obtained a ten percent discount.

на-торг-овáть, *v.p.,* на-торг-óвывать, *v.i.,* + *acc.,* + *gen.,* на + *acc.,* to sell for a certain sum; gain by trading. Онú сегóдня мнóго наторговáли: на 1000 рублéй, business was good today, they made 1,000 rubles.

по-торг-овáть, *v.p.,* торг-овáть, *v.i.,* + *instr.,* to trade, deal, sell. Сегóдня мы хорошó поторговáли, we had a good business day today. По-торг-овáть-ся, *v.p.r.,* to bargain. Я поторговáлся и получúл скúдку, I bargained and obtained a discount.

при-торг-овáть, *v.p.,* при-торг-óвывать, *v.i.,* + *acc.,* to negotiate successfully. Я приторговáл себé дом, I negotiated successfully for a house. При-торг-овáть-ся, *v.p.r.,* при-торг-óвывать-ся, *v.i.r.,* to negotiate. Я давнó приторгóвываюсь к этому дóму, I've been negotiating for this house for a long time.

про-торг-овáть, *v.p.,* про-торг-óвывать, *v.i.,* + *acc.,* to lose in trade. Он проторговáл 10,0000 рублéй, he lost ten thousand rubles in trade. Он проторговáл недéлю я́блоками, he sold apples the whole week long; he spent a week selling apples. Про-торг-овáть-ся, *v.p. r.,* про-торг- овывать-ся, *v.i.r.,* to bargain for a while; to lose in trading. Он в конéц проторговáлся, his business is utterly ruined. Он проторго-

вáлся цéлый час, he bargained for a whole hour.

с-торг-овáть-ся, *v.p.r.,* с-торг-óвывать-ся, *v.i.r.,* с + *instr.,* на, в + *prep.,* to make a bargain; come to an understanding in trading. Я сторговáлся с ним в ценé, we agreed on the price. С. на 50 рубля́х, to agree on fifty rubles.

тóрж-ище, *n.n.,* (*obs.*), market; market place. Торж-éственный, *adj.,* solemn, pompous; triumphant, gala, ceremonial. Сегóдня т. день, today is a solemn day. Т-ое открытие парлáмента, the ceremonial opening of parliament. Торж-éственно, *adv.,* solemnly, triumphantly. Гóрод т. отпрáздновал столéтие своегó основáния, the city solemnly celebrated the hundredth anniversary of its founding. Торж-éственность, *n.f.,* solemnity, solemnness. Церкóвная слýжба отличáлась торжéственностью, the church service was very majestic. Торж-ествó, *n.n.,* triumph, celebration, victory. Т. добродéтели над порóком, the triumph of virtue over vice.

торж-ествовáть, *v.i.,* над + *instr.,* + *gen.,* по пóводу + *gen.,* to triumph over, exult. Т. по поводу побéды, to celebrate a victory. Онú покá торжествýют над нáми, for the time being they have the upper hand over us. Торж-ествýющий, *adj., part. act. pres.,* triumphant. Т. победúтель вступúл в гóрод, the triumphant victor entered the city. Торж-оствовáние, *n.n.,* triumph. Т. зла не вéчно, the triumph of evil does not last forever.

вос-тóрг, *n.m.,* rapture; delight; exaltation. Он в востóрге от неё, he is enraptured by her.

вос-торг-áть-ся, *v.i.r.,* + *instr.,* to be delighted. Мы восторгáемся красотóй мéстности, we are enraptured with the beauty of the countryside.

вос-тóрж-ен(ный), *adj.,* enthusiastic. У негó востóрженная душá, he has an enthusiastic nature. Вос-тóрж-енность, *n.f.,* exultation, enthusiasm. В. сменúлась разочаровáнием, enthusiasm turned into disappointment.

вос-торж-ествовáть, *v.p.,* над + *instr.,* to triumph. В. над своúми врагáми, to triumph over one's enemies.

ис-торг-áть, *v.i.,* ис-тóрг-нуть, *v.p.,* + *acc.,* to erupt; force out; wrench, wrest. Онú бы́ли истóргнуты из их среды́, they were forced out of their milieu. Ис-торж-éние, *n.n.,* eruption; wresting. Ис-тóрж-енный, *adj., part. pass. past,* extorted. И-ое обещáние недействúтельно по закóну, a forced promise is not valid according to the law.

ТРЕСК-, ТРЕС-, ТРЕЩ-, CRACK, CRACKING

треск, *n.m.,* crack, crash. Дéрево упáло с трéском, the tree fell with a crash. Он с трéском провалѝлся на экзáмене, (*colloq.*), he failed dismally in the examination. Треск-отня́, *n.f.,* rattle, clatter, chirp. В пóле стоя́ла т. кузнéчиков, the chirp of crickets was heard in the field. Треск-ýчий, *adj.,* crashing. Т. морóз, hard (sharp) frost. Т-ие фрáзы, high-flown phrases.

трéск-ать, *v.i.,* по-трéск-ать, *v.p.,* + *acc.,* (*vulgar*), to gobble food. Трéск-ать-ся, *v.i.r.,* по-трéск-ать-ся, *v.p.r.,* to crack, chap. У них рýки трéскаются от хóлода, their hands become chapped from the cold. Трéск-ание, *n.n.,* cracking, splitting.

трéс-нуть, *v.p.smf.,* + *acc.,* to strike hard, deal a heavy blow. Он трéснул егó по головé, (*colloq.*), he gave him a blow on the head. Трéс-нуть, *v.p.,* *intrans., used in 3d pers. only,* to crack, split, chap. От удáра у негó трéснул чéреп, his skull was fractured by the blow. Окóнное стеклó трéснуло, the window pane is cracked. Трéс-нувший, *adj., part. act. past,* cracked. Т-ая стенá, cracked wall. Трéс-нуть-ся, *v.p.r.smf.,* о + *acc.,* to hit against, strike, knock. Он трéснулся об ýгол столá, (*colloq.*), he struck himself against the corner. of the table. Над-трéс-нутый, *adj.,* cracked. Н. кóлокол бóльше не звонѝт, a cracked bell no longer rings.

по-трéск-ивать, *v.i.,* to crackle. Дровá потрéскивают в камѝне, the wood is crackling in the fireplace. По-трéск-ивание, *n.n.,* crackling.

рас-трéск-ивать-ся, *v.i.r.,* рас-трéск-ать-ся, рас-трéс-нуть-ся, *v.p.r.,* to crack to pieces; chap; be covered with cracks; parch. Потолóк нáшей кóмнаты рас-трéскался, the ceiling of our room is covered with cracks. У негó рас-трéскиваются гýбы от жáра, his lips are parched from fever.

трещ-áть, *v.i.,* to creak, rattle; burst, split, Мáчта трещѝт от вéтра, the mast is creaking in the wind. Онá трещѝт без ýмолку, (*colloq.*), she is rattling away. Пóсле вчерáшней попóйки у негó трещѝт головá, (*colloq.*), his head is splitting after last night's drinking bout. Трещ-áние, *n.n.,* crackling, rattling, chattering. Трéщ-ина, *n.f.,* crack, split, rift. На стенé большáя т., there is a large crack in the wall. Трещ-óтка, *n.f.,* child's rattle; (*fig.*), chatterbox. Онá неугомóнная т., (*colloq.*), she is an inveterate chatterbox.

за-трещ-áть, *v.p.,* to begin to rattle, to crack. Стул затрещáл под егó вéсом, the chair began to crack under his weight. В лесý затрещáли пулемёты, machine guns began to rattle in the forest. За-трéщ-ина, *n.f.,* box on the ears; blow; crack on the head. Он дал емý здорóвую затрéщину, (*vulgar*), he boxed his ears.

про-трещ-áть, *v.p.,* to rattle for a while; din. Пулемёты протрещáли и замóлкли, the machine guns rattled for a while, then stopped. Он нам протрещáл э́тим все ýши, (*colloq.*), he has dinned this into our ears.

ТРУД-, ТРУЖ-, ТРУЖД-, LABOR

труд, *n.m.,* labor, work. Физѝческий труд полéзен, physical work is wholesome. Он получѝл э́то без трудá, he obtained this without difficulty. Министéрство Трудá, Ministry of Labor. Трýд-ный, *adj.,* difficult, hard. Онѝ не поддержáли егó в трýдную минýту, they failed to support him in a difficult moment. Настáли трýдные временá, hard times are here. Трýд-но, *adv.,* difficult, hard. Емý óчень трýдно угодѝть, he is hard to please. Этому т. повéрить, this is hard to believe. Трýд-ность, *n.f.,* difficulty, hardship. Труд-новáтый, *adj.,* rather difficult. Труд-новáто, *adv.,* rather difficult. С э́тим спрáвиться т., it is rather hard to manage this.

труд-ѝть-ся, труж-ýсь, *v.i.r.,* над + *instr.,* to work, labor. Онá всю жизнь трудѝлась, she has worked hard all her life. Изобретáтель дóлго трудѝлся над своѝм изобретéнием, the inventor worked for a long time at his invention. Не трудѝтесь, пожáлуйста, Don't trouble yourself, please!

на-труд-ѝть, *v.p.,* на-трýж-ивать, *v.i.,* + *acc.,* (*colloq.*), to fatigue, weary, strain. Он натрудѝл себé колéно, he has strained his knee. На-труд-ѝть-ся, *v.p.r.,* to work to exhaustion, strain oneself, become strained through work.

по-труд-ѝть-ся, *v.p.r.,* to work, take the trouble. Он достáточно потрудѝлся над э́тим, he has worked hard enough at it. Потрудѝтесь, пожáлуйста, сдéлать э́то! Please, take the trouble to do it!

за-труд-нѝть, *v.p.,* за-труд-ня́ть, *v.i.,* +

acc., + *instr.*, to impede, cause difficulties, give trouble; embarrass. Надéюсь, я не затрудню вас своéй прóсьбой, I hope my request will not cause you any trouble. За-труд-нён-ный, *adj.*, *part. pass. past*, impeded, difficult. У больнóго затруднённое дыхáние, the patient is breathing with difficulty. За-труд-ни́ть-ся, *v.p.r.*, за-труд-ня́ть-ся, *v.i.r.*, to be perplexed; experience trouble, difficulty. Он затрудня́ется испóлнить егó прóсьбу, he is having difficulty fulfilling his request. За-трудне́ние, *n.n.*, difficulty; embarrassment, perplexity. Дéнежные затруднéния, financial difficulties. Он вы́вел егó из затруднéния, he helped him out of a predicament. За-труд-ни́тельный, *adj.*, difficult, embarrassing, puzzling. Он нахóдится в óчень затрудни́тельном положéнии, he is in great difficulty. За-труд-ни́тельность, *n.f.*, difficulty. З. положéния, difficulty of situation.

труд-овóй, *adj.*, pertaining to labor; earned through labor. Т. дохóд, (*recent*), earnings from physical work. Т-áя жизнь, a life of hard work. Т-áя пови́нность, (*recent*), labor draft. Не-труд-овóй, *adj.*, (*recent*), not earned through labor. Н. дохóд, (*recent*), unearned income. Труд-о-дéнь, *n.m.*, (*recent*), workday. В колхóзах труд оплáчивается по трудодня́м, on collective farms work is paid for by the work day unit. Труд-о-люби́вый, *adj.*, assiduous, industrious, diligent. Труд-о-люби́во, *adv.*, industriously, assiduously, diligently. Труд-о-лю́бие, *n.n.*, industry, assiduity. Он превосхóдит всех свои́м трудолю́бием, he surpasses everyone in industry. Труд-о-спосóбный, *adj.*, able-bodied; efficient. Труд-о-спосóбность, *n.f.*, capacity for work. Егó т. óчень малá, his capacity for work is very low. Не-труд-о-спосóбный, *adj.*, disabled. Не-труд-о-спосóбность, *n.f.*, disability. Труд-я́щийся, *adj.*, *part. act. pres.*, working, toiling. Т-иеся мáссы, working masses.

труж-еник, *n.m.*, трýж-еница, *n.f.*, hard worker. Т. науки, devoted scientist. Трýж-енический, *adj.*, industrious, toiling. Т-ая жизнь, a life of hard work. у-труждáть, *v.i.*, + *acc.*, + *instr.*, to trouble, inconvenience. Я не стáну у. вас своéй прóсьбой, I will not trouble you with my request. Я не хочý вас у., I do not want to trouble you. У-трудж-áть-ся, *v.i.r.*, (*obs.*), to take the trouble, trouble oneself. Не утруждáйтесь напрáсно! Don't trouble yourself, it will be of no avail.

ТУГ-, ТУЖ-, ТЯГ-, ТЯ-, ТЯЖ-, ТЯЗ-, TIGHTNESSS, STIFFNESS, STRAIN; GRIEF, BURDEN

туг-óй, *adj.*, tight, stiff, taut. Он нóсит т-и́е воротники́, he wears tight collars. Они́ тýги на расплáту, (*colloq.*), they are stingy. Он туг нá ухо, he is deaf. Тýг-о, *adv.*, tightly, stiffly, tautly; slowly. Тýж-е, *adj. and adv. comp.*, tighter, stiffer, more taut; more tightly, more stiffly. Он тýго наби́л чемодáн, he packed his suitcase tightly. Механик тýго натянýл прóволоку, the mechanic stretched the wire tightly. Емý прихóдится тýго, he is in straitened circumstances. Стяни́те тýже пóяс, tighten your belt. Туг-о-вáтый, *adj.*, rather tight. Он туговáт нá ухо, he is hard of hearing. Туг-о-плáвкий, *adj.*, refractory. Туг-о-ýздый, *adj.*, hard-mouthed (of a horse). Тýг-ость, *n.f.*, slowness; tautness. Т. слýха, deafness. Тýг-а, *n.f.*, (*obs.*), grief, regret, sorrow. Т. разлилáсь по рýсской землé, (*obs. poet.*), sorrow overwhelmed all of Russia.

туж-и́ть, туж-ý, *v.i.*, (*colloq.*), to grieve, regret. Нéчего вам тужи́ть, you must not grieve. Туж-и́ть-ся, *v.i.r.*, на + *acc.*, to grieve, regret. Он тýжится на свою́ несчáстную судьбý, he grieves over his miserable fate.

тýж-ить-ся, *v.i.r.*, по-тýж-ить-ся, *v.p.r.*, to make an effort, strain. Он тýжится подня́ть э́тот кáмень, he is straining to lift this stone. По-тýг-а, *n.f.*, straining effort (*as in childbirth*). Бесплóдные потýги, vain efforts.

на-тýж-ить-ся, *v.p.r.*, to make an effort, strain. По-на-тýж-ить-ся, *v.p.r.*, to strain for a while. Он понатýжился и реши́л задáчу, he made an effort and solved the problem. На-тýг-а, *n.f.*, effort, strain. Заболéть от натýги, to become ill from overstraining.

за-туж-и́ть, *v.p.*, (*colloq.*), to begin to grieve. Затужи́ла бéдная дéвушка, the poor girl began to grieve.

по-туж-и́ть, *v.p.*, (*colloq.*), to grieve a little. Он потужи́л, потужи́л и утéшился, he grieved a little, then consoled himself.

тя́г-а, *n.f.*, draft, pull, traction; migration (*as* of birds). В печи́ плохáя тя́га, there is too little draft in the stove.

тяг-áть, *v.i.*, + *acc.*, (*colloq.*), to drag. Т. тяжёлые мешки́, to drag heavy bags. Он тягáл их по судáм, (*colloq.*), he dragged them through the courts. Тяг-áть-ся, *v.i.r.*, с + *instr.*, to litigate; compete with. С ним трýдно т., it is hard to compete with him. Тяг-áние, *п.п.*, litigation, competition. Т. по судам очень неприятно, litigation is very unpleasant. Тяг-ло, *п.п.*, (*hist.*), land allotted to peasant families and subject to taxation. Тяг-лый, *adj.*, pertaining to peasant taxes; pertaining to a burden. Т. скот, beasts of burden. Тяг-ость, *n.f.*, тяг-ота, *n.f.*, burden, weight, load, heaviness. Мы были в тягость ему, we were a burden to him. Т. жизни, burdens of life. Тяг-остный, *adj.*, burdensome; painful. Т-ое впечатление, painful impression.

тяг-от-еть, *v.i.*, к + *dat.*, над + *instr.*, to gravitate towards, be attracted to; weigh over, hang over. Он тяготеет к науке, he is attracted to science. Над ними тяготеет проклятие, a curse hangs over them. Тяг-отение, *п.п.*, gravitation; attraction. Ньютонов закон тяготения, Newton's law of gravitation.

тяг-от-й-ть, тяг-ощу, *v.i.*, + *acc.*, overwhelm, overburden, hang heavy on, be a burden. Совершённое преступление тяготит его совесть, the committed crime hangs heavy on him.

тяг-отйть-ся, *v.i.r.*, + *instr.*, to feel the weight, the burden. Он тяготится зависимостью от них, his dependence on them is hard on him.

о-тяг-от-йть, *v.p.*, о-тяг-ощать, *v.i.*, + *acc.*, + *instr.*, to burden, load. Его отягощала большая семья, he was burdened by a large family. О-тяг-ощение, *п.п.*, burdening. Это большое о. для него, this is a heavy burden for him. О-тяг-отйтельный, *adj.*, heavy, difficult, burdensome, irksome. Эта служба отяготительна для него, this job irks him.

тя-ну́-ть (*from* тяг-ну́ть), тя-ну́, *v.i.*, тяг-ивать, *v.i.*, + *acc.*, to delay, prolong. Рыбаки тянут сети, the fishermen are dragging the nets. Он тянет его за волосы, he is pulling him by the hair. Нас тянет домой, we are longing to go home. Они тянут наше дело, they are delaying our case. Тя-ну́ть-ся, *v.i.r.*, to stretch; run along; spread, extend; last; strive for. Дорога тянется вдоль леса, the road skirts the woods. Он не может тянуться за ними, he cannot keep up with them. Его болезнь тянется очень долго, his illness is dragging on. Время тянется, time drags on. Тяг-учий, *adj.*, ductile; viscous; wearisome. Они затянули тягучую песнь, they started a slow, drawn out song. Т-ее вещество, viscous substance. Тяг-учесть, *n.f.*, ductility, malleability. Т. меди, the malleability of copper. Тя-ну́чка, *n.f.*, tof-

fee. Тянучки делают из сахара, сливок и масла, toffee is made from sugar, cream and butter.

в-тя-ну́ть, *v.p.*, в-тяг-ивать, *v.i.*, + *acc.*, to draw in, pull in; involve. Лёгкие втягивают воздух, the lungs draw in air. Его втянули в невыгодную сделку, he has become involved in an unprofitable transaction. В-тя-ну́ть-ся, *v.p.r.*, в-тяг-ивать-ся, *v.i.r.*, в + *acc.*, to become accustomed to. Он втянулся в работу, he got used to the work.

вы́-тя-ну́ть, *v.p.*, вы-тяг-ивать, *v.i.*, + *acc.*, to stretch out; extract. Змея вытянула шею и зашипела, the snake stretched its neck and hissed. Вы́-тя-ну́ть-ся, *v.p.r.*, вы-тяг-ивать-ся, *v.i.r.*, to be stretched, lengthened, pulled out. Он вытянулся на постели, he stretched out on the bed. Вы́-тяж-ка, *n.f.*, extract. В. из щитовидной железы, thyroid extract. Стоять на вытяжку, to stand at attention.

до-тя-ну́ть, *v.p.*, до-тяг-ивать, *v.i.*, до + *gen.*, to drag to; live till; last; postpone. В этом селе никогда не дотягивают до нового урожая, in this village grain never lasts until the new harvest comes in. Он вряд-ли дотянет до утра, he will hardly live through the night. До-тя-ну́ть-ся, *v.p.r.*, до-тяг-ивать-ся, *v.i.r.*, до + *gen.*, to reach; drag oneself as far as. Раненый еле дотянулся до лазарета, the wounded man was hardly able to reach the dressing station.

за-тя-ну́ть, *v.p.*, за-тяг-ивать, *v.i.*, + *acc.*, to tighten, draw tight; drag out, delay. З. узел, to tighten the knot. Они затягивают наше дело, they are delaying our case. За-тя-ну́ть-ся, *v.p.r.*, за-тяг-ивать-ся, *v.i.r.*, to be laced tight; be delayed; heal; inhale. Болезнь затянулась, the illness prolonged itself. Его рана не затягивается, his wound is not healing. Не затягивайся! Do not inhale! За-тяж-ка, *n.f.*, tightening; delay; inhaling. З. времени, delay. Он сделал глубокую затяжку, he inhaled deeply. За-тяж-ной, *adj.*, slow, lingering. Болезнь приняла з. характер, the disease developed into a lingering malady.

на-тя-ну́ть, *v.p.*, на-тяг-ивать, *v.i.*, + *acc.*, на + *acc.*, to stretch, draw on, pull on. Н. перчатки, to pull on gloves. Н. вожжи, to pull the reins. На-тя-ну́ть-ся, *v.p.r.*, на-тяг-ивать-ся, *v.i.r.*, to be stretched; stretch. Струны скрипки натягиваются при помощи колков, the violin strings are stretched by means of pegs. На-тяж-ение, *п.п.*, pulling; tension. Чрезмерное н. троса, привело́ к его́ разры́ву, excessive tension caused the cable to break. На-тя́ж-ка, *n.f.*, stretched interpretation. На-тя́-нутость, *n.f.*, tension; stiffness; strain. Н. отноше́ний, strained relations. На-тя́-нутый, *adj., part. pass. past*, tense, stiff; forced. Н-ые отноше́ния, strained relations. Н-ая любе́зность, stiff politeness. Н-ое сравне́ние, farfetched comparison. Н-ые стру́ны, taut strings.

об-тя-ну́ть, *v.p.*, об-тя́г-ивать, *v.i.*, + *acc.*, + *instr.*, to stretch; cover; upholster. О. дива́н кре́тоном, to cover a sofa with cretonne. Об-тя́ж-ка, *n.f.*, stretching, covering; close fit. На ней бы́ло пла́тье в обтя́жку, she wore a close-fitting dress.

от-тя-ну́ть, *v.p.smf.*, от-тя́г-ивать, *v.i.*, + *acc.*, + *gen.*, to pull away, draw off; delay. Неприя́тель оттяну́л свой войска́ от реки́, the enemy withdrew his troops from the river. От-тя́ж-ка, *n.f.*, delay, procrastination. Это то́лько о. кри́зиса, this is only a delay of the crisis.

пере-тя-ну́ть *v.p.*, пере-тя́г-ивать, *v.i.*, + *acc.*, + *instr.*, to outweigh, overbalance; prevail; overpower; win over; gird, fasten. Он перетяну́л их на свою́ сто́рону, he won them over. Он ту́го перетяну́л чемода́н ремнём, he fastened the suitcase with a leather strap.

по-тя-ну́ть, *v.p.*, по-тя́г-ивать, *v.i.*, + *acc.*, to pull, draw inhale; sip. Потяни́те дверь за ру́чку, pull the door towards you. Он потя́гивал вино́, he was sipping wine. Друзья́ потяну́ли его́ в теа́тр, his friends dragged him off to the theatre. Тя́нут-потя́нут, вы́тянуть не мо́гут, (*folklore*), they tug and tug and cannot pull it out. По-тя-ну́ть-ся, *v.p.r.*, по-тя́г-ивать-ся, *v.i.r.*, to stretch oneself; last, endure. Потяну́лись бесконе́чные до́лгие дни, the days dragged on endlessly. У́тром он потя́гивается, in the morning he stretches himself. По-тя́г-ивание, *n.n.*, act of stretching oneself out.

под-тя-ну́ть, *v.p.*, под-тя́г-ивать, *v.i.*, + *acc.*, to pull up, haul; draw up; join in a song, take in hand; accompany with the voice. Солда́т подтяну́л подпру́гу, the soldier tightened the girth of the saddle. Он пел, а они́ подтя́гивали, he sang and they joined in. Под-тя-ну́ть-ся, *v.p.r.*, под-тя́г-ивать-ся, *v.i.r.*, to pull oneself together, take oneself in hand; be tightened; draw near. По́сле вы́говора он подтяну́лся, after the reprimand he took himself in hand. Он подтяну́лся на трапе́ции, he pulled himself up on the trapeze. Под-тя́ж-ки, *n.f.pl.*, suspenders. Он но́сит брю́ки на подтя́жках, he wears his trousers on suspenders.

при-тя-ну́ть, *v.p.*, при-тя́г-ивать, *v.i.*, + *acc.*, к + *dat.*, to draw to oneself, attract; prosecute, arraign. Магни́т притя́гивает желе́зо, a magnet draws iron to itself. П. к отве́тственности, (*colloq.*), to bring to book. Он всех притя́гивает к себе́, he attracts everyone. При-тя-ну́ть-ся, *v.p.r.*, при-тя́г-ивать-ся, *v.i.r.*, + *instr.*, to be drawn, be attracted. Земля́ притя́гивается со́лнцем, the earth is attracted by the sun. При-тяг-а́тельный, *adj.*, attracting, attractive. Э́тот магни́т облада́ет грома́дной притяга́тельной си́лой, this magnet has an enormous power of attraction. При-тяж-а́тельный, *adj.*, possessive. "Мой - притяжа́тельное местоиме́ние "my" is a possessive pronoun. При-тяж-е́ние, *n.n.*, attraction. Магни́тное п., magnetic attraction.

про-тя-ну́ть, *v.p.*, про-тя́г-ивать, *v.i.*, + *acc.*, to stretch out, extend, reach out, draw through; proffer. По оде́жке протя́гивай но́жки, (*prov.*), cut your coat according to your cloth. П. про́волоку, to stretch a wire. П. ни́тку сквозь иго́лку, to thread a needle. Он до́лго не протя́нет, (*colloq.*), he won't last long. Она́ протяну́ла ему́ ру́ку, she extended her hand to him. П. но́ги, (*colloq.*), to die. Про-тя-ну́ть-ся, *v.p.r.*, про-тя́г-ивать-ся, *v.i.r*, to be extended, reached; to be stretched. По стране́ протяну́лась железнодоро́жная сеть, a network of railroads has been extended over the country. Про-тя́ж-ность, *n.f.*, slowness (*as of speech*); drawl. Про-тя́ж-но, *adv.*, in a drawling way. Говори́ть п., to drawl. Про-тя́ж-ный, *adj.*, lasting, lengthy, long; drawling. П. гудо́к, long blast.

рас-тя-ну́ть, *v.p.*, рас-тя́г-ивать, *v.i.*, + *acc.*, to lengthen, stretch; sprain; drawl; extend. Они́ сли́шком растяну́ли свой фронт, they have overextended their front. Он растяну́л себе́ сухожи́лие, he strained a tendon. Рас-тя-ну́ть-ся, *v.p.r.*, рас-тя́г-ивать-ся, *v.i.r.*, to stretch, be stretched, lengthened; sprawl, fall. Рези́на растя́гивается, rubber stretches. Рас-тяж-е́ние, *n.n.*, expansion; extension; strain; sprain. Р. му́скула боле́зненно, spraining a muscle is painful. Рас-тяж-и́мость, *n.f.*, extensibility, elasticity, tensility. Рас-тяж-и́мый, *adj.*, extensible, elastic, tensile. Р-ое определе́ние, elastic definition. Рас-тя́ж-ка, *n.f.*, stretching, extending. Дать сапоги́ на растя́жку, to have one's shoes stretched.

с-тя-ну́ть, *v.p.,* с-тя́г-ивать, *v.i.,* + *acc.,* to draw together, constrict, tighten; strap, tie, bind; (*mil.*), gather up forces; to pull off. Неприя́тель стя́гивает войска́ в э́том ме́сте, the enemy is concentrating his troops in this place. Он стяну́л чемода́н ремня́ми, he strapped his suitcase. С. сапоги́ с ног, to pull the boots off one's feet. С-тя-ну́ть, *v.p.,* + *acc.,* с + *instr.,* to filch, pilfer; pull off, away. Кто́-то стяну́л мои́ часы́ в толпе́ (*fig.*), someone in the crowd filched my watch. С-тя-ну́ть-ся, *v.r.r.,* с-тя́г-ивать-ся, *v.i.r.,* to be drawn together, be tightened. Пла́тье стя́гивается по́ясом, the dress is held by a belt.

с-тяж-а́ть, *v.p.,* + *acc.,* (*obs.*), to acquire, obtain. До́брыми дела́ми он стяжа́л о́бщую любо́вь, he was generally loved for his good deeds. С-тяж-а́ние, *п.п.,* acquisition; unscrupulous acquisition of money. С-тяж-а́тель, *п.т.,* (*obs.*), one who acquires something through unscrupulous means. Не бу́дьте стяжа́телями, don't be a money grabber. С-тяж-а́тельный, *adj.,* grasping, greedy, avaricious. С-тяж-а́тельство, *n.f.,* money grabbing; greed, greediness.

у-тя-ну́ть, *v.p.,* у-тя́г-ивать, *v.i.,* + *acc.,* to draw away by force; decrease; steal, pilfer. Мы торгова́лись и он рубль утяну́л, we bargained and he gave a ruble less.

тяж, *п.т.,* trace (harness).

тя́ж-б-а, *n.f.,* (*obs.*), lawsuit, litigation; court action. Она́ ведёт тя́жбу про́тив него́, she is prosecuting him in court. Тя́ж-ебный, *adj.,* (*obs.*), pertaining to a lawsuit; litigious. Это сло́жное т-ое де́ло, this is a complicated lawsuit. Тя́жущийся, *adj., part. act. pres.,* used as *n.,* (*obs.*) litigant. Пригласи́те тя́жущихся! Invite the litigants!

тяж-ел-е́ть, *v.i.,* to grow, become heavy. Ребёнок тяжеле́ет с ка́ждым ме́сяцем, this child is growing heavier every month. Тяж-ёлый, *adj.,* heavy, weighty, hard. Т. чемода́н, heavy suitcase. Т-ое положе́ние, difficult situation. Тяжело́, *adv.,* heavily, weightily, painfully, hard. Т. нагружённый ваго́н, heavily loaded car. Т. вздыха́ть, to sigh heavily. Мне т. расста́ться с ва́ми, it is hard for me to leave you. Тяж-ело́-, *a combining form meaning* heavy. Тяжел-о-ве́сный, *adj.,* heavy, ponderous. Т. стиль, ponderous style. Тяжел-о-во́з, *п.т.,* draft horse. Тяжел-о-ду́м, slow-thinking (*of a person*). Тяж-елова́тый, *adj.,* rather heavy; (*fig.*), hard. Он тяжелова́т на

подъём, he is rather difficult to rouse to action.

о-тяж-ел-е́ть, *v.p.,* to become heavy. Он отяжеле́л не по года́м, he became too stout for his years.

тяж-есть, *n.f.,* heaviness, weight, gravity. Он снял с меня́ э́ту т., he took this burden off my shoulders. Центр тя́жести, center of gravity.

тяж-кий, *adj.,* grave, weighty serious; grievous. Т-ая боле́знь, severe illness. Тя́ж-ко, *adv.,* grievously, seriously, sadly, badly, painfully. Он т. заболе́л, he became seriously ill. Мне бы́ло т. ви́деть э́то, it was painful for me to see this.

ис-тяз-а́ть, *v.i.,* + *acc.,* to torture, torment. Нельзя́ и. ко́шек и соба́к, do not torment cats and dogs. Ис-тяз-а́ние, *п.п.,* torture, torment. И. пле́нных, torture of prisoners. Ис-тяз-а́тель, *п.т.,* torturer, tormentor.

при-тяз-а́ть, *v.p.,* на + *acc.,* to pretend, lay claim to. Я не притяза́ю на ва́шу благода́рность, I do not expect thanks from you. При-тяз-а́ние, *п.п.,* pretension, claim. При-тяз-а́тельный, *adj.,* exacting, exigent; pretentious. Не-притяз-а́тельный, *adj.,* easily pleased. Эта я́блоня непритяза́тельна, this apple tree does not require much care.

У

УЗ-, УЖ-, NARROWNESS, TIGHTNESS

у́з-к-ий, *adj.,* narrow, tight. У. пиджа́к, tight, narrow coat. У. кругозо́р, narrow-minded view. У. челове́к, narrow-minded person. У. круг друзе́й, intimate circle of friends. У-ое ме́сто, tight place, bottleneck, narrow spot. В у́зких грани́цах, within narrow bounds. Узе́нький, *adj.,* (*dim.*), narrow, tight. Уз-кова́тый, *adj.,* rather narrow, tight. Уз-кость, *n.f.,* narrowness, tightness. У. взгля́дов, narrow-mindedness of views, of opinions. Уз-ко, *adv.,* narrowly, tightly. Уж-е, *adj. and adv. comp.,* narrower, tighter; more narrowly, more tightly. Уз-ко-, *a combining form meaning* narrow. Узко-го́рлый, *adj.,* narrow-necked. Узко-ло́бый, *adj.,* narrow-headed, narrow-minded. Узко-гру́дый, *adj.,* having narrow shoulders. Узкоплечий, *adj.,* slight of build around the shoulders.

у́з-и-ть, у́ж-у, *v.i.,* + *acc.,* to tighten, make narrow. Этот фасо́н блу́зки у́зит пле́чи, the cut of this blouse makes the shoulders look narrow.

об-у́з-ить, *v.p.,* об-у́ж-ивать, *v.i.,* + *acc.,* to tighten, make narrow. Портни́ха

обузила мне платье, the seamstress made my dress too tight.
с-уз-и́ть, *v.p.,* с-уж-ива́ть, *v.i.,* + *acc.,* to tighten, make narrow. С. глаза́, to squint. С-уж-е́ние, *n.n.,* contracting, shrinking, narrowing, tightening. С. зрачка́, contraction of the pupil of the eye. С-у́ж-енный, *adj., part. pass. past,* narrowed. С-ые глаза́, squinting eyes.

УК-, УЧ-, ЫК- (ВЫК-), ЫЧ- (ВЫЧ-), LEARNING, TEACHING; KNOWLEDGE, ERUDITION

на-у́к-а, *n.f.,* science. В университе́те изуча́ют разли́чные нау́ки, in the university various sciences are studied.
на-у́ч-ный, *adj.,* scientific. Н-ая кни́га, scientific book. На-у́ч-но, *adv.,* scientifically. На-у́ч-ность, *n.f.,* state of being scientific; scientific value. Н. тео́рии, scientific value of a theory.
уч-ёб-а, *n.f., (colloq.),* studies, studying. Ма́льчика посла́ли на учёбу, the boy was sent away for schooling. Уч-е́бник, *n.m.,* textbook. У. хи́мии, textbook of chemistry. Уч-е́бный, *adj.,* pertaining to studies; educational. У. год, school year. У-ое заведе́ние, educational institution. У-ые часы́, school hours, class hours.
уч-е́ние, уч-е́нье, *n.n.,* teaching, learning, practice; doctrine; apprenticeship. Уче́нье свет, а неуче́нье тьма, *(prov.).* learning is light, ignorance is darkness. Без уче́нья нет уме́нья, *(saying),* practice makes perfect. Социалисти́ческое уче́ние, socialist doctrine. Уч-ени́к, *n.m.,* уч-ени́ца, *n.f.,* student, pupil, disciple, apprentice. Уч-ени́ческий, *adj.,* of or pertaining to a pupil; *(fig.),* crude, unskilled. Учени́ческая рабо́та, student's work. Уч-ени́чество, *n.n.,* period of training, apprenticeship. Он прошёл стаж учени́чества, he completed his term of apprenticeship. Учёный, *adj., also used as n.,* scientist, scientific, learned; scholar, savant. Па́влов - вели́кий учёный, Pavlov is a great scientist. У-ая сте́пень, academic degree, scientific degree. Не-уч-ёный, *adj.,* uneducated. Не́-уч, *n.m.,* ignoramus. Уч-ёность, *n.f.,* learning, erudition. Он челове́к большо́й учёности, he is a man of great erudition.
уч-и́л-ище, *n.n.,* school, educational institution. Вое́нное у., military academy.
уч-и́тель, *n.m.,* уч-и́тельница, *n.f.,* teacher, schoolmaster, schoolmistress. Она́ на́ша учи́тельница ру́сского языка́, she is our teacher of Russian. Он учи́тель му́зыки, he is a teacher of music. Уч-и́тельский, *adj.,* teaching,

tutorial. Уч-и́тельская, *adj., used as n.f.,* faculty room. У. персона́л, the teaching staff.
уч-и́тель-ств-ова-ть, *v.i.,* to be a teacher, teach. Она́ учи́тельствует в сре́дней шко́ле, she teaches in a high school.
уч-и́ть, *v.i.,* + *acc.,* + *dat.,* + *inf.,* to teach, instruct, train, drill. Она́ у́чит меня́ му́зыке, she teaches me music. Она́ у́чит меня́ игра́ть на скри́пке, she is teaching me to play the violin. Уч-и́ть-ся, *v.i.r.,* to learn, study. Я учу́сь в шко́ле ру́сскому языку́, I am studying Russian in school. Век живи́, век учи́сь, *(prov.),* live and learn.
вы́-уч-ить, *v.p.,* вы-у́ч-ивать, *v.i.,* + *acc.,* to teach, learn thoroughly. Учени́к хорошо́ вы́учил уро́к, the student learned his lesson well. Он бы́стро выу́чивал стихи́, he used to learn poems quickly. Вы́-уч-ить-ся, *v.p.r.,* вы-у́ч-ивать-ся, *v.i.r.,* + *inf.,* + *dat.,* to learn; teach oneself. Он вы́учился пла́вать, he learned to swim. Де́ти легко́ выу́чиваются англи́йскому языку́, children learn English quickly. Вы́-уч-ка, *n.f.,* apprenticeship. Роди́тели о́тдали ма́льчика на вы́учку к сапо́жнику, the parents apprenticed the boy to a shoemaker.
до-уч-и́ть, *v.p.,* до-у́ч-ивать, *v.i.,* + *acc.,* to complete learning, teaching. Он доучи́л свой уро́к, he finished his lesson, (task, assignment). До-уч-и́ть-ся, *v.p.r.,* до-у́ч-ивать-ся, *v.i.r.,* to complete one's education, finish school, complete one's studies. Он не доучи́лся, he did not finish school. Не-до-у́ч-ка, *n.m., and n.f.,* half-educated person. Он оста́лся недоу́чкой, he remained a half-educated person.
за-уч-и́ть *v.p.,* за-у́ч-ивать, *v.i.,* + *acc.,* to learn by rote, memorize. З. приме́ры, to memorize examples. За-уч-и́ть-ся, *v.p.r.,* за-у́ч-ивать-ся, *v.i.r.,* to overstudy, to be memorized. З. до поте́ри па́мяти, to study to the point of exhaustion.
из-уч-и́ть, *v.p.,* из-уч-а́ть, *v.i.,* + *acc.,* to study, master, know well. Он изуча́ет ру́сскую литерату́ру, he is studying Russian literature, Из-уч-е́ние, *n.n.,* study. Институ́т славяноведе́ния, institute of Slavic studies.
на-уч-и́ть, *v.p.,* на-уч-а́ть, *v.i.,* + *acc.,* + *inf.,* + *dat.,* to teach. Он научи́л их пла́вать, he taught them to swim. Он научи́л их но́вым та́нцам, he taught them new dances. На-уч-и́ть-ся, *v.p.r.,* на-уч-а́ть-ся, *v.i.r.,* + *inf.,* + *dat.,* to learn. Н. англи́йскому произноше́нию тру́дно, it is difficult to learn English pronunciation.

об-уч-и́ть, *v.p.,* об-уч-а́ть, *v.i.,* + *acc.,* + *dat.,* to teach, instruct, train, drill. Солда́т обуча́ли стрельбе́, the soldiers were drilled in marksmanship. Об-уч-и́ть-ся, *v.p.r.,* об-уч-а́ть-ся, *v.i.r.,* + *dat.,* to be taught, learn. Он обуча́лся портня́жному де́лу, he was taught the tailor's trade. Об-уч-е́ние, *п.п.,* teaching, instruction, training, education. В шко́лах бы́ло введено́ совме́стное о., co-education was introduced into schools. Не-об-у́ч-енный, *adj., part. pass. past,* untrained, unskilled.

от-уч-и́ть, *v.p.,* от-уч-а́ть, *v.i.,* + *acc.,* от + *gen.,* to break (*as* a habit). О. дете́й от ша́лости, break the children of the habit of playing pranks. От-уч-и́ть-ся, *v.p.r.,* от-уч-а́ть-ся, *v.i.r.,* от + *gen.,* to lose a habit, be broken of a habit. Ребёнок отучи́лся соса́ть па́лец, the child was broken of the habit of sucking its thumb.

пере-уч-и́ть, *v.p.,* пере-у́ч-ивать, *v.i.,* + *acc.,* to teach anew, learn over again. Но́вому учи́телю пришло́сь переу́чивать ученико́в, the new teacher had to correct the errors of previous teaching. Пере-уч-и́ть-ся, *v.p.r.,* пере-у́ч-ивать-ся, *v.i.r.,* to learn something over again; study too much. Рабо́чему на́до переу́чиваться для рабо́ты на но́вых маши́нах, the workman must relearn his trade in order to work on new machines. Он переучи́лся, he studied too much.

по-уч-и́ть, *v.p.,* + *acc.,* to teach a little. Поучи́те его́ му́зыке, teach him a little music. Ма́льчик поучи́л стихи́, но не вы́учил их, the boy studied the poems for a while, but did not learn them. По-уч-а́ть, *v.i.,* + *acc.,* to preach, teach a doctrine; lecture, admonish. Стари́к всё вре́мя поуча́л нас, the old man preached to us all the time. По-уч-и́ть-ся, *v.p.,* to learn a little. Пуска́й поу́чится немно́го, let him do a little studying. По-уч-а́ть-ся, *v.i.r.,* to be preached to, be sermonized, admonished. Лю́ди поуча́ются не слова́ми, а само́й жи́знью, people learn not from words, but from life itself. Смотри́те и поуча́йтесь, look and learn. По-уч-е́ние, *п.п.,* lesson, precept, sermon, admonishment. Увы́, он забы́л поуче́ния роди́телей, alas, he has forgotten the teachings of his parents. Ра́ди поуче́ния, for the sake of preaching, of edification. По-уч-и́тельный, *adj.,* edifying. Это о́чень п. расска́з, this is a very edifying story.

под-уч-и́ть, *v.p.,* под-уч-а́ть, под-у́ч-ивать, *v.i.,* + *acc.,* + *dat.,* + *inf.,* to teach a little; prompt, egg on, put up to. Его́ подучи́ли това́рищи сде́лать э́ту прока́зу, his comrades taught him how to do this trick. Под-уч-и́ть-ся, *v.p.r.,* под-у́ч-ивать-ся, *v.i.r.,* + *dat.,* to learn a little, receive some training, increase one's knowledge. Он подучи́лся и тепе́рь ко́е-как справля́ется с рабо́той, he got some training and now he can manage after a fashion.

при-уч-и́ть, *v.p.,* при-уч-а́ть, *v.i.,* + *acc.,* к + *dat.,* + *inf.,* to accustom, teach the habit of, train. Мать приучи́ла ребёнка скла́дывать игру́шки в я́щик, the mother taught her child the habit of putting away his toys. При-уч-и́ть-ся, *v.p.r.,* при-у́ч-ивать-ся, *v.i.r.,* при-уч-а́ть-ся, *v.i.r.,* к + *dat.,* + *inf.,* to become accustomed to, inure oneself. Ему́ прихо́дится приуча́ться к чёрной рабо́те, he has to inure himself to drudgery. При-уч-е́ние, при-у́ч-ивание, *п.п.,* accustoming, training.

про-уч-и́ть, *v.p.,* про-у́ч-ивать, *v.i.,* про-уч-а́ть, *v.i.,* + *acc.,* to teach a good lesson, spend time studying. Я хорошо́ проучи́л э́того неве́жу, I taught this boor a good lesson.

раз-уч-и́ть, *v.p.,* раз-у́ч-ивать, *v.i.,* + *acc.,* to learn (*as* a role). Актри́са разу́чивала свою́ роль, the actress was learning her role. Она́ разу́чит сона́ту, she will learn the sonata. Раз-у́ч-ивание, *п.п.,* learning, (*as* a role). Р. роле́й отнима́ло у них мно́го вре́мени, it took them a long time to learn their roles. Раз-уч-и́ть-ся, *v.p.r.,* раз-у́ч-ивать-ся, *v.i.r.,* to forget something one has learned. Он разучи́лся говори́ть по-ру́сски, he forgot how to speak Russian.

на́-вык, *п.т.,* habit, practice; experience. У него́ нет на́выка к физи́ческой рабо́те, he is not used to manual labor.

об-ык-н-ов-е́ние, *п.п.,* habit, custom, way. Он по обыкнове́нию опозда́л, as usual, he was late. Об-ык-нове́нный, *adj.,* ordinary, customary, usual. Это са́мая о-ая исто́рия, it's the usual story. Об-ык-нове́нно, *adv.,* usually, habitually, as a rule. О. мы обе́даем в семь часо́в, we usually dine at seven o'clock. Не-об-ык-нове́нный, *adj.,* unusual, uncommon, extraordinary. Это н. слу́чай, this is an unusual occurrence. Не-об-ык-нове́нно, *adv.,* unusually. Он н. хоро́ший челове́к, he is an unusually good man.

об-ы́ч-ай, *п.т.,* custom. Тако́в у них обы́чай, such is their custom. Они́ соблюда́ют обы́чаи пре́дков, they observe the customs of their ancestors. Об-ы́ч-ный, *adj.,* habitual, usual, customary. О. порядок, usual order. Об-ы́ч-но, *adv.*, usually, generally. О. он приезжа́л сюда́ на́ лето, he usually arrived here for the summer. Не-об-ыч-а́йный, *adj.*, unusual, rare, extraordinary. У него́ н-ое музыка́льное дарова́ние, he has a rare musical talent. Не-об-ыч-а́йно, *adv.*, unusually. Сего́дня н. жесто́кий моро́з, it's unusually cold today. Не-об-ы́ч-ность, *n.f.*, unusualness, singularity. Н. его́ ви́да порази́ла всех, everyone was surprised by the uniqueness of his appearance.

от-вы́-кнуть, *v.p.,* от-вык-а́ть, *v.i.,* от + *gen.,* to be out of practice, lose the habit, become unaccustomed. Я отвы́к писа́ть пи́сьма, I have lost the habit of writing letters. От-вы́ч-ка, *n.p.,* loss of a habit. На привы́чку есть отвы́чка, *(saying)*, it is possible to break any habit.

при-вы́к-нуть, *v.p.,* при-вык-а́ть, *v.i.,* к + *dat.,* to become accustomed, used to, inure oneself, become inured. Нам не привыка́ть ста́ло к таки́м поря́дкам, *(colloq.)*, that is one thing we are already used to. При-вы́ч-ка, *n.f.,* habit. П. - втора́я нату́ра, *(saying)*, habit is second nature. Дурны́е привы́чки, bad habits. При-вы́ч-ный, *adj.,* habitual, usual. Не-при-вы́ч-ный, *adj.,* unusual, unaccustomed.

с-вы́к-нуть-ся, *v.p.r.,* с-вык-а́ть-ся, *v.i.r.,* с + *instr.,* to accustom oneself, become familiar. Она постепе́нно свыка́ется со свое́й го́рькой судьбо́й, she is gradually becoming used to her bad luck.

чрез-выч-а́йный, *adj.,* extraordinary, extreme. Чрезвыча́йный посо́л, ambassador extraordinary. Чрез-выч-а́йно, *adv.,* extremely, exceedingly. Мне ч. приско́рбно слы́шать э́то, I am extremely sorry to hear this.

УМ-, УМ(Л)-, INTELLECT, MIND, REASON, UNDERSTANDING

ум, *n.m.,* mind, intellect, reason, wit, understanding, intelligence. Ум хорошо́, а два лу́чше, *(saying)*, two heads are better than one. Ум доро́же де́нег, *(saying)*, a good mind is worth more than money. У него́ проница́тельный ум, he has a penetrating mind. Ги́бкий ум, flexible mind. Живо́й ум, lively mind. Острый ум, sharp, keen mind. Взя́ться за ум, *(idiom.)*, to become wiser, more reasonable. Мне пришло́ на ум, it occurred to me. Ума́ не приложу́, *(idiom.)*, I cannot understand. Он без ума́ от неё, he

is out of his mind about her. Ты с ума́ сошёл? Are you out of your mind? Have you gone out of your mind? Это не его́ ума́ де́ло, it's too much for him. Это сво́дит меня́ с ума́, it drives me mad. Это у меня́ с ума́ нейдёт, I cannot forget it. Он не в своём уме́, he is out of his wits. Он себе́ на уме́, he is cunning. У него́ друго́е на уме́, he has something else at the back of his mind. Ру́сский челове́к за́дним умо́м кре́пок, *(saying)*, a Russian is wiser after the event. Ум-ный, *adj.,* intelligent, sensible. Она́ у́мная же́нщина, she is a clever woman. Ум-но́, *adv.,* cleverly, intelligently. Он поступи́л у., he acted intelligently.

без-у́м-ец, *n.m.,* madman, maniac, fanatic. Без-у́м-ие, *n.n.,* insanity, madness, extreme foolishness, fanaticism. Без-у́м-ный, *adj.,* crazy, insane, mad. Б-ые глаза́, eyes of a madman. Без-у́м-но, *adv.,* insanely, madly, awfully. Я б. уста́л, I am awfully tired.

ра́з-ум, *n.m.,* intellect, reason, sense, mind. Он утра́тил ра́зум, he has lost his mind. "Кри́тика чи́стого ра́зума," напи́сана Ка́нтом, "The Critique of Pure Reason" was written by Kant. Раз-у́м-ный, *adj.,* rational, reasonable, intelligent, sensible. Это р. план, this is a sensible plan. Р. челове́к, a sensible man. Раз-у́м-но, *adv.,* reasonably, sensibly. Он рассужда́л весьма́ р., he talked very sensibly.

не-раз-у́м-ие, *n.n.,* lack of reason. Не-раз-у́м-ный, *adj.,* senseless, foolish, unwise. Не-раз-у́м-но, *adv.,* unwisely. С его́ стрны́ бы́ло н. сде́лать э́то, it was not wise of him to do this.

с-ум-а-сбро́дничать, *v.p.,* с-ум-а-сбро́дствовать, с-ум-а-сбро́дить, *v.i.,* to behave wildly, extravagantly. Переста́нь с., stop behaving so extravagantly. С-ум-а-сбро́д, *n.m.,* с-ум-а-сбро́дка, *n.f.,* madcap. Он невероя́тный с. he is an incredible madcap. С-ум-а-сбро́дный, *adj.,* extravagant, crazy, wild. Это како́й-то с. прое́кт, this is a crazy plan. С-ум-а-сбро́дство, *n.n.,* extravagance, folly. Его́ с. не́которым нра́вилось, some people liked his foolish behavior.

с-ум-а-сше́ствовать, *v.i.,* to act foolishly, irrationally. С-ум-а-сше́ствие, *n.n.,* insanity, madness. Его́ с. при́няло опа́сную фо́рму, he became dangerously insane. С-ум-а-сше́дший, *adj.,* *used as n.,* insane, madman. С. не до́лжен быть на свобо́де, a madman should not be at large. Душевнобольно́го отпра́вили в сумасше́дший дом, the insane man was sent to an asylum.

ум-é-ть, *v.i.,* + *inf.,* to know how, have the skill. Умéете-ли вы писáть? Do you know how to write? Он умéет плáвать, he knows how to swim. Он умéет быть приятным, he knows how to be pleasant. Я сдéлаю это, как умéю, I shall do it as best I can. Ум-éлый, *adj.,* skillful, expert. Он у. игрóк, he is a skillful player. Ум-éло, *adv.,* skillfully, expertly. Он у. взялся за дéло, he went at it skillfully. Ум-éние, *п.п.,* skill, ability, dexterity.

не-ум-éл-ость, *п.f.,* want of skill, clumsiness, inability. Он показáл в рабóте свою н., he exhibited a lack of skill in his work. Не-ум-éлый, *adj.,* unskillful, clumsy. Н. рабóтник, a clumsy worker. Не-ум-éнье, не-ум-éние, *п.п.,* ignorance, unskillfulness, inability. Он показáл своё н., he showed his ignorance.

не-до-ум-евá-ть, *v.i.,* to be perplexed, puzzled, be at a loss. Они недоумевáли по пóводу егó отсýтствия, they were puzzled by his absence. Не-до-ум-éние, *п.п.,* perplexity, bewilderment. Не-до-ум-ённый, *adj.,* perplexed, puzzled. Н. вопрóс, (*recent*) a perplexing question. Н. взгляд, a bewildered look.

раз-ум-éть, *v.i.,* + *acc.,* to understand, comprehend. Пей, да дéло разумéй! (*saying*), Drink, but do not lose your reason! Раз-ум-éть-ся, *v.i.r.,* used in 3d pers. only, to stand to reason. Это самó собóй разумéется, it stands to reason; it goes without saying. Раз-ум-éет-ся, (*parenthetical word*), of course. Раз-ум-éние, *п.п.,* understanding, cognition. Нáдо всё дéлать с разумéнием, everything must be done with understanding.

с-ум-éть, *v.p.,* + *inf.,* to be able, succeed; *see* умéть, *v.i.,* Ученик не сумéл решить задáчу, the pupil failed to solve the problem. Он сумéл убедить меня, he managed to persuade me.

из-ум-йть, из-ум-л-ю, *v.p.,* из-ум-л-ять, *v.i.,* + *acc.,* to strike dumb, surprise, amaze. Ваш постýпок меня изумляет, your conduct amazes me. Из-ум-йть-ся, *v.p.r.,* из-ум-л-ять-ся, *v.i.r.,* + *dat.,* to be dumbfounded, be surprised, amazed, astonished. Из-ум-йтельный, *adj.,* wonderful, amazing. У негó и-ая пáмять, he has an amazing memory. Из-ум-йтельно, *adv.,* wonderfully, amazingly. Онá и. красива, she is incredibly beautiful. Из-ум-лéние, *п.п.,* surprise, amazement, consternation. Егó неожйданный отъéзд вызвал óбщее и., his unexpected departure caused general consternation. Из-ум-л-ённый, *adj., part. pass. past,* surprised,

astonished, amazed. Поразйтельная картйна открылась пéред егó изумлённым взóром, a wonderful picture appeared before his astonished eyes.

на-до-ýм-ить, *v.p.,* на-до-ý-ливать, *v.i.,* + *acc.,* to suggest, advise. Он надоýмил её сдéлать это, he suggested that she do it.

ум-н-éть, *v.i.,* to grow wiser, become more intelligent. С годáми ребёнок умнéет, with years a child becomes more intelligent.

по-ум-н-éть, *v.p.,* to grow wiser, become more intelligent; *see* умнéть. Он замéтно поумнéл с тех пор, he has become much wiser since then.

ým-н-ич-ать, *v.i.,* to show off one's intelligence; split hairs. Он любит у., he likes to show off his intelligence. Ум-ничание, *п.п.,* philosophizing. Егó постоянное у. скýчно, his constant philosophizing is tedious.

ум-о-, *a combining form meaning* mind. Ум-о-заключáть, *v.i.,* to conclude, deduce. Ум-о-заключéние, *п.п.,* conclusion, deduction. Ум-о-зрéние, *п.п.,* speculation. Ум-о-зрительный, *adj.,* speculative, theoretical. Ум-о-исступлéние, *п.п.,* rage, delirium, frenzy. Ум-о-помешáтельство, *п.п.,* madness, insanity. Ум-о-помрачéние, *п.п.,* temporary insanity. Ум-о-помрачительный, *adj.,* tremendous, stupendous. У. успéх, tremendous success.

ým-ств-ен-ный, *adj.,* mental, intellectual. У. труд, intellectual work. Ум-ствено, *adv.,* mentally. Это у. отстáлый ребёнок, this child is mentally backward.

ým-ств-ова-ть, *v.i.,* (*obs.*), to speculate, reason. Он óчень любит у., he likes to speculate. Ум-ствование, *п.п.,* rationalizing, philosophizing, reasoning. У. не довелó егó до добрá, his theorizing (philosophizing) did not do him any good.

без-ým-ств-ова-ть, *v.i.,* to act insanely, in a frenzied manner. В отчáянии он безýмствовал, in despair he behaved like a frenzied man. Без-ým-ство, *п.п.,* insanity, frenzy, folly. Безýмству хрáбрых поём мы пéсню, (*Gorky*), We sing a song to the mad daring of the brave.

X

ХВАЛ-, PRAISE, EULOGY, COMMENDATION

хвал-й-ть, *v.i.,* + *acc.,* за + *acc.,* to praise, laud, commend. Учйтель хвáлит ученикá, the teacher is praising the pupil. Всякий купец свой товар хвалит, (saying), every cook praises his own broth. Его расхвалили до небес, he was praised to the skies. Хвал-иться, v.i.r., по-хвал-иться, v.p.r., + instr., to boast, swagger. Он хвалится своими успехами, he boasts of his successes. Хвал-а, n.f., praise, laudation. X. и честь ему! Praise and honor to him! Хвал-ебный, adj., laudatory, eulogistic. Х-ые речи, laudatory speeches. Хвал-ебно, adv., in praise. Хвал-ёный, adj., praised, vaunted. X. товар оказался вовсе не первого качества, this vaunted merchandise turned out to be inferior.

вос-хвал-ить, v.p., вос-хвал-ять, v.i., + acc., (rel.), to laud, praise, extol. Все праведные восхвалят Господа, all the righteous will praise the Lord. Восхвал-ение, n.n., eulogy, praise, praising.

за-хвал-ить, v.p., за-хвал-ивать, v.i., + acc., to overpraise, overwhelm with praise. Газеты захвалили его, the newspapers all praised him.

на-хвал-иться, v.p.r., to praise to the skies, express pride in. Учитель не нахвалится своими учениками, the teacher cannot praise his pupils enough.

пере-хвал-ить, v.p., пере-хвал-ивать, v.i., + acc., to extol, praise too much, overpraise. Она перехвалила своего сына, she has overpraised her son.

по-хвал-ить, v.p., хвал-ить, v.i., по-хвал-ивать, v.i., (colloq.), to praise, laud, praise occasionally. Учитель время от времени похваливал своих учеников, from time to time the teacher used to praise his pupils. Похвали меня, Praise me, give me my due. По-хвал-иться, v.p.r., по-хвал-иться-ся, v.i.r., + instr., to boast, brag, Я не могу похвалиться своей квартирой, I cannot boast about my flat. По-хвал-а, n.f., praise, commendation, compliment, eulogy, panegyric. "Похвала глупости," (Erasmus), "In Praise of Folly." Он был выше всякой похвалы, he was above all praise. По-хвал-ь-ба, n.f., bragging, boasting. С похвальбой далеко не уедешь (saying), bragging will not get you far. По-хвал-ьный, adj., laudable, praiseworthy. Это п-ое желание, this is a praiseworthy desire. П. лист, honorable mention. По-хвал-ь-но, adv., with praise.

рас-хвал-ить, v.p., рас-хвал-ивать, v.i., + acc., to lavish praise. В газетах расхвалили новую книгу, the newspapers praised the new book.

ХВАТ-, ХВАЧ-, APPROPRIATION, SEIZURE, GRASPING

хват-а-ть, v.i., с-хват-ить, v.p., + acc., за + acc., to seize, grab, grasp, snatch. Мальчик хватает мяч руками, the boy is seizing the ball with his hands. Он звёзд с неба не хватает, (fig.), he is not intelligent.

хват-й-ть, v.p., хват-ать, v.i., impers., used only in 3d pers., to suffice, be sufficient, last. Этого мне хватит на месяц, this will last me a month.

хват-ить, хвач-у, v.p., + acc. + gen., (colloq.), to whack, hit. Он хватил его по голове, he whacked him over the head. Они хватили через край, (colloq.), they went too far. X. лишнего, to have one drink too many. Хват-ь, abbrev. of хватил. Хват-иться-ся, v.p.r., хват-аться-ся, v.i.r., за + acc., to grip, grasp, snatch. Утопающий хватается за соломинку, (fig.), a drowing man grasps at a straw. Он хватился, но поздно, he noticed it, but too late. Хват-ка, n.f., grasp, grip; bite. Мёртвая х., deadly grip.

вы-хват-ить, v.p., вы-хват-ывать, v.i., + acc., из + gen., to snatch out of. Он выхватил револьвер из кармана, he drew his gun out of his pocket. В. цитату, to quote at random. Вы-хват-ывание, n.n., snatching out.

за-хват-ить, v.p., за-хват-ывать, v.i., + acc., to seize, take possession. З. государственную власть, to seize power. Он захватил собственность своего брата, he has appropriated his own brother's property. Дождь захватил меня на дороге, the rain caught me en route. У меня захватило дух, it took my breath away. За-хват-ывающий, adj., part. act. pres., overwhelming, seizing. За-хвач-енный, adj., part. pass., past, seized, confiscated. З-ое имущество, confiscated property. За-хват, n.m., seizure, seizing, usurpation. З. власти, seizure of power. За-хват-нический, adj., seizing, grasping. З-ая политика, policy of encroachment. За-хват-чик, n.m., one who grabs, confiscator. З. власти, usurper of power.

на-хват-ать, v.p., на-хват-ывать, v.i., + gen., to grab in quantity. Н. раков, to grab crawfish. Н. цитат, to compile quotations. На-хват-анный, adj., part. pass. past, grabbed, seized in quantity. Н-ое имущество, seized property. На-хват-ать-ся, v.p.r., + gen., to get a smattering of, grasp superficially. Он нахватался разных поверхностных знаний, he acquired a smattering of all kinds of knowledge.

не-хват-а́ть, *v.i.,* не-хват-и́ть, *v.p.,* + *gen., impers., used in 3d pers. only,* to be wanting, fall short, be insufficient. Мне нехвата́ет слов, words fail me. Нам нехвати́ло де́нег, we did not have enough money. Этого ещё нехвата́ло! (*idiom.*), That's the limit! Не-хва́т-ка, *n.f.,* lack, shortage, scarcity. Постро́йка останови́лась из-за нехва́тки материа́лов, construction stopped for lack of materials.

о-хват-и́ть, *v.p.,* о-хва́т-ывать, *v.i.,* + *acc.,* to envelop, include, embrace, encompass; understand. Пла́мя охвати́ло дом, the flames enveloped the house. О-хва́ч-ен, *adj., part. pass. past,* seized, enveloped, embraced. Он был о. у́жасом, he was seized with terror. О-хва́т, *n.m.,* reach, scope, range. О-хва́тывать, *v.i.r.,* + *instr.,* to be enveloped, included, embraced.

об-хват-и́ть, *v.p.,* об-хва́т-ывать, *v.i.,* + *acc.,* to clasp, girth, encompass, surround. Это де́рево так велико́, что три челове́ка не мо́гут обхвати́ть его́, this tree is so large, three men cannot encircle it. Об-хва́т, *n.m.,* girth, circumference, compass. Де́рево два ме́тра в обхва́те, a tree two meters in circumference.

от-хват-а́ть, *v.p.,* от-хват-и́ть, *v.p.,* от-хва́т-ывать, *v.i.,* + *acc.,* (*colloq.*), to snap off, cut, bite away, bite off; chop off. Пёс отхвати́л большо́й кусо́к мя́са, the dog bit off a large piece of meat.

пере-хват-а́ть, *v.p.,* пере-хват-и́ть, *v.p.,* пере-хва́т-ывать, *v.i.,* + *acc.,* to catch, intercept; overshoot a mark; borrow; gird; take a bite. Всех граби́телей перехвата́ли, all the burglars were caught. Они́ перехва́тывали телегра́ммы, they tapped the wires. Они́ перехвати́ли его́ письмо́, they intercepted his letter. Он перехвати́л че́рез край, (*colloq.*), he overshot the mark. Он перехвати́л немно́го де́нег, (*colloq.*), he borrowed a little money. В го́рле перехвати́ло, it stopped my breath. Пере-хва́т, *n.m.,* waist. Он был широ́к в плеча́х и то́нок в перехва́те, he had wide shoulders and a narrow waist. Пере-хва́т-ывание, *n.n.,* interception.

по-хват-а́ть, *v.p.,* + *acc.* (*colloq.*), to seize several times, catch in quantity, arrest one after another. Поли́ция похвата́ла мно́го люде́й, the police arrested many people.

под-хват-и́ть, *v.p.,* под-хва́т-ывать, *v.i.,* + *acc.,* to pick up, catch up, snatch up. Он упа́л бы, е́сли бы его́ не подхвати́ли, he would have fallen, if they had not caught him. Ло́шади подхвати́ли, the horses bolted. Хор подхвати́л мело́дию, the chorus picked up the tune.

при-хват-и́ть, *v.p.,* при-хва́т-ывать, *v.i.,* + *acc.,* (*colloq.*), to touch, take along. Он прихвати́л с собо́ю прия́теля, he took along a friend.

про-хват-и́ть, *v.p.,* про-хва́т-ывать, *v.i.,* + *acc.,* (*colloq.*), to chill; penetrate; drag through. Его́ прохвати́ло ве́тром, he was chilled by the wind. Его́ прохвати́ли в газе́тах, (*fig.*), he was harshly criticized in the press.

рас-хват-а́ть, *v.p.,* рас-хва́т-ывать, *v.i.,* + *acc.,* to buy up, snatch away, grab away. Пе́рвое изда́ние расхвата́ли в два дня, the first edition was sold out in two days. Рас-хва́т-ан(ный), *adj., part. pass. past,* snatched up, grabbed up. На распрода́же все пла́тья бы́ли бы́стро расхва́таны, at the sale the dresses were all snatched up (sold). Рас-хва́т, *n.m.,* рас-хва́т-ывание, *n.n.,* snatching, grabbing. Нарас-хва́т, *adv.,* in great demand. Кни́га продава́лась н., the book sold like hot cakes. Ра-хва́т-ывать-ся, *v.i.r.,* + *instr.,* to be snatched up, bought up. На я́рмарке това́ры бы́стро расхва́тываются, merchandise is bought up quickly at the fair.

с-хват-и́ть, *v.p.,* с-хва́т-ывать, *v.i.,* + *acc.,* to seize, grasp. С. ка́мень и бро́сить в кого́-нибудь, to seize a stone and throw it at someone. Он схвати́л его́ за ши́ворот, he seized him by the collar. Ребёнок схвати́л на́сморк, the child caught a cold. Он бы́стро схва́тывает, he is quick-witted. С-хват-и́ть-ся, *v.p.r.,* с-хва́т-ывать-ся, *v.i.r.,* + *instr.,* to quarrel, come to words, come to blows. Они́ поссо́рились и схвати́лись друг с дру́гом, they quarrelled and came to blows. Он схвати́лся с ме́ста, he jumped up from his seat. С-хва́т-ка, *n.f.,* scuffle, skirmish, melee; (*tech.*), brace. Ме́жду ни́ми была́ с., there was a scuffle between them. Это их после́дняя с., this is their final encounter.

у-хват-и́ть, *v.p.,* у-хва́т-ывать, *v.i.,* to grasp, seize, grip, lay hold of. Он ухвати́л его́ за пле́чи, he seized him by the shoulders. Он сра́зу ухвати́л мою́ мысль, he grasped my idea at once. У-хват-и́ть-ся, *v.p.r.,* у-хва́т-ывать-ся, *v.i.r.,* + *acc.,* to catch, lay hold of, grip, grasp, snatch. Он ухвати́лся за бро́шенную ему́ верёвку, he grasped the rope that was thrown to him. Он ухвати́лся за моё предложе́ние, he jumped at my proposal. Они́ ухвати́лись за подверну́вшийся слу́чай, they seized the opportunity. У-хва́т, *n.m.*, fork used in placing pots into an oven. У-хва́т-ка, *n.f.*, way, manner; trick. Брось свой хулига́нские ухва́тки! Quit roughhousing!

ХИТ-, ХИЩ-, RAPACITY, PLUNDER

хищ-е́ние, *n.n.*, plunder, rapine; stealing, embezzlement, misappropriation. Его́ посади́ли в тюрьму́ за растра́ты и хище́ния, he was imprisoned for embezzlement.

вос-хит-и́ть, вос-хищ-у́, *v.p.*, вос-хищ-а́ть, *v.i.*, + *acc.*, to carry away; (*fig.*), to delight, enrapture, ravish. Её пе́ние вас восхити́т, her singing will delight you. Нас восхища́ет иску́сство дре́вних, we admire ancient art. Вос-хит-и́ть-ся, *v.p.r.*, вос-хищ-а́ть-ся, *v.i.r.*, + *instr.*, to admire, be enraptured, be delighted. Все им восхища́ются, everyone admires him. Мы восхища́лись его́ игро́й, we admired his playing. Вос-хит-и́тельный, *adj.*, charming, delightful, ravishing, delicious. Вос-хит-и́тельно, *adv.*, charmingly, delightfully, ravishingly, deliciously. Он восхити́тельно игра́л на скри́пке, he played the violin delightfully. Вос-хищ-е́ние, *n.n.*, admiration, rapture, ravishment, delight. Быть в восхище́нии от кого́-либо (чего́-либо), to be in rapture over someone (something). Смотре́ть с восхище́нием, to look admiringly. Вос-хищ-ённый, *adj.*, *part. pass. past*, enraptured. В. взгляд, admiring look. по-хи́т-ить, *v.p.*, по-хищ-а́ть, *v.i.*, + *acc.*, to kidnap, abduct; steal. П. карти́ну из музе́я, to steal a painting from a museum. По-хит-и́тель, *n.m.*, abductor, kidnapper, thief. В го́роде ору́довала ша́йка похити́телей дете́й, a gang of kidnappers was operating in the city. По-хищ-е́ние, *n.n.*, theft, abduction, kidnapping. Карти́на Ру́бенса "Похище́ние Саби́нянок," Rubens' painting, "The Abduction of the Sabine Women." П. докуме́нтов, theft of documents. По-хищ-а́ть-ся, *v.p.r.*, + *instr.*, to be stolen, kidnapped, abducted. Де́ньги нере́дко похища́ются из ба́нка, money is often stolen from banks. рас-хи́т-ить, *v.p.*, рас-хищ-а́ть, *v.i.*, + *acc.*, to plunder, pillage. Р. иму́щество, to plunder property. Рас-хищ-а́ть-ся, *v.i.r.*, + *instr.*, to be plundered, pillaged. Иму́щество ча́сто расхища́ется, property is often stolen. Рас-хит-и́тель, *n.m.*, plunderer. Расхити́тели наро́дного достоя́ния, plunderers of national property. Рас-хищ-е́ние, *n.n.*, pillage, plunder. Вла́сти веду́т борьбу́ с расхище́нием, the authorities are waging battle against plunder. хи́щ-нич-ать, *v.i.*, to engage in plunder, be rapacious, predatory. Челове́к мо́жет хи́щничать ху́же хи́щного живо́тного, man can be more rapacious than beasts of prey. Хи́щ-ник, *n.m.*, хи́щ-ница, *n.f.*, beast of prey; (*fig.*), plunderer, spoiler. Львы - хи́щники, lions are predatory animals. Хи́щнический, *adj.*, predatory, rapacious, plundering. Х-ие инсти́нкты, predatory instincts. Х-ая ру́бка лесо́в, indiscriminate cutting of forests. Хи́щ-ничество, *n.n.*, rapaciousness, predatoriness. Хи́щ-ность, *n.f.*, rapacity. Хи́щ-ный, *adj.*, rapacious, predatory. Х. взгляд, predatory look. Я́стреб - хи́щная пти́ца, the hawk is a bird of prey.

ХЛАД-, ХЛАЖ-, ХЛАЖД-, ХОЛОД-, ХОЛАЖ-, ХОЛОЖ-, COLD, COLDNESS

хлад, *n.m.*, (*obs.*), cold, coldness. Смерте́льный х. объя́л его́, (*poet.*), a deathly chill seized him. Хла́д-ный, *adj.*, (*obs.*), cold. Хлад-но-кро́вие, *n.n.*, coolness, composure, equanimity. Он сохраня́ет х. в бою́, he keeps his composure in battle. Хлад-но-кро́вный, *adj.*, cool, composed. Он х. челове́к, he is a composed man. Хлад-но-кро́вно, *adv.*, coolly, in cold blood. о-хлад-е́-ть, *v.p.*, о-хлад-ева́ть, *v.i.*, к + *dat.*, to become cool, cold; lose interest, become indifferent. Он охладе́л к свое́й рабо́те, he has lost interest in his work. о-хлад-и́-ть, о-хлаж-у́, *v.p.*, о-хлажд-а́ть, *v.i.*, to cool, chill, refrigerate. О. пи́во, to cool beer. Неуда́чи охлади́ли его́ рве́ние, failures have cooled his enthusiasm. О-хлажд-ённый, *adj.*, *part. pass. past*, cooled. О. пар, condensed steam. О-хлад-и́ть-ся, *v.p.r.*, о-хлажд-а́ть-ся, *v.i.r.*, to grow, become cool, cold. Во́здух охлажда́лся к ве́черу, the air grew cooler towards evening. О-хлад-и́тель, *n.m.*, (*tech.*), cooler, refrigerator. О-хлад-и́тельный, *adj.*, cooling. О-ые напи́тки, cooling beverages, cool beverages. О-хлажд-е́ние, *n.n.*, cooling, condensation. О. напи́тков, chilling of beverages. Ме́жду ни́ми наступи́ло о., their feelings for one another have cooled. про-хлад-и́ть, *v.p.*, про-хлажд-а́ть, *v.i.*, + *acc.*, to cool, refresh. Све́жий во́здух его́ прохла́дит, the fresh air will refresh him. Про-хлад-и́ть-ся, *v.p.r.*, про-хлажд-а́ть-ся, *v.i.r.*, (*colloq.*), to refresh oneself; be idle, idle. Они́ прохлажда́лись в саду́, they refreshed themselves in the garden. Довóльно вам прохлаждáться! (colloq.), Enough of this idling! Про-хлáд-а, n.f., coolness, freshness. Вечéрняя п., the cool of evening. С мóря повéяло прохлáдой, a cool breeze was blowing in from the sea. Про-хлáд-ца, n.f., coolness, used only in expression: Онú рабóтают с прехлáдцой, they work leisurely. Про-хлад-úтельный, adj., refreshing, cooling. П-ое питьё, refreshing drink. Про-хлáд-ный, adj., cool, fresh. Сегóдня прохлáдная погóда, it is cool today. П-ые отношéния, (colloq.), cool relations. Про-хлáд-но, adv., coolly. В кóмнате п., it is cool in the room.

хóлод, n.m., cold, coldness. Зúмний х., winter cold. Стоя́т хóлода, we are having cold weather. Холóд-ный, adj., cold. Х-ое пúво, cold beer. Х-ая войнá, (polit.), cold war. Он хóлоден, как лёд, he has a heart of ice. Он вы́лил на негó ушáт холóдной воды́, (also fig.), he threw cold water upon him. Хóлод-но, adv., coldly. Мне х., I am cold. Сегóдня х., it is cold today. Онú обошлúсь с ним х., they treated him coldly. Холод-новáтый, adj., rather cold; chilly. Сегóдня х. день, today is a cool day. Холод-новáто, adv., rather coldly. Здесь х., it is rather cold here. Холод-но-крóвный, adj., cold-blooded. Лягýшка х-ое живóтное, the frog is a cold-blooded animal. Холóд-ность, n.f., coldness. Вáша х. меня́ огорчáет, your coldness grieves me.

холод-á-ть, v.p., по-холод-áть, v.i., impers., to grow cold (as the weather). К вéчеру холодáет, it grows cold towards evening. Сегóдня похолодáло, it is colder today.

холод-éть, v.p., по-холод-éть, v.i., to become cold; chill. От стрáха у неё рýки холодéют, her hands grow cold from fright. Холод-éющий, adj., part. act. pres., cooling, becoming cold. Х. труп, a corpse which is becoming cold. Холод-éц, n.m., aspic. Онú лю́бят х. из ры́бы, they like aspic made of fish.

за-холод-éть, v.p., to begin to get cold (as the weather). В вóздухе захолодéло, óсень приближáлась, the air was getting cold, autumn was approaching.

холод-úть, v.i., + acc., to cool, chill, refrigerate. Лёд холодúт во рту, ice makes the mouth cold. Холод-úльник, n.m., refrigerator, cooler. Вагóн-холод-úльник, refrigerated car. Хранéние продýктов в холодúльниках, cold storage of products. Холод-úльный, adj., refrigerative.

вы́-холод-ить, v.p., вы-холáж-ивать, v.i., + acc., to make cool; chill thoroughly.

Он вы́холодил нам кóмнаты, he has cooled our rooms.

за-холо-нýть, v.p., (colloq.), to make cold; chill. Сéрдце захолонýло от стрáха, (colloq., fig.), my heart stood still with fear.

рас-холод-úть, v.p., рас-холáж-ивать, v.i., to dampen one's feelings. Её измéна окончáтельно расхолодúла меня́, her infidelity has definitely cooled me towards her. Рас-холáж-ивание, n.n., cooling, chilling.

ХОД-, ХОЖ-, ХАЖ-, ХОЖД-, ШЕД-, ШЕ-, LOCOMOTION ON FOOT, MOTION, MOVEMENT

ход, n.m., course, motion, march, movement; speed; passage, entrance; lead. Парáдный ход, front entrance. Х. пóезда, speed of a train. Тúхий х., slow speed. Крéстный х., religious procession. Паровóз дал зáдний ход, the locomotive was moving in reverse. Лóвкий ход, master stroke. Свобóдный ход, free wheeling. Он пришёл чёрным хóдом, he came through the back entrance. Их интересýет ход собы́тий, they are interested in the course of events. Чей тепéрь ход? Whose move is it? Пустúть дéло в ход, to start a business, get matters under way. Он вскочúл в автóбус на ходý, he jumped on the bus while it was in motion. В большóм ходý, selling well. Емý не даю́т хóду, they are not promoting him Онú знáют все ходы́ и вы́ходы, they know all the ins and outs. Пар-о-хóд, n.m., steamer. Скор-о-хóд, n.m., fast walker, runner. Сапогú-скорохóды, (folklore), seven-league boots. Сам-о-хóд-ный, (mil.), self-propelling, motorized. С-ая артиллéрия, motorized artillery.

ход-ú-ть, хож-ý, v.i., indet., to go, walk, attend; visit; tend, nurse; wear. ид-тú, v.i.det. Я чáсто хожý в теáтр, I often go to the theatre. Онú хóдят пóд руку, they walk arm in arm. Ходúть за больны́м, to take care of a sick person. Он всегдá хóдит в пальтó, he always wears an overcoat. Он ходúл пó-миру, (colloq.), he was a beggar. Хóдит слух, it is rumored. Онá ходúла к сестрé кáждый день, she visited her sister every day. Рубль не хóдит за предéлами Совéтского Сою́за, the ruble is not current outside the Soviet Union. Ходúть на зáдних лáпках, (fig.), to be subservient. Хóдкий, adj., salable, marketable, selling well; fast. Это óчень х. товáр, this merchandise sells well. Это х-ое парусное сýдно, this ship sails well. Ход-

овóй, *adj.*, salable, marketable. Ходо-
вóй сорт, a salable category. Ход-óк,
n.m., walker; (*pre-Rev.*), representative
of a village community delegated to
find new regions for emigration. Хорóший х., a good walker. Ход-ýли,
n.m.pl., stilts. Ходить на ходýлях, to
walk on stilts. Ход-ýльность, *n.f.*, pompousness, stiltedness. Егó х. вызывáет
смех, his pompousness provokes
laughter. Ход-ýльный, *adj.*, stilted,
pompous. Х-ая речь, stilted speech.
Ход-ýн, *n.m.*, *used only in expression*:
Ходить ходунóм, (*colloq.*), to shake,
tremble; be in continual motion. Пол
ходунóм хóдит, the floors seem to
rise and fall. Ход-ь-бá, *n.f.*, walking.
Отсюда 10 минýт ходьбы, it is a ten
minute walk from here. Ход-ячий, *adj.*,
walking, current. Наш учитель х-ая
энциклопéдия, our teacher is a walking
encyclopedia. Зóлото не является
бóльше ходячей монéтой, gold is no
longer a medium of exchange.

ход-áтай-ство-вать, *v.i.*, по-ход-áтай-
ствовать, *v.p.*, о + *prep.*, за + *acc.*, to
solicit, intercede, petition. Х. за дрýга,
to intercede for a friend Походáтай-
ствуйте за меня, intercede for me. Ход-
áтайство, *n.n.*, application, petition, intercession. Подáть х., to file a petition.
Удовлетворить х., to comply with a
request, a petition. Отказáть в ходá-
тайстве, to refuse a request, a petition.
Ход-áтай, *n.m.*, intercessor; (*legal*,
obs.), agent, solicitor.

ход-ь-бá, *n.f.*, walking, pacing. Х. взад
и вперёд, pacing back and forth.
Полчасá ходьбы, a half an hour's
walk.

хожд-éние, *n.n.*, walking, going; pilgrimage; attending; circulation of currency. "Хождéние в нарóд," a slogan
of the Populists (*literally*: a going to
the people). Х. на лéкции, attending of
lectures. Х. по монастырям, pilgrimage
to monasteries.

шéд-ший, *adj.*, *part. act. past*, of идти,
v.i.det., that was going. Пóезд,
шéдший пéред нáми, the train ahead
of us.

шé-(д)-ств-ова-ть, *v.i.*, to march, take
part in a procession. Они вáжно
шéствовали впереди всех, they
marched pompously ahead of all the
others. Шé-ствие, *n.n.*, procession,
cortège. Похорóнное ш., funeral procession. Шé-ствуя, *adv.*, *part. pres.*,
while marching.

в-ход-ить, *v.i.*, войти, *v.p.*, в + *acc.*, to
enter, come in, penetrate. Это не
вхóдит в мои рассчёты, this does not

enter into my estimates. Кáждое ýтро
учитель быстро входил в класс и
сейчáс же начинáл урóк, each morning
the teacher used to enter the classroom
and begin the lesson immediately.
Нóвое слóво вхóдит в употреблéние,
a new word has come into use. Во-
шéд-ший, *adj.*, *part. act. past*, (*from*
войти) that has entered. В. в кóмнату поклонился и сел, the person who
entered the room bowed and sat down.
В-ход, *n.m.*, entrance. Вход и выход,
entrance and exit. Вход воспрещáется,
entrance is forbidden. В-ход-нóй, *adj.*,
pertaining to entrance. В. билéт,
entrance, admission ticket. В-ход-ящий,
adj., *part. act. pres.*, incoming, entering.
В. журнáл, office record. В-хожд-éние,
n.n., walking in, entering.

вос-ход-ить, *v.i.*, на + *acc.*, to rise,
ascend; return to. Сóлнце восхóдит в
5 часóв, the sun rises at five o'clock.
Изучéние геомéтрии восхóдит к дрéв-
ности, the study of geometry goes back
to antiquity. Вос-ход-ящий, *adj.*, *part.
act. pres.*, ascending, rising. Он - в-ее
светило, he is a rising star. Вос-хóд,
n.m., rising. В. сóлнца, sunrise. Лéтом
мы встаём с восхóдом сóлнца, in
summer we rise at sunrise. Вос-хожд-
éние, *n.n.*, ascent. В. на Эльборýс
óчень трýдно, the ascent of Mt. Elbrus
is very difficult. Вос-шéствие, *n.n.*,
accession. В. на престóл, accession to
the throne.

вс-ход-ить, *v.i.*, взойти, *v.p.*, на + *acc.*,
to ascend; sprout, germinate. В. нá
гору, to climb a mountain. Сóлнце
всхóдит и захóдит, the sun rises and
sets. Тéсто всхóдит мéдленно, dough
rises slowly. Пшеница всхóдит, the
wheat is coming up. Взо-шёл, *m.*, взошлá, *f.*, *past tense of* взойти. Рожь
ещё не взошлá, the rye has not yet
sprouted. Взо-шéдший, *adj. part.
past*, that which has risen. В-ая лунá
освещáла ýлицу, the ascending moon
lighted up the street. Вс-ход, *n.m.*,
sprout, shoot. Всхóды пшеницы, shoots
of wheat. Вс-хóж-есть, *n.f.*, germination. В семян, germination of seeds.

вы-ход-ить, *v.i.*, выйти, *v.p.*, из + *gen.*,
в + *acc.*, на + *acc.*, to go out, come
out, get out; be issued; step out. Он
выхóдит из дóма, he is going out of
the house. Корáбль выхóдит в мóре,
the ship is putting out to see. Он
выхóдит в отстáвку, he is retiring;
he is resigning from office. Он вышел
в люди, (*colloq.*), he has risen in life;
he has made something of himself. Рекá
вышла из берегóв, the river overflowed its banks. В. из затруднитель-

ного положе́ния, to get out of an embarrassing situation. В. сухи́м из воды́, (*colloq.*), to go scot-free; get out of a scrape. В. за́муж, to marry (for a woman). Из него́ вы́йдет де́льный инжене́р, he will make a good engineer. Он не выхо́дит из ко́мнаты, he never leaves his room. Ко́мната выхо́дит о́кнами на у́лицу, the windows of the room overlook the street. У нас выхо́дит мно́го электри́чества, we use a good deal of electricity. Из э́того ничего́ не вы́йдет, nothing will come of it. Вы́шел прика́з, an order has been issued. Он вы́шел из крестья́н, he is a peasant by origin. Всё вы́шло о́чень хорошо́, everything turned out very well. Вы-хо́д-ящий, *adj., part. act. pres.,* going out, overlooking. Улица, в-ая на Арба́т, a street off the Arbat. Вы́-шед-ший, *adj., part. act. past,* that has gone out, come out; *see* вы́йти. Вы́-ход, *n.m.,* exit, way out; issue. Где здесь вы́ход? Where is the exit? В. в отста́вку, to resign, retire. В. за́муж, marriage (*of* a woman). Он дал вы́ход своему́ чу́вству, he gave vent to his feelings. По́сле вы́хода кни́ги, after the book was published. Вы́-ход-ец, *n.m.,* (*obs.*), emigrant. Вы́ходцы из Росси́и, Russian emigrants. В. с того́ све́та, apparition, ghost. Вы́-ход-ка, *n.f.,* trick, prank. Я не ожида́л от него́ тако́й вы́ходки, I did not expect such behavior on his part. Вы-ход-но́й, (*recent*), *adj.,* free, leisure. Сего́дня у него́ в. день, today is his day off. В-о́е посо́бие, severance pay.

вы́-ход-ить, выхож-у́, *v.p.,* вы-ха́ж-ивать, *v.i.,* + *acc.,* to rear, tend; pull through, nurse back to health. Она́ выходи́ла всех дете́й, she has brought up all the children. В. теля́т и жеребя́т, to tend calves and foals. Вы-ха́ж-ивать-ся, *v.i.r.,* + *instr.,* to be reared, tended.

до-ход-и́ть, *v.i.,* дойти́, *v.p.,* до + *gen.,* to go as far as, walk up to, walk as far as, come to; reach; obtain; amount to; total; ripen. Мы ча́сто доходи́ли до реки́, we often walked as far as the river. Это дохо́дит до неле́пости, this amounts to absurdity. Счёт доходи́л до 1000 рубле́й, the bill came to 1,000 rubles. Он дошёл до по́лного изнеможе́ния, he is completely exhausted. Письмо́ не дошло́ по а́дресу, the letter was delivered to the wrong address. До-ше́д-ший, *adj., part. act. past,* that has come to, reached; *see* дойти́. Д-ие до нас све́дения оказа́лись неве́рными, the information that reached us proved to be untrue. До-хо́д, *n.m.,*

income, revenue, profit, receipts. Валово́й д., gross income. Чи́стый д., net income. Нетрудово́й д., (*recent*), unearned income. До-хо́д-ность, *n.f.,* net income from a business; profit. До-хо́д-ный, *adj.,* profitable, lucrative, gainful. Д-ое де́ло, a profitable business. Без-до-хо́д-ный, *adj.,* profitless, unprofitable. Это де́ло б-ое, this is an unprofitable business.

за-ход-и́ть, *v.i.,* за-ха́ж-ивать, *v.i., iter.,* зайти́, *v.p.,* to set; put in; call for, drop in; go beyond. Со́лнце захо́дит в 6 часо́в, the sun sets at six o'clock. Он ча́сто заха́живал к нам, he often used to drop in on us. Парохо́д зашёл в га́вань, the ship put in at the port. Ме́сяц зашёл за ту́чу, the moon disappeared behind a cloud. Он зашёл за мной, he called for me. Они́ зашли́ сли́шком далеко́, they went too far. За-ше́д-ший, *adj., part. act. past,* that has set; *see* зайти́. Заше́дшее со́лнце, the sun which has set. За-хо́д, *n.m.,* going in, going to; calling for; setting. З. со́лнца, sunset; setting of the sun.

ис-ход-и́ть, *v.p.,* ис-ха́ж-ивать, *v.i. iter.,* + *acc.,* to cover all the roads. Он исходи́л все доро́ги, he has covered all the roads on foot.

ис-ход-и́ть, *v.i.,* из + *gen.,* to be issued; emanate, originate. Этот за́пах исхо́дит из э́тих цвето́в, this fragrance comes from these flowers. Это исхо́дит из предположе́ния, this proceeds from a conjecture.

ис-ход-и́ть, *v.i.,* изо-йти́, *v.p.,* + *instr.,* to bleed, cry one's heart out. Он исхо́дит кро́вью, he is bleeding. Она́ изошла́ слеза́ми, she cried her heart out. Ис-хо́д-ящий, *adj., part. act. pres.,* outgoing, originating from. И-ие бума́ги, outgoing dispatches. За́пах и. из лаборато́рии, a smell from a laboratory. Ис-хо́д, *n.m.,* issue; outlet; result, outcome "Исхо́д - одна́ из библе́йских книг, "Exodus" is one of the books of the Bible. Он прие́дет на исхо́де неде́ли, he will arrive by the end of the week. Запа́с хле́ба на исхо́де, the bread supply is coming to an end. Ис-хо́д-ный, *adj.,* initial; pertaining to departure. И-ая то́чка, point of departure.

про-ис-ход-и́ть, *v.i.,* произойти́, *v.p.,* от + *gen.,* to be descended from; proceed, result, spring, arise; descend from; issue from; happen, occur, take place. Что там происхо́дит? What is going on over there? Пожа́р происхо́дит от небре́жности, the fire is due to negligence. Про-ис-хо́д-ящий, *adj., part. act. pres.,* occurring, proceeding. П-ие собы́тия, current events. Всё происшéдшее бы́ло давнó подготóвлено, all that happened had been prepared for long ago. Про-ис-хожд-éние, *n.n.*, origin, descent; parentage. Учéние Дарви́на о происхождéнии ви́дов, Darwin's theory of the origin of species. Егó происхождéние неизвéстно, his parentage is unknown. Про-ис-шéствие, *n.n.*, incident, occurrence, accident, event. Ужáсное п., terrible accident.

на-ход-и́ть, *v.i.,* найти́, *v.p.,* + *acc.,* на + *acc.,* to find, discover; come upon; consider. Н. дéньги, to find money. Я нахожý э́ти усло́вия приéмлемыми, I find these terms acceptable. Он найдёт своё призвáние, he will find his vocation. Онá нахóдит удовóльствие в хождéнии по магази́нам, she takes pleasure in shopping around. На негó нахóдит тоскá, he has fits of depression. На-ход-и́ть-ся, *v.i.r.,* найти́сь, *v.p.r., used only in 3d pers.,* to be found. Потéрянная кни́га не нахóдится, the lost book cannot be found. Рабóта найдётся, work will be found. На-хóд-ка, *n.f.,* find, object found; windfall, godsend. Он не вернýл своéй нахóдки, he has not returned the found thing. Какáя н. э́то плáтье! What a find—this dress! Нахóд-чивость, *n.f.,* resourcefulness. Он показáл большýю н. he showed great resourcefulness. На-хóд-чивый, *adj.,* resourceful, quick-witted. Н. человéк, resourceful man. Егó отвéты бы́ли óчень нахóдчивы, his replies were very much to the point. На-хóд-чиво, *adv.,* wittily, quickly. На-хожд-éние, *n.n.,* finding; state of being at a given place. Н. э́того мéтода произвелó переворóт в наýке, the discovery of this new method revolutionized science.

на-ход-и́ть-ся, *v.i.r.,* в, на + *prep.,* to be located. Кни́ги нахóдятся на пóлке, the books are on the shelf. Я нахожýсь в затрудни́тельном положéнии, I find myself in a predicament. Дерéвня э́та нахóдится в 15 киломéтрах от гóрода, this village is located 15 kilometers from the city. Он нахóдится под судóм, he is on trial. Мéсто-на-хождéние, *n.n.,* location.

на-ход-и́ть-ся, *v.p.r.,* to tire oneself by walking. Они́ находи́лись вдóволь, they tired themselves by walking.

на-шé-ствие, *n.n.,* invasion. Н. Наполеóна на Росси́ю в 1812 г., Napoleon's invasion of 1812.

нис-ход-и́ть, *v.i.,* низойти́, *v.p.,* на + *acc.,* (*poet.*), to descend. Вдохновéние

нисхóдит на худóжника, inspiration descends upon the artist. Нис-ходя́щий, *adj., part. act. pres.,* descending; decreasing. Чи́сла располагáются в нисходя́щем поря́дке, the numbers are set down in a descending order. Нисшéд-ший, *adj., part. act. past,* (*obs.*), that which has descended; *see* низойти́.

с-нис-ход-и́ть, *v.i.,* снизойти́, *v.p.,* к + *dat.,* to condescend, be indulgent, lenient; make allowances. Мы должны́ с. к человéческим слáбостям, we must be indulgent towards human weaknesses. С-нис-ход-и́тельность, *n.f.,* condescendence, indulgence; leniency. Снис-ход-и́тельный, *adj.,* condescending, indulgent; lenient. С. начáльник, lenient superior. С-нис-ход-и́тельно, *adv.,* condescendingly, leniently. Относи́ться с. к комý-нибудь, to be lenient towards someone. С-нис-хождéние, *n.n.,* leniency; allowance. Заслýживать с-ия, to deserve leniency.

об-ход-и́ть, *v.i.,* обойти́, *v.p.,* to go round, make rounds; visit; deceive, pass by, over; deprive. Он обхóдит всех знакóмых, he is making the rounds of all his friends. Неприя́тель обошёл нас с флáнга, the enemy outflanked us. Он хитрó обошёл меня́, (*colloq.*), he was clever in getting around me. Кри́тики обхóдят егó молчáнием, the critics ignore him. Емý дáли повышéние, а меня́ обошли́, they promoted him, but passed me by. Об-ход-и́ть-ся, *v.i.r.,* обойти́сь, *v.p.r.,* в + *acc.,* с + *instr.,* без + *gen.,* to cost, come to; treat; dispense with; do, go without something; get used to. Пальтó обхóдится тепéрь в 1500 рублéй, the coat now costs 1,500 rubles. Он óчень хорошó обходи́лся с ней, he treated her very well. Они́ обошли́сь без егó пóмощи, they managed without his help. Всё обойдётся, (*idiom.*), everything will turn out well. Об-хóд, *n.m.,* beat, round, circuit; evasion; by-pass. О. препя́тствий, by-passing of obstacles. Врач дéлает обхóд больны́х, the doctor is making his rounds. Идти́ в о., to go in a round-about way; to make (watchman's) rounds. Об-ход-и́тельный, *adj.,* courteous, obliging. Он óчень о. человéк, he is a very courteous man. Об-ход-и́тельность, *n.f.,* courtesy, amiability. Егó о. подкупáет всех, his courtesy wins everyone over. Об-хóдный, *adj.,* roundabout, circuitous. Нáша часть произвелá о-ое движéние, (*mil.*), our detachment made an encircling maneuver. Об-хожд-éние, *n.n.,* treatment, manner(s), way. Быть прия́тным в о., to have pleasant manners.

от-ход-и́ть, *v.i.i.,* отойти́, *v.р.,* от + *gen,* to withdraw, move away; pass away, die, depart; calm down. Он отошёл от окна́, he withdrew from the window. По́езд отхо́дит в 9 часо́в ве́чера, the train leaves at 9 p.m. Больно́й отошёл сего́дня но́чью, the patient passed away last night. Он рассерди́лся, но пото́м отошёл, he became angry, but then he calmed down. Ви́шни отошли́, the cherry season is over. От-хо́д, *n.m.,* withdrawal, departure; waste. Я пришёл за 10 мину́т до отхо́да по́езда, I arrived 10 minutes before the train left. Отхо́д на пре́жние пози́ции, withdrawal to former positions. Отхо́ды та́кже шли впрок, the waste products were also used. От-ход-на́я, *adj.,* a prayer for the dying. От-хо́д-чивый, *adj.,* easily appeased; capable of easily regaining composure. У него́ о-ое се́рдце, he regains his composure easily. От-хо́ж-ий, *adj.,* far from home. Отхо́жие про́мыслы, seasonal work away from home. О-ее ме́сто, *(folk.),* toilet, rest room.

пере-ход-и́ть, *v.i.,* перейти́, *v.р.,* + *асс.,* в, на + *асс.,* к + *dat.,* to cross; develop into; be converted; change hands; pass. Неприя́тель перехо́дит в наступле́ние, the enemy is taking the offensive. Това́р перехо́дит из рук в ру́ки, the merchandise passes through many hands. Это вещество́ перешло́ из жи́дкого состоя́ния в твёрдое, this substance changed from a liquid to a solid. Пере-хо́д, *n.m.,* transition; passage; march; conversion. П. че́рез Альпы, the crossing over the Alps. Они́ де́лали коро́ткие перехо́ды, *(mil.),* they advanced by short stages. Пере-хо́д-ный, пере-ход-но́й, *adj.,* transitional. Он получи́л п. балл (отме́тку), he received a passing mark. Это то́лько п-ая ста́дия, this is only a transitional stage. Пере-ход-я́щий, *adj., part. act. pres.,* transitory; pertaining to crossing. Пешехо́ды, переходя́щие че́рез мост, пла́тят за э́то, the pedestrians who cross the bridge pay a toll. Пре-ход-я́щий, *adj.,* *(obs.),* transient. Всё преходя́ще на э́том све́те, all is transient in this life.

по-ход-и́ть, *v.р.,* по-ха́ж-ивать, *v.i. iter.,* to walk a little, walk about. Он немно́го походи́л и уста́л, he walked a little and became tired. Ма́тушка по са́дику поха́живает, *(folksong),* mother is walking about the garden. По-хо́д, *n.m.,* campaign, march. Кресто́вый п., Crusade. Войска́ вы́ступили в п., the troops took to the field. По-хо́д-ка, *n.f.,*

walk, gait. Я узнаю́ его́ по похо́дке, I recognize him by his gait. По-хо́д-ный, *adj.,* pertaining to a campaign. П-ая крова́ть, camp cot. По́-ход-я, *adv., (colloq.),* on the march, on the go, offhand. Вре́дно есть п., one should not eat while walking. По-хожд-е́ния, *n.n. plur.,* adventure. П-ия Кота́-Мурлы́ки, the adventures of Purring Tom.

по-ход-и́ть, *v.i.,* на + *асс.,* to resemble, be like, look like. Она́ походи́ла на свою́ мать, she resembled her mother. По-хо́ж-ий, *adj.,* similar, like, resembling. Они́ похо́жи друг на дру́га, как две ка́пли воды́, they are as much alike, as two drops of water. Ты сам на себя́ не похо́ж, *(fig.),* you are not like yourself. По-хо́ж-е, *adv.,* like. П. на дождь, it looks like rain. Это ни на что не п., this doesn't look like anything. Не-по-хо́ж-ий, *adj.,* dissimilar, unlike.

под-ход-и́ть, *v.i.,* подойти́, *v.р.,* к + *dat.,* to come near, approach; suit, fit. По́езд подхо́дит к ста́нции, the train approaches the station. Сад подходи́л к са́мому ле́су, the garden stretched as far as the woods. Он подходи́л к вопро́су с но́вой то́чки зре́ния, he treated the question from a new point of view. Ключ не подхо́дит к замку́, the key does not fit the lock. Эти цвета́ не подхо́дят, these colors do not match. Они́ хорошо́ подхо́дят друг к дру́гу, they suit each other perfectly. Под-ход-я́щий, *adj., part. act. pres.,* suitable, fitting, right, proper. Вы са́мый п. челове́к для э́той рабо́ты, You are indeed the right man in the right place.

при-ход-и́ть, *v.i.,* прийти́, *v.р.,* к + *dat.,* в, на + *асс.,* to come, arrive. Мне прихо́дит в го́лову, it comes to my mind. Он наконе́ц пришёл в себя́, he finally came to his senses, regained his consciousness. Учи́тель прихо́дит в класс в 8 часо́в утра́, the teacher comes into the classroom at eight o'clock in the morning. Он пришёл к концу́ ле́кции, he came towards the end of the lecture. Я прихожу́ в отча́яние от всего́ ви́денного, Everything I've seen makes me despair. Мне пришло́ на па́мять, I recalled. При-ход-я́щий, *adj., part. act. pres.,* coming, arriving. П. учени́к, day pupil. При-шёд-ший, *adj., part. act. past,* that has come, arrived. П. друг утеша́л его́, the friend who had come was consoling him. При-ход-и́ть-ся, *v.i.r.,* прийти́сь, *v.р.r.,* к + *dat,* с + *gen.,* to fit; be obliged; have to. Ключ прихо́дится к

замку́, the key fits the lock. Он при-
хо́дится ей сродни́, he is related to
her. Вся́кому прихо́дится отвеча́ть
за свою́ рабо́ту, everyone has to be
responsible for his work. Ему́ пло́хо
пришло́сь, he has been hard pressed.
Мне пришло́сь заплати́ть вдво́е, I had
to pay double. При-хо́д, *n.m.,* coming,
arrival, advent; receipts; parish. Мы
ждём прихо́да по́езда, we are awaiting
the arrival of the train. Расхо́д превы-
ша́ет прихо́д, the expenses exceed the
the receipts. У э́той це́ркви большо́й
прихо́д, this church has a large parish.
При-хо́д-ный, *adj.,* receipt. Прихо́дно-
расхо́дная кни́га, account book. При-
хо́д-ский, *adj.,* parochial. Это на́ша
п-ая це́рковь, this is our parish church.
Он наш прихо́дский свяще́нник, he
is our parish priest. При-хо́ж-ая, *adj.,*
used as n.f., anteroom, lobby, hallway,
vestibule. П. полна́ люде́й, the hall is
crowded with people. При-ше́-лец, *n.m.,*
(obs.), newcomer, stranger, alien. Он
был прише́льцем среди́ нас, he was a
stranger among us. При-ше́-ствие, *n.n.,*
advent, coming. Второ́е п. бу́дет днём
Стра́шного Суда́, the second coming
will be Judgment Day.
про-ход-и́ть, *v.p.,* to spend time in
walking. Мы проходи́ли всё у́тро по
го́роду, we spent all morning walking
about town.
про-ход-и́ть, *v.p.,* про-ха́ж-ивать, *v.i.,* to
cover by walking, walk a certain
distance; walk a horse. Мы проходи́ли
до 20 верст в день, we used to cover
up to twenty versts a day. Про-ха́ж-
ивать-ся, *v.i.r.,* пройти́сь, *v.p.r.,* to per-
ambulate, stroll. Больны́е проха́жи-
ваются по́ саду, the patients are
strolling in the garden. Пройди́тесь
по го́роду! Take a stroll through the
city!
про-ход-и́ть, *v.i.,* пройти́, *v.p.,* to pass,
go through; elapse; learn, study, cover;
be held. Доро́га прохо́дит че́рез лес,
the road goes through the woods.
Лёд прошёл, the ice has passed. Он
прошёл ого́нь и во́ду, *(fig.),* he went
through fire and water, he had a difficult time. Мо́жно здесь пройти́? May
one pass through here? Это не пройдёт! This will not pass! Это прохо́дит
кра́сной ни́тью, *(fig.),* it is emphasized
throughout. П. физиоло́гию, to study
physiology. Проходи́те, пожа́луйста,
pass on, please. Это ему́ да́ром не
пройдёт, he will not get away with
this. Го́ды прохо́дят незаме́тно, the
years pass imperceptibly. Боль прош-
ла́, the pain has passed. Что вы
прохо́дите по грамма́тике? What are

you covering in grammar? Про-ход-
и́ть-ся, *v.i.r.,* used only in 3d pers., to
be studied. Когда́ прохо́дится полити́-
ческая эконо́мия? When is political
economics studied? Про-хо́д, *n.m.,*
aisle, passage; avenue; gate; *(anat.),*
duct. Все места́ бы́ли за́няты, он
стоя́л в прохо́де, all the seats were
occupied, he stood in the aisle. У него́
зало́жен слухово́й прохо́д, his ear
passage is clogged. Про-ход-и́мец,
n.m., rogue, adventurer. Про-ход-
и́мый, *adj., part. pres. pass.,* passable,
practicable. Доро́га проходи́ма, the
road is passable. Про-ход-и́мость, *n.f.,*
passability, practicability; free passage.
Не-про-ход-и́мый, *adj.,* impassable, impenetrable. Они́ попа́ли в н-ые боло́та,
they stumbled on impassable swamps.
Не-про-ход-и́мо, *adv.,* abysmally. Он н.
глуп, he is abysmally stupid. Про-ход-
но́й, *adj.,* pertaining to passage; transit.
На э́той у́лице мно́го прохо́дны́х
дворо́в, there are many passage ways
on this street. Про-хожд-е́ние, *n.n.,*
passing, going through; studying,
learning. П. че́рез лес бы́ло тру́дно,
going through the woods was difficult.
П. хи́мии дли́тся не́сколько семе́-
стров, the study of chemistry takes
several semesters. Про-хо́ж-ий, *n.m.,*
passer-by. Все п-ие обраща́ли на него́
внима́ние, all the passers-by turned
their attention to him. Про-ше́д-ший,
adj., part. act. past, bygone. Про-
ше́дшее вре́мя, *(gram.),* past tense.
Про́-шл-ый, *adj.,* past, bygone, last. Он
посети́л нас на про́шлой неде́ле, he
visited us last week. Не вызыва́йте
воспомина́ний про́шлых лет, do not
evoke memories of times past. Про́-шл-
ое, *n.n.,* the past. Его́ п. не говори́т в
его́ по́льзу, his past is against him.
пут-е-ше́-ствовать, *v.i.,* to travel. Анг-
лича́не лю́бят путеше́ствовать, Eng-
lishmen like to travel. Пут-е-ше́-
ственник, *n.m.,* путеше́ственница, *n.f.,*
traveller, tourist. Пут-е-ше́ствие, *n.n.,*
journey. Это п. меня́ утоми́ло, this trip
has tired me. Мы должны́ бы́ли
предприня́ть далёкое п., We were
obliged to take a long journey.
рас-ха́ж-ивать, *v.i.,* по + *dat.,* to walk
about, stroll about. Он расха́живал
взад и вперёд по ко́мнате, he was
walking up and down the room. Рас-
ха́ж-ивание, *n.n.,* walking about, strolling about.
рас-ход-и́ть, *v.p.,* + *acc., (rare),* to
limber up by walking. Он расходи́л
свою́ одеревене́вшую но́гу, he limbered up his benumbed leg by walking.
Рас-ходи́ть-ся, *v.p.r.,* to be limbered

up by walking; lose one's self-control.
Моя́ нога́ постепе́нно расхо́дится, my
leg is gradually limbering up. Он ча́сто
расходи́лся, he frequently lost his self-
control. Рас-ход-и́ть-ся, *v.i.r.*, разойти́сь.
v.p.r., to part, separate, break up;
dissent. Они́ попроща́лись и разошли́сь, they said good-bye and went their
separate ways. Они́ разошли́сь че́рез
год по́сле сва́дьбы, they separated one
year after the wedding. Мне́ния по
э́тому вопро́су расхо́дятся, opinions
vary on this subject. На́ши пи́сьма
разошли́сь, our letters crossed. Рас-
хожд-е́ние, *п.п.*, divergence, discord. У
них глубо́кое р. во взгля́дах, their
opinions are very divergent. Рас-хо́д,
п.т., expense, expenditure. У нас
больши́е расхо́ды, we have large expenses.

рас-хо́д-овать, *v.i.*, + *acc.*, to spend,
consume, use up. Р. де́ньги, to spend
money. Они́ расхо́довали ста́рые
запа́сы, they were using up old stores.
Рас-хо́д-овать-ся, *v.i.r.*, to be spent,
expended. Всё расхо́дуется на воо-
руже́ние, everything is spent for armament. Рас-хо́д-ный, *adj.*, for expenses;
pertaining to expenditures. Р-ая кни́га,
a book for entering expenditures. Рас-
ход-ование, *п.п.*, expense, expenditure,
spending. Р. де́нег, spending of money.

из-рас-хо́д-овать, *v.p.*, + *acc.*, to spend,
consume, use up. Они́ израсхо́довали
все материа́лы, they have consumed all
the materials. Из-рас-хо́д-овать-ся,
v.p.r., (*colloq.*), to spend too much. Я
израсхо́довался, I am short of money,
out of funds.

пере-рас-хо́д-овать, *v.p.*, to spend excessively; overdraw. Они́ перерасхо́до-
вали сверх сме́ты, they have exceeded
the estimate. Пере-рас-хо́д, *п.т.*, overdraft. У него́ получи́лся большо́й п.,
he had a large overdraft.

с-ход-и́ть, *v.p.*, в, на + *acc.*, to walk there
and back; fetch. Мне на́до с. на ры́нок,
I have to go to the market, make a trip
to the market. Сходи́те за врачо́м,
fetch the doctor.

с-ход-и́ть, *v.i.*, сойти́, *v.p.*, с + *gen.*, to
go off, go down; descend. Он схо́дит
с ле́стницы, he is descending the stairs.
Он сошёл с авто́буса, he alighted from
the bus. Он сошёл с ума́, he went out
of his mind. Эти су́ммы сошли́ на
нет, the sums dwindled to nothing.
Он сошёл за меня́, he passed for me.
По́езд сошёл с ре́льсов, the train was
derailed. Снег сошёл, the snow has
melted. Кра́ска сошла́, the color has
faded. Это сло́во не схо́дит у него́ с
языка́, this word is always on his lips.

Это сошло́ ему́ с рук, he got away
with it. Всё сошло́ благополу́чно, all
went off very well. Сойдёт! It will
pass! Он написа́л запи́ску, не сходя́
с ме́ста, he wrote a note on the spot.
С-ход-и́ть-ся, *v.i.r.*, сойти́сь, *v.p.r.*, с
+ *instr.*, to meet, join, come together;
live together; cohabit; agree. Заго-
во́рщики сходи́лись тайко́м за́ городом, the conspirators used to meet
secretly in a suburb. Мой жиле́т не
схо́дится, my vest doesn't meet. Она́
сошла́сь с ним, (*colloq.*), she became
intimate with him. Они́ бли́зко
сошли́сь друг с дру́гом, they have become close friends. На́ши взгля́ды не
схо́дятся, your opinions do not agree
with mine. Они́ сошли́сь в цене́, they
agreed on the price. Я ви́жу, мы не
сойдёмся, I see that we shall never
arrive at an agreement. С-ход, *п.т.*,
descent, descending; meeting. С. с горы́
был тру́ден, the descent was difficult.
Се́льский с., (*pre-Rev.*), village assembly. С-хо́д-ка, (*pre-Rev.*), meeting. Сту-
де́нческая с., (*pre-Rev.*), student meeting. С-хо́д-ни, *n.f.pl.*, gangway. С. уже́
у́браны, the gangway has been hoisted.
С-хо́д-ный, *adj.*, analogous, similar,
alike; reasonable. Он схо́ден с ни́ми,
he is like them. Я купи́л э́то по
схо́дной цене́, I bought this at a
reasonable price. С-хо́д-ство, *п.п.*,
likeness, resemblance, similarity. У них
семе́йное с., there is a family resemblance between them. С-хо́ж-ий, *adj.*,
(*colloq.*), like, alike, similar. Они́ все
схо́жи друг с дру́гом, they all resemble each other. Со-ше́д-ший, *adj.*, *part.
act. past*, gone down, descended. С. со
сце́ны арти́ст, the artist who has left
the stage. Со-ше́-ствие, *п.п.*, (*rel.*),
descent. Сего́дня пра́здник Соше́ст-
вия Свято́го Ду́ха, today we celebrate
the Descent of the Holy Ghost.

у-ха́ж-ивать, *v.i.*, за + *instr.*, to tend,
nurse, take care; court, woo, make
love to. Сёстры милосе́рдия уха́жи-
вали за больны́ми, the nurses took
care of the patients. Он уха́живал за
ней ещё студе́нтом, he wooed her
while he was still a student. У-ха́ж-
иватель, *п.т.*, (*colloq.*), suitor, wooer.
За ней волочи́лась толпа́ уха́жива-
телей, a crowd of suitors paid court to
her. У-ха́ж-ивание, *п.п.*, nursing,
tending; courting, courtship, wooing.
Не́жное у. жениха́, the tender courtship
of a fiance. У. за больны́ми - её приз-
ва́ние, nursing is her vocation.

у-ход-и́ть, *v.i.*, уйти́, *v.p.*, + *acc.*, to
go away, walk away, depart,
leave; pass. Он ухо́дит в 8 часо́в

утрá, he leaves at eight o'clock in the morning. Врéмя ухóдит, time is passing. Лисúца ушлá в норý, the fox disappeared into its den. Это от вас не уйдёт, you will receive it sooner or later. Он ушёл домóй, he went home. Врéмя ещё не ушлó, there is still time. Сýдно ушлó в мóре, the ship put forth to sea. Пóезд ушёл, the train has pulled out. Молокó ушлó, the milk has boiled over. У-хóд, *n.m.,* departure, doing away, going out, going off, leaving; care, nursing. У. сýдна в мóре назнáчен на зáвтра, the departure of the ship is fixed for tomorrow. У. егó с дóлжности отлóжен, his retirement from office has been postponed. У. за больнúми трéбует терпéния, nursing requires patience. Здесь нет дóлжного ухóда за машúнами, the machines here are not properly taken care of.

у-ход-úть, *v.p.,* + *acc., (colloq),* to tire, exhaust, wear out. Онá уходúла егó свонúми капрúзами, she has tired him to death with her whims. У-ход-úть-ся, *v.p.r., (colloq.),* to calm down; become exhausted. Наконéц, он уходúлся, finally, he calmed down.

ХОТ-, ХОЧ-, DESIRE, WISH, WANT; INCLINATION, PREDILECTION

хот-é-ть, хоч-ý, *v.i.,* за-хот-éть, *v.p.,* + *gen.,* + *inf.,* to wish, want, desire. Х. хлéба, to want some bread. Я хочý вас вúдеть, I want to see you. Я хотéл бы, чтóбы вы знáли э́то, I would like you to know it. Дéлайте, как хотúте, do as you like. Хóчешь, не хóчешь, — э́то нáдо сдéлать, willy-nilly, this must be done. Хот-éть-ся, *v.i.r.,* + *dat.,* + *inf.,* + *gen.,* to like, have a desire, wish. Мне хóчется поговорúть с ним, I would like to talk with him. Мне совсéм не хóчется слúшать об э́том, I have no desire to hear about is. Мне хóчется спать, I am sleepy, Емý хóчется чегó-нибудь слáдкого, he feels like having something sweet. Хотéние, *n.n.,* wishing, desire, willing. На всáкое х. есть терпéние, *(prov.)* if you want it badly enough, you'll work for it. Хот-ь, хот-я́, *conj.,* though, although. Хóть-бы он ушёл, I wish he would go. Хоть убéй, не пóмню, *(colloq.),* I cannot for the life of me remember it. Он пáрень хоть кудá, *(colloq.),* he is a first-rate chap. Мне необходúмо хотя́ бы два свобóдных дня, I must have at least two free days. Он ушёл, хотя́ егó просúли остáться, he departed, although he was asked to stay.

за-хот-éть, *v.p.,* + *gen.,* + *inf.,* to develop a desire, a wish. Он всё мóжет сдéлать, стóит лишь емý з., he can do everything and anything, if he wants to badly enough. Ребёнок захотéл морóженого, the child would like some ice cream. За-хот-éть-ся, *v.p.r.,* + *gen.,* + *inf.,* to like, have a desire. Мне захотéлось фрýктов, I suddenly felt I wanted some fruit. Емý захóчется есть, he will feel like eating. Нé-хот-я, *adv.,* unwillingly, reluctantly. Онá н. согласúлась, she agreed reluctantly.

о-хóт-ить-ся, о-хóч-усь, *v.i.r.,* на + *gen.,* за + *instr.,* to hunt with a purpose of catching; hunt, shoot, chase. Я охóчусь на лисúц, I hunt foxes. Мáльчики охóтились за скворцáми, the boys were out catching finches. Он охóтился за рéдкими мáрками, he was looking for rare stamps. Полúция охóтилась за грабúтелями, the police were looking for the burglars. О-хóт-а, *n.f.,* hunt, hunting, shooting; desire, inclination. О. егó люби́мый спорт, hunting is his favorite sport. Охóта пýще невóли, *(saying),* desire is more effective than compulsion. Охóта тебé спóрить с ним! What's the use of arguing with him! О-хóт-ник, *n.m.,* hunter, gunner; volunteer; amateur. "Запúски Охóтника," *(Turgenev),* "A Sportsman's Sketches." Он стрáстный о., he is an inveterate hunter. Офицéр вúзвал охóтников, the officer called for volunteers. О-хóт-ничий, *adj.,* hunting, sporting. О-ье ружьё, fowling piece. О-ья собáка, hunting dog. О-хóт-ный, *adj.,* poultry, game. О. ряд, poultry and game market. О-хóт-но, *adv.,* willingly, readily. Он о. э́то сдéлает для вас, he will willingly do it for you.

на-о-хóт-ить-ся, *v.p.r.,* to have one's fill of hunting. Я вдóволь наохóтился сегóдня, I've hunted enough today. Не-о-хóт-а, *n.f.,* disinclination, reluctance. Мне н. идтú к немý, *(colloq.),* I do not want to go with him. Не-о-хóт-ный, *adj.,* unwilling, reluctant. Не-о-хóт-но, *adv.,* unwillingly, reluctantly; backwardly. Он óчень н. взя́лся за э́то дéло, he has undertaken this task very reluctantly.

по-о-хóт-ить-ся, *v.p.r.,* to hunt a little. Мне хóчется п., I want to do a little hunting. По-о-хóт-ничьи, *adv.,* like a hunter. Онú вúпили и закусúли п., they had a drink and ate like hunters.

при-о-хóт-и-ть, *v.p.,* при-о-хóч-ивать, *v.i.,* + *acc.,* к + *dat.,* to give one a liking for; inculcate a taste for. Онú приохóтили егó к винý и кáртам, they've given him a liking for drink and cards. При-о-хо́т-ить-ся, *v.p.r.*, при-о-хо́ч-ивать-ся, *v.i.r.*, к + *dat.*, to conceive a liking for, take to.

по́-хот-ь, *n.f.*, lust, desire. Была́ ли э́то любо́вь и́ли то́лько по́хоть; What was it — love, or only lust? По-хот-ли́вый, *adj.*, lascivious, lustful, wanton. По-хот-ли́вость, *n.f.*, lasciviousness, lust; voluptuousness. По-хот-ли́во, *adv.*, lasciviously, lustfully.

рас-хот-е́ть, *v.p.*, (*colloq.*), to have a change of heart, lose one's desire, feel disinclined, lose one's zest for, change one's wish. Он расхоте́л писа́ть свою́ кни́гу, he has lost his desire to write a book. Рас-хот-е́ть-ся, *v.p.r.*, + *dat.*, *used only in 3d pers.*, to lose one's desire. Ему́ расхоте́лось спать, he is no longer sleepy.

ХИТР-, ХИЩР-, CUNNING, CRAFT, CUNNINGNESS, CRAFTINESS

хитр-и́ть, *v.i.*, с + *instr.*, to dodge, be evasive; act slyly, act with cunning, be foxy. Он всегда́ хитри́т с на́ми, he is always foxy with us. Хитр-е́ц, *n.m.*, crafty person, dodger; fox. Хитр-еца́, *n.f.*, slyness, craftiness, *only in expression*: Он с хитрецо́й, (*colloq.*), he is a deep one. Хи́тр-ость, *n.f.*, cunning, artfulness, craftiness, slyness; stratagem. В ней мно́го же́нской хи́трости, she has much feminine cunning. Хитр-о́, *adv.*, cunningly, craftily, slyly; adroitly. Он вёл себя́ х., he behaved craftily. Хитр-о-сплете́ние, *n.n.*, work of craftiness, of slyness, of cunning. Хитр-о-у́мие, *n.n.*, finesse, artfulness. Хитр-о-у́мный, *adj.*, artful, cunning, crafty. Х. план, crafty plan. Хи́тр-ый, *adj.*, sly, cunning, artful, crafty; intricate, involved. Х. приём, sly trick. Это не х-ая шту́ка, this doesn't require any inventiveness.

бес-хи́тр-остный, *adj.*, artless, unsophisticated. Бес-хи́тр-остность, *n.f.*, artlessness, lack of sophistication. Его́ б. погуби́ла его́, his simple-mindedness ruined him. Бес-хи́тр-остно, *adv.*, artlessly. Она́ б. всё рассказа́ла, she told everything simply.

пере-хитр-и́ть, *v.p.*, пере-хитр-я́ть, *v.i.*, + *acc.*, to outwit. Куту́зов перехитри́л Наполео́на, Kutuzov outwitted Napoleon.

с-хитр-и́ть, *v.p.*, to act slyly. Он схитри́л, но неуда́чно, he acted slyly, but unsuccessfully.

у-хитр-и́ть-ся, у-хитр-ю́сь, *v.p.r.*, у-хитр-я́ть-ся, у-хитр-я́ю-сь, *v.i.r.*, to contrive; manage, make a shift. Он

ухитри́лся бежа́ть из концентрацио́нного ла́геря, he managed to escape from a concentration camp.

у-хищр-и́ть-ся, *v.p.r.*, у-хищр-я́ть-ся, *v.i.r.*, to manage, succeed to. Он ухищря́ется жить почти́ без де́нег, he manages to live almost without money. У-хищр-е́ние, *n.n.*, shift, device, contrivance, artifice. Враг потерпе́л пораже́ние, несмотря́ на все ухищре́ния, despite all his dodges, the enemy was defeated. У-хищр-ённый, *adj.*, artful, cunning. У. план, cunning plan.

ХРАН-, ХОРОН-, CONCEALMENT, HIDING, INTERMENT, BURIAL

хран-и́ть, *v.i.*, + *acc.*, to hide; keep. Х. та́йну, to keep a secret. Что име́ем не храни́м; потеря́вши, пла́чем, (*prov.*), good fortune is never appreciated until it is gone. Да храни́т вас Госпо́дь! May the Lord keep you! В музе́е храня́тся драгоце́нные ру́кописи, precious manuscripts are kept in the museum. Хран-е́ние, *n.n.*, keeping, custody, storing, storage. Отдава́ть на х., to place in storage. Хран-и́лище, *n.n.*, repository, depository, storehouse. Публи́чная Библиоте́ка - х. книг и ру́кописей, the Public Library is a rich depository of books and manuscripts. Хран-и́тель, *n.m.*, keeper, custodian, curator. Х. преда́ний старины́, keeper of ancient traditions. А́нгел-храни́тель, guardian angel. Он был помо́щником храни́теля музе́я, he was an assistant to the curator of the museum.

о-хран-и́ть, *v.p.*, о-хран-я́ть, *v.i.*, + *acc.*, (*rare*), to guard, keep watch over; defend, preserve. О. грани́цы, to guard the frontiers. О-хран-я́ть-ся, *v.i.r.*, + *instr.*, to be guarded, watched. Запа́сы зерна́ охраня́ются сторожа́ми, the grain reserves are guarded by guards. О-хра́н-а, *n.f.*, guard, escort. Это его́ ли́чная о., this is his personal bodyguard. О. труда́, safeguarding of labor. Он нахо́дится под охра́ной та́йной поли́ции, he is being guarded by the secret police. О-хран-е́ние, *n.n.*, guarding, conservation, keeping. О. лесо́в необходи́мо, the conservation of forests is imperative. О. обще́ственного поря́дка, safeguarding of public order. О-хран-и́тельный, *adj.*, (*obs.*), protective, precautionary. О-ые ме́ры, protective measures, precautionary measures. О-хра́н-ка, *n.f.*, (*obs.*), department of secret police. О-хра́нник, *n.m.*, member of the secret police. О-хра́н-ный, *adj.*, protective. О-ая грáмота, (*hist.*), charter establishing the protection of the State.

пред-о-хран-и́ть, *v.p.,* пред-о-хран-я́ть, *v.i.,* + *acc.,* от + *gen.,* to protect, preserve, safeguard. Непромокáемый плащ предохраня́ет от дождя́, the raincoat is protecting from the rain. Пред-о-хран-éние, *n.n.,* prevention, protection, prophylaxis. Приви́вка для п. от бéшенства, vaccine for the prevention of rabies. Пред-о-храни́тель, *n.m.,* protector, preservative, guard; fuse. Перегорéл п., the fuse is burned out. Пред-о-храни́тельный, *adj.,* preservative, precautionary, preventive, protective. П. клáпан, safety valve. П-ые мéры, precautionary measures. П-ая приви́вка, preventive vaccination.

со-хран-и́ть, *v.p.,* со-хран-я́ть, *v.i.,* + *acc.,* to conserve, maintain, keep; observe. Он сохраня́ет хладнокрóвне в бою́, he is cool headed under fire. Он сохрани́л за собóй прáво передáть квартúру, he reserved the right to sublet the apartment. Со-хран-и́ть-ся, *v.p.r.,* со-хран-я́ть-ся, *v.i.r.,* to last, be well preserved. Мехá хорошó сохраня́ются в холóдном помещéнии, furs are well preserved in cold storage. Онá хорошó сохрани́лась, she is well preserved. Со-хран-éние, *n.n.,* preservation, conservation, custody, reservation. Закóн сохранéния энéргии, the law of the conservation of energy. Отдáть вéщи на сохранéние, to place things for safekeeping. Со-хрáн-ность, *n.f.,* safety; integrity; preservation. Я вам отдáм кни́гу в цéлости и сохрáнности, I shall return the books safely and in good condition. Посы́лка пришлá в цéлости и сохрáнности, (*idiom.*), the parcel arrived safe and sound. Со-хрáн-ный, *adj.,* safe, secure. Спря́тать в сохрáнном мéсте, (*obs.*), to hide in a safe place.

хорон-и́ть, *v.i.,* + *acc.,* to bury; hide, conceal. Вчерá хорони́ли извéстного писáтеля, yesterday a famous writer was buried. Они́ умéют хорони́ть концы́ (*fig.*), they know how to remove what might serve as evidence against them. Хорон-и́ть-ся, *v.i.r.,* от + *gen.,* to hide oneself, conceal oneself. Лиси́ца хорóнится в норé от гóнчих, the fox hides itself from the hounds in its den.

по-хорон-и́ть, *v.p.,* + *acc.,* to bury. по-хорóн-ен (*part-pass-past*) was buried. Достоéвский был похорóнен в Петербýрге, Dostoyevsky was buried in St. Petersburg. Пó-хорон-ы, *n.f.pl.,* funeral, burial, interment. Пойти́ на п., to go to a funeral. По-хорóн-ный, *adj.,* funeral. П. звон, funeral knell. П. марш, funeral march. Учáстник похорóнного шéствия, mourner. Владéлец похорóнного бюрó, undertaker, mortician.

Ц

ЦВЕТ-, ЦВЕСТ-, ЦВЕЛ-, ЦВЕЧ-, FLOWER, BLOSSOM; COLOR

цвет, *n.m.,* color; flower; (*fig.*), pick, prime; blossom. цвет-á, *pl.,* colors; цвет-ы́, *pl.,* flowers. Какóго цвéта вáше нóвое пальтó? What color is your new coat? Цвет кóжи, the color of skin. У неё хорóший ц. лицá, she has a good complexion. Он ýмер во цвéте лет, he died in the prime of life. Рóзы в пóлном цветý, the roses are in full bloom. Яблоня облúта цвéтом, the apple tree is covered with blossoms. Цвет-éние, *n.n.,* flowering. Ц. сирéни, lilac time. Цвет-и́стый, *adj.,* flowery, florid. Ц. платóк, flowered kerchief. Употребля́ть ц-ые выражéния, to use florid expressions. Цвет-и́сто, *adv.,* flowery. Писáть ц., to write in a flowery style. Цвет-нóй, *adj.,* colored. Ц-áя матéрия, colored material. Ц-áя капýста, cauliflower. Ц-ы́е метáллы, nonferrous metals. Цвет-óк, *n.m.,* flower, blossom. Они́ сорвáли по цветкý, each picked a flower. Он нóсит цветóк в петли́це, he wears a flower in his buttonhole. Живы́е или искýсственные цветы́, natural or artificial flowers. Убрáть кóмнату цветáми, to decorate the room with flowers. Разведéние цветóв, floriculture. Цвéт-ик, цвет-óчек, *n.m.,* (*dim.*), small flower, floweret. Онá далá емý на пáмять э́тот цветóчек, she has given him this little flower as a keepsake. Цвет-ни́к, *n.m.,* flower-bed; parterre. Цвет-ничёк, *n.m.,* small flower-bed. Цвет-о-, *a combining form meaning* flower. Цвет-о-ви́дный, *adj.,* flower-shaped. Цвет-о-вóд, *n.m.,* florist, floriculturist. Цвет-о-вóдство, *n.n.,* floriculture. Цвет-о-расположéние, *n.n.,* inflorescence. Зóнтичное ц., umbel. Цвет-óчный, *adj.,* floral. Ц. ры́нок, flower market. На óкнах стоя́т ц-ые горшки́, there are flower pots on the windows. Цвет-óчник, *n.m.,* florist. Цвет-óчница, *n.f.,* flower girl.

цвест-и́, *v.i.,* to bloom, flower, flourish; become moldy. Сирéнь цветёт рáнней веснóй, lilacs bloom early in spring. Вáше варéнье ужé цветёт, your preserves are getting moldy. Цветýт нáуки и искýсства, the sciences and arts are flourishing. Цвет-у́щий, *adj.*, *part. pres. act.*, flowering, blossoming. Ц. сад, garden in bloom. Ц. вид страны́, prosperous look of a country. Ц-ее здоро́вье, splendid health.

вы́-цвест-и, *v.p.*, вы-цвет-а́ть, *v.i.*, to lose color, fade. Занаве́ски вы́цвели, the drapes have faded. Вы-цвет-а́ние, *п.п.*, discoloration, fading. Это вещество́ предупрежда́ет в. мате́рии, this chemical substance makes the material sunfast. Вы́-цвет-ший, *adj.*, *part. act. past*, discolored, faded. Она́ ходи́ла в вы́цветшем пла́тье, she wore a faded dress.

за-цвест-й, *v.p.*, за-цвет-а́ть, *v.i.*, to start to bloom, to flower; break out into blossom; become moldy. Ви́шня зацвета́ет, the cherry tree is beginning to bloom. Варе́нье зацвело́, the preserves have become moldy. Цвел-ь, *п.f.*, mold. Стена́ покры́лась цве́лью, the wall is covered with mold. Цвёл-ый, *adj.*, moldy. Это ц-ое я́блоко, this apple is moldy.

от-цвест-й, *v.p.*, от-цвет-а́ть, *v.i.*, to finish flowering, blossoming. Красота́ бы́стро отцвета́ет, beauty fades quickly. От-цвет-а́ние, *п.п.*, withering, fading. О. дере́вьев, fading of tree blossoms.

про-цвест-й, *v.p.*, про-цвет-а́ть, *v.i.*, to thrive, prosper, flourish. Дела́ на́ши процвета́ют, our business is thriving. Про-цвет-а́ющий, *adj.*, *part. act. pres.*, prosperous. Это процвета́ющее предприя́тие, this is a prosperous enterprise. Про-цвет-а́ние, *п.п.*, flourishing, thriving; prosperity, well-being. Пери́од процвета́ния, period of prosperity.

рас-цвест-й, *v.p.*, рас-цвет-а́ть, *v.i.*, to blossom, burst into bloom; flourish, prosper. Ро́зы расцвели́, the roses have blossomed. Её лицо́ расцвело́ улы́бкой, her face broke into a smile. Рас-цве́т, *п.т.*, full blossom, blossoming; opening; prosperity. Р. жи́зни, prime of life. Эпо́ха Возрожде́ния - пери́од расцве́та иску́сства, the Renaissance was a period of the flourishing of the arts. Он в расцве́те сил, he is in the prime of life. Рас-цвет-а́ние, *п.п.*, blossoming, blooming; opening. Со́лнце и тёплые дожди́ ускори́ли р. дере́вьев, the sun and warm rains hastened the blossoming of the trees. Рас-цве́т-ший, *adj.*, *part. act. past*, opened, blossomed out. Р-ая ро́за, full-blown rose, rose in full blossom.

рас-цвет-и́ть, *v.p.*, рас-цве́ч-ивать, *v.i.*, + *acc.*, + *instr.*, to paint, decorate, adorn in gay colors. Прика́зано в пра́здники расцве́чивать дома́ фла́гами, on holidays the people are ordered to deck the houses with flags. Рас-цвет-и́ть-ся, *v.p.r.*, рас-цве́ч-ивать-ся, *v.i.r.*, + *instr.*, to be painted in gay colors; be decorated, dressed. Все суда́ расцве́чены фла́гами, all the ships are decked out in flags. Рас-цве́т-ка, *п.f.*, painting in colors. Мне не нра́вится я́ркая и пёстрая р. шка-ту́лки, I don't like the garish colors of this box.

ЦЕЛ-, ENTIRETY, WHOLE

це́л-ый, *adj.*, whole, entire, integral, unbroken, intact; full. Он рабо́тает по це́лым дням, he works the whole day long. Цел и невреди́м, (*idiom.*), safe and sound. Уходи́ пока́ ещё цел! (*colloq.*), Off with you while there's still time! Цела́-ли ва́ша маши́на? Is your car undamaged? Вот уже́ це́лых 10 дней, как его́ нет, he has been missing for ten whole days. Це́лое число́, integral number. Це́л-ое, *п.п.*, the whole, total totality. В це́лом э́то составна́я часть це́лого, this is an integral part of a whole. В. це́лом э́то составля́ет 100 рубле́й, all in all this amounts to 100 rubles. Цел-ко́вый, *adj.*, used as n., (*colloq.*), one ruble. Цел-ко́вик, *п.т.*, (*colloq.*), one ruble. Это обошло́сь ему́ в 100 целко́вых, it cost him 100 rubles. Цел-ико́м, *adv.*, wholly, totally, entirely, completely; altogether. Он ц. посвяти́л себя́ му́зыке, he devoted himself entirely to music. Цел-ина́, *п.f.*, virgin soil. Поселе́нцы подыма́ют целину́, the settlers are plowing virgin soil. Цел-о-му́дрие, *п.п.*, цел-о-му́дренность, *п.f.*, chastity, continence. Дух целому́дрия, the spirit of chastity. Цел-о-му́дренный, *adj.*, chaste, continent, pure. Она́ целому́дренная молода́я же́нщина, she is a chaste young woman. Це́л-остный, *adj.*, complete, entire, undivided, whole. Ц. проце́сс, a whole process. Це́л-остность, *п.f.*, completeness, wholeness, entirety. Ц. ми́ра ясна́, the wholeness of the universe is evident. Це́л-ость, *п.f.*, wholeness, integrity, entirety. Сохрани́те мне э́ту карти́ну в це́лости, keep this picture safe for me. Он сохрани́л це́лость хара́ктера, he has preserved the integrity of his character. Це́л-ь-ный, *adj.*, whole, entire, integral, total, pure. Он ц. челове́к, he is a man of integrity. Эта ста́туя сде́лана из це́льного куска́ мра́мора, this statue is made of one block of marble. Это це́льное молоко́, this is whole milk.

цел-и́-ть, *v.p.,* + *acc.,* (*obs.*), to heal, cure. Это сре́дство цели́т ра́ны, this remedy heals wounds. Цел-и́тель, *n.m.,* healer. Св. Пантелеймон цели́тель, St. Panteleimon, the Healer. Цел-е́бный, цел-и́тельный, *adj.,* healing, curative, medicinal, salubrious. Это хорошо́ изве́стное ц-ое сре́дство, this is a well-known curative remedy. На ю́ге Кры́ма во́здух цели́телен, the air of Southern Crimea is salubrious. Цел-е́бность, цел-и́тельность, *n.f.,* healing quality. Цели́тельность мно́гих трав при́знана тепе́рь нау́кой, the healing quality of many herbs is now recognized by science.

ис-цел-и́ть, *v.p.,* ис-цел-я́ть, *v.i.,* + *acc., instr.,* to heal, cure. Это лече́ние его́ исцели́ло, this treatment has cured him. Ис-цел-е́ние, *n.n.,* healing, cure; recovery. Ис-цел-и́мый, *adj.,* curable. Не-ис-цел-и́мый, *adj.,* incurable. Н-ая боле́знь, incurable disease. Ис-цел-и́тель, *n.m.,* healer. Вре́мя - вели́кий исцели́тель, time is a great healer.

цел-ова́-ть, *v.i.,* + *acc.,* to kiss. Ц. кого́-нибудь, to kiss someone. Цел-ова́ть-ся, *v.i.r.,* с + *instr.,* to kiss each other, be kissed. Цел-ова́ние, *n.n.,* kissing. Ц. креста́ в знак прися́ги бы́ло обы́чно в Моско́вской Руси́, kissing the cross as a sign of allegiance was customary in medieval Russia. Цел-ова́льник, *n.m.,* (*obs.*), tapster, barkeeper. Ц. стоя́л за сто́йкой, the barkeeper was standing behind the counter.

за-цел-ова́ть, *v.p.,* + *acc.,* to overwhelm, cover with kisses. Мать зацелова́ла ребёнка, the mother covered her child with kisses.

на-цел-ова́ть-ся, *v.p.r.,* to kiss enough, have one's fill of kissing. По́сле до́лгой разлу́ки, они́ не могли́ нацелова́ться, after a long separation they couldn't kiss enough.

пере-цел-ова́ть *v.p.,* + *acc.,* to kiss everyone. Мать перецелова́ла всех дете́й, the mother kissed all her children. Пере-цел-ова́ть-ся, *v.p.r.,* to kiss each other. На Па́сху все в це́ркви перецелова́лись, on Easter Day in church people all kissed each other.

по-цел-ова́ть, *v.p.,* + *acc.,* to kiss. Она́ поцелова́ла его́, she kissed him. По-цел-ова́ть-ся, *v.p.r.,* с + *instr.,* to exchange kisses. Они́ поцелова́лись друг с дру́гом, they exchanged kisses; they kissed each other. По-цел-у́й, *n.m.,* kiss. Пе́рвый п. весны́, (*fig.*), first kiss of spring.

рас-цел-ова́ть, *v.p.,* + *acc.,* to kiss; smother with kisses. Он расцелова́л

своего́ дру́га, he kissed his friend exuberantly. Рас-цел-ова́ть-ся, *v.p.r.,* с + *instr.,* to exchange kisses. Они́ кре́пко расцелова́лись, they kissed each other heartily.

ЦЕН-, WORTH, VALUE

цен-а́, *n.f.,* price, cost, value. Ве́щи про́даны по высо́кой цене́, the things were sold for a high price. Ц. без запро́са и ски́дки, net price. Ц. на аукцио́не, bid. Ры́ночная ц., market price. Уме́ренная ц., reasonable price, moderate price. Фабри́чная ц., factory price. Кака́я цена́? What is the price? What does it cost? Това́р па́дает в цене́, goods are decreasing in price. Это поднима́ется в цене́, this is increasing in price. Я гото́в добы́ть э́то любо́й цено́й, I am ready to pay any price for it. Сба́вка с цены́, reduction in price. Ски́дка с цены́, discount. Назнача́ть це́ну на това́р, to fix the price of merchandise. Снижа́ть (уменьша́ть) це́ну, to lower the price. Он зна́ет себе́ це́ну, he knows his worth

цен-и́ть, *v.i.,* + *acc.,* to value, estimate, appreciate, rate. Я ценю́ ва́шу дру́жбу, I value your friendship. Сли́шком высоко́ ц., to overestimate. Сли́шком ни́зко ц., to underestimate. Во ско́лько це́ните вы э́ту кни́гу? At what do you value this book? Его́ не це́нят, he is not appreciated. Цен-и́ть-ся, *v.i.r.,* в + *acc.,* to be rated, valued, estimated, appreciated. Во ско́лько це́нится э́тот дом? How much is this house worth? Це́н-ность, *n.f.,* value, worth, price. Высо́кая ц., high value. Це́н-ный, *adj.,* valuable, costly. Ц. вклад, valuable contribution. Ц-ая вещь, valuable object. Они́ посла́ли э́ти ве́щи це́нной посы́лкой, they have sent these things by insured parcel post.

бес-це́н-ный, *adj.,* inestimable, invaluable, priceless. Ты мой б. друг, you are a valued friend. Бес-це́н-ок, *n.m.,* absurdly low price. Прода́ть что́ ли́бо за бесце́нок, to sell something for a trifle, for a song.

драг-о-це́н-ный, *adj.,* precious, invaluable. Зо́лото д. мета́лл, gold is a precious metal. Д. ка́мень, precious stone, jewel, gem. Драг-о-це́н-ность, *n.f.,* jewel, gem; precious thing, object.

о-цен-и́ть, *v.p.,* о-це́н-ивать, *v.i.,* + *acc.,* to appraise, value, estimate, appreciate. Они́ оцени́ли дом в 10,000 рубле́й, they appraised the house at 10,000 rubles. Я оцени́л его́ доброту́, I appreciated his kindness. О-це́н-ивать-ся, *v.i.r.,* to be evaluated, appraised. Этот участок оценивается в 2,000 рублей, this lot is valued at 2,000 rubles. О-цен-ка, *n.f.*, evaluation, appraisal. Эта о. слишком низка, this appraisal is too low. О-цен-очный, *adj.*, appraised, assessed. О-ая комиссия, appraisal commission. О-ая цена, assessed price. О-цен-щик, *n.m.*, appraiser, assessor. Он присяжный о., he is a certified appraiser.

пере-о-цен-и́ть, *v.p.,* пере-о-це́н-ивать, *v.i.,* + *acc.,* to overestimate, overrate; revalue. Он переоце́нивает свои силы, he overestimates his strength. Им пришло́сь переоцени́ть иму́щество, they had to revalue the estate. Пере-о-цен-ка, *n.f.,* overrating, revaluation. В обще́ственном мне́нии происхо́дит п. це́нностей, social values are being reassessed.

при-цен-и́ть-ся, *v.p.r.,* при-це́н-иваться, *v.i.r.,* к + *dat.,* to consider the price before buying. Он до́лго прицени́вался, пока́ купи́л, he considered the price for a long time before buying.

рас-цен-и́ть, *v.p.,* рас-це́н-ивать, *v.i.,* + *acc.,* to estimate, value, appraise, assess; set a price; consider. Комиссия расцени́ла дом в 20,000 рубле́й, the commission asssessed the house at 20,000 rubles. Торго́вец расце́нивает това́ры, the merchant is setting a price on his goods. Как вы расце́ниваете собы́тия? How do these events strike you? Рас-це́н-ивать-ся, *v.i.r.,* to be estimated, appraised, assessed. Это предприя́тие расце́нивается в миллио́н рубле́й, this concern is appraised at one million rubles. Рас-це́н-ивание, *n.n.,* рас-це́н-ка, *n.f.,* evaluation, appraisement, tariff, rate. Р. иму́щества, the appraisal of an estate. Эта расце́нка не соотве́тствует действи́тельной це́нности, this evaluation does not correspond to the real value. Рас-це́н-очный, *adj.,* evaluating, appraising. Р. отде́л, department of assessments. Рас-це́н-щик, *n.m.,* assessor, appraiser. Он р. нало́гового отде́ла, he is an assessor in the department of taxation.

Ч

ЧА-, ЧАЙ-, EXPECTATION, HOPE

ча́-я-ть, *v.i.,* + *gen.,* (*obs.*), to expect, hope. Ча́ю воскресе́ния мёртвых, (*rel.*), I believe in the resurrection of the dead. Не ча́ял я тако́й встре́чи, I did not expect to meet you here. Мать души́ в сы́не не ча́ет, (*idiom.*). the mother dotes on her son. Ча́-яние, *n.n.,* expectation, hope. Он жил в

ча́янии бу́дущих благ, he lived in hope of future blessings. Не-ча́-янный, *adj.,* unexpected, inadvertent, unhoped for. Н-ая встре́ча, unexpected meeting. Н-ое движе́ние, inadvert move, motion. Не-ча́-янно, *adv.,* incidentally, by chance, accidentally, unexpectedly; inadvertently. Он н. разби́л ва́зу, he broke the vase accidentally.

чай, (*folk.*), probably, possibly, apparently. Ты, чай, проголода́лся, you are probably hungry.

от-ча́-ять-ся, *v.p.r.,* от-ча́-ивать-ся, *v.i.r.,* to despair, lose courage. Он отча́ялся оста́ться в живы́х, he lost hope of survival. Вы не должны́ отча́иваться, you must not despair. Не отча́ивайтесь, do not despair. От-ча́-яние, *n.n.,* despair; despondency. Он приво́дит нас в о., he is driving us to despair. Нельзя́ впада́ть в тако́е о., you must not be so discouraged. От-ча́-янный, *adj.,* desperate, reckless. Сего́дня о-ая пого́да, the weather today is unbearable. Это о-ое реше́ние, this is a desperate decision. Он о. ездо́к, he is a reckless rider. От-ча́-янно, *adv.,* recklessly. Он о. сме́лый охо́тник на медве́дей, he is a fearless bear hunter. От-ча́-янность, *n.f.,* recklessness. Все бы́ли удивлены́ его́ отча́янностью, everyone was astonished by his recklessness.

ЧА-, ЧН-, ЧИН-, BEGINNING, CONCEPTION, INCEPTION, COMMENCEMENT; DEGREE, RANK; CAUSE

за-ча́-ть, *v.p.,* + *acc.,* to conceive; become pregnant. За-чин-а́ть, *v.i.,* + *acc.,* (*colloq.*), see начина́ть, За-ча́-тие, *n.n.,* conception. Непоро́чное з., Immaculate Conception. За-ча́-ток, *n.m.,* embryo; sprout; source, rudiment. З. расте́ния, sprout of a plant. План провали́лся в са́мом зача́тке, the plan failed in the very beginning. За-ча́-точный, *adj.,* embryonic, rudimentary. Де́ло ещё нахо́дится в зача́точном состоя́нии, the matter, business is still in its embryonic stage. За-чин, *n.m.,* (*folk.*), beginning. З. пе́сни (были́ны), the opening stanza of a Russian folk ballad, song. За-чи́н-щик, *n.m.,* inciter, instigator. З. бу́нта, instigator of a revolt.

на-ча́-ть, на-чн-у́, *v.p.,* на-чин-а́ть, *v.i.,* + *acc.,* с + *gen.,* to begin, commence, start. Мы начина́ем рабо́тать в 8 часо́в утра́, we begin to work at eight o'clock in the morning. Я на́чал писа́ть письмо́, I began to write a letter. Нача́ть с того́, что э́то неве́рно, to begin with, it is wrong. Они́ на́чали избира́-

тельную кампа́нию, they started an election campaign. Начина́й! Begin! На-ча́-ть-ся, *v.p.r.*, на-чин-а́ть-ся, *v.i.r.*, + *instr.*, to begin, be begun, started. Опера начина́ется увертю́рой, the opera begins with an overture. Уро́к начина́ется в 10 часо́в, the class begins at ten o'clock. На-чин-а́ние, *п.п.*, beginning; undertaking. На-чин-а́ю-щий, *adj.*, *part. act. pres.*, *also used as n.*, beginning, starting; beginner, tyro. Это специа́льный курс для начина́ющих, this is a special course for beginners. На-чин-а́ющийся, *adj.*, *part. act. pres.*, beginning, incipient. Н-аяся мете́ль заста́вила нас верну́ться, the coming on of a snowstorm forced us to return. На-ча́-ло, *п.п.*, beginning, start; origin, source; principle, basis. Н. спекта́кля, beginning of a performance. Нева́ берёт н. в Ла́дожском Озере, the Neva originates in Lake Ladoga. До́брое н. полде́ла откача́ло, (*saying*), well begun is half done. От нача́ла до конца́, from beginning to end; through and through. Он пришёл в нача́ле тре́тьего, he came a few minutes past two. Под нача́лом, under a command. На-ча́-льный, *adj.*, initial, first, elementary, rudimentary. Н-ая бу́ква, initial letter. Н-ое образова́ние, elementary education. Н-ая шко́ла, elementary school, grammar school. На-ча́-ток, *п.т.*, rudiment, element. Это то́лько нача́тки зна́ний, these are only the rudiments of knowledge. На-ча́-ль-ств-ова-ть, *v.i.*, над + *instr.*, to command, head. Он нача́льствует над все́ми, he commands them all. На-ча́-льствование, *п.п.*, command, commanding. На-ча́-льник, *п.т.*, head, chief, superior. Н. ста́нции, station master. Н. учи́лища, principal of a school. На-ча́-льнический, на-ча́-льственный, *adj.*, domineering, dictatorial. Все они́ говоря́т нача́льническим то́ном, they all speak in a dictatorial voice. На-ча́-льство, *п.п.*, authorities, heads, chiefs; command. Они́ состоя́т под его́ нача́льством, they are under his command.

без-на-ча́-лие, *п.п.*, anarchy; disorder. Здесь по́лное б., there is total anarchy here. Без-на-ча́-льный, *adj.*, anarchical. Б. и бесконе́чный, having neither beginning nor end. Без-на-ча́-льственный, *adj.*, without command, devoid of authorities. Б-ое о́бщество, a society without authorities.

по-ча́-ть, *v.p.*, по-чин-а́ть, *v.i.*, + *acc.*, (*colloq.*), *see* начина́ть. По-ча́-ток, *п.т.*, (*bot.*), cob, ear; (*text.*), cop. Поча́тки кукуру́зы, corn cobs, ears of corn. По-ча́-тый, по-чато́й, *adj.*, *part. pass. past*, commenced, begun. Не-поча́тый, *adj.*, entire, unbroken; not begun. Н. край, (*idiom.*), plenty, very much. По-чи́н, *п.т.*, beginning, start. Он сде́лал нам п., he was our first customer; he gave us our beginnings.

чин, *п.т.*, rank, grade. Ему́ да́ли но́вый чин, they promoted him to a new rank. Како́й у него́ чин? What rank does he have? Генера́льский чин, rank of general. Во́инские чины́, military ranks. У нас, пожа́луйста, без чино́в, please, do not stand on ceremony. Чин чи́на почита́й, (*saying*), each rank must honor its superior rank. Чин креще́ния, ceremony of baptism. Чи́н-ный, *adj.*, decorous; sedate. Чи́н-ность, *n.f.*, decorum. Чи́н-но, *adv.*, decorously; sedately. Все ч. сиде́ли за столо́м, they were all sitting sedately at the table. Чин-о́вник, *п.т.* (*pre-Rev.*), official, civil servant, functionary. В кабине́т вошёл ч., into the office walked an official. Ме́лкий ч., petty official. Он ч. до мо́зга косте́й, he is a bureaucrat to the core. Чино́внический, *adj.*, bureaucratic. Ч. приём, bureaucratic manners. Чино́вничий, *adj.*, (*colloq.*), official, bureaucratic. Ч-ья душа́, bureaucratic soul. Чин-о́вничество, *п.п.* (*pre-Rev.*), officialdom, bureaucracy. Городско́е ч., municipal bureaucracy. Чин-о́вный, *adj.*, (*obs.*), of high rank. Он о́чень ч-ое лицо́, he is a person of very high rank. Чин-о-нача́лие, *п.п.*, hierarchy; subordination. Чин-о-нача́льник, *п.т.*, person of superior rank. Чин-о-положе́ние, *п.п.*, ecclesiastical order, rites. Чин-о-почита́ние, *п.п.*, respect due rank. Чин-о-произ-во́дство, *п.п.*, advancement in rank. Чин-у́ша, *п.т.*, (*derog.*), petty bureaucrat, official.

чин-и́-ть, *v.i.*, + *acc.*, to impede; administer; mend, repair; sharpen. Они́ чи́нят нам вся́ческие препя́тствия, they are putting all sorts of obstacles in our way. Никому́ я зла не чини́л, I have not harmed anyone. Чини́ть суд и распра́ву, (*idiom.*), to judge and punish. Они́ чи́нят кры́шу до́ма, they are repairing the roof of the house. Шко́льник чи́нит свой каранда́ш, the schoolboy is sharpening his pencil. Перо-чи́н-ный нож, penknife. Чин-и́ть-ся, *v.i.r.*, (*colloq.*), to be placed in the way; be administered; be sharpened; stand on ceremony; be mended, repaired. Что э́то он так чи́нится пе́ред ва́ми? Why is he acting so humble to you? Мой часы́ чи́нятся, my watch is being repaired.

за-чин-и́ть, *v.p.,* за-чин-я́ть, *v.i.,* (*colloq.*), to mend. Она́ зачини́ла ему́ разо́рванный рука́в, she mended his torn sleeve.

на-чин-и́ть, *v.p.,* на-чин-я́ть, *v.i.,* + *acc.,* + *instr.,* to stuff, fill. По́вар начини́л у́тку я́блоками, the cook stuffed the duck with apples. На-чи́н-ка, *n.f.,* stuffing. Н. из гуси́ных печёнок, stuffing of goose livers.

о-чин-и́ть, *v.p.,* о-чин-я́ть, *v.i.,* + *acc.,* to sharpen. Очини́те мне каранда́ш, please sharpen my pencil.

по-чин-и́ть, *v.p.,* по-чин-я́ть, (чин-и́ть), *v.i.,* + *acc.,* to mend, repair. Часово́й ма́стер цочини́л мне часы́, the watchmaker repaired my watch. По-чи́н-ка, *n.f.,* mending, repairing, darning, repairs. Я о́тдал свой велосипе́д в почи́нку, my bicycle is being mended.

под-чин-и́ть, *v.p.,* под-чин-я́ть, *v.i.,* + *acc.,* + *dat.,* to subordinate, subdue, subjugate, conquer. Они́ подчини́ли себе́ весь наро́д, they subjugated the entire nation. Под-чин-и́ть-ся, *v.p.r.,* под-чин-я́ть-ся, *v.i.r.,* + *dat.,* to submit, obey; be subordinated, subjugated. Пришло́сь подчини́ться си́ле, one had to submit to force. Под-чин-е́ние, *n.n.,* под-чин-ённость, *n.f.,* subordination, subjugation. Он в подчине́нии у свое́й жены́, he is henpecked. Под-чин-ённый, *adj., part. pass. past, also used as n.,* subordinated, subjugated, subordinate, inferior; underling, subaltern. Он приказа́л свои́м подчинённым, he ordered his subordinates.

при-чин-и́ть, *v.p.,* при-чин-я́ть, *v.i.,* + *acc.,* + *dat.,* to cause, do. П. больши́е убы́тки, to cause great damage. При-чин-ённый, *adj., part. pass. past,* caused. П. пожа́ром, caused by fire. При-чи́н-а, *n.f.,* cause, reason. Причи́ны и сле́дствия, causes and effects. Всему́ своя́ причи́на, everything has its reason. Ближа́йшая п., immediate cause. По причи́не, because of, for the reason, owing to, on account of. Нет де́йствия, без причи́ны, there is no effect without cause. При-чин-е́ние, *n.n.,* causing, causation, cause. При-чи́н-ность, *n.f.,* causality. Зако́ны причи́нности, laws of causality. При-чи́н-ный, *adj.,* causal, causative.

рас-чин-и́ть, *v.p.,* рас-чин-я́ть, *v.i.,* + *acc.,* to knead. Р. те́сто, to knead dough.

со-чин-и́ть, *v.p.,* со-чин-я́ть, *v.i.,* + *acc.,* to write, compose; fib. Кто сочини́л "Анну Каре́нину?", who wrote "Anna Karenina?" С. исто́рии, to tell stories, fib. Со-чин-е́ние, *n.n.,* composition,

theme, work. По́лное собра́ние сочине́ний, the complete works. Со-чин-и́тель, *n.m.,* со-чин-и́тельница, *n.f.,* author, writer, composer; storyteller, liar. Пу́шкин - с. по́вести "Капита́нская до́чка," Pushkin is the author of the novel, "The Captain's Daughter." Он большо́й с., he tells tall tales.

ЧАСТ-, ЧАЩ-, FREQUENCY; PART, PORTION

ча́ст-о, *adv.,* often, frequently; close; thickly. Ча́сто-ли вы быва́ете в теа́тре? Do you often go to the theatre? Ча́щ-е, *adv. comp.,* more often, more frequently; more thickly. Ч. всего́ он рабо́тает в библиоте́ке, most often he works in the library. Приходи́те к нам, как мо́жно ча́ще, come to visit us as often as possible. Част-е́нько, *adv.,* (*colloq.*), pretty often. Част-ёхонько, *adv.,* (*colloq.*), very often. Част-ота́, *n.f.,* frequency; thickness, closeness. Ч. колеба́ний, frequency of vibrations. Част-о-ко́л, *n.m.,* picket fence; stockade. Обнесён частоко́лом, surrounded by a picket fence. Ча́ст-ый, *adv.,* frequent; thick, close. Ча́стые переме́ны, frequent changes. Ч. гре́бень, fine tooth comb. Ч. лес, thick wood. Руба́ха из ча́стой тка́ни, shirt of close woven fabric. Ча́стые посеще́ния, frequent visits. Част-у́шка, *n.f.,* ditty; popular song composed on a topic of the day, on the theme of love.

за-част-и́ть, за-чащ-у́, *v.p.,* to come often.

у-част-и́ть, *v.p.,* у-чащ-а́ть, *v.i.,* to make more frequent, increase the frequency; thicken. У. колеба́ния, to increase the frequency of vibrations, of oscillations. У-част-и́ть-ся, *v.p.r.,* у-чащ-а́ть-ся, *v.i.r.,* to be increased. У-чащ-ённый, *adj., part. pass. past,* increased in frequency. У-чащ-е́ние, *n.n.,* increase of frequency. Ча́щ-а, *n.f.,* thicket, brushwood. Лесна́я ч., in the thick of a forest.

част-ь, *n.f.,* part, share, portion. Ч. насле́дствия, share of an inheritance. Ч. све́та, part of the world, of the globe. Запасны́е ча́сти, spare parts. Полице́йская ч., (*pre-Rev.*), police department, station. Это не по мое́й ча́сти, (*colloq.*), this is not in my line. По частя́м, by instalments. Часть ре́чи, (*gram.*), part of speech. Ча́ст-ью, *adv.,* partly. Эта вещь сде́лана ч. из де́рева, ч. из желе́за, this thing is made partly of wood, partly of iron. Бо́льшей ча́стью он отсу́тствовал, the greater part of the time he was absent. Частйца, *n.f.*, particle, bit; grain; fraction; (*gram.*), particle. Част-и́чный, *adj.*, partial. Ч. успе́х, partial success. Част-и́чно, *adv.*, partly. Ча́ст-очка, *n.f.*, particle of the host, of Eucharistic bread.

ча́ст-ный, *adj.*, private; informal; particular. Ч-ая со́бственность, private ownership. Ч. дом, private house. Ч-ое лицо́, private individual. Ч-ое де́ло, private matter. Ча́стным о́бразом, confidentially, informally, unofficially. Ча́ст-ник, *n.m.*, (*recent*), owner of a private enterprise. Ча́стность, *n.f.*, particularity. В ча́стности, in particular. Не бу́дем остана́вливаться на ча́стностях, let us not dwell on details.

от-ча́ст-и, *adv.*, partly. О. из-за боле́зни, partly because of illness.

при-част-и́ть, *v.p.*, при-чащ-а́ть, *v.i.*, + *acc.*, to give communion. Сего́дня причаща́ли дете́й, today children received communion. При-част-и́ть-ся, *v.p.r.*, при-чащ-а́ть-ся, *v.i.r.*, to go to communion, receive communion. Прича́ст-ие, *n.n.*, communion; the Sacrament; (*gram.*), participle. П. настоя́щего вре́мени, present active participle. При-ча́ст-ник, *n.m.*, communicant.

с-ча́ст-ье, *n.n.*, luck, happiness. Это ва́ше с.! That's your luck! С. ему́ измени́ло, his luck failed him. Ему́ во всем с., he is always lucky. Всяк молоде́ц своего́ сча́стья кузне́ц, (*prov.*), every man is the architect of his own fate (happiness). Они́ ему́ пожела́ли сча́стья, they wished him luck (happiness). С-част-ли́вец, *n.m.*, с-част-ли́вица, *n.f.*, a lucky person. С-част-ли́вый, *adj.*, happy, lucky, fortunate. С-ые часо́в не наблюда́ют, (*saying*), happiness takes no account of time. С-ого пути́, bon voyage. С-част-ли́во, *adv.*, happily, luckily. Счастли́во! Good luck! Всё обошло́сь с., everything went off very well.

не-с-ча́ст-ье, *n.n.*, misfortune, ill luck; unhappiness. Большо́е н., great misfortune. К несча́стью, unfortunately. Не-с-част-ли́вый, *adj.*, luckless, unlucky, unhappy, unfortunate. Не-с-ча́стный, *adj.*, luckless, unlucky, unhappy, unfortunate. Несча́стлив в бра́ке, his marriage is unhappy. На́до име́ть сострада́ние к несча́стным, one must have compassion for the unfortunate.

у-ча́ст-вовать, *v.i.*, в + *prep.*, to participate, have a share in. Он уча́ствует в э́той конфере́нции, he is participating in this conference. У. на ра́вных права́х, to share alike. Я не уча́ствовал в э́том, I did not participate in this.

У-ча́ст-ие, *n.n.*, share, sharing, part; participation, partnership; sympathy, interest, concern. Принима́ть у., to take part, participate. У. в при́былях, to share in the profits. При уча́стии, with the assistance, the participation. Прояви́ть уча́стие, to show sympathy. Приня́ть у., to take an interest. У-ча́ст-ливый, *adj.*, sympathetic, solicitous, compassionate. У-ча́ст-ливость, *n.f.*, sympathy, solicitude, compassion. У. к заключённым, compassion towards prisoners. У-ча́ст-ливо, *adv.*, sympathetically, compassionately. У-ча́ст-ник, *n.m.*, participant, partner, sharer; member. У. това́рищества, partner in a partnership. У-ча́ст-ок, *n.m.*, part, section; tract of land, lot, parcel of land. У-част-ко́вый, *adj.*, (*pre-Rev.*), pertaining to a district. У. врач, district physician. У-част-ь, *n.f.*, lot, destiny, fate. Её пости́гла го́рькая у., a sad lot has befallen her.

без-у-ча́сти-ие, *n.n.*, без-у-ча́ст-ность, *n.f.*, indifference, unconcern. Без-у-ча́стный, *adj.*, indifferent, unconcerned, impassive. Б. взгляд, indifferent look. Б-ое отноше́ние, к + *dat.*, indifferent attitude. Без-у-ча́ст-но, *adv.*, indifferently, unsympathetically.

со-у-ча́ст-вовать, *v.i.*, с + *instr.*, в + *prep.*, to participate, cooperate, collaborate. Он соуча́ствовал с ни́ми в их преступле́ниях, he was an accomplice in their crimes. Со-у-ча́ст-ие, *n.n.*, participation, co-operation, collaboration. Со-у-ча́ст-ник, *n.m.*, participant, associate, collaborator. Со-уча́стники восста́ния, participants in an uprising.

ЧЕРК-, ЧЕРЧ-, ЧЕРТ-, DELINEATION, DEPICTION, PORTRAYAL

чёрк-ать, (черк-а́ть), *v.i.*, черк-ну́ть, *v.p.*, + *acc.*, to scribble, jot down, write. Что вы там чёркаете? What are you scribbling there? Черкни́те мне не́сколько слов, write me a few words.

вы́-черк-нуть, *v.p.*, вы-чёрк-ивать, *v.i.*, + *acc.*, to strike out, cross out, rule out, delete. Он вы́черкнул не́сколько фраз, he deleted a number of sentences. Я вы́черкнул его́ из па́мяти, I wiped him out of my life. Вы-чёрк-ивание, *n.n.*, striking out, crossing out, expunction, deletion. В. ва́жных фраз испо́ртило мою́ ру́копись, the deletion of important sentences ruined my manuscript. Вы-чёрк-ивать-ся, *v.i.r.*, to be crossed out.

за-черк-ну́ть, *v.p.*, за-чёрк-ивать, *v.i.*, +

acc., to cross out, strike out, scratch out, blot out. Учитель зачёркивает ошибки, the teacher is crossing out the mistakes. За-чёрк ивание, *п.п.*, crossing out. З. слов, crossing out of words.

ис-чёрк-ать, (ис-черк-а́ть), *v.p.*, ис-чёрк-ивать, *v.i.*, (*colloq.*), to cross out in many places, crisscross with corrections. Он исчерка́л весь мой чертёж, he marked up my whole draft.

от-чёрк-ну́ть, *v.p.*, от-чёрк-ивать, *v.i.*, + *acc.*, to mark off, underline. О. не́которые места́, to mark certain passages. От-чёрк-нутый, *adj., part. pass. past*, marked off. Перечита́йте отчёркнутые места́, read again the marked passages.

пере-черк-а́ть, *v.p.*, пере-черк-ну́ть, *v.p.*, пере-чёрк-ивать, *v.i.*, + *acc.*, to cover with lines, cross out, mark up. Он перечерка́л всю страни́цу, he marked up the whole page.

по-черк-а́ть, *v.p.*, + *acc.*, to cover with lines, marks, remarks. Он почерка́л библиоте́чную кни́гу, he marked the library book with marginal comments. По́-черк, *п.т.*, handwriting. Хоро́ший по́черк, good hand, good handwriting. Неразбо́рчивый п., illegible handwriting.

под-черк-ну́ть, *v.p.*, под-чёрк-ивать, *v.i.*, + *acc.*, + *instr.*, to underline, underscore; emphasize, stress. Учи́тель подчёркивает ошибки, the teacher is underlining the mistakes. Кри́тик подчеркну́л нау́чный хара́ктер рабо́ты, the critic emphasized the scientific character of the work. Под-чёрк-ивание, *п.п.*, underlining, underscoring; emphasis, stress. П. ошибок, underlining of mistakes. Под-чёрк-ивать-ся, *v.i.r.*, + *instr.*, to be underlined, underscored; be emphasized. Ощи́бки подчёркиваются учи́телем, mistakes are underlined by the teacher.

рас-черк-а́ть, *v.p.*, рас-чёрк-ивать, *v.i.*, + *acc.*, to crisscross, cover with remarks, marks, designs. Он расчерка́л весь лист, he covered the whole sheet with lines.

ро́с-черк, *п.т.*, flourish, stroke (*in penmanship*). Одни́м ро́счерком пера́, with one stroke of the pen.

черт-а́, *n.f.*, line; feature, trait. Провести́ черту́, to draw a line. Пограни́чная ч., border line, frontier. Ч. осе́длости, (*obs.*), pale of settlement. Вне черты́ го́рода, beyond the city limits. Отличи́тельная ч., characteristic trait. В о́бщих черта́х, in general terms.

черт-и́ть, черч-у́, *v.i.*, + *acc.*, to draft, sketch, trace. Землеме́р черти́т план,

the surveyor is drafting a map. Черч-е́ние, *п.п.*, drawing, sketching, drafting. Он занима́ется черче́нием карт, he is occupied drawing maps.

вы́-черт-ить, *v.p.*, вы-черч-ивать, *v.i.*, to trace, delineate, draw. Чертёжник вычёрчивает сло́жный чертёж, the draftsman is drawing a complicated draft. Вы́-черч-енный, *adj., part. pass. past*, traced, drawn, delineated.

до-черт-и́ть, *v.p.*, до-черч-ивать, *v.i.*, + *acc.*, to complete a draft, a plan. Он по́здно но́чью дочёрчивал свой чертёж, late at night he was completing his draft.

за-черт-и́ть, *v.p.*, за-черч-ивать, *v.i.*, + *acc.*, to begin to trace, to draw; cover with lines, strokes. Он зачерти́л свой рису́нок причу́дливыми ли́ниями, he covered the entire design with fantastic lines.

ис-черт-и́ть, *v.p.*, ис-че́рч-ивать, *v.i.*, + *acc.*, to doodle; cover with lines. Он исчерти́л всю бума́гу, he lined the whole sheet of paper.

на-черт-а́ть, *v.p.*, + *acc.*, to trace, inscribe, write. На-черт-а́ние, *п.п.*, tracing, inscription, writing. На-черт-а́тельный, *adj.*, graphic, descriptive. Н-ая геоме́трия, descriptive geometry.

на-черт-и́ть, на-черч-у́, *v.p.*, на-че́рч-ивать, *v.i.*, + *acc.*, to draw, trace, sketch, outline. Он начерти́л ка́рту Кавка́за, he drew a map of the Caucasus. Он начерти́л свой пла́ны на бу́дущее, he outlined his plans for the future.

о-черт-и́ть, *v.p.*, о-че́рч-ивать, *v.i.*, + *acc.*, to trace, draw, sketch; describe. О. положе́ние, to describe a situation. О. рису́нок черни́лами, to retrace a sketch with ink. О-черк, *п.т.*, essay; outline, sketch.

об-черт-и́ть, *v.p.*, об-че́рч-ивать, *v.i.*, + *acc.*, to draw a line round, contour, frame by means of a design. О. рису́нок орна́ментом, to frame a picture with an ornament. О-черт-а́ние, *п.п.*, outline. О. лица́, outline of a face.

пере-черт-и́ть, *v.p.*, пере-че́рч-ивать, *v.i.*, + *acc.* to draw again; retrace. П. чертёж, to redraw a draft.

рас-черт-и́ть, *v.p.*, рас-че́рч-ивать, *v.i.*, + *acc.*, to rule, trace lines. Рас-че́рч-енный, *adj., part. pass. past*, drawn, traced with lines. Р-ая бума́га, lined paper.

с-черт-и́ть, *v.p.*, с-че́рч-ивать, *v.i.*, + *acc.*, to copy by tracing, drawing, drafting. Этот студе́нт счерти́л свой чертёж с чертежа́ своего́ това́рища, this student has copied his classmate's draft.

ЧЕР(Н)-, ЧЕР(Т)-, ЧОР-(Т)-, BLACK, BLACKNESS; DEVIL, DEMON

чер-н-е́ть, *v.i.,* по-чер-не́ть, *v.p.,* to become black; loom. Серебро́ чернеет, the silver is becoming tarnished. Черне́ть-ся, *v.i.r, used only in 3d pers.,* to appear black. Что́-то черне́лось вдали́, something loomed black in the distance. **чёр-ный,** *adj.,* black; sad; fatal; unlucky. Ч. каранда́ш, black pencil. Ч-ые во́лосы, black, dark hair. Он ви́дит всё в чёрном све́те, (*fig.*), he sees everything in dark colors. Ч. как смоль, black as tar; jet black. Она́ хо́дит в чёрном, she wears black. Ч-ая неблагода́рность, (*fig.*), black ingratitude. Он откла́дывает на чёрный день, he is putting something aside for a rainy day. Ч. ход, back entrance. Ч-ая ле́стница, back stairs. Ч-ая рабо́та, menial labor. Ме́жду ни́ми пробежа́ла чёрная ко́шка, (*fig.*), there is a coolness between them. Чёрное духове́нство, monks; monastic clergy. Чёрное мо́ре, Black Sea. Ч-ые ту́чи, heavy clouds, dark clouds. Чёр-ненький, *adj.,* (*dim.*), black. Черн-о́, чер-н-ёхонько, черны́м-черно́, *adv.,* black, dark; pitch dark. В ко́мнате бы́ло черно́ от ды́ма, the room was black with smoke. Черно́-, *a combining form meaning* black, dark. Черно-боро́дый, *adj.,* black-bearded. Черно-бро́вый, *adj.,* black-browed. Черно-бу́рый, *adj.,* dark brown. Ч-ая лиси́ца, silver fox. Черново-воло́сый, *adj.,* black-haired. Черно-гла́зый, *adj.,* black-eyed. Черно-голо́вый, *adj.,* black-headed. Черно-гри́вый, *adj.,* black-maned. Черно-зём, *n.m.,* black soil. Черно-кни́жие, *n.n.,* (*obs.*), magic, necromancy. Черно-кни́жник, *n.m.,* necromancer. Черно-ко́жий, *adj.,* also used as n., black-skinned, black. Черно-ле́сье, *n.n.,* deciduous forest. Черно-ма́зый, *adj.,* (*colloq.*), swarthy, dark-skinned. Черно-о́кий, *adj.,* black-eyed. Черно-рабо́чий, *n.m.,* unskilled laborer. Черно-ри́зец, *n.m.,* (*obs.*), monk. Черно-сли́в, *n.m.,* prunes. Черно-ва́тый, *adj.,* blackish. Черн-о-ви́к, *n.m.,* rough draft, copy. Черн-ово́й, *adj.,* preliminary draft. Ч-а́я рабо́та, preliminary work. Черн-ота́, *n.f.,* blackness. Черн-а́вка, (*folk.*), black-haired and black-eyed woman; black cow. Де́вка-черна́вка, (*folklore*), swarthy girl.

чер-н-и́ть, *v.i.,* + *acc.,* to blacken; blackmail, slander; soil. Он черни́т свои́ сапоги́, he is blackening his boots. Не черни́те меня́ напра́сно, don't slander me without cause. Чер-н-ёный, *adj.,* in-

laid, decorated with niello. Чер-н-и́ка, *n.f.,* blueberry, whortleberry, bilberry. Чер-н-и́чный, *adj.,* made of bilberries. Чер-н-и́ла, *n.n.pl.,* ink. Кра́сные ч., red ink. Чер-н-и́льница, *n.f.,* inkwell, inkstand. Чер-н-и́льный, *adj.,* ink. Ч-ое пятно́, ink stain. Чер-н-у́шка, *n.f.,* (*colloq.*), brunette; (*bot.*), fennel flower. Чер-н-ь, *n.f.,* niello; black enamel work; rabble, mob.

за-чер-н-и́ть, *v.p.,* + *acc.,* to blacken, paint black. Он зачерни́л свою́ пе́чурку, he blackened his little stove. **о-чер-н-и́ть,** *v.p.,* + *acc.,* to slander. Они́ очерни́ли его́, they slandered him. **по-чер-н-и́ть,** *v.p.,* + *acc.,* to blacken. Почерни́те мои́ сапоги́, blacken my boots.

чор-т, *n.m.,* devil. Не так стра́шен чорт, как его́ малю́ют, (*saying*), the devil is not as black as they paint him. Чорт возьми́, the devil take it. Чорт побери́, the devil take it. Сам чорт не разберёт, who knows; there's no making heads or tails of it. Сам чорт но́гу сло́мит, there's no making heads or tails of it. В ти́хом о́муте че́рти во́дятся (*saying*), still waters sometimes run deep. Чо́рта с два, not for the world. Како́го чо́рта, (*slang*) why; for what reason. Жить у чо́рта на кули́чках (на рога́х), (*saying*), to live at the world's end. Это ни черта́ не сто́ит, (*slang*), it isn't worth anything. Убира́йся к чо́рту, get out; may the devil take you. До-чо́рт-а, *adv.,* (*slang*) very much. Чо́рт-ов, *adj.,* the devil's own. Это чо́ртова вы́думка, (*colloq.*), this is a devilish invention. Чо́ртов мост в Альпах, the Devil's Bridge in the Alps.

чер-т-о́вка, *n.f.,* devil, wicked woman; hag. Черт-о́вский, *adj.,* devilish, diabolical. Ч. план, diabolical plan. Чер-т-о́вски, *adv.,* devilishly, diabolically. Чер-т-о́вщина, *n.f.,* deviltry. Что за чертовщина! what kind of deviltry is this! Чер-т-ополо́х, *n.m.,* (*bot.*), thistle. Уса́дьба заросла́ чертополо́хом, the garden is overgrown with thistle. Чер-т-ыха́ться, *v.i.r.,* (*slang*), to swear, curse. Да, что ты всё чертыха́ешься, Why are you always swearing?

ЧИСТ-, ЧИЩ-, CLEANNESS, PURITY

чи́ст-ить, чищ-у, *v.i.,* + *acc.,* + *instr.,* to clean; brush, polish; purge. Ч. башмаки́, to clean (polish) shoes. Чи́стишь-ли ты зу́бы? Do you brush your teeth? Чи́ст-ить-ся, *v.i.r.,* от + *gen.,* to clean, brush oneself; be cleaned, brushed. Эта мате́рия пло́хо чи́стится, this material is difficult to clean. Чи́ст-ый, *adj.*, clean, neat; pure; sheer. Ч-ая ска́терть, clean tablecloth. Ч-ый дохо́д, clean profit, net income. Это ч-ая пра́вда, this is the bare truth. Бриллиа́нт чи́стой воды́, a diamond of the first water. Ч-ое недоразуме́ние, pure misunderstanding. До́-чист-а, *adv.*, completely. Его́ обокра́ли д., (*colloq.*), he was robbed of everything. Чи́ст-енький, *adj.*, neat, tidy. Чист-ёха, *n.m. and f.*, (*colloq.*), meticulously clean and tidy person. Чист-и́лище, *n.n.*, purgatory. Чист-и́лищный, *adj.*, purgatorial. Чист-и́льщик, *n.m.*, cleaner. Ч. печны́х труб трубочи́ст, chimney sweep. Чи́ст-ка, *n.f.*, cleaning, cleansing; (*fig.*), purging. Он о́тдал пальто́ в чи́стку, he has sent his coat to the cleaner's. Ч. па́ртии, party purge. Чи́ст-о, *adv.*, neatly, cleanly, purely. Он всегда́ оде́т чи́сто, he is always neatly dressed. Чист-ови́к, *n.m.*, (*colloq.*), clean copy. Чист-ово́й, *adj.*, pertaining to a clean copy. Ч-а́я тетра́дь, this is a clean copybook. Чист-о-га́н, *n.m.*, (*colloq.*), cash, cash payment. Заплати́ть ч-ом сто рубле́й, to pay a hundred rubles cash down. Чист-о-кро́вный, *adj.*, thoroughbred, pure-blooded. Ч-ая ло́шадь, thoroughbred horse. Чист-о-, *a combining form meaning* clean, pure. Чист-о-писа́ние, *n.n.*, penmanship. Чист-о-пло́тный, *adj.*, clean, neat. Ч. челове́к, neat person. Чист-о-пло́тность, *n.f.*, cleanliness, neatness. Чист-о-серде́чный, *adj.*, candid, sincere, frank, open-hearted. Чист-о-серде́чность, *n.f.*, candor, sincerity, frankness, openness. Чист-о-серде́чно, *adv.*, candidly, sincerely, frankly, open-heartedly. Чист-ота́, *n.f.*, cleanliness, cleanness, neatness; purity, clarity. Кака́я у них ч.! How clean their home is! Ч. во́здуха, pureness of air. Чист-о-те́л, *n.m.*, (*bot.*), celandine.

вы́-чист-ить, вы́-чищ-у, *v.p.*, вы-чищ-а́ть, *v.i.*, + *acc.*, to clean out, clean; purge; expel. В. пла́тье, to clean a dress. Его́ вы́чистили из па́ртии, (*recent*), he was expelled from the party. Вы́-чистить-ся, *v.p.r.*, вы-чищ-а́ть-ся, *v.i.r.*, to be cleaned, be removed, be purged. Из па́ртии вычища́ются уклони́сты, (*recent*), deviationists are purged from the Party. Это пятно́ не вычища́ется, this stain does not come out.

на-чи́ст-ить, *v.p.*, на-чищ-а́ть, *v.i.*, + *acc.*, to clean, polish, brush; to peel. Н. карто́шки, to peel a quantity of potatoes. На́-чист-о, *adv.*, flatly, thoroughly;

bluntly. Перепиши́те ва́шу рабо́ту н., rewrite your work in a clean copy. Ему́ отка́зано н., he was flatly refused. На-чист-оту́, *adv.*, above board. Он поговори́л с ним н., he talked to him frankly.

о-чи́ст-ить, *v.p.*, о-чищ-а́ть, *v.i.*, от + *gen.*, to clean out, cleanse, purify, refine. О. ка́ссу, (*fig., colloq.*), to clean out, rob a cash box. О. гру́шу, to peel a pear. О-чи́щ-енный, *adj., part. pass. past*, peeled, refined, purified. О. спирт, purified alcohol. О-чи́ст-ить-ся, *v.p.r.*, о-чищ-а́ть-ся, *v.i.r.*, от + *gen.*, to clean oneself, be cleaned, purified, refined. Река́ очи́стилась от льда, the river became free of ice. О-чист-и́тель, *n.m.*, purifier, cleanser, refining agent. О-чист-и́тельный, *adj.*, cleansing, purifying; expiatory. О-чи́ст-ка, *n.f.*, о-чищ-е́ние, *n.n.*, clearance, cleansing, clearing; purification, refining; expiation, justification. О. у́лиц, street cleaning. Для очи́стки со́вести, to clear one's conscience.

от-чи́ст-ить, *v.p.*, от-чищ-а́ть, *v.i.*, от + *gen.*, to clean off, scour, brush away. От-чи́ст-ить-ся, *v.p.r.*, от-чищ-а́ть-ся, *v.i.r.*, to be cleaned out, brushed away; come out. Таки́е пя́тна легко́ отчища́ются, such spots come out easily.

пере-чи́ст-ить, *v.p.*, пере-чищ-а́ть, *v.i.*, + *acc.*, to clean everything; clean anew. На́до п. э́то пальто́, the coat must be cleaned again. На́до п. все зи́мние ве́щи, the winter things must all be cleaned.

по-чи́ст-ить, *v.p.*, + *acc.*, to clean; *see* чи́стить. П. зу́бы, to brush one's teeth. По-чи́ст-ить-ся, *v.p.r.*, to clean oneself. Я до́лжен п. по́сле пы́льной доро́ги, I must spruce up after a dusty journey.

под-чи́ст-ить, *v.p.*, под-чищ-а́ть, *v.i.*, + *acc.*, to clean up; erase, rub out; trim; (*fig.*), eat up. П. не́сколько слов, to erase a few words. П. сад, to trim a garden. Под-чи́ст-ить-ся, *v.p.r.*, под-чищ-а́ть-ся, *v.i.r.*, (*colloq.*), to be cleaned up; be erased, rubbed out; be trimmed. Улицы подчища́ются ка́ждый день, the streets are cleaned every day. Под-чи́ст-ка, *n.f.*, erasure; erased word. В э́той бума́ге нет подчи́сток, there are no erasures on this paper.

про-чи́ст-ить, *v.p.*, про-чищ-а́ть, *v.i.*, + *acc.*, to clean, cleanse thoroughly; (*med.*), purge. Водопрово́дчик прочи́стил засори́вшуюся трубу́, the plumber has cleaned out the clogged pipe. Про-чи́ст-ить-ся, *v.p.r.*, про-чищ-а́ть-ся, *v.i.r.*, to be cleaned through; clear up. Не́бо прочи́стилось, the sky has cleared. Трубы прочищаются едким натром, pipes are cleaned with caustic soda. Про-чист-ка, *n.f.*, scouring, cleaning through; chimney sweeping. Про-чищ-ающий, *adj.*, *part. act. pres.*, *also used as n.*, cathartic. П-ее, cathartic.

рас-чист-ить, *v.p.*, рас-чищ-ать, *v.i.*, + *acc.*, to clear away, free from obstruction. Р. снег, to clear away snow. Р. дорогу в толпе, to clear one's way through a crowd. Рас-чищ-енный, *adj.*, *part. pass. past*, cleaned, cleared. Р-ая дорога, cleared road. Рас-чист-ка, *n.f.*, clearing. Р. пути, clearing of a road.

с-чист-ить, *v.p.*, с-чищ-ать, *v.i.*, + *acc.*, to clean, clear off; brush off. С. снег с крыши, to shovel snow off a roof. С. ошибочно написанное слово, to erase an incorrectly written word. С-чист-ить-ся, *v.p.r.*, с-чищ-ать-ся, *v.i.r.*, to be cleaned, cleared off; be erased, rubbed out, rubbed off. С этой бумаги плохо счищаются ошибки, it is hard to erase mistakes on this paper.

ЧТ-, ЧИТ-, ЧЕТ-, ЧЕСТ-, ЧЕЩ-, READING, COUNTING; RESPECT, REGARD, HONOR

чт-ение, *n.n.*, reading. Я провожу вечера за чтением, I spend my evenings reading. Ч. лекций, lecturing. Беглое ч., fluent reading. Чт-ец, *n.m.*, чт-йца, *n.f.*, reader. Чёт-кий, *adj.*, legible, clear. Ч. почерк, legible handwriting. Ч-ая работа, precise work. Чёт-кость, *n.f.*, legibility, clearness. Ч. почерка, legibility of handwriting. Чёт-ко, *adv.*, legibly, clearly. Эта рукопись написана чётко, this manuscript is written legibly. Не-чёт-кий, *adj.*, illegible. Н. почерк, illegible handwriting. Н-ая формулировка, unprecise formulation. Не-чёт-кость, *n.f.*, illegibility; lack of precision. Не-чёт-ко, *adv.*, illegibly, unprecisely. От-чёт-ливость, *n.f.*, precision, accuracy. О. аргументации, accuracy of argumentation. От-чёт-ливый, *adj.*, clear, distinct, sharp. О-ые очертания, distinctness of outline. От-чёт-ливо, *adv.*, clearly, distinctly, with precision. Говорить о., to speak distinctly.

чит-ать, *v.i.*, + *acc.*, to read. Он читает лекции по зоологии, he lectures on zoology. Я читаю книгу, I am reading a book. Чит-ать-ся, *v.i.r.*, *used only in 3d pers.*, to be read. Этот роман легко читается, this novel reads easily. Чит-альный, *adj.*, reading. Ч. зал, reading

room. Чит-альня, *n.f.*, reading room. Чит-атель, *n.m.*, чит-ательница, *n.f.*, reader. В этой библиотеке много читателей, in this library there are many readers.

в-чит-ать-ся, *v.p.r.*, в-чит-ывать-ся, *v.i.r.*, в + *acc.*, to read attentively, obtain a thorough understanding of a text through reading. **вы-чит-ать**, *v.p.*, вы-чит-ывать, *v.i.*, в + *prep.*, to find out by reading. Я вычитал это в каком-то журнале, I read this in some magazine. **вы-чит-ать**, *v.i.*, вы-чест-ь, *v.p.*, + *acc.*, to subtract.

до-чит-ать, *v.p.*, до-чит-ывать, *v.i.*, + *acc.*, to read to the end. Я не мог дочитать его книгу до конца, I could not read his book to the end. До-чит-ать-ся, *v.p.r.*, до-чит-ывать-ся, *v.i.r.*, до + *gen.*, to be read to the end, to read oneself blind. Он дочитался до отупения, he read himself into a stupor.

за-чит-ать, *v.p.*, за-чит-ывать, *v.i.*, + *acc.*, to read aloud; appropriate a borrowed book; mark a book by handling it carelessly. З. протокол допроса в суде, (*recent*), to read an official report in court. Он зачитал мою книгу, he appropriated my book. За-чит-ать-ся, *v.p.r.*, за-чит-ывать-ся, *v.i.r.*, + *instr.*, to read with delight, be engrossed in reading. Она зачитывается французскими романами, she revels in French novels.

на-чит-ать-ся, *v.p.r.*, на-чит-ывать-ся, *v.i.r.*, + *gen.*, to read widely. Он начитался политической литературы, he has read widely in political literature. На-чёт-чик, *n.m.*, (*obs.*), well-read person. На-чит-анный, *adj.*, *part. pass. past*, well-read. Н. человек, well-read person. На-чит-анность, *n.f.*, reading, erudition, scholarship. Это учёный большой начитанности, he is a scholar of great erudition.

от-чит-ать, *v.p.*, от-чит-ывать, *v.i.*, + *acc.*, to reprimand formally, rebuke, scold. Здорово ты его отчитал, (*colloq.*), you certainly gave it to him. От-чит-ать-ся, *v.p.r.*, от-чит-ывать-ся, *v.i.r.*, to render an account, give a report.

пере-чит-ать, *v.p.*, пере-чест-ь, *v.p.*, пере-чит-ывать, *v.i.*, + *acc.*, to reread; revise; read in sequence. Он два раза перечитал (перечёл) эту статью, he has reread this article twice. Я перечитала все эти книги, I have read through all these books.

пере-чест-ь, пере-счит-ать, *see* пере-считать.

по-чит-áть, *v.p.,* по-чи́т-ывать, *v.i.,* + *acc.,* to read for a while, read now and then. Врéмя от врéмени он почи́тывал нóвые кни́ги, now and then he would read new books.

по-чит-áть, *see* почти́ть, почéсть.

под-чит-áть, *v.p.,* под-чи́т-ывать, *v.i.,* + *acc.,* to read in addition; check an original with a copy. Нáдо ещё подчитáть прéжде чем читáть лéкцию, It is necessary to read a little more before delivering the lecture.

при-чит-áть, *v.i.,* to lament. Бáбы причитáли над покóйником, the women were lamenting over the deceased. При-чит-áние, *n.n.,* lamentation, wailing. Похорóнное п., funeral lamentation. При-чит-áть-ся, *v.i.r.,* + *dat.,* с + *gen.,* за + *acc., impers.,* to be due. За рабóту емý причитáется 100 рублéй, he has 100 rubles coming for his work.

про-чит-áть, *v.p.,* про-чéст-ь, *v.p.,* про-чи́т-ывать, *v.i.,* + *acc.,* to read through; spend time reading. Могý-ли я прочéсть вáшу кни́гу? May I read your book? Он прочитáл всю ночь напролёт, he sat up all night reading. Про-чёт, *n.m., see* просчитáться.

чёт, *n.m.,* pair; even number.

не-чёт, *n.m.,* odd number. Чёт-ный, *adj.,* even. Два - чётное числó, two is an even number. Не-чёт-ный, *adj.,* odd. Н-ое числó, odd number.

чет-á, *n.f.,* pair, couple; match, equal. Они́ óчень счастли́вая ч., they are a happy couple. Он не четá тебé (*colloq.*), he is no match for you. Чёт-ки, *n.f.pl.,* rosary beads.

с-чёт, *n.m.,* numeration, arithmetic; score; account, bill. Учи́ться счёту, to study arithmetic. Счёт в умé, counting mentally. Игроки́ вели́ счёт очкóв, the players kept score. Мóжете быть спокóйны на э́тот счёт, you may rest easy on that score. Текýщий с., checking account. Постáвьте э́то на мой счёт, charge it to me. На чужóй счёт, at someone else's expense. Принеси́те с., please bring me the check. Крýглым счётом, in round figures, round numbers. Он на хорóшем счетý, he has a good reputation. У меня́ с ним счёты, I have a bone to pick with him. С-чёт-ный, *adj.,* pertaining to an account. С-ая кни́га, account book. С-ая маши́на, adding machine. С-ая часть, bookkeeping department. С-чет-о-вóд, *n.m.,* bookkeeper, accountant. С-чет-о-вóдство, *n.n.,* bookkeeping, accountancy. С-чёт-чик, *n.m.,* meter, register, recorder, indicator. Электри́ческий с., electric meter. С-чёт-ы,

n.m.pl., abacus. Прики́нуть на счётах, to count on an abacus.

с-чит-áть, *v.i.,* с-чест-ь, *v.p.,* + *acc.,* to count, compute, reckon, score; hold, regard, think, consider. Он считáет свою́ при́быль, he is counting his profit. Они́ считáют голосá, they are counting the votes. Он считáет, что всё потéряно, he thinks all is lost. Считáю свои́м дóлгом, I consider it my duty. С-чит-áя, *adv. part. pres.,* apart from, exclusive of. С-чит-áть-ся, *v.i.r.,* to be reckoned, counted, computed; be regarded, considered, thought, held. Он считáется ýмным человéком, he is regarded as an intelligent man. Он с э́тим не считáется, he does not take this into account. Не считáясь с э́тим, in spite of this.

вы-с-чит-ать, *v.p.,* вы-с-чи́т-ывать, *v.i.,* + *acc.,* to reckon, compute, estimate. Он вы́считал стóимость пострóйки, he estimated the cost of the construction.

вы-чест-ь, вы́-чт-у, *v.p.,* вы-чит-áть, *v.i.,* + *acc.,* из + *gen.,* to deduct, subtract. Из пяти́ вы́честь три - бýдет два, three subtracted from five leaves two. Вы́чет, *n.m.,* deduction, subtraction. В. из плáты, deduction from wages. Вы-чит-áемое, *n.n.,* (*math.*), subtrahend. Вы-чит-áние, *n.n.,* (*math.*), deduction, subtraction. В. труднéе сложéния, subtraction is more difficult than addition.

за-с-чит-áть, *v.p.,* за-чéст-ь, *v.p.,* за-(с)чи́т-ывать, *v.i.,* + *acc.,* to reckon; register in an account; take into consideration; credit. За-чт-ён-(ный), *adj., part. pass. past,* credited. Емý бы́ло зачтенó врéмя предвари́тельного заключéния, he was credited with the time spent in prison. За-чёт, *n.m.,* academic credit; part payment. Сдавáть з-ы, (*recent*), to pass course examinations. Рабóчие получáют продýкты в зачёт плáты, the workers receive goods in part payment of their wages. За-чёт-ный, *adj.,* pertaining to credit. З-ая кни́жка, (*recent*), students' record book.

на-с-чит-áть, *v.p.,* на-чéст-ь, *v.p.,* на-счи́т-ывать, *v.i.,* + *acc.,* to count; overcharge; number. Н. ли́шнее, to overcharge. На-с-чи́т-ывать-ся, *v.i.r., used only in 3d pers.,* to amount, number. В э́том гóроде насчи́тывается 50,000 населéния, the population of this city amounts to fifty thousand. На-чёт, *n.m.,* deficit, deficiency; unauthorized expenditure; misjudgment. На негó сдéлан крýпный н., he had to pay a fine for an unauthorized expenditure.

На-чёт-истый, *adj.*, expensive; disadvantageous.

об-с-чит-а́ть, *v.p.*, об-с-чи́т-ывать, *v.i.*, + *acc.*, to cheat. О. кого́-нибудь, to cheat someone. Об-с-чит-а́ть-ся, *v.p.r.*, об-с-чи́т-ывать-ся, *v.i.r.*, to miscalculate. Об-че́ст-ь-ся, *v.p.r.*, (*colloq.*), to miscount, miscalculate. Он обсчита́лся в свои́х расчётах, he miscalculated in his count. Раз, два, и обчёлся, (*idiom.*), there was very little to count.

от-с-чит-а́ть, *v.p.*, от-с-чи́т-ывать, *v.i.*, + *acc.*, to count off. Он отсчита́л ему́ 10 рубле́й, а остальны́е де́ньги оста́вил себе́, he counted out ten rubles and left the rest for himself. От-(с)-чит-а́ть-ся, *v.p.r.*, от-(с)-чи́т-ывать-ся, *v.i.r.*, в, на + *prep.*, пе́ред + *instr.*, to render an account; to be deducted. Он не мог отсчита́ться в полу́ченных су́ммах, he could not account for the sum he had received. 10% жа́лования отсчи́тываются на пе́нсию, 10% of the salary is deducted for the pension. От-с-чи́т-ывание, *n.n.*, counting off, reckoning. От-чёт, *n.m.*, account, report. От него́ потре́бовали отчёта, they demanded an accounting from him. Годово́й о., annual report. От-чёт-ность, *n.f.*, accounts, account books. От-чёт-ный, *adj.*, pertaining to accounts. О. год, fiscal year.

пере-с-чит-а́ть, *v.p.*, пере-че́ст-ь, *v.p.*, пере-с-чи́т-ывать, *v.i.*, + *acc.*, to count again, recount. Я да́же их могу́ по па́льцам перече́сть (*Krylov*), I can even count them on my fingers. Пере-с-чи́т-ывать-ся, *v.i.r.*, to be counted again, be recounted. Пере-чёт, *n.m.*, re-counting, recount. На-пере-чёт, *adv.*, thoroughly, through and through; *pred.*, few, not many. Таки́е лётчики, как он, наперечёт, there are few pilots like him.

по-с-чит-а́ть, *v.p.*, с-чит-а́ть, *v.i.*, + *acc.*, (*colloq.*), to count. Посчита́йте сда́чу, count the change. По-с-чит-а́ть-ся, *v.p.r.*, с + *instr.*, (*colloq.*), to get even with. Я ещё с ним посчита́юсь, I shall get even with him yet.

по-че́ст-ь, *v.p.*, по-чит-а́ть, *v.i.*, + *acc.*, + *instr.*, (*obs.*), to consider: *see* почти́ть. Он почёл свои́м до́лгом э́то сде́лать, he considered it his duty to do it. Почита́й, *parenthetical expression*, it seems. П., всё забра́ли, (*folk.*), they've taken everything, it seems. По-чт-й, *adv.*, almost, nearly. Моя́ рабо́та п. гото́ва, my work is almost ready. Э́то почти́ то́же са́мое, this is practically the same thing. У него́ почти́что ничего́ нет, he has almost nothing.

под-с-чит-а́ть, *v.p.*, под-с-чи́т-ывать, *v.i.*, + *acc.*, to calculate, count, reckon. П. голоса́, to count votes. Под-с-чёт, *n.m.*, returns; count of votes. Результа́ты подсчёта, the results of the count.

при-с-чит-а́ть, *v.p.*, при-с-чи́т-ывать, *v.i.*, + *acc.*, to add while counting. По оши́бке касси́р присчита́л ли́шние 2 рубля́, the cashier added two rubles by mistake.

про-с-чит-а́ть, *v.p.*, про-с-чи́т-ывать, *v.i.*, + *acc.*, to count through; check a calculation; spend time counting. П. це́лый день, to spend a whole day counting. Он ещё раз просчита́л их подсчёты, he checked their calculations once more. Про-с-чит-а́ть-ся, *v.p.r.*, про-с-чи́т-ывать-ся, *v.i.r.*, to make an error in counting, miscalculate. Про-(с)-чёт, *n.m.*, error in accounting. У него́ ча́сто быва́ют просчёты, he often makes errors in accounting.

рас-с-чит-а́ть, *v.p.*, рас-с-чи́т-ывать, *v.i.*, + *acc.*, на + *acc.*, to calculate, reckon, figure; expect; depend on, count on; dismiss. Р. констру́кцию моста́, to work out the construction of a bridge. Р. что́-нибудь копе́йка в копе́йку, to figure something out down to a penny. Он не рассчита́л свои́х сил, he overestimated his strength. Не рассчи́тывайте на меня́, please don't count on me. Рас-с-чи́т-ан(ный), *adj.*, *part. pass. past*, calculated, reckoned; dismissed. Э́тот слу́жащий был рассчи́тан, this employee was dismissed. Рас-с-чи́т-ывающий, *adj.*, *part. act. pres.*, counting on, calculating. Рас-с-чит-а́ть-ся, *v.p.r.*, рас-с-чи́т-ывать-ся, *v.i.r.*, с + *instr.*, to settle with; defray; obtain satisfaction. Рас-чёт, *n.m.*, calculation, account; clearing; consideration; dismissal. Его́ р. был непра́вилен, his calculations were wrong. Прими́те э́то в р., take this into consideration. Нет расчёта э́то де́лать, it does not pay to do it. Он обману́лся в свои́х расчётах, he backed the wrong horse. Рас-чёт-ный, *adj.*, pay; settling, clearing. Р. день, payday. Р-ая пала́та, (*obs.*), clearing house.

у-чи́т-ывать, *v.i.*, у-че́ст-ь, *v.p.*, + *acc.*, to take into account, into consideration; take stock of; discount. Он учи́тывает обстоя́тельства, he takes circumstances into consideration. Он учёл ве́ксель в ба́нке, the bank discounted his note. У-чёт, *n.m.*, calculation; accounting; discount. У. сто́имости, cost accounting. У. това́ра, inventory. Э́то не поддаётся учёту, this is beyond all calculation. У-чёт-ный, *adj.*, discount. У. проце́нт, rate of discount.

У-чи́т-ывание, *n.n.*, taking into account, into consideration; discounting.

пере-у-че́ст-ь, *v.p.*, пере-у-чи́т-ывать, *v.i.*, + *acc.*, to take inventory; rediscount. Ба́нки переучи́тывают векселя́, banks re-discount notes. Пере-у-чёт, *n.m.*, accounting, rediscount. П. това́ров, inventory.

че́ст-вовать, *v.i.*, + *acc.*, to honor, celebrate. Почита́тели че́ствовали писа́теля банке́том, his admirers honored the writer with a banquet. Че́ст-вование, *n.n.*, celebration; honoring.

чест-и́ть, *v.i.*, + *acc.*, (*colloq.*), to abuse, scold.

чест-ь, *n.f.*, honor. Его́ ч. заде́та, his honor is at stake. Я не име́ю че́сти знать вас, I do not have the honor of knowing you. Это де́ло че́сти, this is a matter of honor. Всё прошло́ честь че́стью, (*idiom.*), all was as it should be. Кляну́сь че́стью, upon my honor. Че́ст-ный, *adj.*, honest, honorable; fair, square. Ч-ая игра́, fair play. Ч-ое сло́во, word of honor. Че́ст-ность, *n.f.*, honesty, probity, integrity, rectitude. Че́ст-но, *adv.*, fairly, squarly, honorably. Чест-о-лю́бие, *n.n.*, ambition. Чест-о-люби́вый, *adj.*, ambitious. Чест-о-лю́бец, *n.m.*, ambitious person.

бес-че́ст-ить, бес-че́щ-у, *v.i.*, + *acc.*, to dishonor, disgrace; blot; bring disrepute. Его́ поведе́ние бесче́стит его́, his behavior is a disgrace. Бес-че́ст-ящий, *adj.*, *part. act. pres.*, dishonoring. Б. посту́пок, dishonorable act. Бес-че́ст-ие, *n.n.*, dishonor, infamy, disgrace. Бес-че́ст-ный, *adj.*, dishonorable, dishonest. Б. посту́пок, dishonest action. Бес-че́ст-ность, *n.f.*, dishonesty, lack of integrity.

о-бес-че́ст-ить, *v.p.*, о-бес-че́щ-ивать, *v.i.*, + *acc.*, to dishonor; disgrace, discredit; ruin. Он обесче́стил своё и́мя, he disgraced his name. О-бес-че́щ-енный, *adj.*, *part. pass. past*, dishonored. О-ая де́вушка поко́нчила с собо́й, the disgraced girl committed suicide.

не-че́ст-ный, *adj.*, dishonest, unfair. Н-ая игра́, unfair play. Не-че́ст-но, *adv.*, dishonestly, unfairly. Не-че́ст-ность, *n.f.*, dishonesty.

чт-ить, *v.i.*, + *acc.*, to respect, revere, honor. Ч. свои́х роди́телей, to honor, respect one's parents. Чт-и́ть-ся, *v.i.r.*, (*obs.*) to be honored, revered. Он чти́тся свои́ми ученика́ми, he is respected by his pupils. У-чт-и́вость, *n.f.*, politeness, courtesy. У-чт-и́вый, *n.f.*, polite, courteous. У-чт-и́во, *adv.*, politely, courteously.

по-чт-и́ть, *v.p.*, по-чит-а́ть, *v.i.*, + *acc.*, to honor, respect, esteem, revere. Я почита́ю э́того челове́ка, I respect this man. Почти́ть па́мять встава́нием, to stand in honor of someone's memory. По-чит-а́ние, *n.n.*, honoring, respecting, reverence, veneration. П. роди́телей, honoring one's parents. По-чит-а́тель, *n.m.*, по-чит-а́тельница, *n.f.*, admirer. Она́ больша́я почита́тельница его́ тала́нта, she is a great admirer of his talent. По-чт-е́ние, *n.n.*, respect, esteem, honor. Моё п.! (*colloq.*), My compliments! Остаю́сь с соверше́нным почте́нием, (*obs.*), I remain very respectfully (in letters). По-чт-е́нный, *adj.*, honorable, respectable, venerable. 90 лет - это п. во́зраст, ninety is a venerable age. По-чт-е́нно, *adv.*, respectably. П. жить, to live respectably. По-чт-и́тельный, *adj.*, respectful. П. сын, respectful son. На почти́тельном расстоя́нии, at a respectful distance; at arm's length. По-чт-и́тельность, *n.f.*, respect, deference. По-чт-и́тельно, *adv.*, respectfully. Относи́ться п., to show respect.

по́-чест-ь, *n.f.*, honor, distinction, respect, esteem. По-чёт, *n.m.*, honor, respect, esteem. По́льзоваться почётом и любо́вью, to be esteemed and beloved. По-чёт-ный, *adj.*, honorable; honorary. П. член, honorary member. П.-ое ме́сто, place of honor.

по́-тч-евать, (*from* по́-чт-евать), *v.i.*, по-по́-тч-евать, *v.p.*, + *acc.*, + *instr.*, (*obs.*), to regale, treat. П. госте́й пирога́ми, to treat guests with pies.

ЧУД-, MIRACLE, MARVEL, WONDER

чу́д-о, *n.n.*, чуд-еса́, *pl.*, wonder, miracle. Соверша́ть чудеса́, to perform miracles. Страна́ чуде́с, wonderland. Чу́до иску́сства, miracle of art. Чу́д-ный, *adj.*, wonderful, beautiful, marvelous; lovely. Он ч. муж и оте́ц, he is a wonderful husband and father. "Я по́мню чу́дное мгнове́нье: пе́редо мно́й яви́лась ты...," (*Pushkin*), "A moment I recall entrancing, before my eyes thy form arose." Чу́д-но, *adv.*, wonderfully, beautifully, marvelously. Чуд-е́сный, *adj.*, wonderful, miraculous; lovely, fine, splendid. Ч. вид, splendid appearance. Ч-ое избавле́ние, miraculous escape. Чуд-о́вище, *n.n.*, monster. Морско́е ч., sea monster. Чуд-о́вищ-ность, *n.f.*, monstrosity; enormity. Чуд-о́вищный, *adj.*, monstrous. Ч-ые преступле́ния, monstrous crimes. Чуд-о-де́йствовать, *v.i.*, to work miracles. Этот хиру́рг пря́мо чудоде́йствует, this surgeon performs miracles. Чуд-

о-де́йственный, *adj.*, wonder-working.
Ч-ое лека́рство, miraculous medicine,
remedy. Чуд-о-тво́рец, *n.m.*, (*rel.*),
miracle-worker. Чуд-о-тво́рный, *adj.*,
(*rel.*), miracle-working. Ч.-ая ико́на,
miracle-working icon.

чуд-и́ть, чуд-е́сить, *v.i.*, (*colloq.*), to
behave strangely, endeavor to be
original. Он сно́ва на́чал чуди́ть, he
again began to behave strangely.
Чу́д-ить-ся, *v.i.r.*, по-чу́д-ить-ся, *v.p.r.*,
used only in 3d pers., + *dat.*, (*colloq.*),
to seem, appear. Мне чу́дится повсю́ду
её о́браз, it seems to me I see her
image everywhere. Чуд-и́ть-ся, *v.i.r.*, +
dat., (*folk.*), to wonder. Все чуди́лись
его́ необыкнове́нной си́ле, everyone
wondered at his unusual strength.
Чуд-а́к, *n.m.*, чуд-а́чка, *n.f.*, queer person, eccentric. Како́й ты чуда́к! What
a queer one you are! Чуд-а́чество,
n.n., eccentricity.

на-чуд-и́ть, *v.p.*, чуд-и́ть, *v.i.*, (*colloq.*),
to behave strangely, be eccentric, play
strange tricks. На-чуд-и́ть-ся, *v.p.*, +
dat., to wonder much. Они́ не могли́
начуди́ться его́ неожи́данному выздо-
ровле́нию, they could not wonder
enough at his unexpected recovery.

по-чу́д-ить-ся, *v.p.r.*, + *dat.*, *used only
in 3rd pers.*, to seem, appear. Ему́
почу́дилось, что кто́-то вхо́дит, it did
seem to him that someone was coming
in.

при-чу́д-ить-ся, *v.p.r.*, + *dat.*, *used only
in 3d pers.*, to seem, appear. Это вам
причу́дилось, you must have dreamed
it. При-чу́д-а, *n.f.*, whim, whimsy,
fancy, caprice, oddity. Он челове́к с
причу́дами, he is a whimsical man.
При-чу́д-ник, *n.m.*, при-чу́д-ница, *n.f.*,
whimsical person. При-чу́д-ливый, *adj.*,
fantastic, fanciful, whimsical. П. узо́р,
fantastic design. При-чу́д-ливо, *adv.*,
fantastically, fancifully, whimsically.
При-чу́д-ливость, *n.f.*, fantasy, fanciful-
ness.

**ЧУЖ-, ЧУЖД-, EXTRANEOUSNESS,
EXTRINSICALITY; ALIEN, FOREIGN-
ER, STRANGER**

чуж-о́й, *adj.*, alien, foreign, strange;
also used as n., alien, stranger. Ч-о́е
бога́тство в прок не идёт, (*prov.*),
someone else's wealth does one no
good. Он присво́ил себе́ чужу́ю
мысль, he plagiarized the idea. Чуж-е-
зе́мец *n.m.*, чуж-е-стра́нец, *n.m.*, чуж-
е-стра́нка, *n.f.*, foreigner, alien. Он
счита́ет себя́ чужестра́нцем, he con-
siders himself a foreigner. Чуж-е-
зе́мный, чуж-е-стра́нный, *adj.*, foreign,

alien; outlandish. Ч-ое расте́ние,
foreign plant. Чуж-би́на, *n.f.*, foreign
land, strange land. Го́рек хлеб на
чужби́не, (*saying*), bitter is the lot
of one who has to earn a living in a
foreign land.

чужд-а́ть-ся, *v.i.*, + *gen.*, to avoid, shun.
Он всех чужда́ется, he shuns every-
body. Чу́жд-ый, *adj.*, strange, alien.
Он чужд интри́г, he shuns intrigues.

от-чужд-а́ть, *v.i.*, от-чуд-и́ть, *v.p.*, +
acc., y + *gen.*, (*law*), to alienate,
estrange; buy, take under the privilege
of eminent domain; requisition. Пра-
ви́тельство отчуди́ло у них всё их
иму́щество, the government requisitioned all their property. От-чужд-
ённый, *adj.*, *part. pass. past*, requisitioned. О-ая полоса́ земли́, a requisitioned strip of land. От-чужд-ённо,
adv., apart from. Он живёт о., he lives
alone, away from people. От-чужд-
а́емый, *adj.*, *part. pass. pres.*, that is
being requisitioned. О-ая земля́, land
that is being requisitioned. От-чужд-
а́емость, *n.f.*, (*law*), requisition under
the privilege of eminent domain. Нет
преде́лов для отчужда́емости, there
are no limits to what can be requisitioned under the privilege of eminent
domain. От-чужд-е́ние, *n.n.*, requisition; estrangement, alienation. Под-
лежи́т-ли э́то отчужде́нию? Is this
subject to requisition? От-чужд-
ённость, *n.f.*, estrangement; aloofness.
О. отноше́ний, estrangement in relations. Не-от-чужд-а́емость, *n.f.*, inalienability. Н. ли́чных прав, inalienability of personal rights. Не-от-чужд-
а́емый, *adj.*, *part. pass. pres.*, inalienable. Это его́ н-ое пра́во, this is an
inalienable right.

**ЧУ-, ЧУ(Т)-, ЧУ(В)-, PERCEPTION,
FEELING, SENSIBILITY, SENSITIVE-
NESS**

чу́-ять, *v.i.*, по-чу́-ять, *v.p.*, + *acc.*, to
smell, scent; feel; have a feeling, a presentiment, a foreboding. Чу́ет моё
се́рдце беду́, (*folk.*), I have a foreboding. Соба́ка чу́ет след зве́ря, the
dog scents traces of the beast.

чу́-т-кий, *adj.*, sensitive, delicate; tactful,
considerate. Ч. сон, light sleep. Он ч.
челове́к, he is a sensitive man. Чу́-т-ко,
adv., sensitively, keenly. Ч. прислу́ши-
ваться, to listen attentively. Чу́-т-кость,
n.f., quickness, sensitiveness; tact.
Чу́-т-очку, чу-т-ь-чуть, *adv.*, a little,
wee bit; very slightly. Ни чу́точки, ни-
чу́ть, *adv.*, not in the least, not at all.
Чу-ть, *adv.*, hardly, barely, scarcely.

Чуть не, *adv.*, nearly, almost, within an ace; on the verge. Да́йте мне чу́точку отдохну́ть, let me rest a bit. Мы вста́ли чуть свет, when we got up it was hardly daybreak. Чуть что, она́ се́рдится, she flares up at every trifle. Я чуть не упа́л, I nearly fell. Чуть-ё, *п.п.*, scent, hearing, sense. Худо́жественное ч., sense of the artistic. У э́той соба́ки хоро́шее ч., this dog has a good nose.

за-чу́-ять, *v.p.*, по-чу́-ять, *v.p.*, + *acc.*, to scent, smell; hear; feel, have a presentiment. Соба́ки зачу́яли во́лка, the dogs scented the wolf.

у-чу́-ять, *v.p.*, + *acc.*, (*folk.*), to scent, feel; suspect. Он учу́ял что́-то нела́дное, he suspected something had gone wrong.

чу́-в-ство-вать, *v.i.*, + *acc.*, to feel, have a sensation. Я чу́вствую го́лод, I feel hungry. Он чу́вствует себя́ больны́м, he feels ill. Чу́-в-ствовать-ся, *v.i.r.*, по-чу́-в-ствовать-ся, *v.p.r.*, *used in 3d pers. only*, to be felt. Чу́вствуется приближе́ние весны́, one feels the approach of spring. Чу́-в-ство, *п.п.*, feeling, sense, sensation. Ч. жа́лости, a feeling of pity. Он пришёл в чу́вство, he recovered his senses. Она́ лежа́ла без чувств, she lay unconscious. Чу́-в-ственный, *adj.*, sensual, voluptuous. Чу́-в-ственность, *п.f.*, sensuality. Чу-в-стви́тельный, *adj.*, sensitive, receptive; sentimental; painful. Хими́ческие весы́ о́чень чувстви́тельны, chemical scales are highly sensitive. Ч. уда́р, painful stroke, blow. Чу-в-стви́тельность, *п.f.*, sensitiveness, susceptibility. Изли́шняя ч., extreme sensitiveness.

бес-чу́-в-ственный, *adj.*, lacking feeling, sensitivity; unfeeling; callous. Б-ое состоя́ние, unconsciousness. Быть в б-ом состоя́нии, to be unconscious. Бес-чу́-в-ственность, *п.f.*, бес-чу́-в-ствие, *п.п.*, apathy, insensibility; callousness. Бес-чу́-в-ственно, *adv.*, insensitively, apathetically, callously.

пере-чу́-в-ствовать, *v.p.*, + *acc.*, to feel anew, feel once more. Он ещё раз всё перечу́вствовал, he lived the experience over again.

по-чу́-в-ствовать, *v.p.*, + *acc.*, to feel, experience; have a sensation. Он дал им почу́вствовать свою́ си́лу, he permitted them to feel his strength.

пред-чу́-в-ствовать, *v.i.*, + *acc.*, to have a foreboding, a premonition. Моё се́рдце предчу́вствует беду́, I have a premonition, a foreboding. Пред-чу́-в-ствие, *п.п.*, presentiment, premonition,

foreboding. П. не обману́ло меня́, my premonition turned out to be true.

про-чу́-в-ствовать, *v.p.*, + *acc.*, to feel something keenly. П. утра́ту, to feel the loss keenly. Про-чу́-в-ствованный, *adj.*, *part. pass. past*, heartfelt, full of feeling. П-ая речь, emotional, heartfelt speech. Про-чу́-в-ствованность, *п.f.*, emotion. П. звуча́ла в ка́ждом его́ сло́ве, emotion rang in his every word. Про-чу́-в-ствованно, *adv.*, with emotion, with deep feeling. Говори́ть п., to speak with deep emotion.

рас-чу́-в-ствовать, *v.p.*, + *acc.*, to affect, move deeply. Рас-чу́-в-ствовать-ся, *v.p.r.*, to be affected, moved. Они́ расчу́вствовались от его́ не́жности, they were moved by his tenderness.

со-чу́-в-ствовать, *v.i.*, + *dat.*, to sympathize, feel for. Я сочу́вствую ему́, I sympathize with him. Со-чу́-в-ствие, *п.п.*, sympathy, compassion. Слу́шать с сочу́вствием, to listen with sympathy. Со-чу́-в-ственный, *adj.*, sympathetic. С-ая реце́нзия, sympathetic review. Со-чу́-в-ственно, *adv.*, sympathetically. Она́ с. отзыва́ется о нём, she speaks sympathetically of him. Со-чу́-в-ствующий, *adj.*, *part. act. pres.*, *also used as n.*, sympathetic, compassionate; sympathizer. С-ие друзья́, compassionate friends. Мно́го сочу́вствующих пришло́ проводи́ть его́, many sympathizers came to see him off.

Ш

ШАГ-, ШАЖ-, STEP, PACE, STRIDE, GAIT

шаг, *п.т.*, step, stride, pace. Ме́дленный шаг, slow stride. Ме́рные шаги́, measured steps. Ло́вкий шаг, (*fig.*), clever maneuver. Полити́ческий (дипломати́ческий), шаг, political (diplomatic) move. Идти́ ти́хими шага́ми, to walk slowly. Бе́глым ша́гом, with rapid strides. Ускори́ть шаг, приба́вить ша́гу, to quicken one's step. Замедля́ть шаги́, to slacken one's pace. Шаг за ша́гом, step by step. Ни на шаг, not even a move; not a move, not a step. Это большо́й шаг вперёд, this is a great step forward. Сде́лать пе́рвый шаг, (*fig.*), to take one's first step. Продвига́ться бы́стрыми шага́ми, (*fig.*), to make rapid progress. От вели́кого до смешно́го оди́н шаг, it is but a step from the sublime to the ridiculous. В двух шага́х, (*idiom.*), within a stone's throw. Звук шаго́в, sound of footsteps. Ни ша́гу да́льше, not a step further. Шаг-о-ме́р, *п.т.*, pedometer. Ша́г-ом, *adv.*, at a walk.

Вести лóшадь шáгом, to walk a horse.
Ехать шáгом, to drive, ride at a walk.
Шáгом марш! Forward march!

шаж-óк, *n.m.,* (*dim.*), small step, short
stride. Идти мéлкими шажкáми, to
walk slowly, take short strides.

шаг-áть, *v.i.,* шаг-нýть, *v.p.smf.,* to stride,
walk with long strides; step. "Сол-
дáты... мéдленно шагáли по пы́льной
дорóге," (*Tolstoy*), "the soldiers marched slowly along the dusty road." Он
шагáл из углá в у́гол, he paced the
room from corner to corner. Шагнýть
вперёд, to step forward. Шаг-áние,
n.n., striding, pacing, stepping. Шаг-
и́стика, *n.f.,* (*sarc.*), military forma-
tions. Шаг-áя, *adv., part. pres.,* striding.
Шаг-áющий, *adj., part. act. pres.,*
striding.

до-шаг-áть, *v.p.,* до-шаг-нýть, *v.p.smf.,*
до + *gen.,* to step to, reach on foot.
С трудóм шагáя, он дошагáл до
порóга, walking with difficulty, he
reached the threshold. Дошагнýть до
цéли, (*fig.*), to reach the goal.

за-шаг-áть, *v.p.,* to begin to stride, to
pace. З. по кóмнате, to begin to pace
a room.

пере-шáг-ивать, *v.i.,* (*obs.*), пере-шаг-
нýть, *v.p. smf.,* чéрез + *acc.,* to over-
step, step over, step across. П. порóг
дóма (чéрез порóг), to cross a threshold of a house. П. чéрез ручéек, to
step over a brook. П. чéрез препя́т-
ствие, to surmount an obstacle.

по-шаг-áть, *v.p.,* to walk a little with long
strides. По-шаг-áв, *adv. part. perf.,*
having walked, having paced. В
раздýмьи пошагáв по кóмнате, having
paced the room in deep thought.

про-шаг-áть, *v.p.,* to spend time in
walking. П. нéсколько часóв подря́д
на воéнных заня́тиях - довóльно уто-
ми́тельно, it is rather tiring to drill
for several hours at a time.

ШИБ-, BLOW, STROKE, ACT OF DELIVERING

шиб-анýть, *v.p.,* + *acc.,* (*slang*), to hit,
knock, deal a blow; give a push. Как
шибанёт он меня! (*slang*), How he hit
me!

ши́б-кий, *adj.,* (*colloq.*), fast, rapid,
quick. Слишком ши́бкая ездá запре-
щенá, speeding is prohibited. Ши́б-ко,
adv., quickly, rapidly; very much.
Ши́б-че, *adv.,* quicker, more quickly.

вы́-шиб-ить, *v.p.,* вы-шиб-áть, *v.i.,* +
acc., из + *gen.,* to knock out, throw
out, expel. Он вы́шиб ему́ зуб, he
knocked his tooth out. Егó вы́шибли
из шкóлы, (*colloq.*), they expelled him
from school. Вы-шиб-áть-ся, *v.i.r.,* to

be off; get away. Вы-шиб-áйтесь!
(*slang*), Go away! Off with you! Вы-
шиб-áние, *n.n.,* knocking out, driving
out. Вы-шиб-áла, *n.m.,* вы-шиб-áйло,
n.m., (*slang*), bouncer.

за-шиб-и́ть, *v.p.,* за-шиб-áть, *v.i.,* +
acc., (*colloq.*), to hurt, bruise; drink to
excess. Он зашиб себé глаз, he has
bruised his eye. Он си́льно зашибáет
врéмя от врéмени, he drinks hard from
time to time.

о-шиб-и́ть-ся, *v.p.r.,* о-шиб-áть-ся, *v.i.r.,*
в + *prep.,* to make a mistake, be mistaken, err. Не ошибáетесь-ли вы? Are
you not mistaken? Я оши́бся, I made a
mistake; I am wrong. О-ши́б-ка, *n.f.,*
error, mistake, fault. В этом сочи-
нéнии мнóго ошибóк, there are many
mistakes in this composition. По
оши́бке, by mistake. Сдéлать оши́бку,
to make a mistake. О-ши́б-очный, *adj.,*
erroneous, mistaken. О-ое мнéние,
erroneous opinion. О-ши́б-очно, *adv.,*
by mistake, erroneously. О. поня́ть, to
misunderstand, misinterpret. О-ши́б-
очность, *n.f.,* erroneousness, faultiness,
fallacy. Без-о-ши́б-очный, *adj.,* fault-
less; correct. Без-о-ши́б-очность, *n.f.,*
faultlessness. Без-о-ши́б-очно, *adv.,*
faultlessly, infallibly, correctly.

от-шиб-и́ть, *v.p.,* от-шиб-áть, *v.i.,* to
strike off, knock off. У негó отши́бло
пáмять, (*colloq.*), he has lost his memory.

пере-шиб-и́ть, *v.p.,* пере-шиб-áть, *v.i.,* +
acc., to fracture, break. Ему́ перешиб-
ли рýку, they broke his arm. Пере-
ши́б, *n.m.,* (*colloq.*), fracture, break.
П. ноги́, fracture of a leg.

под-шиб-и́ть, *v.p.,* под-шиб-áть, *v.i.,* +
acc., to give a blow. Он подши́б ему́
глаз, he blackened his eye.

при-шиб-и́ть, *v.p.,* при-шиб-áть, *v.i.,* +
acc., to hurt, bruise; deject. Он бóльно
пришиб егó, he struck him brutally.
При-шиб-л-енный, *adj., part. pass.
past,* discouraged, dejected. Этот мáльчик слóвно п., this boy is simply crest-
fallen.

про-шиб-и́ть, *v.p.,* про-шиб-áть, *v.i.,* +
acc., to break through, crack. Они́
проши́бли ему́ гóлову, they cracked
his skull. Меня́ прошибáет пот при
однóй мы́сли об этом, I break into a
cold sweat at the very thought of it.
Лбом стéну не прошибёшь, (*saying*),
you cannot break through a stone wall.

рас-шиб-и́ть, *v.p.,* рас-шиб-áть, *v.i.,* +
acc., (*colloq.*), to bruise badly; to strike
hard. Уйди́, а то расшибý! Clear out,
else I'll strike you! Онá расши́бла себé
колéно, she bruised her knee very
badly. Рас-шиб-и́ть-ся, *v.p.r.,* рас-шиб-

а́ть-ся, *v.i.r.*, to hurt oneself seriously. Она́ вы́бросилась из окна́ и расшиби́лась на́ смерть, she threw herself out of the window and injured herself fatally.

с-шиб-и́ть, *v.p.*, с-шиб-а́ть, *v.i.*, + *acc.*, to knock, strike down, off. Он сшиб меня́ с ног, he knocked me down. Они́ сши́бли их всех в одну́ ку́чу, they pushed them all together into one heap. С-шиб-и́ть-ся, *v.p.r.*, с-шиб-а́ть-ся, *v.i.r.*, to be knocked down; collide. Испу́ганные о́вцы сши́блись в ку́чу, the frightened sheep huddled together.

у-шиб-ить, *v.p.*, у-шиб-а́ть, *v.i.*, + *acc.*, to hurt, bruise. Я уши́бла но́гу, I've bruised my leg. У-шиб-и́ть-ся, *v.p.r.*, у-шиб-а́ть-ся, *v.i.r.*, + *instr.*, об + *acc.*, to be hurt, be bruised; hurt, bruise oneself. Ребёнок уши́бся голово́й об у́гол стола́, the child bruised its head against the corner of a table. У-ши́б, *n.m.*, bruise, contusion. У меня́ нога́ распу́хла от уши́ба, my leg has swollen from a bruise.

ШИ-, ШЬ-, ШЕЙ-, ШВ-, ШОВ-, SEWING; SEAM, STITCH

ши-ть, шь-ю, *v.i.*, с-ши-ть, *v.p.*, + *acc.*, + *instr.*, на + *prep.*, to sew, stitch, embroider. Шить пла́тье, to sew a dress. Ш. ни́тками, to sew with thread. Ш. шёлком, to sew with silk. Ш. зо́лотом, to embroider with gold. Ш. иглой, to sew with a needle. Ш. на маши́не, to sew on a machine. Ш. на живу́ю ни́тку, (*idiom.*), to sew hastily, carelessly. Ши́-ть-ся, *v.i.r.*, с-ши́-ть-ся, *v.p.r.*, to be sewed, embroidered. Ши́тый, *adj.*, *part. pass. past*, sewn, embroidered. Воротни́к, ш. зо́лотом, collar embroidered in gold. Это бе́лыми ни́тками ши́то, (*saying*), this is obvious. Ши-тьё, *n.n.*, sewing, stitching, needlework, embroidery. Ш. зо́лотом, gold embroidery.

в-ши-ть, во-шь-ю́, *v.p.*, в-ши-ва́ть, *v.i.*, + *acc.*, to sew in. В. рука́в, to sew in a sleeve. В-ши́-ть-ся, *v.p.r.*, в-ши-ва́ть-ся, *v.i.r.*, to be sewed in, stitched in. В-ши́-тый, *adj.*, *part. pass. past*, sewed in. В-ши-вно́й, *adj.*, sewed in. В-ы́е карма́ны, sewed in pockets.

до-ши́-ть, *v.p.*, до-ши-ва́ть, *v.i.*, + *acc.*, to finish sewing. К ве́черу э́ти брю́ки на́до д., these pants must be sewed by evening. Портно́й уже́ дошива́ет моё пальто́, the tailor is finishing my coat. До-ши́-ть-ся, *v.p.r.*, до-ши-ва́ть-ся, *v.i.r.*, to be sewed completely. Прида́ное спе́шно дошива́ется ко дню сва́дьбы, the trousseau is being finished in a hurry for the wedding day. До-ши́-тый, *adj.*, *part. pass. past*, completely sewed. Не-до-ши́-тый, *adj.*, *part. pass. past*, not sewed completely. Н. костю́м, unfinished suit.

за-ши́-ть, *v.p.*, за-ши-ва́ть, *v.i.*, + *acc.*, to mend, sew up. З. проре́ху (ды́рку), to mend a tear (a hole). З. ра́ну, (*med.*), to sew a wound. За-ши́-ть-ся, *v.p.r.*, за-ши-ва́ть-ся, *v.i.r.*, to be mended, sewed up. Ды́рки на чулка́х зашива́ются што́пальными ни́тками, holes in stockings are darned with yarn. Заши́ться на рабо́те, (*slang*), to be unable to complete a task. З. на экза́мене, (*slang*), to fail an examination. За-ши́-тый, *adj.*, *part. pass. past*, sewed up, mended. Не-за-ши́-тый, *adj.*, *part. pass. past*, unmended, not sewed up. Н.-ая ды́рка, unsewed hole, unmended hole.

на-ши́-ть, *v.p.*, на-ши-ва́ть, *v.i.*, + *acc.*, to sew on; trim; sew in quantity Н. кружева́ на пла́тье, to trim a dress with lace. На-ши́-ть-ся, *v.p.r.*, на-шива́ть-ся, *v.i.r.*, на + *acc.*, to be sewed on; be sewed in quantity. Галу́н нашива́ется на рукава́, the braid is being sewed on the sleeves. На-ши́-тый, *adj.*, *part. pass. past*, sewed on. Ордена́, наши́тые на мунди́ре, decorations sewed on a uniform. На-ши́-вка, *n.f.*, anything sewed on; (*mil.*), chevron, stripe.

об-ши́-ть, *v.p.*, об-ши-ва́ть, *v.i.*, + *acc.*, to trim, border, bind; make clothes, sew; panel, face, line, plate. О. подо́л ю́бки тесьмо́й, to bind a skirt with tape. О. блу́зку кружева́ми, to trim a blouse with lace. Мать обши́ла дете́й к зиме́, the mother sewed all the winter clothes for the children. Эта портни́ха обшива́ет на́шу семью́, this seamstress sews all the clothes for our family. Об-ши́-ть-ся, *v.p.r.*, об-шива́ть-ся, *v.i.r.*, + *instr.*, to be trimmed, edged; to sew one's clothes; be panelled, faced. Сиро́ты обшива́ются покрови́тельницами сиро́тского прию́та, the orphans have their clothes sewn for them by the patrons of the orphanage. Об-ши́-тый, *adj.*, *part. pass. past*, trimmed, edged, faced; plated. Об-ши́-вка, *n.f.*, trimming, edging, sheathing, boarding, steel plating. О. до́сками, boarding. О. фане́рой, veneering. Стальна́я о., steel plating. Об-шивно́й, *adj.*, trimming, panelling, sheathing, plating.

от-ши́-ть, *v.p.*, от-ши-ва́ть, *v.i.*, (*slang*), to refuse. Е́сли он бу́дет наха́льничать, то я его́ сра́зу отошью́, if he is brazen, I will turn him down immediately.

пере-ши́-ть, *v.p.,* пере-ши-ва́ть, *v.i.,* + *acc.,* to alter, sew again; sew everything. Пальто́ отца́ на́до переш́и́ть на сы́на, the father's coat must be altered to fit the son. Все зака́зы мы уже́ переши́ли, all the orders (for dresses) have been completed. Пере-ши́-ть-ся, *v.p.r.,* пере-ши-ва́ть-ся, *v.i.r.,* to be altered, be sewed again. Мой костю́м перешива́лся не́сколько раз, my suit was altered several times. Пере-шива́ние, *n.n.,* пере-ши́-вка, *n.f.,* alteration, altering, Пере-ши́-тый, *adj., part. pass. past,* altered, sewed over. Пиджа́к, п. из ста́рого, a coat made over from an old one.

по-ши́-ть, *v.p.,* + *acc.,* to sew for a while. Мать поши́ла часа́ два, а зате́м ста́ла гото́вить обе́д, the mother sewed for a while, then began to prepare dinner. По-ши́-вка, *n.f.,* (*colloq.*), sewing. Отда́ть костю́м в поши́вку, to order a suit. По-ши́-вочный, *adj.,* sewing. П-ая мастерска́я, garment workshop.

под-ши́-ть, *v.p.,* под-ши-ва́ть, *v.i.,* + *acc.,* to turn a hem; line. П. подкла́дку под пальто́, to line an overcoat. П. подо́л пла́тья, to hem a dress. П. бума́ги, to file papers. Под-ши́-ть-ся, *v.p.r.,* под-ши-ва́ть-ся, *v.i.r.,* to be hemmed, lined; be filed. Этот докуме́нт подошьётся к суде́бному де́лу, this document will be filed with the other papers pertaining to the case. Под-ши́-тый, *adj., part. pass. past,* lined, hemmed. Под-ши-ва́ние, *n.n.,* под-ши́-вка, *n.f.,* lining, hemming; filing. Купи́те сати́ну на подши́вку, buy some satin for a lining.

при-ши́-ть, *v.p.,* при-ши-ва́ть, *v.i.,* + *acc.,* к + *dat.,* (*colloq.*), to sew on; accuse. П. пу́говицу к пиджаку́, to sew a button to a coat. При-ши́-ть-ся, *v.p.r.,* при-ши-ва́ть-ся, *v.i.r.,* + *instr.,* к + *dat.,* to be sewed on. Воротни́к к пальто́ пришива́ется кре́пкими ни́тками, the collar is sewed to the overcoat with a strong thread. При-ши́-тый, *adj., part. pass. past,* sewed to. При-ши-ва́ние, *n.n.,* при-ши́-вка, *n.f.,* the action of sewing to, sewing on. При-ши-вно́й, *adj.,* pertaining to sewing on; that which is sewed on, that which can be sewed on.

про-ши́-ть, *v.p.,* про-ши-ва́ть, *v.i.,* + *acc.,* to sew through; stitch; sew for a while. Портно́й проши́л пять часо́в без переры́ва, the tailor sewed for five hours without a break. Про-ши́-вка, *n.f.,* sewing through, stitching. Блу́зка с проши́вками, a blouse with stitching.

Про-ши́тый, *adj., part. pass. past,* sewed through.

рас-ши́-ть, *v.p.,* рас-ши-ва́ть, *v.i.* + *acc.,* to embroider, adorn with needlework; rip. Р. полоте́нце цветны́м узо́ром, to embroider a towel with a colored pattern. Р. все швы, to rip all the seams. Рас-ши́-ть-ся, *v.p.r.,* рас-ши-ва́ть-ся, *v.i.r.,* + *instr.,* to become undone, ripped; be embroidered. Рас-ши-ва́ние, *n.n.,* embroidering. Р. узо́ров, embroidery of designs. Рас-ши́-тый, *adj., part. pass. past,* embroidered. Рас-ши́-ва, *n.f.,* a decked barge on the Volga.

с-ши́-ть, *v.p.,* с-ши-ва́ть, *v.i.,* + *acc.,* to sew; seam; tack; patch. Сшить но́вый костю́м, to sew a new suit. С. одея́ло из ра́зных кусо́чков мате́рии, to sew a quilt from pieces of material. С. кра́я ра́ны, to suture the edges of a wound. С. куски́, to piece together. С-ши́-ть-ся, *v.p.r.,* с-ши-ва́ть-ся, *v.i.r.,* to be sewed, hemmed, tacked together. С-ши-ва́ние, *n.n,* с-ши́-вка, *n.f.,* sewing, piecing, tacking. С-ши-вно́й, *adj.,* sewed, pieced together. С-ши́-тый, *adj., part. pass. past,* sewed together.

у-ши́-ть, *v.p.,* у-ши-ва́ть, *v.i.,* + *acc.,* to take in. Эта ю́бка широка́ для меня́, на́до её уши́ть, this skirt is too wide for me, it must be taken in. У-ши́-ть-ся, *v.p.r.,* у-ши-ва́ть-ся, *v.i.r.,* to be taken in. Когда́ э́тот шов ушьётся, тогда́ пла́тье бу́дет лу́чше сиде́ть на мне, when this seam is taken in, the dress will fit me better. У-ши-ва́ние, *n.n.,* у-ши́-вка, *n.f.,* taking in. У-ши́-тый, *adj., part. pass. past,* taken in.

шв-ея́, *n.f.,* шв-е́йка, *n.f.,* (*derog.*), seamstress. Шв-е́йный, *adj.,* pertaining to sewing. Ш-ая маши́на, sewing machine. Ш-ая промы́шленность, sewing industry.

шов, *n.m.,* seam; joint; (*med.*), suture. Пере́дний (боково́й) шов, front (side) seam. Без шва, seamless. Чулки́ без шва, seamless hosiery.

ши́-ворот, *n.m.,* (*colloq.*), collar. Взять за ш., to seize by the collar. Ши́ворот-навы́ворот, (*idiom.*), topsy-turvy; upside down; inside out.

ши́-ло, *n.n.,* awl. Ши́-льце, *n.n.,* (*dim.*), cobbler's awl. Пло́ское ши́ло, broad awl. Ши́ла в мешке́ не утаи́шь, (*saying*), murder will out; a strong passion always betrays itself. Ши-ло-ви́дный, *adj.,* awl-shaped.

ШИР-, BREADTH, WIDTH, LATITUDE

шир-о́кий, *adj.,* broad, wide; unrestrained. Ш. путь, wide, broad way. Ш-ая пу́блика, the public at large. Ш-ое пла́тье, loose dress. Ш-ие пле́чи, broad shoulders. Ш-ие интере́сы, wide interests. Жить на ш-ую но́гу, to live in a grand manner. Шѝр-е, *adj. and adv. comp.*, wider, broader; more widely, more broadly. Шир-оча́йший, *adj. superl.*, the widest, the broadest, extremely wide. Широче́нный, *adj.* (*colloq.*), very wide. Шир-ина́, *n.f.*, breadth, width. В ширину́, in breadth, in width. Три фу́та ширины́ и шесть длины́, three feet wide and six feet long. Шир-око́, *adv.*, broadly, widely. Две́ри бы́ли ш. раскры́ты, the doors were wide open. Широко-, *a combining form meaning* wide, broad. Широко-веща́ние, *n.n.*, broadcast, broadcasting. Широко-веща́тельный, *adj.*, broadcasting. Широко-гру́дый, *adj.*, broadchested. Широко-коле́йный, *adj.*, broad gauge. Широко-ко́стный, *adj.*, bigboned. Широко-ли́стный, *adj.*, broadleaved. Широко-ли́цый, *adj.*, broadfaced. Широко-кры́лый, *adj.*, widewinged. Широко-пле́чий, *adj.*, broadshouldered. Широко-по́лый, *adj.*, widebrimmed. Шир-ота́, *n.f.*, latitude. Ш. взгля́дов, (*fig.*), breath of view. Ш. кругозо́ра, breadth of vision. Шир-потре́б, (*recent*), *abbr.* of това́ры широ́кого потребле́ния, articles of mass consumption, consumer goods. Ни́зкие широ́ты, low latitudes. Шир-ь, *n.f.*, breadth, width. Круго́м ширь и просто́р, all around wide open spaces. **ши́р-ить**, *v.i.*, рас-ши́р-йть, *v.p.*, + *acc.*, to widen, broaden; spread. Р. кругозо́р, to broaden one's horizon. Шѝр-ить-ся, *v.i.r.*, to become wider, broader. Интере́с к э́тому ши́рится, interest in this is increasing. **рас-ши́р-ить**, *v.p.*, рас-шир-я́ть, *v.i.*, + *acc.*, to widen, expand; dilate; extend. Теплота́ расширя́ет все тела́, heat expands all bodies. Р. грани́цы, to extend the frontiers, the boundaries. Р. круг зна́ний, to broaden one's knowledge. Рас-ши́р-ить-ся, *v.p.r.*, рас-шир-я́ть-ся, *v.i.r.*, to be expanded, extended, spread. Рас-шир-е́ние, *n.n.*, expansion, widening, increase, dilation, enlargement. Р. се́рдца, enlargement of the heart. Коэфицие́нт расшире́ния, coefficient of expansion. Рас-ши́р-енный, *adj., part. pass. past*, widened, dilated. Р-ые зрачки́, dilated pupils. Рас-шир-я́ющийся, *adj., part. act. pres.*, expanding. Р-аяся промы́шленность, expanding industry. **об-ши́р-ный**, *adj.*, ample, spacious, vast, broad, extensive, wide, big. "война́ и Мир" - обши́рный труд Толсто́го,

"War and Peace" is a vast work by Tolstoy. О-ое знако́мство, large circle of acquaintances. Об-ши́р-ность, *n.f.*, spaciousness, vastness, expanse. О ми́ра, vastness of the world. О позна́ний, vastness of knowledge.

Щ

ЩАД-, ЩАЖ-, CLEMENCY, MERCY

щад-и́ть, щаж-у́, *v.i.*, + *acc.*, to spare, have mercy. Щ. побеждённых, to spare the conquered. Я щажу́ его́ самолю́бие, I am sparing his selfrespect, his pride.
по-щад-и́ть, *v.p.*, + *acc.*, to spare, have mercy. Они́ не пощади́ли его́ жи́зни, they did not spare his life. По-ща́д-а, *n.f.*, mercy; pardon; quarter. Ему́ не бу́дет поща́ды, there will be no pardon for him. Он напра́сно проси́л поща́ды, he pleaded in vain for mercy.
бес-по-ща́д-ный, *adj.*, merciless, pitiless, cruel. Б. враг, cruel enemy. Бес-поща́д-но, *adv.*, mercilessly, pitilessly, cruelly. Всех пле́нных б. расстреля́ли all the prisoners were shot down in cold blood. Бес-по-ща́д-ность, *n.f.*, mercilessness. Гражда́нская война́ отлича́ется свое́ю беспоща́дностью, civil war is characterized by mercilessness.

ЩЕДР-, GENEROSITY, MUNIFICENCE

ще́др-ый, *adj.*, generous, lavish; unsparing, free-handed. Ще́дрой руко́й with a generous hand, generously. Он щедр на обеща́ния, he is generous with promises. Ще́др-о, *adv.*, generously. Она́ щ. помога́ла бе́дным, she helped the poor generously. Ще́др-ость, *n.f.*, generosity. Его́ щ. созда́ла ему́ мно́го друзе́й, his generosity made him many friends. Ще́др-о́ты, *n.f.pl.* (*obs.*), bounty.
рас-ще́др-ить-ся, *v.p.r.*, рас-ще́др-ивать-ся, *v.i.r.*, to do something in a burst of generosity. Расще́дрился и дал рубль ни́шему, he became generous and gave the beggar a ruble.

ЩИТ-, ЩИЩ-, DEFENSE, PROTECTION

щит, *n.m.*, shield, screen; switchboard control panel. На стене́ виси́т стари́нный щит, an ancient shield hangs on the wall. Щит от огня́, firescreen. Щит стекля́нный у автомоби́ля windshield of an automobile. Щит черепа́хи, turtle shell. Щит управле́ния, control panel. Распредели́тель ный щит, switchboard. Щит-о-но́сец, *п.т.*, (*hist.*), shield-bearer. Щит-о-ви́дный, *adj.*, shield-like; thyroid. Щит-о́к, *п.т.*, (*bot.*), corymb.

а-щит-и́ть, за-щищ-у́, *v.р.*, за-щищ-а́ть, *v.i.*, + *acc.*, to defend, protect; support, advocate, plead for. Армия защища́ет свою́ страну́, the army defends its country. Адвока́т о́чень хорошо́ защища́л его́, his lawyer defended him well. Тёплое пла́тье защища́ет нас от хо́лода, warm clothing protects us against the cold. За-щит-и́ть-ся, *v.р.r.*, за-щищ-а́ть-ся, *v.i.r.*, to be protected, defended. Кре́пость защища́ется тяжёлой артилле́рией, a fortress is defended by heavy artillery. За-щищ-ённый, *adj.*, *part. pass. past*, defended, protected. Мы защищены́ зо́нтиком от дождя́, we are protected from the rain by an umbrella. За-щи́т-а, *n.f.*, defense; protection; safeguard. З. страны́, defense of a country. Я обраща́юсь к ва́шей защи́те, I appeal to you for protection. За-щи́т-ник, *п.т.*, за-щи́т-ница, *n.f.*, defender, protector; lawyer, barrister, counsel for the defense. Армия - защи́тник страны́, the army is the defender of the country. Она́ его́ неизме́нная защи́тница, she is his unfailing supporter. За-щит-и́тельный, *adj.*, pertaining to defense. З-ая речь, a speech in defense. За-щи́т-ный, *adj.*, protective; khaki. Мно́гие насеко́мые име́ют защи́тную окра́ску, many insects have a protective coloring.

ез-за-щи́т-ный, *adj.*, defenseless, unprotected. Б-ая страна́, defenseless country. Без-за-щи́т-ность, *n.f.*, defenselessness.

юд-за-щи́т-ный, *adj.*, *also used as п.*, entrusted; client. Адвока́т всегда́ защища́ет интере́сы свои́х подзащи́тных, a lawyer always defends the interests of his clients.

Ю

ЮН-, YOUTH

ю-ость, *n.f.*, youth, youthfulness. В ю́ности он подава́л больши́е наде́жды, as a youth he gave promise of great things. Цвету́щая ю., blooming youth. Произведе́ние "Де́тство, О́трочество и Ю́ность" напи́сано Толсты́м, "Childhood, Boyhood and Youth" was written by Tolstoy. Ю́ный, *adj.*, young, youthful. Ю. во́зраст, youthful age. Ю. геро́й, young hero. Юн-оша, *п.т.*, youth, young man. Ю. преврати́лся в мужчи́ну, the youth became a man. Юн-ошество, *п.п.*, young people, youth. Кни́ги для ю́ношества, juvenile books, children's books. Юн-ошеский, *adj.*, youthful, juvenile. Ю. задо́р, youthful zest. Ю-ие мечты́, dreams of youth.

юн-е́ть, *v.i.*, to grow young, revive. С молодёжью и старики́ юне́ют, in the company of youth even oldsters grow young. Юн-е́ц, *п.т.*, youth. Юн-кор, (*recent*), *abbr. of* ю́ный корреспонде́нт, juvenile reporter. Юн-се́кция, *n.f.*, (*recent*), young people's section of an organization. Юн-на́ты, *n.pl.* (*recent*), *abbr. of* ю́ные натурали́сты, Young Naturalists, members of Soviet Youth organization who study nature and science.

ЮТ-, ЮЧ-, SHELTER; HUDDLING, NESTLING

ют-и́ть-ся, юч-у́сь, *v.i.r.*, to huddle, nestle; find, seek shelter. "На высо́ком отло́гом берегу́ живопи́сно юти́тся село́," (*Chekhov*), "a village nestles picturesquely on the high sloping bank." Все де́ти юти́лись в одно́м углу́, all the children were huddling in one corner.

при-ют-и́ть, *v.р.*, + *acc.*, to shelter, give refuge. П. сироту́, to give refuge to an orphan. При-ют-и́ть-ся, *v.р.r.*, to take shelter. Ла́сточка приюти́лась под кры́шей, a swallow nestled under the roof. При-ют, *п.т.*, asylum, refuge, shelter. Сиро́тский п., orphan asylum, orphanage. Роди́льный п., lying-in-home, maternity home. П. для престаре́лых, old people's home. Приютский, *adj.*, pertaining to an orphanage. П-ое зда́ние, orphanage building. П-ие де́ти, children in an orphanage.

бес-при-ют-н-ый, *adj.*, homeless. "Бесприю́тного малю́тку приюти́ и обогре́й," (*poet.*), give shelter and warmth to a homeless infant. Бес-при-ю́т-ность, *n.f.*, homelessness.

у-ю́т, *п.т.*, comfort, coziness. Дома́шний у., coziness of a house, a home. Созда́ть у. в до́ме, to make a home, a house cozy. У-ю́т-ность, *n.f.*, coziness. У. обстано́вки соде́йствует о́тдыху, coziness of surroundings is conducive to rest. У-ю́т-ный, *adj.*, snug, cozy, comfortable. У. до́мик, cozy little house. У-ая кварти́ра, cozy apartment.

Я

ЯВ-, ЯВ(Л)-, APPEARANCE

яв-и́ть, яв-л-ю́, *v.i.*, яв-л-я́ть, *v.р.*, + *acc.*, (*obs.*), to show, display. Яви́те мне такýю мѝлость (*obs.*), do me the favor. Он явѝл примéр рéдкого беспристрáстия, he gave proof of rare impartiality. Яв-ѝть-ся, *v.p.r.*, яв-л-ѧ́ть-ся, *v.i.r.*, + *dat.*, + *instr.*, to be; occur, appear, arrive. Онá явѝлась емý во сне, she appeared to him in a dream. Он не явѝлся в суд, he failed to appear in court. У менѧ́ явѝлась мысль поéхать заграницу, I have thought of going abroad. Он явля́ется крýпным авторитéтом в наýке, he appears to be (is) a great authority on science. Яв-ка, *n.f.*, appearance, presence. Вáша ѧ́вка обязáтельна, your presence is obligatory. Яв-л-éние, *n.n.*, appearance, phenomenon; occurrence; scene. Комéта - рéдкое явлéние прирóды, a comet is a rare phenomenon. В. э́том дéйствии нéсколько явлéний, there are several scenes in this act. Яв-ный, *adj.*, evident, obvious. Я-ая ложь, obvious lie. Я вздор, downright nonsense. Я-ое презрéние, open contempt. Яв-но, *adv.*, obviously, evidently. Он ѧ́вно не желáл говорѝть с ним, he obviously did not want to talk to him. Явно-брáчное растéние, (*bot.*) phanerogamous plant. Яв-ность, *n.f.*, evidence, obviousness. Я. улѝк, obviousness of evidence.

яв-ствовать, *v.i.*, из + *gen.*, to be clear, be obvious. Из э́того ѧ́вствует, что он прав, it is clear from this that he is right. Яв-ственный, *adj.*, clear, distinct. Я-ая ошѝбка, obvious mistake. Явственно, *adv.*, clearly, distinctly, obviously. Онá я. не симпатизѝрует емý, she is clearly out of sympathy with him. Яв-ственность, *n.f.*, clearness, distinctness, obviousness. Яв-ь *n.f.*, reality. Явь это былá йли сон? Was it reality, or a dream? На-яв-ý, *adv.*, in reality, in one's waking hours. Это был сон н., it was a waking dream. Грéзить н., to daydream.

вы́-яв-ить, *v.p.*, вы-яв-л-ѧ́ть, *v.i.*, + *acc.*, to show, make apparent, expose. Он вы́явил все её недостáтки, he exposed all her defects. Вы́-яв-ить-ся, *v.p.r.*, вы-яв-л-ѧ́ть-ся, *v.i.r.*, to become apparent, be exposed. Все бóлее и бóлее выявлѧ́лась ложь, the lie became more and more apparent.

за-яв-ѝть, *v.p.*, за-яв-л-ѧ́ть, *v.i.*, + *acc.*, + *dat.*, о + *prep.*, to state, declare, announce officially. Издáтель заявлѧ́ет, что кнѝга вы́йдет в срок, the publisher announces that the book will appear on time. За-яв-ѝтель, *n.m.*, deponent. За-ѧ́в-ка, *n.f.*, (*recent*), statement of claim. Он сдéлал заѧ́вку на дровá, he laid claim to the firewood.

За-яв-л-éние, *n.n.*, statement, deposition, declaration, announcement. Вам нáдо подáть з., you must file a statement. Он сдéлал лóжное з., he misrepresented the facts; he made a false declaration.

из-ъ-яв-ѝть, *v.p.*, изъ-яв-л-ѧ́ть, *v.i.*, + *acc.*, to express. Онѝ изъявѝли своё соглáсие, they have expressed their consent. Из-ъ-яв-ѝтельный, *adj.*, indicative. И-ое наклонéние, (*gram.*), indicative mood.

об-ъ-яв-ѝть, *v.p.*, объ-яв-л-ѧ́ть, *v.i.*, + *acc.*, to announce, advertise, state, notify, proclaim, declare. Я объявѝл об э́том в газéте, I announced this in the newspaper. Странá объявѝла войнý, the country declared war. Об-ъ-яв-ѝтель, *n.m.*, announcer, advertiser. Числó объявѝтелей в э́той газéте увелѝчилось, the number of advertisers in this paper has increased. Об-ъ-яв-л-éние, *n.n.*, announcement, advertisement; statement, declaration; bill, poster. Поместѝте о. в газéте, place an advertisement in the newspaper. О. войны́, declaration of war.

от-ъ-ѧ́в-л-енный, *adj.*, acknowledged; confounded, out and out; arrant.

по-яв-ѝть-ся, *v.p.r.*, по-яв-л-ѧ́ть-ся, *v.i.r.*, to appear, make an appearance; show oneself, emerge. Сóлнце появѝлось из-за облакóв, the sun appeared through the clouds. По-яв-л-éние, *n.n.*, appearance. П. певцá на сцéне встрéчено бýрными аплодисмéнтами, the appearance of the singer on the stage was greeted with loud applause.

предъ-яв-ѝть, *v.p.*, предъ-яв-л-ѧ́ть, *v.i.*, + *acc.*, + *dat.*, to produce, present; lay claim to. П. докумéнты, to present documents. Предъ-ѧ́в-л-ен, *part. pass. past, pred.*, produced, presented. Емý бы́ло предъѧ́влено обвинéние, a charge was brought against him. Пáспорт предъявлѧ́ется на границе, a passport is presented at the frontier. Предъ-яв-ѝтель, *n.m.*, предъ-яв-ѝтельница, *n.f.*, bearer. П. йска, plaintiff. Предъ-яв-л-éние, *n.n.*, presentation. По предъявлéнию, on sight, upon presentation.

про-яв-ѝть, *v.p.*, про-яв-л-ѧ́ть, *v.i.*, + *acc.*, to manifest, display, show. Он нáчал проявлѧ́ть прѝзнаки безýмия, he began to show signs of insanity. П. инициатѝву, to show initiative. П. сѝлу, to display one's strength. П. себѧ́ хорóшим рабóтником, to prove to be an efficient worker. П. плёнки, to develop films. Про-яв-ѝть-ся, *v.p.r.*, про-яв-л-ѧ́ть-ся, *v.i.r.*, в + *prep.*, to be manifested, displayed, shown. В чём проявля́ется его́ боле́знь? What symptoms does he manifest? Про-яв-и́тель, *n.m.*, developer. Про-яв-л-е́ние, *n.n.*, manifestation, display, show; development П. свобо́ды, exercise of freedom. П. сни́мков, development of films.

ЯР-, BRIGHTNESS, CLEARNESS; VIOLENCE; ARDOR

я́р-кий, *adj.*, bright, clear, resplendent. Я. цвет, bright color. Я. ого́нь, blazing fire. Я. приме́р, striking example. Я. тала́нт, brilliant talent. Я-ая кра́ска, bright color. Я-ая красота́, dazzling beauty. Яр-че, *adj., and adv. comp.*, brighter, clearer. Яр-кость, *n.f.*, brightness, clearness, gaudiness. Я. приро́ды, brightness of nature. Я. описа́ния, vividness of description. Яр-ко, *adv.*, brightly, clearly, vividly. Со́лнце све́тит я., the sun is shining brightly. Ярко-зелёный, vivid green. Ярко-кра́сный, bright red.

я́р-ый, *adj.*, violent, raging; zealous, ardent, passionate; vehement. Я. покло́нник, ardent admirer. Я. рабо́тник, zealous worker. Яр-о, *adv.*, in a rage, furiously, violently. Я. защища́ть свои права́, to defend one's rights furiously.

я́р-остный, *adj.*, furious, violent, raging. Я. припа́док, violent attack. Я. гнев, violent rage. Я-ые ата́ки, furious attacks. Я. напо́р волн, furious onslaught of waves. Яр-ость, *n.f.*, fury, rage. Приводи́ть в я., to infuriate, enrage. Приходи́ть в я., to fly into a rage. Вне себя́ от я́рости, in a rage. Я. ве́тра, fury of the wind. Я. волн, violence of waves.

разъ-яр-и́ть, *v.p.*, разъ-яр-я́ть, *v.i.*, + *acc.*, to enrage, infuriate, make mad. Разъ-яр-и́ть-ся, *v.p.r.*, разъ-яр-я́ть-ся, *v.i.r.*, to become furious. Разъ-яр-ённый, *adj., part. pass. past*, infuriated, enraged. Р. лев, enraged lion.

яр-ово́й, *adj.*, vernal. Я-а́я посе́в, spring sowing. Я-а́я пшени́ца, spring wheat. Убо́рка яровы́х, harvest of summer grain crops. Яр-ь, *n.f.*, spring grain.

яр-овиза́тор, *n.m.*, (*agric., recent*), specialist in vernalization. Ку́рсы яровиза́торов, courses for vernalization specialists. Яр-овиза́ция, *n.f.*, vernalization. Я. семя́н, vernalization of seed. Яр-овизи́рованный, *adj., part. pass. past*, vernalized.

яр-овизи́ровать, *v.i.*, про-яр-овизи́ровать, *v.p.*, + *acc.*, (*recent*), to vernalize. Я. семена́, to vernalize seeds. Яр-овизи́ровать-ся, *v.i.r., and v.p.r.*, to be vernalized.

я́р-ка, *n.f.*, young ewe. Яр-очка, *n.f.*, (*dim.*), young ewe.

по-я́р-ковый, *adj.*, pertaining to felt, to lamb's wool. П-ая шля́па, felt hat. По-я́р-ок, *n.m.*, felt.

Яр-и́ло, *n.m.*, (*myth.*), ancient Slavic sun god.

ЯЗЫК- ЯЗЫЧ-, TONGUE, LANGUAGE

язы́к, *n.m.*, language, tongue; (*anat.*), tongue. Язы́к - о́рган ре́чи, the tongue is an organ of speech. Дли́нный я., long tongue. Обло́женный я., coated tongue. Бо́льно прикуси́ть я., to bite one's tongue till it hurts. Показа́ть кому́-нибудь я., to stick one's tongue out at someone. Иностра́нный я., foreign language. Родно́й я., native tongue. Держа́ я. за зуба́ми, hold your tongue. Свобо́дно владе́ть иностра́нным языко́м, to speak a foreign language fluently. Язы́к до Ки́ева доведёт, (*saying*), if you don't know, ask. Газе́тный язы́к, journalese. Язы́к Пу́шкина, Pushkin's language. Злой я., bitter, spiteful tongue. Острый я., sharp tongue. Живо́й (мёртвый) я., living (dead) language. Что у пья́ного на уме́, то и на языке́, (*saying*), in wine there is truth. Язык-о-ве́д, *n.m.*, linguist, philologist. Язык-о-ве́дение, *n.n.*, philology, linguistics. Язык-о-зна́ние, *n.n.*, linguistics. Язык-о́вый, *adj.*, lingual. Ино-язы́ч-ный, *adj.*, foreign. И. наро́д, foreign nation. Много-язы́чный, *adj.*, polyglot. Косн-о-язы́чный, *adj.*, tongue-tied.

язы́ч-о́к, *n.m.*, (*dim.*), small tongue; (*anat.*), uvula. Язы́ч-ко́вый, *adj.*, pertaining to reed. Я-ые инструме́нты, reed instruments.

язы́ч-ник, *n.m.*, heathen, pagan. Язы́ч-ество, *n.n.*, paganism. Язы́ч-еский, *adj.*, heathen, pagan. Я. мир, pagan world. Я. бог, idol, pagan god.

ЯС-, BRIGHTNESS, CLEARNESS, SERENITY

я́с-ный, *adj.*, clear, bright. Я. день, clear, bright day. Я-ая пого́да, clear weather. Я. ум, lucid mind. Я. свет, bright, clear light. Я-ые зву́ки, distinctly audible sounds. Я-ое изложе́ние, lucid explanation. Я-ое де́ло, (*colloq.*), of course, naturally. Яс-ность, *n.f.*, clarity, brightness. Я. не́ба, brightness of the sky. Я. взо́ра, clarity of a look. Внести́ во что́-нибудь я., to make something clear. Яс-но, *adv.*, clearly, brightly, evidently; yes, of course. Я. све́тит со́лнце, the sun is shining brightly. Я. вѝдно, it is clearly seen. Я. говорѝть, to speak clearly. Всем ясно, it is clear to everyone. Если я напишу́ тебѐ, ты отвѐтишь? Ясно, отвѐчу, If I write, will you answer? Of course, I'll answer. Ясно-вѝдение, *п.п.*, clairvoyance, second-sight. Ясно-вѝдец, *п.m.*, ясно-вѝдица, *n.f.*, clairvoyant. Ясно-вѝдящий, *adj., part. act. pres.*, used as n., clairvoyant. Яс-о́чка, *п.m., and n.f.*, (*colloq.*), darling. Я. ты моя́, my darling.

яс-нѐть, *v.i.*, to brighten, become bright, clear.

вы́-яс-нить, *v.p.*, вы-яс-ня́ть, *v.i.*, + *acc.*, to clarify, explain, find out, ascertain. В. положѐние дѐла, to clarify a case, a matter. В. вопро́с, to clarify a question, an issue, a problem. Вы́-яс-нить-ся, *v.p.r.*, вы-яс-ня́ть-ся, *v.i.r.*, to be explained, clarified. Дѐло вы́яснилось, the case was clarified. Вы́яснилось, что подсудѝмый невино́вен, it became clear that the accused was innocent. Вы-яс-нѐние, *п.п.*, clarification, ascertainment.

объ-яс-нѝть, *v.p.*, объ-яс-ня́ть, *v.i.*, + *acc.*, + *dat.*, to explain, elucidate, clarify thoroughly. О. уро́к, to explain a lesson. О. свою́ мысль, to explain one's idea. Объ-яс-нѝть-ся, *v.p.r.*, объ-яс-ня́ть-ся, *v.i.r.*, to explain oneself, to be explained, expounded, elucidated. О. на иностра́нном языкѐ, to explain in a foreign language. О. в любвѝ, to declare one's love. Этим объясня́ется стра́нность его́ поведѐния, this accounts for the strangeness of his behavior. Объ-яс-нѐние, *п.п.*, explana-

tion. Дать о., to give an explanation. О. зада́чи, explanation of a problem. Объ-яс-нѝмый, *adj., part. pass. pres.*, explicable. Объ-яс-нѝтельный, *adj.*, explanatory. О-ая запѝска, memorandum.

по-яс-нѝть, *v.p.*, по-яс-ня́ть, *v.i.*, + *acc.*, to explain, elucidate, expound, illustrate. П. пра́вило (мысль) примѐрами, to illustrate a rule (thought) through examples. По-яс-нѐние, *п.п.*, explanation, illustration. По-яс-нѝтельный, *adj.*, explanatory, illustrative.

про-яс-нѝть, *v.p.*, про-яс-ня́ть, *v.i.*, + *acc.*, to deepen, make the outlines of a design clearer. П. конту́ры на рису́нке, to make the outlines of a design clearer. Про-яс-нѐть, *v.p.*, to clear off, clear up; brighten. На дворѐ проясне́ло, it cleared outside. Про-яс-нѝть-ся, *v.p.r.*, про-яс-ня́ть-ся, *v.i.r.*, to become clear, bright; clear, brighten. Нѐбо прояснѝлось, the sky became clear. Его́ голова́ прояснѝлась, his mind became clear. Лицо́ прояснѝлось, his face brightened. Про-яс-нѐние, *п.п.*, clearing up, brightening. Про-яс-нён-ный, *adj., part. pass. past,* brightened.

у-яс-нѝть, *v.p.*, у-яс-ня́ть, *v.i.*, + *acc.*, + *dat.*, to make out, cause to realize, cause to understand. У. себѐ положѐние, to understand, realize a situation. У. себѐ вопро́с, to clarify a problem to oneself. У-яс-нён-ный, *adj., part. pass. past,* understood, realized. У-яс-ня́ть-ся, *v.i.r.*, у-яс-нѝть-ся, *v.p.r.*, to be realized, understood, clarified. У-яс-нѐние, *п.п.*, elucidation, explanation; realization, understanding.

DUE